T0135321

Lecture Notes in Computer Science　　13686

More information about this series at https://link.springer.com/bookseries/558

Shai Avidan · Gabriel Brostow ·
Moustapha Cissé · Giovanni Maria Farinella ·
Tal Hassner (Eds.)

Computer Vision – ECCV 2022

17th European Conference
Tel Aviv, Israel, October 23–27, 2022
Proceedings, Part XXVI

 Springer

Editors
Shai Avidan
Tel Aviv University
Tel Aviv, Israel

Gabriel Brostow 🆔
University College London
London, UK

Moustapha Cissé
Google AI
Accra, Ghana

Giovanni Maria Farinella 🆔
University of Catania
Catania, Italy

Tal Hassner 🆔
Facebook (United States)
Menlo Park, CA, USA

ISSN 0302-9743 ISSN 1611-3349 (electronic)
Lecture Notes in Computer Science
ISBN 978-3-031-19808-3 ISBN 978-3-031-19809-0 (eBook)
https://doi.org/10.1007/978-3-031-19809-0

This Springer imprint is published by the registered company Springer Nature Switzerland AG
The registered company address is: Gewerbestrasse 11, 6330 Cham, Switzerland

Foreword

Organizing the European Conference on Computer Vision (ECCV 2022) in Tel-Aviv during a global pandemic was no easy feat. The uncertainty level was extremely high, and decisions had to be postponed to the last minute. Still, we managed to plan things just in time for ECCV 2022 to be held in person. Participation in physical events is crucial to stimulating collaborations and nurturing the culture of the Computer Vision community.

There were many people who worked hard to ensure attendees enjoyed the best science at the 16th edition of ECCV. We are grateful to the Program Chairs Gabriel Brostow and Tal Hassner, who went above and beyond to ensure the ECCV reviewing process ran smoothly. The scientific program includes dozens of workshops and tutorials in addition to the main conference and we would like to thank Leonid Karlinsky and Tomer Michaeli for their hard work. Finally, special thanks to the web chairs Lorenzo Baraldi and Kosta Derpanis, who put in extra hours to transfer information fast and efficiently to the ECCV community.

We would like to express gratitude to our generous sponsors and the Industry Chairs, Dimosthenis Karatzas and Chen Sagiv, who oversaw industry relations and proposed new ways for academia-industry collaboration and technology transfer. It's great to see so much industrial interest in what we're doing!

Authors' draft versions of the papers appeared online with open access on both the Computer Vision Foundation (CVF) and the European Computer Vision Association (ECVA) websites as with previous ECCVs. Springer, the publisher of the proceedings, has arranged for archival publication. The final version of the papers is hosted by SpringerLink, with active references and supplementary materials. It benefits all potential readers that we offer both a free and citeable version for all researchers, as well as an authoritative, citeable version for SpringerLink readers. Our thanks go to Ronan Nugent from Springer, who helped us negotiate this agreement. Last but not least, we wish to thank Eric Mortensen, our publication chair, whose expertise made the process smooth.

October 2022

Rita Cucchiara
Jiří Matas
Amnon Shashua
Lihi Zelnik-Manor

Preface

Welcome to the proceedings of the European Conference on Computer Vision (ECCV 2022). This was a hybrid edition of ECCV as we made our way out of the COVID-19 pandemic. The conference received 5804 valid paper submissions, compared to 5150 submissions to ECCV 2020 (a 12.7% increase) and 2439 in ECCV 2018. 1645 submissions were accepted for publication (28%) and, of those, 157 (2.7% overall) as orals.

846 of the submissions were desk-rejected for various reasons. Many of them because they revealed author identity, thus violating the double-blind policy. This violation came in many forms: some had author names with the title, others added acknowledgments to specific grants, yet others had links to their github account where their name was visible. Tampering with the LaTeX template was another reason for automatic desk rejection.

ECCV 2022 used the traditional CMT system to manage the entire double-blind reviewing process. Authors did not know the names of the reviewers and vice versa. Each paper received at least 3 reviews (except 6 papers that received only 2 reviews), totalling more than 15,000 reviews.

Handling the review process at this scale was a significant challenge. To ensure that each submission received as fair and high-quality reviews as possible, we recruited more than 4719 reviewers (in the end, 4719 reviewers did at least one review). Similarly we recruited more than 276 area chairs (eventually, only 276 area chairs handled a batch of papers). The area chairs were selected based on their technical expertise and reputation, largely among people who served as area chairs in previous top computer vision and machine learning conferences (ECCV, ICCV, CVPR, NeurIPS, etc.).

Reviewers were similarly invited from previous conferences, and also from the pool of authors. We also encouraged experienced area chairs to suggest additional chairs and reviewers in the initial phase of recruiting. The median reviewer load was five papers per reviewer, while the average load was about four papers, because of the emergency reviewers. The area chair load was 35 papers, on average.

Conflicts of interest between authors, area chairs, and reviewers were handled largely automatically by the CMT platform, with some manual help from the Program Chairs. Reviewers were allowed to describe themselves as senior reviewer (load of 8 papers to review) or junior reviewers (load of 4 papers). Papers were matched to area chairs based on a subject-area affinity score computed in CMT and an affinity score computed by the Toronto Paper Matching System (TPMS). TPMS is based on the paper's full text. An area chair handling each submission would bid for preferred expert reviewers, and we balanced load and prevented conflicts.

The assignment of submissions to area chairs was relatively smooth, as was the assignment of submissions to reviewers. A small percentage of reviewers were not happy with their assignments in terms of subjects and self-reported expertise. This is an area for improvement, although it's interesting that many of these cases were reviewers hand-picked by AC's. We made a later round of reviewer recruiting, targeted at the list of authors of papers submitted to the conference, and had an excellent response which helped provide enough emergency reviewers. In the end, all but six papers received at least 3 reviews.

The challenges of the reviewing process are in line with past experiences at ECCV 2020. As the community grows, and the number of submissions increases, it becomes ever more challenging to recruit enough reviewers and ensure a high enough quality of reviews. Enlisting authors by default as reviewers might be one step to address this challenge.

Authors were given a week to rebut the initial reviews, and address reviewers' concerns. Each rebuttal was limited to a single pdf page with a fixed template.

The Area Chairs then led discussions with the reviewers on the merits of each submission. The goal was to reach consensus, but, ultimately, it was up to the Area Chair to make a decision. The decision was then discussed with a buddy Area Chair to make sure decisions were fair and informative. The entire process was conducted virtually with no in-person meetings taking place.

The Program Chairs were informed in cases where the Area Chairs overturned a decisive consensus reached by the reviewers, and pushed for the meta-reviews to contain details that explained the reasoning for such decisions. Obviously these were the most contentious cases, where reviewer inexperience was the most common reported factor.

Once the list of accepted papers was finalized and released, we went through the laborious process of plagiarism (including self-plagiarism) detection. A total of 4 accepted papers were rejected because of that.

Finally, we would like to thank our Technical Program Chair, Pavel Lifshits, who did tremendous work behind the scenes, and we thank the tireless CMT team.

October 2022

Gabriel Brostow
Giovanni Maria Farinella
Moustapha Cissé
Shai Avidan
Tal Hassner

Organization

General Chairs

Rita Cucchiara   University of Modena and Reggio Emilia, Italy
Jiří Matas   Czech Technical University in Prague, Czech Republic
Amnon Shashua   Hebrew University of Jerusalem, Israel
Lihi Zelnik-Manor   Technion – Israel Institute of Technology, Israel

Program Chairs

Shai Avidan   Tel-Aviv University, Israel
Gabriel Brostow   University College London, UK
Moustapha Cissé   Google AI, Ghana
Giovanni Maria Farinella   University of Catania, Italy
Tal Hassner   Facebook AI, USA

Program Technical Chair

Pavel Lifshits   Technion – Israel Institute of Technology, Israel

Workshops Chairs

Leonid Karlinsky   IBM Research, Israel
Tomer Michaeli   Technion – Israel Institute of Technology, Israel
Ko Nishino   Kyoto University, Japan

Tutorial Chairs

Thomas Pock   Graz University of Technology, Austria
Natalia Neverova   Facebook AI Research, UK

Demo Chair

Bohyung Han   Seoul National University, Korea

Social and Student Activities Chairs

Tatiana Tommasi   Italian Institute of Technology, Italy
Sagie Benaim   University of Copenhagen, Denmark

Diversity and Inclusion Chairs

Xi Yin   Facebook AI Research, USA
Bryan Russell   Adobe, USA

Communications Chairs

Lorenzo Baraldi   University of Modena and Reggio Emilia, Italy
Kosta Derpanis   York University & Samsung AI Centre Toronto,
                             Canada

Industrial Liaison Chairs

Dimosthenis Karatzas   Universitat Autònoma de Barcelona, Spain
Chen Sagiv   SagivTech, Israel

Finance Chair

Gerard Medioni   University of Southern California & Amazon,
                             USA

Publication Chair

Eric Mortensen   MiCROTEC, USA

Area Chairs

Lourdes Agapito   University College London, UK
Zeynep Akata   University of Tübingen, Germany
Naveed Akhtar   University of Western Australia, Australia
Karteek Alahari   Inria Grenoble Rhône-Alpes, France
Alexandre Alahi   École polytechnique fédérale de Lausanne,
                             Switzerland
Pablo Arbelaez   Universidad de Los Andes, Columbia
Antonis A. Argyros   University of Crete & Foundation for Research
                             and Technology-Hellas, Crete
Yuki M. Asano   University of Amsterdam, The Netherlands
Kalle Åström   Lund University, Sweden
Hadar Averbuch-Elor   Cornell University, USA

Hossein Azizpour   KTH Royal Institute of Technology, Sweden
Vineeth N. Balasubramanian   Indian Institute of Technology, Hyderabad, India
Lamberto Ballan   University of Padova, Italy
Adrien Bartoli   Université Clermont Auvergne, France
Horst Bischof   Graz University of Technology, Austria
Matthew B. Blaschko   KU Leuven, Belgium
Federica Bogo   Meta Reality Labs Research, Switzerland
Katherine Bouman   California Institute of Technology, USA
Edmond Boyer   Inria Grenoble Rhône-Alpes, France
Michael S. Brown   York University, Canada
Vittorio Caggiano   Meta AI Research, USA
Neill Campbell   University of Bath, UK
Octavia Camps   Northeastern University, USA
Duygu Ceylan   Adobe Research, USA
Ayan Chakrabarti   Google Research, USA
Tat-Jen Cham   Nanyang Technological University, Singapore
Antoni Chan   City University of Hong Kong, Hong Kong, China
Manmohan Chandraker   NEC Labs America, USA
Xinlei Chen   Facebook AI Research, USA
Xilin Chen   Institute of Computing Technology, Chinese
                                     Academy of Sciences, China
Dongdong Chen   Microsoft Cloud AI, USA
Chen Chen   University of Central Florida, USA
Ondrej Chum   Vision Recognition Group, Czech Technical
                                     University in Prague, Czech Republic
John Collomosse   Adobe Research & University of Surrey, UK
Camille Couprie   Facebook, France
David Crandall   Indiana University, USA
Daniel Cremers   Technical University of Munich, Germany
Marco Cristani   University of Verona, Italy
Canton Cristian   Facebook AI Research, USA
Dengxin Dai   ETH Zurich, Switzerland
Dima Damen   University of Bristol, UK
Kostas Daniilidis   University of Pennsylvania, USA
Trevor Darrell   University of California, Berkeley, USA
Andrew Davison   Imperial College London, UK
Tali Dekel   Weizmann Institute of Science, Israel
Alessio Del Bue   Istituto Italiano di Tecnologia, Italy
Weihong Deng   Beijing University of Posts and
                                     Telecommunications, China
Konstantinos Derpanis   Ryerson University, Canada
Carl Doersch   DeepMind, UK

Matthijs Douze	Facebook AI Research, USA
Mohamed Elhoseiny	King Abdullah University of Science and Technology, Saudi Arabia
Sergio Escalera	University of Barcelona, Spain
Yi Fang	New York University, USA
Ryan Farrell	Brigham Young University, USA
Alireza Fathi	Google, USA
Christoph Feichtenhofer	Facebook AI Research, USA
Basura Fernando	Agency for Science, Technology and Research (A*STAR), Singapore
Vittorio Ferrari	Google Research, Switzerland
Andrew W. Fitzgibbon	Graphcore, UK
David J. Fleet	University of Toronto, Canada
David Forsyth	University of Illinois at Urbana-Champaign, USA
David Fouhey	University of Michigan, USA
Katerina Fragkiadaki	Carnegie Mellon University, USA
Friedrich Fraundorfer	Graz University of Technology, Austria
Oren Freifeld	Ben-Gurion University, Israel
Thomas Funkhouser	Google Research & Princeton University, USA
Yasutaka Furukawa	Simon Fraser University, Canada
Fabio Galasso	Sapienza University of Rome, Italy
Jürgen Gall	University of Bonn, Germany
Chuang Gan	Massachusetts Institute of Technology, USA
Zhe Gan	Microsoft, USA
Animesh Garg	University of Toronto, Vector Institute, Nvidia, Canada
Efstratios Gavves	University of Amsterdam, The Netherlands
Peter Gehler	Amazon, Germany
Theo Gevers	University of Amsterdam, The Netherlands
Bernard Ghanem	King Abdullah University of Science and Technology, Saudi Arabia
Ross B. Girshick	Facebook AI Research, USA
Georgia Gkioxari	Facebook AI Research, USA
Albert Gordo	Facebook, USA
Stephen Gould	Australian National University, Australia
Venu Madhav Govindu	Indian Institute of Science, India
Kristen Grauman	Facebook AI Research & UT Austin, USA
Abhinav Gupta	Carnegie Mellon University & Facebook AI Research, USA
Mohit Gupta	University of Wisconsin-Madison, USA
Hu Han	Institute of Computing Technology, Chinese Academy of Sciences, China

Bohyung Han	Seoul National University, Korea
Tian Han	Stevens Institute of Technology, USA
Emily Hand	University of Nevada, Reno, USA
Bharath Hariharan	Cornell University, USA
Ran He	Institute of Automation, Chinese Academy of Sciences, China
Otmar Hilliges	ETH Zurich, Switzerland
Adrian Hilton	University of Surrey, UK
Minh Hoai	Stony Brook University, USA
Yedid Hoshen	Hebrew University of Jerusalem, Israel
Timothy Hospedales	University of Edinburgh, UK
Gang Hua	Wormpex AI Research, USA
Di Huang	Beihang University, China
Jing Huang	Facebook, USA
Jia-Bin Huang	Facebook, USA
Nathan Jacobs	Washington University in St. Louis, USA
C.V. Jawahar	International Institute of Information Technology, Hyderabad, India
Herve Jegou	Facebook AI Research, France
Neel Joshi	Microsoft Research, USA
Armand Joulin	Facebook AI Research, France
Frederic Jurie	University of Caen Normandie, France
Fredrik Kahl	Chalmers University of Technology, Sweden
Yannis Kalantidis	NAVER LABS Europe, France
Evangelos Kalogerakis	University of Massachusetts, Amherst, USA
Sing Bing Kang	Zillow Group, USA
Yosi Keller	Bar Ilan University, Israel
Margret Keuper	University of Mannheim, Germany
Tae-Kyun Kim	Imperial College London, UK
Benjamin Kimia	Brown University, USA
Alexander Kirillov	Facebook AI Research, USA
Kris Kitani	Carnegie Mellon University, USA
Iasonas Kokkinos	Snap Inc. & University College London, UK
Vladlen Koltun	Apple, USA
Nikos Komodakis	University of Crete, Crete
Piotr Koniusz	Australian National University, Australia
Philipp Kraehenbuehl	University of Texas at Austin, USA
Dilip Krishnan	Google, USA
Ajay Kumar	Hong Kong Polytechnic University, Hong Kong, China
Junseok Kwon	Chung-Ang University, Korea
Jean-Francois Lalonde	Université Laval, Canada

Ivan Laptev	Inria Paris, France
Laura Leal-Taixé	Technical University of Munich, Germany
Erik Learned-Miller	University of Massachusetts, Amherst, USA
Gim Hee Lee	National University of Singapore, Singapore
Seungyong Lee	Pohang University of Science and Technology, Korea
Zhen Lei	Institute of Automation, Chinese Academy of Sciences, China
Bastian Leibe	RWTH Aachen University, Germany
Hongdong Li	Australian National University, Australia
Fuxin Li	Oregon State University, USA
Bo Li	University of Illinois at Urbana-Champaign, USA
Yin Li	University of Wisconsin-Madison, USA
Ser-Nam Lim	Meta AI Research, USA
Joseph Lim	University of Southern California, USA
Stephen Lin	Microsoft Research Asia, China
Dahua Lin	The Chinese University of Hong Kong, Hong Kong, China
Si Liu	Beihang University, China
Xiaoming Liu	Michigan State University, USA
Ce Liu	Microsoft, USA
Zicheng Liu	Microsoft, USA
Yanxi Liu	Pennsylvania State University, USA
Feng Liu	Portland State University, USA
Yebin Liu	Tsinghua University, China
Chen Change Loy	Nanyang Technological University, Singapore
Huchuan Lu	Dalian University of Technology, China
Cewu Lu	Shanghai Jiao Tong University, China
Oisin Mac Aodha	University of Edinburgh, UK
Dhruv Mahajan	Facebook, USA
Subhransu Maji	University of Massachusetts, Amherst, USA
Atsuto Maki	KTH Royal Institute of Technology, Sweden
Arun Mallya	NVIDIA, USA
R. Manmatha	Amazon, USA
Iacopo Masi	Sapienza University of Rome, Italy
Dimitris N. Metaxas	Rutgers University, USA
Ajmal Mian	University of Western Australia, Australia
Christian Micheloni	University of Udine, Italy
Krystian Mikolajczyk	Imperial College London, UK
Anurag Mittal	Indian Institute of Technology, Madras, India
Philippos Mordohai	Stevens Institute of Technology, USA
Greg Mori	Simon Fraser University & Borealis AI, Canada

Vittorio Murino	Istituto Italiano di Tecnologia, Italy
P. J. Narayanan	International Institute of Information Technology, Hyderabad, India
Ram Nevatia	University of Southern California, USA
Natalia Neverova	Facebook AI Research, UK
Richard Newcombe	Facebook, USA
Cuong V. Nguyen	Florida International University, USA
Bingbing Ni	Shanghai Jiao Tong University, China
Juan Carlos Niebles	Salesforce & Stanford University, USA
Ko Nishino	Kyoto University, Japan
Jean-Marc Odobez	Idiap Research Institute, École polytechnique fédérale de Lausanne, Switzerland
Francesca Odone	University of Genova, Italy
Takayuki Okatani	Tohoku University & RIKEN Center for Advanced Intelligence Project, Japan
Manohar Paluri	Facebook, USA
Guan Pang	Facebook, USA
Maja Pantic	Imperial College London, UK
Sylvain Paris	Adobe Research, USA
Jaesik Park	Pohang University of Science and Technology, Korea
Hyun Soo Park	The University of Minnesota, USA
Omkar M. Parkhi	Facebook, USA
Deepak Pathak	Carnegie Mellon University, USA
Georgios Pavlakos	University of California, Berkeley, USA
Marcello Pelillo	University of Venice, Italy
Marc Pollefeys	ETH Zurich & Microsoft, Switzerland
Jean Ponce	Inria, France
Gerard Pons-Moll	University of Tübingen, Germany
Fatih Porikli	Qualcomm, USA
Victor Adrian Prisacariu	University of Oxford, UK
Petia Radeva	University of Barcelona, Spain
Ravi Ramamoorthi	University of California, San Diego, USA
Deva Ramanan	Carnegie Mellon University, USA
Vignesh Ramanathan	Facebook, USA
Nalini Ratha	State University of New York at Buffalo, USA
Tammy Riklin Raviv	Ben-Gurion University, Israel
Tobias Ritschel	University College London, UK
Emanuele Rodola	Sapienza University of Rome, Italy
Amit K. Roy-Chowdhury	University of California, Riverside, USA
Michael Rubinstein	Google, USA
Olga Russakovsky	Princeton University, USA

Mathieu Salzmann   École polytechnique fédérale de Lausanne,
                                    Switzerland
Dimitris Samaras   Stony Brook University, USA
Aswin Sankaranarayanan   Carnegie Mellon University, USA
Imari Sato   National Institute of Informatics, Japan
Yoichi Sato   University of Tokyo, Japan
Shin'ichi Satoh   National Institute of Informatics, Japan
Walter Scheirer   University of Notre Dame, USA
Bernt Schiele   Max Planck Institute for Informatics, Germany
Konrad Schindler   ETH Zurich, Switzerland
Cordelia Schmid   Inria & Google, France
Alexander Schwing   University of Illinois at Urbana-Champaign, USA
Nicu Sebe   University of Trento, Italy
Greg Shakhnarovich   Toyota Technological Institute at Chicago, USA
Eli Shechtman   Adobe Research, USA
Humphrey Shi   University of Oregon & University of Illinois at
                                    Urbana-Champaign & Picsart AI Research,
                                    USA
Jianbo Shi   University of Pennsylvania, USA
Roy Shilkrot   Massachusetts Institute of Technology, USA
Mike Zheng Shou   National University of Singapore, Singapore
Kaleem Siddiqi   McGill University, Canada
Richa Singh   Indian Institute of Technology Jodhpur, India
Greg Slabaugh   Queen Mary University of London, UK
Cees Snoek   University of Amsterdam, The Netherlands
Yale Song   Facebook AI Research, USA
Yi-Zhe Song   University of Surrey, UK
Bjorn Stenger   Rakuten Institute of Technology
Abby Stylianou   Saint Louis University, USA
Akihiro Sugimoto   National Institute of Informatics, Japan
Chen Sun   Brown University, USA
Deqing Sun   Google, USA
Kalyan Sunkavalli   Adobe Research, USA
Ying Tai   Tencent YouTu Lab, China
Ayellet Tal   Technion – Israel Institute of Technology, Israel
Ping Tan   Simon Fraser University, Canada
Siyu Tang   ETH Zurich, Switzerland
Chi-Keung Tang   Hong Kong University of Science and
                                    Technology, Hong Kong, China
Radu Timofte   University of Würzburg, Germany & ETH Zurich,
                                    Switzerland
Federico Tombari   Google, Switzerland & Technical University of
                                    Munich, Germany

James Tompkin   Brown University, USA
Lorenzo Torresani   Dartmouth College, USA
Alexander Toshev   Apple, USA
Du Tran   Facebook AI Research, USA
Anh T. Tran   VinAI, Vietnam
Zhuowen Tu   University of California, San Diego, USA
Georgios Tzimiropoulos   Queen Mary University of London, UK
Jasper Uijlings   Google Research, Switzerland
Jan C. van Gemert   Delft University of Technology, The Netherlands
Gul Varol   Ecole des Ponts ParisTech, France
Nuno Vasconcelos   University of California, San Diego, USA
Mayank Vatsa   Indian Institute of Technology Jodhpur, India
Ashok Veeraraghavan   Rice University, USA
Jakob Verbeek   Facebook AI Research, France
Carl Vondrick   Columbia University, USA
Ruiping Wang   Institute of Computing Technology, Chinese
                                 Academy of Sciences, China
Xinchao Wang   National University of Singapore, Singapore
Liwei Wang   The Chinese University of Hong Kong,
                                 Hong Kong, China
Chaohui Wang   Université Paris-Est, France
Xiaolong Wang   University of California, San Diego, USA
Christian Wolf   NAVER LABS Europe, France
Tao Xiang   University of Surrey, UK
Saining Xie   Facebook AI Research, USA
Cihang Xie   University of California, Santa Cruz, USA
Zeki Yalniz   Facebook, USA
Ming-Hsuan Yang   University of California, Merced, USA
Angela Yao   National University of Singapore, Singapore
Shaodi You   University of Amsterdam, The Netherlands
Stella X. Yu   University of California, Berkeley, USA
Junsong Yuan   State University of New York at Buffalo, USA
Stefanos Zafeiriou   Imperial College London, UK
Amir Zamir   École polytechnique fédérale de Lausanne,
                                 Switzerland
Lei Zhang   Alibaba & Hong Kong Polytechnic University,
                                 Hong Kong, China
Lei Zhang   International Digital Economy Academy (IDEA),
                                 China
Pengchuan Zhang   Meta AI, USA
Bolei Zhou   University of California, Los Angeles, USA
Yuke Zhu   University of Texas at Austin, USA

Todd Zickler   Harvard University, USA
Wangmeng Zuo   Harbin Institute of Technology, China

Technical Program Committee

Davide Abati
Soroush Abbasi
    Koohpayegani
Amos L. Abbott
Rameen Abdal
Rabab Abdelfattah
Sahar Abdelnabi
Hassan Abu Alhaija
Abulikemu Abuduweili
Ron Abutbul
Hanno Ackermann
Aikaterini Adam
Kamil Adamczewski
Ehsan Adeli
Vida Adeli
Donald Adjeroh
Arman Afrasiyabi
Akshay Agarwal
Sameer Agarwal
Abhinav Agarwalla
Vaibhav Aggarwal
Sara Aghajanzadeh
Susmit Agrawal
Antonio Agudo
Touqeer Ahmad
Sk Miraj Ahmed
Chaitanya Ahuja
Nilesh A. Ahuja
Abhishek Aich
Shubhra Aich
Noam Aigerman
Arash Akbarinia
Peri Akiva
Derya Akkaynak
Emre Aksan
Arjun R. Akula
Yuval Alaluf
Stephan Alaniz
Paul Albert
Cenek Albl

Filippo Aleotti
Konstantinos P.
    Alexandridis
Motasem Alfarra
Mohsen Ali
Thiemo Alldieck
Hadi Alzayer
Liang An
Shan An
Yi An
Zhulin An
Dongsheng An
Jie An
Xiang An
Saket Anand
Cosmin Ancuti
Juan Andrade-Cetto
Alexander Andreopoulos
Bjoern Andres
Jerone T. A. Andrews
Shivangi Aneja
Anelia Angelova
Dragomir Anguelov
Rushil Anirudh
Oron Anschel
Rao Muhammad Anwer
Djamila Aouada
Evlampios Apostolidis
Srikar Appalaraju
Nikita Araslanov
Andre Araujo
Eric Arazo
Dawit Mureja Argaw
Anurag Arnab
Aditya Arora
Chetan Arora
Sunpreet S. Arora
Alexey Artemov
Muhammad Asad
Kumar Ashutosh

Sinem Aslan
Vishal Asnani
Mahmoud Assran
Amir Atapour-Abarghouei
Nikos Athanasiou
Ali Athar
ShahRukh Athar
Sara Atito
Souhaib Attaiki
Matan Atzmon
Mathieu Aubry
Nicolas Audebert
Tristan T.
    Aumentado-Armstrong
Melinos Averkiou
Yannis Avrithis
Stephane Ayache
Mehmet Aygün
Seyed Mehdi
    Ayyoubzadeh
Hossein Azizpour
George Azzopardi
Mallikarjun B. R.
Yunhao Ba
Abhishek Badki
Seung-Hwan Bae
Seung-Hwan Baek
Seungryul Baek
Piyush Nitin Bagad
Shai Bagon
Gaetan Bahl
Shikhar Bahl
Sherwin Bahmani
Haoran Bai
Lei Bai
Jiawang Bai
Haoyue Bai
Jinbin Bai
Xiang Bai
Xuyang Bai

Yang Bai
Yuanchao Bai
Ziqian Bai
Sungyong Baik
Kevin Bailly
Max Bain
Federico Baldassarre
Wele Gedara Chaminda
  Bandara
Biplab Banerjee
Pratyay Banerjee
Sandipan Banerjee
Jihwan Bang
Antyanta Bangunharcana
Aayush Bansal
Ankan Bansal
Siddhant Bansal
Wentao Bao
Zhipeng Bao
Amir Bar
Manel Baradad Jurjo
Lorenzo Baraldi
Danny Barash
Daniel Barath
Connelly Barnes
Ioan Andrei Bârsan
Steven Basart
Dina Bashkirova
Chaim Baskin
Peyman Bateni
Anil Batra
Sebastiano Battiato
Ardhendu Behera
Harkirat Behl
Jens Behley
Vasileios Belagiannis
Boulbaba Ben Amor
Emanuel Ben Baruch
Abdessamad Ben Hamza
Gil Ben-Artzi
Assia Benbihi
Fabian Benitez-Quiroz
Guy Ben-Yosef
Philipp Benz
Alexander W. Bergman

Urs Bergmann
Jesus Bermudez-Cameo
Stefano Berretti
Gedas Bertasius
Zachary Bessinger
Petra Bevandić
Matthew Beveridge
Lucas Beyer
Yash Bhalgat
Suvaansh Bhambri
Samarth Bharadwaj
Gaurav Bharaj
Aparna Bharati
Bharat Lal Bhatnagar
Uttaran Bhattacharya
Apratim Bhattacharyya
Brojeshwar Bhowmick
Ankan Kumar Bhunia
Ayan Kumar Bhunia
Qi Bi
Sai Bi
Michael Bi Mi
Gui-Bin Bian
Jia-Wang Bian
Shaojun Bian
Pia Bideau
Mario Bijelic
Hakan Bilen
Guillaume-Alexandre
  Bilodeau
Alexander Binder
Tolga Birdal
Vighnesh N. Birodkar
Sandika Biswas
Andreas Blattmann
Janusz Bobulski
Giuseppe Boccignone
Vishnu Boddeti
Navaneeth Bodla
Moritz Böhle
Aleksei Bokhovkin
Sam Bond-Taylor
Vivek Boominathan
Shubhankar Borse
Mark Boss

Andrea Bottino
Adnane Boukhayma
Fadi Boutros
Nicolas C. Boutry
Richard S. Bowen
Ivaylo Boyadzhiev
Aidan Boyd
Yuri Boykov
Aljaz Bozic
Behzad Bozorgtabar
Eric Brachmann
Samarth Brahmbhatt
Gustav Bredell
Francois Bremond
Joel Brogan
Andrew Brown
Thomas Brox
Marcus A. Brubaker
Robert-Jan Bruintjes
Yuqi Bu
Anders G. Buch
Himanshu Buckchash
Mateusz Buda
Ignas Budvytis
José M. Buenaposada
Marcel C. Bühler
Tu Bui
Adrian Bulat
Hannah Bull
Evgeny Burnaev
Andrei Bursuc
Benjamin Busam
Sergey N. Buzykanov
Wonmin Byeon
Fabian Caba
Martin Cadik
Guanyu Cai
Minjie Cai
Qing Cai
Zhongang Cai
Qi Cai
Yancheng Cai
Shen Cai
Han Cai
Jiarui Cai

Bowen Cai
Mu Cai
Qin Cai
Ruojin Cai
Weidong Cai
Weiwei Cai
Yi Cai
Yujun Cai
Zhiping Cai
Akin Caliskan
Lilian Calvet
Baris Can Cam
Necati Cihan Camgoz
Tommaso Campari
Dylan Campbell
Ziang Cao
Ang Cao
Xu Cao
Zhiwen Cao
Shengcao Cao
Song Cao
Weipeng Cao
Xiangyong Cao
Xiaochun Cao
Yue Cao
Yunhao Cao
Zhangjie Cao
Jiale Cao
Yang Cao
Jiajiong Cao
Jie Cao
Jinkun Cao
Lele Cao
Yulong Cao
Zhiguo Cao
Chen Cao
Razvan Caramalau
Marlène Careil
Gustavo Carneiro
Joao Carreira
Dan Casas
Paola Cascante-Bonilla
Angela Castillo
Francisco M. Castro
Pedro Castro

Luca Cavalli
George J. Cazenavette
Oya Celiktutan
Hakan Cevikalp
Sri Harsha C. H.
Sungmin Cha
Geonho Cha
Menglei Chai
Lucy Chai
Yuning Chai
Zenghao Chai
Anirban Chakraborty
Deep Chakraborty
Rudrasis Chakraborty
Souradeep Chakraborty
Kelvin C. K. Chan
Chee Seng Chan
Paramanand Chandramouli
Arjun Chandrasekaran
Kenneth Chaney
Dongliang Chang
Huiwen Chang
Peng Chang
Xiaojun Chang
Jia-Ren Chang
Hyung Jin Chang
Hyun Sung Chang
Ju Yong Chang
Li-Jen Chang
Qi Chang
Wei-Yi Chang
Yi Chang
Nadine Chang
Hanqing Chao
Pradyumna Chari
Dibyadip Chatterjee
Chiranjoy Chattopadhyay
Siddhartha Chaudhuri
Zhengping Che
Gal Chechik
Lianggangxu Chen
Qi Alfred Chen
Brian Chen
Bor-Chun Chen
Bo-Hao Chen

Bohong Chen
Bin Chen
Ziliang Chen
Cheng Chen
Chen Chen
Chaofeng Chen
Xi Chen
Haoyu Chen
Xuanhong Chen
Wei Chen
Qiang Chen
Shi Chen
Xianyu Chen
Chang Chen
Changhuai Chen
Hao Chen
Jie Chen
Jianbo Chen
Jingjing Chen
Jun Chen
Kejiang Chen
Mingcai Chen
Nenglun Chen
Qifeng Chen
Ruoyu Chen
Shu-Yu Chen
Weidong Chen
Weijie Chen
Weikai Chen
Xiang Chen
Xiuyi Chen
Xingyu Chen
Yaofo Chen
Yueting Chen
Yu Chen
Yunjin Chen
Yuntao Chen
Yun Chen
Zhenfang Chen
Zhuangzhuang Chen
Chu-Song Chen
Xiangyu Chen
Zhuo Chen
Chaoqi Chen
Shizhe Chen

Xiaotong Chen
Xiaozhi Chen
Dian Chen
Defang Chen
Dingfan Chen
Ding-Jie Chen
Ee Heng Chen
Tao Chen
Yixin Chen
Wei-Ting Chen
Lin Chen
Guang Chen
Guangyi Chen
Guanying Chen
Guangyao Chen
Hwann-Tzong Chen
Junwen Chen
Jiacheng Chen
Jianxu Chen
Hui Chen
Kai Chen
Kan Chen
Kevin Chen
Kuan-Wen Chen
Weihua Chen
Zhang Chen
Liang-Chieh Chen
Lele Chen
Liang Chen
Fanglin Chen
Zehui Chen
Minghui Chen
Minghao Chen
Xiaokang Chen
Qian Chen
Jun-Cheng Chen
Qi Chen
Qingcai Chen
Richard J. Chen
Runnan Chen
Rui Chen
Shuo Chen
Sentao Chen
Shaoyu Chen
Shixing Chen

Shuai Chen
Shuya Chen
Sizhe Chen
Simin Chen
Shaoxiang Chen
Zitian Chen
Tianlong Chen
Tianshui Chen
Min-Hung Chen
Xiangning Chen
Xin Chen
Xinghao Chen
Xuejin Chen
Xu Chen
Xuxi Chen
Yunlu Chen
Yanbei Chen
Yuxiao Chen
Yun-Chun Chen
Yi-Ting Chen
Yi-Wen Chen
Yinbo Chen
Yiran Chen
Yuanhong Chen
Yubei Chen
Yuefeng Chen
Yuhua Chen
Yukang Chen
Zerui Chen
Zhaoyu Chen
Zhen Chen
Zhenyu Chen
Zhi Chen
Zhiwei Chen
Zhixiang Chen
Long Chen
Bowen Cheng
Jun Cheng
Yi Cheng
Jingchun Cheng
Lechao Cheng
Xi Cheng
Yuan Cheng
Ho Kei Cheng
Kevin Ho Man Cheng

Jiacheng Cheng
Kelvin B. Cheng
Li Cheng
Mengjun Cheng
Zhen Cheng
Qingrong Cheng
Tianheng Cheng
Harry Cheng
Yihua Cheng
Yu Cheng
Ziheng Cheng
Soon Yau Cheong
Anoop Cherian
Manuela Chessa
Zhixiang Chi
Naoki Chiba
Julian Chibane
Kashyap Chitta
Tai-Yin Chiu
Hsu-kuang Chiu
Wei-Chen Chiu
Sungmin Cho
Donghyeon Cho
Hyeon Cho
Yooshin Cho
Gyusang Cho
Jang Hyun Cho
Seungju Cho
Nam Ik Cho
Sunghyun Cho
Hanbyel Cho
Jaesung Choe
Jooyoung Choi
Chiho Choi
Changwoon Choi
Jongwon Choi
Myungsub Choi
Dooseop Choi
Jonghyun Choi
Jinwoo Choi
Jun Won Choi
Min-Kook Choi
Hongsuk Choi
Janghoon Choi
Yoon-Ho Choi

Yukyung Choi
Jaegul Choo
Ayush Chopra
Siddharth Choudhary
Subhabrata Choudhury
Vasileios Choutas
Ka-Ho Chow
Pinaki Nath Chowdhury
Sammy Christen
Anders Christensen
Grigorios Chrysos
Hang Chu
Wen-Hsuan Chu
Peng Chu
Qi Chu
Ruihang Chu
Wei-Ta Chu
Yung-Yu Chuang
Sanghyuk Chun
Se Young Chun
Antonio Cinà
Ramazan Gokberk Cinbis
Javier Civera
Albert Clapés
Ronald Clark
Brian S. Clipp
Felipe Codevilla
Daniel Coelho de Castro
Niv Cohen
Forrester Cole
Maxwell D. Collins
Robert T. Collins
Marc Comino Trinidad
Runmin Cong
Wenyan Cong
Maxime Cordy
Marcella Cornia
Enric Corona
Huseyin Coskun
Luca Cosmo
Dragos Costea
Davide Cozzolino
Arun C. S. Kumar
Aiyu Cui
Qiongjie Cui

Quan Cui
Shuhao Cui
Yiming Cui
Ying Cui
Zijun Cui
Jiali Cui
Jiequan Cui
Yawen Cui
Zhen Cui
Zhaopeng Cui
Jack Culpepper
Xiaodong Cun
Ross Cutler
Adam Czajka
Ali Dabouei
Konstantinos M. Dafnis
Manuel Dahnert
Tao Dai
Yuchao Dai
Bo Dai
Mengyu Dai
Hang Dai
Haixing Dai
Peng Dai
Pingyang Dai
Qi Dai
Qiyu Dai
Yutong Dai
Naser Damer
Zhiyuan Dang
Mohamed Daoudi
Ayan Das
Abir Das
Debasmit Das
Deepayan Das
Partha Das
Sagnik Das
Soumi Das
Srijan Das
Swagatam Das
Avijit Dasgupta
Jim Davis
Adrian K. Davison
Homa Davoudi
Laura Daza

Matthias De Lange
Shalini De Mello
Marco De Nadai
Christophe De
　　Vleeschouwer
Alp Dener
Boyang Deng
Congyue Deng
Bailin Deng
Yong Deng
Yc Deng
Zhuo Deng
Zhijie Deng
Xiaoming Deng
Jiankang Deng
Jinhong Deng
Jingjing Deng
Liang-Jian Deng
Siqi Deng
Xiang Deng
Xueqing Deng
Zhongying Deng
Karan Desai
Jean-Emmanuel Deschaud
Aniket Anand Deshmukh
Neel Dey
Helisa Dhamo
Prithviraj Dhar
Amaya Dharmasiri
Yan Di
Xing Di
Ousmane A. Dia
Haiwen Diao
Xiaolei Diao
Gonçalo José Dias Pais
Abdallah Dib
Anastasios Dimou
Changxing Ding
Henghui Ding
Guodong Ding
Yaqing Ding
Shuangrui Ding
Yuhang Ding
Yikang Ding
Shouhong Ding

Haisong Ding
Hui Ding
Jiahao Ding
Jian Ding
Jian-Jiun Ding
Shuxiao Ding
Tianyu Ding
Wenhao Ding
Yuqi Ding
Yi Ding
Yuzhen Ding
Zhengming Ding
Tan Minh Dinh
Vu Dinh
Christos Diou
Mandar Dixit
Bao Gia Doan
Khoa D. Doan
Dzung Anh Doan
Debi Prosad Dogra
Nehal Doiphode
Chengdong Dong
Bowen Dong
Zhenxing Dong
Hang Dong
Xiaoyi Dong
Haoye Dong
Jiangxin Dong
Shichao Dong
Xuan Dong
Zhen Dong
Shuting Dong
Jing Dong
Li Dong
Ming Dong
Nanqing Dong
Qiulei Dong
Runpei Dong
Siyan Dong
Tian Dong
Wei Dong
Xiaomeng Dong
Xin Dong
Xingbo Dong
Yuan Dong

Samuel Dooley
Gianfranco Doretto
Michael Dorkenwald
Keval Doshi
Zhaopeng Dou
Xiaotian Dou
Hazel Doughty
Ahmad Droby
Iddo Drori
Jie Du
Yong Du
Dawei Du
Dong Du
Ruoyi Du
Yuntao Du
Xuefeng Du
Yilun Du
Yuming Du
Radhika Dua
Haodong Duan
Jiafei Duan
Kaiwen Duan
Peiqi Duan
Ye Duan
Haoran Duan
Jiali Duan
Amanda Duarte
Abhimanyu Dubey
Shiv Ram Dubey
Florian Dubost
Lukasz Dudziak
Shivam Duggal
Justin M. Dulay
Matteo Dunnhofer
Chi Nhan Duong
Thibaut Durand
Mihai Dusmanu
Ujjal Kr Dutta
Debidatta Dwibedi
Isht Dwivedi
Sai Kumar Dwivedi
Takeharu Eda
Mark Edmonds
Alexei A. Efros
Thibaud Ehret

Max Ehrlich
Mahsa Ehsanpour
Iván Eichhardt
Farshad Einabadi
Marvin Eisenberger
Hazim Kemal Ekenel
Mohamed El Banani
Ismail Elezi
Moshe Eliasof
Alaa El-Nouby
Ian Endres
Francis Engelmann
Deniz Engin
Chanho Eom
Dave Epstein
Maria C. Escobar
Victor A. Escorcia
Carlos Esteves
Sungmin Eum
Bernard J. E. Evans
Ivan Evtimov
Fevziye Irem Eyiokur
    Yaman
Matteo Fabbri
Sébastien Fabbro
Gabriele Facciolo
Masud Fahim
Bin Fan
Hehe Fan
Deng-Ping Fan
Aoxiang Fan
Chen-Chen Fan
Qi Fan
Zhaoxin Fan
Haoqi Fan
Heng Fan
Hongyi Fan
Linxi Fan
Baojie Fan
Jiayuan Fan
Lei Fan
Quanfu Fan
Yonghui Fan
Yingruo Fan
Zhiwen Fan

Zicong Fan
Sean Fanello
Jiansheng Fang
Chaowei Fang
Yuming Fang
Jianwu Fang
Jin Fang
Qi Fang
Shancheng Fang
Tian Fang
Xianyong Fang
Gongfan Fang
Zhen Fang
Hui Fang
Jiemin Fang
Le Fang
Pengfei Fang
Xiaolin Fang
Yuxin Fang
Zhaoyuan Fang
Ammarah Farooq
Azade Farshad
Zhengcong Fei
Michael Felsberg
Wei Feng
Chen Feng
Fan Feng
Andrew Feng
Xin Feng
Zheyun Feng
Ruicheng Feng
Mingtao Feng
Qianyu Feng
Shangbin Feng
Chun-Mei Feng
Zunlei Feng
Zhiyong Feng
Martin Fergie
Mustansar Fiaz
Marco Fiorucci
Michael Firman
Hamed Firooz
Volker Fischer
Corneliu O. Florea
Georgios Floros

Wolfgang Foerstner
Gianni Franchi
Jean-Sebastien Franco
Simone Frintrop
Anna Fruehstueck
Changhong Fu
Chaoyou Fu
Cheng-Yang Fu
Chi-Wing Fu
Deqing Fu
Huan Fu
Jun Fu
Kexue Fu
Ying Fu
Jianlong Fu
Jingjing Fu
Qichen Fu
Tsu-Jui Fu
Xueyang Fu
Yang Fu
Yanwei Fu
Yonggan Fu
Wolfgang Fuhl
Yasuhisa Fujii
Kent Fujiwara
Marco Fumero
Takuya Funatomi
Isabel Funke
Dario Fuoli
Antonino Furnari
Matheus A. Gadelha
Akshay Gadi Patil
Adrian Galdran
Guillermo Gallego
Silvano Galliani
Orazio Gallo
Leonardo Galteri
Matteo Gamba
Yiming Gan
Sujoy Ganguly
Harald Ganster
Boyan Gao
Changxin Gao
Daiheng Gao
Difei Gao

Chen Gao
Fei Gao
Lin Gao
Wei Gao
Yiming Gao
Junyu Gao
Guangyu Ryan Gao
Haichang Gao
Hongchang Gao
Jialin Gao
Jin Gao
Jun Gao
Katelyn Gao
Mingchen Gao
Mingfei Gao
Pan Gao
Shangqian Gao
Shanghua Gao
Xitong Gao
Yunhe Gao
Zhanning Gao
Elena Garces
Nuno Cruz Garcia
Noa Garcia
Guillermo
    Garcia-Hernando
Isha Garg
Rahul Garg
Sourav Garg
Quentin Garrido
Stefano Gasperini
Kent Gauen
Chandan Gautam
Shivam Gautam
Paul Gay
Chunjiang Ge
Shiming Ge
Wenhang Ge
Yanhao Ge
Zheng Ge
Songwei Ge
Weifeng Ge
Yixiao Ge
Yuying Ge
Shijie Geng

Zhengyang Geng
Kyle A. Genova
Georgios Georgakis
Markos Georgopoulos
Marcel Geppert
Shabnam Ghadar
Mina Ghadimi Atigh
Deepti Ghadiyaram
Maani Ghaffari Jadidi
Sedigh Ghamari
Zahra Gharaee
Michaël Gharbi
Golnaz Ghiasi
Reza Ghoddoosian
Soumya Suvra Ghosal
Adhiraj Ghosh
Arthita Ghosh
Pallabi Ghosh
Soumyadeep Ghosh
Andrew Gilbert
Igor Gilitschenski
Jhony H. Giraldo
Andreu Girbau Xalabarder
Rohit Girdhar
Sharath Girish
Xavier Giro-i-Nieto
Raja Giryes
Thomas Gittings
Nikolaos Gkanatsios
Ioannis Gkioulekas
Abhiram
    Gnanasambandam
Aurele T. Gnanha
Clement L. J. C. Godard
Arushi Goel
Vidit Goel
Shubham Goel
Zan Gojcic
Aaron K. Gokaslan
Tejas Gokhale
S. Alireza Golestaneh
Thiago L. Gomes
Nuno Goncalves
Boqing Gong
Chen Gong

Yuanhao Gong
Guoqiang Gong
Jingyu Gong
Rui Gong
Yu Gong
Mingming Gong
Neil Zhenqiang Gong
Xun Gong
Yunye Gong
Yihong Gong
Cristina I. González
Nithin Gopalakrishnan
    Nair
Gaurav Goswami
Jianping Gou
Shreyank N. Gowda
Ankit Goyal
Helmut Grabner
Patrick L. Grady
Ben Graham
Eric Granger
Douglas R. Gray
Matej Grcić
David Griffiths
Jinjin Gu
Yun Gu
Shuyang Gu
Jianyang Gu
Fuqiang Gu
Jiatao Gu
Jindong Gu
Jiaqi Gu
Jinwei Gu
Jiaxin Gu
Geonmo Gu
Xiao Gu
Xinqian Gu
Xiuye Gu
Yuming Gu
Zhangxuan Gu
Dayan Guan
Junfeng Guan
Qingji Guan
Tianrui Guan
Shanyan Guan

Denis A. Gudovskiy
Ricardo Guerrero
Pierre-Louis Guhur
Jie Gui
Liangyan Gui
Liangke Gui
Benoit Guillard
Erhan Gundogdu
Manuel Günther
Jingcai Guo
Yuanfang Guo
Junfeng Guo
Chenqi Guo
Dan Guo
Hongji Guo
Jia Guo
Jie Guo
Minghao Guo
Shi Guo
Yanhui Guo
Yangyang Guo
Yuan-Chen Guo
Yilu Guo
Yiluan Guo
Yong Guo
Guangyu Guo
Haiyun Guo
Jinyang Guo
Jianyuan Guo
Pengsheng Guo
Pengfei Guo
Shuxuan Guo
Song Guo
Tianyu Guo
Qing Guo
Qiushan Guo
Wen Guo
Xiefan Guo
Xiaohu Guo
Xiaoqing Guo
Yufei Guo
Yuhui Guo
Yuliang Guo
Yunhui Guo
Yanwen Guo

Akshita Gupta
Ankush Gupta
Kamal Gupta
Kartik Gupta
Ritwik Gupta
Rohit Gupta
Siddharth Gururani
Fredrik K. Gustafsson
Abner Guzman Rivera
Vladimir Guzov
Matthew A. Gwilliam
Jung-Woo Ha
Marc Habermann
Isma Hadji
Christian Haene
Martin Hahner
Levente Hajder
Alexandros Haliassos
Emanuela Haller
Bumsub Ham
Abdullah J. Hamdi
Shreyas Hampali
Dongyoon Han
Chunrui Han
Dong-Jun Han
Dong-Sig Han
Guangxing Han
Zhizhong Han
Ruize Han
Jiaming Han
Jin Han
Ligong Han
Xian-Hua Han
Xiaoguang Han
Yizeng Han
Zhi Han
Zhenjun Han
Zhongyi Han
Jungong Han
Junlin Han
Kai Han
Kun Han
Sungwon Han
Songfang Han
Wei Han

Xiao Han
Xintong Han
Xinzhe Han
Yahong Han
Yan Han
Zongbo Han
Nicolai Hani
Rana Hanocka
Niklas Hanselmann
Nicklas A. Hansen
Hong Hanyu
Fusheng Hao
Yanbin Hao
Shijie Hao
Udith Haputhanthri
Mehrtash Harandi
Josh Harguess
Adam Harley
David M. Hart
Atsushi Hashimoto
Ali Hassani
Mohammed Hassanin
Yana Hasson
Joakim Bruslund Haurum
Bo He
Kun He
Chen He
Xin He
Fazhi He
Gaoqi He
Hao He
Haoyu He
Jiangpeng He
Hongliang He
Qian He
Xiangteng He
Xuming He
Yannan He
Yuhang He
Yang He
Xiangyu He
Nanjun He
Pan He
Sen He
Shengfeng He

Songtao He
Tao He
Tong He
Wei He
Xuehai He
Xiaoxiao He
Ying He
Yisheng He
Ziwen He
Peter Hedman
Felix Heide
Yacov Hel-Or
Paul Henderson
Philipp Henzler
Byeongho Heo
Jae-Pil Heo
Miran Heo
Sachini A. Herath
Stephane Herbin
Pedro Hermosilla Casajus
Monica Hernandez
Charles Herrmann
Roei Herzig
Mauricio Hess-Flores
Carlos Hinojosa
Tobias Hinz
Tsubasa Hirakawa
Chih-Hui Ho
Lam Si Tung Ho
Jennifer Hobbs
Derek Hoiem
Yannick Hold-Geoffroy
Aleksander Holynski
Cheeun Hong
Fa-Ting Hong
Hanbin Hong
Guan Zhe Hong
Danfeng Hong
Lanqing Hong
Xiaopeng Hong
Xin Hong
Jie Hong
Seungbum Hong
Cheng-Yao Hong
Seunghoon Hong

Yi Hong
Yuan Hong
Yuchen Hong
Anthony Hoogs
Maxwell C. Horton
Kazuhiro Hotta
Qibin Hou
Tingbo Hou
Junhui Hou
Ji Hou
Qiqi Hou
Rui Hou
Ruibing Hou
Zhi Hou
Henry Howard-Jenkins
Lukas Hoyer
Wei-Lin Hsiao
Chiou-Ting Hsu
Anthony Hu
Brian Hu
Yusong Hu
Hexiang Hu
Haoji Hu
Di Hu
Hengtong Hu
Haigen Hu
Lianyu Hu
Hanzhe Hu
Jie Hu
Junlin Hu
Shizhe Hu
Jian Hu
Zhiming Hu
Juhua Hu
Peng Hu
Ping Hu
Ronghang Hu
MengShun Hu
Tao Hu
Vincent Tao Hu
Xiaoling Hu
Xinting Hu
Xiaolin Hu
Xuefeng Hu
Xiaowei Hu

Yang Hu
Yueyu Hu
Zeyu Hu
Zhongyun Hu
Binh-Son Hua
Guoliang Hua
Yi Hua
Linzhi Huang
Qiusheng Huang
Bo Huang
Chen Huang
Hsin-Ping Huang
Ye Huang
Shuangping Huang
Zeng Huang
Buzhen Huang
Cong Huang
Heng Huang
Hao Huang
Qidong Huang
Huaibo Huang
Chaoqin Huang
Feihu Huang
Jiahui Huang
Jingjia Huang
Kun Huang
Lei Huang
Sheng Huang
Shuaiyi Huang
Siyu Huang
Xiaoshui Huang
Xiaoyang Huang
Yan Huang
Yihao Huang
Ying Huang
Ziling Huang
Xiaoke Huang
Yifei Huang
Haiyang Huang
Zhewei Huang
Jin Huang
Haibin Huang
Jiaxing Huang
Junjie Huang
Keli Huang

Lang Huang
Lin Huang
Luojie Huang
Mingzhen Huang
Shijia Huang
Shengyu Huang
Siyuan Huang
He Huang
Xiuyu Huang
Lianghua Huang
Yue Huang
Yaping Huang
Yuge Huang
Zehao Huang
Zeyi Huang
Zhiqi Huang
Zhongzhan Huang
Zilong Huang
Ziyuan Huang
Tianrui Hui
Zhuo Hui
Le Hui
Jing Huo
Junhwa Hur
Shehzeen S. Hussain
Chuong Minh Huynh
Seunghyun Hwang
Jaehui Hwang
Jyh-Jing Hwang
Sukjun Hwang
Soonmin Hwang
Wonjun Hwang
Rakib Hyder
Sangcck Hyun
Sarah Ibrahimi
Tomoki Ichikawa
Yerlan Idelbayev
A. S. M. Iftekhar
Masaaki Iiyama
Satoshi Ikehata
Sunghoon Im
Atul N. Ingle
Eldar Insafutdinov
Yani A. Ioannou
Radu Tudor Ionescu

Umar Iqbal
Go Irie
Muhammad Zubair Irshad
Ahmet Iscen
Berivan Isik
Ashraful Islam
Md Amirul Islam
Syed Islam
Mariko Isogawa
Vamsi Krishna K. Ithapu
Boris Ivanovic
Darshan Iyer
Sarah Jabbour
Ayush Jain
Nishant Jain
Samyak Jain
Vidit Jain
Vineet Jain
Priyank Jaini
Tomas Jakab
Mohammad A. A. K.
  Jalwana
Muhammad Abdullah
  Jamal
Hadi Jamali-Rad
Stuart James
Varun Jampani
Young Kyun Jang
YeongJun Jang
Yunseok Jang
Ronnachai Jaroensri
Bhavan Jasani
Krishna Murthy
  Jatavallabhula
Mojan Javaheripi
Syed A. Javed
Guillaume Jeanneret
Pranav Jeevan
Herve Jegou
Rohit Jena
Tomas Jenicek
Porter Jenkins
Simon Jenni
Hae-Gon Jeon
Sangryul Jeon

Boseung Jeong
Yoonwoo Jeong
Seong-Gyun Jeong
Jisoo Jeong
Allan D. Jepson
Ankit Jha
Sumit K. Jha
I-Hong Jhuo
Ge-Peng Ji
Chaonan Ji
Deyi Ji
Jingwei Ji
Wei Ji
Zhong Ji
Jiayi Ji
Pengliang Ji
Hui Ji
Mingi Ji
Xiaopeng Ji
Yuzhu Ji
Baoxiong Jia
Songhao Jia
Dan Jia
Shan Jia
Xiaojun Jia
Xiuyi Jia
Xu Jia
Menglin Jia
Wenqi Jia
Boyuan Jiang
Wenhao Jiang
Huaizu Jiang
Hanwen Jiang
Haiyong Jiang
Hao Jiang
Huajie Jiang
Huiqin Jiang
Haojun Jiang
Haobo Jiang
Junjun Jiang
Xingyu Jiang
Yangbangyan Jiang
Yu Jiang
Jianmin Jiang
Jiaxi Jiang

Jing Jiang
Kui Jiang
Li Jiang
Liming Jiang
Chiyu Jiang
Meirui Jiang
Chen Jiang
Peng Jiang
Tai-Xiang Jiang
Wen Jiang
Xinyang Jiang
Yifan Jiang
Yuming Jiang
Yingying Jiang
Zeren Jiang
ZhengKai Jiang
Zhenyu Jiang
Shuming Jiao
Jianbo Jiao
Licheng Jiao
Dongkwon Jin
Yeying Jin
Cheng Jin
Linyi Jin
Qing Jin
Taisong Jin
Xiao Jin
Xin Jin
Sheng Jin
Kyong Hwan Jin
Ruibing Jin
SouYoung Jin
Yueming Jin
Chenchen Jing
Longlong Jing
Taotao Jing
Yongcheng Jing
Younghyun Jo
Joakim Johnander
Jeff Johnson
Michael J. Jones
R. Kenny Jones
Rico Jonschkowski
Ameya Joshi
Sunghun Joung

Felix Juefei-Xu
Claudio R. Jung
Steffen Jung
Hari Chandana K.
Rahul Vigneswaran K.
Prajwal K. R.
Abhishek Kadian
Jhony Kaesemodel Pontes
Kumara Kahatapitiya
Anmol Kalia
Sinan Kalkan
Tarun Kalluri
Jaewon Kam
Sandesh Kamath
Meina Kan
Menelaos Kanakis
Takuhiro Kaneko
Di Kang
Guoliang Kang
Hao Kang
Jaeyeon Kang
Kyoungkook Kang
Li-Wei Kang
MinGuk Kang
Suk-Ju Kang
Zhao Kang
Yash Mukund Kant
Yueying Kao
Aupendu Kar
Konstantinos Karantzalos
Sezer Karaoglu
Navid Kardan
Sanjay Kariyappa
Leonid Karlinsky
Animesh Karnewar
Shyamgopal Karthik
Hirak J. Kashyap
Marc A. Kastner
Hirokatsu Kataoka
Angelos Katharopoulos
Hiroharu Kato
Kai Katsumata
Manuel Kaufmann
Chaitanya Kaul
Prakhar Kaushik

Yuki Kawana
Lei Ke
Lipeng Ke
Tsung-Wei Ke
Wei Ke
Petr Kellnhofer
Aniruddha Kembhavi
John Kender
Corentin Kervadec
Leonid Keselman
Daniel Keysers
Nima Khademi Kalantari
Taras Khakhulin
Samir Khaki
Muhammad Haris Khan
Qadeer Khan
Salman Khan
Subash Khanal
Vaishnavi M. Khindkar
Rawal Khirodkar
Saeed Khorram
Pirazh Khorramshahi
Kourosh Khoshelham
Ansh Khurana
Benjamin Kiefer
Jae Myung Kim
Junho Kim
Boah Kim
Hyeonseong Kim
Dong-Jin Kim
Dongwan Kim
Donghyun Kim
Doyeon Kim
Yonghyun Kim
Hyung-Il Kim
Hyunwoo Kim
Hyeongwoo Kim
Hyo Jin Kim
Hyunwoo J. Kim
Taehoon Kim
Jaeha Kim
Jiwon Kim
Jung Uk Kim
Kangyeol Kim
Eunji Kim

Daeha Kim
Dongwon Kim
Kunhee Kim
Kyungmin Kim
Junsik Kim
Min H. Kim
Namil Kim
Kookhoi Kim
Sanghyun Kim
Seongyeop Kim
Seungryong Kim
Saehoon Kim
Euyoung Kim
Guisik Kim
Sungyeon Kim
Sunnie S. Y. Kim
Taehun Kim
Tae Oh Kim
Won Hwa Kim
Seungwook Kim
YoungBin Kim
Youngeun Kim
Akisato Kimura
Furkan Osman Kınlı
Zsolt Kira
Hedvig Kjellström
Florian Kleber
Jan P. Klopp
Florian Kluger
Laurent Kneip
Byungsoo Ko
Muhammed Kocabas
A. Sophia Koepke
Kevin Koeser
Nick Kolkin
Nikos Kolotouros
Wai-Kin Adams Kong
Deying Kong
Caihua Kong
Youyong Kong
Shuyu Kong
Shu Kong
Tao Kong
Yajing Kong
Yu Kong

Zishang Kong
Theodora Kontogianni
Anton S. Konushin
Julian F. P. Kooij
Bruno Korbar
Giorgos Kordopatis-Zilos
Jari Korhonen
Adam Kortylewski
Denis Korzhenkov
Divya Kothandaraman
Suraj Kothawade
Iuliia Kotseruba
Satwik Kottur
Shashank Kotyan
Alexandros Kouris
Petros Koutras
Anna Kreshuk
Ranjay Krishna
Dilip Krishnan
Andrey Kuehlkamp
Hilde Kuehne
Jason Kuen
David Kügler
Arjan Kuijper
Anna Kukleva
Sumith Kulal
Viveka Kulharia
Akshay R. Kulkarni
Nilesh Kulkarni
Dominik Kulon
Abhinav Kumar
Akash Kumar
Suryansh Kumar
B. V. K. Vijaya Kumar
Pulkit Kumar
Ratnesh Kumar
Sateesh Kumar
Satish Kumar
Vijay Kumar B. G.
Nupur Kumari
Sudhakar Kumawat
Jogendra Nath Kundu
Hsien-Kai Kuo
Meng-Yu Jennifer Kuo
Vinod Kumar Kurmi

Yusuke Kurose
Keerthy Kusumam
Alina Kuznetsova
Henry Kvinge
Ho Man Kwan
Hyeokjun Kweon
Heeseung Kwon
Gihyun Kwon
Myung-Joon Kwon
Taesung Kwon
YoungJoong Kwon
Christos Kyrkou
Jorma Laaksonen
Yann Labbe
Zorah Laehner
Florent Lafarge
Hamid Laga
Manuel Lagunas
Shenqi Lai
Jian-Huang Lai
Zihang Lai
Mohamed I. Lakhal
Mohit Lamba
Meng Lan
Loic Landrieu
Zhiqiang Lang
Natalie Lang
Dong Lao
Yizhen Lao
Yingjie Lao
Issam Hadj Laradji
Gustav Larsson
Viktor Larsson
Zakaria Laskar
Stéphane Lathuilière
Chun Pong Lau
Rynson W. H. Lau
Hei Law
Justin Lazarow
Verica Lazova
Eric-Tuan Le
Hieu Le
Trung-Nghia Le
Mathias Lechner
Byeong-Uk Lee

Chen-Yu Lee
Che-Rung Lee
Chul Lee
Hong Joo Lee
Dongsoo Lee
Jiyoung Lee
Eugene Eu Tzuan Lee
Daeun Lee
Saehyung Lee
Jewook Lee
Hyungtae Lee
Hyunmin Lee
Jungbeom Lee
Joon-Young Lee
Jong-Seok Lee
Joonseok Lee
Junha Lee
Kibok Lee
Byung-Kwan Lee
Jangwon Lee
Jinho Lee
Jongmin Lee
Seunghyun Lee
Sohyun Lee
Minsik Lee
Dogyoon Lee
Seungmin Lee
Min Jun Lee
Sangho Lee
Sangmin Lee
Seungeun Lee
Seon-Ho Lee
Sungmin Lee
Sungho Lee
Sangyoun Lee
Vincent C. S. S. Lee
Jaeseong Lee
Yong Jae Lee
Chenyang Lei
Chenyi Lei
Jiahui Lei
Xinyu Lei
Yinjie Lei
Jiaxu Leng
Luziwei Leng

Jan E. Lenssen
Vincent Lepetit
Thomas Leung
María Leyva-Vallina
Xin Li
Yikang Li
Baoxin Li
Bin Li
Bing Li
Bowen Li
Changlin Li
Chao Li
Chongyi Li
Guanyue Li
Shuai Li
Jin Li
Dingquan Li
Dongxu Li
Yiting Li
Gang Li
Dian Li
Guohao Li
Haoang Li
Haoliang Li
Haoran Li
Hengduo Li
Huafeng Li
Xiaoming Li
Hanao Li
Hongwei Li
Ziqiang Li
Jisheng Li
Jiacheng Li
Jia Li
Jiachen Li
Jiahao Li
Jianwei Li
Jiazhi Li
Jie Li
Jing Li
Jingjing Li
Jingtao Li
Jun Li
Junxuan Li
Kai Li

Kailin Li
Kenneth Li
Kun Li
Kunpeng Li
Aoxue Li
Chenglong Li
Chenglin Li
Changsheng Li
Zhichao Li
Qiang Li
Yanyu Li
Zuoyue Li
Xiang Li
Xuelong Li
Fangda Li
Ailin Li
Liang Li
Chun-Guang Li
Daiqing Li
Dong Li
Guanbin Li
Guorong Li
Haifeng Li
Jianan Li
Jianing Li
Jiaxin Li
Ke Li
Lei Li
Lincheng Li
Liulei Li
Lujun Li
Linjie Li
Lin Li
Pengyu Li
Ping Li
Qiufu Li
Qingyong Li
Rui Li
Siyuan Li
Wei Li
Wenbin Li
Xiangyang Li
Xinyu Li
Xiujun Li
Xiu Li

Xu Li
Ya-Li Li
Yao Li
Yongjie Li
Yijun Li
Yiming Li
Yuezun Li
Yu Li
Yunheng Li
Yuqi Li
Zhe Li
Zeming Li
Zhen Li
Zhengqin Li
Zhimin Li
Jiefeng Li
Jinpeng Li
Chengze Li
Jianwu Li
Lerenhan Li
Shan Li
Suichan Li
Xiangtai Li
Yanjie Li
Yandong Li
Zhuoling Li
Zhenqiang Li
Manyi Li
Maosen Li
Ji Li
Minjun Li
Mingrui Li
Mengtian Li
Junyi Li
Nianyi Li
Bo Li
Xiao Li
Peihua Li
Peike Li
Peizhao Li
Peiliang Li
Qi Li
Ren Li
Runze Li
Shile Li

Sheng Li
Shigang Li
Shiyu Li
Shuang Li
Shasha Li
Shichao Li
Tianye Li
Yuexiang Li
Wei-Hong Li
Wanhua Li
Weihao Li
Weiming Li
Weixin Li
Wenbo Li
Wenshuo Li
Weijian Li
Yunan Li
Xirong Li
Xianhang Li
Xiaoyu Li
Xueqian Li
Xuanlin Li
Xianzhi Li
Yunqiang Li
Yanjing Li
Yansheng Li
Yawei Li
Yi Li
Yong Li
Yong-Lu Li
Yuhang Li
Yu-Jhe Li
Yuxi Li
Yunsheng Li
Yanwei Li
Zechao Li
Zejian Li
Zeju Li
Zekun Li
Zhaowen Li
Zheng Li
Zhenyu Li
Zhiheng Li
Zhi Li
Zhong Li

Zhuowei Li
Zhuowan Li
Zhuohang Li
Zizhang Li
Chen Li
Yuan-Fang Li
Dongze Lian
Xiaochen Lian
Zhouhui Lian
Long Lian
Qing Lian
Jin Lianbao
Jinxiu S. Liang
Dingkang Liang
Jiahao Liang
Jianming Liang
Jingyun Liang
Kevin J. Liang
Kaizhao Liang
Chen Liang
Jie Liang
Senwei Liang
Ding Liang
Jiajun Liang
Jian Liang
Kongming Liang
Siyuan Liang
Yuanzhi Liang
Zhengfa Liang
Mingfu Liang
Xiaodan Liang
Xuefeng Liang
Yuxuan Liang
Kang Liao
Liang Liao
Hong-Yuan Mark Liao
Wentong Liao
Haofu Liao
Yue Liao
Minghui Liao
Shengcai Liao
Ting-Hsuan Liao
Xin Liao
Yinghong Liao
Teck Yian Lim

Che-Tsung Lin
Chung-Ching Lin
Chen-Hsuan Lin
Cheng Lin
Chuming Lin
Chunyu Lin
Dahua Lin
Wei Lin
Zheng Lin
Huaijia Lin
Jason Lin
Jierui Lin
Jiaying Lin
Jie Lin
Kai-En Lin
Kevin Lin
Guangfeng Lin
Jiehong Lin
Feng Lin
Hang Lin
Kwan-Yee Lin
Ke Lin
Luojun Lin
Qinghong Lin
Xiangbo Lin
Yi Lin
Zudi Lin
Shijie Lin
Yiqun Lin
Tzu-Heng Lin
Ming Lin
Shaohui Lin
SongNan Lin
Ji Lin
Tsung-Yu Lin
Xudong Lin
Yancong Lin
Yen-Chen Lin
Yiming Lin
Yuewei Lin
Zhiqiu Lin
Zinan Lin
Zhe Lin
David B. Lindell
Zhixin Ling

Zhan Ling
Alexander Liniger
Venice Erin B. Liong
Joey Litalien
Or Litany
Roee Litman
Ron Litman
Jim Little
Dor Litvak
Shaoteng Liu
Shuaicheng Liu
Andrew Liu
Xian Liu
Shaohui Liu
Bei Liu
Bo Liu
Yong Liu
Ming Liu
Yanbin Liu
Chenxi Liu
Daqi Liu
Di Liu
Difan Liu
Dong Liu
Dongfang Liu
Daizong Liu
Xiao Liu
Fangyi Liu
Fengbei Liu
Fenglin Liu
Bin Liu
Yuang Liu
Ao Liu
Hong Liu
Hongfu Liu
Huidong Liu
Ziyi Liu
Feng Liu
Hao Liu
Jie Liu
Jialun Liu
Jiang Liu
Jing Liu
Jingya Liu
Jiaming Liu

Jun Liu
Juncheng Liu
Jiawei Liu
Hongyu Liu
Chuanbin Liu
Haotian Liu
Lingqiao Liu
Chang Liu
Han Liu
Liu Liu
Min Liu
Yingqi Liu
Aishan Liu
Bingyu Liu
Benlin Liu
Boxiao Liu
Chenchen Liu
Chuanjian Liu
Daqing Liu
Huan Liu
Haozhe Liu
Jiaheng Liu
Wei Liu
Jingzhou Liu
Jiyuan Liu
Lingbo Liu
Nian Liu
Peiye Liu
Qiankun Liu
Shenglan Liu
Shilong Liu
Wen Liu
Wenyu Liu
Weifeng Liu
Wu Liu
Xiaolong Liu
Yang Liu
Yanwei Liu
Yingcheng Liu
Yongfei Liu
Yihao Liu
Yu Liu
Yunze Liu
Ze Liu
Zhenhua Liu

Zhenguang Liu
Lin Liu
Lihao Liu
Pengju Liu
Xinhai Liu
Yunfei Liu
Meng Liu
Minghua Liu
Mingyuan Liu
Miao Liu
Peirong Liu
Ping Liu
Qingjie Liu
Ruoshi Liu
Risheng Liu
Songtao Liu
Xing Liu
Shikun Liu
Shuming Liu
Sheng Liu
Songhua Liu
Tongliang Liu
Weibo Liu
Weide Liu
Weizhe Liu
Wenxi Liu
Weiyang Liu
Xin Liu
Xiaobin Liu
Xudong Liu
Xiaoyi Liu
Xihui Liu
Xinchen Liu
Xingtong Liu
Xinpeng Liu
Xinyu Liu
Xianpeng Liu
Xu Liu
Xingyu Liu
Yongtuo Liu
Yahui Liu
Yangxin Liu
Yaoyao Liu
Yaojie Liu
Yuliang Liu

Yongcheng Liu
Yuan Liu
Yufan Liu
Yu-Lun Liu
Yun Liu
Yunfan Liu
Yuanzhong Liu
Zhuoran Liu
Zhen Liu
Zheng Liu
Zhijian Liu
Zhisong Liu
Ziquan Liu
Ziyu Liu
Zhihua Liu
Zechun Liu
Zhaoyang Liu
Zhengzhe Liu
Stephan Liwicki
Shao-Yuan Lo
Sylvain Lobry
Suhas Lohit
Vishnu Suresh Lokhande
Vincenzo Lomonaco
Chengjiang Long
Guodong Long
Fuchen Long
Shangbang Long
Yang Long
Zijun Long
Vasco Lopes
Antonio M. Lopez
Roberto Javier
    Lopez-Sastre
Tobias Lorenz
Javier Lorenzo-Navarro
Yujing Lou
Qian Lou
Xiankai Lu
Changsheng Lu
Huimin Lu
Yongxi Lu
Hao Lu
Hong Lu
Jiasen Lu

Juwei Lu
Fan Lu
Guangming Lu
Jiwen Lu
Shun Lu
Tao Lu
Xiaonan Lu
Yang Lu
Yao Lu
Yongchun Lu
Zhiwu Lu
Cheng Lu
Liying Lu
Guo Lu
Xuequan Lu
Yanye Lu
Yantao Lu
Yuhang Lu
Fujun Luan
Jonathon Luiten
Jovita Lukasik
Alan Lukezic
Jonathan Samuel Lumentut
Mayank Lunayach
Ao Luo
Canjie Luo
Chong Luo
Xu Luo
Grace Luo
Jun Luo
Katie Z. Luo
Tao Luo
Cheng Luo
Fangzhou Luo
Gen Luo
Lei Luo
Sihui Luo
Weixin Luo
Yan Luo
Xiaoyan Luo
Yong Luo
Yadan Luo
Hao Luo
Ruotian Luo
Mi Luo

Tiange Luo
Wenjie Luo
Wenhan Luo
Xiao Luo
Zhiming Luo
Zhipeng Luo
Zhengyi Luo
Diogo C. Luvizon
Zhaoyang Lv
Gengyu Lyu
Lingjuan Lyu
Jun Lyu
Yuanyuan Lyu
Youwei Lyu
Yueming Lyu
Bingpeng Ma
Chao Ma
Chongyang Ma
Congbo Ma
Chih-Yao Ma
Fan Ma
Lin Ma
Haoyu Ma
Hengbo Ma
Jianqi Ma
Jiawei Ma
Jiayi Ma
Kede Ma
Kai Ma
Lingni Ma
Lei Ma
Xu Ma
Ning Ma
Benteng Ma
Cheng Ma
Andy J. Ma
Long Ma
Zhanyu Ma
Zhiheng Ma
Qianli Ma
Shiqiang Ma
Sizhuo Ma
Shiqing Ma
Xiaolong Ma
Xinzhu Ma

Gautam B. Machiraju
Spandan Madan
Mathew Magimai-Doss
Luca Magri
Behrooz Mahasseni
Upal Mahbub
Siddharth Mahendran
Paridhi Maheshwari
Rishabh Maheshwary
Mohammed Mahmoud
Shishira R. R. Maiya
Sylwia Majchrowska
Arjun Majumdar
Puspita Majumdar
Orchid Majumder
Sagnik Majumder
Ilya Makarov
Farkhod F.
   Makhmudkhujaev
Yasushi Makihara
Ankur Mali
Mateusz Malinowski
Utkarsh Mall
Srikanth Malla
Clement Mallet
Dimitrios Mallis
Yunze Man
Dipu Manandhar
Massimiliano Mancini
Murari Mandal
Raunak Manekar
Karttikeya Mangalam
Puneet Mangla
Fabian Manhardt
Sivabalan Manivasagam
Fahim Mannan
Chengzhi Mao
Hanzi Mao
Jiayuan Mao
Junhua Mao
Zhiyuan Mao
Jiageng Mao
Yunyao Mao
Zhendong Mao
Alberto Marchisio

Diego Marcos
Riccardo Marin
Aram Markosyan
Renaud Marlet
Ricardo Marques
Miquel Martí i Rabadán
Diego Martin Arroyo
Niki Martinel
Brais Martinez
Julieta Martinez
Marc Masana
Tomohiro Mashita
Timothée Masquelier
Minesh Mathew
Tetsu Matsukawa
Marwan Mattar
Bruce A. Maxwell
Christoph Mayer
Mantas Mazeika
Pratik Mazumder
Scott McCloskey
Steven McDonagh
Ishit Mehta
Jie Mei
Kangfu Mei
Jieru Mei
Xiaoguang Mei
Givi Meishvili
Luke Melas-Kyriazi
Iaroslav Melekhov
Andres Mendez-Vazquez
Heydi Mendez-Vazquez
Matias Mendieta
Ricardo A. Mendoza-León
Chenlin Meng
Depu Meng
Rang Meng
Zibo Meng
Qingjie Meng
Qier Meng
Yanda Meng
Zihang Meng
Thomas Mensink
Fabian Mentzer
Christopher Metzler

Gregory P. Meyer
Vasileios Mezaris
Liang Mi
Lu Mi
Bo Miao
Changtao Miao
Zichen Miao
Qiguang Miao
Xin Miao
Zhongqi Miao
Frank Michel
Simone Milani
Ben Mildenhall
Roy V. Miles
Juhong Min
Kyle Min
Hyun-Seok Min
Weiqing Min
Yuecong Min
Zhixiang Min
Qi Ming
David Minnen
Aymen Mir
Deepak Mishra
Anand Mishra
Shlok K. Mishra
Niluthpol Mithun
Gaurav Mittal
Trisha Mittal
Daisuke Miyazaki
Kaichun Mo
Hong Mo
Zhipeng Mo
Davide Modolo
Abduallah A. Mohamed
Mohamed Afham
   Mohamed Aflal
Ron Mokady
Pavlo Molchanov
Davide Moltisanti
Liliane Momeni
Gianluca Monaci
Pascal Monasse
Ajoy Mondal
Tom Monnier

Aron Monszpart
Gyeongsik Moon
Suhong Moon
Taesup Moon
Sean Moran
Daniel Moreira
Pietro Morerio
Alexandre Morgand
Lia Morra
Ali Mosleh
Inbar Mosseri
Sayed Mohammad
   Mostafavi Isfahani
Saman Motamed
Ramy A. Mounir
Fangzhou Mu
Jiteng Mu
Norman Mu
Yasuhiro Mukaigawa
Ryan Mukherjee
Tanmoy Mukherjee
Yusuke Mukuta
Ravi Teja Mullapudi
Lea Müller
Matthias Müller
Martin Mundt
Nils Murrugarra-Llerena
Damien Muselet
Armin Mustafa
Muhammad Ferjad Naeem
Sauradip Nag
Hajime Nagahara
Pravin Nagar
Rajendra Nagar
Naveen Shankar Nagaraja
Varun Nagaraja
Tushar Nagarajan
Seungjun Nah
Gaku Nakano
Yuta Nakashima
Giljoo Nam
Seonghyeon Nam
Liangliang Nan
Yuesong Nan
Yeshwanth Napolean

Dinesh Reddy
   Narapureddy
Medhini Narasimhan
Supreeth
   Narasimhaswamy
Sriram Narayanan
Erickson R. Nascimento
Varun Nasery
K. L. Navaneet
Pablo Navarrete Michelini
Shant Navasardyan
Shah Nawaz
Nihal Nayak
Farhood Negin
Lukáš Neumann
Alejandro Newell
Evonne Ng
Kam Woh Ng
Tony Ng
Anh Nguyen
Tuan Anh Nguyen
Cuong Cao Nguyen
Ngoc Cuong Nguyen
Thanh Nguyen
Khoi Nguyen
Phi Le Nguyen
Phong Ha Nguyen
Tam Nguyen
Truong Nguyen
Anh Tuan Nguyen
Rang Nguyen
Thao Thi Phuong Nguyen
Van Nguyen Nguyen
Zhen-Liang Ni
Yao Ni
Shijie Nie
Xuecheng Nie
Yongwei Nie
Weizhi Nie
Ying Nie
Yinyu Nie
Kshitij N. Nikhal
Simon Niklaus
Xuefei Ning
Jifeng Ning

Yotam Nitzan
Di Niu
Shuaicheng Niu
Li Niu
Wei Niu
Yulei Niu
Zhenxing Niu
Albert No
Shohei Nobuhara
Nicoletta Noceti
Junhyug Noh
Sotiris Nousias
Slawomir Nowaczyk
Ewa M. Nowara
Valsamis Ntouskos
Gilberto Ochoa-Ruiz
Ferda Ofli
Jihyong Oh
Sangyun Oh
Youngtaek Oh
Hiroki Ohashi
Takahiro Okabe
Kemal Oksuz
Fumio Okura
Daniel Olmeda Reino
Matthew Olson
Carl Olsson
Roy Or-El
Alessandro Ortis
Guillermo Ortiz-Jimenez
Magnus Oskarsson
Ahmed A. A. Osman
Martin R. Oswald
Mayu Otani
Naima Otberdout
Cheng Ouyang
Jiahong Ouyang
Wanli Ouyang
Andrew Owens
Poojan B. Oza
Mete Ozay
A. Cengiz Oztireli
Gautam Pai
Tomas Pajdla
Umapada Pal

Simone Palazzo
Luca Palmieri
Bowen Pan
Hao Pan
Lili Pan
Tai-Yu Pan
Liang Pan
Chengwei Pan
Yingwei Pan
Xuran Pan
Jinshan Pan
Xinyu Pan
Liyuan Pan
Xingang Pan
Xingjia Pan
Zhihong Pan
Zizheng Pan
Priyadarshini Panda
Rameswar Panda
Rohit Pandey
Kaiyue Pang
Bo Pang
Guansong Pang
Jiangmiao Pang
Meng Pang
Tianyu Pang
Ziqi Pang
Omiros Pantazis
Andreas Panteli
Maja Pantic
Marina Paolanti
Joao P. Papa
Samuele Papa
Mike Papadakis
Dim P. Papadopoulos
George Papandreou
Constantin Pape
Toufiq Parag
Chethan Parameshwara
Shaifali Parashar
Alejandro Pardo
Rishubh Parihar
Sarah Parisot
JaeYoo Park
Gyeong-Moon Park

Hyojin Park
Hyoungseob Park
Jongchan Park
Jae Sung Park
Kiru Park
Chunghyun Park
Kwanyong Park
Sunghyun Park
Sungrae Park
Seongsik Park
Sanghyun Park
Sungjune Park
Taesung Park
Gaurav Parmar
Paritosh Parmar
Alvaro Parra
Despoina Paschalidou
Or Patashnik
Shivansh Patel
Pushpak Pati
Prashant W. Patil
Vaishakh Patil
Suvam Patra
Jay Patravali
Badri Narayana Patro
Angshuman Paul
Sudipta Paul
Rémi Pautrat
Nick E. Pears
Adithya Pediredla
Wenjie Pei
Shmuel Peleg
Latha Pemula
Bo Peng
Houwen Peng
Yue Peng
Liangzu Peng
Baoyun Peng
Jun Peng
Pai Peng
Sida Peng
Xi Peng
Yuxin Peng
Songyou Peng
Wei Peng

Weiqi Peng
Wen-Hsiao Peng
Pramuditha Perera
Juan C. Perez
Eduardo Pérez Pellitero
Juan-Manuel Perez-Rua
Federico Pernici
Marco Pesavento
Stavros Petridis
Ilya A. Petrov
Vladan Petrovic
Mathis Petrovich
Suzanne Petryk
Hieu Pham
Quang Pham
Khoi Pham
Tung Pham
Huy Phan
Stephen Phillips
Cheng Perng Phoo
David Picard
Marco Piccirilli
Georg Pichler
A. J. Piergiovanni
Vipin Pillai
Silvia L. Pintea
Giovanni Pintore
Robinson Piramuthu
Fiora Pirri
Theodoros Pissas
Fabio Pizzati
Benjamin Planche
Bryan Plummer
Matteo Poggi
Ashwini Pokle
Georgy E. Ponimatkin
Adrian Popescu
Stefan Popov
Nikola Popović
Ronald Poppe
Angelo Porrello
Michael Potter
Charalambos Poullis
Hadi Pouransari
Omid Poursaeed

Shraman Pramanick
Mantini Pranav
Dilip K. Prasad
Meghshyam Prasad
B. H. Pawan Prasad
Shitala Prasad
Prateek Prasanna
Ekta Prashnani
Derek S. Prijatelj
Luke Y. Prince
Véronique Prinet
Victor Adrian Prisacariu
James Pritts
Thomas Probst
Sergey Prokudin
Rita Pucci
Chi-Man Pun
Matthew Purri
Haozhi Qi
Lu Qi
Lei Qi
Xianbiao Qi
Yonggang Qi
Yuankai Qi
Siyuan Qi
Guocheng Qian
Hangwei Qian
Qi Qian
Deheng Qian
Shengsheng Qian
Wen Qian
Rui Qian
Yiming Qian
Shengju Qian
Shengyi Qian
Xuelin Qian
Zhenxing Qian
Nan Qiao
Xiaotian Qiao
Jing Qin
Can Qin
Siyang Qin
Hongwei Qin
Jie Qin
Minghai Qin

Yipeng Qin
Yongqiang Qin
Wenda Qin
Xuebin Qin
Yuzhe Qin
Yao Qin
Zhenyue Qin
Zhiwu Qing
Heqian Qiu
Jiayan Qiu
Jielin Qiu
Yue Qiu
Jiaxiong Qiu
Zhongxi Qiu
Shi Qiu
Zhaofan Qiu
Zhongnan Qu
Yanyun Qu
Kha Gia Quach
Yuhui Quan
Ruijie Quan
Mike Rabbat
Rahul Shekhar Rade
Filip Radenovic
Gorjan Radevski
Bogdan Raducanu
Francesco Ragusa
Shafin Rahman
Md Mahfuzur Rahman
    Siddiquee
Hossein Rahmani
Kiran Raja
Sivaramakrishnan
    Rajaraman
Jathushan Rajasegaran
Adnan Siraj Rakin
Michaël Ramamonjisoa
Chirag A. Raman
Shanmuganathan Raman
Vignesh Ramanathan
Vasili Ramanishka
Vikram V. Ramaswamy
Merey Ramazanova
Jason Rambach
Sai Saketh Rambhatla

Clément Rambour
Ashwin Ramesh Babu
Adín Ramírez Rivera
Arianna Rampini
Haoxi Ran
Aakanksha Rana
Aayush Jung Bahadur
    Rana
Kanchana N. Ranasinghe
Aneesh Rangnekar
Samrudhdhi B. Rangrej
Harsh Rangwani
Viresh Ranjan
Anyi Rao
Yongming Rao
Carolina Raposo
Michalis Raptis
Amir Rasouli
Vivek Rathod
Adepu Ravi Sankar
Avinash Ravichandran
Bharadwaj Ravichandran
Dripta S. Raychaudhuri
Adria Recasens
Simon Reiß
Davis Rempe
Daxuan Ren
Jiawei Ren
Jimmy Ren
Sucheng Ren
Dayong Ren
Zhile Ren
Dongwei Ren
Qibing Ren
Pengfei Ren
Zhenwen Ren
Xuqian Ren
Yixuan Ren
Zhongzheng Ren
Ambareesh Revanur
Hamed Rezazadegan
    Tavakoli
Rafael S. Rezende
Wonjong Rhee
Alexander Richard

Christian Richardt
Stephan R. Richter
Benjamin Riggan
Dominik Rivoir
Mamshad Nayeem Rizve
Joshua D. Robinson
Joseph Robinson
Chris Rockwell
Ranga Rodrigo
Andres C. Rodriguez
Carlos Rodriguez-Pardo
Marcus Rohrbach
Gemma Roig
Yu Rong
David A. Ross
Mohammad Rostami
Edward Rosten
Karsten Roth
Anirban Roy
Debaditya Roy
Shuvendu Roy
Ahana Roy Choudhury
Aruni Roy Chowdhury
Denys Rozumnyi
Shulan Ruan
Wenjie Ruan
Patrick Ruhkamp
Danila Rukhovich
Anian Ruoss
Chris Russell
Dan Ruta
Dawid Damian Rymarczyk
DongHun Ryu
Hyeonggon Ryu
Kwonyoung Ryu
Balasubramanian S.
Alexandre Sablayrolles
Mohammad Sabokrou
Arka Sadhu
Aniruddha Saha
Oindrila Saha
Pritish Sahu
Aneeshan Sain
Nirat Saini
Saurabh Saini

Takeshi Saitoh
Christos Sakaridis
Fumihiko Sakaue
Dimitrios Sakkos
Ken Sakurada
Parikshit V. Sakurikar
Rohit Saluja
Nermin Samet
Leo Sampaio Ferraz
    Ribeiro
Jorge Sanchez
Enrique Sanchez
Shengtian Sang
Anush Sankaran
Soubhik Sanyal
Nikolaos Sarafianos
Vishwanath Saragadam
István Sárándi
Saquib Sarfraz
Mert Bulent Sariyildiz
Anindya Sarkar
Pritam Sarkar
Paul-Edouard Sarlin
Hiroshi Sasaki
Takami Sato
Torsten Sattler
Ravi Kumar Satzoda
Axel Sauer
Stefano Savian
Artem Savkin
Manolis Savva
Gerald Schaefer
Simone Schaub-Meyer
Yoni Schirris
Samuel Schulter
Katja Schwarz
Jesse Scott
Sinisa Segvic
Constantin Marc Seibold
Lorenzo Seidenari
Matan Sela
Fadime Sener
Paul Hongsuck Seo
Kwanggyoon Seo
Hongje Seong

Dario Serez
Francesco Setti
Bryan Seybold
Mohamad Shahbazi
Shima Shahfar
Xinxin Shan
Caifeng Shan
Dandan Shan
Shawn Shan
Wei Shang
Jinghuan Shang
Jiaxiang Shang
Lei Shang
Sukrit Shankar
Ken Shao
Rui Shao
Jie Shao
Mingwen Shao
Aashish Sharma
Gaurav Sharma
Vivek Sharma
Abhishek Sharma
Yoli Shavit
Shashank Shekhar
Sumit Shekhar
Zhijie Shen
Fengyi Shen
Furao Shen
Jialie Shen
Jingjing Shen
Ziyi Shen
Linlin Shen
Guangyu Shen
Biluo Shen
Falong Shen
Jiajun Shen
Qiu Shen
Qiuhong Shen
Shuai Shen
Wang Shen
Yiqing Shen
Yunhang Shen
Siqi Shen
Bin Shen
Tianwei Shen

Xi Shen
Yilin Shen
Yuming Shen
Yucong Shen
Zhiqiang Shen
Lu Sheng
Yichen Sheng
Shivanand Venkanna
  Sheshappanavar
Shelly Sheynin
Baifeng Shi
Ruoxi Shi
Botian Shi
Hailin Shi
Jia Shi
Jing Shi
Shaoshuai Shi
Baoguang Shi
Boxin Shi
Hengcan Shi
Tianyang Shi
Xiaodan Shi
Yongjie Shi
Zhensheng Shi
Yinghuan Shi
Weiqi Shi
Wu Shi
Xuepeng Shi
Xiaoshuang Shi
Yujiao Shi
Zenglin Shi
Zhenmei Shi
Takashi Shibata
Meng-Li Shih
Yichang Shih
Hyunjung Shim
Dongseok Shim
Soshi Shimada
Inkyu Shin
Jinwoo Shin
Seungjoo Shin
Seungjae Shin
Koichi Shinoda
Suprosanna Shit

Palaiahnakote
  Shivakumara
Eli Shlizerman
Gaurav Shrivastava
Xiao Shu
Xiangbo Shu
Xiujun Shu
Yang Shu
Tianmin Shu
Jun Shu
Zhixin Shu
Bing Shuai
Maria Shugrina
Ivan Shugurov
Satya Narayan Shukla
Pranjay Shyam
Jianlou Si
Yawar Siddiqui
Alberto Signoroni
Pedro Silva
Jae-Young Sim
Oriane Siméoni
Martin Simon
Andrea Simonelli
Abhishek Singh
Ashish Singh
Dinesh Singh
Gurkirt Singh
Krishna Kumar Singh
Mannat Singh
Pravendra Singh
Rajat Vikram Singh
Utkarsh Singhal
Dipika Singhania
Vasu Singla
Harsh Sinha
Sudipta Sinha
Josef Sivic
Elena Sizikova
Geri Skenderi
Ivan Skorokhodov
Dmitriy Smirnov
Cameron Y. Smith
James S. Smith
Patrick Snape

Mattia Soldan
Hyeongseok Son
Sanghyun Son
Chuanbiao Song
Chen Song
Chunfeng Song
Dan Song
Dongjin Song
Hwanjun Song
Guoxian Song
Jiaming Song
Jie Song
Liangchen Song
Ran Song
Luchuan Song
Xibin Song
Li Song
Fenglong Song
Guoli Song
Guanglu Song
Zhenbo Song
Lin Song
Xinhang Song
Yang Song
Yibing Song
Rajiv Soundararajan
Hossein Souri
Cristovao Sousa
Riccardo Spezialetti
Leonidas Spinoulas
Michael W. Spratling
Deepak Sridhar
Srinath Sridhar
Gaurang Sriramanan
Vinkle Kumar Srivastav
Themos Stafylakis
Serban Stan
Anastasis Stathopoulos
Markus Steinberger
Jan Steinbrener
Sinisa Stekovic
Alexandros Stergiou
Gleb Sterkin
Rainer Stiefelhagen
Pierre Stock

Ombretta Strafforello
Julian Straub
Yannick Strümpler
Joerg Stueckler
Hang Su
Weijie Su
Jong-Chyi Su
Bing Su
Haisheng Su
Jinming Su
Yiyang Su
Yukun Su
Yuxin Su
Zhuo Su
Zhaoqi Su
Xiu Su
Yu-Chuan Su
Zhixun Su
Arulkumar Subramaniam
Akshayvarun Subramanya
A. Subramanyam
Swathikiran Sudhakaran
Yusuke Sugano
Masanori Suganuma
Yumin Suh
Yang Sui
Baochen Sun
Cheng Sun
Long Sun
Guolei Sun
Haoliang Sun
Haomiao Sun
He Sun
Hanqing Sun
Hao Sun
Lichao Sun
Jiachen Sun
Jiaming Sun
Jian Sun
Jin Sun
Jennifer J. Sun
Tiancheng Sun
Libo Sun
Peize Sun
Qianru Sun

Shanlin Sun
Yu Sun
Zhun Sun
Che Sun
Lin Sun
Tao Sun
Yiyou Sun
Chunyi Sun
Chong Sun
Weiwei Sun
Weixuan Sun
Xiuyu Sun
Yanan Sun
Zeren Sun
Zhaodong Sun
Zhiqing Sun
Minhyuk Sung
Jinli Suo
Simon Suo
Abhijit Suprem
Anshuman Suri
Saksham Suri
Joshua M. Susskind
Roman Suvorov
Gurumurthy Swaminathan
Robin Swanson
Paul Swoboda
Tabish A. Syed
Richard Szeliski
Fariborz Taherkhani
Yu-Wing Tai
Keita Takahashi
Walter Talbott
Gary Tam
Masato Tamura
Feitong Tan
Fuwen Tan
Shuhan Tan
Andong Tan
Bin Tan
Cheng Tan
Jianchao Tan
Lei Tan
Mingxing Tan
Xin Tan

Zichang Tan
Zhentao Tan
Kenichiro Tanaka
Masayuki Tanaka
Yushun Tang
Hao Tang
Jingqun Tang
Jinhui Tang
Kaihua Tang
Luming Tang
Lv Tang
Sheyang Tang
Shitao Tang
Siliang Tang
Shixiang Tang
Yansong Tang
Keke Tang
Chang Tang
Chenwei Tang
Jie Tang
Junshu Tang
Ming Tang
Peng Tang
Xu Tang
Yao Tang
Chen Tang
Fan Tang
Haoran Tang
Shengeng Tang
Yehui Tang
Zhipeng Tang
Ugo Tanielian
Chaofan Tao
Jiale Tao
Junli Tao
Renshuai Tao
An Tao
Guanhong Tao
Zhiqiang Tao
Makarand Tapaswi
Jean-Philippe G. Tarel
Juan J. Tarrio
Enzo Tartaglione
Keisuke Tateno
Zachary Teed

Ajinkya B. Tejankar
Bugra Tekin
Purva Tendulkar
Damien Teney
Minggui Teng
Chris Tensmeyer
Andrew Beng Jin Teoh
Philipp Terhörst
Kartik Thakral
Nupur Thakur
Kevin Thandiackal
Spyridon Thermos
Diego Thomas
William Thong
Yuesong Tian
Guanzhong Tian
Lin Tian
Shiqi Tian
Kai Tian
Meng Tian
Tai-Peng Tian
Zhuotao Tian
Shangxuan Tian
Tian Tian
Yapeng Tian
Yu Tian
Yuxin Tian
Leslie Ching Ow Tiong
Praveen Tirupattur
Garvita Tiwari
George Toderici
Antoine Toisoul
Aysim Toker
Tatiana Tommasi
Zhan Tong
Alessio Tonioni
Alessandro Torcinovich
Fabio Tosi
Matteo Toso
Hugo Touvron
Quan Hung Tran
Son Tran
Hung Tran
Ngoc-Trung Tran
Vinh Tran

Phong Tran
Giovanni Trappolini
Edith Tretschk
Subarna Tripathi
Shubhendu Trivedi
Eduard Trulls
Prune Truong
Thanh-Dat Truong
Tomasz Trzcinski
Sam Tsai
Yi-Hsuan Tsai
Ethan Tseng
Yu-Chee Tseng
Shahar Tsiper
Stavros Tsogkas
Shikui Tu
Zhigang Tu
Zhengzhong Tu
Richard Tucker
Sergey Tulyakov
Cigdem Turan
Daniyar Turmukhambetov
Victor G. Turrisi da Costa
Bartlomiej Twardowski
Christopher D. Twigg
Radim Tylecek
Mostofa Rafid Uddin
Md. Zasim Uddin
Kohei Uehara
Nicolas Ugrinovic
Youngjung Uh
Norimichi Ukita
Anwaar Ulhaq
Devesh Upadhyay
Paul Upchurch
Yoshitaka Ushiku
Yuzuko Utsumi
Mikaela Angelina Uy
Mohit Vaishnav
Pratik Vaishnavi
Jeya Maria Jose Valanarasu
Matias A. Valdenegro Toro
Diego Valsesia
Wouter Van Gansbeke
Nanne van Noord

Simon Vandenhende
Farshid Varno
Cristina Vasconcelos
Francisco Vasconcelos
Alex Vasilescu
Subeesh Vasu
Arun Balajee Vasudevan
Kanav Vats
Vaibhav S. Vavilala
Sagar Vaze
Javier Vazquez-Corral
Andrea Vedaldi
Olga Veksler
Andreas Velten
Sai H. Vemprala
Raviteja Vemulapalli
Shashanka
    Venkataramanan
Dor Verbin
Luisa Verdoliva
Manisha Verma
Yashaswi Verma
Constantin Vertan
Eli Verwimp
Deepak Vijaykeerthy
Pablo Villanueva
Ruben Villegas
Markus Vincze
Vibhav Vineet
Minh P. Vo
Huy V. Vo
Duc Minh Vo
Tomas Vojir
Igor Vozniak
Nicholas Vretos
Vibashan VS
Tuan-Anh Vu
Thang Vu
Mårten Wadenbäck
Neal Wadhwa
Aaron T. Walsman
Steven Walton
Jin Wan
Alvin Wan
Jia Wan

Jun Wan

Xiaoyue Wan

Fang Wan

Guowei Wan

Renjie Wan

Zhiqiang Wan

Ziyu Wan

Bastian Wandt

Dongdong Wang

Limin Wang

Haiyang Wang

Xiaobing Wang

Angtian Wang

Angelina Wang

Bing Wang

Bo Wang

Boyu Wang

Binghui Wang

Chen Wang

Chien-Yi Wang

Congli Wang

Qi Wang

Chengrui Wang

Rui Wang

Yiqun Wang

Cong Wang

Wenjing Wang

Dongkai Wang

Di Wang

Xiaogang Wang

Kai Wang

Zhizhong Wang

Fangjinhua Wang

Feng Wang

Hang Wang

Gaoang Wang

Guoqing Wang

Guangcong Wang

Guangzhi Wang

Hanqing Wang

Hao Wang

Haohan Wang

Haoran Wang

Hong Wang

Haotao Wang

Hu Wang

Huan Wang

Hua Wang

Hui-Po Wang

Hengli Wang

Hanyu Wang

Hongxing Wang

Jingwen Wang

Jialiang Wang

Jian Wang

Jianyi Wang

Jiashun Wang

Jiahao Wang

Tsun-Hsuan Wang

Xiaoqian Wang

Jinqiao Wang

Jun Wang

Jianzong Wang

Kaihong Wang

Ke Wang

Lei Wang

Lingjing Wang

Linnan Wang

Lin Wang

Liansheng Wang

Mengjiao Wang

Manning Wang

Nannan Wang

Peihao Wang

Jiayun Wang

Pu Wang

Qiang Wang

Qiufeng Wang

Qilong Wang

Qiangchang Wang

Qin Wang

Qing Wang

Ruocheng Wang

Ruibin Wang

Ruisheng Wang

Ruizhe Wang

Runqi Wang

Runzhong Wang

Wenxuan Wang

Sen Wang

Shangfei Wang

Shaofei Wang

Shijie Wang

Shiqi Wang

Zhibo Wang

Song Wang

Xinjiang Wang

Tai Wang

Tao Wang

Teng Wang

Xiang Wang

Tianren Wang

Tiantian Wang

Tianyi Wang

Fengjiao Wang

Wei Wang

Miaohui Wang

Suchen Wang

Siyue Wang

Yaoming Wang

Xiao Wang

Ze Wang

Biao Wang

Chaofei Wang

Dong Wang

Gu Wang

Guangrun Wang

Guangming Wang

Guo-Hua Wang

Haoqing Wang

Hesheng Wang

Huafeng Wang

Jinghua Wang

Jingdong Wang

Jingjing Wang

Jingya Wang

Jingkang Wang

Jiakai Wang

Junke Wang

Kuo Wang

Lichen Wang

Lizhi Wang

Longguang Wang

Mang Wang

Mei Wang

Min Wang
Peng-Shuai Wang
Run Wang
Shaoru Wang
Shuhui Wang
Tan Wang
Tiancai Wang
Tianqi Wang
Wenhai Wang
Wenzhe Wang
Xiaobo Wang
Xiudong Wang
Xu Wang
Yajie Wang
Yan Wang
Yuan-Gen Wang
Yingqian Wang
Yizhi Wang
Yulin Wang
Yu Wang
Yujie Wang
Yunhe Wang
Yuxi Wang
Yaowei Wang
Yiwei Wang
Zezheng Wang
Hongzhi Wang
Zhiqiang Wang
Ziteng Wang
Ziwei Wang
Zheng Wang
Zhenyu Wang
Binglu Wang
Zhongdao Wang
Ce Wang
Weining Wang
Weiyao Wang
Wenbin Wang
Wenguan Wang
Guangting Wang
Haolin Wang
Haiyan Wang
Huiyu Wang
Naiyan Wang
Jingbo Wang

Jinpeng Wang
Jiaqi Wang
Liyuan Wang
Lizhen Wang
Ning Wang
Wenqian Wang
Sheng-Yu Wang
Weimin Wang
Xiaohan Wang
Yifan Wang
Yi Wang
Yongtao Wang
Yizhou Wang
Zhuo Wang
Zhe Wang
Xudong Wang
Xiaofang Wang
Xinggang Wang
Xiaosen Wang
Xiaosong Wang
Xiaoyang Wang
Lijun Wang
Xinlong Wang
Xuan Wang
Xue Wang
Yangang Wang
Yaohui Wang
Yu-Chiang Frank Wang
Yida Wang
Yilin Wang
Yi Ru Wang
Yali Wang
Yinglong Wang
Yufu Wang
Yujiang Wang
Yuwang Wang
Yuting Wang
Yang Wang
Yu-Xiong Wang
Yixu Wang
Ziqi Wang
Zhicheng Wang
Zeyu Wang
Zhaowen Wang
Zhenyi Wang

Zhenzhi Wang
Zhijie Wang
Zhiyong Wang
Zhongling Wang
Zhuowei Wang
Zian Wang
Zifu Wang
Zihao Wang
Zirui Wang
Ziyan Wang
Wenxiao Wang
Zhen Wang
Zhepeng Wang
Zi Wang
Zihao W. Wang
Steven L. Waslander
Olivia Watkins
Daniel Watson
Silvan Weder
Dongyoon Wee
Dongming Wei
Tianyi Wei
Jia Wei
Dong Wei
Fangyun Wei
Longhui Wei
Mingqiang Wei
Xinyue Wei
Chen Wei
Donglai Wei
Pengxu Wei
Xing Wei
Xiu-Shen Wei
Wenqi Wei
Guoqiang Wei
Wei Wei
XingKui Wei
Xian Wei
Xingxing Wei
Yake Wei
Yuxiang Wei
Yi Wei
Luca Weihs
Michael Weinmann
Martin Weinmann

Congcong Wen
Chuan Wen
Jie Wen
Sijia Wen
Song Wen
Chao Wen
Xiang Wen
Zeyi Wen
Xin Wen
Yilin Wen
Yijia Weng
Shuchen Weng
Junwu Weng
Wenming Weng
Renliang Weng
Zhenyu Weng
Xinshuo Weng
Nicholas J. Westlake
Gordon Wetzstein
Lena M. Widin Klasén
Rick Wildes
Bryan M. Williams
William Williem
Ole Winther
Scott Wisdom
Alex Wong
Chau-Wai Wong
Kwan-Yee K. Wong
Yongkang Wong
Scott Workman
Marcel Worring
Michael Wray
Safwan Wshah
Xiang Wu
Aming Wu
Chongruo Wu
Cho-Ying Wu
Chunpeng Wu
Chenyan Wu
Ziyi Wu
Fuxiang Wu
Gang Wu
Haiping Wu
Huisi Wu
Jane Wu

Jialian Wu
Jing Wu
Jinjian Wu
Jianlong Wu
Xian Wu
Lifang Wu
Lifan Wu
Minye Wu
Qianyi Wu
Rongliang Wu
Rui Wu
Shiqian Wu
Shuzhe Wu
Shangzhe Wu
Tsung-Han Wu
Tz-Ying Wu
Ting-Wei Wu
Jiannan Wu
Zhiliang Wu
Yu Wu
Chenyun Wu
Dayan Wu
Dongxian Wu
Fei Wu
Hefeng Wu
Jianxin Wu
Weibin Wu
Wenxuan Wu
Wenhao Wu
Xiao Wu
Yicheng Wu
Yuanwei Wu
Yu-Huan Wu
Zhenxin Wu
Zhenyu Wu
Wei Wu
Peng Wu
Xiaohe Wu
Xindi Wu
Xinxing Wu
Xinyi Wu
Xingjiao Wu
Xiongwei Wu
Yangzheng Wu
Yanzhao Wu

Yawen Wu
Yong Wu
Yi Wu
Ying Nian Wu
Zhenyao Wu
Zhonghua Wu
Zongze Wu
Zuxuan Wu
Stefanie Wuhrer
Teng Xi
Jianing Xi
Fei Xia
Haifeng Xia
Menghan Xia
Yuanqing Xia
Zhihua Xia
Xiaobo Xia
Weihao Xia
Shihong Xia
Yan Xia
Yong Xia
Zhaoyang Xia
Zhihao Xia
Chuhua Xian
Yongqin Xian
Wangmeng Xiang
Fanbo Xiang
Tiange Xiang
Tao Xiang
Liuyu Xiang
Xiaoyu Xiang
Zhiyu Xiang
Aoran Xiao
Chunxia Xiao
Fanyi Xiao
Jimin Xiao
Jun Xiao
Taihong Xiao
Anqi Xiao
Junfei Xiao
Jing Xiao
Liang Xiao
Yang Xiao
Yuting Xiao
Yijun Xiao

Yao Xiao
Zeyu Xiao
Zhisheng Xiao
Zihao Xiao
Binhui Xie
Christopher Xie
Haozhe Xie
Jin Xie
Guo-Sen Xie
Hongtao Xie
Ming-Kun Xie
Tingting Xie
Chaohao Xie
Weicheng Xie
Xudong Xie
Jiyang Xie
Xiaohua Xie
Yuan Xie
Zhenyu Xie
Ning Xie
Xianghui Xie
Xiufeng Xie
You Xie
Yutong Xie
Fuyong Xing
Yifan Xing
Zhen Xing
Yuanjun Xiong
Jinhui Xiong
Weihua Xiong
Hongkai Xiong
Zhitong Xiong
Yuanhao Xiong
Yunyang Xiong
Yuwen Xiong
Zhiwei Xiong
Yuliang Xiu
An Xu
Chang Xu
Chenliang Xu
Chengming Xu
Chenshu Xu
Xiang Xu
Huijuan Xu
Zhe Xu

Jie Xu
Jingyi Xu
Jiarui Xu
Yinghao Xu
Kele Xu
Ke Xu
Li Xu
Linchuan Xu
Linning Xu
Mengde Xu
Mengmeng Frost Xu
Min Xu
Mingye Xu
Jun Xu
Ning Xu
Peng Xu
Runsheng Xu
Sheng Xu
Wenqiang Xu
Xiaogang Xu
Renzhe Xu
Kaidi Xu
Yi Xu
Chi Xu
Qiuling Xu
Baobei Xu
Feng Xu
Haohang Xu
Haofei Xu
Lan Xu
Mingze Xu
Songcen Xu
Weipeng Xu
Wenjia Xu
Wenju Xu
Xiangyu Xu
Xin Xu
Yinshuang Xu
Yixing Xu
Yuting Xu
Yanyu Xu
Zhenbo Xu
Zhiliang Xu
Zhiyuan Xu
Xiaohao Xu

Yanwu Xu
Yan Xu
Yiran Xu
Yifan Xu
Yufei Xu
Yong Xu
Zichuan Xu
Zenglin Xu
Zexiang Xu
Zhan Xu
Zheng Xu
Zhiwei Xu
Ziyue Xu
Shiyu Xuan
Hanyu Xuan
Fei Xue
Jianru Xue
Mingfu Xue
Qinghan Xue
Tianfan Xue
Chao Xue
Chuhui Xue
Nan Xue
Zhou Xue
Xiangyang Xue
Yuan Xue
Abhay Yadav
Ravindra Yadav
Kota Yamaguchi
Toshihiko Yamasaki
Kohei Yamashita
Chaochao Yan
Feng Yan
Kun Yan
Qingsen Yan
Qixin Yan
Rui Yan
Siming Yan
Xinchen Yan
Yaping Yan
Bin Yan
Qingan Yan
Shen Yan
Shipeng Yan
Xu Yan

Yan Yan
Yichao Yan
Zhaoyi Yan
Zike Yan
Zhiqiang Yan
Hongliang Yan
Zizheng Yan
Jiewen Yang
Anqi Joyce Yang
Shan Yang
Anqi Yang
Antoine Yang
Bo Yang
Baoyao Yang
Chenhongyi Yang
Dingkang Yang
De-Nian Yang
Dong Yang
David Yang
Fan Yang
Fengyu Yang
Fengting Yang
Fei Yang
Gengshan Yang
Heng Yang
Han Yang
Huan Yang
Yibo Yang
Jiancheng Yang
Jihan Yang
Jiawei Yang
Jiayu Yang
Jie Yang
Jinfa Yang
Jingkang Yang
Jinyu Yang
Cheng-Fu Yang
Ji Yang
Jianyu Yang
Kailun Yang
Tian Yang
Luyu Yang
Liang Yang
Li Yang
Michael Ying Yang

Yang Yang
Muli Yang
Le Yang
Qiushi Yang
Ren Yang
Ruihan Yang
Shuang Yang
Siyuan Yang
Su Yang
Shiqi Yang
Taojiannan Yang
Tianyu Yang
Lei Yang
Wanzhao Yang
Shuai Yang
William Yang
Wei Yang
Xiaofeng Yang
Xiaoshan Yang
Xin Yang
Xuan Yang
Xu Yang
Xingyi Yang
Xitong Yang
Jing Yang
Yanchao Yang
Wenming Yang
Yujiu Yang
Herb Yang
Jianfei Yang
Jinhui Yang
Chuanguang Yang
Guanglei Yang
Haitao Yang
Kewei Yang
Linlin Yang
Lijin Yang
Longrong Yang
Meng Yang
MingKun Yang
Sibei Yang
Shicai Yang
Tong Yang
Wen Yang
Xi Yang

Xiaolong Yang
Xue Yang
Yubin Yang
Ze Yang
Ziyi Yang
Yi Yang
Linjie Yang
Yuzhe Yang
Yiding Yang
Zhenpei Yang
Zhaohui Yang
Zhengyuan Yang
Zhibo Yang
Zongxin Yang
Hantao Yao
Mingde Yao
Rui Yao
Taiping Yao
Ting Yao
Cong Yao
Qingsong Yao
Quanming Yao
Xu Yao
Yuan Yao
Yao Yao
Yazhou Yao
Jiawen Yao
Shunyu Yao
Pew-Thian Yap
Sudhir Yarram
Rajeev Yasarla
Peng Ye
Botao Ye
Mao Ye
Fei Ye
Hanrong Ye
Jingwen Ye
Jinwei Ye
Jiarong Ye
Mang Ye
Meng Ye
Qi Ye
Qian Ye
Qixiang Ye
Junjie Ye

Sheng Ye
Nanyang Ye
Yufei Ye
Xiaoqing Ye
Ruolin Ye
Yousef Yeganeh
Chun-Hsiao Yeh
Raymond A. Yeh
Yu-Ying Yeh
Kai Yi
Chang Yi
Renjiao Yi
Xinping Yi
Peng Yi
Alper Yilmaz
Junho Yim
Hui Yin
Bangjie Yin
Jia-Li Yin
Miao Yin
Wenzhe Yin
Xuwang Yin
Ming Yin
Yu Yin
Aoxiong Yin
Kangxue Yin
Tianwei Yin
Wei Yin
Xianghua Ying
Rio Yokota
Tatsuya Yokota
Naoto Yokoya
Ryo Yonetani
Ki Yoon Yoo
Jinsu Yoo
Sunjae Yoon
Jae Shin Yoon
Jihun Yoon
Sung-Hoon Yoon
Ryota Yoshihashi
Yusuke Yoshiyasu
Chenyu You
Haoran You
Haoxuan You
Yang You

Quanzeng You
Tackgeun You
Kaichao You
Shan You
Xinge You
Yurong You
Baosheng Yu
Bei Yu
Haichao Yu
Hao Yu
Chaohui Yu
Fisher Yu
Jin-Gang Yu
Jiyang Yu
Jason J. Yu
Jiashuo Yu
Hong-Xing Yu
Lei Yu
Mulin Yu
Ning Yu
Peilin Yu
Qi Yu
Qian Yu
Rui Yu
Shuzhi Yu
Gang Yu
Tan Yu
Weijiang Yu
Xin Yu
Bingyao Yu
Ye Yu
Hanchao Yu
Yingchen Yu
Tao Yu
Xiaotian Yu
Qing Yu
Houjian Yu
Changqian Yu
Jing Yu
Jun Yu
Shujian Yu
Xiang Yu
Zhaofei Yu
Zhenbo Yu
Yinfeng Yu

Zhuoran Yu
Zitong Yu
Bo Yuan
Jiangbo Yuan
Liangzhe Yuan
Weihao Yuan
Jianbo Yuan
Xiaoyun Yuan
Ye Yuan
Li Yuan
Geng Yuan
Jialin Yuan
Maoxun Yuan
Peng Yuan
Xin Yuan
Yuan Yuan
Yuhui Yuan
Yixuan Yuan
Zheng Yuan
Mehmet Kerim Yücel
Kaiyu Yue
Haixiao Yue
Heeseung Yun
Sangdoo Yun
Tian Yun
Mahmut Yurt
Ekim Yurtsever
Ahmet Yüzügüler
Edouard Yvinec
Eloi Zablocki
Christopher Zach
Muhammad Zaigham
    Zaheer
Pierluigi Zama Ramirez
Yuhang Zang
Pietro Zanuttigh
Alexey Zaytsev
Bernhard Zeisl
Haitian Zeng
Pengpeng Zeng
Jiabei Zeng
Runhao Zeng
Wei Zeng
Yawen Zeng
Yi Zeng

Yiming Zeng
Tieyong Zeng
Huanqiang Zeng
Dan Zeng
Yu Zeng
Wei Zhai
Yuanhao Zhai
Fangneng Zhan
Kun Zhan
Xiong Zhang
Jingdong Zhang
Jiangning Zhang
Zhilu Zhang
Gengwei Zhang
Dongsu Zhang
Hui Zhang
Binjie Zhang
Bo Zhang
Tianhao Zhang
Cecilia Zhang
Jing Zhang
Chaoning Zhang
Chenxu Zhang
Chi Zhang
Chris Zhang
Yabin Zhang
Zhao Zhang
Rufeng Zhang
Chaoyi Zhang
Zheng Zhang
Da Zhang
Yi Zhang
Edward Zhang
Xin Zhang
Feifei Zhang
Feilong Zhang
Yuqi Zhang
GuiXuan Zhang
Hanlin Zhang
Hanwang Zhang
Hanzhen Zhang
Haotian Zhang
He Zhang
Haokui Zhang
Hongyuan Zhang

Hengrui Zhang
Hongming Zhang
Mingfang Zhang
Jianpeng Zhang
Jiaming Zhang
Jichao Zhang
Jie Zhang
Jingfeng Zhang
Jingyi Zhang
Jinnian Zhang
David Junhao Zhang
Junjie Zhang
Junzhe Zhang
Jiawan Zhang
Jingyang Zhang
Kai Zhang
Lei Zhang
Lihua Zhang
Lu Zhang
Miao Zhang
Minjia Zhang
Mingjin Zhang
Qi Zhang
Qian Zhang
Qilong Zhang
Qiming Zhang
Qiang Zhang
Richard Zhang
Ruimao Zhang
Ruisi Zhang
Ruixin Zhang
Runze Zhang
Qilin Zhang
Shan Zhang
Shanshan Zhang
Xi Sheryl Zhang
Song-Hai Zhang
Chongyang Zhang
Kaihao Zhang
Songyang Zhang
Shu Zhang
Siwei Zhang
Shujian Zhang
Tianyun Zhang
Tong Zhang

Tao Zhang
Wenwei Zhang
Wenqiang Zhang
Wen Zhang
Xiaolin Zhang
Xingchen Zhang
Xingxuan Zhang
Xiuming Zhang
Xiaoshuai Zhang
Xuanmeng Zhang
Xuanyang Zhang
Xucong Zhang
Xingxing Zhang
Xikun Zhang
Xiaohan Zhang
Yahui Zhang
Yunhua Zhang
Yan Zhang
Yanghao Zhang
Yifei Zhang
Yifan Zhang
Yi-Fan Zhang
Yihao Zhang
Yingliang Zhang
Youshan Zhang
Yulun Zhang
Yushu Zhang
Yixiao Zhang
Yide Zhang
Zhongwen Zhang
Bowen Zhang
Chen-Lin Zhang
Zehua Zhang
Zekun Zhang
Zeyu Zhang
Xiaowei Zhang
Yifeng Zhang
Cheng Zhang
Hongguang Zhang
Yuexi Zhang
Fa Zhang
Guofeng Zhang
Hao Zhang
Haofeng Zhang
Hongwen Zhang

Hua Zhang	Zhizhong Zhang	Bowen Zhao
Jiaxin Zhang	Qilong Zhangli	Pu Zhao
Zhenyu Zhang	Bingyin Zhao	Bingchen Zhao
Jian Zhang	Bin Zhao	Borui Zhao
Jianfeng Zhang	Chenglong Zhao	Fuqiang Zhao
Jiao Zhang	Lei Zhao	Hanbin Zhao
Jiakai Zhang	Feng Zhao	Jian Zhao
Lefei Zhang	Gangming Zhao	Mingyang Zhao
Le Zhang	Haiyan Zhao	Na Zhao
Mi Zhang	Hao Zhao	Rongchang Zhao
Min Zhang	Handong Zhao	Ruiqi Zhao
Ning Zhang	Hengshuang Zhao	Shuai Zhao
Pan Zhang	Yinan Zhao	Wenda Zhao
Pu Zhang	Jiaojiao Zhao	Wenliang Zhao
Qing Zhang	Jiaqi Zhao	Xiangyun Zhao
Renrui Zhang	Jing Zhao	Yifan Zhao
Shifeng Zhang	Kaili Zhao	Yaping Zhao
Shuo Zhang	Haojie Zhao	Zhou Zhao
Shaoxiong Zhang	Yucheng Zhao	He Zhao
Weizhong Zhang	Longjiao Zhao	Jie Zhao
Xi Zhang	Long Zhao	Xibin Zhao
Xiaomei Zhang	Qingsong Zhao	Xiaoqi Zhao
Xinyu Zhang	Qingyu Zhao	Zhengyu Zhao
Yin Zhang	Rui Zhao	Jin Zhe
Zicheng Zhang	Rui-Wei Zhao	Chuanxia Zheng
Zihao Zhang	Sicheng Zhao	Huan Zheng
Ziqi Zhang	Shuang Zhao	Hao Zheng
Zhaoxiang Zhang	Siyan Zhao	Jia Zheng
Zhen Zhang	Zelin Zhao	Jian-Qing Zheng
Zhipeng Zhang	Shiyu Zhao	Shuai Zheng
Zhixing Zhang	Wang Zhao	Meng Zheng
Zhizheng Zhang	Tiesong Zhao	Mingkai Zheng
Jiawei Zhang	Qian Zhao	Qian Zheng
Zhong Zhang	Wangbo Zhao	Qi Zheng
Pingping Zhang	Xi-Le Zhao	Wu Zheng
Yixin Zhang	Xu Zhao	Yinqiang Zheng
Kui Zhang	Yajie Zhao	Yufeng Zheng
Lingzhi Zhang	Yang Zhao	Yutong Zheng
Huaiwen Zhang	Ying Zhao	Yalin Zheng
Quanshi Zhang	Yin Zhao	Yu Zheng
Zhoutong Zhang	Yizhou Zhao	Feng Zheng
Yuhang Zhang	Yunhan Zhao	Zhaoheng Zheng
Yuting Zhang	Yuyang Zhao	Haitian Zheng
Zhang Zhang	Yue Zhao	Kang Zheng
Ziming Zhang	Yuzhi Zhao	Bolun Zheng

Haiyong Zheng
Mingwu Zheng
Sipeng Zheng
Tu Zheng
Wenzhao Zheng
Xiawu Zheng
Yinglin Zheng
Zhuo Zheng
Zilong Zheng
Kecheng Zheng
Zerong Zheng
Shuaifeng Zhi
Tiancheng Zhi
Jia-Xing Zhong
Yiwu Zhong
Fangwei Zhong
Zhihang Zhong
Yaoyao Zhong
Yiran Zhong
Zhun Zhong
Zichun Zhong
Bo Zhou
Boyao Zhou
Brady Zhou
Mo Zhou
Chunluan Zhou
Dingfu Zhou
Fan Zhou
Jingkai Zhou
Honglu Zhou
Jiaming Zhou
Jiahuan Zhou
Jun Zhou
Kaiyang Zhou
Keyang Zhou
Kuangqi Zhou
Lei Zhou
Lihua Zhou
Man Zhou
Mingyi Zhou
Mingyuan Zhou
Ning Zhou
Peng Zhou
Penghao Zhou
Qianyi Zhou

Shuigeng Zhou
Shangchen Zhou
Huayi Zhou
Zhize Zhou
Sanping Zhou
Qin Zhou
Tao Zhou
Wenbo Zhou
Xiangdong Zhou
Xiao-Yun Zhou
Xiao Zhou
Yang Zhou
Yipin Zhou
Zhenyu Zhou
Hao Zhou
Chu Zhou
Daquan Zhou
Da-Wei Zhou
Hang Zhou
Kang Zhou
Qianyu Zhou
Sheng Zhou
Wenhui Zhou
Xingyi Zhou
Yan-Jie Zhou
Yiyi Zhou
Yu Zhou
Yuan Zhou
Yuqian Zhou
Yuxuan Zhou
Zixiang Zhou
Wengang Zhou
Shuchang Zhou
Tianfei Zhou
Yichao Zhou
Alex Zhu
Chenchen Zhu
Deyao Zhu
Xiatian Zhu
Guibo Zhu
Haidong Zhu
Hao Zhu
Hongzi Zhu
Rui Zhu
Jing Zhu

Jianke Zhu
Junchen Zhu
Lei Zhu
Lingyu Zhu
Luyang Zhu
Menglong Zhu
Peihao Zhu
Hui Zhu
Xiaofeng Zhu
Tyler (Lixuan) Zhu
Wentao Zhu
Xiangyu Zhu
Xinqi Zhu
Xinxin Zhu
Xinliang Zhu
Yangguang Zhu
Yichen Zhu
Yixin Zhu
Yanjun Zhu
Yousong Zhu
Yuhao Zhu
Ye Zhu
Feng Zhu
Zhen Zhu
Fangrui Zhu
Jinjing Zhu
Linchao Zhu
Pengfei Zhu
Sijie Zhu
Xiaobin Zhu
Xiaoguang Zhu
Zezhou Zhu
Zhenyao Zhu
Kai Zhu
Pengkai Zhu
Bingbing Zhuang
Chengyuan Zhuang
Liansheng Zhuang
Peiye Zhuang
Yixin Zhuang
Yihong Zhuang
Junbao Zhuo
Andrea Ziani
Bartosz Zieliński
Primo Zingaretti

Nikolaos Zioulis
Andrew Zisserman
Yael Ziv
Liu Ziyin
Xingxing Zou
Danping Zou
Qi Zou

Shihao Zou
Xueyan Zou
Yang Zou
Yuliang Zou
Zihang Zou
Chuhang Zou
Dongqing Zou

Xu Zou
Zhiming Zou
Maria A. Zuluaga
Xinxin Zuo
Zhiwen Zuo
Reyer Zwiggelaar

Contents – Part XXVI

Contrastive Deep Supervision

Linfeng Zhang[1], Xin Chen[2], Junbo Zhang[1], Runpei Dong[3],
and Kaisheng Ma[1(✉)]

[1] Tsinghua University, Beijing, China
kaisheng@mail.tsinghua.edu.cn
[2] Intel Corporation, Santa Clara, USA
[3] Xi'an Jiaotong University, Xi'an, China

Abstract. The success of deep learning is usually accompanied by the growth in neural network depth. However, the traditional training method only supervises the neural network at its last layer and propagates the supervision layer-by-layer, which leads to hardship in optimizing the intermediate layers. Recently, deep supervision has been proposed to add auxiliary classifiers to the intermediate layers of deep neural networks. By optimizing these auxiliary classifiers with the supervised task loss, the supervision can be applied to the shallow layers directly. However, deep supervision conflicts with the well-known observation that the shallow layers learn low-level features instead of task-biased high-level semantic features. To address this issue, this paper proposes a novel training framework named Contrastive Deep Supervision, which supervises the intermediate layers with augmentation-based contrastive learning. Experimental results on nine popular datasets with eleven models demonstrate its effects on general image classification, fine-grained image classification and object detection in supervised learning, semi-supervised learning and knowledge distillation. Codes have been released in Github.

1 Introduction

Along with the growth in large-scale datasets and computation resources, deep neural networks have become the most dominant models for various tasks [14, 52]. However, the increasing depth of neural networks also introduces challenges in their training process. Traditional supervised training method only applies the supervision to the last layer and then propagates the error from the last layer to the shallow layers (Fig. 1(a)), which leads to hardship in optimizing the intermediate layers such as gradient vanishing [29].

Recently, deep supervision (*a.k.a. deeply-supervised net*) has been proposed to address this issue by optimizing the intermediate layers directly [38]. As shown in Fig. 1(b), deep supervision adds several auxiliary classifiers to the intermediate layers in different depths. During the training phase, these classifiers are optimized with the original final classifier together by the same training loss (*e.g.* cross entropy for classification tasks). Both experimental and theoretical analyses have demonstrated its effectiveness in facilitating model convergence [62].

However, success comes with remaining obstacles. In general, different layers in convolutional neural networks tend to learn features at different levels. Usually,

S. Avidan et al. (Eds.): ECCV 2022, LNCS 13686, pp. 1–19, 2022.
https://doi.org/10.1007/978-3-031-19809-0_1

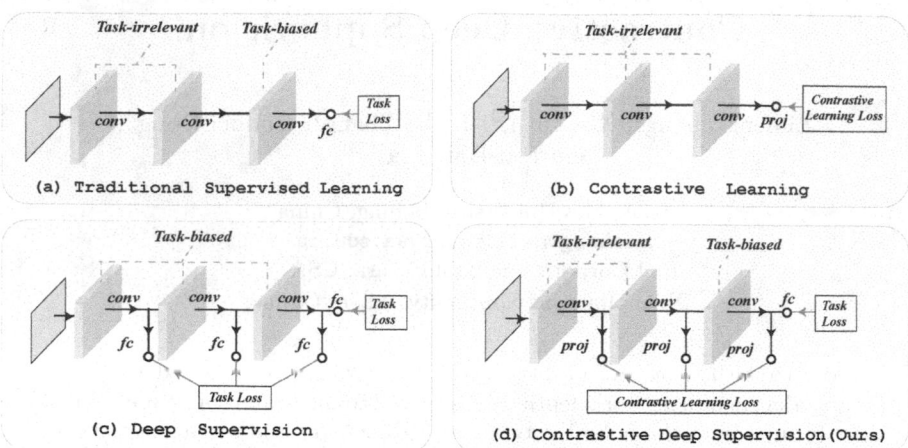

Fig. 1. The overview of the four methods. "→" and "⇢" indicate the path of forward computation and gradients backward computation. "proj" and "fc" indicate the projection heads and the fully connected classifiers, respectively. The gray dash line indicates whether the feature is task-irrelevant or task-biased. (a) Traditional supervised learning only applies supervision to the last layer and propagates it to the previous layers, leading to gradient vanishing. (c) Deep supervision trains both the last layer and the intermediate layers directly, which addresses gradient vanishing but makes all the layers be biased to the task. (d) Our method introduces contrastive learning to supervise the intermediate layer and thus avoid these problems.

the shallow layers learn low-level features such as colors and edges, while the last several layers learn more high-level task-related semantic features such as categorical knowledge for classification tasks [82]. However, deep supervision forces the shallow layers to learn the task-related knowledge, which disobeys the original feature extraction process in neural networks. As pointed out in MSDNet [28], this conflict sometimes leads to accuracy degradation in the final classifier. This observation indicates that the supervised task loss is probably not the best supervision for optimizing the intermediate layers.

In this paper, we argue that *contrastive learning can provide better supervision for intermediate layers than the supervised task loss*. Contrastive learning is one of the most popular and effective techniques in representation learning [7,8,34]. Usually, it regards two augmentations from the same image as a positive pair and different images as negative pairs. In the training period, the neural network is trained to minimize the distance of a positive pair while maximizing the distance of a negative pair. As a result, the network can learn the invariance to various data augmentation, such as Color Jitter and Random Gray Scale. Considering that these data augmentation invariances are usually low-level, task-irrelevant and transferable to various vision tasks [3,64], we argue that they are more beneficial knowledge to be learned by intermediate layers.

Motivated by these observations, we propose a novel training framework named *Contrastive Deep Supervision*. It optimizes the intermediate layers with contrastive learning instead of traditional supervised learning. As shown in Fig. 1(d), several projection heads are attached in the intermediate layers of the neural networks and trained to perform contrastive learning. These projection heads can be discarded in the inference period to avoid additional computation and storage. Different from deep supervision which trains the intermediate layers to learn the knowledge for a specific task, the intermediate layers in our method are trained to learn the invariance to data augmentation, which makes the neural network generalize better. Besides, since contrastive learning can be performed on unlabeled data, the proposed contrastive deep supervision can also be easily extended in the semi-supervised learning paradigm.

Moreover, contrastive deep supervision can be further utilized to boost the performance of another deep learning technique – knowledge distillation. Knowledge distillation (KD) is a popular model compression approach which aims to transfer the knowledge from a cumbersome teacher model to a lightweight student model [2,15,23]. Recently, abundant research finds that distilling the "crucial knowledge" inside the backbone features such as attention and relation [49,58,72] leads to better performance than directly distilling all the backbone features. In this paper, we show that the data augmentation invariances learned by the intermediate layers in contrastive deep supervision are more beneficial knowledge to be distilled. By combining contrastive deep supervision with the naïve feature distillation, the distilled ResNet18 achieves 73.23% accuracy on ImageNet, which outperforms the baseline and the second-best KD method by 4.02% and 2.16%, respectively.

Extensive experiments on nine datasets with eleven neural networks methods have been conducted to evaluate its effectiveness on general image classification, fine-grained image classification, object detection in supervised learning, semi-supervised learning and knowledge distillation, which demonstrates that contrastive deep supervision enables neural networks to learn better visual representation. In the discussion section, we further explain the effectiveness of our method from the perspective of regularization methods, which prevents models from overfitting and leads to better uncertainty estimation. To sum up, the main contributions of our paper can be summarized as follows.

- We propose *contrastive deep supervision*, a neural network training method in which the intermediate layers are directly optimized with contrastive learning. It enables neural networks to learn better visual representation at no expense of additional parameters and computation during inference.
- From the perspective of deep supervision, this paper firstly shows that the intermediate layers can be trained with supervision besides the task loss.
- From the perspective of representation learning, we firstly show that contrastive learning and supervised learning can be combined in a one-stage deep-supervision manner instead of the two-stage "pretrain-finetune" scheme.
- Extensive experiments on nine datasets, eleven neural networks with eleven comparison methods demonstrate the effectiveness of our method on general classification, fine-grained classification and object detection in supervised learning, semi-supervised learning and knowledge distillation.

2 Related Work

2.1 Deep Supervision

Deep neural networks usually contain a large number of layers, which increases the difficulty of optimization. To address this issue, deeply supervised net (*a.k.a.* deep supervision) is proposed to directly supervise the intermediate layers of deep neural networks [38]. Wang *et al.* show that deep supervision can alleviate the vanishing gradient problem and thus leads to significant performance improvements [62]. Usually, deep supervision attaches several auxiliary classifiers at the intermediate layers and supervises these auxiliary classifiers with the task loss (*e.g.* cross-entropy loss in classification). Recently, several methods have been proposed to improve deep supervision with knowledge distillation, which aims to minimize the difference between the prediction of the deepest classifier and the auxiliary classifiers in the intermediate layers [40,55]. Besides classification, abundant research has also demonstrated the effectiveness of deep supervision methods in dynamic neural networks [78], semantic segmentation [51,73,81], object detection [39], knowledge distillation [76] and so on.

2.2 Contrastive Learning

In the last several years, contrastive learning has become the most popular method in representation learning [5,18,24,27,32,60,61,63,68,74]. Oord *et al.* propose the contrastive predictive coding, which aims to predict the low dimension embedding of future signals with an auto-regressive model [47]. He *et al.* propose MoCo, which introduces a dynamic memory bank to record the embeddings of negative samples [9,11,19]. Then, SimCLR is proposed to show the importance of large batch size and long training time in contrastive learning [7,8]. Recently, abundant research has been proposed to study the influence of negative samples further. BYOL is introduced to demonstrate that contrastive learning is effective even without negative samples [16]. SimSiam gives a detailed study on the importance of batch normalization, negative samples, memory bank, and the stop-gradient operation [10]. Besides self-supervised learning, contrastive learning has also shown its power in the traditional supervised learning paradigm. Khosla *et al.* show that state-of-the-art performance can be achieved on ImageNet with the basic contrastive learning in SimCLR by building the positive pairs with label supervision [6,34]. Park *et al.* apply contrastive learning to unpaired image-to-image translation, which breaks the limitation of cycle reconstruction [48].

2.3 Knowledge Distillation

Knowledge distillation, which aims to facilitate the training of a lightweight student model under the supervision of an over-parameterized teacher model, has become one of the most popular methods in model compression. Knowledge distillation is first proposed by Bucilua *et al.* [2] and then expanded by Hinton *et al.* [23], who introduces a temperature-characterized softmax to soften the distribution of teacher logits. Instead of distilling the knowledge of the logits, more and more techniques are proposed to distill the information in teacher features or its variants, such as attention maps [42,72], negative values [22], task-oriented information [76], relational information [43,49,58], Gram matrix [69], mutual information [1], context information [75] and so on. Besides model compression, knowledge distillation has also achieved significant success in self-supervised learning [30,46], semi-supervised learning [37,56], multi-exit neural network [70,77,78], incremental learning [83] and model robustness [65,79].

3   Methodology

3.1   Deep Supervision

In this subsection, we revisit the formulation of deep supervision methods. Let c be a given backbone classifier, deep supervision introduces several shallow classifiers by using the intermediate features in c. More specifically, assume $c = g \circ f$ where g is the final classifier, f is the feature extractor operator and $f = f_K \circ f_{K-1} \circ \cdots f_1$. K denotes the number of convolutional stages in f. At each feature extraction stage i, deep supervision attaches an auxiliary classifier g_i for providing intermediate supervision. Thus, there are K classifiers in total which have the following form:

$$
\begin{aligned}
c_1(x) &= g_1 \circ f_1(x) \\
c_2(x) &= g_2 \circ f_2 \circ f_1(x) \\
&\cdots \\
c_K(x) &= g_K \circ f_K \circ f_{K-1} \circ \cdots \circ f_1(x).
\end{aligned}
\tag{1}
$$

Given a set of training samples $\mathcal{X} = \{x_i\}_{i=1}^n$ and its corresponding labels $\mathcal{Y} = \{y_i\}_{i=1}^n$, the training loss of deep supervision $\mathcal{L}_{\mathrm{DS}}$ can be formulated as

$$
\mathcal{L}_{\mathrm{DS}} = \underbrace{\mathcal{L}_{\mathrm{CE}}(c_K(\mathcal{X}), \mathcal{Y})}_{\text{from standard training}} + \alpha \cdot \sum_{i=1}^{K-1} \underbrace{\mathcal{L}_{\mathrm{CE}}(c_i(\mathcal{X}), \mathcal{Y})}_{\text{from deep supervision}},
\tag{2}
$$

where $\mathcal{L}_{\mathrm{CE}}$ indicates the cross entropy loss. The first and the second item in the loss function indicate the standard training loss and the additional loss from deep supervision for the intermediate layers, respectively. α is a hyper-parameter to balance the two loss items. Recently, some research has been proposed to apply layer-wise consistency on deep supervision, which additionally minimizes the KL divergence between the prediction of auxiliary classifiers and the final classifier [40,55]. These methods can also be considered as the knowledge distillation which regards the final classifier as the teacher and the auxiliary classifiers as the students. Their training loss can be formulated as

$$
\mathcal{L}_{\mathrm{DS}} + \beta \cdot \sum_{i=1}^{K-1} \mathcal{L}_{\mathrm{KL}}(c_i(\mathcal{X}), c_K(\mathcal{X})),
\tag{3}
$$

where β is a hyper-parameter to balance the two loss functions.

3.2   Contrastive Deep Supervision

In this subsection, we first introduce the formulation of contrastive learning. For a minibatch of N images $\{x_1, x_2, ..., x_N\}$, we apply stochastic data augmentation to each image twice, resulting in a batch of $2N$ images. For convenience, we denote x_i and x_{N+i} images as the two augmentations from the same image, which is regarded as a positive pair. Denote $z = c(x)$ as the normalized projection head outputs, contrastive learning loss (*a.k.a.* NT-Xtent [7]) can be formulated as

$$\mathcal{L}_{\text{Contra}} = -\sum_{i=1}^{N} \log \frac{\exp(z_i \cdot z_{i+N})/\tau}{\sum_{k=1}^{2N} \mathbb{1}_{[k \neq i]} \exp(z_i \cdot z_k)/\tau}, \qquad (4)$$

where $\mathbb{1} \in \{0, 1\}$ is an indicator function evaluating to 1 if $k \neq i$ and τ is a temperature hyper-parameter. Intuitively, $\mathcal{L}_{\text{Contra}}$ encourages the encoder network to learn similar representation for different augmentations from the same image while increasing the difference between representations of the augmentations from different images.

The main difference between deep supervision and our method is that deep supervision trains the auxiliary classifiers by the cross entropy loss while our method trains them with the contrastive loss $\mathcal{L}_{\text{Contra}}$. By denoting the contrastive loss at c_i as $\mathcal{L}_{\text{Contra}}(\mathcal{X}; c_i)$, then the training loss of our contrastive deep supervision $\mathcal{L}_{\text{CDS}}$ can be formulated as

$$\mathcal{L}_{\text{CDS}} = \underbrace{\mathcal{L}_{\text{CE}}(c_K(\mathcal{X}), \mathcal{Y})}_{\text{from standard training}} + \lambda_1 \sum_{i=1}^{K-1} \underbrace{\mathcal{L}_{\text{Contra}}(\mathcal{X}; c_i)}_{\text{from our method}}, \qquad (5)$$

where the first and the second item indicate the standard training loss and the additional loss in our method for the intermediate layers, respectively. λ_1 is a hyper-parameter to balance the two loss items.

Based on the above formulation on supervised learning, we can extend contrastive deep supervision in semi-supervised learning and knowledge distillation.

Semi-supervised Learning. In semi-supervised learning, we assume that there is a labeled dataset $\mathcal{X}_1$ with its labels $\mathcal{Y}_1$ and an unlabeled dataset $\mathcal{X}_2$. On the labeled data, contrative deep supervision can be appled directly with $\mathcal{L}_{\text{CDS}}$. On the unlabeled data, due to the lack of labels, contrastive deep supervision only optimize the contrastive learning loss $\mathcal{L}_{\text{Contra}}$, which can be formulated as

$$\mathcal{L}_{\text{CDS}}(\mathcal{X}_1, \mathcal{Y}_1) + \mathcal{L}_{\text{Contra}}(\mathcal{X}_2) \qquad (6)$$

Knowledge Distillation. The intermediate layers in contrastive deep supervision are supervised with contrastive learning and thus they can learn the invariance to different data augmentation. As shown in previous research, these data augmentation invariance is beneficial to various downstream tasks [31]. In this paper, we further propose to improve knowledge distillation with contrastive deep supervision by transferring the data augmentation invariance learned by the teachers to the students. Denote the student model and the teacher model in knowledge distillation as f^S and f^T respectively, the naïve feature-based knowledge distillation directly minimizes the distance between the backbone features of the student and the teacher, which can be formulated as

$$\sum_{i=1}^{K} \|f_i^T(\mathcal{X}) - f_i^S(\mathcal{X})\|_2. \tag{7}$$

In contrast, knowledge distillation with contrastive deep supervision minimizes the distance between the embedding vectors (the output of the projection heads) of the student and the teacher, which can be formulated as

$$\mathcal{L}_{\text{CDS for KD}} = \sum_{i=1}^{K-1} \|c_i^T(\mathcal{X}) - c_i^S(\mathcal{X})\|_2. \tag{8}$$

Now we can formulate the overall training loss of the student as

$$\mathcal{L}_{\text{DCDS}} = \mathcal{L}_{\text{CDS}} + \lambda_2 \cdot \mathcal{L}_{\text{CDS for KD}} + \lambda_3 \cdot \mathcal{L}_{\text{KL}}\left(c_K^T(\mathcal{X}), c_K^S(\mathcal{X})\right), \tag{9}$$

where λ_2 and λ_3 are the hyper-parameters to balance different loss items. Following previous works in deep supervision, we do not set an individual hyper-parameter for each projection head for convenience in hyper-parameter tuning.

3.3 Other Details and Tricks

Design of Projection Heads. In contrastive deep supervision, several projection heads are added to the intermediate layers of neural networks during the training period. These projection heads map the backbone features into a normalized embedding space, where the contrastive learning loss is applied. As discussed in related works, the architecture of the projection head is crucial to model performance [8]. Usually, the projection head is a non-linear projection stacked by two fully connected layers and a ReLU function. However, in contrastive deep supervision, the input feature comes from the intermediate layers instead of the final layer, and thus it is more challenging to project them properly [8]. Hence, we increase the complexity of these projection heads by adding convolutional layers before the non-linear projection.

Contrastive Learning. The proposed contrastive deep supervision is a general training framework and does not depend on a specific contrastive learning method. In this paper, we adopt SimCLR [7] and SupCon [34] as the contrastive learning method in most experiments. We argue that the performance of our method can be further improved by using better contrastive learning method.

Negative Samples. Previous studies show that the number of negative samples has a vital influence on the performance of contrastive learning. Accordingly, a large batch size, a momentum encoder or a memory bank is usually required [7,16,19]. In contrastive deep supervision, we do not use any of these solutions because the supervised loss ($\mathcal{L}_{\text{CE}}$ in Eq. 5) is enough to prevent contrastive learning from converging to the collapsing solutions.

Table 1. Comparison experiments (top-1 accuracy / %) with the other deep supervision methods on CIFAR100.

Method	RNT18	RNT50	RNT101	RXT50	RXT101	WRN50	WRN101	SET18	SET50	PAT18
Base	77.45	77.81	78.65	79.85	80.67	79.46	79.98	77.46	78.02	76.84
DSN	78.30	78.96	79.37	81.02	81.70	80.98	81.30	78.28	79.46	77.40
DKS	78.96	80.95	81.39	82.27	82.98	81.95	82.58	79.32	80.76	78.96
DHM	78.82	81.12	81.27	82.14	83.27	81.76	82.76	79.14	80.72	78.32
Ours	**80.84**	**81.31**	**83.12**	**82.81**	**83.87**	**82.28**	**83.93**	**80.13**	**81.51**	**80.76**

Table 2. Comparison experiments (top-1 accuracy / %) with the other deep supervision methods on CIFAR10.

Method	RNT18	RNT50	RNT101	RXT50	RXT101	WRN50	WRN101	SET18	SET50	PAT18
Base	94.96	95.07	95.13	95.09	95.34	95.01	95.27	94.86	95.11	94.78
DSN	95.31	95.41	95.63	95.39	95.70	95.27	95.78	95.21	95.41	95.13
DKS	95.72	95.90	96.21	95.98	96.10	95.50	96.12	95.74	95.72	95.47
DHM	95.61	95.87	96.04	96.10	96.27	95.62	96.31	95.59	95.77	95.38
Ours	**96.49**	**96.78**	**97.02**	**96.76**	**97.05**	**96.88**	**97.01**	**96.50**	**96.73**	**96.37**

Table 3. Comparison with the other deep supervision methods on ImageNet.

Metric	Model	Baseline	DSN	DKS	DHM	**Ours**
top-1	RNT18	69.21	69.54	71.32	71.29	**72.85**
	RNT34	73.17	73.29	74.01	73.89	**76.19**
	RNT50	75.30	75.37	76.47	76.57	**78.25**
top-5	RNT18	89.01	88.87	89.20	90.06	**91.30**
	RNT34	91.24	91.30	91.87	91.66	**93.08**
	RNT50	92.20	92.49	93.60	93.24	**93.99**

4 Experiment

4.1 Experiment Setting

Common Image Classification. For common image classification, our method has been evaluated on three datasets, including CIFAR10, CIFAR100 and ImageNet [13,36] with kinds of neural networks including ResNet (RNT), ResNeXt (RXT), Wide ResNet (WRN), SENet (SET), PreAct ResNet (PAT), MobileNetv1, MobileNetv2, ShuffleNetv1 and ShuffleNetv2 [20,21,25,26,54,66, 71,80].

Fine-Grained Image Classification. For fine-grained image classification, our method has been evaluated on five popular datasets, including CUB200-2011 [59], Stanford Cars [35], Oxford Flowers [45], Stanford Dogs [33] and FGVC Aircraft [44]. ResNet50 is utilized as the classifier for all the experiments.

Table 4. Experiments on different object detection models on COCO2017. ResNet50 models are pre-trained on ImageNet with different deep supervision methods and then utilized as the backbones of these detectors.

Model	Method	AP	AP_S	AP_M	AP_L
Faster RCNN	Baseline	37.4	21.2	41.0	48.1
	DSN	$37.3_{-0.1}$	$21.0_{-0.2}$	$40.8_{-0.2}$	$48.3_{-0.2}$
	DKS	$37.5_{+0.1}$	$21.2_{+0.0}$	$41.5_{+0.5}$	$47.6_{-0.5}$
	DHM	$37.6_{+0.2}$	$21.3_{+0.1}$	$41.3_{+0.3}$	$48.2_{+0.1}$
	Ours	$\mathbf{38.3_{+0.9}}$	$\mathbf{21.6_{+0.4}}$	$\mathbf{42.0_{+1.0}}$	$\mathbf{50.1_{+2.0}}$
RetinaNet	Baseline	36.5	20.4	40.3	48.1
	DSN	$36.3_{-0.2}$	$20.1_{-0.3}$	$40.0_{-0.3}$	$48.1_{0.0}$
	DKS	$36.7_{+0.2}$	$20.1_{-0.3}$	$40.9_{+0.6}$	$48.2_{+0.1}$
	DHM	$36.7_{+0.2}$	$20.0_{-0.4}$	$40.7_{+0.4}$	$48.5_{+0.4}$
	Ours	$\mathbf{37.3_{+0.8}}$	$\mathbf{21.2_{+0.8}}$	$\mathbf{41.0_{+0.7}}$	$\mathbf{47.9_{-0.2}}$

Table 5. Comparison (top-1 acc. / %) with deep supervision methods with ResNet50 for fine-grained classification. Models are trained from scratch.

Method	CUB	Cars	Flowers	Dogs	Aircrafts
Baseline	60.65	79.86	87.52	64.00	74.07
DSN	$62.37_{+1.72}$	$81.04_{+1.18}$	$88.54_{+1.02}$	$66.32_{+2.32}$	$74.49_{+0.42}$
DKS	$63.59_{+2.94}$	$81.52_{+1.66}$	$88.94_{+0.40}$	$68.31_{+4.31}$	$75.07_{+1.00}$
DHM	$64.01_{+3.36}$	$81.49_{+1.63}$	$89.03_{+1.51}$	$68.38_{+4.38}$	$75.00_{+0.93}$
Ours	cellcolormygray$\mathbf{64.65_{+4.00}}$	$\mathbf{82.07_{+2.21}}$	$\mathbf{89.26_{+1.74}}$	$\mathbf{69.02_{+5.02}}$	$\mathbf{75.43_{+1.36}}$

Table 6. Comparison (top-1 acc. %) with deep supervision methods with ResNet50 for fine-grained classification. Models are finetuned from ImageNet pre-trained weights.

Method	CUB	Cars	Flowers	Dogs	Aircrafts
Baseline	78.50	90.25	97.68	76.47	87.43
DSN	$80.14_{+1.64}$	$91.32_{+1.07}$	$98.64_{+0.96}$	$77.21_{+0.74}$	$89.31_{+1.88}$
DKS	$81.34_{+2.84}$	$92.54_{+2.29}$	$99.01_{+1.33}$	$78.32_{+1.85}$	$89.20_{+1.77}$
DHM	$81.27_{+2.77}$	$92.31_{+2.06}$	$98.84_{+1.16}$	$78.20_{+1.73}$	$89.57_{+2.14}$
Ours	$\mathbf{82.10_{+3.60}}$	$\mathbf{92.90_{+2.65}}$	$\mathbf{99.39_{+1.71}}$	$\mathbf{80.99_{+4.52}}$	$\mathbf{90.52_{+3.09}}$

Object Detection. For object detection, our method has been evaluated on MS COCO2017 [41] with Faster RCNN and RetinaNet by MMdetection [4].

Semi-supervised Learning. Semi-supervised learning experiments have been conducted on CIFAR100, CIFAR10 with ResNet18. For each dataset, we have evaluated our method with 10%, 20%, 30% and 40% labels.

Table 7. Comparison experiments (top-1 and top-5 accuracy / %) with the other eight knowledge distillation methods on ImageNet with ResNet. Numbers in bold indicate the highest.Results marked with † come from the paper of SSKD [67].

Metric	Model	Base	KD	AT	RKD	SP	CRD	CC†	OKD†	SSKD†	Ours
top-1	RNT18	69.21	70.52	70.74	70.63	70.61	71.07	69.96	70.55	71.62	**73.23**
	RNT34	73.17	74.44	74.69	74.61	74.60	74.99	–	–	–	**76.65**
	RNT50	75.30	76.62	76.79	76.92	76.88	77.21	–	–	–	**78.68**
top-5	RNT18	89.01	89.88	90.00	89.71	89.80	91.06	89.17	89.59	90.67	**91.56**
	RNT34	91.24	92.07	92.18	92.14	92.10	92.58	–	–	–	**93.38**
	RNT50	92.20	93.36	93.51	93.60	93.58	93.88	–	–	–	**94.42**

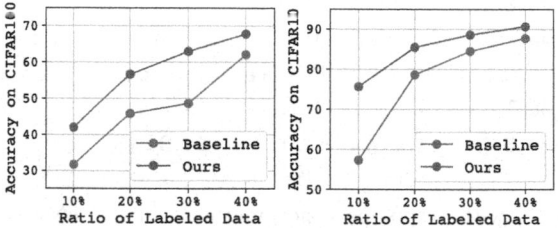

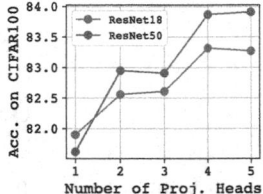

Fig. 2. Experimental results of semi-supervised training on CIFAR100 and CIFAR10 with ResNet18.

Fig. 3. Influence from the number of projection heads.

Comparison Methods. Three previous deep supervision methods are utilized for comparison, including DSN [38], DKS [55] and DHM [40]. In knowledge distillation experiments, we have evaluated our method with nine knowledge distillation methods, including KD [23], FitNet [53], AT [72], RKD [49], SP [58] and CRD [57]. Besides, we also cite results on ImageNet of CC [50], OKD [84], and SSKD [67] from the paper of SSKD.

4.2   Experimental Results

Image Classification. Experimental results on CIFAR100, CIFAR10 and ImageNet are shown in Table 1, Table 2 and Table 3, respectively. It is observed that: **(a)** Our method achieves 3.44% and 1.70% top-1 accuracy improvements on CIFAR100 and CIFAR10 on average, respectively. It consistently outperforms the second-best deep supervision method by 1.05% and 0.90% on the two datasets, respectively. **(b)** On ImageNet, contrastive deep supervision leads to 3.64%, 3.02% and 2.95% top-1 accuracy improvements on ResNet18, ResNet34 and ResNet50, respectively. On average, it outperforms the baseline and the second-best method by 3.20% and 1.83% top-1 accuracy, respectively.

Object Detection. Table 4 shows the performance of our method on object detection. In these experiments, We firstly pretrain the ResNets on ImageNet with standard training (Baseline), three deep supervision methods, and our method, and then finetuning them as the backbone for object detection models,

Table 8. Comparison with the other knowledge distillation methods on CIFAR.

CIFAR100							
Model	Base	KD	FitNet	AT	RKD	SP	CRD	**Ours**
ResNet18	77.45	78.68	78.15	78.09	78.21	78.19	81.41	**83.31**
ResNet50	77.81	79.19	78.42	78.34	78.94	78.81	82.45	**83.53**
ResNet101	78.65	80.40	80.78	80.97	81.24	80.94	82.57	**84.80**
ResNeXt50	79.85	81.41	82.67	82.59	83.71	82.67	83.41	**84.41**
ResNeXt101	80.67	82.03	82.51	82.43	83.01	82.64	84.50	**85.37**
WRNet50	79.46	81.02	81.29	81.16	82.06	82.07	82.94	**84.27**
WRNet101	79.98	81.82	82.07	82.16	82.54	82.49	83.07	**85.04**
SENet18	77.46	78.92	79.09	79.15	79.41	79.31	81.22	**82.68**
SENet50	78.02	79.78	80.13	80.45	80.69	80.71	81.79	**83.36**
SENet101	78.92	80.31	80.54	80.53	80.74	80.52	82.75	**84.15**
MobileNetV1	68.32	70.04	70.25	70.17	70.89	70.19	72.68	**73.79**
MobileNetV2	69.34	70.58	70.64	70.51	70.83	70.68	71.82	**72.61**
ShuffleNetV1	72.46	74.08	74.19	74.11	74.56	74.68	75.11	**75.77**
ShuffleNetV2	72.81	74.39	74.47	74.51	74.82	74.67	75.62	**76.11**
PreActNet18	76.84	78.25	78.34	78.67	79.01	79.12	81.62	**82.83**
PreActNet50	77.31	79.04	79.27	79.54	79.82	79.76	81.27	**83.42**
CIFAR10								
Model	Base	KD	FitNet	AT	RKD	SP	CRD	**Ours**
ResNet18	94.96	95.24	95.31	95.26	95.31	95.27	95.81	**96.84**
ResNet50	95.07	95.31	95.45	95.47	95.33	95.29	96.21	**97.08**
ResNet101	95.13	95.39	95.71	95.49	95.43	95.18	96.37	**97.40**
ResNeXt50	95.09	95.27	95.36	95.68	95.59	95.37	96.49	**97.15**
ResNeXt101	95.34	95.68	95.92	95.78	95.81	95.38	96.51	**97.40**
WRNet50	95.01	95.34	95.38	95.34	95.61	95.73	96.17	**97.37**
WRNet101	95.27	95.51	95.48	95.71	95.99	95.82	96.34	**97.39**
SENet18	94.86	95.21	95.30	95.47	95.34	95.41	96.00	**96.96**
SENet50	95.11	95.39	95.44	95.64	95.57	95.47	96.21	**97.19**
SENet101	95.30	95.64	95.81	95.78	95.81	95.77	96.19	**97.36**
MobileNetV1	90.24	91.27	92.59	92.87	93.01	92.90	93.27	**93.94**
MobileNetV2	90.76	91.09	91.57	91.75	91.82	91.83	92.17	**92.87**
ShuffleNetV1	91.57	91.99	92.30	92.19	92.47	92.38	93.08	**94.04**
ShuffleNetV2	91.19	91.87	92.23	92.41	92.30	92.54	92.90	**93.16**
PreActNet18	94.78	95.08	95.28	95.39	95.51	95.69	96.07	**96.70**
PreActNet50	94.89	95.21	95.57	95.49	95.37	95.48	96.11	**96.93**

including RetinaNet and Faster RCNN on COCO2017 datasets. It is observed that with backbones pre-trained with our method, there are 0.9 and 0.8 AP improvements on Faster RCNN and RetinaNet respectively, which outperforms the second-best method by 0.6 AP, indicating that the representation learned with our method are more beneficial to downstream tasks.

Fine-Grained Image Classification. Experiments on fine-grained image classification are shown in Table 6. It is observed that: **(a)** Contrastive deep supervision leads to consistent and significant accuracy improvements on the five datasets. On average, it leads to 3.80%, 2.43%, 1.73%, 4.77% and 2.25% accuracy improvements on the five datasets, respectively. **(b)** Besides, the benefits of our method in *"finetuning from ImageNet"* and *"training from scratch"* are very similar (except on Aircraft), which indicates that the effectiveness of our method is consistent in different training settings.

Semi-supervised Learning. Experiments on semi-supervised learning with ResNet18 on CIFAR10 and CIFAR100 are shown in Fig. 2. It is observed that: **(a)** Our method leads to consistent accuracy improvements at all the ratios of labeled data. **(b)** The benefits of our method become larger when there is less labeled data, which indicates that our method is effective in using the unlabeled data to optimize the intermediate layers.

Knowledge Distillation. Knowledge distillation experiments on ImageNet and CIFAR are shown in Table 7 and Table 8, respectively. It is observed that: **(a)** Our method achieves 5.07% and 2.20% top-1 accuracy improvements on CIFAR100 and CIFAR10 on average, outperforming the second-best KD method by 1.40% and 0.87% on the two datasets, respectively. **(b)** The similar results can also be observed in ImageNet experiments. Our method leads to 4.02%/2.55%, 3.48%/2.14% and 3.38%/2.22% top-1/top-5 accuracy improvements on ResNet18, ResNet34 and ResNet50, respectively. On average, it outperforms the baseline and the second-best method by 3.62% and 1.76% top-1 accuracy, respectively.

5   Discussion

5.1   Contrastive Deep Supervision as a Regularizer

Loss Curves. Regularization methods in deep learning are usually utilized to avoid model overfitting by introducing additional penalties or loss. In this subsection, we show that the contrastive learning loss introduced by our method in the intermediate layers works as a regularizer. Figure 4 shows the cross entropy loss between predicted results and labels during the training period from two ResNet18 models trained by the standard method and our method, respectively. It is observed that at most of epochs, the baseline model has lower cross entropy loss than our model. When both models are converged (epoch 280–300), the baseline model has only 0.005 loss while our model still has 0.025 loss. These observations

Table 9. Comparison between our method and contrastive learning methods with ResNet50 on ImageNet. Baseline[1] − 2: Two baselines trained with and without AutoAugmentation [12]. SupCon[1−3]: Three models trained by supervised contrastive learning with different hyper-parameters. BYOL: ResNet50 unsupervisedly pre-trained by 1000 epochs and then supervisedly finetuned. BYOL+DSN: ResNet50 pretrained with BYOL and then finetuned with deep supervision. Ours[1,3]: ResNet50 trained with contrastive deep supervision in different settings. Ours[2]: ResNet50 trained with contrastive deep supervision+ knowledge distillation.

Method	Batchsize	Epoch	AutoAug	Top-1 acc. (%)
Baseline[1]	256	90	✗	75.3
Baseline[2]	4096	270	✓	77.6
SupCon[1]	6144	350	✓	78.7
SupCon[2]	512	350	✓	74.5
SupCon[3]	6144	100	✓	77.0
BYOL	1024	1080	✗	77.7
BYOL+DSN	1024	1080	✗	78.2
Ours[1]	256	90	✗	78.3
Ours[2]	256	90	✗	78.7
Ours[3]	256	350	✓	79.8

indicate that there is serve overfitting in the baseline model while deep contrastive supervision can alleviate overfitting and thus improve the accuracy.

Uncertainty Estimation. Besides, the comparison on expected calibrated error (ECE) of models trained with the standard method and our method has been shown in Fig. 5. A lower ECE indicates that the predicted probability of a neural network estimates representative of the true correctness likelihood better [17]. It is observed that compared with the baseline model, our method leads to a lower ECE, indicating better uncertainty estimation and interpretability.

5.2 Comparison with Contrastive Learning

Comparison between our method and two "pretrain & finetune" contrastive learning methods is shown in Table 9. It is observed that without a large batch size and the advanced data augmentation policy (AutoAugment), contrastive deep supervision (Ours[1]) with only 25% training time achieves 0.4% lower accuracy than SupCon[3]. Besides, contrastive deep supervision with the same training time and data augmentation (Ours[3]) achieves 1.1% and 1.6% higher accuracy than SupCon[3] and BYOL+DSN, respectively, which demonstrates the advantage of our method over the traditional contrastive learning methods.

5.3 Ablation Study on Knowledge Distillation

The main difference between the naïve feature distillation and feature distillation with our contrastive deep supervision is *"what to distill"*. Naïve feature distillation distills the backbone features while our method distills the embedding learned by contrastive deep supervision. To further demonstrate its effectiveness, we have trained a ResNet50 model on CIFAR100 with both contrastive deep supervision and distillation on backbone features. Experimental results show this model achieves 82.26% accuracy, which is 1.27% lower than distilling the embedding. These results demonstrate that distilling the embedding learned by contrastive deep supervision is more beneficial.

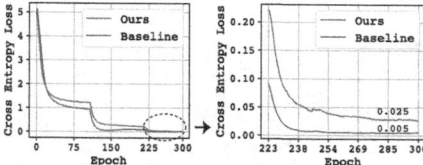 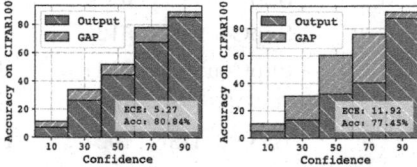

Fig. 4. Comparison on the cross entropy loss between predicted results and labels during the training period. Note that our method also leads to better accuracy (80.84% vs 77.45%)

Fig. 5. Comparison on reliability diagrams. "GAP" indicates the difference between confidence and accuracy. "Output" indicates accuracy. ECE: Expected Calibrated Error (lower is better).

5.4 Sensitivity Study

Where to Apply Projection Heads. We study the influence from the position of projection heads with the following four schemes: (1)*uniform scheme* - applying projection heads into different depths uniformly; (2) *downsampling scheme* - applying projection heds into the layers before downsampling; (3) *shallow scheme* - applying projection heads into only the shallower layers; (4) *deep scheme* - applying projection heads to only the deeper layers; Experimental results on CIFAR100 with ResNet50 show that the four schemes achieves 81.23%, 81.31%, 81.07% and 80.99% accuracy, respectively. It is observed that both *uniform* and *downsampling* schemes leads to excellent performance, indicating our method is not sensitive to where to apply projection heads.

The Number of Projection Heads. We have studied the influence from the number of projection heads in Fig. 3. It is observed that when there are less than five projection heads, more projection heads tend to achieve better performance. The fifth projection head does not leads to more accuracy improvements.

6 Conclusion

This paper proposes *contrastive deep supervision*, a novel training methodology that directly optimizes the intermediate layers of deep neural networks with contrastive learning. It enables the neural network to learn better visual representation without additional computation and storage in inference. Experiments on nine datasets with eleven neural networks have demonstrated its effectiveness in general image classification, fine-grained image classification and object detection for traditional supervised learning, semi-supervised learning and knowledge distillation. It outperforms the previous deep supervision methods, knowledge distillation methods, and contrastive learning methods by a clear margin. Besides, we also show that contrastive deep supervision works as a regularizer to prevent models from overfitting, and thus leads to better uncertainty estimation.

References

1. Ahn, S., Hu, S.X., Damianou, A., Lawrence, N.D., Dai, Z.: Variational information distillation for knowledge transfer. In: Proceedings of the IEEE Conference on Computer Vision and Pattern Recognition, pp. 9163–9171 (2019)
2. Buciluǎ, C., Caruana, R., Niculescu-Mizil, A.: Model compression. In: Proceedings of the 12th ACM SIGKDD International Conference on Knowledge Discovery and Data Mining, pp. 535–541. ACM (2006)
3. Chaitanya, K., Erdil, E., Karani, N., Konukoglu, E.: Contrastive learning of global and local features for medical image segmentation with limited annotations. In: Advances in Neural Information Processing Systems, vol. 33 (2020)
4. Chen, K., et al.: Mmdetection: open mmlab detection toolbox and benchmark. arXiv preprint. arXiv:1906.07155 (2019)
5. Chen, L., Wang, D., Gan, Z., Liu, J., Henao, R., Carin, L.: Wasserstein contrastive representation distillation. In: IEEE Conference on Computer Vision and Pattern Recognition, CVPR 2021, virtual, 19–25 June 2021, pp. 16296–16305. Computer Vision Foundation/IEEE (2021)
6. Chen, L., Wang, D., Gan, Z., Liu, J., Henao, R., Carin, L.: Wasserstein contrastive representation distillation. In: Proceedings of the IEEE/CVF Conference on Computer Vision and Pattern Recognition, pp. 16296–16305 (2021)
7. Chen, T., Kornblith, S., Norouzi, M., Hinton, G.: A simple framework for contrastive learning of visual representations. In: International Conference on Machine Learning, pp. 1597–1607. PMLR (2020)
8. Chen, T., Kornblith, S., Swersky, K., Norouzi, M., Hinton, G.E.: Big self-supervised models are strong semi-supervised learners. In: Advances in Neural Information Processing Systems, vol. 33, pp. 22243–22255 (2020)
9. Chen, X., Fan, H., Girshick, R., He, K.: Improved baselines with momentum contrastive learning. arXiv preprint. arXiv:2003.04297 (2020)
10. Chen, X., He, K.: Exploring simple siamese representation learning. In: Proceedings of the IEEE/CVF Conference on Computer Vision and Pattern Recognition, pp. 15750–15758 (2021)
11. Chen, X., Xie, S., He, K.: An empirical study of training self-supervised visual transformers. arXiv e-prints pp. arXiv-2104 (2021)
12. Cubuk, E.D., Zoph, B., Mane, D., Vasudevan, V., Le, Q.V.: Autoaugment: learning augmentation strategies from data. In: Proceedings of the IEEE/CVF Conference on Computer Vision and Pattern Recognition (CVPR) (2019)
13. Deng, J., et al.: Imagenet: a large-scale hierarchical image database. In: CVPR, pp. 248–255 (2009)

14. Devlin, J., Chang, M.W., Lee, K., Toutanova, K.: Bert: pre-training of deep bidirectional transformers for language understanding. In: NAACL (2018)
15. Furlanello, T., Lipton, Z.C., Tschannen, M., Itti, L., Anandkumar, A.: Born again neural networks. In: ICML (2018)
16. Grill, J.B., et al.: Bootstrap your own latent-a new approach to self-supervised learning. In: Advances in Neural Information Processing Systems, vol. 33, pp. 21271–21284 (2020)
17. Guo, C., Pleiss, G., Sun, Y., Weinberger, K.Q.: On calibration of modern neural networks. In: International Conference on Machine Learning, pp. 1321–1330. PMLR (2017)
18. Han, Z., Fu, Z., Chen, S., Yang, J.: Contrastive embedding for generalized zero-shot learning. In: IEEE Conference on Computer Vision and Pattern Recognition, CVPR 2021, Virtual, 19–25 June 2021, pp. 2371–2381. Computer Vision Foundation/IEEE (2021)
19. He, K., Fan, H., Wu, Y., Xie, S., Girshick, R.: Momentum contrast for unsupervised visual representation learning. In: Proceedings of the IEEE/CVF Conference on Computer Vision and Pattern Recognition, pp. 9729–9738 (2020)
20. He, K., Zhang, X., Ren, S., Sun, J.: Deep residual learning for image recognition. In: CVPR, pp. 770–778 (2016)
21. He, K., Zhang, X., Ren, S., Sun, J.: Identity mappings in deep residual networks. In: Leibe, B., Matas, J., Sebe, N., Welling, M. (eds.) ECCV 2016. LNCS, vol. 9908, pp. 630–645. Springer, Cham (2016). https://doi.org/10.1007/978-3-319-46493-0_38
22. Heo, B., Kim, J., Yun, S., Park, H., Kwak, N., Choi, J.Y.: A comprehensive overhaul of feature distillation. In: Proceedings of the IEEE International Conference on Computer Vision, pp. 1921–1930 (2019)
23. Hinton, G., Vinyals, O., Dean, J.: Distilling the knowledge in a neural network. In: NeurIPS (2014)
24. Hou, J., Graham, B., Nießner, M., Xie, S.: Exploring data-efficient 3d scene understanding with contrastive scene contexts. In: IEEE Conference on Computer Vision and Pattern Recognition, CVPR 2021, Virtual, 19–25 June 2021. pp. 15587–15597. Computer Vision Foundation/IEEE (2021)
25. Howard, A.G., et al.: Mobilenets: efficient convolutional neural networks for mobile vision applications. In: CVPR (2017)
26. Hu, J., Shen, L., Sun, G.: Squeeze-and-excitation networks. In: CVPR, pp. 7132–7141 (2018)
27. Hu, Q., Wang, X., Hu, W., Qi, G.: Adco: adversarial contrast for efficient learning of unsupervised representations from self-trained negative adversaries. In: IEEE Conference on Computer Vision and Pattern Recognition, CVPR 2021, Virtual, 19–25 June 2021, pp. 1074–1083 (2021)
28. Huang, G., Chen, D., Li, T., Wu, F., van der Maaten, L., Weinberger, K.Q.: Multiscale dense networks for resource efficient image classification. In: ICLR (2018)
29. Huang, G., Sun, Yu., Liu, Z., Sedra, D., Weinberger, K.Q.: Deep networks with stochastic depth. In: Leibe, B., Matas, J., Sebe, N., Welling, M. (eds.) ECCV 2016. LNCS, vol. 9908, pp. 646–661. Springer, Cham (2016). https://doi.org/10.1007/978-3-319-46493-0_39
30. Hyun Lee, S., Ha Kim, D., Cheol Song, B.: Self-supervised knowledge distillation using singular value decomposition. In: Proceedings of the European Conference on Computer Vision (ECCV), pp. 335–350 (2018)
31. Jaiswal, A., Babu, A.R., Zadeh, M.Z., Banerjee, D., Makedon, F.: A survey on contrastive self-supervised learning. Technologies 9(1), 2 (2021)

32. Jeon, S., Min, D., Kim, S., Sohn, K.: Mining better samples for contrastive learning of temporal correspondence. In: IEEE Conference on Computer Vision and Pattern Recognition, CVPR 2021, virtual, 19–25 June 2021, pp. 1034–1044 (2021)
33. Khosla, A., Jayadevaprakash, N., Yao, B., Fei-Fei, L.: Novel dataset for fine-grained image categorization. In: First Workshop on Fine-Grained Visual Categorization, IEEE Conference on Computer Vision and Pattern Recognition. Colorado Springs, CO (2011)
34. Khosla, P., Teterwak, P., Wang, C., Sarna, A., Tian, Y., Isola, P., Maschinot, A., Liu, C., Krishnan, D.: Supervised contrastive learning. In: Advances in Neural Information Processing Systems,vol. 33, pp. 18661–18673 (2020)
35. Krause, J., Stark, M., Deng, J., Fei-Fei, L.: 3d object representations for fine-grained categorization. In: 4th International IEEE Workshop on 3D Representation and Recognition (3dRR-13), Sydney, Australia (2013)
36. Krizhevsky, A., Hinton, G.: Learning multiple layers of features from tiny images. Technical report Citeseer (2009)
37. Laine, S., Aila, T.: Temporal ensembling for semi-supervised learning. In: International Conference on Learning Representations (ICLR), vol. 4, p. 6 (2017)
38. Lee, C.Y., Xie, S., Gallagher, P., Zhang, Z., Tu, Z.: Deeply-supervised nets. In: Artificial Intelligence and Statistics, pp. 562–570 (2015)
39. Li, C., Zeeshan Zia, M., Tran, Q.H., Yu, X., Hager, G.D., Chandraker, M.: Deep supervision with shape concepts for occlusion-aware 3d object parsing. In: Proceedings of the IEEE Conference on Computer Vision and Pattern Recognition, pp. 5465–5474 (2017)
40. Li, D., Chen, Q.: Dynamic hierarchical mimicking towards consistent optimization objectives. In: Proceedings of the IEEE/CVF Conference on Computer Vision and Pattern Recognition, pp. 7642–7651 (2020)
41. Lin, T.Y., et al.: Microsoft COCO: common objects in context. In: Fleet, D., Pajdla, T., Schiele, B., Tuytelaars, T. (eds.) ECCV 2014. LNCS, vol. 8693, pp. 740–755. Springer, Cham (2014). https://doi.org/10.1007/978-3-319-10602-1_48
42. Liu, M., Chen, X., Zhang, Y., Li, Y., Rehg, J.M.: Attention distillation for learning video representations. In: BMVC (2020)
43. Liu, Y., Shu, C., Wang, J., Shen, C.: Structured knowledge distillation for dense prediction. IEEE Transactions on Pattern Analysis and Machine Intelligence (2020)
44. Maji, S., Kannala, J., Rahtu, E., Blaschko, M., Vedaldi, A.: Fine-grained visual classification of aircraft. Technical report (2013)
45. Nilsback, M.E., Zisserman, A.: Automated flower classification over a large number of classes. In: 2008 Sixth Indian Conference on Computer Vision, Graphics & Image Processing, pp. 722–729. IEEE (2008)
46. Noroozi, M., Vinjimoor, A., Favaro, P., Pirsiavash, H.: Boosting self-supervised learning via knowledge transfer. In: Proceedings of the IEEE Conference on Computer Vision and Pattern Recognition, pp. 9359–9367 (2018)
47. Oord, A.v.d., Li, Y., Vinyals, O.: Representation learning with contrastive predictive coding. arXiv preprint. arXiv:1807.03748 (2018)
48. Park, T., Efros, A.A., Zhang, R., Zhu, J.-Y.: Contrastive learning for unpaired image-to-image translation. In: Vedaldi, A., Bischof, H., Brox, T., Frahm, J.-M. (eds.) ECCV 2020. LNCS, vol. 12354, pp. 319–345. Springer, Cham (2020). https://doi.org/10.1007/978-3-030-58545-7_19
49. Park, W., Kim, D., Lu, Y., Cho, M.: Relational knowledge distillation. In: Proceedings of the IEEE Conference on Computer Vision and Pattern Recognition, pp. 3967–3976 (2019)

50. Peng, B., et al.: Correlation congruence for knowledge distillation. In: Proceedings of the IEEE International Conference on Computer Vision, pp. 5007–5016 (2019)
51. Reiß, S., Seibold, C., Freytag, A., Rodner, E., Stiefelhagen, R.: Every annotation counts: multi-label deep supervision for medical image segmentation. In: IEEE Conference on Computer Vision and Pattern Recognition, CVPR 2021, virtual, 19–25 June 2021, pp. 9532–9542. Computer Vision Foundation/IEEE (2021)
52. Ren, S., He, K., Girshick, R., Sun, J.: Faster r-cnn: towards real-time object detection with region proposal networks. In: Advances in Neural Information Processing Systems, pp. 91–99 (2015)
53. Romero, A., Ballas, N., Kahou, S.E., Chassang, A., Gatta, C., Bengio, Y.: Fitnets: hints for thin deep nets. In: ICLR (2015)
54. Sandler, M., Howard, A., Zhu, M., Zhmoginov, A., Chen, L.C.: Mobilenetv 2: inverted residuals and linear bottlenecks. In: Proceedings of the IEEE Conference on Computer Vision and Pattern Recognition, pp. 4510–4520 (2018)
55. Sun, D., Yao, A., Zhou, A., Zhao, H.: Deeply-supervised knowledge synergy. In: Proceedings of the IEEE/CVF Conference on Computer Vision and Pattern Recognition, pp. 6997–7006 (2019)
56. Tarvainen, A., Valpola, H.: Mean teachers are better role models: Weight-averaged consistency targets improve semi-supervised deep learning results. In: Advances in Neural Information Processing Systems, pp. 1195–1204 (2017)
57. Tian, Y., Krishnan, D., Isola, P.: Contrastive representation distillation. In: ICLR (2020)
58. Tung, F., Mori, G.: Similarity-preserving knowledge distillation. In: Proceedings of the IEEE International Conference on Computer Vision, pp. 1365–1374 (2019)
59. Wah, C., Branson, S., Welinder, P., Perona, P., Belongie, S.: The caltech-ucsd birds-200-2011 dataset. Technical report, CNS-TR-2011-001, California Institute of Technology (2011)
60. Wang, F., Liu, H.: Understanding the behaviour of contrastive loss. In: IEEE Conference on Computer Vision and Pattern Recognition, CVPR 2021, Virtual, 19–25 June 2021, pp. 2495–2504. Computer Vision Foundation/IEEE (2021)
61. Wang, L., Huang, J., Li, Y., Xu, K., Yang, Z., Yu, D.: Improving weakly supervised visual grounding by contrastive knowledge distillation. In: IEEE Conference on Computer Vision and Pattern Recognition, CVPR 2021, Virtual, 19–25 June 2021, pp. 14090–14100. Computer Vision Foundation/IEEE (2021)
62. Wang, L., Lee, C.Y., Tu, Z., Lazebnik, S.: Training deeper convolutional networks with deep supervision. arXiv preprint. arXiv:1505.02496 (2015)
63. Wang, P., Han, K., Wei, X., Zhang, L., Wang, L.: Contrastive learning based hybrid networks for long-tailed image classification. In: IEEE Conference on Computer Vision and Pattern Recognition, CVPR 2021, Virtual, 19–25 June 2021, pp. 943–952 (2021)
64. Xie, E., et al.: Detco: unsupervised contrastive learning for object detection. arXiv preprint. arXiv:2102.04803 (2021)
65. Xie, Q., Luong, M.T., Hovy, E., Le, Q.V.: Self-training with noisy student improves imagenet classification. In: Proceedings of the IEEE/CVF Conference on Computer Vision and Pattern Recognition, pp. 10687–10698 (2020)
66. Xie, S., Girshick, R., Dollár, P., Tu, Z., He, K.: Aggregated residual transformations for deep neural networks. In: CVPR, pp. 5987–5995 (2017)
67. Xu, G., Liu, Z., Li, X., Loy, C.C.: Knowledge distillation meets self-supervision. In: Vedaldi, A., Bischof, H., Brox, T., Frahm, J.-M. (eds.) ECCV 2020. LNCS, vol. 12354, pp. 588–604. Springer, Cham (2020). https://doi.org/10.1007/978-3-030-58545-7_34

68. Yang, M., Li, Y., Huang, Z., Liu, Z., Hu, P., Peng, X.: Partially view-aligned representation learning with noise-robust contrastive loss. In: IEEE Conference on Computer Vision and Pattern Recognition, CVPR 2021, Virtual, 19–25 June 2021, pp. 1134–1143. Computer Vision Foundation/IEEE (2021)
69. Yim, J., Joo, D., Bae, J., Kim, J.: A gift from knowledge distillation: Fast optimization, network minimization and transfer learning. In: Proceedings of the IEEE Conference on Computer Vision and Pattern Recognition, pp. 4133–4141 (2017)
70. Yu, J., Huang, T.S.: Universally slimmable networks and improved training techniques. In: The IEEE International Conference on Computer Vision (ICCV) (2019)
71. Zagoruyko, S., Komodakis, N.: Wide residual networks. In: BMVC (2016)
72. Zagoruyko, S., Komodakis, N.: Paying more attention to attention: improving the performance of convolutional neural networks via attention transfer. In: ICLR (2017)
73. Zeng, G., Yang, X., Li, J., Yu, L., Heng, P.-A., Zheng, G.: 3D U-net with multi-level deep supervision: fully automatic segmentation of proximal femur in 3d mr images. In: Wang, Q., Shi, Y., Suk, H.-I., Suzuki, K. (eds.) MLMI 2017. LNCS, vol. 10541, pp. 274–282. Springer, Cham (2017). https://doi.org/10.1007/978-3-319-67389-9_32
74. Zhang, H., Koh, J.Y., Baldridge, J., Lee, H., Yang, Y.: Cross-modal contrastive learning for text-to-image generation. In: IEEE Conference on Computer Vision and Pattern Recognition, CVPR 2021, Virtual, 19–25 June 2021, pp. 833–842. Computer Vision Foundation/IEEE (2021)
75. Zhang, L., Kaisheng, M.: Improve object detection with feature-based knowledge distillation: towards accurate and efficient detectors. In: ICLR (2021)
76. Zhang, L., Shi, Y., Shi, Z., Ma, K., Bao, C.: Task-oriented feature distillation. In: NeurIPS (2020)
77. Zhang, L., Song, J., Gao, A., Chen, J., Bao, C., Ma, K.: Be your own teacher: improve the performance of convolutional neural networks via self distillation. In: arXiv preprint:1905.08094 (2019)
78. Zhang, L., Tan, Z., Song, J., Chen, J., Bao, C., Ma, K.: Scan: a scalable neural networks framework towards compact and efficient models. ArXiv abs/1906.03951 (2019)
79. Zhang, L., Yu, M., Chen, T., Shi, Z., Bao, C., Ma, K.: Auxiliary training: Towards accurate and robust models. In: Proceedings of the IEEE/CVF Conference on Computer Vision and Pattern Recognition, pp. 372–381 (2020)
80. Zhang, X., Zhou, X., Lin, M., Sun, J.: Shufflenet: an extremely efficient convolutional neural network for mobile devices. In: Proceedings of the IEEE Conference on Computer Vision and Pattern Recognition, pp. 6848–6856 (2018)
81. Zhang, Y., Chung, A.C.S.: Deep supervision with additional labels for retinal vessel segmentation task. In: Frangi, A.F., Schnabel, J.A., Davatzikos, C., Alberola-López, C., Fichtinger, G. (eds.) MICCAI 2018. LNCS, vol. 11071, pp. 83–91. Springer, Cham (2018). https://doi.org/10.1007/978-3-030-00934-2_10
82. Zhou, B., Khosla, A., Lapedriza, A., Oliva, A., Torralba, A.: Object detectors emerge in deep scene cnns. arXiv preprint. arXiv:1412.6856 (2014)
83. Zhou, P., Mai, L., Zhang, J., Xu, N., Wu, Z., Davis, L.S.: M2kd: multi-model and multi-level knowledge distillation for incremental learning. arXiv preprint. arXiv:1904.01769 (2019)
84. Zhu, X., Gong, S., et al.: Knowledge distillation by on-the-fly native ensemble. In: Advances in Neural Information Processing Systems, vol. 31 (2018)

Discriminability-Transferability Trade-Off: An Information-Theoretic Perspective

Quan Cui[1,2], Bingchen Zhao[1,3], Zhao-Min Chen[1,4], Borui Zhao[1],
Renjie Song[1(✉)], Boyan Zhou[5], Jiajun Liang[1], and Osamu Yoshie[2]

[1] MEGVII Technology, Beijing, China
songrenjie@megvii.com
[2] Waseda University, Tokyo, Japan
cui-quan@toki.waseda.jp
[3] University of Edinburgh, Edinburgh, UK
[4] Wenzhou University, Wenzhou, China
[5] ByteDance, Beijing, China

Abstract. This work simultaneously considers the discriminability and transferability properties of deep representations in the typical supervised learning task, *i.e.*, image classification. By a comprehensive temporal analysis, we observe a trade-off between these two properties. The discriminability keeps increasing with the training progressing while the transferability intensely diminishes in the later training period. From the perspective of information-bottleneck theory, we reveal that the incompatibility between discriminability and transferability is attributed to the over-compression of input information. More importantly, we investigate why and how the InfoNCE loss can alleviate the over-compression, and further present a learning framework, named contrastive temporal coding (CTC), to counteract the over-compression and alleviate the incompatibility. Extensive experiments validate that CTC successfully mitigates the incompatibility, yielding discriminative and transferable representations. Noticeable improvements are achieved on the image classification task and challenging transfer learning tasks. We hope that this work will raise the significance of the transferability property in the conventional supervised learning setting.

Keywords: Information-bottleneck theory · Representation learning · Discriminability · Transferability · Contrastive learning

---

Q. Cui and B. Zhao—Equal contributions.

Supplementary Information The online version contains supplementary material available at https://doi.org/10.1007/978-3-031-19809-0_2.

1   Introduction

In recent decades, great progress has been achieved on learning discriminative representations with deep neural networks in a supervised learning manner. Advanced by such powerful deep representations, performances of many real-world computer vision applications are remarkably improved, *e.g.*, visual categorization [17,20,37], object detection [16,34,46], and semantic segmentation [28,54]. However, the mainstream supervised learning works concentrate on pursuing more discriminative representations, which deserves the most attention for direct effects on model performances. Except for the discriminability, transferability should also be taken into considerations in the conventional supervised learning classification task, which is preferred for many downstream tasks [4,14,49,57,58] yet neglected in the conventional supervised learning setting.

We start this work by investigating the correlation between discriminability and transferability properties of representations in the entire supervised training process. Concretely, in the training process of a deep classification model, we extract representations from each training epoch and respectively assess their discriminability and transferability. Conclusions are generally illustrated in the left part of Fig. 1. We observe that the discriminability keeps getting better, while the transferability intensely diminishes in the later training. It reveals that representations can hardly be discriminative and transferable at the same time in the conventional supervised learning setting, *i.e.*, these two properties could be incompatible. Nevertheless, high-quality representations are expected to possess both properties, and we suppose that the learning mechanism underlying the conventional supervised learning leads to the trade-off.

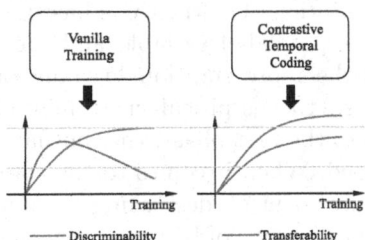

Fig. 1. Considered properties of deep representations. In a vanilla training, we reveal that the discriminability keeps increasing while the transferability first climbs to a peak and then gradually decreases. To address this issue, we propose the contrastive temporal coding, which successfully alleviates the incompatibility between transferability and discriminability.

Interestingly, we notice a concept *Information-Bottleneck (IB) trade-off* in the IB theory [1,39,42], *i.e.*, the network learning can be interpreted by finding the optimal trade-off between input information compression and label-related information enhancement. This IB trade-off intrigues us to explain our observed trade-off between discriminability and transferability. Following IB, we visualize mutual information dynamics [2] in the information plane [39], and reveal the *over-compression* phenomenon, *i.e.*, prolonged input information compression leads to inadequate information on downstream tasks and thus poor transferability.

The above IB-based perspective also provides us an idea to make the discriminability and transferability compatible, *i.e.*, simultaneously training the model with a loss for the specific task and another loss to *counteract the over-compression*. To support this standpoint, we establish the correlation between counteracting over-compression and improving transferability via a principle components analysis (PCA) perspective. We further explore and provide a solution based on the InfoNCE [19,32,40] loss to counteract the over-compression. Concretely, we present a two-stage learning framework, namely Contrastive Temporal Coding (CTC). The learning process of CTC consists of two stages, *i.e.*, the information aggregation and revitalization stages. In the first stage, a classification model is optimized and the last epoch model is stored as the information bank, which aggregates informative representations. In the second stage, we introduce an InfoNCE loss between the current model and the information bank, counteracting the over-compression. As shown in the right part of Fig. 1, our proposed method successfully alleviates the incompatibility, achieving high-quality representations in supervised learning.

2   Related Work

Information-Bottleneck Theory. The information-bottleneck (IB) theory [1, 39,42] provides an information-theoretic principle for encoding the input data into a compressed representation. The theory is based on measuring the mutual information between the input/label variable and the representation variable. It is demonstrated that the representation learning of deep neural networks undergoes two phases, *i.e.*, the empirical error minimization and representation compression phases. In the first phase, the mutual information on the label variable is rapidly increased. When it comes to the compression phase, most of the optimization epochs are spent on decreasing the mutual information on the input variable. From the perspective of IB theory, we analyze the incompatibility between the transferability and the discriminability of learned representations in the common supervised learning, which is mostly ignored by the community. We conjecture and prove that the drop of transferability owes to the prolonged compression phase, *i.e.*, the information relevant to downstream tasks is overly discarded for learning discriminative representations.

Discriminability vs. Transferability. The transferability of deep representations has been studied from various perspectives [3,7,11,23,24,36,43,52]. And many previous works also noticed the correlation between discrimiability and transferability in the domain adaptation area [3,7]. In this work, we venture to study the correlation between discriminability and transferability with from an information-theoretic point of view. It is worth noting that [23] also noticed that better ImageNet classification results (obtained from better loss functions) could lead to worse transfer learning performances, strongly supporting our work.

Contrastive Learning. The main idea of contrastive learning is maximizing the similarity between samples from the same category/view while minimizing the similarity between samples from different categories/views. In recent years, contrastive learning has shown great potentials in self-supervised and unsupervised learning [4,4,5,14,22,32,33,40,41,49,50,57] but is not widely studied in the supervised learning setting [22,38]. Different from these previous works, our method contrasts the representations from the current training against those from the previous training. The contrastive learning objective has been proven to be the lower bound of the mutual information between the two views [32,40,48]. In this work, we utilize this property for optimizing the mutual information between deep representations from different training stages.

3   Discriminability vs. Transferability

In this section, we first reveal the incompatibility between *discriminability* and *transferability* properties of deep representations. Then, we give theoretical and empirical explanations from the information-theoretic perspective.

3.1   Revealing the Incompatibility

We optimize a classification model with the cross-entropy loss on CIFAR-100 [25] and evaluate these properties[1]:

Discriminability. Intuitively, the discriminability of representations is reflected by the classification accuracy. However, the high accuracy only indicates separable representations since a sample can be correctly classified but near located to the decision boundary. Previous work [37,47] pointed out that the discriminability can be better revealed by nearest neighbor search (NNS) algorithms. Besides, a subtle but essential component in a classification model should be considered, *i.e.*, the classifier. Recent works [21,56] revealed that the performance of a classification model is closely related to the quality of its classifier. To precisely quantify the discriminability, we propose to evaluate retrieval and clustering performances of representations, which are built upon classifier-irrelevant NNS algorithms.

To measure discriminability, we evaluate representations with a typical network architecture ResNet18 [17]. Representations from each training epoch are extracted and assessed by retrieval and clustering tasks. Recall@1 ($R@1$) is the evaluation metric for retrieval tasks. Normalized Mutual Information (NMI) is reported to assess clustering performances. Metrics are calculated only by the test set to avoid problems that can be caused by over-fitting the training set.

---

[1] Representations refer to the outputs of the backbone, which are processed with a global average pooling in popular models [17].

Transferability. For measuring the transferability, it is reasonable to transfer learned knowledge to out-of-sample datasets. Given a deep classification model learned on a source dataset, we freeze its backbone network and re-train a classifier on top of the last feature layer on unseen target datasets. Corresponding classification accuracies reveal the transferability.

To measure the transferability, CIFAR-100 is the source dataset, and target datasets are CINIC10 [10] and STL-10 [8], respectively. Following the above experimental settings, ResNet-18 model is utilized.

Trade-Off Between Discriminability and Transferability. As illustrated in Fig. 2, it can be observed that both $R@1$ and NMI have been improved with the training process. However, the continual training in later epochs can significantly hurt the transferability. In all the above experiments, models with the best transferability are mostly located in the middle training stage, rather than the later stage, where the best discriminability is scored. Conclusively, with the training progressing, representations become increasingly discriminative while the transferability remains uncertain, and, more importantly, these two properties could be incompatible in the later training stage.

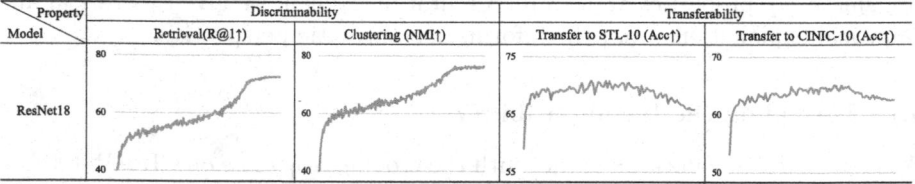

Fig. 2. Temporal analyses of representations in the vanilla training process. In each subfigure, the X-axis is the training epoch, and Y-axis is the evaluated metric (*e.g.*, R@1, NMI, and Top-1 accuracy). "↑" denotes "the higher the better". In the entire training, it can be observed that the discriminability keeps becoming better while the transferability first goes to a peak and then intensely drops in the later training. In a typical supervised training process, discriminability and transferability are incompatible.

3.2   Connection to Information-Bottleneck Trade-Off

The trade-off between discriminability and transferability in Sect. 3.1 motivates us to explain it with the well-known Information-Bottleneck (IB) trade-off [1, 39,42].

Recap of the IB Theory. The IB theory explains the learning of deep neural networks (DNNs) by the Information-Bottleneck trade-off, *i.e.*, the network learning is interpreted by finding the optimal trade-off between input information compression and label-related information enhancement.

An essential viewpoint of IB theory is that, except for the input variable X and label variable Y, the hidden representation layer T is regarded as a variable.

Under these assumptions, the mutual information (MI) between X (or Y) and T is used to describe the trade-off between input information compression and label-related information enhancement. $I(X;T)$ denotes the MI between inputs X and representations T, and $I(T;Y)$ represents the MI between representations T and labels Y. Based on MI, the empirical error minimization (ERM) and representation compression phases are defined. The fast ERM phase rapidly increases $I(T;Y)$, and subsequently, the much longer representation compression phase results in the decrease of $I(X;T)$. These two phases indicate that network first rapidly memorizes label-related information, and then compresses input information for finding an optimal trade-off.

IB Trade-Off Meets Discriminability-Transferability Trade-Off. In the IB trade-off, we suppose that input information could be *overly compressed* on the source dataset. Due to the network focuses on enhancing label-related information, the task-irrelevant information could be discarded. Thus, insufficient information on target datasets brings about the unsatisfactory transferability. In other words, the over-compression results in the aforementioned empirical observation of discriminability-transferability trade-off. To prove this standpoint, we follow IB to calculate MI dynamics on both source and target datasets, capturing the correlation between the information-bottleneck trade-off and discriminability-transferability trade-off[2].

(1) MIs on the source dataset. As shown in Fig. 3, expectedly, $I(T;Y)$ on the source dataset (CIFAR-100) rapidly increases in initial training, corresponding to the fast ERM phase. Then, $I(X;T)$ slowly decreases with the training progressing, matching the representation compression phase. Associated with results in Fig. 2, the discriminability greatly benefits from the representation compression phase.

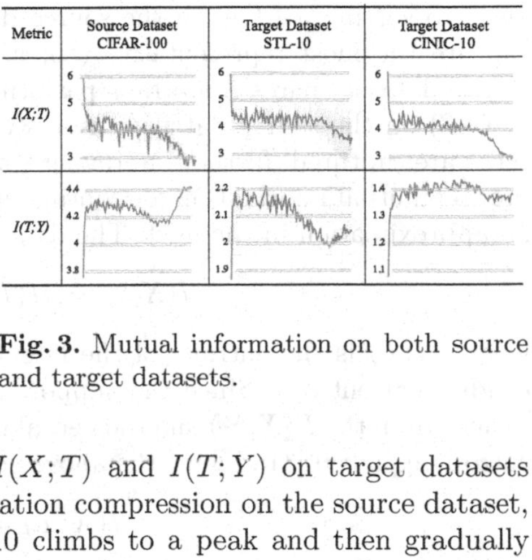

Fig. 3. Mutual information on both source and target datasets.

(2) MIs on the target dataset. Both $I(X;T)$ and $I(T;Y)$ on target datasets are illustrated in Fig. 3. With representation compression on the source dataset, $I(T;Y)$ on both STL-10 and CINIC-10 climbs to a peak and then gradually decreases, consistently acting like the transferring performances in Fig. 2. Meanwhile, $I(X;T)$ on target datasets also gradually decrease with the training progressing, indicating that the information relevant to target datasets is also discarded due to the long representation compression phase.

Over-Compression Leads to the Incompatibility. The above results reveal the *over-compression* issue, which degrades both $I(X;T)$ and $I(T;Y)$ on target

---

[2] We use the Mutual Information Neural Estimation (MINE) [2] method to calculate the mutual information between continuous variables.

datasets in the later training. Driven by the IB trade-off, the transferability can be sacrificed by the supervised leaning to overly compress input-related information for efficient representations. Over-compression results in insufficient information related to target datasets, unsatisfactory transferring performances, and the incompatibility. However, we suppose that high-quality representations are expected to possess both properties, arising our next explorations.

4   Method

4.1   Alleviating the Incompatibility

Understanding the Transferability. Following [29], we hypothesize that the transferability between a source dataset and a target dataset relies on the model learns important representation patterns shared by source and target datasets. Thus, the decrease of transferability is attributed to the information of representations which related to the target dataset is overly compressed.

Counteracting Over-Compression Improves Transferability. To achieve this goal, an intuitive solution is to counteract the decrease of $I(X;T)$ on the source dataset. To support our motivation, we give an explanation from the Principal Components Analysis (PCA) perspective.

Given an example where the model is linear, maximizing $I(X;T)$ is equivalent to solving a PCA on the source dataset[3]. Solving PCA helps the model capture the most representative representations on the source dataset. If the target dataset shares important patterns with the source dataset, maximizing $I(X;T)$ on the source dataset ensures the most important representation patterns are captured, further improving transferring performances. Since calculating the mutual information for continuous variables is challenging, we introduce an approximation in the next. The definition of $I(X;T)$ is as followed:

$$I(X;T) = H(T) - H(T|X),$$

where $H(T)$ is the entropy of the latent representation T and $H(T|X)$ is the conditional entropy. Since the support set of X contains tremendous natural images from the $P(X,Y)$ and the neural network is deterministic, the conditional entropy equals 0 [31]. Thus, the above equation can be re-written as:

$$I(X;T) = H(T),$$

which demonstrates that counteracting the decreasing of $H(T)$ on the source dataset could be a potential way to alleviate over-compression. In the following, we demonstrate how to counteract the decrease of $H(T)$. It is proven in [19, 32,40] that minimizing the InfoNCE loss maximizes a lower bound on mutual information. Given two representation variables T_1 and T_2, the relation between InfoNCE loss and the mutual information $I(T_1;T_2)$ can be derived as:

$$I(T_1;T_2) \geq \log(N) - \mathcal{L}_{\text{InfoNCE}}, \tag{1}$$

---

[3] Proofs are attached in the appendix A.1.

where N is normally the number of samples in a training set. As demonstrated, minimizing the InfoNCE loss would increase the lower bound of $I(T_1; T_2)$. Combining Eq.(1) with the definition of the mutual information:

$$I(T_1; T_2) = H(T_1) + H(T_2) - H(T_1, T_2)$$
$$\leq H(T_1) + H(T_2) - \max(H(T_1), H(T_2)),$$
$$= \min(H(T_1), H(T_2)),$$

the Eq. (1) could be re-written as:

$$\log(N) - \mathcal{L}_{\text{InfoNCE}} \leq \min(H(T_1), H(T_2)). \tag{2}$$

Equation (2) suggests that minimizing InfoNCE loss improves the lower bound of $\min(H(T_1), H(T_2))$, which simultaneously improves lower bounds of $H(T_1)$ and $H(T_2)$. Therefore, we could select the representation T_1 from early training and *fix it as constant*, regard the representation in later training as T_2, and develop an InfoNCE loss between the constant representation T_1 and the later representation T_2, for counteracting the decrease of $H(T_2)$. Inspired by the well-known "memory bank" concept, we name the constant representation T_1 as the *information bank*.

Concretely, in Eq. (2), if $H(T_2) \leq H(T_1)$, the InfoNCE loss would improve the lower bound of $H(T_2)$. If $H(T_2) > H(T_1)$, the objective of counteracting has been reached. In this manner, the loss $\mathcal{L}_{\text{InfoNCE}}$ ensures the representation of later training has a relatively large $H(T)$.

4.2   Contrastive Temporal Coding

Inspired by the above explorations, we propose a two-stage learning framework to alleviate the incompatibility between discriminability and transferability. In the first training stage, named information aggregation stage, the main objective is to obtain the information bank to provide the $H(T_1)$ in Eq. (2). In the second training stage, named information revitalization stage, the main objective is to further counteract the decrease of $H(T_2)$ via Eq. (2).

Information Aggregation Stage (IAS). In this stage, a classification model is trained with a vanilla cross-entropy (CE) loss $\mathcal{L}_{\text{CE}}$ as the main loss function for learning T_1. Equation (2) indicates that, if $H(T_2) \leq H(T_1)$, the InfoNCE loss will improve the lower bound of $H(T_2)$. Thus, it is reasonable to choose the T_1 with a relatively large $H(T_1)$ in this stage. However, experiments in Sect. 3 demonstrate that, only with the CE loss, the information compression is not controllable and predictable, and the last epoch model could still be overly compressed. For practical usage, it is tricky to select a good T_1 among all epochs, and we hope the last model is a satisfactory choice. To this end, we introduce an auxiliary InfoNCE loss $\mathcal{L}_{\text{IAS}}$ for desensitizing the model selection.

Let T_1 denote the representation variable. Similar to IB theory, we regard a memory bank V as a variable, which keeps representations for each training sample and provide contrastive samples. For $t_1 \in T_1$ and $v \in V$ (which are normalized representations), contrastive representation pairs are composed as $\{t_1^i, v^j\}_{i,j=1}^N$, and N is the number of training samples. Positive pairs are constructed by representations of the identical samples, while negative pairs are composed of different samples. Therefore, the loss function of t_1^i can be re-written as:

$$\mathcal{L}_{\text{IAS}} = -\log \frac{\exp(t_1^i \cdot v^i)}{\sum_{j=1}^{N} \exp(t_1^i \cdot v^j)}, \tag{3}$$

where v^i is the positive "key". When the learning process ends, the model of the latest epoch is saved as the information bank $\hat{T}_1$.

Information Revitalization Stage (IRS). Let T_2 denote representation variable of the second stage. In this stage, we continue training the model from the end of the former stage, and develop an InfoNCE loss $\mathcal{L}_{\text{IRS}}$ to counteract the decrease of $H(T_2)$. For $\hat{t}_1 \in \hat{T}_1$ and $t_2 \in T_2$, contrastive representation pairs are composed as $\{\hat{t}_1^i, t_2^j\}_{i,j=1}^{N}$, where t_2 is from the current epoch and $\hat{t}_1$ is from the previously saved information bank. The optimization objective function of t_2^j can be written as:

$$\mathcal{L}_{\text{IRS}} = -\log \frac{\exp(t_2^j \cdot \hat{t}_1^j)}{\sum_{k=1}^{N} \exp(t_2^j \cdot \hat{t}_1^k)}, \tag{4}$$

where $\hat{t}_1^j$ is the positive "key". Consequently, the optimization objective can implicitly counteract the decrease of $H(T_2)$ and over-compression, promoting the transferability of learned representations.

Learning Framework. The learning of the information aggregation stage is driven by a cross-entropy loss function $\mathcal{L}_{\text{CE}}$ and a contrastive loss $\mathcal{L}_{\text{IAS}}$ as:

$$\mathcal{L}_{\text{stage 1}} = \alpha \mathcal{L}_{\text{IAS}} + \mathcal{L}_{\text{CE}}. \tag{5}$$

At the end of this stage, the information bank model is saved. In the information revitalization stage, the learning of the current model is simultaneously motivated by a contrastive learning loss $\mathcal{L}_{\text{IRS}}$ and a cross-entropy loss $\mathcal{L}_{\text{CE}}$. The $\mathcal{L}_{\text{IRS}}$ is calculated with representations from both the current model and the information bank. The loss can be written as:

$$\mathcal{L}_{\text{stage 2}} = \beta \mathcal{L}_{\text{IRS}} + \mathcal{L}_{\text{CE}}. \tag{6}$$

α and β are weighting hyper-parameters, which respectively emphasize the importance of two properties. The general framework could be similar to the well-known knowledge distillation process [13,18,53]; however, learning the first stage without the $\mathcal{L}_{\text{IAS}}$ loss function (which corresponds to the teacher model training) still leads to poor transferability in T_1. Consequently, developing the $\mathcal{L}_{\text{IPS}}$ loss with such T_1 will limit the increasing of T_2.

4.3   Discussions on Self-Supervised Learning (SSL)

We notice that SSL has shown great potential in transfer learning tasks [6,14,49], while linear probing results of these methods still cannot catch up with supervised learning results. It is similar to supervised learning that the transferability and discriminability also cannot be compatible. However, the superiority of SSL in improving transferability drives us to explore the underlying working mechanism.

On Transferability. Mainstream SSL methods depend on InfoNCE loss, and we attempt to formulate its learning target from the information view. In representative works, a dictionary (memory bank [49] or momentum encoder [6,14]) is typically used for providing negative samples for a trainable encoder. We denote the dictionary representation as T_1, and the trainable encoder representation as T_2. Given that T_1 comes from the dictionary, the $H(T_1)$ could be regarded as a constant before being updated. Minimizing the contrastive loss also counteracts the decrease of $H(T_2)$. Thus, the good transferability of SSL methods could also result from the learning target for informative representations.

On Discriminability. Mainstream SSL methods can be interpreted by a $(K+1)$-way softmax-based classification task, where K is the number of negative samples [14]. Intuitively, due to K is a large number, the $(K+1)$-way classification task is more challenging than the conventional supervised image classification. Thus, we conjecture that SSL compresses input information slowly and is inferior to enhance label-related information. We also notice in [6] that longer training will bring in significant discriminability improvement but minor transferability improvement, which suggest that SSL methods could require longer time for compressing input information and enhancing label-related information.

Later experiments will demonstrate that our CTC outperforms SSL methods on the transferability property.

5   Experiments

Experiments and discussions focus on the following two parts: (1) Validating our motivation and (2) Transferring representations learned by our method.

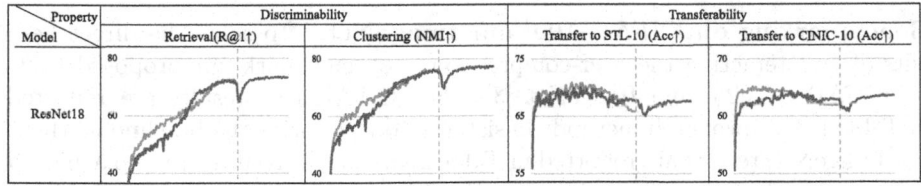

Fig. 4. Temporal analysis of representations in the vanilla and **CTC** training processes. Results of the vanilla and CTC are colored in blue and red, respectively. Two stages are divided by grey dotted lines. Compared with the vanilla training, it can be observed that the transferability is greatly preserved by CTC in later epochs. Furthermore, discriminability is improved by preserving the transferability.

5.1   Motivation Validation and Main Results

Motivation: Counteracting Over-Compression. In this part, we prove our motivation that the proposed method is able to counteract the over-compression.

Following the experimental settings in Sect. 3, we report a temporal analysis of our proposed method. Generally, ResNet18 [17] is trained with CTC on the CIFAR-100 [25] dataset, and representations of each epoch are evaluated and reported afterward. For discriminability, representations of models from each epoch are extracted to perform retrieval and clustering tasks. As to the transferability, we transfer learned representations to STL-10 [8] and CINIC-10 [10].

Evaluations of discriminability

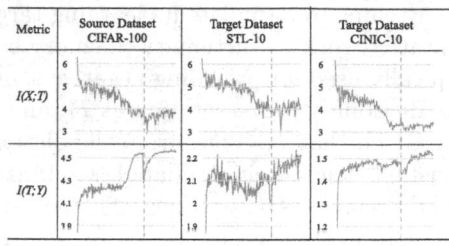

Fig. 5. Mutual information of CTC on both source and target datasets. For better illustration, two stages are split with grey dotted lines. The left and right parts correspond to information aggregation and revitalization stages, respectively. (Color figure online)

and transferability are illustrated in Fig. 4. We divide two stages with a grey dotted line. In the first stage, benefitting from $\mathcal{L}_{\text{IAS}}$, our method (red lines) achieves better transferring results in the last epoch than the baseline (blue lines). The second stage further improves transferring results on target datasets (STL-10 and CINIC-10) by large margins. Mutual information dynamics are provided in Fig. 5. Similar to transferring results, the $I(T; Y)$ on target datasets also keeps increasing in the second stage, showing the information relevant to target datasets is revitalized by our CTC. Meanwhile, the $I(X; T)$ on source and target datasets is also non-decreasing in the second stage. The above results jointly demonstrate that the over-compression has been successfully alleviated by our method. Besides, the discriminability is not damaged, proving the incompatibility is also mitigated.

Benchmarking on CIFAR-100 and ImageNet. To show the direct benefits of counteracting the over-compression, we benchmark our proposed CTC on CIFAR-100 [25] and ImageNet [35]. For CIFAR-100, results are reported in Table 1. Our proposed method consistently outperforms the baseline method. For ImageNet, results are reported in Table 2 and better results are also achieved compared with the vanilla training results. Counteracting the over-compression does not damage the discriminability and conversely benefits the classification performances. Moreover, our CTC brings in no increase on the number of model parameters and FLOPs.

Boosting Transferability with CTC. To further validate that (1) the correctness of the discriminability-transferability trade-off and (2) our method is able to adjust the trade-off, we conduct experiment on sacrificing the discriminability for boosting the transferability. Since the information aggregation stage of CTC decides the lower bound of $H(T)$, we could adjust the hyper-parameter

Table 1. Top-1 accuracies (%) on CIFAR-100 of baseline and CTC (5 runs).

Method	Top-1 Acc. (%)
Res18+CosLr	79.3 ± 0.2
Res18+CTC(Ours)	**80.1** ± 0.3

Table 2. Top-1 accuracies (%) on ImageNet of baseline and CTC (3 runs).

Method	Top-1 Acc. (%)
Res50+CosLr	76.1 ± 0.1
Res50+CTC(Ours)	**76.4** ± 0.1

α for helping the model learn informative representations. Unavoidably, large weight for $\mathcal{L}_{\mathrm{IAS}}$ influences the learning of $\mathcal{L}_{\mathrm{CE}}$. As shown in Table 6 and Fig. 7, increasing α to 0.5 leads to a normal classification accuracy on CIFAR-100, but significantly better transferring results. It also suggests that ending the baseline at an appropriate time is a bad option for enhancing transferability. Moreover, early ending baseline would unavoidably lead to poor discriminability.

method	top-1 acc. (%)
Res18+CosLr	79.3±0.2
Res18+CTC($\alpha = 0.1$)	80.1±0.3
Res18+CTC($\alpha = 0.5$)	79.4±0.3

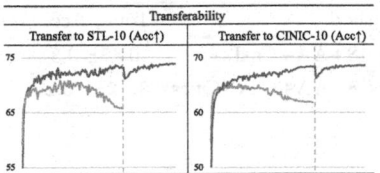

Fig. 6. Top-1 accuracies (%) on CIFAR-100. We adjust the α from 0.1 to 0.5, and the top-1 accuracy is decreased but still better than vanilla training. Transferring results are in the right figure.

Fig. 7. Setting **CTC**'s α to 0.5 (red) leads to greatly better transferring results than vanilla training (blue), showing the over-compression is sufficiently alleviated. (Color figure online)

5.2   Towards Better Transferability

In this part, we study (1) how to get better transferability of representations and (2) how to plug in CTC to further boost the transferability, proving its scalability.

AutoAugment (AA) Contributes to Good Transferability. We suppose that strong augmentations could contribute to good transferability, since strong augmentation can increase the difficulty of information compression, and thus lead to higher $H(T)$. Except for normal crop and resize operations, color normalization and translation operations might be more difficult to learn. Thus, on the CIFAR-100 dataset, we first conduct temporal analysis on representations learned with the AA [9], and results are blue lines in Fig. 8. Similar to results from Sect. 3, the discriminability of representations becomes better with the training progressing. However, it is surprised to notice that the transferability of representations learned with the AA does not diminish as intensely as representations learned without AA, especially in later training epochs. It conveys

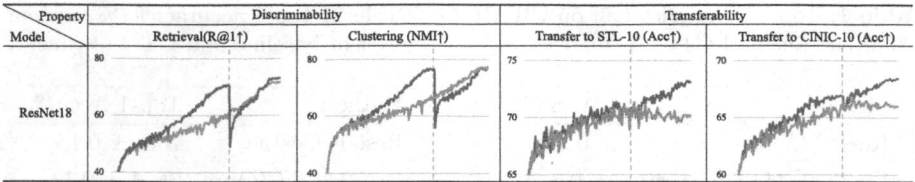

Fig. 8. Temporal analyses of representations in the vanilla and **CTC** training *with the AutoAugment*. Results of the vanilla and CTC are colored in blue and red, respectively. Two stages of CTC (red lines) are separated by the grey dotted line. Compared with the vanilla training (blue lines), it can be observed that the transferability of CTC keeps climbing in the entire learning process. Different to Fig. 4, we train the baseline and CTC with the same number of epochs for fair comparisons. (Color figure online)

Table 3. Top-1 accuracies (%) on CIFAR-100 of baseline and CTC with AA.

Method	Top-1 Acc. (%)
Res18+AA+CosLr	80.4 ± 0.3
Res18+AA+CTC(Ours)	**81.2 ± 0.2**

Table 4. Top-1 accuracies (%) on ImageNet of baseline and CTC with AA.

Method	Top-1 Acc. (%)
Res50+AA+CosLr	76.8 ± 0.1
Res50+AA+CTC(Ours)	**77.2 ± 0.1**

an intuition that strong augmentations could contribute to good transferability, which possibly result from our hypothesis that strong augmentation can increase the difficulty of information compression.

"AA+CTC" Contributes to Better Transferability. Subsequently, we prove our CTC is scalable and orthogonal to other methods. We first optimize the model with CTC and AA, and then report the temporal analysis by red lines in Fig. 8. With the assistance of CTC, discriminability scores higher within expectations. Moreover, the transferability keeps climbing in the entire learning process, eventually achieving the best transferring classification accuracies which can not be achieved only with AA. It further validates our motivation that the transferability could be promoted by counteracting the decrease of representation entropy. For comprehensiveness, we benchmark our CTC with AutoAugment on CIFAR-100 and ImageNet. All experimental settings in this part are the same as those in Sect. 5.1. As reported in Table 3 and 4, superior classification accuracies than the baseline also meet our expectations.

Table 5. COCO object detection and instance segmentation based on Mask-RCNN-FPN with 1× schedule.

Pre-training method	Performance					
	AP^{bbox}	AP^{bbox}_{50}	AP^{bbox}_{75}	AP^{mask}	AP^{mask}_{50}	AP^{mask}_{75}
Res50 random init	30.2	48.9	32.7	28.6	46.6	30.7
Res50+MoCo v2 [6]	38.5	58.3	41.6	33.6	54.8	35.6
Res50+InfoMin [41]	39.0	58.5	42.0	34.1	55.2	**36.3**
Res50+CosLr	38.2	58.2	41.2	33.3	54.7	35.2
Res50+CTC(Ours)	**39.5**	**58.7**	**42.0**	**34.2**	**55.4**	36.2

5.3 Transferring Representations

In this part, we present extensive tasks and datasets to which representations learned by our method can be transferred. Since self-supervised learning methods exceed supervised learning in transferring tasks, we also compare with representative self-supervised learning works [6,14,41].

Object Detection and Instance Segmentation. In this part, we transfer the learned representations of CTC to the object detection and instance segmentation tasks [14,15,46]. Models pre-trained on ImageNet are further fine-tuned with the Mask-RCNN-FPN [16,26] on the MS-COCO dataset [27] in the commonly applied training protocol.

Transferring results are summarized in Table 5. Compared to the vanilla pre-training with cosine learning rate (CosLr), our CTC yields consistently better transfer performances on the COCO dataset. Compared with self-supervised learning methods, *i.e.*, MoCo v2 [6] and InfoMin [41], CTC also achieves comparable or better results on COCO. For one thing, it indicates that our method also preserves information concerning the detection task. For another, the superiority of SSL in transferring tasks is challenged, *i.e.*, our method proves that supervised pre-training has the potential to achieve better results than SSL methods.

Table 6. Top-1 classification accuracies (%) on transferring representations to FGVC datasets. "†" and "‡" denote the backbone network is frozen and unfrozen, respectively.

Pre-training method	CUB200	Aircraft
	Top-1 Acc. (%)	Top-1 Acc. (%)
Res50+CosLr†	62.5	27.8
Res50+CTC(Ours)†	**63.7**	**28.2**
Res50+AA+CosLr†	64.8	31.2
Res50+AA+CTC(Ours)†	**66.1**	**32.1**
Res50+CosLr‡	80.1	82.5
Res50+CTC(Ours)‡	**81.7**	**84.1**
Res50+AA+CosLr‡	81.3	83.4
Res50+AA+CTC(Ours)‡	**83.5**	**85.6**

Fine-Grained Visual Categorization. In this part, representations are transferred to popular fine-grained visual categorization (FGVC) [12,55] datasets. With the backbone network pre-trained on ImageNet frozen and unfrozen, two kinds of transferring experiments are conducted on the CUB-200-2011 (CUB200) [45] and the FGVC-Aircraft (Aircraft) [30] datasets. To compare with SSL methods, we extend the experiment on the large-scale iNaturalist-18 (iNat-18) [44] dataset. Training details are attached in appendix.

Transferring results of CUB200 and Aircraft are reported in Table 6 and 7. By freezing the backbone parameters and training a linear classifier on top of the learned representations, we observe that the representations learned by CTC achieve better performance over the vanilla baseline. Results of training the model with unfrozen backbone are also provided in Table 6. CTC again outperforms the vanilla training, further validating its effectiveness and practicality. Notably, on iNat-18, our method also outperforms the MoCo v1 [14], even the model is pre-trained on the billion-level data Instagram-1B [51]. It further demonstrates that learning transferable representations in the supervised learning is a promising research direction.

Table 7. Top-1 accuracies (%) on iNaturalist and the backbone is frozen. "IN-1M" and "IG-1B" denote pre-training with ImageNet-1M [35] and web Instagram-1B [51] datasets, respectively. All methods (except MoCo v1 IG-1B) are pre-trained on IN-1M.

Pre-training method	Inat-18 Top-1 Acc. (%)
Res50+CosLr	66.1
Res50+MoCo v1 (IN-1M) [14]	65.6
Res50+MoCo v1 (IG-1B) [14]	65.8
Res50+CTC (ours)	**66.4**
Res50+AA+CosLr	66.3
Res50+AA+CTC (ours)	**66.7**

6   Discussion and Conclusion

This study focuses on learning representations with good discriminability and transferability at the same time. The trade-off between these properties is firstly observed by us via a temporal analysis. To explain this incompatibility, we explore the correlation between information-bottleneck trade-off and our observed trade-off, and reveal the over-compression phenomenon. Moreover, we investigate how and why the InfoNCE loss can alleviate the over-compression, and further present the contrastive temporal coding method. Our method successfully make discriminability and transferability compatible. Remarkable transfer learning performances are also achieved. We hope that this work can arouse attentions to the transferability of representations in the conventional supervised learning tasks. In the future, we will explore the existence of over-compression on other popular tasks, e.g., self-supervised learning, object detection and large-scale pre-training.

Acknowledgement. This work was supported in part by the Zhejiang Provincial Natural Science Foundation of China under Grant No. LQ22F020006. We thank anonymous reviewers from ECCV 2022 for insightful comments.

References

1. Alemi, A.A., Fischer, I., Dillon, J.V., Murphy, K.: Deep variational information bottleneck. In: ICLR (2017)
2. Belghazi, M.I., et al.: MINE: mutual information neural estimation. arXiv:1801.04062 (2018)
3. Chen, C., Zheng, Z., Ding, X., Huang, Y., Dou, Q.: Harmonizing transferability and discriminability for adapting object detectors. In: CVPR (2020)
4. Chen, T., Kornblith, S., Norouzi, M., Hinton, G.: A simple framework for contrastive learning of visual representations. In: ICML (2020)
5. Chen, T., Kornblith, S., Swersky, K., Norouzi, M., Hinton, G.: Big self-supervised models are strong semi-supervised learners. In: NeurIPS (2020)
6. Chen, X., Fan, H., Girshick, R., He, K.: Improved baselines with momentum contrastive learning. arXiv:2003.04297 (2020)
7. Chen, X., Wang, S., Long, M., Wang, J.: Transferability vs. discriminability: batch spectral penalization for adversarial domain adaptation. In: ICML (2019)
8. Coates, A., Ng, A., Lee, H.: An analysis of single-layer networks in unsupervised feature learning. In: AISTATS (2011)
9. Cubuk, E.D., Zoph, B., Mane, D., Vasudevan, V., Le, Q.V.: AutoAugment: learning augmentation strategies from data. In: CVPR (2019)
10. Darlow, L.N., Crowley, E.J., Antoniou, A., Storkey, A.J.: CINIC-10 is not ImageNet or CIFAR-10. arXiv:1810.03505 (2018)
11. Feng, Y., Jiang, J., Tang, M., Jin, R., Gao, Y.: Rethinking supervised pre-training for better downstream transferring. In: ICLR (2022)
12. Fu, J., Zheng, H., Mei, T.: Look closer to see better: recurrent attention convolutional neural network for fine-grained image recognition. In: CVPR (2017)
13. Furlanello, T., Lipton, Z., Tschannen, M., Itti, L., Anandkumar, A.: Born again neural networks. In: ICML (2018)
14. He, K., Fan, H., Wu, Y., Xie, S., Girshick, R.: Momentum contrast for unsupervised visual representation learning. In: CVPR (2020)
15. He, K., Girshick, R., Dollár, P.: Rethinking ImageNet pre-training. In: ICCV (2019)
16. He, K., Gkioxari, G., Dollár, P., Girshick, R.: Mask R-CNN. In: ICCV (2017)
17. He, K., Zhang, X., Ren, S., Sun, J.: Deep residual learning for image recognition. In: CVPR (2016)
18. Hinton, G., Vinyals, O., Dean, J.: Distilling the knowledge in a neural network. arXiv:1503.02531 (2015)
19. Hjelm, R.D., et al.: Learning deep representations by mutual information estimation and maximization. In: ICLR (2019)
20. Hu, J., Shen, L., Sun, G.: Squeeze-and-excitation networks. In: CVPR (2018)

21. Kang, B., et al.: Decoupling representation and classifier for long-tailed recognition. In: ICLR (2020)
22. Khosla, P., et al.: Supervised contrastive learning. arXiv preprint arXiv:2004.11362 (2020)
23. Kornblith, S., Chen, T., Lee, H., Norouzi, M.: Why do better loss functions lead to less transferable features? In: NeurIPS (2021)
24. Kornblith, S., Shlens, J., Le, Q.V.: Do better ImageNet models transfer better? In: CVPR (2019)
25. Krizhevsky, A., Hinton, G., et al.: Learning multiple layers of features from tiny images (2009)
26. Lin, T.Y., Dollár, P., Girshick, R., He, K., Hariharan, B., Belongie, S.: Feature pyramid networks for object detection. In: CVPR (2017)
27. Lin, T.Y., et al.: Microsoft COCO: common objects in context. In: ECCV (2014)
28. Long, J., Shelhamer, E., Darrell, T.: Fully convolutional networks for semantic segmentation. In: CVPR (2015)
29. Long, M., Cao, Y., Wang, J., Jordan, M.: Learning transferable features with deep adaptation networks. In: ICML (2015)
30. Maji, S., Rahtu, E., Kannala, J., Blaschko, M., Vedaldi, A.: Fine-grained visual classification of aircraft. arXiv:1306.5151 (2013)
31. Mao, H., Chen, X., Fu, Q., Du, L., Han, S., Zhang, D.: Neuron campaign for initialization guided by information bottleneck theory. In: CIKM (2021)
32. Oord, A.V.D., Li, Y., Vinyals, O.: Representation learning with contrastive predictive coding. arXiv:1807.03748 (2018)
33. Park, T., Efros, A.A., Zhang, R., Zhu, J.Y.: Contrastive learning for unpaired image-to-image translation. In: ECCV (2020)
34. Ren, S., He, K., Girshick, R., Sun, J.: Faster R-CNN: towards real-time object detection with region proposal networks. In: NeurIPS (2015)
35. Russakovsky, O., et al.: ImageNet large scale visual recognition challenge. In: IJCV (2015)
36. Sariyildiz, M.B., Kalantidis, Y., Larlus, D., Alahari, K.: Concept generalization in visual representation learning. In: ICCV (2021)
37. Schroff, F., Kalenichenko, D., Philbin, J.: FaceNet: a unified embedding for face recognition and clustering. In: CVPR (2015)
38. Shao, J., Wen, X., Zhao, B., Xue, X.: Temporal context aggregation for video retrieval with contrastive learning. In: Proceedings of the IEEE/CVF Winter Conference on Applications of Computer Vision (WACV) (2021)
39. Shwartz-Ziv, R., Tishby, N.: Opening the black box of deep neural networks via information. arXiv:1703.00810 (2017)
40. Tian, Y., Krishnan, D., Isola, P.: Contrastive multiview coding. arXiv:1906.05849 (2019)
41. Tian, Y., Sun, C., Poole, B., Krishnan, D., Schmid, C., Isola, P.: What makes for good views for contrastive learning? In: NeurIPS (2020)
42. Tishby, N., Zaslavsky, N.: Deep learning and the information bottleneck principle. In: ITW (2015)
43. Tripuraneni, N., Jordan, M., Jin, C.: On the theory of transfer learning: The importance of task diversity. In: NeurIPS (2020)
44. Van Horn, G., et al.: The INaturalist species classification and detection dataset. In: CVPR (2018)
45. Wah, C., Branson, S., Welinder, P., Perona, P., Belongie, S.: The caltech-ucsd birds-200-2011 dataset (2011)

46. Wang, X., Zhang, R., Shen, C., Kong, T., Li, L.: Dense contrastive learning for self-supervised visual pre-training. arXiv:2011.09157 (2020)
47. Wen, Y., Zhang, K., Li, Z., Qiao, Y.: A discriminative feature learning approach for deep face recognition. In: ECCV (2016)
48. Wu, M., Zhuang, C., Mosse, M., Yamins, D., Goodman, N.: On mutual information in contrastive learning for visual representations. arXiv:2005.13149 (2020)
49. Wu, Z., Xiong, Y., Yu, S.X., Lin, D.: Unsupervised feature learning via non-parametric instance discrimination. In: CVPR (2018)
50. Xiao, T., Li, S., Wang, B., Lin, L., Wang, X.: Joint detection and identification feature learning for person search. In: CVPR (2017)
51. Yalniz, I.Z., Jégou, H., Chen, K., Paluri, M., Mahajan, D.: Billion-scale semi-supervised learning for image classification. arXiv:1905.00546 (2019)
52. You, K., Liu, Y., Wang, J., Long, M.: LogME: practical assessment of pre-trained models for transfer learning. In: ICML (2021)
53. Zhao, B., Cui, Q., Song, R., Qiu, Y., Liang, J.: Decoupled knowledge distillation. In: CVPR (2022)
54. Zhao, H., Shi, J., Qi, X., Wang, X., Jia, J.: Pyramid scene parsing network. In: CVPR (2017)
55. Zheng, H., Fu, J., Mei, T., Luo, J.: Learning multi-attention convolutional neural network for fine-grained image recognition. In: ICCV (2017)
56. Zhou, B., Cui, Q., Wei, X.S., Chen, Z.M.: BBN: bilateral-branch network with cumulative learning for long-tailed visual recognition. In: CVPR (2020)
57. Zhu, R., Zhao, B., Liu, J., Sun, Z., Chen, C.W.: Improving contrastive learning by visualizing feature transformation. In: Proceedings of the IEEE/CVF International Conference on Computer Vision (ICCV) (2021)
58. Zoph, B., et al.: Rethinking pre-training and self-training. In: NeurIPS (2020)

LocVTP: Video-Text Pre-training
for Temporal Localization

Meng Cao[1], Tianyu Yang[2], Junwu Weng[2], Can Zhang[1], Jue Wang[2],
and Yuexian Zou[1,3(✉)]

[1] Scter Engineering, Peking University, Beijing, China
zouyx@pku.edu.cn
[2] Tencent AI Lab, Bellevue, USA
[3] Peng Cheng Laboratory, Shenzhen, China

Abstract. Video-Text Pre-training (VTP) aims to learn transferable representations for various downstream tasks from large-scale web videos. To date, almost all existing VTP methods are limited to *retrieval-based* downstream tasks, *e.g.*, video retrieval, whereas their transfer potentials on *localization-based* tasks, *e.g.*, temporal grounding, are underexplored. In this paper, we experimentally analyze and demonstrate the incompatibility of current VTP methods with localization tasks, and propose a novel **Loc**alization-oriented **V**ideo-**T**ext **P**re-training framework, dubbed as **LocVTP**. Specifically, we perform the fine-grained contrastive alignment as a complement to the coarse-grained one by a clip-word correspondence discovery scheme. To further enhance the temporal reasoning ability of the learned feature, we propose a context projection head and a temporal aware contrastive loss to perceive the contextual relationships. Extensive experiments on four downstream tasks across six datasets demonstrate that our LocVTP achieves state-of-the-art performance on both retrieval-based and localization-based tasks. Furthermore, we conduct comprehensive ablation studies and thorough analyses to explore the optimum model designs and training strategies. Codes are available at https://github.com/mengcaopku/LocVTP.

1 Introduction

Video-Text Pre-training (VTP) [4,26,30,31,39,49,54,67] has attracted increasing attention with the aim to learn generic and transferable *joint* video-language (VL) representations. Compared to the conventional *separate* pre-training on each single modality, *e.g.*, video features are pre-trained under the action recognition datasets (Kinetics [23], Sport1M [22]), VTP has several advantages: 1) It

---

M. Cao—Work done during an internship at Tencent AI Lab.

Supplementary Information The online version contains supplementary material available at https://doi.org/10.1007/978-3-031-19809-0_3.

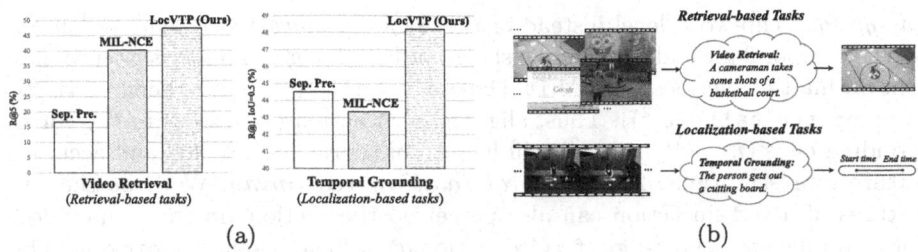

(a)   (b)

Fig. 1. (a) Video retrieval and temporal grounding performance using different pre-trained features. Sep.Pre. means separately pre-training, *i.e.*, the video encoder supervisedly pre-trained on Kinetics [23] and text encoder taken from BERT [12]. **MIL-NCE** and our **LocVTP** are VTP methods pre-trained on HowTo100M [39]. For video retrieval, we use COOT [16] as the downstream method and evaluate on YouCook2 [75] dataset with R@5. For temporal grounding, we take 2D-TAN [74] as the downstream method and evaluate on ActivityNet Captions [24] dataset with R@1, IoU = 0.5. **(b) Retrieval-based and localization-based downstream tasks.** We take video retrieval and temporal grounding as typical examples, respectively. The former needs video-level classification while the latter requires clip-level or frame-level localization.

leverages large-scale unlabeled narrated video data with automatically generated corresponding text data for video-text correspondence pre-training. 2) It tries to map different modality features into a shared latent space, which reduces the difficulties of the cross-modal feature interaction. Thanks to these advantages, VTP has significantly improved the performance of many downstream VL tasks. For example, as illustrated in [16], the video retrieval performance using features pre-trained with the VTP method MIL-NCE [38] is much higher than that using separately pre-trained way (cf. Fig. 1a (left)).

Despite their encouraging performance, we find that most current VTP methods are applicable to limited downstream tasks, *i.e.*, they focus on *retrieval-based* tasks which require video-level predictions, *e.g.*, video retrieval [64], video captioning [45], and video question answering [21]. In contrast, there exists another mainstream *localization-based* tasks which expect more fine-grained clip-level or frame-level predictions, *e.g.*, temporal grounding [15], action segmentation [51], action step localization [77] (cf. Fig. 1b). Unfortunately, through experiments, we find their poor generalization abilities on this type of downstream tasks. For example, on temporal grounding, even pre-trained with a much larger dataset HowTo100M [39], the VTP method MIL-NCE still performs worse than the separately pre-trained counterpart (cf. Fig 1a (right)).

In this paper, we analyze that this poor transfer ability on localization-based tasks is due to the absence of two indispensable characteristics: **1)** *Fine-grained alignment*: We contend that the alignment should be conducted on more *fine-grained* clip-word level instead of the *coarse-grained* video-sentence[1] level. As the temporal grounding example shown in Fig. 2, a given query sentence may contain multiple actions (*e.g.*, "hit the golf ball" (q^{s1}) and "bend down to pick up the ball" (q^{s2})). Thus, aligning each action (or words) to the corresponding clips (*i.e.*, v^{t1} and v^{t2}) will help to obtain more detailed and accurate feature representations. **2)** *Temporal relation reasoning*: We hope the clip features of a certain action can also perceive other actions in the same video. For example, for a typical golf video, action q^{s2} ("bend down to pick up the ball") always occurs shortly after action q^{s1} ("hit the golf ball"). Thus, incorporating such temporal relationship into VTP can help to improve the temporal awareness of video features

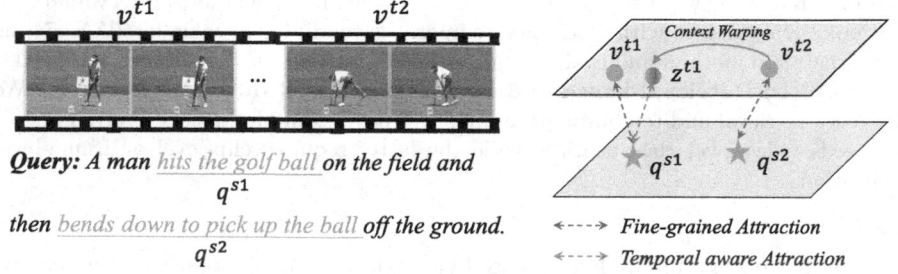

Query: *A man* hits the golf ball *on the field and*
                     q^{s1}

then bends down to pick up the ball *off the ground.*
                     q^{s2}

←---→ *Fine-grained Attraction*

←---→ *Temporal aware Attraction*

Fig. 2. Fine-grained video-text alignment: positive clip-word pairs are selected via cosine similarity and are then forced to be close to each other, *i.e.*, $v^{t1} \leftrightarrow q^{s1}$, $v^{t2} \leftrightarrow q^{s2}$; **Temporal relation reasoning:** a context warping head reconstructs v^{t1} conditioned on v^{t2} and distance $t2 - t1$ while maintaining the cross-modal alignment unchanged, *i.e.*, $z^{t1} = \mathrm{warp}(v^{t2}, t2 - t1) \leftrightarrow q^{s1}$.

Based on these observations, we propose a novel video-text pre-training framework for localization tasks, dubbed as LocVTP. By considering both above-mentioned characteristics, LocVTP achieves state-of-the-art performance not only on the widely studied retrieval-based tasks, but also on the less-focused localization-based tasks. Specifically, **for fine-grained alignment**, we extend the coarse-grained contrastive training with video-sentence alignment to a fine-grained one with clip-word alignment. Since there are no clip-word correspondence annotations in existing large-scale datasets, we utilize the latent space established by the coarse-grained contrastive learning to estimate the clip-word similarity, and then select the clip-word pairs with high similarities as positive samples. To further illustrate this, as shown in Fig. 2 (right), suppose $\{v^{t1}, q^{s1}\}$ and $\{v^{t2}, q^{s2}\}$ are two matched clip-word feature pairs. Semantic embeddings in each pair are mapped to be close to each other, *i.e.*, $v^{t1} \leftrightarrow q^{s1}$, $v^{t2} \leftrightarrow q^{s2}$. **For temporal relation reasoning**, we propose a new pretext task called *context warping*. Here we use Fig. 2 (right) for illustration. Context warping is designed

---

[1] Here we use "sentence" to represent the whole paired text for each video, such as the ASR in HowTo100M [39] or query language in ActivityNet Caption [24].

to generate a new temporally relevant clip features z^{t1}, which imitates v^{t1}, conditioned on another clip v^{t2} and the relative distance $t2 - t1$ in time, $i.e.$, $z^{t1} = \text{warp}(v^{t2}, t2 - t1)$. The predicted relevant clip feature z^{t1} is enforced to maintain the original established cross-modal correspondence unchanged, $i.e.$, $z^{t1} \leftrightarrow q^{s1}$. In this manner, we simulate the contextual reasoning process and enhance the temporal awareness of video features.

We conduct extensive experiments on four downstream tasks ($i.e.$, video retrieval, temporal grounding, action step localization, and action segmentation) across six datasets. The results on both retrieval-based and localization-based tasks demonstrate the superiority and the generalization ability of our LocVTP.

In summary, we make three contributions in this paper:

- We propose a localization-oriented video-text pre-training framework, LocVTP, which benefits both retrieval-based and the less-explored localization-based downstream tasks.
- We pinpoint two crucial designs in LocVTP, $i.e.$, fine-grained video-text alignment and temporal relation reasoning.
- Experimental results show that our LocVTP significantly outperforms previous state-of-the-art methods when transferred to various downstream tasks.

2   Related Work

Video-Text Pre-training (VTP). With the release of the large-scale instructional dataset HowTo100M, VTP has spurred significant interest in the community. Overall, the mainstream methods can be broadly classified into two classes: 1) Generative methods: Several methods [11,20,28,31,34,50,55,56] try to extend BERT [53] to the cross-modal domain, $i.e.$, they accept both visual and textual tokens as input and perform the masked-token prediction task. 2) Discriminative methods. These methods [4,26,30,41] learn representations by differentiating input samples using objectives such as the metric loss [19,58] or contrastive loss [9,18]. ClipBert [26] enables affordable pre-training from sparsely sampled frames. Frozen [4] adapts the recent ViT [13] as the visual encoder and is flexible to be trained on both image and video datasets. T2VLAD [56] and FCA [17] also perform the fine-grained interactions between video clips and phrases. However, both of them resort to additional overload, $e.g.$, k-means cluster or graph auto-encoder. In contrast, our LocVTP explicitly models the clip-word matching with a more light-weighted similarity comparison manner.

Pre-training for Localization Tasks. Compared to the retrieval tasks [21,45, 64] which only require only video-level predictions, localization tasks [15,51,77] are essentially different since they need dense clip-level or frame-level predictions and thus the pre-training for these tasks is more challenging. In the pure video domain, this gap has been noticed and several pre-training works [2,65,66,73] tailored for action localization have been proposed. BSP [65] synthesizes temporal boundaries using existing action recognition datasets and conducts boundary type classification to generate localization-friendly features. TSP [2] trains video encoders to be temporally sensitive by predicting the foreground clip label and classifying whether a clip is inside or outside the action. As for the video-language domain, our LocVTP is the first pre-training framework designed for localization tasks. Besides, compared to TSP and BSP which require label information for supervised pre-training, our LocVTP can directly learn from narrated videos.

3   Approach

3.1   Overview of LocVTP

An overview of LocVTP is illustrated in Fig. 3. We firstly feed the video and language modalities to their respective encoders $f_v(\cdot)$ and $f_q(\cdot)$ to obtain embedded features. We follow the sparse sampling spirit in [26] and sample T clips for each video, yielding the encoded video $v = \{v^t\}_{t=1}^T$, where $v^t \in \mathbb{R}^D$ is the tth clip feature and D is the feature dimension. The text embedding is represented as $q = \{q^s\}_{s=1}^{S_q}$, where $q^s \in \mathbb{R}^D$ is the sth word embedding and S_q is the word length of q.

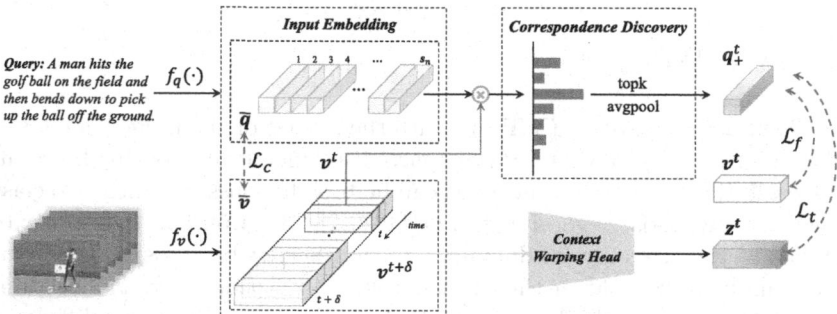

Fig. 3. An overview of LocVTP. $f_v(\cdot)$ and $f_q(\cdot)$ are video and language encoders, respectively. **1)** Coarse-grained contrastive loss $\mathcal{L}_c$ matches the global video and sentence representations $\bar{v}$ and $\bar{q}$. **2)** The clip-word correspondence is firstly built by similarity computing and then fine-grained contrastive loss $\mathcal{L}_f$ conducts detailed cross-modal alignment. Note that for clarity, we only present the correspondence discovery for the clip v^t. **3)** A context warping head is employed to warp the contextual feature $v^{t+\delta}$ and a temporal aware contrastive loss $\mathcal{L}_t$ is applied based on the warped feature z^t.

Three types of contrastive methods are then performed to learn cross-modal features: 1) The coarse-grained contrastive loss builds the video-sentence level alignment; 2) A correspondence discovery strategy is proposed to build clip-word relations, based on which the fine-grained contrastive loss is applied; 3) Temporal aware contrastive loss with the context warping pretext task is proposed to encode temporal information into video representations.

3.2 Coarse-Grained Contrastive Learning

We firstly conduct contrastive alignment at the global video-sentence level. Specifically, to obtain the video and sentence level features, we average pool v and q along the temporal and word index dimension, respectively. The global features are represented as $\bar{v}$, $\bar{q} \in \mathbb{R}^D$. Then we formulate this video-sentence alignment into the contrastive framework [18] as follows:

$$\mathcal{L}_c = -\log \frac{\exp(\bar{v} \cdot \bar{q}/\tau)}{\sum_{i=1}^{N} \exp(\bar{v} \cdot \bar{q}_i/\tau)}, \tag{1}$$

where $\bar{q}_i, i \in [1, N]$, is the sentence feature for other samples within the batch. N denotes the batch size and τ is the temperature parameter. The coarse-grained contrastive loss $\mathcal{L}_c$ serves as a base loss to conduct video-sentence level constraint and induces a basic latent space where the detailed cross-modal matching is achieved. Though usually coarse and noisy, this latent space encodes prior for fine-grained clip-word correspondence discovery. In Sect. 4.6, we design and analyze three potential ways to use this cross-modal matching prior.

3.3 Fine-Grained Contrastive Learning

Beyond the coarse-grained video-sentence alignment, we propose to conduct contrastive learning in a fine-grained manner, *i.e.*, clip-word matching. We contend that introducing such alignment learning into the pre-training stage could narrow down its gap with downstream localization tasks and calibrate the pre-trained feature to be more temporally aware.

Clip-Word Correspondence Discovery. Before performing fine-grained contrastive learning, we firstly need to estimate the clip-word correspondences from video-sentence pairs. Thanks to the priors well established by the coarse-grained contrastive learning, we compute the cosine similarities between the video clips and their corresponding caption words in the pre-built latent space and choose the most similar K words as the correspondence for each video clip. Note that we select multiple positive words rather than simply pick one with the highest similarity because individual words may have vague meanings while sense-group[2] conveys more precise information (cf. Sect. 4.7).

Given the video sentence pair $\{v, q\}$, for the encoded t^{th} video clip v^t, we compute its cosine similarities with the sth word embedding q^s and apply the topk operation to select the most matched K ones. Following [57], these K selected items are average pooled to form the final positive sample:

$$q_+^t = \text{avgpool}\left(\arg\text{topk}_{s \in [1, S_q]} (v^t \cdot q^s)\right), \tag{2}$$

where q_+^t is the final positive sample for v^t. $(u \cdot v) = u^\top v / \|u\| \|v\|$ represents the cosine similarity between ℓ_2 normalized u and v. This process can be efficiently performed for all the video clips using matrix operations.

---

[2] A group or sequence of words conveying a particular meaning or idea in linguistics..

Fine-Grained Contrastive Loss. With the selected clip-word correspondence as positive pairs, we perform fine-grained representation learning following the cross-modal InfoNCE [18] loss (cf. Fig. 4a). The negative samples are taken from the other words within the batch. Therefore, the fine-grained contrastive loss is defined as follows.

$$\mathcal{L}_f = \frac{1}{T} \sum_{t=1}^{T} -\log \frac{\exp(\boldsymbol{v}^t \cdot \boldsymbol{q}_+^t / \tau)}{\sum_{i=1}^{N} \sum_{s=1}^{S_{q_i}} \exp(\boldsymbol{v}^t \cdot \boldsymbol{q}_i^s / \tau)}, \tag{3}$$

where $\boldsymbol{q}_i^s$ is the sth word feature of the ith sentence $\boldsymbol{q}_i$.

3.4 Temporal Aware Contrastive Learning

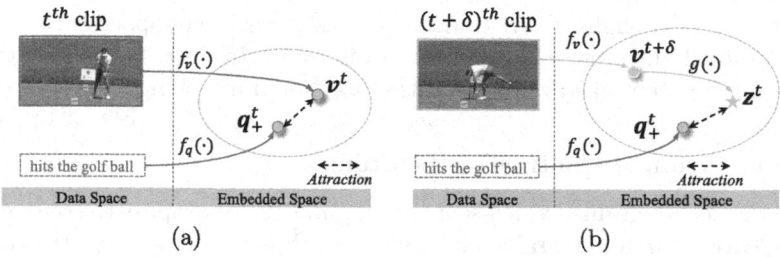

(a)   (b)

Fig. 4. Illustrations of (a) fine-grained contrastive Loss and (b) temporal aware contrastive loss. $\boldsymbol{v}^t$ is the tth clip of video $\boldsymbol{v}$. $\boldsymbol{q}_+^t$ is the pooled positive word features. $\boldsymbol{z}^t$ is the warped feature. We only present positive samples and omit negative ones.

Compared with the video-level retrieval task, which favors temporal invariant features [40,42], the clip-level localization task [6–8,33,60,61,70–72] prefers temporal aware video embeddings. Specifically, correlated actions in the same video should perceive each other. This characteristic is however not embodied in the aforementioned contrastive learning.

Context Warping Head. To alleviate this, we set up a *context-warping* operation to enforce the video clip to perceive the context. For the video clip $\boldsymbol{v}^t$ in a matched clip-word pair $\{\boldsymbol{v}^t, \boldsymbol{q}_+^t\}$ (cf. Sect. 3.3), we warp its contextual video clip with δ temporal distance, *i.e.*, $\boldsymbol{v}^{t+\delta}$, to "reconstruct" itself. To supervise this warping process, we set up a temporal aware contrastive loss to maintain the established correspondence. Specifically, we propose a *context warping head* $g(\cdot)$ to instantiate this warping process, by taking the context clip feature $\boldsymbol{v}^{t+\delta}$ and temporal distance δ as input.

$$\begin{aligned} \boldsymbol{z}^t &= g(\boldsymbol{v}^{t+\delta}; \delta) \\ &= \text{ReLU}\left(W[\boldsymbol{v}^{t+\delta}, \text{sgn}(\delta), |\delta|] \right), \end{aligned} \tag{4}$$

where $\boldsymbol{z}^t$ is the warped feature. $W \in \mathbb{R}^{(D+2) \times D}$ are the trainable weights. δ is randomly sampled within the range of $[-\delta_{max}, \delta_{max}]$. $\text{sgn}(\cdot)$ is the sign function which returns 1 for positive values and -1 for negative ones. Here $\mathrm{sgn}(\delta)$ and $|\delta|$ indicate the direction and distance of the temporal difference δ, respectively.

Temporal Aware Contrastive Loss. Through the context warping head, the warped feature $\boldsymbol{z}^t$ should mimic the reference feature $\boldsymbol{v}^t$. Since $\boldsymbol{v}^t$ has the clip-word alignment with $\boldsymbol{q}^t_+$, such correspondence should be preserved between the warped feature $\boldsymbol{z}^t$ and $\boldsymbol{q}^t_+$ (cf. Fig. 4b).

$$\mathcal{L}_t = \frac{1}{T} \sum_{t=1}^{T} - \log \frac{\exp(\boldsymbol{z}^t \cdot \boldsymbol{q}^t_+ / \tau)}{\sum_{i=1}^{N} \sum_{s=1}^{S_{q_i}} \exp(\boldsymbol{z}^t \cdot \boldsymbol{q}^s_i / \tau)}. \tag{5}$$

This process enforces video features to learn the ability of temporally reasoning, thus leading to more localization-friendly video features.

Integrating the above constraints, our final loss function is as follows.

$$\mathcal{L} = \lambda_c \mathcal{L}_c + \lambda_f \mathcal{L}_f + \lambda_t \mathcal{L}_t, \tag{6}$$

where λ_c, λ_f, and λ_t balance the focus on different constraints during training.

4 Experiments

4.1 Settings of Pre-training

Datasets. We pre-trained our model on three public datasets: **1)** HowTo100M [39]. It consists of more than 1.2M videos accompanied with ASR-generated speech transcription. The provided transcription is used to create video-sentence pairs separated by each timestamp. **2)** WebVid-2M [39]. It contains about 2.5M well-aligned web video-text pairs. **3)** Google Conceptual Captions [48]. It contains 3.3M image and description pairs harvested from the web.

Encoders. Following [4,54,67], we adopted ViT-B/16 [13] with space-time attention [5] as the video encoder. The spatial attention weights in the transformer were initialized with ImageNet-21k pre-trained weights while the temporal attention weights were set to zero. We chose a lightweight DistilBERT [47] as the language encoder. Following [3,4,41,52], the language encoder was initialized with the weights pre-trained on English Wikipedia and Toronto Book Corpus.

Implementation Details. For the video in each video-sentence pair, we sampled 8 clips of 16 frames equidistantly and fed them to the video encoder to obtain clip-level features. All frames were resized to 224×224. For downstream transfer, we extracted video features with the well-trained model in a dense manner, i.e., every 16 consecutive frames were grouped to compute one clip feature.

Experiments were conducted on 64 V100 GPUs with a batch size of 256 and lasted for 200 epochs. We used Adam [32] with the initial learning rate 10^{-4} as the optimizer. The learning rate decayed by 0.1 at the 100th and 160th epoch. Random flip, random crop, and color jitter for video data augmentation were included. The loss balance factors λ_c, λ_f, and λ_t were set to 0.5, 1, 1, respectively. The temperature factor τ used in contrastive learning was set to 0.07 following [43,59] and K in Eq.(2) was set to 3. Features in all three contrastive losses were ℓ_2-normalized before computation (Table 1).

4.2   Transfer Results on Video Retrieval

Datasets. We evaluate our LocVTP on the widely-used benchmark **MSR-VTT** dataset [64]. It is composed of 10K YouTube videos (9K for training and 1K for test). We report results on the train/test splits introduced in [69].

Results. 1) As can be seen, we achieve state-of-the-art performance under both sets of data, *i.e.*, HowTo100M and CC3M+WV2M. Specifically, when pre-trained on CC3M+WV2M, LocVTP outperforms Frozen [4] by an absolute lift of 4.8% on R@5. **2)** It should be pointed out that although using RGB data only, our LocVTP achieves better performance than the methods using multi-modal expert features including motion, face, and speech, *c.g.*, MMT [14]. **3)** The recent work CLIP [43] provides a stronger vision encoder and we also evaluate the performance based on it. It is shown that the CLIP's weights greatly improve the performance of LocVTP with R@5 achieving 72.8%, surpassing top-performing

Table 1. Video retrieval performance on MSR-VTT. Vis Enc. Init.: Datasets used for pre-training visual encoders. Methods using multi-modal features are grayed out. COCO: Coco Captions [10]; VGen: Visual genome [25]; CC3M: Conceptual captions [48]; WV2M: WebVid-2M [4]; † denotes the technical report available on ArXiv.

Method	Vis Enc. Init.	Pre-trained Data	#pairs	R@1	R@5	R@10	MdR
UniVL [35]	-	HowTo100M	136M	21.2	49.6	63.1	6.0
ClipBERT [26]	-	COCO, VGen	5.6M	22.0	46.8	59.9	6.0
CE [31]	Multi-modal	HowTo100M	136M	20.9	48.8	62.4	6.0
MMT [14]	Multi-modal	HowTo100M	136M	26.6	57.1	69.6	4.0
HIT [30]	Multi-modal	HowTo100M	136M	30.7	60.9	73.2	2.6
Clip4clip† [36]	CLIP	HowTo100M	136M	44.5	71.4	81.6	2.0
VideoClip [63]	CLIP	HowTo100M	136M	30.9	55.4	66.8	-
OA-Trans [54]	CLIP	CC3M, WV2M	5.5M	40.9	70.4	80.3	2.0
Frozen [4]	ImageNet	CC3M, WV2M	5.5M	31.0	59.5	70.5	3.0
ActBERT [76]	VisGenome	HowTo100M	136M	16.3	42.8	56.9	10.0
SupportSet [41]	IG65M, ImageNet	HowTo100M	136M	30.1	58.5	69.3	3.0
HERO [27]	ImageNet, Kinetics	HowTo100M	136M	16.8	43.4	57.7	-
AVLnet [46]	ImageNet, Kinetics	HowTo100M	136M	27.1	55.6	66.6	4.0
NoiseEstimation [3]	ImageNet, Kinetics	HowTo100M	136M	17.4	41.6	53.6	8.0
DECEMBER [52]	ImageNet, Kinetics	HowTo100M	136M	30.7	60.9	73.2	2.6
OA-Trans [54]	ImageNet	CC3M, WV2M	5.5M	35.8	63.4	76.5	3.0
RegionLearner† [67]	ImageNet	CC3M, WV2M	5.5M	36.3	63.9	72.5	3.0
LocVTP (Ours)	ImageNet	HowTo100M	136M	37.4	66.6	80.5	3.0
LocVTP (Ours)	CLIP	HowTo100M	136M	46.3	72.8	82.0	2.0
LocVTP (Ours)	**ImageNet**	**CC3M,WV2M**	**5.5M**	**36.5**	**64.3**	**76.8**	**3.0**
Zero-shot							
SupportSet [41]	IG65M, ImageNet	HowTo100M	136M	8.7	23.0	31.1	31.0
Frozen [4]	ImageNet	CC3M, WV2M	5.5M	18.7	39.5	51.6	10.0
OA-Trans [54]	ImageNet	CC3M, WV2M	5.5M	23.4	47.5	55.6	8.0
OA-Trans [54]	CLIP	CC3M, WV2M	5.5M	31.4	55.3	64.8	4.0
LocVTP (Ours)	ImageNet	HowTo100M	136M	24.7	48.9	56.1	8.0
LocVTP (Ours)	CLIP	HowTo100M	136M	32.7	55.7	64.9	4.0
LocVTP (Ours)	**ImageNet**	**CC3M,WV2M**	**5.5M**	**22.1**	**48.0**	**55.3**	**8.0**

CLIP-based methods. **4)** Our LocVTP also outperforms previous methods under the zero-shot setting, showing its generalization ability.

4.3 Transfer Results on Temporal Grounding

Settings. We validate the performance of pre-trained representations on temporal grounding, which aims to localize actions corresponding to the sentence from an untrimmed video. Specifically, we re-train the mainstream temporal grounding method 2D-TAN [74][3] by only replacing the original input features with pre-trained ones. For ease of feature extraction, we choose representative VTP methods with publicly-available codes for comparisons.

Datasets and Metrics. **1)** ActivityNet Captions (ANet) [24]. It contains 20K untrimmed videos with 100K descriptions. By convention, we use 37,417 video-query pairs for training, 17,505 pairs for validation, and 17,031 pairs for testing. **2)** Charades-STA [15]. Following the official split, 12,408 video-query pairs are used for training, and 3,720 pairs for testing. **3)** TACoS [44]. It has 10,146 video-query pairs for training, 4,589 pairs for validation, and 4,083 pairs for testing.

Following prior works, we adopt R@n, IoU@m (abbreviated as R_n^m) as the metric, Specifically, R_n^m is defined as the percentage of at least one of top-n retrieved moments having IoU with the ground-truth moment larger than m.

Table 2. Temporal grounding performances using pre-trained representations. Sep.Pre.: separately pre-training, *i.e.*, the video encoder supervisedly pretrained on Kinetics and text encoder taken from BERT. We retrain the temporal grounding method 2D-TAN [74] using the pre-trained features. HT: HowTo100M; CO: Coco Captions [10]; VG: Visual genome [25]; CC: Conceptual captions [48]; WV: WebVid-2M [4]; **HT** ‡: the subset of HowTo100M with the same training volume as Kinetics (300K pairs). Methods with * are not open source and we implement them ourselves. † denotes the technical report available on ArXiv.

Models	PT Data	ANet Captions				Charades-STA				TACoS			
		$R_1^{0.5}$	$R_1^{0.7}$	$R_5^{0.5}$	$R_5^{0.7}$	$R_1^{0.5}$	$R_1^{0.7}$	$R_5^{0.5}$	$R_5^{0.7}$	$R_1^{0.3}$	$R_1^{0.5}$	$R_5^{0.3}$	$R_5^{0.5}$
Sep.Pre. [74]	Kinetics	44.4	27.1	77.6	62.1	39.7	23.8	79.6	52.3	37.2	25.6	58.2	45.5
LocVTP (Ours)	**HT‡**	**45.2**	**27.1**	**78.3**	**63.5**	**40.3**	**24.2**	**80.6**	**52.7**	**38.4**	**25.9**	**59.0**	**45.9**
VideoBERT*[49]	HT	37.2	21.0	66.7	53.6	32.7	19.5	68.1	46.2	33.8	22.2	51.6	41.0
MIL-NCE [38]	HT	41.8	24.5	73.5	57.7	37.0	21.2	74.3	50.4	35.1	23.5	53.7	42.5
UniVL [35]	HT	42.2	25.4	75.3	60.5	38.2	22.7	77.2	51.4	35.7	23.7	55.8	43.7
SupportSet* [41]	HT	41.9	25.2	74.7	58.3	37.4	21.6	75.6	50.9	35.5	23.5	54.2	43.2
LocVTP (Ours)	HT	48.2	30.5	80.1	64.7	43.6	26.3	81.9	55.3	41.6	28.9	61.4	47.6
Frozen [4]	CC,WV	43.3	25.8	75.8	59.3	38.8	22.9	77.6	50.3	35.7	23.5	54.4	43.7
OA-Trans*[54]	CC, WV	43.6	25.9	76.5	60.2	39.2	22.6	78.5	50.8	35.2	22.5	53.4	42.6
LocVTP (Ours)	**CC,WV**	**46.1**	**27.6**	**78.9**	**63.7**	**41.2**	**24.8**	**81.3**	**53.5**	**39.6**	**27.8**	**60.4**	**47.9**
December [52]	HT	43.0	25.1	76.0	60.2	37.2	21.6	78.3	50.6	34.8	22.9	55.1	43.9
ClipBERT [26]	CO,VG	42.6	24.6	75.3	59.7	37.0	20.8	77.7	50.2	33.7	21.0	54.3	43.3

---

[3] We choose 2D-TAN since it is relatively simple without too many dataset-specific parameters, which can fairly verify the effectiveness of pre-training features. Results on more advanced baselines are available in the supplementary material.

Results. 1) As shown in Table 2, even trained with a much larger dataset, the current popular video-text pre-training frameworks achieve inferior performance compared to the separately pre-trained one. For example, Frozen [4] reaches 43.3% at $R_1^{0.5}$ on ANet Captions, which is 1.1% absolute value lower than the separately pre-trained counterpart. 2) Either pre-trained on HowTo100M or CC + WV, our LocVTP outperforms both video-text pre-training methods by a large margin on all three datasets. For example, pre-trained on HowTo100M, LocVTP surpasses the separately pre-trained method by 3.8% on $R_1^{0.5}$ of ANet Captions. 3) For more fair comparisons, we sample a subset of HowTo100M by selecting the same training sample as Kinetics [23] (300K training pairs), denoted as HT‡ in Table 2. Although using noisy ASR captions, the results demonstrates that under the same training data volume, our LocVTP still shows better performance compared to the separately pre-trained method. This manifests that our performance improvement is brought by the sound architecture design rather than just the use of the large-scale dataset.

4.4 Transfer Results on Action Step Localization

Settings. In action step localization, each video belongs to a task and is annotated with multiple action steps described with short natural languages. The goal is to align each frame with the correct step in the text form. Following [35,39,68,76], we take [77] as the downstream localization method. Specifically, we compute the similarity between each frame and the action step descriptions in feature space to find the optimal frame-wise order of action steps for a video.

Datasets and Metrics. We experiment on the instructional video dataset CrossTask [77], which includes 83 tasks and 4.7K videos. Each task is described with an ordered list of steps with manual natural language descriptions. We perform the same evaluation protocol as in [77] by reporting the average recall (CTR).

Results. Table 3 reports the action step localization performance on CrossTask dataset. Our LocVTP pre-trained feature achieves state-of-the-art performance with CTR reaching 51.7%, surpassing the previous method VideoClip by 4.4%. Our competitive performance demonstrates that LocVTP features can effectively perceive detailed action steps.

Table 3. Comparison results of action step localization (CTR: average recall) and action segmentation (FA: frame-wise accuracy).

Method	CTR	FA
Zhukov et al. [77]	31.6	–
NN-Viterbi [1]	–	21.2
CBT [38]	–	53.9
MIL-NCE [38]	40.5	61.0
ActBERT [76]	41.4	57.0
UniVL [35]	42.0	70.0
TACo [68]	42.5	68.4
VideoClip [63]	47.3	68.7
VLM [62]	46.5	68.4
LocVTP (Ours)	**51.7**	**72.9**

4.5   Transfer Results on Action Segmentation

Settings. We assess our LocVTP on action segmentation, which aims to predict the action label frame-wisely for each video frame. It is a pure vision task without the use of the text encoder. Following [35,68,76], we encode the input video frames with the well-trained video encoder and apply a linear classifier upon the features to predict action labels.

Datasets and Metrics. We conduct experiments on the widely used COIN dataset [51] and the frame-wise accuracy (FA) is taken as the evaluation metric.

Results. As shown in Table 3, our LocVTP achieves state-of-the-art performance with FA reaching 72.9%. This further demonstrates the superiority of our feature in localization tasks even in the absence of language guidance.

4.6   Ablation Study on Training Objective[4]

Training Strategy. Coarse-grained contrastive alignment loss $\mathcal{L}_c$ provides a basic cross-modal matching prior and we introduce three potential ways to use it: **1)** *multi-stage training*: first perform coarse-grained training and then use the trained model to initialize other stages. **2)** *warm-up training*: decrease λ_c exponentially from 1 to 0 throughout the training process. **3)** *weighted training*: set λ_c to a constant value. Here we set $\lambda_c = 0.5$. As shown in Table 4a, we find the weighted training strategy achieves the best performance and warm-up training is slightly behind. Multi-stage training is the least effective one.

Loss Component. We present the loss component ablations in Table 4b. As shown, both fine-grained loss $\mathcal{L}_f$ and temporal aware loss $\mathcal{L}_t$ are crucial. For example, compared to the full version (exp.#1), removing $\mathcal{L}_f$ and $\mathcal{L}_t$ brings about 1.4% and 1.5% performance degradation on the $R_1^{0.5}$ metric, respectively.

More Downstream Temporal Grounding Baselines. We take another temporal grounding method CSMGAN [29] as the downstream baseline. As shown in Table. 4c, our LocVTP pre-trained feature consistently benefits this more advanced baseline.

4.7   Ablations on Fine-grained Contrastive Loss (see Footnote 4)

Correspondence Discovery Strategies. We experiment four potential strategies to extract cross-modal correspondences: **1)** *random*: randomly select K words for each clip; **2)** *2d-topk*: select the most similar $K \times T$ clip-word pairs; **3)** *word-topk*: select the most similar K clips for each word; **4)** *clip-topk*: select the most similar K words for each clip, namely the method illustrated in Sect. 3.3. As indicated in Table 5a, the *random* and *2d-topk* matching strategies are the

---

[4] If not specified, all ablation studies are conducted on the downstream temporal grounding task at ActivityNet Captions dataset. We use LocVTP pre-trained on HowTo100M with ImageNet initialization..

Table 4. Ablations studies of (a) training strategies; (b) loss component; (c) comparison results on temporal grounding method CSMGAN [29]. Sep.Pre.: separately pretraining, *i.e.*, the video encoder supervisedly pre-trained on Kinetics and text encoder taken from BERT.

Mode	$R_1^{0.5}$	$R_1^{0.7}$
multi-stage	47.4	29.7
warm-up	47.7	30.1
weighted	**48.2**	**30.5**

(a)

	$\mathcal{L}_c$	$\mathcal{L}_f$	$\mathcal{L}_t$	$R_1^{0.5}$	$R_1^{0.7}$
#1	✓	✓	✓	**48.2**	**30.5**
#2	✓	✓		$46.7_{-1.5}$	$29.4_{-1.1}$
#3	✓		✓	$46.8_{-1.4}$	$29.6_{-0.9}$
#4	✓			$45.6_{-2.6}$	$29.0_{-1.5}$

(b)

Method	$R_1^{0.5}$	$R_1^{0.7}$
Sep.Pre. [29]	48.9	29.0
Frozen [4]	47.3	26.8
LocVTP	**53.9**	**34.6**

(c)

two worst options. For the *word-topk* matching, it is also sub-optimal, which can be attributed to the possibility of introducing words without concrete meanings (*e.g.*, articles or pronouns) into matched pairs.

Number of Selected Pairs K. We further ablate the hyper-parameter K used in the *clip-topk* strategy. Table 5b shows that the performance saturates at $K = 3$ and slightly decreases for $K = 4$. We conjecture that this may be because too few words have vague meanings while too large K value leads to the inability to establish accurate correspondences.

4.8 Ablations on Temporal Aware Contrastive Loss (see Footnote 4)

Table 5. Ablations studies of (a) correspondence discovery strategies; (b) selected pair number K; (c) context projection head. sgn(δ), $|\delta|$ denotes the direction and distance; (d) the maximum bias distance; (e) intra-modal *v.s.* cross-modal $\mathcal{L}_t$; (f) linear localization accuracy. $Accu_o$ and $Accu_d$ are order and distance prediction accuracy.

	$R_1^{0.5}$	$R_1^{0.7}$
random	42.0	25.8
2d-topk	44.8	27.2
word-topk	47.0	28.7
clip-topk	**48.2**	**30.5**

(a)

K	$R_1^{0.5}$	$R_1^{0.7}$
1	46.3	28.8
2	47.5	29.7
3	**48.2**	**30.5**
4	48.0	29.8

(b)

sgn(δ)	$|\delta|$	$R_1^{0.5}$	$R_1^{0.7}$
✓	✓	**48.2**	**30.5**
✓	✗	47.3	29.3
✗	✓	47.1	29.0
✗	✗	46.2	28.1

(c)

δ_{max}	$R_1^{0.5}$	$R_1^{0.7}$
2	47.6	29.2
3	47.8	29.5
4	**48.2**	**30.5**
5	47.7	28.9

(d)

$\mathcal{L}_c$ Mode	$R_1^{0.5}$	$R_1^{0.7}$
intra-modal	47.7	29.8
cross-modal	**48.2**	**30.5**

(e)

Method	$Accu_o$	$Accu_d$
LocVTP (w/ $\mathcal{L}_c$)	**72.8**	**58.2**
LocVTP (w/o $\mathcal{L}_c$)	69.0	56.5
UniVL [35]	64.2	52.8
MIL-NCE [38]	61.3	51.4

(f)

Context Projection Head Components. In Eq. (4), the warped feature is generated based on both the direction sgn(δ) and distance $|\delta|$. Here we investigate eliminating either of them to see the difference. We observe in Table. 5c that removing either component decreases the performance, which indicates that both the direction and distance of bias δ are crucial for feature warping.

Maximum Bias Distance δ_{max}. Here we ablate different values for δ_{max}. From Table 5d, we can see that $\delta_{max} = 4$ achieves the best performance. This may be because that small bias makes the model unable to perceive enough context, while a large bias makes contextual reasoning too difficult.

Intra-modal *v.s.* Cross-modal Constraint. In Sect. 3.4, given the matched clip-word pair $\{v^t, q_+^t\}$ and the warped feature z^t, we force the *cross-modal* supervision, *i.e.*, $z^t \leftrightarrow q_+^t$. Here, we apply the temporal aware contrastive loss $\mathcal{L}_t$ in a *intra-modal* manner which regards z^t and v^t as positive pairs, *i.e.*, $z^t \leftrightarrow v^t$. The results in Table 5 e show that our adopted cross-modal mode outperforms the intra-modal one.

Temporal Sensitivity Analysis. As a sanity check, we devise two proxy tasks to evaluate the temporal sensitivity of pre-trained video features. As shown in Fig. 5a, n equidistantly sampled clips from one video are fed into the frozen video backbone to extract their corresponding features. Two linear classifiers are trained to perform two tasks: *order prediction* and *distance estimation*. The first task predicts the temporal index while the second one estimates the temporal distance of two clips. The results in Table 5f show that our LocVTP with temporal aware loss $\mathcal{L}_t$ outperforms the variant without it as well as two typical VTP methods (*i.e.*, UniVL and MIL-NCE), which shows that $\mathcal{L}_t$ clearly contributes to the localization ability.

4.9   Visualization[5]

Cross-modal Correspondence Visualizations. Figure 5b shows two frames[6] and their corresponding similarity scores with caption words. The top K highest scored words are marked with red ($K = 3$). Frame #1 and frame #2 have similar appearance views yet correspond to different action processes. Our method pinpoints the subtle differences and accurately finds the most relevant words.

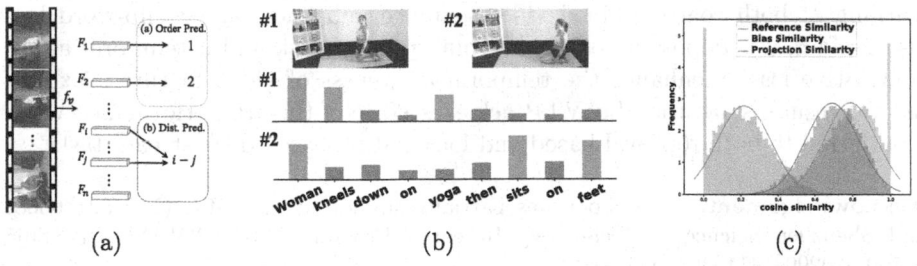

(a)   (b)   (c)

Fig. 5. (a) Linear localization evaluations including order and distance prediction; (b) Cross-modal correspondence visualizations. Top K responsive words are marked with red. (c) Gaussian distributions of the reference, biased, and projected similarities. (Color figure online)

---

[5] More visualizations are left in the supplementary materials..

[6] Here we use "frame" to indicate the center frame of a video snippet.

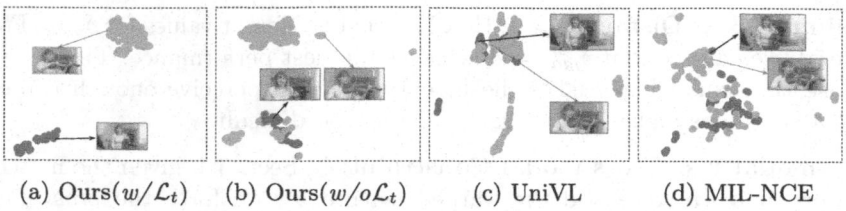

(a) Ours($w/\mathcal{L}_t$)   (b) Ours($w/o\mathcal{L}_t$)   (c) UniVL   (d) MIL-NCE

Fig. 6. UMAP visualizations. Clips corresponding to ground-truth caption are marked with green while others are with gray. (Color figure online)

UMAP Visualizations. As shown in Fig. 6, we provide UMAP [37] visualizations for *fused* multi-modal features, which are generated by multiplying the extracted video feature by one query feature. With the temporal aware loss $\mathcal{L}_t$, our LocVTP shows more separable distributions compared with LocVTP w/o $\mathcal{L}_t$, manifesting that $\mathcal{L}_t$ helps distinguish action-of-interest from background.

Similarity Distribution Visualizations. In Eq.(4), context projection head warps contextual clip $v^{t+\delta}$ to the reference one v^t. Here we collect 10K paired training samples and compute three sets of cosine similarities: reference similarity (v^t, q_+^t), bias similarity $(v^{t+\delta}, q_+^t)$, and projection similarity (z^t, q_+^t). Figure 5c plots the histogram of these similarities. We can see that the distribution of projection similarity is close to that of reference similarity while far away from that of bias similarity. This demonstrates that our context projection head can effectively warp contextual features conditioned on the temporal information.

5   Conclusions

In this paper, we propose LocVTP, the first video-text pre-training framework for temporal localization tasks. Specifically, we apply cross-modal contrastive learning at both coarse-grained video-sentence and fine-grained clip-word levels. Besides, we propose a context warping pretext task and a temporal aware contrastive loss to enhance the temporal awareness of video features. Experimental results show that LocVTP achieves state-of-the-art performance when transferred to both retrieval-based and localization-based downstream tasks.

Acknowledgement. This paper was partially supported by NSFC (No: 62176008) and Shenzhen Science & Technology Research Program (No: GXWD20201231165 807007-20200814115301001).

References

1. Alayrac, J.B., Bojanowski, P., Agrawal, N., Sivic, J., Laptev, I., Lacoste-Julien, S.: Unsupervised learning from narrated instruction videos. In: Proceedings of the IEEE Conference on Computer Vision and Pattern Recognition, pp. 4575–4583 (2016)

2. Alwassel, H., Giancola, S., Ghanem, B.: TSP: temporally-sensitive pretraining of video encoders for localization tasks. In: Proceedings of the IEEE/CVF International Conference on Computer Vision, pp. 3173–3183 (2021)

3. Amrani, E., Ben Ari, R., Rotman, D., Bronstein, A.: Noise estimation using density estimation for self-supervised multimodal learning. arXiv preprint arXiv:2003.03186 (2020)

4. Bain, M., Nagrani, A., Varol, G., Zisserman, A.: Frozen in time: a joint video and image encoder for end-to-end retrieval. arXiv preprint arXiv:2104.00650 (2021)

5. Bertasius, G., Wang, H., Torresani, L.: Is space-time attention all you need for video understanding? arXiv (2021)

6. Cao, M., Chen, L., Shou, M.Z., Zhang, C., Zou, Y.: On pursuit of designing multimodal transformer for video grounding. EMNLP (2021)

7. Cao, M., Zhang, C., Chen, L., Shou, M.Z., Zou, Y.: Deep motion prior for weakly-supervised temporal action localization. arXiv preprint arXiv:2108.05607 (2021)

8. Chen, L., et al.: Rethinking the bottom-up framework for query-based video localization. In: AAAI, pp. 10551–10558 (2020)

9. Chen, T., Kornblith, S., Norouzi, M., Hinton, G.: A simple framework for contrastive learning of visual representations. In: ICML, pp. 1597–1607 (2020)

10. Chen, X., et al.: Microsoft COCO captions: data collection and evaluation server. arXiv preprint arXiv:1504.00325 (2015)

11. Chen, Y.-C., et al.: UNITER: UNiversal image-TExt representation learning. In: Vedaldi, A., Bischof, H., Brox, T., Frahm, J.-M. (eds.) ECCV 2020. LNCS, vol. 12375, pp. 104–120. Springer, Cham (2020). https://doi.org/10.1007/978-3-030-58577-8_7

12. Devlin, J., Chang, M.W., Lee, K., Toutanova, K.: BERT: pre-training of deep bidirectional transformers for language understanding. arXiv preprint arXiv:1810.04805 (2018)

13. Dosovitskiy, A., et al.: An image is worth 16×16 words: transformers for image recognition at scale. In: ICLR (2021)

14. Gabeur, V., Sun, C., Alahari, K., Schmid, C.: Multi-modal transformer for video retrieval. In: Vedaldi, A., Bischof, H., Brox, T., Frahm, J.-M. (eds.) ECCV 2020. LNCS, vol. 12349, pp. 214–229. Springer, Cham (2020). https://doi.org/10.1007/978-3-030-58548-8_13

15. Gao, J., Sun, C., Yang, Z., Nevatia, R.: TALL: temporal activity localization via language query. In: ICCV, pp. 5267–5275 (2017)

16. Ging, S., Zolfaghari, M., Pirsiavash, H., Brox, T.: COOT: cooperative hierarchical transformer for video-text representation learning. In: Advances in Neural Information Processing Systems, vol. 33, pp. 22605–22618 (2020)

17. Han, N., Chen, J., Xiao, G., Zhang, H., Zeng, Y., Chen, H.: Fine-grained cross-modal alignment network for text-video retrieval. In: Proceedings of the 29th ACM International Conference on Multimedia, pp. 3826–3834 (2021)

18. He, K., Fan, H., Wu, Y., Xie, S., Girshick, R.: Momentum contrast for unsupervised visual representation learning. In: Proceedings of the IEEE/CVF Conference on Computer Vision and Pattern Recognition, pp. 9729–9738 (2020)

19. Hoffer, E., Ailon, N.: Deep metric learning using triplet network. In: Feragen, A., Pelillo, M., Loog, M. (eds.) SIMBAD 2015. LNCS, vol. 9370, pp. 84–92. Springer, Cham (2015). https://doi.org/10.1007/978-3-319-24261-3_7

20. Hu, R., Singh, A.: Transformer is all you need: Multimodal multitask learning with a unified transformer. arXiv (2021)

21. Jang, Y., Song, Y., Yu, Y., Kim, Y., Kim, G.: TGIF-QA: toward spatio-temporal reasoning in visual question answering. In: Proceedings of the IEEE Conference on Computer Vision and Pattern Recognition, pp. 2758–2766 (2017)
22. Karpathy, A., et al.: Large-scale video classification with convolutional neural networks. In: CVPR (2014)
23. Kay, W., et al.: The kinetics human action video dataset. arXiv (2017)
24. Krishna, R., Hata, K., Ren, F., Fei-Fei, L., Carlos Niebles, J.: Dense-captioning events in videos. In: ICCV, pp. 706–715 (2017)
25. Krishna, R., et al.: Visual genome: connecting language and vision using crowd-sourced dense image annotations. IJCV **123**, 32–73 (2017)
26. Lei, J., et al.: Less is more: ClipBERT for video-and-language learning via sparse sampling. In: Proceedings of the IEEE/CVF Conference on Computer Vision and Pattern Recognition, pp. 7331–7341 (2021)
27. Li, L., Chen, Y.C., Cheng, Y., Gan, Z., Yu, L., Liu, J.: Hero: hierarchical encoder for video+ language omni-representation pre-training. arXiv preprint arXiv:2005.00200 (2020)
28. Li, L.H., Yatskar, M., Yin, D., Hsieh, C.J., Chang, K.W.: VisualBERT: a simple and performant baseline for vision and language. arXiv (2019)
29. Liu, D., Qu, X., Liu, X.Y., Dong, J., Zhou, P., Xu, Z.: Jointly cross-and self-modal graph attention network for query-based moment localization. In: ACM MM, pp. 4070–4078 (2020)
30. Liu, S., Fan, H., Qian, S., Chen, Y., Ding, W., Wang, Z.: HiT: hierarchical transformer with momentum contrast for video-text retrieval. arXiv preprint arXiv:2103.15049 (2021)
31. Liu, Y., Albanie, S., Nagrani, A., Zisserman, A.: Use what you have: Video retrieval using representations from collaborative experts. arXiv preprint arXiv:1907.13487 (2019)
32. Loshchilov, I., Hutter, F.: Decoupled weight decay regularization. arXiv (2017)
33. Lu, C., Chen, L., Tan, C., Li, X., Xiao, J.: DEBUG: a dense bottom-up grounding approach for natural language video localization. In: EMNLP, pp. 5147–5156 (2019)
34. Lu, J., Batra, D., Parikh, D., Lee, S.: ViLBERT: pretraining task-agnostic visiolinguistic representations for vision-and-language tasks. In: NeurIPS (2019)
35. Luo, H., et al.: UniVL: a unified video and language pre-training model for multi-modal understanding and generation. arXiv preprint arXiv:2002.06353 (2020)
36. Luo, H., et al.: CLIP4Clip: an empirical study of clip for end to end video clip retrieval. arXiv preprint arXiv:2104.08860 (2021)
37. McInnes, L., Healy, J., Melville, J.: UMAP: uniform manifold approximation and projection for dimension reduction. arXiv preprint arXiv:1802.03426 (2018)
38. Miech, A., Alayrac, J.B., Smaira, L., Laptev, I., Sivic, J., Zisserman, A.: End-to-end learning of visual representations from uncurated instructional videos. In: Proceedings of the IEEE/CVF Conference on Computer Vision and Pattern Recognition, pp. 9879–9889 (2020)
39. Miech, A., Zhukov, D., Alayrac, J.B., Tapaswi, M., Laptev, I., Sivic, J.: HowTo100M: learning a text-video embedding by watching hundred million narrated video clips. In: Proceedings of the IEEE/CVF International Conference on Computer Vision, pp. 2630–2640 (2019)
40. Pan, T., Song, Y., Yang, T., Jiang, W., Liu, W.: VideoMoCo: contrastive video representation learning with temporally adversarial examples. In: Proceedings of the IEEE/CVF Conference on Computer Vision and Pattern Recognition, pp. 11205–11214 (2021)

41. Patrick, M., et al.: Support-set bottlenecks for video-text representation learning. arXiv preprint arXiv:2010.02824 (2020)
42. Qian, R., et al.: Spatiotemporal contrastive video representation learning. In: Proceedings of the IEEE/CVF Conference on Computer Vision and Pattern Recognition, pp. 6964–6974 (2021)
43. Radford, A., et al.: Learning transferable visual models from natural language supervision. arXiv preprint arXiv:2103.00020 (2021)
44. Regneri, M., Rohrbach, M., Wetzel, D., Thater, S., Schiele, B., Pinkal, M.: Grounding action descriptions in videos. TACL 1, 25–36 (2013)
45. Rohrbach, A., Rohrbach, M., Tandon, N., Schiele, B.: A dataset for movie description. In: Proceedings of the IEEE Conference on Computer Vision and Pattern Recognition, pp. 3202–3212 (2015)
46. Rouditchenko, A., et al.: AVLnet: learning audio-visual language representations from instructional videos. arXiv preprint arXiv:2006.09199 (2020)
47. Sanh, V., Debut, L., Chaumond, J., Wolf, T.: DistilBERT, a distilled version of BERT: smaller, faster, cheaper and lighter. arXiv preprint arXiv:1910.01108 (2019)
48. Sharma, P., Ding, N., Goodman, S., Soricut, R.: Conceptual captions: a cleaned, hypernymed, image alt-text dataset for automatic image captioning. In: ACL, pp. 2556–2565 (2018)
49. Sun, C., Myers, A., Vondrick, C., Murphy, K., Schmid, C.: VideoBERT: a joint model for video and language representation learning. In: Proceedings of the IEEE/CVF International Conference on Computer Vision, pp. 7464–7473 (2019)
50. Tan, H., Bansal, M.: LXMERT: learning cross-modality encoder representations from transformers. In: EMNLP (2019)
51. Tang, Y., et al.: Coin: a large-scale dataset for comprehensive instructional video analysis. In: Proceedings of the IEEE/CVF Conference on Computer Vision and Pattern Recognition, pp. 1207–1216 (2019)
52. Tang, Z., Lei, J., Bansal, M.: DeCEMBERT: learning from noisy instructional videos via dense captions and entropy minimization. In: Proceedings of the 2021 Conference of the North American Chapter of the Association for Computational Linguistics: Human Language Technologies, pp. 2415–2426 (2021)
53. Vaswani, A., et al.: Attention is all you need. In: NeurIPS (2017)
54. Wang, A.J., et al.: Object-aware video-language pre-training for retrieval. In: Proceedings of the IEEE/CVF Conference on Computer Vision and Pattern Recognition (2022)
55. Wang, W., et al.: Dig into multi-modal cues for video retrieval with hierarchical alignment. In: IJCAI (2021)
56. Wang, X., Zhu, L., Yang, Y.: T2VLAD: global-local sequence alignment for text-video retrieval. In: Proceedings of the IEEE/CVF Conference on Computer Vision and Pattern Recognition, pp. 5079–5088 (2021)
57. Wang, X., Zhang, R., Shen, C., Kong, T., Li, L.: Dense contrastive learning for self-supervised visual pre-training. In: Proceedings of the IEEE/CVF Conference on Computer Vision and Pattern Recognition, pp. 3024–3033 (2021)
58. Wu, C.Y., Manmatha, R., Smola, A.J., Krahenbuhl, P.: Sampling matters in deep embedding learning. In: Proceedings of the IEEE International Conference on Computer Vision, pp. 2840–2848 (2017)
59. Wu, Z., Xiong, Y., Yu, S.X., Lin, D.: Unsupervised feature learning via non-parametric instance discrimination. In: Proceedings of the IEEE Conference on Computer Vision and Pattern Recognition, pp. 3733–3742 (2018)
60. Xiao, S., Chen, L., Shao, J., Yueting, Z., Xiao, J.: Natural language video localization with learnable moment proposals. In: EMNLP (2021)

61. Xiao, S., et al.: Boundary proposal network for two-stage natural language video localization. In: AAAI (2021)
62. Xu, H., et al.: VLM: task-agnostic video-language model pre-training for video understanding. arXiv preprint arXiv:2105.09996 (2021)
63. Xu, H., et al.: VideoCLIP: contrastive pre-training for zero-shot video-text understanding. arXiv preprint arXiv:2109.14084 (2021)
64. Xu, J., Mei, T., Yao, T., Rui, Y.: MSR-VTT: a large video description dataset for bridging video and language. In: Proceedings of the IEEE Conference on Computer Vision and Pattern Recognition, pp. 5288–5296 (2016)
65. Xu, M., et al.: Boundary-sensitive pre-training for temporal localization in videos. In: Proceedings of the IEEE/CVF International Conference on Computer Vision, pp. 7220–7230 (2021)
66. Xu, M., Perez Rua, J.M., Zhu, X., Ghanem, B., Martinez, B.: Low-fidelity video encoder optimization for temporal action localization. In: Advances in Neural Information Processing Systems, vol. 34 (2021)
67. Yan, R., Shou, M.Z., Ge, Y., Wang, A.J., Lin, X., Cai, G., Tang, J.: Video-text pre-training with learned regions. arXiv preprint arXiv:2112.01194 (2021)
68. Yang, J., Bisk, Y., Gao, J.: TACo: token-aware cascade contrastive learning for video-text alignment. In: Proceedings of the IEEE/CVF International Conference on Computer Vision, pp. 11562–11572 (2021)
69. Yu, Y., Kim, J., Kim, G.: A joint sequence fusion model for video question answering and retrieval. In: Ferrari, V., Hebert, M., Sminchisescu, C., Weiss, Y. (eds.) ECCV 2018. LNCS, vol. 11211, pp. 487–503. Springer, Cham (2018). https://doi.org/10.1007/978-3-030-01234-2_29
70. Yuan, Y., Lan, X., Wang, X., Chen, L., Wang, Z., Zhu, W.: A closer look at temporal sentence grounding in videos: datasets and metrics. arXiv (2021)
71. Zhang, C., Cao, M., Yang, D., Chen, J., Zou, Y.: CoLA: weakly-supervised temporal action localization with snippet contrastive learning. In: CVPR, pp. 16010–16019 (2021)
72. Zhang, C., Cao, M., Yang, D., Jiang, J., Zou, Y.: Synergic learning for noise-insensitive Webly-supervised temporal action localization. Image Vis. Comput. **113**, 104247 (2021)
73. Zhang, C., Yang, T., Weng, J., Cao, M., Wang, J., Zou, Y.: Unsupervised pre-training for temporal action localization tasks. In: Proceedings of the IEEE/CVF Conference on Computer Vision and Pattern Recognition, pp. 14031–14041 (2022)
74. Zhang, S., Peng, H., Fu, J., Luo, J.: Learning 2d temporal adjacent networks for moment localization with natural language. In: AAAI, pp. 12870–12877 (2020)
75. Zhou, L., Xu, C., Corso, J.J.: Towards automatic learning of procedures from web instructional videos. In: Thirty-Second AAAI Conference on Artificial Intelligence (2018)
76. Zhu, L., Yang, Y.: ActBERT: learning global-local video-text representations. In: Proceedings of the IEEE/CVF Conference on Computer Vision and Pattern Recognition, pp. 8746–8755 (2020)
77. Zhukov, D., Alayrac, J.B., Cinbis, R.G., Fouhey, D., Laptev, I., Sivic, J.: Cross-task weakly supervised learning from instructional videos. In: Proceedings of the IEEE/CVF Conference on Computer Vision and Pattern Recognition, pp. 3537–3545 (2019)

Few-Shot End-to-End Object Detection via Constantly Concentrated Encoding Across Heads

Jiawei Ma$^{(\boxtimes)}$ (iD), Guangxing Han(iD), Shiyuan Huang(iD), Yuncong Yang(iD),
and Shih-Fu Chang

Columbia University, New York, NY 10027, USA
{jiawei.m,gh2561,shiyuan.h,yy3035,sc250}@columbia.edu

Abstract. Few-shot object detection (FSOD) aims to detect objects of new classes and learn effective models without exhaustive annotation. The end-to-end detection framework has been proposed to generate sparse proposals and set a stack of detection heads to improve the performance. For each proposal, the predictions at lower heads are fed into deeper heads. However, the deeper head may not concentrate on the detected objects and then degrades, resulting in inefficient training and further limiting the performance gain in few-shot scenario. In this paper, we propose a few-shot adaptation strategy, Constantly Concentrated Encoding across heads (CoCo-RCNN), for the end-to-end detectors. For each class, we gather the encodings which detect on its object instances and then train them to be discriminative to avoid degraded prediction. In addition, we embed the class-relevant encodings to the learnable proposals to facilitate the adaptation at lower heads. Extensive experimental results show that our model brought clear gain on benchmarks. Detailed ablation studies are provided to justify the selection of each component.

Keywords: End-to-end detector · Constantly concentrated encoding

1 Introduction

Deep convolution neural networks have achieved impressive successes in general object detection. Learning a deep detector typically requires sufficient annotated training instances, and the detection performance is far from satisfactory when the annotated samples are extremely limited. As such, few-shot object detection has been studied to mimic human vision system which has remarkable ability to learn the object visual appearance for new (*novel*) classes with a few instances.

Recently, the end-to-end framework [1,32,42] has been proposed for object detection. Different from the conventional methods [12–14,28,29] which generate dense proposals from the anchor boxes, the end-to-end framework sets a few

Supplementary Information The online version contains supplementary material available at https://doi.org/10.1007/978-3-031-19809-0_4.

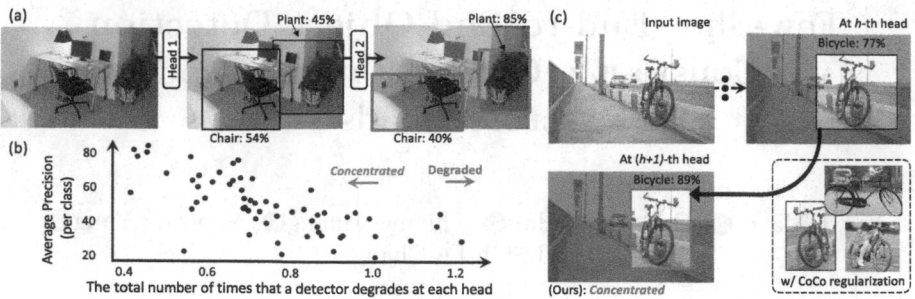

Fig. 1. (a) Within an end-to-end object detector, the prediction from a lower head can be fed into a deeper head. For each proposal, the prediction can be improved (green) when the detector concentrates on the object that has been detected or degraded (red) when it is distracted by other patterns. (b) Comparison between the detection precision and the total number of times that an object detector degrades at each head. For each class, the precision can be high when the detector can keep concentrating on the previously detected object instances and improve the performance (more details can be found in Supp.). (c) Comparing with conventional finetuning baseline, we add constantly concentrated encoding regularization to make the detector concentrated (Color figure online)

learnable proposal vectors to generate sparse proposals for each image dynamically. Each vector is learned as part of the model parameters and serves as a proposal encoding to predict an object encoding in one detection head. Then, similar to the Faster-RCNN [29], a detection module is set for classification and bounding box regression while the prediction from different proposals are supposed to be diverse. To improve the performance, a small number of heads are stacked. As shown in Fig. 1(a, green), the predictions from lower heads are fed into deeper heads for refinement. In this way, all heads can make predictions and the detection from deeper heads are closer to the groundtruth on average [1,32], *i.e.*, more accurate classification and higher intersection over union (IoU).

Though the detection precision of a deeper head is generally higher, for each proposal, as shown in Fig. 1(a, red), the prediction can still *degrade*. For example, given a proposal, the detection at lower heads may be close to one object in image, the prediction can then be *distracted* by other patterns in deeper heads. Meanwhile, by breaking down the detection scores for each class separately, as shown in Fig. 1(b), when the detector can keep *concentrating* on the objects in its input at each head, the detection can be refined constantly and the final detection precision is high. As such, even if the end-to-end object detector has achieved superior performance under large-scale training, adapting it for few-shot novel classes is still challenging, as it is hard to maintain the detector constantly concentrate on instances of novel classes in the data-hunger scenario.

As an end-to-end object detector makes sparse proposals to detect all object instances over the full image, at each head, the object encodings are supposed to be different from each other to avoid similar/overlapping predictions. Recent work has observed that an adapted object detector can properly localize novel instances [2,31], while a discriminative object encoding is important for strengthening the detection results [32,42]. Then, at each head, to make the model improve its input, *i.e.*, the detection at the previous head, it is important to make the detector concentrate on the class-relevant components and avoid being distracted. Thus, for each proposal, the object encodings from all heads are supposed to be discriminative such that the classification is accurate and consistent and the detection at each head can be refined continuously.

In this paper, as shown in Fig. 1(c), we propose CoCo-RCNN, a simple yet effective strategy for few-shot adaptation, for the end-to-end object detectors. We design the Constantly Concentrated Encoding (CoCo) regularization based on the supervised contrastive learning [20], aiming to make the object encodings discriminative and have high similarity with the groundtruth encodings of the same class. Different from the conventional supervised contrastive learning which performs augmentation through manipulation on the pixels, within the end-to-end object detector where multiple heads are stacked, the object encodings from different heads can be treated as the augmentation at feature-level. We use Sparse-RCNN as our baseline and first pre-train it on the classes with abundant annotated samples (*base*). Then, we adapt the base detector to novel classes by finetuning on only a few examples as well as minimizing the CoCo loss and detection losses. Meanwhile, as the proposal vectors are class-irrelevant and the model is difficult to concentrate on objects at lower heads, we also embed class-relevant information by adding each of the class encodings on a sub-group of proposal vectors. The contributions of this paper are as follows:

- We propose CoCo-RCNN, a few-shot adaptation strategy for end-to-end object detectors. At each head, for each proposal, the model is trained to concentrate on the object detected at previous head when the training data is limited.
- We design the constantly concentrated encoding loss, incorporating the supervised contrastive loss to make the object encodings discriminative. To encourage the detector to concentrate on object instances at lower heads, we additionally embed class-relevant information to the learnable proposals.
- We use Sparse-RCNN as a baseline model, and show that our CoCo-RCNN consistently achieves performance gain on PASCAL VOC and MSCOCO. We also provide comprehensive ablation studies to justify the design of each component and demonstrate its effect in large-scale training.

2   Related Work

Object detection methods with dense proposals, have been widely used in many related tasks and the most representative method is Faster-RCNN [29]. Given the feature maps of a full image, a detector first uses the region proposal network (RPN) [29] to generate dense proposals ($\sim 10^5$). Each proposal is paired with an objectness score to indicate the possibility for the existence of objects. Then, the proposals ($\sim 1,000$) with high objectness scores are kept and used to extract object encodings from the original feature maps through RoI pooling [29]. Finally, the object encodings are used for detection, *i.e.*, classification and bounding box regression. As such, these methods are all termed two-stage detectors. In practice, each proposal is predicted w.r.t. an anchor box while each anchor box is determined by the spatial position, size, and aspect ratio. Thus, a large number of anchor boxes are manually defined to densely cover the full image, resulting in heavy computation. To improve the detection speed and training efficiency, methods such as YoLo [28] and SSD [26] have been proposed to directly predict the class and location of objects from the image feature maps in a single stage. However, all of the methods mentioned above need to generate dense candidates ($\geq 1,000$). Thus, the non-maximum suppression (NMS) [7] is required to fuse the detection results and obtain clean & sparse predictions.

End-to-end object detection methods, in contrast, set a few learnable proposals. Each proposal is represented as a vector and learned as part of the model parameters. The representative methods include Detr [1], Deformable Detr [42], and Sparse-RCNN [32]. Within a detection head, each proposal vector, serving as a proposal encoding, is used to make one prediction. Typically, a correlation module is set to connect each proposal encoding with the image feature maps and extract an object encoding. The correlation modules include cross-attention [34] and dynamic instance interaction [32]. The cross-attention module flattens the feature maps into a set of vision encodings and measures the affinity scores with the proposal encodings pair-wisely. For each proposal encoding, the visual encodings with high attention scores are kept in the corresponding object encoding. For Sparse-RCNN, instead, each proposal vector is paired with a learnable bounding box (part of model parameters). Then, the dynamic instance interaction will perform RoI pooling on the feature maps using the paired bounding box and connect the pooled feature with the proposal encoding to predict an object encoding. In this way, each proposal encoding is only compared with the feature maps of a sub-region. As a result, Sparse-RCNN is more efficient than other methods, *e.g.*, variants of Detr [1]. For the sake of training efficiency and low computational workload, we choose Sparse-RCNN [32] as our baseline.

The end-to-end object detectors are trained to generate sparse predictions such that manual intervention including NMS is no longer needed. The predictions by various proposals are supposed to be different such that all objects appearing in the image can still be detected. To improve the detection precision, multiple detection heads are stacked & cascaded where the predictions at lower heads are used as inputs at deeper heads. To balance the computational workload and performance, the number of heads is usually set as six for a fair comparison. For Sparse-RCNN, the object encodings and bounding boxes predicted by the current head are used as inputs for the next head. For the convenience of description, we omit description for bounding boxes but just mention that the object encodings are reused as proposal encodings in the stacked heads.

Few-shot object detection (FSOD) learns to detect objects of novel classes by only training on a few annotated instances (support). Different from the few-shot classification which can directly compare the global image features [18, 27, 30, 33, 41], FSOD is additionally supposed to localize the objects in images and distinguish the objects from the background. The methods for FSOD are mostly developed on the framework with dense proposals and can be roughly categorized into meta-learning-based and finetuning-based.

The *meta-learning-based* methods aim to learn a class-agnostic meta-learner and improve the detection performance by learning to align the support samples with the objects in testing images [9]. As the few support instances may be of various viewpoints or shapes, how to effectively extract the discriminative components and align the support with objects in test images is important. First, given the support samples, re-weighting the image feature maps is an effective strategy [19]. Then, FewX [6] obtains an attention-based meta-learner for RPN such that the class-relevant proposals are generated for further detection. The following works dig into this problem and propose attentive feature alignment module [9], query-adaptive heterogeneous graph convolution [8] and fully cross-transformer [10] to improve the performance. Meanwhile, *Han et al.* [11] propose to exploit class semantic information to assist in FSDO. The meta-learning-based method is a promising solution for transferring meta-knowledge from base classes to novel classes, and has shown its strength in extremely few-shot cases (*e.g.*, 1-shot) on challenging datasets (*e.g.*, MS COCO [25]).

The *finetuning-based* methods first obtain an initialization by pre-training the object detector with sufficient *base* samples and then finetune the model a few support samples for *novel* classes. In this way, the finetuning-based methods aim to adapt a pre-trained model to novel classes efficiently, which has drawn increasing attention thanks to its simplicity. Recently, TFA [35] has shown that finetuning on a few data is a strong baseline. Then, by learning to detect objects from multiple scales, MPSR [39] has improved the performance further. In addition, FSCE [31] builds upon TFA and improves the detection performance by learning to obtain discriminative object encodings for FSOD. Different from the previous methods, the end-to-end object detector applies multiple heads to refine the detection progressively where our focus is to keep the detector concentrating on the detected objects during the refinement process to learn the adapted model efficiently.

3   Preliminary

3.1   Learning-Task Formulation

In FSOD, we are first given a *base* dataset $\mathcal{D}_{base}$, including abundant amount of annotated object instances from *base* classes $\mathcal{C}_{base}$. For each instance, the annotation consists of a class label c, and a bounding box (bbox) $u = (x, y, w, h)$ in the image. An image may contain multiple (N_T) instances from different classes, *i.e.*, $\mathcal{T} = \{(c_t, u_t)\}_{t=1}^{N_T}$. Then, we are given a *novel* set $\mathcal{D}_{novel}$ and the instances are from the novel classes $\mathcal{C}_{novel}$.

For an N_C-way K-shot FSOD task, there are N_C novel classes $|\mathcal{C}_{novel}| = N_C$ and each class has K annotated instances. The class sets for *base* and *novel* are disjoint, *i.e.*, $\mathcal{C}_{base} \cap \mathcal{C}_{novel} = \varnothing$. Following most finetuning-based methods [31,35], we first pre-train our object detector on $\mathcal{D}_{base}$ to obtain a base model and then finetune the model on $\mathcal{D}_{novel}$ for adaptation. Finally, we evaluate the adapted model on a test set.

3.2 End-to-End Object Detection

Conventional object detectors predict dense proposals w.r.t. each anchor box and filter out the proposals with low objectness scores. In contrast, the end-to-end framework sets a few learnable proposals to generate sparse predictions. As illustrated in Fig. 2, a proposal is represented as a proposal vector and learned as part of model parameters. Given the image feature maps, a proposal vector serves as a proposal encoding and is used to generate one object encoding for the image within one head, which is further used for detection. To improve the performance, multiple (N_H) heads are stacked and learned jointly.

In detail, at the h-th head where $h \in \{1...N_H\}$, a d-dim proposal encoding $\mathbf{p}_n^h \in \mathcal{R}^d$ is fed into a correlation module $f_a^h(\cdot, \cdot)$ to generate an object encoding $\mathbf{o}_n^h = f_a^h(\mathbf{p}_n^h, f_f(I)) \in \mathcal{R}^d$. The feature maps for image I is extracted by $f_f(\cdot)$ and the $n \in \{1...N_P\}$ indexes the encodings. The object encoding is then used for classification and bbox regression through a detection module $f_d^h(\cdot)$. When multiple heads are stacked, the object encoding $\mathbf{o}_n^h$ at the h-th head is directly used as the proposal encoding for the $(h+1)$-th head, i.e., $\mathbf{p}_n^{h+1} = \mathbf{o}_n^h$. Then, only $\{\mathbf{p}_n^1\}_{n=1}^{N_P}$ in the first head are model parameters (learnable proposal vectors).

During training, at h-th head, we calculate the matching costs between the predictions $\{f_d^h(\mathbf{o}_n^h)\}_{n=1}^{N_P}$ and annotated instances $\mathcal{T}$ pair-wisely. The matching cost between t-th instance and n-th prediction $l^h(n, t)$ is a weighted sum of costs for classification and localization. Then, we find the bipartite matching such that the average matching cost is minimum and assign the labels to each prediction. We usually set $N_T < N_P$, and only N_T predictions at each head are assigned with the object instances (positive) while the rest $(N_P\text{-}N_T)$ predictions are supposed to be background. For example, $t = m^h(n|I)$ means the t-th instance in image I is assigned to the prediction originating from the n-th proposal vector $\mathbf{p}_n^1$ while $t > N_T$ means the assigned label is background.

4 CoCo-RCNN for Few-Shot Object Detection

In this section, we present the proposed CoCo-RCNN to adapt the pre-trained base detector to novel classes efficiently and effectively. We first review the supervised contrastive learning in Sect. 4.1 and then explain the detailed strategy for constantly concentrated encoding regularization in Sect. 4.2. During adaptation, the CoCo loss is jointly minimized with the detection losses.

4.1 Supervised Contrastive Learning

Supervised contrastive learning (SupCT) is proposed to extract discriminative encodings for image classification. Given a batch $\mathcal{B}$ with N_B images, i.e., $|\mathcal{B}| = N_B$, each image $\mathcal{B}(i)$ where $i \in \mathcal{I} \equiv \{1...N_B\}$ is used as an anchor. Then, a positive index set $\mathcal{I}_i' \subset \mathcal{I} \setminus \{i\}$ is selected, such that all images $\mathcal{B}(j)$ for $j \in \mathcal{I}_i'$ are of the same class as $\mathcal{B}(i)$. Then, the SupCT loss is defined as

$$\mathcal{L}_{SupCT}(\mathcal{B}) = \sum_{i \in I} \frac{-1}{|\mathcal{I}_i'|} \sum_{j \in \mathcal{I}_i'} \log \frac{\exp(\mathbf{z}_i \cdot \mathbf{z}_j / \tau)}{\sum_{a \in \mathcal{I} \setminus \{i\}} \exp(\mathbf{z}_i \cdot \mathbf{z}_a / \tau)} \tag{1}$$

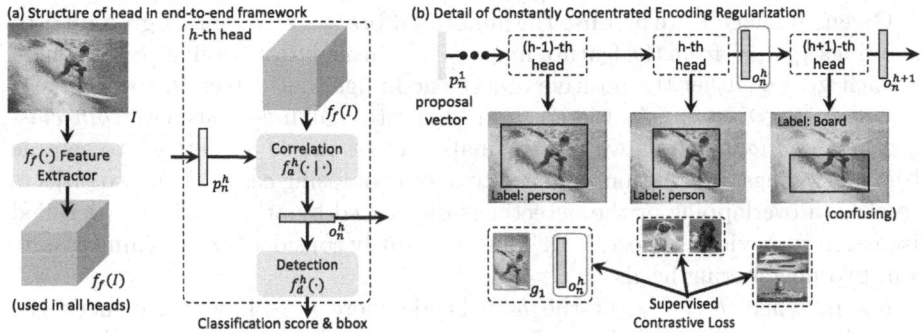

(a) Structure of head in end-to-end framework   (b) Detail of Constantly Concentrated Encoding Regularization

Fig. 2. (a): A correlation module is set to connect the proposal encoding with image feature maps and obtain an object encoding for detection. (b) When multiple heads are stacked/cascaded, the object encodings at each head are used as proposal encodings in the next head, our method will sample the object encodings whose prediction are similar as the prediction of input and then perform supervised contrastive learning. We use the assigned labels after bipartite matching as references and specifically highlight $\mathbf{o}_n^h$ and $\mathbf{o}_n^{h+1}$ for better illustration

where $\mathbf{z}_i \in \mathcal{R}^d$ is the encoding for image $\mathcal{B}(i)$ after l_2-normalization and τ is a temperature hyperparameter used to rescale the affinity score. Minimizing $\mathcal{L}_{SupCT}(\mathcal{B})$ trains the feature extractor to maximize the similarity between features of the same class (positive pairs) while pushing away the features from different classes (negative pairs). Usually, to ensure at least one positive pair can be built for each anchor image in the batch, we set B as large as possible or perform data augmentation to each sample in the batch. As noted in [20], then, the SupCT is in effect performing pair-wise comparison where the disagreement between the two encodings in a positive pair is induced by the variation between image instances and difference resulting from augmentation.

4.2 Constantly Concentrated Encoding

At the h-th head, the f_a^h models the correlation between a proposal encoding $\mathbf{p}_n^h$ and the image feature maps $f_f(I)$. The features with high co-attention is kept in the object encoding $\mathbf{o}_n^h$. When the prediction $f_d^{h-1}(\mathbf{o}_n^{h-1})$ has been close to an object $\mathcal{T}(t)$ in the image, *i.e.*, $t = m^{h-1}(n|I)$ and $t < N_T$, as $\mathbf{p}_n^h = \mathbf{o}_n^{h-1}$, under the <u>Co</u>nstantly <u>Co</u>ncentrated encoding (CoCo) regularization, the detector is trained to still concentrate on the discriminative component of object $\mathcal{T}(t)$, such that the prediction $f_d^h(\mathbf{o}_n^h)$ can be improved w.r.t. $f_d^{h-1}(\mathbf{o}_n^{h-1})$. Different from the classification task, being close to an object means both the confidence score for classification and the IoU with annotated boxes for localization are high. As a discriminative object encoding is important to improve detection result [32,42] while no spatial prior is available for learnable proposals, CoCo regularization applies supervised contrastive learning and designs an encoding selection strategy correspondingly to build positive and negative pairs.

Given an image I, we first use the annotated bboxes $\mathcal{T}$ to extract groundtruth encodings $\{\mathbf{g}_t\}_{t=1}^{N_T}$ from the feature maps $f_f(I)$ through RoI pooling [7,15]. Then, for each $\mathbf{g}_t$, we gather the positive object encodings that detect the object $\mathcal{T}(t)$ for calculating $\mathcal{L}_{SupCT}$. As the costs in bipartite matching considers *both classification and localization*, we use the matching results as a reference to sample object encodings. In addition, we need to avoid confusing cases when two objects are of high overlapping or the detector is distracted by other patterns (detailed discussion is provided in Sect. 5.3). Thus, we jointly consider the matching results from two neighboring heads.

For $\mathbf{g}_t$ where $t \leq N_T$, at the h-th head where $h > 1$, we first check the prediction from the proposal encodings, *i.e.*, the labels assigned at the $(h-1)$-th head, and find the $\mathbf{p}_n^h$ where $t = m^{h-1}(n|I)$. Then, the object encoding $\mathbf{o}_n^h$ will be treated as positive if $\mathcal{T}(t)$ is also assigned to its prediction $f_d^h(\mathbf{o}_n^h)$, *i.e.*,

$$m^h(n|I) = m^{h-1}(n|I) \tag{2}$$

or matching cost between $\mathcal{T}(t)$ and $f_d^h(\mathbf{o}_n^h)$ is smaller, *i.e.*,

$$l^h(n,t) < l^{h-1}(n,t) \tag{3}$$

After checking all heads, we have the object encodings $\mathcal{P}_t$ for $\mathbf{g}_t$ and each encoding in $\mathcal{P}_t$ is of class c_t. In practice, the condition in Eq. 2 has been enough for FSOD. However, as the bipartite matching is obtained when the global matching cost is minimum, it is still possible that $l^h(n,t) < l^{h-1}(n,t)$ though $m^h(n|I) \neq t$. As such, we avoid false negative cases by considering Eq. 3 and it is useful in large-scale training. As mentioned above, we ignore the object encoding $\mathbf{o}_n^h$ that $m^{h-1}(n|I) \neq m^h(n|I)$ and $(m^{h-1}(n|I) - t)(m^h(n|I) - t) = 0$ as it is confusing. Thus, it is possible that none of Eqs. 2 and 3 is met at some heads, and we have $|\mathcal{P}_t| \leq N_T$ (including $\mathcal{P}_t = \varnothing$, *i.e.*, no object encodings selected for $\mathbf{g}_t$).

Though the matching results can help the selection at h-th heads where $h > 1$, the proposal vectors $\{\mathbf{p}_n^1\}_{n=1}^{N_P}$ are not trained to be class-specific. Then, the $\{\mathbf{o}_n^1\}_{n=1}^{N_P}$ cannot be directly determined and the model may not be capable to concentrate on relevant objects at lower heads. Thus, we add class encodings to the learnable proposal vectors to embed class-specific information.

For the convenience of implementation, we directly crop the annotated instances out of the few images used in finetuning and use a frozen ResNet-101 [16] (pretrained on ImageNet [3]) to extract a visual feature for each instance. Then, we average the visual features for each class c as class encodings. During adaptation, we also learn an MLP to post-process the class encodings such that the dimension is the same as the proposal vectors, *i.e.*, $\mathbf{s}_c \in \mathcal{R}^d$. Then, for each class c, we randomly select a subset of $\{\mathbf{p}_n^1\}_{n=1}^{N_P}$ and add the encoding $\mathbf{s}_c$ to each of the selected proposal vectors. Thus, the object encoding $\mathbf{o}_n^1$ will be selected in $\mathcal{P}_t$ with $\mathbf{g}_t$ when both $m^1(n|I) = t$ and the encoding added to $\mathbf{p}_n^1$ is of class c_t.

After gathering $\mathcal{P}_t$ for each $\mathbf{g}_t$ from all heads, we calculate SupCT loss on all selected encodings $\cup_{t=1}^{N_T}\{\{\mathbf{g}_t\} \cup \mathcal{P}_t\}$. In this way, comparing with the conventional SupCT learning which directly performs augmentation on the low-level image pixels, we perform augmentation at the feature-level for each $\mathbf{g}_t$. As the

Table 1. Performance comparison on the PASCAL VOC dataset (nAP$_{50}$)

Method	Venue	Split 1					Split 2					Split 3				
		1	2	3	5	10	1	2	3	5	10	1	2	3	5	10
YOLOv2-ft [36]	ICCV'19	6.6	10.7	12.5	24.8	38.6	12.5	4.2	11.6	16.1	33.9	13.0	15.9	15.0	32.2	38.4
MetaYOLO [19]	ICCV'19	14.8	15.5	26.7	33.9	47.2	15.7	15.3	22.7	30.1	40.5	21.3	25.6	28.4	42.8	45.9
Meta R-CNN [40]	ICCV'19	19.9	25.5	35.0	45.7	51.5	10.4	19.4	29.6	34.8	45.4	14.3	18.2	27.5	41.2	48.1
TFA-w/ fc [35]	ICML'20	36.8	29.1	43.6	55.7	57.0	18.2	29.0	33.4	35.5	39.0	27.7	33.6	42.5	48.7	50.2
TFA-w/ cos [35]	ICML'20	39.8	36.1	44.7	55.7	56.0	23.5	26.9	34.1	35.1	39.1	30.8	34.8	42.8	49.5	49.8
MPSR [39]	ECCV'20	41.7	–	51.4	55.2	61.8	24.4	–	39.2	39.9	47.8	35.6	–	42.3	48.0	49.7
CGDP+FSCN [23]	CVPR'21	40.7	45.1	46.5	57.4	62.4	27.3	31.4	40.8	42.7	46.3	31.2	36.4	43.7	50.1	55.6
CME (MPSR) [22]	CVPR'21	41.5	47.5	50.4	58.2	60.9	27.2	30.2	41.4	42.5	46.8	34.3	39.6	45.1	48.3	51.5
FSCE [31]	CVPR'21	44.2	43.8	51.4	61.9	63.4	27.3	29.5	43.5	44.2	50.2	37.2	41.9	47.5	54.6	58.5
SVD (FSCE) [38]	NeurIPS'21	46.1	43.5	48.9	60.0	61.7	25.6	29.9	44.8	47.5	48.2	39.5	45.4	48.9	53.9	56.9
FSOD-Up [37]	ICCV'21	43.8	47.8	50.3	55.4	61.7	31.2	30.5	41.2	42.2	48.3	35.5	39.7	43.9	50.6	53.5
CoCo-RCNN		43.9	44.5	53.1	64.6	65.5	29.4	31.3	43.8	44.3	51.8	39.1	43.9	47.2	54.7	60.3
TFA w/ cos † [35]	ICML'20	25.3	36.4	42.1	47.9	52.8	18.3	27.5	30.9	34.1	39.5	17.9	27.2	34.3	40.8	45.6
FSCE † [31]	CVPR'21	32.9	44.0	46.8	52.9	59.7	23.7	30.6	38.4	43.0	48.5	22.6	33.4	39.5	47.3	54.0
Sparse-RCNN †		28.2	39.5	45.1	51.1	56.3	21.1	30.5	34.1	37.6	43.2	21.4	30.8	37.5	43.7	49.6
CoCo-RCNN †		**33.5**	**44.2**	**50.2**	**57.5**	**63.3**	**25.3**	**31.0**	**39.6**	**43.8**	**50.1**	**24.8**	**36.9**	**42.8**	**50.8**	**57.7**

More comparison can be found in Supp.. †: The performance averaged from multiple runs.

groundtruth encodings $\{\mathbf{g}_t\}_{t=1}^{N_T}$ are obtained through RoI pooling instead of correlation module, we set a linear layer to process $\{\mathbf{g}_t\}_{t=1}^{N_T}$. Also, as the object encodings are obtained from different heads, we also set a linear layer (projector) to process the object encodings for each head.

5 Experiment

5.1 Benchmark Datasets and Implementation Detail

PASCAL VOC consists of 20 classes where the class split for $\mathcal{C}_{base}$ and $\mathcal{C}_{novel}$ are 15 and 5 separately. The base training data $\mathcal{D}_{base}$ are from PASCAL VOC 07+12 trainval sets [4,5]. The novel set $\mathcal{D}_{novel}$ are randomly sampled where $K = \{1, 2, 3, 5, 10\}$. Following [35], we conduct experiments on three standard base-novel class partitions which are marked as $\{1, 2, 3\}$. In each partition, for fair comparison, we use the same sampled novel instances and report the AP$_{50}$ for novel detections (nAP$_{50}$) on PASCAL VOC 2007 test set [4].

MS COCO is derived from COCO14 [25] consisting of 80 classes where the split for $\mathcal{C}_{base}$ and $\mathcal{C}_{novel}$ are 60 and 20. The 20 classes is in common with PASCAL VOC. The train set $\mathcal{D}_{base}$ and $\mathcal{D}_{novel}$ are from COCO14 train set. We set $K = \{1, 10, 30\}$ and report scores of novel detection on COCO 14 val dataset.

Implementation Details. We build CoCo-RCNN based on Sparse-RCNN and use ResNet-101 with FPN [24] as backbone to extract feature maps. For fair comparison, we set $N_H = 6$ and all heads are stacked/cascaded. (*Class encodings*) Following the standard few-shot finetuning pipeline, we also include a few instances of base classes during finetuning. Thus, we gather class encodings for each class

Table 2. Performance comparison of *novel* detection on the MS COCO dataset

Method	Venue	1-shot	10-shot						30-shot					
		nAP	nAP	nAP$_{50}$	nAP$_{75}$	nAPs	nAPm	nAPl	nAP	nAP$_{50}$	nAP$_{75}$	nAPs	nAPm	nAPl
MetaYOLO [19]	ICCV'19		5.6	12.3	4.6	0.9	3.5	10.5	9.1	19.0	7.6	0.8	4.9	16.8
MetaDet [36]†	ICCV'19		7.1	14.6	6.1	1.0	4.1	12.2	11.3	21.7	8.1	1.1	6.2	17.3
Meta R-CNN [40]	ICCV'19		8.7	19.1	6.6	2.3	7.7	14	12.4	25.3	10.8	2.8	11.6	19.0
TFA w/ fc [35]†	ICML'20	2.9	9.1	17.3	8.5	–	–	–	12.2	22.2	11.8	–	–	–
TFA w/ cos [35]†	ICML'20	3.4	9.1	17.1	8.8	–	–	–	12.1	22.0	12.0	–	–	–
MPSR [39]	ECCV'20	2.3	9.8	17.9	9.7	3.3	9.2	16.1	14.1	25.4	14.2	4.0	12.9	23.0
FSCE [31]†	CVPR'21		11.1	–	9.8	–	–	–	15.3	–	14.2	–	–	–
CME [22]	CVPR'21		15.1	24.6	16.4	4.6	16.6	26.0	16.9	28.0	17.8	4.6	18.0	29.2
TIP [21]†	CVPR'21		16.3	33.2	14.1	5.4	17.5	25.8	18.3	35.9	16.9	6.0	19.3	29.2
DCNet [17]†	CVPR'21		12.8	23.4	11.2	4.3	13.8	21	18.6	32.6	17.5	0.9	16.5	27.1
FSOD-UP [37]	ICCV'21		11.0	–	10.7	4.5	11.2	17.3	15.6	–	15.7	4.7	15.1	25.1
SVD (FSCE) [38]	NeurIPS'21		12.0	–	10.4	4.2	12.1	18.9	16.0	–	15.3	6.0	16.8	24.9
SVD (MPSR) [38]	NeurIPS'21		11.0	–	10.6	4.4	11.5	17.1	16.2	–	15.9	4.6	14.6	26.6
CoCo-RCNN†		**5.2**	**16.4**	26.5	**16.5**	**5.4**	13.4	**27.8**	**19.2**	32.9	**21.0**	5.8	18.1	**32.8**

The full table can be found in Supp. †: The performance averaged from multiple runs.

from $\mathcal{C}_{base} \cup \mathcal{C}_{novel}$. (*Background encodings*) The GPU memory usage for object detection is huge, *i.e.*, each GPU can hold at most four images, and the end-to-end object detector is characterized by generating sparse proposals. Thus, the encoding pairs built in each batch is limited, which is different from the related literature [20, 31] (*e.g.*, 1024^2 pairs per batch) and results in less efficient training. To mitigate this issue, we include the object encodings of background, *i.e.*, low classification score for all classes and low IoU with all objects in the image, into CoCo regularization. These object encodings are only used to build negative pairs in SupCT loss and none of them is used as an anchor. (*Multiple runs*) Finally, for each base-novel class split, we average the performance over 10 runs and report the average detection score. More details can be found in Supp.

5.2   Comparison with State-of-the-Arts

As shown in Table 1, we compare CoCo-RCNN with the finetuning-based adaptation methods. For fair comparison, we first show the baseline performance by directly finetuning Sparse-RCNN on the novel instances without any regularization. Benefiting from the multi-head structure, the Sparse-RCNN baseline outperforms the Faster-RCNN baseline TFA [35].

FSCE [31] improves detection precision by learning discriminative encodings (obtained through RoI pooling) and also use the IoU between proposals and annotated bbox to modify the SupCT loss. Instead, we perform comparison on object encodings and each encoding is output by the correlation module without explicit spatial prior. With our CoCo regularization, for each proposal, the object encoding in deeper head is trained to still concentrate on the object detected at lower heads. In this way, we can improve the adaptation performance clearly and keep achieving clear gain upon a stronger baseline. Meanwhile, as the end-to-end object detector can predict high-quality bboxes and the correlation module can generalize to new classes, in Table 2, CoCo-RCNN achieves high score in nAP$_{75}$ and the challenging 1-shot scenario.

Table 3. Ablation study on the constantly concentrated encoding regularization

Method	VOC 10-shot			MS COCO 10-shot			MS COCO 30-shot		
	nAP	nAP_{50}	nAP_{75}	nAP	nAP_{50}	nAP_{75}	nAP	nAP_{50}	nAP_{75}
Hard-deepest	13.0	16.8	14.1	2.7	7.5	1.4	3.1	5.2	3.0
Hard-lowest	18.5	25.0	20.3	3.4	9.2	1.9	6.7	10.0	6.5
Distillation	43.1	59.4	46.5	15.9	28.1	15.9	16.8	28.0	17.4
Contrastive	44.5	62.1	48.2	17.0	29.2	16.8	18.7	30.4	19.4
Iou-supct	46.0	61.8	51.0	17.7	29.6	17.8	20.0	31.0	19.8
Input-supct	43.3	60.2	47.7	17.3	30.0	17.2	19.1	30.7	19.9
CoCo-RCNN	47.2	65.5	51.5	18.1	30.4	18.2	20.6	33.8	21.4

5.3 Ablation on Constantly Concentrated Encoding

Different from the conventional object detectors which directly predict the class and location for each object, the end-to-end object detectors in effect improve the detection for each proposal across heads. Thus, we set constantly concentrated encoding regularization to prevent the object encodings from being distracted.

At each head, an object encoding will be selected as positive when the assigned labels before and after the head is consistent. In this way, for each proposal, our loss serves as a soft regularization where we do not force the model to make consistent prediction at all heads. Then, we discuss relevant alternatives for the regularization and summarize the results on Table 3.

- (*hard-deepest*) We assign the same label for predictions originating from the same proposal and use the matching results at the last head to assign labels.
- (*hard-lowest*) Similar to *hard-deepest*, we use the bipartite matching result at the first head as reference to assign labels for all heads.
- (*distillation*) At each head, the predictions are used as soft-labels to supervise the previous head. Thus, we minimize the kl-divergence loss between the probability distribution of h-th head and $(h - 1)$-th head (for classification) and the $l1$ loss between the predicted bboxes (for localization).
- (*contrastive*) We perform contrastive learning among the sampled object encodings where only encodings in $\mathcal{P}_t \cup \{\mathbf{g}_t\}$, *i.e.*, corresponding to the same object, will be treated as positive to each other.
- (*iou-supct*) Use contrastive proposal encoding (CPE) proposed in FSCE [31] for the constantly concentrated encoding regularization.
- (*input-supct*) At each head, use the label assigned to the prediction at the previous head to select the object encoding in $\mathcal{P}_t$ for $\mathbf{g}_t$.

As the learnable proposals are class-irrelevant, it is hard for the object encodings at lower heads to detect discriminative components of objects. Thus, the predictions by the lowest head and the deepest head vary, resulting in disparate label assignments. Then, when we naively use the same label-prediction assignment across all heads, the precision drops clearly (*hard-deepest, hard-lowest*).

Instead of doing the hard-label assignment, *distillation* adds soft labels to the original detection losses. At each head, we observe the $l1$ loss for localization is small and the main contribution is thus from the classification. In particular, the classification logits can indicate the relationships between classes. Then, combining one-hot labels and soft labels will help with the classifier training.

Thus, the model could be confused and the object encodings is less discriminative. However, since we have limited positive pairs within each batch, it is rare to have different object instances of the same class within one batch. As such, the features can still be trained to be discriminative, and the precision drop w.r.t. the full method is not huge.

For *iou-supct*, the CPE differs from SupCT by using the IoU to reweight the loss for each anchor feature. Then, in CPE, the loss from an anchor encoding will contribute less to the detector update if the IoU is low. In FSCE, as the proposal encodings are extracted by RoI pooling the image feature maps, the IoU between the proposal and groundtruth bbox can thus be directly calculated. However, for the end-to-end object detectors, each object encoding is obtained through a correlation module and no spatial prior is available, we thus use the predicted bbox as a reference to calculate the IoU as weights. Then, replacing SupCT with CPE does not result in significant difference. After all, as the object encodings are not directly pooled from the feature maps, the referred bbox may not be precise. Meanwhile, for the selected positive object encodings, we observed that the IoU of the predicted bbox is high. Thus, CPE is similar to that of SupCT.

Lastly, *input-supct* adjusts the sampling strategy by only using the label assignment at the current head for selection. Then, the object encodings at lower heads will always be selected. However, the encodings at lower heads may not be discriminative in nature, and enforcing CoCo loss on those object encodings may confuse the model, *e.g.*, the two objects with high overlapping (a child is playing with a dog) can only be distinguished at deeper heads. Besides, when the object encoding is distracted by objects of different classes, applying CoCo loss will also be risky, *e.g.*, for the same proposal, the 'chair' is initially detected at lower heads but the encodings at deeper heads are distracted by 'couch'. In addition, as the object encoding at the h-th head could succeed in detecting large objects but may fail in finding tiny instances, our sampling strategy in effect dynamically determines the object encodings used for comparison.

5.4   Discussion

Ablation study of our full method is summarized in Table 4. Compared with baseline (Row$_1$), adding class encodings to proposal vectors (Row$_2$) or performing SupCT among object encodings from the 2nd to 6th heads (Row$_3$) can clearly facilitate the final detection, while combining them can further improve the detection precision (Row$_4$). As the pairs to be sampled from each batch are limited, we thus include negative object encodings of background in the regularization, which mitigates the training inefficiency. By comparing the anchor feature and the background encodings during the network training, the object encodings can be more discriminative and we are thus capable to improve the

Table 4. Ablation study of the full method

2nd-6th heads	Class encoding	Negative	VOC 10-shot			MS COCO 10-shot			MS COCO 30-shot		
			nAP	nAP$_{50}$	nAP$_{75}$	nAP	nAP$_{50}$	nAP$_{75}$	nAP	nAP$_{50}$	nAP$_{75}$
			45.0	58.1	48.9	13.5	22.7	13.6	16.3	26.3	16.8
	✓		42.3	61.2	45.8	14.9	24.9	15.3	17.3	28.3	17.9
✓			45.2	63.5	49.2	16.8	28.4	16.8	19.2	31.1	19.7
✓	✓		47.0	65.3	51.0	17.4	29.4	17.4	20.1	32.6	20.6
✓		✓	46.2	64.5	50.8	17.6	30.2	17.4	19.9	32.7	20.7
✓	✓	✓	47.2	65.5	51.5	18.1	30.4	18.2	20.6	33.8	21.4

Table 5. Multiple runs for class encodings

Run	1	2	3	4	5
VOC 10-shot	65.5	65.3	65.4	65.5	65.5
MS COCO 30-shot	20.6	20.6	20.9	20.4	20.5

Table 6. Ablation study of projector

Project	Separate	Shared
VOC 10-shot	65.5	64.0
MS COCO 30-shot	20.6	19.8

performance. To note, even though each proposal vector $\mathbf{p}_n^1$ is added with an encoding of class c, $\mathbf{p}_n^1$ is not trained to predict the objects of class c specifically. After all, through self-attention [32,34], the discriminate components shared between two classes can benefit each other, *e.g.*, cats and dogs have four legs.

During testing, we randomly assign the proposal vectors for each class. As we have 300 learnable proposal vectors, each class encoding is added to at least 3 (10) proposal vectors for MS COCO (Pascal VOC). However, as compared in Table 5, the overall performance is stable.

Large-scale Object Detection. Besides the FSOD task, our constantly concentrated encoding can also benefit large-scale object detection. As the parameters are completely trained from scratch, we do not add class encodings on the proposal vectors and the object encodings are only sampled from the 2nd to 6th heads. As shown in Fig. 3(a), the detection AP at early checkpoints grows faster and the final detection performance is also improved from 46.3 AP to 47.5 AP. Meanwhile, as the bipartite matching is performed for each head separately, for a proposal whose prediction at h-th head is assigned to t-th instance, *i.e.*, $m^h(n|I) = t$ and $t \leq N_T$, its prediction at $(h+1)$-th head can be assigned to the background though the prediction is closer to that instance, *i.e.*, $m^h(n|I) > N_T$ and $l^h(n,t) < l^{h-1}(n,t)$. Thus, including Eq. 3 can contribute 0.8 AP gain.

Deep supervision, *i.e.*, supervising the prediction at each head separately, is important for end-to-end detectors [1]. As shown in Fig. 3(b), it is also necessary for few-shot finetuning. With deep supervision, the lower detection heads can also be tuned to adapt to the novel classes such that the object encodings are lower heads can learn to concentrate on the novel object instances. However, when deep supervision is removed, performance by the deepest head drops significantly. Furthermore, we vary the number of heads in the end-to-end object detector and

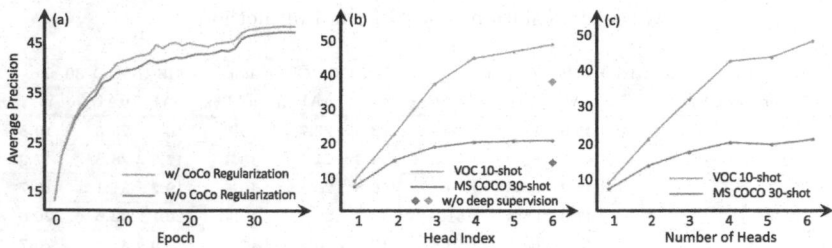

Fig. 3. (a) Testing curve on COCO17 (large-scale). (b) Detection precision at each head of an adapted six-head model. (c) Detection precision by detectors with different number of stacked heads

retrain the model on VOC and MS COCO. As summarized in Fig. 3(c), when fewer heads are set in the framework, the adaptation precision is even worse. It might because the gradient from deeper heads can also benefit the adaptation of lower heads. As such, when fewer heads are set, the precision is compromised.

Projectors are the linear layers set to map the object encodings to a common feature space such that the SupCT loss can be calculated. As the object encodings are sampled from all heads, we set a separate projector at each head. Then, as shown in Table 6, we observed that the detection score will drop a bit when we share the parameters across all projectors. Even though a few more parameters are introduced, sharing the parameters will assume that the object encodings will exactly be in the same space. Instead, setting separate sets of parameters will be more flexible. However, we can still see that the object encodings are similar to each other as the performance drop is not significant.

6   Conclusion

In this paper, we have proposed CoCo-RCNN, an adaptation strategy of end-to-end object detectors for FSOD. As a degraded prediction at each head may result in inefficient adaptation when the training data is limited, we design the constantly concentrated encoding regularization. We use the label assignments at neighboring heads as references to gather object encodings, and then perform supervised contrastive learning to make them discriminative. In this way, the detector is trained to keep concentrating on the objects that have been detected and constantly improve the detection precision. Experiments on two datasets demonstrate the effectiveness of CoCo-RCNN. Detailed ablation study is provided to compare the potential variances of CoCo regularization and ours also benefits the large-scale training. In addition to make the encodings at each head discriminative, the relationship between encodings of different heads will be studied in the future to further explore the strength of end-to-end detectors.

Acknowledgments. This material is based on research sponsored by Air Force Research Laboratory (AFRL) under agreement number FA8750-19-1-1000. The U.S. Government is authorized to reproduce and distribute reprints for Government purposes notwithstanding any copyright notation therein. The views and conclusions contained herein are those of the authors and should not be interpreted as necessarily representing the official policies or endorsements, either expressed or implied, of Air Force Laboratory, DARPA or the U.S. Government.

References

1. Carion, N., Massa, F., Synnaeve, G., Usunier, N., Kirillov, A., Zagoruyko, S.: End-to-end object detection with transformers. In: Vedaldi, A., Bischof, H., Brox, T., Frahm, J.-M. (eds.) ECCV 2020. LNCS, vol. 12346, pp. 213–229. Springer, Cham (2020). https://doi.org/10.1007/978-3-030-58452-8_13
2. Dai, Z., Cai, B., Lin, Y., Chen, J.: Up-detr: unsupervised pre-training for object detection with transformers. In: Proceedings of the IEEE/CVF Conference on Computer Vision and Pattern Recognition, pp. 1601–1610 (2021)
3. Deng, J., Dong, W., Socher, R., Li, L.J., Li, K., Fei-Fei, L.: Imagenet: a large-scale hierarchical image database. In: 2009 IEEE Conference on Computer Vision and Pattern Recognition, pp. 248–255. IEEE (2009)
4. Everingham, M., Van Gool, L., Williams, C.K.I., Winn, J., Zisserman, A.: The PASCAL Visual Object Classes Challenge 2007 (VOC2007) Results. www.pascal-network.org/challenges/VOC/voc2007/workshop/index.html
5. Everingham, M., Van Gool, L., Williams, C.K.I., Winn, J., Zisserman, A.: The PASCAL Visual Object Classes Challenge 2012 (VOC2012) Results. www.pascal-network.org/challenges/VOC/voc2012/workshop/index.html
6. Fan, Q., Zhuo, W., Tang, C.K., Tai, Y.W.: Few-shot object detection with attention-rpn and multi-relation detector. In: Proceedings of the IEEE/CVF Conference on Computer Vision and Pattern Recognition, pp. 4013–4022 (2020)
7. Girshick, R.: Fast R-CNN. In: Proceedings of the IEEE International Conference on Computer Vision, pp. 1440–1448 (2015)
8. Han, G., He, Y., Huang, S., Ma, J., Chang, S.F.: Query adaptive few-shot object detection with heterogeneous graph convolutional networks. In: Proceedings of the IEEE/CVF International Conference on Computer Vision, pp. 3263–3272 (2021)
9. Han, G., Huang, S., Ma, J., He, Y., Chang, S.F.: Meta faster R-CNN: towards accurate few-shot object detection with attentive feature alignment. In: Proceedings of the AAAI Conference on Artificial Intelligence, vol. 36, pp. 780–789 (2022)
10. Han, G., Ma, J., Huang, S., Chen, L., Chang, S.F.: Few-shot object detection with fully cross-transformer. In: Proceedings of the IEEE/CVF Conference on Computer Vision and Pattern Recognition, pp. 5321–5330 (2022)
11. Han, G., Ma, J., Huang, S., Chen, L., Chellappa, R., Chang, S.F.: Multimodal few-shot object detection with meta-learning based cross-modal prompting. arXiv preprint arXiv:2204.07841 (2022)
12. Han, G., Zhang, X., Li, C.: Revisiting faster R-CNN: a deeper look at region proposal network. In: International Conference on Neural Information Processing, pp. 14–24 (2017)
13. Han, G., Zhang, X., Li, C.: Single shot object detection with top-down refinement. In: 2017 IEEE International Conference on Image Processing (ICIP), pp. 3360–3364. IEEE (2017)

14. Han, G., Zhang, X., Li, C.: Semi-supervised DFF: decoupling detection and feature flow for video object detectors. In: Proceedings of the 26th ACM International Conference on Multimedia, pp. 1811–1819 (2018)

15. He, K., Gkioxari, G., Dollár, P., Girshick, R.: Mask R-CNN. In: Proceedings of the IEEE International Conference on Computer Vision, pp. 2961–2969 (2017)

16. He, K., Zhang, X., Ren, S., Sun, J.: Deep residual learning for image recognition. In: Proceedings of the IEEE Conference on Computer Vision and Pattern Recognition, pp. 770–778 (2016)

17. Hu, H., Bai, S., Li, A., Cui, J., Wang, L.: Dense relation distillation with context-aware aggregation for few-shot object detection. In: Proceedings of the IEEE/CVF Conference on Computer Vision and Pattern Recognition, pp. 10185–10194 (2021)

18. Huang, S., Ma, J., Han, G., Chang, S.F.: Task-adaptive negative envision for few-shot open-set recognition. In: Proceedings of the IEEE/CVF Conference on Computer Vision and Pattern Recognition, pp. 7171–7180 (2022)

19. Kang, B., Liu, Z., Wang, X., Yu, F., Feng, J., Darrell, T.: Few-shot object detection via feature reweighting. In: Proceedings of the IEEE/CVF International Conference on Computer Vision, pp. 8420–8429 (2019)

20. Khosla, P., et al.: Supervised contrastive learning. Adv. Neural. Inf. Process. Syst. **33**, 18661–18673 (2020)

21. Li, A., Li, Z.: Transformation invariant few-shot object detection. In: Proceedings of the IEEE/CVF Conference on Computer Vision and Pattern Recognition, pp. 3094–3102 (2021)

22. Li, B., Yang, B., Liu, C., Liu, F., Ji, R., Ye, Q.: Beyond max-margin: class margin equilibrium for few-shot object detection. In: Proceedings of the IEEE/CVF Conference on Computer Vision and Pattern Recognition, pp. 7363–7372 (2021)

23. Li, Y., et al.: Few-shot object detection via classification refinement and distractor retreatment. In: Proceedings of the IEEE/CVF Conference on Computer Vision and Pattern Recognition, pp. 15395–15403 (2021)

24. Lin, T.Y., Dollár, P., Girshick, R., He, K., Hariharan, B., Belongie, S.: Feature pyramid networks for object detection. In: Proceedings of the IEEE Conference on Computer Vision and Pattern Recognition, pp. 2117–2125 (2017)

25. Lin, T.-S., et al.: Microsoft COCO: common objects in context. In: Fleet, D., Pajdla, T., Schiele, B., Tuytelaars, T. (eds.) ECCV 2014. LNCS, vol. 8693, pp. 740–755. Springer, Cham (2014). https://doi.org/10.1007/978-3-319-10602-1_48

26. Liu, W., et al.: SSD: single shot multiBox detector. In: Leibe, B., Matas, J., Sebe, N., Welling, M. (eds.) ECCV 2016. LNCS, vol. 9905, pp. 21–37. Springer, Cham (2016). https://doi.org/10.1007/978-3-319-46448-0_2

27. Ma, J., Xie, H., Han, G., Chang, S.F., Galstyan, A., Abd-Almageed, W.: Partner-assisted learning for few-shot image classification. In: Proceedings of the IEEE/CVF International Conference on Computer Vision, pp. 10573–10582 (2021)

28. Redmon, J., Divvala, S., Girshick, R., Farhadi, A.: You only look once: Unified, real-time object detection. In: Proceedings of the IEEE Conference on Computer Vision and Pattern Recognition, pp. 779–788 (2016)

29. Ren, S., He, K., Girshick, R., Sun, J.: Faster R-CNN: towards real-time object detection with region proposal networks. In: Advances in Neural Information Processing Systems, vol. 28 (2015)

30. Snell, J., Swersky, K., Zemel, R.: Prototypical networks for few-shot learning. In: Advances in Neural Information Processing Systems, vol. 30 (2017)

31. Sun, B., Li, B., Cai, S., Yuan, Y., Zhang, C.: FSCE: few-shot object detection via contrastive proposal encoding. In: Proceedings of the IEEE/CVF Conference on Computer Vision and Pattern Recognition, pp. 7352–7362 (2021)

32. Sun, P., et al.: Sparse R-CNN: end-to-end object detection with learnable proposals. In: Proceedings of the IEEE/CVF Conference on Computer Vision and Pattern Recognition, pp. 14454–14463 (2021)
33. Tian, Y., Wang, Y., Krishnan, D., Tenenbaum, J.B., Isola, P.: Rethinking few-shot image classification: a good embedding is all you need? In: Vedaldi, A., Bischof, H., Brox, T., Frahm, J.-M. (eds.) ECCV 2020. LNCS, vol. 12359, pp. 266–282. Springer, Cham (2020). https://doi.org/10.1007/978-3-030-58568-6_16
34. Vaswani, A., et al.: Attention is all you need. In: Advances in Neural Information Processing Systems, vol. 30 (2017)
35. Wang, X., Huang, T., Gonzalez, J., Darrell, T., Yu, F.: Frustratingly simple few-shot object detection. In: International Conference on Machine Learning, pp. 9919–9928. PMLR (2020)
36. Wang, Y.X., Ramanan, D., Hebert, M.: Meta-learning to detect rare objects. In: Proceedings of the IEEE/CVF International Conference on Computer Vision, pp. 9925–9934 (2019)
37. Wu, A., Han, Y., Zhu, L., Yang, Y.: Universal-prototype enhancing for few-shot object detection. In: Proceedings of the IEEE/CVF International Conference on Computer Vision, pp. 9567–9576 (2021)
38. Wu, A., Zhao, S., Deng, C., Liu, W.: Generalized and discriminative few-shot object detection via SVD-dictionary enhancement. In: Advances in Neural Information Processing Systems, vol. 34 (2021)
39. Wu, J., Liu, S., Huang, D., Wang, Y.: Multi-scale positive sample refinement for few-shot object detection. In: Vedaldi, A., Bischof, H., Brox, T., Frahm, J.-M. (eds.) ECCV 2020. LNCS, vol. 12361, pp. 456–472. Springer, Cham (2020). https://doi.org/10.1007/978-3-030-58517-4_27
40. Yan, X., Chen, Z., Xu, A., Wang, X., Liang, X., Lin, L.: Meta R-CNN: towards general solver for instance-level low-shot learning. In: Proceedings of the IEEE/CVF International Conference on Computer Vision, pp. 9577–9586 (2019)
41. Ypsilantis, N.A., Garcia, N., Han, G., Ibrahimi, S., Van Noord, N., Tolias, G.: The met dataset: instance-level recognition for artworks. In: Thirty-fifth Conference on Neural Information Processing Systems Datasets and Benchmarks Track (Round 2) (2021)
42. Zhu, X., Su, W., Lu, L., Li, B., Wang, X., Dai, J.: Deformable DETR: deformable transformers for end-to-end object detection. In: International Conference on Learning Representations (2020)

Implicit Neural Representations
for Image Compression

Yannick Strümpler[1]([✉]) [iD], Janis Postels[1] [iD], Ren Yang[1] [iD], Luc Van Gool[1],
and Federico Tombari[2,3] [iD]

[1] ETH Zurich, Zürich, Switzerland
y.struempler@gmail.com
[2] Technical University of Munich, Munich, Germany
[3] Google, Mountain View, USA

Abstract. Implicit Neural Representations (INRs) gained attention as
a novel and effective representation for various data types. Recently,
prior work applied INRs to image compressing. Such compression algorithms are promising candidates as a general purpose approach for any
coordinate-based data modality. However, in order to live up to this
promise current INR-based compression algorithms need to improve their
rate-distortion performance by a large margin. This work progresses on
this problem. First, we propose meta-learned initializations for INR-
based compression which improves rate-distortion performance. As a
side effect it also leads to leads to faster convergence speed. Secondly,
we introduce a simple yet highly effective change to the network architecture compared to prior work on INR-based compression. Namely, we
combine SIREN networks with positional encodings which improves rate
distortion performance. Our contributions to source compression with
INRs vastly outperform prior work. We show that our INR-based compression algorithm, meta-learning combined with SIREN and positional
encodings, outperforms JPEG2000 and Rate-Distortion Autoencoders on
Kodak with 2x reduced dimensionality for the first time and closes the
gap on full resolution images. To underline the generality of INR-based
source compression, we further perform experiments on 3D shape compression where our method greatly outperforms Draco - a traditional
compression algorithm.

1 Introduction

Living in a world where digitalization is ubiquitous and important decisions are
based on big data analytics, the problem of how to store information effectively

---

Y. Strümpler and J. Postels—Equal contribution.

Supplementary Information The online version contains supplementary material
available at https://doi.org/10.1007/978-3-031-19809-0_5.

is more important than ever. Source compression is the generalized term for representing data in a compact form, that either preserves all the information (lossless compression) or sacrifices some information for even smaller file sizes (lossy compression). It is a key component to tackle the flood of image and video data that is uploaded, transmitted and downloaded from the internet every day. While lossless compression is arguably more desirable, it has a fundamental theoretical limit, namely Shannon's entropy [47]. Therefore, lossy compression aims at trading off a file's quality with its size - called rate-distortion trade-off.

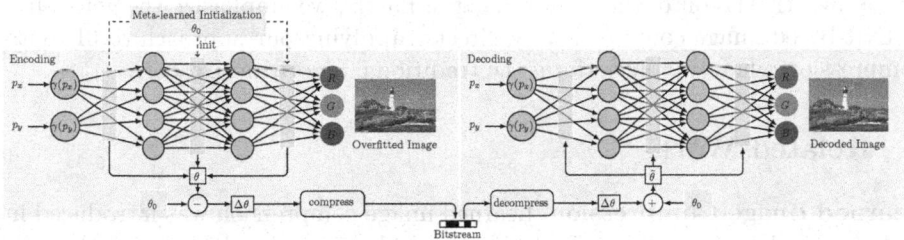

Fig. 1. Method overview: we summarize our approach to use INRs for compression by using the model weights θ as the representation for an image. We also visualize how a meta-learned initialization θ_0 is used in the encoding and decoding process in order to compress only the weight update $\Delta\theta$ into the bitstream

Apart from traditional hand-designed algorithms tuned for particular data modalities, e.g. audio, images or video, machine learning research has recently developed promising learned approaches to source compression by leveraging the power of neural networks. Such methods typically build on the well-known autoencoder [28] by implementing a constrained version of it. These so-called Rate-Distortion Autoencoders (RDAEs) [5,6,25,37] jointly optimize the quality of the decoded data sample and its encoded file size.

This work sidesteps the prevalent approach of RDAEs and investigates a novel paradigm for source compression - particularly focusing on image compression. Recently, INRs gained popularity as a flexible, multi-purpose data representation that is able to produce high-fidelity samples on images [49], 3D shapes [44,49] and scenes [40]. In general, INRs represent data that lives on an underlying regular grid by learning a mapping between the grid's coordinates and the corresponding data values (e.g. RGB values) and have even been hypothesized to yield well compressed representations [49]. Due to their generality and concurrent early attempts to leverage them for compression [11,19,20], INRs denote a promising candidate as a general purpose compression algorithm.

Currently there are two main challenges for INR-based compression algorithms: (1) Straightforward approaches struggle to compete even with the simplest traditional algorithms [19]. (2) Since INRs encode data by overfitting to particular instances, the encoding time is perceived impractical. To this end, we make two contributions. Firstly, we propose meta-learned initializations for INR-based compression. We exploit recent advances in meta-learning for INRs [48,52] based on Model-Agnostic Meta-Learning (MAML) [22] to find weight initializations that can compress data with fewer gradient updates as well as yield better rate-distortion performance. Secondly, we combine SIREN with positional encodings for INR-based compression which greatly improves rate-distortion performance. While we focus on images, we emphasize that our proposed method can easily be adapted to any coordinate-based data modality. Overall, we introduce a compression pipeline that vastly outperforms the recently proposed COIN [19] and is competitive with traditional compression algorithms for images. Moreover, we demonstrate that meta-learned INRs already outperform JPEG2000 and a few RDAEs on downsampled images. Lastly, we emphasize the generality of INR-based image compression by directly applying our approach to 3D data compression where we outperform the traditional algorithm Draco.

2   Related Work

Learned Image Compression. Learned image compression was introduced in [6] by proposing an end-to-end autoencoder and entropy model that jointly optimizes rate and distortion. In the following, [7] extends this approach by adding a scale hyperprior, and then [33,37,41] propose employing autoregressive entropy models to further improve the compression performance. Later, Hu et al. [29] propose a coarse-to-fine hierarchical hyperprior, and Cheng et al. [14] achieve further improvements by adding attention modules and using a Gaussian Mixture Model (GMM) to estimate the distribution of latent representations. The current state-of-the art is achieved by [58]: They propose an invertible convolutional network, and apply residual feature enhancement as pre-processing and post-processing. Moreover, there are also plenty of methods aiming at variable rate compression, mainly including RNN-based autoencoders [30,54,55] and conditional autoencoders [15]. Besides, [4,38] propose image compression with Generative Adversarial Networks (GAN) to optimize perceptual quality.

Implicit Neural Representations. One of the early works on INRs is DeepSDF [45] which is a neural network representation for 3D shapes. In particular, they use a Signed Distance Function (SDF) to represent the shape by a field where every point in space holds the distance to the shape's surface. Concurrently to DeepSDF, multiple works propose similar approaches to represent 3D shapes with INRs, e.g. , the occupancy network [39] and the implicit field decoder [13]. Besides, INRs have also been used for scene representation [40], image representation [12,50] and compact representation [17].

Model Compression. In the past decades, there has been a plethora of works on model compression [36]. For instance, [26] proposes sequentially applying pruning, quantization and entropy coding combined with retraining in between the steps. Later, [2] suggests an end-to-end learning approach using a rate-distortion objective. To optimize performance under quantization, several works [18,24,56,57] use mixed-precision quantization, while others [10,21,31,35,42,43] propose post-quantization optimization techniques.

Model Weights for Instance-Adaptive Compression. Recently, [46] suggests finetuning the decoder weights of an RDAE on a per-instance basis and appending the weight update to the latent vector, thereby improving RDAEs. It is related to our work in that model weights are included in the representation, however the RDAE architecture fundamentally differs from ours. Most recently, Dupont *et al.* [19] propose the first INR-based image compression approach COIN, which overfits an INR's model weights to represent single images and compresses the INR using quantization. Importantly, COIN does not use meta-learning for initializing INRs, positional encodings for SIREN, post-quantization retraining and entropy coding. Furthermore, [9] recently proposed a compression algorithm for entire scenes based on compressing the weights of NeRF [40]. Moreover, concurrently NeRV [11] proposed to compress videos using INRs. While they use another data modality and neither use post-quantization retraining nor meta-learned initializations, their work shows the potential of INR-based compression of coordinate-based data. In another concurrent work, [20] also proposes to apply meta-learning to INR-based compression in an effort to extend COIN. However, unlike this work they do not outperform JPEG on the full resolution images on KODAK. Their performance is similar to our method absent of meta-learning and positional encodings (see Fig. 7).

3   Method

3.1   Background

INRs store coordinate-based data such as images, videos and 3D shapes by representing data as a continuous function from coordinates to values. For example, an image is a function of a horizontal and vertical coordinate (p_x, p_y) and maps to a color vector within a color space such as RGB:

$$I : (p_x, p_y) \to (R, G, B) \tag{1}$$

This mapping can be approximated by a neural network f_θ, typically a Multi Layer Perceptron (MLP) with parameters θ, such that $I(p_x, p_y) \approx f_\theta(p_x, p_y)$. Since these functions are continuous, INRs are resolution agnostic, *i.e.*, they can be evaluated on arbitrary coordinates within the normalized range $[-1, 1]$. To express a pixel based image tensor $\mathbf{x}$, we evaluate the image function on a uniformly spaced coordinate grid $\mathbf{p}$ such that $\mathbf{x} = I(\mathbf{p}) \in \mathbb{R}^{W \times H \times 3}$ with

$$\mathbf{p}_{ij} = \left(\frac{2i}{W - 1} - 1, \frac{2j}{H - 1} - 1 \right) \in [-1, 1]^2 \tag{2}$$
$$\forall\, i \in \{0, \dots, W - 1\}, j \in \{0, \dots, H - 1\}.$$

Note that each coordinate vector is mapped independently:

$$f_\theta(\mathbf{p}) = \begin{bmatrix} f_\theta(\mathbf{p}_{11}) & \cdots & f_\theta(\mathbf{p}_{1H}) \\ \vdots & \ddots & \vdots \\ f_\theta(\mathbf{p}_{W1}) & \cdots & f_\theta(\mathbf{p}_{WH}) \end{bmatrix}. \tag{3}$$

Rate-Distortion Autoencoders. The predominant approach in learned source compression are RDAEs: An encoder network produces a compressed representation, typically called a latent vector $z \in \mathbb{R}^d$, which a jointly trained decoder network uses to reconstruct the original input. Early approaches enforce compactness of z by limiting its dimension d [27]. Newer methods constrain the representation by adding an entropy estimate, the so-called rate loss, of z to the loss. This rate term, reflecting the storage requirement of z, is minimized jointly with a distortion term, that quantifies the compression error.

3.2 Image Compression Using INRs

In contrast to RDAEs, INRs store all information implicitly in the network weights θ. The input to the INR itself, *i.e.*, the coordinate, does not contain any information. The encoding process is equivalent to training the INR. The decoding process is equivalent to loading a set of weights into the network and evaluating on a coordinate grid. We can summarize this as:

$$\arg \min_{\theta} \mathcal{L}(\mathbf{x}, f_\theta(\mathbf{p})) = \theta^\star \xrightarrow[\text{transmit } \theta^\star]{} \widehat{\mathbf{x}} = f_{\theta^\star}(\mathbf{p}). \tag{4}$$

Thus, we only need to store $\theta^\star$ to reconstruct a distorted version of the original image $\mathbf{x}$. With our approach, we describe a method to find $\theta^\star$ to achieve compact storage and good reconstruction at the same time.

Architecture. We use SIREN, namely a MLP using sine activations with a frequency $\omega = 30$ as proposed originally in [49], which has recently shown good performance on image data. We adopt the initialization scheme suggested by the authors. Since we aim to evaluate our method at multiple bitrates, we vary the model size to obtain a rate-distortion curve. We also provide an ablation on how to vary the model size to achieve optimal rate-distortion performance (see supplementary material) and on the architecture of the INR (see Sect. 4.4).

Input Encoding. An input encoding transforms the input coordinate to a higher dimension, which has been shown to improve perceptual quality [40,53]. Notably, to the best of our knowledge we are the first to combine SIREN with an input encoding - previously input encodings have only been used for INRs based on the Rectified Linear Unit (ReLU) activation functions. We apply an adapted version of the positional encoding presented in [40], where we introduce the scale parameter σ to adjust the frequency spacing (similarly to [53]) and concatenate the frequency terms with the original coordinate p (as in the SIREN codebase[1]):

$$\gamma(p) = (p, \sin(\sigma^0 \pi p), \cos(\sigma^0 \pi p), \ldots,$$
$$\sin(\sigma^{L-1} \pi p), \cos(\sigma^{L-1} \pi p)). \tag{5}$$

where L is the number of frequencies used. We investigate the impact of the input encoding in Sect. 4.4.

---

[1] https://github.com/vsitzmann/siren.

3.3 Compression Pipeline for INRs

This section introduces our INR-based compression pipeline. First, we describe our basic approach based on randomly initialized INRs (Sect. 3.3). Then, we propose meta-learned initializations to improve the rate-distortion performance and encoding time of INR-based compression (Sect. 3.3). The entire pipeline is depicted in Fig. 2 and a higher level overview is shown in Fig. 1.

Basic Approach Using Random Initialization. Stage 1: Overfitting. First, we overfit the INR f_θ to a data sample at test time. This is equivalent to calling the encoder of other learned methods. We call this step overfitting to emphasize that the INR is trained to only represent a single image. Given an image $\mathbf{x}$ and a coordinate grid $\mathbf{p}$, we minimize the objective:

$$\arg\min_\theta \mathcal{L}_{\mathrm{MSE}}(\mathbf{x}, f_\theta(\mathbf{p})). \tag{6}$$

We use the Mean Squared Error (MSE) as the loss function to measure similarity of the ground-truth target and the INRs output:

$$\mathcal{L}_{\mathrm{MSE}}(\mathbf{x}, \widehat{\mathbf{x}}) = \sum_i^W \sum_j^H \frac{\|\mathbf{x}_{ij} - \widehat{\mathbf{x}}_{ij}\|_2^2}{WH}. \tag{7}$$

Note that $\mathbf{x}_{ij} \in \mathbb{R}^3$ is the color vector of a single pixel.

Regularization. In image compression, we aim at minimizing distortion (*e.g.*, MSE) as well as bitrate simultaneously. Since the model entropy is not differentiable, we can not directly use it in gradient-based optimization. One option that has been used in literature is to use a differentiable entropy estimator during training [2]. We however choose to use a regularization term that approximately induces lower entropy. In particular, we apply L_1 regularization to the model weights. Overall, this yields the following optimization objective:

$$\mathcal{L}(\mathbf{x}, f_\theta(\mathbf{p})) = \mathcal{L}_{\mathrm{MSE}}(\mathbf{x}, f_\theta(\mathbf{p})) + \lambda \|\theta\|_1 \tag{8}$$

where λ determines the importance of the L_1 regularization which induces sparsity. Our regularization term is related to the sparsity loss employed in [46]: we have the same goal of limiting the entropy of the weights, however we apply this to an INR, whereas they apply it to a traditional explicit decoder.

Stage 2: Quantization. Typically, the model weights resulting from overfitting are single precision floating point numbers requiring 32 bits per weight. To reduce the memory requirement, we quantize the weights using the AI Model Efficiency Toolkit (AIMET)[2]. We employ quantization specific to each weight tensor such that the uniformly-spaced quantization grid is adjusted to the value range of the tensor. The bitwidth determines the number of discrete levels, *i.e.*, quantization

---

[2] https://quic.github.io/.

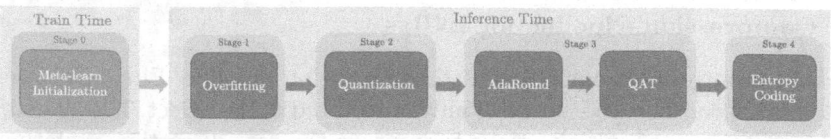

Fig. 2. Overview of INR-based compression pipeline. Blue: the basic compression pipeline comprising overfitting, quantization, AdaRound, QAT and entropy coding. Green: Additional meta-learning of initializations at training time (Color figure online)

bins. We find empirically that bitwidths in the range of 7–8 lead to optimal rate-distortion performance for our models as shown in the supplement.

Stage 3: Post-Quantization Optimization. Quantization reduces the models performance by rounding the weights to their nearest quantization bin. We leverage two methods to mitigate this effect. First, we employ *AdaRound* [42], which is a second-order optimization method to decide whether to round a weight up or down. The core idea is that the traditional nearest rounding is not always the best choice, as shown in [42]. Subsequently, we fine-tune the quantized weights using Quantization Aware Training (QAT). This step aims to reverse part of the quantization error. Quantization is non-differentiable and we thus rely on the Straight Through Estimator (STE) [8] for the gradient computation, essentially bypassing the quantization operation during backpropagation.

Stage 4: Entropy Coding. Finally, we perform entropy coding to further losslessly compress weights. In particular, we use a binarized arithmetic coding algorithm to losslessly compress the quantized weights.

Meta-Learned Initializations for Compressing INRs. Directly applying INRs to compression has two severe limitations: firstly, it requires overfitting a model from scratch to a data sample during the encoding step. Secondly, it does not allow embedding inductive biases into the compression algorithm (*e.g.*, knowledge of a particular image distribution). To this end, we apply meta-learning, i.e. Model Agnostic Meta-Learning (MAML) [23], for learning a weight initialization that is close to the weight values and entails information of the distribution of images. Previous work on meta-learning for INRs has aimed at improving mainly convergence speed [52]. The learned initialization θ_0 is claimed to be closer in weight space to the final INR. We want to exploit this fact for compression under the hypothesis that the update $\Delta\theta = \theta - \theta_0$ requires less storage than the full weight tensor θ. We thus fix θ_0 and include it in the decoder such that it is sufficient to transmit $\Delta\theta$, or, to be precise, the quantized update $\Delta\tilde{\theta}$. The decoder can then reconstruct the image by computing:

$$\tilde{\theta} = \theta_0 + \Delta\tilde{\theta}, \quad \hat{\mathbf{x}} = f_{\tilde{\theta}}(\mathbf{p}). \tag{9}$$

We expect the value range occupied by the weight updates $\Delta\theta$ to be significantly smaller than that of the full weights θ. The range between the lowest and highest quantization bin can thus be smaller when quantizing the weight updates. At a fixed bitwidth, the stepsize in-between quantization bins will be smaller in the case of weight updates and, thus, the average rounding error is also smaller.

Note that the initialization is only learned once per distribution $\mathcal{D}$ prior to overfitting a single image. Thus, we introduce it as Stage 0. Stage 0 happens at training time, is performed on many images and is not part of inference. Stages 1–4 happen at inference time and aim at compressing a single image. Consequently, using meta-learned initializations does not increase inference time.

Integration into a Compression Pipeline. When we want to encode only the update $\Delta\theta$, we need to adjust our compression pipeline accordingly. During overfitting we change the objective to:

$$\mathcal{L}(\mathbf{x}, f_\theta(\mathbf{p})) = \mathcal{L}_{\mathrm{MSE}}(\mathbf{x}, f_\theta(\mathbf{p})) + \lambda \left\| \Delta\theta \right\|_1 \tag{10}$$

thus, the regularization term now induces the model weights to stay close to the initialization. Also, we directly apply quantization to the update $\Delta\theta$. In order to perform AdaRound and QAT, we apply a decomposition to all linear layers in the MLP to separate initial values from the update:

$$
\begin{aligned}
\mathbf{W}\mathbf{x} + \mathbf{b} &= (\mathbf{W}_0 + \Delta\mathbf{W})\mathbf{x} + (\mathbf{b}_0 + \Delta\mathbf{b}) \\
&= \underbrace{(\mathbf{W}_0\mathbf{x} + \mathbf{b}_0)}_{\text{fix}} + \underbrace{(\Delta\mathbf{W}\mathbf{x} + \Delta\mathbf{b})}_{\text{quantize \& retrain}} .
\end{aligned} \tag{11}
$$

This is necessary, because optimizing the rounding and QAT require the original input-output function of each linear layer. Splitting it up into two parallel linear layers, we can fix the linear layer containing $\mathbf{W}_0$ and $\mathbf{b}_0$ and apply quantization, AdaRound and QAT to the update parameters $\Delta\mathbf{W}$ and $\Delta\mathbf{b}$.

INRs for 3D Shape Compression. The proposed INR-based compression pipeline is applicable to any coordinate based data modality with minimal modification. We demonstrate this for 3D shapes. A 3D shape can be represented as a signed distance function:

$$SDF : (p_x, p_y, p_z) \to d \tag{12}$$

i.e., we assign a signed distance d between each point (p_x, p_y, p_z) in 3D space and the shape surface. Here, the sign of the distance indicates whether we are inside (negative) or outside of the shape (positive). We can now simply train our INR to approximate the SDF:

$$f_\theta(\mathbf{p}) \approx SDF(\mathbf{p}). \tag{13}$$

When training INRs to estimate SDFs accurate predictions close to the surface are most important. Therefore, we adopt the sampling strategy proposed in [51].

4   Experiments

Datasets. The **Kodak** [1] dataset is a collection of 24 images containing various objects, people or landscapes. This dataset has a resolution of 768×512 pixels (vertical × horizontal). The **DIV2K** dataset introduced in [3] contains 1000 high resolution images with a width of ≈ 2000 pixels. The dataset is split into 800 training, 100 validation and 100 test images. For our purpose of meta-learning the initialization, we resize the DIV2K images to the same resolution as Kodak (768×512). **CelebA** [34] is a dataset containing over 200'000 images of celebrities with a resolution of 178×218. We evaluate our method on 100 images that are randomly sampled from the test set. For our 3D shape compression experiment we use 5 high resolution meshes from the **Stanford 3D Scanning Repository** [16], which we normalize such that they fit into a unit cube prior to training. More details are in the supplement.

Metrics. We evaluate two metrics to analyze performance in terms of rate and distortion. We measure the rate as the total number of bits required to store the representation divided by the number of pixels $W \cdot H$ of the image:

$$\text{bitrate} = \frac{\text{total number of bits}}{WH} \quad \text{[bpp]}. \tag{14}$$

We measure distortion in terms of MSE and convert it to the Peak Signal to Noise Ratio (PSNR) using the formula:

$$\text{PSNR} = 10 \log_{10} \left(\frac{1}{MSE} \right) \quad \text{[dB]}. \tag{15}$$

Baselines. We compare our method against traditional codecs, INR based compression and learned approaches based on RDAEs.

- Traditional image compression codecs: JPEG, JPEG2000, BPG
- INR-based image compression: Dupont *et al.* [19] (COIN)
- RDAE-based image compression: Ballé *et al.* [6], Xie *et al.* [58]
- 3D mesh compression: Draco[3]

Optimization and Hyperparameters. We use a default set of hyperparameters throughout the experiment section unless mentioned otherwise. In particular, we use INRs with 3 hidden layers and sine activations combined with the positional encoding using $\sigma = 1.4$. On the higher resolution Kodak dataset, we set the number of frequencies to $L = 16$, whereas on CelebA we set $L = 12$. We vary the number of hidden units per layer M, *i.e.*, the width of the MLP, to evaluate performance at different rate-distortion operating points. We refer to our method with random initialization as the *basic* approach whereas the method including meta-learned initialization is called *meta-learned*. We found the optimal bitwidth to be $b = 7$ for the *meta-learned* approach and $b = 8$ for the *basic* approach. For additional details on the training and hyperparameters we refer to the supplementary material.

---

[3] https://github.com/google/draco.

4.1 Comparison with State-of-the-Art

Full Resolution. Figure 4 depicts our results on CelebA/Kodak respectively. The proposed *basic* approach can already outperform COIN clearly over the whole range of bitrates. It is also better than JPEG for most bitrates, except the highest setting on CelebA. With our proposed *meta-learned* approach we improve over the *basic* approach at all bitrates. Between the two datasets, the difference is noticeably greater on the CelebA dataset. At the lowest bitrate examined the meta-learned approach reaches the performance of JPEG2000, however our approach cannot keep up with JPEG2000 at higher bitrates. On the CelebA dataset, the meta-learned approach also almost reaches the performance of an autoencoder with a factorized prior [6] at lower bitrates. Towards higher bitrates, the advantage of the autoencoder becomes clearer. BPG as well as the state-of-the-art RDAE [58] clearly outperform our method on both datasets (Fig. 3).

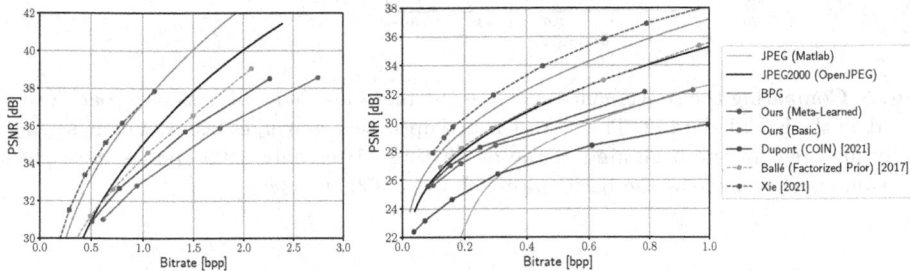

Fig. 3. Performance overview over image compression approaches including conventional (solid line), learned autoencoder (dashed line) and learned INR methods (solid line with dots) evaluated on the **CelebA** (left) **Kodak** (right) dataset

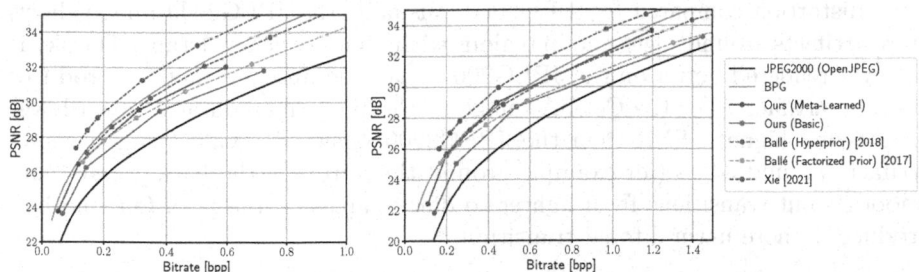

Fig. 4. Image compression approaches including conventional (solid line), RDAEs (dashed line) and learned INR-based methods (solid line with dots) evaluated on the **Kodak** dataset with image resolution reduced by a factor of two (left) and four (right). Meta-learned INRs show competitive performance in this regime

Reduced Image Resolution. We further compare our *basic* and *meta-learned* approach with other methods on Kodak with reduced resolution (2x/4x). These image are comprised of 384 × 256, resp. 192 × 128, pixels. We observe that the *meta-learned* approach again performs strictly better than the *basic* approach. Moreover, our *meta-learned* approach demonstrates competitive performance for this image resolution outperforming all other methods, except BPG and Xie *et al.* , over the entire range of bitrates.

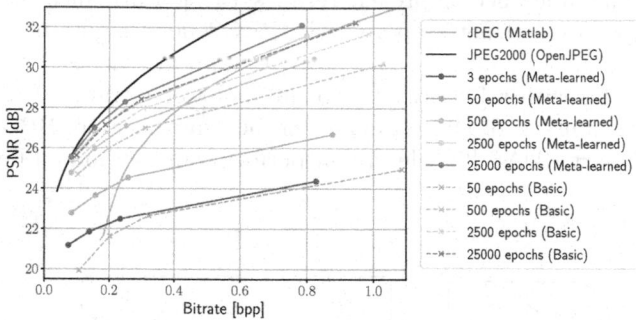

Fig. 5. Comparing the convergence speed of the meta-learned and basic approach evaluated on the Kodak dataset. The meta-learned approach converges faster, which is especially apparent in the beginning of the overfitting. After only 2500 epochs it reaches the same performance as the basic approach after 25000 epochs

4.2   Visual Comparison to JPEG and JPEG2000

We compare compressed images of our meta-learned approach with the codecs JPEG and JPEG2000 in Fig. 6. We visually confirm that our model significantly improves over JPEG: Our model produces an overall more pleasing image with better detail and less artifacts although we operate at a lower bitrate on both images. For the Kodak image in Fig. 6 we achieve a slightly lower bitrate at the same distortion compared to JPEG2000. Visually, the JPEG2000 image shows more artifacts around edges and in regions with high frequency details. The sky is however rendered better on the JPEG2000 image because our model introduces periodic artifacts. For the CelebA image in Fig. 6 our method achieves a lower bitrate and higher PSNR than the JPEG2000 image. JPEG2000 again shows artifacts around edges (for example around the letters in the background) and smoothes out transitions from lighter to darker areas on the face. Our method produces a more natural tonal transition.

4.3   Convergence Speed

In Fig. 5 we show how the basic and meta-learned approach compare over different numbers of epochs. Especially in the beginning of the overfitting, the meta-learned approach shows significantly faster convergence. Already after the first

3 epochs, we obtain better performance than what the basic approach achieves after 50 epochs. Convergence slows down as we approach the final performance of the respective model, while the meta-learned approach maintains the advantage: It achieves the same performance after 2500 epochs as the basic approach after 25000 epochs. This amounts to a reduction in training time of 90%.

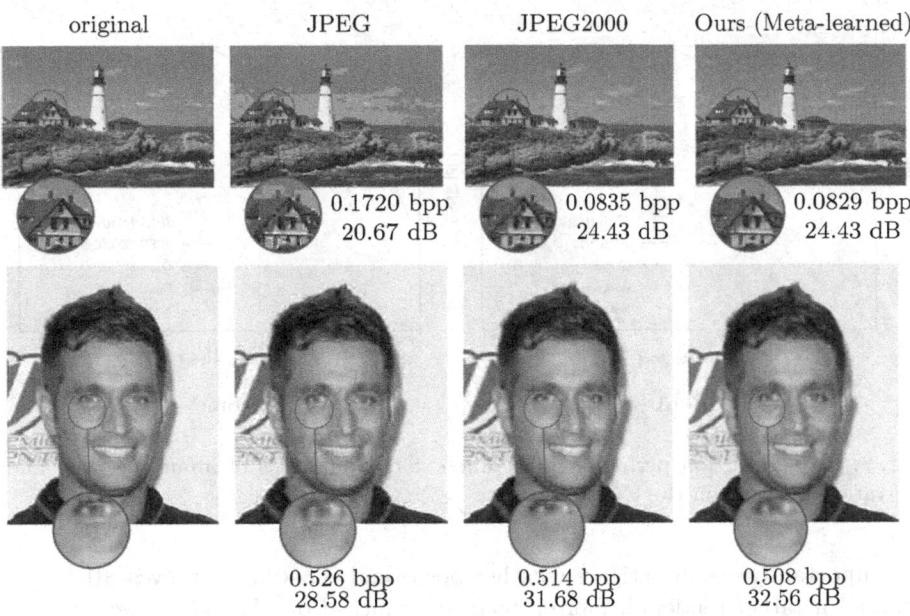

Fig. 6. Visual comparison of images compressed with JPEG (quality factor 1/13), JPEG2000 (compression factor 287/47) and our meta-learned approach on Kodak/CelebA (top/bottom). We use a model with a hidden dimension of $M = 32/24$. JPEG introduces heavy block artifacts and loss of color information resulting in the worst image in comparison. JPEG2000 shows blurring and blocking around edges. Our method maintains better local contrast but shows periodic artifacts visible in the sky as well as smearing at some edges

4.4 Choosing Input Encoding and Activation

An important architecture choice is the combination of input encoding and the activation function used. We compare against the Gaussian encoding proposed in [53]. For this encoding we use the same number of frequencies as hidden dimensions ($L = M$) as in [53] and a standard deviation of $\sigma = 4$. We train models with different hidden dimensions ($M \in \{32, 48, 64, 96, 128\}$) and different input encodings on the Kodak dataset starting from random initializations using the regularization parameter $\lambda = 10^{-6}$.

Looking at Fig. 7a, compared to Fig. 7b we can see that the sine activation outperforms the ReLU activation in every configuration, especially at higher bitrates. The best overall input encoding is *positional* encoding beating *Gaussian* for both activations. The MLP without input encoding and sine activations, the SIREN architecture, performs significantly better than its ReLU counterpart but still cannot reach the performance of the models with input encoding.

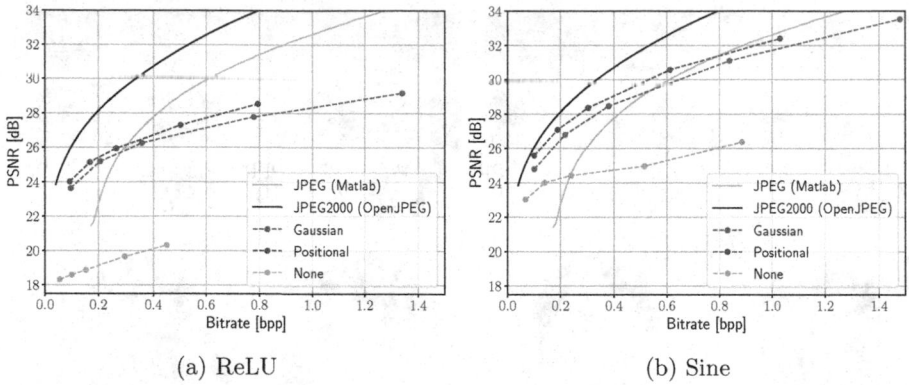

(a) ReLU   (b) Sine

Fig. 7. Rate-distortion performance of different combinations of input encoding and activation function on the Kodak dataset

Importantly, we investigate whether positional encoding improves SIREN in general or rather renders it more robust to quantization. Therefore, we measure the quantization error of our basic approach for different bitwidths. The result is depicted in Fig. 8. ReLU and sine activations both show a reduced quantization error when trained with positional encoding. However, the effect is most obvious in the case of SIREN. Comparing the PSNR-delta of SIREN with and without positional encoding in Fig. 8 with Fig. 7 (b) reveals that applying positional encoding makes SIREN predominantly more robust to quantization.

4.5   3D Shape Compression

To demonstrate that our algorithm is applicable to coordinate-based data beyond images, we provide an additional experiment showing its performance on the task of 3D shape compression. Since the main goal of this experiment is to show the transferability of INRs-based compression, we only train our basic approach without meta-learning on 3D shapes. We plot the chamfer distance averaged over all shapes against the storage required in Fig. 9 and compare to the algorithm Draco which is based on mesh quantization. We focus on the comparison with mesh-based compression algorithms because they also preserve a continuous surface unlike the alternative approach of point cloud compression. We require much fewer bits to encode a shape of similar quality than Draco. Further details regarding this experiment are in the supplement.

5   Conclusion

Overall, INRs demonstrated great potential as a compressed representation for images. Our main contributions, the use of meta-learned initializations and SIREN combined with positional encodings, largely improve rate-distortion performance compared to previous methods [19] performing image compression based on INRs. Moreover, our approach is the first INRs-based method that is competitive with traditional codecs over a large portion of bitrates.

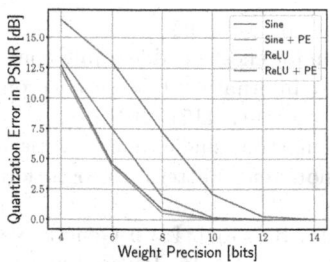

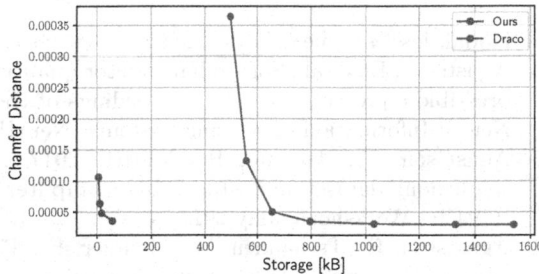

Fig. 8. Quantization error of our basic model using ReLU/sine activations with/without positional encoding (PE)

Fig. 9. Rate-Distortion performance for 3D shape compression of our method (basic) and the traditional algorithm Draco. We clearly outperform Draco

Meta-learned initializations are superior to random initializations. Specifically, they reduce the bitrate at the same reconstruction quality. This supports the hypothesis that weight updates are more compressible. In particular, the performance gain is larger on the CelebA dataset, where the initializations are trained on an image distribution that is more similar to the test set. Moreover, the distribution of faces has less variation than the distribution of natural scenes which eases learning a single strong initialization. Consequently, we make our compression algorithm adaptive to a certain distribution by including *a priori* knowledge into the initialization.

Moreover, meta-learned initializations are a potential solution for long encoding times of INR-based compression: Our meta-learned approach can reduce training time by up to 90% at a fixed performance.

We also highlight the importance of applying input encodings in INR-based compression (see Fig. 7). This demonstrates significance of choosing the correct inductive biases for compression and is another promising future research avenue. Furthermore, the observation that input encodings render INRs more robust to quantization (see Fig. 8) has potential applications beyond compression.

Interestingly, the here proposed INR-based compression technique is competitive on lower resolution images (see Sect. 4.1). However, the performance falls short of RDAEs and BPG on higher resolution images. We hypothesize that processing pixels independently has inefficient scaling properties. Therefore, it is crucial for future research to develop novel architectures for INRs beyond the MLP that mitigate the current deficits at at high resolution images.

Lastly, our basic approach outperforms the traditional algorithm Draco on 3D mesh compression (see Sect. 4.5). Thus conducting further research into 3D shape compression based on INRs denotes a promising direction.

Acknowledgements. This work was partially supported by Google.

References

1. Kodak lossless true color image suite. www.r0k.us/graphics/kodak/
2. Agustsson, E., et al.: Soft-to-hard vector quantization for end-to-end learning compressible representations. In: Proceedings of the 31st International Conference on Neural Information Processing Systems (NeurIPS), pp. 1141–1151 (2017)
3. Agustsson, E., Timofte, R.: NTIRE 2017 challenge on single image super-resolution: dataset and study. In: Computer Vision and Pattern Recognition (CVPR) Workshops, July 2017
4. Agustsson, E., Tschannen, M., Mentzer, F., Timofte, R., Gool, L.V.: Generative adversarial networks for extreme learned image compression. In: Proceedings of the IEEE/CVF International Conference on Computer Vision (ICCV), pp. 221–231 (2019)
5. Alemi, A., Poole, B., Fischer, I., Dillon, J., Saurous, R.A., Murphy, K.: Fixing a broken ELBO. In: Dy, J., Krause, A. (eds.) Proceedings of the 35th International Conference on Machine Learning. Proceedings of Machine Learning Research, vol. 80, pp. 159–168. PMLR. 10–15 July 2018. www.proceedings.mlr.press/v80/alemi18a.html
6. Ballé, J., Laparra, V., Simoncelli, E.P.: End-to-end optimized image compression. In: International Conference on Learning Representations (ICLR) (2017)
7. Ballé, J., Minnen, D., Singh, S., Hwang, S.J., Johnston, N.: Variational image compression with a scale hyperprior. In: International Conference on Learning Representations (ICLR) (2018)
8. Bengio, Y.: Estimating or propagating gradients through stochastic neurons (2013)
9. Bird, T., Ballé, J., Singh, S., Chou, P.A.: 3d scene compression through entropy penalized neural representation functions. In: 2021 Picture Coding Symposium (PCS), pp. 1–5. IEEE (2021)
10. Chai, S.M.: Quantization-guided training for compact TinyML models. arXiv preprint arXiv:2103.06231 (2021)
11. Chen, H., He, B., Wang, H., Ren, Y., Lim, S.N., Shrivastava, A.: NeRV: neural representations for videos. In: Thirty-Fifth Conference on Neural Information Processing Systems (2021)
12. Chen, Y., Liu, S., Wang, X.: Learning continuous image representation with local implicit image function. In: Conference on Computer Vision and Pattern Recognition (CVPR) (2021)
13. Chen, Z., Zhang, H.: Learning implicit fields for generative shape modeling. In: Conference on Computer Vision and Pattern Recognition (CVPR) (2019)
14. Cheng, Z., Sun, H., Takeuchi, M., Katto, J.: Learned image compression with discretized gaussian mixture likelihoods and attention modules. In: Conference on Computer Vision and Pattern Recognition (CVPR) (2020)

15. Choi, Y., El-Khamy, M., Lee, J.: Variable rate deep image compression with a conditional autoencoder. In: Proceedings of the IEEE/CVF International Conference on Computer Vision (ICCV), pp. 3146–3154 (2019)
16. Curless, B., Levoy, M.: A volumetric method for building complex models from range images. In: Proceedings of the 23rd Annual Conference on Computer Graphics and Interactive Techniques (1996)
17. Davies, T., Nowrouzezahrai, D., Jacobson, A.: On the effectiveness of weight-encoded neural implicit 3D shapes (2021)
18. Dong, Z., Yao, Z., Gholami, A., Mahoney, M.W., Keutzer, K.: HAWQ: hessian aware quantization of neural networks with mixed-precision. In: International Conference on Computer Vision (ICCV) (2019)
19. Dupont, E., Golinski, A., Alizadeh, M., Teh, Y.W., Doucet, A.: COIN: compression with implicit neural representations. In: Neural Compression, From Information Theory to Applications - Workshop (ICLR) (2021)
20. Dupont, E., Loya, H., Alizadeh, M., Goliński, A., Teh, Y.W., Doucet, A.: Coin++: data agnostic neural compression. arXiv preprint arXiv:2201.12904 (2022)
21. Fan*, A., et al.: Training with quantization noise for extreme model compression (2020)
22. Finn, C., Abbeel, P., Levine, S.: Model-agnostic meta-learning for fast adaptation of deep networks. In: International Conference on Machine Learning (ICLR) (2017)
23. Finn, C., Abbeel, P., Levine, S.: Model-agnostic meta-learning for fast adaptation of deep networks. In: International Conference on Machine Learning, pp. 1126–1135. PMLR (2017)
24. Habi, H.V., Jennings, R.H., Netzer, A.: HMQ: hardware friendly mixed precision quantization block for CNNs. In: European Conference on Computer Vision (ECCV) (2020)
25. Habibian, A., Rozendaal, T.V., Tomczak, J.M., Cohen, T.S.: Video compression with rate-distortion autoencoders. In: Proceedings of the IEEE/CVF International Conference on Computer Vision, pp. 7033–7042 (2019)
26. Han, S., Mao, H., Dally, W.J.: Deep compression: compressing deep neural network with pruning, trained quantization and huffman coding. In: International Conference on Learning Representations, (ICLR) (2016)
27. Hinton, G.E., Salakhutdinov, R.R.: Reducing the dimensionality of data with neural networks. Science 313(5786), 504-507 (2006)
28. Hinton, G.E., Zemel, R.S.: Autoencoders, minimum description length, and helmholtz free energy. Advances in neural information processing systems 6, 3–10 (1994)
29. Hu, Y., Yang, W., Liu, J.: Coarse-to-fine hyper-prior modeling for learned image compression. In: Conference on Artificial Intelligence (AAAI) (2020)
30. Johnston, N., et al.: Improved lossy image compression with priming and spatially adaptive bit rates for recurrent networks. In: Proceedings of the IEEE Conference on Computer Vision and Pattern Recognition (CVPR), pp. 4385–4393 (2018)
31. Kim, T., Yoo, Y., Yang, J.: FrostNet: towards quantization-aware network architecture search (2020)
32. Kingma, D.P., Ba, J.L.: Adam: a method for stochastic gradient descent. In: Proceedings of the International Conference on Learning Representations (ICLR), pp. 1–15 (2015)
33. Lee, J., Cho, S., Beack, S.K.: Context-adaptive entropy model for end-to-end optimized image compression. In: Proceedings of the International Conference on Learning Representations (ICLR) (2019)

34. Liu, Z., Luo, P., Wang, X., Tang, X.: Deep learning face attributes in the wild. In: International Conference on Computer Vision (ICCV), December 2015
35. Louizos, C., Reisser, M., Blankevoort, T., Gavves, E., Welling, M.: Relaxed quantization for discretized neural networks. In: International Conference on Learning Representations (ICLR) (2019)
36. Menghani, G.: Efficient deep learning: a survey on making deep learning models smaller, faster, and better (2021)
37. Mentzer, F., Agustsson, E., Tschannen, M., Timofte, R., Van Gool, L.: Conditional probability models for deep image compression. In: Proceedings of the IEEE Conference on Computer Vision and Pattern Recognition (CVPR), pp. 4394–4402 (2018)
38. Mentzer, F., Toderici, G.D., Tschannen, M., Agustsson, E.: High-fidelity generative image compression. In: Advances in Neural Information Processing Systems (NeuIPS), vol. 33 (2020)
39. Mescheder, L., Oechsle, M., Niemeyer, M., Nowozin, S., Geiger, A.: Occupancy networks: learning 3d reconstruction in function space. In: Proceedings of the IEEE/CVF Conference on Computer Vision and Pattern Recognition (CVPR), pp. 4460–4470 (2019)
40. Mildenhall, B., Srinivasan, P.P., Tancik, M., Barron, J.T., Ramamoorthi, R., Ng, R.: Nerf: representing scenes as neural radiance fields for view synthesis. In: European Conference on Computer Vision (ECCV) (2020)
41. Minnen, D., Ballé, J., Toderici, G.: Joint autoregressive and hierarchical priors for learned image compression. In: Advances in Neural Information Processing Systems (NeurIPS) (2018)
42. Nagel, M., Amjad, R.A., van Baalen, M., Louizos, C., Blankevoort, T.: Up or down? adaptive rounding for post-training quantization (2020)
43. Nagel, M., van Baalen, M., Blankevoort, T., Welling, M.: Data-free quantization through weight equalization and bias correction. In: International Conference on Computer Vision (ICCV) (2019)
44. Park, J.J., Florence, P., Straub, J., Newcombe, R., Lovegrove, S.: DeepSDF: learning continuous signed distance functions for shape representation. In: Proceedings of the IEEE/CVF Conference on Computer Vision and Pattern Recognition, pp. 165–174 (2019)
45. Park, J.J., Florence, P., Straub, J., Newcombe, R., Lovegrove, S.: DeepSDF: learning continuous signed distance functions for shape representation. In: Conference on Computer Vision and Pattern Recognition (CVPR) (2019)
46. van Rozendaal, T., Huijben, I.A., Cohen, T.: Overfitting for fun and profit: instance-adaptive data compression. In: International Conference on Learning Representations (ICLR) (2021)
47. Shannon, C.A.: A mathematical theory of communication. Bell Syst. Tech. J. 27(3), 379–423 (1948)
48. Sitzmann, V., Chan, E.R., Tucker, R., Snavely, N., Wetzstein, G.: MetaSDF: meta-learning signed distance functions. In: Advances in Neural Information Processing Systems (NeurIPS) (2020)
49. Sitzmann, V., Martel, J.N., Bergman, A.W., Lindell, D.B., Wetzstein, G.: Implicit neural representations with periodic activation functions. In: Advances in Neural Information Processing Systems (NeurIPS) (2020)
50. Skorokhodov, I., Ignatyev, S., Elhoseiny, M.: Adversarial generation of continuous images. In: Conference on Computer Vision and Pattern Recognition (CVPR) (2021)

51. Takikawa, T., et al.: Neural geometric level of detail: real-time rendering with implicit 3D shapes. In: Proceedings of the IEEE/CVF Conference on Computer Vision and Pattern Recognition (CVPR) (2021)
52. Tancik, M., et al.: Learned initializations for optimizing coordinate-based neural representations. In: CVPR (2021)
53. Tancik, M., et al.: Fourier features let networks learn high frequency functions in low dimensional domains. In: Advances in Neural Information Processing Systems (NeurIPS) (2020)
54. Toderici, G., et al.: Variable rate image compression with recurrent neural networks. In: Proceedings of the International Conference on Learning Representations (ICLR) (2016)
55. Toderici, G., et al.: Full resolution image compression with recurrent neural networks. In: Proceedings of the IEEE Conference on Computer Vision and Pattern Recognition (CVPR), pp. 5306–5314 (2017)
56. Uhlich, S., et al.: Mixed precision DNNs: all you need is a good parametrization. In: International Conference on Learning Representations (ICLR) (2019)
57. Wang, K., Liu, Z., Lin, Y., Lin, J., Han, S.: HAQ: hardware-aware automated quantization with mixed precision. In: Conference on Computer Vision and Pattern Recognition (CVPR) (2019)
58. Xie, Y., Cheng, K.L., Chen, Q.: Enhanced invertible encoding for learned image compression. In: ACM International Conference on Multimedia (2021)

LiP-Flow: Learning Inference-Time Priors for Codec Avatars via Normalizing Flows in Latent Space

Emre Aksan[1(✉)], Shugao Ma[3], Akin Caliskan[2], Stanislav Pidhorskyi[3],
Alexander Richard[3], Shih-En Wei[3], Jason Saragih[3], and Otmar Hilliges[1]

[1] ETH Zürich, Zürich, Switzerland
eaksan@inf.ethz.ch
[2] CVSSP, University of Surrey, Guildford, UK
[3] Meta Reality Labs Research, Pittsburgh, USA

Abstract. Neural face avatars that are trained from multi-view data captured in camera domes can produce photo-realistic 3D reconstructions. However, at inference time, they must be driven by limited inputs such as partial views recorded by headset-mounted cameras or a front-facing camera, and sparse facial landmarks. To mitigate this asymmetry, we introduce a prior model that is conditioned on the runtime inputs and tie this prior space to the 3D face model via a normalizing flow in the latent space. Our proposed model, LiP-Flow, consists of two encoders that learn representations from the rich training-time and impoverished inference-time observations. A normalizing flow bridges the two representation spaces and transforms latent samples from one domain to another, allowing us to define a latent likelihood objective. We trained our model end-to-end to maximize the similarity of both representation spaces and the reconstruction quality, making the 3D face model aware of the limited driving signals. We conduct extensive evaluations where the latent codes are optimized to reconstruct 3D avatars from partial or sparse observations. We show that our approach leads to an expressive and effective prior, capturing facial dynamics and subtle expressions better. Check out our project page for an overview.

1 Introduction

VR telepresence promises immersive social interactions. To experience the presence of others as genuine, such a system must provide photo-realistic 3D renderings, capture fine-grained details such as pores and hair, and produce subtle facial dynamics. Codec Avatars [32,47] have been shown to be a promising

E. Aksan and A. Caliskan—This work was performed during an internship at Meta Reality Labs Research.

Supplementary Information The online version contains supplementary material available at https://doi.org/10.1007/978-3-031-19809-0_6.

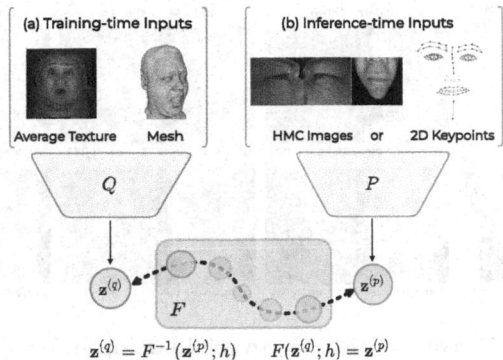

$$\mathbf{z}^{(q)} = F^{-1}(\mathbf{z}^{(p)}; h) \qquad F(\mathbf{z}^{(q)}; h) = \mathbf{z}^{(p)}$$

Fig. 1. Information asymmetry between the (a) training- and (b) inference-time observations. We learn a normalizing flow model (F) across latent spaces, minimizing the discrepancy between the base network's Deep Appearance Model (DAM) encoder [32], DAM-encoder (Q), and an inference-time encoder (P), namely the HMC-encoder or KPT-encoder conditioned on partial head-mounted camera (HMC) images or sparse 2D keypoints (KPT), respectively.

direction towards this goal. Such systems implement 3D avatars via the decoder network of a variational auto-encoder (VAE) [26]. Per subject, high-quality 3D face avatars are trained with multi-view imagery from a 40+ camera dome [32].

In prior work [8,16,32,33,40], the network learns to decode latent codes into shape and view-conditioned appearance. Importantly, each latent code is a projection of the geometry and unwrapped texture which are only available during *training* (Fig. 1-a). At *inference-time*, the driving signal is impoverished – consisting of a set of partial face images captured from cameras mounted on a VR headset [47], facial landmarks [13] (Fig. 1-b) or a single-view from a frontal camera [12]. To maximize the reconstruction quality, the avatar model is often trained in isolation, and typically a separate run-time encoder for the driving signal is used. We show that this separate training scheme limits performance since the constrained run-time conditions are not considered during decoder training.

In this work, we introduce LiP-Flow, a learned inference-time prior, based on normalizing flows, to bridge this information gap for 3D face models. Specifically, we incorporate a prior model into the Deep Appearance Model (DAM) pipeline [32] with minimal modifications such that the decoder's high reconstruction quality is preserved. We make use of this prior model in *inference-time* optimization tasks. This allows us to optimize latent codes to capture facial dynamics and subtle expressions even when only impoverished inputs are available (Fig. 2). It is effective even on less challenging neutral expressions, while it is more pronounced on peak expressions. We simulate the run-time conditions via sparse 2D keypoints (KPT) and synthetically generated partial head-mounted camera (HMC) images, allowing to define (virtual) correspondences between training and inference data and to run tightly controlled evaluations in all settings.

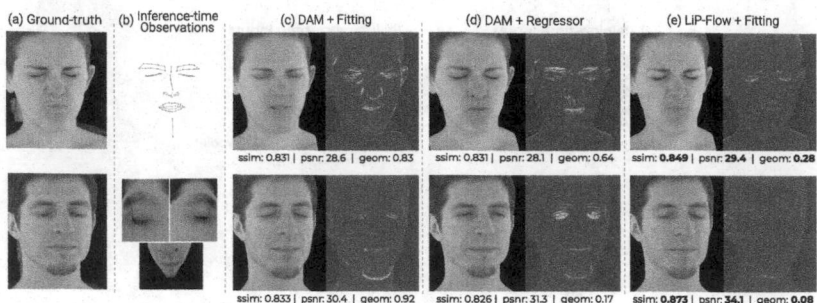

Fig. 2. Driving a 3D avatar with impoverished inputs. For the DAM (c) and our proposed model LiP-Flow (e), we first optimize latent codes to reconstruct the inference-time observations (b), and then reconstruct the full face. In (d), we train a regressor to directly predict latent codes from the inference-time inputs (b) by using the pretrained DAM-encoder (Q) in (c).

Data-driven priors have many uses in under-constrained problems. Given partial or imperfect observations, the task is the reconstruction of a clean signal or inference of the latent factors leading to it. This task has been studied in the context of related areas, amongst others 3D lifting [10,36], 3D pose and shape estimation from images [14,37,44,52], and refining [31], image editing [6,35], or prediction of the next step from the past in sequence models [2,3, 16,29,37]. Our focus lies particularly on learning latent priors conditioned on limited observations [2,17,37] and using prior models for inference in a more compact representation space [14,28,36,37]. In our work, we learn a prior that is conditioned on the HMC views or facial landmarks. We aim to regularize the main avatar model by incorporating the run-time observations into the training pipeline and increase reconstruction quality in inference-time optimization.

Our work introduces a novel approach for learning of conditional priors. To minimize the discrepancy between the training- and inference-time representations, we learn a mapping across the two latent spaces via a conditional normalizing flow (Fig. 1) [7,49]. It is noteworthy to mention that both the training- and inference-time encoders, our latent flow network as well as the decoder are jointly trained. Our training objective consists of reconstruction terms for appearance and geometry, and a latent likelihood term, replacing the KL-divergence (KL-D) term in the VAE framework. Specifically, we optimize the likelihood of the latent samples from the DAM-encoder (Q) under the learned inference-time prior (LiP) distribution estimated from the HMC views or 2D keypoints. This is enabled by the bijective nature of the underlying flow, allowing us to map samples from one space to another. We note that the information asymmetry is pronounced in our task both in terms of modality and amount of carried information (*i.e.*, geometry and texture vs. HMC images or keypoints). The KL-D objective enforces distribution similarity between the latent-spaces which we show experimentally may be a too strong of an assumption, given the differences in input distributions. We relax this assumption by leveraging a normalizing flow to bridge between the latent spaces without enforcing distributional similarity. We show that our approach constitutes a powerful means to deal with such large discrepancies.

We first demonstrate how our latent space formulation improves the reconstruction performance of the base DAM network. Next, we compare different approaches for learning a prior model conditioned on the HMC images or 2D keypoints. We evaluate the quality of the prior models via an analysis-by-synthesis technique [14,34]. More specifically, we aim to recover the underlying latent code from HMC images or facial landmarks. We treat the pre-trained decoder (*i.e.*, the 3D face model) as a black box renderer to produce an image for a given latent code, view direction, and camera pose. In this task, in addition to a reconstruction objective, we also leverage the learned prior via a likelihood objective on the latent codes. We show that our flow-based prior model yields latent codes that reconstruct the 3D face faithfully (Fig. 2). Our contributions can be summarized as follows: (1) a novel approach for learning conditional priors that can be integrated seamlessly into a base architecture for the task of 3D face avatar generation and animation, (2) a more expressive and flexible representation space compared to KL-D driven latent spaces, (3) better reconstruction quality than the baseline approaches in tightly controlled extensive evaluations.

2 Related Work

3D Face Appearance Models. Modeling of 3D human faces for animation has long been an active area of research. Early work models 3D human faces with linear combinations of blendshape vectors representing meshes and texture (*e.g.*[9]). We refer to Lewis *et al.* [30] for a review. Such models are limited in their expressiveness: a large number of blendshapes are needed to create high-fidelity animations. Recent works [11,20] leverages 3D parametric face models to predict texture and shape for novel identities. Many deep appearance face models utilize deep generative neural networks such as VAEs [5,13,32,33,45] or GANs [1,15,41,42] with facial expressions represented as compact *latent codes*.

In particular *Codec Avatars* [32,33] trained with high resolution multi-view images can photo-realistically render human faces. Face animations can also be generated when conditioned on HMC images [16,47], frontal-view images [12] or even audio [39]. However, the significant discrepancy between training- and inference-time inputs is a key challenge for achieving high fidelity facial animation for telepresence applications. To alleviate this problem, we explore novel approaches augmenting the Codec Avatar pipeline via conditional priors..

Latent Code Optimization. Generative models like GANs [22] and VAEs [26] can represent the underlying data manifold in a latent space. They have been used as data-driven priors in solving inverse problems, via optimization in the more abstract latent space. The standard Gaussian latent prior of a VAE [36] and a hierarchical VAE [31] replace a GMM prior in the output space [10] for modeling and reconstructing 3D human pose. Chen *et al.* [14] also use a VAE

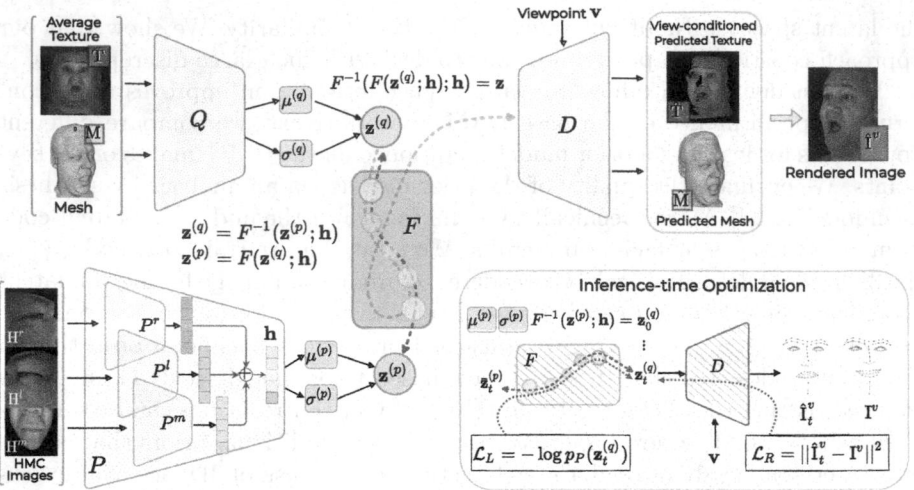

Fig. 3. LiP-Flow with HMC inputs. Without losing generality, we introduce an HMC-encoder (P), treated as a prior model conditioned on the HMC images, which can be replaced with a KPT-encoder (P) conditioned on 2D keypoints. The prior model (P) is trained end-to-end with the base DAM-encoder (Q) and the decoder (D). The bijective function (F) learns to map samples from one space to another. We train the decoder (D) with latent samples $\mathbf{z}^{(q)}$ only. To get the reconstruction training signal in the flow (F), the input code follows the flow cycle $\mathbf{z} = F^{-1}(F(\mathbf{z}^{(q)}; \mathbf{h}); \mathbf{h})$. **Inference-time Optimization.** To faithfully reconstruct the 3D face only from runtime inputs, we optimize the latent codes to fit the observations such as HMC images or 2D key-points. We first estimate a prior distribution (P) with the inference-time encoders HMC-encoder or KPT-encoder. We then use this prior to initialize the latent code $\mathbf{z}_0$ and evaluate the likelihood of the latent code $\mathbf{z}_t$ where t corresponds to the optimization step. The red dashed lines denote the gradients of the respective objective terms, namely the latent likelihood $\mathcal{L}_L$ (Eq. 9) and the reconstruction loss $\mathcal{L}_R$.

decoder and regularize the latent codes explicitly by evaluating the latent likelihood under the VAE prior. In [6,35], GANs and in [23], denoising autoencoders are treated as a block-box sample generator for image in-painting and denoising tasks. Similarly, GANFit [21] models facial texture via a GAN, and jointly optimizes the corresponding latent code and parameters of a 3D morphable model. Our work differs from those in that we learn a conditional prior model allowing us to calculate the likelihood of the latent code during optimization. HuMoR [37] also provides a learned prior that affords likelihood evaluation. It is conditioned on the 3D pose in the previous frame and regularized via KL-D. Instead, we propose a flow-based approach for learning conditional priors in settings where the inference-time data differs significantly from the training data.

Normalizing flow priors have been proposed for inverse problems [4,48,51]. In [4], an invertible Glow model [25] replaces GANs for image inpainting. Similarly in [28], a normalizing flow model is used for 2D-3D lifting. Zanfir et al.[51]

introduce a 3D human pose prior by learning a mapping between a Gaussian latent space and 3D human poses via normalizing flows. These works make use of the generative nature of unconditional flows and replace GANs or VAEs 1-to-1. The LSGM [46] learns an invertible mapping between a standard Normal prior and an encoder space via a diffusion process. In our work, we introduce a different setting where we jointly learn separate representation spaces with a large discrepancy in the inputs and the mapping between them.

3   Method

Our work extends the Deep Appearance Model (DAM) [32] by introducing a run-time encoder (LiP-encoder) that is conditioned on the impoverished inference-time inputs. We aim to learn models that are capable of driving avatars via partial HMC images or sparse facial landmarks. Our paper showcases two modalities for different yet related tasks, including but not limited to HMC- and KPT-encoder taking HMC views (see Fig. 3) and 2D keypoints, respectively. In the remainder of the paper, the LiP-encoder term refers to either of the HMC- or KPT-encoder. We treat a LiP-encoder as a conditional prior and train it end-to-end together with the DAM network via our flow-based latent space formulation.

In the following sections, we first explain the problem setup and provide an overview of the base 3D face model, DAM [32], in Sect. 3.1. We then present our approach, LiP-Flow, in Sect. 3.3 along with the HMC- and KPT-encoder networks in Sect. 3.2. We also describe alternative techniques to drive the avatar with inference-time inputs in Sect. 4. Architecture details are in the supp. mat.

3.1   Background: Deep Appearance Model

We follow the data preprocessing steps described in [32] and use the same data, and training routines for all the models. Specifically, frames are unwarped into a texture, using the tracked geometry. The DAM-encoder (Q) (Fig. 4-a) takes the geometry $\mathbf{M} \in \mathbb{R}^{7306 \times 3}$ and the average texture across all the views $\bar{\mathbf{T}} \in \mathbb{R}^{3 \times 1024 \times 1024}$, and parameterizes a Normal distribution of latent codes $\mathbf{z} \in \mathbb{R}^{256}$:

$$\boldsymbol{\mu}^{(q)}, \boldsymbol{\sigma}^{(q)} = Q(\bar{\mathbf{T}}, \mathbf{M}), \quad \mathbf{z} \sim \mathcal{N}(\boldsymbol{\mu}^{(q)}, \boldsymbol{\sigma}^{(q)}). \tag{1}$$

The decoder D decodes a latent sample $\mathbf{z}$ for a given camera view-vector $\mathbf{v}$ into geometry $\hat{\mathbf{M}}$ and view-specific texture $\bar{\mathbf{T}}^v$ accounting for view-dependent effects by $\hat{\mathbf{M}}, \bar{\mathbf{T}}^v = D(\mathbf{z}, \mathbf{v})$. The reconstructed image is rendered with the decoded texture, mesh, and camera pose information. The training objective consists of reconstruction and latent space regularization terms with separate weights:

$$\mathcal{L} = \sum_v \lambda_I \mathcal{L}_I + \lambda_M \mathcal{L}_M + \lambda_L \mathcal{L}_L, \tag{2}$$

$$\mathcal{L}_I = \left\| \left(\mathbf{I}^v - \hat{\mathbf{I}}^v \right) \odot \mathbf{W}^v \right\|^2, \quad \mathcal{L}_M = \left\| \mathbf{M} - \hat{\mathbf{M}} \right\|^2, \tag{3}$$

$$\mathcal{L}_L = D_{KL} \left(\mathcal{N}(\boldsymbol{\mu}^{(q)}, \boldsymbol{\sigma}^{(q)}) \, \| \, \mathcal{N}(\mathbf{0}, \mathbf{I}) \right), \tag{4}$$

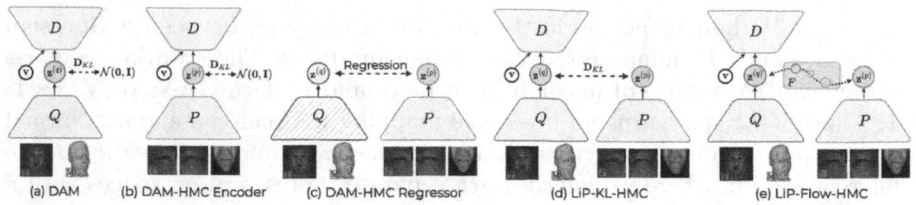

Fig. 4. An overview of latent space concepts. Note that the models are depicted with HMC inputs. The same concepts also apply to the KPT-encoder with keypoint inputs. Details are skipped for brevity. The decoder D decodes a view-specific texture and mesh for a given view vector $\mathbf{v}$ and a latent code z. (a) The Deep Appearance Model (DAM) following the conditional VAE framework with $\mathcal{N}(0, I)$ prior. (b) Replacing the DAM-encoder Q with the HMC-encoder P. The face avatar model (i.e., the decoder) is trained with the HMC images directly. (c) Learning to regress the latent codes for HMC views by using a pretrained DAM-encoder Q. (d) Training the HMC-encoder as a conditional prior model by minimizing the KL-divergence objective. (e) Our LiP-Flow introduces a normalizing flow bridging the latent space of Q and P.

where $\mathcal{L}_I$ is the image reconstruction loss between the rendered $\hat{\mathbf{I}}^v$ and the ground-truth image $\mathbf{I}^v \in \mathbb{R}^{3 \times 1334 \times 2048}$, given view $\mathbf{v}$. The view-dependent image masks $\mathbf{W}^v$ removes the background. We apply additional supervision for the predicted mesh via a geometry reconstruction loss $\mathcal{L}_M$. DAM uses a standard Gaussian prior (Fig. 4-a) where its latent space is regularized via KL-D ($\mathcal{L}_L$). This formulation already achieves high-quality reconstructions during training. However, we show that the prior $\mathcal{N}(\mathbf{0}, \mathbf{I})$ is not effective enough when recovering underlying latent codes only from the impoverished observations (see Fig. 2-c). for the latent code fitting task with only partial observations (see Fig. 2-c).

3.2   Inference-time Encoders (LiP-encoder)

We define the HMC- and the KPT-encoders conditioned on the HMC images and the 2D keypoints, respectively. Note that these networks are also used in the baselines illustrated in Fig. 4-b and Fig. 4-c.

HMC-encoder. The set of HMC views at every frame consists of partial and non-overlapping images of mouth $\mathbf{H}^m$, left eye $\mathbf{H}^l$ and right eye $\mathbf{H}^r$ regions (Fig. 5) where $\mathbf{H}^* \in \mathbb{R}^{480 \times 640}$. The HMC-encoder consists of small networks for each view which are then fused via a 3-channel attention operation:

$$\mathbf{h}^* = P^*(\mathbf{H}^*), \qquad \mathbf{h} = \text{Attention}(\mathbf{h}^m, \mathbf{h}^l, \mathbf{h}^r; \mathbf{W}^A), \tag{5}$$

where $\mathbf{h}^*$ denotes the representations for each HMC view. The hidden representation and the attention weights are of shape $\mathbf{h} \in \mathbb{R}^{1024}$ and $\mathbf{W}^A \in \mathbb{R}^{1024 \times 3}$, respectively. The attention weights are data-agnostic trainable parameters. The attention operation learns a weighted mixture of HMC views.

KPT-encoder. 2D keypoint samples, $\mathbf{K}$, are in pixel coordinates normalized between 0 and 1, consisting of facial landmarks except the iris (Fig. 5) where $\mathbf{K} \in \mathbb{R}^{136 \times 2}$. We pass the keypoint samples to a ResNet [24] with fully connected

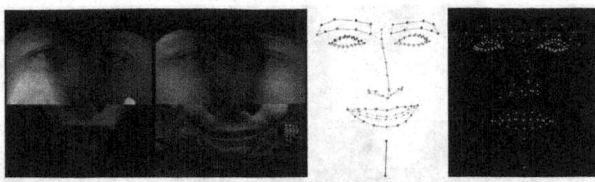

Fig. 5. Driving signals. Synthetic HMC images with lighting and background augmentations (left) and 2D keypoints (right).

layers. Our KPT-encoder maps the keypoint inputs to a an over-parameterized representation $\mathbf{h} \in \mathbb{R}^{1024}$.

Latent Space. We model a probabilistic latent space and parameterize a Gaussian distribution as a function of the run-time input context $\mathbf{h}$:

$$\boldsymbol{\mu}^{(p)}, \boldsymbol{\sigma}^{(p)} = P(\mathbf{h}), \quad \mathbf{z}^{(p)} \sim \mathcal{N}(\boldsymbol{\mu}^{(p)}, \boldsymbol{\sigma}^{(p)}). \tag{6}$$

Without loss of generality, P encapsulates the HMC- and KPT-encoders and the layers that compute $\boldsymbol{\mu}^{(p)}$ and $\boldsymbol{\sigma}^{(p)}$.

3.3 Learning Conditional Priors

Instead of a standard Gaussian prior, we propose a learned prior, which has been shown to be more expressive [17,43]. Here, the prior model is conditioned on the HMC images or 2D keypoints. We also study several architectures for this task, illustrated in Fig. 4 and explained in Sect. 4.

LiP-KL (Fig. 4-d). In previous studies [2,17,37,43], conditional priors replace the VAE's isotropic Gaussian prior with a learned prior. Similarly in our work, the latent objective $\mathcal{L}_L$ in Eq. 4 takes the form of

$$\mathcal{L}_L = D_{KL} \left(\mathcal{N}(\boldsymbol{\mu}^{(q)}, \boldsymbol{\sigma}^{(q)}) \parallel \mathcal{N}(\boldsymbol{\mu}^{(p)}, \boldsymbol{\sigma}^{(p)}) \right), \tag{7}$$

where the KL-D objective D_{KL} enforces similarity between Q and P. We build a variant of our model with the KL objective (see Fig. 4-d). Ground-truth correspondences between the inputs of the LiP-encoders and the DAM-encoder allow us to learn a mapping between the latent spaces. Note that the distributional similarity is a plausible assumption in the prior works where the inputs are often consecutive timesteps. However, in our case, the discrepancy between the Q and the P inputs is considerably larger than in prior work.

LiP-Flow (Fig. 4-e). To further mitigate the asymmetry of the Q and P spaces, we propose to bridge the two spaces and remove the assumption that they must be the same (*i.e.*, KL-D). To achieve this, we introduce a normalizing flow network F to transform latent samples from one space to another (Fig. 4-e). Normalizing flows are typically used to represent complex and intractable data

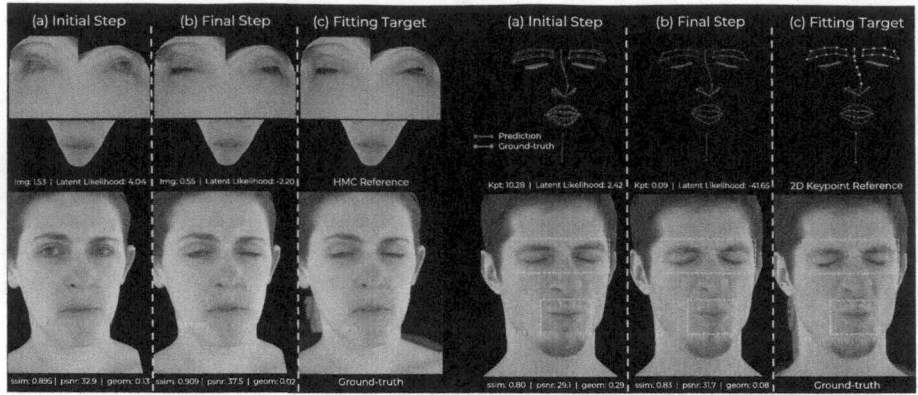

Fig. 6. Reconstruction from inference-time observations with LiP-Flow. We optimize a latent code to reconstruct the 3D avatar (bottom) from imperfect fitting targets (c), such as HMC images (left) or 2D keypoints (right). The latent code is initialized with a sample from the HMC-encoder's or the KPT-encoder's prior. We provide the renderings from the initial latent code in columns (a) both in the target's representation and in the frontal view. The optimization considers the fitting loss between the targets and the HMC (*i.e.* "Img" loss) or 2D keypoint (*i.e.* "Kpt" loss) projections (Eq. 11), and the latent likelihood under the corresponding prior model (Eq. 12). Renderings after the optimization are in the "Final Step" columns (b).

distributions with a simple parametric distribution such as the standard Gaussian [18,19,25,38]. In our work, we use a conditional normalizing flow [7,18,49] enabling the transformation:

$$\bar{\mathbf{z}}^{(p)} = F(\mathbf{z}^{(q)}; \mathbf{h}), \quad F = f_K \circ \cdots \circ f_2 \circ f_1, \tag{8}$$

where the bijection $F : Q \to P$ is a composition of K transformations f_k. For a given pair of inference- and training-time inputs, we first draw a $\mathbf{z}^{(q)}$ sample (Eq. 1) and estimate a prior distribution by using the LiP-encoder, parameterizing it as a Gaussian (Eq. 6). The $\mathbf{z}^{(q)}$ sample is then transformed to the P space corresponding to $\bar{\mathbf{z}}^{(p)}$ (Eq. 8). Finally, we calculate the log-likelihood of the latent sample $\mathbf{z}^{(q)}$ under the prior distribution P such that:

$$\log p_P(\mathbf{z}^{(q)}) = \log p_P(\bar{\mathbf{z}}^{(p)}) + \log \left(\det \left| \frac{\partial F(\mathbf{z}^{(q)}; \mathbf{h})}{\partial \mathbf{z}^{(q)}} \right| \right), \tag{9}$$

where $\log p_P(\bar{\mathbf{z}}^{(p)}) = \log \mathcal{N}(\bar{\mathbf{z}}^{(p)}; \boldsymbol{\mu}^{(p)}, \boldsymbol{\sigma}^{(p)})$ (see Eq. 6).

In LiP-Flow, the latent training objective $\mathcal{L}_L$ then becomes the negative log-likelihood $-\log p_P(\mathbf{z}^{(q)})$ in Eq. 9, replacing the D_{KL} term. We use the flow F to project the sample $\mathbf{z}^{(q)}$ onto the P space. Hence, this objective enforces $\mathbf{z}^{(p)}$ and $\bar{\mathbf{z}}^{(p)}$ to be similar *after* the transformation of $\mathbf{z}^{(q)}$ via F (Eq. 8). However, the formulation does not restrict Q or P to any particular structure.

We would like to note that this likelihood can increase arbitrarily by contracting the P distribution, resulting in a trivial solution. This behavior is prevented by the determinant of the Jacobian term in Eq. 9, penalizing the contraction and encouraging expansion [18].

To keep the modifications to the base model at a minimum, the decoder D is trained with samples from the DAM-encoder Q only, as in the original pipeline. We do not use any samples from the LiP-encoders P. In other words, the LiP-encoders learn to complete the partial observations via the latent objective (Eq. 9). Finally, to attain the reconstruction signal in our LiP-Flow's latent flow network F, the decoder's latent code $\mathbf{z}$ follows the flow cycle: $\mathbf{z} = F^{-1}(F(\mathbf{z}^{(q)}; \mathbf{h}); \mathbf{h})$. We provide ablations in Sect. 4.4.

4   Results

We experimentally answer the following questions: (1) How does end-to-end training of the conditional priors affect the base model's performance? (2) What is the most effective approach of leveraging limited driving signals? (3) Which of the priors is the most useful in inference-time optimization tasks?

The base DAM network consists of a view-conditioned decoder and an encoder expecting rich training data. To evaluate the DAM in run-time conditions, we follow analysis-by-synthesis and optimize latent codes to reconstruct impoverished inference-time observations. For a fair comparison, we also introduce the HMC- or the KPT-encoders into the DAM, leveraging the run-time inputs in different ways and allowing us to make latent code predictions directly.

DAM with an Inference-Time Encoder (Fig. 4-b). The naive way to attain a face avatar from the inference-time inputs is to use the ground-truth correspondences between the multi-view images and the synthetic HMC data or 2D keypoints. To do so, we replace the DAM-encoder with an HMC- or a KPT-encoder and train a conditional VAE as before. We use this model to verify the hypothesis that the limited run-time observations do not carry enough information to faithfully build a high-quality avatar model.

Inference-Time Encoder as Regressor (Fig. 4-c). To analyse the effectiveness of treating the inference-time encoders as a prior and inference-time optimization, we train the KPT- and HMC-encoders to regress the latent codes of the pre-trained DAM-encoder. We follow the probabilistic approach in Eq. 6 and use the negative log-likelihood training objective.

In our work, the latent space formulation is the only difference across models (Fig. 4). To tightly control the settings and simulate the application conditions, we introduce facial landmark and synthetic HMC datasets (Fig. 5). The synthetic HMC images are generated by re-projecting the multi-view camera images into virtual head-mounted camera views with various lighting, background and headset slop augmentations. For the 2D keypoints, we project a predetermined set of mesh vertices onto the image plane. Both the 2D keypoints and synthetic HMC images provide correspondences to ground truth 3D full face observations, enabling careful study of the methods. We report average performance over 4 subjects in the PSNR and SSIM image metrics, and per vertex geometry loss.

Table 1. Reconstruction. We evaluate the DAM-encoder (Q) and the decoder (D) by reconstructing the latent codes estimated from the training-time inputs to see how the inference-time encoder affects the base model, DAM. We report the performance with both the HMC-encoder and the KPT-encoder (Fig. 4). The DAM-HMC Enc. and the DAM-KPT Enc. baselines (b) take HMC images and 2D keypoints as inputs, respectively.

Models	Decoding DAM-encoder (Q)		
	PSNR ↑	SSIM ↑	Geom ↓
(a) DAM	36.05	0.893	0.015
(b) DAM-HMC Enc.	33.93	0.872	0.186
(c) DAM-HMC Reg.	n/a	n/a	n/a
(d) LiP-KL-HMC	35.79	0.890	0.018
(e) LiP-Flow-HMC	**36.21**	**0.895**	**0.014**
(b) DAM-KPT Enc.	33.50	0.866	0.142
(c) DAM-KPT Reg.	n/a	n/a	n/a
(d) LiP-KL-KPT	35.71	0.888	0.021
(e) LiP-Flow-KPT	**36.22**	**0.895**	**0.014**

In Sect. 4.1, we present reconstruction performance of the models in the training setup. We then compare our model LiP-Flow against the baselines via inference-time optimization with limited observations in Sect. 4.2. We report the performance of the models with both the HMC-encoder and KPT-encoder as the prior model. Finally, we provide insights on dynamics of our model in Sect. 4.3.

In our supp. mat., we provide experiment details, additional evaluations (Sect. B), qualitative results (Sect. E) and an ablation (Sect. A) where we use our flow-based formulation with a $\mathcal{N}(\mathbf{0}, \mathbf{I})$ instead of a conditional prior.

4.1   Reconstruction Quality

We evaluate the reconstruction performance of the 3D face model in the training setup. More specifically, the decoder (D) reconstructs the latent codes from the DAM-Encoder (Q) where we pass the average texture and the 3D geometry (Eq. 1). We aim to find the effect of end-to-end training of the conditional priors on the base model. Table 1 provides the reconstruction results when the HMC- and KPT-encoders are treated as priors and trained along with the DAM.

In both setups, our LiP-Flow outperforms the baselines. The LiP-KL reduces the reconstruction performance of the base model DAM, suggesting that the combination of conditional prior (P) and the KL objective are detrimental. In contrast, our flow-based prior improves the performance of the DAM, implying that LiP-Flow learns a more expressive latent space than the LiP-KL. Also note the consistent performance of our flow-based formulation in the HMC- and KPT-encoder settings. Our learned conditional priors tackle the difficulty of modeling the limited inference-time data, and the base model's DAM-encoder (Q) and

Table 2. HMC inputs. We use the HMC-encoder (P) to estimate a prior distribution from the HMC images. For the baselines (b) and (c), a latent sample is decoded directly, whereas for (a), (d) and (e), the latent code is first optimized to reconstruct the given HMC images (Fig. 6).

Models	HMC Observations		
	PSNR ↑	SSIM ↑	Geom ↓
(a) DAM	31.65	0.858	0.676
(b) DAM-HMC Enc.	33.93	0.872	0.186
(c) DAM-HMC Reg.	34.16	0.872	0.248
(d) LiP-KL-HMC	34.36	0.881	0.090
(e) LiP-Flow-HMC	34.98	0.885	0.087

Table 3. 2D keypoint inputs. We use the KPT-encoder (P) to estimate a prior distribution from the keypoints. For the baselines (b) and (c), a latent sample is decoded directly, whereas for (a), (d) and (e), the latent code is first optimized to reconstruct the given keypoints (Fig. 6).

Models	Keypoint (KPT) Observations		
	PSNR ↑	SSIM↑	Geom ↓
(a) DAM	31.62	0.865	0.431
(b) DAM-KPT Enc.	33.50	0.866	0.142
(c) DAM-KPT Reg.	33.67	0.864	0.151
(d) LiP-KL-KPT	35.08	0.886	0.089
(e) LiP-Flow-KPT	35.55	0.891	0.053

the decoder (D) enjoy a more expressive latent space. Since the HMC- and KPT-encoders are required to extract the relevant information only from the limited inputs, the "DAM-HMC Enc." and "DAM-KPT Enc." baselines suffer from underfitting, degrading the performance of the DAM.

4.2 Inference-time Optimization

Here, we analyze the models in the inference-time conditions. We treat the pre-trained decoder as a black box renderer for a given latent code, view direction, and camera pose and fit the latent code to reconstruct the given target:

$$\mathbf{z} = \arg\min_{\mathbf{z}} \mathcal{L}_R + \lambda_L \mathcal{L}_L, \tag{10}$$

$$\mathcal{L}_R = \left\| \left(\mathbf{I}^v - \hat{\mathbf{I}}^v \right) \odot \mathbf{W}^v \right\|^2, \tag{11}$$

$$\mathcal{L}_L = -\log p_P(\mathbf{z}) = -\log \mathcal{N}(\mathbf{z}; \boldsymbol{\mu}^{(p)}, \boldsymbol{\sigma}^{(p)}), \tag{12}$$

where $\boldsymbol{\mu}^{(p)}$ and $\boldsymbol{\sigma}^{(p)}$ are predicted by the HMC- or KPT-encoders. The learned prior is leveraged via the latent likelihood term $\mathcal{L}_L$ (Eq. 12). Similarly, the latent codes are initialized with the predicted mean $\mu^{(p)}$. Note that for the base model DAM (Fig. 4-a), the prior is a standard Gaussian. In this task, we use only the HMC- or KPT-encoders and the decoder (D) and report the performance on the fully rendered images including the parts that are not visible in the fitting targets (see Fig. 6). Evaluations without $\mathcal{L}_L$ is provided in Secr. B in supp. mat.

For all models, we assume that the decoder's input z stems from Q. Hence, in LiP-Flow, the initial latent sample is mapped to the Q space via the inverse of Eq. 8. The likelihood is computed via Eq. 8 and Eq. 9 (cf. Fig. 3).

Table 4. Fitting to frontal-view images. We evaluate all the models (a-e) in the inference-time optimization task with frontal-view targets. First, the latent codes are fitted to the frontal-view images and then evaluated by decoding in left, right, and frontal views. Note that the prior input is different from the fitting targets. It is conditioned on the HMC images or 2D keypoints.

Models	Frontal-view Fitting		
	PSNR ↑	SSIM ↑	Geom ↓
(a) DAM	35.16	0.888	0.212
(b) DAM-HMC Enc.	35.36	0.883	0.047
(c) DAM-HMC Reg.	36.28	0.895	0.057
(d) LiP-KL-HMC	36.08	0.892	0.039
(e) LiP-Flow-HMC	**36.50**	**0.898**	**0.022**
(b) DAM-KPT Enc.	34.75	0.874	0.059
(c) DAM-KPT Reg.	36.31	0.895	0.030
(d) LiP-KL-KPT	35.94	0.890	0.041
(e) LiP-Flow-KPT	**36.53**	**0.898**	**0.025**

HMC Targets. We use the partial HMC views as the fitting target and use the HMC-conditioned priors (see Fig. 6-left). We decode the latent code z for 3 view vectors and render with the corresponding HMC parameters. For each rendered HMC view, the image fitting objective $\mathcal{L}_R$ (Eq. 11) is calculated on the visible HMC regions only. This task evaluates the models in terms of multi-view consistency under partial views and the reconstruction quality from incomplete observations. The prior term $\mathcal{L}_L$ (Eq. 12) is of higher importance in this task as the HMC views are unseen and very different from the decoder's training views.

In Table 2, our flow-based (e) LiP-Flow outperforms the baselines in both the image and geometry metrics. We observe a significant gap between the base model DAM and the models with a learned prior, showing that the standard Gaussian prior is not effective for optimization when only partial information is available. This is partly mitigated by the variants (b) DAM-HMC Enc. and (c) DAM-HMC Reg. which estimate latent codes directly from the observations.

2D Keypoint Targets. We evaluate the models by fitting the latent codes to sparse 2D keypoint observations where the priors and the inference-time encoders

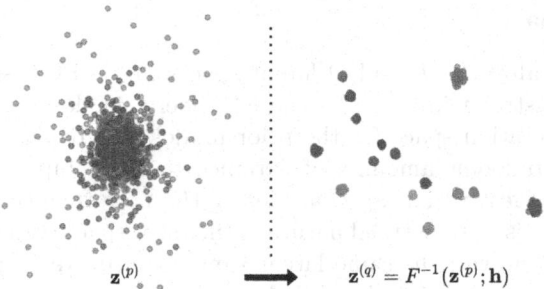

Fig. 7. Latent space visualization in PCA (Left) Samples in the P space. (Right) Same samples in the Q space after applying our latent transformation via flow F. For a given HMC sample (color-coded), the HMC-encoder predicts a prior distribution. For each of the 15 HMC inputs, we visualize 100 latent codes (see Sect. C in supp. mat.) (Color figure online).

are also conditioned on the keypoints (see Fig. 6-right). After decoding a latent code, a predetermined set of vertices on the predicted mesh is projected onto the image plane. The reconstruction term L_R in Eq. 11 is the ℓ^2 norm between the given and the projected keypoints. This means that the latent code is optimized solely based on the geometry and the improved image quality can be attributed to the learned correlations between the texture and the geometry.

The evaluations on keypoints in Table 3 are inline with the HMC setup (Table 2) where our (e) LiP-Flow achieves the best performance again, demonstrating the generalization ability of our flow-based latent formulation. Moreover, the geometry error is improved for all the models as the underlying prior model and the fitting objective ($\mathcal{L}_R + \mathcal{L}_L$) explicitly use geometric cues.

Frontal-view Targets. In this task, we use frontal-view images as the fitting targets for all the models. The models have access to the frontal views targets, and depending on the configuration, the HMC images or the 2D keypoints as the driving signal. This setup allows us to evaluate the models with more informative observations and assess the learned priors when the fitting target is different from the prior inputs. Table 4 summarizes the results for both the HMC- and KPT-encoders as well as the base DAM. Our LiP-Flow achieves the best performance in both image and geometry metrics. The DAM's performance significantly improves when the fitting target is more informative frontal views, implying that the DAM is not able to handle impoverished observations. We also evaluate the DAM baselines (b and c) via latent code fitting. Similar to the DAM, (b) the DAM-HMC Enc. and the DAM-KPT Enc. use a standard Gaussian prior. Our proposed LiP-Flow outperforms the DAM and its variants, showing the advantage of our flow-based conditional prior over the $\mathcal{N}(\mathbf{0}, \mathbf{I})$ prior.

4.3 Latent Space

In Fig. 7, we visualize the P and Q latent spaces in 2D PCA space. Removing the similarity constraint imposed by the KL-divergence loss results in a highly distorted representation space for the prior model (P). It also allows the prior model to assign different amounts of variance to the samples (*i.e.*, the green sample has the largest variance). Considering the performance of our model in the fitting tasks, this unstructured nature of the prior space seems to be effective. In the Q space, however, the same latent samples form well-separated clusters for different inputs, indicating that LiP-Flow captures semantics in Q.

4.4 Ablations

In Table 5, we ablate our learned prior in the HMC fitting task. It significantly improves the performance when the latent codes are initialized from the prior and the latent likelihood is considered. Random initializations from the $\mathcal{N}(\mathbf{0}, \mathbf{I})$ causes higher geometry error while the latent likelihood $\mathcal{L}_L$ is highly important for image quality. We also present two variants of our model. We first train "LiP-Flow + Decoding P" by decoding samples both from the P and Q spaces, causing a detrimental effect. This setup encourages the LiP-encoders (P) to predict the incomplete information in the output space rather than the more compact latent space, limiting the prior's capacity. We then train "LiP-Flow - Flow Cycle" by ignoring the flow cycle (cf. Figure 3) and decoding Q samples directly. The reconstruction signal helps the latent flow network to learn transformations that are more accurately reflected in the output space.

Table 5. Ablation. (Top) Training our model by ignoring the flow cycle $\mathbf{z} = F^{-1}(F(\mathbf{z}^{(q)}; \mathbf{h}); \mathbf{h})$, and decoding latent samples from the P space as well. (Bottom) Evaluating our LiP-Flow by not using initializations from the learned prior and the latent likelihood objective $\mathcal{L}_L$ (Eq. 12). Ablation is performed on one subject.

Models	HMC Fitting		
	PSNR ↑	SSIM ↑	Geom ↓
DAM	31.09	0.850	0.522
LiP-Flow−Flow Cycle	33.07	0.856	0.108
LiP-Flow+Decoding P	33.03	0.862	0.125
LiP-Flow−prior init−$\mathcal{L}_L$	28.51	0.821	0.841
LiP-Flow−prior init	32.29	0.862	0.405
LiP-Flow−$\mathcal{L}_L$	30.34	0.845	0.212
LiP-Flow	**33.61**	**0.874**	**0.060**

4.5 Discussion

Our evaluations provide evidence for the effectiveness of our LiP-Flow. When evaluated with the limited inference-time observations, our proposed conditional prior via our flow-based formulation is superior compared to the standard Normal prior (see Tables 2 and 3, and Fig. 2). This is achieved without sacrificing the base DAM's performance in training-time setup (Table 1). We show that the DAM's performance can be improved by leveraging the inference-time encoders. However, learning an inference-time regressor (DAM-HMC Reg. or DAM-KPT Reg.) separately is not as effective as end-to-end training of the inference-time encoders by treating them as priors. Our LiP-Flow yields consistently the best results via inference-time optimization, indicating that our flow-based formulation improves both the prior's and the decoder's performance.

5   Limitations and Future Work

Learning conditional priors relies on the correspondences between the training and inference data, which is not always feasible. For example, in VR telepresence with head-worn displays, we expect a domain gap when attempting to directly replace synthetic HMC images with real ones. Considering the extensive use of synthetic data in other domains [27,50], we think that introducing domain adaptation techniques [32,47] to our pipeline could be a promising direction to make use of unpaired HMC data. Another potential direction is a temporal extension where our flow network considers latent samples from the past frames.

6   Conclusion

Our work introduces a novel representation learning approach to bridge the information asymmetry between the training and inference domains for 3D face avatar models. We propose end-to-end training of the inference-time models as a prior together with the main avatar model to make it aware of the impoverished driving signals. Our prior model is tied to the main model via a normalizing flow which learns to map samples from the prior's representation space to the main model's, allowing us to define a latent likelihood objective. We present two related tasks where we augment a 3D face avatar model via a learned prior conditioned on either partial HMC images or sparse 2D keypoints. We experimentally show that our formulation yields an expressive and flexible latent space. In tightly controlled evaluations, our model LiP-Flow outperforms the base model as well as a set of carefully designed baselines in reconstruction and various inference-time optimization tasks. Importantly, our approach does not require modifications to the base model or additional training objectives.

Acknowledgments. This project is partially funded by the European Research Council (ERC) under the European Union's Horizon 2020 research and innovation programme grant agreement No. 717054.

References

1. Abrevaya, V.F., Boukhayma, A., Wuhrer, S., Boyer, E.: A decoupled 3d facial shape model by adversarial training. In: Proceedings of the IEEE/CVF International Conference on Computer Vision (ICCV), October 2019
2. Aksan, E., Hilliges, O.: STCN: stochastic temporal convolutional networks. arXiv preprint arXiv:1902.06568 (2019)
3. Aksan, E., Pece, F., Hilliges, O.: DeepWriting: making digital ink editable via deep generative modeling. In: Proceedings of the 2018 CHI Conference on Human Factors in Computing Systems, pp. 1–14 (2018)
4. Asim, M., Daniels, M., Leong, O., Ahmed, A., Hand, P.: Invertible generative models for inverse problems: mitigating representation error and dataset bias. In: International Conference on Machine Learning. pp. 399–409. PMLR (2020)
5. Bagautdinov, T., Wu, C., Saragih, J., Fua, P., Sheikh, Y.: Modeling facial geometry using compositional VAEs In: Proceedings of the IEEE Conference on Computer Vision and Pattern Recognition (CVPR), June 2018
6. Bau, D., et al.: Semantic photo manipulation with a generative image prior. arXiv preprint arXiv:2005.07727 (2020)
7. Bhattacharyya, A., Hanselmann, M., Fritz, M., Schiele, B., Straehle, C.N.: Conditional flow variational autoencoders for structured sequence prediction. arXiv preprint arXiv:1908.09008 (2019)
8. Bi, S., et al.: Deep relightable appearance models for animatable faces. ACM Trans. Graph. (TOG) **40**(4), 1–15 (2021)
9. Blanz, V., Vetter, T.: A morphable model for the synthesis of 3d faces. In: Proceedings of the 26th Annual Conference on Computer Graphics and Interactive Techniques, SIGGRAPH 1999, pp. 187–194 (1999)
10. Bogo, F., Kanazawa, A., Lassner, C., Gehler, P., Romero, J., Black, M.J.: Keep It SMPL: automatic estimation of 3d human pose and shape from a single image. In: Leibe, B., Matas, J., Sebe, N., Welling, M. (eds.) ECCV 2016. LNCS, vol. 9909, pp. 561–578. Springer, Cham (2016). https://doi.org/10.1007/978-3-319-46454-1_34
11. Bühler, M.C., Meka, A., Li, G., Beeler, T., Hilliges, O.: VariTex: variational neural face textures. In: Proceedings of the IEEE/CVF International Conference on Computer Vision, pp. 13890–13899 (2021)
12. Cao, C., et al.: Real-time 3d neural facial animation from binocular video. ACM Trans. Graph. (TOG) **40**(4), 1–17 (2021)
13. Chandran, P., Bradley, D., Gross, M., Beeler, T.: Semantic deep face models. In: 2020 International Conference on 3D Vision (3DV), pp. 345–354. IEEE (2020)
14. Chen, X., Dong, Z., Song, J., Geiger, A., Hilliges, O.: Category level object pose estimation via neural analysis-by-synthesis. In: Vedaldi, A., Bischof, H., Brox, T., Frahm, J.-M. (eds.) ECCV 2020. LNCS, vol. 12371, pp. 139–156. Springer, Cham (2020). https://doi.org/10.1007/978-3-030-58574-7_9
15. Cheng, S., Bronstein, M., Zhou, Y., Kotsia, I., Pantic, M., Zafeiriou, S.: MeshGAN: non-linear 3d morphable models of faces (2019)
16. Chu, H., Ma, S., De la Torre, F., Fidler, S., Sheikh, Y.: Expressive telepresence via modular codec avatars. In: Vedaldi, A., Bischof, H., Brox, T., Frahm, J.-M. (eds.) ECCV 2020. LNCS, vol. 12357, pp. 330–345. Springer, Cham (2020). https://doi.org/10.1007/978-3-030-58610-2_20
17. Chung, J., Kastner, K., Dinh, L., Goel, K., Courville, A.C., Bengio, Y.: A recurrent latent variable model for sequential data. Adv. Neural Inf. Process. Syst. **28**, 2980–2988 (2015)

18. Dinh, L., Krueger, D., Bengio, Y.: Nice: non-linear independent components estimation. arXiv preprint arXiv:1410.8516 (2014)
19. Dinh, L., Sohl-Dickstein, J., Bengio, S.: Density estimation using real NVP. arXiv preprint arXiv:1605.08803 (2016)
20. Feng, Y., Feng, H., Black, M.J., Bolkart, T.: Learning an animatable detailed 3d face model from in-the-wild images. ACM Trans. Graph. (TOG) **40**(4), 1–13 (2021)
21. Gecer, B., Ploumpis, S., Kotsia, I., Zafeiriou, S.: GANFIT: generative adversarial network fitting for high fidelity 3d face reconstruction. In: Proceedings of the IEEE/CVF Conference on Computer Vision and Pattern Recognition, pp. 1155–1164 (2019)
22. Goodfellow, I., et al.: Generative adversarial nets. In: Advances in Neural Information Processing Systems, pp. 2672–2680 (2014)
23. Guo, B., Han, Y., Wen, J.: AGEM: solving linear inverse problems via deep priors and sampling. Adv. Neural Inf. Process. Syst. **32**, 547–558 (2019)
24. He, K., Zhang, X., Ren, S., Sun, J.: Deep residual learning for image recognition. In: Proceedings of the IEEE Conference on Computer Vision and Pattern Recognition, pp. 770–778 (2016)
25. Kingma, D.P., Dhariwal, P.: Glow: generative flow with invertible 1 x 1 convolutions. arXiv preprint arXiv:1807.03039 (2018)
26. Kingma, D.P., Welling, M.: Auto-encoding variational bayes. arXiv preprint arXiv:1312.6114 (2013)
27. Kocabas, M., Huang, C.H.P., Tesch, J., Muller, L., Hilliges, O., Black, M.J.: Spec: seeing people in the wild with an estimated camera. In: Proceedings of the IEEE/CVF International Conference on Computer Vision, pp. 11035–11045 (2021)
28. Kolotouros, N., Pavlakos, G., Jayaraman, D., Daniilidis, K.: Probabilistic modeling for human mesh recovery. In: Proceedings of the IEEE/CVF International Conference on Computer Vision, pp. 11605–11614 (2021)
29. Lai, G., Li, B., Zheng, G., Yang, Y.: Stochastic wavenet: a generative latent variable model for sequential data. arXiv preprint arXiv:1806.06116 (2018)
30. Lewis, J.P., Anjyo, K., Rhee, T., Zhang, M., Pighin, F., Deng, Z.: Practice and theory of blendshape facial models. In: Eurographics (2014)
31. Li, J., et al.: Task-generic hierarchical human motion prior using VAEs. In: 2021 International Conference on 3D Vision (3DV), pp. 771–781. IEEE (2021)
32. Lombardi, S., Saragih, J., Simon, T., Sheikh, Y.: Deep appearance models for face rendering. ACM Trans. Graph. (TOG) **37**(4), 1–13 (2018)
33. Ma, S., et al.: Pixel codec avatars. In: Proceedings of the IEEE/CVF Conference on Computer Vision and Pattern Recognition, pp. 64–73 (2021)
34. Nair, V., Susskind, J., Hinton, G.E.: Analysis-by-synthesis by learning to invert generative black boxes. In: Kůrková, V., Neruda, R., Koutník, J. (eds.) ICANN 2008. LNCS, vol. 5163, pp. 971–981. Springer, Heidelberg (2008). https://doi.org/10.1007/978-3-540-87536-9_99
35. Pan, X., Zhan, X., Dai, B., Lin, D., Loy, C.C., Luo, P.: Exploiting deep generative prior for versatile image restoration and manipulation. IEEE Trans. Pattern Anal. Mach. Intell. **44**(11), 7474–7489 (2021)
36. Pavlakos, G., et al.: Expressive body capture: 3d hands, face, and body from a single image. In: Proceedings of the IEEE/CVF Conference on Computer Vision and Pattern Recognition, pp. 10975–10985 (2019)
37. Rempe, D., Birdal, T., Hertzmann, A., Yang, J., Sridhar, S., Guibas, L.J.: Humor: 3d human motion model for robust pose estimation. arXiv preprint arXiv:2105.04668 (2021)

38. Rezende, D., Mohamed, S.: Variational inference with normalizing flows. In: International Conference on Machine Learning, pp. 1530–1538. PMLR (2015)
39. Richard, A., Lea, C., Ma, S., Gall, J., De la Torre, F., Sheikh, Y.: Audio-and gaze-driven facial animation of codec avatars. In: Proceedings of the IEEE/CVF Winter Conference on Applications of Computer Vision, pp. 41–50 (2021)
40. Schwartz, G., et al.: The eyes have it: an integrated eye and face model for photo-realistic facial animation. ACM Trans. Graph. (TOG) **39**(4), 91:1-91:15 (2020)
41. Shamai, G., Slossberg, R., Kimmel, R.: Synthesizing facial photometries and corresponding geometries using generative adversarial networks. ACM Trans. Multimedia Comput. Commun. Appl. **15**(3s), 1–24 (2019)
42. Slossberg, R., Shamai, G., Kimmel, R.: High quality facial surface and texture synthesis via generative adversarial networks. In: Proceedings of the European Conference on Computer Vision (ECCV) Workshops, September 2018
43. Sohn, K., Lee, H., Yan, X.: Learning structured output representation using deep conditional generative models. Adv. Neural Inf. Process. Syst. **28**, 3483–3491 (2015)
44. Spurr, A., Song, J., Park, S., Hilliges, O.: Cross-modal deep variational hand pose estimation. In: Proceedings of the IEEE Conference on Computer Vision and Pattern Recognition, pp. 89–98 (2018)
45. Tewari, A., et al.: MoFA: model-based deep convolutional face autoencoder for unsupervised monocular reconstruction. In: The IEEE International Conference on Computer Vision (ICCV) (2017)
46. Vahdat, A., Kreis, K., Kautz, J.: Score-based generative modeling in latent space. Adv. Neural Inf. Process. Syst. **34**, 11287–11302 (2021)
47. Wei, S.E., et al.: VR facial animation via multiview image translation. ACM Trans. Graph. (TOG) **38**(4), 1–16 (2019)
48. Whang, J., Lindgren, E., Dimakis, A.: Composing normalizing flows for inverse problems. In: International Conference on Machine Learning, pp. 11158–11169. PMLR (2021)
49. Winkler, C., Worrall, D., Hoogeboom, E., Welling, M.: Learning likelihoods with conditional normalizing flows. arXiv preprint arXiv:1912.00042 (2019)
50. Wood, E., Baltrusaitis, T., Hewitt, C., Dziadzio, S., Cashman, T.J., Shotton, J.: Fake it till you make it: face analysis in the wild using synthetic data alone. In: Proceedings of the IEEE/CVF International Conference on Computer Vision, pp. 3681–3691 (2021)
51. Zanfir, A., Bazavan, E.G., Xu, H., Freeman, W.T., Sukthankar, R., Sminchisescu, C.: Weakly supervised 3d human pose and shape reconstruction with normalizing flows. In: Vedaldi, A., Bischof, H., Brox, T., Frahm, J.-M. (eds.) ECCV 2020. LNCS, vol. 12351, pp. 465–481. Springer, Cham (2020). https://doi.org/10.1007/978-3-030-58539-6_28
52. Zhou, X., Leonardos, S., Hu, X., Daniilidis, K.: 3d shape estimation from 2d landmarks: a convex relaxation approach. In: proceedings of the IEEE Conference on Computer Vision and Pattern Recognition, pp. 4447–4455 (2015)

Learning to Drive by Watching YouTube Videos: Action-Conditioned Contrastive Policy Pretraining

Qihang Zhang[1], Zhenghao Peng[1], and Bolei Zhou[2(✉)]

[1] The Chinese University of Hong Kong, Hong Kong SAR, China
[2] University of California, Los Angeles, USA
bolei@cs.ucla.edu

Abstract. Deep visuomotor policy learning, which aims to map raw visual observation to action, achieves promising results in control tasks such as robotic manipulation and autonomous driving. However, it requires a huge number of online interactions with the training environment, which limits its real-world application. Compared to the popular unsupervised feature learning for visual recognition, feature pretraining for visuomotor control tasks is much less explored. In this work, we aim to pretrain policy representations for driving tasks by watching hours-long uncurated YouTube videos. Specifically, we train an inverse dynamic model with a small amount of labeled data and use it to predict action labels for all the YouTube video frames. A new contrastive policy pretraining method is then developed to learn action-conditioned features from the video frames with pseudo action labels. Experiments show that the resulting action-conditioned features obtain substantial improvements for the downstream reinforcement learning and imitation learning tasks, outperforming the weights pretrained from previous unsupervised learning methods and ImageNet pretrained weight. Code, model weights, and data are available at: https://metadriverse.github.io/ACO/.

Keywords: Learning from unlabeled data · Feature Pretraining

1 Introduction

Deep policy learning makes promising progress to many visuomotor control tasks ranging from robotic manipulation [20,22,25,38] to autonomous driving [5,47]. By learning to map visual observation directly to control action through a deep neural network, it mitigates the manual design of controller, lowers the system complexity, and improves generalizability. However, the sample efficiency of the underlying algorithms such as reinforcement learning or imitation learning remains low. It requires a significant amount of online interactions or expert demonstrations in the training environment thus limits its real-world applications.

Supplementary Information The online version contains supplementary material available at https://doi.org/10.1007/978-3-031-19809-0_7.

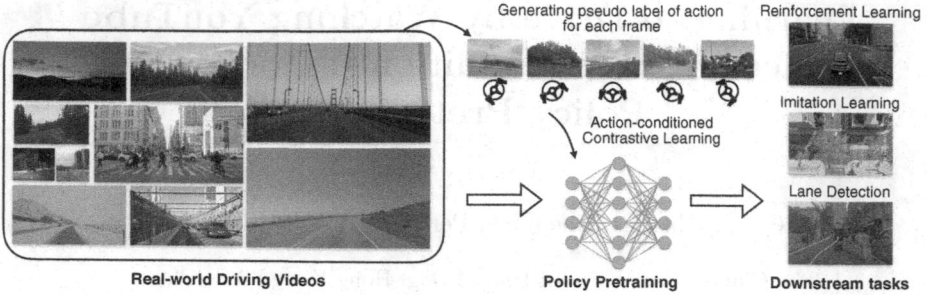

Fig. 1. Hours-long YouTube videos contain a huge variety of driving scenes. By developing an action-conditioned contrastive learning algorithm, our work aims to pretrain the visual representations with pseudo action labels on the diverse real-world data and improve sample efficiency, feature generalizability, and performance of the downstream tasks

Many recent works use unsupervised learning and data augmentation to improve the sample efficiency by pretraining the neural representations before policy learning. For example, random background videos are incorporated in the policy feature pretraining [16,17,43]. However, the augmented data with random background videos shifts drastically from the original data distribution, which degrades the overall performance of the model. Also, it remains challenging to generalize the learned weights to real world as it is hard to design augmentations that reflect the real-world diversity. In this work, we explore pretraining the neural representation on massive amount of real-world data directly. Figure 1 shows some uncurated YouTube videos, which contain driving scenes all over the world with diverse conditions such as different weathers, urban and rural environments, and various traffic densities. We show that exploiting such real-world data in deep policy learning can substantially improve the generalizability of the learned weight and benefit various downstream tasks.

Learning deep representations from unlabeled data is a popular topic in visual recognition. The learned representations are shown to be generalizable across visual tasks ranging from image classification, semantic segmentation, to object detection [7,13,18,39,42]. However, these methods are mainly designed for learning visual features for recognition tasks, which are different from control tasks where an agent takes actions in uncertain environment. In control tasks, visual information such as the abstraction of appearance and texture of the scene may not be useful for decision making. For example, visual elements like lighting and weather are usually irrelevant to the driving task and might even become confounders in policy learning, negatively affecting the driving performance [46]. On the contrary, it is crucial to learn the features that matter to the output action. For example, at the driving junction, the traffic light and the driving lane occupy only a few pixels in the visual observation but has a significant impact on the driver's actions.

In this paper, we propose a novel action-conditioned policy pretraining paradigm, which learns to capture important features in the neural representation relevant to decision making and benefits downstream tasks. As shown in Fig. 1, we first collect a large corpus of driving videos from YouTube which are recorded in 68 cities all over the world with a wide range of visual appearances. We then train an inverse dynamics model with a small amount of labeled data and use it to generate pseudo action labels for each video frame. We finally develop a novel policy pretraining method called **A**ction-conditioned **CO**ntrastive Learning (**ACO**) that incorporates the action information in the representation learning. The motivation is to learn the discriminative features of video frames most related to driving actions. Specifically, instead of contrasting images based on different augmented views [18], we define a new contrastive pair conditioned on action similarity. By learning with those action-conditioned contrastive pairs, the representation captures visual elements that are highly correlated to the output actions.

We evaluate the effectiveness of the action-conditioned pretraining for a variety of tasks, such as policy learning through Imitation Learning (IL) and Reinforcement Learning (RL) in end-to-end autonomous driving, and Lane Detection (LD). The experimental results show that ACO successfully learns generalizable features for the downstream tasks. Our contributions are summarized below:

1. We propose a new paradigm of policy pretraining on a massive amount of real-world driving videos.
2. We develop a novel action-conditioned contrastive learning approach ACO to learn action-related features.
3. Experiments of various pretraining methods in downstream policy learning tasks show that the feature resulting from the proposed method achieves sufficient performance gain in the driving tasks.

2   Related Work

2.1   Image-Based Policy Learning

Learning with Auxiliary Task. Reconstruction tasks [15,24,44], self-supervised objectives [23,33], and future prediction objectives [1,12,15,29,41] are proposed to mitigate the gap between state-based and image-based Reinforcement Learning (RL). However, unsupervised learning based on visual information may not lead to optimal policy learning performance since the irrelevant visual features might become confounders in the representation and distract policy learning [46].

Augmenting the Input Distribution. Data augmentations like random shift [17,43] and inserting random videos at background [16,17] can improve policy robustness and generalization ability. Visual and physical attributes of the environment and the agent can be randomized through domain randomization [2,28,35]. However, it is hard to design augmentations that cover real world's variations. Significant computational resources are also required to train the policy with augmented input [35].

Decoupling Visual-Level and Policy-Level Learning. Chen *et al.* [5] first train a policy with full state observation and then use this cheating policy as a teacher to train an image-based policy. Similar teacher-student architecture is adopted in [6] to learn visuomotor grasping policy. These methods decouple visual knowledge and policy knowledge and learn in a two-stage fashion. However, they require accessing the underlying proprioceptive state as observation to train the teacher agent.

Pretraining. Several works pretrain policies on offline demonstrations [37,45]. However, the training data is from the policy learning environment and requires expert policy to collect trajectories, limiting the scalability and efficiency. On the contrary, RRL [32] pretrains ResNet on ImageNet dataset as image encoder and freezes it in following policy learning process. Xiao *et al.* [40] pretrain on in-the-wild frames via masked image modeling. Our proposed ACO conducts pretraining based on YouTube videos which are captured in real world. We train an inverse dynamics model to create pseudo action labels and perform contrastive learning conditioned on these pseudo action labels. As a concurrent work, VPT [3] similarly pretrains on online videos (game playing of Minecraft) and gets pseudo action labels from a trained inverse dynamics model. VPT pretrains by behavior cloning, different from contrastive learning used in our method.

2.2   Contrastive Learning

Contrastive learning [18,39] is a popular pretext task for self-supervised learning. It creates supervisory labels via considering each image (instance) in the dataset forms a unique category and applies the learning objective of instance discrimination. Previous works [7,13,18,39] in computer vision use contrastive learning to learn general vision knowledge that transfers well to various downstream tasks. In reinforcement learning, CURL [23] and ATC [33] leverage contrastive learning as an additional signal to learn representation with environmental reward.

Common practice [18] considers two views, *i.e.* different augmentations, of a single image as a positive pair and views of different images as negative pairs. We call this type of positive/negative pair as Instance Contrastive Pair (ICP). However, ICP only preserves knowledge for visual discriminability without task-relevant information. We introduce Action Contrastive Pair (ACP) that contrasts images based on the underlying actions. Learning together with ACP and ICP will force the representation to focus on the visual elements most relevant to the decision-making process.

3   Method

We aim to learn generalizable visual feature for visuomotor policy learning, by pretraining on large amounts of uncurated real-world driving videos. We propose a novel contrastive learning algorithm called **A**ction-Conditioned **CO**ntrastive Learning (**ACO**).

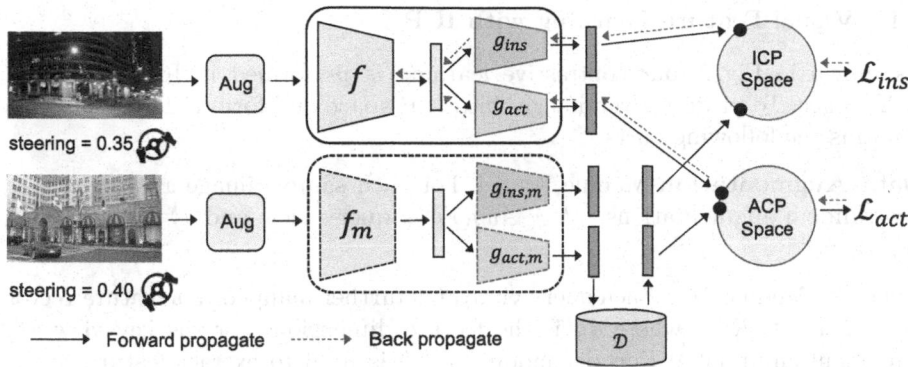

Fig. 2. In the training pipeline of ACO, we form both ICP and ACP for the input images and update the model with contrastive losses in ICP space and ACP space. The upper branch shows the calculation flow of query images and the lower shows the flow to generate the features of key images. History key features $\mathcal{D}$ are stored in a key dictionary and re-used later

The essential of ACO is that we define two types of contrastive pair: Instance Contrastive Pair (ICP) and Action Contrastive Pair (ACP). Two views of a single image form a positive ICP, while two views of different images form a negative ICP. Only pretraining with ICP may make the representation include unnecessary information for downstream policy learning tasks. For example, visual cues like weather and lighting conditions are essential for forming ICP but contribute little to decision-making in autonomous driving. To focus the feature on policy-relevant properties, we introduce another type of contrastive pair called Action Contrastive Pair (ACP). Positive ACP is composed of two different images showing scenarios where the drivers' actions are similar. As an example, the two real-world snapshots in Fig. 2 form a positive ACP, both showing the first-view images when the drivers are turning left. ACO learns representation based on both ICP and ACP, where ICP focuses on learning discriminative general visual feature and ACP focuses on policy-relevant feature.

Figure 2 illustrates the training pipeline of ACO. In upper branch, we first augment the given images twice to create query and key views and form ICPs. As discussed in Sect. 3.1, the ICPs are used to compute the ICP loss for visual discriminative feature learning. We create another learning flow based on ACP. To create ACP, each frame in the dataset is tagged with a pseudo action label as introduced in Sect. 3.2. In Sect. 3.3, the action labels are used to form ACPs between different images and compute the ACP loss for policy feature learning.

3.1 Visual Feature Learning with ICP

As shown in Fig. 2, our contrastive learning is performed in ICP space and ACP space. To project given images into ICP space and form ICP, our pipeline contains the following parts:

Data Augmentation Module $Aug(\cdot)$. For each sample image x, we generate two random augmentations, $x^q = Aug(x)$ as query view and $x^k = Aug(x)$ as key view.

Encoder Module $f(\cdot)$. Each query view x^q is further mapped to a feature vector $v^q = f(x^q) \in \mathcal{R}^{d_E}$, where d_E is the feature dimension. For the key view x^k, a momentum-updated Encoder module $f_m(\cdot)$ is used to extract feature vector $v^k = f_m(x^k) \in \mathcal{R}^{d_E}$. The update rule of the encoder's parameters is:

$$\theta_{f_m} \leftarrow \alpha\theta_{f_m} + (1 - \alpha)\theta_f, \tag{1}$$

where α is the momentum coefficient and θ_f, θ_{f_m} are the parameters of f and f_m, respectively. The output of encoder module is the representation passed to policy head in downstream task.

Projector Module $g_{ins}(\cdot)$. We map key and query feature v^q and v^k to instance-contrastive space:

$$z^q_{ins} = g_{ins}(v^q), \qquad z^k_{ins} = g_{ins,m}(v^k), \tag{2}$$

where $z^q_{ins}, z^k_{ins} \in \mathcal{R}^{d_P}$ and d_P is the dimension of the projected vector. z^q_{ins} and z^k_{ins} are further normalized to the unit hypersphere in R^{d_P}. The projector $g_{ins,m}$ for key representation is also updated in a momentum way:

$$\theta_{g_{ins,m}} \leftarrow \alpha\theta_{g_{ins,m}} + (1 - \alpha)\theta_{g_{ins}}. \tag{3}$$

Key Dictionary Module $\mathcal{D}$. Following [18], we use a key dictionary to store historical encoded key z^k_{ins} to enable larger contrastive batchsize. Concretely, we generate key features z^k of images following the lower branch in Fig. 2. These key features not only form positive pairs with query features at current training epoch, but are also stored into $\mathcal{D}$ and used to form negative pairs at future training, if sampled. The samples in the dictionary are progressively replaced if $\mathcal{D}$ exceeds its maximum size.

At each iteration of training, a batch of images are sampled from dataset. The images are sequentially processed by Data Augmentation, Encoder and Projector modules to get query and key features. The query-key pair forms positive ICP since they come from the same image. To create negative ICP, we sample a batch (num=N) of key features from $\mathcal{D}$ and form negative pairs with current queries. The negative keys are concatenated with current key features to form the key set K. Current key features are inserted into key dictionary for later use. Then we perform contrastive learning on ICP between query and key features.

The ICP loss for visual feature learning is computed as:

$$\mathcal{L}_{ins} = -\log \frac{\sum_{z^+ \in P_{ins}(z^q_{ins})} \exp(z^q_{ins} \cdot z^+/\tau)}{\sum_{z^- \in N_{ins}(z^q_{ins})} \exp(z^q_{ins} \cdot z^-/\tau)},$$

$$P_{ins}(z^q) = \{z \mid id(z) = id(z^q), z \in K\},$$

$$N_{ins}(z^q) \equiv K \backslash P_{ins}(z^q). \tag{4}$$

The symbol $\cdot$ denotes inner (dot) product, $id(z^q) = x$ returns the image from which the projected vector is generated, $P_{ins}(z^q)$ and $N_{ins}(z^q)$ are the sets of keys of all positive and negative ICP, respectively. Notice that $P_{ins}(z^q)$ only contains one sample and $N_{ins}(z^q)$ contains N samples. This is because only one element in key set comes from the anchor image x while other key features are sampled from $\mathcal{D}$.

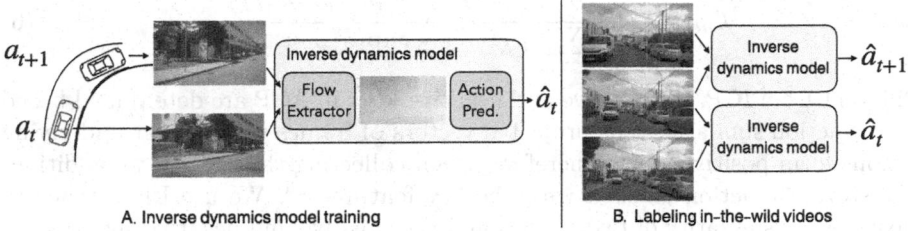

A. Inverse dynamics model training   B. Labeling in-the-wild videos

Fig. 3. A. We use real-world driving dataset to train an inverse dynamics model. The inverse dynamics model is composed of a frozen flow extractor and action prediction head. **B.** We use the trained inverse dynamics model to label actions on large corpus of in-the-wild first view driving videos

3.2 Generating Pseudo Labels for Video Frames

We propose to conduct contrastive learning based on drivers' actions. However, uncurated videos on the web do not contain any ground-truth action. We thus train an inverse dynamics model ϕ to predict the pseudo action label [21,36] $\hat{a}_t$ that has happened between two consecutive frames I_t and I_{t+1}. Nevertheless, many visual cues, such as weather and lighting, are irrelevant to action prediction. Using two RGB frames as input may introduce unnecessary distractions to the inverse dynamics model. Instead, we find that employing optical flow, the concise description of interframe movement, improves action prediction accuracy.

As illustrated in Fig. 3A, we first extract the optical flow between frames by using an off-the-shelf algorithm RAFT [34]. We then use the optical flow as the input to the inverse dynamics model ϕ to predict the action. We choose NuScenes [4] dataset which contains consecutive first-view driving scenes with labeled steering action to perform supervised learning of ϕ. L1 loss between ground truth action a_t from the dataset and predicted $\hat{a}_t$ is optimized. As shown in Fig. 3B, we then use the extracted optical flow together with the learned ϕ to label action for each frame in YouTube videos. The pseudo action labels are further used to formulate ACPs to be introduced in the next section.

3.3 Policy Feature Learning with ACP

Based on the pseudo action labels, we conduct contrastive learning on ACP space to discover policy-relevant representation. We share the Data Augmentation and Encoder modules with ICP learning in Sect. 3.1. During learning with ACP, the projector $g_{act}(\cdot)$ shares the same architecture as ICP's, but not the weights. A momentum-updated ACP projector $g_{act,m}(\cdot)$ is updated in a similar way as ICP projector in Eq. 3. Thus the key and query vectors in action-contrastive space are computed as:

$$z_{act}^{q} = g_{act}(v^{q}) = g_{act}(f(x^{q})), \qquad z_{act}^{k} = g_{act,m}(v^{k}) = g_{act,m}(f_{m}(x^{k})). \qquad (5)$$

We also sample a batch of key features from $\mathcal{D}$ and concatenate them with current key features to form key set K. The ACP loss is computed as:

$$\mathcal{L}_{act} = -\log \frac{\sum_{z^{+} \in P_{act}(z_{act}^{q})} \exp(z_{act}^{q} \cdot z^{+}/\tau)}{\sum_{z^{-} \in N_{act}(z_{act}^{q})} \exp(z_{act}^{q} \cdot z^{-}/\tau)}. \qquad (6)$$

Different from ICP, the positive and negative keys in ACP are determined based on the action similarity. The projected vectors of frames with similar underlying actions form positive pairs. Therefore, when collecting the key set, we additionally store the action labels $\hat{a}$ with the key features z^{k}. We use L1 distance to measure the similarity of two actions and the positive and negative key sets are determined as:

$$P_{act}(z^{q}) = \{z \mid \|\hat{a} - \hat{a}^{q}\| < \epsilon, (z, \hat{a}) \in K\},$$
$$N_{act}(z^{q}) \equiv K \backslash P_{act}(z^{q}), \qquad (7)$$

where $\hat{a}^{q}$ is the predicted pseudo action label of the query image and ϵ is the action distance threshold.

3.4 Loss

The overall contrastive loss of ACO is:

$$\mathcal{L} = \lambda_{ins}\mathcal{L}_{ins} + \lambda_{act}\mathcal{L}_{act}, \qquad (8)$$

where λ_{ins} and λ_{act} are weighted factors to balance ICP and ACP.

4 Experiments

We evaluate the pretrained feature from our method on two main policy learning tasks: Imitation Learning (IL) and Reinforcement Learning (RL) in end-to-end driving. We also evaluate on one related visual recognition task: Lane Detection (LD). Section 4.1 lists the compared baselines. The main experimental results with a comparison of different pretraining methods are presented in Sect. 4.2 for IL, in Sect. 4.3 for RL, and in Sect. 4.4 for LD. Section 4.5 gives a qualitative analysis of the learned action-conditioned representation. Ablation study and further discussion are included in Sect. 4.6.

YouTube Driving Dataset. We crawl first-view driving videos from YouTube. 134 videos with a total length of over 120 h are collected. As shown in Fig. 1, these videos cover different driving scenes with various weather conditions (sunny, rainy, snowy, etc.) and regions (rural and urban areas). We sample one frame every one second, resulting to a dataset of 1.30 million frames. We split the YouTube driving dataset into training set with 70% data and test set with 30% data and conduct the training of ACO on the training set.

Inverse Dynamics Model. An inverse dynamics model with ResNet-34 architecture is used to predict action labels for frames in YouTube driving dataset. We use RAFT [34] as the optical flow extractor and apply Adam optimizer with learning rate of 0.001 and weight decay of 0.001 to learn the model on the training set of NuScenes [4]. We normalize steering value between 0 and 1. In our preliminary experiments, the L1 error of steering prediction averaged over the test set of NuScenes [4] is 0.10 when using consecutive images as input, and 0.04 when using optical flow. Using optical flow as the input brings better inverse dynamics prediction performance as it is more invariant to the image content. Figure 4 shows some sampled frames. The steering action is predicted accurately under different visual conditions.

Fig. 4. Exemplar video frames organized by their pseudo labels. We use the inverse dynamics model to label each frame's action. The predicted action is mostly correct despite diverse visual variations of the image content

Pretraining. In the representation learning, we largely follow the hyperparameters from the official implementation of MoCo-v2 [8]. We optimize the model with synchronized SGD over 8 GPUs with a weight decay of 0.0001, a momentum of 0.9, and a batch size of 32 on each GPU. We perform 100 epochs optimization with an initial learning rate of 0.03 and a cosine learning rate schedule. Two projectors for ICP and ACP are both instantiated as two-layer MLPs. We maintain a memory queue of 40,960 samples as the Key Dictionary $\mathcal{D}$. The momentum coefficient in Eq. 1 and Eq. 3 is set to 0.999 for updating the key encoder and projector.

Data Augmentations. During pretraining, we follow MoCo-v2 [8] and use image augmentations to generate key and query views of an image. Specifically, we apply random gray scaling, color jittering and Gaussian blurring. Random resized cropping and horizontal flipping are excluded because we find that they will largely change the scene's semantic, thus degrading the overall performance, as shown in the ablation study.

Table 1. Success Rate of Imitation Learning. We evaluate the performance of different pretrained models under IL tasks with different scales of dataset

Pretrain method	IL demonstration size ($\times 40K$)			
	10%	20%	40%	100%
Random	0.0 ± 0.0	0.0 ± 0.0	37.3 ± 6.6	81.3 ± 5.2
AutoEncoder	0.0 ± 0.0	4.0 ± 3.3	6.7 ± 2.5	46.0 ± 5.9
ImageNet	21.3 ± 7.5	52.7 ± 13.1	72.0 ± 4.3	90.7 ± 7.4
MoCo	19.3 ± 3.4	60.3 ± 8.2	76.0 ± 9.1	80.7 ± 2.5
ACO	**30.7 ± 3.4**	**66.0 ± 5.7**	**82.0 ± 5.0**	**96.0 ± 3.3**

4.1 Baselines

We choose ResNet-34 as the backbone (encoder) architecture and compare the downstream tasks' performance when using different pretrained models as the initial parameters of the backbone network. Different pretraining methods are as follows:

Random. The backbone's parameters are initialized randomly. Specifically, we use Kaiming normalization [19] to initialize convolution layers. Constant initialization is applied to batchnorm layer (1 for weight and 0 for bias).

ImageNet. We use official ImageNet's pretrain weights to initialize the backbone. This is considered as the most common approach for current image-based policy learning [32].

AutoEncoder. We train an autoencoder on the collected YouTube videos and use the encoder to initialize the backbone, which has been used in previous policy learning work [14].

MoCo. As a straightforward comparison to our method, contrastive learning is conducted following MoCo-v2 [8] on the collected YouTube videos. As a baseline, we only use ICP to conduct contrastive learning and set $\lambda_{act} = 0$ in Eq. 8.

4.2 Imitation Learning

Setup. We evaluate the performance of different pretrained weights for Imitation Learning in the open-source CARLA [11] simulator. We use the original CARLA [11] benchmark (also known as CORL2017) and collect 50 trajectories of expert demonstration, which amount to 40K transitions, in Town01 with train weather. Town02 with test weather is used for evaluation. The expert is a rule-based PID controller with injected noise [9]. We adopt CILRS [10], a conditional behavior clonning algorithm, to train policies based on different pretrained models. The backbone network is fine-tuned during policy learning. We also conduct IL with frozen backbone and conclude the result in Appendix. All experiments are repeated three times with different random seeds. Information about other hyper-parameters is given in Appendix.

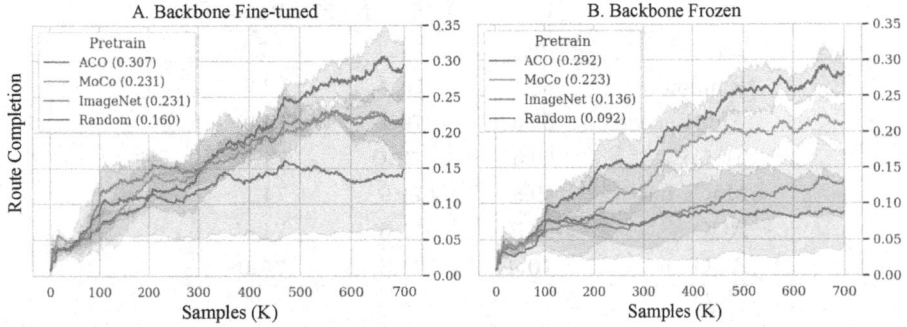

Fig. 5. Route completion curves for PPO [31] with different pretrain weights. In the left panel, the backbone is actively updated during policy learning. In the right panel, the backbone is frozen and not updated. The proposed ACO outperforms all baselines

Results. To see how pretrained models improve IL tasks, we experiment on the expert datasets with 10%, 20%, 40% and 100% of all 40K samples. As shown in Table 1, ACO outperforms all other baselines in datasets of all scales. Notably, AutoEncoder is less competitive even compared to random initialization. This is because pixel reconstruction target is misaligned with policy learning target and makes the encoder pay more attention to areas with larger size like buildings and the sky, which however are useless for imitation learning. MoCo and ImageNet perform well at full dataset but have degraded performance when dataset size is reduced. ACO-pretrained models consistently outperform baselines at all different dataset sizes.

4.3 Reinforcement Learning

Setup. Similar to Imitation Learning, we also use CARLA [11] as the simulator for evaluating pretrained models in Reinforcement Learning. We use Town01 in NoCrash benchmark [10] as the environment and evaluate the performance of Proximal Policy Optimization (PPO) [31] with different pretrained weights.

Results. As shown in Fig. 5A, PPO with ACO initialization introduces a clear improvement of 7% route completion compared to other baselines when the backbone is fine-tuned during policy learning. This suggests that incorporating policy-relevant objects into pretraining stage benefits downstream RL's performance. ImageNet and MoCo, which only learn visual knowledge, are less competitive compared to ACO. For random initialization, we observe a poor 15% route completion, in which case the agent can only drive in straight road but fails to learn turning.

Table 2. F1 metric of lane detection

Pretrain method	LD method		
	UFLD [30]	SCNN [27]	RESA [48]
ImageNet	*70.9*	*74.1*	*76.1*
Random	68.4	70.4	73.9
AutoEncoder	68.6	70.1	74.0
MoCo	69.5	**72.0**	74.1
MoCo-bn	69.8	71.9	74.1
ACO	69.5	71.6	74.5
ACO-bn	**70.4**	71.8	**75.0**

To further understand the importance of considering policy-relevant information in pretraining, we freeze the backbone and only finetune the policy head during RL. As shown in Fig. 5B, compared to backbone fine-tuned case, the performance of PPO declines dramatically when using ImageNet pretraining. This indicates that ImageNet pretrained weight lacks the essential knowledge for policy learning thus leads to a poor RL performance. ACO's and MoCo's performance are not affected when freezing the backbone.

4.4 Lane Detection

Setup. To further prove that the representation learned by ACO is generalizable, we conduct lane detection experiments. We train three popular lane detection methods on CULane dataset [27]: UFLD [30], SCNN [27], and RESA [48]. All of these methods employ backbone networks with ResNet architecture. We use ACO and other baselines to initialize the backbone's parameters before training. We adopt the training settings (*e.g.* learning rate) of three LD methods fine-tuned on ImageNet pretrained backbone. Better performance is expected after tunning the hyper-parameters for different pretrained methods respectively. MoCo [18] suggests that a batch normalization layer after backbone can alleviate the gap between contrastive learning and supervised learning caused by different parameters' distribution. We thus follow this procedure on ACO and MoCo baseline and present the results with "-bn" suffix.

Results. As shown in Table 2, ImageNet pretraining achieves the best performance among all candidates. Although trained in an object-centric dataset, ImageNet still provides high quality feature for lane detection learning. Within the self-supervised baselines, ACO outperforms others in UFLD [30] and RESA [48]. In SCNN [27], ACO is on par with MoCo. Introducing batch normalization improves the performance of ACO.

4.5   Visualization

We perform t-SNE [26] analysis on features extracted by different layers of ACO and compare them with that of MoCo. We randomly select frames from the test set and divide them into three categories: *left turn*, *right turn*, and *go straight*. Each category has 25 examples. Images within same category form positive ACPs with one another. To build positive ICPs, we sample the previous and next frame of chosen samples and consider them as positive pairs.

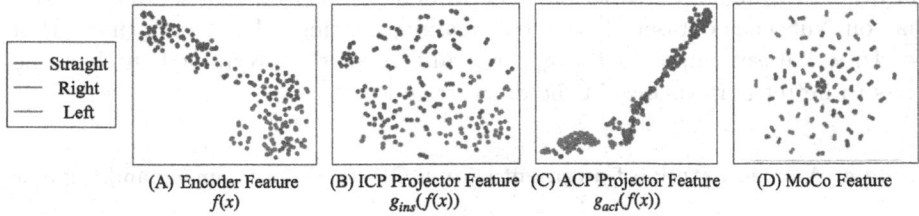

(A) Encoder Feature $f(x)$ (B) ICP Projector Feature $g_{ins}(f(x))$ (C) ACP Projector Feature $g_{act}(f(x))$ (D) MoCo Feature

Fig. 6. t-SNE [26] visualization of extracted features. Red, green, and blue dots indicate frames under *left turn*, *right turn*, and *go straight* scenarios respectively (Color figure online)

Table 3. Ablation study of pretraining datasets. We use ACO to pretrain models on our YouTube dataset and the NuScenes dataset respectively, and conduct IL training on CARLA

Pretraining dataset	Frame num (M)	IL Demonstration size ($\times 40K$)			
		10%	20%	40%	100%
NuScenes [4]	0.19 @ 10Hz	13.3±3.4	27.3±10.4	67.3±9.0	82.7±8.4
YouTube	**1.30@1Hz**	**30.7**±3.4	**66.0**±5.7	**82.0**±5.0	**96.0**±3.3

As shown in Fig. 6**A**, features extracted by ACO's encoder, which will be passed to policy head in downstream task, form separable clusters and have clear semantics related to the possible actions of drivers. On the contrary, the action-conditioned clustering does not emerge in MoCo in Fig. 6**D**. Instead, we find that MoCo feature demonstrates the *instance clustering phenomenon*, where the features of three temporal neighboring frames lay closely and form a clique in the t-SNE visualization.

Diving into the contrastive learning modules, we find the ICP projector demonstrates instance clustering as in Fig. 6**B**. The phenomenon does not exist in ACP projected features in Fig. 6**C**, where features cluster more tightly according to action information instead of temporal relationship. t-SNE visualization shows that ICP and ACP in ACO both achieve their respective goals: ICP endows features with the capacity to discriminate across instances, whereas ACP creates features that tightly couple with action information.

4.6   Ablation Study

We conduct ablation studies that examine the effectiveness of collecting and labeling YouTube driving videos rather than using NuScenes dataset [4] and the impact of geometric-aware augmentations (cropping and flipping).

YouTube Dataset. To highlight the importance of collecting large dataset from YouTube, we train IL agents based on models pretrained on different datasets and compare the success rate on IL benchmark. As shown in Table 3, the size of our collected YouTube dataset is six times larger than NuScenes dataset [4] even though we sample frames 1 Hz from the video, compared 10 Hz of NuScenes. The imitation learning performance of ACO trained on YouTube dataset outperforms that on NuScenes dataset [4] at all IL training settings. The result shows that YouTube dataset improves the generalizability of the pretrained models and leads to better performance in the downstream task.

Table 4. Ablation study of augmentations. CF stands for Cropping and Flipping

Methods	IL Demonstration Size ($\times 40K$)			
	10%	20%	40%	100%
MoCo w/ CF	19.3 ± 3.4	60.3 ± 8.2	76.0 ± 9.1	80.7 ± 2.5
MoCo w/o CF	13.3 ± 3.4	47.3 ± 13.7	72.7 ± 9.0	84.0 ± 4.9
ACO w/ CF	27.3 ± 0.9	36.0 ± 5.9	74.0 ± 7.5	89.3 ± 5.0
ACO w/o CF	$\mathbf{30.7 \pm 3.4}$	$\mathbf{66.0 \pm 5.7}$	$\mathbf{82.0 \pm 5.0}$	$\mathbf{96.0 \pm 3.3}$

Augmentations. We conduct imitation learning experiments to discover the impact of two augmentations, cropping and flipping frames (CF in the following for lucidity). As shown in Table 4, the performance of MoCo without CF is significantly lower than MoCo with these two augmentations, showing that CF is important for instance discriminative learning. However, the result suggests ACO is incompatible with CF. Excluding CF in ACO will affect the feature's instance discriminative ability but improve the overall performance in downstream driving tasks with action-conditioned contrastive learning.

5   Conclusion and Discussion

In this paper, we propose a novel contrastive policy pretraining method ACO using hours-long uncurated YouTube videos. By learning action-conditioned features from unlabeled video frames with pseudo action labels, our methods greatly improve the generalizability of the learned representation and brings substantial improvements to downstream tasks.

Limitations. Despite the generalizable representation provided by pretraining with action information, we incorporate a strong assumption: only one action corresponds to each driving scene in a single video frame. This does not hold true as drivers may have various driving intentions in complex scenarios. Future study will concentrate on how to label frames more accurately, *e.g.* labeling each frame with an action distribution, to produce more precise action contrastive pairs. Besides, action-conditioned contrastive learning has conflict with widely used geometric-aware augmentations like cropping and flipping, suppressing feature's instance discrimination ability. We leave this problem for future study.

References

1. Agrawal, P., Nair, A.V., Abbeel, P., Malik, J., Levine, S.: Learning to poke by poking: Experiential learning of intuitive physics. Adv. Neural Inf. Process. Syst. **29**, 5074–5082 (2016)
2. Andrychowicz, O.M., et al.: Learning dexterous in-hand manipulation. Int. J. Robot. Res. **39**(1), 3–20 (2020)
3. Baker, B., et al.: Video pretraining (VPT): learning to act by watching unlabeled online videos. arXiv preprint arXiv:2206.11795 (2022)
4. Caesar, H., et al.: nuScenes: a multimodal dataset for autonomous driving. In: Proceedings of the IEEE/CVF conference on computer vision and pattern recognition. pp. 11621–11631 (2020)
5. Chen, D., Zhou, B., Koltun, V., Krähenbühl, P.: Learning by cheating. In: Conference on Robot Learning, pp. 66–75. PMLR (2020)
6. Chen, T., Xu, J., Agrawal, P.: A system for general in-hand object re-orientation. In: Conference on Robot Learning, pp. 297–307. PMLR (2022)
7. Chen, T., Kornblith, S., Norouzi, M., Hinton, G.: A simple framework for contrastive learning of visual representations. In: International Conference on Machine Learning, pp. 1597–1607. PMLR (2020)
8. Chen, X., Fan, H., Girshick, R., He, K.: Improved baselines with momentum contrastive learning. arXiv preprint arXiv:2003.04297 (2020)
9. Codevilla, F., Müller, M., López, A., Koltun, V., Dosovitskiy, A.: End-to-end driving via conditional imitation learning. In: 2018 IEEE International Conference on Robotics and Automation (ICRA), pp. 4693–4700. IEEE (2018)

10. Codevilla, F., Santana, E., López, A.M., Gaidon, A.: Exploring the limitations of behavior cloning for autonomous driving. In: Proceedings of the IEEE/CVF International Conference on Computer Vision, pp. 9329–9338 (2019)
11. Dosovitskiy, A., Ros, G., Codevilla, F., López, A.M., Koltun, V.: CARLA: an open urban driving simulator. CoRR abs/1711.03938 (2017), arxiv.org/abs/1711.03938
12. Finn, C., Tan, X.Y., Duan, Y., Darrell, T., Levine, S., Abbeel, P.: Learning visual feature spaces for robotic manipulation with deep spatial autoencoders. arXiv preprint arXiv:1509.06113 25 (2015)
13. Grill, J.B., et al.: Bootstrap your own latent-a new approach to self-supervised learning. Adv. Neural Inf. Process. Syst. **33**, 21271–21284 (2020)
14. Ha, D., Schmidhuber, J.: World models. arXiv preprint arXiv:1803.10122 (2018)
15. Hafner, D., Lillicrap, T., Fischer, I., Villegas, R., Ha, D., Lee, H., Davidson, J.: Learning latent dynamics for planning from pixels. In: International Conference on Machine Learning, pp. 2555–2565. PMLR (2019)
16. Hansen, N., et al.: Self-supervised policy adaptation during deployment. arXiv preprint arXiv:2007.04309 (2020)
17. Hansen, N., Wang, X.: Generalization in reinforcement learning by soft data augmentation. In: 2021 IEEE International Conference on Robotics and Automation (ICRA), pp. 13611–13617. IEEE (2021)
18. He, K., Fan, H., Wu, Y., Xie, S., Girshick, R.: Momentum contrast for unsupervised visual representation learning. In: Proceedings of the IEEE/CVF Conference on Computer Vision and Pattern Recognition, pp. 9729–9738 (2020)
19. He, K., Zhang, X., Ren, S., Sun, J.: Delving deep into rectifiers: surpassing human-level performance on ImageNet classification. In: Proceedings of the IEEE International Conference on Computer Vision, pp. 1026–1034 (2015)
20. Kalashnikov, D., et al.: Scalable deep reinforcement learning for vision-based robotic manipulation. In: Conference on Robot Learning, pp. 651–673. PMLR (2018)
21. Kumar, A., Gupta, S., Malik, J.: Learning navigation subroutines by watching videos. corr abs/1905.12612 (2019) (1905)
22. Lange, S., Riedmiller, M., Voigtländer, A.: Autonomous reinforcement learning on raw visual input data in a real world application. In: The 2012 International Joint Conference on Neural Networks (IJCNN), pp. 1–8. IEEE (2012)
23. Laskin, M., Srinivas, A., Abbeel, P.: Curl: contrastive unsupervised representations for reinforcement learning. In: International Conference on Machine Learning, pp. 5639–5650. PMLR (2020)
24. Lee, A.X., Nagabandi, A., Abbeel, P., Levine, S.: Stochastic latent actor-critic: deep reinforcement learning with a latent variable model. Adv. Neural Inf. Process. Syst. **33**, 741–752 (2020)
25. Levine, S., Finn, C., Darrell, T., Abbeel, P.: End-to-end training of deep visuomotor policies. J. Mach. Learn. Res. **17**(1), 1334–1373 (2016)
26. Van der Maaten, L., Hinton, G.: Visualizing data using t-SNE. J. Mach. Learn. Res. **9**(11), 2579–2605 (2008)
27. Pan, X., Shi, J., Luo, P., Wang, X., Tang, X.: Spatial as deep: Spatial CNN for traffic scene understanding. In: Proceedings of the AAAI Conference on Artificial Intelligence, vol. 32 (2018)
28. Peng, X.B., Andrychowicz, M., Zaremba, W., Abbeel, P.: Sim-to-real transfer of robotic control with dynamics randomization. In: 2018 IEEE International Conference on Robotics and Automation (ICRA), pp. 3803–3810. IEEE (2018)

29. Pinto, L., Gandhi, D., Han, Y., Park, Y.-L., Gupta, A.: The curious robot: learning visual representations via physical interactions. In: Leibe, B., Matas, J., Sebe, N., Welling, M. (eds.) ECCV 2016. LNCS, vol. 9906, pp. 3–18. Springer, Cham (2016). https://doi.org/10.1007/978-3-319-46475-6_1
30. Qin, Z., Wang, H., Li, X.: Ultra fast structure-aware deep lane detection. In: Vedaldi, A., Bischof, H., Brox, T., Frahm, J.-M. (eds.) ECCV 2020. LNCS, vol. 12369, pp. 276–291. Springer, Cham (2020). https://doi.org/10.1007/978-3-030-58586-0_17
31. Schulman, J., Wolski, F., Dhariwal, P., Radford, A., Klimov, O.: Proximal policy optimization algorithms. arXiv preprint arXiv:1707.06347 (2017)
32. Shah, R., Kumar, V.: RRL: Resnet as representation for reinforcement learning. arXiv preprint arXiv:2107.03380 (2021)
33. Stooke, A., Lee, K., Abbeel, P., Laskin, M.: Decoupling representation learning from reinforcement learning. In: International Conference on Machine Learning, pp. 9870–9879. PMLR (2021)
34. Teed, Z., Deng, J.: RAFT: recurrent all-pairs field transforms for optical flow. In: Vedaldi, A., Bischof, H., Brox, T., Frahm, J.-M. (eds.) ECCV 2020. LNCS, vol. 12347, pp. 402–419. Springer, Cham (2020). https://doi.org/10.1007/978-3-030-58536-5_24
35. Tobin, J., Fong, R., Ray, A., Schneider, J., Zaremba, W., Abbeel, P.: Domain randomization for transferring deep neural networks from simulation to the real world. In: 2017 IEEE/RSJ International Conference on Intelligent Robots and Systems (IROS), pp. 23–30. IEEE (2017)
36. Torabi, F., Warnell, G., Stone, P.: Behavioral cloning from observation. In: IJCAI (2018)
37. Wang, C., Luo, X., Ross, K., Li, D.: Vrl3: a data-driven framework for visual deep reinforcement learning. arXiv preprint arXiv:2202.10324 (2022)
38. Wu, B., Nair, S., Fei-Fei, L., Finn, C.: Example-driven model-based reinforcement learning for solving long-horizon visuomotor tasks. arXiv preprint arXiv:2109.10312 (2021)
39. Wu, Z., Xiong, Y., Yu, S.X., Lin, D.: Unsupervised feature learning via nonparametric instance discrimination. In: Proceedings of the IEEE Conference on Computer Vision and Pattern Recognition, pp. 3733–3742 (2018)
40. Xiao, T., Radosavovic, I., Darrell, T., Malik, J.: Masked visual pre-training for motor control. arXiv preprint arXiv:2203.06173 (2022)
41. Yan, W., Vangipuram, A., Abbeel, P., Pinto, L.: Learning predictive representations for deformable objects using contrastive estimation. arXiv preprint arXiv:2003.05436 (2020)
42. Yang, C., Wu, Z., Zhou, B., Lin, S.: Instance localization for self-supervised detection pretraining. In: Proceedings of the IEEE/CVF Conference on Computer Vision and Pattern Recognition, pp. 3987–3996 (2021)
43. Yarats, D., Kostrikov, I., Fergus, R.: Image augmentation is all you need: regularizing deep reinforcement learning from pixels. In: International Conference on Learning Representations (2020)
44. Yarats, D., Zhang, A., Kostrikov, I., Amos, B., Pineau, J., Fergus, R.: Improving sample efficiency in model-free reinforcement learning from images. arXiv preprint arXiv:1910.01741 (2019)
45. Zhan, A., Zhao, P., Pinto, L., Abbeel, P., Laskin, M.: A framework for efficient robotic manipulation. arXiv preprint arXiv:2012.07975 (2020)

46. Zhang, A., McAllister, R., Calandra, R., Gal, Y., Levine, S.: Learning invariant representations for reinforcement learning without reconstruction. arXiv preprint arXiv:2006.10742 (2020)
47. Zhang, Z., Liniger, A., Dai, D., Yu, F., Van Gool, L.: End-to-end urban driving by imitating a reinforcement learning coach. In: Proceedings of the IEEE/CVF International Conference on Computer Vision (ICCV) (2021)
48. Zheng, T., et al.: Resa: Recurrent feature-shift aggregator for lane detection (2020)

Learning Ego 3D Representation as Ray Tracing

Jiachen Lu[1], Zheyuan Zhou[1], Xiatian Zhu[2], Hang Xu[3], and Li Zhang[1]([✉])

[1] School of Data Science, Fudan University, Shanghai, China
`lizhangfd@fudan.edu.cn`
[2] University of Surrey, Guildford, UK
[3] Huawei Noah's Ark Lab, Shanghai, Canada
`https://fudan-zvg.github.io/Ego3RT`

Abstract. A self-driving perception model aims to extract 3D semantic representations from multiple cameras collectively into the bird's-eye-view (BEV) coordinate frame of the ego car in order to ground downstream planner. Existing perception methods often rely on error-prone depth estimation of the whole scene or learning sparse virtual 3D representations without the target geometry structure, both of which remain limited in performance and/or capability. In this paper, we present a novel end-to-end architecture for ego 3D representation learning from an arbitrary number of unconstrained camera views. Inspired by the ray tracing principle, we design a polarized grid of "imaginary eyes" as the learnable ego 3D representation and formulate the learning process with the adaptive attention mechanism in conjunction with the 3D-to-2D projection. Critically, this formulation allows extracting rich 3D representation from 2D images without any depth supervision, and with the built-in geometry structure consistent *w.r.t* BEV. Despite its simplicity and versatility, extensive experiments on standard BEV visual tasks (*e.g.*, camera-based 3D object detection and BEV segmentation) show that our model outperforms all state-of-the-art alternatives significantly, with an extra advantage in computational efficiency from multi-task learning.

Keywords: 3D object detection · BEV segmentation · Multi-camera

1 Introduction

Taking an image as input, existing vision models usually either ignore (*e.g.*, image classification [6,10,26]) or consume directly (*e.g.*, object detection [17,22, 41], image segmentation [3,13,38]) the coordinate frame of input during results prediction. Nonetheless, this paradigm does not match the perception circumstance of self-driving out-of-the-box, where the input source is multiple cameras

---

Supplementary Information The online version contains supplementary material available at https://doi.org/10.1007/978-3-031-19809-0_8.

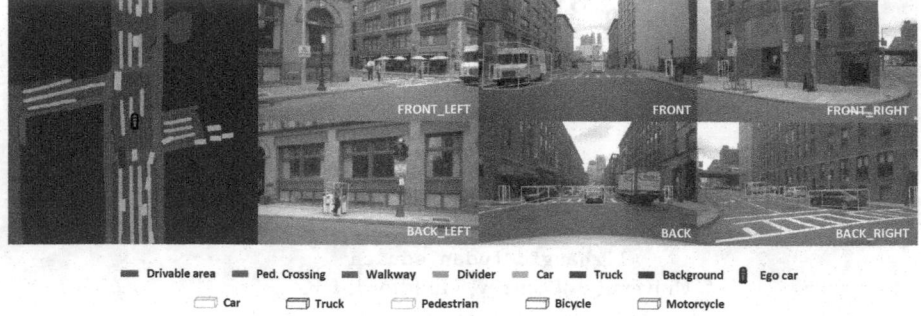

Fig. 1. We propose an ego 3D representation learning method that extracts 3D representation in bird's-eye-view (BEV) from multi-view cameras (*right*). With the aid of our 3D representation, multiple tasks can be executed efficiently in a single model: BEV segmentation (*left*) and 3D object detection (*right*).

each with a specific coordinate frame, and the perception models for downstream tasks (*e.g.*, 3D object detection, lane segmentation) need to make predictions in the coordinate frame of the ego car, totally *different* from all the input frames. That is, a self-driving perception model needs to reason about 3D semantics from 2D visual representations of multi-view images, which is non-trivial and highly challenging.

In the literature, existing methods mostly take the following two strategies. The *first* strategy show in Fig. 2(a) (*e.g.*, LSS [20], CaDDN [21]) relies on pixel-level depth estimation, as it can be used to project the 2D visual representation to the ego coordinate frame alongside intrinsic and extrinsic projection. Often, the depth prediction is end-to-end learned within the model without supervision [20], or with extra 3D supervision [21]. A downside of these methods is that depth estimation in unconstrained scenes is typically error-prone, which would be further propagated down to the subsequent components. This is also known as the *error propagation* problem, largely inevitable for such pipelines.

To solve this above issue, the *second* strategy (*e.g.*, Image2Map [25], OFT [24], DETR3D [32]) eliminates the depth dimension via directly learning 3D representations from 2D images through architecture innovation. This approach has shown to be superior over depth-estimation based counterparts, implying that learning 3D representation is a superior general strategy. In particular, Image2Map [25] and PON [23] leverage a Transformer or FC layer to learn the projection from 2D image frame to the bird's-eye-view (BEV) coordinate frame forwardly. As is shown in Fig. 2(b), However, their 3D representation is structurally inconsistent with 2D counterparts as no rigorous intrinsic and extrinsic projection can be leveraged, *i.e.*, no explicit one-one correspondence relation across the coordinate frames, consequently resulting in sup-optimal solutions. The recent state-of-the-art DETR3D [32] formulates a 3D representation learning model with a Transformer model, inspired by contemporary image based object detection models [2]. However, its 3D representation is not only *sparse*, but *virtual* in the sense of no geometry structure explicitly involved *w.r.t* the ego coordinate frame, and is thus unable to conduct dense prediction tasks such as segmentation.

In this work, we present a novel ego 3D representation learning method that overcomes all the aforementioned limitations in an end-to-end formulation. This is inspired by the ray tracing principle [33] in computer graphics, which simulates the light transport process from the sources to human eyes in graphic rendering. Rather than taking the optical sources as inception, ray tracing *backtracks* the optical paths from the imaginary eyes to the objects in an opposite way. Analogously, we start with introducing a polarized grid of dense "imaginary eyes" for BEV representation, with each eye naturally occupying a specific geometry location with the depth information involved. As is shown in Fig. 2(c), for learning 3D representation including height information intrinsically absent in BEV, we initialize each eye using a uniform value and leave the eyes to look backward surrounding 2D visual representations subject to the intrinsic and extrinsic 3D-to-2D projection. With the adaptive attention mechanism, eyes focus dynamically on 2D representations and directly learn to approximate missing height information in a data driven manner. Critically, our architecture can be applied for both sparse (*e.g.*, 3D object detection) and dense (*e.g.*, BEV semantic segmentation) prediction tasks. We term our method *Ego 3D representation learning as Ray Tracing* (**Ego3RT**).

We make the following **contributions**: (**1**) We propose a novel ego 3D representation learning architecture, inspired by the ray tracing perspective. (**2**) Without depth supervision, our method can learn geometrically structured and dense 3D representations from arbitrary camera rigs *w.r.t* the ego car coordinate frame, subject to the intrinsic and extrinsic 3D-to-2D projection. This is achieved by adapting the ray tracing concept, where we first introduce a polarized grid of "imaginary eyes" as the learnable BEV representation, and then trace them *backwards* to camera rigs by formulating the learning process of this 3D representation into an adaptive attention framework. (**3**) Expensive experiments on 3D object detection and lane segmentation self-driving tasks validate the superiority of our method over state-of-the-art alternative methods, often by a large performance gap. In particular, Ego3RT enables multi-task learning by representation sharing between object detection and BEV segmentation whilst still yielding superior performance, hence more computationally efficient and economically scalable for self-driving.

2 Related Work

Depth-Based Strategy. Benefited from well-studied depth estimation, Pseudo-lidar [31], Pseudo-lidar++ [37] and AM3D [16] separate the 3D representation learning into monocular depth estimation and 3D detection. CaDDN [21] uses a supervised depth estimation network to accumulate a more precise position of each voxel from the front-view features. These dual-step methods rely on extra depth estimation data and are not end-to-end trainable. LSS [20] and

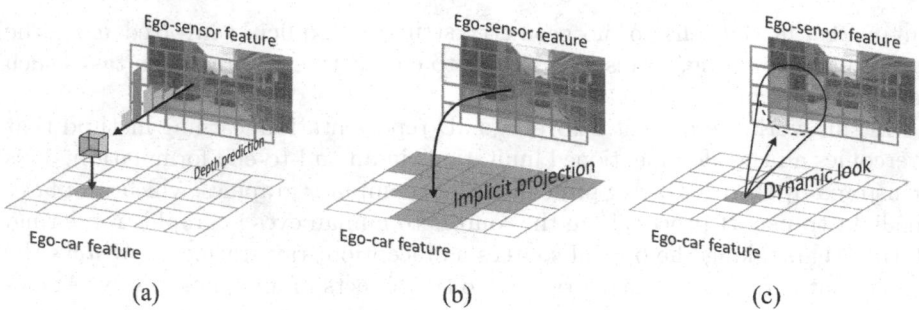

Fig. 2. Comparison of dense 3D representation learning strategies. (a) The *first* strategy, represented by LSS [20], CaDDN [21], is based on dense pixel-level depth estimation. (b) The *second* strategy represented by PON [23] bypasses the depth estimation by learning implicit 2D-3D projection. (c) *Our* strategy that backtracks 2D information from "imaginary" eyes specially designed in the BEV's geometry.

FIERY [11] achieve the front-view features lifting in an end-to-end manner with the depth distribution prediction to generate the intermediate 3D representations. However, weakly-constrained depth estimation is error-prone, with the depth error propagated to limit the subsequent 3D localization.

Depth-Free Strategy. OFT [24] simply hypothesizes a uniform distribution over the depth, leading to poor performance in the 3D detection task. Rather than predicting depth, [4, 23, 25, 35] opt to exploit the 3D-to-2D projection process. PYVA [35] shows that the correspondence between 2D features and 3D features can be implicitly learned by cross attention. NEAT [4] further proposes a variation of cross attention for the same purpose. PON [23] and Image2Map [25] resort to a Transformer or FC layer to learn a correspondence between images and 3D features. While decently estimating the 3D-to-2D relationship, a clear limitation is that these models ignore the intrinsic one-one correspondence. Recently, DETR3D [32] learns sparse 3D representations with a Transformer by using sparse queries to detect 3D objects. However, this 3D representation has no geometry structure, making it incapable of performing dense prediction tasks. In this work, we present Ego3RT, a novel end-to-end trainable ego 3D representation learning architecture that solves all the above limitations. Critically, it can learn 3D ego representation from unconstrained camera rigs without any 3D or depth supervision, achieving superior performance on BEV visual tasks even in a more efficient multi-task model design.

3   Method

Our architecture can be divided into two components: (1) ego 3D representation learning (***Ego3RT***) and (2) downstream task head.

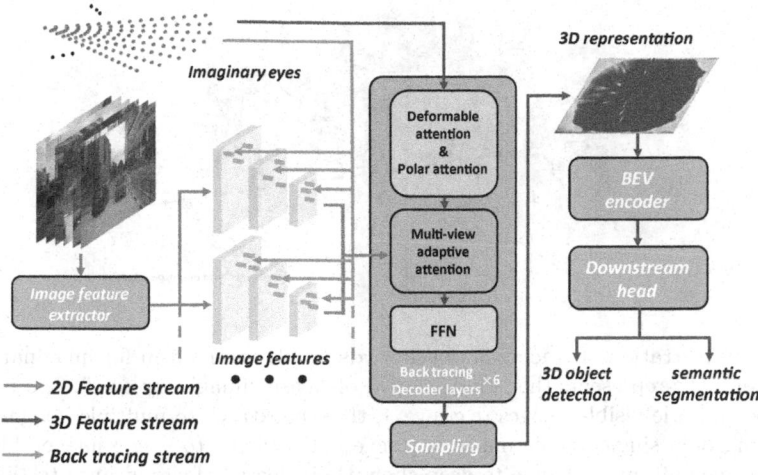

Fig. 3. Our pipeline comprises two stages: learning ego 3D representation from 2D features and executing multiple downstream tasks based on 3D representation. The gray lines represent the 2D feature stream while the blue lines represent the 3D feature stream. Besides, the orange lines specify our back tracing path. (Color figure online)

3.1 Ego3RT: Ego 3D Representation Learning

Ego3RT consists of two parts: image feature extractor and back tracing decoder. In addition, to illustrate back tracing decoder clearly, we will first introduce its components – imaginary eyes, tracing 3D backwards to 2D mechanism and multi-view multi-scale adaptive attention.

Image Feature Extractor. Given a set of images $\mathcal{I} = \{\mathbf{p}_1, \mathbf{p}_2, \cdots \mathbf{p}_{N_{\text{view}}}\}$ from multiple camera sensors (*i.e.*, multiple views), where each image $\mathbf{p}_t \in \mathbb{R}^{H \times W \times 3}$ with t the index of surrounding cameras (*e.g.*, $N_{\text{view}} = 6$ for nuScenes). These images are then encoded by a single shared ego-sensor feature extractor, including a CNN and a transformer encoder. ResNet [10] is used to extract image feature maps at N_{scale} spatial resolutions. To capture global context information, we further apply a transformer encode [41] at each resolution individually. As a result, we obtain the multi-view multi-scale self-attentive 2D representation $\{\mathbf{x}_l^{(t)}\}_{l=1}^{N_{\text{scale}}}$, where $\mathbf{x}_l^{(t)} \in \mathbb{R}^{H_l \times W_l \times C_l}$, $H_l = \frac{H}{4*2^l}$, $W_l = \frac{W}{4*2^l}$, $t \in [1, \cdots, N_{\text{view}}]$.

Imaginary Eyes. From this part, we will specify how Ego3RT learning 3D representation from 2D. To avoid exhaustive pixel-level prediction and inconsistent coordinate projection, we draw an analogue in the back tracing idea from ray tracing [33]. We start with introducing a polarized grid of dense "imaginary eyes" shown in Fig. 4, for BEV representation, with each eye naturally occupying a specific geometry location with built-in depth information. The grid of eyes are in size of $N_{\text{eyes}} = R \times S$, where R is the number of eyes on each polar ray, and

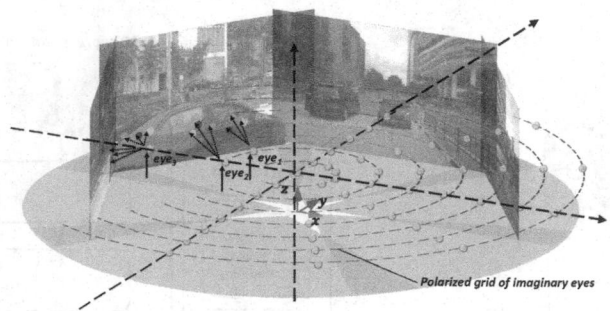

Fig. 4. An illustration of tracing 3D backwards to 2D mechanism for imaginary eyes. The golden balls represents the polarized grid of dense "imaginary eyes". Specially, for eyes have multiple visible images (e.g. eye_3), they backtrack to multiple images, while eyes having only single visible image (e.g. eye_1) backtrack to single image. The blue points on image from light blue to deep show their degree of significance to their eye, thus facilitating the adaptive attention. (Color figure online)

S is the number of these polar rays. To construct or, "render" our BEV representation, these imaginary eyes send rays *backwards* to 2D visual representation following the above 3D-2D projection routine (which will be described later). Since each eye only occupies a single, fixed geometry location, tracing back at its corresponding 2D position alone is less informative due to limited local observation. To solve this problem, we propose to encourage the eyes look around to focus adaptively on pivotal feature points across multiple scale per image and multiple camera views. This results in our multi-view multi-scale adaptive attention module (MVAA). And finally, the features of these imaginary eyes will be the final 3D representation.

Tracing 3D Backwards to 2D. To specify the tracing back mechanism, we first illustrate coordinate transformation between 3D and 2D. In typical cases, we usually have one LIDAR coordinate (3D), N_{view} camera coordinate (3D) and N_{view} image coordinate (2D). A 3D point $\mathbf{x}_{lidar}$ can be projected to image point $\mathbf{x}_{img}^{(t)}$ of tth camera by the projection matrix $\mathbf{M}^{(t)} = \mathbf{M}_{in}^{(t)}\mathbf{M}_{ex}^{(t)}$. Details of projection matrix will be illustrated in supplement. If the $\mathbf{x}_{img}$ is inside the image, we say that the image is visible to the corresponding $\mathbf{x}_{lidar}$. In our method, imaginary eyes are encouraged to "look" around their 2D projection point in each image coordinate. We denote the set of visible images of the qth eyes as $\mathcal{I}_q \subset \mathcal{I}$.

Multi-view Multi-scale Adaptive Attention (MVAA). MVAA is the core of transferring 2D representation into 3D. We formulate the learning of these imaginary eyes in an adaptive self-attention detection framework [41]. This is based on an idea of *regarding the eyes as object queries*, denoted as $\mathbf{y} \in \mathbb{R}^{C \times N_{eye}}$. Let $\mathbf{r} \in \mathbb{R}^{3 \times N_{eye}}$ be the location of eyes in ego car coordinate. Formally, each eye (*i.e.*, query) will dynamically choose N_{point} feature points at every scale of 2D image representation. This gives us a total of $N_{\text{scale}} \times |\mathcal{I}_q| \times N_{\text{point}}$ feature points. Our MVAA then chooses the most significant feature points from them and fuse them across multiple scales and views into the desired 3D representation. The process can be expressed as

$$
\text{MVAA}(\mathbf{y}_q, \mathbf{r}_q, \{\{\mathbf{x}_l^{(t)}\}_{l=1}^{N_{\text{scale}}}\}_{t=1}^{N_{\text{view}}})
$$

$$
= \underset{h \in \{N_h\}}{\text{concat}} \mathbf{W}_h \left[\sum_{l \in \{N_{\text{scale}}\}} \sum_{t \in \mathcal{I}_q} \sum_{k \in \{N_{\text{point}}\}} \mathbf{A}_{hltk} \cdot \mathbf{W}_h' \phi \left(x_l^{(t)}, \mathbf{M}^{(t)} \mathbf{r} + \Delta \mathbf{r}_{hvlk} \right) \right]
$$

$$
(1)
$$

Vector $\mathbf{y}_q$ is the qth query (eye), $\mathbf{r}_q$ is its position, N_h is the head number, $\mathbf{M}^{(t)}$ is the projection matrix. $\mathbf{A}$ and $\Delta \mathbf{r}$ are conditioned on $\mathbf{y}_q$ by learnable parameters:

$$
\mathbf{A} = \text{softmax}_{tk}(\mathbf{W}_q^{(\mathbf{A})} \mathbf{y}_q) \tag{2}
$$

with learnable parameter $\mathbf{W}_q^{(\mathbf{A})} \in \mathbb{R}^{N_h \times N_{\text{scale}} \times |\mathcal{I}_q| \times N_{\text{point}} \times C}$, and

$$
\Delta \mathbf{r} = \mathbf{W}_q^{(\mathbf{r})} \mathbf{y}_q + \mathbf{b}_q^{(\mathbf{r})} \tag{3}
$$

with learnable parameter $\mathbf{W}_q^{(\mathbf{r})} \in \mathbb{R}^{N_h \times N_{\text{scale}} \times |\mathcal{I}_q| \times N_{\text{point}} \times 2 \times C}$, and fixed parameter $\mathbf{b}_q^{(\mathbf{r})} \in \mathbb{R}^{N_h \times N_{\text{scale}} \times |\mathcal{I}_q| \times N_{\text{point}} \times 2}$. To avoid these N_{point} feature points collapse into one point, $\mathbf{b}_q^{(\mathbf{r})}$ is initialized with $|\mathbf{b}_q^{(\mathbf{r})}[\cdot, \cdot, \cdot, k]| = k$, so that the more N_{point}, the larger offset of these feature points can be achieved. Therefore, N_{point} can be utilized to control the receptive field. $\phi(x, r)$ represents access r^{th} feature points from x by index. For adaptively assigning the significance to $N_{\text{scale}} \times |\mathcal{I}_q| \times N_{\text{point}}$ points, the $\mathtt{Softmax}$ function is applied across all the attended feature points, scales, and views:

$$
\sum_{l \in \{N_{\text{scale}}\}} \sum_{t \in \mathcal{I}_q} \sum_{k \in \{N_{\text{point}}\}} \mathbf{A}_{hltk} = 1 \tag{4}
$$

Back Tracing Decoder. Technically, back tracing decoder takes randomly initialized features of imaginary eyes and scales of 2D feature provided by image feature extractor as input, and finally outputs the fine-grained features of imaginary eyes as 3D representation. Back tracing decoder is made up with a stack of attention layers adapted from the transformer decoder layers [17]. As shown in Fig. 3, each layer stacks two self-attention modules and one cross-attention module in order: deformable attention module [41], polar attention and MVAA. Compared to self-attention, deformable attention is more memory efficient. On the on 3D representation, we apply a standard self-attention on the eyes of same polar ray for polar attention. Also, the feed-forward network (FFN) block is equipped with a depth-wise convolution like [30]. As illustrated before, MVAA is responsible for back tracing 2D features into 3D representation.

Table 1. Comparison of different paradigms on the nuScenes val set. FCOS3D† is trained with 1x learning schedule, depth weight 0.2 and is finetuned on another FCOS3D checkpoint. PGD† is trained with 2x learning schedule, depth weight 0.2 on another PGD checkpoint. DETR3D† and Ego3RT† are initialized from the same pretrained FCOS3D checkpoint. Ego3RT‡ is initialized from the pretrained DD3D checkpoint.

Methods	mATE↓	mASE↓	mAOE↓	mAVE↓	mAAE↓	mAP↑	NDS↑
FCOS3D [29]	0.790	**0.261**	0.499	1.286	**0.167**	0.298	0.377
DETR3D [32]	0.860	0.278	**0.327**	**0.967**	0.235	0.303	0.374
PGD [28]	0.732	0.263	0.423	1.285	0.172	0.336	0.409
Ego3RT(Ours)	**0.714**	0.275	0.421	0.988	0.292	**0.355**	**0.409**
FCOS3D† [29]	0.754	**0.260**	0.486	1.331	**0.158**	0.321	0.395
DETR3D† [32]	0.765	0.267	0.392	0.876	0.211	0.347	0.422
PGD† [28]	0.667	0.264	0.435	1.276	0.177	0.358	0.425
Ego3RT(Ours)†	**0.657**	0.268	**0.391**	**0.850**	0.206	**0.375**	**0.450**
Ego3RT(Ours)‡	**0.582**	0.272	**0.316**	**0.683**	0.202	**0.478**	**0.534**

3.2 Downstream Task Head Design

BEV Sampling. Before the features of imaginary eyes being processed at downstream task, we first grid sample the polarized features into the rectangular ego car coordinate system to match with dataset annotation.

BEV Encoder. To encode the 3D representation for multiple tasks, we adopt the same BEV encoder module from OFT [24]. This kind of sub-network is also widely used in the LiDAR-based 3D detector [12,34].

Downstream Task Head. While the previously mentioned stage has generated a dense BEV features, we adopt the popular 3D detection head from Center-Point [36] for our detection task. For the BEV segmentation task, we choose a group of progressive up-sampling convolution-based semantic segmentation decoder heads. Details are shown in Supplement.

4 Experiments

4.1 Setup

Dataset. We evaluate the proposed model on the nuScenes [1] dataset, a large-scale autonomous driving dataset with 1000 driving scenes. Specifically, for multi-camera 3d object detection, it provides streams of images of 6 cameras covering all round from these 1000 scenes, which are then split into 700/150/150 scenes respectively for training, validation, and testing. nuScenes also provide informative annotations of the map. We choose 5 segmentation tasks: drivable area, pedestrian crossing, walkway, carpark, and divider.

Table 2. Comparisons to top-performing works on the nuScenes `test` set. ‡ represents that the method uses external data other than nuScenes 3D box annotations. DD3D‡ uses extra data for depth estimation. DETR3D‡ and Ego3RT‡ are initialized from the pre-trained DD3D checkpoint.

Methods	mATE↓	mASE↓	mAOE↓	mAVE↓	mAAE↓	mAP↑	NDS↑
MonoDIS	0.738	0.263	0.546	1.553	0.134	0.304	0.384
CenterNet [39]	0.658	0.255	0.629	1.629	0.142	0.338	0.400
FCOS3D [29]	0.690	0.249	0.452	1.434	**0.124**	0.358	0.428
PGD [28]	0.626	**0.245**	**0.451**	1.509	0.127	0.386	**0.448**
Ego3RT(Ours)	**0.599**	0.268	0.470	**1.169**	0.172	**0.389**	0.443
DD3D‡ [19]	0.572	**0.249**	**0.368**	1.014	**0.124**	0.418	0.477
DETR3D‡ [32]	0.641	0.255	0.394	**0.845**	0.133	0.412	**0.479**
Ego3RT(Ours)‡	**0.549**	0.264	0.433	1.014	0.145	**0.425**	0.473

Metrics. To evaluate performance, mean Average Precision (mAP) [8] and NuScenes Detection Score (NDS) [1] are reported. The segmentation task uses Intersection over Union(IoU) to assess the performance. As done by the LSS [20], we create a binary image for each element based on a specific threshold to evaluate with the ground truth image.

Implementation Details. Following FCOS3D [29] and DETR3D [32], ResNet-101 [10], with 3rd and 4th stages equipped with deformable convolutions is applied as our image backbone. The following deformable DETR encoder then utilizes multi-scale feature maps from the 2nd, 3rd, and 4th stages of the backbone. We use eyes of density 80×256 for Ego3RT and be sampled to rectangular 160×160 grids by BEV sampling. For the BEV encoder, we use 8 Bottleneck block [10] identical to OFT [24]. In the segmentation task, we set our ground-truth BEV segmentation map of 480×480 size with $0.2\,\mathrm{m/pixel}$ resolution. Therefore, 1 block of the upsampling module with the bilinear upsampling ratio of $3\times$ is adopted to mitigate lossing details of the screen. Additionally, loss functions are illustrated in supplement.

Training and Testing. Our models are trained 24 epoch with `AdamW` [14] of base learning rate 2.5×10^{-4} and weightdecay 0.01. Especially, the learning rate of the backbone is 1/10 of the global learning rate and the parameter of batch normalizations of backbone still participate in fine-tuning. To avoid over-fitting, we apply an early stop at 16 epoch. Since a total batch size of 48 across six cameras on eight NVIDIA A6000 GPUs is used, we apply synchronized implementation for every batch normalization. During the training process, we use the input image of 1500×900 resolution with only photometric distortion augmentation. Random flip, random rotation, and random scaling are applied to the 3D feature. Our 3D detection head is trained with class-balanced grouping

Table 3. Comparison of BEV semantic segmentation IoU on the nuScenes `val` set. Multi means wether generate a full surrounded BEV segmentation map from multi-view images. "-" represents the unprovided result. Single-task version Ego3RT uses EfficientNet-B0 [27] as the image backbone to align with OFT [24] and LSS [20]. Multi-task version Ego3RT¶ means we only train the segmentation head with the pretrained detection model frozen

Method	multi?	Drivable	Crossing	Walkway	Carpark	Divider
VED [15]	✗	54.7	12.0	20.7	13.5	–
VPN [18]	✗	58.0	27.3	29.4	12.3	–
PON [23]	✗	60.4	28.0	31.0	18.4	–
OFT [24]	✗	62.4	30.9	34.5	23.5	–
LSF [7]	✗	61.1	33.5	37.8	25.4	–
Image2Map [25]	✗	74.5	**36.6**	35.9	31.3	–
OFT [24]	✓	71.7	–	–	–	18.0
LSS [20]	✓	72.9	–	–	–	20.0
Ego3RT(Ours)	✓	**79.6**	**48.3**	**52.0**	**50.3**	**47.5**
Ego3RT(Ours) ¶	✓	**74.6**	33.0	**42.6**	**44.1**	**36.6**

method [40] (but no DS sampling) as default. After the detection head is well trained, we fix the parameters of Ego3RT and fine-tune our segmentation head for multi-task.

4.2   Comparison with State of the Art

3D Object Detection. We compare our model with previous state-of-the-art methods on both nuScenes validation set and test set. Following FCOS3D [29] and DETR3D [32], all our experiments are trained using ResNet-101 with deformable convolution as backbone for prototype verification. Models without special notification is initialized from a ResNet-101 checkpoint which pretrained on ImageNet [5]. We also present the result of our model on pre-trained checkpoints from FCOS3D [29] and DD3D [19]. In specific, the DD3D [19] fintunes on extra DDAD15M [9] dataset. **To be noted, the monocular-camera paradigms [28,29] and the multi-camera ones can be fairly compared.** They all take 6 cameras as input, but the monocular paradigms process these input images independently while the multi-view paradigms process these input images simultaneously.

Table 1 summarizes our multi-camera 3D object detection results on the nuScenes `validation` set. The upward arrow means the large the better while the downward one means the small the better. Our method leads in both `mAP` and `NDS`. Specially, it achieves the best in **transition error** (`mATE`), proving back tracing strategy's ability in localization reasoning. Just with simple attention, Ego3RT outperforms localization prediction than the well-designed PGD.

Table 4. Comparisons of detection performance in non-overlap region and overlap region. FCOS3D is trained with 1x learning schedule, depth weight 0.2 and is finetuned on another FCOS3D checkpoint. PGD is trained with 2x learning schedule, depth weight 0.2 and is finetuned on another PGD checkpoint. DETR3D and Ego3RTare initialized from a same pretrained FCOS3D checkpoint.

Methods	overlap?	mATE↓	mASE↓	mAOE↓	mAVE↓	mAAE↓	mAP↑	NDS↑
FCOS3D [29]	✗	0.747	**0.260**	0.487	1.351	**0.156**	0.320	0.395
PGD [28]	✗	0.658	0.263	0.425	1.290	0.178	0.357	0.426
DETR3D [32]	✗	0.769	0.267	**0.390**	0.893	0.215	0.343	0.419
Ego3RT(Ours)	✗	**0.655**	0.267	0.395	**0.854**	0.208	**0.371**	**0.448**
FCOS3D [29]	✓	0.816	0.272	0.571	1.084	**0.173**	0.229	0.329
PGD [28]	✓	0.768	0.274	0.495	1.090	0.186	0.255	0.354
DETR3D[32]	✓	0.807	0.273	0.453	**0.788**	0.184	0.268	0.384
Ego3RT(Ours)	✓	**0.671**	**0.268**	**0.347**	0.797	0.212	**0.298**	**0.420**

Table 5. Ablation on the effectiveness of adaptive attention mechanism

Adaptive?	mATE↓	mASE↓	mAOE↓	mAVE↓	mAAE↓	mAP↑	NDS↑
✗	0.688	0.272	0.403	**0.835**	0.217	0.365	0.441
✓	**0.657**	**0.268**	**0.391**	0.850	**0.206**	**0.375**	**0.450**

Table 2 shows our results on the nuScenes **test** set. The training sets are the same as the validation set. The least **transition error** (mATE) also reflects the overwhelming localization power of back tracing mechanism. We achieve the best mAP but the NDS is hindered by the attribute error. We have to say that the 2D representation has a manifest advantage on classification over 3D representation.

BEV Segmentation. Table 3 summarizes our BEV segmentation results on nuScenes **validation** set. We achieve the best performance in all tasks except the pedestrian crossing, but its overwhelming advantage in other tasks still proves its success. We also present single-task version using ImageNet pre-trained Efficient-B0 [27] as our image backbone to make a fair comparison with OFT [24] and LSS [20]. In terms of the single-task version, Ego3RT leads the board with huge superiority.

Table 6. Ablations on polarized grid of imaginary eyes

Polarized Grid?	Polar Attention?	mATE↓	mASE↓	mAOE↓	mAVE↓	mAAE↓	mAP↑	NDS↑
✗	✗	0.673	0.271	0.397	0.901	0.211	0.365	0.437
✓	✗	**0.656**	0.271	0.397	0.881	**0.206**	0.362	0.440
✓	✓	0.657	**0.268**	**0.391**	**0.850**	**0.206**	**0.375**	**0.450**

Table 7. (a) Results with different density of imaginary eyes. (b) Results with different height above the ground of imaginary eyes in meter

#Eyes	96 × 256	64 × 256	80 × 224	80 × 256
mAP ↑	0.372	0.366	0.372	**0.375**
NDS ↑	0.447	0.444	0.445	**0.450**

Height	0 m	0.4 m	0.8 m
mAP ↑	0.375	0.375	0.375
NDS ↑	0.445	0.437	**0.450**

4.3 Qualitative Results

We present our visualization in Fig. 5. The structural similarity to the ground-truth highlights the superiority of our Ego3RT, which simultaneously generates dynamic object detection and static semantic segmentation results from the 3D representation. In specific, we project all bounding boxes of class *vehicle* in nuScenes from the detection head onto the generated BEV segmentation map for a clear comparison. As can be seen from the perspective of images, our detection results demonstrate appealing localization ability even in distance situations. More qualitative results are shown in supplement.

4.4 Ablation Studies

In this section, we will figure out how the performance is established and prove the effectiveness of our innovation. Additional studies are shown in the supplement.

Back Tracing Mechanism. Here, we prove that the back tracing mechanism posses superiority in localization. To eliminate interference of multi-view mechanism, in the top part of Table 4, hence, we validate the 3D detection result only at the non-overlap region where only a monocular camera is used. We show advantage in overall mAP, NDS metrics at monocular region. Specially, the lowest transition error mATE proves the best localization reasoning of Ego3RT .

Multi-view Mechanism. We will prove the superiority of the multi-view mechanism over the former monocular ones. In the bottom part of Table 4, we validate the 3D detection result at region where only multiple cameras are used. We find that multi-view methods DETR3D and our Ego3RT outperform mono-view methods FCOS3D [29] and PGD [28] remarkably in all metrics. Additionally, Ego3RT achieves overwhelming performance over the other methods in both mAP and NDS.

Adaptive Attention Mechanism. We state in the method section that the adaptive attention mechanism can approximate missing height information. All the other conditions remaining the same, we switch off the adaptive attention module by fixing learnable parameter $\mathbf{W}_q^{(r)}\mathbf{y}_q$ in Eq. (3) to prove its effectiveness. The results shown in Table 5 prove our statement.

Table 8. Comparison of the efficiency and the performance of different configurations of Ego3RT and the other methods. "FPS" is a metric for efficiency standing for frames per second. "Resolution" represents input image shape. "FFN" represents the channel expansion dimension of FFN in Back tracing decoder. "Blocks" notes the number of blocks in BEV encoder. "$\star$" means we test the speed at 1600×900

Methods	Resolution	Eyes density	FFN	#Blocks	FPS↑	mAP↑	NDS↑
FCOS3D [29]	1600×900	–	–	–	2.0	0.321	0.395
PGD [28]	1600×900	–	–	–	1.5	0.358	0.425
DETR3D [32]	1600×900	–	–	–	**3.0**	0.347	0.422
Ego3RT(Ours)	$1600 \times 900^{\star}$	80×256	1024	8	1.7	**0.375**	**0.450**
Ego3RT(Ours)	1280×768	72×192	1024	8	2.3	0.372	0.438
Ego3RT(Ours)	1280×768	64×128	256	2	**3.0**	0.355	0.423

Polarized Grid of Imaginary Eyes. We apply a polarized grid of "imaginary eyes" rather than a rectangular grid. Here, we compare these two settings in Table 6. The first line and the second line compare the grid type of eyes without polar attention. Although the polarized grid doesn't show manifest superiority over the rectangular grid, the polarized grid achieves a remarkable advantage in localization prediction (mATE). Finally, with the help of polar attention on the eyes of each polar ray, the model achieves the best.

Imaginary Eyes. Table 7 studies density and height of imaginary eyes. Lower density will lead to coarser feature maps while the higher density imposes a burden on optimization, so a balance should be achieved. Table 7(a) shows that our final choice 80×256 is the optimal choice. Table 7(b) shows that no significant difference exists among the different choices of height.

Efficiency of Ego3RT. In Table 8, our Ego3RT (of main configuration) achieves the best mAP and 3rd FPS, and Ego3RT with smaller input image size and imaginary eyes density barely looses its performance while achieves a better efficiency. When Ego3RT further reduces its eyes density, FFN channel expansion dimension and BEV encoder blocks, it reaches the best trade-off between accuracy and efficiency.

Fig. 5. Qualitative results on nuScenes dataset. *Left* is the BEV segmentation map with projected *vehicle* 3D bounding boxes result from detection head. *Right* are in image perspective with prediction results. Different colors stand for different categories. (Color figure online)

5   Conclusion

In this work, we have presented Ego3RT, a novel end-to-end architecture for ego 3D representation learning given multiple unconstrained camera views. In the absence of depth or 3D supervision, it can learn rich and semantic 3D representation with multi-view images efficiently in the ego car coordinate frame. This is realized by drawing an analog from the ray tracing concept, where we create a polarized grid of learnable "imaginary eyes" as the ego 3D representation and formulate the learning with the adaptive attention mechanism subject to the 3D-to-2D projection. It is easy to implement and able to support multiple different tasks. Extensive experiments validate the superiority of our Ego3RT in comparison to state-of-the-art alternatives in terms of both accuracy and versatility.

Acknowledgments. This work was supported in part by National Natural Science Foundation of China (Grant No. 6210020439), Lingang Laboratory (Grant No. LG-QS-202202–07), Natural Science Foundation of Shanghai (Grant No. 22ZR1407500).

References

1. Caesar, H., et al.: nuScenes: a multimodal dataset for autonomous driving. In: CVPR (2020)
2. Carion, N., Massa, F., Synnaeve, G., Usunier, N., Kirillov, A., Zagoruyko, S.: End-to-end object detection with transformers. In: Vedaldi, A., Bischof, H., Brox, T., Frahm, J.-M. (eds.) ECCV 2020. LNCS, vol. 12346, pp. 213–229. Springer, Cham (2020). https://doi.org/10.1007/978-3-030-58452-8_13

3. Chen, L.C., Papandreou, G., Schroff, F., Adam, H.: Rethinking atrous convolution for semantic image segmentation. arXiv preprint (2017)
4. Chitta, K., Prakash, A., Geiger, A.: Neat: neural attention fields for end-to-end autonomous driving. In: ICCV (2021)
5. Deng, J., Dong, W., Socher, R., Li, L.J., Li, K., Fei-Fei, L.: ImageNet: a large-scale hierarchical image database. In: CVPR (2009)
6. Dosovitskiy, A., et al.: An image is worth 16x16 words: transformers for image recognition at scale. In: ICLR (2021)
7. Dwivedi, I., Malla, S., Chen, Y.T., Dariush, B.: Bird's eye view segmentation using lifted 2d semantic features. In: BMVC (2021)
8. Everingham, M., Van Gool, L., Williams, C.K., Winn, J., Zisserman, A.: The pascal visual object classes (voc) challenge. In: IJCV (2010)
9. Guizilini, V., Ambrus, R., Pillai, S., Raventos, A., Gaidon, A.: 3d packing for self-supervised monocular depth estimation. In: CVPR (2020)
10. He, K., Zhang, X., Ren, S., Sun, J.: Deep residual learning for image recognition. In: CVPR (2016)
11. Hu, A., et al.: Fiery: future instance prediction in bird's-eye view from surround monocular cameras. In: CVPR (2021)
12. Lang, A.H., Vora, S., Caesar, H., Zhou, L., Yang, J., Beijbom, O.: Pointpillars: fast encoders for object detection from point clouds. In: CVPR (2019)
13. Long, J., Shelhamer, E., Darrell, T.: Fully convolutional networks for semantic segmentation. In: CVPR (2015)
14. Loshchilov, I., Hutter, F.: Decoupled weight decay regularization. In: ICLR (2019)
15. Lu, C., van de Molengraft, M.J.G., Dubbelman, G.: Monocular semantic occupancy grid mapping with convolutional variational encoder-decoder networks. IEEE Robot. Autom. Lett. 4(2), 445–452 (2019)
16. Ma, X., Wang, Z., Li, H., Zhang, P., Ouyang, W., Fan, X.: Accurate monocular 3D object detection via color-embedded 3D reconstruction for autonomous driving. In: ICCV (2019)
17. Misra, I., Girdhar, R., Joulin, A.: An end-to-end transformer model for 3D object detection. In: ICCV (2021)
18. Pan, B., Sun, J., Leung, H.Y.T., Andonian, A., Zhou, B.: Cross-view semantic segmentation for sensing surroundings. IEEE Robotics and Automation Letters (2020)
19. Park, D., Ambrus, R., Guizilini, V., Li, J., Gaidon, A.: Is pseudo-lidar needed for monocular 3D object detection? In: ICCV (2021)
20. Philion, J., Fidler, S.: Lift, splat, shoot: encoding images from arbitrary camera rigs by implicitly unprojecting to 3D. In: Vedaldi, A., Bischof, H., Brox, T., Frahm, J.-M. (eds.) ECCV 2020. LNCS, vol. 12359, pp. 194–210. Springer, Cham (2020). https://doi.org/10.1007/978-3-030-58568-6_12
21. Reading, C., Harakeh, A., Chae, J., Waslander, S.L.: Categorical depth distribution network for monocular 3D object detection. In: CVPR (2021)
22. Ren, S., He, K., Girshick, R., Sun, J.: Faster R-CNN: towards real-time object detection with region proposal networks. In: NeurIPS (2015)
23. Roddick, T., Cipolla, R.: Predicting semantic map representations from images using pyramid occupancy networks. In: CVPR (2020)
24. Roddick, T., Kendall, A., Cipolla, R.: Orthographic feature transform for monocular 3D object detection. In: BMVC (2019)
25. Saha, A., Maldonado, O.M., Russell, C., Bowden, R.: Translating images into maps. arXiv preprint arXiv:2110.00966 (2021)

26. Simonyan, K., Zisserman, A.: Very deep convolutional networks for large-scale image recognition. In: ICLR (2015)
27. Tan, M., Le, Q.: EfficientNet: rethinking model scaling for convolutional neural networks. In: ICML (2019)
28. Wang, T., Xinge, Z., Pang, J., Lin, D.: Probabilistic and geometric depth: detecting objects in perspective. In: Conference on Robot Learning (2022)
29. Wang, T., Zhu, X., Pang, J., Lin, D.: Fcos3D: fully convolutional one-stage monocular 3D object detection. In: CVPR (2021)
30. Wang, W., Xie, E., Li, X., Fan, D.P., Song, K., Liang, D., Lu, T., Luo, P., Shao, L.: PVT v2: improved baselines with pyramid vision transformer. In: Computational Visual Media, pp. 415–424 (2022)
31. Wang, Y., Chao, W.L., Garg, D., Hariharan, B., Campbell, M., Weinberger, K.Q.: Pseudo-lidar from visual depth estimation: bridging the gap in 3D object detection for autonomous driving. In: CVPR (2019)
32. Wang, Y., Guizilini, V.C., Zhang, T., Wang, Y., Zhao, H., Solomon, J.: Detr3D: 3D object detection from multi-view images via 3D-to-2D queries. In: Conference on Robot Learning (2022)
33. Whitted, T.: An improved illumination model for shaded display. In: ACM Siggraph 2005 Courses (2005)
34. Yan, Y., Mao, Y., Li, B.: Second: sparsely embedded convolutional detection. Sensors (2018)
35. Yang, W., Li, Q., Liu, W., Yu, Y., Ma, Y., He, S., Pan, J.: Projecting your view attentively: Monocular road scene layout estimation via cross-view transformation. In: CVPR (2021)
36. Yin, T., Zhou, X., Krahenbuhl, P.: Center-based 3D object detection and tracking. In: CVPR (2021)
37. You, Y., et al.: Pseudo-LiDAR++: accurate depth for 3D object detection in autonomous driving. In: ICLR (2019)
38. Zheng, S., et al.: Rethinking semantic segmentation from a sequence-to-sequence perspective with transformers. In: CVPR (2021)
39. Zhou, X., Wang, D., Krähenbühl, P.: Objects as points. arXiv preprint arXiv:1904.07850 (2019)
40. Zhu, B., Jiang, Z., Zhou, X., Li, Z., Yu, G.: Class-balanced grouping and sampling for point cloud 3D object detection. arXiv preprint (2019)
41. Zhu, X., Su, W., Lu, L., Li, B., Wang, X., Dai, J.: Deformable DETR: deformable transformers for end-to-end object detection. In: ICLR (2021)

Static and Dynamic Concepts
for Self-supervised Video Representation
Learning

Rui Qian[1], Shuangrui Ding[2], Xian Liu[1], and Dahua Lin[1,3](✉)

[1] The Chinese University of Hong Kong, Hong Kong, China
{qr021,lx021}@ie.cuhk.edu.hk
[2] Shanghai Jiao Tong University, Shanghai, China
dsr1212@sjtu.edu.cn
[3] Shanghai Artificial Intelligence Laboratory, Shanghai, China
dhlin@ie.cuhk.edu.hk

Abstract. In this paper, we propose a novel learning scheme for self-supervised video representation learning. Motivated by how humans understand videos, we propose to first learn general visual concepts then attend to discriminative local areas for video understanding. Specifically, we utilize static frame and frame difference to help decouple static and dynamic concepts, and respectively align the concept distributions in latent space. We add diversity and fidelity regularizations to guarantee that we learn a compact set of meaningful concepts. Then we employ a cross-attention mechanism to aggregate detailed local features of different concepts, and filter out redundant concepts with low activations to perform local concept contrast. Extensive experiments demonstrate that our method distills meaningful static and dynamic concepts to guide video understanding, and obtains state-of-the-art results on UCF-101, HMDB-51, and Diving-48.

Keywords: Video representation · Visual concepts · Local contrast

1 Introduction

Self-supervised representation learning has been an exciting problem in computer vision, which aims to encode robust representations that can be transferred to various downstream tasks without human labeling. A prevalent strategy is to design pretext tasks and acquire pseudo labels as self-supervision [7,24] or employ contrastive learning to discriminate instances [8,12,29]. However, this learning scheme is inconsistent with how humans learn from the world. To be specific, instead of solely learning from labels or contrasting global features, humans

---

Supplementary Information The online version contains supplementary material available at https://doi.org/10.1007/978-3-031-19809-0_9.

can typically conclude some general basic concepts from detailed observations, then make predictions based on these concepts [6,38,62]. For example, we identify an airplane through its wings and rudder; and recognize the action of playing soccer through the ball as well as running and kicking movement as in Fig 1. To this end, it would be promising to automatically formulate transferable concepts to guide detailed local feature perception and improve the representations.

There have been some works exploring learning interpretable visual concepts for particular tasks [6,13,38,78]. But in unsupervised video representation learning, how to formulate meaningful visual concepts and efficiently leverage local cues remains unsolved. The difficulty lies in two aspects: Videos contain more redundancy on temporal dimension. Besides, we lack fine-grained supervision on the potential visual concepts. Most of the recent state-of-the-art works on video representation learning inherit contrastive learning framework [22,28,58], which projects the global pooled feature vectors into a latent space and performs instance discrimination. Compared with the aforementioned human perception, this formulation explicitly contrasts high-level global feature vectors but has difficulty dealing with detailed local features. Some works propose region-based local feature contrast but could result in high redundancy [73,83]. In order to effectively utilize the detailed local features, we propose a novel learning strategy for self-supervised video representation learning. We aggregate local features that present similar concepts, and then perform the concept-level alignment.

(a) Soccer Juggling

(b) Basketball

Fig. 1. Visualization of visual concept attention maps. Each column corresponds to the same concept, the former two columns describe static concepts and the latter three present dynamic concepts. The same visual concept highlights similar visual patterns, e.g., spherical objects, grass land, foot movement, leg movement, arm movement

Concretely, we propose to form a latent space consisting of the learned visual concepts, and leverage the latent concept distributions as self-supervision to jointly optimize feature representations and concept descriptions. However, since the feature attributes are highly entangled in the high-level representation, it is nontrivial to directly obtain general concepts without annotations. To solve this, we divide the learning concepts into two general divisions, i.e., static scenes and dynamic motions. Those two concepts are proved to be complementary but orthogonal for video representation learning [32]. Static scenes focus on background cues while dynamic motions lay more emphasis on object's movement. In practice, we use the simple static frame and frame difference to naturally decouple these two aspects and ameliorate the entanglement of high-level feature. Further, we define the projection head as a cosine classifier to generate concept latent codes, with each class corresponding to a potential static or dynamic local concept. We respectively align the static (dynamic) concept latent codes between original video and static frame (frame difference), and encourage sparsity in the latent space to guarantee diversity of learned concepts. Besides, to make the projection head preserve necessarily relevant information and reduce redundancy, we regard the latent codes as information bottleneck, where they are expected to reconstruct the initial feature vectors. Thus, we apply a light-weight MLP to achieve the fidelity regularization. By doing so, we establish a concept-based latent space consisting of general static and dynamic visual concepts.

With these learned concept prototypes, we attend to local concepts in each spatio-temporal area to improve the detailed local feature modeling. Specifically, we use cross-attention to aggregate local features, then output a set of features belonging to different concepts like Fig. 1. By referring to the concept latent code, we select a series of visual concepts with high activations as valid ones and filter out the redundant feature pairs. Contrastive loss is applied to these valid pairs for fine-grained alignment. In this way, we seamlessly integrate general concept learning with detailed local feature perception to enhance video representations.

To sum up, our contributions are: (1) We propose a novel self-supervised video representation learning scheme, where we formulate general concepts to guide concept-level detailed local feature alignment. (2) We employ cross-attention to aggregate detailed features of different concepts, and filter out redundant local features by concept latent codes. In this way, we achieve efficient local concept contrast. (3) We achieve state-of-the-art results on downstream action recognition and video retrieval across UCF-101, HMDB-51 and Diving-48 datasets.

2   Related Work

Self-supervised Learning. Self-supervised learning aims to make full use of large-scale unlabelled data without resorting to human annotations. Some works design pretext tasks, e.g., image rotation [24], colorization [37], clustering [7,60], to obtain pseudo labels and guide representation learning. Another line of works introduce contrastive learning to build robust feature representations [20,52,75]. They employ noise contrastive estimation [25] to compare feature representations and discriminate different instances [12,29,65]. Technically, these methods rely on nonlinear projection head to project the extracted features into a latent space for contrastive loss computation to reduce information loss. However, without explicit constraint on the projection head, what information is preserved and contrasted in the latent space is unclear, and the learning process is of low interpretability. More recently, [21] employs whitening to analyze the latent feature space. [8] assigns features to prototype vectors and contrasts cluster assignments in the latent space. In contrast, in this work, we enforce the projection heads to learn potential visual concepts and formulate an interpretable latent space, where we contrast the concept distributions to guide general representation learning.

Video Representation Learning. Representation learning in video domain requires the model to capture crucial spatio-temporal relationships in video sequences. Early works employ the temporal transformation [5,11,35,51,79–81], spatio-temporal jigsaw [36,69], temporal cycle-consistency [33,42,72], future prediction [4,49] as pretext tasks. Later, [22,30,44–46,55,58,70] expand contrastive learning framework to video and audio-video domain. Further, [17,18,31,34,39] utilize the internal temporal structure to generate richer positive samples. [2,28,41,50,54] contrast temporally aligned multi-modal inputs to learn complementary information. These works explicitly contrast the global representations of video clips, but pay little attention to detailed local features. To this end, [26,27] propose to predict dense feature maps in future timestamps. [3,15,56,59] contrast short and long clips on each timestamp to attend to fine-grained temporal features, but still fail to utilize detailed spatial cues. [10,83] rely on bounding boxes or segmentation masks to align semantically related local areas. While in our work, we use simple static frame and frame difference to distill static and dynamic visual concepts, based on which we aggregate relevant information from each spatio-temporal area to enhance detailed content modeling.

Concept Learning. Recently, there have emerged a line of works that learn human-specified visual concepts to solve downstream visual tasks [6,13,16,38,47]. They design concept bottlenecks models to first predict concepts then use these concepts to make final predictions. Comparing to end-to-end deep models, concept bottleneck models are more interpretable but require extra concept annotations. To tackle this problem, [1,61] develop various regularizations to constrain the concept bottleneck and obtain potential concepts. [78] points out that one-hot category labels are not optimal concept descriptions, and devises an exploration-experience loss to alternatively update feature representation and concept description. To our best knowledge, we are the first to integrate concept learning into self-supervised video representation learning. We utilize static and dynamic visual concepts to learn both general and detailed video representations.

3   Method

Our framework is shown in Fig. 2. For simplicity, we show detailed procedures for video clip v, while static frame s and d are processed similarly. Specifically, we first propose decoupled concept alignment (Sect. 3.1) with regularizations (Sect. 3.2) to jointly optimize the extracted features and concept descriptions. Then referring to learned concepts, we employ cross-attention to aggregate detailed local features of different concepts, filter out redundant concepts with low activations and perform concept-level alignment (Sect. 3.3).

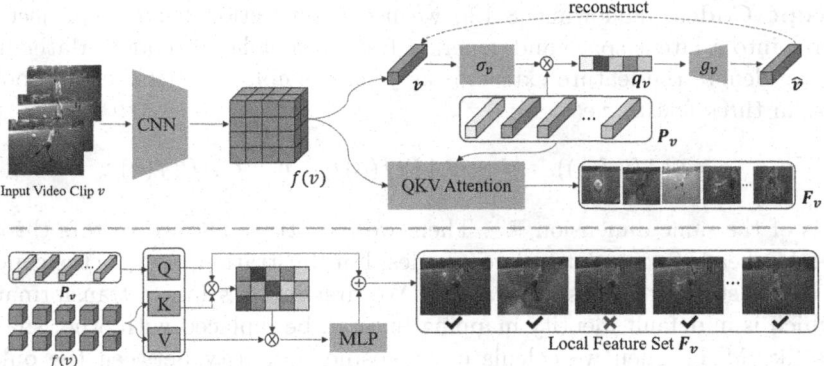

Fig. 2. Overview of the framework. We take the original input video clip v for illustration. In the upper branch, we calculate cosine similarity between concept prototypes $\boldsymbol{P}_v$ and transformed video feature $\sigma_v(\boldsymbol{v})$ as concept latent code $\boldsymbol{q}_v$, which is then passed through simple MLP to reconstruct the original feature vector. In the lower branch, we use QKV attention with residue to aggregate local features of different concepts and refer to $\boldsymbol{q}_v$ to avoid redundant local concept contrast

3.1 Decoupled Concept Learning

Videos typically possess two complementary concepts, static concepts that indicate background scene attributes, and dynamic concepts that reveal human or object movements. Given a video sequence v, since various visual concepts are highly entangled, it is nontrivial to directly learn meaningful visual concepts without resorting to human annotations. But it is practical to decouple the static and dynamic information in the input stage, i.e., we randomly select a static frame s and calculate frame difference d to respectively carry static and dynamic attributes. Then, an intuitive idea is to learn potential static concepts from v and s, extract dynamic concepts from v and d, and respectively perform static and dynamic concept alignment.

Concept Prototypes. To formulate the latent concept space, we propose to learn several prototypes, each corresponding to a static or dynamic concept. Specifically, we define three sets of prototypes respectively for s, d, v as:

$$\boldsymbol{P}_s \in \mathbb{R}^{K_s \times C}, \quad \boldsymbol{P}_d \in \mathbb{R}^{K_d \times C}, \quad \boldsymbol{P}_v \in \mathbb{R}^{(K_s + K_d) \times C}, \tag{1}$$

where C denotes channel dimension, K_s is the number of static concepts, K_d is the number of dynamic concepts. We use these concept prototypes to generate latent concept activation codes and retrieve relevant local features in later stage.

Concept Codes. Following [8,12], we use a projection head to project the features into a latent space and generate the concept latent codes. Mathematically, we denote the feature extractor as f, and employ global average pooling to obtain three feature vectors[1]:

$$s = GAP(f(s)), \quad d = GAP(f(d)), \quad v = GAP(f(v)), \quad (2)$$

each is of the same dimension $\mathbb{R}^C$. Then, we pass these feature vectors through projection heads to calculate concept codes. For illustration, we take the concept code q_s for static frame as an example. We first input s into a transformation σ_s, which is in default identity mapping but can be replaced with other shallow layers like MLP. Then we calculate the cosine similarity between the output vector and each prototype to form q_s:

$$q_s^{(k)} = \frac{P_s^{(k)}\sigma_s(s)^T}{||P_s^{(k)}||_2||\sigma_s(s)||_2}, \quad q_s \in \mathbb{R}^{K_s}, \quad (3)$$

where the superscript (k) indicates k-th channel. Similarly, we obtain concept codes $q_d \in \mathbb{R}^{K_d}$ and $q_v \in \mathbb{R}^{K_s+K_d}$ in the same manner.

Concept Alignment. Since the video and static frame share the same static attributes, while video and frame difference have the same dynamic attributes, we propose to respectively align the static and dynamic concepts through Eq. 4.

$$\mathcal{L}_{aln} = -\sum_{k=1}^{K_s}\left(\overline{q_s}^{(k)}\log\frac{\exp(q_v^{s\,(k)}/\tau)}{\sum_{k'}\exp(q_v^{s\,(k')}/\tau)} + \overline{q_v^s}^{(k)}\log\frac{\exp(q_s^{(k)}/\tau)}{\sum_{k'}\exp(q_s^{(k')}/\tau)}\right)$$
$$-\sum_{k=1}^{K_d}\left(\overline{q_d}^{(k)}\log\frac{\exp(q_v^{d\,(k)}/\tau)}{\sum_{k'}\exp(q_v^{d\,(k')}/\tau)} + \overline{q_v^d}^{(k)}\log\frac{\exp(q_d^{(k)}/\tau)}{\sum_{k'}\exp(q_d^{(k')}/\tau)}\right),$$

$$(4)$$

For simplicity, we divide q_v into two parts, the former K_s channels as q_v^s indicating static concepts, and the latter K_d channels as q_v^d for dynamic concepts. Similar to SWAV [8], we assume the concepts follow a uniform distribution over the whole dataset, and use Sinkhorn-Knopp algorithm [14] to generate the soft code $\overline{q}$. Then we calculate the cross-entropy between $\overline{q}$ and the latent concept distribution by taking softmax with temperature τ on q. By minimizing $\mathcal{L}_{aln}$, we respectively align static and dynamic concept distributions, and jointly optimize feature representations and concept descriptions from large-scale video data.

---

[1] For simplicity, we use the same symbol to denote the backbone for s, d, v.

3.2   Concept Bottleneck Constraint

However, the decoupled concept alignment objective alone cannot guarantee that each of the learned prototype corresponds to a meaningful concept. Motivated by [1], the general concepts should possess fidelity and diversity. That is, the concepts should preserve much relevant information from the inputs, and the inputs can be described by a few concepts. To this end, we devise two constraints on the concept latent codes as follows.

The first constraint is the sparsity regularization term as Eq. 5 to enforce diversity of learned concepts. We employ $\mathcal{L}_1$ norm regularization to encourage sparsity of concept latent codes, so that each input activates only a few concepts.

$$\mathcal{L}_{div} = \|q_s\|_1 + \|q_d\|_1 + \|q_v\|_1 . \tag{5}$$

The second constraint is a reconstruction loss as Eq. 6 to ensure fidelity and reduce redundancy. We borrow the idea from autoencoder to reconstruct the feature vectors. Since the channel dimension of concept code is smaller than the feature vector, we regard q as information bottleneck and pass them through two-layer MLP g for reconstruction. We use $\mathcal{L}_2$ loss for optimization, and stop gradient on the original features. In this way, the concept prototypes cover a wide range of important information with low redundancy.

$$\mathcal{L}_{fid} = \|g_s(q_s) - s\|_2^2 + \|g_d(q_d) - d\|_2^2 + \|g_v(q_v) - v\|_2^2 . \tag{6}$$

Relation to SWAV. Our concept code formulation is similar to SWAV [8], both using cosine similarity between feature vectors and prototypes. But the motivations and technical designs are different. In terms of the motivation, SWAV is essentially over-clustering and the prototypes are cluster centroids, the number of which is set as 3,000 in default, much greater than semantic categories. While in our method, the prototypes project the feature vectors into the low dimensional space, which interprets the concept activations instead of the instance discrimination. Through regularizations and activation alignment, our prototypes are an ordered set of interpretable concepts each presenting a visual attribute. In terms of technical design, our method only conducts spatio-temporal cropping due to multiple modalities while SWAV requires stronger augmentation to make the pretraining task harder and improve the representation quality.

3.3   Local Concept Contrast

The global concept code alignment serves as an effective supervision to learn spatio-temporal characters in videos, but does not make use of detailed local features which are crucial for video understanding. Some existing works in image domain first match corresponding local areas then make contrast [73,77], but they have difficulty expanding to videos because of the redundancy on time dimension. [83] employs bounding boxes for region-based contrast between video clips, but requires prior to filter redundant background areas. In order to better utilize the detailed local contents, we need to generate a compact set of local features with low redundancy. Therefore, we propose to leverage the learned prototypes to retrieve detailed local features that are relevant to particular concepts, and output an ordered set of local features for effective contrast.

Local Feature Attention. Motivated by the success of attention mechanism in local feature aggregation [19,23,67,71], we employ widely used cross-attention mechanism to retrieve detailed local features that are relevant to specific visual concepts. As illustrated in Fig. 2, we linearly project the concept prototypes as query tokens, and project the feature maps to formulate key and value tokens. Then QKV attention with residue is applied to aggregate local features related to the query. We still use the local features on static frame as an example:

$$F_s = QKV(P_s, f(s), f(s)), \quad F_s \in \mathbb{R}^{K_s \times C}. \tag{7}$$

We obtain $F_d \in \mathbb{R}^{K_d \times C}$ and $F_v \in \mathbb{R}^{(K_s+K_d) \times C}$ in the same manner. Similar to the separation on q_v, we also divide F_v into $F_v^s \in \mathbb{R}^{K_s \times C}$ and $F_v^d \in \mathbb{R}^{K_d \times C}$.

Since each prototype corresponds to a potential static or dynamic concept, each generated attention map highlights local areas that contain particular concepts as shown in Fig. 1, where each column belongs to the same concept. Therefore, it is intuitive to apply contrastive loss on the aggregated features of the matching concepts to further enhance detailed local representations.

Local Feature Contrast. Recall that each input is representable with a few concepts, we need to first filter out a set of valid concepts that exist in the input sample. To do this, we resort to the previously obtained concept latent codes q, which figure out which concepts are activated in each training sample. Mathematically, we take local features of static concepts for illustration. Given concept latent codes q_s, q_v^s and local features F_s, F_v^s, we select top-K indexes of each latent code and take the intersection as the valid static concept indexes:

$$idx_s = \text{top-k}(q_s, K) \cap \text{top-k}(q_v^s, K). \tag{8}$$

The valid local feature pairs are denoted as $\{(F_s^{(k)}, F_v^{s\,(k)}) | k \in idx_s\}$, with the superscript (k) indicating local feature of k-th concept.

These local features of the same static (dynamic) concept from the same video are expected to represent exactly the same appearances (movements), thus should be aligned. To this end, we apply contrastive margin loss in Eq. 9 to contrast the local features of valid concept indexes. To be specific, we employ the valid local feature pair from the same video as positive samples, and use local features of corresponding concept from other videos in the mini-batch to form negative samples. We minimize the $\mathcal{L}_2$ distance between positive feature pairs, and push the distance between negative pairs to a large margin:

$$l(\boldsymbol{F_s}, \boldsymbol{F_v^s}) = \sum_{k \in idx_s} \left[\left\| \boldsymbol{F_s}^{(k)} - \boldsymbol{F_v^s}^{(k)} \right\|_2^2 + \sum_{\tilde{F} \in \mathcal{N}} \max \left(\lambda - \left\| \boldsymbol{F_s}^{(k)} - \boldsymbol{\tilde{F}_v^s}^{(k)} \right\|_2, 0 \right)^2 \right], \qquad (9)$$

where λ is the margin hyper-parameter, and $\mathcal{N}$ is the set of negative samples in the mini-batch. We use similar techniques to process local features of dynamic concepts, and the final local concept contrast learning objective is formulated as

$$\mathcal{L}_{loc} = l(\boldsymbol{F_s}, \boldsymbol{F_v^s}) + l(\boldsymbol{F_v^s}, \boldsymbol{F_s}) + l(\boldsymbol{F_d}, \boldsymbol{F_v^d}) + l(\boldsymbol{F_v^d}, \boldsymbol{F_d}). \qquad (10)$$

By minimizing $\mathcal{L}_{loc}$, we build a concept-level self-supervision to make use of detailed local features and improve video representations. Comparing to previous methods using similar techniques to contrast local features [74,83], our method does not rely on prior or complex post-processing to filter out redundant feature pairs. The integration of general concept learning and detailed local feature contrast leads to higher learning efficiency and more comprehensive representations.

Overall Learning Objective. The overall training objective can be written as

$$\mathcal{L} = \mathcal{L}_{aln} + \alpha \mathcal{L}_{loc} + \beta \mathcal{L}_{fid} + \gamma \mathcal{L}_{div}, \qquad (11)$$

where the balancing hyper-parameters are respectively set to $\alpha = \beta = 1, \gamma = 0.01$ in default. Since the formulation of $\mathcal{L}_{loc}$ relies on the concept codes to filter out valid pairs, in the first few epochs (5 epochs in default), we do not include $\mathcal{L}_{loc}$ to prevent random selection and stabilize training.

4 Experiment

4.1 Dataset

We use 4 popular video datasets, Kinetics-400 [9], UCF-101 [63], HMDB-51 [40] and Diving-48 [43]. **Kinetics-400** [9] is a widely used benchmark for self-supervised video representation learning, with 240K video clips covering 400 human action classes. **UCF-101** [63] covers 101 action categories and more than 13K annotated clips. **HMDB-51** [40] contains around 7k clips covering 51 action classes. **Diving-48** [43] contains 48 different diving actions. Different action classes in Diving-48 mainly vary in motion patterns and the backgrounds are quite similar.

4.2   Implementation Details

We choose R(2+1)D-18 [66] with 14.4M parameters, and S3D [76] as the video encoder. We empirically find that using separate networks or sharing the same network to extract RGB/static frame/frame difference features leads to similar performance. But using shared backbone results in higher learning efficiency, so we use the same backbone for all in default. Given a video clip, we randomly select a frame and repeat 16 times on the temporal axis to construct static frame input, and use the difference between adjacent frames to form the frame difference input. The resolution of each input sequence is $16 \times 112 \times 112$ if not specially motioned. We pretrain the model for 200 epochs on UCF-101 or 100 epochs on Kinetics-400. We adopt SGD optimizer with the initial learning rate of 10^{-2} and weight decay of 10^{-4}. We set the number of static or dynamic concepts to $K_s = K_d = 50$, and the ratio of valid local concepts to 10%, $K = 5$ in default.

4.3   Evaluation on Downstream Tasks

Action Recognition. We first present action recognition in Table 1. We report *linear probe* and *finetune* Top-1 accuracy. For fair comparison, we exclude the works with different evaluation settings and much deeper backbone [22,58] or rely on audio and text [50,59]. The † means jointly utilizing RGB and optical flow for pretraining, and the final performance is tested with RGB only.

In *linear probe* settings, our method achieves state-of-the art results on both two datasets. It is worth noting that our UCF-101 pretrained model even outperforms most RGB-based methods pretrained on Kinetics-400, which indicates the high data efficiency of our learning framework. Regarding to comparison with CoCLR [28] pretrained with RGB and Flow, we reach higher accuracy with fewer frames in each clip. It indicates that simple frame difference could replace computationally expensive optical flow to improve dynamic attribute learning.

In *finetune*, ours also achieves the best results among RGB-only methods, and is comparable with RGB-Flow two-stream models. Among these method, [11,31,34,35] carefully design temporal transformations to enhance temporal perception in videos, [3,15] employ short and long clips to attend to fine-grained temporal features, [28,68] utilize complementary information between RGB and Flow to enhance video representations. While our method proposes to formulate general static and dynamic concepts to guide detailed local feature perception, the performance demonstrates the effectiveness of our new learning scheme.

Table 1. Results on action recognition downstream task. We present the backbone encoder, pretrain dataset, spatio-temporal resolution of each method. Freeze (tick) indicates *linear probe*, and no freeze (cross) denotes *end-to-end finetune*

Method	Backbone	Pretrain Dataset	Frames	Res.	Freeze	UCF-101	HMDB-51
CBT [64]	S3D	Kinetics-600	16	112	✓	54.0	29.5
RSPNet [11]	R3D	Kinetics-400	16	112	✓	61.8	42.8
MLRep [57]	R3D	Kinetics-400	16	112	✓	63.2	33.4
CoCLR† [28]	S3D	Kinetics-400	32	128	✓	74.5	46.1
Ours	R(2+1)D	UCF-101	16	112	✓	67.4	40.7
Ours	R(2+1)D	Kinetics-400	16	112	✓	72.1	45.9
Ours	S3D	Kinetics-400	16	128	✓	75.1	47.4
TempTrans [35]	R(2+1)D	UCF-101	16	112	✗	81.6	46.4
LSFD [3]	R3D	UCF-101	32	112	✗	77.2	53.7
STS† [68]	R(2+1)D	UCF-101	16	112	✗	77.8	40.7
CoCLR† [28]	S3D	UCF-101	32	128	✗	81.4	52.1
Ours	R(2+1)D	UCF-101	16	112	✗	82.1	49.7
Ours	S3D	UCF-101	32	128	✗	83.7	53.8
ASCNet [31]	R3D	Kinetics-400	16	112	✗	80.5	52.3
Pace [70]	R(2+1)D	Kinetics-400	16	112	✗	77.1	36.6
VideoMoCo [53]	R(2+1)D	Kinetics-400	32	112	✗	78.7	49.2
RSPNet [11]	R(2+1)D	Kinetics-400	16	112	✗	81.1	44.6
TCLR [15]	R(2+1)D	Kinetics-400	16	112	✗	84.3	54.2
TimeEq [34]	S3D-G	Kinetics-400	32	128	✗	86.9	63.5
STS† [68]	S3D-G	Kinetics-400	64	224	✗	89.0	62.0
CoCLR† [28]	S3D	Kinetics-400	32	128	✗	87.9	54.6
Ours	R(2+1)D	Kinetics-400	16	112	✗	86.1	54.8
Ours	S3D	Kinetics-400	16	128	✗	88.3	56.4

Video Retrieval. We show the performance on video retrieval with R@k in Table 2. All models are pretrained on UCF-101 with resolution 112×112 for fair comparison. Generally, our method achieves superior results over both RGB-only and RGB-Flow two-stream methods, especially when k is small. It indicates that our method encodes desired characteristics into a more compact manifold.

4.4 Concept Analysis

Intuitively, actions can be represented by some general concepts, and the detailed feature description of these concepts help to discriminate similar action classes. To this end, in this section, we reveal how the learned static and dynamic concepts influence downstream action recognition.

Table 2. Results on video retrieval downstream task. We report R@k (k = 1,5,10,20), † means pretrained with RGB and optical flow

Method	Backbone	UCF-101				HMDB-51			
		R@1	R@5	R@10	R@20	R@1	R@5	R@10	R@20
VCP [48]	R3D	18.6	33.6	42.5	53.3	7.6	24.4	36.3	53.6
MLRep [57]	R3D	39.6	57.6	69.2	78.0	18.8	39.2	51.0	63.7
VCLR [39]	R2D-50	46.8	61.8	70.4	79.0	17.6	38.6	51.1	67.6
PRP [82]	R(2+1)D	20.3	34.0	41.9	51.7	8.2	25.3	36.2	51.0
STS† [68]	R(2+1)D	38.1	58.9	68.9	77.2	16.4	36.9	50.5	65.4
CoCLR† [28]	S3D	53.3	69.4	76.6	82.0	23.3	43.2	53.5	65.5
Ours	R(2+1)D	55.6	70.1	77.4	83.1	24.4	45.1	54.5	66.4

Table 3. Results of static and dynamic concept analysis. The models in first two rows and the third row are respectively pretrained on Kinetics-400 and Diving-48

Feature	v	q_v	q_v^s	q_v^d	F_v	F_v^s	F_v^d
UCF-101	72.1	66.3	61.4	62.6	72.7	68.3	69.8
HMDB-51	45.9	43.8	42.9	40.1	46.3	45.7	44.2
Diving-48	73.4	59.4	26.7	64.8	72.5	31.1	74.1

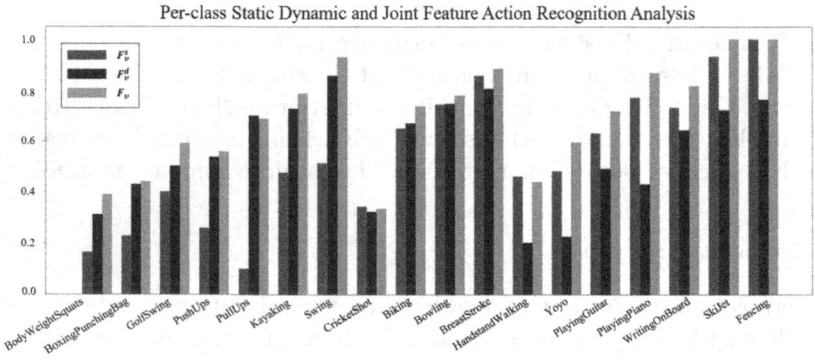

Fig. 3. Per-class action recognition accuracy analysis. We compare the performance of using static, dynamic and joint concept related local feature set, namely F_v^s, F_v^d, F_v

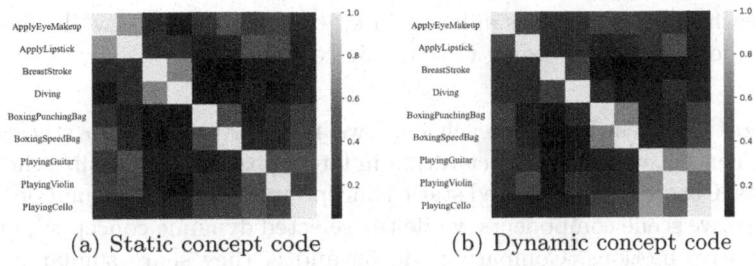

(a) Static concept code   (b) Dynamic concept code

Fig. 4. Decoupled concept code similarity. We respectively average static and dynamic concept latent codes, q_v^s and q_v^d, within each category, then calculate cosine similarity

Decoupled Concept for Action Recognition. We first quantitatively analyze the static and dynamic concepts and their relevant local features on action recognition. We adopt different outputs from our learning framework and pass them through linear classifier to do action classification on UCF-101, HMDB-51 and Diving-48. Specifically, in default evaluation settings, we use the global average pooled v as input to the classifier. We also compare using the concept latent codes or the local feature set for recognition. Note that when using the local feature set, e.g., F_v, we first filter out Top-10% concepts from q_v, then average the corresponding local features for classification. From Table 3, we have several observations. First, using concept latent code for classification leads to performance drop, while the local feature set slightly improves performance. This is because we learn limited number of general concepts and could lose detailed information. While the local feature set effectively aggregates detailed information and drops redundant features, which helps to improve action recognition. Second, on UCF-101 and HMDB-51, static and dynamic concepts are almost of equal significance, and jointly utilizing static and dynamic concepts leads to best performance. Third, the dynamic concepts dominate action recognition on Diving-48, and the static concepts are nearly useless as expected. This is because different diving classes share the same background scene and only differ in motions, the static concepts could disturb motion pattern discrimination.

To further analyze the impact of the decoupled concepts on specific action categories, we select some typical classes from UCF-101 and visualize the per-class accuracy under different settings in Fig. 3. Among the selected action categories, the blue ones are highly dominated by motions, the red ones may have ambiguous motion patterns but can be easily recognized by appearance, and for the purple ones, both static appearance and dynamic motion are discriminative. The per-class accuracy with different feature input is in line with our expectations, which indicates the decoupled concepts respectively reveal static and dynamic attributes. Besides, we analyze the inter-class similarity in static and dynamic concept latent space. In Fig. 4, we visualize the similarity between different actions. Intuitively, some actions share similar background but with different motions, e.g., breaststroke and diving, while some possess similar movement but diverse appearances, e.g., playing different instruments. As expected, the former ones have higher inter-class similarity in static concept space while the latter ones are more similar regarding to dynamic concepts.

Visualization Results. For each clip, we respectively select a static and a dynamic concept with highest activation in latent space, and visualize the attention maps. Generally, the selected static concept attends to foreground objects or representative scene components, while the selected dynamic concepts highlights discriminative motions. Comparing Fig. 5a and c, they share similar dynamic attributes, i.e., almost synchronized forearm movements, but can be discriminated by static objects. Regarding to Figs 5b and d, they happen in similar pools, but the dynamic concept helps to figure out distinct motion patterns. It reveals that the we learn meaningful static and dynamic concepts that focus on different aspects, these two jointly facilitate video understanding.

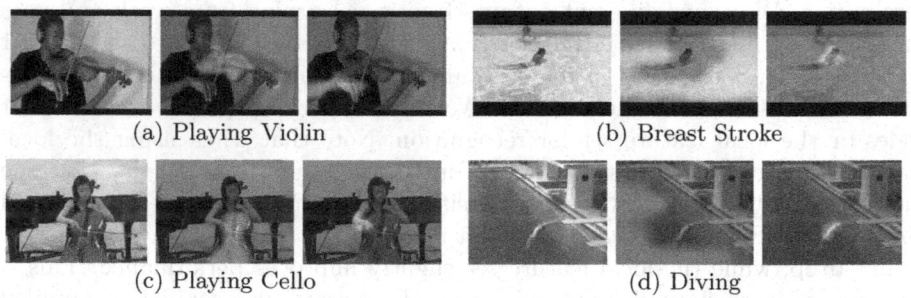

(a) Playing Violin   (b) Breast Stroke

(c) Playing Cello   (d) Diving

Fig. 5. Visualization of static and dynamic concept attention maps. Each subfigure left to right is: original frame, static concept attention map, dynamic concept attention map

4.5 Ablation Study

We perform ablation studies on the loss function designs and crucial hyper-parameters. More ablative experiments please refer to Supplementary Material.

Table 4. Ablation study on loss functions. We pretrain on Kinetics-400

$\mathcal{L}_{aln}$	$\mathcal{L}_{fid}$	$\mathcal{L}_{div}$	$\mathcal{L}_{loc}$	UCF-101		HMDB-51	
				Linear	Finetune	Linear	Finetune
✓				61.4	76.3	40.3	44.7
✓	✓	✓		68.1	80.1	43.2	47.9
✓			✓	67.4	78.9	43.3	46.4
✓	✓	✓	✓	72.1	82.1	45.9	49.7

Overall Framework. We first validate the effectiveness of the loss functions in Table 4. The model is pretrained with default concept numbers, $K_s = K_d = 50$, and the decoupled concept alignment objective $\mathcal{L}_{aln}$ serves as the baseline. We can observe that the two regularizations $\mathcal{L}_{fid}$ and $\mathcal{L}_{div}$ significantly improve the performance. This is because these two terms reduce redundancy in the learned concept prototypes and contribute to more compact and diverse concept formulation, which effectively guides representation learning. And regarding to $\mathcal{L}_{loc}$, it also brings significant improvement since this objective explicitly contrasts local features of valid concepts and facilitates detailed local feature perception.

Table 5. Ablation study on concept numbers. We report linear probe accuracy

K_s	K_d	UCF-101		HMDB-51	
		$w/\mathcal{L}_{loc}$	w/o $\mathcal{L}_{loc}$	w/ $\mathcal{L}_{loc}$	w/o $\mathcal{L}_{loc}$
25	25	70.3	61.2	43.0	39.4
25	50	71.7	66.3	44.1	40.8
50	25	71.3	65.2	44.8	42.4
50	50	72.1	68.1	45.9	43.2
100	100	72.3	68.8	45.8	44.3
200	200	72.3	69.4	45.6	44.1

Number of Concepts. We also explore the impact of different concept numbers in Table 5. With the help of $\mathcal{L}_{loc}$, the performance slightly improves when K_s and K_d increases, and maintains stable in range of 50 to 200. While without $\mathcal{L}_{loc}$, the performance dramatically drops when the concept numbers become small. Because when K_s and K_d are small, the latent space captures general concepts but loses detailed information to discriminate similar actions. But when combined with $\mathcal{L}_{loc}$, the model adaptively attends to detailed local features with desired concepts, which makes up for the information loss to a large extent.

5   Conclusion

In this paper, we propose to learn general static and dynamic visual concepts to guide self-supervised video representation learning. We design decoupled concept alignment objective with regularizations to jointly optimize feature representations and concept distributions. Then we refer to the learned concepts to aggregate detailed local features corresponding to different concepts. We utilize the concept latent code to filter out redundant concepts with low activations, and perform concept-level local feature contrast for detailed video understanding. We achieve state-of-the-art results on UCF-101, HMDB-51 and Diving-48. The ablation studies demonstrate that the integration of general concept learning and detailed local feature contrast improves video representation learning.

Acknowledgments. This work is supported by GRF 14205719, TRS T41-603/20-R, Centre for Perceptual and Interactive Intelligence, and CUHK Interdisciplinary AI Research Institute.

References

1. Alvarez Melis, D., Jaakkola, T.: Towards robust interpretability with self-explaining neural networks. In: Advances in Neural Information Processing Systems 31 (2018)
2. Asano, Y.M., Patrick, M., Rupprecht, C., Vedaldi, A.: Labelling unlabelled videos from scratch with multi-modal self-supervision. arXiv preprint arXiv:2006.13662 (2020)
3. Behrmann, N., Fayyaz, M., Gall, J., Noroozi, M.: Long short view feature decomposition via contrastive video representation learning. In: Proceedings of the IEEE/CVF International Conference on Computer Vision, pp. 9244–9253 (2021)
4. Behrmann, N., Gall, J., Noroozi, M.: Unsupervised video representation learning by bidirectional feature prediction. In: Proceedings of the IEEE/CVF Winter Conference on Applications of Computer Vision, pp. 1670–1679 (2021)
5. Benaim, S., et al.: Learning the speediness in videos. In: Proceedings of the IEEE/CVF Conference on Computer Vision and Pattern Recognition, pp. 9922–9931 (2020)
6. Bucher, M., Herbin, S., Jurie, F.: Semantic bottleneck for computer vision tasks. In: Jawahar, C.V., Li, H., Mori, G., Schindler, K. (eds.) ACCV 2018. LNCS, vol. 11362, pp. 695–712. Springer, Cham (2019). https://doi.org/10.1007/978-3-030-20890-5_44
7. Caron, M., Bojanowski, P., Joulin, A., Douze, M.: Deep clustering for unsupervised learning of visual features. In: Ferrari, V., Hebert, M., Sminchisescu, C., Weiss, Y. (eds.) Computer Vision – ECCV 2018. LNCS, vol. 11218, pp. 139–156. Springer, Cham (2018). https://doi.org/10.1007/978-3-030-01264-9_9
8. Caron, M., Misra, I., Mairal, J., Goyal, P., Bojanowski, P., Joulin, A.: Unsupervised learning of visual features by contrasting cluster assignments. arXiv preprint arXiv:2006.09882 (2020)
9. Carreira, J., Zisserman, A.: Quo vadis, action recognition? a new model and the kinetics dataset. In: Proceedings of the IEEE/CVF Conference on Computer Vision and Pattern Recognition, pp. 6299–6308 (2017)
10. Chen, B., Selvaraju, R.R., Chang, S.F., Niebles, J.C., Naik, N.: Previts: contrastive pretraining with video tracking supervision. arXiv preprint arXiv:2112.00804 (2021)
11. Chen, P., et al.: RSPNet: relative speed perception for unsupervised video representation learning. In: Proceedings of the AAAI Conference on Artificial Intelligence, vol. 1 (2021)
12. Chen, T., Kornblith, S., Norouzi, M., Hinton, G.: A simple framework for contrastive learning of visual representations. In: International conference on machine learning, pp. 1597–1607. PMLR (2020)
13. Chen, Z., Bei, Y., Rudin, C.: Concept whitening for interpretable image recognition. Nat. Mach. Intell. **2**(12), 772–782 (2020)
14. Cuturi, M.: Sinkhorn distances: lightspeed computation of optimal transport. In: NIPS. vol. 2, p. 4 (2013)
15. Dave, I., Gupta, R., Rizve, M.N., Shah, M.: TCLR: temporal contrastive learning for video representation. arXiv preprint arXiv:2101.07974 (2021)

16. De Fauw, J., et al.: Clinically applicable deep learning for diagnosis and referral in retinal disease. Nat. Med. **24**(9), 1342–1350 (2018)

17. Ding, S., et al.: Motion-aware contrastive video representation learning via foreground-background merging. In: Proceedings of the IEEE/CVF Conference on Computer Vision and Pattern Recognition, pp. 9716–9726 (2022)

18. Ding, S., Qian, R., Xiong, H.: Dual contrastive learning for spatio-temporal representation. arXiv preprint arXiv:2207.05340 (2022)

19. Dosovitskiy, A., et al.: An image is worth 16x16 words: Transformers for image recognition at scale. arXiv preprint arXiv:2010.11929 (2020)

20. Dosovitskiy, A., Springenberg, J.T., Riedmiller, M., Brox, T.: Discriminative unsupervised feature learning with convolutional neural networks. In: Advances in neural information processing systems 27 (2014)

21. Ermolov, A., Siarohin, A., Sangineto, E., Sebe, N.: Whitening for self-supervised representation learning. In: International Conference on Machine Learning, pp. 3015–3024. PMLR (2021)

22. Feichtenhofer, C., Fan, H., Xiong, B., Girshick, R., He, K.: A large-scale study on unsupervised spatiotemporal representation learning. In: Proceedings of the IEEE/CVF Conference on Computer Vision and Pattern Recognition, pp. 3299–3309 (2021)

23. Gao, P., Lu, J., Li, H., Mottaghi, R., Kembhavi, A.: Container: context aggregation network. arXiv preprint arXiv:2106.01401 (2021)

24. Gidaris, S., Singh, P., Komodakis, N.: Unsupervised representation learning by predicting image rotations. arXiv preprint arXiv:1803.07728 (2018)

25. Gutmann, M., Hyvärinen, A.: Noise-contrastive estimation: a new estimation principle for unnormalized statistical models. In: Proceedings of the Thirteenth International Conference on Artificial Intelligence and Statistics, pp. 297–304. JMLR Workshop and Conference Proceedings (2010)

26. Han, T., Xie, W., Zisserman, A.: Video representation learning by dense predictive coding. In: Proceedings of the IEEE International Conference on Computer Vision Workshops (2019)

27. Han, T., Xie, W., Zisserman, A.: Memory-augmented dense predictive coding for video representation learning. In: Vedaldi, A., Bischof, H., Brox, T., Frahm, J.-M. (eds.) ECCV 2020. LNCS, vol. 12348, pp. 312–329. Springer, Cham (2020). https://doi.org/10.1007/978-3-030-58580-8_19

28. Han, T., Xie, W., Zisserman, A.: Self-supervised co-training for video representation learning. arXiv preprint arXiv:2010.09709 (2020)

29. He, K., Fan, H., Wu, Y., Xie, S., Girshick, R.: Momentum contrast for unsupervised visual representation learning. In: Proceedings of the IEEE/CVF Conference on Computer Vision and Pattern Recognition, pp. 9729–9738 (2020)

30. Hu, D., et al.: Discriminative sounding objects localization via self-supervised audiovisual matching. Adv. Neural. Inf. Process. Syst. **33**, 10077–10087 (2020)

31. Huang, D., et al.: ASCNet: self-supervised video representation learning with appearance-speed consistency. arXiv preprint arXiv:2106.02342 (2021)

32. Huang, L., Liu, Y., Wang, B., Pan, P., Xu, Y., Jin, R.: Self-supervised video representation learning by context and motion decoupling. In: Proceedings of the IEEE/CVF Conference on Computer Vision and Pattern Recognition, pp. 13886–13895 (2021)

33. Jabri, A., Owens, A., Efros, A.A.: Space-time correspondence as a contrastive random walk. arXiv preprint arXiv:2006.14613 (2020)

34. Jenni, S., Jin, H.: Time-equivariant contrastive video representation learning. In: Proceedings of the IEEE/CVF International Conference on Computer Vision, pp. 9970–9980 (2021)
35. Jenni, S., Meishvili, G., Favaro, P.: Video representation learning by recognizing temporal transformations. In: Vedaldi, A., Bischof, H., Brox, T., Frahm, J.-M. (eds.) ECCV 2020. LNCS, vol. 12373, pp. 425–442. Springer, Cham (2020). https://doi.org/10.1007/978-3-030-58604-1_26
36. Kim, D., Cho, D., Kweon, I.S.: Self-supervised video representation learning with space-time cubic puzzles. In: Proceedings of the AAAI Conference on Artificial Intelligence, vol. 33, pp. 8545–8552 (2019)
37. Kim, D., Cho, D., Yoo, D., Kweon, I.S.: Learning image representations by completing damaged jigsaw puzzles. In: 2018 IEEE Winter Conference on Applications of Computer Vision (WACV), pp. 793–802. IEEE (2018)
38. Koh, P.W., et al.: Concept bottleneck models. In: International Conference on Machine Learning, pp. 5338–5348. PMLR (2020)
39. Kuang, H., et al.: Video contrastive learning with global context. In: Proceedings of the IEEE/CVF International Conference on Computer Vision, pp. 3195–3204 (2021)
40. Kuehne, H., Jhuang, H., Garrote, E., Poggio, T., Serre, T.: HMDB: a large video database for human motion recognition. In: 2011 International Conference on Computer Vision, pp. 2556–2563. IEEE (2011)
41. Li, R., Zhang, Y., Qiu, Z., Yao, T., Liu, D., Mei, T.: Motion-focused contrastive learning of video representations. In: Proceedings of the IEEE/CVF International Conference on Computer Vision, pp. 2105–2114 (2021)
42. Li, X., Liu, S., De Mello, S., Wang, X., Kautz, J., Yang, M.H.: Joint-task self-supervised learning for temporal correspondence. arXiv preprint arXiv:1909.11895 (2019)
43. Li, Y., Li, Y., Vasconcelos, N.: RESOUND: towards action recognition without representation bias. In: Ferrari, V., Hebert, M., Sminchisescu, C., Weiss, Y. (eds.) ECCV 2018. LNCS, vol. 11210, pp. 520–535. Springer, Cham (2018). https://doi.org/10.1007/978-3-030-01231-1_32
44. Liu, X., et al.: Visual sound localization in the wild by cross-modal interference erasing. arXiv preprint arXiv:2202.06406 (2022)
45. Liu, X., et al.: Learning hierarchical cross-modal association for co-speech gesture generation. In: Proceedings of the IEEE/CVF Conference on Computer Vision and Pattern Recognition, pp. 10462–10472 (2022)
46. Liu, X., Xu, Y., Wu, Q., Zhou, H., Wu, W., Zhou, B.: Semantic-aware implicit neural audio-driven video portrait generation. arXiv preprint arXiv:2201.07786 (2022)
47. Losch, M., Fritz, M., Schiele, B.: Interpretability beyond classification output: semantic bottleneck networks. arXiv preprint arXiv:1907.10882 (2019)
48. Luo, D., et al.: Video cloze procedure for self-supervised spatio-temporal learning. In: Proceedings of the AAAI Conference on Artificial Intelligence, vol. 34, pp. 11701–11708 (2020)
49. Luo, Z., Peng, B., Huang, D.A., Alahi, A., Fei-Fei, L.: Unsupervised learning of long-term motion dynamics for videos. In: Proceedings of the IEEE international conference on computer vision, pp. 2203–2212 (2017)
50. Miech, A., Alayrac, J.B., Smaira, L., Laptev, I., Sivic, J., Zisserman, A.: End-to-end learning of visual representations from uncurated instructional videos. In: Proceedings of the IEEE/CVF Conference on Computer Vision and Pattern Recognition, pp. 9879–9889 (2020)

51. Misra, I., Zitnick, C.L., Hebert, M.: Shuffle and learn: unsupervised learning using temporal order verification. In: Leibe, B., Matas, J., Sebe, N., Welling, M. (eds.) ECCV 2016. LNCS, vol. 9905, pp. 527–544. Springer, Cham (2016). https://doi.org/10.1007/978-3-319-46448-0_32
52. van den Oord, A., Li, Y., Vinyals, O.: Representation learning with contrastive predictive coding. arXiv preprint arXiv:1807.03748 (2018)
53. Pan, T., Song, Y., Yang, T., Jiang, W., Liu, W.: Videomoco: contrastive video representation learning with temporally adversarial examples. In: Proceedings of the IEEE/CVF Conference on Computer Vision and Pattern Recognition, pp. 11205–11214 (2021)
54. Piergiovanni, A., Angelova, A., Ryoo, M.S.: Evolving losses for unsupervised video representation learning. In: Proceedings of the IEEE/CVF Conference on Computer Vision and Pattern Recognition, pp. 133–142 (2020)
55. Qian, R., Hu, D., Dinkel, H., Wu, M., Xu, N., Lin, W.: Multiple sound sources localization from coarse to fine. In: Vedaldi, A., Bischof, H., Brox, T., Frahm, J.-M. (eds.) ECCV 2020. LNCS, vol. 12365, pp. 292–308. Springer, Cham (2020). https://doi.org/10.1007/978-3-030-58565-5_18
56. Qian, R., et al.: Exploring temporal granularity in self-supervised video representation learning. arXiv preprint arXiv:2112.04480 (2021)
57. Qian, R., et al.: Enhancing self-supervised video representation learning via multi-level feature optimization. arXiv preprint arXiv:2108.02183 (2021)
58. Qian, R., et al.: Spatiotemporal contrastive video representation learning. arXiv preprint arXiv:2008.03800 (2020)
59. Recasens, A., et al.: Broaden your views for self-supervised video learning. In: Proceedings of the IEEE/CVF International Conference on Computer Vision, pp. 1255–1265 (2021)
60. Regatti, J.R., Deshmukh, A.A., Manavoglu, E., Dogan, U.: Consensus clustering with unsupervised representation learning. arXiv preprint arXiv:2010.01245 (2020)
61. Sawada, Y., Nakamura, K.: Concept bottleneck model with additional unsupervised concepts. arXiv preprint arXiv:2202.01459 (2022)
62. Seel, N.M.: Encyclopedia of the sciences of learning, 1st edn. Springer (2011). https://doi.org/10.1007/978-1-4419-1428-6
63. Soomro, K., Zamir, A.R., Shah, M.: UCF101: a dataset of 101 human actions classes from videos in the wild. arXiv preprint arXiv:1212.0402 (2012)
64. Sun, C., Baradel, F., Murphy, K., Schmid, C.: Learning video representations using contrastive bidirectional transformer. arXiv preprint arXiv:1906.05743 (2019)
65. Tian, Y., Krishnan, D., Isola, P.: Contrastive multiview coding. In: Vedaldi, A., Bischof, H., Brox, T., Frahm, J.-M. (eds.) ECCV 2020. LNCS, vol. 12356, pp. 776–794. Springer, Cham (2020). https://doi.org/10.1007/978-3-030-58621-8_45
66. Tran, D., Wang, H., Torresani, L., Ray, J., LeCun, Y., Paluri, M.: A closer look at spatiotemporal convolutions for action recognition. In: Proceedings of the IEEE conference on Computer Vision and Pattern Recognition, pp. 6450–6459 (2018)
67. Vaswani, A., et al.: Attention is all you need. In: Advances in Neural Information Processing Systems 30 (2017)
68. Wang, J., Jiao, J., Bao, L., He, S., Liu, W., Liu, Y.: Self-supervised video representation learning by uncovering spatio-temporal statistics. arXiv preprint arXiv:2008.13426 (2020)
69. Wang, J., Jiao, J., Bao, L., He, S., Liu, Y., Liu, W.: Self-supervised spatio-temporal representation learning for videos by predicting motion and appearance statistics. In: Proceedings of the IEEE/CVF Conference on Computer Vision and Pattern Recognition, pp. 4006–4015 (2019)

70. Wang, J., Jiao, J., Liu, Y.-H.: Self-supervised video representation learning by pace prediction. In: Vedaldi, A., Bischof, H., Brox, T., Frahm, J.-M. (eds.) ECCV 2020. LNCS, vol. 12362, pp. 504–521. Springer, Cham (2020). https://doi.org/10.1007/978-3-030-58520-4_30

71. Wang, X., Girshick, R., Gupta, A., He, K.: Non-local neural networks. In: Proceedings of the IEEE Conference on Computer Vision and Pattern Recognition, pp. 7794–7803 (2018)

72. Wang, X., Jabri, A., Efros, A.A.: Learning correspondence from the cycle-consistency of time. In: Proceedings of the IEEE/CVF Conference on Computer Vision and Pattern Recognition, pp. 2566–2576 (2019)

73. Wang, X., Zhang, R., Shen, C., Kong, T., Li, L.: Dense contrastive learning for self-supervised visual pre-training. In: Proceedings of the IEEE/CVF Conference on Computer Vision and Pattern Recognition, pp. 3024–3033 (2021)

74. Weinzaepfel, P., Lucas, T., Larlus, D., Kalantidis, Y.: Learning super-features for image retrieval. arXiv preprint arXiv:2201.13182 (2022)

75. Wu, Z., Xiong, Y., Yu, S.X., Lin, D.: Unsupervised feature learning via non-parametric instance discrimination. In: Proceedings of the IEEE conference on computer vision and pattern recognition, pp. 3733–3742 (2018)

76. Xie, S., Sun, C., Huang, J., Tu, Z., Murphy, K.: Rethinking spatiotemporal feature learning: speed-accuracy trade-offs in video classification. In: Ferrari, V., Hebert, M., Sminchisescu, C., Weiss, Y. (eds.) ECCV 2018. LNCS, vol. 11219, pp. 318–335. Springer, Cham (2018). https://doi.org/10.1007/978-3-030-01267-0_19

77. Xie, Z., Lin, Y., Zhang, Z., Cao, Y., Lin, S., Hu, H.: Propagate yourself: exploring pixel-level consistency for unsupervised visual representation learning. In: Proceedings of the IEEE/CVF Conference on Computer Vision and Pattern Recognition, pp. 16684–16693 (2021)

78. Xiong, S., Tan, Y., Wang, G.: Explore visual concept formation for image classification. In: International Conference on Machine Learning, pp. 11470–11479. PMLR (2021)

79. Xu, D., Xiao, J., Zhao, Z., Shao, J., Xie, D., Zhuang, Y.: Self-supervised spatiotemporal learning via video clip order prediction. In: Proceedings of the IEEE/CVF Conference on Computer Vision and Pattern Recognition, pp. 10334–10343 (2019)

80. Yang, C., Xu, Y., Dai, B., Zhou, B.: Video representation learning with visual tempo consistency. arXiv preprint arXiv:2006.15489 (2020)

81. Yao, T., Zhang, Y., Qiu, Z., Pan, Y., Mei, T.: SeCo: exploring sequence supervision for unsupervised representation learning. arXiv preprint arXiv:2008.00975 (2020)

82. Yao, Y., Liu, C., Luo, D., Zhou, Y., Ye, Q.: Video playback rate perception for self-supervised spatio-temporal representation learning. In: Proceedings of the IEEE/CVF Conference on Computer Vision and Pattern Recognition, pp. 6548–6557 (2020)

83. Yuan, L., et al.: Contextualized spatio-temporal contrastive learning with self-supervision. arXiv preprint arXiv:2112.05181 (2021)

SphereFed: Hyperspherical Federated Learning

Xin Dong[1][(✉)] [iD], Sai Qian Zhang[1] [iD], Ang Li[2], and H.T. Kung[1] [iD]

[1] Harvard University, Cambridge, USA
xindong@g.harvard.edu
[2] UT Dallas, Richardson, USA

Abstract. Federated Learning aims at training a global model from multiple decentralized devices (*i.e.* clients) without exchanging their private local data. A key challenge is the handling of non-*i.i.d.* (independent identically distributed) data across multiple clients that may induce disparities of their local features. We introduce the Hyperspherical Federated Learning (SphereFed) framework to address the non-*i.i.d.* issue by constraining learned representations of data points to be on a unit hypersphere shared by clients. Specifically, all clients learn their local representations by minimizing the loss with respect to a fixed classifier whose weights span the unit hypersphere. After federated training in improving the global model, this classifier is further calibrated with a closed-form solution by minimizing a mean squared loss. We show that the calibration solution can be computed efficiently and distributedly without direct access of local data. Extensive experiments indicate that our SphereFed approach is able to improve the accuracy of multiple existing federated learning algorithms by a considerable margin (up to 6% on challenging datasets) with enhanced computation and communication efficiency across datasets and model architectures.

Keywords: Federated learning · Efficient classifier calibration

1 Introduction

Federated learning (FL) is an emerging machine learning paradigm in which distributed clients learn on private data and communicate with a coordinating server to train a single global model that generalizes well across local data [51,69]. One of its major challenges is the handling of non-*i.i.d.* (independent identically distributed) local data across clients [32,40,42]. Non-*i.i.d.* local data leads to disparity of local models after learning on private data [94]. For instance, different feature[1] extractors in local models may learn biased and discrepant input-to-feature mapping functions for the same class [18,41,89]. This obstructs the convergence of collaborative training.

---

[1] The terms representation and feature are used interchangeably.

Supplementary Information The online version contains supplementary material available at https://doi.org/10.1007/978-3-031-19809-0_10.

Existing federated learning algorithms primarily tackle the non-*i.i.d.* problem in two phases: (i) *In the local learning phase*, regularization terms [2,43,80] and additive objectives [41,84,97] are used to control distances among local models by constraining the learning process. (ii) *In the post-learning phase*, the inevitable divergence of local models is corrected with additional information exchange [24,32,66,79,82] and advanced aggregation strategies such as normalized averaging [76], distillation [39], and so on [3,5,60,87].

In this work, we argue that federated learning can also be improved *in the pre-learning phase*; this is a novel research direction complementary to existing approaches. A key insight is the use of a fixed classifier (*e.g.*, the last fully-connected layer) that serves as a template of the feature extractor's output for all clients. Note the loss function is often computed on the inner product between the feature vector (*i.e.*, output of the feature extractor) and the classifier's weight vectors. During local training, the feature extractor is optimized to project data from the i-th class to feature vectors that have the maximum inner product with the i-th of row of the classifier. We refer to the classifier as learning target of the feature extractor. However, higher data heterogeneity leads to a larger disparity of classifiers (in terms of both norms and directions) across clients. In this regard, if the local classifiers can be aligned, clients would have more consistent learning targets without modifying the learning procedure. Unfortunately, a real-time classifier synchronization carries prohibitively high communication overhead for federated learning. To avoid this communication cost, we use instead, for all clients, a fixed classifier constructed from orthonormal basis vectors.

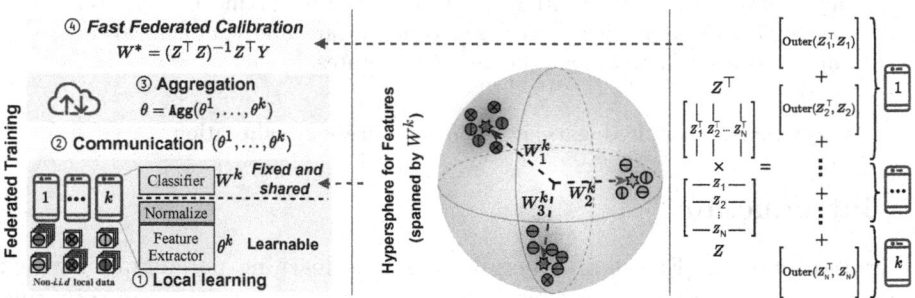

Fig. 1. *Left*: An overview of SphereFed (Hyperspherical Federated Learning). Before federated training starts, we construct a fixed shared classifier whose weight vectors span an unit hypersphere. After federated training ends, we calibrate the classifier in a distributed manner. *Middle*: All clients share the same hypersphere and learn to map local samples (markers represent clients) from the same class (colors represent classes) to the same area on the hypersphere whose centroid (the pentagram) corresponds to a weight vector. *Right*: Leveraging the linearity of the classifier, we derive its closed-form optimum which can be precisely computed by distributed clients. $Z^\top Z$ and $Z^\top Y$ are computed distributively because a matrix multiplication can be implemented as an accumulation of outer products and each outer product depends only on one client. (Color figure online)

Motivated by this insight, we propose to construct a classifier whose weight vectors span an unit hypersphere *before the federated training starts*. Throughout federated training, this classifier is fixed and shared by all clients. Meanwhile, we also normalize the feature representation to the same hypersphere. During local learning, clients' feature extractors learn to map data samples from the *same* class to the *same* area on the hypersphere whose centriod is the corresponding row vector of the classifier. As a result, the local features learned by different clients for data belonging to the same class are better aligned and the interference among local models are reduced, leading to an improved accuracy of the global model.

We name our approach *Hyperspherical Federated Learning* (SphereFed), which is a generic framework compatible with existing federated learning algorithms. An overview of the framework is illustrated in Fig. 1. SphereFed does **not** introduce extra hyper-parameters nor requiring additional computation. In fact, a pre-defined classifier eliminates the need of communication and brings improved efficiency to the system. Given that the classifiers are frozen during federated training, we propose to calibrate the classifier after federated training to achieve its optimum in a provable and lightweight manner. We first derive the closed-form optimum of the classifier leveraging its linearity and find that this closed-form solution can be precisely computed in a distributed manner without direct access to the private features (or data). We name this calibration method *Fast Federated Calibration* (FFC), which is provable and efficient compared with state-of-the-art methods (*e.g.*, [48]) that depend on synthetically generated virtual features.

We conduct extensive experiments to demonstrate that the proposed SphereFed method is compatible with and complementary to several existing federated learning algorithms, capable of introducing up to 6% improvement on testing accuracy. Further experiments show that our proposed calibration achieves a performance gain comparable to the oracle fine-tuning with real features, verifying its theoretical optimality. A set of ablation studies are further presented to understand the efficacy of each design component in SphereFed.

2   Related Work

Standard Federated Learning. Federated learning (FL) was originally proposed by [51,69]. To address the non-*i.i.d.* problem, works have been pursued in two directions: imposing additional constraints in the local learning phase [64,66] and conducting weight correction in the post learning phase [48,60,76,87]. There have also been studies that tackle the non-*i.i.d.* issue by augmenting the on-client and on-server data with public [39] or synthetic [85,97] samples.

Personalized Federated Learning. Personalized federated learning (pFL) differs from FL, by relaxing the setting of standard FL to allow each client to have its personalized local model via, e.g., additional local epochs after standard FL [11,44]. In general, a personalized local model is more likely to obtain better accuracy on a local test set than the single global model, but the personalized local model could be more biased and less general to data from other sources [29,77]. So, pFL and FL has different use focuses and application scenarios. Inspired from transfer learning [57,86], a line of pFL methods learns local private parameters for the classifier but uses a shared feature extractor [7,15,70]. A concurrent and most related work is FedBABU [54] which finds that fixing the classifier during collaborative learning is beneficial to the personalization process. Although this finding is consistent to our observations, our contribution is substantially different from FedBABU. First, we focus on FL while FedBABU focuses on pFL. Second, we ensure a stable performance gain resulting from an in-depth analysis on the benefit of fixing classifier. Third, we further propose a provable calibration method to improve the classifier after federated training.

Decoupling Layers for Federated Learning. Dealing layers at different depths with varying strategies has demonstrated effectiveness for many tasks in centralized training [23], like few-shot learning [65,83], domain adaption [28,75] and meta-learning [55,59]. Such layer decoupling studies could also benefit federated learning applications. For instance, parameters from different layers can be updated and synchronized with different frequency to save communication cost [12,13,16]. FedRecon [68] splits a model into global/local parts and reconstructs the local part on clients in each round to improve privacy and reduce communication. FedUFO [89] resorts an adversary module to reduce the divergence of feature extractors on clients. A most related work is CCVR [48] which also focuses on the classifier. CCVR conducts on-server calibration for the classifier by fine-tuning it with virtual features sampled from Gaussian distributions. This work uses fundamentally different methodologies for the classifier (closed-form classifier fine tuning), and has higher performance gains and less communication/computation costs against CCVR.

Hyperspherical Representation. To the best of our knowledge, this is the first work introducing hyperspherical representation to address the non-$i.i.d.$ challenge in FL. This combination is not trivial but motivated by analytical justifications and empirical supports as elaborated in the remaining sections. Hyperspherical representation has been widely adapted by studies on face recognition [45,95], long-tail recognition [31], regression [52], metric learning [88,96] and contrastive learning [33] to enhance the discriminative power of features. In this work, under the context of FL, we use hyperspherical features with fixed targets to align the learning objectives and minimize cross-party interference.

3   Federated Learning with Non-$i.i.d.$ Clients

3.1   Terminologies

We consider K clients and a central server in a federated learning system. Each client $k \in [K]$ has a local and private dataset $\mathcal{D}^k$. We focus on the non-$i.i.d.$ data setting where local datasets could have heterogeneous distributions [40]. The goal is to train a single global classification model collaboratively which performs well on the global test set. The loss function is represented using $\mathcal{L}(\cdot,\cdot)$.

For a single training example $(\mathbf{x}, y)$, let $\mathbf{z} = f_\theta(\mathbf{x}) \in \mathbb{R}^l$ denote the l-dimension feature vector given a feature extractor $f_\theta(\cdot)$ parameterized by θ. The classifier $h_\mathbf{W}(\cdot)$ takes $\mathbf{z}$ as input and makes the final prediction after a linear transformation $\mathbf{o} = h_\mathbf{W}(\mathbf{z}) = \mathbf{W}\mathbf{z} + \mathbf{b}$ with a weight matrix $\mathbf{W} \in \mathbb{R}^{C \times l}$, where C is the number of classes. For simplicity, we omit the bias term $\mathbf{b}$ in future equations.

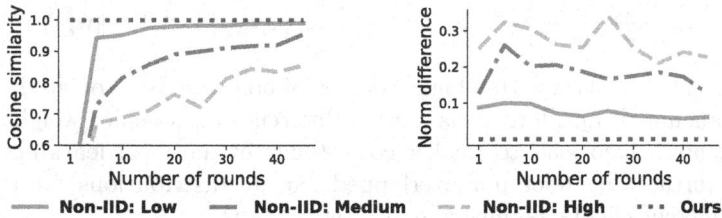

Fig. 2. Direction and norm alignment of classifiers' weights across clients. For the sake of simplicity, we train ResNet18 on CIFAR-100 with 10 clients for 50 rounds, using FedAvg in this empirical study. The non-$i.i.d.$ level is controlled by the concentration parameter of a Dirichlet distribution [32,40,42]. There is a clear negative correlation between non-$i.i.d.$ level and consistency of classifiers' weights across clients, which incurs inconsistent local learning targets.

3.2   Non-$i.i.d.$ Data Leads to Inconsistent Local Learning Targets

In each round of standard federated learning, each client optimizes the feature extractor and the classifier $(\theta, \mathbf{W})$ jointly. Then each client sends its updated feature extractor and classifier $(\theta^k, \mathbf{W}^k)$ to the central server which aggregates ($e.g.$, averages [51]) all received local models into a single global one used for the next round. Prior studies [40] focus on either the local training loss function or an advanced aggregation strategy.

In this work, we pay special attention to the classifier. A classifier is the closet layer to the loss function and the i-th row of its weights $\mathbf{w}_i^k$ acts as a feature template and the learning target of the i-th class for the feature extractor. As a result, the disparity of classifiers across clients induces inconsistent local learning targets and further engenders local feature extractors' disparity. A performance degradation may occur after aggregation in the central server.

The above hypothesis is verified by empirical observations. To show that, we rewrite the output of the classifier as,

$$\mathbf{W}^k \mathbf{z} = \left[\mathbf{w}_1^k \mathbf{z}, \dots, \mathbf{w}_i^k \mathbf{z}, \dots, \mathbf{w}_C^k \mathbf{z} \right], \text{ where } \mathbf{w}_i^k \mathbf{z} = \|\mathbf{w}_i^k\| \|\mathbf{z}\| \cdot \cos\left(\angle\left(\mathbf{w}_i^k, \mathbf{z}\right)\right) . \quad (1)$$

$\angle(\cdot, \cdot)$ denotes the angle between two vectors and $\|\cdot\|$ is the euclidean norm of a vector. A local feature extractor f_θ^k learns to maximize the output of the ground-truth class, $\mathbf{w}_i^k \mathbf{z}$, $\forall i = y$, and minimize outputs of other classes $\mathbf{w}_j^k \mathbf{z}$, $\forall j \neq y$. In summary, Eq. (1) highlights that both norms and directions of classifier's weight vectors impact the optimization of feature extractor and thus (at least partially) effect the distribution of features generated by the feature extractor.

We empirically find that there is a clear negative correlation between non-$i.i.d.$ degree and the consistency of classifiers' weights (in terms of both norm and direction) across clients. We compute the cosine similarity (Eq. (2) and Fig. 2, *Left*) and norm difference (Eq. (3) and Fig. 2, *Right*) of classifier weight vectors for the same class but from arbitrary two different clients ($k_1 \neq k_2$ and $1 \leq k_1, k_2 \leq K$) using FedAvg [51].

$$\mathbb{E}_{c \sim [C], k_1 \neq k_2} \left[\frac{\mathbf{w}_c^{k_1} \cdot \mathbf{w}_c^{k_2}}{\|\mathbf{w}_c^{k_1}\| \|\mathbf{w}_c^{k_2}\|} \right] \quad (2) \qquad \mathbb{E}_{c \sim [C], k_1 \neq k_2} \left[|\|\mathbf{w}_c^{k_1}\| - \|\mathbf{w}_c^{k_2}\|| \right] \quad (3)$$

According to Fig. 2, data with a higher degree of non-$i.i.d.$ is associated with less direction alignment and larger magnitude difference of classifier weight vectors among clients, which lead to weaker consistency of the local learning targets. This will further engender non-overlapped feature distributions for the same class on different clients as illustrated in Fig. 3 (*Left*).

4 Hyperspherical Federated Learning

4.1 Hyperspherical Representation

A simple yet effective tweak to bypass the aforementioned issue is to align features from clients on a hypersphere, aided by a fixed classifier. In Eq. (1), we show that both the norm and the direction of k-th weight vector $\mathbf{w}_i^k$ play crucial roles in the learning of f_{θ^k} but a non-$i.i.d.$ data distribution causes a disorder of norms and directions. To tackle this problem, we consider to construct $\mathbf{W}^k = \{\mathbf{w}_i^k\}_{i=1}^C$ manually, which has a unit norm and orthogonal components,

$$\mathbf{W}^k = \{\mathbf{w}_i^k\}_{i=1}^C, \quad \text{where } \|\mathbf{w}_i^k\| = 1 \text{ and } \mathbf{w}_i^k \perp \mathbf{w}_j^k, \forall i = j. \quad (4)$$

Note that $\{\mathbf{w}_i^k\}_{i=1}^C$ span an l-dimension unit hypersphere. The orthogonality among $\{\mathbf{w}_i^k\}_{i=1}^C$ ensures the maximum separation between arbitrary pair of classes. In addition, the uniformly unit norm guarantees balance in classes. Feature normalization is further adapted to project feature vectors on the same unit hypersphere, $\tilde{\mathbf{z}} = \mathbf{z}/\|\mathbf{z}\|$. Normalizing features enables f_θ^k to focus on learning feature vectors' directions and makes federated training process more robust to feature magnitude. Given a data point $(\mathbf{x}, y)$, a feature extractor f_{θ^k} maps the input $\mathbf{x}$ to a feature vector $f_{\theta^k}(\mathbf{x})/\|f_{\theta^k}(\mathbf{x})\|$ on the unit hypersphere, using the corresponding weights $\mathbf{w}_y^k$ as the target of mapping.

To ensure that all clients have the same learning targets (*i.e.*, the same classifier $h_{\mathbf{W}^k}$), we share the constructed $\mathbf{W}^k$ with all clients and keep the shared $\mathbf{W}^k$ fixed throughout the federated training process. By doing this, local classifiers become consistent automatically without costly frequent inter-client synchronization. Since all clients now share the same learning targets, different local feature extractors on clients learn to map local data samples from the i-th class to the same area on the hypersphere with $\mathbf{w}_i^k$ as the centroid of that area. As a result, the norms and directions of local features are aligned with reduced interference across clients. In addition, the features from different classes have minimized overlaps and balanced magnitudes. An illustration of hyperspherical features can be found in Fig. 1 (Middle).

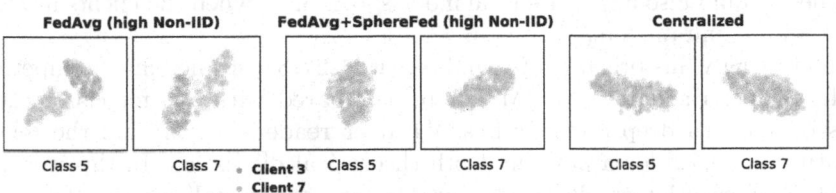

Fig. 3. A qualitative study of Hyperspherical Federated Learning (SphereFed). In the left and middle sub-figures, dots in different colors represent features of the same class but generated by local models f_{θ^k} of different clients. SphereFed encourages consistency among clients' features by aligning local learning targets (Color figure online).

The benefits of adapting the proposed hyperspherical features (and each design component described above) are revealed in a qualitative evaluation (Fig. 3). For more detailed ablation study including quantitative results, please refer to Sect. 5.3. In Fig. 3, we plot a certain class's features from different clients to visualize local features alignment across clients. Three kinds of methods are compared including FedAvg [51] (with conventional classifier), standard centralized training, and SphereFed. We use MobileNetV2 for all three methods. For FedAvg and SphereFed, we partition the CIFAR-100 dataset to 10 clients according to the Dirichlet distribution with the concentration parameter α set as 0.1 to simulate the high non-$i.i.d.$ scenario. For the sake of visualization, we randomly select two clients (*e.g.*, the 3-rd and 7-th clients in Fig. 3) and use their local models (at the 90-th round) to generate features of two random classes (*e.g.*, the class 5 and 7 in Fig. 3). For centralized training, we train MobileNetV2 for 120 epochs to convergence and use the learnt model to generate features. The dimension of raw features is 1280 and we use t-SNE [49] to reduce the dimension to 2 for visualization. According to Fig. 3, in FedAvg, local models learn divergent mapping functions and thus features from the same class but different clients are biased to different distributions (*i.e.*, non-overlapped clusters in Fig. 3). While, our hyperspherical features aligns well across clients as the centralized training (*i.e.*, fused clusters in Fig. 3).

4.2   Using Mean Squared Error Loss on Hyperspherical Features

A widely accepted training method for classification tasks is to apply the softmax function [6] to the classifier output $\mathbf{W}^k\mathbf{z}$ before calculating the cross entropy (CE) loss. Combination of CE and softmax function is known to be sensitive to the scale of its input [23,74]. However, in SphereFed, the classifier's output, has less-than-one scale because of unit weights and hyperspherical features. To mitigate such a scaling issue, prior work for centralized training adopts either a pre-defined [14,74] or a learnable [23,31] scaling parameter τ in $\tau \cdot \mathbf{W}^k \mathbf{z}$ (*i.e.*, temperature) to stabilize optimization. Unfortunately, performing a grid search on the scaling hyper-parameter would add significant communication and computation overheads in the setting of federated learning. A freely learnable scaling parameter could also aggravate local models' disparity when the clients have different scaling parameters.

Interestingly, historical [19,63] and recent [4,27,34] studies show competitive results of mean square error (MSE) [10] compared with CE for classification tasks on modern deep architectures. We refer readers to [53] and the related literature [8,50,72] for a more in-depth theoretical discussion. In this work, we use MSE to learn hyperspherical features to bypass the scaling issue of CE, *i.e.*,

$$\mathcal{L}_{\mathrm{MSE}}(\mathbf{W}^k \mathbf{z}, \ y) = \tfrac{1}{C} \|\mathbf{W}^k \mathbf{z} - \mathtt{one\_hot}(y)\|^2 = \tfrac{1}{C} \sum_{i=1}^C \left(\mathbf{w}_i^k \mathbf{z} - \mathbf{1}(i = y)\right)^2, \quad (5)$$

where $\mathbf{1}(i = y)$ is equal to 1 if and only if $i = y$, C is the number of classes, and $\mathtt{one\_hot}(\cdot)$ is the one-hot vector representation of a label.

4.3   Fast Federated Calibration (FFC)

Throughout federated training of the hyperspherical representation, the weight of classifier $\mathbf{W}^k$ is fixed to help align learning targets of local features. So naturally, after federated training, a calibration on the classifier could be useful in improving the accuracy of the resulting global model. We, in turn, fix the learnt global feature extractor and calibrate the global classifier to boost the performance of the global model.

An interesting effect of using MSE loss in conjunction with a linear classifier is that we are able to calculate the unique closed-form optimum of classifier's weight matrix given the input of the linear classifier. Formally, the objective of calibrating the classifier $\mathbf{W}$ is,

$$\arg\min_{\mathbf{W}} \ \mathbb{E}_{(\mathbf{x},y) \sim \mathcal{D}} \left[\mathcal{L}_{\mathrm{MSE}}(\mathbf{W}\mathbf{z}, \ y)\right], \quad \text{where } \mathbf{z} = f_\theta(\mathbf{x})/\|f_\theta(\mathbf{x})\| \text{ and } \mathcal{D} = \bigcup_{k \in [K]} \mathcal{D}^k \ .$$
$$(6)$$

We temporarily remove the superscripts of $(\theta, \mathbf{W})$ to emphasize that we consider the global feature extractor and global classifier. We refer to $\mathcal{D}$ as the whole dataset which consists of all local training data. Equation (6) is essentially a least square problem, which has a closed-form solution, *i.e.*,

$$\mathbf{W}^* = (\mathbf{Z}^\top \mathbf{Z})^{-1} \mathbf{Z}^\top \mathbf{Y} \ . \quad (7)$$

The i-th row of $\mathbf{Z}$ is the normalized feature vector $\mathbf{z}_i$ corresponding to the i-th sample $\mathbf{x}_i$ in $\mathcal{D}$. Similarly, the i-th row of $\mathbf{Y}$ is the one-hot target vector $\mathtt{one\_hot}(y_i)$ corresponding to $\mathbf{x}_i$.

Obtaining $\mathbf{Z}$ (and $\mathbf{Y}$) requires all clients to upload their features (and corresponding labels). However, in the context of federated learning, sharing features and labels will cause prohibitively expensive communication overheads and potential model inversion attack [17,93]. To achieve efficient and privacy-enhanced calibration, we propose to compute $\mathbf{W}^*$ in a distributed manner. It is inspired by that matrix multiplication can be implemented by a sum of outer products [46,92]. Take $\mathbf{Z}^\top\mathbf{Z}$ as an example. We can rewrite the $\mathbf{Z}^\top\mathbf{Z}$ as a sum of outer products between columns of $\mathbf{Z}^\top$ and rows of $\mathbf{Z}$ such that

$$\mathbf{Z}^\top\mathbf{Z} = \underbrace{n\ \mathbf{z}_1^\top \otimes n\ \mathbf{z}_1}_{\text{Client 1}} + \cdots \cdots \cdots + \underbrace{\cdots \cdots \cdots}_{\text{Client } k} + \underbrace{n\ \mathbf{z}_{|\mathcal{D}|}^\top \otimes n\ \mathbf{z}_{|\mathcal{D}|}}_{\text{Client } K}. \qquad (8)$$

As a result, to calculate $\mathbf{Z}^\top\mathbf{Z}$, each client can complete a fraction of sum over their local features (as shown in Eq. (8)) and upload the intermediate results to the sever to finish the computation, rather than upload private local features $\mathbf{z}_i$. In addition, the computation of $\mathbf{Z}^\top\mathbf{Y}$ in Eq. (7) can be calculated in the same way. See Fig. 1 (*Right*) for a vivid illustration.

Algorithm. We elaborate the FFC algorithm below:

1. On clients: Each client receives the latest global feature extractor f_θ from the server and computes the $\mathbf{V}^k \in \mathbb{R}^{l \times l}$, $\mathbf{U}^k \in \mathbb{R}^{l \times C}$ on its local data $\mathcal{D}^k$,

$$\mathbf{V}^k = \sum_{i=1}^{|\mathcal{D}^k|} \mathbf{z}_i^\top \mathbf{z}_i, \quad \mathbf{U}^k = \sum_{i=1}^{|\mathcal{D}^k|} \mathbf{z}_i^\top \text{one\_hot}(y_i), \qquad (9)$$

where $\mathbf{z}_i = f_\theta(\mathbf{x}_i)/\|f_\theta(\mathbf{x}_i)\|$ and $(\mathbf{x}_i, y_i) \sim \mathcal{D}^k$.

2. On server: The server receives all $\{(\mathbf{V}^k, \mathbf{U}^k) \mid k \in [K]\}$ from clients and computes the closed-form weights optimum,

$$\mathbf{W}^* = \left(\sum_{k=1}^K \mathbf{V}^k\right)^{-1} \left(\sum_{k=1}^K \mathbf{U}^k\right). \qquad (10)$$

Table 1. Comparison of communication and computation costs for the classifier over 10 clients for 100 rounds. We assume that communicated weights are in 32-bit. The number of FLOPs is computed by considering both clients ("(C)") and the server ("(S)"). Since all approaches require forward of the classifier, we exclude it from calculation. "Every" (and "Once") means communicating at every round (and only once).

Method	Communication			Computation		Accuracy
	Objects	Frequency	Size (MB)	Operation	FLOPs (G)	
FedAvg	$\mathbf{W} \in \mathbb{R}^{l \times C}$	Every	102	Update $\mathbf{w}$ (S)	1.9×10^4	68.78
				Avg (S)		
CCVR	$\mathbf{W} \in \mathbb{R}^{l \times C}$	Every	758	GMM fitting (C)	2.1×10^4	69.14
	$\mu \in \mathbb{R}^{l \times C}$	Once		Sampling&Tukey (S)		
	$\mathbf{\Sigma} \in \mathbb{R}^{l \times l \times C}$			Fine-tuning (S)		
SphereFed (Ours)	$\mathbf{U} \in \mathbb{R}^{l \times C}$	Once	7	Eq. (9) (C)	1.7×10^2	71.85
	$-\mathbf{V} \in \mathbb{R}^{l \times l}$			Eq. (10) (S)		

Communication and Computation. FFC introduces much lighter communication and computation overhead to clients/server compared with state-of-the-art calibration methods like CCVR [48]. For instance, computing Eq. (9) on one client requires $2l|\mathcal{D}^k|(l + C)$ FOLPs which is less than the total computation of the classifier's local training for one round. In addition, the communication amount of FFC is $l(l + C)$ parameters. In Table 1, we compare the communication and computation amount for the classifier of FFC against baselines (e.g., FedAvg [51] and CCVR [48]) over 100 rounds with MobileNetV2 and CIFAR-100. As depicted in Table 1, SphereFed and FFC are more efficient than both FedAvg and CCVR in terms of communication and computation. In Sect. 5.4, we also provide latency comparison measured on a real embedded hardware.

5   Experiments

5.1   Experimental Setup

Baselines. Our proposed methods (i.e., SphereFed and FFC) are compatible with and complementary to several existing federated learning algorithms like FedAvg [51], FedProx [43], FedNova [76], FedOpt [60] and so on. We refer to those algorithms as "base algorithms" in the remaining of this paper. We test five widely used models including a seven-layer ConvNet [85,90] and other modern deep architectures like MobileNetV2 [62], ResNet18 [22], VGG13 [36,67], SENet [26]. For all models, we refer to the last fully-connected layer as the classifier and all the other layers as the feature extractor.

Benchmarks. Following prior literature [40,41,84], we consider two representative and challenging image classification tasks for federated learning, CIFAR-100 [35] and TinyImageNet [37]. CIFAR-100 has 50,000 training samples from 100 classes. Prior method [48] obtains relatively small improvement against base algorithms on CIFAR-100 because the virtual features sampled from the classwise Gaussian Mixture Model (GMM) are less separable when the number of class increases, thereby constraining its practicality for realistic applications. In this work, we show that our proposed methods are able to achieve superior performance for such many-class classification tasks. For example, we evaluate our methods on TinyImageNet which is larger than CIFAR-100 in terms of the input size, the number of samples, and the number of classes, as a more challenging dataset. Empirical results indicate that our proposed methods provide consistent improvements across multiple base algorithms, model architectures and datasets.

Like previous studies [20,30,41], we partition the training set of CIFAR-100 and TinyImageNet to K clients according to a Dirichlet distribution with a concentration parameter α to simulate the data distribution of federated learning. The default number of client is set to $K = 10$. A smaller concentration parameter will result in higher non-i.i.d. degree of partitioning. For example, when $\alpha = 0.1$, one client could have less than ten data samples in some classes. We consider three different non-i.i.d. degrees for CIFAR-100 to study how data heterogeneity degree impacts methods' performance. For fair comparison, we use exactly the same partitioning for all methods. The original test sets of CIFAR-100 and TinyImageNet are used to measure the resulted global model's testing accuracy.

Implementation. We use the SGD optimizer with a momentum 0.9 and a weight decay 10^{-5} for all approaches. Since we change the loss function from cross entropy to mean square error and these two loss functions have different magnitude, we tune the learning rate for both baselines and our methods using grid search. We note that SphereFed and FFC do not introduce any extra hyper-parameter to base algorithms. In addition, we observe that our methods are more robust to various learning rates than base algorithms in Sect. 5.3. For baselines with extra hyper-parameters, we either use the recommended values from their papers [48, 76] or carefully tune them [43, 60]. To tune hyper-parameters, we use a 15% of training data for validation. We train all approaches for 100 rounds and decay the learning rate every round using a cosine annealing schedule [47]. We use $B = 64$ local batch size and $E = 10$ local epochs unless otherwise stated. In Appendix A, we further test our methods on different federated learning settings by varying local training epochs, number of clients, clients' participating rate, and learning rate scheduling strategies. We observe similar trends as shown in the following sections.

Table 2. Accuracy (%) on CIFAR-100 and TinyImageNet with different degrees of non-*i.i.d.*. "+" means applying a considered method (CCVR, BABU and Ours) to a base FL algorithm (FedAvg, FedProx, FedNova and FedOpt). "↑" (and "↓") means accuracy improvement (and degradation) compared with the corresponding base algorithm.

Model	Method	IID	$\alpha = 0.5$	$\alpha = 0.1$	TinyImageNet
MobileNetV2	FedAvg	71.86	68.78	63.90	29.95
	+ CCVR	72.09 (↑0.23)	69.14 (↑0.36)	64.05 (↑0.15)	31.41 (↑1.46)
	+ BABU	71.84 (↓0.02)	69.35 (↑0.57)	64.91 (↑1.01)	28.38 (↓1.57)
	+ Ours	**73.56** (↑**1.72**)	**71.85** (↑**3.07**)	**66.52** (↑**2.62**)	**34.72** (↑**4.76**)
ResNet	FedProx	70.19	67.50	65.63	30.55
	+ CCVR	71.31 (↑0.12)	67.89 (↑0.39)	66.09 (↑0.46)	32.56 (↑2.01)
	+ BABU	71.66 (↑1.47)	69.62 (↑2.12)	67.90 (↑2.27)	31.87 (↑0.32)
	+ Ours	**73.41** (↑**3.22**)	**72.20** (↑**4.70**)	**69.19** (↑**3.56**)	**35.21** (↑**4.66**)
VGG13	FedNova	62.12	60.49	57.20	39.63
	+ CCVR	62.53 (↑0.41)	61.61 (↑1.12)	58.13 (↑0.93)	40.12 (↑0.49)
	+ BABU	62.03 (↓0.09)	60.54 (↑0.05)	58.95 (↑1.75)	40.87 (↑1.24)
	+ Ours	**65.50** (↑**3.38**)	**65.12** (↑**4.63**)	**62.54** (↑**5.34**)	**45.21** (↑**5.58**)
SENet	FedOpt	61.89	59.60	57.46	24.29
	+ CCVR	61.97 (↑0.08)	60.42 (↑0.82)	57.93 (↑0.47)	25.01 (↑0.72)
	+ BABU	62.27 (↑0.38)	59.69 (↑0.09)	56.75 (↓0.71)	25.34 (↑1.05)
	+ Ours	**65.15** (↑**3.26**)	**65.69** (↑**6.09**)	**62.61** (↑**5.15**)	**29.84** (↑**5.55**)

5.2   Results

We present in Table 2 the test accuracy of various base algorithms before and after applying our methods (*i.e.*, SphereFed and FFC) and two state-of-the-art baselines (*i.e.*, CCVR [48] and BABU [54]). Our proposed methods improve these base algorithms consistently across model architectures and datasets.

CCVR estimates Gaussian Mixture Model (GMM) for features on the class granularity on clients and samples virtual features from the GMM to fine-tune the classifier on the server. However, when the number of classes is relatively large (*e.g.*, 100 for CIFAR-100 and 200 for TinyImageNet), class-wise GMMs are not sufficiently separable to facilitate the fine-tuning. As a result, the improvement brought by CCVR is relatively small [48].

BABU [54] keeps the classifier fixed after random initialization during federated training and then fine-tunes on each client's local dataset individually for personalization. Two evaluation metrics are considered in BABU: (i) initial accuracy which is calculated with the single global model on the global test set and (ii) personalized accuracies measured with personalized models on local test sets over clients. As mentioned previously, we focus on the former (*i.e.*, initial accuracy) rather than personalized federated learning, while an analysis on how our method helps personalized federated learning is provided in Appendix B.

An interesting finding is that our methods tend to bring more accuracy gains when the non-*i.i.d.* degree is higher. This confirms our observation that a higher non-*i.i.d.* degree leads to more severe issues on classifier disparity and inconsistent local learning targets. With our methods, the performance gap between *i.i.d.* and non-*i.i.d.* data is reduced. For instance, the performance gap between "IID" and "$\alpha = 0.1$" is 4.92% for base algorithm FedNova, while this gap is reduced to 2.96% after applying the proposed approaches.

Table 3. Quantitative ablation study of Hyperspherical Federated Learning (SphereFed). We investigate the effectiveness of each design component by applying them individually using FedAvg as the base algorithm on MobileNetV2 and CIFAR-100 ($\alpha = 0.5$). "Fix (R)" ("Fix (OU)") means fixing the classifier with random (orthogonal and unit-norm) initialization. "Norm" represents normalizing features.

	FedAvg	+ Fix (R)	+ Fix (OU)	+ Norm	+ Fix (OU) +Norm
CE	68.78	69.35 (↑0.57)	69.65 (↑0.87)	69.76 (↑0.98)	70.87 (↑2.09)
MSE	66.42 (↓2.36)	67.05 (↓1.73)	67.21 (↓1.57)	Diverging	**71.85 (↑3.07)**

5.3   Ablation Studies

Besides overall effectiveness, we perform several ablation experiments which help understand the significance of each component in the proposed method.

The Importance of Ortho-normalization. In Table 3, we first compare different initializations of the fixed classifier. For the orthogonal and unit-norm

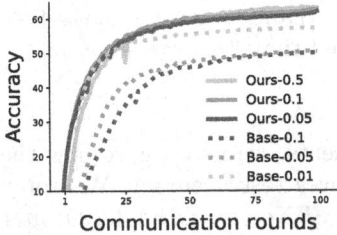

Fig. 4. The impact of different learning rates for "FedNova" and "FedNova + SphereFed".   After applying SphereFed, training becomes more robust to different learning rates.

Table 4. Ablation study for FFC. Both CCVR and FFC methods exhibit performance gain on non-*i.i.d.* data. For sanity check, we collect local train sets to fine-tune the classifier. FFC is able to achieve a larger accuracy improvement than CCVR with significantly less communication and computation overheads (Table 1).

Calibration	IID	$\alpha = 0.1$
W/o	65.07	61.66
CCVR	65.03 ($\downarrow$0.04)	62.09 ($\uparrow$0.43)
FFC	**65.15** ($\uparrow$**0.08**)	**62.61** ($\uparrow$**0.95**)
Sanity check	65.17 ($\uparrow$0.10)	62.64 ($\uparrow$0.98)

initialization ("+ Fix (OU)"), we generate orthogonal weight matrix via the classic Gram-Schmidt process [1,58]. Other generation methods [52,71] are also considered in the appendix and no significant differences are observed. For the random initialization ("+ Fix (R)"), we instantiate it with He Initialization [21] which is the default initialization method in widely used packages such as PyTorch [56]. Random initialization achieves a comparable but slightly lower accuracy gain because two random vectors tend to be more orthogonal when their dimensionality increases [38,54], while orthogonal initialization directly ensures that.

In addition, SphereFed also normalizes features before feeding them to the classifier (denoted "Norm" in Table 3). After normalization, features are in the same unit hypersphere as the row vectors of classifier's weight and the feature extractor can focus on learning features' directions with the guidance of the fixed classifier. Applying feature normalization for the "Fix (OU)" completes the construction of hyperspherical representation and leads to about 1.22 accuracy gain. More importantly, we show that "Fix (OU)" and feature normalization work better with MSE than CE in the following discussion.

The Superiority of Mean-Square-Error Loss. We evaluate both CE and MSE loss functions in Table 3 to validate our choice of MSE loss. We confirm that replacing CE with MSE improves the accuracy by a considerable margin. The reasons are stated in Sect. 4.3 that MSE avoids the scaling issue and fully exploits the benefit of "Fix (OU) + Norm". For "CE + Fix (OU) + Norm", we find that it is quite sensitive to the scaling hyper-parameter (*i.e.*, temperature). Although we carefully tune the scaling factor τ and report the best result in Table 3, it is difficult and expensive to find the optimal τ in practice.

The Robustness of SphereFed Training. Compared with base algorithms, SphereFed does not introduce any extra hyper-parameters. Since the CE and MSE losses have different magnitudes, we tune their learning rates respectively from a set of candidate learning rates. Interestingly, we observe that SphereFed is more robust than the corresponding base algorithm. In Fig. 4, we test three different learning rates for "FedNova" (as the base algorithm) and "FedNova + SphereFed" with VGG13 on CIFAR-100 ($\alpha = 0.1$). It is observed that "FedNova + SphereFed" is less sensitive to different learning rates.

How Beneficial is FFC? In this set of experiments, we investigate how the closed-form classifier calibration (*i.e.*, FFC) improves test accuracy. We apply CCVR and FFC individually for the classifier of SENet on CIFAR-100 after federated learning with "FedOpt + SphereFed". As a sanity check, we collect all local train sets to fine-tune the classifier only. To ensure the sanity check truly reveals the upper bound of classifier calibration, we experiment different loss functions (*i.e.*, CE and MSE) and learning rates for the sanity fine-tuning and report the best results we get. It can be seen from Table 4 that both CCVR and FFC achieve performance gains on non-*i.i.d.* data while FFC is able to improve accuracy more. CCVR estimates a GMM distribution for each class's features and sample virtual features for model fine-tuning on the server. However, such a class-wise method has relatively high communication and computation complexities (which scale linearly with number of classes). Moreover, GMMs of different classes could be less separable when the number of classes increases, thereby further limiting CCVR's effectiveness. In contrast, FFC, with provable formulations, is agnostic to number of classes and more suitable for realistic many-class federated learning tasks [25,81]. It is expected that FFC obtains comparable results as the sanity check because solving a linear classifier with either closed-form equations or SGD will converge to similar optimums [9,61].

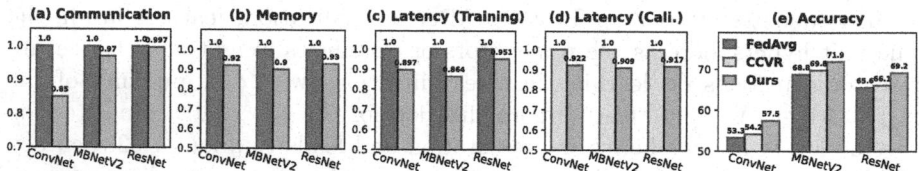

Fig. 5. Efficiency comparison measured on a neural network accelerator [78,91] with three models and CIFAR-100. (a) The normalized total communication amount. (b) The normalized peak memory consumption during local training. (c) The normalized latency for one-round local training. (d) The normalized latency for classifier calibration. (e) The test accuracy.

5.4   Efficient Communication and Computation

Besides accuracy gain, Hyperspherical Federated Learning also brings communication and computation savings depending on the size of classifier.

In Table 1, we compare the communication and computation costs related to the classifier for FedAvg, CCVR and our methods on MobileNetV2 and CIFAR-100. As seen in Table 1, SphereFed eliminates the need of updating and communicating (neither uploading nor downloading), resulting over two orders of magnitude communication and computation savings compared to FedAvg and CCVR.

Figure 5 depicts the relative computational savings of different approaches during the federated training process, measured on a DNN training accelerator built on Xilinx VC707 FPGA evaluation board [78,91]. Detailed settings about the DNN training accelerator are described in the appendix. SphereFed enables us to skip gradient computing for the classifier and thus to release some intermediate tensors used by gradient computing earlier. Overall, SphereFed achieves up to 10.5% and 13.6% savings on memory consumption and processing latency compared with FedAvg, respectively. SphereFed achieves a greater saving of training latency on MobileNetV2 than ConvNet and ResNet. This is because the computation workload associated with the convolutional layers are smaller in MobileNetV2 due to the usage of the depthwise separable operations [62], leading to a greater relative savings when the classifier is skipped during the local training. We also measure the latency of classifier calibration using CCVR and our Fast Federated Calibration in Fig. 5 (d). Since calibration-related computation happens on both clients and the server, the reported latency consists of both the average latency on one client and the on-server latency. Our closed-form calibration saves up to 9.1% latency against CCVR and this efficiency improvement will be more pronounced when number of classes increases as analysed above.

6 Conclusions

We presented the Hyperspherical Federated Learning (SphereFed) framework to address the non-*i.i.d.* issue. The proposed method focuses on the pre-learning phase and is complementary to existing federated learning methods. The hyperspherical representation is learned against a frozen classifier composed of orthonormal basis vectors, and the classifier is calibrated after training. We show that a mean squared loss is more suitable to hyperspherical representation as opposed to a cross-entropy loss due to the scaling issues. A Fast Federated Calibration (FFC) approach is proposed based on the mean squared loss. Extensive experiments indicate that SphereFed improves multiple existing federated learning algorithms by considerable margins.

Acknowledgements. This research was supported in part by the Air Force Research Laboratory under award number FA8750-18-1-0112.

References

1. Torch.linalg.qr. https://pytorch.org/docs/stable/generated/torch.linalg.qr.html
2. Acar, D.A.E., Zhao, Y., Matas, R., Mattina, M., Whatmough, P., Saligrama, V.: Federated learning based on dynamic regularization. In: International Conference on Learning Representations (2021). https://openreview.net/forum?id=B7v4QMR6Z9w
3. Acar, D.A.E., et al.: Debiasing model updates for improving personalized federated training. In: International Conference on Machine Learning, pp. 21–31. PMLR (2021)

4. Achille, A., Golatkar, A., Ravichandran, A., Polito, M., Soatto, S.: LQF: linear quadratic fine-tuning. In: Proceedings of the IEEE/CVF Conference on Computer Vision and Pattern Recognition, pp. 15729–15739 (2021)
5. Al-Shedivat, M., Gillenwater, J., Xing, E., Rostamizadeh, A.: Federated learning via posterior averaging: a new perspective and practical algorithms. In: International Conference on Learning Representations (ICLR) (2021)
6. Anzai, Y.: Pattern Recognition and Machine Learning. Elsevier, Amsterdam (2012)
7. Arivazhagan, M.G., Aggarwal, V., Singh, A.K., Choudhary, S.: Federated learning with personalization layers. arXiv preprint arXiv:1912.00818 (2019)
8. Belkin, M.: Fit without fear: remarkable mathematical phenomena of deep learning through the prism of interpolation. arXiv preprint arXiv:2105.14368 (2021)
9. Boyd, S., Boyd, S.P., Vandenberghe, L.: Convex Optimization. Cambridge University Press, Cambridge (2004)
10. Brier, G.W., et al.: Verification of forecasts expressed in terms of probability. Mon. Weather Rev. **78**(1), 1–3 (1950)
11. Bui, D., et al.: Federated user representation learning. arXiv preprint arXiv:1909.12535 (2019)
12. Chen, C., et al.: Communication-efficient federated learning with adaptive parameter freezing. In: 2021 IEEE 41st International Conference on Distributed Computing Systems (ICDCS), pp. 1–11. IEEE (2021)
13. Chen, Y., Sun, X., Jin, Y.: Communication-efficient federated deep learning with layerwise asynchronous model update and temporally weighted aggregation. IEEE Trans. Neural Netw. Learn. Syst. **31**(10), 4229–4238 (2019)
14. Cheraghian, A., Rahman, S., Fang, P., Roy, S.K., Petersson, L., Harandi, M.: Semantic-aware knowledge distillation for few-shot class-incremental learning. In: Proceedings of the IEEE/CVF Conference on Computer Vision and Pattern Recognition, pp. 2534–2543 (2021)
15. Collins, L., Hassani, H., Mokhtari, A., Shakkottai, S.: Exploiting shared representations for personalized federated learning. In: International Conference on Machine Learning, pp. 2089–2099. PMLR (2021)
16. Diao, E., Ding, J., Tarokh, V.: HeteroFL: computation and communication efficient federated learning for heterogeneous clients. In: International Conference on Learning Representations (2021)
17. Dong, X., Yin, H., Alvarez, J.M., Kautz, J., Molchanov, P.: Deep neural networks are surprisingly reversible: a baseline for zero-shot inversion. arXiv preprint arXiv:2107.06304 (2021)
18. Duan, J.-H., Li, W., Lu, S.: FedDNA: federated learning with decoupled normalization-layer aggregation for non-IID data. In: Oliver, N., Pérez-Cruz, F., Kramer, S., Read, J., Lozano, J.A. (eds.) ECML PKDD 2021. LNCS (LNAI), vol. 12975, pp. 722–737. Springer, Cham (2021). https://doi.org/10.1007/978-3-030-86486-6_44
19. Golik, P., Doetsch, P., Ney, H.: Cross-entropy vs. squared error training: a theoretical and experimental comparison. In: InterSpeech, vol. 13, pp. 1756–1760 (2013)
20. He, C., et al.: FedML: a research library and benchmark for federated machine learning. arXiv preprint arXiv:2007.13518 (2020)
21. He, K., Zhang, X., Ren, S., Sun, J.: Delving deep into rectifiers: surpassing human-level performance on imagenet classification. In: Proceedings of the IEEE International Conference on Computer Vision, pp. 1026–1034 (2015)
22. He, K., Zhang, X., Ren, S., Sun, J.: Deep residual learning for image recognition. In: Proceedings of the IEEE Conference on Computer Vision and Pattern Recognition, pp. 770–778 (2016)

23. Hoffer, E., Hubara, I., Soudry, D.: Fix your classifier: the marginal value of training the last weight layer. In: International Conference on Learning Representations (2018)
24. Hsu, T.M.H., Qi, H., Brown, M.: Measuring the effects of non-identical data distribution for federated visual classification. arXiv preprint arXiv:1909.06335 (2019)
25. Hsu, T.-M.H., Qi, H., Brown, M.: Federated visual classification with real-world data distribution. In: Vedaldi, A., Bischof, H., Brox, T., Frahm, J.-M. (eds.) ECCV 2020. LNCS, vol. 12355, pp. 76–92. Springer, Cham (2020). https://doi.org/10. 1007/978-3-030-58607-2_5
26. Hu, J., Shen, L., Sun, G.: Squeeze-and-excitation networks. In: Proceedings of the IEEE Conference on Computer Vision and Pattern Recognition, pp. 7132–7141 (2018)
27. Hui, L., Belkin, M.: Evaluation of neural architectures trained with square loss vs cross-entropy in classification tasks. In: ICLR (2020)
28. Jain, V., Learned-Miller, E.: Online domain adaptation of a pre-trained cascade of classifiers. In: CVPR 2011, pp. 577–584. IEEE (2011)
29. Jiang, Y., Konečný, J., Rush, K., Kannan, S.: Improving federated learning personalization via model agnostic meta learning. arXiv preprint arXiv:1909.12488 (2019)
30. Kairouz, P., et al.: Advances and open problems in federated learning. arXiv preprint arXiv:1912.04977 (2019)
31. Kang, B., et al.: Decoupling representation and classifier for long-tailed recognition. In: International Conference on Learning Representations (2020)
32. Karimireddy, S.P., Kale, S., Mohri, M., Reddi, S., Stich, S., Suresh, A.T.: Scaffold: stochastic controlled averaging for federated learning. In: International Conference on Machine Learning, pp. 5132–5143. PMLR (2020)
33. Khosla, P., et al.: Supervised contrastive learning. Adv. Neural. Inf. Process. Syst. **33**, 18661–18673 (2020)
34. Kornblith, S., Chen, T., Lee, H., Norouzi, M.: Why do better loss functions lead to less transferable features? Adv. Neural Inf. Process. Syst. **34** (2021)
35. Krizhevsky, A.: Learning multiple layers of features from tiny images. Technical report (2009)
36. Kuangliu: Pytorch-cifar/vgg.py. https://github.com/kuangliu/pytorch-cifar/blob/ master/models/vgg.py
37. Le, Y., Yang, X.S.: Tiny imagenet visual recognition challenge (2015)
38. Lezama, J., Qiu, Q., Musé, P., Sapiro, G.: Ole: orthogonal low-rank embedding - a plug and play geometric loss for deep learning. In: Proceedings of the IEEE Conference on Computer Vision and Pattern Recognition, pp. 8109–8118 (2018)
39. Li, D., Wang, J.: FedMD: heterogenous federated learning via model distillation. In: NeurIPS 2019 Workshop on Federated Learning for Data Privacy and Confidentiality (2019)
40. Li, Q., Diao, Y., Chen, Q., He, B.: Federated learning on non-IID data silos: an experimental study. In: IEEE International Conference on Data Engineering (2021)
41. Li, Q., He, B., Song, D.: Model-contrastive federated learning. In: Proceedings of the IEEE/CVF Conference on Computer Vision and Pattern Recognition, pp. 10713–10722 (2021)
42. Li, T., Sahu, A.K., Talwalkar, A., Smith, V.: Federated learning: challenges, methods, and future directions. IEEE Sig. Process. Mag. **37**(3), 50–60 (2020)
43. Li, T., Sahu, A.K., Zaheer, M., Sanjabi, M., Talwalkar, A., Smith, V.: Federated optimization in heterogeneous networks. Proc. Mach. Learn. Syst. **2**, 429–450 (2020)

44. Liang, P.P., et al.: Think locally, act globally: federated learning with local and global representations. arXiv preprint arXiv:2001.01523 (2020)
45. Liu, W., Wen, Y., Yu, Z., Li, M., Raj, B., Song, L.: SphereFace: deep hypersphere embedding for face recognition. In: Proceedings of the IEEE Conference on Computer Vision and Pattern Recognition, pp. 212–220 (2017)
46. Liu, X., Tang, Z., Huang, H., Zhang, T., Yang, B.: Multiple learning for regression in big data. In: 2019 18th IEEE International Conference On Machine Learning And Applications (ICMLA), pp. 587–594. IEEE (2019)
47. Loshchilov, I., Hutter, F.: SGDR: stochastic gradient descent with warm restarts. arXiv preprint arXiv:1608.03983 (2016)
48. Luo, M., Chen, F., Hu, D., Zhang, Y., Liang, J., Feng, J.: No fear of heterogeneity: classifier calibration for federated learning with non-IID data. IN: 35th Conference on Neural Information Processing Systems (2021)
49. van der Maaten, L., Hinton, G.: Visualizing data using t-SNE. J. Mach. Learn. Res. **9**(86), 2579–2605 (2008). http://jmlr.org/papers/v9/vandermaaten08a.html
50. Mai, X., Liao, Z.: High dimensional classification via empirical risk minimization: improvements and optimality. arXiv preprint arXiv:1905.13742 (2019)
51. McMahan, B., Moore, E., Ramage, D., Hampson, S., Arcas, B.A.: Communication-efficient learning of deep networks from decentralized data. In: Artificial Intelligence and Statistics, pp. 1273–1282. PMLR (2017)
52. Mettes, P., van der Pol, E., Snoek, C.: Hyperspherical prototype networks. Adv. Neural Inf. Process. Syst. **32** (2019)
53. Muthukumar, V., Narang, A., Subramanian, V., Belkin, M., Hsu, D., Sahai, A.: Classification vs regression in overparameterized regimes: does the loss function matter? J. Mach. Learn. Res. **22**(222), 1–69 (2021)
54. Oh, J., Kim, S., Yun, S.Y.: FedBABU: towards enhanced representation for federated image classification. In: International Conference on Learning Representations (2021)
55. Oh, J., Yoo, H., Kim, C., Yun, S.Y.: Boil: towards representation change for few-shot learning. In: International Conference on Learning Representations (2021)
56. Paszke, A., et al.: PyTorch: an imperative style, high-performance deep learning library. Adv. Neural Inf. Process. Syst. **32** (2019)
57. Puigcerver, J., et al.: Scalable transfer learning with expert models. In: International Conference on Learning Representations (2021)
58. Pursell, L., Trimble, S.: Gram-Schmidt orthogonalization by gauss elimination. Am. Math. Mon. **98**(6), 544–549 (1991)
59. Raghu, A., Raghu, M., Bengio, S., Vinyals, O.: Rapid learning or feature reuse? Towards understanding the effectiveness of MAML. In: International Conference on Learning Representations (2019)
60. Reddi, S., et al.: Adaptive federated optimization. In: International Conference on Learning Representations (2021)
61. Saad, D.: Online algorithms and stochastic approximations. Online Learning **5**, 6–3 (1998)
62. Sandler, M., Howard, A., Zhu, M., Zhmoginov, A., Chen, L.C.: MobileNetv 2: inverted residuals and linear bottlenecks. In: Proceedings of the IEEE Conference on Computer Vision and Pattern Recognition, pp. 4510–4520 (2018)
63. Sangari, A., Sethares, W.: Convergence analysis of two loss functions in soft-max regression. IEEE Trans. Sig. Process. **64**(5), 1280–1288 (2015)
64. Shamir, O., Srebro, N., Zhang, T.: Communication-efficient distributed optimization using an approximate newton-type method. In: International Conference on Machine Learning, pp. 1000–1008. PMLR (2014)

65. Shao, S., Xing, L., Wang, Y., Xu, R., Zhao, C., Wang, Y., Liu, B.: MHFC: multi-head feature collaboration for few-shot learning. In: Proceedings of the 29th ACM International Conference on Multimedia, pp. 4193–4201 (2021)
66. Shoham, N., et al.: Overcoming forgetting in federated learning on non-IID data. In: NeurIPS 2019 Workshop on Federated Learning for Data Privacy and Confidentiality (2019)
67. Simonyan, K., Zisserman, A.: Very deep convolutional networks for large-scale image recognition. arXiv preprint arXiv:1409.1556 (2014)
68. Singhal, K., Sidahmed, H., Garrett, Z., Wu, S., Rush, J., Prakash, S.: Federated reconstruction: partially local federated learning. Adv. Neural Inf. Process. Syst. **34** (2021)
69. Smith, V., Chiang, C.K., Sanjabi, M., Talwalkar, A.S.: Federated multi-task learning. Adv. Neural Inf. Process. Syst. **30** (2017)
70. Sun, B., Huo, H., Yang, Y., Bai, B.: PartialFED: cross-domain personalized federated learning via partial initialization. Adv. Neural Inf. Process. Syst. **34** (2021)
71. Tammes, P.M.L.: On the origin of number and arrangement of the places of exit on the surface of pollen-grains. Recueil des travaux botaniques néerlandais **27**(1), 1–84 (1930)
72. Thrampoulidis, C., Oymak, S., Soltanolkotabi, M.: Theoretical insights into multi-class classification: a high-dimensional asymptotic view. Adv. Neural Inf. Process. Syst. (2020)
73. Trefethen, L.N., Bau III, D.: Numerical Linear Algebra, vol. 50. SIAM (1997)
74. Vaswani, A., et al.: Attention is all you need. In: Advances in Neural Information Processing Systems, pp. 5998–6008 (2017)
75. Venkat, N., Kundu, J.N., Singh, D., Revanur, A., et al.: Your classifier can secretly suffice multi-source domain adaptation. Adv. Neural. Inf. Process. Syst. **33**, 4647–4659 (2020)
76. Wang, J., Liu, Q., Liang, H., Joshi, G., Poor, H.V.: Tackling the objective inconsistency problem in heterogeneous federated optimization. Adv. Neural Inf. Process. Syst. (2020)
77. Wang, K., Mathews, R., Kiddon, C., Eichner, H., Beaufays, F., Ramage, D.: Federated evaluation of on-device personalization. arXiv preprint arXiv:1910.10252 (2019)
78. Xilinx: Xilinx virtex-7 fpga vc707 evaluation kit. https://www.xilinx.com/products/boards-and-kits/ek-v7-vc707-g.html
79. Xu, A., Huang, H.: Coordinating momenta for cross-silo federated learning. In: Proceedings of the AAAI Conference on Artificial Intelligence, vol. 36, pp. 8735–8743 (2022)
80. Xu, C., Hong, Z., Huang, M., Jiang, T.: Acceleration of federated learning with alleviated forgetting in local training. In: International Conference on Learning Representations (2021)
81. Yang, K., Fan, T., Chen, T., Shi, Y., Yang, Q.: A quasi-newton method based vertical federated learning framework for logistic regression. In: The 2nd International Workshop on Federated Learning for Data Privacy and Confidentiality, in Conjunction with NeurIPS 2019 (2019)
82. Yao, X., Sun, L.: Continual local training for better initialization of federated models. In: 2020 IEEE International Conference on Image Processing (ICIP), pp. 1736–1740. IEEE (2020)
83. Ye, H.J., Hu, H., Zhan, D.C.: Learning adaptive classifiers synthesis for generalized few-shot learning. Int. J. Comput. Vision **129**(6), 1930–1953 (2021)

84. Yoon, J., Jeong, W., Lee, G., Yang, E., Hwang, S.J.: Federated continual learning with weighted inter-client transfer. In: International Conference on Machine Learning, pp. 12073–12086. PMLR (2021)
85. Yoon, T., Shin, S., Hwang, S.J., Yang, E.: Fedmix: approximation of mixup under mean augmented federated learning. In: International Conference on Learning Representations (2021)
86. You, K., Liu, Y., Wang, J., Long, M.: Logme: practical assessment of pre-trained models for transfer learning. In: International Conference on Machine Learning, pp. 12133–12143. PMLR (2021)
87. Yuan, H., Zaheer, M., Reddi, S.: Federated composite optimization. In: International Conference on Machine Learning, pp. 12253–12266. PMLR (2021)
88. Zhai, A., Wu, H.Y.: Classification is a strong baseline for deep metric learning. arXiv preprint arXiv:1811.12649 (2018)
89. Zhang, L., Luo, Y., Bai, Y., Du, B., Duan, L.Y.: Federated learning for non-IID data via unified feature learning and optimization objective alignment. In: Proceedings of the IEEE/CVF International Conference on Computer Vision, pp. 4420–4428 (2021)
90. Zhang, S.Q., Lin, J., Zhang, Q.: A multi-agent reinforcement learning approach for efficient client selection in federated learning. arXiv preprint arXiv:2201.02932 (2022)
91. Zhang, S.Q., McDanel, B., Kung, H.: Fast: DNN training under variable precision block floating point with stochastic rounding. In: International Symposium on High-Performance Computer Architecture (2021)
92. Zhang, T., Yang, B.: Box-cox transformation in big data. Technometrics **59**(2), 189–201 (2017)
93. Zhao, N., Wu, Z., Lau, R.W., Lin, S.: What makes instance discrimination good for transfer learning? In: International Conference on Learning Representations (2021)
94. Zhao, Y., Li, M., Lai, L., Suda, N., Civin, D., Chandra, V.: Federated learning with non-IID data. arXiv preprint arXiv:1806.00582 (2018)
95. Zheng, Y., Pal, D.K., Savvides, M.: Ring loss: convex feature normalization for face recognition. In: Proceedings of the IEEE Conference on Computer Vision and Pattern Recognition, pp. 5089–5097 (2018)
96. Zhu, Y., Bai, Y., Wei, Y.: Spherical feature transform for deep metric learning. In: Vedaldi, A., Bischof, H., Brox, T., Frahm, J.-M. (eds.) ECCV 2020. LNCS, vol. 12364, pp. 420–436. Springer, Cham (2020). https://doi.org/10.1007/978-3-030-58529-7_25
97. Zhu, Z., Hong, J., Zhou, J.: Data-free knowledge distillation for heterogeneous federated learning. In: International Conference on Machine Learning, pp. 12878–12889. PMLR (2021)

Hierarchically Self-supervised Transformer for Human Skeleton Representation Learning

Yuxiao Chen[1]([✉]), Long Zhao[2], Jianbo Yuan[3], Yu Tian[3], Zhaoyang Xia[1], Shijie Geng[1], Ligong Han[1], and Dimitris N. Metaxas[1]

[1] Rutgers University, Piscataway, USA
yc984@cs.rutgers.edu
[2] Google Research, Los Angeles, USA
[3] ByteDance Incorporated, Seattle, USA

Abstract. Despite the success of fully-supervised human skeleton sequence modeling, utilizing self-supervised pre-training for skeleton sequence representation learning has been an active field because acquiring task-specific skeleton annotations at large scales is difficult. Recent studies focus on learning video-level temporal and discriminative information using contrastive learning, but overlook the hierarchical spatial-temporal nature of human skeletons. Different from such superficial supervision at the video level, we propose a self-supervised hierarchical pre-training scheme incorporated into a hierarchical Transformer-based skeleton sequence encoder (Hi-TRS), to explicitly capture spatial, short-term, and long-term temporal dependencies at frame, clip, and video levels, respectively. To evaluate the proposed self-supervised pre-training scheme with Hi-TRS, we conduct extensive experiments covering three skeleton-based downstream tasks including action recognition, action detection, and motion prediction. Under both supervised and semi-supervised evaluation protocols, our method achieves the state-of-the-art performance. Additionally, we demonstrate that the prior knowledge learned by our model in the pre-training stage has strong transfer capability for different downstream tasks. The source code can be found at https://github.com/yuxiaochen1103/Hi-TRS.

Keywords: Skeleton representation learning · Self-supervised learning · Action recognition · Action detection · Motion prediction

1 Introduction

Human skeleton data [25,26,37] are sequences of human body joints with 2D or 3D coordinates that are extracted from human activity videos. Compared with data from other modalities such as RGB frames [9,44] and depth images

---

Supplementary Information The online version contains supplementary material available at https://doi.org/10.1007/978-3-031-19809-0_11.

S. Avidan et al. (Eds.): ECCV 2022, LNCS 13686, pp. 185–202, 2022.
https://doi.org/10.1007/978-3-031-19809-0_11

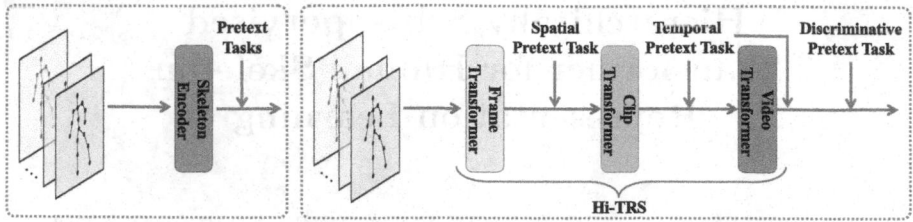

Fig. 1. Comparison of pre-training strategies. **Left:** Previous methods apply pretext tasks to supervise the final output of a skeleton encoder. **Right:** We propose to hierarchically supervise outputs of the encoder at different levels during pre-training

[47,48], human skeletons are light-weight and more robust against variations in illumination, texture, and background [15,40]. Therefore, leveraging skeletons as the input in deep neural networks to understand human activities has become prevalent recently [15,20,40,46,52,56].

Different from other modalities, skeletons have naturally inherent spatial-temporal hierarchies. The main challenge of skeleton-based methods is how to properly capture the domain knowledge (*i.e.*, the correlations among the joints in the spatial and temporal domains) while extract effective feature representations from skeletons. Recent studies [38,40,50] have achieved remarkable performance improvement by learning skeleton encoders in a fully-supervised manner. These methods require massive skeleton training data with task-specific annotations which are expensive and labor-intensive to be collected. Some studies [22,24, 43] tackle the problem by directly applying the self-supervised learning scheme designed for videos or images to skeleton data. Their pretext tasks extract video-level temporal and discriminative information but are only employed to supervise the final encoder outputs, as shown in Fig. 1 (Left). However, these approaches do not consider the hierarchical nature of human skeletons and thus ignore the structural domain knowledge carried by them.

To address the above limitations, we propose a novel skeleton representation learning framework to capture the hierarchical spatial-temporal domain knowledge of human skeletons. As shown in Fig. 1 (Right), it consists of (1) a hierarchical Transformer-based skeleton sequence encoder, namely *Hi-TRS*, incorporating with (2) a hierarchical self-supervised pre-training scheme.

Specifically, the proposed Hi-TRS models skeleton sequence in three levels. Given a skeleton sequence, the Frame Transformer *(F-TRS)* and the Clip Transformer *(C-TRS)* learn the spatial structures (**frame level**) and short-term fine-grained temporal dynamic dependencies (**clip level**) among the skeleton joints by applying self-attentions [45] on the spatial and temporal domains, respectively. Then, the clip-level embeddings are fed to the Video Transformer *(V-TRS)* to summarize long-term abstract information from clips (**video level**) and produce the feature representation of the skeleton sequence. The clip-level embeddings can be applied to short-term skeleton-based tasks, such as action detection [23,25], while embeddings from V-TRS can be used in long-term skeleton-based tasks, such as action recognition [50] and motion prediction [28].

Instead of only supervising the final output of the encoder as in previous work [22,24,43], our framework leverages different pretext tasks to supervise the encoder at different levels. As a result, the encoder acquires different types and levels of prior knowledge on human skeletons. To be specific, the *spatial pretext task* infers the information of one joint conditioned on the other joints from the same time step. It is applied to the output of the F-TRS for learning the spatial dependencies among joints. The *temporal pretext task* assists our model to capture the temporal dynamic prior by distinguishing between valid and invalid motion patterns. It supervises the outputs of C-TRS and V-TRS. The *discriminative pretext task* captures discriminative information for supervising the output of V-TRS, which enforces the model to predict future information in a contrastive manner.

We conduct extensive experiments covering a wide range of tasks and problem settings to evaluate the proposed method. Our approach outperforms the state-of-the-art skeleton representation learning methods on three downstream tasks, including *action recognition*, *action detection*, and *motion prediction*, under both *semi-supervised* and *supervised learning* evaluation protocols. Most noticeably, Hi-TRS improves previous state-of-the-art methods on action recognition by 5.8% (semi-supervised), by 8.1% (supervised) on action detection, and by 4.2% (4.6mm) (semi-supervised) on motion prediction. Additionally, we conclude the following key observations: (1) With the help of our hierarchical supervision, the prior knowledge learned during pre-training is more versatile to support downstream tasks at different levels than prior work using contrastive learning only on the video level (see Sects. 4.5 and 4.6); (2) Our approach demonstrates strong transfer capability under the transfer learning setting, where we achieve significant improvement on action recognition, action detection, and motion prediction tasks by 5%, 4.5%, and 11.7% (12.3 mm), respectively; (3) Our ablation study shows that pre-training at lower levels is beneficial to higher level downstream tasks. Interestingly, we observe similar improvement obtained on lower level downstream tasks when leveraging higher level pre-training.

2 Related Work

Self-supervised Learning. Self-supervised learning targets learning effective feature representations from unlabeled data. It trains the model to solve pre-designed pretext tasks, where labels are automatically generated from data without human efforts. Great efforts have been made in previous work to design pretext tasks [7,33,53]. In computer vision, colorizing grayscale images [53], image inpainting [33], and image jigsaw puzzles [31] are proposed to learn image feature representations. Motion prediction [12], temporal jigsaw puzzle recognition [31], clip orders prediction [49], and sequential verification [29] tasks are employed to learn temporal dynamic information in videos. Recently, contrastive-based pretext tasks [4,13] are introduced to learn instance discriminative information. On the other hand, language-based pre-training objectives are widely used in language domains [2,7,34]. Motivated by the success of these methods, our work leverages in-domain pretext tasks to supervise the encoder at different levels.

Skeleton Representation Learning. Early skeleton representation learning methods [5,11,19,42,55] are mainly based on the encoder-decoder architecture. Zheng *et al.* [55] trained a GAN-based model to reconstruct the original skeleton information from the corrupted input. Su *et al.* [42] trained the model to decode the future motion of the input skeleton sequences. Recent studies adopt the self-supervised learning schemes designed for videos or images to skeleton data. Lin *et al.* [24] trained the model to jointly solve motion prediction, temporal jigsaw puzzle, and contrastive learning discriminative tasks. Li *et al.* [22] presented a memory augmented contrastive learning framework and further improved its performance by pursuing cross-view consistency constraints. Su *et al.* [43] guided the model to learn motion consistency and continuity from videos. A shortcoming of these methods is that they do not explicitly encourage the model to learn the spatial structure of skeletons. Yang *et al.* [51] proposed to represent skeleton sequences as skeleton clouds and learn the spatial and temporal information of skeletons by solving the skeleton cloud colorization problem. However, it required training two different models to learn the spatial and temporal information, respectively. Different from these methods, we use multiple pretext tasks hierarchically to train our model so that the spatial structure, temporal dynamics, and discriminative information can be learned simultaneously.

Downstream Tasks. *Action recognition* aims to predict the action category of a skeleton sequence. Studies in this area mainly focus on designing skeleton-specific architectures for feature encoding. Early methods [16,17,20,40,52,56] applied CNNs or RNNs to extract the representation of skeleton data. Recent methods [38,50] modeled the skeleton data as spatial-temporal graphs and extracted skeleton embeddings from graphs by Graph Convolutional Networks [18]. More recent studies [6,36] leveraged the self-attention mechanism to extract global dependencies among joints. In this work, we use this task to evaluate the effectiveness of skeleton representation learning methods for long-term discriminative tasks. *Action detection* temporally localizes and recognizes the presence of the action in untrimmed videos [23,25,41]. Studies in this area can be categorized into two streams. The first stream [23,25] formulates the task as a frame prediction problem, and generates detection results directly from the predicted categories of each frame in a skeleton sequence. The second stream [21,41] first generates action proposals, and then recognizes action categories from them. This paper follows the first stream to evaluate skeleton representation learning methods for short-term discriminative tasks. *Motion prediction* targets predicting future human poses based on a short observation of human motion [1,3,27,54]. Previous methods employed RNNs to encode observed information and predict future motions [10,28]. These models are trained to generate deterministic results. Recent work incorporated VAEs or GANs to decode multiple possible motions [1,3,27,35]. To evaluate the effectiveness of learned prior knowledge, we fine-tune models to predict deterministic motion in generation tasks.

3 Our Method

3.1 Hierarchical Transformer-Based Encoder

The Hi-TRS model consists of three components: F-TRS, C-TRS, and V-TRS. Given a skeleton sequence, the F-TRS first learns the spatial dependencies among the joints by applying the self-attention operation on the spatial domain. Then, the obtained results are fed to the C-TRS model to further encode the temporal fine-grained dynamics dependencies among joints and extract a feature representation at the clip level. Finally, the V-TRS infers the temporal relations among the clips and extracts the embedding of the input skeleton sequence. In the following sections, we provide details on each component.

Frame Transformer (F-TRS). Given a skeleton sequence, the positional feature of each joint is first extracted from its coordinates by a fully-connected layer with the GELU activation [14]. F-TRS utilizes the positional features from all the joints within a frame of the skeleton sequence as input. It is composed of a stack of F-TRS layers, each of which encodes the spatial dependencies among the joints based on the self-attention mechanism.

To be specific, in the l-th F-TRS layer, the model starts by projecting the input feature of each joint to query, key, and value vectors [45] by three learnable project matrices $\mathbf{W}_Q^l$, $\mathbf{W}_K^l$, and $\mathbf{W}_V^l$, respectively, as described by the following equation:

$$\mathbf{Q}_t^l = \mathbf{W}_Q^l \mathbf{X}_t^{l-1}, \ \mathbf{K}_t^l = \mathbf{W}_K^l \mathbf{X}_t^{l-1}, \ \mathbf{V}_t^l = \mathbf{W}_V \mathbf{X}_t^{l-1}, \tag{1}$$

where $\mathbf{X}_t^{l-1}$ is the matrix of the input features. When $l = 1$, it consists of the positional features of the joints at the t-th frame; otherwise, it is the output of the previous F-TRS layer. $\mathbf{Q}_t^l$, $\mathbf{K}_t^l$ and $\mathbf{V}_t^l$ are the transformed outputs of query, key, and value vectors, respectively. We note that the i-th rows of these four matrices are correspondent to the i-th joint in the skeleton.

The dot-product between each pair of query and key vectors is then calculated and scaled by the dimension number of the key or value vectors. Finally, the attention weights are obtained by normalizing the scaled dot-product with a Softmax function. This process is defined in the following equation:

$$\mathbf{A}_t^l = \text{Softmax}(\frac{\mathbf{Q}_t^l (\mathbf{K}_t^l)^T}{\sqrt{d_k}}), \tag{2}$$

where $(\mathbf{K}_t^l)^T$ is the transpose of $\mathbf{K}_t^l$; d_k is the dimension number of key or value vectors; $\mathbf{A}_t^l$ is the matrix of spatial attention weights among the joints at the t-th frame, and its element at the i-th row and j-th column is the attention weight of the i-th joint with respect to the j-th joint. These attention weights can be regarded as the measure of the spatial dependencies among the joints. The output feature of each joint is updated as the weighted sum of the value vectors, as shown in the following equation:

$$\mathbf{X}_t^l = \mathbf{A}_t^l \mathbf{V}_t^l. \tag{3}$$

As a result, the spatial dependence among joints is encoded into their features.

Following the multi-head attention mechanism [45], the above self-attention operation is performed h times with h different learnable projection matrices $\mathbf{W}_Q^l$, $\mathbf{W}_K^l$, $\mathbf{W}_V^l$, and the obtained h outputs for each joint are concatenated. The results are then fed to the Feedforward Network (FFN) [45], generating the final output of the l-th F-TRS laye.

Clip Transformer (C-TRS). Since a skeleton sequence typically contains a large number of joints and the self-attention operation scales quadratically with respect to the number of joints, learning the fine-grained temporal dependencies over the entire skeleton sequence using self-attention is computationally expensive. To alleviate this problem, we temporally split a skeleton sequence into a sequence of clips C with a sliding window. Then, the temporal dependencies among the joints within each clip of C are learned using the C-TRS model.

Specifically, the input of C-TRS contains the spatial features of the joints within a clip and a [CLS] token [7]. The [CLS] token summarizes useful information from all the joints of the clip, because its output embedding is the weighted sum of all joints features, where the weights are calculated using self-attention [7,8]. The output of the [CLS] token from the C-TRS model is used as the feature representation of the entire clip. The C-TRS model is composed of a stack of C-TRS layers, each of which learns the temporal dependencies among joints by applying the multi-head self-attention mechanism on the temporal domain. We leverage the following equation to compute the attention weights $\mathbf{A}_c$:

$$\mathbf{A}_c = \text{Softmax}(\text{Mask}(\frac{\mathbf{Q}_c(\mathbf{K}_c)^T}{\sqrt{d_k}})), \tag{4}$$

where $\mathbf{Q}_c$ and $\mathbf{K}_c$ are the matrices of the query and key vectors for all the joints within the c-th skeleton clip of C, which are generated following the same way as Eq. 1. More importantly, the Mask function is used for discarding spatial attention weights. It achieves this by setting the scaled dot-product among the joints from the same frame as the negative infinity, and keeps the other joints unchanged. After Softmax, all spatial attention weights in $\mathbf{A}_c$ are equal to 0.

The joint features are updated following the same method as in Eq. 3 to further encode the temporal dependencies information. The output clip-level embeddings of all the clips in C are fed to the V-TRS model to extract the feature representation of the skeleton sequence.

Video Transformer (V-TRS). The V-TRS model summarizes the long-term abstracted video level information. It consists of stacked standard transformer encoder layers [45] and takes clip-level embeddings of all the clips in C together with a [CLS] token as inputs. Each of the V-TRS layers learns the temporal dependencies among the clips. The output embedding of the [CLS] token is used as the feature representation of the skeleton sequence.

3.2   Hierarchical Self-supervised Pre-training

In this section, we introduce the proposed pre-training tasks and describe how they can be applied to supervise the training of the proposed model.

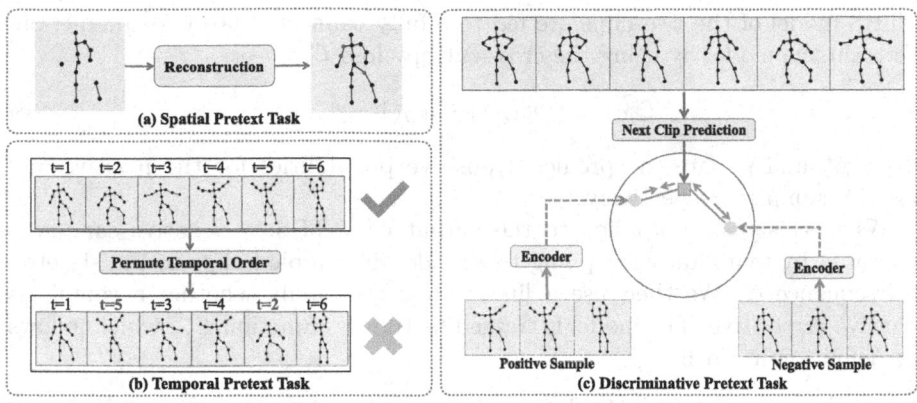

Fig. 2. Overview of our pre-training tasks which include: (**a**) Spatial pretext task: predicting the 3D coordinates of joints based on those of other joints from the same time step; (**b**) Temporal pretext task: predicting whether the temporal dynamic pattern of a skeleton clip or sequence is valid; (**c**) Discriminative pretext task: forecasting the embedding of the next clip of a skeleton sequence

Spatial Pretext Task. The spatial task is to predict the coordinates of a joint based on other joints from the same time step, as shown in Fig. 2(a). Given a skeleton sequence, we first randomly sample 15% of the joints and replace the coordinate of the i-th sampled joints by: (1) the randomly generated coordinate 80% of the time, (2) the coordinate randomly sampled from other joints 10% of the time, and (3) the unchanged coordinate 10% of the time. These strategies are inspired by the masking strategies in BERT [7]. The modified skeleton sequence is fed to the F-TRS model, and then the extracted spatial embeddings of the modified joints are fed to a fully-connected layer to regress their original coordinates. The model is trained to minimize the absolute error between the predicted and ground truth coordinates by the following L1 loss $\mathcal{L}_S$:

$$\mathcal{L}_S = \frac{1}{|M|} \sum_{i \in M} ||\bar{y}_i - y_i||_1, \tag{5}$$

where M is the set of modified joints; $|M|$ is the size of M; $\bar{y}_i$ and y_i are the predicted and ground truth coordinates of the i-th modified joint, respectively.

Temporal Pretext Task. The temporal task requires the model to determine whether the temporal dynamic pattern of a skeleton clip or sequence is valid, as shown in Fig. 2(b). This is a binary classification problem, where the positive samples are the original skeleton sequences or the skeleton clips cropped from the original skeleton sequences, while negative samples are generated by permuting the temporal order of the positive samples. It guides the model to learn the prior knowledge of temporal dynamics. When this task is applied to the output of C-TRS, a positive skeleton clip is generated by temporally cropping a few frames from the skeleton sequence, while the negative sample is created by swapping two randomly sampled frames of the positive clips. The output embeddings from the

C-TRS model of the two clips are fed to a fully connected layer for prediction. We train the model by using the cross-entropy loss $\mathcal{L}_T^C$:

$$\mathcal{L}_T^C = -(log(p^+) + log(1 - p^-)), \tag{6}$$

where p^+ and p^- are the predicted positive possibilities for the positive and negative samples, respectively.

When this task is applied to the output of V-TRS, a negative sample is generated by temporally swapping two randomly sampled clips in the skeleton clip sequence C. We then use a linear layer to classify whether a sample is negative or positive. The model is trained by the loss function $\mathcal{L}_T^V$, which follows the definition in Eq. 6.

Discriminative Pretext Task. This task predicts the embedding of the future clip of a skeleton sequence, as shown in Fig. 2(c). It encourages the model to learn discriminative information by supervising the task in a contrastive way. Specifically, the model is trained to predict the embedding of the last clip in C based on the information from all other clips in C. The output from the C-TRS model of the last clip is used as the ground truth, and all other clips are fed to the V-TRS to extract a video-level embedding, which encodes the past information of the last clip. The obtained video-level embedding is fed to a fully-connected layer to regress the feature of the last clip. The model is trained by using the InfoNCE loss [32] $\mathcal{L}_D$:

$$\mathcal{L}_D = \frac{exp(\bar{e}_i \cdot e_i / \tau)}{\sum_{j=1}^{B} exp(\bar{e}_i \cdot e_j / \tau)}, \tag{7}$$

where $\bar{e}_i$ and e_i are the predicted and ground truth embedding of the last clip of the i-th video, respectively; τ is a temperature hyper-parameter [33]; B is batch size. $\mathcal{L}_D$ enforces the predicted embedding of a sample to be more similar to its ground truth than to those of other negative samples. Compared with previous studies where the contrastive learning methods are based on data augmentation [22,24], our method potentially requires lower computation as it does not require encoding augmented views of input data.

Full Pre-training Objective. The full objective of the proposed hierarchical self-supervised pre-training framework $\mathcal{L}_H$ is: $\mathcal{L}_H = \mathcal{L}_S + \mathcal{L}_T^C + \mathcal{L}_T^V + \mathcal{L}_D$.

4   Experiments

To evaluate the proposed method, we begin by introducing the datasets, evaluation protocols, and implementation details in Sects. 4.1, 4.2, and 4.3, respectively. We then compare our method with the state-of-the-art skeleton representation learning approaches for the action recognition, action detection, and motion prediction tasks in Sects. 4.4, 4.5, and 4.6, respectively. We further evaluate the transfer capability of the learned prior knowledge on human skeletons through pre-training in Sect. 4.7. Finally, we conduct an ablation study to evaluate the proposed pre-training strategy in Sect. 4.8.

4.1 Datasets

NTU RGB+D 60 Dataset (NTU-60). The NTU-60 dataset [37] contains 56,880 videos of 60 action categories. These videos are performed by 40 actors and captured by three Microsoft Kinect v2 cameras from different views. Each video contains at most two subjects. A subject has 25 joints per frame. The 3D joint locations of these joints are extracted by the Microsoft Kinect cameras. Two common evaluation benchmarks [37] are recommended on this dataset. In Cross-Subject (xsub) benchmark, the training videos are from 20 selected subjects, and the testing videos are from the other 20 subjects. In Cross-View (xview) benchmark, the videos from the second and third cameras are used for training, while the videos from the first camera are used for evaluation purpose.

NTU RGB+D 120 Dataset (NTU-120). The NTU-120 dataset [26] is an extended version of the NTU-60 dataset. It contains 113,945 skeleton sequences from 120 action categories. There are two common protocols [26] for this dataset. In Cross-Subject (xsub) benchmark, the samples of the selected 53 subjects are used for training, and the samples of the remaining subjects are used for testing. In Cross-Setup (xset) benchmark, the samples with even setup IDs are used for training, and those with odd setup IDs are used for testing.

PKU Multi-Modality Dataset (PKUMMD). PKUMMD [25] is a new large-scale benchmark for continuous multi-modality 3D human action understanding. It contains almost 20,000 action instances and 5.4 million frames from 52 action categories. Actions are labeled at frame level [25]. The 3D joints are also extracted via the Microsoft Kinect v2 cameras. PKUMMD consists of two subsets: Part I and Part II. Following the common settings [24,25], the training and testing data are split under the Cross-Subject [25] protocol for each subset.

4.2 Evaluation Protocol

Following previous work [22,51], our model is evaluated under two settings: (1) the supervised setting and (2) the semi-supervised setting. Under the supervised setting, the pre-trained encoder is jointly fine-tuned with a linear classifier or a LSTM-based motion decoder [28] for downstream tasks using all the labeled pre-training data. Under the semi-supervised setting, we use the same setup as the supervised setting described above except that the amount of annotated training samples used for fine-tuning is limited.

4.3 Implementation Details

In the F-TRS, C-TRS, and V-TRS models, the number of their layers, attention heads, and dimensions of query vectors are all set as 2, 8, and 64, respectively. The input and output dimensions of the F-TRS, C-TRS, and V-TRS model are 128, 256, and 512, respectively. Before being fed to F-TRS, the input 3D coordinates of each joint are projected to 128 dimensions by a fully connected layer with the GELU activation [14]. The output of F-TRS and C-TRS are

Table 1. Top-1 classification accuracy (%) for action recognition on the NTU-60 and NTU-120 datasets under the supervised setting. "-2S" and "-3S" mean two-stream and three-stream based models, respectively. The best results are highlighted in bold

Method	NTU-60		NTU-120	
	xsub	xview	xsub	xview
MS^{2}L [24] (ACMMM'20)	78.8	81.8	–	–
VPD [30] (ECCV'20)	–	81.4	–	–
MCC [43] (ICCV'21)	83.0	89.7	77.0	77.8
MCC-2S [43] (ICCV'21)	89.7	**96.3**	81.3	83.3
CrosSCLR-3S [22] (CVPR'21)	86.2	92.5	80.5	80.4
SCC-3S [51] (ICCV'21)	88.0	94.9	–	–
Hi-TRS (Ours)	86.0	93.0	80.6	81.6
Hi-TRS-2S (Ours)	89.2	95.1	84.7	86.6
Hi-TRS-3S (Ours)	**90.0**	95.7	**85.3**	**87.4**

fed into a fully-connected layer to increase feature dimension to 256 and 512, respectively, before being fed into C-TRS and V-TRS. Positional encodings [45] are added to the joint features or clip features to retain their spatial identity and temporal information. Specifically, standard learnable 1D positional embeddings [8] are added to the input of F-TRS and V-TRS, while learnable 2D positional embeddings [8] are used for the input of C-TRS. More details can be found in the supplementary materials.

4.4   Results on Action Recognition

In this section, we evaluate our method on the action recognition task. Given a skeleton sequence, the entire Hi-TRS model is used as the encoder, and the outputs from the V-TRS model are fed into a linear classifier (*i.e.*, a fully-connected layer) to predict action categories. For a fair comparison with the two-streams (2S) and three-streams (3S) based methods [22,43,51], we implement a 2S and a 3S version of our method. Specifically, we train three individual models from three different views of skeleton sequences, including joints, motions, and bones following [22]. During the evaluation, the 3S prediction results are obtained by fusing the prediction scores of the three models [22], while the 2S prediction results are obtained by fusing the results of the joint and bone models [22,43].

Supervised Setting. We compare the proposed Hi-TRS with other approaches on NTU-60 and NTU-120 under the supervised setting. The top-1 classification accuracy is reported on each benchmark. The obtained results are shown in Table 1. We can see that our 3S method achieves the state-of-art performance on NTU-60 and NTU-120. Note that the encoders used by several previous methods achieve better performance than our model when the parameters are randomly initialized. For example, when trained from scratch , MCC outperforms the proposed Hi-TRS by 1.9% under the cross-subject setting on the NTU-60 dataset,

Table 2. Top-1 classification accuracy (%) for action recognition on the NTU-60 dataset under the semi-supervised setting. "-2S" and "-3S" mean two-stream and three-stream based models. The best results are highlighted in bold

Method	1% data		5% data		10% data	
	xsub	xview	xsub	xview	xsub	xview
ASSL [39] (ECCV'20)	–	–	57.3	63.6	64.3	69.8
MS²L [24] (ACMMM20)	33.1	–	–	–	65.2	–
MCC-2S [43] (ICCV21)	–	–	47.4	53.3	60.8	65.8
CrosSCLR-3S [22] (CVPR21)	**51.1**	50.0	–	–	74.4	77.8
SCC-3S [51] (ICCV21)	48.3	**52.5**	65.7	70.3	71.7	78.9
Hi-TRS (Ours)	39.1	42.9	63.3	68.3	70.7	74.8
Hi-TRS-3S (Ours)	49.3	51.5	**71.5**	**74.8**	**77.7**	**81.1**

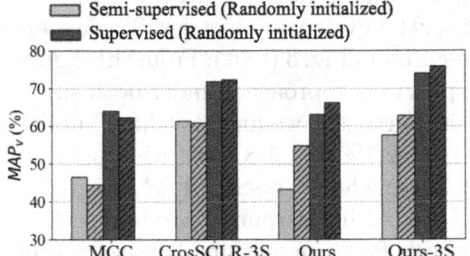 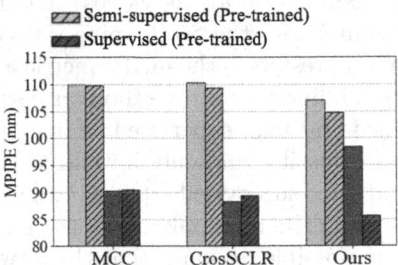

Fig. 3. Left: mAP$_v$ (%) results on the action detection task (the higher the better). **Right**: MPJPE (mm) results on the motion prediction task (the lower the better). We note that the reported results of both MCC [43] and CrosSCLR [22] are based on our implementation. Please refer to the supplementary material for the implementation details and exact numbers of each model

and the 3S-encoders used by CrosSCLR outperforms Hi-TRS by around 3% on the NTU-120 dataset. However, our method is able to outperform them when the models are pre-trained. These results demonstrate that the proposed hierarchical pre-training scheme enables Hi-TRS to learn powerful prior knowledge on human skeletons which can be successfully leveraged in the downstream task.

Semi-Supervised Setting. Following the standard setup in [22,24,51], we fine-tune our pre-trained encoder and the randomly initialized linear classifier with randomly sampled 1%, 5%, and 10% of the training data on the NTU-60 dataset, respectively. From the results reported in Table 2, we observe that the proposed Hi-TRS outperforms the state of the art by a large margin under the 5% and 10% settings. On the other hand, we note that our model performs slightly worse under 1% setting. We hypothesize this is due to the fact that 1% of the training data is insufficient to train Transformer-based encoders with a large number of parameters as explained in [45].

4.5 Results on Action Detection

In this section, we compare our method with previous approaches on the action detection task. This experiment aims to evaluate the effectiveness of the learned skeleton representations for short-term discriminative tasks.

We formulate the action detection task as a per-frame classification problem following the setting in [23,25]. Given one certain frame, we extract a short clip that contains its surrounding information from the entire skeleton sequence. (Due to space limitation, please refer to the supplementary material for more details on how video clips are extracted). The obtained video clip is then fed into F-TRS and C-TRS to extract its feature representation. Finally, a linear classifier is applied to predict the action category of the input frame based on the obtained feature representation.

Following the evaluation setting of [22,23,38], the experiments are conducted on PKUMMD Part I subset. According to [25], we adopt mAP_v (mean average precision of different videos) and mAP_a (mean average precision of different actions) with the overlapping ratio of 0.5 as the evaluation metrics. The experimental results of the mAP_v metric are presented in Fig. 3 (Left). From this figure, we can find that our method outperforms previous approaches under both supervised and semi-supervised settings. More importantly, we find that MCC underperforms its randomly initialized encoder by 2.1% and 1.8% in the supervised and semi-supervised settings, respectively. Meanwhile, CrosSCLR-3S also underperforms its randomly initialized encoder by 0.5% in the semi-supervised setting. One possible reason is that these two methods focus on learning long-term temporal representations [22,43]. As a result, their learned prior knowledge is not effective for short-term downstream tasks. In contrast, the proposed Hi-TRS surpasses its randomly initialized counterpart by a large margin. This demonstrates that our method can capture powerful prior knowledge for short-term downstream tasks, thanks to the proposed hierarchical pre-training strategy. We also have the same observations when the mAP_a metric is utilized, and please refer to the supplementary material for the corresponding results and qualitative analysis.

4.6 Results on Motion Prediction

In this task, the model is trained to predict the motions in the future 400 milliseconds based on an observation of two seconds, following the short-term motion prediction protocol defined in [28]. We adopt this task to evaluate the effectiveness of learned prior knowledge for generation tasks.

Specifically, the observed skeletons are fed into the proposed Hi-TRS to extract feature representations. The outputs of the V-TRS model are fed into a GRU-based decoder [28] to predict the joint coordinates of skeletons for the future 400 ms. The model is then trained to minimize the Euclidean distance between the predicted poses and ground truths.

Following previous work [3,54], we employ MPJPE (mm) as the evaluation metric, which measures the distance between the ground truths and the generated results. The experiments are conducted on the NTU-60 cross-subject

Table 3. Results of motion prediction, action recognition, and action detection under the transfer learning setting. The best results are highlighted in bold

Pre-training Dataset	PKU Part II		PKU Part I	
	MPJPE ↓	Accuracy ↑	mAP$_a$ ↑	mAP$_v$ ↑
Randomly Initialized Encoder	105.4	50.9	53.4	63.2
NTU-60-xsub	94.2	55.0	55.2	66.6
NTU-120-xsub	**93.1**	**55.9**	**57.9**	**67.3**

benchmark as shown in Fig. 3 (Right). From this figure, we can find that our method outperforms previous methods by a large margin under both supervised and semi-supervised settings. Additionally, the learned prior knowledge of the previous methods is not useful under the semi-supervised setting. On the other hand, our method significantly outperforms the randomly initialized counterpart under different settings. It is consistent with the observations on the action detection task, demonstrating that our learned prior knowledge is more versatile to support different downstream tasks than the previous approaches. We also provide qualitative results in the supplementary material.

4.7 Evaluation of Transfer Learning

In this section, we evaluate whether the learned knowledge of Hi-TRS through the pre-training process is transferable across datasets. To this end, we first pre-train two encoders under the cross-subject protocol on NTU-60 and NTU-120, respectively. The pre-trained encoders are then fine-tuned on PKUMMD Part I and PKUMMD Part II for action detection, action recognition, and motion prediction. The obtained results are then compared with the ones of a randomly initialized encoder. These results are reported in Table 3. We can observe that pre-training can improve performance for different-level downstream tasks by a large margin, because the learned prior knowledge is transferable and versatile. Additionally, from the results of "NTU-120-xsub" and "NTU-60-xsub", we find that pre-training on larger datasets can further improve transfer capability.

4.8 Ablation Study

In this section, we evaluate the effectiveness of the proposed hierarchical pre-training strategy. This is achieved by comparing the performance of the encoders that are pre-trained on different levels.

We first show how pre-training on low levels affects the performance of the high-level downstream tasks. The experiments are conducted on the NTU-60 cross-subject benchmark for action recognition and motion prediction under the supervised protocol. The obtained results are reported in Table 4. We find that pre-training on each level (frame level, clip level, and video level) can achieve performance improvement over the randomly initialized encoder, thanks to the

Table 4. Results of the ablation study under the supervised setting on the NTU-60 cross-subject benchmark for action recognition and motion prediction. "-" means the encoder's parameters are randomly initialized. F, C, and V mean that the pre-training tasks are applied on the output of F-TRS, C-TRS, and V-TRS, respectively. The best results are highlighted in bold

Pre-trained Level	–	F	C	V	F+C	F+V	C+V	F+C+V
Accuracy(%) ↑	79.6	80.8	81.1	82.0	83.9	84.1	84.0	**86.0**
MPJPE(mm) ↓	98.4	97.3	96.7	88.1	95.4	87.4	90.2	**85.6**

Table 5. Results of the ablation study under the supervised setting on the PKUMMD Part I subset for action detection. "-" means that the encoder's parameters are randomly initialized. F, C, and V mean that the pre-training tasks are applied on the output of F-TRS, C-TRS, and V-TRS, respectively. The best results are in boldface

Pre-trained Level	–	F+C	F+C+V
mAP_a	53.4	55.6	**58.4**
mAP_v	63.2	65.1	**66.3**

powerful prior knowledge learned from the pre-training tasks of each level. Additionally, pre-training on any combination of two levels achieves higher performance improvement than pre-training on only one level. More importantly, the best improvement is achieved when the encoder is pre-trained on all levels. This confirms the fact that our full model manages to combine prior knowledge containing spatial structure, temporal dynamics, and discriminative information for human skeletons during the pre-training stage.

To further explore how the high-level pre-training tasks affect the low-level downstream tasks, we conduct experiments on the PKUMMD Part I subset for action detection. The results are shown in Table 5. Please refer to the supplementary material for the results of more model variants. We can see that pre-training on high level (video level) leads to performance improvement on the low level downstream task as well, since it can introduce temporal dynamic information and complementary discriminative information.

5   Conclusion

In this work, we proposed a novel method that encodes skeleton sequences using a hierarchical Transformer-based encoder and designed a pre-training scheme consisting of three pretext tasks at three different levels. We conducted extensive experiments under different learning settings. For the supervised and semi-supervised settings, our method achieves the state-of-the-art performance against competitive baselines. Moreover, the learned prior knowledge through hierarchical pre-training shows strong transfer learning capability for downstream tasks at different levels. The experimental results demonstrate that our method is an effective way for learning feature representations of skeleton data.

References

1. Barsoum, E., Kender, J., Liu, Z.: HP-GAN: probabilistic 3D human motion prediction via gan. In: Proceedings of the IEEE conference on computer vision and pattern recognition workshops, pp. 1418–1427 (2018)
2. Bojanowski, P., Grave, E., Joulin, A., Mikolov, T.: Enriching word vectors with subword information. Trans. Assoc. Comput. Linguist. **5**, 135–146 (2017)
3. Cai, Y., et al.: A unified 3D human motion synthesis model via conditional variational auto-encoder. In: Proceedings of the IEEE/CVF International Conference on Computer Vision, pp. 11645–11655 (2021)
4. Chen, T., Kornblith, S., Norouzi, M., Hinton, G.: A simple framework for contrastive learning of visual representations. In: International conference on machine learning, pp. 1597–1607. PMLR (2020)
5. Chen, Y., Zhao, L., Peng, X., Yuan, J., Metaxas, D.N.: Construct dynamic graphs for hand gesture recognition via spatial-temporal attention. In: BMVC (2019)
6. Cheng, Y.B., Chen, X., Chen, J., Wei, P., Zhang, D., Lin, L.: Hierarchical transformer: Unsupervised representation learning for skeleton-based human action recognition. In: 2021 IEEE International Conference on Multimedia and Expo (ICME), pp. 1–6. IEEE (2021)
7. Devlin, J., Chang, M.W., Lee, K., Toutanova, K.: BERT: pre-training of deep bidirectional transformers for language understanding. arXiv preprint arXiv:1810.04805 (2018)
8. Dosovitskiy, A., et al.: An image is worth 16x16 words: transformers for image recognition at scale. arXiv preprint arXiv:2010.11929 (2020)
9. Feichtenhofer, C., Fan, H., Malik, J., He, K.: Slowfast networks for video recognition. In: Proceedings of the IEEE/CVF International Conference on Computer Vision, pp. 6202–6211 (2019)
10. Fragkiadaki, K., Levine, S., Felsen, P., Malik, J.: Recurrent network models for human dynamics. In: Proceedings of the IEEE International Conference on Computer Vision, pp. 4346–4354 (2015)
11. Gui, L.-Y., Wang, Y.-X., Liang, X., Moura, J.M.F.: Adversarial geometry-aware human motion prediction. In: Ferrari, V., Hebert, M., Sminchisescu, C., Weiss, Y. (eds.) ECCV 2018. LNCS, vol. 11208, pp. 823–842. Springer, Cham (2018). https://doi.org/10.1007/978-3-030-01225-0_48
12. Han, T., Xie, W., Zisserman, A.: Video representation learning by dense predictive coding. In: Proceedings of the IEEE/CVF International Conference on Computer Vision Workshops (2019)
13. He, K., Fan, H., Wu, Y., Xie, S., Girshick, R.: Momentum contrast for unsupervised visual representation learning. In: Proceedings of the IEEE/CVF Conference on Computer Vision and Pattern Recognition, pp. 9729–9738 (2020)
14. Hendrycks, D., Gimpel, K.: Gaussian error linear units (gelus). arXiv preprint arXiv:1606.08415 (2016)
15. Hussein, M.E., Torki, M., Gowayyed, M.A., El-Saban, M.: Human action recognition using a temporal hierarchy of covariance descriptors on 3D joint locations. In: Twenty-Third International Joint Conference on Artificial Intelligence (2013)
16. Ke, Q., Bennamoun, M., An, S., Sohel, F., Boussaid, F.: A new representation of skeleton sequences for 3d action recognition. In: Proceedings of the IEEE conference on computer vision and pattern recognition, pp. 3288–3297 (2017)
17. Kim, T.S., Reiter, A.: Interpretable 3D human action analysis with temporal convolutional networks. In: 2017 IEEE Conference on Computer Vision and Pattern Recognition Workshops (CVPRW), pp. 1623–1631. IEEE (2017)

18. Kipf, T.N., Welling, M.: Semi-supervised classification with graph convolutional networks. arXiv preprint arXiv:1609.02907 (2016)
19. Kundu, J.N., Gor, M., Uppala, P.K., Radhakrishnan, V.B.: Unsupervised feature learning of human actions as trajectories in pose embedding manifold. In: 2019 IEEE Winter Conference on Applications of Computer Vision (WACV), pp. 1459–1467. IEEE (2019)
20. Li, C., Zhong, Q., Xie, D., Pu, S.: Skeleton-based action recognition with convolutional neural networks. In: 2017 IEEE International Conference on Multimedia & Expo Workshops (ICMEW), pp. 597–600. IEEE (2017)
21. Li, C., Zhong, Q., Xie, D., Pu, S.: Co-occurrence feature learning from skeleton data for action recognition and detection with hierarchical aggregation. arXiv preprint arXiv:1804.06055 (2018)
22. Li, L., Wang, M., Ni, B., Wang, H., Yang, J., Zhang, W.: 3D human action representation learning via cross-view consistency pursuit. In: Proceedings of the IEEE/CVF Conference on Computer Vision and Pattern Recognition, pp. 4741–4750 (2021)
23. Li, Y., Lan, C., Xing, J., Zeng, W., Yuan, C., Liu, J.: Online human action detection using joint classification-regression recurrent neural networks. In: Leibe, B., Matas, J., Sebe, N., Welling, M. (eds.) ECCV 2016. LNCS, vol. 9911, pp. 203–220. Springer, Cham (2016). https://doi.org/10.1007/978-3-319-46478-7_13
24. Lin, L., Song, S., Yang, W., Liu, J.: MS2L: multi-task self-supervised learning for skeleton based action recognition. In: Proceedings of the 28th ACM International Conference on Multimedia, pp. 2490–2498 (2020)
25. Liu, C., Hu, Y., Li, Y., Song, S., Liu, J.: PKU-MMD: a large scale benchmark for continuous multi-modal human action understanding. arXiv preprint arXiv:1703.07475 (2017)
26. Liu, J., Shahroudy, A., Perez, M., Wang, G., Duan, L.Y., Kot, A.C.: NTU RGB + D 120: a large-scale benchmark for 3D human activity understanding. IEEE Trans. Pattern Anal. Mach. Intell. 42(10), 2684–2701 (2019)
27. Mao, W., Liu, M., Salzmann, M.: Generating smooth pose sequences for diverse human motion prediction. In: Proceedings of the IEEE/CVF International Conference on Computer Vision, pp. 13309–13318 (2021)
28. Martinez, J., Black, M.J., Romero, J.: On human motion prediction using recurrent neural networks. In: Proceedings of the IEEE Conference on Computer Vision and Pattern Recognition, pp. 2891–2900 (2017)
29. Misra, I., Zitnick, C.L., Hebert, M.: Shuffle and learn: unsupervised learning using temporal order verification. In: Leibe, B., Matas, J., Sebe, N., Welling, M. (eds.) ECCV 2016. LNCS, vol. 9905, pp. 527–544. Springer, Cham (2016). https://doi.org/10.1007/978-3-319-46448-0_32
30. Nie, Q., Liu, Z., Liu, Y.: Unsupervised 3D human pose representation with viewpoint and pose disentanglement. In: Vedaldi, A., Bischof, H., Brox, T., Frahm, J.-M. (eds.) ECCV 2020. LNCS, vol. 12364, pp. 102–118. Springer, Cham (2020). https://doi.org/10.1007/978-3-030-58529-7_7
31. Noroozi, M., Favaro, P.: Unsupervised learning of visual representations by solving jigsaw puzzles. In: Leibe, B., Matas, J., Sebe, N., Welling, M. (eds.) ECCV 2016. LNCS, vol. 9910, pp. 69–84. Springer, Cham (2016). https://doi.org/10.1007/978-3-319-46466-4_5
32. van den Oord, A., Li, Y., Vinyals, O.: Representation learning with contrastive predictive coding. arXiv preprint arXiv:1807.03748 (2018)

33. Pathak, D., Krahenbuhl, P., Donahue, J., Darrell, T., Efros, A.A.: Context encoders: feature learning by inpainting. In: Proceedings of the IEEE conference on computer vision and pattern recognition, pp. 2536–2544 (2016)
34. Pennington, J., Socher, R., Manning, C.D.: Glove: global vectors for word representation. In: Proceedings of the 2014 conference on empirical methods in natural language processing (EMNLP), pp. 1532–1543 (2014)
35. Petrovich, M., Black, M.J., Varol, G.: Action-conditioned 3D human motion synthesis with transformer VAE. In: Proceedings of the IEEE/CVF International Conference on Computer Vision, pp. 10985–10995 (2021)
36. Plizzari, C., Cannici, M., Matteucci, M.: Spatial temporal transformer network for skeleton-based action recognition. In: Del Bimbo, A., et al. (eds.) ICPR 2021. LNCS, vol. 12663, pp. 694–701. Springer, Cham (2021). https://doi.org/10.1007/978-3-030-68796-0_50
37. Shahroudy, A., Liu, J., Ng, T.T., Wang, G.: NTU RGB+ D: a large scale dataset for 3D human activity analysis. In: Proceedings of the IEEE Conference on Computer Vision and Pattern Recognition, pp. 1010–1019 (2016)
38. Shi, L., Zhang, Y., Cheng, J., Lu, H.: Two-stream adaptive graph convolutional networks for skeleton-based action recognition. In: Proceedings of the IEEE/CVF Conference on Computer Vision and Pattern recognition, pp. 12026–12035 (2019)
39. Si, C., Nie, X., Wang, W., Wang, L., Tan, T., Feng, J.: Adversarial self-supervised learning for semi-supervised 3D action recognition. In: Vedaldi, A., Bischof, H., Brox, T., Frahm, J.-M. (eds.) ECCV 2020. LNCS, vol. 12352, pp. 35–51. Springer, Cham (2020). https://doi.org/10.1007/978-3-030-58571-6_3
40. Song, S., Lan, C., Xing, J., Zeng, W., Liu, J.: An end-to-end spatio-temporal attention model for human action recognition from skeleton data. In: Proceedings of the AAAI Conference on Artificial Intelligence (2017)
41. Song, S., Lan, C., Xing, J., Zeng, W., Liu, J.: Spatio-temporal attention-based LSTM networks for 3D action recognition and detection. IEEE Trans. Image Process. **27**(7), 3459–3471 (2018)
42. Su, K., Liu, X., Shlizerman, E.: Predict & cluster: Unsupervised skeleton based action recognition. In: Proceedings of the IEEE/CVF Conference on Computer Vision and Pattern Recognition, pp. 9631–9640 (2020)
43. Su, Y., Lin, G., Wu, Q.: Self-supervised 3D skeleton action representation learning with motion consistency and continuity. In: Proceedings of the IEEE/CVF International Conference on Computer Vision, pp. 13328–13338 (2021)
44. Tran, D., Bourdev, L., Fergus, R., Torresani, L., Paluri, M.: Learning spatiotemporal features with 3D convolutional networks. In: Proceedings of the IEEE International Conference on Computer Vision, pp. 4489–4497 (2015)
45. Vaswani, A., et al.: Attention is all you need. In: Advances in Neural Information Processing Systems, pp. 5998–6008 (2017)
46. Vemulapalli, R., Arrate, F., Chellappa, R.: Human action recognition by representing 3D skeletons as points in a lie group. In: Proceedings of the IEEE Conference on Computer Vision and Pattern Recognition, pp. 588–595 (2014)
47. Wang, P., Li, W., Gao, Z., Zhang, J., Tang, C., Ogunbona, P.O.: Action recognition from depth maps using deep convolutional neural networks. IEEE Trans. Human-Mach. Syst. **46**(4), 498–509 (2015)
48. Xiao, Y., Chen, J., Wang, Y., Cao, Z., Zhou, J.T., Bai, X.: Action recognition for depth video using multi-view dynamic images. Inf. Sci. **480**, 287–304 (2019)
49. Xu, D., Xiao, J., Zhao, Z., Shao, J., Xie, D., Zhuang, Y.: Self-supervised spatiotemporal learning via video clip order prediction. In: Proceedings of the IEEE/CVF Conference on Computer Vision and Pattern Recognition, pp. 10334–10343 (2019)

50. Yan, S., Xiong, Y., Lin, D.: Spatial temporal graph convolutional networks for skeleton-based action recognition. In: Thirty-second AAAI Conference on Artificial Intelligence (2018)
51. Yang, S., Liu, J., Lu, S., Er, M.H., Kot, A.C.: Skeleton cloud colorization for unsupervised 3d action representation learning. In: Proceedings of the IEEE/CVF International Conference on Computer Vision, pp. 13423–13433 (2021)
52. Zhang, P., Lan, C., Xing, J., Zeng, W., Xue, J., Zheng, N.: View adaptive recurrent neural networks for high performance human action recognition from skeleton data. In: Proceedings of the IEEE International Conference on Computer Vision, pp. 2117–2126 (2017)
53. Zhang, R., Isola, P., Efros, A.A.: Colorful image colorization. In: Leibe, B., Matas, J., Sebe, N., Welling, M. (eds.) ECCV 2016. LNCS, vol. 9907, pp. 649–666. Springer, Cham (2016). https://doi.org/10.1007/978-3-319-46487-9_40
54. Zhao, L., Peng, X., Tian, Y., Kapadia, M., Metaxas, D.N.: Semantic graph convolutional networks for 3D human pose regression. In: Proceedings of the IEEE/CVF Conference on Computer Vision and Pattern Recognition, pp. 3425–3435 (2019)
55. Zheng, N., Wen, J., Liu, R., Long, L., Dai, J., Gong, Z.: Unsupervised representation learning with long-term dynamics for skeleton based action recognition. In: Proceedings of the AAAI Conference on Artificial Intelligence (2018)
56. Zhu, W., et al.: Co-occurrence feature learning for skeleton based action recognition using regularized deep lstm networks. In: Proceedings of the AAAI Conference on Artificial Intelligence (2016)

Posterior Refinement on Metric Matrix Improves Generalization Bound in Metric Learning

Mingda Wang, Canqian Yang, and Yi Xu[✉]

MoE Key Lab of Artificial Intelligence, AI Institute, Shanghai Jiao Tong University,
Shanghai, China
{597924594,charles.young,xuyi}@sjtu.edu.cn

Abstract. Deep metric learning (DML) attempts to learn a representation model as well as a metric function with a limited generalization gap, so that the model trained on finite known data can achieve similitude performance on infinite unseen data. While considerable efforts have been made to bound the generalization gap by enhancing the model architecture and training protocol a priori in the training phase, none of them notice that a lightweight posterior refinement operation on the trained metric matrix can significantly improve the generalization ability. In this paper, we attempt to fill up this research gap and theoretically analyze the impact of the refined metric matrix property on the generalization gap. Based on our theory, two principles, which suggest a smaller trace or a smaller Frobenius norm of the refined metric matrix, are proposed as guidance for the posterior refinement operation. Experiments on three benchmark datasets verify the correctness of our principles and demonstrate that a pluggable posterior refinement operation is potential to significantly improve the performance of existing models with negligible extra computation burden.

Keywords: Deep metric learning · Generalization · Metric matrix · Posterior refinement

1 Introduction

Deep metric learning (DML) attempts to map instances onto an embedding space, in which similar instances are closer to each other by means of a predefined distance metric function. The most studied metric is Mahalanobis distance, which is parameterized by a metric matrix learned automatically from the data. To enhance the discriminability of the learned metric, recent works focus on the constraints on the embedding space, such as the loss functions [6,11,14,20,21,26,27] which provide direct criterion to learn powerful embedding

---

Supplementary Information The online version contains supplementary material available at https://doi.org/10.1007/978-3-031-19809-0_12.

space, the mining strategies [7,9,25,29] which select training samples contributing significantly to the training procedure, and topology-based methods [30,32] which considers prior knowledge about the data manifold.

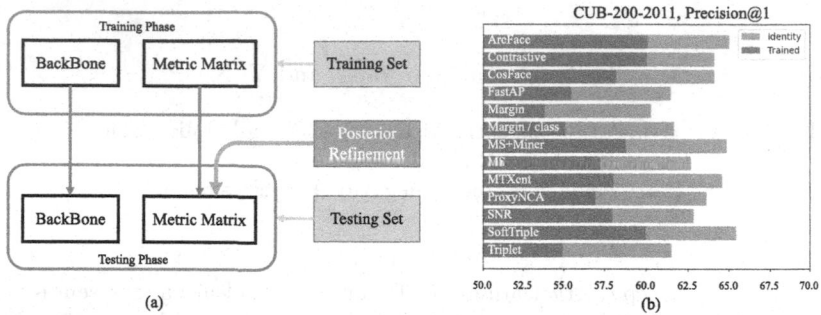

(a)   (b)

Fig. 1. (a) Demonstration about the standard pipeline of training and testing phase for DML models (in blue boxes and arrows). Posterior refinement (red box) can serve as a data-free pluggable operation on the trained metric matrix before the testing phase. (b) Comparison between the standard pipeline (evaluated by the *trained* metric directly) and refining the metric matrix to one *identity* metric matrix (Color figure online)

In the common scenarios of DML, there is no overlap in the data category between the training set and the testing set, which implies extreme data distribution shift. Therefore, achieving good generalization ability of the learned metric is one crucial problem for DML. The generalization ability can be quantified by the generalization gap, which is the difference between the evaluation error on the training set (called *empirical risk error*) and the whole space of possible data (called *expected risk error*), measures the capacity that the metric learned on the finite training set can yield approximate performance on infinite unseen data. The generalization gap is proven to be influenced by the training hypothesis [4] and model magnitude [8]. Accordingly, several methods with theoretical guarantee and practical achievement, including more effective training strategies [4,13] and model regularizer [2,18], are proposed to provide prior guidance **during the training phase** to improve the generalization ability of the trained model.

Despite the efforts mentioned above to learn a more discriminative and generative metric, we uncover an important fact that, even though trained by state-of-the-art DML methods, the trained metric matrix still generalizes no better than an identity matrix as shown in Fig. 1(b). Compared to the standard evaluation pipeline of DML, evaluating with identity metric matrix can be viewed as an additional operation that refines the learned metric matrix before the testing phase as shown in Fig. 1(a) (in this case, the learned metric matrix is refined to be an identity matrix). Such discovery implies that there exists a certain refinement operation on the learned metric matrix which can reduce the generalization gap efficiently. We call these operations as *posterior refinement*, since they are data-free methods that enhance the property of the metric matrix **after the**

training phase. As far as we know, there is no existing work investigating in this subject. Therefore, in this paper, we try to fill up this research gap and provide a theoretical explanation of our discovery. To this end, we establish an upper bound of the generalization gap, which suggests that a smaller trace or smaller Frobenius norm of the refined metric matrix facilitates the generalization ability and vice versa. Based on our formula of the generalization gap, two principles are proposed to serve as the foundation of future posterior refinement operations. The contributions of this paper are three-fold. (1) We indicate the fact that posterior refinement on the metric matrix can improve generalization ability in DML. (2) We provide two principles, which suggest a smaller trace or smaller Frobenius norm of the refined metric matrix, to guide the conduction of the posterior refinement operation and corresponding theoretical analysis to support these principles. (3) We conduct comprehensive experiments to verify the correctness of the proposed principles and demonstrate the effectiveness of the posterior refinement operations.

2 Preliminaries

2.1 Notation

Let $D_n = \{(I_1, y_1), (I_2, y_2), \ldots, (I_n, y_n)\}$ denote a dataset with n instances, where $I_i \in \mathcal{I}$ is the input image sampled from an unknown distribution space $\mathcal{I}$ and y_i is the category label of I_i. For simplicity, we assume that each category contains m instances and there are totally n/m different categories in D_n. Let f denote a feature extractor model parameterized by θ, which maps an image to a d dimensional embedding vector x_i, denoted as $x_i := f(I_i, \theta)$. We assume that x_i is independently and identically distributed (i.i.d.) sampled from an unknown distribution space, $x_i \in \mathcal{X} \subseteq \mathbb{R}^d$. Let $X_n = [x_1, x_2, \ldots, x_n]$ denote the matrix of embedding vectors extracted from the images in D_n, then $X_n \in \mathcal{X}^n \subseteq \mathbb{R}^{d \times n}$. Let $M \in \mathcal{M} \subset \mathbb{R}^{d \times d}$ denote a trainable metric matrix, where $\mathcal{M}$ denotes the space of symmetric positive semi-definite matrices.

Given a dataset D_n, a feature extractor model f and a metric matrix M, the evaluation error of DML model, denoted as $L(X_n, M)$, can be derived as follows. Let $sim(x_i, x_j, M)$ denote the similarity between the embedding vectors of two instances under the metric of M. Let $\mathcal{T}$ denote the set of all possible data triplets collected from D_n, where each data triplet $t = \{i, j, k\} \in \mathcal{T}$ is composed of the instance index of an anchor instance i, a positive instance j and a negative instance k. $sim(x_i, x_j, M)$ is supposed to overpass $sim(x_i, x_k, M)$. In practice, the positive instance is generally sampled from the instance set sharing the same category with the anchor, and the negative instance belongs to another different category. Let $l(t, M) = max\{sim(x_i, x_k, M) - sim(x_i, x_j, M), 0\}$ denote the error caused by one data triplet. When $l(t, M) = 0$, the similarity between positive data pairs has surpassed that of negative pairs so there is no error. Otherwise, a bigger $l(t, M)$ implies a relatively higher degree that the model deviates from the successful discrimination of data triplet t. Then, the evaluation error $L(X_n, M)$

can be expressed as the expected error for all data triplets

$$L(X_n, M) = \underset{t \in \mathcal{T}}{\mathbb{E}}[l(t, M)] = \frac{1}{|\mathcal{T}|} \sum_{t \in \mathcal{T}} l(t, M) \tag{1}$$

where $|\mathcal{T}|$ denotes the number of data triplets in $\mathcal{T}$.

Now we rewrite Eq. 1 in the form of matrices. Let $S = X_n^T M X_n$ denote the pairwise similarity matrix of X_n, where each element of S is equal to the similarity of two instances, $s_{ij} = x_i^T M x_j = sim(x_i, x_j, M)$. For each data triplet $t = \{i, j, k\}$, a $n \times n$ sparse sampling matrix C^t is generated, where $c_{ji}^t = -1$, $c_{ki}^t = 1$ and all other elements are zero. Let $A := SC^t$, so the diagonal elements of matrix A are all zero except $a_{ii} = sim(x_i, x_k, M) - sim(x_i, x_j, M)$. Let Λ^t denote a sparse matrix where $\lambda_{ii} = 1$ if $a_{ii} > 0$ and $\lambda_{ii} = 0$ otherwise. Therefore, $l(t, M)$ can be rewritten in the form of matrices as $l(t, M) = tr(A\Lambda^t) = tr(X_n^T M X_n C^t \Lambda^t)$.

However, consider one case that $M_1 = 2M_2$, then $l(t, M_1) = 2l(t, M_2)$, but the performance of M_1 and M_2 will be exactly the same because the similarity ranking of data pairs are not changed. To eliminate the influence of the scalar on the metric matrix, we introduce $P(M)$ to $l(t, M)$, defining the error as $l(t, M) := tr(X_n^T M X_n C^t \Lambda^t)/P(M)$, where $P(M)$ represents a certain property of the metric matrix. It is easy to verify that in the case of $M_1 = 2M_2$, if we define the property function as the Frobenius norm $P(M) := \|M\|_F$, then $l(t, M_1) = l(t, M_2)$. Thus, in this paper we will only discuss the reduction of generalization gap **on condition that** $P(M)$ **is fixed**.

Then, $L(X_n, M)$ can be rewritten as

$$L(X_n, M) = \frac{1}{P(M)|\mathcal{T}|} \sum_{t \in \mathcal{T}} tr(X_n^T M X_n C^t \Lambda^t) \tag{2}$$

$$= \frac{1}{P(M)|\mathcal{T}|} tr(X_n^T M X_n (\sum_{t \in \mathcal{T}} C^t \Lambda^t))$$

$$= \frac{1}{P(M)|\mathcal{T}|} tr(X_n^T M X_n C_n)$$

where $C_n := \sum_{t \in \mathcal{T}} C^t \Lambda^t$ is named as the *similarity sampling matrix* for D_n.

In the general protocol of DML, two datasets sharing non-overlap in class category are collected, namely the training set D_{tr} and the testing set D_{te}. For simplicity, in this paper the instance numbers of D_{tr} and D_{te} are both assumed to be n and each category is assumed to contain m instances, which is generally the case of DML benchmark datasets as described in Sect. 4.1. This assumption means that $\mathcal{T}$ and $|\mathcal{T}|$ are exactly the same for D_{tr} and D_{te}. Therefore, in the rest of this paper we will not distinguish these symbols separately for the training set and testing set.

2.2   Generalization Gap of DML

Given a training set D_{tr} and a metric matrix M, the empirical risk error is defined as the evaluation error of the current model on D_{tr}, which can be represented as *empirical   risk   error* $:= L(X_{tr}, M)$. According to the empirical risk minimization (ERM) optimization principle, the task of the DML training procedure is to obtain optimal parameters for feature extractor function θ^* and an optimal metric matrix M^* such that

$$\theta^*, M^* = \arg\min_{\theta, M} L(X_{tr}, M)$$

The training procedure of the DML model attempts to minimize the empirical risk error via a certain optimization algorithm, such as gradient descent (GD).

Since we concern more about the performance of the trained model on unseen data, the expected risk error, which refers to the evaluation error on the whole space of all possible data, is wished to approximate the empirical error which has been reduced during the training procedure. Therefore, a good DML model should have a small generalization gap, which is the difference between the empirical risk error and expected risk error. Let $L(\mathcal{X}, M^*)$ denote the expected risk error, the generalization gap $G(\mathcal{X}, M^*)$ of DML is denoted as

$$G(\mathcal{X}, M^*) := L(\mathcal{X}, M^*) - L(X_{tr}, M^*) \tag{3}$$

The previous works [2,4,8,18] attempt to study $G(\mathcal{X}, M^*)$ directly. To reach a tighter bound of $G(\mathcal{X}, M^*)$, these works study the impact of property of M^* and θ^* on $G(\mathcal{X}, M^*)$, proposing restraints or training protocols to adjust the property of optimal M^* *a priori* in the training phase. Orthogonal to these works, in this paper we investigate in the impact of *posterior* refinement operation on the metric matrix. Suppose that an optimal metric matrix M^* and corresponding θ^* have been obtained via certain optimization procedure, before evaluating the learned metric in the testing phase, we further refine the trained metric matrix $M' = g(M^*)$ by a matrix refinement operation $g : \mathcal{M} \rightarrow \mathcal{M}$. M' is assumed to be still symmetric positive semi-definite, which is the prerequisite that one square matrix can serve as a metric matrix. Then, our objective generalization gap $G(\mathcal{X}, M', M*)$ is represented as

$$G(\mathcal{X}, M', M^*) := L(\mathcal{X}, M') - L(X_{tr}, M^*) \tag{4}$$

which is the difference between the expected risk error under the metric of M' and the empirical error under the metric of M^*. Since by definition, posterior refinement will not consider the improvement of θ^* or M^*, θ^* and M^* can be regarded as constant variables, thus $L(X_{tr}, M^*)$ can be regarded as one definite and constant number. Then the upper bound of $G(\mathcal{X}, M', M^*)$ is purely determined by $L(\mathcal{X}, M')$. In the next section, we will analyze the upper bound of $L(\mathcal{X}, M')$, which has only one constant difference to the generalization gap.

3   Upper Bound of the Generalization Gap

In this section, we will derive the formula of the expected risk error under the posterior refined metric matrix $L(\mathcal{X}, M')$, and establish the link from its upper bound to the property of the refined metric matrix. Finally, based on our theorem, we will point out two principles to reduce the upper bound of $L(\mathcal{X}, M')$, which also lowers the upper bound of the generalization gap.

3.1   Formula of Expected Risk Error

Consider the general evaluation pipeline to evaluate a trained metric M on distribution $\mathcal{X}$. First, n instances are newly sampled to form the reference set denoted as D_{ref}. None of the instances in D_{ref} has been used for training. Let $X_{ref} = [x_1^{ref}, x_2^{ref}, \ldots, x_n^{ref}]$ denote the embedding matrix of D_{ref} generated by feature extractor function f. In practice, the testing set can be regarded as the reference set. Then, let $x_i' \in \mathcal{X}$ denote a random variable which is supposed to share the same category as x_i^{ref}. Let $X_i = [x_1^{ref}, x_2^{ref}, \ldots, x_{i-1}^{ref}, x_i', x_{i+1}^{ref}, \ldots, x_n^{ref}]$ denote the embedding matrix which is prepared to evaluate the error caused by x_i' and let C_i denote the corresponding similarity sampling matrix. X_i only differs X_{ref} in the ith column. Then, the error on random variable x_i' can be denoted as $L(X_i, M')$. Therefore, the expected risk error can be represented as the expectation of the error caused by all x_i'.

$$L(\mathcal{X}, M') = \mathbb{E}_i[L(X_i, M')] = \frac{1}{n} \sum_{i=1}^{n} L(X_i, M') \tag{5}$$

For $L(X_i, M')$, notice that X_i is a finite set with only one random variable x_i'. Then, $L(X_i, M')$ can be represented as the expectation over this random variable

$$L(X_i, M') = \frac{1}{P(M')|T|} \int_{x_i' \in \mathcal{X}} p(x_i') tr(X_i^T M' X_i C_i) dx_i' \tag{6}$$

where $p(x_i')$ is the probability density function (PDF) of x_i'. Carrying Eq. 6 into Eq. 5, we get

$$L(\mathcal{X}, M') = \frac{1}{nP(M')|T|} \sum_{i=1}^{n} \int_{x_i' \in \mathcal{X}} p(x_i') tr(X_i^T M' X_i C_i) dx_i' \tag{7}$$

Let $X' = [x_1', x_2', \ldots, x_n']$ denote the embedding matrix of n random variables. Since x_i' is i.i.d., then $p(X') = p(x_1')p(x_2')\ldots p(x_n')$. Also notice that $\forall i, \int_{x_i' \in \mathcal{X}} p(x_i') dx_i' = 1$, thus we can always attach an additional integral on x_j' such that the following equation holds

$$\int_{x_i' \in \mathcal{X}} p(x_i') tr(X_i^T M' X_i C_i) dx_i' = \int_{x_i' \in \mathcal{X}, x_j' \in \mathcal{X}} p(x_i') p(x_j') tr(X_i^T M' X_i C_i) dx_i' dx_j'$$
$$\tag{8}$$

Then, Eq. 7 can be further rewritten as

$$L(\mathcal{X}, M') = \frac{1}{nP(M')|T|} \sum_{i=1}^{n} \int_{x_1', \ldots, x_n' \in \mathcal{X}} p(x_1') \ldots p(x_n') tr(X_i^T M' X_i C_i) dx_1' \ldots dx_n'$$

$$= \frac{1}{nP(M')|T|} \sum_{i=1}^{n} \int_{X' \in \mathcal{X}^n} p(X') tr(X_i^T M' X_i C) dX'$$

$$= \int_{X' \in \mathcal{X}^n} p(X') \frac{1}{n} \sum_{i=1}^{n} \left(\frac{1}{P(M')|T|} tr(X_i^T M' X_i C_i) \right) dX'. \tag{9}$$

The last equality switch the order of $\frac{1}{n}\sum_{i=1}^{n}$ and $\int_{X' \in \mathcal{X}^n} p(X')$, because these two components are separable.

Equation 9 points out the difference between the evaluation error on the testing set $L(X_{te}, M')$ and the expected error $L(\mathcal{X}, M')$. Consider the standard evaluation procedure of DML models. For each instance in the testing set, the rest of the testing set is regarded as the reference set. Then the set prepared to evluate the error of ith testing instance is $X_{te_i} = [x_1^{ref}, \ldots, x_{i-1}^{ref}, x_i^{te}, x_{i+1}^{ref}, \ldots x_n^{ref}] = X_{te} = X_{ref}$, here by assumption the testing set is used as the reference set. Thus the error caused by the ith testing instance is $L(X_{te_i}, M') = \frac{1}{P(M')|T|}tr(X_{ref}^T M' X_{ref} C)$. The evaluation error on the testing set is the expected error across all testing instances, denoted as $L(X_{te}, M') = \frac{1}{n}\sum_{i=1}^{n}\left(\frac{1}{P(M')|T|}tr(X_{ref}^T M' X_{ref} C)\right) = \frac{1}{P(M')|T|}tr(X_{ref}^T M' X_{ref} C)$. Therefore, from Eq. 9, we known that actually, there is a gap between $L(X_{te}, M')$ and $L(\mathcal{X}, M')$, where $L(\mathcal{X}, M')$ further requires an integral over X'. Such a gap is caused by the oversight of the current evaluation procedure that, when evaluating the error of x_i^{te}, it should be regarded as a random variable instead of one fixed variable. Therefore, to give a more fundamental theoretical analysis of the generalization gap, we will analyze and try to reduce the upper bound of $L(\mathcal{X}, M')$ instead of $L(X_{te}, M')$.

For the upper bound of $L(\mathcal{X}, M')$, we only need to analysis the upper bound of $\frac{1}{n}\sum_{i=1}^{n}\left(\frac{1}{P(M')|T|}tr(X_i^T M' X_i C_i)\right)$, since in Eq. 9 (1) $p(X')$ is determined by the intrinsic distribution of image space and the model parameters θ^*, thus changing the property of M' will not influence $p(X')$. So we neglect the impact of $p(X')$ on the upper bound of $L(\mathcal{X}, M')$. (2) $p(X')$ is a non-negative function, so the upper bound of $L(\mathcal{X}, M')$ is positively correlated to the upper bound of $\frac{1}{n}\sum_{i=1}^{n}\left(\frac{1}{P(M')|T|}tr(X_i^T M' X_i C_i)\right)$. Then, in the following the upper bound of $\frac{1}{n}\sum_{i=1}^{n}\left(\frac{1}{P(M')|T|}tr(X_i^T M' X_i C_i)\right)$ will be linked to the property of M'.

3.2 Upper Bound of Expected Error

In the following the uniform upper bound u of $tr(X_i^T M' X_i C_i)/P(M')$ across the index i will be derived, denoted as $tr(X_i^T M' X_i C_i)/P(M') \leq u$. Then the objective formula can be upper bounded by $\frac{1}{n}\sum_{i=1}^{n}\left(\frac{1}{P(M')|T|}tr(X_i^T M' X_i C_i)\right) \leq \frac{u}{|T|}$. Therefore, eliminating u can reach a tighter upper bound of expected risk error $L(\mathcal{X}, M')$. Suppose $|x_i' - x_i^{ref}|_2 \leq \epsilon_1$, where $|x|_2$ denote the L2 norm of vector x. Let $\|X\|_F$ denote the Frobenius norm of matrix X. First, consider the most simple and general case that $P(M') := \|M'\|_F$, then

Theorem 1. $tr(X_i^T M' X_i C_i)/\|M'\|_F$ is upper bounded by

$$tr(X_i^T M' X_i C_i)/\|M'\|_F \leq \delta_1 \delta_2 tr(M')/\|M'\|_F \quad (10)$$

where $\delta_1 := (\|X_{ref}\|_F + \epsilon_1)^2$, $\delta_2 := \sqrt{\frac{n}{m}(m-n)^2 + \frac{n^2-n}{m^2}(m-1)^2}$

Proof. See Supplementary ??

Except $tr(M')/\|M'\|_F$, the dominating factors of other components, including $\epsilon_1, \delta_1, \delta_2$, are not related to the property of M'. Observing Eq. 10, it is easy to verify that reducing the trace of the learned metric matrix will result in a relative smaller $tr(M')/\|M'\|_F$. Then the first principle to guide the posterior refinement operation on the metric matrix can be summarized as

Principle 1. *If the refined matrix is symmetric positive semi-definite, then reducing the trace of the learned metric matrix leads to a tighter upper bound for expected risk error under the metric of the refined matrix.*

Theorem 1 points out the correlation of the generalization ability and the trace of the refined metric matrix. Since $tr(M')$ can also eliminate the influence of matrix scalar, in the following, we attempt to derive another upper bound of $tr(X_i^T M' X_i C_i)/P(M')$ when $P(M') := tr(M')$. The following theorem holds

Theorem 2. $tr(X_i^T M' X_i C_i)/tr(M')$ *is upper bounded by*

$$tr(X_i^T M' X_i C_i)/tr(M') \leq \delta_3 \|M'\|_F /tr(M') \tag{11}$$

where $\delta_3 = \epsilon_1 \sqrt{\delta_1} \delta_2 + \epsilon_1^2 \delta_2 + \delta_2 \|X_{ref}\|_F^2$.

Proof. See supplementary ??.

The Theorem 2 is simple and straightforward. Since δ_3 is not dominated by the metric matrix anymore, it is easy to draw the following second principle

Principle 2. *If the refined matrix is symmetric, then fixing the trace and reducing the Frobenius norm of the learned metric matrix leads to a tighter upper bound for expected risk error under the metric of the refined matrix.*

4   Experiments

4.1   Experiment Setup

Dataset. We conduct experiments on three widely-used benchmark datasets for deep metric learning: CUB-200-2011 (CUB) [28], Cars196 (Cars) [12] and Stanford Online Products (SOP) [16]. For CUB, we use the first half split of 100 classes with 5, 864 images for training and 5, 924 images from the last half split for testing. Similarly, for Cars, 8, 054 images of the first 98 classes are used for training and 8, 131 images of the rest classes are used for testing. For SOP, we follow the official dataset split using the first 11, 318 classes with 59, 551 images for training and the rest 11, 316 classes with 60, 502 instances for testing. Therefore, for the training set and testing set, neither the total instance number nor the class number differs much, supporting our assumption about DML datasets in Sect. 2.1.

Trained Models. All the evaluated models have already been trained under the constraint of a certain loss function following the training protocols on powerful-benchmarker [15], a fair comparison platform for deep metric learning. To be more specific, BN-Inception [10] pretrained on ImageNet dataset [3] is adopted as the backbone model with output embedding dimension of 1024. A Multi-layer Perceptron (MLP) as the neck model further reduces the embedding dimension to 128. All mini-batches are constructed by arbitrarily sampling 32 (or 8) classes and 1 (or 4) instances per class for training data, resulting in a mini-batch size of 32. As for image augmentation, all images are resized into 256×256 pixels and then randomly cropped to patches of 227×227 pixels during training. RMSprop [22] under a fixed learning rate of 10^{-6} is employed to train the backbone model and the neck model simultaneously. The training is terminated when no improvement is gained on the validation set. 50 iterations of Bayesian optimization are run to find the best hyperparameters of the DML methods compared in [15]. Each iteration consists of 4-fold cross-validation. Therefore, the best performance yielded by the Bayesian optimization measures the upper bound of the discrimination ability that the corresponding DML method can achieve. We refer the readers to [15] for more details about the training protocol.

Evaluation Protocol. Each run of the experiment consists of 4-fold cross-validation, generating 4 different packages of model, each model package contains the checkpoints of one backbone model and one neck model. For each fold, the accuracy of the corresponding model package is obtained, and therefore we can obtain 4 different accuracies for each DML method. Then the average of these 4 accuracies is reported as the final accuracy for this run.

For each DML method, the hyperparameters and the corresponding model checkpoints for the highest-accuracy run are provided by [15]. We directly fetch these checkpoints and follow the above-mentioned evaluation protocol to compare the testing accuracy under different posterior refinement methods.

4.2   Posterior Refinement Methods

From the view of deep metric learning, the backbone model serves as the feature extractor, mapping an input sample I_i to an embedding vector $x_i \in R^d$. Let $W \in R^{d' \times d}$ denote the weight of the neck model which conducts linear dimension reduction from d to d'. The similarity of two samples (I_i, I_j) can be represented as the inner product of two d' dimensional embeddings, denoted as $x_i^T (W^T W) x_j$. Therefore, the symmetric positive semi-definite matrix $M^* := W^T W$ can serve as the metric matrix, which is trainable as model parameters during the training procedure. To verify the correctness of our principles, we implement several refinement operations on the trained metric matrix M^*, namely

1. **Diagonal Restraint** which randomly restrains the diagonal elements of M^* to be zero. To be more specific, given a hyperparameter $0 \leq r \leq 1$, we

randomly set one non-zero diagonal element of M^* to be zero and repeated this operation until $tr(M') \leq (1-r)tr(M^*)$. In the extreme case when $r = 1$, all the diagonal elements of M^* are set to zero. Diagonal restraint is prepared to evaluate the correctness of Principle 1.

2. **Random Restraint** which randomly restrains the non-diagonal elements of M^* to be zero. Analogous to diagonal restraint, we randomly select an index pair $\{i, j\}(i \neq j)$, and set two elements to be zeros $m_{ij} = 0$, $m_{ji} = 0$. This operation is repeated until $\|M_{off}'\|_F \leq (1-r)\|M_{off}^*\|_F$, where M_{off} denote the off-diagonal part of the matrix. Random restraint is prepared to evaluate the correctness of Principle 2. To decouple the effect of matrix trace, we avoid setting the diagonal elements to zero, so that the accuracy diversification can be purely traced to $\|M'\|_F$.

3. **Identity Refinement** which set M' to be a $d \times d$ identity matrix regardless of M^*.

The above three restraint methods can satisfy the precondition in two principles as discussed in Section ??, thus they can be used to verify the correctness of two principles. For diagonal restraint and random restraint, the hyperparameter r controls the degree to which the matrix restraint is carried out. A relative larger r requests that we have to restrain more elements of M^* to be zero, resulting in smaller $tr(M')$ for diagonal restraint, or smaller $\|M'\|_F$ for random restraint.

After the refinement operation, on the testing set we collect the embedding vectors generated by the trunk model, compute the pairwise similarity under the refined metric matrix, and compute the accuracy via a KNN classifier just as the standard evaluation pipeline.

Table 1. Comparison between the trained metric, identity matrix (marked as *) and the best refined matrix under random restraint or diagonal restraint (marked as †). The superscript $D/R, r$ represents such best refinement method is **D**iagonal or **R**andom restraint with restraint degree r. The best and the second best metric for each DML method is highlighted in red and blue, respectively

Methods	CUB			Cars			SOP		
	MAP	Pre@1	RP	MAP	Pre@1	RP	MAP	Pre@1	RP
ArcFace[23]	21.51	60.12	32.39	17.48	72.88	27.66	42.23	71.98	45.15
ArcFace*	24.20	65.06	35.05	18.10	78.79	27.78	42.18	72.28	44.93
ArcFace†	24.18	64.90	35.03^{R,1}	18.66	78.80	28.55^{D,1}	43.08	73.02	45.88^{D,1}
ProxyNCA[14]	19.39	56.99	30.18	18.85	73.91	29.43	41.90	71.51	44.86
ProxyNCA*	22.16	63.64	33.03	18.43	80.10	28.27	41.96	71.79	44.75
ProxyNCA†	22.16	63.55	33.03^{R,1}	19.58	79.82	29.76^{D,1}	42.80	72.48	45.65^{D,1}
Triplet[27]	18.29	54.95	29.09	15.35	64.92	26.14	38.50	67.96	41.75
Triplet*	21.16	61.52	32.07	16.90	74.86	27.21	40.33	70.49	43.33
Triplet†	21.16	61.61	32.08^{R,1}	17.16	72.53	27.82^{D,1}	40.45	70.28	43.55^{D,1}

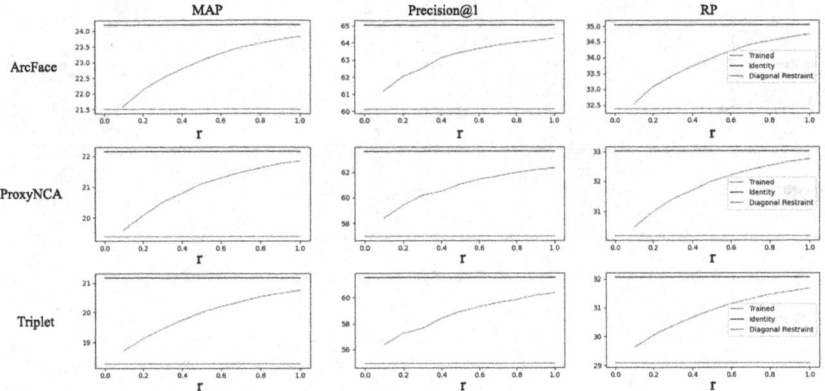

Fig. 2. Ablation of the restraint degree r for diagonal restraint on three DML methods. From left to right column enumerates the accuracy of MAP, Precision@1 and RP. Models are trained by ArcFace, ProxyNCA and Triplet

4.3 Problem Observation

Recall that the motivation of this paper is founded on one observation that the identity matrix generalizes better than the trained metric matrix. To reveal this observation more comprehensively and specifically, in Table 1 we compare the performance of the trained metric, the identity matrix and the best performance of diagonal restraint or random restraint based metric matrix among three DML methods over three benchmark datasets. Of the three methods, ArcFace [23] is the SOTA method on CUB, ProxyNCA is a classical classification-based method, and Triplet loss is one classical pair-based method. Please refer to supplementary for full comparison across all methods in [15]. As can be clearly observed, for each DML method, the performance of identity matrix or restrained based metric has a remarkable margin in advance of the trained metric. Roughly speaking, the refined matrices improves MAP by 3%, precision@1 by 5%, RP by 3% on CUB, MAP by 1%, precision@1 by 7%, RP by 0.5% on Cars, and MAP by 1%, precision@1 by 2%, RP by 1% on SOP. Since identity refinement can be regarded as one special case of posterior refinement operation, we claim that there exist lightweight posterior refinement operations which can boost the performance of the trained metric significantly.

4.4 Verification of Two Principles

Principle 1. To evaluate the correctness of Principle 1, we conduct ablation study about the restraint degree r for diagonal restraint. A relatively larger r means that we have to set more diagonal elements of M' to be zero, leading to a relatively smaller $tr(M')/\|M'\|_F$. According to Principle 1, this will result in a tighter upper bound for the expected risk error, thus increasing the accuracy in practice. Therefore, we conduct diagonal restraint under different restraint

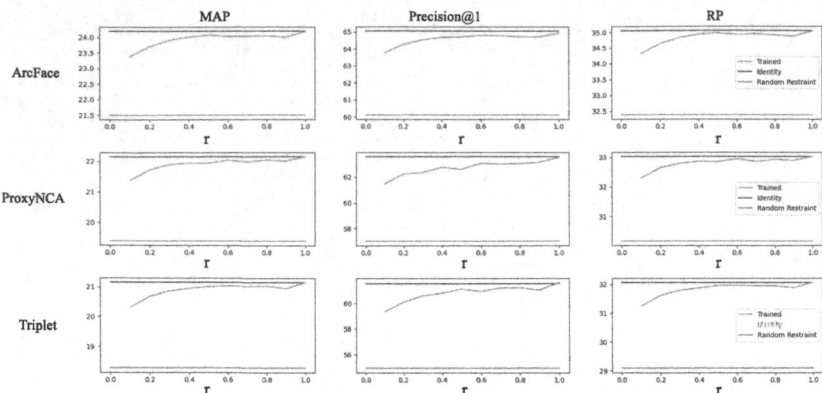

Fig. 3. Ablation of the restraint degree r for random restraint on three DML methods. From left to right column enumerates the accuracy of MAP, Precision@1 and RP. Models are trained by ArcFace, ProxyNCA and Triplet

degrees r on the metric matrix trained by ArcFace, ProxyNCA and Triplet on CUB, and then compute the accuracy under the metric of the refined metric. As depicted in Fig. 2, better performance is achieved as r increases on three datasets consistently, which exactly follows the tendency in Principle 1.

Principle   2. A relatively larger restraint degree r for random restraint leads to a smaller Frobenius norm of M' while $tr(M')$ is fixed. According to Principle 2, this will lead to a tighter upper bound of the generalization gap, thus reflected as advanced performance. As illustrated in Fig. 3, all the DML methods benefit from a relative larger r. Also, notice that in the extreme case of $r = 1$ when all off-diagonal elements are all restrained to zero, random restraint converges to an identity matrix. Such observation implies the reason that the identity matrix generalizes better than the trained matrix because it has a reduced Frobenius norm. In the next we will give a more concrete discussion on the identity matrix.

4.5   Discussion of Identity Matrix

Based on the theoretical analysis and experimental results above, we attempt to explain the most original question that why an identity matrix generalizes better than the trained metric. Let M^* denote the metric matrix trained by ArcFace on CUB, and I denote an identity matrix having the same shape as M^*. In practice, $tr(M^*) = 42.72$ and $\|M^*\|_F^2 = 16.03$. In the following, we will compare the property of M^* and aI, where $a > 0$ is a scalar to preserve several properties consistent between M^* and aI, so that we can decouple the impact of two objective factors (trace and Frobenius norm) discovered in this paper. A numerical analysis to verify whether aI follows two principles is given as

1. Principle 1 To control $\|aI\|_F = \|M^*\|_F$, then we have $a = \frac{\|M^*\|_F}{\sqrt{1024}}$. Thus the trace of $tr(aI) = \sqrt{1024}\|M^*\|_F > tr(M^*)$, which means that the identity matrix actually violates Principle 1.

2. Principle 2 To control $tr(aI) = tr(M^*)$, then we have $a = \frac{tr(M^*)}{1024}$. Thus the Frobenius norm of $\|aI\|_F = \frac{tr(M^*)}{32} < \|M^*\|_F$. Therefore, identity matrix follows Principle 2. Such conclusion can also be confirmed by such observation that, for random restraint when $r = 1$, all off-diagonal elements are restrained to zero, then the refined matrix approximates an identity matrix. Correspondingly, as depicted in Fig. 2 random restraint will converge to identity matrix as restraint degree increases.

Therefore, one conclusion can be drawn that an identity matrix generalizes better than a trained metric because it has a limited Frobenius norm. It is worth noticing that one good posterior refinement operation does not have to follow two principles at the same time. As long as one principle is followed, a relatively tighter upper bound of the generalization gap can be established.

5 Related Work

5.1 Classical DML Methods

Deep metric learning attempts to learn a powerful embedding space where instances can be discriminated based on the inter-instance similarity. Early metric learning losses, such as contrastive loss [6] and triplet loss [27], construct instance pairs from the training set, maximizing the similarity of positive pairs while minimizing that of negative ones. These methods are known as *pair-based method*. Some of the recent pair-based methods attempt to consider adaptive margin for flexible expected gap between the similarity of positive pairs and negative pairs [24,29], whereas others construct more data pairs to consider denser relationships among data [16,19]. At the same time, some studies [20,26] provide efficient approaches for collecting and weighting informative pairs based on gradient analysis. Meanwhile, other methods leverage concepts defined in signal processing to devise new similarity functions [1,31]. However, pair-based methods are known to suffer from the slow convergence speed, which is caused by the manner of learning on enormous but low informative data pairs [29].

In contrast to pair-based methods, another mainstream of studies, called *proxy-based method*, resolve such problem by introducing learnable category representations (called proxies) into the organization of the loss formula. These methods only consider data-to-proxy relations, which significantly reduces the computation burden since the number of objective proxy-data pairs is much less than data pairs. ProxyNCA [14] is one of the first studies to introduce this paradigm. ProxyNCA++ [21] and proxy anchor loss [11] integrate several improvements into Proxynca, including backbone enhancement, carefully designed learning rate scheduler, temperature scaling and denser proxy-to-data relations. Moreover, GS-TRS loss [5] and softtriple [17] loss attempt to construct multiple-center embedding structure such that intra-class variance and inter-class diversity can be handled separately.

5.2   Generalization Bound of DML

Despite the remarkable success the popular DML methods have achieved, there are no theoretical guarantees that these methods have strong generalization ability, which refers to the capacity that the trained metric can yield approximate performance on unseen data. Recently, a few works attempt to theoretically analyze the generalization ability of DML methods and propose several principles to reduce the upper bound of the generalization gap. Some of these works propose regularizers on the learned metric. Cao *et al.* [2] first proposes to learn a sparse metric via L1 norm regularization. Roth *et al.* [18] conduct comprehensive experiments to show that ranking-based DML methods are hurt by the excessive compressed level of instance representation, thus proposing a simple technique to regularize the compression of the learned embedding space. Others consider the impact of several important components of the backbone model. Huai *et al.* [8] involve dropout into the generalization bound, thus proving the benefit of taking an adaptive dropout into account during the training process. Further, Dong *et al.* [4] suggests that early stopping as well as the Lipschitz smooth loss function and classifier has a positive influence on the generalization error.

The existing DML generalization theorems all assume that the trained metric will be directly employed in evaluation. Therefore, they propose methods to introduce the discovered prior knowledge about the generalization into the training procedure to enhance the current DML pipeline. Orthogonality to these methods, in this paper we investigate in the impact of the posterior refinement on the metric matrix, which is a lightweight data-free operation but also significantly improves the generalization ability of the trained metric.

6   Conclusion

In this paper, we uncover an observation that, before the testing phase, a lightweight posterior refinement operation on the learned metric can significantly improve the generalization ability of the deep metric learning models. Based on the theoretical analysis of the generalization bound the refined matrix, we propose two simple principles to guide the refinement operations, and conduct experiments on three benchmark datasets to verify the correctness of these principles. The theories and experiments prove that posterior refinement can serve as a lightweight plug-in to boost the performance of DML models dramatically.

Acknowledgements. Yi Xu is supported in part by the National Natural Science Foundation of China (62171282, 111 project BP0719010, STCSM 18DZ2270700), the Shanghai Municipal Science and Technology Major Project (2021SHZDZX0102).

References

1. Cakir, F., He, K., Xia, X., Kulis, B., Sclaroff, S.: Deep metric learning to rank. In: CVPR, pp. 1861–1870 (2019)
2. Cao, Q., Guo, Z.C., Ying, Y.: Generalization bounds for metric and similarity learning. Mach. Learn. **102**(1), 115–132 (2016)
3. Deng, J., Dong, W., Socher, R., Li, L.J., Li, K., Fei-Fei, L.: Imagenet: a large-scale hierarchical image database. In: 2009 IEEE Conference on Computer Vision and Pattern Recognition, pp. 248–255. IEEE (2009)
4. Dong, M., Yang, X., Zhu, R., Wang, Y., Xue, J.H.: Generalization bound of gradient descent for non-convex metric learning. Adv. Neural. Inf. Process. Syst. **33**, 9794–9805 (2020)
5. Em, Y., Gag, F., Lou, Y., Wang, S., Huang, T., Duan, L.Y.: Incorporating intraclass variance to fine-grained visual recognition. In: 2017 IEEE International Conference on Multimedia and Expo (ICME), pp. 1452–1457. IEEE (2017)
6. Hadsell, R., Chopra, S., LeCun, Y.: Dimensionality reduction by learning an invariant mapping. In: CVPR, vol. 2, pp. 1735–1742. IEEE (2006)
7. Harwood, B., Kumar BG, V., Carneiro, G., Reid, I., Drummond, T.: Smart mining for deep metric learning. In: ICCV, pp. 2821–2829 (2017)
8. Huai, M., et al.: Deep metric learning: the generalization analysis and an adaptive algorithm. In: IJCAI, pp. 2535–2541 (2019)
9. Huang, C., Loy, C.C., Tang, X.: Local similarity-aware deep feature embedding. arXiv preprint arXiv:1610.08904 (2016)
10. Ioffe, S., Szegedy, C.: Batch normalization: accelerating deep network training by reducing internal covariate shift. arXiv preprint arXiv:1502.03167 (2015)
11. Kim, S., Kim, D., Cho, M., Kwak, S.: Proxy anchor loss for deep metric learning. In: Proceedings of the IEEE/CVF Conference on Computer Vision and Pattern Recognition, pp. 3238–3247 (2020)
12. Krause, J., Stark, M., Deng, J., Fei-Fei, L.: 3D object representations for fine-grained categorization. In: ICCV Workshops, pp. 554–561 (2013)
13. Liu, K., Bellet, A.: Escaping the curse of dimensionality in similarity learning: efficient frank-wolfe algorithm and generalization bounds. Neurocomputing **333**, 185–199 (2019)
14. Movshovitz-Attias, Y., Toshev, A., Leung, T.K., Ioffe, S., Singh, S.: No fuss distance metric learning using proxies. In: ICCV, pp. 360–368 (2017)
15. Musgrave, K., Belongie, S., Lim, S.N.: A metric learning reality check. arXiv preprint arXiv:2003.08505 (2020)
16. Oh Song, H., Xiang, Y., Jegelka, S., Savarese, S.: Deep metric learning via lifted structured feature embedding. In: CVPR, pp. 4004–4012 (2016)
17. Qian, Q., Shang, L., Sun, B., Hu, J., Li, H., Jin, R.: Softtriple loss: deep metric learning without triplet sampling. In: ICCV, pp. 6450–6458 (2019)
18. Roth, K., Milbich, T., Sinha, S., Gupta, P., Ommer, B., Cohen, J.P.: Revisiting training strategies and generalization performance in deep metric learning. In: International Conference on Machine Learning, pp. 8242–8252. PMLR (2020)
19. Sohn, K.: Improved deep metric learning with multi-class n-pair loss objective. NIPS **29**, 1857–1865 (2016)
20. Sun, Y., et al.: Circle loss: a unified perspective of pair similarity optimization. In: CVPR, pp. 6398–6407 (2020)
21. Teh, E.W., DeVries, T., Taylor, G.W.: Proxynca++: revisiting and revitalizing proxy neighborhood component analysis. arXiv preprint arXiv:2004.01113 (2020)

22. Tieleman, T., Hinton, G.: Lecture 6.5–RmsProp: divide the gradient by a running average of its recent magnitude. In: COURSERA: Neural Networks for Machine Learning (2012)
23. Wang, F., Cheng, J., Liu, W., Liu, H.: Additive margin softmax for face verification. IEEE Signal Process. Lett. **25**(7), 926–930 (2018)
24. Wang, J., Zhou, F., Wen, S., Liu, X., Lin, Y.: Deep metric learning with angular loss. In: ICCV, pp. 2593–2601 (2017)
25. Wang, X., Hua, Y., Kodirov, E., Hu, G., Robertson, N.M.: Deep metric learning by online soft mining and class-aware attention. In: Proceedings of the AAAI Conference on Artificial Intelligence, vol. 33, pp. 5361–5368 (2019)
26. Wang, X., Han, X., Huang, W., Dong, D., Scott, M.R.: Multi-similarity loss with general pair weighting for deep metric learning. In: CVPR, pp. 5022–5030 (2019)
27. Weinberger, K.Q., Blitzer, J., Saul, L.K.: Distance metric learning for large margin nearest neighbor classification. In: NIPS, pp. 1473–1480 (2006)
28. Welinder, P., et al.: Caltech-UCSD Birds 200. Technical report, CNS-TR-2010-001, California Institute of Technology (2010)
29. Wu, C.Y., Manmatha, R., Smola, A.J., Krahenbuhl, P.: Sampling matters in deep embedding learning. In: ICCV, pp. 2840–2848 (2017)
30. Yang, F., Wang, Z., Xiao, J., Satoh, S.: Mining on heterogeneous manifolds for zero-shot cross-modal image retrieval. In: Proceedings of the AAAI Conference on Artificial Intelligence, vol. 34, pp. 12589–12596 (2020)
31. Yuan, T., Deng, W., Tang, J., Tang, Y., Chen, B.: Signal-to-noise ratio: a robust distance metric for deep metric learning. In: CVPR, pp. 4815–4824 (2019)
32. Zhu, Y., Yang, M., Deng, C., Liu, W.: Fewer is more: a deep graph metric learning perspective using fewer proxies. In: Larochelle, H., Ranzato, M., Hadsell, R., Balcan, M.F., Lin, H. (eds.) Advances in Neural Information Processing Systems, vol. 33, pp. 17792–17803. Curran Associates, Inc. (2020)

Balancing Stability and Plasticity Through Advanced Null Space in Continual Learning

Yajing Kong[1], Liu Liu[1], Zhen Wang[1], and Dacheng Tao[1,2(✉)]

[1] The University of Sydney, Darlington, NSW 2008, Australia
{ykon9947,liuliu1,zwan4121}@sydney.edu.au, dacheng.tao@gmail.com
[2] JD Explore Academy, Beijing, China

Abstract. Continual learning is a learning paradigm that learns tasks sequentially with resources constraints, in which the key challenge is stability-plasticity dilemma, i.e., it is uneasy to simultaneously have the stability to prevent catastrophic forgetting of old tasks and the plasticity to learn new tasks well. In this paper, we propose a new continual learning approach, Advanced Null Space (AdNS), to balance the stability and plasticity without storing any old data of previous tasks. Specifically, to obtain better stability, AdNS makes use of low-rank approximation to obtain a novel null space and projects the gradient onto the null space to prevent the interference on the past tasks. To control the generation of the null space, we introduce a non-uniform constraint strength to further reduce forgetting. Furthermore, we present a simple but effective method, intra-task distillation, to improve the performance of the current task. Finally, we theoretically find that null space plays a key role in plasticity and stability, respectively. Experimental results show that the proposed method can achieve better performance compared to state-of-the-art continual learning approaches.

Keywords: Continual learning · Catastrophic forgetting · Null space

1 Introduction

Humans have excellent abilities in learning new knowledge while maintaining the knowledge learned from past experience through their lifelong time. Continual learning aims at developing algorithms for neural networks with the same capabilities from a stream of data [34,48]. However, although deep neural networks have made impressive achievements across various domains, they easily suffer performance degradation on the previous tasks when applied to sequential tasks without any access to historical data. The problem, referred to as catastrophic forgetting, is a key challenge in continual learning [16,21,30,34,38,48].

Supplementary Information The online version contains supplementary material available at https://doi.org/10.1007/978-3-031-19809-0_13.

This problem is closely related to the stability-plasticity dilemma [31,32]. Specifically, when learning in a sequential fashion, the network is required to have the plasticity to integrate new knowledge well and the stability to prevent the forgetting of previous tasks. However, the stability-plasticity dilemma indicates that it is hard to simultaneously have high plasticity and high stability. To relieve the dilemma, a growing body of continual learning methods are introduced. These method can be roughly divided into four categories: architecture-based methods expand the network or allocate new neurons for new tasks [13,28,42,60]; replayed-based methods interleave old data with current data by storing historical data in a buffer or generating virtual old data [4,8,12,39,40]; regularization-based methods penalize the update of important parameters of previous tasks [1,17,21,58]; algorithm-based methods modify the update rule of parameters to prevent the interference across tasks [7,26,43,47,49].

For algorithm-based methods, one of the classical approaches is to project the gradient onto the approximation null space of all previous tasks, in which the gradient has little interference on the performance of previous tasks [43,49,57]. However, despite the impressive performance achieved by these methods, there are still some challenges that impede the null space methods to achieve satisfactory stability-plasticity trade-off. First, the null space methods are based on the finding that the model modifies the parameters in the exact null space of previous tasks. However, due to the approximation of null space, the model will occur in interference on the previous tasks. Moreover, the interference would affect the subsequent approximation of null space of past tasks, thus leading to more information deficiency of null space of previous tasks. Therefore, the stability of the model will be unsatisfactory. Second, the model update is based on the gradient projection on the null space of previous task, preventing the model from learning the current task well, i.e., resulting in worse plasticity.

To address the above challenges, we propose a new algorithm-based continual learning approach, Advanced Null Space (AdNS), to achieve a good balance between stability and plasticity. Specifically, to alleviate the impact of approximation on the stability, AdNS makes use of the low-rank approximation to extract the shared null space between the previous null space and the current candidate null space. Unlike existing works that only focus on the current candidate null space [43,57], AdNS projects the gradient onto the shared null space, which contains the core spaces between null spaces, and thus could mitigate the information deficiency of the previous null spaces and reduce forgetting. Moreover, we present a constraint to control the approximation of null space and propose non-uniform constraint strength, which monotonically decreases with the number of tasks increasing, to further relieve the forgetting. What's more, to improve the performance of the current task, we leverage a simple method, intra-task distillation, to self-distill the knowledge of the current task. The procedure of the proposed method is shown in Fig. 1.

Finally, although various algorithms about null space have been proposed, few efforts were spent on the theoretical foundations. Therefore, in this paper, we theoretically analyze the impact of null space and present two theorems to

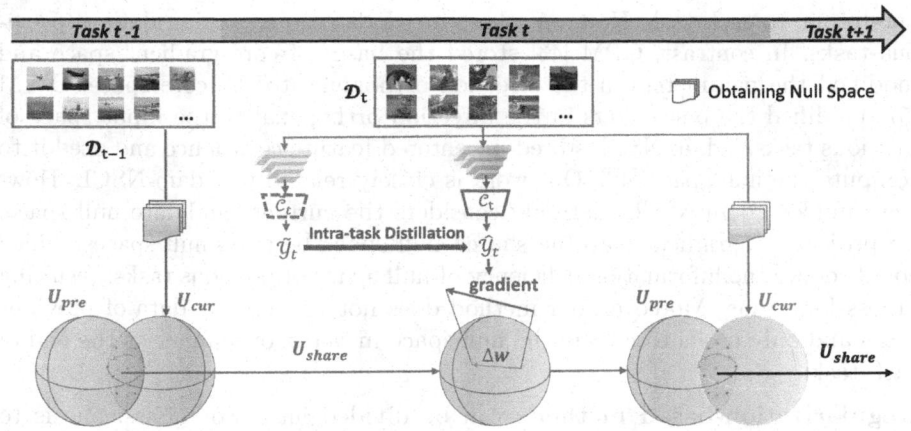

Fig. 1. The pipeline of the proposed method. Left: At the task $\mathcal{T}_{t-1}$, we obtain the shared low-rank null space $\mathbf{U}_{\text{share}}$ based on $\mathbf{U}_{\text{pre}}$ and $\mathbf{U}_{\text{cur}}$. Middle: We project the gradient at each layer onto the shared low-rank null space. Right: $\mathbf{U}_{\text{share}}$ is used for the next task $\mathcal{T}_{t+1}$ as $\mathbf{U}_{\text{pre}}$. Note at the task $\mathcal{T}_t$ ($t>1$), we conduct Intra-task Distillation between $\tilde{y}_t$ and $\hat{y}_t$

prove that null space plays a key role in stability and plasticity. The theoretical finding indicates the inherent properties of the stability-plasticity dilemma, in which it is hard to have high plasticity and high stability simultaneously. To summarize, our contributions are threefolds:

- To address the stability-plasticity dilemma, we propose a new algorithm-based continual learning approach, AdNS, which projects the gradient into the shared null space under non-uniform constraint strength to reduce forgetting, and uses intra-task distillation to improve the tasks' performance.
- We present two theorems from the perspective of stability and plasticity, which show that the null space plays a key role in balancing the stability-plasticity dilemma. Specifically, the larger the dimension of the null space, the better the plasticity, the worse the stability.
- We validate the proposed method in several benchmarks, and the empirical results show that the proposed method can outperform related state-of-the-art continual learning methods.

2   Related Work

Algorithms-based methods design the update rule to decrease the interference of parameter update on the performance of old tasks [6,7,24,26,43,47,49, 54]. For example, GEM [26] and A-GEM [7] used the historical samples to compute the gradients of old tasks and proposed inequality constraints of gradients to avoid the increase of losses of past tasks. *Arslan et al.* [6] manually divided a random orthonormal space into several subspaces and allocated these subspaces one-to-one to each task. However, these methods require storing data of previous tasks. In contrast, GPM [43] stored the bases of core gradient space and modified the parameters in the direction orthogonal to the core space. OWM [57] modified the parameters in the direction orthogonal to the input space of previous tasks. Adam-NSCL stored uncentered feature covariance and used it to compute the null space [49]. Our work is closely related to Adam-NSCL. However, unlike Adam-NSCL that only considers the current candidate null space, we project the gradient onto the shared null space between null spaces, which could relieve the information deficiency of null space of previous tasks, resulting in less forgetting. Moreover, our method does not rely on any data of previous tasks and only needs to update the null space in one shot manner at the end of each task.

Regularization-based methods can be divided into two classes: one is to distill knowledge from the previous model which is trained on the previous tasks [14,15,23,36,52,59]; another is to explicitly use a regularizer to penalize the update of important parameters of previous tasks, preventing the model from deviating too much from the previous one to avoid forgetting [19,21,33,35,58]. For example, for the first class, LwF [23] distills the knowledge by using the previous model outputs as soft labels and penalizing the distillation term between the current and recorded output. For the latter one, EWC [17] used the diagonal of the Fisher information matrix as the importance.

Other Approaches. Architecture-based methods allocate different parameters or add new parameters for the new task, while sharing parameters across tasks to reduce the interference of previous tasks [3,22,27–29,41,42,44,53,56,60]. However, such methods may lead to a cumbersome and complex network if new tasks continually arrive. Replayed-based methods leverage episodic memory to store representative history data or generate virtual data via a generative model, and replay these samples with current data [2,7,8,12,26,37,39,40,45,50,51]. However, replayed-based methods may bring some problems since storing old data will result in data imbalance, and the generative model would be large and expensive if it synthesizes the historical data reasonably.

3   Preliminaries

3.1   Settings and Notations

In this part, we present the settings and notations. We consider a sequence of tasks $\mathcal{T}_t, t \in \{1, ..., T\}$, where T is the total number of tasks. Let $\mathcal{D}_t = \{\mathcal{X}_t, \mathcal{Y}_t\}$ be the dataset of task $\mathcal{T}_t$, where $\mathcal{X}_t$ and $\mathcal{Y}_t$ are the corresponding inputs set and label set. In continual learning, the model is trained on these datasets sequentially. Let $\mathbf{w} = \{w^1, ..., w^L\}$ be the parameters of L-layer neural network, where w^l is the parameter vector of the l-th layer, $l \in \{1, ..., L\}$. Let $\hat{L}_t(\mathbf{w})$ be the empirical loss of task $\mathcal{T}_t$ with parameters $\mathbf{w}$. Define $\tilde{\mathbf{w}}_t$ as the convergence parameters after the model has been trained on the task $\mathcal{T}_t$. Rank(·) denotes the rank of a matrix, and [·, ·] denotes the concatenation of vectors or matrices. $\| \cdot \|_F$ denotes Frobenius norm, $\| \cdot \|_1$ denotes L$_1$ norm, and $\| \cdot \|_2$ denotes L$_2$ norm.

3.2   Null Space

Let Δw^l be the parameter update for l-th layer for the current step. If Δw^l lies in the null space of previous tasks at each training step for the l-th layer, $l \in \{1, ..., L\}$, then the stability can be guaranteed, which is illustrated by the following lemma.

Lemma 1. *[49] Define $X_{p,p}^l$ as the input feature of l-th layer when the network is fed with data $\mathcal{X}_p$ after training on the task $\mathcal{T}_p$. Let $\mathcal{N}(\tilde{\mathbf{w}}_t; \mathcal{X}_p)$ be the output of the L-layer network with parameters $\tilde{\mathbf{w}}_t$ when the network is fed with data $\mathcal{X}_p$. If at each training step of task $\mathcal{T}_t$, Δw^l lies in the null space of $X_{t-1}^l = [X_{1,1}^l, ..., X_{t-1,t-1}^l]$, i.e.,*

$$X_{t-1}^l \Delta w^l = \mathbf{0}, \quad l = 1, ..., L, \tag{1}$$

then we have $\mathcal{N}(\tilde{\mathbf{w}}_t; \mathcal{X}_p) = \mathcal{N}(\tilde{\mathbf{w}}_p; \mathcal{X}_p)$ for all $p \in \{1, ..., t-1\}$.

According to Lemma 1, if the parameters are modified in the null space of X_{t-1}^l, then the training loss of previous tasks will be retained and the forgetting can be avoid. Nevertheless, it is unrealistic to expect the existence of the null space, thus previous works [43, 49, 57] use the approximation null space instead. However, the approximation will cause that Eq. (1) no longer holds and result in the occurrence of interference on previous tasks. Moreover, the interference would affect the subsequent approximation of null space of past tasks, leading to more performance degradation on past tasks, i.e., catastrophic forgetting.

4   Methodology

In this section, we propose a new continual learning method, Advanced Null Space (AdNS), involving shared low-rank null space (Sect. 4.1), non-uniform constraint strength (Sect. 4.2), and intra-task distillation (Sect. 4.3), to balance the stability and plasticity. The procedure of AdNS is shown in Fig. 1 and the algorithm is shown in Algorithm 1.

4.1   Shared Low-Rank Null Space

In this part, we introduce a noval null space, the shared low-rank null space, which extracts the shared null spaces between the previous null space and the current candidate null space based on low-rank approximation.

When training on the current task $\mathcal{T}_t$ ($t>1$), the gradient of l-th layer is projected onto the null space of previous tasks, which is spanned by the columns of $\mathbf{U}_{\text{pre}}^l$[1], $l \in \{1, ..., L\}$ and $\mathcal{U}_{\text{pre}} = \{\mathbf{U}_{\text{pre}}^1, ..., \mathbf{U}_{\text{pre}}^L\}$ is the set containing the previous null spaces of L layers. After training the current task, the current candidate null space $\mathcal{U}_{\text{cur}} = \{\mathbf{U}_{\text{cur}}^1, ..., \mathbf{U}_{\text{cur}}^L\}$ could be obtained based on the

---

[1] We use the matrix whose columns are consisted of the orthonormal basis of the null space to represent null space.

Algorithm 1. Advanced Null Space (AdNS)

Input: Network $\mathcal{N}$ with parameters $\mathbf{w}$
Output: Target network $\mathcal{N}$
  for $t = 1, 2, .., T$ **do**
    if $t = 1$ **then**
      while not converged **do**
        Update the gradient according to $\hat{L}_1(\mathbf{w})$
      end while
      $\tilde{X}_1^l \leftarrow (X_{1,1}^l)^\top X_{1,1}^l$
      $\mathbf{U}^l \leftarrow$ Null space of $\tilde{X}_1^l$ based on (3)
      $\mathbf{U}_{\text{pre}}^l \leftarrow \mathbf{U}^l$
      Break   ▷ Return to the next task
    end if
    $\tilde{\mathcal{Y}}_t \leftarrow \mathcal{N}(\mathbf{w}; \mathcal{X}_t)$ after updating the classifier $\tilde{C}_t$
    while not converged **do**
      Update the gradient in the null space at each layer based on $\mathcal{U} = \{\mathbf{U}^1, ..., \mathbf{U}^L\}$
  according to (5)
    end while
    $\tilde{X}_t^l \leftarrow \tilde{X}_{t-1}^l + (X_{t,t}^l)^\top X_{t,t}^l$
    $\mathbf{U}_{\text{cur}}^l \leftarrow$ Null space of $\tilde{X}_t^l$ based on (3)
    $\tilde{\mathbf{U}}^l = [\mathbf{U}_{\text{pre}}^l, \mathbf{U}_{\text{cur}}^l]$, $l = 1, ..., L$
    $\mathbf{U}^l \leftarrow$ The shared low-rank null space obtained in (P4.1)
    $\mathbf{U}_{\text{pre}}^l \leftarrow \mathbf{U}^l$
  end for
  return $\mathcal{N}$

---

input features of tasks seen so far. Specifically, we use the uncentered feature covariance, i.e., $\tilde{X}_t^l = (X_t^l)^\top X_t^l$, to compute the current candidate null space [49]. Such process has moderate memory consumption since the dimension of $\tilde{X}_t^l$ is irrelevant to the size of data. It can be easily proved that the null space of $\tilde{X}_t^l$ is equal to X_t^l. We update the input features of each layer by $\tilde{X}_t^l \leftarrow \tilde{X}_{t-1}^l + (X_{t,t}^l)^\top X_{t,t}^l$, where $X_{t,t}^l$ is the input feature of l-th layer when the network is fed with data $\mathcal{X}_t$ after training on the task $\mathcal{T}_t$, and then obtain the current candidate null space at the end of task.

To alleviate the impact of approximation on the stability, rather than using $\mathcal{U}_{\text{cur}}$, we extract the shared null space between $\mathcal{U}_{\text{pre}}$ and $\mathcal{U}_{\text{cur}}$ by solving the problem of low-rank approximation for the concatenation matrix $\tilde{\mathbf{U}}^l = [\mathbf{U}_{\text{pre}}^l, \mathbf{U}_{\text{cur}}^l]$:

$$\text{minimize}_{\hat{\mathbf{U}}^l} \quad \|\tilde{\mathbf{U}}^l - \hat{\mathbf{U}}^l\|_F \quad s.t. \quad \text{Rank}(\hat{\mathbf{U}}^l) \leq k_l, \quad l = 1, ..., L, \tag{P2}$$

where k_l is the rank of the shared null space of l-th layer. The optimization problem (P2) has analytic solutions in terms of the singular value decomposition. Because we want to project the gradient onto an orthonormal space, according to the properties of singular value decomposition, the objective matrix $\mathbf{U}^l$, i.e., the shared low-rank null space of l-th layer, can be constructed by the singular vectors of $\hat{\mathbf{U}}^l$ rather than using $\hat{\mathbf{U}}^l$ directly. The implementation details can be found in the Appendix.

The shared low-rank null space, which is the range space of $\mathbf{U}^l$, contains the shared information of the previous null space and the current null space. Thus, projecting the gradient onto the shared low-rank space could relieve catastrophic forgetting. In formal, we project g^l as the following projection operation:

$$\Delta w^l = \mathbf{U}^l (\mathbf{U}^l)^\top g^l, \quad l = 1, ..., L, \tag{2}$$

and the parameter is updated by $w^l \leftarrow w^l - \eta \Delta w^l$, where η is the learning rate.

Regarding the computing complexity, let the dimension of the feature at l-th layer be d^l and the dimension of $\tilde{\mathbf{U}}^l$ be $\tilde{k}_l$, where $\tilde{k}_l < d^l$. Then the complexity of computing the current candidate null space $\mathcal{O}((d^l)^3)$ is larger than the complexity of the low-rank approximation $\mathcal{O}(d^l (\tilde{k}_l)^2)$. Therefore, the time consumption of our proposed method is comparable to previous works [43,49]. The comparisons of running time can be reffed to Appendix.

4.2 Non-uniform Constraint Strength

In continual learning, it is essential to balance the importance of previous tasks and the current task to achieve satisfying performance [19,21,58]. For example, if the model puts too much weight on the current task, it may suffer significant performance degradation on the prior tasks and vice-versa. Therefore, to make a trade-off between the importance of previous tasks and current task, i.e., stability and plasticity, we rewrite the constraint $X_{t-1}^l \Delta w^l = \mathbf{0}$ for $l \in \{1, ..., L\}$ to $\|X_{t-1}^l \Delta w^l\|_1 \leq \epsilon$, where ϵ is a factor controlling the strength of constraint. Such a constraint is reasonable for the following two reasons: (a) In practice, it is unrealistic to expect that there exists a null space satisfying $X_{t-1}^l \Delta w^l = \mathbf{0}$ for $l \in \{1, ..., L\}$. (b) Although the constraint $X_{t-1}^l \Delta w^l = \mathbf{0}$ could guarantee that the model would not suffer from catastrophic forgetting, it would result in poor performance of the current task because the constraint is too strict for the parameter update of the current task. In contrast, introducing the balance factor ϵ allows us to make a trade-off between stability and plasticity flexibly.

Moreover, with new tasks occurring, the number of previous tasks increases, resulting in a greater impact of previous tasks on the final performance than the current task [19,21,58]. Hence, with the growth of observed tasks, it is necessary to pay more attention to previous tasks to relieve the catastrophic forgetting. Therefore, we propose non-uniform constraint strength following a common assumption that the importance of previous tasks is related to the number of tasks seen so far. In particular, the non-uniform constraint strength can be represented as

$$\|X_{t-1}^l \Delta w^l\|_1 \leq \epsilon(t), \quad \text{for} \quad l = 1, ..., L, \tag{3}$$

where $\epsilon(t)$ is a function monotonically decreasing with the number of tasks seen so far. With new tasks continually coming, the constraint strength becomes more restrictive, and thus the model pays more attention to preserving the performance of previous tasks, achieving better stability.

4.3   Intra-task Distillation

To further address the plasticity-stability dilemma, we leverage knowledge distillation of the current task, called intra-task distillation, to improve the performance of the current task. In particular, as shown in Fig. 1, before training the task T_t, we first freeze the backbone, which is learned on the previous $t-1$ tasks sequentially, and only train the classifier $\tilde{C}_t$ of the task T_t. Then we store the outputs $\tilde{\mathcal{Y}}_t$ for the current task T_t. The frozen backbone and the classifier absorb the information of prior tasks and the current task, respectively. Therefore, by penalizing the difference between the record outputs $\tilde{\mathcal{Y}}_t$ from the classifier $\tilde{C}_t$ and the current outputs $\hat{\mathcal{Y}}_t$ from the classifier C_t, intra-task distillation could improve the performance of the current task while preserving the acquired knowledge from previous tasks.

Specifically, we use the modified cross-entropy loss as the distillation loss. When training on the task T_t, the distillation loss can be represented as:

$$\hat{L}_d(\tilde{y}_t, \hat{y}_t) = -\sum_{c=1}^{C_t} \tilde{y}_t^{\prime(c)} \log \hat{y}_t^{\prime(c)}, \tag{4}$$

where $\tilde{y}_t^{\prime(c)} = \frac{\exp(\tilde{y}_t^{(c)}/\tau)}{\sum_i \exp(\tilde{y}_t^{(i)}/\tau)}, \hat{y}_t^{\prime(c)} = \frac{\exp(\hat{y}_t^{(c)}/\tau)}{\sum_i \exp(\hat{y}_t^{(i)}/\tau)}$, C_t is the number of classes of task T_t, τ is the temperature factor; $\tilde{y}_t^{(c)}$ and $\hat{y}_t^{(c)}$ are the recorded and current outputs of a sample x_t in task T_t, respectively. We set $\tau = 2$ by default.

In summary, when training on the task T_t ($t>1$), the optimization problem including (P2) and (2)–(4), which is represented as:

$$\begin{aligned}
\underset{\mathbf{w}}{\text{minimize}} \quad & \hat{L}_t(\mathbf{w}) + \beta \hat{L}_d(\tilde{\mathcal{Y}}_t, \hat{\mathcal{Y}}_t), \\
s.t. \quad & \text{Rank}(h(X_{t-1}^l)) \le k_l, \|X_{t-1}^l \Delta w^l\|_1 \le \epsilon(t), \quad l = 1, ..., L,
\end{aligned} \tag{5}$$

where $\hat{L}_t(\mathbf{w})$ is the cross-entropy loss for the current task and β is a coefficient that balances the importance between the cross-entropy loss and the distillation loss $\hat{L}_d(\tilde{\mathcal{Y}}_t, \hat{\mathcal{Y}}_t)$; $\mathbf{w}$ is the network parameters and $\epsilon(t)$ is the constraint strength which impacts the trade-off between the stability and plasticity; $h(X)$ denotes X is mapped to its approximation null space which satisfies the constraint; k_l is used to control the rank of the matrix of l-th layer.

5   Analysis

In this section, we present two theorems to theoretically prove that the null space plays a key role in the stability-plasticity dilemma. Theorem 1 is in terms of plasticity and Theorem 2 is in terms of stability. The proof can be found in Appendix. Before introducing the two theorems, we first present three assumptions. Comparable assumptions are also made in existing studies on continual learning [55].

Assumption 1. $\hat{L}_t(\mathbf{w})$ is L_f-smooth, i.e., $\hat{L}_t(\mathbf{w}) \leq \hat{L}_t(\mathbf{v}) + \langle \nabla \hat{L}_t(\mathbf{v}), \mathbf{w} - \mathbf{v} \rangle + \frac{L_f}{2} \|\mathbf{w} - \mathbf{v}\|_2^2$, $t \in \{1, ..., T\}$, for any $\mathbf{v}, \mathbf{w} \in \mathbb{R}^d$.

Assumption 2. For each task $\mathcal{T}_t$, $t \in \{1, ..., T\}$, the number of iterations is bounded by an integer S.

Assumption 3. $\hat{L}_t$ has the σ^2-uniformly bounded gradient variance, i.e.,

$$\|\nabla \hat{L}_t(\mathbf{w}; x, y) - \nabla \hat{L}_t(\mathbf{w}; \mathcal{X}_t, \mathcal{Y}_t)\|_2^2 \leq \sigma^2, (x, y) \in \mathcal{D}_t, t \in \{1, ..., T\}.$$

Based on the assumptions, we derive the following two Theorems regarding the plasticity and stability. Specifically, we obtain the upper bound of the loss of the current task and forgetting.

Theorem 1. *(Plasticity). Suppose Assumptions 1, 2, and 3 hold. Let $\mathbf{w}_{t,s}$ be the parameters on task $\mathcal{T}_t$ at the s-th step and η be the learning rate. Let the range of space of $\mathbf{U}^l$ be the null space of previous tasks for l-th layer, then the loss of the current task $\mathcal{T}_t$ is upper bound by*

$$\hat{L}_t(\mathbf{w}_{t,S}) \leq \hat{L}_t(\mathbf{w}_{t,0}) + \frac{\eta}{2} \sum_{s=0}^{S-1} \sum_{l=1}^{L} \|(I - \mathbf{U}^l(\mathbf{U}^l)^\top) g_{t,s}^l\|_2^2 - \frac{\eta}{2} \sum_{s=0}^{S-1} \|\nabla \hat{L}_t(\mathbf{w}_{t,s})\|_2^2 + \frac{SL_f \eta^2 \sigma^2}{2},$$

where $g_{t,s}^l$ is l-th layer gradient of $\hat{L}_t(\mathbf{w}_{t,s})$.

Theorem 2. *(Stability). Suppose Assumptions 1, 2, and 3 hold. Let $\mathbf{w}_{t,s}$ be the parameters on task $\mathcal{T}_t$ at the s-th and η be the learning rate. Let $\hat{L}_{1:t-1}$ be the sum of empirical loss function of previous $t - 1$ tasks and $g_{1:t-1,s}^l$ is its gradient of l-th layer at $\mathbf{w}_{t,s}$. Let $g_{t,s}^l$ be the gradient of the current task at $\mathbf{w}_{t,s}$ of l-th layer. Let the range of space of $\mathbf{U}^l$ be the null space of previous tasks for l-th layer, then the forgetting of the previous $t - 1$ tasks generated by training on the task $\mathcal{T}_t$ is upper bound by*

$$\hat{L}_{1:t-1}(\mathbf{w}_{t,S}) - \hat{L}_{1:t-1}(\mathbf{w}_{t,0}) \leq \eta \sum_{s=0}^{S-1} \sum_{l=1}^{L} \|\mathbf{U}^l(\mathbf{U}^l)^\top\|_2 \|g_{t,s}^l\|_2 \|g_{1:t-1,s}^l\|_2$$

$$+ \frac{L_f}{2} \eta^2 \sum_{s=0}^{S-1} \sum_{l=1}^{L} \|\mathbf{U}^l(\mathbf{U}^l)^\top\|_2^2 \|g_{t,s}^l\|_2^2.$$

Remark 1. From Theorems 1 and 2, we could conclude that $\mathbf{U}^l$ plays a key role in the stability and plasticity. According to Theorem 1, if the rank of the null space is larger, then the term $\|(I - \mathbf{U}^l(\mathbf{U}^l)^\top) g_{t,s}^l\|_2^2$ will be smaller and the upper bound of $\hat{L}_t(\mathbf{w}_{t,S})$ will be smaller. Therefore, the model could learn the current task better, indicating better plasticity. However, according to Theorem 2, the larger the rank of the null space, the larger the term $\|\mathbf{U}^l(\mathbf{U}^l)^\top\|_2^2$. Therefore, the upper bound of the forgetting would be larger, resulting in poorer stability. The two theorems indicate the inherent properties of the stability-plasticity dilemma that it is hard to have high plasticity and high stability simultaneously.

6   Experiments

6.1   Experimental Setup

Datasets and Architecture. Following [49], we perform experiments on three continual learning benchmarks: 10-Split CIFAR-100 (10-S-CIFAR100), 20-Split-CIFAR-100 (20-S-CIFAR100), and 25-Spilt TinyImageNet (25-S-TinyImageNet). Specifically, 10-Split CIFAR-100 and 20-Split CIFAR-100 are constructed by splitting CIFAR100 [18] into 10 and 20 sequential tasks, respectively. Each task contains the same classes without replacement out of the total 100 classes. Similarly, 25-Spilt TinyImageNet is constructed by splitting 200 classes of TinyImageNet [46] into 25 sequential tasks, where each task has 8 classes. We use ResNet-18 [11] as the backbone [4,6,10,11]. All tasks share the same backbone, while each task has its separate classifier.

Baselines. We compare the proposed method against competitive and well-established methods[2], including 5 regularization-based methods using importance measure (EWC [17], MAS [1], MUC-MAS [25], SI [58], and CPR [5]), 2 regularization-based methods using knowledge distillation (LwF [23] and GD-WILD [20]), 1 architecture-based method (InstAParam [9]), and 6 algorithm-based methods (GEM [26], A-GEM [7], MEGA [10], OWM [57], GPM [43], and Adam-NSCL [49]). We also provide a lower bound performance of Vanilla which trains tasks sequentially without any countermeasure to forgetting.

Performance Metrics. To evaluate the performance, we use two standard metrics: a) Average accuracy (ACC) [26,32] is the average test accuracy evaluated on all tasks after learning all tasks sequentially; b) Backward Transfer (BWT) [7,26] is the average performance decrease of the network on previous tasks after new learning. In formal, ACC and BWT are defined as: $ACC = \frac{1}{T}\sum_{i=1}^{T} A_{T,i}$, $BWT = \frac{1}{T-1}\sum_{i=1}^{T-1}(A_{T,i} - A_{i,i})$, where T is the total number of tasks and $A_{j,i}$ is the accuracy of task $\mathcal{T}_i$ after training on the task $\mathcal{T}_j$ sequentially. The larger the two metrics, the better the model. If the performances of ACC are similar, then the method with a larger value of BWT is better [26].

Implementation Details. When obtaining the null space at the end of each task, we approximate the constraint $\|X_{t-1}^l \Delta w^l\|_1 \leq \epsilon(t)$ like [49]. Specifically, when computing the current candidate null space, we approximate the current candidate null space with the singular values satisfying $\lambda \in \{\tilde{\lambda}|\tilde{\lambda} \leq \alpha(t)\lambda_{\min}^l\}$, where $\lambda_{\min}^l$ is the smallest singular value of $\tilde{X}_{t-1}^l$ and $\alpha(t)$ is a positive value which balances the stability and plasticity. For the non-uniform constraint strength, we use a simple strategy that $\alpha(t)$ linearly decreases with task number t observed so far. We perform experiments on the 10-Split CIFAR-100 and 20-Split CIFAR-100 5 runs, and 25-Spilt TinyImageNet 3 runs. Note that the update of the null space in our method is only performed at the end of task, and no data of old data are stored during training. More implementation details, including the hyperparameters settings, can be found in Appendix.

---

[2] We do not compare with replay-based methods because they store the data of previous tasks, which is out of the scope of this paper's setting.

6.2   Performance Comparison

We show the comparison results of the proposed method and baselines in Table 1. The results except Vanilla, CPR, and GPM are from [49]. According to Table 1, our method achieves the highest average accuracy (ACC) with comparable forgetting (BWT) on all benchmarks.

Compared with regularization-based methods, the proposed method achieves over 5% ACC higher with less forgetting than EWC and MAS on all benchmarks. Although MUC-MAS and SI obtained comparable forgetting on the 25-Spilt TinyImageNet, their ACCs are lower than 50%, largely below AdNS's ACC (59.77%). The forgetting of CPR on the 20-Split CIFAR-100 and 25-Spilt Tiny-ImageNet are less, while its performance of ACC is worse than the proposed method on all benchmarks. For the regularization-based methods using knowledge distillation, the ACCs of LwF and GD-WILD are comparable to the proposed method on the 20-Split CIFAR-100 while their stability is very poor. For the architecture-based method, AdNS is significantly better than InstAParam, e.g., over 25% ACC higher on three benchmarks.

Table 1. Results of ACC (%) and BWT (%) evaluated on the all tasks after finishing learning all tasks. [↑] higher is better

Method	10-S-CIFAR-100		20-S-CIFAR-100		25-S-TinyImagNet	
	ACC [↑]	BWT [↑]	ACC [↑]	BWT [↑]	ACC [↑]	BWT [↑]
Vanilla	34.91	−60.96	30.48	−65.90	16.96	−66.06
EWC [17]	70.77	−2.83	71.66	−3.72	52.33	−6.71
MAS [1]	66.93	−4.03	63.84	−6.29	47.96	−7.04
MUC-MAS [25]	63.73	−3.38	67.22	−5.72	41.18	−4.03
SI [58]	60.57	−5.17	59.76	−8.62	45.27	−4.45
CPR [5]	74.56	−2.51	72.98	−2.32	58.01	−2.45
LwF [23]	70.70	−6.27	74.38	−9.11	56.57	−11.19
GD-WILD [20]	71.27	−18.24	77.16	−14.85	42.74	−34.58
InstAParam [9]	47.84	−11.92	51.04	−4.92	34.64	−10.05
GEM [26]	49.48	2.77	68.89	−1.2	-	-
A-GEM [7]	49.57	−1.13	61.91	−6.88	53.32	−7.68
MEGA [10]	54.17	−2.19	64.98	−5.13	57.12	−5.90
OWM [57]	68.89	−1.88	68.47	−3.37	49.98	−3.64
GPM [43]	73.66	−2.20	75.20	−7.58	58.96	−6.96
Adam-NSCL [49]	75.03	−2.98	75.59	−3.66	59.10	−7.19
AdNS (Ours)	**77.21**	−2.32	**77.33**	−3.25	**59.77**	−4.58

Now we compare AdNS with algorithm-based methods. On the 10-Split CIFAR-100, although the forgetting of GEM, A-GEM, MEGA, OWM, and GPM is slightly better than our method, their ACCs are largely below the proposed method. It is also observed that our method can obtain better performance with less forgetting than Adam-NSCL. As shown in Table 1, the ACCs of the proposed method are 2.18%, 1.74%, and 0.66% higher than Adam-NSCL on the 10-Split CIFAR-100, 20-Split CIFAR-100, and 25-Spilt TinyImageNet, respectively. As for forgetting, the BWTs of the proposed method are 0.66%, 0.41%, and 2.61% better than Adam-NSCL on the three benchmarks, respectively. It is because AdNS considers the shared null space between null spaces and also leverages knowledge distillation to further mitigate the stability-plasticity dilemma.

Table 2. Different methods to obtain the shared null space. "Random" obtains the shared null space with the dimensions randomly from $\mathbf{U}_{pre}^l$ and $\mathbf{U}_{cur}^l$

Method	10-S-CIFAR-100		20-S-CIFAR-100		25-S-TinyImageNet	
	ACC [↑]	BWT [↑]	ACC [↑]	BWT [↑]	ACC [↑]	BWT [↑]
Random	76.10	−4.13	75.70	−5.81	59.07	−6.78
Low-Rank	**76.45**	**−2.87**	**76.31**	**−3.66**	**59.26**	**−5.77**

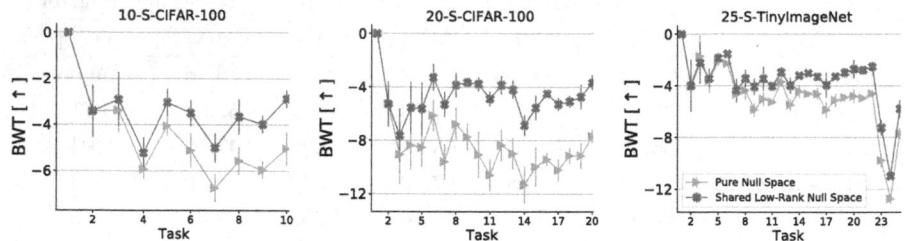

Fig. 2. Comparison of forgetting between the pure null space and the shared low-rank null space. The results are the curves of BWT when the network has been trained on each task ([↑] Higher BWT indicates less forgetting)

6.3   Ablation Studies and Analyses

Effect of Low-Rank. First, we compare the forgetting of using shared low-rank null space and pure null space, in which pure null space projects the gradient onto the current candidate null space instead of the shared null space. According to Fig. 2, with new tasks continually coming, the superiority of the shared low-rank null space on alleviating forgetting becomes more and more obvious than the pure null space, validating that our shared low-rank null space can relieve the catastrophic forgetting due to null space approximation. Next, we validate whether it is effective to use low-rank approximation to obtain the shared space.

Table 3. Effect of each component. "NS" denotes "Null Space", "LR" denotes "Low-Rank", "NCS" denotes "Non-uniform Constraint Strength", and "ID" denote Intra-task Distillation

Module				10-S-CIFAR-100		20-S-CIFAR-100		25-S-TinyImagnet	
NS	LR	NCS	ID	ACC [↑]	BWT [↑]	ACC [↑]	BWT [↑]	ACC [↑]	BWT [↑]
✓				76.11	−5.02	75.53	−7.67	59.20	−7.69
✓	✓			76.45	−2.87	76.31	−3.66	59.26	−5.77
✓		✓		76.15	−4.98	75.66	−7.36	59.42	−5.07
✓	✓	✓		76.45	−2.84	76.34	−3.55	59.27	−5.11
✓			✓	76.99	−4.36	77.04	−6.09	**60.00**	−6.98
✓	✓	✓	✓	**77.21**	**−2.32**	**77.33**	**−3.25**	59.77	**−4.58**

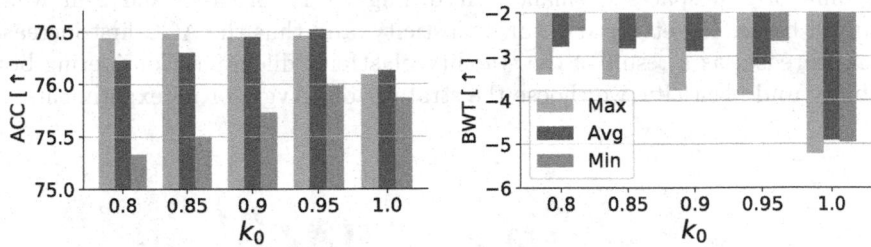

Fig. 3. The effect of k. The dataset is 10-Split CIFAR-100. [↑] higher is better

To realize this, we compare the performance of the shared low-rank null space with the method that obtains the shared null space by extracting dimensions randomly from $\mathbf{U}_{\text{pre}}^l$ and $\mathbf{U}_{\text{cur}}^l$[3]. For a fair comparison, intra-task distillation is excluded, and all the settings including the constraints are the same. According to Table 2, using low-rank approximation can achieve higher ACC and better BWT on all benchmarks. Especially for BWT, "Low-Rank" is at least 1% better than the method of "Random", indicating the effectiveness of low-rank approximation.

Effect of Each Component. We now validate the effect of each component to demonstrate that AdNS could achieve better stability-plasticity trade-off. From Table 3, we can find that (1) Both "Low-Rank" and "Non-uniform Constraint Strength" decrease forgetting significantly with better performance. Especially, on the 20-Split CIFAR-100, the shared low-rank null space ("NS" + "LR") is 4.01% BWT better and 0.78% ACC higher than the pure null space ("NS"). On the 25-Spilt TinyImageNet, adding non-uniform constraint strength ("NS"

---

[3] We extract $k_l/2$ dimensions randomly from $\mathbf{U}_{\text{pre}}^l$ and another $k_l/2$ dimensions randomly from $\mathbf{U}_{\text{cur}}^l$. If the dimension of $\mathbf{U}_{\text{pre}}^l$ or $\mathbf{U}_{\text{cur}}^l$ is smaller than $k_l/2$, to make up k_l dimensions, we concatenate the whole matrix and the rest dimensions randomly extracted from another matrix.

+ "NCS") increases BWT 2.62%. (2) Intra-task Distillation improves ACC significantly with better BWT. For example, on the 20-Split CIFAR-100, adding intra-task distillation ("NS" + "ID") increases ACC 1.51 % with less forgetting. (3) Combing all modules can achieve better stability and plasticity simultaneously. For example, on 20-Spilt CIFAR100, combing all modules is 1.8% ACC higher and 4.42% BWT better than the pure null space ("NS").

Effect of k. Now we explore the effect of k. We use k to denote k_l because we apply the same operation for k_l at each layer. Assume that the dimensions of $\mathbf{U}_{pre}^l$ and $\mathbf{U}_{cur}^l$ are p and q, respectively. Then "Max", "Avg", and "Min"[4] means that $k = \mathrm{Max}(p, q) \times k_0$, $k = \mathrm{Avg}(p, q) \times k_0$, and $k = \mathrm{Min}(p, q) \times k_0$, respectively, where k_0 is used to adjust the value of k. As shown in Fig. 3, for all strategies, with the decrease of k_0, forgetting continually decreases while ACC first increases and then decreases. It is because with the decrease of k_0, k becomes smaller and the rank of null spaces is smaller. According to Theorems 1 and 2, it would result in better forgetting and worse plasticity, and thus the ACC first increases then decreases as a result of the stability-plasticity dilemma. Considering both stability and plasticity, we choose the strategy of "Avg" for all experiments.

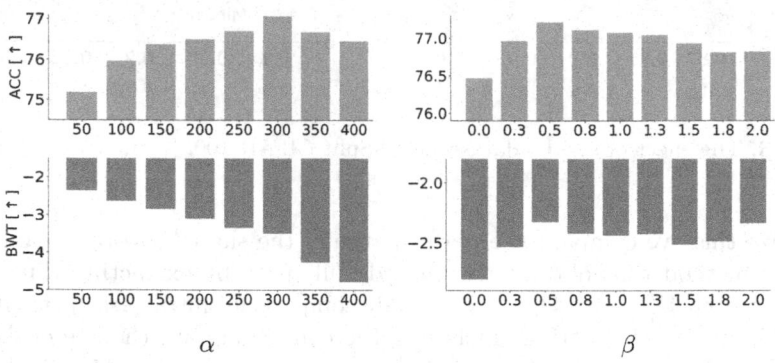

Fig. 4. The effect of α and β. The dataset is 10-Split CIFAR-100. [↑] higher is better

Effect of α and β. Finally, we explore the effect of α in constraint and β in intra-task distillation, respectively. For simplification, we apply constant α for all tasks. Larger α indicates looser constraint in (3). As shown in Fig. 4, with the increase of α, BWT becomes worse, and ACC first increases and then decreases as a result of the stability-plasticity dilemma. The results agree with the theoretical analysis that larger null space (looser constraint) leads to better plasticity and worse stability and vice-versa. For intra-task distillation, as shown in Fig. 4, with proper β, it could mitigate the forgetting and achieve a good balance between stability and plasticity. Too large or too small β will have a negative impact on the performance.

---

[4] $\mathrm{Max}(\cdot), \mathrm{Avg}(\cdot)$, and $\mathrm{Min}(\cdot)$ are functions that compute the maximum, average, and minimum values over inputs, respectively.

7 Conclusion

To relieve the stability-plasticity dilemma, we propose a new algorithm-based continual learning method, Advanced Null Space (AdNS). Specifically, AdNS extracts the shared low-rank null space based on low-rank approximation and projects the gradient onto the null space to reduce forgetting. Moreover, we introduce non-uniform constraint strength to further alleviate the catastrophic forgetting, and present intra-task distillation to improve performance. Furthermore, we provide theoretical findings of the impact of null space on the stability and plasticity, respectively. Empirical results validate that the proposed algorithm could achieve a better stability-plasticity trade-off.

Acknowledgements. Ms Yajing Kong and Dr Liu Liu are supported by ARC FL-170100117 and DP-180103424.

References

1. Aljundi, R., Babiloni, F., Elhoseiny, M., Rohrbach, M., Tuytelaars, T.: Memory aware synapses: learning what (not) to forget. In: Proceedings of the European Conference on Computer Vision (ECCV), pp. 139–154 (2018)
2. Aljundi, R., et al.: Online continual learning with maximal interfered retrieval. In: Advances in Neural Information Processing Systems, pp. 11849–11860 (2019)
3. Aljundi, R., Chakravarty, P., Tuytelaars, T.: Expert gate: lifelong learning with a network of experts. In: Proceedings of the IEEE Conference on Computer Vision and Pattern Recognition, pp. 3366–3375 (2017)
4. Buzzega, P., Boschini, M., Porrello, A., Abati, D., Calderara, S.: Dark experience for general continual learning: a strong, simple baseline. arXiv preprint arXiv:2004.07211 (2020)
5. Cha, S., Hsu, H., Hwang, T., Calmon, F.P., Moon, T.: CPR: classifier-projection regularization for continual learning. arXiv preprint arXiv:2006.07326 (2020)
6. Chaudhry, A., Khan, N., Dokania, P.K., Torr, P.H.: Continual learning in low-rank orthogonal subspaces. arXiv preprint arXiv:2010.11635 (2020)
7. Chaudhry, A., Ranzato, M., Rohrbach, M., Elhoseiny, M.: Efficient lifelong learning with a-gem. arXiv preprint arXiv:1812.00420 (2018)
8. Chaudhry, A., et al.: Continual learning with tiny episodic memories (2019)
9. Chen, H.J., Cheng, A.C., Juan, D.C., Wei, W., Sun, M.: Mitigating forgetting in online continual learning via instance-aware parameterization. In: Advances in Neural Information Processing Systems, vol. 33 (2020)
10. Guo, Y., Liu, M., Yang, T., Rosing, T.: Improved schemes for episodic memory based lifelong learning algorithm. In: Conference on Neural Information Processing Systems (2020)
11. He, K., Zhang, X., Ren, S., Sun, J.: Identity mappings in deep residual networks. In: Leibe, B., Matas, J., Sebe, N., Welling, M. (eds.) ECCV 2016. LNCS, vol. 9908, pp. 630–645. Springer, Cham (2016). https://doi.org/10.1007/978-3-319-46493-0_38
12. Isele, D., Cosgun, A.: Selective experience replay for lifelong learning. In: Proceedings of the AAAI Conference on Artificial Intelligence, vol. 32 (2018)
13. Jerfel, G., Grant, E., Griffiths, T., Heller, K.A.: Reconciling meta-learning and continual learning with online mixtures of tasks. In: Advances in Neural Information Processing Systems, pp. 9122–9133 (2019)

14. Jing, Y., Yang, Y., Wang, X., Song, M., Tao, D.: Amalgamating knowledge from heterogeneous graph neural networks. In: CVPR (2021)
15. Jung, H., Ju, J., Jung, M., Kim, J.: Less-forgetting learning in deep neural networks. arXiv preprint arXiv:1607.00122 (2016)
16. Kemker, R., McClure, M., Abitino, A., Hayes, T., Kanan, C.: Measuring catastrophic forgetting in neural networks. In: Proceedings of the AAAI Conference on Artificial Intelligence, vol. 32 (2018)
17. Kirkpatrick, J., et al.: Overcoming catastrophic forgetting in neural networks. Proc. Natl. Acad. Sci. **114**(13), 3521–3526 (2017)
18. Krizhevsky, A., Hinton, G., et al.: Learning multiple layers of features from tiny images (2009)
19. Lee, J., Hong, H.G., Joo, D., Kim, J.: Continual learning with extended kronecker-factored approximate curvature. In: Proceedings of the IEEE/CVF Conference on Computer Vision and Pattern Recognition, pp. 9001–9010 (2020)
20. Lee, K., Lee, K., Shin, J., Lee, H.: Overcoming catastrophic forgetting with unlabeled data in the wild. In: Proceedings of the IEEE/CVF International Conference on Computer Vision, pp. 312–321 (2019)
21. Lee, S.W., Kim, J.H., Jun, J., Ha, J.W., Zhang, B.T.: Overcoming catastrophic forgetting by incremental moment matching. In: Advances in Neural Information Processing Systems, pp. 4652–4662 (2017)
22. Li, X., Zhou, Y., Wu, T., Socher, R., Xiong, C.: Learn to grow: a continual structure learning framework for overcoming catastrophic forgetting. arXiv preprint arXiv:1904.00310 (2019)
23. Li, Z., Hoiem, D.: Learning without forgetting. IEEE Trans. Pattern Anal. Mach. Intell. **40**(12), 2935–2947 (2017)
24. Lin, S., Yang, L., Fan, D., Zhang, J.: TRGP: trust region gradient projection for continual learning (2022)
25. Liu, Yu., Parisot, S., Slabaugh, G., Jia, X., Leonardis, A., Tuytelaars, T.: More classifiers, less forgetting: a generic multi-classifier paradigm for incremental learning. In: Vedaldi, A., Bischof, H., Brox, T., Frahm, J.-M. (eds.) ECCV 2020. LNCS, vol. 12371, pp. 699–716. Springer, Cham (2020). https://doi.org/10.1007/978-3-030-58574-7_42
26. Lopez-Paz, D., Ranzato, M.: Gradient episodic memory for continual learning. In: Advances in Neural Information Processing Systems, pp. 6467–6476 (2017)
27. Mallya, A., Davis, D., Lazebnik, S.: Piggyback: adapting a single network to multiple tasks by learning to mask weights. In: Proceedings of the European Conference on Computer Vision (ECCV), pp. 67–82 (2018)
28. Mallya, A., Lazebnik, S.: Packnet: adding multiple tasks to a single network by iterative pruning. In: Proceedings of the IEEE Conference on Computer Vision and Pattern Recognition, pp. 7765–7773 (2018)
29. Masse, N.Y., Grant, G.D., Freedman, D.J.: Alleviating catastrophic forgetting using context-dependent gating and synaptic stabilization. Proc. Natl. Acad. Sci. **115**(44), E10467–E10475 (2018)
30. McCloskey, M., Cohen, N.J.: Catastrophic interference in connectionist networks: the sequential learning problem. In: Psychology of Learning and Motivation, vol. 24, pp. 109–165. Elsevier (1989)
31. Mirzadeh, S.I., Farajtabar, M., Ghasemzadeh, H.: Dropout as an implicit gating mechanism for continual learning. In: Proceedings of the IEEE/CVF Conference on Computer Vision and Pattern Recognition Workshops, pp. 232–233 (2020)

32. Mirzadeh, S.I., Farajtabar, M., Pascanu, R., Ghasemzadeh, H.: Understanding the role of training regimes in continual learning. In: Advances in Neural Information Processing Systems, vol. 33 (2020)
33. Nguyen, C.V., Li, Y., Bui, T.D., Turner, R.E.: Variational continual learning. arXiv preprint arXiv:1710.10628 (2017)
34. Parisi, G.I., Kemker, R., Part, J.L., Kanan, C., Wermter, S.: Continual lifelong learning with neural networks: a review. Neural Netw. **113**, 54–71 (2019)
35. Park, D., Hong, S., Han, B., Lee, K.M.: Continual learning by asymmetric loss approximation with single-side overestimation. In: Proceedings of the IEEE International Conference on Computer Vision, pp. 3335–3344 (2019)
36. Rannen, A., Aljundi, R., Blaschko, M.B., Tuytelaars, T.: Encoder based lifelong learning. In: Proceedings of the IEEE International Conference on Computer Vision, pp. 1320–1328 (2017)
37. Rao, D., Visin, F., Rusu, A., Pascanu, R., Teh, Y.W., Hadsell, R.: Continual unsupervised representation learning. In: Advances in Neural Information Processing Systems, pp. 7647–7657 (2019)
38. Rebuffi, S.A., Kolesnikov, A., Sperl, G., Lampert, C.H.: ICARL: incremental classifier and representation learning. In: Proceedings of the IEEE Conference on Computer Vision and Pattern Recognition, pp. 2001–2010 (2017)
39. Riemer, M., et al.: Learning to learn without forgetting by maximizing transfer and minimizing interference. arXiv preprint arXiv:1810.11910 (2018)
40. Rolnick, D., Ahuja, A., Schwarz, J., Lillicrap, T., Wayne, G.: Experience replay for continual learning. In: Advances in Neural Information Processing Systems, pp. 350–360 (2019)
41. Rosenfeld, A., Tsotsos, J.K.: Incremental learning through deep adaptation. IEEE Trans. Pattern Anal. Mach. Intell. **42**(3), 651–663 (2018)
42. Rusu, A.A., et al.: Progressive neural networks. arXiv preprint arXiv:1606.04671 (2016)
43. Saha, G., Garg, I., Roy, K.: Gradient projection memory for continual learning. In: International Conference on Learning Representations (2021). https://openreview. net/forum?id=3AOj0RCNC2
44. Serra, J., Suris, D., Miron, M., Karatzoglou, A.: Overcoming catastrophic forgetting with hard attention to the task. In: International Conference on Machine Learning, pp. 4548–4557. PMLR (2018)
45. Shin, H., Lee, J.K., Kim, J., Kim, J.: Continual learning with deep generative replay. In: Advances in Neural Information Processing Systems, pp. 2990–2999 (2017)
46. Stanford: Tiny ImageNet Challenge (CS231n) (2015). https://tiny-imagenet.hero kuapp.com/
47. Tang, S., Chen, D., Zhu, J., Yu, S., Ouyang, W.: Layerwise optimization by gradient decomposition for continual learning. In: Proceedings of the IEEE/CVF Conference on Computer Vision and Pattern Recognition, pp. 9634–9643 (2021)
48. Tani, J.: Exploring Robotic Minds: Actions, Symbols, and Consciousness as Self-organizing Dynamic Phenomena. Oxford University Press, Oxford (2016)
49. Wang, S., Li, X., Sun, J., Xu, Z.: Training networks in null space of feature covariance for continual learning. In: Proceedings of the IEEE/CVF Conference on Computer Vision and Pattern Recognition (CVPR), pp. 184–193, June 2021
50. Wang, Z., Liu, L., Duan, Y., Kong, Y., Tao, D.: Continual learning with lifelong vision transformer. In: Proceedings of the IEEE/CVF Conference on Computer Vision and Pattern Recognition (CVPR), pp. 171–181, June 2022

51. Wang, Z., Liu, L., Duan, Y., Tao, D.: Continual learning through retrieval and imagination. In: Proceedings of the AAAI Conference on Artificial Intelligence, vol. 36, no. 8, pp. 8594–8602 (2022). https://doi.org/10.1609/aaai.v36i8.20837. https://ojs.aaai.org/index.php/AAAI/article/view/20837

52. Wang, Z., Liu, L., Tao, D.: Deep streaming label learning. In: International Conference on Machine Learning (ICML), vol. 119, pp. 9963–9972 (2020)

53. Wu, L., Liu, B., Stone, P., Liu, Q.: Firefly neural architecture descent: a general approach for growing neural networks. In: Advances in Neural Information Processing Systems, vol. 33 (2020)

54. Yiduo, G., Wenpeng, H., Dongyan, Z., Bing, L.: Adaptive orthogonal projection for continual learning. In: AAAI (2022)

55. Yin, D., Farajtabar, M., Li, A., Levine, N., Mott, A.: Optimization and generalization of regularization-based continual learning: a loss approximation viewpoint (2020)

56. Yoon, J., Kim, S., Yang, E., Hwang, S.J.: Scalable and order-robust continual learning with additive parameter decomposition. arXiv preprint arXiv:1902.09432 (2019)

57. Zeng, G., Chen, Y., Cui, B., Yu, S.: Continual learning of context-dependent processing in neural networks. Nat. Mach. Intell. (NMI) **1**(8), 364–372 (2019)

58. Zenke, F., Poole, B., Ganguli, S.: Continual learning through synaptic intelligence. In: International Conference on Machine Learning, pp. 3987–3995. PMLR (2017)

59. Zhang, J., et al.: Class-incremental learning via deep model consolidation. In: Proceedings of the IEEE/CVF Winter Conference on Applications of Computer Vision, pp. 1131–1140 (2020)

60. Zhou, G., Sohn, K., Lee, H.: Online incremental feature learning with denoising autoencoders. In: Artificial Intelligence and Statistics, pp. 1453–1461 (2012)

DisCo: Remedying Self-supervised Learning on Lightweight Models with Distilled Contrastive Learning

Yuting Gao[1], Jia-Xin Zhuang[1,2], Shaohui Lin[3], Hao Cheng[4], Xing Sun[1], Ke Li[1(✉)], and Chunhua Shen[5]

[1] Tencent Youtu Lab, Shanghai, China
{yutinggao,tristanli}@tencent.com
[2] Hong Kong University of Science and Technology, Kowloon, Hong Kong
[3] East China Normal University, Shanghai, China
[4] University of California, Santa Cruz, Santa Cruz, USA
[5] Zhejiang University, Hangzhou, China

Abstract. While Self-Supervised Learning (SSL) has received widespread attention from the community, recent researches argue that its performance often suffers a cliff fall when the model size decreases. Since current SSL methods mainly rely on contrastive learning to train the network, we propose a simple yet effective method termed **Dis**tilled **Co**ntrastive Learning (DisCo) to ease this issue. Specifically, we find that the final inherent embedding of the mainstream SSL methods contains the most important information, and propose to distill the final embedding to maximally transmit a teacher's knowledge to a lightweight model by constraining the last embedding of the student to be consistent with that of the teacher. In addition, we find that there exists a phenomenon termed Distilling BottleNeck and propose to enlarge the embedding dimension to alleviate this problem. Since the MLP only exists during the SSL phase, our method does not introduce any extra parameters to lightweight models for the downstream task deployment. Experimental results demonstrate that our method surpasses the state-of-the-art on many lightweight models by a large margin. Particularly, when ResNet-101/ResNet-50 is used respectively as a teacher to teach EfficientNet-B0, the linear result of EfficientNet-B0 on ImageNet is improved by 22.1% and 19.7%, respectively, which is very close to ResNet-101/ResNet-50 with much fewer parameters. Code is available at https://github.com/Yuting-Gao/DisCo-pytorch.

Keywords: Self-supervised learning · Distillation

Y. Gao and J.-X. Zhuang—Contributed equally. This work was done when Jia-Xin Zhuang was an intern at Tencent Youtu Lab.

Supplementary Information The online version contains supplementary material available at https://doi.org/10.1007/978-3-031-19809-0_14.

1 Introduction

Deep learning has achieved great success in computer vision tasks, including image classification, object detection, and semantic segmentation. Such success relies heavily on manually labeled datasets, which are time-consuming and expensive to obtain. Therefore, more and more researchers begin to explore how to make better use of off-the-shelf unlabeled data. Among them, SSL is an effective way to explore the information contained in the data itself by using proxy signals as supervision. Usually, after pre-training the network on massive unlabeled data with self supervised methods and fine-tuning on downstream tasks, the performance of downstream tasks will be significantly improved. Hence, SSL has attracted widespread attention from the community, and many methods have been proposed [6,7,11,14,15,21,25,27]. Among them, methods based on contrastive learning are becoming the mainstream due to their superior results. These methods are constantly refreshing the SOTA results with relatively large networks, but are unsatisfactory on some lightweight models at the same time. For example, the number of parameters of MobileNet-v3-Large/ResNet-152 is 5.2M/57.4M [17,20], and the corresponding linear evaluation top-1 accuracy on ImageNet [30] using MoCo-V2 [8] is 36.2%/74.1%. Compared to their fully supervised counterparts 75.2%/78.57%, the results of MobileNet-v3-Large is far from satisfying. Meanwhile in real scenarios, sometimes only lightweight models can be deployed due to the limited hardware resources. Therefore, improving the ability of self-supervised learning on small models is of great significance (Fig. 1).

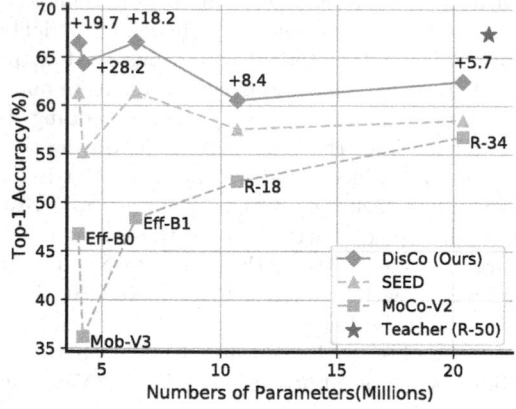

Fig. 1. ImageNet top-1 linear evaluation accuracy on different network architectures. Our method significantly exceeds the result of using MoCo-V2 directly, and also surpasses the state-of-the-art SEED by a large margin. Particularly, the result of EfficientNet-B0 is quite close to the teacher ResNet-50, while the number of parameters of EfficientNet-B0 is only 16.3% of ResNet-50. The improvement brought by DisCo is compared to the MoCo-V2 baseline

Knowledge distillation [19] is an effective way to transfer the knowledge learned by a large model (teacher) to a small model (student). Recently, some self-supervised learning methods use knowledge distillation to improve the efficacy of small models. SimCLR-V2 [7] uses logits in the fine-tuning stage to transfer the knowledge in a task-specific way. CompRess [1] and SEED [13] mimic the similarity score distribution between a teacher and a student model over a dynamically maintained queue. Though distillation is effective, two factors affect the result prominently, *i.e.*, *which* knowledge is most needed by the student, and *how* to deliver it. We propose new insights into these two aspects.

In the current mainstream contrastive learning based SSL methods, a multilayer perceptron (MLP) is added after the encoder to obtain a low-dimensional embedding. Training loss and the accuracy evaluation are both performed on this embedding. We thus hypothesize that this final embedding contains the most fruitful knowledge and should be regarded as the first choice for knowledge transfer. To achieve this, we propose a simple yet effective DisCo framework to transfer this knowledge from large models to lightweight models in the pre-training stage. Specifically, DisCo takes the MLP embedding obtained by the teacher as the knowledge and injects it into the student by constraining the corresponding embedding of the student to be consistent with that of the teacher using MSE loss. In addition, we find that a budgeted dimension of the hidden layer in the MLP of the student may cause a knowledge transmission bottleneck. We term this phenomenon as *Distilling Bottleneck* and present to enlarge the embedding dimension to alleviate this problem. This simple yet effective operation relates to the capability of model generalization in the setting of self-supervised learning from the Information BottleNeck [33] perspective. It is worth noting that our method only introduces a small number of additional parameters in the pre-training phase, but during the fine-tuning and deployment stage, there is no extra computational burden since the MLP layer is removed.

Experimental results demonstrate that DisCo can effectively transfer the knowledge from the teacher to the student, making the representations extracted by the student more generalized. Our approach is simple and incorporate it into existing contrastive based SSL methods can bring significant gains. Our contributions are summarized as follows:

- We propose a simple yet effective self-supervised distillation method to boost the representation abilities of lightweight models.
- We discover that there exists a phenomenon termed Distilling BottleNeck in the self-supervised distillation stage and propose to enlarge the embedding dimension to alleviate this problem.
- We achieve state-of-the-art SSL results on lightweight models. Particularly, the linear evaluation results of EfficientNet-B0 [32] on ImageNet is quite close to ResNet-101/ResNet-50, while the number of parameters of EfficientNet-B0 is only 9.4%/16.3% of ResNet-101/ResNet-50.

2   Related Work

2.1   Self-supervised Learning

SSL is a generic framework that learns high semantic patterns from data without any tags from human beings. Current methods mainly rely on three paradigms, *i.e.*, pretext tasks based, contrastive learning based, and clustering based.

Pretext Tasks Based. Approaches based on pretext paradigm first design surrogate tasks, e.g., Rotation [21], Jigsaw [25], and then train the network to solve.

Contrastive Learning Based. Contrastive learning based approaches have shown impressive performance on self-supervised learning, which enforce different views of the same input to be closer in feature space [6–9,14,15,18,34,35]. SimCLR-V2 indicates that SSL can be boosted by applying strong data augmentation, training with larger batch size, and adding projection head after the global average pooling. However, SimCLR relies on a very large batch size to achieve comparable performance. MoCo-V2 considers contrastive learning as a look-up dictionary, using a memory bank to maintain consistent representations of negative samples. Thus, MoCo can achieve superior performance without a large batch size, which is more feasible to implement. DINO [5] applies contrastive learning to vision transformers.

Clustering Based. Clustering is a kind of promising approach for unsupervised representation learning [2,3]. SwAV [4] maps representations to prototype vectors and is capable to scale to larger datasets.

Mainstream methods from different self-supxervised categories have four things in common: 1) two views for each input image, 2) two encoders for feature extraction, 3) two projection heads to map the representations into a lower dimension space, and 4) the two low-dimensional embeddings are regarded as a pair of positive samples and are pulled closer during training, which can be considered as a contrast process. However, all of these methods suffer a performance cliff fall that is way much more severe than expected on lightweight models, which is what we try to remedy in this work.

2.2   Knowledge Distillation

Knowledge distillation tries to transfer the knowledge from a larger teacher model to a smaller student model. The form of knowledge can be classified into three categories, logits-based, feature-based, and relation-based. Logits-based method KD [19] proposes to make the student mimic the logits of the teacher by minimizing the KL-divergence of the class distribution. Feature-based methods [29,36] directly transfer the knowledge from the intermediate layers of the teacher to the student. AT [36] proposes to use the spatial attention of the teacher as the knowledge and let the student pay attention to the area that the teacher is concerned about. Relation-based approaches explore the relationship between data instead of the output of a single instance. RKD [26] transfers the mutual relationship of the input data within one batch from the teacher to the student. In this work, we use feature-based distillation methods.

2.3 SSL Meets KD

CompRess [1] and SEED [13] try to employ knowledge distillation as a means to improve the representation capability of small models in self-supervised learning, which utilize the negative sample queue in MoCo-V2 to constrain the distribution of positive sample over negative samples of the student to be consistent with that of the teacher. However, both methods heavily rely on MoCo-V2, which means that a memory bank has to be preserved during the distillation process. Our method also aims to boost the self-supervised learning ability on lightweight models by distilling, however, we do not restrict the self-supervised framework and thus are more flexible. Furthermore, our method surpasses SEED with a large margin on all lightweight models under the same setting.

3 Method

In this section, we introduce the proposed *Distilled Contrastive Learning* (DisCo) framework for lightweight models. We first give some preliminaries on contrastive based SSL and then introduce the overall architecture of DisCo and how DisCo transfers the knowledge from the teacher to the student. Finally, we present how DisCo can be combined with the existing contrastive based SSL methods.

3.1 Preliminary on Contrastive Learning Based SSL

Mainstream contrastive learning-based SSL methods have four commonalities.

Two Views: one input image x is transformed into two views v and v' by two drastic data augmentation operations.

Two Encoders: two augmented views are input to two encoders of the same structure, one is a learnable base encoder $s(\cdot)$ and the other $m(\cdot)$ is updated according to the base encoder, either shared or momentum updated. The encoder here can use any network architecture, such as the commonly used ResNet. Given an input image, the extracted representation obtained from the last global average pooling of the encoder is denoted as Z, and its dimension is D.

Projection Head: both encoders are followed by a small projection head $p(\cdot)$ that maps the representation Z to a low-dimensional embedding E, which contains several linear layers. This procedure can be formulated as $E = p(Z) = W_{(n)} \cdots (\sigma(W_{(1)}Z))$, where W is the weight parameter of the linear layer, n is the number of layers, which is greater than or equal to 1, and σ is the non-linear function ReLU. The importance the of projection head has been addressed in SimCLR-V2 and MoCo-V2. Following MoCo-V2, the default configuration of the projection head is two linear layers, in which the first layer maintains the original feature dimension D, and the second layer reduces the dimension to 128.

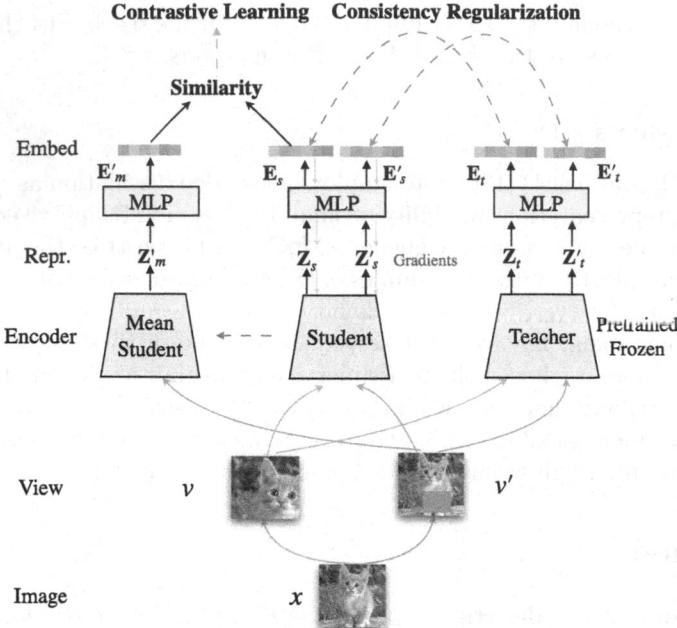

Fig. 2. The framework of the proposed method DisCo. One image is first transformed into two views by two drastic data augmentation operations. In addition to the original contrastive SSL part, a self-supervised pre-trained teacher is introduced, and the final embeddings obtained by the learnable student and the frozen teacher are required to be consistent for each view. Repr. stands for representation

Loss Function: after obtaining the final embeddings of these two views, they are regarded as a pair of positive samples to calculate the loss.

3.2   Overall Architecture

The framework of DisCo is shown in Fig. 2, consisting of three encoders followed by the projection head. The *Student* $s(\cdot)$ in center is the encoder that we want to improve, the *Mean Student* $m(\cdot)$ is updated according to $s(\cdot)$, and *Teacher* $t(\cdot)$ is the self-supervised pre-trained large encoder that is used as teacher in distillation.

For each input image x, it is first transformed into two views v and v' by two drastic data augmentation operations. On the one hand, v is input to $s(\cdot)$ and $t(\cdot)$, generating two representations $Z_s = s(v)$, $Z_t = t(v)$, then after the projection head, these two representations are mapped to low-dimensional embeddings, $E_s = p_s(Z_s)$, $E_t = p_t(Z_t)$ respectively. On the other hand, v' is input to $s(\cdot)$, $m(\cdot)$ and $t(\cdot)$ simultaneously, after encoding and projecting, three low-dimensional vectors $E'_s = p_s(s(v'))$, $E'_m = p_m(m(v'))$, and $E'_t = p_t(t(v'))$ are obtained.

E'_m and E_s are the embeddings of two different views, which are regarded as a pair of positive samples and are pulled together in the existing SSL methods. E_s

and E_t, E_s' and E_t' are two pairs of embeddings of the student and the teacher of the same view, and each pair is constrained to be consistent during the distilling.

3.3 Distilling Procedure

In most contrastive based SSL methods, the calculation of loss function and the evaluation of accuracy are performed at the final embedding vector E. Therefore, we hypothesize that the last embedding E contains the most fruitful knowledge and should be primarily considered when distilling.

For a self-supervised pre-trained teacher model, we distill the knowledge in the last embedding into the student, that is, for view v and view v', the embedding vector output by the frozen teacher and the learnable student should be consistent. Specifically, we use a consistency regularization term to pull the embedding vector E_s closer to E_t and E_s' closer to E_t'. Formally,

$$\mathcal{L}_{dis} = ||E_s - E_t||^2 + ||E_s' - E_t'||^2 \tag{1}$$

To verify that the embedding E contains the most meaningful knowledge, we experiment with several other commonly used distillation schemes in Table 5. The results prove that the knowledge we transmitted and the way it is transferred are indeed the most effective.

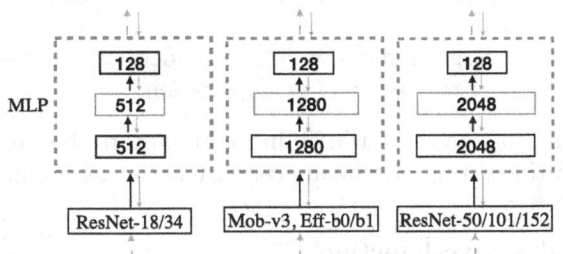

Fig. 3. Default MLP of multiple networks

Distilling Bottleneck. In our distillation experiment, we found an interesting phenomenon. When the encoder of the student is ResNet-18/34 and the default MLP configuration is adopted, that is, the dimension of embedding output by the encoder is projected from D to D and then to 128, the results of DisCo are not satisfactory. We assume that this degradation is caused by the fact that the dimension of the hidden layer in the MLP is too small, and term this phenomenon as *Distilling Bottleneck*. In Fig. 3, we exhibit the default configuration of the projection head of ResNet-18/34, EfficientNet-B0/B1, MobileNet-v3-Large, and ResNet-50/101/152. It can be seen that the dimension of the hidden layer of ResNet-18/34 is too small compared to other networks.

To alleviate the Distilling Bottleneck problem, we expand the dimension of the hidden layer in MLP. It's worth noting that this operation only introduces a small number of parameters at the self-supervised distillation stage, and the MLP will be directly discarded during fine-tuning and deployment, which means no extra computational burden is brought. We experimentally verified that such a simple operation can bring significant gains in Table 4.

This operation can be explained from the Information Bottleneck (IB) [33] perspective. IB is utilized in [10,31] to understand how deep networks work by visualizing mutual information ($I(X;T)$ and $I(T;Y)$) in the information plane, where $I(X;T)$ is the mutual information between input and output, and $I(T;Y)$ is the mutual information between output and label. The training of deep networks can be described by two phases: the first *fitting phase*, where the network memorizes the information of input, resulting in the growth of $I(X;T)$ and $I(T;Y)$; the subsequent *compression phase*, where the network removes irrelevant information of input for better generalization, resulting in the decrease of $I(X;T)$. Generally, in the *compression phase*, $I(X;T)$ can present the model's capability of generalization while $I(T;Y)$ can present the model's capability of fitting label [10]. We visualize the *compression phase* of our model with different dimensions of the hidden layer in the pre-training distillation stage in the information plane on one downstream transferring classification task. The results in Fig. 6 shows two interesting phenomenons:

i. Models with different dimensions of the hidden layer have very similar $I(T;Y)$, suggesting that models have nearly equal capability of fitting the labels.
ii. The Model with a larger dimension in the hidden layer has smaller $I(X;T)$, suggesting a stronger capability of generalization.

These phenomenons show that MLP indeed relates to the capability of model generalization in the setting of self-supervised transfer learning.

3.4   Overall Objective Function

The overall objective function is defined as follows:

$$\mathcal{L} = \mathcal{L}_{dis} + \lambda \mathcal{L}_{co} \tag{2}$$

where $\mathcal{L}_{dis}$ comes from the distillation part, $\mathcal{L}_{co}$ can be the contrastive loss of any SSL method, and λ is a hyper-parameter that controls the weights of the distillation loss and contrastive loss. In our experiments, λ is set to 1. Due to the simplicity of implementation, we use MoCo-V2 as the testbed in the experiments without additional explanation.

4   Experiments

4.1   Settings

Dataset. All the self-supervised pre-training experiments are conducted on ImageNet [30]. For downstream classification tasks, experiments are carried out on

Cifar10 and Cifar100 [22]. For downstream detection tasks, experiments are conducted on PASCAL VOC [12] and MS-COCO [23], with train+val/test and train2017/val2017 for training/testing respectively. For downstream segmentation tasks, the proposed method is verified on MS-COCO.

Teacher Encoders. Four large encoders are used as teachers, ResNet-50(22.4M), ResNet-101(40.5M), ResNet-152(55.4M), and ResNet-50*2(55.5M), where X(Y) denotes that the encoder X has Y millions of parameters and the Y does not consider the linear layer.

Student Encoders. Five widely used small yet effective networks are used as student, EfficientNet-B0(4.0M), MobileNet-v3-Large(4.2M), EfficientNet-B1(6.4M), ResNet-18(10.7M) and ResNet-34(20.4M).

Teacher Pre-training Setting. ResNet-50/101/152 are pre-trained using MoCo-V2 with default hyper-parameters. Following SEED, ResNet-50/101 are trained for 200 epochs, and ResNet-152 is trained for 400 epochs. ResNet-50*2 is pre-trained by SwAV, which is an open-source model[1] and trained for 800 epochs.

Self-supervised Distillation Setting. The projection head of all the student networks has two linear layers, with the dimension being 2048 and 128. The configuration of the learning rate and optimizer is set the same as MoCo-V2, and without a specific statement, the model is trained for 200 epochs. During the distillation stage, the teacher is frozen.

Student Fine-Tuning Setting. For linear evaluation on ImageNet, the student is fine-tuned for 100 epochs. Initial learning rate is 3 for EfficientNet-B0/EfficientNet-B1/MobileNet-v3-Large, and 30 for ResNet-18/34. For linear evaluation on Cifar10 and Cifar100, the initial learning rate is 3 and all the models are fine-tuned for 100 epochs. SGD is adopted as the optimizer and the learning rate is decreased by 10 at 60 and 80 epochs for linear evaluation. For downstream detection and segmentation tasks, following SEED [13], all parameters are fine-tuned. For the detection task on VOC, the initial learning rate is 0.1 with 200 warm-up iterations and decays by 10 at 18k, 22.2k steps. The detector is trained for 48k steps with a batch size of 32. Following SEED, the scales of images are randomly sampled from [400, 800] during the training and is 800 at the inference. For the detection and instance segmentation on COCO, the model is trained for 180k iterations with the initial learning rate 0.11, and the scales of images are randomly sampled from [600, 800] during the training.

4.2   Linear Evaluation

We conduct linear evaluation on ImageNet to validate the effectiveness of our method. As shown in Table 1, student models distilled by DisCo outperform the counterparts pre-trained by MoCo-V2 (Baseline) with a large margin. Besides, DisCo surpasses the state-of-the-art SEED over various student models with

---

[1] https://github.com/facebookresearch/swav

Table 1. ImageNet test accuracy (%) using linear classification on different student architectures. ◊ denotes the models are pre-trained with MoCo-V2, which is our implementation and †means the teacher is pre-trained by SwAV, which is an open-source model. When using R50*2 as the teacher, SEED distills 800 epochs while DisCo distills 200 epochs. Subscript in green represents the improvement compared to MoCo-V2

Method	S / T	Eff-b0		Eff-b1		Mob-v3		R-18		R-34	
		T-1	T-5	T-1	T-5	T-1	T-5	T-1	T-5	T-1	T-5
Supervised		77.1	93.3	79.2	94.4	75.2	-	72.1	-	75.0	-
Self-supervised											
MoCo-V2 (Baseline)◊		46.8	72.2	48.4	73.8	36.2	62.1	52.2	77.6	56.8	81.4
SSL Distillation											
SEED[13]	R-50 (67.4)	61.3	82.7	61.4	83.1	55.2	80.3	57.6	81.8	58.5	82.6
DisCo (ours)	R-50 (67.4)◊	**66.5**	**87.6**	**66.6**	**87.5**	**64.4**	**86.2**	**60.6**	**83.7**	**62.5**	**85.4**
		(19.7↑)	(15.4↑)	(18.2↑)	(13.7↑)	(28.2↑)	(24.1↑)	(8.4↑)	(6.1↑)	(5.7↑)	(4.0↑)
SEED [13]	R-101 (70.3)	63.0	83.8	63.4	84.6	59.9	83.5	58.9	82.5	61.6	84.9
DisCo (ours)	R-101 (69.1)◊	**68.9**	**88.9**	**69.0**	**89.1**	**65.7**	**86.7**	**62.3**	**85.1**	**64.4**	**86.5**
		(22.1↑)	(16.7↑)	(20.6↑)	(15.3↑)	(29.5↑)	(24.6↑)	(10.1↑)	(7.5↑)	(7.6↑)	(5.1↑)
SEED [13]	R-152 (74.2)	65.3	86.0	67.3	86.9	61.4	84.6	59.5	83.3	62.7	85.8
DisCo (ours)	R-152 (74.1)◊	**67.8**	**87.0**	**73.1**	**91.2**	**63.7**	**84.9**	**65.5**	**86.7**	**68.1**	**88.6**
		(21.0↑)	(14.8↑)	(24.7↑)	(17.4↑)	(27.5↑)	(22.8↑)	(13.3↑)	(9.1↑)	(11.3↑)	(7.2↑)
SEED [13]	R50*2 (77.3†)	67.6	87.4	68.0	87.6	68.2	88.2	63.0	84.9	65.7	86.8
DisCo (ours)	R50*2 (77.3)†	**69.1**	**88.9**	64.0	84.6	58.9	81.4	**65.2**	**86.8**	**67.6**	**88.6**
		(22.3↑)	(17.7↑)	(15.6↑)	(10.8↑)	(22.7↑)	(19.3↑)	(13↑)	(9.2↑)	(10.8↑)	(7.2↑)

teacher ResNet-50/101/152 under the same setting, especially on MobileNet-v3-Large distilled by ResNet-50 with a difference of 9.2% at top-1 accuracy. When using R50*2 as the teacher, SEED distills 800 epochs while DisCo still distills 200 epochs, but the results of EfficientNet-B0, ResNet-18, and, ResNet-34 using DisCo also exceed that of SEED. The performance on EfficientNet-B1 and MobileNet-v3-Large is closely related to the epochs of distillation. For example, when EfficientNet-B1 is distilled for 290 epochs, the top-1 accuracy becomes 70.4%, which surpasses SEED and when MobileNet-v3-Large is distilled for 340 epochs, the top-1 accuracy becomes 64%. We believe that when DisCo distills 800 epochs, the results will be further improved. Moreover, since CompRess uses a better teacher which trained 600 epochs longer and distills 400 epochs longer than SEED and ours, it's not fair to compare thus we do not report the result in the table.

In addition, when DisCo uses a larger model as the teacher, the student will be further improved. For instance, using ResNet-152 instead of ResNet-50 as the teacher, ResNet-34 is improved from 62.5% to 68.1%. It's worth noting, when using ResNet-101/ResNet-50 as the teacher, the linear evaluation result of EfficientNet-B0 is very close to the teacher, while the number of parameters of EfficientNet-B0 is only 9.4%/16.3% of ResNet-101/ResNet-50.

4.3   Semi-supervised Linear Evaluation

Following SEED, we evaluate our method under the semi-supervised setting. Two 1% and 10% sampled subsets of ImageNet training data (∼12.8 and ∼128 images

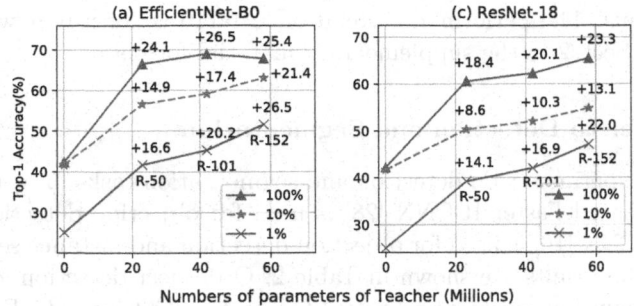

Fig. 4. ImageNet top-1 accuracy (%) of semi-supervised linear evaluation with 1%, 10% and 100% training data. Points where the number of teacher network parameters are 0 are the results of the MoCo-V2 without distillation

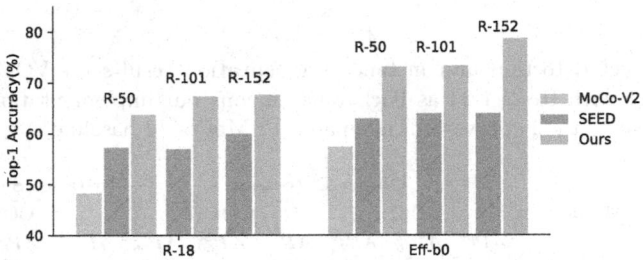

Fig. 5. Top-1 accuracy of students transferred to Cifar100 with and without distillation from different teachers

per class respectively) [6] are used for fine-tuning the student models. As is shown in Fig. 4, student models distilled by DisCo outperform baseline under any amount of labeled data. Furthermore, DisCo also shows the consistency under different fractions of annotations, that is, students always benefit from larger models as teachers. More labels will be helpful to improve the final performance of the student model, which is expected.

4.4 Transfer to Cifar10/Cifar100

In order to analyze the generalization of representations obtained by DisCo, we further conduct linear evaluation on Cifar10 and Cifar100 with ResNet-18/EfficientNet-B0 as student and ResNet-50/ResNet101/ResNet152 as a teacher. Since the image resolution of the Cifar dataset is 32×32, all the images are resized to 224×224 with bicubic re-sampling before feeding into the model, following [13]. The results are shown in Fig. 5, it can be seen that the proposed DisCo surpasses the MoCo-V2 baseline by a large margin with different student and teacher architectures on and Cifar100. In addition, our method also has a significant improvement compared to the-state-of-art method SEED. It is worth noting that as the teacher becomes better, the improvement brought by DisCo is more obvious. The performance trend on Cifar10 is consistent with that on Cifar100, see Sect. 2 in the supplementary material for details.

4.5   Transfer to Detection and Segmentation

We conduct experiments on detection and segmentation tasks for generalization analysis. C4-based Faster R-CNN [28] is used for objection detection on VOC and Mask R-CNN [16] is used for objection detection and instance segmentation on COCO. The results are shown in Table 2. On object detection, our method can bring obvious improvement on both VOC and COCO datasets. Furthermore, as SEED [13] claimed, the improvement on COCO is relatively minor compared to VOC since COCO training dataset has 118k images while VOC has only 16.5k training images, thus, the gain brought by weight initialization is relatively small. On the instance segmentation task, DisCo also shows superiority.

Table 2. Object detection and instance segmentation results on VOC07 test and COCO val2017 with ResNet-34 as backbone. ‡means our implementation. Subscript in green represents the improvement compared to MoCo-V2 baseline

S	T	Method	Object Detection						Instance Segmentation		
			VOC			COCO			COCO		
			AP^{bb}	AP^{bb}_{50}	AP^{bb}_{75}	AP^{bb}	AP^{bb}_{50}	AP^{bb}_{75}	AP^{mk}	AP^{mk}_{50}	AP^{mk}_{75}
R-34	×	MoCo-V2‡	53.6	79.1	58.7	38.1	56.8	40.7	33.0	53.2	35.3
	R-50	SEED [13]	53.7	79.4	59.2	38.4	57.0	41.0	33.3	53.2	35.3
		DisCo (ours)	**56.5**	**80.6**	**62.5**	**40.0**	**59.1**	**43.4**	**34.9**	**56.3**	**37.1**
			(2.9↑)	(1.5↑)	(3.8↑)	(1.9↑)	(2.3↑)	(2.7↑)	(1.9↑)	(3.1↑)	(1.8↑)
	R-101	SEED [13]	54.1	79.8	59.1	38.5	57.3	41.4	33.6	54.1	35.6
		DisCo (ours)	**56.1**	**80.3**	**61.8**	**40.0**	**59.1**	**43.2**	**34.7**	**55.9**	**37.4**
			(2.5↑)	(1.2↑)	(3.1↑)	(1.9↑)	(2.3↑)	(2.5↑)	(1.9↑)	(2.7↑)	(1.8↑)
	R-152	SEED [13]	54.4	80.1	59.9	38.4	57.0	41.0	33.3	53.7	35.3
		DisCo (ours)	**56.6**	**80.8**	**63.4**	**39.4**	**58.7**	**42.7**	**34.4**	**55.4**	**36.7**
			(3.0↑)	(1.7↑)	(5.7↑)	(1.3↑)	(1.9↑)	(2.0↑)	(1.4↑)	(2.2↑)	(1.4↑)

Table 3. Linear evaluation top-1 accuracy (%) on ImageNet

Method	Eff-b0	Mob-v3	R-18	R-34
SEED	61.3	55.2	57.6	58.5
DisCo*	65.6	63.8	57.1	58.9
DisCo	**66.5**(0.9↑)	**64.4**(0.6↑)	**60.6**(3.5↑)	**62.5**(3.6↑)

4.6   Distilling BottleNeck Phenomenon

In the self-supervised distillation stage, we first tried to distill small models with default MLP configuration of MoCo-V2 using ResNet-50 as a teacher, and the results are shown in Table 3, denoted by DisCo*. It is worth noting that the

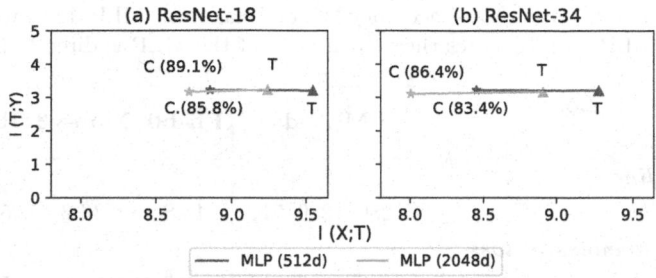

Fig. 6. Mutual information paths from transition points to convergence points in the compression phase of training. T denotes transition points, and C(X%) denotes convergent points with X% top-1 accuracy on Cifar10. Points with similar I(T;Y) but smaller I(X;T) are better generalized

dimensions of the hidden layer in DisCo* are exactly as same as SEED. It can be seen that compared to SEED, DisCo* shows superior results on EfficientNet-B0, and MobileNet-v3-Large, and has comparable results on ResNet-18. Then we expand the dimension of the hidden layer in the MLP of the student to be consistent with that of the teacher, that is, $2048D$, it can be seen that the results can be further improved, which is recorded in the third row. This expansion operation brings 3.5% and 3.6% gains for ResNet-18 and ResNet-34 respectively.

Theoretical Analysis from IB Perspective. In Fig. 6, on the downstream Cifar10 classification task, we visualize the *compression phase* of ResNet-18/34 with different hidden dimensions distilled by the same teacher in the information plane. Following [10], we use binning strategy [24] to estimate mutual information. It can be seen that when we adjust the hidden dimension in the MLP of ResNet-18 and ResNet-34 from $512D$ to $2048D$, the value of $I(X;T)$ becomes smaller while $I(T;Y)$ is basically unchanged, which suggests that enlarging the hidden dimension can make the student model more generalized in the setting of self-supervised transfer learning.

4.7 Ablation Study

In this section, we testify the effectiveness of two important modules in DisCo, i.e. the distillation loss and the expansion of the hidden dimension of MLP, and the results are shown in Table 4. It can be seen that distillation loss can bring about essential changes, and the result will be greatly improved. Even with only distillation loss, good results can be achieved. Furthermore, as the hidden dimension increases, the top-1 accuracy also increases, but when the dimension is already large, the growth trend will slow down.

4.8 Comparison Against Other Distillation

We compare with three widely used distillation schemes, namely, 1) *Attention transfer* denoted by AT [36], 2) *Relational knowledge distillation* denoted by

Table 4. Linear evaluation top-1 accuracy (%) on ImageNet. MLP-d means the hidden dimension of MLP and - denotes the hidden layer of the MLP is directly removed

Loss		MLP-d	Eff-b0	Mob-v3	R-18
L_{co}	L_{dis}				
Baseline					
✓		1280/1280/512	46.8	36.2	52.2
Effectiveness of loss					
	✓	1280/1280/512	65.6	58.9	54.5
✓	✓	1280/1280/512	65.6	63.7	57.1
Effectiveness of MLP-d					
✓	✓	-/-/-	52.5	60.3	52.5
✓	✓	512/512/512	62.5	62.8	57.1
✓	✓	1024/1024/1024	65.0	63.8	59.2
✓	✓	2048/2048/2048	**66.5**	**64.4**	**60.6**

RKD [26] 3) *Knowledge distillation* denoted by KD [19]. AT and RKD are feature-based and relation-based respectively, which can be utilized during the self-supervised pre-training stage. KD is a logits-based method, which can only be used at the supervised fine-tuning stage. The comparison results are shown in Table 5. *Singe-Knowledge* means using one of these approaches individually, and it can be seen that all distillation approaches can bring improvement to the baseline but the gain from DisCo is the most significant, which indicates the knowledge that DisCo has chosen to transfer and the way of transmission is indeed more effective. Then, we also try to transfer multi-knowledge from teacher to student by combining DisCo with other schemes. It can be seen that integrating DisCo with AT/RKD/KD can boost the performance a lot, which further proves the effectiveness of DisCo.

4.9 More SSL Methods

We further experiment with two SSL methods that are quite different from the MoCo-V2. i) SwAV is used to testify to the compatibility of the learning paradigm, in which the difference is measured between clusters instead of instances (see supplementary Sect. 3). ii) DINO is used to testify the compatibility towards the backbone type, in which the encoder is a vision transformer instead of CNN, as is shown in Table 3 in the supplemental material. DisCo can bring significant improvement under most of the popular SSL frameworks.

Table 5. Top-1 accuracy (%) on ImageNet compared with various distillation methods

Method	Eff-b0	Eff-b1	Mob-v3	R-18
Baseline				
MoCo-V2	46.8	48.4	36.2	52.2
Single-Knowledge				
AT	57.1	58.2	51.0	56.2
RKD	48.3	50.3	36.9	56.4
KD	46.5	48.5	37.3	51.5
DisCo (ours)	**66.5**	**66.6**	**64.4**	**60.6**
Multi-Knowledge				
AT + DisCo	66.7	66.3	64.1	60.0
RKD + DisCo	**66.8**	**66.5**	64.4	**60.6**
KD + DisCo	65.8	65.9	**65.2**	**60.6**

5   Conclusion

In this paper, we propose DisCo to remedy self-supervised learning on lightweight models. The proposed method constraints the final embedding of the lightweight student to be consistent with that of the teacher to maximally transmit the teacher's knowledge. DisCo is not limited to specific contrastive learning methods and can remedy student performance by a large margin.

Acknowledgements. This paper is sponsored by the National Natural Science Foundation of China (NO. 62102151), Shanghai Sailing Program (21YF1411200), and CAAI-Huawei MindSpore Open Fund (CAAIXSJLJJ-2021-031A).

References

1. Abbasi Koohpayegani, S., Tejankar, A., Pirsiavash, H.: Compress: self-supervised learning by compressing representations. In: NeurIPS, pp. 12980–12992 (2020)
2. Asano, Y.M., Rupprecht, C., Vedaldi, A.: Self-labelling via simultaneous clustering and representation learning. In: ICLR (2020)
3. Caron, M., Bojanowski, P., Joulin, A., Douze, M.: Deep clustering for unsupervised learning of visual features. In: ECCV, pp. 132–149 (2018)
4. Caron, M., Misra, I., Mairal, J., Goyal, P., Bojanowski, P., Joulin, A.: Unsupervised learning of visual features by contrasting cluster assignments. In: NeurIPS, pp. 9912–9924 (2020)
5. Caron, M., et al.: Emerging properties in self-supervised vision transformers (2021)
6. Chen, T., Kornblith, S., Norouzi, M., Hinton, G.: A simple framework for contrastive learning of visual representations. In: ICML, pp. 1597–1607 (2020)
7. Chen, T., Kornblith, S., Swersky, K., Norouzi, M., Hinton, G.: Big self-supervised models are strong semi-supervised learners. In: NeurIPS, pp. 22243–22255 (2020)
8. Chen, X., Fan, H., Girshick, R., He, K.: Improved baselines with momentum contrastive learning. In: CVPR, pp. 9729–9738 (2020)

9. Chen, X., He, K.: Exploring simple siamese representation learning. arXiv preprint arXiv:2011.10566 (2020)
10. Cheng, H., Lian, D., Gao, S., Geng, Y.: Evaluating capability of deep neural networks for image classification via information plane. In: ECCV, pp. 168–182 (2018)
11. Doersch, C., Gupta, A., Efros, A.A.: Unsupervised visual representation learning by context prediction. In: ICCV, pp. 1422–1430 (2015)
12. Everingham, M., Van Gool, L., Williams, C.K., Winn, J., Zisserman, A.: The pascal visual object classes challenge, vol. 88, pp. 303–338 (2010)
13. Fang, Z., Wang, J., Wang, L., Zhang, L., Yang, Y., Liu, Z.: Seed: self-supervised distillation for visual representation. In: ICLR (2021)
14. Grill, J.B., et al.: Bootstrap your own latent: a new approach to self-supervised learning. In: NeurIPS, pp. 21271–21284 (2020)
15. He, K., Fan, H., Wu, Y., Xie, S., Girshick, R.: Momentum contrast for unsupervised visual representation learning. In: CVPR, pp. 9729–9738 (2020)
16. He, K., Gkioxari, G., Dollár, P., Girshick, R.: Mask R-CNN. In: ICCV, pp. 2961–2969 (2017)
17. He, K., Zhang, X., Ren, S., Sun, J.: Deep residual learning for image recognition. In: CVPR, pp. 770–778 (2016)
18. Henaff, O.: Data-efficient image recognition with contrastive predictive coding. In: ICML, pp. 4182–4192 (2020)
19. Hinton, G., Vinyals, O., Dean, J.: Distilling the knowledge in a neural network. In: NeurIPSW (2015)
20. Howard, A., et al.: Searching for mobilenetv3. In: ICCV, pp. 1314–1324 (2019)
21. Komodakis, N., Gidaris, S.: Unsupervised representation learning by predicting image rotations. In: ICLR (2018)
22. Krizhevsky, A., Hinton, G.: Learning multiple layers of features from tiny images. Citeseer (2009)
23. Lin, T.-Y., et al.: Microsoft COCO: common objects in context. In: Fleet, D., Pajdla, T., Schiele, B., Tuytelaars, T. (eds.) ECCV 2014. LNCS, vol. 8693, pp. 740–755. Springer, Cham (2014). https://doi.org/10.1007/978-3-319-10602-1_48
24. Murphy, K.P.: Machine Learning: A Probabilistic Perspective. MIT Press, Cambridge (2012)
25. Noroozi, M., Favaro, P.: Unsupervised learning of visual representations by solving jigsaw puzzles. In: Leibe, B., Matas, J., Sebe, N., Welling, M. (eds.) ECCV 2016. LNCS, vol. 9910, pp. 69–84. Springer, Cham (2016). https://doi.org/10.1007/978-3-319-46466-4_5
26. Park, W., Kim, D., Lu, Y., Cho, M.: Relational knowledge distillation. In: CVPR, pp. 3967–3976 (2019)
27. Pathak, D., Krahenbuhl, P., Donahue, J., Darrell, T., Efros, A.A.: Context encoders: feature learning by inpainting. In: CVPR, pp. 2536–2544 (2016)
28. Ren, S., He, K., Girshick, R., Sun, J.: Faster R-CNN: towards real-time object detection with region proposal networks, vol. 39, pp. 1137–1149 (2015)
29. Romero, A., Ballas, N., Kahou, S.E., Chassang, A., Gatta, C., Bengio, Y.: Fitnets: hints for thin deep nets. In: ICLR (2014)
30. Russakovsky, O., et al.: ImageNet large scale visual recognition. Challenge 115, 211–252 (2015)
31. Shwartz-Ziv, R., Tishby, N.: Opening the black box of deep neural networks via information (2017)
32. Tan, M., Le, Q.: Efficientnet: rethinking model scaling for convolutional neural networks. In: ICML, pp. 6105–6114 (2019)

33. Tishby, N., Pereira, F.C., Bialek, W.: The information bottleneck method (2000)
34. Wang, J., et al.: Enhancing unsupervised video representation learning by decoupling the scene and the motion (2020)
35. Wang, J., Gao, Y., Li, K., Lin, Y., Ma, A.J., Sun, X.: Removing the background by adding the background: towards background robust self-supervised video representation learning (2020)
36. Zagoruyko, S., Komodakis, N.: Paying more attention to attention: Improving the performance of convolutional neural networks via attention transfer. In: ICLR (2017)

CoSCL: Cooperation of Small Continual Learners is Stronger Than a Big One

Liyuan Wang[1,2,3], Xingxing Zhang[3], Qian Li[1,2], Jun Zhu[3(✉)],
and Yi Zhong[1,2(✉)]

[1] School of Life Sciences, IDG/McGovern Institute for Brain Research,
Tsinghua University, Beijing, China
wly19@mails.tsinghua.edu.cn, {liqian8,zhongyithu}@tsinghua.edu.cn
[2] Tsinghua-Peking Center for Life Sciences, Beijing, China
[3] Department of Computer Science Technology, Institute for AI, BNRist Center,
THBI Lab, Tsinghua University, Beijing, China
xxzhang2020@mails.tsinghua.edu.cn, dcszj@tsinghua.edu.cn

Abstract. Continual learning requires incremental compatibility with a
sequence of tasks. However, the design of model architecture remains an
open question: In general, learning all tasks with a shared set of parameters suffers from severe interference between tasks; while learning each
task with a dedicated parameter subspace is limited by scalability. In
this work, we theoretically analyze the generalization errors for learning plasticity and memory stability in continual learning, which can be
uniformly upper-bounded by (1) discrepancy between task distributions,
(2) flatness of loss landscape and (3) cover of parameter space. Then,
inspired by the robust biological learning system that processes sequential experiences with multiple parallel compartments, we propose Cooperation of Small Continual Learners (CoSCL) as a general strategy for
continual learning. Specifically, we present an architecture with a fixed
number of narrower sub-networks to learn all incremental tasks in parallel, which can naturally reduce the two errors through improving the
three components of the upper bound. To strengthen this advantage, we
encourage to cooperate these sub-networks by penalizing the difference of
predictions made by their feature representations. With a fixed parameter budget, CoSCL can improve a variety of representative continual
learning approaches by a large margin (e.g., up to 10.64% on CIFAR-
100-SC, 9.33% on CIFAR-100-RS, 11.45% on CUB-200-2011 and 6.72%
on Tiny-ImageNet) and achieve the new state-of-the-art performance.
Our code is available at https://github.com/lywang3081/CoSCL.

Keywords: Continual learning · Catastrophic forgetting · Ensemble
model

L. Wang and X. Zhang—Contributed equally.

Supplementary Information The online version contains supplementary material
available at https://doi.org/10.1007/978-3-031-19809-0_15.

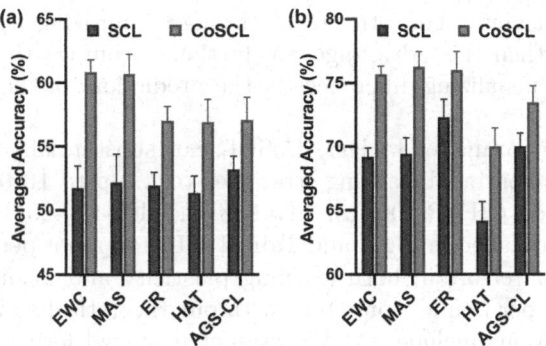

Fig. 1. Comparison of a single continual learner (SCL) and CoSCL (Ours) on (a) CIFAR-100-SC and (b) CIFAR-100-RS

1 Introduction

The ability to incrementally learn a sequence of tasks is critical for artificial neural networks. Since the training data distribution is typically dynamic and unpredictable, this usually requires a careful trade-off between learning plasticity and memory stability. In general, excessive plasticity in learning new tasks leads to the catastrophic forgetting of old tasks [25], while excessive stability in remembering old tasks limits the learning of new tasks. Most efforts in continual learning either use a single model to learn all tasks, which has to sacrifice the performance of each task to find a shared solution [33]; or allocate a dedicated parameter subspace for each task to overcome their mutual interference [14,39], which usually lacks scalability. Recent work observed that a wider network can suffer from less catastrophic forgetting [26], while different components such as batch normalization, skip connections and pooling layers play various roles [27]. Thus, how to achieve effective continual learning in terms of model architecture remains an open question.

In contrast, the robust biological learning system applies multiple compartments (i.e., sub-networks) to process sequential experiences in parallel, and integrates their outputs in a weighted-sum fashion to guide adaptive behaviors [3,9,30]. This provides a promising reference for artificial neural networks.

In this work, we first theoretically analyze the generalization errors of learning plasticity and memory stability in continual learning. We identify that both aspects can be uniformly upper-bounded by (1) *discrepancy between task distributions*, (2) *flatness of loss landscape* and (3) *cover of parameter space*. Inspired by the biological strategy, we propose a novel method named Cooperation of Small Continual Learners (CoSCL). Specifically, we design an architecture with multiple narrower sub-networks[1] to learn all incremental tasks in parallel, which

---

[1] In contrast to a single continual learning model with a wide network, we refer to such narrower sub-networks as "small" continual learners.

can naturally alleviate the both errors through improving the three components. To strengthen this advantage, we further encourage the cooperation of sub-networks by penalizing differences in the predictions of their feature representations.

With a fixed parameter budget, CoSCL can substantially boost a variety of representative continual learning strategies (e.g., up to **10.64%** on CIFAR-100-SC, **9.33%** on CIFAR-100-RS, **11.45%** on CUB-200-2011 and **6.72%** on Tiny-ImageNet, detailed in Fig. 1 and Table 1). The superior performance comes from reducing the errors in both learning plasticity and memory stability by tightening the upper bound, consistent with our theoretical analysis.

Our contributions include: (1) We present a unified form of generalization bounds for learning plasticity and memory stability in continual learning; (2) The generalization bounds suggest that the two aspects are not necessarily in conflict, but can be simultaneously enhanced in a compatible parameter space of a well-designed model architecture; (3) To achieve this goal, we draw inspirations from the biological strategy and propose to cooperate multiple (small) continual learners; (4) Extensive experiments validate the efficacy and generality of our proposal, which can be adapted to a variety of representative continual learning approaches and improve their performance by a large margin.

2   Related Work

Continual Learning requires effective learning of incremental tasks without severe catastrophic forgetting. Representative strategies include weight regularization [1,18,50], memory replay [34,42,44], parameter isolation [17,39] and dynamic architecture [14,48]. These strategies either learn all tasks with a single model, which have to compromise the performance of each task to obtain a shared solution [33]; or allocate parameter subspace for each task to prevent mutual interference, yet limited by scalability. Several recent work tried to improve continual learning in terms of architecture, such as by using neural architecture search [32] or learning an additional set of shared parameters [16], but to a limited extent. [33] proposed a model zoo that incrementally adds sub-networks to learn new tasks, which had to store a large amount of old training samples.

Flatness of Loss Landscape provides a conceptual explanation of generalization for deep neural networks, which is recently introduced to understand catastrophic forgetting in continual learning [6,11,23,29,40]. The core idea is that convergence to a smooth region will be more robust to (mild) parameter changes. [12,29] analyzed that the forgetting of old tasks in continual learning can be bounded by the variation of parameters between tasks and the eigenvalues of the Hessian matrix, where the lower eigenvalues indicate a flatter curvature of the solution. [6,11,40] explicitly encouraged the network to find a flat minima and empirically validated its efficacy in continual learning.

Ensemble Model is a powerful architecture to improve generalization, but is still under explored in continual learning. Most current applications focus on learning each single task with a sub-network [2,37,47], which can be seen as a special case of dynamic architecture. The main limitation is that the total amount of parameters (resp., the storage and computational cost) might grow linearly with the number of incremental tasks. [45] proposed an efficient ensemble strategy to reduce extra parameter cost for task-specific sub-networks. Similar to ours, a *concurrent* work [13] also observed that ensemble of multiple continual learning models brings huge benefits. They further exploited recent advances of mode connectivity [28] and neural network subspace [46] to save computational cost, but had to use old training samples [13]. Besides, [20] achieved more effective weight regularization by ensemble of multiple auxiliary classifiers learned from extra out-of-distribution data (e.g., SVHN [31] for CIFAR-100 [19]).

Main Advantages of Our Work are summarized in three aspects: (1) The generalization bounds presented in our work demonstrate the *direct* link between continual learning performance and flatness of loss landscape (as well as other components). (2) We use a *fixed* number of sub-networks, which are all continual learners rather than single-task learners, and adjust their width accordingly, so no additional or growing parameters are needed. (3) We mainly focus on a restrict setting where old training samples or extra data sources are *not* needed, which is more general and realistic for continual learning.

3 Preliminary Analysis

In this section, we first introduce the problem formulation and representative continual learning strategies, and then present the generalization bounds.

3.1 Problem Formulation

Let's consider a general setting of continual learning: A neural network with parameter θ incrementally learns T tasks, called a *continual learner*. The training set and test set of each task follow the same distribution $\mathbb{D}_t$ ($t = 1, 2, ..., T$), where the training set $D_t = \{(x_{t,n}, y_{t,n})\}_{n=1}^{N_t}$ includes N_t data-label pairs. For classification task, it might include one or several classes. After learning each task, the performance of all the tasks ever seen is evaluated on their test sets. Although D_t is only available when learning task t, an ideal continual learner should behave as if training them jointly. To achieve this goal, it is critical to balance learning plasticity of new tasks and memory stability of old tasks. Accordingly, the loss function for continual learning can typically be defined as

$$L_{\mathrm{CL}}(\theta) = L_t(\theta) + \lambda \hat{L}_{1:t-1}(\theta), \tag{1}$$

where $L_t(\cdot)$ is the task-specific loss for learning task t (e.g., cross-entropy for supervised classification), and $\hat{L}_{1:t-1}(\cdot)$ provides the constraint to achieve a proper trade-off between new and old tasks. For example, $\hat{L}_{1:t-1}(\theta) = \sum_i I_{1:t-1,i}(\theta_i - \theta^*_{1:t-1,i})^2$ for weight regularization [1,18,50], where $\theta^*_{1:t-1}$ denotes the continually-learned solution for old tasks and $I_{1:t-1}$ indicates the "importance" of each parameter. $\hat{L}_{1:t-1}(\theta) = \sum_{k=1}^{t-1} L_k(\theta; \hat{D}_k)$ for memory replay

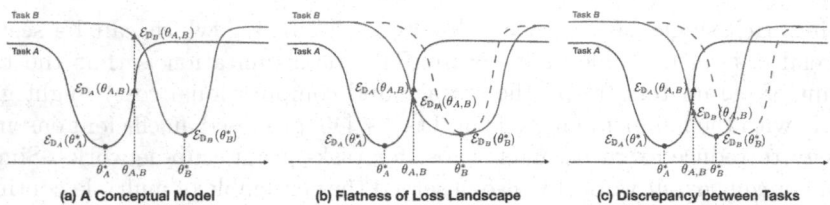

Fig. 2. A conceptual model of two tasks (the learning order of Task A and Task B does not matter). The dashed line in (b) and (c) is the original solution in (a), where finding a flatter solution or reducing the discrepancy between tasks help to mitigate the generalization errors of a shared solution $\theta_{A,B}$

[34,42,44], where $\hat{D}_k$ is an approximation of D_k through storing old training samples or learning a generative model. For parameter isolation [17,39], $\theta = \{\bigcup_{k=1}^{t-1} \hat{\theta}_k, \hat{\theta}_{\text{free}}\}$ is dynamically isolated as multiple task-specific subspaces $\hat{\theta}_k$, while $\hat{\theta}_{\text{free}}$ denotes the "free" parameters for current and future tasks. So $\hat{L}_{1:t-1}(\theta)$ usually serves as a sparsity regularizer to save $\hat{\theta}_{\text{free}}$. For dynamic architecture [14,48], $\theta = \{\bigcup_{k=1}^{t-1} \hat{\theta}_k, \hat{\theta}_t\}$ attempts to add a new subspace $\hat{\theta}_t$ on the basis of the previous ones, and $\hat{L}_{1:t-1}(\theta)$ should limit the amount of extra parameters.

3.2   Generalization Bound for Continual Learning

Formally, the goal of continual learning is to find a solution θ in a parameter space Θ that can generalize well over a set of distribution $\mathbb{D}_t$ and $\mathbb{D}_{1:t-1} := \{\mathbb{D}_k\}_{k=1}^{t-1}$. Let's consider a bounded loss function $\ell : \mathcal{Y} \times \mathcal{Y} \to [0, c]$ (where $\mathcal{Y}$ denotes a label space and c is the upper bound), such that $\ell(y_1, y_2) = 0$ holds if and only if $y_1 = y_2$. Then, we can define a population loss over the distribution $\mathbb{D}_t$ by $\mathcal{E}_{\mathbb{D}_t}(\theta) = \mathbb{E}_{(x,y)\sim\mathbb{D}_t}[\ell(f_\theta(x), y)]$, where $f_\theta(\cdot)$ is the prediction of an input parameterized by θ. Likewise, the population loss over the distribution of old tasks is defined by $\mathcal{E}_{\mathbb{D}_{1:t-1}}(\theta) = \frac{1}{t-1} \sum_{k=1}^{t-1} \mathbb{E}_{(x,y)\sim\mathbb{D}_k}[\ell(f_\theta(x), y)]$. To minimize both $\mathcal{E}_{\mathbb{D}_t}(\theta)$ and $\mathcal{E}_{\mathbb{D}_{1:t-1}}(\theta)$, a continual learning model (i.e., a continual learner) needs to minimize an empirical risk over the current training set D_t in a constrained parameter space, i.e., $\min_{\theta\in\Theta} \hat{\mathcal{E}}_{D_t}(\theta)$. Specifically, $\hat{\mathcal{E}}_{D_t}(\theta) = \frac{1}{N_t} \sum_{n=1}^{N_t} \ell(f_\theta(x_{t,n}), y_{t,n})$, and the constrained parameter space Θ depends on the previous experience carried by parameters, data, and/or task labels, so as to prevent catastrophic forgetting. Likewise, $\hat{\mathcal{E}}_{D_{1:t-1}}(\theta)$ denotes an empirical risk over the old tasks. In practice, sequential learning of each task by minimizing the empirical risk $\hat{\mathcal{E}}_{D_t}(\theta)$ in Θ can find multiple solutions, but provides significantly different generalizability on $\mathcal{E}_{\mathbb{D}_t}(\theta)$ and $\mathcal{E}_{\mathbb{D}_{1:t-1}}(\theta)$. Several recent studies suggested that a flatter solution is more robust to catastrophic forgetting [6,11,23,29,40]. To find such a flat solution, we define a robust empirical risk by the worst case of the neighborhood in parameter space as $\hat{\mathcal{E}}_{D_t}^b(\theta) := \max_{\|\Delta\|\le b}\hat{\mathcal{E}}_{D_t}(\theta + \Delta)$ [5], where b is the radius around θ and $\|\cdot\|$ denotes the L2 norm, likewise for the old tasks as $\hat{\mathcal{E}}_{D_{1:t-1}}^b(\theta) := \max_{\|\Delta\|\le b}\hat{\mathcal{E}}_{D_{1:t-1}}(\theta + \Delta)$. Then, solving the constrained robust empirical risk

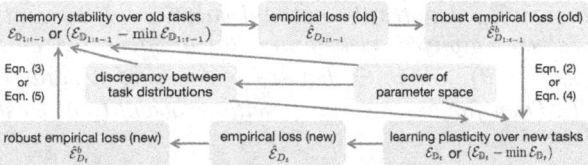

Fig. 3. Illustration of simultaneously promoting learning plasticity and memory stability in continual learning, where arrows represent the tightening process

minimization, i.e., $\min_{\theta \in \Theta} \hat{\mathcal{E}}^b_{D_t}(\theta)$, will find a near solution of a flat optimum showing better generalizability. In particular, the minima found by the empirical loss $\hat{\mathcal{E}}_{D_t}(\theta)$ will also be the minima of $\hat{\mathcal{E}}^b_{D_t}(\theta)$ if the "radius" of its loss landscape is sufficiently wider than b. Intuitively, such a flat solution helps to mitigate catastrophic forgetting since it is more robust to parameter changes.

However, this connection is not sufficient. If a new task is too different from the old tasks, the parameter changes to learn it well might be much larger than the "radius" of the old minima, resulting in catastrophic forgetting. On the other hand, staying around the old minima is not a good solution for the new task, limiting learning plasticity. Let $\mathcal{E}_{\mathbb{D}_t}(\theta_{1:t})$ and $\mathcal{E}_{\mathbb{D}_{1:t-1}}(\theta_{1:t})$ denote the generalization errors of performing the new task and old tasks, respectively. Inspired by the PAC-Bayes theory [24] and previous work in domain generalization [4,5], we present the upper bounds of these two errors as follows (proof in Appendix A):

Proposition 1. *Let Θ be a cover of a parameter space with VC dimension d. If $\mathbb{D}_1, \cdots, \mathbb{D}_t$ are the distributions of the continually learned $1:t$ tasks, then for any $\delta \in (0,1)$ with probability at least $1 - \delta$, for every solution $\theta_{1:t}$ of the continually learned $1:t$ tasks in parameter space Θ, i.e., $\theta_{1:t} \in \Theta$:*

$$\mathcal{E}_{\mathbb{D}_t}(\theta_{1:t}) < \hat{\mathcal{E}}^b_{D_{1:t-1}}(\theta_{1:t}) + \frac{1}{2(t-1)} \sum_{k=1}^{t-1} \mathrm{Div}(\mathbb{D}_k, \mathbb{D}_t) + \sqrt{\frac{d \ln(N_{1:t-1}/d) + \ln(1/\delta)}{N_{1:t-1}}}, \quad (2)$$

$$\mathcal{E}_{\mathbb{D}_{1:t-1}}(\theta_{1:t}) < \hat{\mathcal{E}}^b_{D_t}(\theta_{1:t}) + \frac{1}{2(t-1)} \sum_{k=1}^{t-1} \mathrm{Div}(\mathbb{D}_t, \mathbb{D}_k) + \sqrt{\frac{d \ln(N_t/d) + \ln(1/\delta)}{N_t}}, \quad (3)$$

where $\mathrm{Div}(\mathbb{D}_i, \mathbb{D}_j) := 2 \sup_{h \in \mathcal{H}} |\mathcal{P}_{\mathbb{D}_i}(I(h)) - \mathcal{P}_{\mathbb{D}_j}(I(h))|$ is the $\mathcal{H}$-divergence for the distribution $\mathbb{D}_i$ and $\mathbb{D}_j$ ($I(h)$ is the characteristic function). $N_{1:t-1} = \sum_{k=1}^{t-1} N_k$ is the total number of training samples over all old tasks.

It can be concluded from Proposition 1 that, the generalization errors over the new task and old tasks are uniformly constrained by three components: (1) *discrepancy between task distributions*; (2) *flatness of loss landscape*; and (3) *cover of parameter space*. By the optimal solution for (robust) empirical loss, we further demonstrate that the generalization gaps of the new task and old tasks are upper bounded as follows (proof in Appendix A):

Proposition 2. *Let $\hat{\theta}^b_{1:t}$ denotes the optimal solution of the continually learned $1:t$ tasks by robust empirical risk minimization over the current task, i.e., $\hat{\theta}^b_{1:t} = \arg\min_{\theta \in \Theta} \hat{\mathcal{E}}^b_{D_t}(\theta)$, where Θ denotes a cover of a parameter space with VC dimension d. Then for any $\delta \in (0,1)$, with probability at least $1 - \delta$:*

$$\mathcal{E}_{D_t}(\hat{\theta}^b_{1:t}) - \min_{\theta \in \Theta} \mathcal{E}_{D_t}(\theta) \leq \min_{\theta \in \Theta} \hat{\mathcal{E}}^b_{D_{1:t-1}}(\theta) - \min_{\theta \in \Theta} \hat{\mathcal{E}}_{D_{1:t-1}}(\theta) + \frac{1}{t-1} \sum_{k=1}^{t-1} \mathrm{Div}(\mathbb{D}_k, \mathbb{D}_t) + \lambda_1,$$

$$(4)$$

$$\mathcal{E}_{D_{1:t-1}}(\hat{\theta}^b_{1:t}) - \min_{\theta \in \Theta} \mathcal{E}_{D_{1:t-1}}(\theta) \leq \min_{\theta \in \Theta} \hat{\mathcal{E}}^b_{D_t}(\theta) - \min_{\theta \in \Theta} \hat{\mathcal{E}}_{D_t}(\theta) + \frac{1}{t-1} \sum_{k=1}^{t-1} \mathrm{Div}(\mathbb{D}_t, \mathbb{D}_k) + \lambda_2,$$

$$(5)$$

where $\lambda_1 = 2\sqrt{\frac{d \ln(N_{1:t-1}/d) + \ln(2/\delta)}{N_{1:t-1}}}$, $\lambda_2 = 2\sqrt{\frac{d \ln(N_t/d) + \ln(2/\delta)}{N_t}}$, and $\mathrm{Div}(\mathbb{D}_i, \mathbb{D}_j) := 2\sup_{h \in \mathcal{H}} |\mathcal{P}_{\mathbb{D}_i}(I(h)) - \mathcal{P}_{\mathbb{D}_j}(I(h))|$ is the $\mathcal{H}$-divergence for the distribution $\mathbb{D}_i$ and $\mathbb{D}_j$ ($I(h)$ is the characteristic function).

Likewise, the generalization gaps over the new and old tasks are also constrained by the three components above. In particular, learning plasticity and memory stability in continual learning can be simultaneously promoted by using a more compatible parameter space, as illustrated in Fig. 3. Specifically, compatibility with the new task can facilitate a smaller robust empirical risk on the old tasks as well as improve task discrepancy, then tightening the generalization bound for learning plasticity through Eq. (2)/Eq. (4), and vice versa tightening the generalization bound for memory stability through Eq. (3)/Eq. (5).

4   Method

Unlike artificial neural networks, the robust biological learning system, such as that of fruit flies, processes sequential experiences with multiple parallel compartments (i.e., sub-networks) [3,9]. These compartments are modulated by dopaminergic neurons (DANs) that convey valence (i.e., supervised signals), and their outputs are integrated in a weighted-sum fashion to guide adaptive behaviors [3,9,30] (detailed in Fig. 4, a). Inspired by this, we propose to cooperate multiple (small) continual learners as a simple yet effective method for continual learning. We present our proposal in Sect. 4.1, and validate this idea both theoretically (Sect. 4.2) and empirically (Sect. 5).

4.1   Cooperation of (Small) Continual Learners

Instead of learning all tasks with a single continual learner, we design a bio-inspired architecture to coordinate multiple continual learners. Specifically, each continual learner is implemented with a sub-network $f_{\phi_i}(\cdot), i = 1, ..., K$ in a parameter space for learning all incremental tasks, where the dedicated output

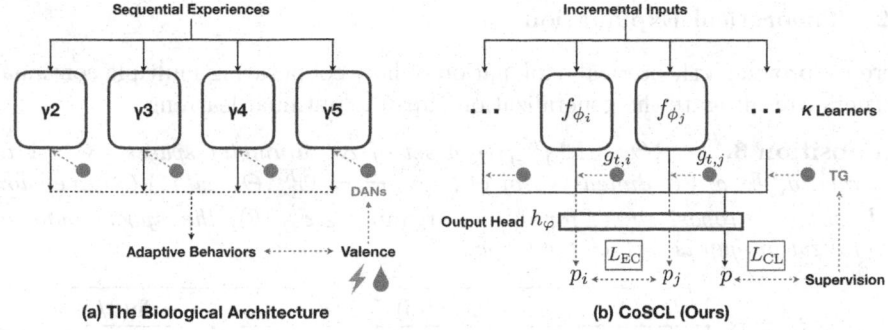

Fig. 4. (a) Fruit flies learn sequential experiences with multiple parallel compartments (γ 2-5), under the modulation of dopaminergic neurons (DANs) that convey valence. The figure is modified from [9]. (b) Inspired by the biological learning system, we propose a general strategy of cooperating multiple (small) continual learners

head is removed and the output of the previous layer is weighted by a set of learnable parameters (usually a fully connected layer). Then, these outputs are fed into a shared output head $h_\varphi(\cdot)$ for prediction. For a regular classifier, this is equivalent to making predictions on a weighted-sum of feature representations, so we refer to this strategy as *feature ensemble* (FE).

When task labels are available, our architecture can more effectively incorporate task-specific information by learning an additional set of *task-adaptive gates* (TG) for each continual learner's output. Such a gate is defined as $g_{t,i} = \sigma(s \cdot \alpha_{t,i})$ for learner i to perform task t, where $\alpha_{t,i}$ is a learnable parameter, s is a scale factor and σ denotes the sigmoid function. Therefore, the final prediction becomes $p(\cdot) = h_\varphi(\sum_{i=1}^{K} g_{t,i} f_{\phi_i}(\cdot))$, and all optimizable parameters include $\bar\theta = \{\bigcup_{i=1}^{K} \phi_i, \bigcup_{i=1}^{K} \alpha_{t,i}, \varphi\}$.

To strengthen the advantage of feature ensemble, we encourage to cooperate the continual learners by penalizing differences in the predictions of their feature representations (e.g., $\boldsymbol{p}_i$ and $\boldsymbol{p}_j$). We choose the widely-used Kullback Leibler (KL) divergence and define an *ensemble cooperation* (EC) loss as

$$
\begin{aligned}
L_{\mathrm{EC}}(\bar\theta) &= \frac{1}{K} \sum_{i=1, j\neq i}^{K} D_{KL}(\boldsymbol{p}_i \| \boldsymbol{p}_j) = \frac{1}{K} \frac{1}{N_t} \sum_{i=1, j\neq i}^{K} \sum_{n=1}^{N_t} p_i(x_{t,n}) \log \frac{p_i(x_{t,n})}{p_j(x_{t,n})} \\
&= \frac{1}{K} \frac{1}{N_t} \sum_{i=1, j\neq i}^{K} \sum_{n=1}^{N_t} h_\varphi(g_{t,i} f_{\phi_i}(x_{t,n})) \log \frac{h_\varphi(g_{t,i} f_{\phi_i}(x_{t,n}))}{h_\varphi(g_{t,j} f_{\phi_j}(x_{t,n}))}.
\end{aligned}
\tag{6}
$$

In practice, we reduce the sub-network width to save parameters, so we call our method "Cooperation of Small Continual Learners (CoSCL)". Taking Eq. (1) and Eq. (6) together, the objective of CoSCL is defined as

$$
L_{\mathrm{CoSCL}}(\bar\theta) = L_{\mathrm{CL}}(\bar\theta) + \gamma L_{\mathrm{EC}}(\bar\theta).
\tag{7}
$$

4.2   Theoretical Explanation

Here we provide a theoretical explanation of how cooperating multiple continual learners can mitigate the generalization gaps in continual learning:

Proposition 3. *Let $\{\Theta_i \in \mathbb{R}^r\}_{i=1}^K$ be a set of K parameter spaces ($K > 1$ in general), d_i be a VC dimension of Θ_i, and $\Theta = \cup_{i=1}^K \Theta_i$ with VC dimension d. Based on Proposition 2, for $\hat{\theta}_{1:t}^b = \arg\min_{\bar{\theta} \in \Theta} \hat{\mathcal{E}}_{D_t}^b(\bar{\theta})$, the upper bound of generalization gap is further tighter with*

$$\lambda_1 = \max_{i \in [1,K]} \sqrt{\frac{d_i \ln(N_{1:t-1}/d_i) + \ln(2K/\delta)}{N_{1:t-1}}} + \sqrt{\frac{d \ln(N_{1:t-1}/d) + \ln(2/\delta)}{N_{1:t-1}}}, \quad (8)$$

$$\lambda_2 = \max_{i \in [1,K]} \sqrt{\frac{d_i \ln(N_t/d_i) + \ln(2K/\delta)}{N_t}} + \sqrt{\frac{d \ln(N_t/d) + \ln(2/\delta)}{N_t}}. \quad (9)$$

Comparing Proposition 3 and Proposition 2, we conclude that cooperating K continual learners facilitates a smaller generalization gap over the new and old tasks in continual learning than a single one. Due to the space limit, we leave more details of Proposition 3 in Appendix A, where we also analyze how a compatible parameter space of a well-designed model architecture can improve the discrepancy between task distributions, thus further tightening the generalization bounds. Next, we empirically validate our proposal as detailed below.

5   Experiment

In this section, we extensively evaluate CoSCL on visual classification tasks. All results are averaged over 5 runs with different random seeds and task orders.

Benchmark: We consider four representative continual learning benchmarks. The first two are with CIFAR-100 dataset [19], which includes 100-class colored images of the size 32×32. All classes are split into 20 incremental tasks, based on random sequence (RS) or superclass (SC). The other two are with larger-scale datasets, randomly split into 10 incremental tasks: CUB-200-2011 [41] includes 200 classes and 11,788 bird images of the size 224×224, and is split as 30 images per class for training while the rest for testing. Tiny-ImageNet [10] is derived from iILSVRC-2012 [36], consisting of 200-class natural images of the size 64×64.

Implementation: We mainly focus on the task-incremental setting used in [6,17,39,43] and follow their implementation for most experiments if not specified. For all the baselines, we apply a 6-layer CNN architecture for CIFAR-100-SC and CIFAR-100-RS, and an AlexNet-based architecture for CUB-200-2011 and Tiny-ImageNet.[2] Since our method consists of multiple continual learners, we use a similar architecture for each sub-network and accordingly

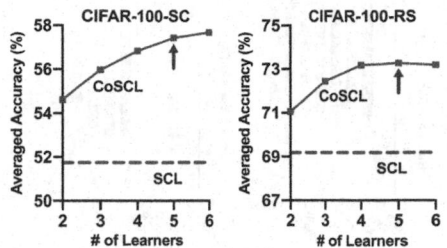

Fig. 5. Trade-off between learner number and width with a fixed parameter budget

reduce the width (i.e., using fewer channels) to keep the total number of parameters comparable to other baselines, so as to make the comparison as fair as possible. Then, there is an intuitive trade-off between the number and width of learners. According to our theoretical analysis in Proposition 1 and 2, the choice for the number of learners (i.e., parameter spaces) K is *independent* of the training data distribution under a limited parameter budget. Also, we empirically validate that this trade-off is only moderately sensitive (see Fig. 5). So we simply set $K = 5$ for all experiments. The learners' training differs only in random initialization of the parameters. The implementations are further detailed in Appendix B.

Table 1. Averaged accuracy (%) of all the tasks learned so far in continual learning (A_t for t tasks). All results are cited from [6,17,43] or reproduced from their officially-released code for a fair comparison. CoSCL cooperates 5 continual learners with similar architectures as other baselines, while reducing the sub-network width accordingly to keep the total amount of parameters comparable

Methods	CIFAR-100-SC		CIFAR-100-RS		CUB-200-2011		Tiny-ImageNet	
	A_{10}	A_{20}	A_{10}	A_{20}	A_5	A_{10}	A_5	A_{10}
SI [50]	52.20 ±4.37	51.97 ±2.07	68.72 ±1.11	69.21 ±0.77	33.08 ±4.05	42.03 ±3.06	45.61 ±2.05	46.00 ±1.13
RWALK [7]	50.51 ±4.53	49.62 ±3.28	66.02 ±1.89	66.90 ±0.29	32.56 ±3.76	41.94 ±2.35	49.69 ±1.47	48.12 ±0.96
P&C [38]	53.48 ±2.79	52.88 ±1.68	70.10 ±1.22	70.21 ±1.22	33.88 ±4.48	42.79 ±3.29	51.71 ±1.58	50.33 ±0.86
EWC [18]	52.25 ±2.99	51.74 ±1.74	68.72 ±0.24	69.18 ±0.69	32.90 ±2.98	42.29 ±2.34	50.92 ±1.86	48.38 ±0.86
w/ AFEC [43]	56.28 ±3.27	55.24 ±1.61	72.36 ±1.23	72.29 ±1.07	34.36 ±4.39	43.05 ±3.00	51.34 ±1.62	50.58 ±0.74
w/ CPR [6]	54.60 ±2.51	53.37 ±2.06	71.12 ±1.82	70.25 ±1.33	33.36 ±3.25	42.51 ±2.31	50.12 ±1.43	50.29 ±0.89
w/ CoSCL (Ours)	**62.89** ±3.05	**60.84** ±0.95	**78.08** ±1.25	76.05 ±0.65	**44.35** ±3.59	48.53 ±2.21	**56.10** ±1.77	55.10 ±1.02
MAS [1]	52.76 ±2.85	52.18 ±2.22	67.60 ±1.85	69.41 ±1.27	31.68 ±2.37	42.56 ±1.84	49.69 ±1.50	50.20 ±0.82
w/ AFEC [43]	55.26 ±4.14	54.89 ±2.23	69.57 ±1.73	71.20 ±0.70	34.08 ±3.80	42.93 ±3.51	51.35 ±1.75	50.90 ±1.08
w/ CPR [6]	52.90 ±1.62	53.63 ±1.31	70.69 ±1.85	72.06 ±1.86	33.49 ±2.46	43.07 ±2.56	50.82 ±1.94	51.24 ±1.26
w/ CoSCL (Ours)	62.55 ±1.94	60.69 ±1.53	76.93 ±1.94	**76.29** ±2.33	43.67 ±3.73	**49.48** ±2.40	55.43 ±1.48	**55.11** ±0.89

---

[2] A concurrent work observed that the regular CNN architecture indeed achieves better continual learning performance than more advanced architectures such as ResNet and ViT with the same amount of parameters [27].

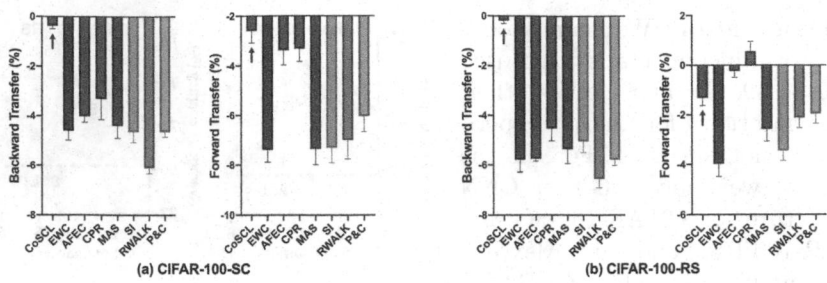

Fig. 6. Comparison of backward transfer (BWT) and forward transfer (FWT)

Overall Performance: We first adapt CoSCL to representative continual learning strategies, including weight regularization such as EWC [18] and MAS [1], parameter isolation such as HAT [39] and AGS-CL [17], and experience replay (ER) of old training samples (20 images per class) [35]. As shown in Fig. 1, our proposal that cooperates multiple continual learners with narrower sub-networks can largely improve their performance. Then, we compare with the state-of-the-art (SOTA) methods under a realistic restriction that old training samples or additional data sources are *not* available, as detailed below.

First, we compare with the SOTA methods that can be plug-and-play with weight regularization baselines, such as AFEC [43] and CPR [6]. AFEC [43] encouraged the network parameters to resemble the optimal solution for each new task to mitigate potential negative transfer, while CPR [6] added a regularization term that maximized the entropy of output probability to find a flat minima. In contrast, CoSCL can more effectively improve the weight regularization baselines and achieve the new SOTA performance (detailed in Table 1).

Table 2. Averaged accuracy (%) of architecture-based methods on CIFAR-100-RS. Here we use EWC as the default continual learning method for CoSCL

Methods	# Param	20-split	50-split
HAT [39]	6.8M	76.96	80.46
MARK [16]	4.7M	78.31	–
BNS [32]	6.7M	–	82.39
CoSCL (Ours)	4.6M	**79.43** ±1.01	**87.88** ±1.07

At the same time, we consider the SOTA methods that improve continual learning in terms of architecture, such as BNS [32] and MARK [16]. BNS applied neural structure search to build a network for preventing catastrophic forgetting and promoting knowledge transfer, while MARK achieved this goal by learning an additional set of shared weights among tasks.[3] With a smaller parameter budget, ours largely outperforms the two recent strong baselines (see Table 2).

Detailed Analysis: Now, we use EWC [18] as the default continual learning method and provide a detailed analysis for the superior performance of CoSCL. First, we analyze the **knowledge transfer** among tasks by evaluating the metrics of backward transfer (BWT), which is the averaged influence of learning each new task to the old tasks, and forward transfer (FWT), which is the averaged influence of remembering the old tasks to each new task [22]. As shown in Fig. 6, CoSCL substantially improves both BWT and FWT of the default method, and in general far exceeds other representative baselines implemented in a single model. In particular, CoSCL raises BWT to almost zero, which means that catastrophic forgetting can be completely avoided. We also evaluate the **expertise** of each continual learner across tasks in Appendix C.1. The predictions made by each continual learner's representations differ significantly and complement with each other. The functional diversity can be naturally obtained from the randomness in architecture, such as the use of dropout and a different random initialization for each learner, and is explicitly regulated by our ensemble cooperation loss (Fig. 7, a, discussed later).

Table 3. Ablation study. A_t: averaged accuracy (%) of t tasks learned so far. TG: task-adaptive gates; EC: ensemble cooperation loss

Methods	#Param	CIFAR-100-SC		CIFAR-100-RS	
		A_{10}	A_{20}	A_{10}	A_{20}
Single Continual Learner	837K	52.25 ±2.99	51.74 ±1.74	68.72 ±0.24	69.18 ±0.69
Classifier Ensemble	901K	50.08 ±1.65	43.88 ±0.79	66.80 ±1.45	55.65 ±0.32
Feature Ensemble	773K	58.76 ±3.72	57.69 ±1.42	73.57 ±0.50	73.01 ±1.22
Feature Ensemble + EC	773K	61.12 ±3.11	59.49 ±1.59	75.46 ±1.35	74.76 ±0.84
Feature Ensemble + TG	799K	62.01 ±3.36	59.85 ±1.77	76.11 ±0.98	74.78 ±0.41
Feature Ensemble + EC + TG	799K	62.89 ±3.05	60.84 ±0.95	78.08 ±1.25	76.05 ±0.65

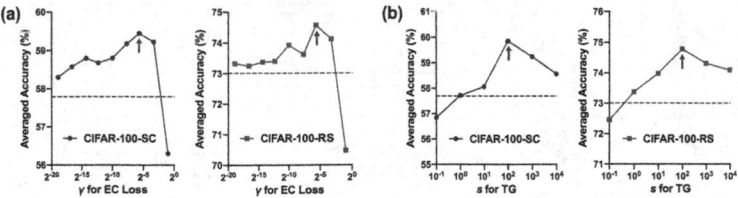

Fig. 7. Effects of hyperparameters in CoSCL. (a) γ for ensemble cooperation (EC) loss; (b) s for task-adaptive gates (TG). The dashed lines indicate the performance w/o EC or TG in corresponding benchmarks. The arrows denote the chosen values

---

[3] They both are performed against a similar AlexNet-based architecture.

Next, we present the results of an **ablation study** in Table 3. We first consider a naive baseline that averages the predictions of multiple independently-trained small continual learners, referred to as the "classifier ensemble (CE)". However, such a naive baseline even underperforms the single continual learner (SCL). In contrast, the proposed feature ensemble (FE) of multiple small continual learners can naturally achieve a superior performance, where the ensemble cooperation loss (EC) and the task-adaptive gates (TG) bring obvious benefits by properly adjusting for functional diversity among learners and exploiting the additional information from task labels, respectively. Then we evaluate the effect of **hyperparameters** in Fig. 7. The hyperparameters of EC and TG are only moderately sensitive within a wide range. In this case, an appropriate (positive) strength of EC constrains the excessive diversity of predictions to improve the performance, while the continual learners will lose diversity if EC is too strong, resulting in a huge performance drop. If CoSCL cannot obtain sufficient diversity from the randomness of its architecture, the use of negative strength of EC can naturally serve this purpose, left for further work.

Moreover, we empirically validate our theoretical analysis as below. We first evaluate the $\mathcal{H}$-divergence of feature representations between tasks, which relies on the capacity of a hypothesis space to distinguish them [21]. Specifically, the $\mathcal{H}$-divergence can be empirically approximated by training a discriminator to distinguish if the features of input images belong to a task or not, where a larger discrimination loss indicates a smaller $\mathcal{H}$-divergence. As shown in Fig. 8, a, the proposed FE together with EC can largely decrease the $\mathcal{H}$-divergence while TG has a moderate benefit (there is a saturation effect when they are combined together). Meanwhile, we evaluate the **curvature of loss landscape** for the continually-learned solution by permuting the parameters to ten random directions [11], where the solution obtained by CoSCL enjoys a clearly flatter loss landscape than SCL (Fig. 8, b).

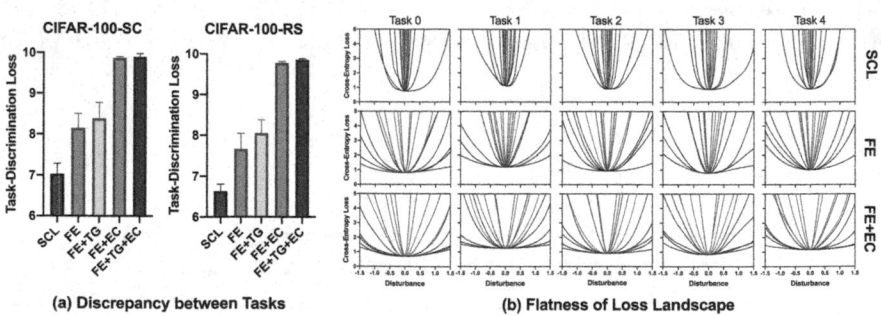

(a) Discrepancy between Tasks   (b) Flatness of Loss Landscape

Fig. 8. Empirical validation of our theoretical analysis. (a) Task-discrimination loss in feature space. Larger loss indicates a smaller $\mathcal{H}$-divergence. (b) Curvature of the test loss landscape for the first five incremental tasks on CIFAR-100-SC. Each line indicates the result of a random direction

Taking all results together, cooperating multiple small continual learners can mitigate the discrepancy between tasks in feature space and improve flatness of the continually-learned solution (Fig. 8), thus facilitating both FWT and BWT (Fig. 6). This is consistent with our theoretical analysis, suggesting that learning plasticity and memory stability are *not* necessarily conflicting in continual learning, but can be simultaneously enhanced by a well-designed model architecture.

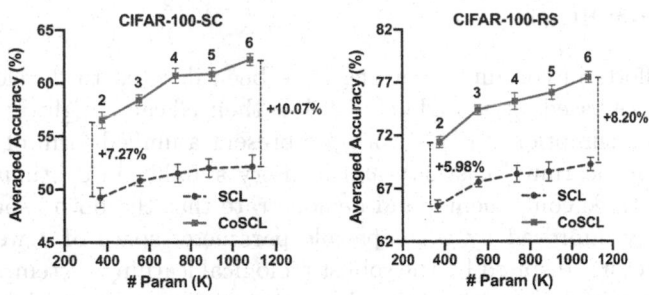

Fig. 9. Adding continual learners in CoSCL is more effective than widening the network of a single continual learner (SCL). We present the results of cooperating 2–6 continual learners with the same sub-network width, while accordingly adjust the size of SCL for a fair comparison

Adding Continual Learners is More Effective than Widening a Single Network: All of the above experiments are performed under a *fixed* parameter budget. A recent work observed that a wider network usually suffers from less catastrophic forgetting [26], providing an initial exploration of the effects of architecture in continual learning. Here we argue that adding continual learners with CoSCL is a better choice. In Fig. 9 we compare the performance of using an increasing number of continual learners (the width is the same as that used in Table 1) and accordingly widening the network of a single continual learner (SCL). It can be clearly seen that the performance gap between CoSCL and SCL is growing when more parameters are used. Therefore, CoSCL presents a promising direction for continual learning that can leverage network parameters in an efficient and scalable way.

Unsupervised Continual Learning (UCL): has the unique property of being naturally robust to catastrophic forgetting when fine-tuning on incremental unlabeled data [15, 23]. An empirical explanation is that UCL achieves a flatter loss landscape and more meaningful

Table 4. Averaged accuracy (%) of unsupervised continual learning on CIFAR-100-RS. The results are reproduced from the officially-released code of [23]

Methods	SimSiam [8]	BarlowTwins [49]
Finetune	41.38 ±0.80	63.29 ±0.38
w/ CoSCL	**46.33** ±0.51	**74.03** ±0.36

feature representations [23], which is consistent with our analysis. We further validate this idea by adapting CoSCL to UCL[4], where we follow the UCL setting of [23] for CIFAR-100-RS and use a similar architecture as Table 1. As shown in Table 4, CoSCL can significantly improve the performance of UCL with two strong unsupervised learning strategies such as SimSiam [8] and BarlowTwins [49].

6   Conclusion

Numerous efforts in continual learning have been devoted to developing effective approaches based on a single model, but their efficacy might be limited by such a priori assumption. In this work, we present a unified form of generalization bounds for learning plasticity and memory stability in continual learning, consisting of three components, and demonstrate that the both aspects can be simultaneously improved by a compatible parameter space of a well-designed mode architecture. Inspired by the robust biological learning system, we propose to cooperate multiple (small) continual learners, which can naturally tighten the generalization bounds through improving the three components. Our method can substantially enhance the performance of representative continual learning strategies by improving both learning plasticity and memory stability. We hope that this work can serve as a strong baseline to stimulate new ideas for continual learning from an architecture perspective. A promising direction is to cooperate a variety of continual learning approaches with properly-designed architectures, so as to fully leverage task attributes for desired compatibility.

Acknowledgements. This work was supported by the National Key Research and Development Program of China (2017YFA0700904, 2020AAA0106000, 2020AAA01 04304, 2020AAA0106302, 2021YFB2701000), NSFC Projects (Nos. 62061136001, 62106123, 62076147, U19B2034, U1811461, U19A2081, 61972224), Beijing NSF Project (No. JQ19016), BNRist (BNR2022RC01006), Tsinghua-Peking Center for Life Sciences, Tsinghua Institute for Guo Qiang, Beijing Academy of Artificial Intelligence (BAAI), Tsinghua-OPPO Joint Research Center for Future Terminal Technology, the High Performance Computing Center, Tsinghua University, and China Postdoctoral Science Foundation (Nos. 2021T140377, 2021M701892).

References

1. Aljundi, R., Babiloni, F., Elhoseiny, M., Rohrbach, M., Tuytelaars, T.: Memory aware synapses: learning what (not) to forget. In: Proceedings of the European Conference on Computer Vision, pp. 139–154 (2018)
2. Aljundi, R., Chakravarty, P., Tuytelaars, T.: Expert gate: lifelong learning with a network of experts. In: Proceedings of the IEEE Conference on Computer Vision and Pattern Recognition, pp. 3366–3375 (2017)
3. Aso, Y., et al.: The neuronal architecture of the mushroom body provides a logic for associative learning. Elife **3**, e04577 (2014)

---

[4] Here we only use feature ensemble (FE) with ensemble cooperation loss (EC).

4. Ben-David, S., Blitzer, J., Crammer, K., Kulesza, A., Pereira, F., Vaughan, J.W.: A theory of learning from different domains. Mach. Learn. **79**(1), 151–175 (2010)
5. Cha, J., et al.: Swad: domain generalization by seeking flat minima. arXiv preprint arXiv:2102.08604 (2021)
6. Cha, S., Hsu, H., Hwang, T., Calmon, F., Moon, T.: CPR: classifier-projection regularization for continual learning. In: Proceedings of the International Conference on Learning Representations (2020)
7. Chaudhry, A., Dokania, P.K., Ajanthan, T., Torr, P.H.: Riemannian walk for incremental learning: Understanding forgetting and intransigence. In: Proceedings of the European Conference on Computer Vision, pp. 532–547 (2018)
8. Chen, X., He, K.: Exploring simple siamese representation learning. In: Proceedings of the IEEE/CVF Conference on Computer Vision and Pattern Recognition, pp. 15750–15758 (2021)
9. Cohn, R., Morantte, I., Ruta, V.: Coordinated and compartmentalized neuromodulation shapes sensory processing in drosophila. Cell **163**(7), 1742–1755 (2015)
10. Delange, M., et al.: A continual learning survey: defying forgetting in classification tasks. IEEE Trans. Pattern Anal. Mach. Intell. **44**(7), 3366–3385 (2021)
11. Deng, D., Chen, G., Hao, J., Wang, Q., Heng, P.A.: Flattening sharpness for dynamic gradient projection memory benefits continual learning. In: Proceedings of the Advances in Neural Information Processing Systems, vol. 34 (2021)
12. Dinh, L., Pascanu, R., Bengio, S., Bengio, Y.: Sharp minima can generalize for deep nets. In: Proceedings of the International Conference on Machine Learning, pp. 1019–1028. PMLR (2017)
13. Doan, T., Mirzadeh, S.I., Pineau, J., Farajtabar, M.: Efficient continual learning ensembles in neural network subspaces. arXiv preprint arXiv:2202.09826 (2022)
14. Fernando, C., et al.: Pathnet: evolution channels gradient descent in super neural networks. arXiv preprint arXiv:1701.08734 (2017)
15. Hu, D., et al.: How well self-supervised pre-training performs with streaming data? arXiv preprint arXiv:2104.12081 (2021)
16. Hurtado, J., Raymond, A., Soto, A.: Optimizing reusable knowledge for continual learning via metalearning. In: Proceedings of the Advances in Neural Information Processing Systems, vol. 34 (2021)
17. Jung, S., Ahn, H., Cha, S., Moon, T.: Continual learning with node-importance based adaptive group sparse regularization. arXiv e-prints pp. arXiv-2003 (2020)
18. Kirkpatrick, J., et al.: Overcoming catastrophic forgetting in neural networks. Proc. Natl. Acad. Sci. **114**(13), 3521–3526 (2017)
19. Krizhevsky, A., Hinton, G., et al.: Learning multiple layers of features from tiny images. Technical report, Citeseer (2009)
20. Liu, Yu., Parisot, S., Slabaugh, G., Jia, X., Leonardis, A., Tuytelaars, T.: More classifiers, less forgetting: a generic multi-classifier paradigm for incremental learning. In: Vedaldi, A., Bischof, H., Brox, T., Frahm, J.-M. (eds.) ECCV 2020. LNCS, vol. 12371, pp. 699–716. Springer, Cham (2020). https://doi.org/10.1007/978-3-030-58574-7_42
21. Long, M., Cao, Y., Wang, J., Jordan, M.: Learning transferable features with deep adaptation networks. In: Proceedings of the International Conference on Machine Learning, pp. 97–105. PMLR (2015)
22. Lopez-Paz, D., et al.: Gradient episodic memory for continual learning. In: Proceedings of the Advances in Neural Information Processing Systems, pp. 6467–6476 (2017)

23. Madaan, D., Yoon, J., Li, Y., Liu, Y., Hwang, S.J.: Rethinking the representational continuity: Towards unsupervised continual learning. arXiv preprint arXiv:2110.06976 (2021)
24. McAllester, D.A.: PAC-Bayesian model averaging. In: Proceedings of the Twelfth Annual Conference on Computational Learning Theory, pp. 164–170 (1999)
25. McCloskey, M., Cohen, N.J.: Catastrophic interference in connectionist networks: the sequential learning problem. In: Psychology of Learning and Motivation, vol. 24, pp. 109–165. Elsevier (1989)
26. Mirzadeh, S.I., Chaudhry, A., Hu, H., Pascanu, R., Gorur, D., Farajtabar, M.: Wide neural networks forget less catastrophically. arXiv preprint arXiv:2110.11526 (2021)
27. Mirzadeh, S.I., et al.: Architecture matters in continual learning. arXiv preprint arXiv:2202.00275 (2022)
28. Mirzadeh, S.I., Farajtabar, M., Gorur, D., Pascanu, R., Ghasemzadeh, H.: Linear mode connectivity in multitask and continual learning. arXiv preprint arXiv:2010.04495 (2020)
29. Mirzadeh, S.I., Farajtabar, M., Pascanu, R., Ghasemzadeh, H.: Understanding the role of training regimes in continual learning. In: Proceedings of the Advances in Neural Information Processing Systems, vol. 33, pp. 7308–7320 (2020)
30. Modi, M.N., Shuai, Y., Turner, G.C.: The drosophila mushroom body: from architecture to algorithm in a learning circuit. Annu. Rev. Neurosci. **43**, 465–484 (2020)
31. Netzer, Y., Wang, T., Coates, A., Bissacco, A., Wu, B., Ng, A.Y.: Reading digits in natural images with unsupervised feature learning (2011)
32. Qin, Q., Hu, W., Peng, H., Zhao, D., Liu, B.: BNS: building network structures dynamically for continual learning. In: Proceedings of the Advances in Neural Information Processing Systems, vol. 34 (2021)
33. Ramesh, R., Chaudhari, P.: Model zoo: a growing brain that learns continually. In: NeurIPS 2021 Workshop on Distribution Shifts: Connecting Methods and Applications (2021)
34. Rebuffi, S.A., Kolesnikov, A., Sperl, G., Lampert, C.H.: ICARL: incremental classifier and representation learning. In: Proceedings of the IEEE Conference on Computer Vision and Pattern Recognition, pp. 2001–2010 (2017)
35. Riemer, M., et al.: Learning to learn without forgetting by maximizing transfer and minimizing interference. arXiv preprint arXiv:1810.11910 (2018)
36. Russakovsky, O., et al.: Imagenet large scale visual recognition challenge. Int. J. Comput. Vision **115**(3), 211–252 (2015)
37. Rusu, A.A., et al.: Progressive neural networks. arXiv preprint arXiv:1606.04671 (2016)
38. Schwarz, J., et al.: Progress & compress: a scalable framework for continual learning. In: Proceedings of the International Conference on Machine Learning, pp. 4528–4537. PMLR (2018)
39. Serra, J., Suris, D., Miron, M., Karatzoglou, A.: Overcoming catastrophic forgetting with hard attention to the task. In: Proceedings of the International Conference on Machine Learning, pp. 4548–4557. PMLR (2018)
40. Shi, G., Chen, J., Zhang, W., Zhan, L.M., Wu, X.M.: Overcoming catastrophic forgetting in incremental few-shot learning by finding flat minima. In: Proceedings of the Advances in Neural Information Processing Systems, vol. 34 (2021)
41. Wah, C., Branson, S., Welinder, P., Perona, P., Belongie, S.: The caltech-UCSD birds-200-2011 dataset (2011)

42. Wang, L., Yang, K., Li, C., Hong, L., Li, Z., Zhu, J.: Ordisco: effective and efficient usage of incremental unlabeled data for semi-supervised continual learning. In: Proceedings of the IEEE/CVF Conference on Computer Vision and Pattern Recognition, pp. 5383–5392 (2021)
43. Wang, L., et al.: AFEC: active forgetting of negative transfer in continual learning. In: Proceedings of the Advances in Neural Information Processing Systems, vol. 34 (2021)
44. Wang, L., et al.: Memory replay with data compression for continual learning. In: Proceedings of the International Conference on Learning Representations (2021)
45. Wen, Y., Tran, D., Ba, J.: Batchensemble: an alternative approach to efficient ensemble and lifelong learning. In: Proceedings of the International Conference on Learning Representations (2020)
46. Wortsman, M., Horton, M.C., Guestrin, C., Farhadi, A., Rastegari, M.: Learning neural network subspaces. In: Proceedings of the International Conference on Machine Learning, pp. 11217–11227. PMLR (2021)
47. Wortsman, M., et al.: Supermasks in superposition. In: Proceedings of the Advances in Neural Information Processing Systems, vol. 33, pp. 15173–15184 (2020)
48. Yan, S., Xie, J., He, X.: DER: dynamically expandable representation for class incremental learning. arXiv preprint arXiv:2103.16788 (2021)
49. Zbontar, J., Jing, L., Misra, I., LeCun, Y., Deny, S.: Barlow twins: self-supervised learning via redundancy reduction. In: Proceedings of the International Conference on Machine Learning, pp. 12310–12320. PMLR (2021)
50. Zenke, F., Poole, B., Ganguli, S.: Continual learning through synaptic intelligence. In: Proceedings of the International Conference on Machine Learning, pp. 3987–3995. PMLR (2017)

Manifold Adversarial Learning for Cross-domain 3D Shape Representation

Hao Huang[1,2,3,4], Cheng Chen[1,3,4], and Yi Fang[1,2,3,4(✉)]

[1] NYU Multimedia and Visual Computing Lab, Abu Dhabi, UAE
[2] NYUAD Center for Artificial Intelligence and Robotics, Abu Dhabi, UAE
[3] NYU Tandon School of Engineering, New York University, New York, USA
[4] New York University, Abu Dhabi, UAE
{hh1811,cc6858,yfang}@nyu.edu

Abstract. On a variety of 3D vision tasks, deep neural networks (DNNs) for point clouds have outperformed the conventional non-learning-based methods. However, generalization to out-of-distribution 3D point clouds remains challenging for DNNs. As annotating large-scale point clouds is prohibitively expensive or even impossible, strategies for generalizing DNN models to unseen domains of point clouds without access to those domains during training are urgently needed but have yet to be substantially investigated. In this paper, we design an adversarial learning scheme to learn point cloud representation on a seen source domain and then generalize the learned knowledge to an unseen target domain. Specifically, we unify several geometric transformations into a manifold-based framework under which a distance between transformations is well-defined. Measured by the distance, adversarial samples are mined to form *intermediate domains* and retained in an adaptive replay-based memory. We further provide theoretical justification for the intermediate domains to reduce the generalization error of the DNN models. Experimental results on synthetic-to-real datasets illustrate that our method outperforms existing 3D deep learning models for domain generalization.

Keywords: 3D point cloud · Domain generalization · Adversarial learning · Manifold and memory

1 Introduction

If a 3D point cloud classifier was trained on intact point clouds, would it work on partial point clouds? What if a neural network trained on point clouds uniformly sampled from clean CAD models is tested on real-scanned point clouds

Supplementary Information The online version contains supplementary material available at https://doi.org/10.1007/978-3-031-19809-0_16.

containing noise? Is it possible to deploy a classification model trained on point clouds with a certain prior under a wild condition where all point clouds are randomly collected from the Internet? Answers to these questions heavily depend on the capability of the classification models to deal with the *domain shift* problem, which refers to the distribution shift/discrepancy between the samples from training (source) domain and those from testing (target) domain [3,24,47].

Although DNNs have been successful in various applications and separately obtained state-of-the-art classification results in both synthetic and real-scanned point clouds datasets [5,21,25,26], studies in [16, 27] suggest that deep learning models' performance degrades significantly on out-of-distribution (OOD) datasets. Most statistical learning models, including DNNs, strongly rely on an over-simplified assumption, *i.e.*, the source and target samples are drawn from independent and identically (*i.i.d.*) distributions,

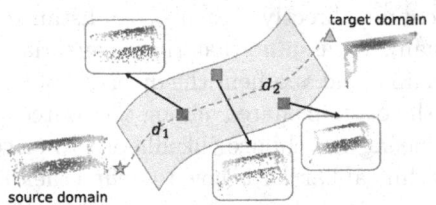

Fig. 1. Three intermediate domains consist of adversarial samples transformed from source point clouds. The distances between the transformed point cloud to the source and target are d_1 and d_2.

while ignoring OOD scenarios commonly encountered in real world. A straightforward solution to deal with domain shift is to collect samples from the target domain to fine-tune a source-domain-trained model. Such a schema is denoted as *domain adaptation* (DA) [28] which is infeasible when target samples are inaccessible or even unknown in advance. To resolve the domain shift and the absence of target data simultaneously, *domain generalization* (DG) [4] is introduced. The goal of DG is to train a DNN model on a single or multiple source domains such that the trained DNN can still perform well on a previously unseen OOD target domain. Despite that DG has received increasing attention in 2D vision tasks [9,30,45], few literature [16] focuses on DG (or DA [27]) in 3D vision. The recent work MetaSets [16] aims to train a classification model on source (synthetic) point clouds such that the trained model can also performance well on target (real-scanned) point clouds which are inaccessible during training. By applying a collection of specifically designed geometric transformations to source point clouds, the transformed point clouds imitate the real-world scenarios of occlusions, missing parts, and variations in scanning density, thus expanding the source domain towards the target domain.

In this work, we explore adversarial training [14,31], whose main goal in previous literature is to increase the robustness of neural network models against fluctuations in the input. Distinct to imperceptible attacks utilized in conventional adversarial training, we instead aim to train DNN models which are robust to OOD samples which bridge the distribution gap between the source and target domains. In other word, we generate "fictitious" yet "challenging" point clouds in an adversarial way to mimic virtual *intermediate domains* as an expansion of the source domain, driving the model to learn domain-invariant features to improve its generalization performance, as illustrated in Fig. 1 conceptually. To utilize the adversarial samples in intermediate domains to the maximum extent, we design an adaptive replay-based memory mechanism to select and retain some more effective adversarial samples, *i.e.*, the ones pushing the intermediate domains *far* away from the source domain and moving *close* towards the target domain. Despite that the target domain is inaccessible during training and thus we cannot directly measure the distance of an adversarial sample to the target domain, we assume that the adversarial samples which are far from the source domain could augment the diversity of the source domain, consequently, increasing the overlap shared among the source and the target domains, and potentially increasing the chance (likelihood) to close the gap between these two domains. A technical barrier is how to define the distance between domains (induced from the distance between samples in these domains) as measurement of *farness* and *closeness*. To circumvent this barrier, we unify the geometric transformations proposed in [16] in a manifold-based framework in which each transformation and the corresponding transformed point cloud are regard as points on the manifolds and the distance between points (on the manifolds) are well-defined.

Our contributions are: 1). We propose adversarial training to generate adversarial point clouds to form intermediate domains for tackling the DG problem in 3D vision; 2). We introduce a manifold-based framework to unify different geometric transformations and define distance between transformations to facilitate the construction of intermediate domains; 3). We design an adaptive memory to fully utilize the adversarial samples in intermediate domains for domain-invariant 3D point cloud feature learning. We validate our method on two Sim-to-Real benchmarks [16] and observe that our proposed method outperforms previous approaches for point clouds representation learning under DG settings.

2　Related Work

Cross-Domain Representation Learning (for both DA and DG) has been extensively studied in 2D visionll tasks [12,13,15,44], but has not yet been fully explored for 3D models. MetaSets [16] designs several geometric transformations for data augmentation based on the priors of real-scanned point clouds, aiming to bridge domain gaps. Our work is built upon [16] but instead we explore adversarial point clouds to construct intermediate domains for generalizable point cloud representation learning. **Adversarial learning** [14,23] aims to increase the robustness of DNNs to adversarial examples with imperceptible perturbations added to the inputs. Previous works in 2D vision explore to adopt adversarial learning to train models that are robust to significant perturbations, *i.e.*, OOD samples [17,31,34,35,46]. These works show that adversarial domain augmentation (ADA) can effectively improve the generalization performance and robustness of models However, few work has explored ADA for cross-domain generalizable point cloud representation learning. To our best knowledge, we are among the first to extend ADA for point cloud representation learning for DG. We refer the reader to *supplementary material* for detailed related work.

3   Method

We first give a brief introduction of some mathematical tools based which we formulate our manifold-based framework to measure point cloud transformations in Sect. 3.1. Then, we unify different types of transformations under this framework in Sect. 3.2. Next, we describe our adversarial learning and adaptive memory for intermediate domains in 3.4. Lastly, we depict the learning scheme to train our DNN in Sec. 3.5. A schematic illustration of our method is shown in Fig. 2.

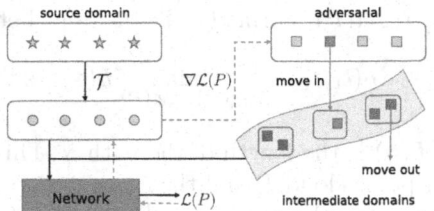

Fig. 2. Point clouds from a source domain are transformed by $\mathcal{T}$ and fed into to a network. The gradient of loss $\nabla \mathcal{L}(P)$ are used to generated adversarial samples on a manifold. The adversarial samples are retained in a memory as intermediate domains to close the source and target domain gap.

3.1   Manifolds of Transformation and Point Cloud

Let $\mathcal{T}$ be a Lie group consisting of geometric transformations and $t \in \mathcal{T}$ be a specific transformation. The dimensionality of $\mathcal{T}$ equals to the number of free parameters of t. For instance, $\mathcal{T}$ can be 3D rotation group SO(3) and $t \in$ SO(3) : $\mathbb{R}^3 \rightarrow \mathbb{R}^3$, parameterized by a vector $\theta_t \in \Theta \subset \mathbb{R}^3$ representing three rotation angles. We interpret t as a mapping from one point cloud to another. More specifically, we define a point cloud P with N points as a square integrable function $P = \sum_i^N p_i \delta_{p_i} : \mathbb{R}^{3 \times N} \rightarrow \mathbb{R}^{3 \times N}$ where δ_p denotes a Dirac delta function placed at a location $p = (x, y, z) \in \mathbb{R}^3$. The action of t on P is denoted as P_t, which can be regarded as a function that maps elements in the Lie group $\mathcal{T}$ to elements in a space of the transformed point clouds from P, denoted as $P_t : \mathcal{T} \rightarrow \mathbb{L}^2$, where $\mathbb{L}^2$ is the space of square integrable functions.

Given a Lie group $\mathcal{T}$, the function $d(t_1, t_2) : \mathcal{T} \times \mathcal{T} \rightarrow \mathbb{R}$ defines a metric to measure the distance between the two transformations t_1 and t_2. A native option is to instantiate $d(t_1, t_2) = \|t_1 - t_2\|_{L^2}$. However, this metric is inaccurate as it fails to consider the point cloud on which these transformations act. For instance, $d(\vec{0}_{\times 3}, [0, 0, 2\pi]) = 2\pi$, however, rotating any point cloud by 2π along any axis leaving the point cloud unchanged. Another instantiation $d(t_1, t_2) = \|P_{t_1} - P_{t_2}\|_{L^2}$ considers both the transformations and the point cloud, but it requires per-point correspondences to make the minus operation well-defined.

Geodesic Distance, the length of the shortest path between $t_1, t_2 \in \mathcal{T}$, is a metric to measure the distance between the two transformations. This metric is valid only if a Riemannian metric is defined for $\mathcal{T}$. Inspired by [18,19,36], we formulate such a Riemannian metric by mapping $\mathcal{T}$ to the set of transformed point clouds of P: $\mathcal{M}(P) = \{P_t : t \in \mathcal{T}\}$. This set forms a manifold and we name it *Point Cloud Appearance Manifold* (PCAM). The Riemannian metric on $\mathcal{T}$ can be chosen such that the length of a path on $\mathcal{T}$, $\gamma(t) : [0, 1] \rightarrow \mathcal{T}$, equals to the length of the mapped path on $\mathcal{M}(P)$, $P_\gamma(t) : [0,1] \to \mathcal{M}(P)$. The geodesic distance between $t_1, t_2 \in \mathcal{T}$ thus equals to the geodesic distance between $P_{t_1}, P_{t_2} \in \mathcal{M}(P)$. Formally, the distance between $t_1, t_2 \in \mathcal{T}$ can be defined as:

$$d_P(t_1, t_2) = \min_{\gamma:[0,1]\to\mathcal{M}(P)} L(\gamma) \quad \text{s.t.} \quad \gamma(0) = P_{t_1}, \gamma(1) = P_{t_2} , \qquad (1)$$

where $L(\gamma)$ is the length of the path γ. This metric depends on both the transformed point cloud P and the characteristics of the transformations t_1 and t_2.

By varying the parameter θ_t of a transformation t that controls the appearance of each point cloud, e.g., location and orientation, we can get different point clouds transformed from the original one. In DG, we assume point clouds in the target domain $\mathbb{T}$ are transformed from the corresponding ones in the source domain $\mathbb{S}$ by a collection of unknown transformations $\mathcal{T}_{\mathbb{S}\to\mathbb{T}}$. (Notice that $\mathcal{T}_{\mathbb{S}\to\mathbb{T}}$ is not exactly the same as SO(3), but can be parameterized using SO(3) as formulated in Sec. 3.2.) Given two point clouds P in $\mathbb{S}$ and P' in $\mathbb{T}$, satisfying $P' = P_t$ where $t \in \mathcal{T}_{\mathbb{S}\to\mathbb{T}}$ is unknown, we define the distance of t relative to $\mathbb{S}$ as $d_P(e, t)$ where e is an identity transformation that keeps any point cloud unchanged, i.e., $P_e = P$. The larger $d_P(e, t)$, the further distance of t relative to $\mathbb{S}$.

3.2   Geometric Transformation Unification

The distribution shift between source and target domains is usually caused by (unknown) geometric transformations. As indicated in [16,40], occlusions, density changes, and scanning noises mainly contribute to the point cloud geometric variations. The work MetaSets [16] proposes three types of transformations to mimic these geometric variations in real-scanned point clouds. Similarly, we train a DNN model on a collection of transformed point clouds that covers a wide range of feasible variations across the source and the target domains to enhance the DNN model's generalization capability. Distinct from [16] where each type of transformation is parameterized by different transformation-specific hyper-parameters, we unify all three transformations by parameterizing them using a direct product of SO(3) and $\mathbb{R}$, i.e., SO(3) $\times \mathbb{R}$ which is still a Lie group. Utilizing the tools defined in Sect. 3.1, we can qualitatively measure the distance between transformations relative to the source domain, and thus mine effective adversarial samples based on the distance as described in Sect. 3.3 and 3.4. For the integrity

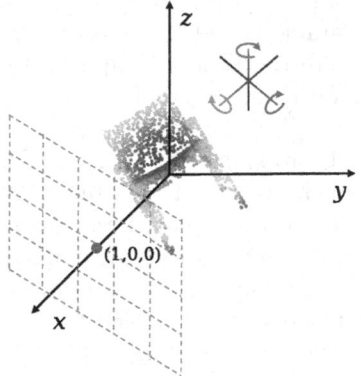

Fig. 3. Illustration of the unification of all transformations using a direct product of SO(3) and $\mathbb{R}$.

of the paper, we cite and briefly review the three transformations formulated in [16] and refer the reader to [16] for detailed descriptions.

Non-uniform Density (p_1, g). First, randomly select a point p_1 from a unit sphere outside point cloud P and calculate its distances to each point in P. Then, the distances are normalized to $[0, 1]$ and multiplied by a multiplier $g > 1$. The resultant values are used as dropping rates of each point in P and discard points according to the dropping rates.

Dropping $(p_2, x\%)$. First, randomly select a point p_2 in point cloud P and then drop the nearest $x\%$ points in P. Broken or missing parts in real-world scanned objects can be simulated by this type of transformation.

Self-Occlusion $(\vec{v}, W)$. First, a plane outside point cloud P is chosen and all points in P are projected onto the plane along its normal vector $\vec{v}$. The minimum distance between each candidate plane and P is the same for all. Then, equal-sized grids are drawn on the chosen plane with the size W. Only the nearest points to the chosen plane along the normal vector are retained in each grid.

For the three types of geometric transformations described above, the geometric shifts of self-occlusions, density changes, and missing assemblies are simulated and controlled by hyper-parameters $(p_1, g, p_2, x\%, \vec{v}, W)$. Distinct from [16] which samples discrete values of these hyper-parameters randomly and individually, we unify all the three transformations using a direct product of SO(3) and $\mathbb{R}$, and impose a manifold structure on the set of transformations. Specifically, as illustrated in Fig. 3, we centerize point cloud P and normalize it within a unit sphere. For ***non-uniform density*** (s, r), we fix p_1 as an anchor point $p_1 = (1, 0, 0)$ and rotate P by $s \in$ SO(3). Then, we calculate the distances between the anchor point to each point in P. The distances are normalized to $[0, 1]$ and multiplied by a multiplier $r > 1$, resulting the dropping rates of each point in P. For ***dropping*** $(s, r\%)$, we fix an anchor vector $\vec{e} = (1, 0, 0)$ and rotate P by $s \in$ SO(3). Then, we choose the point $p_{\vec{e}}$ in P with the minimal angle with the anchor vector and drop the nearest $r\%$ points around $p_{\vec{e}}$ in P. For ***self-occlusion*** (s, r), we first fix a plane parallel to yz-plane with the coordinate $x > 1$. We do not specify the concrete plane's x coordinate only if $x > 1$ as the projection is orthogonal. Then, we rotate P by $s \in$ SO(3) and only keep the point with minimal distance to the plane within each grid with the grid size of r along its normal vector. In sum, we unify all the three transformations parameterized by a direct product of SO(3) and $\mathbb{R}$ as $\mathcal{T} = \{(s, r) \mid s \in \text{SO}(3), r \in \mathbb{R}\}$, which achieves the same transformation effect as in [16]. We overload the notations in Sect. 3.1 and denote the set of unified transformations as $\mathcal{T}$ in which $\theta_t = [\theta_s : r] \in \Theta \subset \mathbb{R}^4$ for $t \in \mathcal{T}$ and the symbol : denotes concatenation.

3.3 Adversarial Point Cloud Generation

We first review the generic additive adversarial point cloud generation under supervised settings. Let P be a training sample with N points and y be the corresponding label. A supervised learning model is denoted as $f_w : P \mapsto y$

where w parameterizes the model. An *adversarial sample* P^a is the worst-case example by adding perturbation to each point in P which maximizes the loss of the given model f_w [20,39,42]:

$$P^a = P + \alpha \mathbf{sign}(\nabla_P \mathcal{L}(P, y; w)) \text{ s.t. } \|p_i - p'_i\|_{L^2} \leq \epsilon \ \forall i \in \{1, 2, \cdots, N\} , \quad (2)$$

where $\mathcal{L}$ is the supervised loss (*e.g.*, cross-entropy) and the condition term prevents the adversarial sample P^a from significantly deteriorating the original P.

However, the generic additive adversarial samples generated using Eq. 2 is purely driven by loss without considering the transformations towards shrinking the domain gap, thus not applicable to DG. We propose to search for the adversarial samples of a given transformed point cloud P_t maximizing the loss while still staying on PCAM. The searching process consists of two steps: 1) choosing the searching movement

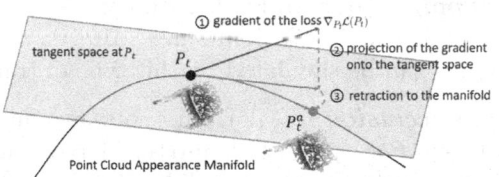

Fig. 4. Gradient computed at a given point P_t on PCAM is first projected to the tangent space. This projected gradient is then retracted to a point on the manifold, resulting in an adversarial sample P_t^a.

direction, and 2) mapping this movement back onto PCAM [1,2,19]. The idea is illustrated in Fig. 4 conceptually. Mathematically, let $\mathcal{L}(P_t)$ represent the loss evaluated at P_t of the model f_w, and we choose the direction maximizing the loss, *i.e.*, the direction of the gradient $\nabla_{P_t} \mathcal{L}(P_t)$. However, as we need to stay on the manifold $\mathcal{M}(P)$, we project the gradient $\nabla_{P_t} \mathcal{L}(P_t)$ onto the tangent space at P_t and such a tangent space is denoted as $T_{P_t}\mathcal{M}$ [1,2]. The projection of $\nabla_{P_t} \mathcal{L}(P_t)$ onto $T_{P_t}\mathcal{M}$ is evaluated as [6,19]:

$$g = \mathcal{J}_{P_t}^+ \nabla_{P_t} \mathcal{L}(P_t) \approx \arg\min_{x} \|\mathcal{J}_{P_t} x - \nabla_{P_t} \mathcal{L}(P_t)\| \in \mathbb{R}^4 , \quad (3)$$

where $\mathcal{J}_{P_t} \in \mathbb{R}^{(N \times 3) \times 4}$ is the Jacobian matrix of P_t (described below) whose columns form a basis of the tangent space at P_t, and $\mathcal{J}_{P_t}^+$ is the pseudo-inverse of $\mathcal{J}_{P_t}$. Due to the complexity of computing pseudo-inverse, the projection $g \in T_{P_t}\mathcal{M}$ can be approximated using the least squares method [6] as in Eq. 3.

To numerically define Jacobian matrix $\mathcal{J}_P$ of a point cloud P in Eq. 3, we first define the *difference field* of P relative to another point cloud P' as:

$$\Delta P_{\to P'} \triangleq \{\Delta p_{\to P'} \mid p \in P\} = \{\arg\min_{p'} \|p - p'\|_{L^2} - p \mid p \in P, p' \in P'\} . \quad (4)$$

That is, for each point $p \in P$, we find the nearest point (under the L^2 metric in Euclidean space) $p' \in P'$ and then use the *difference vector* $p' - p$ to measure the *change* of p from P to P'. Gathering all difference vectors of each point in P, we form the difference field of P denoting the changes from P to P'. Equipped with the difference field defined in Eq. 4, we can define the Jacobian matrix $\mathcal{J}_P$. For a point cloud P_t, we add a small $\Delta\theta$ to the parameters θ_t of the transformation t, and then the (i,j)-th entry of the Jacobian $\mathcal{J}_{P_t}$ is defined as:

$$\mathcal{J}_{P_t}[i,j] = \frac{\Delta p_{i \to P'_t}}{\Delta\theta[j]} \, , \tag{5}$$

where $p_i \in P_t$, P'_t is the point cloud transformed from P by $t \circ \Delta t$ (*i.e.*, changing the parameters from θ_t to $\theta_t + \Delta\theta$), and $\Delta\theta[j]$ is the j-th entry of $\Delta\theta$.

After generating the searching direction g, we update the parameter θ_t of the current transformation t to generate an adversarial transformation t^a parameterized by θ_t^a using gradient ascent:

$$\theta_t^a = \theta_t + \alpha \cdot g \, , \tag{6}$$

where $\alpha \in (0, +\infty) \subset \mathbb{R}$ is ascent rate. Once computing the adversarial transformation parameter θ_t^a, the next step is to map θ_t^a back onto $\mathcal{M}(P)$ using *retraction* [1,2,19], an operation of mapping a vector in a tangent space of a manifold back to the manifold. Here we focus on recover $s^a \in SO(3)$ from $\theta_s^a = \{\theta_t^a[j] \mid j = 0,1,2\} \in \mathbb{R}^3$ and leave $r^a = \theta_t^a[3] \in \mathbb{R}$ unchanged.

Let G_i be the basis of the tangent space $T_e SO(3)$ at the identity element e of the 3D rotation group $SO(3)$ (see *supplementary materials*), the steps of retraction are summarized as: 1) mapping θ_s^a to a tangent vector in $T_e SO(3)$ using G_i; 2) mapping the resultant tangent vector in $T_e SO(3)$ to a rotation $s^a \in SO(3)$, and 3) mapping the resultant transformation $t^a = (s^a, r^a) \in \mathcal{T}$ back to the manifold $\mathcal{M}(P)$. Formally, retraction $R_{P_t} : T_{P_t}\mathcal{M} \to \mathcal{M}(P)$ at $P_t \in \mathcal{M}(P)$ is defined as:

$$R_{P_t}(\alpha \cdot g) = P_{t^a}, \quad \text{s.t.} \quad t^a = (s^a, r^a) \text{ and } s^a = \exp(\sum_{j=0}^{2} \theta_s^a[j]G_j) \, , \tag{7}$$

where $\theta_s^a[j]$ is the j-th entry of θ_s^a, also the coefficient w.r.t. the basis G_j. Thus, the adversarial sample from P_t can be defined as $P_t^a = R_P(t^a) = P_{t^a}$ as in Eq. 7.

3.4 Adaptive Memory for Intermediate Domains

We describe an adaptive memory mechanism for determining which adversarial samples to be retained in an external memory [38] as intermediate domains. Adversarial samples from different types of transformations are grouped into different intermediate domains. This mechanism jointly considers the transformation distances relative to the source domain as

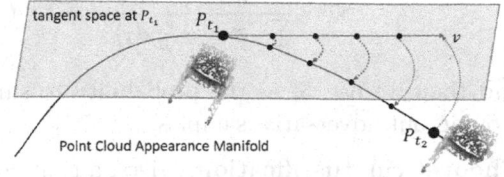

Fig. 5. Illustration of computing geodesic distance between $P_1, P_2 \in \mathcal{M}(P)$ using direct path with $N = 5$ segments

shown in Fig. 1 and the intermediate domain sizes. We first estimate the probability of a current adversarial sample to move in memory and then choose a sample in memory to move it out simultaneously. Let M_i denotes the i-th intermediate domains formed by the adversarial samples transformed by the i-th type of transformation and retained in memory M; $n_i = |M_i|$ denotes the number of samples in domain M_i; and $n = |M|$ denotes the total number of samples in memory, satisfying $n = \sum_{i=1}^{3} n_i$.

Probability of New Adversarial Sample Moving into Memory. When a new adversarial sample $P_{t_i}^a$ is generated through transformation t_i, the chance of $P_{t_i}^a$ being moved into memory is estimated, with the central principle being the further distance from $P_{t_i}^a$ to the source domain, the higher probability of $P_{t_i}^a$ being retained. The probability is positively correlated to the geodesic distance $d_P(e, t_i)$. Furthermore, to avoid imbalance of samples among intermediate domains, we enforce the move-in probability to be inversely proportional to n_i.

Algorithm 1. A sketch of training scheme

Input: $\mathbb{S} = \{D_{\mathbb{S}}^{tr}, D_{\mathbb{S}}^{val}\}$, T, M, f_w, batch size B
1: **while** $\mathcal{L}^{val} < \epsilon$ **do**
2:     ▷ Training phase
3:     Sample $\{P_i\}_{i=1}^{B}$ from $D_{\mathbb{S}}^{tr}$, $\{t_i\}_{i=1}^{B}$ from T
4:     Apply $\{t_i\}_{i=1}^{B}$ to $\{P_i\}_{i=1}^{B}$ to get $\{P_{t_i}\}_{i=1}^{B}$
5:     Sample $\{P_i^a\}_{i=1}^{B}$ from M
6:     Compute $\mathcal{L}^{tr}(P) = f_w(\{P_i\}_{i=1}^{B} \cup \{P_i^a\}_{i=1}^{B})$
7:     Compute projected gradient using Eq. 3
8:     Generate adversarial $\{P_i^a\}_{i=1}^{M}$ using Eq. 7
9:     Compute $d_P(e, t_i)$ using Eq. 13
10:    Compute move-in/out prob. as in Sec. 3.4
11:    Add some adversarial $\{P_i^a\}_{i=1}^{m}$ into M
12:    ▷ Validation phase
13:    Sample $\{P_i\}_{i=1}^{B}$ from $D_{\mathbb{S}}^{val}$, $\{t_i\}_{i=1}^{B}$ from T
14:    Compute $\mathcal{L}^{val}(P) = f_w(\{P_i\}_{i=1}^{B})$
15: **end while**

Probability of Existing Adversarial Sample Moving Out of Memory. To move an existing adversarial sample out of memory, we perform a hierarchical sampling as proposed in [38] by first selecting an intermediate domain based on a score and then randomly move out a sample in the selected domain. The score for each domain is negatively correlated to the average geodesic distance of all samples in the domain. For the same reason as above, we enforce the score to be proportional to n_i. Formally, the score for the i-th intermediate domain is:

$$S_i = \frac{\exp(-\frac{n_i}{n}\bar{d}_i)}{\sum_j \exp(-\frac{n_j}{n}\bar{d}_j)}, \quad \text{s.t. } \bar{d}_i = \frac{1}{n_i}\sum_{k=1}^{n_i} d_P(e, t_k) \ , \tag{8}$$

and then we use S_i as the probability to sample intermediate domain M_i for moving out adversarial samples.

Theoretical Justification. Given a source domain $\mathbb{S}$ and a target domain $\mathbb{T}$, the error of a classifier h on the target domain $\epsilon_{\mathbb{T}}(h)$ can be bounded by the sum of the source domain error $\epsilon_{\mathbb{S}}(h)$, the divergence between the distributions $\mathcal{D}_{\mathbb{S}}$ and $\mathcal{D}_{\mathbb{T}}$, and a constant C which is independent of h [3,27]:

$$\epsilon_{\mathbb{T}}(h) < \epsilon_{\mathbb{S}}(h) + d_1(\mathcal{D}_{\mathbb{S}}, \mathcal{D}_{\mathbb{T}}) + C \ , \tag{9}$$

where $d_1(\mathcal{D}_{\mathbb{S}}, \mathcal{D}_{\mathbb{T}})$ is the total variation divergence (or L^1 distance when each set is countable) for distributions. In previous literature [3,8,27,29], $\mathcal{H}\Delta\mathcal{H}$-distance $d_{\mathcal{H}\Delta\mathcal{H}}(\cdot, \cdot)$, an upper bound of $d_1(\cdot, \cdot)$, is adopted in place of the total variation divergence in Eq. 9 for analysis. However, as indicated in [33], there exists a connection between the total variation divergence and transportation theory:

$$d_1(\mathcal{D}_{\mathbb{S}}, \mathcal{D}_{\mathbb{T}}) = \frac{1}{2}\|\mathcal{D}_{\mathbb{S}} - \mathcal{D}_{\mathbb{T}}\|_{L^1} = \inf_{\pi} \mathbb{E}_{\pi}[c(x, y)] \ , \tag{10}$$

where $x \sim \mathcal{D}_{\mathbb{S}}$, $y \sim \mathcal{D}_{\mathbb{T}}$, $c(x, y)$ is a cost function, and the expectation is taken w.r.t. the probability measure π on the space where (x, y) lives. In transportation theory, the cost function $c(x, y)$ is proportional to the distance between x and y. In our setting, we choose the cost function to be the geodesic distance between two point clouds, $i.e.$, $c(P_{t_1}, P_{t_2}) = d_P(t_1, t_2)$. Denoting intermediate domains as $\mathbb{M}$, to minimize the right-hand side of Eq. 9, we have:

$$
\begin{aligned}
&\min d_1(\mathcal{D}_{\mathbb{S}}, \mathcal{D}_{\mathbb{T}}) \Rightarrow \min d_1(\mathcal{D}_{\mathbb{S}\cup\mathbb{M}}, \mathcal{D}_{\mathbb{T}}) && \triangleright \text{M is an expansion of S} \\
&\Rightarrow \min \inf_{\pi} \mathbb{E}_{\pi}[c(P_{t_1} \in \mathbb{S} \cup \mathbb{M}, P_{t_2} \in \mathbb{T})] && \\
&\Rightarrow \min \inf_{\pi} \mathbb{E}_{\pi}[c(P_{t_1} \in \mathbb{M}, P_{t_2} \in \mathbb{T})] && \triangleright \text{S is given and fixed} \\
&\Rightarrow \min \inf_{\pi} \mathbb{E}_{\pi}[d_P(t_{\mathbb{S}\to\mathbb{M}}, t_{\mathbb{S}\to\mathbb{T}})] && \triangleright t_1 := t_{\mathbb{S}\to\mathbb{M}} \text{ and } t_2 := t_{\mathbb{S}\to\mathbb{T}} \\
&\Rightarrow \min \inf_{\pi} \mathbb{E}_{\pi}[d_P(e, t_{\mathbb{S}\to\mathbb{T}}) - d_P(e, t_{\mathbb{S}\to\mathbb{M}})] && \triangleright d_P(e, t_{\mathbb{S}\to\mathbb{T}}) = d_P(e, t_{\mathbb{S}\to\mathbb{M}}) + d_P(t_{\mathbb{S}\to\mathbb{M}}, t_{\mathbb{S}\to\mathbb{T}}) \\
&\Rightarrow \max \inf_{\pi} \mathbb{E}_{\pi}[d_P(e, t_{\mathbb{S}\to\mathbb{M}})] && \triangleright t_{\mathbb{S}\to\mathbb{T}} \text{ is unknown and assumed fixed} \quad (11)
\end{aligned}
$$

The fourth comment assumes $d_P(e, t_{\mathbb{S}\to\mathbb{M}}) = d_1$ and $d_P(t_{\mathbb{S}\to\mathbb{M}}, t_{\mathbb{S}\to\mathbb{T}}) = d_2$, as shown in Fig. 1. We select the adversarial sample with the maximum geodesic distance of $d_P(e, t_{\mathbb{S}\to\mathbb{M}})$ and store it into the corresponding intermediate domain.

We now describe how to calculate the geodesic distance $d_P(t_1, t_2)$. Assuming $P_{t_1}, P_{t_2} \in \mathcal{M}(P)$, we adopt the *direct path* method [19] to approximately measure the geodesic distance between these two points as follows. First, map P_{t_2} to the tangent space at P_{t_1} as vector $v = \theta_{t_2} - \theta_{t_1}$, dividing v into smaller vector segments and re-map these segments back onto the manifold. Then, $d_P(t_1, t_2)$ is computed as the sum of distances between these interval points on $\mathcal{M}(P)$. Mathematically, the direct path from P_{t_1} to P_{t_2} can be estimated using retraction as:

$$\gamma(\tau) = R_{P_{t_1}}(\tau v) = P_{t_\tau} \in \mathcal{M}(P), \quad \text{s.t.} \ \theta_{t_\tau} = \theta_{t_1} + \tau v \text{ and } \tau \in [0, 1] \ . \tag{12}$$

For a pre-defined number of steps N, v can be divided into segments as $\hat{v} = \frac{v}{N}$, the geodesic distance can be measured as:

$$d_P(t_1, t_2) = d(P_{t_1}, P_{t_2}) = \sum_{i=1}^{N}\|R_{P_{t_1}}(i\hat{v}) - R_{P_{t_1}}((i-1)\hat{v}))\|_d = \sum_{i=1}^{N}\|P_{t_i} - P_{t_{i-1}}\|_d \ , \tag{13}$$

where $\theta_{t_i} = \theta_{t_1} + i\hat{v}$. In our case, we estimate $d_P(t_1, t_2)$ as $d(P_{t_1}, P_{t_2})$, since from Eq. 1, the distance between two transformations on $\mathcal{T}$ is defined as the distance between their transformed point clouds on PCAM $\mathcal{M}(P)$. Using the difference vectors defined in Eq. 4, we can induce a metric on $\mathcal{M}(P)$ defined as:

$$\|P - P'\|_d = \frac{1}{N}\sum_{p\in P}\|\Delta_{p\to P'}\|_{L^2} \ , \tag{14}$$

where N is number of points in P. $\|P - P'\|_d = 0$ if and only if P and P' are the same. Plugging Eq. 14 into the right-hand side of Eq. 13, we can approximate the geodesic distance between t_1 and t_2.

3.5   Training Scheme

We sketch key steps of our training scheme in Algorithm 1. We split data in the source domain into training and validation sets, and apply transformations to a batch of sampled data in each iteration. The loss is applied to generate adversarial samples as in Sect. 3.3. We compute move-in/out probabilities of the adversarial samples based on geodesic distances as in Sec. 3.4 and move some samples into and/or out of the memory. We refer the reader to *supplementary materials* for a detailed training scheme.

4   Experiment

Dataset and Implementation. We evaluate our model on the two Sim-to-Real benchmarks proposed in [16] in which two synthetic datasets, ModelNet [41] and ShapeNet [7], and a real-scanned dataset ScanObjectNN [32] are calibrated to serve as three domains. We use the common categories shared across each dataset. We refer the reader to *supplementary materials* and [16] for detailed description about the Sim-to-Real benchmarks. We split each source domain into training and validation sets with a ratio of 5 : 1 as in [11,16]. We implement f_w using a meta-learning algorithm [10,17] with first-order approximation. The parameter $\theta_s \in \mathbb{R}^3$ for $s \in SO(3)$ are optimized in adversarial learning without bounds, while the parameter $r \in \mathbb{R}$ are constrained using upper and lower bounds to avoid significantly deteriorating point clouds as suggested in [16].

4.1   Visualization of Adversarial Point Clouds

Figure 6 shows several adversarial samples that are generated for three types of transformations in experiments. We notice that compared to the clean and intact point clouds in synthetic ModelNet40 and ShapeNet datasets, real-scanned point clouds in ScanObjectNN are partial and noisy, raising the distribution shift issue that a model trained only using naive initial data from ModelNet40 or ShapeNet cannot perform well on ScanObjectNN as the target domain. By generating adversarial samples diverting away from synthetic clean data and towards partial and noisy data, the distributions of point clouds in the source and the target domains could gradually align. For instance, the sofa in ScanObjectNN contains a missing part (a hole) on its back, the transformed sofa also produces a hole on the back, making the training data geometrically closer to the testing one.

4.2   ModelNet40 to ScanObjectNN

We select 11 shared categories across ModelNet40 and ScanObjectNN datasets. We train the networks on ModelNet40 and evaluate the performance on ScanObjectNN. Our method is compared against the following classification models: PointNet [25], PointNet++ [26], DGCNN [37], ConvPoint [5], LDGCNN [43], PointCNN [22], PointDAN [27] and MetaSets [16]. Note that PointDAN is a DA method which utilizes unlabeled point clouds from the target domain during training. From Table 1, our approach outperforms all the compared methods for cross-domain point cloud classification in DG settings. Our superior performance over previous single-domain approaches (line 1–6) is attributed to the intermediate domain expanding the source domain and aligning data distribution with the target domain. Compare with DA and DG approaches (line 7–9), we still achieve optimal performance. Distinct from [16] which generates data for augmentation using random transformation parameters, our method produces adversarial transformations in a principle manner, *i.e.*, the transformed samples are more challenging w.r.t. the network and have further distances relative to the source domain. Moreover, the adaptive memory retains some adversarial samples during training to alleviate the potential *forgetting* problem in the network. We have to mention that superiority of adversarial learning could be partially countered, however, if massive amounts of data are transformed arbitrarily and encompass a broad spectrum of transformation possibilities.

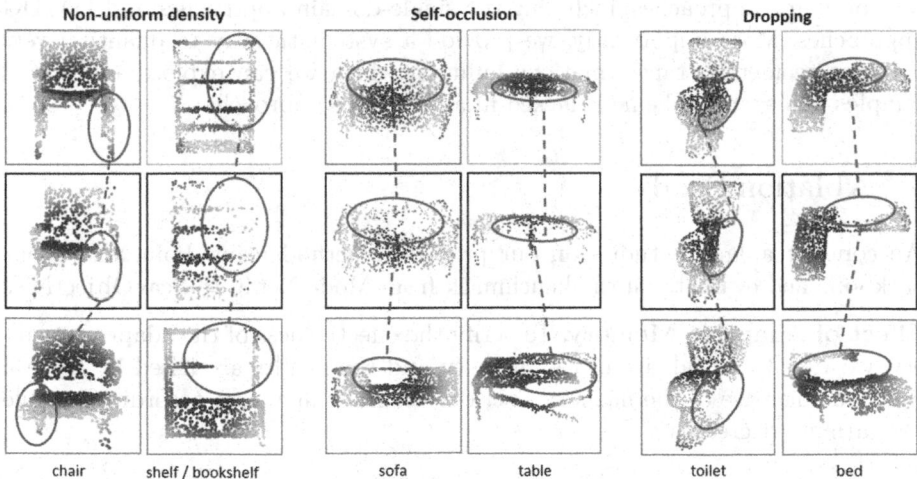

Fig. 6. Blue boxes: point clouds from ModelNet40 as the source domain. Orange boxes: point clouds from ShapeNet as the source domain. Black boxes: adversarial samples generated from the corresponding source domain point clouds (above). Green boxes: point clouds from ScanobjectNN as the target domain. The adversarially transformed point clouds form the intermediate domains closing the geometric gap between intact point clouds in the source domain and incomplete point clouds in the target domain (Color figure online)

Table 1. Accuracy (%) on the benchmark: ModelNet40 → ScanObjectNN.

Method	Object	Object & background
PointNet [25]	55.90 ± 1.47	49.48 ± 2.28
PointNet++ [26]	47.30 ± 0.53	40.42 ± 1.17
ConvPoint [5]	57.40 ± 0.44	55.44 ± 0.32
DGCNN [21]	61.68 ± 1.26	57.61 ± 0.44
PointCNN [22]	50.32 ± 0.43	46.11 ± 0.43
LDGCNN [21]	62.29 ± 0.22	58.83 ± 0.43
PointDAN [27] with PointNet	63.32 ± 0.85	55.13 ± 0.97
MetaSets [16] with PointNet	68.28 ± 0.79	57.19 ± 1.23
MetaSets [16] with DGCNN	72.42 ± 0.21	65.66 ± 1.06
Ours with PointNet	69.84 ± 0.56	58.36 ± 0.94
Ours with DGCNN	**73.83 ± 0.48**	**66.71 ± 0.97**

4.3   ShapeNet to ScanObjectNN

Similar to Sect. 4.2, we select 9 categories shared across ShapeNet and ScanObjectNN, and train our model on ShapeNet and evaluate on ScanObjectNN. We compare our method with the same state-of-the-art approaches as forementioned and the results are listed in Table 2. Our method still outperforms all the compared approaches, including the single-domain approaches and DA/DG approaches. More importantly, we provide a systematic way to quantitatively measure geometric transformations built on which we can explore adversarial samples and such a scheme is lacked in all previous approaches.

5   Ablation Study

We conduct ablative studies on our proposed method using PointNet as our backbone and evaluate on the benchmark from ModelNet40 to ScanObjectNN.

Effect of Adaptive Memory. To verify the effectiveness of the adaptive memory, we vary the total size of the memory and the results are listed in Table 3. With the increase of the memory size, the accuracy increases accordingly while the variance decreases.

Table 2. Accuracy (%) on the benchmark: ShapeNet → ScanObjectNN.

Method	Object	Object & background
PointNet [25]	54.00 ± 0.32	45.50 ± 0.99
PointNet++ [26]	45.50 ± 0.64	43.25 ± 1.23
ConvPoint [5]	52.58 ± 0.58	50.67 ± 0.88
DGCNN [21]	57.42 ± 1.01	54.42 ± 0.80
PointCNN [22]	49.42 ± 0.29	43.92 ± 0.63
LDGCNN [21]	57.92 ± 0.63	52.50 ± 0.25
PointDAN [27] with PointNet	54.95 ± 0.87	43.00 ± 0.95
MetaSets [16] with PointNet	55.25 ± 0.35	49.50 ± 0.43
MetaSets [16] with DGCNN	60.92 ± 0.76	59.08 ± 1.01
Ours with PointNet	57.03 ± 0.47	51.35 ± 0.46
Ours with DGCNN	**62.21 ± 0.49**	**61.13 ± 0.86**

Effect of Manifold-Based Adversarial Samples. We validate our manifold-based adversarial samples against the additive adversarial samples generated using Eq. 2 and the results are listed in Table 4. By varying ϵ, we control the *adversarialness*. Note that when the adversarialness increases, the performance even drops, as the per-point adversarial acts as noise and fails to bridge domain gaps as our proposed adversarial samples.

Table 3. Effect of the memory size on the benchmark: ModelNet40 → ScanObjectNN.

Method	Object	Object & background
PointNet ($n = 100$)	69.22 ± 0.74	57.94 ± 1.15
PointNet ($n = 300$)	69.51 ± 0.69	58.17 ± 1.08
PointNet ($n = 500$)	69.84 ± 0.56	58.36 ± 0.94

Table 4. Effect of additive adversarial on benchmark: ModelNet40 → ScanObjectNN.

Method	Ours	$\epsilon = 0.1$	$\epsilon = 0.25$	$\epsilon = 0.5$
PointNet on **Object**	69.84 ± 0.56	68.31 ± 0.46	64.29 ± 0.51	58.37 ± 0.74

6 Conclusions

This work presents a 3D point cloud representation learning method for domain generation. We construct a point cloud appearance manifold on which different types of geometric transformations can be unified and quantitatively measured using geodesic distance. The geodesic distance is then utilized to generate and select adversarial samples which are retained in an adaptive memory as intermediate domains to reduce domain shift. We evaluate our method on two Sim-to-Real benchmarks and achieve superior performance. The manifold-based framework can be extended to domain adaption by measuring the distance from the source to the target domains, which is left for future work.

Acknowledgments. The authors appreciate the generous support provided by Inception Institute of Artificial Intelligence (IIAI) in the form of NYUAD Global Ph.D. Student Fellowship. This work was also partially supported by the NYUAD Center for Artificial Intelligence and Robotics (CAIR), funded by Tamkeen under the NYUAD Research Institute Award CG010.

References

1. Absil, P.A., Mahony, R., Sepulchre, R.: Optimization algorithms on matrix manifolds. Princeton University Press (2009)
2. Absil, P.A., Mahony, R., Sepulchre, R.: Optimization on manifolds: methods and applications. In: Recent Advances in Optimization and Its Applications in Engineering, pp. 125–144. Springer (2010). https://doi.org/10.1007/978-3-642-12598-0_12
3. Ben-David, S., Blitzer, J., Crammer, K., Kulesza, A., Pereira, F., Vaughan, J.W.: A theory of learning from different domains. Mach. Learn. **79**(1), 151–175 (2010)
4. Blanchard, G., Lee, G., Scott, C.: Generalizing from several related classification tasks to a new unlabeled sample. In: Advances in Neural Information Processing Systems, vol. 24 (2011)
5. Boulch, A.: Convpoint: Continuous convolutions for point cloud processing. Comput. Graph. **88**, 24–34 (2020)
6. Buss, S.R.: Introduction to inverse kinematics with jacobian transpose, pseudoinverse and damped least squares methods. J. Robotics Automat. **17**(1–19), 16 (2004)
7. Chang, A.X., et al.: Shapenet: An information-rich 3d model repository. arXiv preprint arXiv:1512.03012 (2015)
8. Chen, Y., Li, W., Sakaridis, C., Dai, D., Van Gool, L.: Domain adaptive faster r-cnn for object detection in the wild. In: Proceedings of the Conference on Computer Vision and Pattern Recognition, pp. 3339–3348 (2018)
9. Fan, X., Wang, Q., Ke, J., Yang, F., Gong, B., Zhou, M.: Adversarially adaptive normalization for single domain generalization. In: Proceedings of the Conference on Computer Vision and Pattern Recognition, pp. 8208–8217 (2021)
10. Finn, C., Abbeel, P., Levine, S.: Model-agnostic meta-learning for fast adaptation of deep networks. In: International Conference on Machine Learning, pp. 1126–1135. PMLR (2017)
11. Ghifary, M., Kleijn, W.B., Zhang, M., Balduzzi, D.: Domain generalization for object recognition with multi-task autoencoders. In: Proceedings of the International Conference on Computer Vision, pp. 2551–2559 (2015)
12. Gong, B., Shi, Y., Sha, F., Grauman, K.: Geodesic flow kernel for unsupervised domain adaptation. In: Proceedings of the Conference on Computer Vision and Pattern Recognition, pp. 2066–2073. IEEE (2012)

13. Gong, R., Li, W., Chen, Y., Gool, L.V.: Dlow: Domain flow for adaptation and generalization. In: Proceedings of the Conference on Computer Vision and Pattern Recognition, pp. 2477–2486 (2019)
14. Goodfellow, I.J., Shlens, J., Szegedy, C.: Explaining and harnessing adversarial examples. In: International Conference on Learning Representations (2015)
15. Gopalan, R., Li, R., Chellappa, R.: Domain adaptation for object recognition: An unsupervised approach. In: Proceedings of the International Conference on Computer Vision, pp. 999–1006. IEEE (2011)
16. Huang, C., Cao, Z., Wang, Y., Wang, J., Long, M.: Metasets: Meta-learning on point sets for generalizable representations. In: Proceedings of the Conference on Computer Vision and Pattern Recognition, pp. 8863–8872 (2021)
17. Huang, Z., Wang, H., Xing, E.P., Huang, D.: Self-challenging Improves cross-domain generalization. In: Vedaldi, A., Bischof, H., Brox, T., Frahm, J.-M. (eds.) ECCV 2020. LNCS, vol. 12347, pp. 124–140. Springer, Cham (2020). https://doi. org/10.1007/978-3-030-58536-5_8
18. Jacques, L., De Vleeschouwer, C.: A geometrical study of matching pursuit parametrization. Trans. Signal Process. **56**(7), 2835–2848 (2008)
19. Kanbak, C., Moosavi-Dezfooli, S.M., Frossard, P.: Geometric robustness of deep networks: analysis and improvement. In: Proceedings of the Conference on Computer Vision and Pattern Recognition, pp. 4441–4449 (2018)
20. Kim, M., Tack, J., Hwang, S.J.: Adversarial self-supervised contrastive learning. Adv. Neural. Inf. Process. Syst. **33**, 2983–2994 (2020)
21. Li, G., Muller, M., Thabet, A., Ghanem, B.: Deepgcns: Can gcns go as deep as cnns? In: Proceedings of the International Conference on Computer Vision, pp. 9267–9276 (2019)
22. Li, Y., Bu, R., Sun, M., Wu, W., Di, X., Chen, B.: Pointcnn: Convolution on x-transformed points. In: Advances in Neural Information Processing Systems, vol. 31 (2018)
23. Madry, A., Makelov, A., Schmidt, L., Tsipras, D., Vladu, A.: Towards deep learning models resistant to adversarial attacks. In: International Conference on Learning Representations (2018)
24. Moreno-Torres, J.G., Raeder, T., Alaiz-Rodríguez, R., Chawla, N.V., Herrera, F.: A unifying view on dataset shift in classification. Pattern Recogn. **45**(1), 521–530 (2012)
25. Qi, C.R., Su, H., Mo, K., Guibas, L.J.: Pointnet: Deep learning on point sets for 3d classification and segmentation. In: Proceedings of the Conference on Computer Vision and Pattern Recognition (2017)
26. Qi, C.R., Yi, L., Su, H., Guibas, L.J.: Pointnet++: Deep hierarchical feature learning on point sets in a metric space. In: Advances in Neural Information Processing Systems (2017)
27. Qin, C., You, H., Wang, L., Kuo, C.C.J., Fu, Y.: Pointdan: A multi-scale 3d domain adaption network for point cloud representation. In: dvances in Neural Information Processing Systems, vol. 32 (2019)
28. Saenko, K., Kulis, B., Fritz, M., Darrell, T.: Adapting visual category models to new domain. In: Daniilidis, K., Maragos, P., Paragios, N. (eds.) ECCV 2010. LNCS, vol. 6314, pp. 213–226. Springer, Heidelberg (2010). https://doi.org/10.1007/978-3-642-15561-1_16
29. Saito, K., Watanabe, K., Ushiku, Y., Harada, T.: Maximum classifier discrepancy for unsupervised domain adaptation. In: Proceedings of the Conference on Computer Vision and Pattern Recognition, pp. 3723–3732 (2018)

30. Shu, Y., Cao, Z., Wang, C., Wang, J., Long, M.: Open domain generalization with domain-augmented meta-learning. In: Proceedings of the Conference on Computer Vision and Pattern Recognition, pp. 9624–9633 (2021)
31. Sinha, A., Namkoong, H., Duchi, J.: Certifiable distributional robustness with principled adversarial training. In: International Conference on Learning Representations (2018)
32. Uy, M.A., Pham, Q.H., Hua, B.S., Nguyen, T., Yeung, S.K.: Revisiting point cloud classification: A new benchmark dataset and classification model on real-world data. In: Proceedings of the International Conference on Computer Vision, pp. 1588–1597 (2019)
33. Villani, C.: Optimal transport: old and new, vol. 338. Springer (2009) https://doi.org/10.1007/978-3-540-71050-9
34. Volpi, R., Murino, V.: Addressing model vulnerability to distributional shifts over image transformation sets. In: Proceedings of the International Conference on Computer Vision, pp. 7980–7989 (2019)
35. Volpi, R., Namkoong, H., Sener, O., Duchi, J.C., Murino, V., Savarese, S.: Generalizing to unseen domains via adversarial data augmentation. In: Advances in Neural Information Processing Systems, vol. 31 (2018)
36. Wakin, M.B., Donoho, D.L., Choi, H., Baraniuk, R.G.: The multiscale structure of non-differentiable image manifolds. In: Optics & Photonics, vol. 5914, p. 59141B. International Society for Optics and Photonics (2005)
37. Wang, Y., Sun, Y., Liu, Z., Sarma, S.E., Bronstein, M.M., Solomon, J.M.: Dynamic graph cnn for learning on point clouds. Trans. Graph. **38**(5), 1–12 (2019)
38. Wang, Z., Duan, T., Fang, L., Suo, Q., Gao, M.: Meta learning on a sequence of imbalanced domains with difficulty awareness. In: Proceedings of the International Conference on Computer Vision, pp. 8947–8957 (2021)
39. Wen, Y., Lin, J., Chen, K., Chen, C.P., Jia, K.: Geometry-aware generation of adversarial point clouds. Trans. Pattern Anal. Mach. Intell. **44**, 2984–2999 (2020)
40. Wu, B., Zhou, X., Zhao, S., Yue, X., Keutzer, K.: Squeezesegv 2: Improved model structure and unsupervised domain adaptation for road-object segmentation from a lidar point cloud. In: International Conference on Robotics and Automation, pp. 4376–4382. IEEE (2019)
41. Wu, Z., et al.: 3d shapenets: A deep representation for volumetric shapes. In: Proceedings of the Conference on Computer Vision and Pattern Recognition, pp. 1912–1920 (2015)
42. Xiang, C., Qi, C.R., Li, B.: Generating 3d adversarial point clouds. In: Proceedings of the Conference on Computer Vision and Pattern Recognition, pp. 9136–9144 (2019)
43. Zhang, K., Hao, M., Wang, J., de Silva, C.W., Fu, C.: Linked dynamic graph cnn: Learning on point cloud via linking hierarchical features. arXiv preprint arXiv:1904.10014 (2019)
44. Zhang, L., Wang, S., Huang, G.B., Zuo, W., Yang, J., Zhang, D.: Manifold criterion guided transfer learning via intermediate domain generation. Trans. Neural Netw. Learn. Syst. **30**(12), 3759–3773 (2019)
45. Zhang, X., Cui, P., Xu, R., Zhou, L., He, Y., Shen, Z.: Deep stable learning for out-of-distribution generalization. In: Proceedings of the Conference on Computer Vision and Pattern Recognition, pp. 5372–5382 (2021)
46. Zhao, L., Liu, T., Peng, X., Metaxas, D.: Maximum-entropy adversarial data augmentation for improved generalization and robustness. Adv. Neural. Inf. Process. Syst. **33**, 14435–14447 (2020)

47. Zhou, K., Liu, Z., Qiao, Y., Xiang, T., Loy, C.C.: Domain generalization in vision: A survey. arXiv preprint arXiv:2103.02503 (2021)

Fast-MoCo: Boost Momentum-Based Contrastive Learning with Combinatorial Patches

Yuanzheng Ci[1], Chen Lin[2], Lei Bai[3(✉)], and Wanli Ouyang[1,3]

[1] SenseTime Computer Vision Group, The University of Sydney,
Camperdown, Australia
{yuanzheng.ci,wanli.ouyang}@sydney.edu.au
[2] University of Oxford, Oxford, England
chen.lin@eng.ox.ac.uk
[3] Shanghai AI Laboratory, Shanghai, China
bailei@pjlab.org.cn

Abstract. Contrastive-based self-supervised learning methods achieved great success in recent years. However, self-supervision requires extremely long training epochs (e.g., 800 epochs for MoCo v3) to achieve promising results, which is unacceptable for the general academic community and hinders the development of this topic. This work revisits the momentum-based contrastive learning frameworks and identifies the inefficiency in which two augmented views generate only one positive pair. We propose Fast-MoCo - a novel framework that utilizes combinatorial patches to construct multiple positive pairs from two augmented views, which provides abundant supervision signals that bring significant acceleration with neglectable extra computational cost. Fast-MoCo trained with **100** epochs achieves **73.5%** linear evaluation accuracy, similar to MoCo v3 (ResNet-50 backbone) trained with 800 epochs. Extra training (**200** epochs) further improves the result to **75.1%**, which is on par with state-of-the-art methods. Experiments on several downstream tasks also confirm the effectiveness of Fast-MoCo. (Code and pretrained models are available at https://github.com/orashi/Fast-MoCo.)

Keywords: Self-supervised learning · Contrastive learning

1 Introduction

Self-supervision is crucial in some of the most remarkable achievements from natural language processing (NLP) [2,10] to computer vision [6]. In particular, recent advances in contrastive learning produced state-of-the-art results on self-supervised learning benchmarks [9,15,29]. Contrastive learning performs an

Supplementary Information The online version contains supplementary material available at https://doi.org/10.1007/978-3-031-19809-0_17.

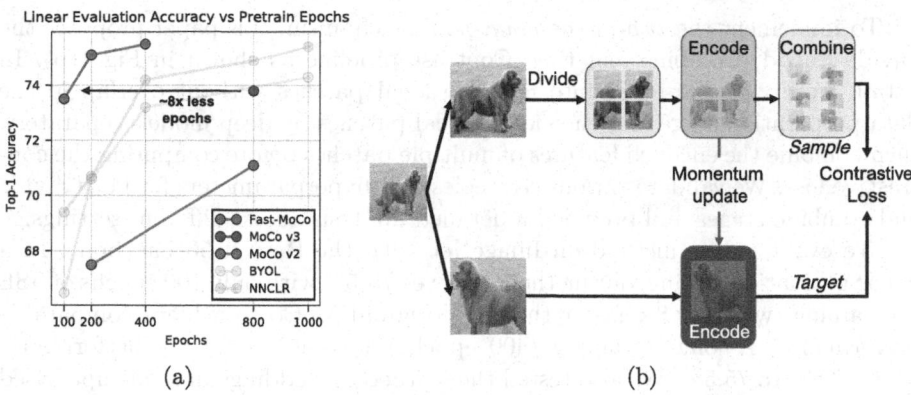

Fig. 1. (a): Comparison with state-of-the-arts on ImageNet. All methods uses ResNet-50 encoders and are measured with Top-1 linear evaluation accuracy. (b): Overview of Fast-MoCo that includes the Split-Encode-Combine pipeline.

instance discrimination pretext task by attracting the embedding of positive samples closer while encouraging the negative samples to be further apart. Some methods opt to make the sample pairs asymmetric with tools such as momentum encoder [18], predictor [15] and `stop-grad` [8] to provide more flexibility for architecture design [13,15].

While great advances have been achieved in the self-supervised learning area in the past two years, a major concern about these works is the extremely long training steps to get a promising performance(e.g., normally 800 epochs, and even 1000 epochs for some methods [9,11,15,32]), which makes it hard or even impossible for many academics to contribute to this area. High training cost also posts challenges when dealing with large industry scale datasets [1,17]. In order to accelerate training, we spotted one limitation of recent momentum based contrastive learning methods [7,15,18], which is the *two-image-one-pair* strategy. In this strategy, two images (or two augmented views of the same image) are fed to the deep models separately and then used as one pair for contrastive learning in [7,9,11,18]. Although symmetric loss designs are normally employed to improve the sample efficiency, we argue that the *two-image-one-pair* mechanism is sub-optimal. To overcome this issue, we propose combinatorial patches, a novel mechanism to efficiently generate feature embeddings for arbitrary combination of local patches. In this strategy, an image pair can be used for generating multiple positive pairs for contrastive learning. Therefore, in contrast to the *two-image-one-pair* mechanism in existing works, our combinatorial patches enable the *two-image-multi-pair* mechanism. With more pairs used for contrastive learning using this *two-image-multi-pair* mechanism, our Fast-MoCo method trained using 100 epochs based on MoCo v3 (*two-image-one-pair* mechanism) for ResNet50 can achieve on-par accuracy when compared with MoCo v3 trained using 800 epochs, as shown in Fig. 1(a).

To implement the *two-image-multi-pair* mechanism, this paper proposes the Divide-Encode-Combine and then Contrast pipeline as shown in Fig. 1(b). In detail, we divide the input into multiple local patches without overlap in the data preparation stage and encode the local patches by deep models separately, then combine the encoded features of multiple patches before computing the contrastive loss. We validate various strategies and hyperparameters for both divide and combine stages and provided a detailed analysis across different settings.

We evaluate our method on ImageNet with the ResNet-50 backbone. In a linear evaluation setting, our method achieves 73.5% with only 100 epochs of SSL pretraining, which is 8× faster than the original MoCo to achieve comparable performance. A longer training (400 epochs) further boosts the performance from 73.5% to 75.5%. We also tested the learned embeddings in semi-supervised learning, object detection, and instance segmentation. Our method performs better than previous approaches in both settings, which suggests the embeddings learned with our method are general and transferable.

2   Related Works

2.1   Patch Based Representation Learning

Various self-supervised learning methods [1,5,13,17,21,25–27] manipulates image patches. A common way to incorporate patches is to encode them separately [13,21,25,26], while Jigsaw Clustering [5] encodes multiple patches at the same time: patches are augmented independently and stitched to form a new image for encoding, the encoded features are then separated spatially before pooling to get the embedding for each patch. Either way, the encoded embeddings can then be used for solving jigsaw puzzles [5,25], contrastive prediction [5,21,26] or bag-of-word reconstruction [13]. On the other hand, Context encoder [27] encodes an image with random masking and then learns to reconstruct the missing part with a decoder. With a ViT encoder, BEiT [1] and MAE [17] split the image into a grid of patches and mask out some of them, the rest patches are gathered and forwarded to get encoded embeddings. They are then optimized for reconstructing the missing patches at feature-level [1] or pixel-level [17]. However, these methods do not construct multiple pairs of samples from combinatorial patches and thus are different from our Divide-Encode-Combine pipeline.

2.2   Contrastive Learning

Contrastive learning methods [3,6,16] have attracted many attentions for their simplicity and performance. They retrieve useful representations by promoting instance discrimination, where the positive samples are generated by applying different data augmentations to the same image while having an identical spatial size. SwAV [3] and NNCLR [11] further extend the semantic gap between a positive pair with a target embedding being replaced by a learned cluster center and a neighborhood embedding. Since the methods in [3,6,11,16] are not momentum-based learning, our method does not aim at improving them. Besides, our proposed Divide-Encode-Combine scheme is not investigated in them.

Momentum-based contrastive learning methods adopt an asymmetric forward path. On the online path, an input image is fed into the encoder. On the target path, another input image is fed into a slowly moving momentum encoder [7,9,18]. The two encoded samples from these two paths form a pair for contrastive learning, which has been proven to be effective in many scenarios [4,13,15]. However, these works adopt the *two-image-one-pair* mechanism. In contrast, our Fast-MoCo adopts a *two-image-multi-pair* mechanism. At almost the same training cost of the *two-image-one-pair* mechanism, Fast-MoCo generates more sample pairs in a mini-batch for efficiency.

3 Method

In this Section, we first give preliminaries about MoCo, which is adopted as our baseline. Then, we introduce the design of combinatorial patches, which boost both the learning process and performance. Finally, we discuss how the proposed approach will affect the performance and computation.

3.1 Preliminaries About MoCo

MoCo is a highly recognized framework for self-supervised learning, which has three versions, i.e., MoCo [18], MoCo v2 [7], and MoCo v3 [9], which gradually incorporate some of the best practice in the area. Specifically, MoCo v3 pipeline has two branches, i.e., an online branch and a target branch. The online branch consists of an encoder f (e.g., ResNet50), a projector g, follow by a predictor q. The target branch only contains the encoder and projector with the same structure as in the online branch and its parameters are updated through an exponential moving average process as follows:

$$\theta_t^f \leftarrow \alpha\theta_t^f + (1-\alpha)\theta_o^f, \quad \theta_t^g \leftarrow \alpha\theta_t^g + (1-\alpha)\theta_o^g, \tag{1}$$

where θ_o^f and θ_o^g are parameters for encoder and projector in the online branch, θ_t^f and θ_t^g are parameters for encoder and projector in the target branch. This asymmetric architecture design and the use of moving average for target branch parameters updating have been shown to help the model avoid collapse [15].

Given an image x, two different views are generated through two different augmentations a and a', which are then forward to the encoders in the online and target branches respectively to retrieve the encoded embeddings as a positive pair $(v_o^a, v_t^{a'})$. These embeddings are then projected to vectors $z_o^a = q(g(v_o^a; \theta_o^g); \theta_o^q)$ and $z_t^{a'} = g(v_t^{a'}; \theta_t^g)$. Finally, the loss function for this pair $(z_o^a, z_t^{a'})$ is formulated by InfoNCE [26] as follows:

$$\mathcal{L}_{ctr}(z_o^a, \mathbf{z}_t^{a'}) = -log\frac{exp(z_o^a \cdot z_t^{a'}/\tau)}{\sum_{z \in \mathbf{z}_t^{a'}} exp(z_o^a \cdot z/\tau)}, \tag{2}$$

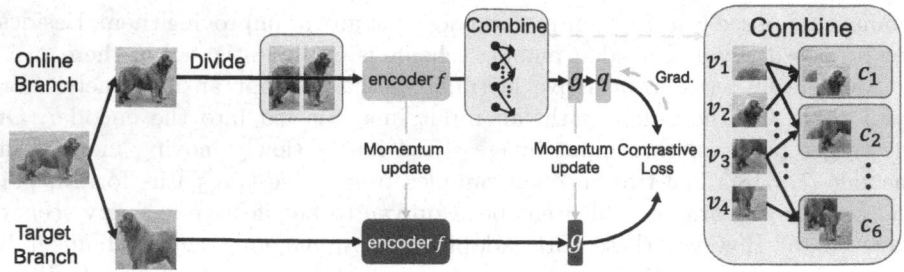

Fig. 2. Overview of Fast-MoCo framework. It consists of four steps: 1) *Divide* step, where the input image in the online branch is divided into multiple patches; 2) *Encode* step, which the encoder f encodes the features of the patches separately; 3) *Combine* step, which combines the encoded features (at the last layer of the neural network); 4) the combined features are fed into projector g, predictor q, and contrastive loss for contrastive learning. Compared with MoCo, we add the Divide step and Combine Step in the online branch, with details in Sect. 3.2. The target branch is the same as MoCo.

where $\mathbf{z}_t^{a'}$ denotes the set of target representations for all images in the batch. Note that vectors z, z_o^a, and $z_t^{a'}$ are l_2 normalized before computing the loss. Besides, for every sample image x, this loss is symmetrized as:

$$\mathcal{L}_x = \frac{1}{2}(\mathcal{L}_{ctr}(z_o^a, \mathbf{z}_t^{a'}) + \mathcal{L}_{ctr}(z_o^{a'}, \mathbf{z}_t^a)). \tag{3}$$

3.2 Fast-MoCo

In this section, we introduce Fast-MoCo, a simple method that can greatly improve the training efficiency of self-supervised learning with negligible extra cost. An overview of Fast-MoCo is shown in Fig. 2. With MoCo v3 as the baseline, Fast-MoCo only makes three modifications, 1) add a *Divide* step to divide an image into multiple patches before sending the patches to the encoder[1] of the online branch, 2) insert a *Combine* step (e.g., Combine) immediately behind the encoder to combine patches, and 3) a slightly modified definition of positive and negative pairs corresponding to the divide and combine operations. In the following, we illustrate the Divide step, Combine step, and the modified loss function in detail.

Divide Step. For the online branch, instead of directly feed the given the augmented image x^a into the encoder, we first divide it into a $m \times m$ grid of patches $\{x_p | p \in \{1, \ldots, m^2\}\}$ as shown in Fig. 2, with $\mathbf{p}$ denotes the set of patch index $\{p\}$. The influence of m in will be analyzed in Sect. 5.4.

---

[1] In this paper, we only explore the ResNet50 as the encoder while leaving the evaluation of ViT version MoCo v3 as our future work.

Combine Step. Instead of directly using the encoded embedding of each patch individually for further step, we combine multiple (less than m^2) patch embeddings v_p to form combined embeddings c before sending them to further step, i.e., the projector.

To form a combined embedding, we take a subset of n indices from the patch index set $\mathbf{p}$, noted as $\mathbf{p}_n (\subseteq \mathbf{p})$, and collect their corresponding features $\mathbf{v_{p_n}} = \{v_p | p \in \mathbf{p}_n\}$. While there could be diverse options to combine multiple embeddings (e.g., concatenate, sum), we empirically found that simply averaging the selected features works reasonably well and is computationally efficient. Thus, in the Combine step, we generate the combined embedding by:

$$c = \frac{1}{n} \sum_{p \in \mathbf{p}_n} v_p. \tag{4}$$

To improve the sample utilization efficiency, we take all possible n-combinations of patch embeddings for supervisions, leading to the combined embedding set $\mathbf{c} = \{c_i | i \in \{1, \ldots, C_{m^2}^n\}\}$, where $C_m^n = \frac{m!}{n!(m-n)!}$. In this way, we can generate many samples by the averaging operation in Eq. 4 with negligible extra cost and ensure the sample and the target have a sufficient information gap since the combined patch embeddings only covers part of the image information.

After the Combine step, the projector and the predictor in the online branch transfer each combined embedding c to vector z_o^c in a sequential manner. On the other hand, the target branch maps the other input view to $z_t^{a'}$ in the same manner as the basic MoCo v3 without modification. They are then L2-normalized and used for computing contrastive loss.

Loss Functions. Like MoCo v3, we still utilize the contrastive loss (Eq. 2) to optimize the encoder, projector, and predictor. Compared with MoCo v3, Fast-MoCo does not include any extra parameters to be learned, the only difference is that there are multiple ($C_{m^2}^n$) combined patch embeddings z_o^c instead of one image embedding z_o^a corresponding to a target branch image embedding $z_t^{a'}$. We directly adapt the original loss function by averaging the contrastive losses from $C_{m^2}^n$ positive pairs between the combined patch embeddings z_o^c and target image embedding z_t. Similarly, the negative pairs are defined between the combined patch embedding and the embedding of other images in the target branch.

3.3   Discussion

In this section, we present some intuitive analysis about why Fast-MoCo can improve training efficiency, which will be further demonstrated with empirical results in Sect. 4. The primary component that makes Fast-MoCo converge faster is the utilization of a set of combined patch embeddings, which significantly increase the number of positive pairs. Take $m = 2$ and $n = 2$ as an example, Fast-MoCo will divide the input image in the online branch into four patches and then combine their four embeddings into six, each of which represents two patches, directly expanding the number of positive pairs six times more than MoCo v3.

Thus, Fast-MoCo can get more supervision signals in each iteration compared to MoCo v3 and thus achieves promising performance with fewer iterations.

At the same time, the introduced operations in Fast-MoCo, i.e., divide an image into patches and average the representation of several patches, are extremely simple and only require negligible extra computation. The major computational cost is introduced by additional forwards over the projector and the predictor in the online branch. However, they only involve the basic linear transformations, which contributes little cost when compared to the backbone. Thus, the total overhead of Fast-MoCo accounts for 7% extra training time compared to MoCo v3 (38.5 h on 16 V100 GPUs for 100 epochs, by contrast, MoCo v3 costs 36 h under the same setting)

Besides, since the combined patch embeddings only contain part of the information in the whole image, pulling the partially combined patches closer to the target view that contains the whole image information is more challenging than pulling the original image pairs and implicitly increasing the asymmetric of the network structure, which have been demonstrated beneficial for increasing the richness of feature representations and improve the self-supervised learning performance [11,15,22]. Owing to these merits, Fast-MoCo can achieve high sample utilization efficiency with marginal extra computational cost and thus obtain promising performance with much less training time. Experimental results in Sect. 5.2 and 5.4 below will validate these analysis.

4   Experimental Results

4.1   Implementation Details

The backbone encoder f is a ResNet-50 [20] network excluding the classification layer. Following SimSiam [8] and MoCo v3 [9], projector g and predictor h are implemented as MLP, with the detailed configuration identical to [8]. For self-supervised pretraining, we use SGD optimizer with batch size 512, momentum 0.9, and weight decay $1e^{-4}$. The learning rate has a cosine decay schedule from 0.1 to 0 with one warm-up epoch starting from 0.025. We use the same augmentation configurations as in SimSiam [8] (see supplementary material).

4.2   Results

ImageNet Linear Evaluation. Following [6,8,15], we evaluate our method with a linear classifier on top of frozen embeddings obtained from self-supervised pretraining. The classifier is finetuned with LARS optimizer [31] with configurations same as SimSiam [8] excepting the learning rate which we set as $lr = 0.8$. We compare with existing methods in Table 1, Our Fast-MoCo achieved 75.5% linear evaluation result with only 400 epochs of training, which shows obvious improvement of our Fast-Moco compared with all methods using two augmented views for supervision. When considering the same amount of training epoch, our result also surpass SwAV [3] and DINO [4] even including the use

Table 1. ImageNet-1k linear evaluation results for existing methods and our Fast-MoCo using ResNet-50. Best results are in **bold**. Fast-MoCo can achieve similar performance as MoCo v3 with only 100 epochs. When trained for 200 epochs, Fast-MoCo performances better than MoCo v3 trained for 800 epochs and is comparable with state-of-the-arts (`multi-crop` is not used in Fast-MoCo for a fair comparison).

Method	100 ep	200 ep.	400 ep.	800 ep.	1000 ep
SimCLR [6]	64.8	67.0	68.3	69.1	–
MoCo v2 [7]	-	67.5	-	71.1	–
BYOL [15]	66.5	70.6	73.2	–	74.3
SwAV [3]	–	–	70.1	–	–
BarlowTwins [32]	–	–	–	–	73.2
SimSiam [8]	68.1	70.0	70.8	71.3	–
MoCo v3 [9]	-	-	-	73.8	–
NNCLR [11]	69.4	70.7	74.2	74.9	75.4
OBoW [13]	-	73.8	–	–	–
Fast-MoCo	**73.5**	**75.1**	**75.5**	–	–
SwAV [3] (w/ `multi-crop`)	72.1	73.9	-	75.3	–
DINO [4] (w/ `multi-crop`)	–	–	–	75.3	–
NNCLR [11] (w/ `multi-crop`)	–	–	–	**75.6**	–

of `multi-crop` [3]. Note that our new design is orthogonal to `multi-crop` [3] (details in Sect. 5.3) and the novel designs in SwAV, DINO and NNCLR.

Semi-supervised Learning. Following the semi-supervised learning setting in [6], we fine-tune our model pretrained by 400 epochs with 1% and 10% of the data split. The results are shown in Table 2. Our method performs better than all compared methods w/o `multi-crop` and is on par with SwAV using `multi-crop`.

Transfer Learning. Table 3 shows experimental results evaluating the effectiveness of the learned model when transferred to detection and segmentation tasks. For object detection on PASCAL-VOC [12], with Faster R-CNN [28] framework, we have all weights finetuned on the `trainval07+12` dataset and evaluated on the `test07` dataset. For detection and instance segmentation on COCO [23], we finetune our weights with Mask R-CNN [19] on the `train` set and report results on the `val` split. The results in Table 3 show that our Fast-MoCo performs on par with or better than the state-of-the-arts in localization tasks.

5   Analysis

5.1   Same or Different Augmented Views

Recent works [6,15] have indicated that contrastive methods are sensitive to augmentations, especially spatial transformations [6]. Compared with the con-

Table 2. Semi-supervised learning results on ImageNet-1K with ResNet-50 backbone. We report Top-1 and Top-5 accuracies for models finetuned with 1% and 10% labeled data. Detailed configuration can be found in supplementary material.

Method	1%		10%	
	Top-1	Top-5	Top-1	Top-5
Supervised	25.4	48.4	56.4	80.4
InstDisc [30]	–	39.2	–	77.4
PIRL [24]	–	57.2	–	83.8
SimCLR [6]	48.3	75.5	65.6	87.8
BYOL [15]	53.2	78.4	68.8	89.0
Barlow Twins [32]	55.0	79.2	69.7	89.3
NNCLR [11]	56.4	80.7	69.8	89.3
Fast-MoCo	**56.5**	**81.1**	**70.3**	**89.4**
SwAV [3] (w/ multi-crop)	53.9	78.5	70.2	89.9

Table 3. VOC and COCO object detection (det) and instance segmentation (seg) results. We report results measured by Average Precision (AP) using ResNet50 with the C4 backbone variant [14]. For VOC dataset, we train on trainval07+12 and evaluate on test07 by running three trials and report the averaged results.

Method	VOC det			COCO det			COCO seg		
	AP_{all}	AP_{50}	AP_{75}	AP_{all}^{bb}	AP_{50}^{bb}	AP_{75}^{bb}	AP_{all}^{mk}	AP_{50}^{mk}	AP_{75}^{mk}
Supervised	53.5	81.3	58.8	38.2	58.2	41.2	33.3	54.7	35.2
MoCo V2 [7]	57.4	82.5	64.0	39.3	58.9	42.5	34.4	55.8	36.5
SimSiam [8]	57	82.4	63.7	39.2	**59.3**	42.1	34.4	**56.0**	36.7
Barlow Twins [32]	56.8	82.6	63.4	39.2	59.0	42.5	34.3	**56.0**	36.5
Fast-MoCo	**57.7**	**82.7**	**64.4**	**39.5**	59.2	**42.6**	**34.6**	55.9	**36.9**
SwAV [3] (w/ multi-crop)	56.1	82.6	62.7	38.4	58.6	41.3	33.8	55.2	35.9

ventional settings of having different augmented view (73.5% on ImageNet for 100-epoch training of Fast-MoCo), we observe severe drop of accuracy (48.5%) if the positive embedding pair in Eq. (5) are from the same augmented view, i.e. $a' = a$. When the same augmented view is used, the detrimental non-semantic information contained in patches would be exposed to its contrastive target, which causes the significant drop of accuracy. These results show the importance of using appropriate targets for contrastive learning.

5.2 Comparison on Patch Encoding Approaches

Apart from our proposed Fast-MoCo pipeline, there is also a number of alternatives [1,5,13,17,21,25–27] that falls into the same category with our Fast-MoCo which does not apply the *two-image-one-pair* mechanism. In this Section, we provide a detailed comparison on these variants.

Sample-Encode-Combine. The compared settings contain cases where patches can not be generated from dividing a 224×224 view. Apart from the Fast-MoCo baseline, we set up a Sample-Encode-Combine (SEC) configuration for fair comparison. In SEC configuration, we replace the 'Divide' step in Fast-MoCo by randomly and independently sampling patches. In contrast to Fast-MoCo with 2×4 patches divided from two 224×224 views, for SEC we have eight independently sampled patches :$\{x_p | p \in \{1, \ldots, 8\}\}$ and two 224×224 target $\{x_t^a, x_t^{a'}\}$. As x_p for SEC are not devided from the target views x_t. The embeddings of all eight x_p can be combined with each other to get combined embedding c, we have the amount of combination increased from $2C_4^2 = 12$ to $C_8^2 = 28$. The loss function for SEC is written as follows:

$$\mathcal{L}_x = \frac{1}{2C_8^2} \sum_{c \in \mathbf{c}} (\mathcal{L}_{ctr}(z_c, \mathbf{z}_t^a) + \mathcal{L}_{ctr}(z_c, \mathbf{z}_t^{a'})), \tag{5}$$

Table 4. (a) Comparison of patch encoding approaches. Results are based on ImageNet linear evaluation, all models are pretrained for 100 epochs. (b) Relationship with `multi-crop`. 'Comb.' denotes the usage of combinatorial patches. Results are linear evaluation on ImageNet, all models are pretrained for 100 epochs.

Method	Num. of Samples	Top-1
Encode Only	4	68.9
Sample-Combine-Encode	4	71.2
Divide-Combine-Encode	4	71.8
Montage-Encode-Divide-Combine	28	70.4
Sample-Encode-Combine	28	72.9
Fast-MoCo	12	73.5

Case	multi-crop	Comb.	Top-1
MoCo v3	–	–	70.3
(i)	✓	-	73.1
(ii)	–	✓	73.5
(iii)	✓	✓	74.2

It obtains 72.8%, which is the second-best among all variants in Table 4(a).

Encode Only. A widely adopted way to encode patches is to encode them separately [13,21,25,26], which do not include the 'Divide' step or 'Combine' step in our Fast-MoCo as depicted in Fig. 2. For a fair comparison, the patch used for encoding should contain approximately the same amount of information as two 112×112 patches combined, so we set the spatial size of the patch as 158×158. In doing so, we can no longer retrieve these patches by dividing a 224×224 that we use for contrastive target, thus they are independently generated by augmentation as described in Sect. 4.1. We generate four 158×158 patches $\{x_p\}$ and two 224×224 target $\{x_t^a, x_t^{a'}\}$, for each image x we have:

$$\mathcal{L}_x = \frac{1}{8} \sum_{z_p \in \mathbf{z}_p} (\mathcal{L}_{ctr}(z_p, \mathbf{z}_t^a) + \mathcal{L}_{ctr}(z_p, \mathbf{z}_t^{a'})), \tag{6}$$

where $\mathbf{z}_{target}$ denotes the target vectors in a mini-batch and $\mathbf{z}_p$ denotes the features of the four patches sampled from the image x. As shown in Table 4(a), the result of Encode Only is 68.9%.

Divide(Sample)-Combine-Encode. While Fast-MoCo encodes the small divided patches independently and combines them at embedding level; one can also combine them at image level with patches placed in their original positions, thus preserving the relative positional information among patches. Note that if the stitched image is not in a rectangular shape, the redundant computational cost would be hard to avoid for a CNN encoder. In the Divide step, we divide a 224×224 image vertically and horizontally to get four 112×112 patches. In the Combine step for Divide-Combine-Encode, two 112×112 patches are stitched to 112×224 or 224×112 at image level. The Divide step, Encode step, and losses are the same as Fast-MoCo. As shown by Divide-Combine-Encode in Table 4(a), compared to Encode Only with four squared 158×158 crops, these rectangular crops with less locally-bounded features is preferred with a +2.9 gain. Divide-Combine-Encode can also be viewed as bringing the Combine step of our Fast-MoCo pipeline before the encoding step. Compared with the Fast-MoCo pipeline, 1) the Fast-MoCo Divide-Combine-Encode pipeline generates fewer target-sample pairs for the same computational cost, and 2) does not include sufficiently difficult target-sample pairs (more discussion in Sect. 5.4).

For the *Sample-Combine-Encode* in Table 4(a), we generate the 112×112 rectangular patches independently, and find its +2.3 gain over Encode Only. Sample-Combine-Encode performs worse than Divide-Combine-Encode because the divided patches in Divide-Combine-Encode have no overlap, which maximizes the diversity of the combined patches, but Sample-Combine-Encode cannot guarantee non-overlapping patches.

Montage-Encode-Divide-Combine. JigClu [5] proposed a patch encoding technique with montage image. Given a batch of K images, four patches are generated from each image with different augmentations, resulting in a mini-batch of $4K$ patches. Then K montage images of size 224×224 are generated by stitching four patches randomly selected (without replacement) from the mini-batch of $4K$ patches. The encoder adds an additional step before average pooling to divide K montage feature maps back to $4K$ patch features to get their encoded embeddings. We replaced our Divide-Encode steps with this Montage-Encode-Divide approach, forming a Montage-Encode-Divide-Combine pipeline. The result of this approach in Table 4(a) shows that it is not as good as the relatively simpler Fast-MoCo approach.

Analysis. All in all, our Fast-MoCo outperform other variants with a steady margin. The Encode Only baseline achieves 68.9%. If we combine inputs before the encoding mechanism, the performance improved to 71.2% and 71.8% for inputs obtained by random cropping and dividing respectively. If we combine the embedding after encoding inputs, the performance improved to 72.9% (sample by random cropping) and 73.5% (Fast-MoCo). The Montage strategy achieves 70.4%. We find that the Sample (random cropping) always performs worse than

Divide, and combine after encoding always better than before encoding in our experiments. Based on these results, we found non-overlapping patches(Divide) and Combine after encoding to be the best practice.

5.3   Relationship with Multi-crop

Multi-crop is a technique proposed in SwAV [3]. In addition to two 224×224 crops, multi-crop additionally adds six 96×96 patches as samples so that the encoder is trained with samples that have multiple resolutions and hard samples. However, the additional samples also needs more computation. While both Fast-MoCo and mulit-crop use small patches as their input, Fast-MoCo is not trained with samples of multiple resolutions. Except the (iii) in Table 4(b), all reported results in this paper for Fast-MoCo are w/o mulit-crop. Nevertheless, as shown by (ii) in Table 4(b), Fast-MoCo w/o mulit-crop is 0.4 better than MoCo v3 w/ mulit-crop. Fast-MoCo w/ mulit-crop (see supplementary material for details), i.e. (iii) in Table 4(b), further improves the result of Fast-MoCo by 0.7, which shows that our contribution is orthogonal to mulit-crop.

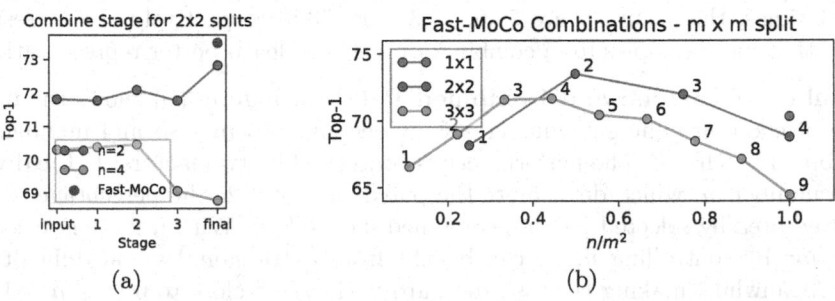

(a)   (b)

Fig. 3. (a): ImageNet linear evaluation accuracy (Y-axis) when different ResNet stages (X-axis) are selected for combining $n = 2$ divided patches or $n = 4$ divided patches in the Divide step. (b): ImageNet accuracy (Y-axis) when n/m^2 (X-axis) patches are combined for $m \times m$ (1×1, 2×2, 3×3) divided patches. Annotations represent the number of combined samples n.

5.4   Ablation on Fast-MoCo

Combine Stage and Task Difficulty. In our Fast-MoCo pipeline, a 224×224 cropped image is divided into four patches. The embeddings of these four patches are combined at the final layer of the ResNet encoder. In this Section, we investigate the influence of combining $n = 2$ patches or $n = 4$ patches. When $n = 2$, there is an information gap between sample and target because the sample only has half of its patches used for contrastive loss. When $n = 4$, all information within the original image is preserved. When combining two patches (or their feature maps) before the last stage, as it is difficult to handle non-rectangle input for CNN, we only stitch them vertically and horizontally with respect to their original position as described in Sect. 5.2. Since convolution layers are computationally heavy, we do not reuse patches/patch feature maps, so uniformly, we have two target-sample pairs per image when $n = 2$. In the case of the final layer, for a fair comparison, we adopt the same sample pair selected as in previous stages, which means two target-sample pairs per image.

In Fig. 3(a), the results show that when the Combine step took place at the embedding level, i.e., the elimination of relative positional information between patches at later stages, it is beneficial when there is an information gap between sample and target ($n = 2$). However, it will be harmful when there is no gap ($n = 4$). On the other hand, we can see the training does benefit from a harder task, i.e., presence of information gap between sample and target when $n = 2$. While for our Fast-MoCo, it will further improve the result as more samples are generated with the help of embedding level combination.

Number of Combined Samples. Given $m^2 = 4$ divided patches and $n = 2$ patches to be combined, we have $C_{m^2}^n = 6$ target-sample pairs, but is it necessary to use them all? From these 6 target-sample pairs, when we use 2, 4, and 6 target-sample pairs per image and ensure all patches are selected for combination for equal times, the accuracy are 72.6, 73.3, and 73.5, respectively. These results show that more samples from combination helps to learn better representations.

Number of Divided and Combined Patches. Figure 3(b) shows the influence of choosing different numbers of divided patches $m \times m$ and numbers of combined patches n. The performance is controlled by two factors: 1) the divide base number m, which determines the patch size, and 2) the percentage of the covered area by selected patches combined, i.e., n/m^2. With a proper selection of n/m^2 by controlling n, we can benefit from extra samples and difficulty it self. Meanwhile, making the task too hard with n/m^2 close to 0 (e.g. $n = 1$ for $m^2 = 2 \times 2$), or making the actual patches too small, e.g. 3×3 are both harmful to the performance. We find choosing 2×2 split with $n = 2$ have a good trade-off for these factors, which is used for our key results. When n is close to the optimal choice, i.e. $n = 2$ for $m^2 = 2 \times 2$ or $n = 3$ for $m^2 = 3 \times 3$, the small variation of n (e.g. $n = 4$ for $m^2 = 3 \times 3$) does not lead to large variation of ImageNet top-1 accuracy, showing Fast-MoCo is relatively stable to the variation of n and m.

5.5   Combination Method

In this section we discuss different combination choices in the Combine step. We consider two alternatives: weighted average and merge by max operation.

Weighted Average. Consider the case of combining 2 patches p and p' from the 2×2 divided patches, for patch embeddings v_p and $v_{p'}$ of patches p and p' respectively, we have:

$$c = \gamma v_p + (1 - \gamma)v_{p'}, \tag{7}$$

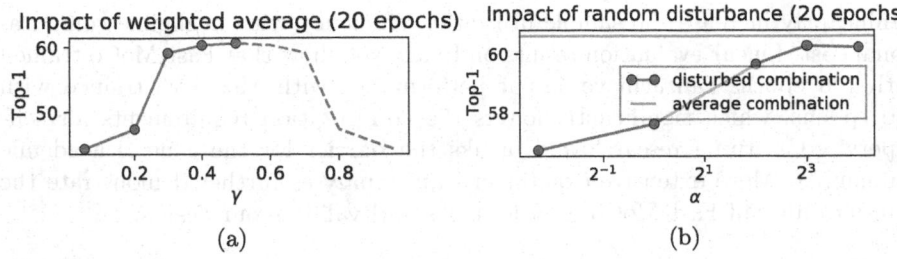

Fig. 4. (a): Random weighted average - fix value. (b): Random weighted average - Beta distribution.

where $p' \neq p$ and every patch is selected for equal times. By adjusting γ within the range of $[0.5, 1)$, we create a continuous transition between using patch embeddings separately and combinatorial patches with four combinations. The results are shown in Fig. 4(a), from which we can see the best setting is to have $\gamma = 0.5$, which assigns equal weights for both patches. Therefore, equal weight for Fast-MoCo is the default setting in other experimental results. The transition is idiosyncratic when the weight for either feature is close to zero.

Weighted Average with Weight from Random Sampling. Apart from weighted combining with fixed weights, we also investigated the case when γ is randomly sampled from beta distribution; we have $\gamma \sim Beta(\alpha, \alpha)$ with $\alpha \in \{0.2, 1, 4, 8, 16\}$. As shown in Fig. 4(b), The result gradually approaches average combination as randomness is suppressed by higher α. We conclude that the combination of patch embedding is best done with its patch members contributing equally to the combined embedding.

Max Operation. As for combination with max operation, for each feature channel i, we have:

$$c^{(i)} = \max_{v \in \{v_p, v_{p'}\}} v^{(i)}. \tag{8}$$

The 100-epoch linear evaluation result when the max operation is used at the Combine step is 64.6, which is significantly lower than the result of 73.5 for the Fast-MoCo counterpart with weighted average.

6   Conclusion

In this work, a simple yet effective self-supervised learning method, i.e., Fast-MoCo, is proposed to boost the training speed of the momentum-based contrastive learning method. By extending the MoCo v3 baseline with our proposed divide and combine steps, Fast-MoCo can construct multiple positive pairs with moderately more challenging optimization objectives for each input, which could significantly increase the sample utilization efficiency with negligible computational cost. Linear evaluation results on ImageNet show that Fast-MoCo trained with 100 epochs can achieve on-par performance with MoCo v3 trained with 800 epochs, which significantly lowers the computation requirements for self-supervised learning research and breaks the barrier for the general academic community. More extensive experiments and analyses further demonstrate the transferability of Fast-MoCo to other tasks and validate our design.

Acknowledgement. This work was supported by the Australian Research Council Grant DP200103223, Australian Medical Research Future Fund MRFAI000085, CRC-P Smart Material Recovery Facility (SMRF) – Curby Soft Plastics, and CRC-P ARIA - Bionic Visual-Spatial Prosthesis for the Blind.

References

1. Bao, H., Dong, L., Wei, F.: Beit: Bert pre-training of image transformers. arXiv preprint arXiv:2106.08254 (2021)
2. Brown, T., et al.: Language models are few-shot learners. In: Advances in neural Information Processing Systems, vol. 33, pp. 1877–1901 (2020)
3. Caron, M., Misra, I., Mairal, J., Goyal, P., Bojanowski, P., Joulin, A.: Unsupervised learning of visual features by contrasting cluster assignments. In: Advances in Neural Information Processing Systems, vol. 33, pp. 9912–9924 (2020)
4. Caron, M., et al.: Emerging properties in self-supervised vision transformers. In: Proceedings of the IEEE/CVF International Conference on Computer Vision, pp. 9650–9660 (2021)
5. Chen, P., Liu, S., Jia, J.: Jigsaw clustering for unsupervised visual representation learning. In: Proceedings of the IEEE/CVF Conference on Computer Vision and Pattern Recognition, pp. 11526–11535 (2021)
6. Chen, T., Kornblith, S., Norouzi, M., Hinton, G.: A simple framework for contrastive learning of visual representations. In: International Conference on Machine Learning, pp. 1597–1607. PMLR (2020)
7. Chen, X., Fan, H., Girshick, R., He, K.: Improved baselines with momentum contrastive learning. arXiv preprint arXiv:2003.04297 (2020)
8. Chen, X., He, K.: Exploring simple siamese representation learning. In: Proceedings of the IEEE/CVF Conference on Computer Vision and Pattern Recognition, pp. 15750–15758 (2021)
9. Chen, X., Xie, S., He, K.: An empirical study of training self-supervised vision transformers. In: Proceedings of the IEEE/CVF International Conference on Computer Vision, pp. 9640–9649 (2021)
10. Devlin, J., Chang, M.W., Lee, K., Toutanova, K.: Bert: Pre-training of deep bidirectional transformers for language understanding. arXiv preprint arXiv:1810.04805 (2018)
11. Dwibedi, D., Aytar, Y., Tompson, J., Sermanet, P., Zisserman, A.: With a little help from my friends: Nearest-neighbor contrastive learning of visual representations. In: Proceedings of the IEEE/CVF International Conference on Computer Vision, pp. 9588–9597 (2021)
12. Everingham, M., Van Gool, L., Williams, C.K., Winn, J., Zisserman, A.: The pascal visual object classes (voc) challenge. Int. J. Comput. Vision **88**(2), 303–338 (2010)

13. Gidaris, S., Bursuc, A., Puy, G., Komodakis, N., Cord, M., Perez, P.: Obow: Online bag-of-visual-words generation for self-supervised learning. In: Proceedings of the IEEE/CVF Conference on Computer Vision and Pattern Recognition, pp. 6830–6840 (2021)
14. Girshick, R., Radosavovic, I., Gkioxari, G., Dollár, P., He, K.: Detectron (2018)
15. Grill, J.B., et al.: Bootstrap your own latent-a new approach to self-supervised learning. In: Advances in Neural Information Processing Systems, vol. 33, pp. 21271–21284 (2020)
16. Hadsell, R., Chopra, S., LeCun, Y.: Dimensionality reduction by learning an invariant mapping. In: 2006 IEEE Computer Society Conference on Computer Vision and Pattern Recognition (CVPR 2006), vol. 2, pp. 1735–1742. IEEE (2006)
17. He, K., Chen, X., Xie, S., Li, Y., Dollár, P., Girshick, R.: Masked autoencoders are scalable vision learners. arXiv preprint arXiv:2111.06377 (2021)
18. He, K., Fan, H., Wu, Y., Xie, S., Girshick, R.: Momentum contrast for unsupervised visual representation learning. In: Proceedings of the IEEE/CVF Conference on Computer Vision and Pattern Recognition, pp. 9729–9738 (2020)
19. He, K., Gkioxari, G., Dollár, P., Girshick, R.: Mask r-cnn. In: Proceedings of the IEEE International Conference on Computer Vision, pp. 2961–2969 (2017)
20. He, K., Zhang, X., Ren, S., Sun, J.: Deep residual learning for image recognition. In: Proceedings of the IEEE Conference on Computer Vision and Pattern Recognition, pp. 770–778 (2016)
21. Henaff, O.: Data-efficient image recognition with contrastive predictive coding. In: International Conference on Machine Learning, pp. 4182–4192. PMLR (2020)
22. Koohpayegani, S.A., Tejankar, A., Pirsiavash, H.: Mean shift for self-supervised learning. In: Proceedings of the IEEE/CVF International Conference on Computer Vision, pp. 10326–10335 (2021)
23. Lin, T.-Y., et al.: Microsoft COCO: Common objects in context. In: Fleet, D., Pajdla, T., Schiele, B., Tuytelaars, T. (eds.) ECCV 2014. LNCS, vol. 8693, pp. 740–755. Springer, Cham (2014). https://doi.org/10.1007/978-3-319-10602-1_48
24. Misra, I., Maaten, L.v.d.: Self-supervised learning of pretext-invariant representations. In: Proceedings of the IEEE/CVF Conference on Computer Vision and Pattern Recognition, pp. 6707–6717 (2020)
25. Noroozi, M., Favaro, P.: Unsupervised learning of visual representations by solving Jigsaw Puzzles. In: Leibe, B., Matas, J., Sebe, N., Welling, M. (eds.) ECCV 2016. LNCS, vol. 9910, pp. 69–84. Springer, Cham (2016). https://doi.org/10.1007/978-3-319-46466-4_5
26. Van den Oord, A., Li, Y., Vinyals, O.: Representation learning with contrastive predictive coding. arXiv e-prints pp. arXiv-1807 (2018)
27. Pathak, D., Krahenbuhl, P., Donahue, J., Darrell, T., Efros, A.A.: Context encoders: Feature learning by inpainting. In: Proceedings of the IEEE Conference on Computer Vision and Pattern Recognition, pp. 2536–2544 (2016)
28. Ren, S., He, K., Girshick, R., Sun, J.: Faster r-cnn: Towards real-time object detection with region proposal networks. In: Advances in Neural Information Processing Systems, vol. 28 (2015)
29. Wang, Y., et al.: Revisiting the transferability of supervised pretraining: an mlp perspective. In: Proceedings of the IEEE/CVF Conference on Computer Vision and Pattern Recognition, pp. 9183–9193 (2022)
30. Wu, Z., Xiong, Y., Yu, S.X., Lin, D.: Unsupervised feature learning via non-parametric instance discrimination. In: Proceedings of the IEEE Conference on Computer Vision and Pattern Recognition, pp. 3733–3742 (2018)

31. You, Y., Gitman, I., Ginsburg, B.: Large batch training of convolutional networks. arXiv preprint arXiv:1708.03888 (2017)
32. Zbontar, J., Jing, L., Misra, I., LeCun, Y., Deny, S.: Barlow twins: Self-supervised learning via redundancy reduction. In: International Conference on Machine Learning, pp. 12310–12320. PMLR (2021)

LoRD: Local 4D Implicit Representation for High-Fidelity Dynamic Human Modeling

Boyan Jiang[1], Xinlin Ren[1], Mingsong Dou[2], Xiangyang Xue[1(✉)],
Yanwei Fu[1(✉)], and Yinda Zhang[2(✉)]

[1] Fudan University, Shanghai, China
yanweifu@fudan.edu.cn
[2] Google, California, USA

Abstract. Recent progress in 4D implicit representation focuses on globally controlling the shape and motion with low dimensional latent vectors, which is prone to missing surface details and accumulating tracking error. While many deep local representations have shown promising results for 3D shape modeling, their 4D counterpart does not exist yet. In this paper, we fill this blank by proposing a novel **Lo**cal 4D implicit **R**epresentation for **D**ynamic clothed human, named **LoRD**, which has the merits of both 4D human modeling and local representation, and enables high-fidelity reconstruction with detailed surface deformations, such as clothing wrinkles. Particularly, our key insight is to encourage the network to learn the latent codes of local part-level representation, capable of explaining the local geometry and temporal deformations. To make the inference at test-time, we first estimate the inner body skeleton motion to track local parts at each time step, and then optimize the latent codes for each part via auto-decoding based on different types of observed data. Extensive experiments demonstrate that the proposed method has strong capability for representing 4D human, and outperforms state-of-the-art methods on practical applications, including 4D reconstruction from sparse points, non-rigid depth fusion, both qualitatively and quantitatively.

1 Introduction

Dynamic 3D human modeling has been a long-standing challenge to 3D vision and graphics communities, as it is critical to various applications, such as

---

B. Jiang, X. Ren and X. Xue are with School of Computer Science, Fudan University. Yanwei Fu is with School of Data Science, Fudan University.

Supplementary Information The online version contains supplementary material available at https://doi.org/10.1007/978-3-031-19809-0_18.

VR/AR, animation and robot simulation. Traditional methods leverage well-designed parametric model [2] and physics-based simulation [20,22,60,66] to model the inner human body and deformable outer cloth separately, but they typically demand huge engineering efforts and expensive computational cost. Recently, many learning based methods have been proposed [4,11,25,32,35,36, 43,59]; unfortunately, some of these methods can not model fine-grained geometry details beyond inner body, while the others only support frame-wise reconstruction to produce dynamic sequence.

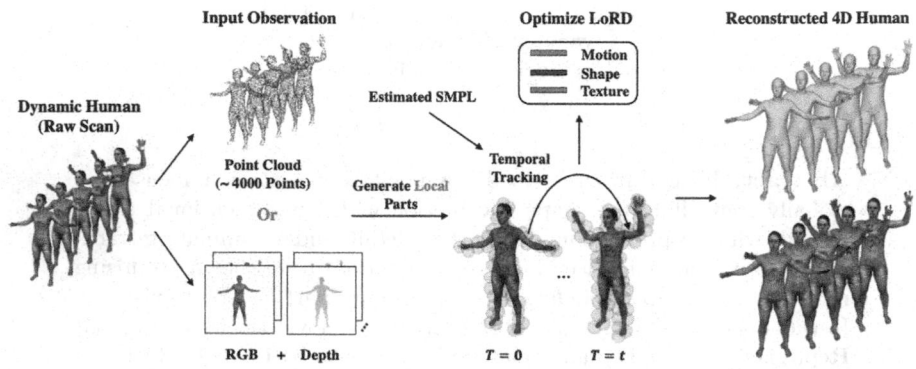

Fig. 1. LoRD represents dynamic human with a set of overlapping local parts. Each part is temporally tracked with the estimated SMPL meshes, and contains low-dimensional latent codes of motion, canonical shape and texture (optional), which can be decoded to recover the detailed temporal changing of local surface patches by a 4D implicit network. During the test-time, these latent codes are optimized based on the different types of input observations, such as sparse point clouds and monocular RGB-D video to produce high-fidelity 4D human reconstruction.

The key challenge of dynamic human modeling is to find a way to model 4D representations for both surface geometry and temporal motion. Typically, existing 4D human representation methods infer the single *holistic* latent code/vector to control global motion and shape, which unfortunately are prone to over-smoothing shapes and missing fine-grained surface details. Recent efforts are made on inferring local representations for 3D modeling [6,15,19,30,53]. Typically, these methods utilize a set of local parts to model the geometry of local surface regions for reconstructing complete 3D shapes. Such local formulation improves the model capacity in recovering the detailed geometry with a stronger generalization ability than global free-form modeling [44,48,51]. However, it is nontrivial to directly enable these local methods to support the 4D scenario of modeling a dynamic 3D human with temporal motions, as their naïve extension to do per-frame reconstruction can not maintain the desirable properties of 4D modeling, such as temporal inter-/extrapolation, 4D spatial completion.

To this end, this paper proposes a **Lo**cal 4D implicit **R**epresentation for **D**ynamic human, named **LoRD**, which combines the merits of 4D human modeling and local representation. The LoRD is capable to produce high-fidelity human mesh sequence. Given a dynamic clothed human sequence over a time span $T \in [0, 1]$, we decouple its temporal evolution into two factors: inner body skeleton motion and outer surface deformation. We handle the skeleton motion with the widely-used SMPL parametric model [40], which uses a shape parameter and a series of pose parameters to represent the temporal changing of inner body. On the other hand, for outer surface deformation, we resort to a local implicit framework. Specifically, we sample a bunch of local parts on the inner body mesh of the canonical frame $(T = 0)$, each part is represented by a 3D sphere with the intrinsic parameters (not camera intrinsics) of radius and transformation with respect to the world coordinate frame, and latent codes encoding local deformation and canonical shape information. Since SMPL models have the unified mesh topology, we can find the correspondence in subsequent frames and temporally align the local coordinate systems for each part. Then we use a 4D local implicit network to model the surface deformation within each part conditioned on their latent codes. Such representation utilizes inner body model to handle the global skeleton motion, and leaves the detailed surface dynamics to the powerful local implicit network. This facilitates the dynamic human modeling with high-quality geometry.

Technically, our local representation is learned on 100 human sequences with ground truth mesh and its corresponding inner body mesh, each sequence contains $L = 17$ frames. For each training sequence, we first sample the local parts on the surface of inner body mesh and randomly initialize the latent codes. Then we use objective function introduced by IGR [23] to optimize the local implicit network and latent codes. During the test-time, we fix the local implicit network to support a particular application (e.g., 4D reconstruction from sparse points, non-rigid depth fusion) via the auto-decoding method [51]. To obtain the inner body mesh, we use the existing work H4D [29] to provide plausible body estimation. Moreover, our representation can combine with the H4D motion model to conduct body reference optimization introduced by PaMIR [77], and support inner body refining to handle the imperfect body estimation (detailed in Sec. 3.4). This improves the robustness of LoRD against inaccurate inner body tracking.

To summarize, the main contributions of our work are: 1) We propose a novel local 4D implicit representation, which divides surface of a dynamic human into a collection of local parts and supports high-fidelity dynamic human modeling; 2) To temporally align each part for training and test-time optimization, we leverage inner SMPL body mesh for local part tracking; 3) We design an inner body refining strategy based on our local representation to optimize imperfect initial body estimation; 4) Our representation only requires a small set of data for training, and outperforms the state-of-the-art methods on practical applications, e.g. 4D reconstruction from sparse points, non-rigid depth fusion.

2   Related Work

4D Representation. Deep learning methods have shown impressive results on 3D-related tasks based on various representations, such as voxels [12,21,69], point clouds [1,18,55,56], meshes [7,24,31,37,68] and neural implicit surfaces [6,9,10,17,19,30,44,51]. While great success has achieved for static 3D object, recent works [28,48,57] attempt to investigate elegant 4D representation of modeling dynamic 3D object with an additional temporal dimension. When targeting the dynamic human, recent methods [28,48] always suffer from missing surface details and inaccurate motion due to the global shape modeling and lack of human motion prior. In contrast, the proposed local 4D representation leverages inner body tracking to handle the global skeleton motion and leaves the detailed dynamics to a set of local parts, which is effective to recover high-fidelity surface deformation, and generalize well to the novel sequences.

Local Shape Representation. The implicit representations conditioned on a global latent vector [44,51] often produce over-smooth results and have failed to recover detailed geometry such as human hands and clothing wrinkles. To tackle this problem, some recent works utilize local implicit representation for shape modeling [14,19,30,53] and neural rendering [39,52], but none of them has used it to build 4D representation that represents how 3D geometry deforms *continuously* over time. Similar to us, there is a family of work [8,67] building human avatar which supports shape generation under arbitrary body poses. However, they process different timestamps independently and do not explicitly estimate temporal correspondences, which are shown to be important for recovering geometry details from multiple input frames or applications like motion completion/prediction. In contrast, our method extends the local representation to 4D scenario by combining the human prior model and 4D implicit network, which can directly produce 4D results with one-shot optimization process.

Dynamic Human Modeling. When it comes to capturing the dynamic human, some methods [26,27,73] require a pre-scanned template as a good initialization to obtain results from monocular color information. Recent methods [46,61,74,76] utilize depth sensors to achieve real-time speed based on the classical deformation graph [62] and volumetric fusion [47], which get rid of subject-specific template. Since these methods are conducted in a frame-by-frame manner without intermediate motion representation, they are prone to error accumulation and hard to recover from tracking failures. Most recently, NDG [5] learns a globally-consistent deformation graph to facilitate non-rigid reconstruction, but requires per-sequence retraining and relies on multi-view depth sensors, which is inconvenient in the actual usage. As a popular line of works, NeRF-based [45] human modeling methods [52,54] typically do not satisfy both local and temporal modeling. Most similar to us, Zheng et al. [75] propose a structured temporal NeRF for dynamic human rendering. We note that these methods mainly focus on rendering quality but usually produce unsatisfactory geometry. In contrast, LoRD models motion and shape jointly with local representation, so that information from two domains can be exchanged through the 4D model and benefit each other, which produces high-fidelity geometry results.

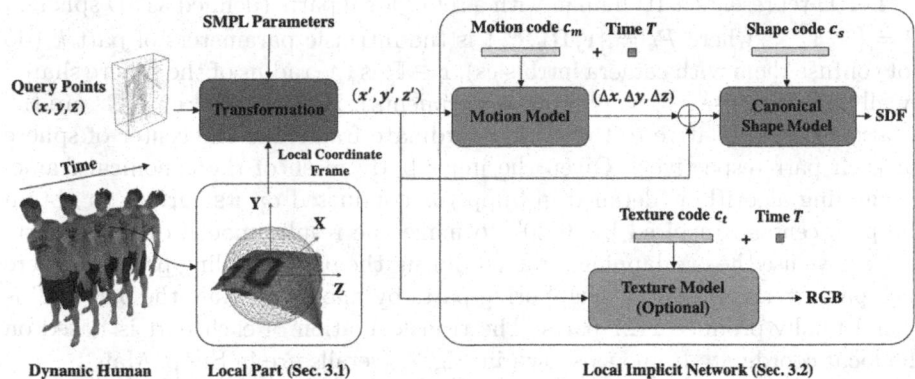

Fig. 2. Overview of our framework. We use a set of spherical parts to model the local surface deformation of dynamic human. Given a 3D point (x, y, z) under the world coordinate frame, we determine which part it falls into and transform it into the local coordinate frame, i.e. (x', y', z'), according to the estimated SMPL parameters. The transformed point is queried into a local implicit network, which is conditioned on the latent codes of local part, to obtain signed distance and RGB (optional) value. Note that our local implicit network is shared by all parts. Meshes are extracted with Marching Cubes [41].

3   Method

Our framework is overviewed in Fig. 2: given a 3D clothed human mesh sequence of length $L = 17$ frames that performs some motions in a normalized time span $[0, 1]$, we first define a set of local parts (Sect. 3.1) around inner body surface of the canonical frame ($T = 0$ in our setup). Then we temporally track these parts which are controlled by the skeleton motion of the inner body model (SMPL). Note that we use the ground truth SMPL mesh during training, whereas the SMPL parameters are estimated with the off-the-shelf method [29] at test-time. Each part contains a motion code c_m, a shape code c_s and a texture code c_t (optional), which can be decoded by our local implicit network (Sect. 3.2) to obtain the reconstructed surface. Overall, we utilize the inner body model to track global skeleton motion and leave the detailed temporal deformation, geometry and texture of the local surface patch to the local implicit network. Training and test-time optimization are discussed in Sect. 3.3 and Sect. 3.4, respectively.

3.1   Local Part Formulation

Inner body model There are many ways to track the global skeleton motion of a dynamic human, e.g. optical/scene flow [38,65], dense human correspondence

[64,71], and deformation graph [62]. In our formulation, we choose the widely-used SMPL model [40] as it naturally provides surface correspondence between frames and its low-dimensional representations are easily to be optimized.

LoRD represents a 4D human with a set of local parts (defined as 3D spheres) $\mathcal{P} = \{\mathcal{P}_k\}_{k=1}^{K}$, where $\mathcal{P}_k = \{\mathbf{r}, \mathbf{R}_k, \mathbf{c}_k\}$ is the intrinsic parameters of part k (do not confuse them with camera intrinsics); $\mathbf{r} \in \mathbb{R}$ is the radius of the sphere shared by all parts (we use $r = 5cm$ in our experiments); $\mathbf{R}_k \in \mathbb{R}^9$ and $\mathbf{c}_k \in \mathbb{R}^3$ are the rotation matrix relative to the world coordinate frame and the center of sphere for each part respectively. Given the inner body mesh of the canonical frame, a sampling algorithm (detailed in Supp.) is conducted on its surface to obtain the part centers. Inspired by [6,30], to make the result smooth over the parts border, we use the overlapping strategy during the part sampling process, where each part overlaps with its neighboring parts by maximum 1.5× the part radius $\mathbf{r}$, and finally produce 2127 parts. The transformation of each part is based on the local coordinate frame as shown in Fig. 2. Details are in Supp. Mat.

3.2   Local Implicit Network

Besides the intrinsic parameters, each local part also has the latent parameters as low-dimensional codes c_m, c_s and c_t, which encode respectively the information of the local surface deformation, canonical geometry and texture. The goal of the local parts is to represent the detailed temporal deformation and geometry of the local surface patches. To this end, we follow D-NeRF [54] and use a 4D implicit network, which consists of a motion model and a canonical shape model. Moreover, if the observed data contain texture information, the additional texture model would be triggered to predict colors for the vertices of reconstructed mesh. Note that the implicit network is shared by all local parts. Next, We briefly introduce each model and the detailed architecture can be found in Supp. Mat.

Motion Model. As shown in Fig. 2, we formulate the motion model $f^m(\mathbf{x}, T \mid c_m)$ as a 4D function conditioned by the motion code $c_m \in \mathbb{R}^{128}$, which takes a 3D point $\mathbf{x} = (x, y, z)$ in the local coordinate frame and a time value T (normalized to $[0, 1]$) as input, and predicts a deformation vector $\Delta \mathbf{x}$ that transforms this point to the canonical frame, i.e. $T = 0$, by $\mathbf{x}^* = \mathbf{x} + \Delta \mathbf{x}$. We adopt the network architecture of IM-Net [9], and reduce the feature dimension of each hidden layer by 4 fold [30] to obtain an efficient motion model.

Canonical Shape Model. The canonical shape model $f^s(\mathbf{x} \mid c_s)$ is a neural signed distance function, which only holds a static implicit geometry of the canonical frame as the temporal deformation is handled by the motion model. Specifically, given a 3D query point at time T, we first obtain its position in the space of the canonical frame with the motion model, and then use the canonical shape model that is conditioned on a canonical shape latent code $c_s \in \mathbb{R}^{128}$ to predict the signed distance of the given point towards the surface. The same network architecture as DeepSDF [51] is adopted for canonical shape model. For training and testing efficiency, we reduce the number of layers and the feature channels for each layer to 6 and 256 respectively. During inference, we compute the bounding box of human based on the inner body mesh for each frame, and utilize the Marching Cubes algorithm [41] to extract the iso-surface.

Texture Model. If the input data contains texture information, e.g. colored point clouds, our representation can be extended to support surface texture inference. We achieve this by learning a function $f^t(\mathbf{x}, T \mid c_t)$ to predict the 4D texture field [49,58,59] of the dynamic local surface conditioned on a texture code $c_t \in \mathbb{R}^{128}$. It takes a 3D point $\mathbf{x}$ in the local coordinate frame and a time value T, and outputs the RGB value of this point. We use the architecture of TextureField [49] decoder for our texture model. Please refer Supp. Mat. for the detailed network architecture. Note that we use our texture model in a per-sequence fashion during the test-time without pre-training, i.e. fit the input sequence with updating the network parameters, for better visualization results.

3.3 Training

Thank to our local formulation, the training of our model is very data efficient. We only use 100 sequences of length $L = 17$ frames from CAPE dataset [42] to learn our representation. During training, we adopt the auto-decoding method [51] and optimize our motion model, canonical shape model, and the latent codes for training parts. Specifically, given a training sequence that contains ground truth clothed meshes and the corresponding inner body meshes, we first sample a bunch of local parts on the surface of the inner body mesh of the first frame. Since the SMPL mesh has the unified surface topology, we can obtain the rotations and locations of each part in the following time steps, thus align their local coordinate frames. Next, we initialize the motion code and canonical shape code for each part with the vectors randomly sampled from $N(0, 0.01)$, these codes are optimized with the network parameters during training. To train our implicit networks, the query points are sampled from three sources, i.e. surface, near surface space and free space in the bounding box.

Loss Functions. The point sets sampled on-surface and off-surface are denoted as $\mathcal{X}$ and $\bar{\mathcal{X}}$ respectively. We optimize our 4D implicit function $f(\cdot)$ base on the loss functions introduced by IGR [23]:

$$\mathcal{L}_s = \frac{1}{|\mathcal{X}|} \sum_{x \in \mathcal{X}} f(\boldsymbol{x}) + \|\nabla_x f(\boldsymbol{x}) - \boldsymbol{n}(\boldsymbol{x})\|, \quad \mathcal{L}_e = \frac{1}{|\bar{\mathcal{X}}|} \sum_{x \in \bar{\mathcal{X}}} (\|\nabla_x f(\boldsymbol{x})\| - 1)^2$$

where $\mathcal{L}_s$ ensures the zero signed distance values for on-surface points and their normals aligned with the ground truth. $\mathcal{L}_e$ is the regularization term encouraging the learned function to satisfy the Eikonal equation [13]. In addition, we also add a latent regularization term $\mathcal{L}_c = \|c_m\|_2 + \|c_s\|_2$ to constrain the learning of latent spaces. The final objective function for training is $\mathcal{L} = \lambda_1 \mathcal{L}_s + \lambda_2 \mathcal{L}_e + \lambda_3 \mathcal{L}_c$. We use $\lambda_1 = 1.0$, $\lambda_2 = 1e^{-1}$, $\lambda_3 = 1e^{-3}$ in our experiment.

Evaluate SDF for Query Points. During the training process, the sampled points are only evaluated by the local parts that cover them. In our case, "point x is covered by part k" means the Euclidean distance between x and the center of part c_k is less than or equal to the pre-defined part radius $\mathbf{r}$, i.e. $d(\mathbf{x}, c_k) \leq \mathbf{r}$. The sampled parts are highly overlapping, thus for one query point, we randomly choose n parts that covered this point to evaluate its SDF, and then average n SDF values ($n = 4$ in our experiments) as the final output. This could encourage the network to produce the smooth results in the overlapping regions. If some points are not covered by any parts, e.g. points sampled in the free space far from surface, then it will choose n-nearest parts to obtain the SDF prediction. Note that this is important for reconstructing complete results, since we cannot ensure the local parts sampled from inner body mesh would completely cover the surface of the clothed human.

3.4 Test-Time Optimization

After learning our local representation, we can then conduct the test-time optimization to reconstruct the dynamic human based on the given observations. In our experiments, we mainly focus on recovering 4D humans from complete point clouds or partial depth sequences. Generally speaking, the test-time optimization is similar to the training process, which performs backward optimization with the auto-decoding fashion, except that we fix the network parameters and only update the latent codes for each local part. Since we leverage the loss functions from IGR [23], and directly perform optimization based on the point clouds with local-based representation, the geometry covered by each part is a non-watertight surface, which causes the extracted surface contains artificial interior back-faces. We borrow the post-processing algorithm from LIG [30] to remove such artifacts. The details about the post-processing algorithm and the choices of hyper-parameters can be found in Supp. Mat. In addition, there are some technical details that we want to clarify below.

Inner Body Estimation. Given a testing sequence, we first need to estimate inner body meshes to sample local parts. As the temporal consistency could facilitate our reconstruction, we use the recent motion based human body estimation method H4D [29] to fit the SMPL parameters via backward optimization.

Inner Body Refining. The fitting results of H4D [29] are accurate enough in most cases, but still imperfect on some sequences, which may cause the observations of some local parts vary too much over time. Inspired by PaMIR [77], we propose a strategy to refine the initial inner body fitting from H4D. Specifically, we first sample and track the local parts on the initial body mesh sequence produced by H4D, and optimize the latent codes for each part. Then we fix the latent codes and local parts, query the SMPL vertices into our local implicit network, and optimize the SMPL parameters for shape and initial pose, and latent vector for motion of H4D. We follow the body reference optimization proposed in PaMIR to build the loss functions of our refining process:

$$\mathcal{L}_{\text{SMPL}} = \begin{cases} |f(x)| & f(x) \geq 0 \\ \frac{1}{\eta}|f(x)| & f(x) < 0 \end{cases}, \quad \mathcal{L}_{reg} = \left\| V - V^{init} \right\|_2,$$

where $\eta = 5$, $f(\cdot)$ is our local implicit signed distance function; $V = (\beta, \theta_0, c_m)$ contains the shape parameter, initial pose parameter and latent motion code of H4D, and the superscript "init" means initial estimations. This reflects the fact that, if the body estimation is accurate, then the vertices of the body mesh will get the negative SDF predictions (inside surface). Moreover, we also use an additional observation loss $\mathcal{L}_{\text{obs}}$, which denotes Chamfer loss for the complete point cloud and point-to-surface loss for partial point cloud from the depth image. The final objective function is $\mathcal{L} = \lambda_1 \mathcal{L}_{\text{SMPL}} + \lambda_2 \mathcal{L}_{\text{obs}} + \lambda_3 \mathcal{L}_{reg}$, where $\lambda_1 = 1.0$, $\lambda_2 = 1e^2$ and $\lambda_3 = 1e^{-3}$ in our experiments. We verify the effectiveness of our inner body refining strategy in Sect. 4.4.

Texture Model Optimization. As mentioned in Sect. 3.2, we optimize the texture model for each testing sequence. Given a colored point cloud sequence, we can obtain the ground truth color $C_T(\mathbf{x})$ of a surface point $\mathbf{x}$ in time T. Then we query $\mathbf{x}$ into the texture model conditioned on the texture code c_t^k of part k to get the color prediction. We also use the average of n predicted colors as the final output (Sect. 3.3). To optimize the network parameters and texture codes, we add the L_1-loss $\mathcal{L}_{\text{color}} = |f^c(\mathbf{x}, T \mid c_t) - C_T(\mathbf{x})|$ into the objective function.

OFlow   4D-CR   DeepSDF   NGLoD   Ours

Fig. 3. 4D human fitting. We choose SoTA implicit 3D/4D representations to overfit a given mesh sequence and compare the results with us. The colors on our results indicate the correspondences across different frames, which cannot be obtained by the framewise baselines, i.e. NGLoD, DeepSDF. The zoomed-in part shows we reconstruct better finger details than NGLoD. (Color figure online)

4   Experiments

In this section, we evaluate the representation capability of LoRD and its value in practical applications, i.e. 4D reconstruction and non-rigid depth fusion.

Dataset and Metric. For training and evaluation, we use the CAPE [42] dataset which contains more than 600 motion sequences of 15 persons wearing different types of outfits, and the SMPL registrations are provided. Additionally, some raw scanned sequences with texture information are also available. We choose 100 sub-sequences of length $L = 17$ for training, and use the sub-sequences of novel subjects for testing. To compare with the baseline methods,

Interpolation   **Extrapolation**

Fig. 4. Temporal inter-/extrapolation. Colored meshes are inter-/extrapolated frames. (Color figure online)

we use Chamfer Distance-$L2$ [44], normal consistency [59] (the average $L2$ distance between the normal of given point on the source mesh and the normal of its nearest neighbor on the target mesh), and F-Score [68] as evaluation metrics.

Implementation Details. We use PyTorch with Adam optimizer [34] of learning rate $1e^{-3}$ and batch size 1 for both training and test-time optimization. The experiments are conducted on a single Nvidia 2080Ti GPU. The test-time optimization takes around $15min$ for each 17 frames sequence.

Table 1. Comparisons on 4D human fitting. Left: framewise methods, Right: temporal methods. "Ch.-L_2" and "Normal" mean Chamfer Distance ($\times 10^{-4}\,m^2$) and Surface Normal Consistency respectively. The threshold for computing F-Score is $\tau = 5\,mm$.

Framewise	Ch.-L_2 ↓	Normal ↓	F-Score ↑	Temporal	Ch.-L_2 ↓	Normal ↓	F-Score ↑
DeepSDF [51]	0.846	0.291	0.669	OFlow [48]	0.317	0.312	0.675
				4D-CR [28]	5.249	0.359	0.425
NGLoD [63]	**0.074**	0.135	**0.969**	Ours	0.075	**0.131**	**0.969**

4.1 Representation Capability

4D Human Fitting. We first evaluate the efficacy of LoRD in representing dynamic human by overfitting a given mesh sequence. We select one sequence from the CAPE dataset for this task. For comparison, we choose 3D neural SDF methods DeepSDF [51] and NGLoD [63], DeepSDF is a global representation which represents the complete shape with a single latent code, while NGLoD is a SoTA local neural SDF representation based on the Octree, both of them are 3D representations that need to work with frame-wise manner to produce a temporal sequence. In addition, we choose the SoTA 4D representation methods OFlow [48] and 4D-CR [28] as our baseline.

The quantitative results are shown in Table 1. Our LoRD representation clearly outperforms DeepSDF and all the SoTA 4D representation methods, and performs comparable with framewise method NGLoD. We show the visual results in Fig. 3, the colors of our results indicate the dense correspondences w.r.t the first frame. Specifically, for each vertex on the reconstructed mesh of time T, we use the optimized motion codes to transform it to the first frame, and obtain color value of the nearest vertex. We note that this cannot be achieved by DeepSDF or NGLoD, since they do not model temporal information.

Temporal Inter-/extrapolation To further show the superiority of LoRD over the framewise representations, we show the temporal inter-/extrapolation results achieved by our method in Fig. 4. Given a sequence of length $L = 17$ frames, for interpolation, we randomly choose 9 frames as the observations to perform SDF fitting, the goal is to complete the missing frames to obtain a temporally complete sequence. And for extrapolation, we only use the first 9 frames and need predict the future motion of the last 8 frames. Figure 4 shows that LoRD produces the plausible results on both inter- or extra-polation modes. Again, these temporal completion tasks also cannot be achieved by the framewise 3D representations, e.g. DeepSDF, NGLoD. We also provide the results about interpolation of the latent codes in Supp. Mat. (Sect. 2.2) as a sanity check.

4.2   4D Reconstruction from Sparse Points

We then show that LoRD can support various applications. First, we demonstrate that LoRD can achieve high quality 4D reconstruction from sparse point clouds. In this case, we assume the point normal directions are available (oriented point cloud, the same for Poisson Reconstruction [33] and LIG [30]).

Compare to Instance-Level Methods. We first compare LoRD with the instance level methods, the "instance-level" in here means we only overfit one sequence at a time and do not consider generalization to other instances. We choose the traditional Poisson Surface Reconstruction with octree depth value $d = 10$ (PSR10) [33], Alpha Shape [16] and Ball Pivoting [3] as the baseline. Moreover, we also compare with the SoTA network-based surface reconstruction method Deep Hybrid Self-Prior (DHSP), and the non-rigid reconstruction method Neural Deformation Graph (NDG). The quantitative results are show in Fig. 6 (a, I), the leftmost column represents the sampled point cloud density (number of points per square meter of surface), the smaller number corresponds to the sparser point cloud, the surface area of SMPL mesh used for point sampling is around $2 \, m^2$. As can be seen, our method outperforms all the baselines by a large margin. More importantly, the sparser point cloud hardly affects our performance while the baseline methods have been significantly affected, this is because LoRD is a 4D representation, sparse observation from each frame can compensate each other through the motion model. The qualitative comparisons are shown in Fig. 5 (above the solid line), our method can recover geometry details on the face and cloth with high resolution texture, while the baselines only produce over-smooth results due to the limited information from sparse inputs.

Compare to Generalizable Methods. To show the generalization ability of our method, we train LoRD on the training set of 100 sequences, then fix the network parameters and optimize the latent codes of local parts to fit the input point cloud via back-propagation. In this experiment, we use the point

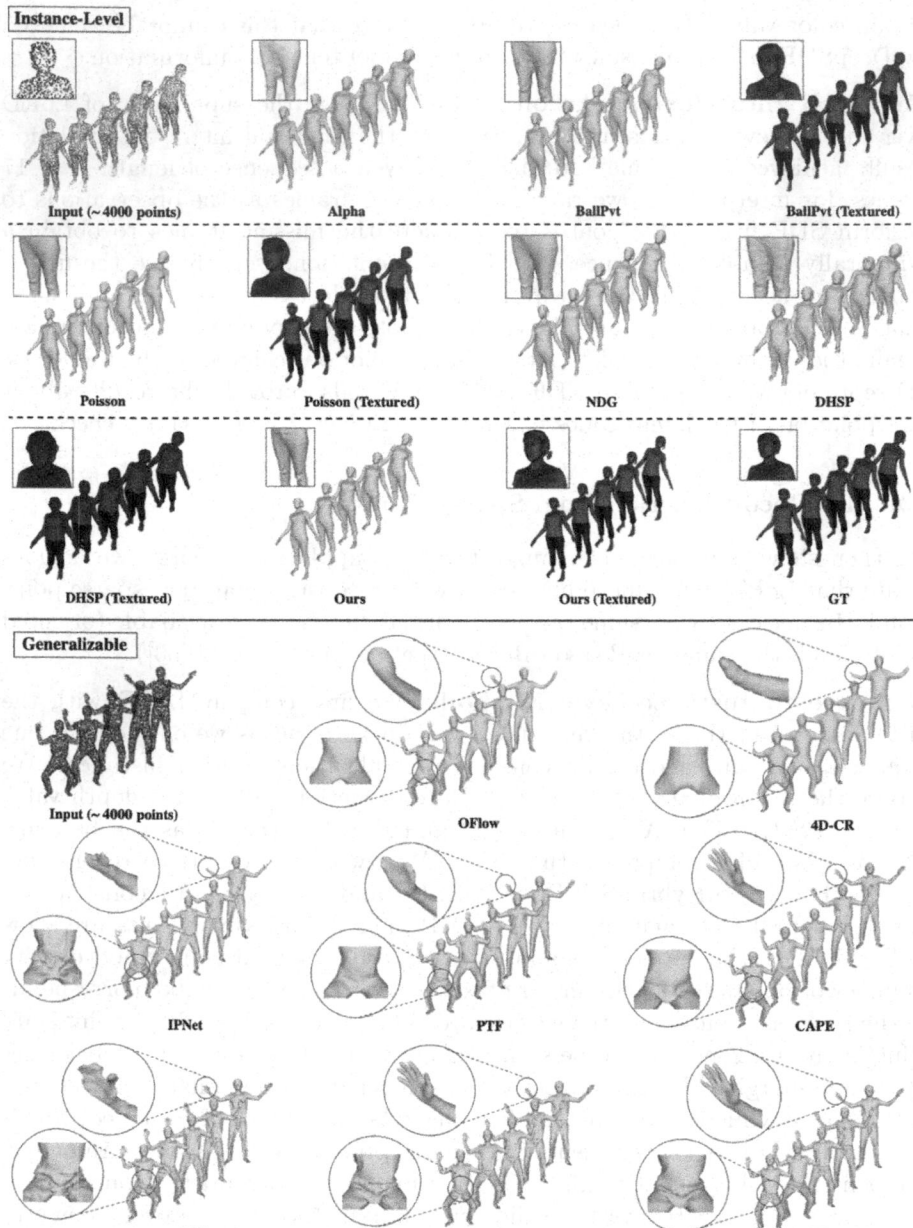

Fig. 5. 4D reconstruction from sparse points. Each input point cloud contains around 4000 points. Note the detailed geometry in the zoomed-in parts and the surface deformation recovered by our method. We provide more qualitative results in Supp. Mat.

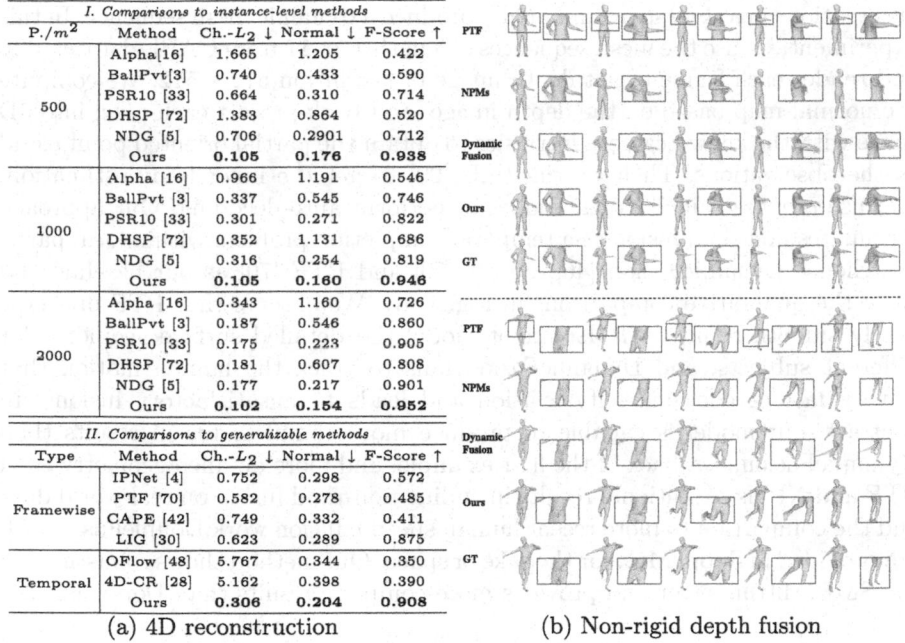

I. Comparisons to instance-level methods

P./m²	Method	Ch.-L_2 ↓	Normal ↓	F-Score ↑
500	Alpha[16]	1.665	1.205	0.422
	BallPvt[3]	0.740	0.433	0.590
	PSR10 [33]	0.664	0.310	0.714
	DHSP [72]	1.383	0.864	0.520
	NDG [5]	0.706	0.2901	0.712
	Ours	**0.105**	**0.176**	**0.938**
1000	Alpha [16]	0.966	1.191	0.546
	BallPvt [3]	0.337	0.545	0.746
	PSR10 [33]	0.301	0.271	0.822
	DHSP [72]	0.352	1.131	0.686
	NDG [5]	0.316	0.254	0.819
	Ours	**0.105**	**0.160**	**0.946**
2000	Alpha [16]	0.343	1.160	0.726
	BallPvt [3]	0.187	0.546	0.860
	PSR10 [33]	0.175	0.223	0.905
	DHSP [72]	0.181	0.607	0.808
	NDG [5]	0.177	0.217	0.901
	Ours	**0.102**	**0.154**	**0.952**

II. Comparisons to generalizable methods

Type	Method	Ch.-L_2 ↓	Normal ↓	F-Score ↑
Framewise	IPNet [4]	0.752	0.298	0.572
	PTF [70]	0.582	0.278	0.485
	CAPE [42]	0.749	0.332	0.411
	LIG [30]	0.623	0.289	0.875
Temporal	OFlow [48]	5.767	0.344	0.350
	4D-CR [28]	5.162	0.398	0.390
	Ours	**0.306**	**0.204**	**0.908**

(a) 4D reconstruction   (b) Non-rigid depth fusion

Fig. 6. (a) Comparisons on 4D reconstruction from sparse points. The leftmost column in Block I represents the sampled point cloud density, the smaller number corresponds to the sparser point cloud. The results in Block II are obtained from the point cloud of density 2000 points/m². (b) Qualitative comparisons on non-rigid depth fusion.

density of 2000 points/m² (same as the results in the last group of Fig. 6 (a, I)), and choose 10 testing sequences of novel subjects for evaluation. As framewise baselines, we choose: IPNet [4] and PTF [70], which takes point cloud as input and output reconstructed mesh via feed forward fashion; CAPE [42] and LIG [30], which obtain reconstructions via the backward optimization similar to us. The OFlow and 4D-CR are still considered as the baseline of temporal methods, we remove their encoders, fix the decoder parameters, and perform backward optimization. For OFlow and 4D-CR, we use the ground truth occupancy instead of oriented point cloud as supervision for more stable results. The results are shown in Fig. 5 (below the solid line) and Fig. 6 (a, II), our method beats all the baselines both qualitatively and quantitatively. We can observe the fine-grained geometry recovered by LoRD in the zoomed-in parts of Fig. 5, as well as detailed clothing deformation, which show that our model trained on small set of data can generalize well to the novel motion sequences. More results are in Supp. Mat.

4.3 Non-Rigid Depth Fusion

We further test LoRD with the application of non-rigid depth fusion. Given a static RGB-D camera, with a person standing in front of it performing different actions, the goal is to accurately track the human motion and merge all depth observations in a time span, and finally produce a dynamic mesh sequence. In this experiment, we use the mesh sequences of length $L = 17$ from CAPE dataset [42], and render each frame to get depth image of resolution 512×512. We compute the normal map based on the depth image, and back-project each pixel into 3D space with the known camera intrinsics to obtain the partial oriented point cloud as the observations. Then we run H4D [29] to get the inner body estimation, and use our pretrained LoRD model to perform auto-decoding. Our approach formulates non-rigid fusion as a temporal completion problem within local parts. We choose DynamicFusion [46], NPMs [50] and PTF [70] as our baseline and show the qualitative comparisons in Fig. 6 (b). We observe that PTF produces overly smooth results, NPMs cannot model the detailed surface geometry for different subjects, and DynamicFusion fails to track the human motion that is very fast or contains self-occlusion and leads to unsatisfactory fusions. In contrast, our model is capable to produce more complete fusion results than DynamicFusion, e.g. back of the first example, and more detailed geometry than PTF and NPMs. Additional results including non-rigid fusion on real-world data and the comparison to more recent human specific fusion work DoubleFusion [74] are provided in Supp. Mat. for the sake of space. Our method shows robustness to the SMPL fitting error and provides more complete results than DoubleFusion.

4.4 Ablation Study

Imperfect Body Tracking. We first provide an ablation study to demonstrate the effectiveness of the proposed inner body refining method. We use the 4D reconstruction task with the point density 2000 point/m^2 for evaluation. Given the initially estimated SMPL inner body, we manually add the random Gaussian noise to it and compare the reconstruction performances before and after refining. Specifically, we perturb the SMPL shape (β) and pose (θ) parameters by $\beta + = \lambda_\beta \cdot \sigma \cdot \mu$ and $\theta + = \lambda_\theta \cdot \sigma \cdot \mu$, where $\mu \in N(0,1)$, $\lambda_\beta = 0.05$, $\lambda_\theta = 0.01$, and $\sigma \in [3,5]$ represents the level of noise. The quantitative results are show in Table 2 (left). Without inner body refining, the reconstruction performance drops fast as the noise level up. And by using our refining method, the performance improves and in general stable on different noise levels.

Local Part Size. We then study the effect of different radii for local part. To this end, we use our pretrained model, and test on the task of 4D reconstruction

Table 2. Ablation study. Left: the effectiveness of the inner body refining on different noise levels; Right: the effect of the part radius. We choose part radius $r = 5cm$ in our experiments. The visualization examples are in Supp. Mat.

Noise σ	Refining	Ch.-L_2 ↓	Normal ↓	F-Score ↑
3	Before	1.980	0.297	0.730
	After	0.628	0.245	0.776
4	Before	5.469	0.382	0.605
	After	0.896	0.256	0.758
5	Before	6.815	0.435	0.528
	After	0.753	0.260	0.733

Radius r	Ch.-L_2 ↓	Normal ↓	F-Score ↑
3 cm	0.406	0.278	0.858
5 cm	**0.306**	**0.204**	**0.908**
8 cm	0.346	0.205	0.905
10 cm	0.373	0.210	0.896

as previous. The comparisons are shown in Table 2 (right). As can be seen, the reconstruction performance is affected by the choice of part radius r. We choose $r = 5cm$ in our experiment for slightly better results. We find that the over-small part is inclined to produce artifacts, possibly due to the limited receptive field within part. And the larger part could lead to overly smooth results.

5 Conclusion

This work introduces LoRD, a local 4D implicit representation for dynamic human, which aims to optimize a part-level temporal network for modeling detailed human surface deformation, e.g. clothing wrinkles. LoRD is learned on a very small set of training data (less than 100 sequences). Once trained, it can be used to fit different types of observed data including sparse point clouds, monocular depth images via auto-decoding. LoRD is capable to reconstruct high-fidelity 4D human and outperforms the state-of-the-art methods.

Acknowledgement. This work was supported by Shanghai Municipal Science and Technology Major Projects (No.2018SHZDZX01, and 2021SHZDZX0103).

References

1. Achlioptas, P., Diamanti, O., Mitliagkas, I., Guibas, L.: Representation learning and adversarial generation of 3d point clouds. arXiv preprint arXiv:1707.02392 2(3), 4 (2017)
2. Anguelov, D., Srinivasan, P., Koller, D., Thrun, S., Rodgers, J., Davis, J.: Scape: shape completion and animation of people. In: ACM SIGGRAPH 2005 Papers, pp. 408–416 (2005)
3. Bernardini, F., Mittleman, J., Rushmeier, H., Silva, C., Taubin, G.: The ball-pivoting algorithm for surface reconstruction. IEEE Trans. Visual Comput. Graphics 5(4), 349–359 (1999)
4. Bhatnagar, B.L., Sminchisescu, C., Theobalt, C., Pons-Moll, G.: Combining implicit function learning and parametric models for 3D human reconstruction. In: Vedaldi, A., Bischof, H., Brox, T., Frahm, J.-M. (eds.) ECCV 2020. LNCS, vol. 12347, pp. 311–329. Springer, Cham (2020). https://doi.org/10.1007/978-3-030-58536-5_19
5. Bozic, A., Palafox, P., Zollhofer, M., Thies, J., Dai, A., Nießner, M.: Neural deformation graphs for globally-consistent non-rigid reconstruction. In: Proceedings of the IEEE/CVF Conference on Computer Vision and Pattern Recognition, pp. 1450–1459 (2021)
6. Chabra, R., et al.: Deep local shapes: learning local SDF priors for detailed 3D reconstruction. In: Vedaldi, A., Bischof, H., Brox, T., Frahm, J.-M. (eds.) ECCV 2020. LNCS, vol. 12374, pp. 608–625. Springer, Cham (2020). https://doi.org/10.1007/978-3-030-58526-6_36
7. ChaoWen, Zhang, Y., Li, Z., Fu, Y.: Pixel2mesh++: Multi-view 3d mesh generation via deformation. In: ICCV (2019)
8. Chen, X., et al.: gdna: Towards generative detailed neural avatars. In: Proceedings of the IEEE/CVF Conference on Computer Vision and Pattern Recognition, pp. 20427–20437 (2022)

9. Chen, Z., Zhang, H.: Learning implicit fields for generative shape modeling. In: CVPR, pp. 5939–5948 (2019)
10. Chibane, J., Alldieck, T., Pons-Moll, G.: Implicit functions in feature space for 3d shape reconstruction and completion. In: Proceedings of the IEEE/CVF Conference on Computer Vision and Pattern Recognition, pp. 6970–6981 (2020)
11. Choi, H., Moon, G., Lee, K.M.: Beyond static features for temporally consistent 3d human pose and shape from a video. In: Conference on Computer Vision and Pattern Recognition (CVPR) (2021)
12. Choy, C.B., Xu, D., Gwak, J.Y., Chen, K., Savarese, S.: 3D-R2N2: A unified approach for single and multi-view 3d object reconstruction. In: Leibe, B., Matas, J., Sebe, N., Welling, M. (eds.) ECCV 2016. LNCS, vol. 9912, pp. 628–644. Springer, Cham (2016). https://doi.org/10.1007/978-3-319-46484-8_38
13. Crandall, M.G., Lions, P.L.: Viscosity solutions of hamilton-jacobi equations. Trans. Am. Math. Soc. **277**(1), 1–42 (1983)
14. Deng, B., Genova, K., Yazdani, S., Bouaziz, S., Hinton, G., Tagliasacchi, A.: Cvxnet: Learnable convex decomposition. In: Proceedings of the IEEE/CVF Conference on Computer Vision and Pattern Recognition, pp. 31–44 (2020)
15. Deng, B., et al.: NASA neural articulated shape approximation. In: Vedaldi, A., Bischof, H., Brox, T., Frahm, J.-M. (eds.) ECCV 2020. LNCS, vol. 12352, pp. 612–628. Springer, Cham (2020). https://doi.org/10.1007/978-3-030-58571-6_36
16. Edelsbrunner, H., Mücke, E.P.: Three-dimensional alpha shapes. ACM Trans. Graph. (TOG) **13**(1), 43–72 (1994)
17. Erler, P., Guerrero, P., Ohrhallinger, S., Mitra, N.J., Wimmer, M.: POINTS2SURF learning implicit surfaces from point clouds. In: Vedaldi, A., Bischof, H., Brox, T., Frahm, J.-M. (eds.) ECCV 2020. LNCS, vol. 12350, pp. 108–124. Springer, Cham (2020). https://doi.org/10.1007/978-3-030-58558-7_7
18. Fan, H., Su, H., Guibas, L.J.: A point set generation network for 3d object reconstruction from a single image. In: Proceedings of the IEEE Conference on Computer Vision and Pattern Recognition, pp. 605–613 (2017)
19. Genova, K., Cole, F., Sud, A., Sarna, A., Funkhouser, T.: Local deep implicit functions for 3d shape. In: Proceedings of the IEEE/CVF Conference on Computer Vision and Pattern Recognition, pp. 4857–4866 (2020)
20. Gillette, R., Peters, C., Vining, N., Edwards, E., Sheffer, A.: Real-time dynamic wrinkling of coarse animated cloth. In: Proceedings of the 14th ACM SIGGRAPH/Eurographics Symposium on Computer Animation, pp. 17–26 (2015)
21. Girdhar, R., Fouhey, D.F., Rodriguez, M., Gupta, A.: Learning a predictable and generative vector representation for objects. In: Leibe, B., Matas, J., Sebe, N., Welling, M. (eds.) ECCV 2016. LNCS, vol. 9910, pp. 484–499. Springer, Cham (2016). https://doi.org/10.1007/978-3-319-46466-4_29
22. Goldenthal, R., Harmon, D., Fattal, R., Bercovier, M., Grinspun, E.: Efficient simulation of inextensible cloth. In: ACM SIGGRAPH 2007 papers, pp. 49-es (2007)
23. Gropp, A., Yariv, L., Haim, N., Atzmon, M., Lipman, Y.: Implicit geometric regularization for learning shapes. arXiv preprint arXiv:2002.10099 (2020)
24. Groueix, T., Fisher, M., Kim, V.G., Russell, B.C., Aubry, M.: Atlasnet: A papier-mâché approach to learning 3d surface generation. arXiv preprint arXiv:1802.05384 (2018)
25. Guler, R.A., Kokkinos, I.: Holopose: Holistic 3d human reconstruction in-the-wild. In: Proceedings of the IEEE/CVF Conference on Computer Vision and Pattern Recognition, pp. 10884–10894 (2019)

26. Habermann, M., Xu, W., Zollhoefer, M., Pons-Moll, G., Theobalt, C.: Livecap: Real-time human performance capture from monocular video. ACM Trans. Graph. (TOG) **38**(2), 1–17 (2019)
27. Habermann, M., Xu, W., Zollhofer, M., Pons-Moll, G., Theobalt, C.: Deepcap: Monocular human performance capture using weak supervision. In: Proceedings of the IEEE/CVF Conference on Computer Vision and Pattern Recognition, pp. 5052–5063 (2020)
28. Jiang, B., Zhang, Y., Wei, X., Xue, X., Fu, Y.: Learning compositional representation for 4d captures with neural ode. In: Proceedings of the IEEE/CVF Conference on Computer Vision and Pattern Recognition, pp. 5340–5350 (2021)
29. Jiang, B., Zhang, Y., Wei, X., Xue, X., Fu, Y.: H4d: Human 4d modeling by learning neural compositional representation. In: Proceedings of the IEEE/CVF Conference on Computer Vision and Pattern Recognition, pp. 19355–19365 (2022)
30. Jiang, C., Sud, A., Makadia, A., Huang, J., Nießner, M., Funkhouser, T.: Local implicit grid representations for 3d scenes. In: Proceedings of the IEEE/CVF Conference on Computer Vision and Pattern Recognition, pp. 6001–6010 (2020)
31. Kanazawa, A., Tulsiani, S., Efros, A.A., Malik, J.: Learning category-specific mesh reconstruction from image collections. In: Ferrari, V., Hebert, M., Sminchisescu, C., Weiss, Y. (eds.) ECCV 2018. LNCS, vol. 11219, pp. 386–402. Springer, Cham (2018). https://doi.org/10.1007/978-3-030-01267-0_23
32. Kanazawa, A., Zhang, J.Y., Felsen, P., Malik, J.: Learning 3d human dynamics from video. In: Proceedings of the IEEE Conference on Computer Vision and Pattern Recognition, pp. 5614–5623 (2019)
33. Kazhdan, M., Hoppe, H.: Screened poisson surface reconstruction. ACM Trans. Graph. (ToG) **32**(3), 1–13 (2013)
34. Kingma, D.P., Ba, J.: Adam: A method for stochastic optimization. arXiv preprint arXiv:1412.6980 (2014)
35. Kocabas, M., Athanasiou, N., Black, M.J.: Vibe: Video inference for human body pose and shape estimation. In: Proceedings of the IEEE/CVF Conference on Computer Vision and Pattern Recognition, pp. 5253–5263 (2020)
36. Lassner, C., Romero, J., Kiefel, M., Bogo, F., Black, M.J., Gehler, P.V.: Unite the people: Closing the loop between 3d and 2d human representations. In: Proceedings of the IEEE Conference on Computer Vision and Pattern Recognition, pp. 6050–6059 (2017)
37. Liao, Y., Donne, S., Geiger, A.: Deep marching cubes: Learning explicit surface representations. In: Proceedings of the IEEE Conference on Computer Vision and Pattern Recognition, pp. 2916–2925 (2018)
38. Liu, X., Qi, C.R., Guibas, L.J.: Flownet3d: Learning scene flow in 3d point clouds. In: Proceedings of the IEEE/CVF Conference on Computer Vision and Pattern Recognition, pp. 529–537 (2019)
39. Lombardi, S., Simon, T., Schwartz, G., Zollhoefer, M., Sheikh, Y., Saragih, J.: Mixture of volumetric primitives for efficient neural rendering. ACM Trans. Graph. (TOG) **40**(4), 1–13 (2021)
40. Loper, M., Mahmood, N., Romero, J., Pons-Moll, G., Black, M.J.: Smpl: A skinned multi-person linear model. ACM Trans. Graph. (TOG) **34**(6), 1–16 (2015)
41. Lorensen, W.E., Cline, H.E.: Marching cubes: A high resolution 3d surface construction algorithm. ACM Siggraph Comput. Graph. **21**(4), 163–169 (1987)
42. Ma, Q., et al.: Learning to Dress 3D People in Generative Clothing. In: Computer Vision and Pattern Recognition (CVPR) (2020)
43. Mehta, D., et al.: Single-shot multi-person 3d pose estimation from monocular rgb. In: 2018 International Conference on 3D Vision (3DV), pp. 120–130. IEEE (2018)

44. Mescheder, L., Oechsle, M., Niemeyer, M., Nowozin, S., Geiger, A.: Occupancy networks: Learning 3d reconstruction in function space. In: Proceedings of the IEEE Conference on Computer Vision and Pattern Recognition, pp. 4460–4470 (2019)

45. Mildenhall, B., Srinivasan, P.P., Tancik, M., Barron, J.T., Ramamoorthi, R., Ng, R.: NeRF: Representing scenes as neural radiance fields for view synthesis. In: Vedaldi, A., Bischof, H., Brox, T., Frahm, J.-M. (eds.) ECCV 2020. LNCS, vol. 12346, pp. 405–421. Springer, Cham (2020). https://doi.org/10.1007/978-3-030-58452-8_24

46. Newcombe, R.A., Fox, D., Seitz, S.M.: Dynamicfusion: Reconstruction and tracking of non-rigid scenes in real-time. In: Proceedings of the IEEE Conference on Computer Vision and Pattern Recognition, pp. 343–352 (2015)

47. Newcombe, R.A., et al.: Kinectfusion: Real-time dense surface mapping and tracking. In: 2011 10th IEEE International Symposium on Mixed and Augmented Reality, pp. 127–136. IEEE (2011)

48. Niemeyer, M., Mescheder, L., Oechsle, M., Geiger, A.: Occupancy flow: 4d reconstruction by learning particle dynamics. In: Proceedings of the IEEE International Conference on Computer Vision, pp. 5379–5389 (2019)

49. Oechsle, M., Mescheder, L., Niemeyer, M., Strauss, T., Geiger, A.: Texture fields: Learning texture representations in function space. In: Proceedings of the IEEE International Conference on Computer Vision, pp. 4531–4540 (2019)

50. Palafox, P., Božič, A., Thies, J., Nießner, M., Dai, A.: Npms: Neural parametric models for 3d deformable shapes. In: Proceedings of the IEEE/CVF International Conference on Computer Vision, pp. 12695–12705 (2021)

51. Park, J.J., Florence, P., Straub, J., Newcombe, R., Lovegrove, S.: Deepsdf: Learning continuous signed distance functions for shape representation. In: Proceedings of the IEEE Conference on Computer Vision and Pattern Recognition, pp. 165–174 (2019)

52. Peng, S., et al.: Neural body: Implicit neural representations with structured latent codes for novel view synthesis of dynamic humans. In: Proceedings of the IEEE/CVF Conference on Computer Vision and Pattern Recognition, pp. 9054–9063 (2021)

53. Peng, S., Niemeyer, M., Mescheder, L., Pollefeys, M., Geiger, A.: Convolutional occupancy networks. In: Vedaldi, A., Bischof, H., Brox, T., Frahm, J.-M. (eds.) ECCV 2020. LNCS, vol. 12348, pp. 523–540. Springer, Cham (2020). https://doi.org/10.1007/978-3-030-58580-8_31

54. Pumarola, A., Corona, E., Pons-Moll, G., Moreno-Noguer, F.: D-nerf: Neural radiance fields for dynamic scenes. In: Proceedings of the IEEE/CVF Conference on Computer Vision and Pattern Recognition, pp. 10318–10327 (2021)

55. Qi, C.R., Liu, W., Wu, C., Su, H., Guibas, L.J.: Frustum pointnets for 3d object detection from RGB-D data. In: CVPR (2018)

56. Qi, C.R., Su, H., Mo, K., Guibas, L.J.: Pointnet: Deep learning on point sets for 3d classification and segmentation. In: CVPR (2017)

57. Rempe, D., Birdal, T., Zhao, Y., Gojcic, Z., Sridhar, S., Guibas, L.J.: Caspr: Learning canonical spatiotemporal point cloud representations. In: Advances in Neural Information Processing Systems, vol. 33 (2020)

58. Saito, S., Huang, Z., Natsume, R., Morishima, S., Kanazawa, A., Li, H.: Pifu: Pixel-aligned implicit function for high-resolution clothed human digitization. In: Proceedings of the IEEE/CVF International Conference on Computer Vision, pp. 2304–2314 (2019)

59. Saito, S., Yang, J., Ma, Q., Black, M.J.: Scanimate: Weakly supervised learning of skinned clothed avatar networks. In: Proceedings of the IEEE/CVF Conference on Computer Vision and Pattern Recognition, pp. 2886–2897 (2021)
60. Selle, A., Su, J., Irving, G., Fedkiw, R.: Robust high-resolution cloth using parallelism, history-based collisions, and accurate friction. IEEE Trans. Visual Comput. Graphics 15(2), 339–350 (2008)
61. Su, Z., Xu, L., Zheng, Z., Yu, T., Liu, Y., Fang, L.: Robustfusion: Human volumetric capture with data-driven visual cues using a rgbd camera. In: Vedaldi, A., Bischof, H., Brox, T., Frahm, J.-M. (eds.) ECCV 2020. LNCS, vol. 12349, pp. 246–264. Springer, Cham (2020). https://doi.org/10.1007/978-3-030-58548-8_15
62. Sumner, R.W., Schmid, J., Pauly, M.: Embedded deformation for shape manipulation. In: ACM Siggraph 2007 Papers, pp. 80-es (2007)
63. Takikawa, T., et al.: Neural geometric level of detail: Real-time rendering with implicit 3d shapes. In: Proceedings of the IEEE/CVF Conference on Computer Vision and Pattern Recognition, pp. 11358–11367 (2021)
64. Tan, F., et al.: Humangps: Geodesic preserving feature for dense human correspondences. In: Proceedings of the IEEE/CVF Conference on Computer Vision and Pattern Recognition, pp. 1820–1830 (2021)
65. Teed, Z., Deng, J.: RAFT: Recurrent all-pairs field transforms for optical flow. In: Vedaldi, A., Bischof, H., Brox, T., Frahm, J.-M. (eds.) ECCV 2020. LNCS, vol. 12347, pp. 402–419. Springer, Cham (2020). https://doi.org/10.1007/978-3-030-58536-5_24
66. Terzopoulos, D., Platt, J., Barr, A., Fleischer, K.: Elastically deformable models. In: Proceedings of the 14th Annual Conference on Computer Graphics and Interactive techniques, pp. 205–214 (1987)
67. Tiwari, G., Sarafianos, N., Tung, T., Pons-Moll, G.: Neural-gif: Neural generalized implicit functions for animating people in clothing. In: Proceedings of the IEEE/CVF International Conference on Computer Vision. pp. 11708–11718 (2021)
68. Wang, N., Zhang, Y., Li, Z., Fu, Y., Liu, W., Jiang, Y.-G.: Pixel2mesh: Generating 3d mesh models from single rgb images. In: Ferrari, V., Hebert, M., Sminchisescu, C., Weiss, Y. (eds.) ECCV 2018. LNCS, vol. 11215, pp. 55–71. Springer, Cham (2018). https://doi.org/10.1007/978-3-030-01252-6_4
69. Wang, P.S., Liu, Y., Guo, Y.X., Sun, C.Y., Tong, X.: O-cnn: Octree-based convolutional neural networks for 3d shape analysis. ACM Trans. Graph. (TOG) 36(4), 72 (2017)
70. Wang, S., Geiger, A., Tang, S.: Locally aware piecewise transformation fields for 3d human mesh registration. In: Proceedings of the IEEE/CVF Conference on Computer Vision and Pattern Recognition, pp. 7639–7648 (2021)
71. Wei, L., Huang, Q., Ceylan, D., Vouga, E., Li, H.: Dense human body correspondences using convolutional networks. In: Proceedings of the IEEE Conference on Computer Vision and Pattern Recognition, pp. 1544–1553 (2016)
72. Wei, X., Chen, Z., Fu, Y., Cui, Z., Zhang, Y.: Deep hybrid self-prior for full 3d mesh generation. In: Proceedings of the IEEE/CVF International Conference on Computer Vision, pp. 5805–5814 (2021)
73. Xu, W., et al.: Monoperfcap: Human performance capture from monocular video. ACM Trans. Graph. (ToG) 37(2), 1–15 (2018)
74. Yu, T., et al.: Doublefusion: Real-time capture of human performances with inner body shapes from a single depth sensor. In: Proceedings of the IEEE Conference on Computer Vision and Pattern Recognition, pp. 7287–7296 (2018)

75. Zheng, Z., Huang, H., Yu, T., Zhang, H., Guo, Y., Liu, Y.: Structured local radiance fields for human avatar modeling. In: Proceedings of the IEEE/CVF Conference on Computer Vision and Pattern Recognition, pp. 15893–15903 (2022)
76. Zheng, Z., et al.: Hybridfusion: Real-time performance capture using a single depth sensor and sparse IMUs. In: Ferrari, V., Hebert, M., Sminchisescu, C., Weiss, Y. (eds.) ECCV 2018. LNCS, vol. 11213, pp. 389–406. Springer, Cham (2018). https://doi.org/10.1007/978-3-030-01240-3_24
77. Zheng, Z., Yu, T., Liu, Y., Dai, Q.: Pamir: Parametric model-conditioned implicit representation for image-based human reconstruction. IEEE Trans. Pattern Anal. Mach. Intell. **44**, 3170–3184 (2021)

On the Versatile Uses of Partial Distance Correlation in Deep Learning

Xingjian Zhen[1]([⊠])(iD), Zihang Meng[1](iD), Rudrasis Chakraborty[2](iD),
and Vikas Singh[1](iD)

[1] University of Wisconsin-Madison, Madison, USA
{xzhen3,zmeng29}@wisc.edu, vsingh@biostat.wisc.edu
[2] Butlr, Burlingame, USA

Abstract. Comparing the functional behavior of neural network models, whether it is a single network over time or two (or more networks) during or post-training, is an essential step in understanding what they are learning (and what they are not), and for identifying strategies for regularization or efficiency improvements. Despite recent progress, e.g., comparing vision transformers to CNNs, systematic comparison of function, especially across different networks, remains difficult and is often carried out layer by layer. Approaches such as canonical correlation analysis (CCA) are applicable in principle, but have been sparingly used so far. In this paper, we revisit a (less widely known) from statistics, called distance correlation (and its partial variant), designed to evaluate correlation between feature spaces of different dimensions. We describe the steps necessary to carry out its deployment for large scale models – this opens the door to a surprising array of applications ranging from conditioning one deep model w.r.t. another, learning disentangled representations as well as optimizing diverse models that would directly be more robust to adversarial attacks. Our experiments suggest a versatile regularizer (or constraint) with many advantages, which avoids some of the common difficulties one faces in such analyses (Code is at https://github.com/zhenxingjian/Partial_Distance_Correlation.).

1 Introduction

The extent to which popular architectures in computer vision even partly mimic human vision continues to be studied (and debated) in our community. But consider the following hypothetical scenario. Let us say that a fully functional *computational* model of the visual system – perhaps a modern version of the Neocognitron [20] – was somehow provided to us. And we wished to "compare" its behavior to modern CNN models [28,33]. To do so, two options appear sensible. The first – inspired by analogies between computational vision and biological vision – would draw a correspondence between how simple/complex cells in the

---

Supplementary Information The online version contains supplementary material available at https://doi.org/10.1007/978-3-031-19809-0_19.

visual cortex process scenes and their induced receptive fields with those of activations of units/blocks in a modern deep neural network architecture [60]. While
this process is often difficult to carry out systematically, it is powerful and, in
some ways, has contributed to interest in biologically inspired deep learning,
see [67]. Updated forms of this intuition – associating different subsets of cells
(or neural network units) to different semantic/visual concepts – remains the
default approach we use in debugging and interpretation. The second option for
tackling the hypothetical setting above is to pose it in an information theoretic
setting. That is, for two models Θ_X and Θ_Y, we ask the following question:
what has Θ_X learned that Θ_Y has not? Or vice versa. The asymmetry is inten-
tional because if we consider two random variables (r.v.) X, Y, the question
simply takes the form of "conditioning", i.e., compare $\mathbb{P}(X)$ versus $\mathbb{P}(X|Y)$.
This form suffices if our interest is restricted to the *predictions* of the two models. If we instead wish to capture the model's behavior more globally – when X
and Y denote the full set of feature responses – we can use divergence measures
on high dimensional probability measures given by the two models (Θ_X and
Θ_Y) responses on the training samples. Importantly, notice that our description
assumes that, at least, the probability measures are defined on the same domain.

More General Use Cases. While the above discussion was cast as comparing
two networks, it is representative of a broad basket of tasks in deep learning. **(a)**
Consider the problem of learning fair representations [17,44,70,71] where the
model must be invariant to one (or more) sensitive attributes. We seek latent
representations, say $\Psi_{\text{pred}}(X)$ for the prediction task, which minimizes mutual
information w.r.t. the latent representation relevant for predicting the sensitive
attribute $\Psi_{\text{sens}}(X)$. Indeed, if information regarding the sensitive attribute is
partially preserved or leaks into $\Psi_{\text{pred}}(X)$, the relative entropy will be low [49].
Observe that this calculation is possible partly because the latent space specifies
the *same probability space* for the two distributions. **(b)** The setting is identical
in common approaches for learning disentangled representations, where disentanglement is measured via various information theoretic measures [1,8,21,61].
If we now segue back to comparing two different networks, but without the convenience of a common coordinate system to measure divergence, the options turn
out to be limited. **(c)** Recently, in trying to understand whether vision Transformers "see" similar to convolutional neural networks [56], one option utilized
recently was a kernel-based representation similarity, in a layer-by-layer manner. What we may actually want is a mechanism for conditioning – for example,
if one of the models is thought of a "nuisance variable", we wish to check the
residual in the other after the first has been controlled for (or marginalized out).
Importantly, this should be possible without assuming that the probability distributions live in the same space (or networks Θ_X and Θ_Y are the same).

A Direct Application of CCA? Consider two different feature spaces ($\mathcal{X}$ and
$\mathcal{Y}$), say in dimensions $\mathbb{R}^p$ and $\mathbb{R}^q$, pertaining to feature activations from two different models. Comparison of these two feature spaces *is* possible. One natural
choice is canonical correlation analysis (CCA) [5], a generalization of correlation,
specifically suited when $p \neq q$. The idea has been utilized for studying repre-

sentation similarity in deep neural network models [48], albeit in a post-training setting for reasons that will be clear shortly, as well as for identifying more efficient training regimes (i.e., can lower layers be sequentially frozen after a certain number of timesteps). CCA has also been shown to be implementable within DNN pipelines for multi-view training, called DeepCCA [4], although efficiency can be a bottleneck limiting its broader deployment. A stochastic version of CCA suitable for DNN training with mini-batches has been proposed very recently, and strong experimental evidence was presented [47], also see [25]. Given that a stochastic CCA is now available, its extensions to the partial CCA setting are not yet available. If successful, this may eventually provide a scheme, suitable for deep learning, for controlling the influence of one model (or a set of variables) on another model.

This Work. The starting point of this work is a less widely used statistical concept to measure the correlation between two different feature spaces $(\mathcal{X}, \mathcal{Y})$ of *different dimensions*, called distance correlation (and the method of dissimilarities). In shallow settings, CCA and distance correlation offers very similar functionality – for the most part, they can be used interchangeably although distance correlation would *also need* specification of distances (or dissimilarities). In other words, CCA may be easier to deploy. On the other hand, deep variants of CCA involve specialized algorithms [4,47]. Further, deep versions of partial CCA have not been reported. In contrast, as long as feature distances *can* be calculated, the differences between the shallow and the deep versions of distance correlation are minimal at best, and adjustments needed are quite minor. These advantages carry over to partial distance correlation, directly enabling conditioning one model w.r.t. another (or using such a term as a regularizer). The main **contribution** of this paper is to study distance correlation (and partial distance correlation) as a powerful measure in a broad suite of tasks in vision. We review the relevant technical steps which enable its instantiation in deep learning settings and show its broad applications ranging from learning disentangled representations to understanding the differences between what two (or more) networks are learning to training "mutually distinct" deep models (akin to earlier works on M best solutions to MAP estimation in graphical models [19,69]) or training M diverse models for foreground-background segmentation as well as other tasks [27].

1.1   Related Works

Four distinct lines of work are related to our development, which we review next.

Similarity Between Networks. Understanding the similarity between different networks is an active topic [24,38,50] also relevant in adversarial models [9,15]. Early attempts to compare neural network representations were approached via linear regression [58], whose applicability to nonlinear models is limited. As noted above, canonical correlation analysis (CCA) [3,31] is a suitable off-the-shelf method for model comparisons. To this end, singular vector

CCA (SVCCA) [55], Projection-Weighted CCA [48], DeepCCA [4], and stochastic CCA [23] are all potentially useful. Recently, [37] studied the invariance properties for a good similarity measurement and proposed the centered kernel alignment (CKA). CKA offers invariance to invertible linear transformations, orthogonal transformations, and isotropic scaling. Separately, [51,56] used CKA to study similarities between deep and wide neural networks and also between different network structures.

Information Theoretic Divergence Measures. Another body of related work pertains to approximately measuring the mutual information [12] to remove this information, mainly in the context of fair representation learning. Here, mutual information (MI) is measured between features and the sensitive attribute [49]. In [63], another information theoretic bound for learning maximally expressive representations subject to the given attributes is presented. In [10], MI between prediction and the sensitive attributes is used to train a fair classifier whereas [2] describes the use of inverse contrastive loss. Group-theoretic approaches have also been described in [11,45]. The work in [41] gives an empirical solution to remove specific visual features from the latent variables using adversarial training.

Repulsion/Diversity. If we consider the ensemble of neural networks, there are several different strategies to maintain functional diversity between ensemble members – we acknowledge these results here because they are loosely related to one of the use cases we evaluate later. SVGD [14] shows the benefits of choosing the kernel to measure the similarity between ensemble members. In [13], the authors introduce a kernelized repulsive term in the training loss, which endows deep ensembles with Bayesian convergence properties. The so-called quality diversity (QD) is interesting: [53] tries to maximize a given objective function with diversity to a set of pre-defined measure functions [22,57]. When both the objective and measure functions in QD are differentiable, [18] offers an efficient way to explore the latent space of the objective w.r.t. the measure functions.

Distance Correlation (DC). The central idea motivating our work is distance correlation described in [65]. It has been used in the analysis of nonlinear dependence in time-series [72], and feature screening in ultra high-dimensional data analysis tasks [42] and we will review it in detail shortly.

2   Review: Distance (and Partial Distance) Correlation

Given two random variables $X, Y \in \mathbb{R}$ (in the same domain), correlation (say, the Pearson correlation) helps measure their association. One can derive meaningful conclusions by statistical testing. As noted in Sect. 1, one generalization of correlation to a higher dimension is CCA, which seeks to find projection matrices such that correlation among the projected data is maximized, see [5].

Benefits of Distance Correlation. In many applications, the notion of distances or dissimilarities appears quite naturally. Motivated by the need for a scheme that can capture both linear and non-linear correlations when provided with such dissimilarity information, in [65], the authors proposed a new measure of dependence between random vectors, called **distance correlation**. The key benefits of distance correlation are:

1. The distance correlation $\mathcal{R}$ satisfies $0 \leq \mathcal{R} \leq 1$, and $\mathcal{R} = 0$ if and only if X, Y are independent.
2. $\mathcal{R}(X, Y)$ is defined for X and Y in **arbitrary dimensions**, e.g., $\mathcal{R}(X, Y)$ is well-defined when X is of dimension p while Y is of dimension q for $p \neq q$.

We focus on empirical distance correlation for n samples drawn from the unknown joint distribution, and review its calculation.

For an observed random sample $(x, y) = \{(X_i, Y_i) : i = 1, \cdots, n\}$ from the joint distribution of random vectors X in $\mathbb{R}^p$ and Y in $\mathbb{R}^q$, define:

$$a_{k,l} = \|X_k - X_l\|, \quad \bar{a}_{k,.} = \frac{1}{n} \sum_{l=1}^{n} a_{k,l}, \quad \bar{a}_{.,l} = \frac{1}{n} a_{k,l},$$

$$\bar{a}_{.,.} = \frac{1}{n^2} \sum_{k,l=1}^{n} a_{k,l}, \quad A_{k,l} = a_{k,l} - \bar{a}_{k,.} - \bar{a}_{.,l} + \bar{a}_{.,.} \tag{1}$$

where $k, l \in \{1, \cdots, n\}$. Similarly, we can define $b_{k,l} = \|Y_k - Y_l\|$, and $B_{k,l} = b_{k,l} - \bar{b}_{k,.} - \bar{b}_{.,l} + \bar{b}_{.,.}$, and based on these quantities we have.

Definition 1. *(Distance correlation) [65]. The empirical distance correlation $\mathcal{R}_n(x, y)$ is the square root of*

$$\mathcal{R}_n^2(x, y) = \begin{cases} \frac{\mathcal{V}_n^2(x,y)}{\sqrt{\mathcal{V}_n^2(x,x)\mathcal{V}_n^2(y,y)}} & , \mathcal{V}_n^2(x,x)\mathcal{V}_n^2(y,y) > 0 \\ 0 & , \mathcal{V}_n^2(x,x)\mathcal{V}_n^2(y,y) = 0 \end{cases} \tag{2}$$

where the empirical distance covariance (variance) $\mathcal{V}_n(x, y), \mathcal{V}_n(x, x)$ are defined as $\mathcal{V}_n^2(x, y) = \frac{1}{n^2} \sum_{k,l=1}^{n} A_{k,l} B_{k,l}, \mathcal{V}_n^2(x, x) = \frac{1}{n^2} \sum_{k,l=1}^{n} A_{k,l}^2$, with A in (1).

Examples. We show a few simple 2D examples to contrast Pearson Correlation and Distance Correlation in Fig. 1. Notice that if the relationship between the two random variables is not linear, Pearson Correlation might be small while Distance Correlation remains meaningful.

Extensions to Conditioning. Given three random variables X, Y, and Z, we want to measure the correlation between X and Y but "controlling for" Z (thinking of it as a nuisance variable), i.e., we want to estimate $\mathcal{R}(X|Z, Y|Z) = \mathcal{R}^*(X, Y; Z)$. Such a quantity is key in existing approaches in disentangled learning, deriving invariant representations and understanding what one or more networks are learning after concepts learned by another network have been accounted for. Consider how this task would be accomplished in linear regression. We would project X and Y into the space of Z, and only use the residuals to measure the correlation. Nonetheless, defining partial distance correlation is more involved – in [64], the authors introduced a new Hilbert space where we can define the projection of distance matrix. To do so, the authors calculate a $\mathcal{U}$-centered matrix $\tilde{A}$ from the distance matrix $(a_{k,l})$ so that the inner product of the $\mathcal{U}$-centered matrices will be the distance covariance.

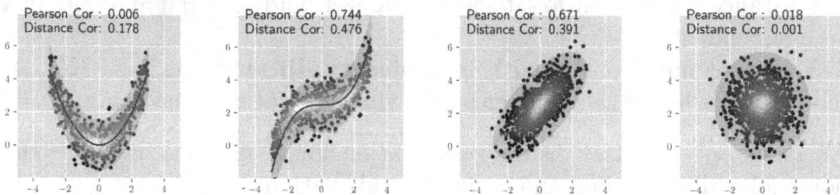

Fig. 1. Examples of Pearson Correlation and Distance Correlation in different settings. (a): $y = 0.5x^2 + 0.75n, n \sim \mathcal{N}(0,1)$; (b): $y = 0.15x^3 + 0.75n + 2.5, n \sim \mathcal{N}(0,1)$; (c): $\begin{bmatrix} x \\ y \end{bmatrix} \sim \mathcal{N}\left(\begin{bmatrix} 0 \\ 2.5 \end{bmatrix}, \begin{bmatrix} 1 & 0.75 \\ 0.75 & 1.25 \end{bmatrix} \right)$; (d): $\begin{bmatrix} x \\ y \end{bmatrix} \sim \mathcal{N}\left(\begin{bmatrix} 0 \\ 2.5 \end{bmatrix}, \begin{bmatrix} 1 & 0 \\ 0 & 1.25 \end{bmatrix} \right)$.

Definition 2. *Let $A = (a_{k,l})$ be a symmetric, real valued $n \times n$ matrix $(n > 2)$ with zero diagonal. Define the $\mathcal{U}$-centered matrix $\tilde{A} = (\tilde{a}_{kl})$ as follows.*

$$
\tilde{a}_{kl} = \begin{cases} a_{k,l} - \dfrac{1}{n-2}\displaystyle\sum_{i=1}^{n} a_{i,l} - \dfrac{1}{n-2}\displaystyle\sum_{j=1}^{n} a_{k,j} + \dfrac{1}{(n-1)(n-2)}\displaystyle\sum_{i,j=1}^{n} a_{i,j} & , k \neq l \\ 0 & , k = l \end{cases} \tag{3}
$$

Further, the inner product between $\tilde{A}, \tilde{B}$ is defined as $(\tilde{A} \cdot \tilde{B}) := \frac{1}{n(n-3)} \sum_{k \neq l} \tilde{A}_{k,l}\tilde{B}_{k,l}$, and is an unbiased estimator of squared population distance covariance $\mathcal{V}^2(x,y)$.

Before defining partial distance covariance formally, we recall the definition of orthogonal projection on these matrices.

Definition 3. *Let $\tilde{A}, \tilde{B}, \tilde{C}$ corresponding to samples x, y, z respectively, and let $P_{z^\perp}(x) = \tilde{A} - \frac{(\tilde{A} \cdot \tilde{C})}{(\tilde{C} \cdot \tilde{C})}\tilde{C}$, $P_{z^\perp}(y) = \tilde{B} - \frac{(\tilde{B} \cdot \tilde{C})}{(\tilde{C} \cdot \tilde{C})}\tilde{C}$ denote the orthogonal projection of $\tilde{A}(x)$ onto $(\tilde{C}(z))^\perp$ and the orthogonal projection of $\tilde{B}(y)$ onto $(\tilde{C}(z))^\perp$.*

Now, we are ready to define the partial distance covariance and the partial distance correlation.

Definition 4. *Let (x,y,z) be a random sample observed from the joint distribution of (X, Y, Z). The sample partial distance covariance is defined by:*

$$
pdCov(x,y;z) = (P_{z^\perp}(x) \cdot P_{z^\perp}(y)) = \frac{1}{n(n-3)}\sum_{i \neq j}(P_{z^\perp}(x))_{i,j}(P_{z^\perp}(y))_{i,j} \tag{4}
$$

And the partial distance correlation is defined as: $\mathcal{R}^{*2}(x,y;z) := \frac{(P_{z^\perp}(x) \cdot P_{z^\perp}(y))}{\|P_{z^\perp}(x)\|\|P_{z^\perp}(y)\|}$ where $\|P_{z^\perp}(x)\| = (P_{z^\perp}(x) \cdot P_{z^\perp}(x))^{1/2}$ is the norm.

Partial distance correlation enables asking various interesting questions. By projecting the original $\mathcal{U}$-centered matrix $\tilde{A}$ onto $\tilde{C}$, the correlation between the residual and $\tilde{B}$ will be a measure of what does X learn that Z does not.

3   Optimizing Distance Correlation in Neural Networks

While distance correlation can be implemented in a differentiable way, and thereby used as an appropriate loss function in a neural network, we must take efficiency into account. For two p dimensional random variables, let the number of samples for the empirical estimate of DC be n. Observe that the total cost for computing $(a_{k,l})$ is $O(n^2 p)$, and the memory to store the intermediate matrices is also $O(n^2)$. So, we use a stochastic estimate of DC by averaging over minibatches, with each minibatch containing m samples. We describe why this approximation is sensible.

Notation. We use Θ_X, Θ_Y to denote the parameters of the neural networks, and X, Y as features extracted by the respective neural networks. Let the minibatch size be m, and the dataset $\mathcal{D} = (\mathcal{D}_\mathcal{X}, \mathcal{D}_\mathcal{Y})$ be of size n. We use $(x_t, y_t)_{t=1}^T, x_t \subset \mathcal{D}_\mathcal{X}, y_t \subset \mathcal{D}_\mathcal{Y}$ to represent the data samples at step t, T is the total number of training steps. The distance matrices A_t, B_t are computed when given X_t, Y_t using (1), which is of dimension $m \times m$ for each minibatch. Further, we use $(X_t)_k$ to represent the kth element in X_t. And $(A_t)_{k,l}$ is the kth row and l^{th} column element in the matrix A_t. The inner-product between two matrices A, B is defined as $\langle A, B \rangle = \sum_{i,j}^m (A)_{i,j}(B)_{i,j}$.

Objective Function. Consider the case where we minimize DC between two networks Θ_X, Θ_Y. Since the parameters between Θ_X, Θ_Y are separable, we can use the block stochastic gradient iteration in [68] with some simple modifications.

To minimize the distance correlation, we need to solve the following problem

$$\min_{\Theta_X, \Theta_Y} \frac{\langle A(\Theta_X; x), B(\Theta_Y; y) \rangle}{\sqrt{\langle A(\Theta_X; x), A(\Theta_X; x) \rangle \langle B(\Theta_Y; y), B(\Theta_Y; y) \rangle}} \tag{5}$$

$$(A)_{k,l} = ||(X)_k - (X)_l||_2, \ X = \Theta_X(x), (B)_{k,l} = ||(Y)_k - (Y)_l||_2, \ Y = \Theta_Y(y)$$

We slightly abuse the notation of $\Theta_X(x)$ as applying the network Θ_X onto data x, and reuse A to simplify the notation $A(\Theta_X; x)$ and the distance matrix. We can rewrite the expression (with A, B defined above) using:

$$\min_{\Theta_X, \Theta_Y} \langle A, B \rangle \ \text{s.t.} \ \max_{x \subset \mathcal{D}_\mathcal{X}} \langle A, A \rangle \leq m; \ \max_{y \subset \mathcal{D}_\mathcal{Y}} \langle B, B \rangle \leq m \tag{6}$$

where (x, y) are the minibatch of samples from the data space $(\mathcal{D}_\mathcal{X}, \mathcal{D}_\mathcal{Y})$.

We can rewrite the above into the following equation similar to (1) in [68].

$$\min_{\Theta_X, \Theta_Y} \Phi(\Theta_X, \Theta_Y) = \mathbb{E}_{x,y} f(\Theta_X, \Theta_Y; x, y) + \gamma(\Theta_X) + \gamma(\Theta_Y) \tag{7}$$

where $f(\Theta_X, \Theta_Y; x, y)$ is $\langle A, B \rangle$ and $\gamma(\Theta_X)$ encodes the convex constraint of network Θ_X: $\max_{x \subset \mathcal{D}_x} \langle A, A \rangle \leq m$. Similarly, $\gamma(\Theta_Y)$ encodes $\max_{y \subset \mathcal{D}_y} \langle B, B \rangle \leq m$. $\Phi(\Theta_X, \Theta_Y)$ is the constrained objective function to be optimized.

Block Stochastic Gradient Iteration. We adjust Algorithm 1 from [68] to our case inAlgorithm 1. Since we will need the entire minibatch (x_t, y_t) to compute the objective function, there will be no mean term when computing the sample gradient $\tilde{\mathbf{g}}_X^t$. Further, since both blocks (Θ_X, Θ_Y) are constrained, line $3, 5$ will use (5) from [68]. The detailed algorithm is presented inAlgorithm 1.

Algorithm 1: Block Stochastic Gradient for Updating Distance Correlation

---

Require: Two neural network with starting point Θ_X^1, Θ_Y^1. Training data $\{(x_t, y_t)\}_{t=1}^T$, step size η_X, η_Y, and batch size m.

Output: $\tilde{\Theta}_X^T, \tilde{\Theta}_Y^T$

1: **for** $t = 1, \cdots, T$ **do**
2:    Compute sample gradient for Θ_X

   $\tilde{\mathbf{g}}_X^t = \nabla_{\Theta_X} f(\Theta_X^t, \Theta_Y^t; x_t, y_t)$

3:    $\Theta_X^{t+1} = \arg\min_{\Theta_X} \langle \tilde{\mathbf{g}}_X^t + \tilde{\nabla}\gamma_X(\Theta_X^t), \Theta_X - \Theta_X^t \rangle + \frac{1}{2\eta_X}\|\Theta_X - \Theta_X^t\|^2$
4:    Compute sample gradient for Θ_Y

   $\mathbf{g}_Y^t = \nabla_{\Theta_Y} f(\Theta_X^{t+1}, \Theta_Y^t; x_t, y_t)$

5:    $\Theta_Y^{t+1} = \arg\min_{\Theta_Y} \langle \tilde{\mathbf{g}}_Y^t + \tilde{\nabla}\gamma_Y(\Theta_Y^t), \Theta_Y - \Theta_Y^t \rangle + \frac{1}{2\eta_Y}\|\Theta_Y - \Theta_Y^t\|^2$
6: **end for**
7: $\tilde{\Theta}_X^T = \frac{1}{T}\sum_{t=1}^T \Theta_X^t$
8: $\tilde{\Theta}_Y^T = \frac{1}{T}\sum_{t=1}^T \Theta_Y^t$

Proposition 1. *After T iterations of Algorithm 1 with step size $\eta_X = \eta_Y = \frac{\eta}{\sqrt{T}} < \frac{1}{L}$, for some positive constant $\eta < \frac{1}{L}$, where L is the Lipschitz constant of the partial gradient of f, by Theorem. 6 in [68], we know there exists an index subsequence $\mathcal{T}$ such that:*

$$\lim_{t \to \infty, t \in \mathcal{T}} \mathbb{E}[dist(\mathbf{0}, \nabla\Phi(\Theta_X^t, \Theta_Y^t))] = 0 \qquad (8)$$

where $dist(\mathbf{y}, \mathcal{X}) = \min_{\mathbf{x} \in \mathcal{X}} \|\mathbf{x} - \mathbf{y}\|$.

But empirically, we find that simply applying Stochastic Gradient Decent (SGD) is sufficient, but this choice is available to the user.

4   Independent Features Help Robustness

Goal. We show how distance correlation can help us train multiple deep networks that learn **mutually independent** features, roughly similar to finding diverse M-best solutions in structured SVM models [59]. We describe how such an approach can lead to better robustness against adversarial attacks.

Rationale. Recently, several efforts have explored generating of adversarial examples that can transfer to different networks and how to defend against such attacks [6,15,62]. It is often observed that an adversarial sample for one trained network is relatively easy to transfer to another network with the same architecture [15]. Here, we show that even for as few as two networks (same architecture; trained on the same data), we can, to some extent, prevent adversarial examples from transferring between them by seeking independent features.

Setup. We formulate the problem considering a classification task as an example. Given two deep neural networks with the same architecture denoted as $f_1(\cdot), f_2(\cdot)$, we train them using image-label pairs (x, y) using the cross-entropy loss $\mathrm{Loss_{CE}}$. If we train f_1 and f_2 using only the cross-entropy loss, the adversarial examples generated on f_1 can relatively easily transfer to f_2 (see the performance of "Baseline" in Table 1). To enforce f_1 and f_2 to learn independent features, let the extracted feature of x in some intermediate layer of f be given as $g(x)$ (in this section we use the feature before the last fully connected layer as an example). We can still train f_1 using $\mathrm{Loss_{CE}}$, and then, we train f_2 using,

$$\mathrm{Loss_{total}} = \mathrm{Loss_{CE}}(f_2(x), y) + \alpha \cdot \mathrm{Loss_{DC}}(g_1(x), g_2(x)) \tag{9}$$

where α is a constant scalar and $\mathrm{Loss_{DC}}$ is the distance correlation from Def. 1. Note that we do not require $g_1(x)$ and $g_2(x)$ to be in the same dimension, so in principle we could easily use features from different layers for these two networks.

Experimental Settings. We first conduct experiments on CIFAR10 [39] using Resnet 18 [28]. We then use four different architectures (mobilenet-v3-small [32], efficientnet-B0 [66], Resnet 34, and Resnet152) and train them on ImageNet [40]. For each network architecture, we first train two networks using only $\mathrm{Loss_{CE}}$. Next, we train a network using only $\mathrm{Loss_{CE}}$ before training a second network using the loss in (9). On CIFAR10, we utilize the SGD optimizer with momentum 0.9 and train for 200 epochs using an initial learning rate 0.1 with a cosine learning rate scheduler [52]. The mini-batch size is set to 128. On ImageNet [40], we train for 40 epochs using an initial learning rate 0.1, which decays by 0.1 every 10 epochs. The mini-batch size is 512. Our α in (9) is set to 0.05 for all cases. For each combination of the dataset and the network architecture, we train two networks f_1 and f_2, after which we generate adversarial examples on f_1 and use them to attack f_2 and measure its classification accuracy. We construct a baseline by training f_1 and $f_{2\mathrm{Baseline}}$ without constraints. And train $f_{2\mathrm{Our}}$ using (9) to learn independent features w.r.t. f_1. We report performance under two widely used attack methods: fast gradient sign method (FGM) [26] and projected gradient descent method (PGD) [46], where the latter is considered among the strongest attacks. The scale ϵ of the adversarial perturbation is chosen from $\{0.03, 0.05, 0.1\}$ and the maximum number of iterations of PGD is set to 40.

Results. The results are shown in Table 1. We see that we get significant improvement in accuracy over the baseline under adversarial attacks, with comparable performance on clean inputs. Notably, our method achieves more than 10% absolute improvement in accuracy under PGD attack on Resnet-18 and Mobilenet-v3-small. This provides evidence supporting the benefits of enforcing the networks to learn independent features using our distance correlation loss.

Table 1. The test accuracy (%) of a model f_2 on the adversarial examples generated using f_1 with the same architecture. "Baseline": train without constraint. "Ours": f_2 is independent to f_1. "Clean": test accuracy without adversarial examples.

Dataset	Network	Method	Clean	FGM$_{\epsilon=0.03}$	PGD$_{\epsilon=0.03}$	FGM$_{\epsilon=0.05}$	PGD$_{\epsilon=0.05}$	FGM$_{\epsilon=0.1}$	PGD$_{\epsilon=0.1}$
CIFAR10	Resnet 18	Baseline	89.14	72.10	66.34	62.00	49.42	48.23	27.41
CIFAR10	Resnet 18	Ours	87.61	**74.76**	**72.85**	**65.56**	**59.33**	**50.24**	**36.11**
ImageNet	Mobilenet-v3-small	Baseline	47.16	29.64	30.00	23.52	24.81	13.90	17.15
ImageNet	Mobilenet-v3-small	Ours	42.34	**34.47**	**36.98**	**29.53**	**33.77**	**19.53**	**28.04**
ImageNet	Efficientnet-B0	Baseline	57.85	26.72	28.22	18.96	19.45	12.04	11.17
ImageNet	Efficientnet-B0	Ours	55.82	**30.42**	**35.99**	**22.05**	**27.56**	**14.16**	**17.62**
ImageNet	Resnet 34	Baseline	64.01	52.62	56.61	45.45	51.11	33.75	41.70
ImageNet	Resnet 34	Ours	63.77	**53.19**	**57.18**	**46.50**	**52.28**	**35.00**	**43.35**
ImageNet	Resnet 152	Baseline	66.88	56.56	59.19	50.61	53.49	40.50	44.49
ImageNet	Resnet 152	Ours	68.04	**58.34**	**61.33**	**52.59**	**56.05**	**42.61**	**47.17**

In Fig. 2, we show correlation results using Picasso [7,29] to lower the dimension of features for each network. The embedding dimension is 2 for visualization. In Fig. 2(a), we show the embedding of different networks. f_1 represents the network to generate the adversarial examples. $f_{2Baseline}$ denotes the baseline network, trained without distance correlation constraint. Also, f_{2Ours} is the same network trained to be independent to f_1. In Fig. 2(b), we visualize the correlation between f_1 and $f_{2Baseline}$ for each dimension, and the correlation between f_1 and f_{2Ours}. If the scatter plot looks circle-like, we can infer that the two models

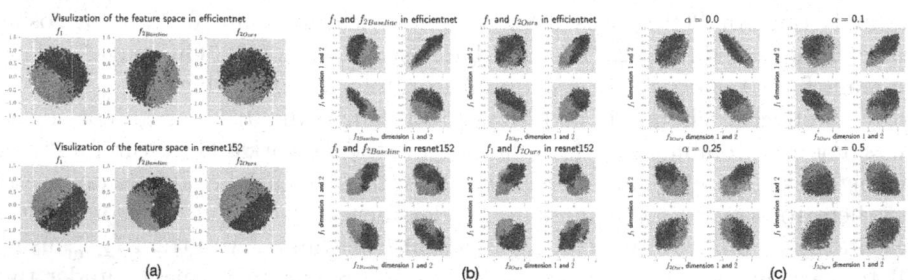

Fig. 2. Picasso visualization of features space and the correlation between different models. **(a)** Feature space distribution. **(b)** Cross-correlation between the feature space of f_1 and f_2 trained with/without DC. We get better independence. **(c)** By increasing the balance parameter α of DC loss, Mobilenet is more independent to f_1.

are independent. We see that in different networks, the use of DC shows stronger independence. From Fig. 2/Table 1, we also see that the more independent the models are, the better is the gain for transferred attack robustness.

5 Informative Comparisons Between Networks

Overview. As discussed in Sect. 1, there is much interest in understanding whether two different models learn similar concepts from the data – for example, whether vision Transformers "see" similar to convolutional neural networks [56]. Here, we first follow [56] and discuss similarities between different layers of ViT and ResNets using distance correlation. Next, we investigate that after taking out the influence of Resnets from ViT (or vice versa), what are the residual learned concepts remaining in the network.

5.1 Measure Similarity Between Neural Networks

Goal. We first want to understand whether ViTs represent features across all layers differently from CNNs (such as Resnets). However, analyzing the features in the hidden layers can be challenging, because the features are spread across neurons. Also, different layers have different numbers of neurons. Recently, [56] applied the Centered Kernel Alignment (CKA) for this task. CKA is effective because it involves no constraint on the number of neurons. It is also independent to the orthogonal transformations of representations. Here, we want to demonstrate that distance correlation is a reasonable alternative for CKA in these settings.

Experimental Settings. First, as described in [56], we show that similarity between layers within a single neural network can be assessed using distance correlation (see Fig. 3(a)). We pick ViT Base with patch 16, and three commonly used Resnets. All networks are pretrained on ImageNet. For ViT, we pick the embedding layer and all the normalization, attention, and fully connected layers within each block. The total number of layers is 63. For Resnets, we use all

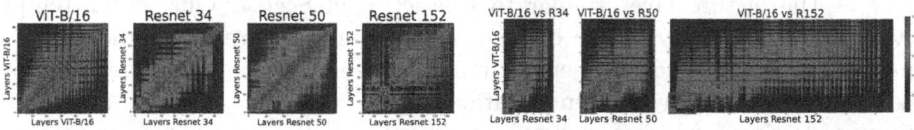

Fig. 3. (a) Left 4: Similarity between layers within one single model. ViT can be split into small blocks and the similarity from shallow layers to the deeper layers is higher. Most Resnet models show few large blocks in the network, and the last few layers share minimal similarity with the shallow layers. **(b) Right 3:** Similarity between layers across ViT and Resnets. In the initial 1/6 layers (highlighted in green), the two networks share high similarity. And the last few layers share the least similarity. (Color figure online)

convolutional layers and the last fully connected layer, which is the same counting method to build Resnet models.

Results (a). Our findings add to those from [56]. Using distance correlation, we find that the ViT layers can be split into small blocks and the similarity between different blocks from shallow layers to the deeper layers is higher. For most Resnets, the feature similarity shows that there are a few large blocks in the network, which contains more than 30 layers each, and the last few layers share minimal similarity with the shallow layers.

Results (b). After within-model distance correlation, we perform across-model distance correlation comparisons between ViT and Resnets, see Fig. 3(b). We notice that in the initial 1/6 layers, the two networks share high similarities. But later, the similarity spreads across all different layers between ViT and Resnets. Notably, the last few layers share the least similarity between two networks.

By using the distance correlation to calculate the heatmap of the similarity matrices, we can qualitatively describe the difference between the patterns of the features in different layers from different networks. What is even more interesting is to quantitatively show the difference, for example, to answer which network contains more information for the ground truth classes. We discuss this next.

5.2   What Remains When "Taking Out" Y from X

Goal. Even measuring information contained in one neural network is challenging, and often tackled by measuring the accuracy on the test dataset. But the association between accuracy and the information contained in a network may be weak. Based on existing literature, conditioning one network w.r.t. another remains unresolved. Despite the above challenges, we can indeed measure the similarity between the features of the network X and the ground truth labels. If the similarity is higher, we can say that the feature space of X contains more information regarding the true labels. Distance correlation enables this. Interestingly, partial distance correlation extends this idea to multiple networks allowing us to approach the "conditioning" question posed above.

Rationale/Setup. Here, we choose the last layer before the final fully-connected layer as the feature layer similar to the setup in Sect. 4. Our first attempt involved directly applying the distance correlation measurement to feature X and the one-hot ground truth embedding. However, the one-hot embedding for the label contains very little information, e.g., it does not show the difference between "cat" vs. "dog" and "cat" vs. "airplane". So, we use the pretrained BERT [16] to linguistically embed the class labels into the hidden space. We then measure the distance correlation between the feature space of X and the pretrained hidden space GT. $\mathcal{R}^2(X, GT) = \frac{m}{n} \sum_{t=1}^{n/m} dCor(x_t, gt_t)$ where x_t is the feature for one minibatch, and gt_t is the BERT embedding vector of the corresponding label. To further extend this metric to measure the "remaining" or residual information, we apply the partial distance correlation calculation by removing Y out of X, or say X conditioned on Y. Then, we have

$\mathcal{R}^2\left((X|Y), GT\right) = \frac{m}{n} \sum_{t=1}^{n/m} dCor\left((x_t|y_t), gt_t\right)$ using (4). This capability has not been shown before.

Table 2. Partial DC between the network Θ_X conditioned on the network Θ_Y, and the ImageNet class name embedding. The higher value indicates the more information.

Network Θ_X	Network Θ_Y	$\mathcal{R}^2(X, GT)$	$\mathcal{R}^2(Y, GT)$	$\mathcal{R}^2((X|Y), GT)$	$\mathcal{R}^2((Y|X), GT)$
ViT[1]	Resnet 18[2]	0.042	0.025	0.035	0.007
ViT	Resnet 50[3]	0.043	0.036	0.028	0.017
ViT	Resnet 152[4]	0.044	0.020	0.040	0.009
ViT	VGG 19 BN[5]	0.042	0.037	0.026	0.015
ViT	Densenet121[6]	0.043	0.026	0.035	0.007
ViT large[7]	Resnet 18	0.046	0.027	0.038	0.007
ViT large	Resnet 50	0.046	0.037	0.031	0.016
ViT large	Resnet 152	0.046	0.021	0.042	0.010
ViT large	ViT	0.045	0.043	0.019	0.013
ViT+Resnet 50[8]	Resnet 18	0.044	0.024	0.037	0.005
Resnet 152	Resnet 18	0.019	0.025	0.013	0.020
Resnet 152	Resnet 50	0.021	0.037	0.003	0.030
Resnet 50	Resnet 18	0.036	0.025	0.027	0.008
Resnet 50	VGG 19 BN	0.036	0.036	0.020	0.019

Accuracy: 1. 84.40%; 2. 69.76%; 3. 79.02%; 4. 82.54%;
5. 74.22%; 6. 75.57%; 7. 85.68%; 8. 84.13%

Experimental Settings. In order to measure the information remaining when conditioning network Θ_Y out of Θ_X, we first use pretrained networks on ImageNet. We use the validation set of the ImageNet for evaluation. We want to evaluate which network contains the richest information regarding linguistic embedding. Interestingly, we can go beyond such an evaluation, instead, asking *the network Θ_X to learn concepts above and beyond what the network Θ_Y has learned*. To do so, we include the partial distance correlation into the loss. Unlike the experiment discussed above (minimizing distance correlation), in this setup, we seek to maximize partial distance correlation. The $\text{Loss}_{\text{total}}$ is

$$\text{Loss}_{\text{CE}}(f_1(x), y) - \alpha \cdot \text{Loss}_{\text{PDC}}\left((g_1(x)|g_2(x)), gt\right) \qquad (10)$$

We take pretrained networks Θ_X, Θ_Y and then finetune Θ_X using (10). The learning rate is set to be $1e-5$ and α in the loss term is 1. To check the benefits of partial DC, we use Grad-CAM [60] to highlight the areas that each network is looking at, together with what Θ_X conditioned on Θ_Y sees then.

Results (a). We first show information comparison between two networks. The details of DC and partial DC are shown in Table 2. The reader will notice that since ViT achieves the best test accuracy, it also contains the most information. Additionally, although better test accuracy normally coincides with more information, this is not always true. Resnet 50 contains more linguistic information than the much deeper Resnet 152, perhaps a compensation mechanism. For Resnet 152, the network is deep enough to focus on local structures that overwhelm the linguistic information (or this information is unnecessary). This experiment suggests a new strategy to compare two networks beyond test accuracy.

Results (b). After using a pretrained network, we can also check that by including the partial distance correlation in the loss, which regions does the model pay attention to, using Grad-CAM. We replace the loss term of Grad-CAM with the partial distance correlation. The results are shown in Fig. 4. We see that the pretrained ViT sees across the whole image in different locations, while the Resnet (VGG) tends to focus on only one area of the image. After training, ViT (conditioned on Resnet) pays more attention to the subjects, especially locations outside the Resnet focus. Such experiments help understand how ViT learns *beyond* Resnets (CNNs).

6 Disentanglement

Overview. This experiment studies disentanglement [8,21,30,36,43]. It is believed that the image data are generated from low dimensional latent variables – but isolating and disentangling the latent variables is challenging. A key in disentangled latent variable learning is to make the factors in the latent variables independent [2]. Distance correlation fits perfectly and can handle a

Fig. 4. Grad-CAM results on ImageNet using ViT, Resnet18 and VGG16. After using Partial DC to remove the information learned by another network, ViT can focus on detail places and Resnet can only look in major spots. Similar issue happens to VGG.

variety of dimensions for the latent variables. When the distance correlation is 0, we know that the two variables are independent.

Experimental Settings. We follow [21] which focuses on semi-supervised disentanglement to generate high-resolution images. In [21], one divides the latent variables into two categories: (a) attributes of interest – a set of semantic and interpretable attributes, e.g. hair color and age; (b) residual attributes – the remaining information. Formally, $x_i = G(f_i^1, ..., f_i^k, r_i)$, where G is the generator that uses the factors of interest f_i^l and the residual to generate image x_i.

In order to enforce the condition that the information regarding the attributes of interest is not leaking into the residual representations, the authors of [21] introduced the loss $L_{res} = \sum_{i=1}^{n} ||r_i||^2$ to limit the residual information. This is sub-optimal as there can be cases where r_i is not 0 but still independent to the factors of interest $(f_i^l)_{l=1}^k$. Thus, we use distance correlation to replace this loss:

$$L_{res} = dCor([f^1; f^2; ...; f^k], r) \tag{11}$$

We use the same structure proposed in [21], while the generator architecture is adopted from StyleGAN2 [35]. The dataset is the human face dataset FFHQ [34], and the attributes are: age, gender, etc. We use CLIP [54] to partially label the attributes to generate the semi-supervised dataset for training. All losses from [21] are used, except that L_{res} is replaced by (11).

Results. (Shown in Fig. 5) Our model shows the ability to change specific attributes without affecting residual features, such as posture (also see supplement).

Fig. 5. Representative generated images using our training on FFHQ. Note that these results only use semi-supervised dataset by CLIP. Our methods shows the ability to disentangle the attributes of interest and the remaining information.

7 Conclusions

In this paper, we studied how distance correlation (and partial distance correlation) has a wide variety of uses in deep learning tasks in vision. The measure offers various properties that are often enforced using alternative means, that are often far more involved. Further, it is extremely simple to incorporate in contrast to various divergence-based measures often used in invariant representation learning. Notably, the use of partial distance correlation offers the ability of conditioning, which is underexplored in the community. We showcase three very different settings, ranging from network comparison to training distinct/different models to disentanglement where the idea is immediately beneficial, and expect that numerous other applications will emerge in short order.

Acknowledgement. Research supported in part by NIH grants RF1 AG059312, RF1 AG062336, and RF1AG059869, and NSF grant CCF #1918211.

References

1. Achille, A., Soatto, S.: Emergence of invariance and disentanglement in deep representations. J. Mach. Learn. Res. **19**(1), 1947–1980 (2018)
2. Akash, A.K., Lokhande, V.S., Ravi, S.N., Singh, V.: Learning invariant representations using inverse contrastive loss. In: Proceedings of the AAAI Conference on Artificial Intelligence, vol. 35, pp. 6582–6591 (2021)
3. Anderson, T.W.: An introduction to multivariate statistical analysis. Technical report (1958)
4. Andrew, G., Arora, R., Bilmes, J., Livescu, K.: Deep canonical correlation analysis. In: International Conference on Machine Learning, pp. 1247–1255. PMLR (2013)
5. Bach, F.R., Jordan, M.I.: A probabilistic interpretation of canonical correlation analysis (2005)
6. Chan, A., Tay, Y., Ong, Y.S.: What it thinks is important is important: robustness transfers through input gradients. In: Proceedings of the IEEE/CVF Conference on Computer Vision and Pattern Recognition, pp. 332–341 (2020)
7. Chari, T., Banerjee, J., Pachter, L.: The specious art of single-cell genomics. bioRxiv (2021)
8. Chen, R.T., Li, X., Grosse, R., Duvenaud, D.: Isolating sources of disentanglement in VAEs. In: Proceedings of the 32nd International Conference on Neural Information Processing Systems, pp. 2615–2625 (2018)
9. Cheng, S., Dong, Y., Pang, T., Su, H., Zhu, J.: Improving black-box adversarial attacks with a transfer-based prior. Adv. Neural. Inf. Process. Syst. **32**, 1–11 (2019)
10. Cho, J., Hwang, G., Suh, C.: A fair classifier using mutual information. In: 2020 IEEE International Symposium on Information Theory (ISIT), pp. 2521–2526. IEEE (2020)
11. Cohen, T., Welling, M.: Group equivariant convolutional networks. In: International Conference on Machine Learning, pp. 2990–2999. PMLR (2016)
12. Cover, T.M.: Elements of Information Theory. John Wiley & Sons, Hoboken (1999)
13. D'Angelo, F., Fortuin, V.: Repulsive deep ensembles are Bayesian. Adv. Neural. Inf. Process. Syst. **34**, 3451–3465 (2021)

14. D'Angelo, F., Fortuin, V., Wenzel, F.: On stein variational neural network ensembles. arXiv preprint arXiv:2106.10760 (2021)
15. Demontis, A., et al.: Why do adversarial attacks transfer? Explaining transferability of evasion and poisoning attacks. In: 28th USENIX Security Symposium (USENIX Security 2019), pp. 321–338 (2019)
16. Devlin, J., Chang, M.W., Lee, K., Toutanova, K.: BERT: pre-training of deep bidirectional transformers for language understanding. arXiv preprint arXiv:1810.04805 (2018)
17. Feldman, M., Friedler, S.A., Moeller, J., Scheidegger, C., Venkatasubramanian, S.: Certifying and removing disparate impact. In: proceedings of the 21th ACM SIGKDD International Conference on Knowledge Discovery and Data Mining, pp. 259–268 (2015)
18. Fontaine, M., Nikolaidis, S.: Differentiable quality diversity. Adv. Neural. Inf. Process. Syst. **34**, 10040–10052 (2021)
19. Fromer, M., Globerson, A.: An LP view of the m-best map problem. Adv. Neural. Inf. Process. Syst. **22**, 567–575 (2009)
20. Fukushima, K., Miyake, S., Ito, T.: NeoCognitron: a neural network model for a mechanism of visual pattern recognition. IEEE Trans. Syst. Man Cybern. **5**, 826–834 (1983)
21. Gabbay, A., Cohen, N., Hoshen, Y.: An image is worth more than a thousand words: towards disentanglement in the wild. Adv. Neural. Inf. Process. Syst. **34**, 9216–9228 (2021)
22. Gaier, A., Asteroth, A., Mouret, J.B.: Discovering representations for black-box optimization. In: Proceedings of the 2020 Genetic and Evolutionary Computation Conference, pp. 103–111 (2020)
23. Gao, C., Garber, D., Srebro, N., Wang, J., Wang, W.: Stochastic canonical correlation analysis. J. Mach. Learn. Res. **20**, 167–1 (2019)
24. Geirhos, R., Rubisch, P., Michaelis, C., Bethge, M., Wichmann, F.A., Brendel, W.: Imagenet-trained CNNs are biased towards texture; increasing shape bias improves accuracy and robustness. In: International Conference on Learning Representations (2019). https://openreview.net/forum?id=Bygh9j09KX
25. Gemp, I., Chen, C., McWilliams, B.: The generalized eigenvalue problem as a Nash equilibrium. arXiv preprint arXiv:2206.04993 (2022)
26. Goodfellow, I.J., Shlens, J., Szegedy, C.: Explaining and harnessing adversarial examples. arXiv preprint arXiv:1412.6572 (2014)
27. Guzman-Rivera, A., Kohli, P., Batra, D., Rutenbar, R.: Efficiently enforcing diversity in multi-output structured prediction. In: Artificial Intelligence and Statistics, pp. 284–292. PMLR (2014)
28. He, K., Zhang, X., Ren, S., Sun, J.: Deep residual learning for image recognition. In: Proceedings of the IEEE Conference on Computer Vision and Pattern Recognition, pp. 770–778 (2016)
29. Henderson, R., Rothe, R.: Picasso: a modular framework for visualizing the learning process of neural network image classifiers. arXiv preprint arXiv:1705.05627 (2017)
30. Higgins, I., et al.: BETA-VAE: learning basic visual concepts with a constrained variational framework (2016)
31. Hotelling, H.: Relations between two sets of variates. In: Kotz, S., Johnson, N.L. (eds.) Breakthroughs in Statistics. Springer Series in Statistics, pp. 162–190. Springer, New York, NY (1992). https://doi.org/10.1007/978-1-4612-4380-9_13
32. Howard, A., et al.: Searching for mobilenetv3. In: Proceedings of the IEEE/CVF International Conference on Computer Vision, pp. 1314–1324 (2019)

33. Iandola, F., Moskewicz, M., Karayev, S., Girshick, R., Darrell, T., Keutzer, K.: DenseNet: implementing efficient convnet descriptor pyramids. arXiv preprint arXiv:1404.1869 (2014)
34. Karras, T., Laine, S., Aila, T.: A style-based generator architecture for generative adversarial networks. In: Proceedings of the IEEE/CVF Conference on Computer Vision and Pattern Recognition, pp. 4401–4410 (2019)
35. Karras, T., Laine, S., Aittala, M., Hellsten, J., Lehtinen, J., Aila, T.: Analyzing and improving the image quality of styleGAN. In: Proceedings of the IEEE/CVF Conference on Computer Vision and Pattern Recognition, pp. 8110–8119 (2020)
36. Kim, H., Mnih, A.: Disentangling by factorising. In: International Conference on Machine Learning, pp. 2649–2658. PMLR (2018)
37. Kornblith, S., Norouzi, M., Lee, H., Hinton, G.: Similarity of neural network representations revisited. In: International Conference on Machine Learning, pp. 3519–3529. PMLR (2019)
38. Kornblith, S., Shlens, J., Le, Q.V.: Do better imagenet models transfer better? In: Proceedings of the IEEE/CVF Conference on Computer Vision and Pattern Recognition, pp. 2661–2671 (2019)
39. Krizhevsky, A., Hinton, G., et al.: Learning multiple layers of features from tiny images (2009)
40. Krizhevsky, A., Sutskever, I., Hinton, G.E.: ImageNet classification with deep convolutional neural networks. Adv. Neural. Inf. Process. Syst. **25**, 1097–1105 (2012)
41. Lample, G., Zeghidour, N., Usunier, N., Bordes, A., Denoyer, L., Ranzato, M.: Fader networks: manipulating images by sliding attributes. In: NIPS (2017)
42. Li, R., Zhong, W., Zhu, L.: Feature screening via distance correlation learning. J. Am. Stat. Assoc. **107**(499), 1129–1139 (2012)
43. Locatello, F., Tschannen, M., Bauer, S., Rätsch, G., Schölkopf, B., Bachem, O.: Disentangling factors of variations using few labels. In: International Conference on Learning Representations (2019)
44. Lokhande, V.S., Akash, A.K., Ravi, S.N., Singh, V.: FairALM: augmented Lagrangian method for training fair models with little regret. In: Vedaldi, A., Bischof, H., Brox, T., Frahm, J.-M. (eds.) ECCV 2020. LNCS, vol. 12357, pp. 365–381. Springer, Cham (2020). https://doi.org/10.1007/978-3-030-58610-2_22
45. Lokhande, V.S., Chakraborty, R., Ravi, S.N., Singh, V.: Equivariance allows handling multiple nuisance variables when analyzing pooled neuroimaging datasets. In: Proceedings of the IEEE/CVF Conference on Computer Vision and Pattern Recognition, pp. 10432–10441 (2022)
46. Madry, A., Makelov, A., Schmidt, L., Tsipras, D., Vladu, A.: Towards deep learning models resistant to adversarial attacks. In: International Conference on Learning Representations (2018). https://openreview.net/forum?id=rJzIBfZAb
47. Meng, Z., Chakraborty, R., Singh, V.: An online Riemannian PCA for stochastic canonical correlation analysis. In: Ranzato, M., Beygelzimer, A., Dauphin, Y., Liang, P., Vaughan, J.W. (eds.) Advances in Neural Information Processing Systems, vol. 34, pp. 14056–14068. Curran Associates, Inc. (2021). https://proceedings.neurips.cc/paper/2021/file/758a06618c69880a6cee5314ee42d52f-Paper.pdf
48. Morcos, A.S., Raghu, M., Bengio, S.: Insights on representational similarity in neural networks with canonical correlation. In: NeurIPS (2018)
49. Moyer, D., Gao, S., Brekelmans, R., Galstyan, A., Ver Steeg, G.: Invariant representations without adversarial training. In: NeurIPS (2018)

50. Neyshabur, B., Sedghi, H., Zhang, C.: What is being transferred in transfer learning? In: Larochelle, H., Ranzato, M., Hadsell, R., Balcan, M., Lin, H. (eds.) Advances in Neural Information Processing Systems, vol. 33, pp. 512–523. Curran Associates, Inc. (2020). https://proceedings.neurips.cc/paper/2020/file/0607f4c705595b911a4f3e7a127b44e0-Paper.pdf

51. Nguyen, T., Raghu, M., Kornblith, S.: Do wide and deep networks learn the same things? uncovering how neural network representations vary with width and depth. In: International Conference on Learning Representations (2020)

52. Paszke, A., et al.: Pytorch: an imperative style, high-performance deep learning library. Adv. Neural. Inf. Process. Syst. **32**, 8026–8037 (2019)

53. Pugh, J.K., Soros, L.B., Stanley, K.O.: Quality diversity: a new frontier for evolutionary computation. Front. Robot. AI **3**, 40 (2016)

54. Radford, A., et al.: Learning transferable visual models from natural language supervision. In: International Conference on Machine Learning, pp. 8748–8763. PMLR (2021)

55. Raghu, M., Gilmer, J., Yosinski, J., Sohl-Dickstein, J.: SVCCA: singular vector canonical correlation analysis for deep learning dynamics and interpretability. In: NIPS (2017)

56. Raghu, M., Unterthiner, T., Kornblith, S., Zhang, C., Dosovitskiy, A.: Do vision transformers see like convolutional neural networks? In: Ranzato, M., Beygelzimer, A., Dauphin, Y., Liang, P., Vaughan, J.W. (eds.) Advances in Neural Information Processing Systems, vol. 34, pp. 12116–12128. Curran Associates, Inc. (2021). https://proceedings.neurips.cc/paper/2021/file/652cf38361a209088302ba2b8b7f51e0-Paper.pdf

57. Rakicevic, N., Cully, A., Kormushev, P.: Policy manifold search: Exploring the manifold hypothesis for diversity-based neuroevolution. In: Proceedings of the Genetic and Evolutionary Computation Conference, pp. 901–909 (2021)

58. Ramsay, J., ten Berge, J., Styan, G.: Matrix correlation. Psychometrika **49**(3), 403–423 (1984)

59. Schiegg, M., Diego, F., Hamprecht, F.A.: Learning diverse models: the coulomb structured support vector machine. In: Leibe, B., Matas, J., Sebe, N., Welling, M. (eds.) ECCV 2016. LNCS, vol. 9907, pp. 585–599. Springer, Cham (2016). https://doi.org/10.1007/978-3-319-46487-9_36

60. Selvaraju, R.R., Cogswell, M., Das, A., Vedantam, R., Parikh, D., Batra, D.: Grad-CAM: visual explanations from deep networks via gradient-based localization. In: Proceedings of the IEEE International Conference on Computer Vision, pp. 618–626 (2017)

61. Shu, R., Chen, Y., Kumar, A., Ermon, S., Poole, B.: Weakly supervised disentanglement with guarantees. In: International Conference on Learning Representations (2019)

62. Shumailov, I., Gao, X., Zhao, Y., Mullins, R., Anderson, R., Xu, C.Z.: Sitatapatra: blocking the transfer of adversarial samples. arXiv preprint arXiv:1901.08121 (2019)

63. Song, J., Kalluri, P., Grover, A., Zhao, S., Ermon, S.: Learning controllable fair representations. In: The 22nd International Conference on Artificial Intelligence and Statistics, pp. 2164–2173. PMLR (2019)

64. Székely, G.J., Rizzo, M.L.: Partial distance correlation with methods for dissimilarities. Ann. Stat. **42**(6), 2382–2412 (2014)

65. Székely, G.J., Rizzo, M.L., Bakirov, N.K.: Measuring and testing dependence by correlation of distances. Ann. Stat. **35**(6), 2769–2794 (2007)

66. Tan, M., Le, Q.: EfficientNet: rethinking model scaling for convolutional neural networks. In: International Conference on Machine Learning, pp. 6105–6114. PMLR (2019)
67. Woźniak, S., Pantazi, A., Bohnstingl, T., Eleftheriou, E.: Deep learning incorporating biologically inspired neural dynamics and in-memory computing. Nat. Mach. Intell. **2020**(2), 325–336 (2020)
68. Xu, Y., Yin, W.: Block stochastic gradient iteration for convex and nonconvex optimization. SIAM J. Optim. **25**(3), 1686–1716 (2015)
69. Yadollahpour, P., Batra, D., Shakhnarovich, G.: Diverse m-best solutions in MRFs. In: Workshop on Discrete Optimization in Machine Learning, NIPS (2011)
70. Zafar, M.B., Valera, I., Rogriguez, M.G., Gummadi, K.P.: Fairness constraints: mechanisms for fair classification. In: Artificial Intelligence and Statistics, pp. 962–970. PMLR (2017)
71. Zemel, R., Wu, Y., Swersky, K., Pitassi, T., Dwork, C.: Learning fair representations. In: International Conference on Machine Learning, pp. 325–333. PMLR (2013)
72. Zhou, Z.: Measuring nonlinear dependence in time-series, a distance correlation approach. J. Time Ser. Anal. **33**(3), 438–457 (2012)

Self-Regulated Feature Learning
via Teacher-free Feature Distillation

Lujun Li[✉][iD]

Chinese Academy of Sciences, Beijing, China
lilujunai@gmail.com

Abstract. Knowledge distillation conditioned on intermediate feature representations always leads to significant performance improvements. Conventional feature distillation framework demands extra selecting/ training budgets of teachers and complex transformations to align the features between teacher-student models. To address the problem, we analyze teacher roles in feature distillation and have an intriguing observation: additional teacher architectures are not always necessary. Then we propose Tf-FD, a simple yet effective **T**eacher-$f$ree **F**eature **D**istillation framework, reusing channel-wise and layer-wise meaningful features within the student to provide teacher-like knowledge without an additional model. In particular, our framework is subdivided into intra-layer and inter-layer distillation. The intra-layer Tf-FD performs feature salience ranking and transfers the knowledge from salient feature to redundant feature within the same layer. For inter-layer Tf-FD, we deal with distilling high-level semantic knowledge embedded in the deeper layer representations to guide the training of shallow layers. Benefiting from the small gap between these self-features, Tf-FD simply needs to optimize extra feature mimicking losses without complex transformations. Furthermore, we provide insightful discussions to shed light on Tf-FD from feature regularization perspectives. Our experiments conducted on classification and object detection tasks demonstrate that our technique achieves state-of-the-art results on different models with fast training speeds. Code is available at https:// lilujunai.github.io/Teacher-free-Distillation/.

Keywords: Feature regularization · Knowledge distillation

1 Introduction

Despite the tremendous success of deep learning in various tasks [2,11,24,53], it is still difficult to employ deep neural networks to solve real-world problems because of the limitations of calculation and memory assets. To alleviate this issue, there have been several efforts [13,28,65,66] to drive down the computational cost of deep neural networks, and Knowledge Distillation (KD) [16] is one of the examples.

Supplementary Information The online version contains supplementary material available at https://doi.org/10.1007/978-3-031-19809-0_20.

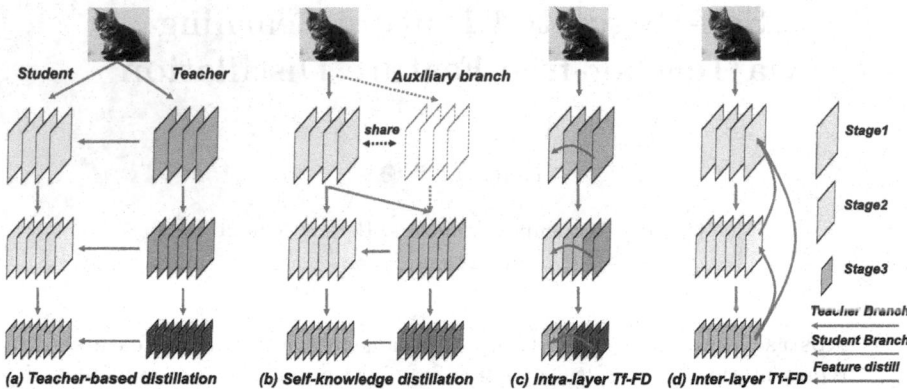

Fig. 1. Comparison of teacher-based distillation (a), self-knowledge distillation (b), our intra-layer Tf-FD (c) and inter-layer Tf-FD (d). We use ResNet-20 as a student model on CIFAR-100. Different teacher architectures, pre-trained ResNet-110/ResNet-20, online ResNet-110/ResNet-20 in (a) and auxiliary branch of ResNet-20 in (b) improve baseline by 1.66%, 1.36%, 1.88%, 1.42% and 0.98% gains for top-1 accuracy, respectively. Our intra-layer and inter-layer Tf-FD obtain 1.42% and 1.25% gains.

KD is an effective training process that achieves a higher precision-efficiency trade-off at runtime by transferring the knowledge learnt by a high-capacity teacher model to a low-capacity student model.

The original KD [16] uses the logit outcomes of the teacher network as knowledge. For further exploiting the knowledge, the feature distillation methods [44,61] enable student to imitate the intermediate feature of the teacher in order to further utilize its knowledge. Subsequent works [1,15,20,22,52,61] focus on extracting and matching informative knowledge conditioned on the feature representations of a pre-defined teacher model. However, the pipeline of these traditional teacher-student learning suffers from three critical problems: (a) It requires substantial efforts and experiments to find proper teacher models, especially for large student models. (b) Training teacher model needs extra training resources, which brings heavy burdens for applications. (c) Teacher-based distillation methods always employ complex feature transformations (*e.g.*, encoder-decoder [22]) or matching strategies [5] to perform better semantic alignment due to the feature gap. These issues limit the extensive application of feature distillation.

A question naturally arises: is an extra teacher model necessary for feature distillation? To make it clear, we investigate behaviours of teacher models in distillation works, including teacher-based distillation methods [16,34] and self-knowledge distillation (self-KD) methods [21,25,31,41,62]. As demonstrated in Fig. 1, for the teacher-based techniques, another high-capability model is typically selected as the teacher model. Meanwhile, self-KD methods obtain the teacher model by constructing auxiliary branches, which share the shallow layer with the student model. Therefore, in these two frameworks, the teacher-student model can be regarded as a super-network [8,18] with a teacher branch and a student branch. We evaluate different types of models as a teacher branch to investigate their effect for feature distillation. The results (see the captions in Fig. 1) indicate that all these various teacher modules can bring considerable distillation gains. That is to say, for the super-network, features located in different branches can play the role of the teacher model for other sub-networks. This observation encourages us to explore whether features from sub-networks in other dimensions (*e.g.*, depth and width) can similarly produce distillation boosts. Consequently, we discard the teacher branch and employ the features located in different layers and channels for distillation (see Fig. 1 (c) and (d)). Magically, such a completely teacher-free feature distillation approach also yields significant performance gains.

Inspired by the above observations, we present a simple yet effective **Teacher-free Feature Distillation** (Tf-FD) framework. Different from the current teacher-student framework, our approach takes supervision from the intermediate features within the student network itself to perform distillation without additional teacher models. Specially, intra-layer Tf-FD and inter-layer Tf-FD are developed in our framework, respectively. For intra-layer Tf-FD, we first reorganize intra-layer features depending on their salience, which is calculated based on the l_p-norm of each feature. These larger l_p-norm features contain more meaningful knowledge [28]. Then, intra-layer Tf-FD allows salient features to distill redundant ones. The inter-layer Tf-FD leverages the fact that deeper layers contain rich contextual information [6] and achieves the knowledge distillation chain from deep to shallow layers by minimizing self-training losses. The merits of Tf-FD lie in three-fold. First, it proposes a simple distillation pipeline that can successfully broaden the usage of distillations without additional teacher seeking and training costs. Second, Tf-FD only needs to employ simple l_2 distances for the feature mimicking loss, which benefits from fast training speed. Third, self-feature knowledge mined by Tf-FD is orthogonal to knowledge from other models and self-logits. Thus, Tf-FD could naturally combine with teacher-based KD, and logit regularizes to obtain additional gains. We further shed light on the Tf-FD from a regularization perspective. In principle, our Tf-FD plays the role of a new regularizer via self-features, which provide semantic disturbance to obtain significant performance gains. Thus, Tf-FD outperforms other regularizers in terms of enhancing the feature consistency of the lightweight model.

Comprehensive experiments are implemented on a variety of deep models and datasets. For performance improvement, our approach surpasses previous regularization techniques with 0.75%~0.99% obvious margins and yields 1.07%~1.56% gains than baseline on CIFAR-100. On the large-scale ImageNet dataset, our approach still achieves 0.71% gains, which outperforms other training techniques. For training efficiency, Tf-FD achieves at least 3× faster training speed than teacher-based KDs. Moreover, Tf-FD with orthogonal logits KD on the outputs surpasses the recent contrastive training distillation (*e.g.*, CRD [50]). On downstream tasks, Tf-FD improves the AP by 0.99 on the Faster R-CNN detector on the MS-COCO dataset, demonstrating the generality of our approach.

In conclusion, we make the following major contributions in this paper:

- By analyzing and exploring teacher models in feature distillation, we point out that the distillation process on intermediate features does not rely on additional teacher architectures. This motivates us to propose a novel Teacher-free Feature Distillation (Tf-FD) framework.

- Tf-FD explores new distillation schemas where the student learns from the salient feature maps in the same layer (intra-layer Tf-FD) and the deeper layers representations (inter-layer Tf-FD) without any additional teacher model and complex transformations. As a result, Tf-FD merits faster training speeds, superior accuracy gains, and extensive generalizability.
- We further discuss the relationship between Tf-FD and feature regularization. Tf-FD implicitly utilizes self-features as regularization distortion by optimizing the distillation loss. We hope this discussion could facilitate future research for feature distillation works to some extent.

2   Related Work

We summarize the current distillation and regularization works in this part.

Feature Distillation vs Feature Regularization. Knowledge distillation use logits [3,16] or feature knowledge [44] from a high-capacity teacher to drive the student's training. The intermediate features of a network contain extensive spatial and structural information regarding image content [7]. Accordingly, feature distillation methods [7,44,57,61] are emphasized in designed to convince the student model to simulate the teacher model's feature representations. As feature maps from different layers of the student and teacher networks typically have non-matching dimensions (e.g., widths, heights, and channels), existing feature distillation methods adopt various transformations to match their dimensions and different distance metrics to measure differences. FitNets [44], for instance, uses l_2-loss to emulate the middle features of teacher-student networks, and AT [61] applies feature distillation on the attention map. However, choosing a suitable teacher model for feature distillation is not easy. In sharp contrast to these methods, Tf-FD is a complete teacher-free feature distillation without any extra structure. It opens up a new avenue for distillation design conditioned on the intermediate representations. Feature regularization methods [10,37,49] can effectively prevent neural network overfitting by injecting noise into feature space. For instance, DropBlock [10] randomly removes some consecutive portions of a feature map, while SpatialDropout [51] randomly abandons the entire channels. However, these methods depend on some unique strategies to avoid severe semantic damage, which will be detrimental to the performance of the CNNs [49]. Our Tf-FD can be regarded as a feature regularization method and uses self-features as a noise, which contains more semantic information than random masks. Tf-FD develops the connections between feature regularization and distillation from this point.

Self-knowledge Distillation vs Teacher-Free Distillation. Some self-knowledge distillation frameworks [21,25,41,62] generate extra auxiliary branches [25,29,47], classifiers [41] and FPN [21] to present online logits distillation. Nevertheless, these methods are not teacher-free distillation methods.

They necessitate careful designing and training of auxiliary structures, which may enable student network optimization challenging [19]. Also, these methods are teacher-based and mainly work on the outputted logits, not the intermediate features. Other Self-KDs [27,59] use additional data views as teachers/peers but may lose helpful information in the augmentation process on some tasks (*e.g.*, object detection). Our Tf-FD does not require any additional teacher structures or additional forward and backward passes. SAD [17] adds attention supervision based on the nature of the feature map on specific lane line detection task. However, it also introduces additional parameters on feature alignment and is not present as a general approach for classification and object detection. Our inter-layer Tf-FD performs dense cross-layer distillation, but only residual supervision exists with SAD [17]. Recent methods [58,63] let the student model learn from the manually designed smooth distribution on the outputted logits like label smoothing [48]. Tf-FD mainly acts on the intermediate features, not the outputs, and can be well combined with these methods, further expanding the family of teacher-free distillations.

3   Teacher-free Feature Distillation

In this section, we first review feature distillation methods with a general formulation in Sect. 3.1. Then, the formulation and insights of our Teacher-free Feature Distillation (Tf-FD) are presented in Sect. 3.2. Finally, we discuss the relationship between Tf-FD and feature regularization in Sect. 3.3.

3.1   Revisiting Conventional Feature Distillation

We first briefly review the fundamental concept of knowledge distillation within the feature level to further comprehend our methodology. Conventional feature distillation methods [44,61], which explicitly optimize the feature distillation loss, promote the student model to learn the feature spaces of the teacher. Given that x stands for the training data and $\mathcal{H}$ for a collection of layer location pairs for feature distillation. The generic objective function for a target student model S with features ψ_S and its teacher model T with features ψ_T is defined as:

$$\mathcal{L}_{\mathrm{S}} = \mathcal{L}_{\mathrm{CE}}(\theta_S, x) + \mu \sum_{h \in \mathcal{H}} \mathcal{D}_f(T_s^h(\psi_S), T_t^h(\psi_T)), \tag{1}$$

where θ_S denotes the parameters of the student model. The student and teacher transformations, T_s and T_t are used to align the feature channel and spatial dimensions. The distance function quantifying the difference of intermediate features is $\mathcal{D}_f(\cdot)$. The weighting factor called μ is used to balance loss terms.

3.2   Formulation of Teacher-free Feature Distillation

Our Tf-FD aims to realize feature distillation via optimizing self-training losses to make the design as general as possible. As illustrated in Fig. 2, merely given

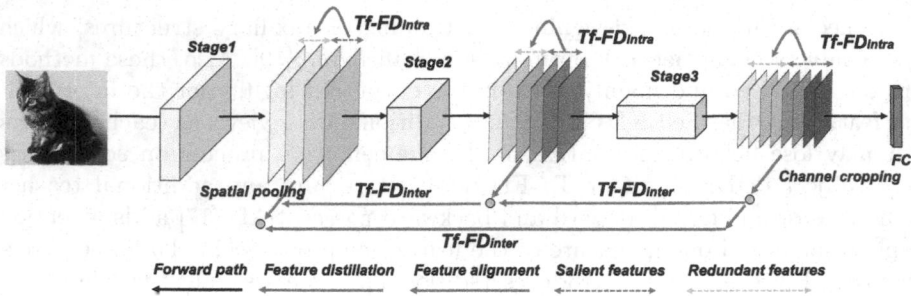

Fig. 2. An illustration of our Tf-FD, including intra-layer and inter-layer parts. In the training phase, for intra-layer Tf-FD, we first rank the features on the same layer according to the feature salience. Then the top half of salient features are leveraged to distill the remaining features. And inter-layer Tf-FD capitalizes on features in deeper layers to supervise shallow ones. In the inference phase, the model can be inferred separately.

a student network and training data, Tf-FD achieves such a goal by learning from the salient feature maps in the same layer (intra-layer distillation) and the deeper layers representations (inter-layer distillation).

Intra-layer Teacher-Free Feature Distillation. Over-parameterized models tend to produce *redundant* features that contain poor visual concepts [28]. We present intra Tf-FD that uses salient features to supervise redundant features to address this problem. Specifically, we first sort the features of the same channel according to the l_p-norm [35,64] ($p = 2$) and then use the top half features to distill the bottom half ones. We reduce shallow features to the same resolution as deep ones for feature alignment via average pooling. For channel alignment, we crop the wider deep features into multiple groups, each having the same number of features as the shallow ones. Then, the intra-layer Tf-FD can directly calculate l_2 loss for $\mathcal{D}_f(\cdot)$, which can be formulated as:

$$\mathcal{L}_{\text{intra}} = \frac{1}{\delta} \sum_{i=1}^{\delta} \mathcal{D}_f\left(\overline{\psi_{S_i}}, \widetilde{\psi_{S_i}}\right) = \frac{1}{\delta} \sum_{i=1}^{\delta} ||\overline{\psi_{S_i}} - \widetilde{\psi_{S_i}}||^2, \tag{2}$$

where δ denotes the number of total layers, $\overline{\psi_{S_i}}$ is the bottom half redundant features and $\widetilde{\psi_{S_i}}$ is the top half salient features. Different from other channel-wise architecture designs (*e.g.*, GhostNet [12]) with extra inference costs, intra-layer Tf-FD is cost-free in inference by optimizing loss rather than changing the model.

Inter-layer Teacher-Free Feature Distillation. There are extensive computer vision applications [9,17,30] and information-bottleneck theory [9,17,55] demonstrating a solid fact: the features of the deep layer contain more task-relevant semantic visual concepts. Thus, deep features always obtain significant gains in the distillation framework [5]. Our inter-layer Tf-FD uses self-features in the deep layer of the student network to supervise shallow ones, which are updated by the l_2 sum loss during back propagation. The loss of inter-layer Tf-FD can be written as:

$$\mathcal{L}_{\text{inter}} = \frac{1}{\gamma} \sum_{i=1}^{L-1} \sum_{j>i}^{L} \mathcal{D}_f\left(T_{s_i}(\psi_{S_i}), T_{s_j}(\psi_{S_j})\right) = \frac{1}{\gamma} \sum_{i=1}^{L-1} \sum_{j>i}^{L} \|T_{s_i}(\psi_{S_i}) - T_{s_j}(\psi_{S_j})\|^2,$$
(3)

where γ denotes the number of pair loss, L is the number of layers of selected features, we use l_2 distance as D_f, and T_s represents feature alignment. In particular, we use a pooling operation and channel cropping to align features in spatial and channel dimensions without complex transformation. To reduce computation and semantic conflicts in dense cross-layer distillation in Tf-FD, we also propose simple inter-layer Tf-FD for the residual feature pairs in i and $i+1$ layers as $\frac{1}{\gamma} \sum_{i=1}^{L-1} \sum_{j=i+1}^{L} \|T_{s_i}(\psi_{S_i}) - T_{s_j}(\psi_{S_j})\|^2$. Note that ψ_{S_j} in Eq. (3) is frozen when updating losses.

Comparison Between Inter-layer Tf-FD with Residual Connection and BYOT. (a) Residual connections alleviate vanishing gradients in deep networks via summation of block-wise cross-layer features. It is adopted in CNN architecture engineering (*e.g.*, ResNet) and cannot be removed in inference. While inter-layer Tf-FD does not exist in inference. (b) The BYOT uses the auxiliary classifier in Deep Supervision [26] to change the original student model into a new multi-exit architecture like ONE [25] and transfers knowledge between these branches. Similar to Deep Supervision, BYOT prevents models from the vanishing gradient problem in terms of optimization. However, shallow classifiers with fewer layers in BYOT have much weaker performance than the student model (41.26% vs 68.12% for ResNet-18 on ImageNet as BYOT reported), and its different optimization properties would affect the optimization of the student network [19]. In sharp contrast, inter-layer Tf-FD improves feature consistency by directly optimizing the cross-layer feature loss without extra parameters.

Overall Optimization Objectives of Tf-FD. In the vanilla Tf-FD method, we train the student network with three losses (α and β are weighting factors):

$$\mathcal{L}_{\text{T}f\text{-FD}} = \mathcal{L}_{\text{CE}}(\theta_S, x) + \beta\mathcal{L}_{\text{intra}} + \alpha\mathcal{L}_{\text{inter}},$$
(4)

Augmenting Tf-FD with Logits Teacher-Based Distillations. Being a generic feature regularizer framework, Tf-FD itself provides a new teacher-free feature KD framework when selecting/training extra teachers are difficult. When pre-trained teachers are available, since different sources of knowledge (other models and self logits), our Tf-FD could naturally combine with teacher-based KD losses $\mathcal{L}_{\text{KD}}$ to train student models. To explore this potential, we apply distillation on the outputted logits from the two heads of the student network to promote the performance of our Tf-FD. We call the resulting method Tf-FD†. Specifically, Tf-FD† performs logits distillation with KL divergence $\mathcal{D}_{kl}(\theta_S\|\theta_T)$, and the total training objective can be expressed as:

$$\mathcal{L}_{\text{T}f\text{-FD}\dagger} = \mathcal{L}_{\text{CE}}(\theta_S, x) + \mathcal{D}_{kl}(\theta_T, \theta_S) + \beta\mathcal{L}_{\text{intra}} + \alpha\mathcal{L}_{\text{inter}},$$
(5)

3.3 Discussion of the Relationships with Feature Regularization

Decoupled from the additional teacher model, our Tf-FD extends the feature distillation to a more generic training method. Tf-FD improves the generalization of the model by supervision of self-features, which can also be considered as feature noise. Therefore, we discuss why Tf-FD works from the perspective of feature regularization. To

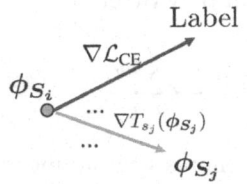

Fig. 3. Illustration of feature updating.

make the analysis process as clear as possible, we select the inter-layer Tf-FD as the distillation function alone. For the ith layer of network, its features ψ_{S_i} are supervised by deeper features $\{\psi_{S_j} | j \in \{i+1, i+2, \cdots, L\}\}$. Thus, updated loss function for i^{th} layer can be defined as $\mathcal{L}_{i^{\text{th}}-layer} = \mathcal{L}_{CE} + \alpha \times \frac{1}{\gamma} \sum_{j>i}^{L} ||T_{s_i}(\psi_{S_i}) - T_{s_j}(\psi_{S_j})||^2$. Similar to the error update formula of the parameters, the ψ_{S_i} is updated as following:

$$\widehat{\psi_{S_i}} = \psi_{S_i} - \eta \nabla \left(\mathcal{L}_{CE}(\theta_S, x) + \alpha \times \frac{1}{\gamma} \sum_{j>i}^{L} ||T_{s_i}(\psi_{S_i}) - T_{s_j}(\psi_{S_j})||^2 \right). \quad (6)$$

where η is the learning rate, and $\widehat{\psi_{S_i}}$ is the updated ψ_{S_i}. As mentioned above, we adopt the simple feature alignment for T_s. Therefore, we simplify its role in the following analysis.

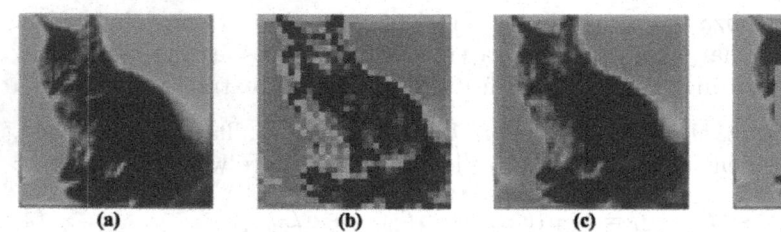

Fig. 4. Schematic diagram of Tf-FD (c) and Dropblock [10] (d) for feature of Conv2_x (a) and Conv3_x (b) of ResNet-18 on ImageNet. Tf-FD implicitly employs Conv3_x features as noises for Conv2_x features when explicitly optimizing this pair of inter Tf-FD loss. Moreover, Dropblock applies a random mask for feature regularization on the Conv2_x features.

As shown in Fig. 3, during the training process, the ψ_{S_i} needs to be updated in the direction of ψ_{S_j} so that feature distillation loss is reduced to make Eq. (6) converge. This illustrates that Tf-FD implicitly applies a feature distortion of ψ_{S_j} to ψ_{S_i} by optimizing the distillation loss. The regularization effect of Tf-FD depends on the feature knowledge contained in ψ_{S_j} and the weighting factor α. Therefore, Tf-FD seeks to leverage privileged within the network itself to maximize regularization gains. As shown in Fig. 4, while Dropblock [10] utilizes random masks that often cause semantic damage, Tf-FD preserves more semantic information. Furthermore, when ψ_{S_j} is features ψ_T from other teacher models, the Eq. (6) reveals the feature regularization role played by general feature distillation. From this perspective, different teacher models in the previous exploration experiments provide feature regularization disturbances and thus all achieve performance gains. This explains why feature distillation could work without additional teacher modules.

Table 1. Top-1 accuracies (%) of teacher-free methods, self-knowledge distillations (self-KD) and teacher-based distillation (Tb-KD) reported in CRD [50] under the same training setting of 240 epochs. Note that teacher models are only for teacher-based distillations, and Tf-FD is completely free of teacher models.

Method	Student	ResNet-20 69.06	ResNet-32 71.14	WRN-16-2 73.26	ResNet-8×4 72.50	VGG-8 70.36
Tf method	Dropout [24]	69.22	71.31	73.31	72.68	70.52
	DropBlock [10]	69.65	71.56	73.42	72.87	70.76
	SAD [17]	69.76	71.48	73.68	72.71	70.72
	LS [48]	69.87	71.86	73.65	72.91	70.87
	Tf-KD [58]	70.02	72.06	73.88	73.05	71.05
	Tf-FD (ours)	**70.62**	**72.55**	**74.33**	**73.62**	**71.62**
Self-KD	CS-KD [59]	70.12	72.26	73.98	73.10	71.26
	BYOT [62]	70.37	72.46	73.70	72.98	70.88
	ONE [25]	70.77	72.78	74.68	73.51	72.01
	Teacher	ResNet-110 74.31	ResNet-110 74.31	WRN-40-2 75.61	ResNet-32×4 79.42	VGG-13 74.64
Tb-KD	FitNets [44]	68.99	71.06	73.58	73.50	71.02
	AT [53]	70.22	72.31	74.08	73.44	71.43
	SP [52]	70.04	72.69	73.83	72.94	72.68
	PKT [38]	70.25	72.61	74.54	73.64	72.88
	AB [15]	69.53	70.98	72.50	73.17	70.94
	NST [20]	69.53	71.96	73.68	73.30	71.53
	KD [16]	70.67	73.08	74.92	73.33	72.98
	CRD [50]	71.46	73.48	75.64	75.51	73.94
	Tf-FD† (ours)	**71.56**	**73.68**	**75.68**	**75.65**	**74.08**

4   Experiments

In this section, we first evaluate our Tf-FD/Tf-FD† on CIFAR-100 in Sect. 4.1 and ImageNet in Sect. 4.2. Apart from image classification, Tf-FD is also effective for downstream tasks, such as object detection in Sect. 4.3. Comprehensive ablation experiments are performed to analyze the key design in Sect. 4.4.

4.1   Experiments on CIFAR-100

Implementation. The CIFAR-100 dataset [23] is used for the trials without extra strong data augmentation. We conduct experiments on ResNets [14], WRNs [60] and VGG [46] with CRD's settings [50], whose training epochs are 240. The weight decay is 5×10^{-4}, and the optimizer is SGD. Initialized at 0.1, the multi-step learning rate increases by 0.1 every 150, 180, and 210 epochs.

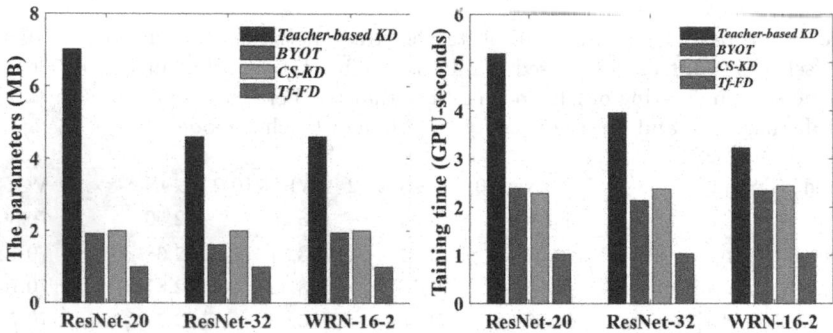

Fig. 5. (Left) The total training parameters and (Right) training time of teacher-based KD [61], BYOT [62], CS-KD [59] and our Tf-FD, which are measured on a single NVIDIA 2080Ti. Number of Y-axis represents the improved ratios compared to baseline.

Comparison Results. In Table 1, we report the results of various regularization, self-KDs, and teacher-based methods on CIFAR-100. For ResNet-like models, Tf-FD obtains 1.12%~1.56% absolute accuracy gains, which shows its practical value for different depth and width networks. Besides, on WRN and VGG, Tf-FD outperforms baselines with 1.07 %~1.26 % margins. Compared to feature regularizers, Tf-FD outperforms DropBlock [10] with 0.75%~0.99% margins. This proves that more semantic feature distortions of Tf-FD can obtain significant performance gains. Furthermore, Tf-FD achieves superior performance than these typical self-distillation methods (*e.g.*, BYOT [62] and CS-KD [59]). Compared to feature distillation methods with a strong pre-trained teacher model, Tf-FD achieves competitive performance gains, indicating that our framework without the teacher model can still effectively boost performance. Tf-FD's basic performance is already better than SOTA teacher-free logits KDs/ regularizers and can be further improved with advanced loss functions, demonstrating its effectiveness. Extra teachers contain richer knowledge than students themselves. Thus, teacher-based KDs usually have superior accuracy than teacher-free KDs (including Tf-FD). In particular, the combination (Tf-FD†) of Tf-FD with logits KD [16] obtains 0.60%~1.22% gains than KD, which illustrate their orthogonality. Compared to recent SOTA teacher-based KDs with contrastive training with pair-wise augmentations (*e.g.*, CRD [50]), Tf-FD† achieves superior accuracy and training efficiency. In summary, our Tf-FD can noticeably improve the performance of the student network without additional overhead, which effectively expands the application of feature distillation.

Training Efficiency. Furthermore, we compare the training cost between Tf-FD and teacher-based feature distillation under the same settings. As shown in Fig. 5, Tf-FD does not introduce additional parameters and achieves $3\times \sim 5\times$ training acceleration than BYOT, CS-KD, and teacher-based KD.

Table 2. Top-1/Top-5 accuracies (%) of teacher-free methods, self-knowledge distillations (self-KD) and teacher-based knowledge distillations (KDs) on ImageNet dataset. Most results of other methods are references to the original paper report. N/A means no published result is available.

Model	ResNet-18 [Student]			Model	ResNet-34 [Teacher]		
Type	Method	Top-1	Top-5	Type	Method	Top-1	Top-5
	Student	69.75	89.07		Teacher	73.31	91.42
Tf-method	Dropout [24]	69.79	89.16	Tb-KD	KD [16]	70.66	89.88
	DropBlock [10]	69.88	89.32		AT [53]	70.70	90.00
	SAD [17]	69.82	89.24		AFD [7]	70.39	N/A
	LS [48]	69.93	N/A		SP [52]	70.62	89.88
	Tf-KD [58]	70.15	N/A		CC [39]	69.96	89.17
	Tf-FD (ours)	**70.46**	**89.72**		VID [1]	70.30	N/A
Self-KD	BYOT [62]	69.84	N/A		FitNets [44]	70.31	N/A
	FRSKD [21]	70.17	N/A		SemCKD [36]	70.87	N/A
	ONE [25]	70.55	N/A		**Tf-FD† (ours)**	**71.00**	**90.22**

4.2   Experiments on ImageNet

Detailed Implementation. The experiments on ImageNet [45] are carried out via ResNet-18 [14]. We use the same training configurations (*e.g.*, 100 training epochs) with most distillation techniques. Warm-up and early-decay schedules are performed for loss weight of Tf-FD.

Comparison Results. Table 2 reports the performance of our approach on ImageNet. Tf-FD improves baseline models of ResNet-18 by 0.71% gains and outperforms regularization approaches and self-KDs methods with 0.29 %~0.61% margins, which supports its superiority on the large-scale dataset. Despite the fact that traditional teacher-based distillation methods use the pre-trained ResNet-34 as a teacher, Tf-FD produces very competitive performance in teacher-free configurations. Equipped with knowledge distillation for outputted logits, Tf-FD† obtains 1.25% gain than baseline and surpasses other teacher-based approaches.

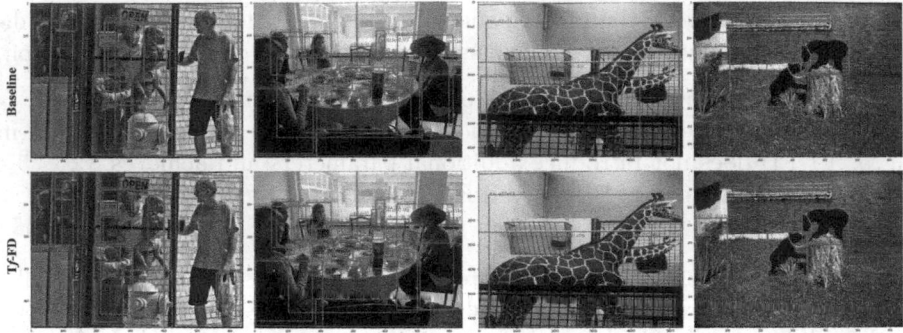

Fig. 6. Visualization of bounding-box detection outputs of Faster R-CNN via ResNet-50 backbone on the MS-COCO2017. The two figures on the left illustrate that Tf-FD is more effective in capturing small objects than baseline. The two figures on the right indicate that fewer false positives occur in Tf-FD.

Table 3. Results on object detection [40]. R50 represents using ResNet-50 as backbone. Note that teacher models are only for other feature distillation methods, and Tf-FD is completely free of teacher models.

Detector	Model	AP	AP_{50}	AP_{75}	AP_L	AP_M	AP_S
Faster R-CNN (R101-FPN)	Teacher baseline	42.04	62.48	45.88	54.60	45.55	25.22
Faster R-CNN (R50-FPN)	Student baseline	37.93	58.84	41.05	49.10	41.14	22.44
	KD [16]	38.35	59.41	41.71	49.48	41.80	22.73
	FitNets [44]	38.76	59.62	41.80	50.70	42.20	22.32
	FGFI [54]	39.44	60.27	43.04	51.97	42.51	22.89
	Tf-FD† (ours)	**38.92**	**59.71**	**41.93**	**50.88**	**41.92**	**21.96**

4.3   Extension to Object Detection

Implementation. We evaluate Tf-FD on MS-COCO2017 dataset [32], which includes more than 120K images encompassing 80 categories. We apply Tf-FD to Faster R-CNN [43] and employ Detectron2 as the baseline. Note that the Tf-FD distillation is carried out at the detection fine-tuning stage with advanced feature losses [54,56]. All models are trained using a 2× learning schedule, and their performance is evaluated on the MS-COCO2017 validation set.

Comparison Results. Table 3 demonstrate that Tf-FD improves the AP 0.99 on Faster R-CNN. Compared with other distillation methods with strong teacher models, Tf-FD outperforms KD [16] and FitNets [44] and obtains competitive gains with FGFI [54], which is particularly designed for object detection. As shown in Fig. 6, visualization results demonstrate the effectiveness of Tf-FD in small object detection and reducing false positives. The success of challenging object detection tasks demonstrates the generality and effectiveness of our approach. Besides this simple extension, we are also designing and investigating

Self-Regulated Feature Learning via Teacher-free Feature Distillation 359

Table 4. Ablation study of each loss added to different blocks of ResNet-20 on CIFAR-100. S2, S3, and S4 refer to Conv2_x features, Conv3_x features, and Conv4_x features, respectively. S3 → S2 means that Conv3_x features are employed to distill Conv2_x features. ↑ refers to the performance gain.

$\mathcal{L}_{inter}$	S3 → S2	✓	×	×	✓	×	×	×	×	✓
	S4 → S3	×	✓	×	✓	×	×	×	×	✓
	S4 → S2	×	×	✓	✓	×	×	×	×	✓
$\mathcal{L}_{intra}$	S2	×	×	×	×	✓	×	×	✓	✓
	S3	×	×	×	×	×	✓	×	✓	✓
	S4	×	×	×	×	×	×	✓	✓	✓
ResNet-20	Top-1 (%)	69.84 (0.78↑)	70.29 (1.23↑)	70.18 (1.12↑)	70.31 (1.25↑)	70.26 (1.20↑)	70.29 (1.23↑)	70.41 (1.35↑)	70.51 (1.45↑)	70.62 (1.56↑)

specially designed feature regularizers for object detection and semantic segmentation [42] following our Tf-FD idea.

4.4 Ablation Study

We concentrate on the effect of each element of our approach in this section.

Design of Each Loss. The ablation research on CIFAR-100 with ResNet-20 is conducted in Table 4 to illustrate the individual efficacy of various components in Tf-FD. It is observed that (a) A single loss of Tf-FD can also obtain 0.78%~1.23% accuracy gains. (b) The intra-layer Tf-FD in the deep layer obtains more obvious performance improvement. This is consistent with the fact that some feature regularization methods [10,49] work well on the final stage of the neural network.

Advanced Feature Mimicking Loss for Tf-FD. In Fig. 7 (b), we explore different feature mimicking losses for Tf-FD for ResNet-20 on CIFAR-100. The AT [61], SP [52] and ICKD [33] achieve more obvious performance than the simple l_2 loss, indicating that the specially designed mimicking loss can further improve the performance of Tf-FD. The AB [15] use complex feature mapping, resulting in the loss of valuable feature knowledge. We adopt the simple l_2 loss for Tf-FD for all previous analyses and experiments.

Sensitivity Study for Hyper-parameters α and β. α and β are loss weights of $\mathcal{L}_{inter}$ and $\mathcal{L}_{intra}$. As shown in Fig. 7, experiments on CIFAR-100 and ResNet-20 are conducted to study their sensitivity. The results demonstrate that (α, β) = (0.0005, 0.0008) is the best solution for the hyper-parameter setting. Even in the worst situation when $\alpha = 0.01$ and $\beta = 0.0001$, Tf-FD still achieves 0.71% accuracy improvements than the baseline and outperforms some KDs (e.g., FitNets [44] and AB [15]) in Table 1.

Attention Map Visualization. Our Tf-FD would help the network pay attention to important information. Figure 8 illustrates that the gradient activation map of Tf -FD is more concerned with the correct region than Dropblock.

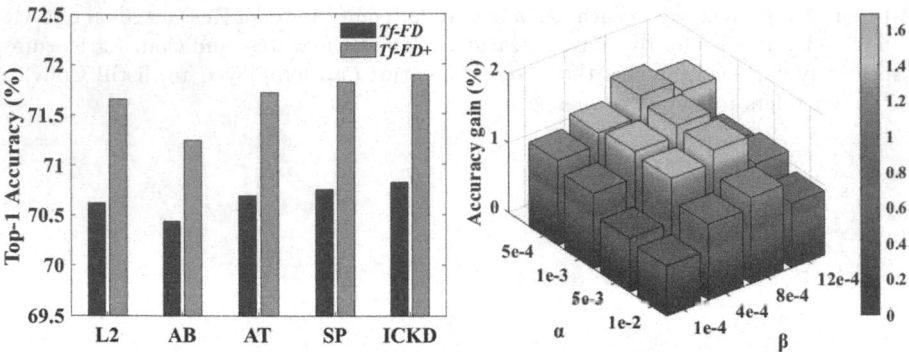

Fig. 7. (Left) Comparison results of different feature mimicking loss for Tf-FD. (Right) Hyper-parameter analysis: the top-1 accuracy (%) of Tf-FD with various α (Y-axis) and β (X-axis) for ResNet-20 trained on CIFAR-100.

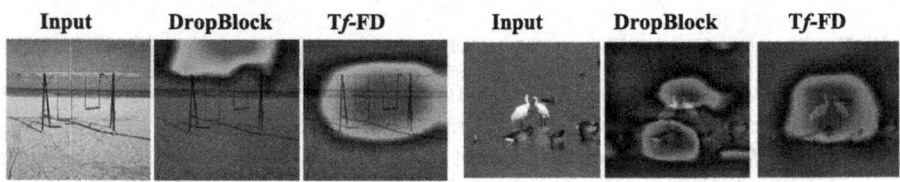

Fig. 8. Comparison on the Grad-CAM++ [4] visualization results between the features of the Dropblock, and Tf-FD on ImageNet.

5   Conclusion

In this Tf-FD work, we develop a novel paradigm for performing feature distillation efficiently without teacher models. Based on our insight that feature distillation does not depend on additional modules, Tf-FD achieves this goal by capitalizing on channel-wise and layer-wise salient self-features without setting complicated feature alignment and assuming additional teacher modules to be available. From the perspective of regularization, Tf -FD exerts meaningful feature perturbations by optimizing the loss. This insight opens new doors for the community to trade technical routes for both feature regularization and distillation. In future work, we will make an effort to analyze Tf-FD from a theoretical perspective and explore its application with unique designs on downstream tasks such as FPN-free detectors, VGG-like model optimization, and weakly supervised semantic segmentation [42], etc. We hope this elegant and practical approach will inspire more investigation into the interpretability and widespread applications of knowledge distillation for feature representations.

References

1. Ahn, S., Hu, S.X., Damianou, A., Lawrence, N.D., Dai, Z.: Variational information distillation for knowledge transfer. In: CVPR (2019)
2. Brown, T.B., et al.: Language models are few-shot learners. arXiv preprint, arXiv:2005.14165 (2020)
3. Bucila, C., Caruana, R., Niculescu-Mizil, A.: Model compression. In: KDD (2006)
4. Chattopadhyay, A., Sarkar, A., Howlader, P., Balasubramanian, V.: Grad-CAM++: Improved visual explanations for deep convolutional networks. In: WACV (2018)
5. Chen, D., Mei, J.P., Zhang, Y., Wang, C., Wang, Z., Feng, Y., Chen, C.: Cross-layer distillation with semantic calibration. arXiv preprint, arXiv:2012.03236 (2020)
6. Cheng, X., Rao, Z., Chen, Y., Zhang, Q.: Explaining knowledge distillation by quantifying the knowledge. In: CVPR (2020)
7. Chung, I., Park, S., Kim, J., Kwak, N.: Feature-map-level online adversarial knowledge distillation. In: ICML (2020)
8. Dong, P., Niu, X., Li, L., Xie, L., Zou, W., Ye, T., Wei, Z., Pan, H.: Prior-guided one-shot neural architecture search. arXiv preprint arXiv:2206.13329 (2022)
9. Dong, Z., Hanwang, Z., Jinhui, T., Xiansheng, H., Qianru, S.: Self-regulation for semantic segmentation. International Conference on Computer Vision (ICCV) (2021)
10. Ghiasi, G., Lin, T.Y., Le, Q.V.: Dropblock: a regularization method for convolutional networks. In: NeurIPS (2018)
11. Girshick, R., Donahue, J., Darrell, T., Malik, J.: Rich feature hierarchies for accurate object detection and semantic segmentation. In: CVPR (2014)
12. Han, K., Wang, Y., Tian, Q., Guo, J., Xu, C., Xu, C.: GhostNet: more features from cheap operations. In: CVPR (2020)
13. Han, S., Pool, J., Tran, J., Dally, W.J.: Learning both weights and connections for efficient neural networks. In: NeurIPS (2015)
14. He, K., Zhang, X., Ren, S., Sun, J.: Deep residual learning for image recognition. In: CVPR (2016)
15. Heo, B., Lee, M., Yun, S., Choi, J.Y.: Knowledge transfer via distillation of activation boundaries formed by hidden neurons. In: AAAI (2019)
16. Hinton, G., Vinyals, O., Dean, J.: Distilling the knowledge in a neural network. arXiv preprint, arXiv:1503.02531 (2015)
17. Hou, Y., Ma, Z., Liu, C., Loy, C.C.: Learning lightweight lane detection CNNS by self attention distillation. In: ICCV (2019)
18. Hu, Y., Wang, X., Li, L., Gu, Q.: Improving one-shot NAS with shrinking-and-expanding supernet. Pattern Recogn. **118**, 108025 (2021)
19. Huang, G., Chen, D., Li, T., Wu, F., van der Maaten, L., Weinberger, K.Q.: Multi-scale dense networks for resource efficient image classification. In: ICLR (2018)
20. Huang, Z., Wang, N.: Like what you like: Knowledge distill via neuron selectivity transfer. arXiv preprint, arXiv:1707.01219 (2017)
21. Ji, M., Shin, S., Hwang, S., Park, G., Moon, I.C.: Refine myself by teaching myself: feature refinement via self-knowledge distillation. arXiv preprint, arXiv:2103.08273 (2021)
22. Kim, J., Park, S., Kwak, N.: Paraphrasing complex network: Network compression via factor transfer. In: NeurIPS (2018)
23. Krizhevsky, A., Hinton, G.: Learning multiple layers of features from tiny images. Technical report (2009)

24. Krizhevsky, A., Sutskever, I., Hinton, G.E.: ImageNet classification with deep convolutional neural networks. In: NeurIPS (2012)
25. Lan, X., Zhu, X., Gong, S.: Knowledge distillation by on-the-fly native ensemble. In: NeurIPS (2018)
26. Lee, C.Y., Xie, S., Gallagher, P., Zhang, Z., Tu, Z.: Deeply-supervised nets. In: AISTATS (2015)
27. Lee, H., Hwang, S.J., Shin, J.: Self-supervised label augmentation via input transformations. In: ICML (2020)
28. Li, H., Kadav, A., Durdanovic, I., Samet, H., Graf, H.P.: Pruning filters for efficient convnets. In: ICLR (2017)
29. Li, L., Shiuan-Ni, L., Yang, Y., Jin, Z.: Boosting online feature transfer via separable feature fusion. In: IJCNN (2022)
30. Li, L., Shiuan-Ni, L., Yang, Y., Jin, Z.: Teacher-free distillation via regularizing intermediate representation. In: IJCNN (2022)
31. Li, L., Wang, Y., Yao, A., Qian, Y., Zhou, X., He, K.: Explicit connection distillation (2020)
32. Lin, T.-Y., et al.: Microsoft COCO: common objects in context. In: Fleet, D., Pajdla, T., Schiele, B., Tuytelaars, T. (eds.) ECCV 2014. LNCS, vol. 8693, pp. 740–755. Springer, Cham (2014). https://doi.org/10.1007/978-3-319-10602-1_48
33. Liu, L., et al.: Exploring inter-channel correlation for diversity-preserved knowledge distillation. In: ICCV (2021)
34. Liu, Y., et al.: Search to distill: Pearls are everywhere but not the eyes. In: CVPR (2020)
35. Liu, Z., Li, J., Shen, Z., Huang, G., Yan, S., Zhang, C.: Learning efficient convolutional networks through network slimming. In: ICCV (2017)
36. Malinin, A., Mlodozeniec, B., Gales, M.: Ensemble distribution distillation. In: ICLR (2020)
37. Pan, H., Jiang, H., Niu, X., Dou, Y.: Dropfilter: A novel regularization method for learning convolutional neural networks. arXiv preprint, arXiv:1811.06783 (2018)
38. Passalis, N., Tefas, A.: Learning deep representations with probabilistic knowledge transfer. In: Ferrari, V., Hebert, M., Sminchisescu, C., Weiss, Y. (eds.) ECCV 2018. LNCS, vol. 11215, pp. 283–299. Springer, Cham (2018). https://doi.org/10.1007/978-3-030-01252-6_17
39. Peng, B., et al.: Correlation congruence for knowledge distillation. In: ICCV (2019)
40. Pengguang, C., Shu, L., Hengshuang, Z., Jia, J.: Distilling knowledge via knowledge review. In: CVPR (2021)
41. Phuong, M., Lampert, C.H.: Distillation-based training for multi-exit architectures. In: ICCV (2019)
42. Qin, J., Wu, J., Xiao, X., Li, L., Wang, X.: Activation modulation and recalibration scheme for weakly supervised semantic segmentation. In: AAAI (2022)
43. Ren, S., He, K., Girshick, R., Sun, J.: Faster R-CNN: towards real-time object detection with region proposal networks. arXiv preprint, arXiv:1506.01497 (2015)
44. Romero, A., Ballas, N., Kahou, S.E., Chassang, A., Gatta, C., Bengio, Y.: Fitnets: Hints for thin deep nets. In: ICLR (2015)
45. Russakovsky, O., et al.: Imagenet large scale visual recognition challenge. IJCV. **115**, 211–252 (2015)
46. Simonyan, K., Zisserman, A.: Very deep convolutional networks for large-scale image recognition. arXiv preprint, arXiv:1409.1556 (2014)
47. Sun, D., Yao, A.: Deeply-supervised knowledge synergy. In: CVPR (2019)
48. Szegedy, C., Vanhoucke, V., Ioffe, S., Shlens, J., Wojna, Z.: Rethinking the inception architecture for computer vision. In: ICCV (2016)

49. Tang, Y., Wang, Y., Xu, Y., Shi, B., Xu, C., Xu, C., Xu, C.: Beyond dropout: feature map distortion to regularize deep neural networks. In: AAAI (2020)
50. Tian, Y., Krishnan, D., Isola, P.: Contrastive representation distillation. In: ICLR (2020)
51. Tompson, J., Goroshin, R., Jain, A., LeCun, Y., Bregler, C.: Efficient object localization using convolutional networks. In: CVPR (2015)
52. Tung, F., Mori, G.: Similarity-preserving knowledge distillation. In: ICCV (2019)
53. Vaswani, A., et al.: Attention is all you need. arXiv preprint, arXiv:1706.03762 (2017)
54. Wang, T., Yuan, L., Zhang, X., Feng, J.: Distilling object detectors with fine-grained feature imitation. In: CVPR (2019)
55. Wolchover, N., Reading, L.: New theory cracks open the black box of deep learning. Quanta Magazine (2017)
56. Yang, Z., et al.: Focal and global knowledge distillation for detectors. In: CVPR (2022)
57. Yim, J., Joo, D., Bae, J., Kim, J.: A gift from knowledge distillation: fast optimization, network minimization and transfer learning. In: CVPR (2017)
58. Yuan, L., Tay, F.E., Li, G., Wang, T., Feng, J.: Revisiting knowledge distillation via label smoothing regularization. In: CVPR (2020)
59. Yun, S., Park, J.S., Lee, K., Shin, J.: Regularizing class-wise predictions via self-knowledge distillation. In: CVPR (2020)
60. Zagoruyko, S., Komodakis, N.: Wide residual networks. In: BMVC (2016)
61. Zagoruyko, S., Komodakis, N.: Paying more attention to attention: improving the performance of convolutional neural networks via attention transfer. In: ICLR (2017)
62. Zhang, L., Song, J., Gao, A., Chen, J., Bao, C., Ma, K.: Be your own teacher: improve the performance of convolutional neural networks via self distillation. In: ICCV (2019)
63. Zhang, Z., Sabuncu, M.R.: Self-distillation as instance-specific label smoothing. arXiv preprint, arXiv:2006.05065 (2020)
64. Zhao, C., Ni, B., Zhang, J., Zhao, Q., Zhang, W., Tian, Q.: Variational convolutional neural network pruning. In: CVPR (2019)
65. Zhou, A., Yao, A., Guo, Y., Xu, L., Chen, Y.: Incremental network quantization: towards lossless CNNs with low-precision weights. In: ICLR (2017)
66. Zhou, S., Yuxin, W., Ni, Z., Zhou, X., Wen, H., Zou, Y.: DoReFa-Net: training low Bitwidth convolutional neural networks with low Bitwidth gradients. arXiv preprint, arXiv:1606.06160 (2016)

Balancing Between Forgetting and Acquisition in Incremental Subpopulation Learning

Mingfu Liang[1], Jiahuan Zhou[2(✉)], Wei Wei[1], and Ying Wu[1]

[1] Northwestern University, Evanston, USA
{mingfuliang2020,weiwei2022}@u.northwestern.edu, yingwu@northwestern.edu
[2] Peking University, Beijing, China
jiahuanzhou@pku.edu.cn

Abstract. The subpopulation shifting challenge, known as some subpopulations of a category that are not seen during training, severely limits the classification performance of the state-of-the-art convolutional neural networks. Thus, to mitigate this practical issue, we explore incremental subpopulation learning (ISL) to adapt the original model via incrementally learning the unseen subpopulations without retaining the seen population data. However, striking a great balance between subpopulation learning and seen population forgetting is the main challenge in ISL but is not well studied by existing approaches. These incremental learners simply use a pre-defined and fixed hyperparameter to balance the learning objective and forgetting regularization, but their learning is usually biased towards either side in the long run. In this paper, we propose a novel two-stage learning scheme to explicitly disentangle the acquisition and forgetting for achieving a better balance between subpopulation learning and seen population forgetting: in the first "gain-acquisition" stage, we progressively learn a new classifier based on the margin-enforce loss, which enforces the hard samples and population to have a larger weight for classifier updating and avoid uniformly updating all the population; in the second "counter-forgetting" stage, we search for the proper combination of the new and old classifiers by optimizing a novel objective based on proxies of forgetting and acquisition. We benchmark the representative and state-of-the-art non-exemplar-based incremental learning methods on a large-scale subpopulation shifting dataset for the first time. Under almost all the challenging ISL protocols, we significantly outperform other methods by a large margin, demonstrating our superiority to alleviate the subpopulation shifting problem (Code is released in https://github.com/wuyujack/ISL).

1 Introduction

For the classification task in computer vision, a category is always consisted of many fine-grained sub-classes which can be called subpopulations. For example, the category "dog" has subpopulations including "Dalmatians", "Poodles"

Supplementary Information The online version contains supplementary material available at https://doi.org/10.1007/978-3-031-19809-0_21.

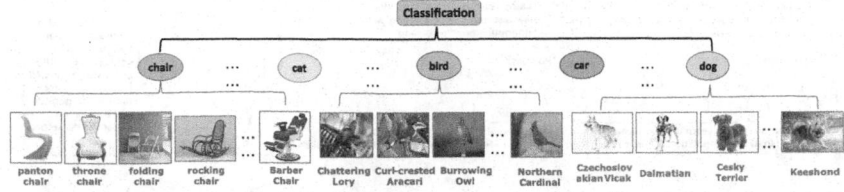

Fig. 1. Subpopulations [28] are widely existed in the real world. A visual category (colored ellipse) contains a large number of subpopulations (denoted by each image) which are semantically similar and share common visual characteristics [28] to be in the same category, while they also have large differences in appearances, shape, context, etc. Each subpopulation [28] is also a distribution with sufficient variations, e.g., cover thousands of distinct objects belonging to this subpopulation in nature.

and "Terriers", etc. (as shown in Fig. 1). However, such kinds of large-scale subpopulations severely limit the discriminative ability of learned models. Recently, Santurkar et al. [28] studied how well a model generalizes to subpopulations that are unseen during training, i.e., whether the model can recognize "Dalmatians" as "dogs" even their training data for "dogs" comprise only the dog's breeds like "Poodles" and "Terriers". Their observations demonstrate that the classification accuracy on those unseen subpopulations drops significantly (mostly more than 30%) compared to the seen population. Such a critical issue is defined as *subpopulation shifting*, caused by the large intra-class variations within a category, or more specifically, the large inter-subclass variations between different subpopulations of a common category in the natural world.

To tackle such a subpopulation shifting problem, a naive solution is to comprehensively collect sufficient data from all subpopulations for learning. However, due to the visual complexity of a category in nature, it is hard to completely cover all the subpopulations during data collection. Therefore, in recent years, more efforts have been paid to leverage the *incremental learning* (IL) technique to improve the generalization ability of an offline learned classification model against the online unseen data. While existing incremental learning methods mostly focus on the data from unseen categories but simply ignore the subpopulation shifting problem within a seen category from the training phase.

Recently, a few works spotlight a scenario where the distributions of seen categories are shifting while the label space is fixed, called incremental domain learning (IDL) [12,32], which mostly targets on two specific cases. Firstly, changing visual domains (e.g., from photo-style to painting-style) of the seen category, known as continual domain adaptation (CDA) [33]; Secondly, adding new poses and environment conditions (e.g., illumination, background) to the seen category, denoted as the new instance (NI) setting [18,20]. However, none of them recognize the critical subpopulation shifting problem caused by the large inter-subclass variations within every specific visual category. Therefore, it is worthwhile to provide a first and comprehensive study of tackling the subpopulation shifting problem in an incremental learning manner, e.g., incrementally learning to recognize the unseen subpopulations of "dog" as "dog", without retaining the

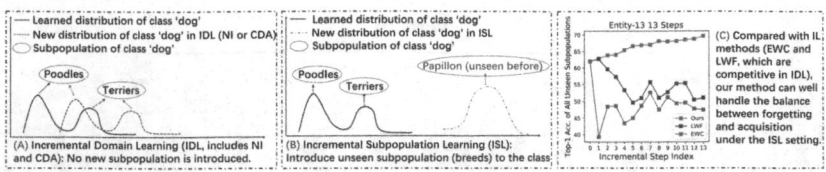

Fig. 2. (A) and (B) show the difference between the ISL and incremental domain learning (IDL): in IDL (includes NI and CDA), the new distribution is only the manipulation of the existing subpopulations' distributions (e.g., the same subpopulation in different visual domains), but no new unseen subpopulations are introduced; Instead in ISL, the new distribution is the totally new and unseen subpopulation [28] that is not existed in the distribution of a category before. Concrete examples are in our supplementary. (C) shows our method can gradually acquire the unseen subpopulations during ISL.

data of seen population. We call this *incremental subpopulation learning* (ISL) and more discussions about the differences with the aforementioned incremental learning settings can be found in Fig. 2 and Sect. 2.

However, as commonly observed in the incremental learning research, a model may be quickly adapted to acquire the unseen task while forgetting the seen tasks gradually, especially without retaining the previous learning data [6,42]. Such a phenomenon significantly limits the final discriminative ability of the model. Thus, *balancing the forgetting and acquisition appropriately in incremental learning* still remains a challenging problem and may be more critical in ISL. The reason is that the unseen subpopulations share common visual characteristics to be grouped in the same category [28]. Such a correlation makes the model being easily transferred to unseen subpopulations in finetuning [28] while forget the seen subpopulations. Currently, general IL solutions design various forgetting regularizations to jointly optimize the acquisition and forgetting [8,11,14,15,17,36,42]. However, they heavily rely on a controller hyperparameter predetermined before incremental learning starts and fixed afterward [6]. Since the relation between forgetting and acquisition is not explicitly modeled, the hyperparameter needs to be subtly tuned based on a held-out test set from each incremental learning phase. This not only introduces large amounts of manual trials and errors, but also has no guarantee to obtain a great balance in the long run, especially when we can not access previous test sets [6].

Therefore, in this paper, we propose a novel two-stage learning scheme to tackle the above forgetting issue from an adversarial perspective, also as a preliminary baseline for ISL. In the first "gain-acquisition" stage, we progressively learn a new classifier using only the learning data from unseen subpopulations without explicitly regularizing the forgetting issue. To do so, we explore the possibility of the feature extractor sharing during incremental learning and achieve a better stability-and-plasticity trade-off [6] by progressively reducing prediction error on the hard samples and classes. To explicitly defy the forgetting issue, we propose a second "counter-forgetting" stage to further achieve a better balance between forgetting and acquisition by encouraging them to compete against each other and linearly combining the old and new classifiers based on an additive parameter α. To achieve this, we leverage a novel objective function to model the confrontation by two proxy estimations of forgetting and acquisition respectively, then search for the proper α by optimizing this objective function.

Our proposed method disentangles the acquisition and forgetting in our two-stage learning scheme to explicitly guarantee the acquisition of knowledge from unseen subpopulations as well as mitigate the forgetting issue of seen subpopulations. To verify this, for the first time, we elaborately design extensive experimental protocols to investigate ISL on the large-scale datasets, i.e., BREEDS [28], which are recently proposed to precisely simulate the subpopulation shifting condition. Extensive empirical results demonstrate that our proposed method outperforms the existing incremental learning approaches by a significant margin under almost all the protocols. Moreover, our further discussions and analyses also show the effectiveness of leveraging incremental learning to alleviate the subpopulation shifting problem. To sum up, our contributions are three-fold: (1) We conduct a first extensive experimental study of representative incremental learning methods on incremental subpopulation learning (ISL) based on a recently proposed large-scale benchmark tailored to subpopulation shifting; (2) We propose a novel two-stage non-exemplar-based (NEB) ISL method to explicitly disentangle the acquisition and forgetting in ISL for achieving a better balance, which outperforms the representative NEB methods by a large margin under different and challenging ISL protocols; (3) We empirically show that incremental learning is promising for alleviating the challenging subpopulation shifting problem, which is worthwhile for future study. Our empirical analyses further enlighten the challenges and future research direction for ISL.

2 Related Works

To highlight the necessity of our proposed ISL, it is essential to compare several related learning scenarios, including our Incremental Subpopulation Learning (ISL), Incremental Domain Learning (IDL) [12,32] that includes New Instance (NI) [18,20] and Continual Domain Adaptation (CDA) [33] settings, Class-Incremental Learning (CIL) [6,21] and Incremental Implicitly-Refined Classification (IIRC) [1]. Please also refer to our supplementary for more discussions.

ISL v.s. IDL (includes NI and CDA): As mentioned in Sect. 1, the input distribution or domain in IDL [12,32] is shifting while the label space is fixed. However, IDL does not propose to introduce any new unseen subpopulations to a category (see Fig. 2). The general IDL methods [12,32] can hardly model the data variation caused by subpopulation shifting and can not balance the forgetting and acquisition without retaining old data. More specifically, NI [18] adds new patterns to the same object by changing the object's poses and image conditions (e.g., illumination). CDA [33] means continually adapting a model to new visual domains (e.g., from photo style to other styles' images). Thus, both NI and CDA can be considered as specific cases of IDL. Although our ISL also does not change the label space and can be generally viewed as a specific case of IDL, ISL has its specific research targets and challenges that are different from the above-mentioned settings. Given that NI and CDA are explicitly framed to specify their identity, it is also of great necessity to frame ISL explicitly.

From the data perspective, datasets [18,33] used in NI or CDA do not have a large scale and precise label hierarchy to define the subpopulations within a category, thus they can not precisely simulate the subpopulation shifting [28]. CORe50 [18] used in NI does have a hierarchy (10 categories, each one has 5 classes), but each class is only a distinct object. The objects are hand held in different views and the environmental conditions are changed to get their new instances. Such a dataset is insatiable to create the subpopulation given its limited diversity and scale (see Fig. 1), and can not simulate the subpopulation shift as the new instances are still belonging to existing seen objects (see Fig. 2 (A)). Recently, [28] proposed a large-scale BREEDS dataset to create the desired hierarchy with large amounts of human efforts and identify for the first time the subpopulation shifting problem to the community. Thus, existing studies in IDL (NI or CDA) are not suitable for ISL. To the best of our knowledge, ISL has rarely been mentioned or studied in the IL literature. The BREEDS benchmark paves the way for our timely study of the subpopulation shifting problem.

ISL v.s. General IL (includes CIL [6] and IIRC [1]): ISL also differs from CIL. In CIL, we continually learn new classes that are disjoint with previous ones. Thus we have a clear boundary between new and old classes and can fix the old classifiers to avoid detrimental updates [6]. In contrast, we only have a fixed size, unified classifier in ISL, and it is unavoidable to update the whole decision boundary. Recently, IIRC [1] is proposed to incrementally learn new classes and also refine the label hierarchy between the seen subclasses and their specific class: A model first learns several classes (e.g., "cat"), where the training data for each class comprises several subclasses. Then the model encounters both new class samples (e.g., "cow") and the seen sample with its subclass label. The model needs to learn the different granularity of labels of a class and the relation between them. Differently, in ISL, we do not introduce new classes, and the new subpopulation needs to be strictly *unseen and disjoint* to the old ones.

Incremental Learning Methods. Given whether the training images can be retained, existing IL methods are divided into exemplar-based (EB) [5,11,13,24] [3,16,31,36] and non-exemplar-based (NEB) methods. However, storing old training data is not privacy-preserved in the real world [6]. NEB methods mostly aim to design better forgetting regularization constraints on parameters [2,14,19,39,40] and model outputs [8,15,35,41]. However, the former needs a well-defined metric to identify the important parameter, which is hard to design [6]; the latter's performance depends largely on the old and new task correlation [6]. Other kinds of NEB methods learn a generative model (GAN) [4,30,34,34] to generate the old images for retraining or dynamically extend the models [5,22,23,37,38]. However, the former requires the GAN to be capable of IL and generate high-quality images, which is still challenging; the latter requires growing memory and is undesirable in the real world. Moreover, all the above NEB methods mostly couple the forgetting and acquisition into a joint optimization problem, where their balance is controlled based on finely-tuned hyperparameters.

Differently, our proposed method disentangles the acquisition and forgetting to explicitly and adaptively control them in a data-driven manner in ISL, which significantly outperforms the representative NEB methods mentioned above.

3 Method

3.1 Terminology and Problem Formulation

Following the terminology in [28], the term "population" is concretely defined as class or super-class, e.g., "cat" and "dog", and the "subpopulation" is defined as the subclass of a specific class, e.g., different "dog" breeds. All subclasses are under the same visual domain (i.e., natural image). Before incremental learning, we have a *base step* to train a model to learn many diverse classes with sufficient data, where the model is called the *base step's model*. Each class is learned by a dataset comprised of different subclasses, e.g., subclasses of "dog" like "Poodles" and "Terriers". These subclasses are labeled as class "dog". Then in each *incremental step*, the model encounters unseen subclasses of existing classes, and it incrementally learns to predict the class label of these unseen subclasses.

Formally, let $t = 0$ denote the *base step*, and let $t = 1, 2, .., T$ denote the *incremental steps*. The training dataset of the t-th incremental step is $D_t^{train} = \{X_t^{train}, S_t^{train}, Y\} = \{x_{t,j}^{train}, s_{t,j}^{train}, y_j\}_{j=1}^{N_t}$, where x, s, y denote the inputs, subclass labels and class labels, respectively. Note that the only supervision is the class label, while the subclass labels will not be used during training but to ensure unseen subclasses differ from all seen subclasses, i.e., $S_t^{train} \cap (\cup_{i=0}^{t-1} S_i^{train}) = \varnothing$. The set of class labels is the same over all steps. At each step we have a corresponding held-out test set $D_t^{test} = \{X_t^{test}, S_t^{test}, Y\}$ to evaluate the performance on the current step, and we also only use the class label Y for evaluation. The model, e.g., CNN, comprises the feature extractor f_θ and classifier G_ϕ, parameterized by θ and ϕ respectively, where G_ϕ refers to the last linear layer of the CNN. After T steps, the model is tested on all the previous steps' held out test sets $D_t^{test}, t = 0, ..., T$ to evaluate the performance over all the learned subclasses.

3.2 A Novel Two-stage Learning Scheme

Here we introduce the proposed two-stage learning method. We argue that the learned CNN feature extractor is capable of extracting discriminative features for each class. Then the potential reason of misclassifying the unseen subclasses is that the final classifier emphasizes the feature that is less discriminative for the unseen subclasses because the classifier may have already biased to the seen subclasses. Therefore, we conjecture that the subpopulation shifting may be alleviated by appropriately updating the classifier to emphasize the proper feature for the unseen subpopulation. To explore this idea, we consider to share a fixed feature extractor after the *base step* and only learn the new classifier as a novel baseline tailored to ISL. Since feature extractor sharing may lead to concerns of stability and plasticity trade-off, thus in our Stage-1 we introduce the

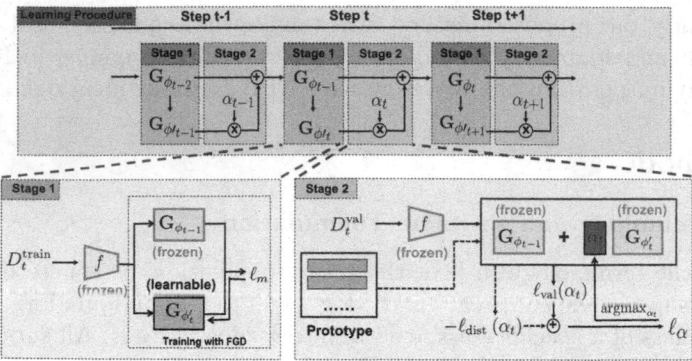

Fig. 3. During the incremental subpopulation learning procedure, in each incremental step t we obtain the classifier G_{ϕ_t} for the model F_t by two stages. In Stage-1, we learn a new classifier $G_{\phi'_t}$ via functional gradient descent (FGD) of Eq. 3. In Stage-2, we obtain G_{ϕ_t} by combining the new and old classifiers linearly via a proper α_t solved by Eq. 10 to balance the acquisition and forgetting approximately.

gradient-based boosting [26] idea to alleviate the issue by progressively reducing the prediction error. In Stage-2 we design a specific objective function to approximately model the balance of acquisition and forgetting and leverage it to achieve our target. Figure 3 provides a systematic view of our design.

Stage-1: Gain-Acquisition. Suppose $Y = \{1, \ldots, C\}$ is the class label for each incremental step in ISL, and $y^k \in \mathbb{R}^C$ is the one-hot vector to represent the class k. We define the margin [26,27] of a sample x to an arbitrary class k as:

$$\mathcal{M}\left(y^k, F(x)\right) = \min_{l \neq k} \frac{1}{2} < y^k - y^l, F(x) > \tag{1}$$

where $F(x) = G_\phi\left(f_\theta(x)\right)$ denotes the model prediction given a sample x and $F(x) \in \mathbb{R}^C$; $\langle ., . \rangle$ denotes the dot-product and $\frac{1}{2}\langle y^k - y^l, F(x)\rangle$ is the l-th margin component of class k, where $y^k F(x)$ is the k-th element of the model's prediction vector. Now we define the margin of the model given the training data $D = \{X, Y\}$ (we omit t and the subclass label S_t as it is not used as supervision):

$$M(D, F) = \min_{(x_i, y^{c_i}) \in D} \mathcal{M}\left(y^{c_i}, F(x_i)\right), \tag{2}$$

where y^{c_i} is the one-hot vector of the ground-truth class label c_i given a sample x_i. $M(D, F)$ measures the distance between the closest sample to each ground-truth class's decision boundary given the model and training data, and we want to encourage the model to have a large $M(D, F)$ such that given a sample, the model prediction of its ground-truth class can be far away from other classes [26, 27]. Hence we define our margin-enforce objective function [27] as:

$$\ell_m(F) = \frac{1}{|D|} \cdot \sum_{(x_i, y^{c_i}) \in D} L_M\left[y^{c_i}, F(x_i)\right], \tag{3}$$

where $|D|$ denotes the size of dataset and the $L_M[.,.]$ should be a differentiable and monotonically decreasing function such that by minimizing Eq. 3, it is equivalent to maximize the margin defined by Eq. 2. This margin-enforce property has a guarantee that the optimal model obtained by minimizing Eq. 3 may have good generalization, as demonstrated in the boosting theory [26]. We consider the default choice in the multi-class boosting theory [26,27] as:

$$L_M[y^c, F(x)] = \sum_{k=1, k \neq c}^{C} e^{-\frac{1}{2}[<y^c, F(x)> - <y^k, F(x)>]}. \tag{4}$$

Then a new model is obtained by the largest decrease of Eq. 3. Such a decrease can be determined by the directional derivative [9] of Eq. 3 along the functional $g : \mathcal{X} \to \mathbb{R}^C$, where $\mathcal{X}$ denotes the input space of the model $F(x)$:

$$\delta \ell_m[F; g] = \left. \frac{\partial \ell_m[F(x) + \epsilon g]}{\partial \varepsilon} \right|_{\varepsilon=0}, \tag{5}$$

called the functional gradient (FG) [9]. By first order Taylor expansion we have:

$$- \delta \ell_m[F; g] = \frac{1}{2|D|} \sum_{i=1}^{|D|} w_i < g(x_i), y^{c_i} - \sum_{k \neq c_i} y^k \tau_k(x_i, c_i) >, \tag{6}$$

where $w_i = \sum_{k \neq c_i} e^{-\frac{1}{2}<y^{c_i} - y^k, F(x_i)>}$ and $\tau_k(x_i, c_i) = \frac{e^{-\frac{1}{2}<y^{c_i} - y^k, F(x_i)>}}{\sum_{k \neq c_i} e^{-\frac{1}{2}<y^{c_i} - y^k, F(x_i)>}}$.

Detailed derivation of Eq. 6 can be found in [26,27]. Finally, we achieve a new model by maximizing the negative functional gradient, i.e., Eq. 6:

$$g(x) = \arg\max_g \sum_{i=1}^{|D|} w_i < g(x_i), y^{c_i} - \sum_{k \neq c_i} y^k \tau_k(x_i, c_i) > . \tag{7}$$

Such an update is known as functional gradient descent (FGD) [26] on Eq. 3. In our work, we integrate the above learning mechanism into incremental subpopulation learning (ISL): Assume we have a model F_{t-1} after $t-1$ incremental steps. For the t-th step, we only use the current step's training data to learn a new model F_t by optimizing Eq. 3 via FGD, which is exactly to solve the Eq. 7 and then $F_t = g$. Since we want to explore the possibility of only updating the classifier of CNN, thus for the model F_t, only the classifier is learnable and the feature extractor f_θ is frozen after the *base step* and shared over each *incremental step*, illustrated in Fig. 3. Thus by FGD, we actually obtain a new classifier $G_{\phi'_t}$ for F_t. To solve the Eq. 7, we initialize g as F_{t-1} and minimize the negative of Eq. 7 by stochastic gradient descent (SGD). We empirically observe that this learning mechanism works smoothly and converges to high accuracy (>90%) on the unseen subpopulation training data after several epochs, which essentially relieves the stability-plasticity concern. This is due to the merit of margin-enforce loss [26,29] that can progressively reduce the training error. Formally, it relates to the reweighting mechanism [26] presented in Eq. 7 and we show that it is also beneficial to ISL: (1) The w_i is a decreasing function of the margin components of the ground-truth class c_i given the sample x_i. Then the w_i is close to 0 when the smallest margin component of class c_i is large and positive, where from Eq. 1 this means the sample x_i is with a large margin and is easy to be predicted since the model prediction of the class c_i, i.e., $y^{c_i} F(x_i)$, is much larger than other classes. Thus, the classifier may receive small updates from easy samples as w_i are small, and large updates from hard samples (i.e., with small margins). *This reweighting mechanism may avoid uniformly updating the decision boundary given every training sample. Meanwhile, it lets the model to focus on hard samples to reduce error progressively. This is crucial for ISL since it avoids unnecessary updates and lead to less forgetting.* (2) The other reweighting can be observed from $< g(x_i), y^{c_i} - \sum_{k \neq c_i} y^k \tau_k(x_i, c_i) >$. We change it to $\sum_{k \neq c} \tau_k(x_i, c_i) [< g(x_i), y^{c_i} - y^k >]$ by taking the $\tau_k(x_i, c_i)$ outside. $\tau_k(x_i, c_i)$ is a weighted average over the margin components of the class c_i, and it will weigh a class k (hard class) more for updating the classifier if the model prediction of it, i.e., $y^k F(x_i)$, is close to the prediction of the class c_i. Hence this reweighting may also avoid uniformly updating the class decision boundaries.

Stage-2: Counter-Forgetting. Although we connect general boosting with incremental learning and show that it is favorable for ISL due to its reweighting mechanisms, the above learning mechanism can not entirely defy the forgetting. The new classifier $G_{\phi_t'}$ is only trained with the current step's unseen subpopulation data while we do not explicitly impose any forgetting control. Therefore, we propose to obtain the final classifier G_{ϕ_t} for model F_t by linear addition:

$$G_{\phi_t} = G_{\phi_{t-1}} + \alpha_t \cdot G_{\phi_t'}. \tag{8}$$

This is also inspired from boosting mechanism, but it is totally different from boosting since the α_t here is for controlling the learning and forgetting, while in boosting we use it to progressively reduce the training error [29]. As the classifier of CNN is a linear layer and in ISL, we do not introduce new classes and the size of this layer is fixed. Thus the linear combination of two linear classifiers is equal to linear combine the weight of them, i.e., $\phi_t = \phi_{t-1} + \alpha_t \cdot \phi_t'$. The key challenge is to determine the proper α_t without storing previous training images since it is infeasible to measure the forgetting only by the current step's training data. To tackle this challenge, we consider obtaining the proxy of forgetting by measuring the relative distance distortion of the class representative prototype between the last step's classifier $G_{\phi_{t-1}}$ and new classifier $G_{\phi_t'}$ under different α_t. The insight is: Since the feature extractor is shared, it can provide consistent transformation for each class's data in the feature space. Thus the class prototype is fixed and consistent for each class during incremental learning. The forgetting can now be disentangled and measured by the distance distortion between the prototype and the changed decision boundary, since the class prediction error is directly related to the change of decision boundary. This differs from the existing non-exemplar-based method, e.g., PASS [42], leveraging the prototype (class mean feature) to create a constraint to train on the new class data to maintain the old decision boundary which is changing dynamically in CIL. After each incremental step, if a class is introduced with unseen subclasses, we obtain one prototype (class mean feature) of that class and add it to the prototype bank, which is the same as the PASS [42] storing one prototype of each new class in CIL. The prototype is calculated by the feature extractor f_θ and thus it has the same input dimension as the classifier. At step t, we denote the relative distance distortion as:

$$l_{\text{dist}}\,(\alpha_t) = \sum_{i=0}^{t-1} \sum_{j \in N_p^i} \frac{1}{C} \cdot \left| \frac{\alpha_t \cdot G_{\phi_t'}\,(K_{i,j})}{G_{\phi_{t-1}}\,(K_{i,j})} \right|_1, \tag{9}$$

where $G_\phi\,(K_{i,j}) \in \mathbb{R}^C$ and $|\cdot|_1$ denotes the L1 norm, $K_{i,j}$ denotes the prototype of class j in step i and N_p^i denotes the set of index of the stored prototype in step i. We do element-wise division here to measure the relative distortion of each class between old and new classifiers under different α_t. The distance is normalized by the size of the label space C. For the acquisition measurement, before training on current step's training data D_t^{train}, we randomly sample a held-out validation set D_t^{val} from D_t^{train} to measure the relative improvement of validation accuracy between $G_{\phi_{t-1}} + \alpha_t \cdot G_{\phi_t'}$ and $G_{\phi_{t-1}}$, denoted as $l_{val}(\alpha_t)$. The proper α_t is obtained by optimizing an objective function modeling the balance:

$$\alpha_t = \arg\max_{\alpha_t} l_\alpha = \arg\max_{\alpha_t} l_{val}\,(\alpha_t) - l_{dist}\,(\alpha_t), \tag{10}$$

which means we want more acquisition while also less forgetting. Note that in Stage-2 we do not update any classifier by backpropagation. Instead we fix both the old and new classifiers, $G_{\phi_{t-1}}$ and $G_{\phi_t'}$, and search for the proper α_t by solving Eq. 10, shown in Fig. 3. The α_t can be readily searched by simple line search. More details and discussions are included in our supplementary.

4   Experiments

Datasets. We leverage the latest BREEDS datasets [28] in our experiments. BREEDS simulates the real-world subpopulation shifting based on the ImageNet [7], and it comprises four different datasets: Entity-13, Entity-30, Living-17, and Non-Living-26, with a total of 0.86 million (M) of images. The dataset configurations and statistics are all included in supplementary. However, BREEDS is not proposed for incremental subpopulation learning (ISL), so we need to further create the ISL-specific benchmark based on it. Since we focus on the incremental learner's performance in the sufficiently long run, hence in present work, our main testbeds are based on Entity-13 and Entity-30 from BREEDS as they have the most number of subclasses, i.e., totally 260 and 240 subclasses respectively, and more than 0.6M images. To the best of our knowledge, this is the first time to leverage such large-scale datasets to investigate the ISL.

Comparison Methods. A strict requirement of ISL is that no previous training images can be retained, thus it is rarely studied before. Moreover, very few methods are proposed tailored to the related Incremental Domain Learning (IDL);

Methods like BOCL [31] for IDL needs to store and use old images during training on new instances, which can not satisfy the ISL requirements. Thus following the works benchmarked the IDL [12,31,32] and other settings, we choose several general and representative non-exemplar-based (NEB) methods [21,42] and benchmark them under BREEDS [28] for the first time. They include EWC [14], LwF [15], LwF-MC [25], MUC [17], LwM [8] and PASS [42]. Among them, EWC and LwF are widely used to benchmark various IL settings including IDL [12,31–33] and achieve comparable results to the state-of-the-art (SOTA). Methods like MUC and PASS were tested in CIL, but as stated in their papers [17,42], they are also *general* for different IL settings including ISL. PASS is the SOTA NEB method in CIL. We also compare the naive baselines, i.e., finetune the whole model ("Finetune All") and finetune only the last layer ("Finetune Last"). The joint training of all the data is the "Oracle".

Evaluation Metrics. We report the common metrics [42] in IL literature for evaluation, i.e., the average top-1 accuracy (%) on all the seen and unseen subclasses we learned for each class (includes the *base step*), denoted as *"All"*, and the average forgetting $\mathbb{F}_i$ to measure the forgetting in previous steps. At step i, the forgetting score on step j is $\mathbf{f}_i^j = \max_{t \in 0,\ldots,i-1} (a_{t,j} - a_{i,j}), \forall j < i$, where $a_{i,j}$ denotes the accuracy of step j after the training of step i. Then $\mathbb{F}_i$ is defined as $\mathbb{F}_i = \frac{1}{i} \sum_{j=0}^{i-1} \mathbf{f}_i^j$. We further define *"Unseen"* as the average test accuracy only on all the unseen subclasses and report it in Tables 1 and 2 to show how well each method acquires the unseen subpopulation after incremental learning.

Experimental Design. Entity-30 and Entity-13 have 30 and 13 classes where each class has 8 and 20 subclasses respectively. We design 3 protocols for each dataset. In the *base step*, the training set of each class comprises data from 4 and 10 subclasses for Entity-30 and Entity-13 respectively, the same as BREEDS to simulate subpopulation shifting. Then we split the rest of 120 and 130 unseen subclasses in each dataset respectively to create different protocols. For Entity-30, we design protocols with 4, 8, 15 incremental steps: in each step, for 4 Steps setup, each class is introduced with 1 unseen subclass; for 8 and 15 Steps setups, we randomly choose 15 and 8 out of 30 classes respectively to introduce with 1 unseen subclass. For Entity-13, we design protocols with 5, 10, 13 incremental steps: in each step, for 5 and 10 Steps setups, we introduce 2 and 1 unseen subclasses for each class respectively; For 13 Steps setup, we randomly sample 10 out of 13 classes to introduce with 1 unseen subclass. These designs simulate two scenarios: (1) all the classes are updated with at least 1 unseen subclass; (2) only a part of classes are updated with unseen subclasses. We denote the former as **even update** and the latter as **uneven update**.

Implementation Details. We use ResNet-18 [10] for all methods as [42]. For a fair comparison, all methods are initialized with the same *base step model* and then start incremental learning. As the first benchmark for ISL, it is essential to compare different methods fairly. Therefore, we use the Continual Hyperparameter Framework (CHF) proposed by [6] to find the hyperparameters for comparison methods, and also use the same data augmentation as in BREEDS [28]

Table 1. Results on Entity-30 benchmark. Smaller $\mathbb{F}_i$ and larger *Unseen/All* is better. Before incremental learning, *"Unseen"* is 50.18 for all the methods.

Method	4 Steps (Even Update)			8 Steps (Uneven Update)			15 Steps (Uneven Update)		
	Unseen	*All*	$\mathbb{F}_4$	*Unseen*	*All*	$\mathbb{F}_8$	*Unseen*	*All*	$\mathbb{F}_{15}$
Oracle	88.03	87.63	–	88.03	87.63	–	88.03	87.63	–
Finetune All	53.72	48.08	47.75	26.45	23.08	73.86	14.68	13.77	84.49
Finetune Last	55.25	58.30	32.43	30.85	32.50	60.82	19.98	21.56	72.40
EWC [14]	56.17	54.10	40.69	30.50	29.00	66.94	22.20	23.68	74.03
LwF [15]	62.67	58.85	32.32	34.52	29.69	64.38	32.62	31.17	62.51
LwF-MC [25]	**68.28**	64.43	28.20	46.93	43.69	50.88	34.53	33.79	62.36
MUC [17]	62.98	59.59	29.45	36.17	31.83	61.49	34.15	32.54	60.65
LwM [8]	63.32	59.20	33.13	42.47	38.90	55.59	33.43	30.78	61.23
PASS [42]	64.50	69.37	21.79	48.85	54.99	40.50	32.13	39.75	58.27
Ours	64.73	**72.88**	**4.16**	**58.63**	**72.14**	**2.30**	**56.87**	**71.69**	**3.48**

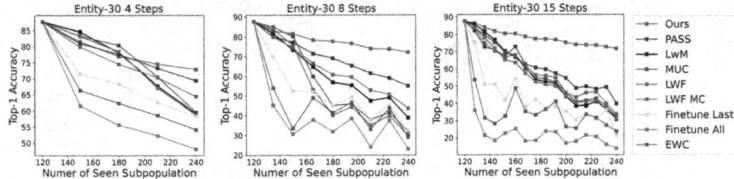

Fig. 4. Average top-1 test accuracy in each step under 3 protocols of Entity-30.

to train both the *base* and *incremental steps* consistently for all methods. All experimental details are in supplementary. The data augmentation comprises random resize crop, random horizontal flip, lighting, color jitter, etc. Note that such a heavy strategy is the same as the domain randomization (DR) method used in continual domain adaptation (CDA) [33] to achieve SOTA results.

4.1 Comparison with the State-of-the-art

From Tables 1 and 2 we observe: when the incremental step is small and the update is even (the 4 Steps Entity-30 and 5 Steps Entity-13), all the NEB methods can improve their accuracy on the unseen subclasses (*"Unseen"*) compared to themselves before incremental learning, reported in the captions of Tables 1 and 2. However, when we compare the performance on all the subclasses (*"All"*), our method exceeds all compared methods with a large margin since those methods forget the learned subpopulations during ISL and thus lead to poor *"All"* performance when average on all the subclasses (as shown in Figs. 4 and 5). This demonstrates that most NEB methods can learn to recognize the unseen subpopulations in small steps but at the cost of forgetting the seen ones. When the incremental steps become large and **uneven update**, e.g., 15 and 13 Steps for Entity-30 and Entity-13, all the compared methods suffer from severe forget-

Table 2. Results on Entity-13 benchmark. Smaller $\mathbb{F}_i$ and larger *Unseen/All* is better. Before incremental learning, "*Unseen*" is 62.03 for all the methods.

Method	5 Steps (Even Update)			10 Steps (Even Update)			13 Steps (Uneven Update)		
	Unseen	*All*	$\mathbb{F}_5$	*Unseen*	*All*	$\mathbb{F}_{10}$	*Unseen*	*All*	$\mathbb{F}_{13}$
Oracle	90.61	90.46	–	90.61	90.46	–	90.61	90.46	–
Finetune All	61.54	59.16	37.79	51.55	50.88	46.76	41.98	41.72	56.97
Finetune Last	65.52	71.15	18.89	61.52	67.37	25.47	49.89	55.23	40.31
EWC [14]	63.85	63.48	32.99	55.63	57.31	36.53	47.51	48.54	50.49
LwF [15]	66.91	64.82	31.47	59.97	50.17	36.26	51.14	51.05	46.31
LwF-MC [25]	67.57	65.96	30.64	59.58	59.22	38.42	59.45	59.70	37.02
MUC [17]	67.51	65.88	30.00	62.17	61.98	31.45	53.58	52.89	43.74
LwM [8]	69.69	67.61	28.22	63.49	62.25	31.72	51.05	50.80	46.31
PASS [42]	**73.12**	75.44	16.73	65.63	68.51	26.55	50.48	52.49	43.76
Ours	72.02	**78.92**	**3.29**	**68.31**	**77.53**	**3.35**	**69.69**	**78.75**	**3.35**

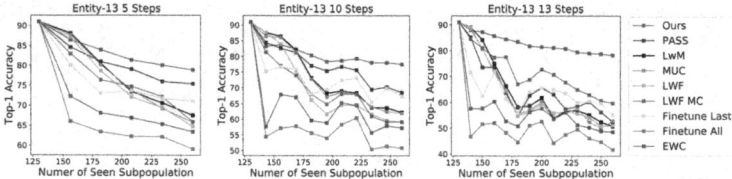

Fig. 5. Average top-1 test accuracy in each step under 3 protocols of Entity-13.

ting on the subpopulations learned in previous steps and perform significantly poorly. The baseline "Finetune Last" almost fails in 15 Steps Entity-30, though it may obtain comparable results to some NEB methods in small steps and even update. This shows it is hard to only fix the feature extractor to achieve excellent results in ISL in the long run. In contrast, our proposed method achieves small average forgetting and great average accuracy even after 13 and 15 steps, outperforming the best existing method by 19.05% and 31.94% on "*All*" respectively. Interestingly, we also observe that our method can have smaller forgetting in longer steps (8 and 15 Steps Entity-30). This is due to the positive transfer in our method shown in Table 4, where the test accuracy of some steps can be improved after ISL and have no forgetting. The reason is our method can gradually learn unseen subpopulations and strike a much better balance between acquisition and forgetting than existing methods. The acquired knowledge from new unseen subpopulations sometimes could be helpful for better distinguishing the old seen subpopulations, which is essential for countering forgetting in ISL.

Further Discussions and Analyses. We further analyze the performance of existing methods in both ISL and other IL settings based on our empirical observation. We highlight our analyses below, and more details are in our supplementary: (1) *ISL provides new challenges for the representative NEB methods.* For instance, EWC and LWF can achieve comparable, or even SOTA results in

Table 3. Ablation study by Entity-13 13 Steps setup

	Unseen	All	$\mathbb{F}_{13}$
Cross Entropy	49.89	55.23	40.31
ℓ_m	53.13	60.38	29.48
ℓ_m + Random α_t	62.60	71.59	5.93
ℓ_m + Fixed $\alpha_t = 1$	63.83	75.24	4.23
ℓ_m + Obtained α_t (Ours)	**69.69**	**78.75**	**3.35**

Table 4. Positive transfer. $\mathbf{f}_{15}^8$ means the forgetting score of 8-th step of overall 15 Step.

	Positive transfer
15 Step Entity-30	$\mathbf{f}_{15}^8 = -0.5$, $\mathbf{f}_{15}^{11} = -2.5$
8 Step Entity-30	$\mathbf{f}_8^2 = -0.8$, $\mathbf{f}_8^4 = -3.73$, $\mathbf{f}_8^6 = -4.4$
10 Step Entity-13	$\mathbf{f}_{10}^6 = -1.5$

the benchmark of IDL [12,32], NI [31] and CDA [33], and the data augmentation strategy is also the same as the DR method proposed in CDA [33] to achieve SOTA results. However, they still suffer largely from forgetting in ISL, especially under **uneven update**. This is caused by the differences between ISL and other settings since the unseen subpopulation may not be simulated by strong augmentation as verified in [28] or only changing the seen subpopulation's views or environments. Thus it is hard to acquire the unseen subpopulations without forgetting the seen ones. (2) All compared methods control the forgetting by one or several hyperparameters. Although some of them may perform well in early steps in Figs. 4 and 5, such a mechanism can not strike a balance in the long run.

4.2   Ablation Study and Analysis

To further explore the proposed method, we investigate the contribution of each model component. As our method is two-stage and also optimizes a new learning objective instead of cross entropy loss, thus we compared our method with: (1) "Cross Entropy": directly finetune the last layer by the cross entropy loss known as the "Finetune Last" in Tables 1 and 2; (2) "ℓ_m": only finetune the last layer by our margin loss from Eq. 3 (only Stage-1); (3) "ℓ_m + Random α_t": use both Stage-1 and 2 but update the model by a random α_t without using Eq. 10; (4) "ℓ_m + Fixed $\alpha_t = 1$": the same as (3) except the α_t is fixed as 1 to equally weight the influence of acquisition and forgetting. We observe from Table 3: (1) The margin loss performs better than the cross entropy, confirming the formal discussion in Sect. 3.2. However, the margin loss can not completely defy the forgetting in the long run and its performance is still far from satisfactory. (2) The proposed Stage-2 further improves the performance of the margin loss, shown in both "ℓ_m + Random α_t" and "ℓ_m + Fixed $\alpha_t = 1$". However, without explicitly optimizing Eq. 10 to obtain the proper α_t, their performance are inferior to "Ours" after the long run. This illustrates the importance of the proposed objective function to search for the proper α_t to achieve a remarkable balance over the long run for ISL. Besides we also find that: (1) the proposed forgetting proxy estimation has a strong statistical correlation with the actual performance drop of the seen subpopulations; (2) our method can robustly perform well for ISL under different sizes of the training dataset in the *base step* and different network structures, which relieves our concern of sharing the feature extractor for ISL. All the details and discussions of limitations are in our supplementary.

5   Conclusion

To alleviate the challenging subpopulation shifting issue, we explore incremental subpopulation learning (ISL) and propose a novel two-stage model to better balance forgetting and acquisition. We provide the first extensive benchmark of existing methods for ISL. Empirical results show that our method outperforms existing ones significantly under different and challenging protocols, which could be a promising baseline for ISL and enlighten future research.

Acknowledgement. This work was supported in part by National Science Foundation grant IIS-1815561 and IIS-2007613.

References

1. Abdelsalam, M., Faramarzi, M., Sodhani, S., Chandar, S.: IIRC: incremental implicitly-refined classification. In: Proceedings of the IEEE/CVF Conference on Computer Vision and Pattern Recognition, pp. 11038–11047 (2021)
2. Ahn, H., Cha, S., Lee, D., Moon, T.: Uncertainty-based continual learning with adaptive regularization. In: Advances in Neural Information Processing Systems, pp. 4392–4402 (2019)
3. Ahn, H., Kwak, J., Lim, S., Bang, H., Kim, H., Moon, T.: SS-IL: separated softmax for incremental learning. In: Proceedings of the IEEE/CVF International Conference on Computer Vision (ICCV), pp. 844–853, October 2021
4. van de Ven, G.M., et al.: Brain-inspired replay for continual learning with artificial neural networks. Nat. Commun. **11**(1), 1–14 (2020)
5. Aljundi, R., Chakravarty, P., Tuytelaars, T.: Expert gate: lifelong learning with a network of experts. In: Proceedings of the IEEE Conference on Computer Vision and Pattern Recognition (CVPR), July 2017
6. Delange, M., et al.: A continual learning survey: defying forgetting in classification tasks. IEEE Trans. Pattern Anal. Mach. Intell. **44**, 3366–3375 (2021)
7. Deng, J., Dong, W., Socher, R., Li, L.J., Li, K., Fei-Fei, L.: ImageNet: a large-scale hierarchical image database. In: 2009 IEEE Conference on Computer Vision and Pattern Recognition, pp. 248–255. IEEE (2009)
8. Dhar, P., Singh, R.V., Peng, K.C., Wu, Z., Chellappa, R.: Learning without memorizing. In: Proceedings of the IEEE Conference on Computer Vision and Pattern Recognition, pp. 5138–5146 (2019)
9. Frigyik, B.A., Srivastava, S., Gupta, M.R.: An introduction to functional derivatives. Technical report, Department of Electronic Engineering, University of Washington, Seattle, WA (2008)
10. He, K., Zhang, X., Ren, S., Sun, J.: Deep residual learning for image recognition. In: Proceedings of the IEEE Conference on Computer Vision and Pattern Recognition, pp. 770–778 (2016)
11. Hou, S., Pan, X., Loy, C.C., Wang, Z., Lin, D.: Learning a unified classifier incrementally via rebalancing. In: Proceedings of the IEEE/CVF Conference on Computer Vision and Pattern Recognition, pp. 831–839 (2019)

12. Hsu, Y.C., Liu, Y.C., Ramasamy, A., Kira, Z.: Re-evaluating continual learning scenarios: a categorization and case for strong baselines. In: NeurIPS Continual Learning Workshop (2018)
13. Kim, C.D., Jeong, J., Kim, G.: Imbalanced continual learning with partitioning reservoir sampling. In: Vedaldi, A., Bischof, H., Brox, T., Frahm, J.-M. (eds.) ECCV 2020. LNCS, vol. 12358, pp. 411–428. Springer, Cham (2020). https://doi.org/10.1007/978-3-030-58601-0_25
14. Kirkpatrick, J., et al.: Overcoming catastrophic forgetting in neural networks. Proc. Natl. Acad. Sci. **114**(13), 3521–3526 (2017)
15. Li, Z., Hoiem, D.: Learning without forgetting. IEEE Trans. Pattern Anal. Mach. Intell. **40**(12), 2935–2947 (2017)
16. Liu, Y., Schiele, B., Sun, Q.: RMM: reinforced memory management for class-incremental learning. Adv. Neural. Inf. Process. Syst. **34**, 3478–3490 (2021)
17. Liu, Y., et al.: More classifiers, less forgetting: a generic multi-classifier paradigm for incremental learning. In: Vedaldi, A., Bischof, H., Brox, T., Frahm, J.-M. (eds.) ECCV 2020. LNCS, vol. 12371, pp. 699–716. Springer, Cham (2020). https://doi.org/10.1007/978-3-030-58574-7_42
18. Lomonaco, V., Maltoni, D.: Core50: a new dataset and benchmark for continuous object recognition. In: Conference on Robot Learning, pp. 17–26. PMLR (2017)
19. Lopez-Paz, D., Ranzato, M.: Gradient episodic memory for continual learning. In: Advances in Neural Information Processing Systems, pp. 6467–6476 (2017)
20. Maltoni, D., Lomonaco, V.: Continuous learning in single-incremental-task scenarios. Neural Netw. **116**, 56–73 (2019)
21. Masana, M., Liu, X., Twardowski, B., Menta, M., Bagdanov, A.D., van de Weijer, J.: Class-incremental learning: survey and performance evaluation on image classification. arXiv preprint arXiv:2010.15277 (2020)
22. Muhlbaier, M.D., Topalis, A., Polikar, R.: Learn ++ .nc: combining ensemble of classifiers with dynamically weighted consult-and-vote for efficient incremental learning of new classes. IEEE Trans. Neural Netw. **20**(1), 152–168 (2008)
23. Polikar, R., Upda, L., Upda, S.S., Honavar, V.: Learn++: an incremental learning algorithm for supervised neural networks. IEEE Trans. Syst. Man Cybern. Part C (App. Rev.) **31**(4), 497–508 (2001)
24. Polikar, R., Upda, L., Upda, S.S., Honavar, V.: Learn++: an incremental learning algorithm for supervised neural networks. IEEE Trans. Syst. Man Cybern. Part C (App. Rev.) **31**(4), 497–508 (2001)
25. Rebuffi, S.A., Kolesnikov, A., Sperl, G., Lampert, C.H.: ICARL: incremental classifier and representation learning. In: Proceedings of the IEEE Conference on Computer Vision and Pattern Recognition (CVPR), July 2017
26. Saberian, M., Vasconcelos, N.: Multiclass boosting: margins, codewords, losses, and algorithms. J. Mach. Learn. Res. **20**(137), 1–68 (2019). https://jmlr.org/papers/v20/17-137.html
27. Saberian, M.J., Vasconcelos, N.: Multiclass boosting: theory and algorithms. In: Advances in Neural Information Processing Systems, pp. 2124–2132 (2011)
28. Santurkar, S., Tsipras, D., Madry, A.: BREEDS: benchmarks for subpopulation shift. In: International Conference on Learning Representations (2021). https://openreview.net/forum?id=mQPBmvyAuk
29. Schapire, R.E., Freund, Y.: Boosting: Foundations and Algorithms. Kybernetes (2013)
30. Shin, H., Lee, J.K., Kim, J., Kim, J.: Continual learning with deep generative replay. In: Advances in Neural Information Processing Systems, pp. 2990–2999 (2017)

31. Tao, X., Hong, X., Chang, X., Gong, Y.: Bi-objective continual learning: Learning 'new'while consolidating 'known'. In: Proceedings of the AAAI Conference on Artificial Intelligence. vol. 34, pp. 5989–5996 (2020)
32. Van de Ven, G.M., Tolias, A.S.: Three scenarios for continual learning. In: NeurIPS - Continual Learning workshop (2018)
33. Volpi, R., Larlus, D., Rogez, G.: Continual adaptation of visual representations via domain randomization and meta-learning. In: Proceedings of the IEEE/CVF Conference on Computer Vision and Pattern Recognition, pp. 4443–4453 (2021)
34. Wu, C., et al.: Memory replay GANs: learning to generate new categories without forgetting. In: Advances in Neural Information Processing Systems, pp. 5962–5972 (2018)
35. Wu, G., Gong, S., Li, P.: Striking a balance between stability and plasticity for class-incremental learning. In: Proceedings of the IEEE/CVF International Conference on Computer Vision (ICCV), pp. 1124–1133, October 2021
36. Wu, Y., et al.: Large scale incremental learning. In: Proceedings of the IEEE/CVF Conference on Computer Vision and Pattern Recognition, pp. 374–382 (2019)
37. Yan, S., Xie, J., He, X.: Der: dynamically expandable representation for class incremental learning. In: Proceedings of the IEEE/CVF Conference on Computer Vision and Pattern Recognition, pp. 3014–3023 (2021)
38. Yoon, J., Yang, E., Lee, J., Hwang, S.J.: Lifelong learning with dynamically expandable networks. In: International Conference on Learning Representations (2018)
39. Yu, L., et al.: Semantic drift compensation for class-incremental learning. In: Proceedings of the IEEE/CVF Conference on Computer Vision and Pattern Recognition, pp. 6982–6991 (2020)
40. Zenke, F., Poole, B., Ganguli, S.: Continual learning through synaptic intelligence. Proc. Mach. Learn. Res. **70**, 3987 (2017)
41. Zhao, B., Xiao, X., Gan, G., Zhang, B., Xia, S.T.: Maintaining discrimination and fairness in class incremental learning. In: Proceedings of the IEEE/CVF Conference on Computer Vision and Pattern Recognition, pp. 13208–13217 (2020)
42. Zhu, F., Zhang, X.Y., Wang, C., Yin, F., Liu, C.L.: Prototype augmentation and self-supervision for incremental learning. In: Proceedings of the IEEE/CVF Conference on Computer Vision and Pattern Recognition, pp. 5871–5880 (2021)

Counterfactual Intervention Feature Transfer for Visible-Infrared Person Re-identification

Xulin Li[1,2], Yan Lu[1,2], Bin Liu[1,2(✉)], Yating Liu[3], Guojun Yin[1,2], Qi Chu[1,2], Jinyang Huang[1,2], Feng Zhu[4], Rui Zhao[4,5], and Nenghai Yu[1,2]

[1] School of Information Science and Technology, University of Science and Technology of China, Hefei, China
{lxlkw,luyan17,gjyin,huangjy}@mail.ustc.edu.cn, {qchu,ynh}@ustc.edu.cn,
flowice@ustc.edu.cn
[2] Key Laboratory of Electromagnetic Space Information, Chinese Academy of Science, Beijing, China
[3] School of Data Science, University of Science and Technology of China, Hefei, China
liuyat@mail.ustc.edu.cn
[4] SenseTime Research, Hong Kong, China
{zhufeng,zhaorui}@sensetime.com
[5] Qing Yuan Research Institute, Shanghai Jiao Tong University, Shanghai, China

Abstract. Graph-based models have achieved great success in person re-identification tasks recently, which compute the graph topology structure (affinities) among different people first and then pass the information across them to achieve stronger features. But we find existing graph-based methods in the visible-infrared person re-identification task (VI-ReID) suffer from bad generalization because of two issues: 1) **train-test modality balance gap**, which is a property of VI-ReID task. The number of two modalities data are balanced in the training stage but extremely unbalanced in inference, causing the low generalization of graph-based VI-ReID methods. 2) **sub-optimal topology structure** caused by the end-to-end learning manner to the graph module. We analyze that the joint learning of backbone features and graph features weaken the learning of graph topology, making it not generalized enough during the inference process. In this paper, we propose a Counterfactual Intervention Feature Transfer (CIFT) method to tackle these problems. Specifically, a Homogeneous and Heterogeneous Feature Transfer (H²FT) is designed to reduce the train-test modality balance gap by two independent types of well-designed graph modules and an unbalanced scenario simulation. Besides, a Counterfactual Relation Intervention (CRI) is proposed to utilize the counterfactual intervention and causal effect tools

---

X. Li and Y. Lu—Equal contribution.

Supplementary Information The online version contains supplementary material available at https://doi.org/10.1007/978-3-031-19809-0_22.

to highlight the role of topology structure in the whole training process, which makes the graph topology structure more reliable. Extensive experiments on standard VI-ReID benchmarks demonstrate that CIFT outperforms the state-of-the-art methods under various settings.

Keywords: Person re-identification · Counterfactual · Cross-modality

1   Introduction

Standard person re-identification (ReID) [5,15,25,26,43] aims to match pedestrian images of the same identity captured by different cameras, which is essentially a single-modality (RGB) retrieval task. However, open-world intelligent monitoring requires methods to retrieve targets captured by infrared or thermal cameras in the dark scenario. Therefore, the research on visible-infrared person re-identification (VI-ReID) has attracted great attention in recent years. Different from standard ReID, large cross-modality discrepancy and intra-modality variations bring new challenges to research on VI-ReID. Most researchers [7,11,37,38, 41,42,49] aimed to embed images of two modalities into the same feature space to tackle this task, which preliminarily solved the modality gap.

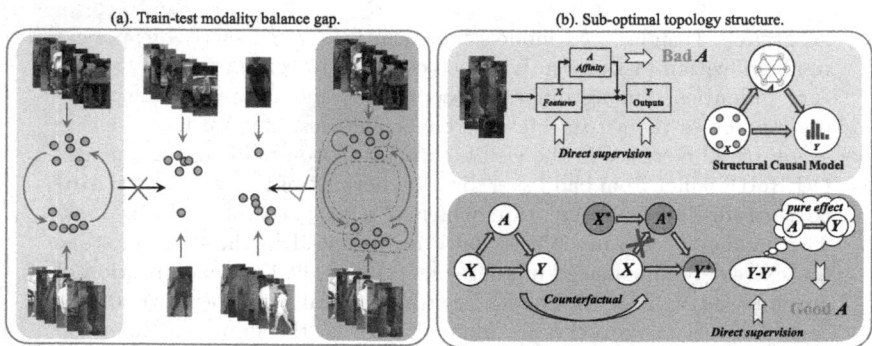

Fig. 1. The red background hints at the existing methods and the green one means our method. (a) Existing graph-based methods trained on modality-balanced data are difficult to transfer to a modality unbalanced scenario. Our method overcomes this problem by unbalanced scenarios simulation and a novel graph module design. (b) Existing training strategies learn the backbone features and the graph outputs jointly, making affinity learning be weakened. Our method uses a counterfactual intervention tool to calculate the pure effect contributed by the affinity changes only, making the model perceive the role of graph topology more direly. (Color figure online)

Graph-based methods have achieved excellent performance on standard person ReID [2,14,23,24]. Generally, they predict the pair-wise similarity as relationships between different samples and then utilize those relationships to propagate messages across samples. This kind of methods can bring a large range of performance gain because the features of one sample not only have the discriminative information of this sample itself but also carry information from other relative samples. So several methods [13,39] attempt to employ graph-based modules to establish relationships and enhance features in the VI-ReID task. But we argue that different from the graph module on the standard Re-ID, the graph methods on VI-ReID suffer bad generalization.

We delve into the graph models pipeline in VI-ReID and summarize two main reasons for the bad generalization: *Train-test modality balance gap* and *Sub-optimal topology structure*. The train-test modality balance gap is a property of VI-ReID task, which means that the number of two modalities data are balanced in the training stage but extremely unbalanced in inference, like Fig. 1 (a) shows. More details about this property will be further introduced in Sect. 3. The sub-optimal structure is another problem but usually ignored by previous methods. It is caused by the end-to-end learning manner of the graph model. We summarize that the existing joint learning process of both the backbone and the graph module would weaken the learning of the graph topology structure, like Fig. 1 (b) shows. They both lead to low generalization of the graph structure predicted by the graph module in inference.

To tackle the aforementioned problems respectively, we propose a Counterfactual Intervention Feature Transfer (CIFT) including one new graph module called Homogeneous and Heterogeneous Feature Transfer (H^2FT) with one additional learning methods Counterfactual Relation Intervention (CRI). The H^2FT aims to reduce the train-test modality balance gap in two ways, training algorithm and model designing. We reorganize the balanced training data to simulate unbalanced modality distributed scenarios and let the H^2FT trained on that environment, which guides the model to adapt to the situation with unbalanced modality distribution. Also, we find that it is hard for the standard graph module to train efficiently on that unbalanced data because the standard message-passing process cannot adapt to the extremely unbalanced modality information. So, we carefully construct the module of the H^2FT which includes two different types of graph modules, to reduce the useless information introduced by the standard graph module and treat the message passing in unbalanced data better, as Fig. 1 (a) shows. Except that, the CRI tackles the sub-optimal graph topology problem by highlighting the role of graph structure (predicted affinity) in the total end-to-end training. We utilize the tools of causal inference to implement that motivation. We first represent our graph module in the Structural Causal Model [19,20] in Fig. 1 (b) and modify the training targets of the graph module from only maximizing the probability likelihood to maximizing the combination of both probability likelihood and the total indirect effect (TIE). The former term guides the whole model to classify the identity of each person image. And the latter one is essentially equal to maximize the difference between the original output and a counterfactual output contributed by the affinity changes only (Fig. 1 (b) green background), which can make the model perceive the function of the graph affinity.

The main contributions of our work are summarized as follows:

- We delve into the existing VI-ReID graph model and find two main reasons for their low generalization: train-test modality balance gap and sub-optimal structure. And we design a novel and effective Counterfactual Intervention Feature Transfer (CIFT) to tackle these problems and achieve the new state of the art.
- We introduce a Homogeneous and Heterogeneous Feature Transfer (H^{2}FT) module including two independent types of well-designed graph module and an unbalanced scenario simulation, which is more suitable for tackling the sample interaction in the scenario with unbalanced modality distribution.
- We propose a novel Counterfactual Relation Intervention (CRI) algorithm to tackle the sub-optimal topology structure problem. It utilizes the counterfactual intervention and causal effect tools to highlight the role of the topology in the feature transfer module, which can train the total module more generalized.

2   Related Work

Visible-Infrared Person Re-ID. Traditional single-modality person Re-ID [15, 26, 43] is limited by the poor illumination conditions at night, so the VI-ReID has received extensive attention in recent years. Many VI-ReID approaches have been proposed to overcome the modality discrepancy produced by different cameras. Wu *et al.* [36] proposed a deep zero-padding network and contribute the first large-scale multiple modality Re-ID dataset named SYSU-MM01.

Many works [7, 10, 11, 37, 38, 41, 42, 49] designed loss functions from the perspective of metric learning to better embed different modalities into the same feature space. Zhu *et al.* [49] proposed the hetero-center loss to reduce the intra-class cross-modality variations. Liu *et al.* [11] proposed the hetero-center triplet loss to relax the strict constraint of traditional triplet loss.

Some methods [4, 31, 32, 34] are based on the generative adversarial network (GAN) [6]. cmGAN [4] adopted generative adversarial training to better distinguish images of different modalities at the feature level. D^{2}RL [34] applied dual-level discrepancy reduction learning based on a bi-directional cycle GAN. Recently, Wu *et al.* [37] introduced a modality alleviation module and a pattern alignment module to discover cross-modality nuances. Hao *et al.* [7] confused two modalities, ensuring that the optimization is explicitly concentrated on the modality-irrelevant perspective. All these methods treat the VI-ReID as an image embedding task and learn to extract features directly from the single image.

Graph-Based Person Re-ID. In the single-modality person Re-ID task, except for the image embedding method, some works [2, 14, 23, 24] pay attention to the relationship between sample pairs. These methods introduced more supervised information of graph relationships into the training stage, while the inference stage also benefits from pair-wise similarity. Besides, some re-ranking [47] and graph neural networks (GNN) [44] methods only treated relational modeling as post-processing to more flexibly adapt to various backbone networks.

In VI-ReID, the large cross-modality discrepancy makes the optimization of the relationship more difficult. Recently, some approaches have explored cross-modality pair-wise relation learning with graph networks. Ye *et al.* [39] introduced cross-modality graph-structured attention to enhance robustness against noisy samples. Lu *et al.* [13] proposed the cross-modality shared-specific feature transfer algorithm that utilizes the graph convolution operator to propagate features over a graph to supplement the information of another modality. These methods utilized the graph network or transformer module to propagate message cross samples to extract stronger features. But they are all suffering from the train-test modality balance gap and sub-optimal topology problems, which limits their applications. In this paper, we propose a novel graph method CIFT to tackle these two problems by both model design and learning algorithm, achieving satisfying generalization on VI-ReID.

Causal Inference in Computer Vision. The causal inference has recently aroused widespread interest, especially in the combination with computer vision [1,12,21,33] to endow models with the ability to pursue the causal effect. Some works [3,17,22,27,28,45] utilized counterfactual to solve problems in various fields of computer vision. Tang *et al.* [27,28] used counterfactual inference in scene graph generation and long-tailed classification to remove bias from training data with long-tailed distributions. Rao *et al.* [22] used counterfactual training in fine-grained image recognition to tackle the bias of the spatial attention caused by the dataset. Niu *et al.* [17] reduce the language bias in visual question answering by subtracting the direct language effect from the total causal effect.

Different from them, we focus on highlighting the affinity of the feature transfer module to address the sub-optimal topology structure due to the graph-based Re-ID model itself, rather than reducing the impact caused by biased data.

3 Delving into Graph-Based Visible-Infrared ReID

In this section, we investigate the influence of graph-based modules in the VI-ReID task. Specifically, we first give a brief review of graph-based VI-ReID methods. Then, we investigate why they suffered by bad generalization. Here, we take cm-SSFT [13] and DDAG [39] as examples for analysis.

3.1 Review of Graph-Based VI-ReID Models

The definition of VI-ReID is essentially a cross-modality retrieval task. So its formula can be written as follow: $\mathcal{R} = \mathcal{M}(q, G)$, where $\mathcal{M}$ is the Re-ID model, used to feedback the ranking list $\mathcal{R}$ between the given query sample q and the gallery set G whose modality is different with the query one. To achieve this pipeline, cm-SSFT [13] and DDAG [39] can be summarized as following:

Step 1: Modality-Invariant Feature Extraction. Give an image x_m whatever its modality m ($m \in \{rgb, ir\}$), utilizing CNNs or other backbones to extract features x for each sample.

Step 2: Feature Enhancement. Build affinities A between all samples in $\{q, G\}$ on their given features X, where $A_{i,j}$ means the relationship between the i-th and the j-th images. After that, messages can be passed and transferred across different samples, leading to stronger features. It can be written as

$$F = A \cdot v(X), \tag{1}$$

where v is a linear learnable function and F stores the output features. This process is essentially equal to constructing a graph whose nodes are person features and edges are affinities and then propagating information based on that graph.

Step 3: Computing Results. After getting enhanced features, different kinds of outputs, e.g. person identities or ranking lists, can be derived.

Step 4: Feature Learning. In the training stage, feature learning algorithms are added on both the backbone features X and graph features F. The classification output Y is derived by F through a classification layer and a cross-entropy loss is used to train it, which makes features carrying identity information.

The most priority of these graph-based modules is passing messages across samples, which mines the potential relationships between different person images. So, they can benefit both training [13,39] and inference [39]. But we find that they are all suffering from bad generalization in VI-ReID.

3.2 Analysis of Bad Generalization of Graph-Based VI-ReID

We summarize that the bad generalization of graph-based VI-ReID is caused by two following problems:

Train-Test Modality Balance Gap. The train-test modality balance gap is caused by the difference of modality information ratio in the training and test stage. Specifically, in the training stage, both cm-SSFT [13] and DDAG [39] pass messages and transfer features on the batch data which includes an equal number of visible and infrared images. So the ratio of two modality information provided in training is 1 : 1. But in inference, the available data is $\{q, G\}$ consisting of one query sample q and a gallery set G. Here, the modality information ratio between two modalities is $1 : N_G$, where N_G is the size of the gallery set. It is clear that the modality information ratio of training and testing is quite different. This is the property of VI-ReID because VI-ReID utilizes the single query evaluation setting which means there is only one query sample available in the inference scenario. It is hard for the model trained on the balanced training data to generalize on the unbalanced inference scenario. The cm-SSFT [13] also provides a series of experiments that demonstrate the unbalanced inference scenario can actually harm the generalization, which brings about 13.9% Rank-1 and 9.1% mAP drops corresponding to a balanced inference one.

Sub-optimal Topology Structure. The affinities A computed by cm-SSFT [13] and DDAG [39] can indicate the relationships between different samples. So the A can be interpreted as a kind of graph topology structure on the given data. But we argue that the structure learned by the existing graph VI-ReID modules are all sub-optimal because of the end-to-end joint learning.

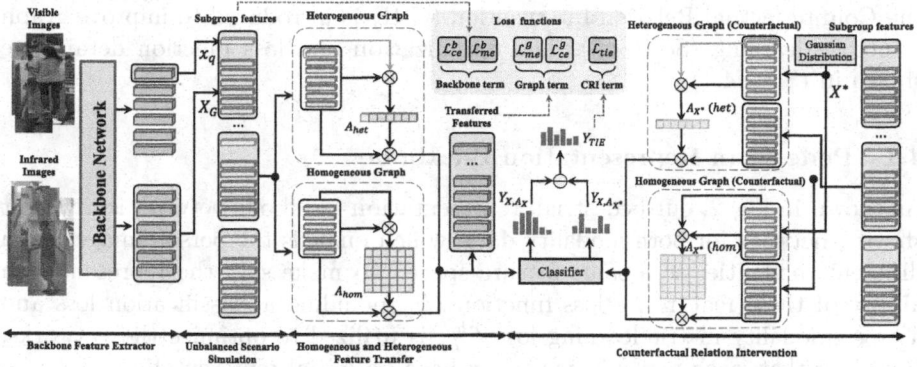

Fig. 2. The Framework of the proposed Counterfactual Intervention Feature Transfer (CIFT). The Homogeneous and Heterogeneous Feature Transfer (H^2FT) module receives features from the backbone feature extractor and simulates unbalanced modality distributed scenarios. It builds homogeneous and heterogeneous message passing for better relationship feature learning under the unbalanced modality distribution. Then, the Counterfactual Relation Intervention (CRI) module calculates total indirect effects to highlight the role of the graph topology and leads to stronger results.

Both cm-SSFT [13] and DDAG [39] add supervisions on backbone features and graph features simultaneously without any constraint on the affinities A, which hurts the generalization. It is common for the graph modules, like transformer [29] or Graph Attention [30], to train the A in an end-to-end joint manner. But the situation is different here, the supervision on the backbone makes the backbone features X discriminative in the training set. At this time, an A with standard quality can make the final output belong to the feature learning constraints[1], so the structure A cannot get much useful guidance. Without further supervision of A, it is hard for the graph module to capture the complex relationships between different samples.

The above analyses reveal that the key to increasing the generalization of graph-based VI-ReID is reducing the modality balance gap between train-test and introducing additional constraints on A in the end-to-end joint learning. Along this direction, we proposed a Counterfactual Intervention Feature Transfer module and show how this model is used to tackle these problems.

4   Counterfactual Intervention Feature Transfer

The overview of our proposed Counterfactual Intervention Feature Transfer (CIFT) is shown in Fig. 2. Visible images and infrared images are first fed into a pedestrian feature extractor to extract the instance-level features. Then these features are sent to the graph module Homogeneous and Heterogeneous Feature Transfer (H^2FT) to extract transferred features (Sect. 4.2). Meanwhile,

---

[1] Further proves could be seen in the supplementary.

the Counterfactual Relation Intervention (CRI) is introduced to improve graph structure learning (Sect. 4.3). The optimization and loss function details are shown in (Sect. 4.4).

4.1 Pedestrian Representation Backbone

As shown in Fig. 2, our pedestrian representation backbone network is a weight sharing network for both modality data, which embeds the person images from different modalities to a same feature space. To make sure the representation ability of those features, a loss function $\mathcal{L}_{ce}^b$ including a classification loss and a cross-modality metric learning loss $\mathcal{L}_{me}^b$ is utilized to optimize the networks. Based on that, each person's image can have an initial representation.

4.2 Homogeneous and Heterogeneous Feature Transfer

For a given batch data including N Visible and N infrared images, we aim to simulate the unbalanced modality distributed scenario to train our model. The batch data is split into a series of groups and each group consists of a single image from one modality (seen as the query q) and N other modality images (seen as the gallery set G). Specifically, each group can have one visible image with N infrared images or one infrared image with N visible images. Every group simulates the scenario with $1 : N$ modality ratio which is similar in the inference setting (one query vs more galleries). So, our H^{2}FT trained under that can adapt on the single query inference without much influence on generalization.

But, under that setting, the modality information is quite imbalanced. The sample seen as the query can only interact with N images from other modality. And for the data seen as gallery, inter-modality interaction is trivial because it just introduces the information provided by the fixed query one, which is redundant even noisy. To avoid this problem, we provide a heterogeneous and a homogeneous graph module for the query data and gallery data separately like Fig. 2 shows. Its equation can be written as:

$$f_q = A_{het} \cdot [v(x_q), v(X_G)], \quad F_G = A_{hom} \cdot v(X_G), \tag{2}$$

where x_q and X_G mean the query feature vector and the gallery features matrix respectively. $[\bullet, \bullet]$ means concatenation in the column dimension. The function $v(\cdot)$, a BNNeck [15] with learnable weights, is used to enhanced the features. f_q and F_G mean the transferred features of the query and the gallery set. A means affinity matrix indicating the relationships between its corresponding samples. To achieve A, we first compute the similarity matrix based on the input features:

$$\mathcal{S}_{ty}^{i,j} = \exp \frac{cos(v(x_i), v(x_j))}{\tau_{ty}}, \quad ty \in \{hom, het\}. \tag{3}$$

$cos(\cdot, \cdot)$ is the cosine distance function to measure the similarity between samples. τ is the temperature parameter to adjust the smoothness of the total similarity distribution. We use different τ for the heterogeneous and homogeneous process because the intra-modality and inter-modality similarities are quite different. To filter out the noisy relationships, we use near neighbor chosen function $\mathcal{T}(\bullet, k)$ [13] to keep the top-k values in each row of similarity matrix: $\mathbf{S}' = \mathcal{T}(\mathbf{S}, k)$. Finally, our affinity matrices are computed as follows:

$$A_{hom} = \mathbf{D}_{hom}^{-1} \cdot \mathbf{S}'_{hom}, \quad A_{het} = \mathbf{D}_{het}^{-1} \cdot \mathbf{S}'_{het}. \tag{4}$$

$\mathbf{D}^{-1}$ is the Laplacian matrix of the $\mathbf{S}'$, used to normalize the total affinities.

Finally, after achieving the final transferred features F, a classification layer derives the logits Y and the cross-entropy loss $\mathcal{L}_{ce}^g$ is utilized to train Y which is equal to maximizing likelihood to keep the features carrying richer identity information. Then metric learning term $\mathcal{L}_{me}^g$ is added to the output to make features carry more discriminative information.

Along that pipeline, the unbalanced scenario simulation makes the model adapt to the single query inference scenario. And the two kinds of message passing processes, heterogeneous and homogeneous, guide the query sample to interact with potential galleries while the gallery data only propagate messages across themselves, which preserves the nontrivial information interaction process in each group data, which is more suitable for tackling this unbalanced situation.

4.3 Counterfactual Relation Intervention

To add additional supervision of the affinities A and keep the whole end-to-end training pipeline, we present to highlight the role of the graph topology structure in the total learning process. For this goal, we bring the tools of causal inference here. We first represent our H^2FT into a Structural Causal Model (SCM) [19,20], like Fig. 1 (b) shows. $X \rightarrow A$ means the affinity computation and $X \rightarrow Y \leftarrow A$ is the message passing process (including the output computation).

It is obvious the process that deriving the output Y from input X can be seen as two types of effects: One is the direct effect $X \rightarrow Y$ and the other is an indirect one $X \rightarrow A \rightarrow Y$. The classification loss for our H^2FT, equal to maximizing the likelihood, would affect the two effects in an end-to-end manner so the A in the indirect effect path cannot be enhanced sufficiently.

To highlight the A in the whole training process, we utilize the Total Indirect Effect (TIE) here. We first give its equation:

$$Y_{TIE} = Y_{X,A_X} - \mathbb{E}_{X^*}[Y_{X,A_{X^*}}]. \tag{5}$$

Y_{X,A_X} is the original output of our graph module, which means feeding forward the different sample features X and computing their outputs. Note that the affinity matrix here is denoted as A_X which means that affinities are computed based on the input features X. $Y_{X,A_{X^*}}$ means computing the results by replacing original affinity A_X to a intervened one A_{X^*}, where X^* is the intervened inputs given manually. It is obvious that $Y_{X,A_{X^*}}$ cannot occur in the real world because features X and affinities A_{X^*} come from different inputs X and X^*, which is called counterfactual intervention. So modification from Y_{X,A_X} to $Y_{X,A_{X^*}}$ is equal to keep all potential variables fixed but only change the affinity A, which can show the pure effect introduced by A. We compute the expectation of that effect to get the more stable one. Intervened input features X^* utilized to compute A_{X^*} are sampled by a Gaussian distribution:

$$X^* = X_\sigma \cdot Z + X_\mu, \tag{6}$$

where Z is the standard random vector whose dimension is same with features X. mean X_μ and stand deviation X_σ are learned by the re-parameterization trick [9] in an end-to-end way.

A cross-entropy loss is added to the TIE: $\mathcal{L}_{tie} = \mathcal{L}_{ce}(Y_{TIE})$. Minimizing that cross-entropy loss is equal to maximizing the Y_{TIE} on the prediction of the correct class, which guides the model to increase the gap between the original output and the counterfactual one. It is clear that the counterfactual classification results should be worse than the original one because the intervened affinities A_{X^*} commonly do not match with inputs X. So an intuitive understanding about maximizing TIE is constraining the model to increase the difference between the outputs derived from good A_X and bad A_{X^*}. Since other variables have been fixed, the model has to change the A_X to increase the original results Y_{X,A_X} for enhancing the gaps, leading to better training of affinity.

4.4 Optimization

The whole model is trained end-to-end and the total loss $\mathcal{L}_{total}$ of our method is defined as:[2]

$$\mathcal{L}_{total} = \underbrace{\mathcal{L}_{ce}^b + \mathcal{L}_{me}^b}_{\text{backbone term}} + \underbrace{\mathcal{L}_{ce}^g + \mathcal{L}_{me}^g}_{\text{graph term}} + \underbrace{\mathcal{L}_{tie}}_{\text{CRI term}} . \tag{7}$$

5   Experiments

5.1   Datasets and Evaluation Protocol

In this section, we conduct comprehensive experiments to evaluate our method on two public datasets, SYSU-MM01 [36] and RegDB [16].

SYSU-MM01 is the first large-scale benchmark dataset for Visible-Infrared ReID. It is collected by four visible and two infrared cameras, in both indoor and outdoor environments. The training set contains 395 identities with 22,258 visible and 11,909 infrared images while the test set contains 96 identities. Concretely, the query set contains 3,803 infrared images and the gallery set contains 301/3010 (single-shot/multi-shot) randomly selected visible images.

RegDB is collected by a dual-camera system(a pair of aligned visible and thermal cameras). It contains 412 people, and each person has 10 visible and 10 far-infrared images. The dataset is divided into training and test splits randomly, the images of 206 identities for training and the rest 206 identities for testing.

---

[2] The details about cross-modality metric learning loss $\mathcal{L}_{me}$ and $\mathcal{L}_{me}$ can be found in the supplementary.

Table 1. Comparison of rank-1 accuracy (%) and mAP accuracy (%) with the state-of-the-art methods on SYSU-MM01 and RegDB. (CIFT[†] means we use backbone features for inference rather than the transferred graph features.)

Method	SYSU-MM01 [36]								RegDB [16]			
	All-search				Indoor-search				Visible to Infrared		Infrared to Visible	
	Single-shot		Multi-shot		Single-shot		Multi-shot					
	rank-1	mAP	rank-1	mAP	rank-1	mAP	rank-1	mAP	rank-1	mAP	rank-1	mAP
Zero-Pad [36]	14.80	15.95	19.13	10.89	20.58	26.92	24.43	18.64	–	–	–	–
cmGAN [4]	26.97	27.80	31.49	22.27	31.63	42.19	37.00	32.76	–	–	–	–
D^{2}RL [34]	28.9	29.2	–	–	–	–	–	–	43.4	44.1	–	–
JSIA-ReID [31]	38.1	36.9	45.1	29.5	43.8	52.9	52.7	42.7	48.5	49.3	48.1	48.9
AlignGAN [32]	42.4	40.7	51.5	33.9	45.9	54.3	57.1	45.3	57.9	53.6	56.3	53.4
AGW [40]	47.5	47.65	–	–	54.17	62.97	–	–	70.05	66.37	–	–
cm-SSFT [13]	61.6	63.2	63.4	62.0	70.5	72.6	73.0	72.4	72.3	72.0	71.0	71.7
cm-SSFT(sq)	47.7	54.1	–	–	57.4	59.1	–	–	65.4	65.6	63.8	64.2
DDAG [39]	54.75	53.02	–	–	61.02	67.98	–	–	69.34	63.46	68.06	61.80
HC [49]	56.96	54.95	62.09	48.02	59.74	64.91	69.76	57.81	–	–	–	–
CIMA [46]	57.2	59.3	60.7	52.6	66.6	74.7	73.8	68.3	78.8	69.4	77.9	69.4
HCT [11]	61.68	57.51	–	–	63.41	68.17	–	–	91.05	83.28	89.30	81.46
MCLNet [7]	65.4	61.98	–	–	72.56	76.58	–	–	80.31	73.07	75.93	69.49
SMCL [35]	67.39	61.78	72.15	54.93	68.84	75.56	79.57	66.57	83.93	79.83	83.05	78.57
MPANet [37]	70.58	68.24	75.58	62.91	76.74	80.95	84.22	75.11	83.7	80.9	82.8	80.7
CIFT[†](Ours)	71.77	67.64	78.00	62.46	78.65	82.11	86.97	77.03	**92.17**	86.96	90.12	84.81
CIFT(Ours)	**74.08**	**74.79**	**79.74**	**75.56**	**81.82**	**85.61**	**88.32**	**86.42**	91.96	**92.00**	**90.30**	**90.78**

Evaluation Protocol. All the experiments follow the standard evaluation protocol in existing Visible-Infrared cross-modality ReID benchmarks. For SYSU-MM01, the original evaluation protocol [36] provides all-search and indoor-search modes for testing. Both search modes have two retrieval settings, single-shot and multi-shot. For RegDB, we follow the widely used evaluation protocol in [16] which contains two modes for testing, Visible to Infrared test mode and Infrared to Visible test mode. We evaluate our model on the 10 trials with different training/test splits to achieve stable performance. For both datasets, the cumulative matching characteristics (CMC) and mean average precision (mAP) are adopted as evaluation metrics.

5.2 Implementation Details

We implement our approach with PyTorch [18] on one NVIDIA Titan Xp GPU. Following the previous ReID methods [15,40], we use ResNet-50 [8] pre-trained on ImageNet as our backbone network. We change the stride of the last convolutional layer in the backbone to 1 and employ the Batch Normalization Neck [15] as the embedding layer. Each person image is resized to commonly used 288 × 144 resolution. We also adopt the random cropping, random horizontal flipping and random erasing [48] for data augmentation. The k in the near neighbor chosen function is set to 4. τ_{hom} and τ_{het} in Eq. 3 are set to 0.4 and 0.2 for the heterogeneous and homogeneous process. The whole model is trained for 120 epochs with the SGD optimizer. The learning rate gradually rises up by the warm-up scheme and decays by a factor of 10 at the 60th and 100th epochs. The batch size is set to 64, containing 32 visible and 32 infrared images from 8 identities. And each identity consists of 4 visible and 4 infrared images.

5.3   Comparison with State-of-the-Art Methods

In this part, we compare our proposed method CIFT with state-of-the-art (SOTA) visible-infrared person Re-ID approaches, including Zero-Pad [36], cmGAN [4], D^{2}RL [34], JSIA-ReID [31], AlignGAN [32], AGW [40], cm-SSFT [13], DDAG [39], HC [49], CIMA [46], HCT [11], MCLNet [7], SMCL [35] and MPANet [37].

Comparison and Analysis. The experimental results are shown in Table 1 and the proposed method outperforms the existing SOTAs on both datasets. In SYSU-MM01 dataset, our CIFT achieves 74.08% rank-1 accuracy and 74.79% mAP accuracy, which surpasses MPANet [37] by 3.50% on rank-1 accuracy and 6.55% on mAP accuracy in the most challenging single-shot all search mode. Even our CIFT† (only uses graph module in training and utilizes the backbone features in inference) outperforms MPANet by 1.19% on rank-1 accuracy. In another popular public RegDB dataset, whether in 'infrared to visible' mode or 'visible to infrared' mode, our CIFT† still achieves the highest scores. The average performances in the two modes are 91.15% rank-1 accuracy and 85.89% mAP accuracy, which surpasses MPANet by a large gain of about 7.90% on rank-1 accuracy and 5.09% on mAP accuracy. This is because the learning of transferred features introduces additional supervision to the model, so that the features of the backbone network are also enhanced.

For the multi-shot setting, the mAP accuracy of all other methods will drop significantly compared with the single-shot evaluation because the model is required to retrieve more positive targets in the multi-shot setting. So it is more challenging for the model to find out all potential targets. But our CIFT is not suffering that bad phenomenon even can achieve better results, which shows that our method is qualitatively different from other methods. When the scale gallery size is larger, our model can extract richer and more discriminate relation features so that the model is more robust to gallery size even benefited by the larger scale one. Compared with cm-SSFT [13] which also obtain relationship from the gallery set, our CIFT improves the mAP accuracy by 0.77% as the gallery size increases (multi-shot versus single-shot), while the cm-SSFT reduces the mAP accuracy by 1.2%. This is because we utilize CRI to highlight the role of topology structure in the whole training process. The affinities are much more accurate so that the final representation is much stronger.

5.4   Comparison with Multi-gallery Matching Methods

To demonstrate the superiority of our CIFT to other graph and post-process VI-ReID methods, we compare it with other multi-gallery matching methods,

Table 2. Compared with other methods that use gallery set information in the inference stage on same backbone networks, *i.e.* AGW [40], HC [49], HCT [11] and our backbone. We report the rank-1 accuracy (%) and the mAP accuracy (%) on the SYSU-MM01 single-shot all search mode. 'train' and 'test' in 'strategy' means the training methods and test methods separately

Row	Strategy	Backbone							
		AGW [40]		HC [49]		HCT [11]		Our backbone	
		rank-1	mAP	rank-1	mAP	rank-1	mAP	rank-1	mAP
1	Backbone	47.22	47.78	54.52	54.06	61.05	56.97	70.49	66.58
2	k-reciprocal [47]	47.63	51.81	53.91	60.03	62.33	62.05	71.47	72.49
3	GNN rerank [44]	46.96	52.01	55.05	59.79	60.52	62.72	70.40	73.21
4	cm-SSFT [13]	48.65	51.76	56.17	61.36	62.27	61.85	69.92	71.77
5	**CIFT**	**52.12**	**56.92**	**61.03**	**64.05**	**66.18**	**68.09**	**74.08**	**74.79**

Table 3. Ablation study on SYSU-MM01. The important modules of the proposed CIFT, *i.e.* H^2FT and CRI are analyzed under different settings.

Row	GFT	UBS	H^2G	CRI	SYSU-MM01	
					rank-1	mAP
1	–	–	–	–	70.49	66.58
2	✓	–	–	–	72.01	72.12
3	✓	✓	–	–	72.90	71.97
4	✓	✓	✓	–	72.29	73.79
5	✓	✓	✓	✓	74.08	74.79

Table 4. Affinity quality statistics on the SYSU-MM01 test set. The value (%) represents the **average error ratio** of the affinity matrix in the entire test set.

Method	All-search		Indoor-search	
	Single-shot	Multi-shot	Single-shot	Multi-shot
w/o CRI	5.16	3.95	6.54	6.15
w/ CRI	3.90	2.76	5.03	4.66

including cm-SSFT [13], k-reciprocal rerank [47], and GNN rerank [44]. We evaluate these methods with our CIFT on different backbone networks including AGW [40], HC [49], HCT [11], and our backbone network, to show the generality of our method under different level baselines. For a fair comparison, we also search the best hyper-parameters for these multi-gallery matching methods, so that they can fit the backbones well. Please note that, to adapt these backbone features format, cm-SSFT is set as only using the shared feature transfer.

Our results are shown in the 5th line in Table 2 and 1st–3rd lines represent different widely used post-processing ways, combining different multi-gallery matching methods with the trained backbone features directly in inference. Comparing with the strongest post-process GNN rerank [44], we achieve averaged 5.12% rank-1 and 4.03% mAP gains on all given backbones. Further, we also compare the single query cm-SSFT (the 4th row) who does additional feature transfer learning corresponding to the aforementioned post-process methods. It only achieves comparable results with GNN rerank in the 3rd line and does not show much more priority of its graph learning. That is because cm-SSFT trains in the case of balanced modality but transferred to modal unbalanced inference scenario, which hurts its generalization. So, with the ability to tackle the inference under unbalanced modality distribution, it is common for CIFT to suppress the cm-SSFT by a large margin. The results in Table 2 show that our method achieves the best performance on all backbone networks, bringing average improvements of 5.03% on rank-1 accuracy and 9.50% on mAP accuracy. This proves that our method is compatible with various backbone networks and can achieve effective improvement.

5.5   Ablation Study

In this section, we conduct ablation studies to prove the effectiveness of each module of the proposed CIFT, $i.e.$ H^2FT and CRI. All ablation experiments are performed on our baseline backbone in the single-shot all search mode of the large-scale dataset SYSU-MM01. The results are shown in Table 3.

Effectiveness of H^2FT. In the proposed CIFT, we introduce a graph-based feature transfer module H^2FT to tackle the train-test modality balance gap. To evaluate the effectiveness of each detailed part in H^2FT, We split the H^2FT into three parts: Graph Feature Transfer (GFT), UnBalanced Scenario simulation (UBS) and Homogeneous&Heterogeneous Graph module (H^2G). GFT is a simple graph module baseline proposed by ourselves, which is used to show the gain introduced by the message passing in the graph module itself. Its details can be seen in the supplementary and we try ourselves to keep other variables not changing. Its performance in the 2nd row shows that the feature transfer can bring about 5.5% gains in mAP. To train the model suitable for the unbalanced inference scenario, we add the UBS on it. But we find that the performance on mAP has a little drop. We think that is caused by the model design who is not fit the unbalanced data. Now, we add the H^2G back in the 3rd line, equal to the complete H^2FT, and achieve additional 1.67% mAP gains. Proving the effectiveness of our H^2FT.

Effectiveness of CRI. The proposed CRI algorithm utilizes the counterfactual intervention to highlight the role of the topology to tackle the sub-optimal topology structure problem. As shown in Table 3, CRI algorithm brings improvements of 1.79% rank-1 accuracy and 1.00% mAP accuracy without any computational costs in the inference stage. In addition, we also do another quantitative analysis of the CRI to demonstrate its contribution. Specifically, we first compute the ideal affinity matrix by the ground-truth label, which uses 1 to indicate the positive pair and 0 as the negative one. And then for the affinity matrix computed by our model, we define the top-4 results in each row as positive. After that, we compute the averaged error rate between the predicted affinities with the ground truths in the entire test set. The results are shown in Table 4. In the single-shot all-search mode, the model without CRI gets for 5.16% error ratio while the model with CRI achieves 3.90%. In other test modes, introducing CRI also significantly reduces the error ratios. This reflects that our CRI has learned a better structure which is more close to the ground-truth one.

6   Conclusion

We propose a Homogeneous and Heterogeneous Feature Transfer (H^2FT) module with a Counterfactual Relation Intervention (CRI) learning method to tackle the Visible-Infrared Person Re-identification. The H^2FT consists of two types of graph modules that can handle the train-test modality balance gap that the previous graph-based model suffered. And CRI introduces the causal inference tool to tackle the sub-optimal topology structure problem and makes our method more generalized.

References

1. Chalupka, K., Perona, P., Eberhardt, F.: Visual causal feature learning. arXiv preprint arXiv:1412.2309 (2014)
2. Chen, D., Xu, D., Li, H., Sebe, N., Wang, X.: Group consistent similarity learning via deep CRF for person re-identification. In: Proceedings of the IEEE Conference on Computer Vision and Pattern Recognition, pp. 8649–8658 (2018)
3. Chen, L., Yan, X., Xiao, J., Zhang, H., Pu, S., Zhuang, Y.: Counterfactual samples synthesizing for robust visual question answering. In: Proceedings of the IEEE/CVF Conference on Computer Vision and Pattern Recognition, pp. 10800–10809 (2020)
4. Dai, P., Ji, R., Wang, H., Wu, Q., Huang, Y.: Cross-modality person re-identification with generative adversarial training. In: IJCAI, vol. 1,p. 2 (2018)
5. Gong, S., Cristani, M., Loy, C.C., Hospedales, T.M.: The re-identification challenge. In: Gong, S., Cristani, M., Yan, S., Loy, C.C. (eds.) Person Re-Identification. ACVPR, pp. 1–20. Springer, London (2014). https://doi.org/10.1007/978-1-4471-6296-4_1
6. Goodfellow, I., et al.: Generative adversarial networks. Commun. ACM **63**(11), 139–144 (2020)
7. Hao, X., Zhao, S., Ye, M., Shen, J.: Cross-modality person re-identification via modality confusion and center aggregation. In: Proceedings of the IEEE/CVF International Conference on Computer Vision, pp. 16403–16412 (2021)
8. He, K., Zhang, X., Ren, S., Sun, J.: Deep residual learning for image recognition. In: Proceedings of the IEEE Conference on Computer Vision and Pattern Recognition, pp. 770–778 (2016)
9. Kingma, D.P., Welling, M.: Auto-encoding variational Bayes. arXiv preprint arXiv:1312.6114 (2013)

10. Ling, Y., Luo, Z., Lin, Y., Li, S.: A multi-constraint similarity learning with adaptive weighting for visible-thermal person re-identification. In: IJCAI, pp. 845–851 (2021)
11. Liu, H., Tan, X., Zhou, X.: Parameter sharing exploration and hetero-center triplet loss for visible-thermal person re-identification. IEEE Trans. Multimedia **23**, 4414–4425 (2020)
12. Lopez-Paz, D., Nishihara, R., Chintala, S., Scholkopf, B., Bottou, L.: Discovering causal signals in images. In: Proceedings of the IEEE Conference on Computer Vision and Pattern Recognition, pp. 6979–6987 (2017)
13. Lu, Y., ot al.: Cross-modality person re-identification with shared-specific feature transfer. In: Proceedings of the IEEE/CVF Conference on Computer Vision and Pattern Recognition, pp. 13379–13389 (2020)
14. Luo, C., Chen, Y., Wang, N., Zhang, Z.: Spectral feature transformation for person re-identification. In: Proceedings of the IEEE/CVF International Conference on Computer Vision, pp. 4976–4985 (2019)
15. Luo, H., Gu, Y., Liao, X., Lai, S., Jiang, W.: Bag of tricks and a strong baseline for deep person re-identification. In: Proceedings of the IEEE/CVF Conference on Computer Vision and Pattern Recognition Workshops (2019)
16. Nguyen, D.T., Hong, H.G., Kim, K.W., Park, K.R.: Person recognition system based on a combination of body images from visible light and thermal cameras. Sensors **17**(3), 605 (2017)
17. Niu, Y., Tang, K., Zhang, H., Lu, Z., Hua, X.S., Wen, J.R.: Counterfactual VQA: a cause-effect look at language bias. In: Proceedings of the IEEE/CVF Conference on Computer Vision and Pattern Recognition, pp. 12700–12710 (2021)
18. Paszke, A., et al.: Automatic differentiation in PyTorch (2017)
19. Pearl, J., Glymour, M.A., Jewell, N.P.: Causal Inference in Statistics: A Primer. Wiley (2016)
20. Pearl, J., Mackenzie, D.: The Book of Why: The New Science of Cause and Effect. Basic Books (2018)
21. Qi, J., Niu, Y., Huang, J., Zhang, H.: Two causal principles for improving visual dialog. In: Proceedings of the IEEE/CVF Conference on Computer Vision and Pattern Recognition, pp. 10860–10869 (2020)
22. Rao, Y., Chen, G., Lu, J., Zhou, J.: Counterfactual attention learning for fine-grained visual categorization and re-identification. In: Proceedings of the IEEE/CVF International Conference on Computer Vision, pp. 1025–1034 (2021)
23. Shen, Y., Li, H., Xiao, T., Yi, S., Chen, D., Wang, X.: Deep group-shuffling random walk for person re-identification. In: Proceedings of the IEEE Conference on Computer Vision and Pattern Recognition, pp. 2265–2274 (2018)
24. Shen, Y., Li, H., Yi, S., Chen, D., Wang, X.: Person re-identification with deep similarity-guided graph neural network. In: Ferrari, V., Hebert, M., Sminchisescu, C., Weiss, Y. (eds.) ECCV 2018. LNCS, vol. 11219, pp. 508–526. Springer, Cham (2018). https://doi.org/10.1007/978-3-030-01267-0_30
25. Sun, Y., et al.: Circle loss: a unified perspective of pair similarity optimization. In: Proceedings of the IEEE/CVF Conference on Computer Vision and Pattern Recognition, pp. 6398–6407 (2020)
26. Sun, Y., Zheng, L., Yang, Y., Tian, Q., Wang, S.: Beyond part models: person retrieval with refined part pooling (and a strong convolutional baseline). In: Ferrari, V., Hebert, M., Sminchisescu, C., Weiss, Y. (eds.) ECCV 2018. LNCS, vol. 11208, pp. 501–518. Springer, Cham (2018). https://doi.org/10.1007/978-3-030-01225-0_30

27. Tang, K., Huang, J., Zhang, H.: Long-tailed classification by keeping the good and removing the bad momentum causal effect. arXiv preprint arXiv:2009.12991 (2020)
28. Tang, K., Niu, Y., Huang, J., Shi, J., Zhang, H.: Unbiased scene graph generation from biased training. In: Proceedings of the IEEE/CVF Conference on Computer Vision and Pattern Recognition, pp. 3716–3725 (2020)
29. Vaswani, A., et al.: Attention is all you need. In: Advances in Neural Information Processing Systems, pp. 5998–6008 (2017)
30. Veličković, P., Cucurull, G., Casanova, A., Romero, A., Lio, P., Bengio, Y.: Graph attention networks. arXiv preprint arXiv:1710.10903 (2017)
31. Wang, G.A., et al.: Cross-modality paired-images generation for RGB-infrared person re-identification. In: Proceedings of the AAAI Conference on Artificial Intelligence, vol. 34, pp. 12144–12151 (2020)
32. Wang, G., Zhang, T., Cheng, J., Liu, S., Yang, Y., Hou, Z.: RGB-infrared cross-modality person re-identification via joint pixel and feature alignment. In: Proceedings of the IEEE/CVF International Conference on Computer Vision, pp. 3623–3632 (2019)
33. Wang, T., Huang, J., Zhang, H., Sun, Q.: Visual commonsense R-CNN. In: Proceedings of the IEEE/CVF Conference on Computer Vision and Pattern Recognition, pp. 10760–10770 (2020)
34. Wang, Z., Wang, Z., Zheng, Y., Chuang, Y.Y., Satoh, S.: Learning to reduce dual-level discrepancy for infrared-visible person re-identification. In: Proceedings of the IEEE/CVF Conference on Computer Vision and Pattern Recognition, pp. 618–626 (2019)
35. Wei, Z., Yang, X., Wang, N., Gao, X.: Syncretic modality collaborative learning for visible infrared person re-identification. In: Proceedings of the IEEE/CVF International Conference on Computer Vision, pp. 225–234 (2021)
36. Wu, A., Zheng, W.S., Yu, H.X., Gong, S., Lai, J.: RGB-infrared cross-modality person re-identification. In: Proceedings of the IEEE International Conference on Computer Vision, pp. 5380–5389 (2017)
37. Wu, Q., et al.: Discover cross-modality nuances for visible-infrared person re-identification. In: Proceedings of the IEEE/CVF Conference on Computer Vision and Pattern Recognition, pp. 4330–4339 (2021)
38. Ye, M., Lan, X., Li, J., Yuen, P.: Hierarchical discriminative learning for visible thermal person re-identification. In: Proceedings of the AAAI Conference on Artificial Intelligence, vol. 32 (2018)
39. Ye, M., Shen, J., J. Crandall, D., Shao, L., Luo, J.: Dynamic dual-attentive aggregation learning for visible-infrared person re-identification. In: Vedaldi, A., Bischof, H., Brox, T., Frahm, J.-M. (eds.) ECCV 2020. LNCS, vol. 12362, pp. 229–247. Springer, Cham (2020). https://doi.org/10.1007/978-3-030-58520-4_14
40. Ye, M., Shen, J., Lin, G., Xiang, T., Shao, L., Hoi, S.C.: Deep learning for person re-identification: a survey and outlook. IEEE Trans. Pattern Anal. Mach. Intell. 44, 2872–2893 (2021)
41. Ye, M., Wang, Z., Lan, X., Yuen, P.C.: Visible thermal person re-identification via dual-constrained top-ranking. In: IJCAI, vol. 1, p. 2 (2018)
42. Zhang, L., Du, G., Liu, F., Tu, H., Shu, X.: Global-local multiple granularity learning for cross-modality visible-infrared person reidentification. IEEE Trans. Neural Netw. Learn. Syst. (2021)
43. Zhang, X., et al.: AlignedReID: surpassing human-level performance in person re-identification. arXiv preprint arXiv:1711.08184 (2017)

44. Zhang, X., Jiang, M., Zheng, Z., Tan, X., Ding, E., Yang, Y.: Understanding image retrieval re-ranking: a graph neural network perspective. arXiv preprint arXiv:2012.07620 (2020)
45. Zhang, Z., Zhao, Z., Lin, Z., He, X., et al.: Counterfactual contrastive learning for weakly-supervised vision-language grounding. Adv. Neural. Inf. Process. Syst. **33**, 18123–18134 (2020)
46. Zhao, Z., Liu, B., Chu, Q., Lu, Y., Yu, N.: Joint color-irrelevant consistency learning and identity-aware modality adaptation for visible-infrared cross modality person re-identification. In: Proceedings of the AAAI Conference on Artificial Intelligence, vol. 35, pp. 3520–3528 (2021)
47. Zhong, Z., Zheng, L., Cao, D., Li, S.: Re-ranking person re-identification with k-reciprocal encoding. In: Proceedings of the IEEE Conference on Computer Vision and Pattern Recognition, pp. 1318–1327 (2017)
48. Zhong, Z., Zheng, L., Kang, G., Li, S., Yang, Y.: Random erasing data augmentation. In: Proceedings of the AAAI Conference on Artificial Intelligence, vol. 34, pp. 13001–13008 (2020)
49. Zhu, Y., Yang, Z., Wang, L., Zhao, S., Hu, X., Tao, D.: Hetero-center loss for cross-modality person re-identification. Neurocomputing **386**, 97–109 (2020)

DAS: Densely-Anchored Sampling
for Deep Metric Learning

Lizhao Liu[1,2], Shangxin Huang[1], Zhuangwei Zhuang[1], Ran Yang[1],
Mingkui Tan[1,3(✉)], and Yaowei Wang[2(✉)]

[1] South China University of Technology, Guangzhou, China
{selizhaoliu,sevtars,z.zhuangwei,msyangran}@mail.scut.edu.cn,
mingkuitan@scut.edu.cn
[2] PengCheng Laboratory, Shenzhen, China
[3] Key Laboratory of Big Data and Intelligent Robot, Ministry of Education,
Guangzhou, China

Abstract. Deep Metric Learning (DML) serves to learn an embedding function to project semantically similar data into nearby embedding space and plays a vital role in many applications, such as image retrieval and face recognition. However, the performance of DML methods often highly depends on sampling methods to choose effective data from the embedding space in the training. In practice, the embeddings in the embedding space are obtained by some deep models, where the embedding space is often with barren area due to the absence of training points, resulting in so called "missing embedding" issue. This issue may impair the sample quality, which leads to degenerated DML performance. In this work, we investigate how to alleviate the "missing embedding" issue to improve the sampling quality and achieve effective DML. To this end, we propose a Densely-Anchored Sampling (DAS) scheme that considers the embedding with corresponding data point as "anchor" and exploits the anchor's nearby embedding space to densely produce embeddings without data points. Specifically, we propose to exploit the embedding space around single anchor with Discriminative Feature Scaling (DFS) and multiple anchors with Memorized Transformation Shifting (MTS). In this way, by combing the embeddings with and without data points, we are able to provide more embeddings to facilitate the sampling process thus boosting the performance of DML. Our method is effortlessly integrated into existing DML frameworks and improves them without bells and whistles. Extensive experiments on three benchmark datasets demonstrate the superiority of our method.

Keywords: Deep metric learning · Missing embedding · Embedding space exploitation · Densely-Anchored Sampling

Supplementary Information The online version contains supplementary material available at https://doi.org/10.1007/978-3-031-19809-0_23.

1   Introduction

Deep Metric learning (DML) is the foundation of various applications, including face recognition, verification [10,42], image retrieval [21], image clustering [17], image classification [12], few-shot learning [32], video representation learning [5] and sound generation [6] *etc.* Since it was introduced, it has sparked considerable interest in the community, where academics have offered a variety of methods [18, 36,38,42,45,53,56] and have made substantial progress [37,41]. The goal of DML is to learn a deep model that is capable of mapping semantically similar data points to similar embeddings in the embedding space. To accomplish this, most existing approaches [7,18,42,48,53,56] train the deep model with loss functions that bring the embeddings from semantically similar data points close to each other and vice versa. However, some embeddings may have limited contribution or bring no improvement to train the deep model [56], or even lead to bad local minima early on in training (such as a collapsed model) [42]. Thus, sampling informative and stable embeddings is very important to facilitate the training of deep model [56]. As a result, improving the sample quality is of significance to achieve effective DML. There are two commonly used measures for this goal: designing more effective sampling methods or providing more embeddings.

Pioneering efforts have made substantial progress toward the design of effective sampling methods upon embedding pairs [41,42,56] or a full batch of embeddings [36,38]. These methods typically perform sampling on a batch of embeddings, which often leads to inaccurate sampling results due to the following reasons. First, the batch size is typically constrained by the memory of a single GPU as the sampling process typically cannot cross different GPU devices [41]. Second, even with GPU that has sufficient memory to support a larger batch size, the embedding space that contains the embeddings embedded by deep models may still with barren area due to the absence of data points, resulting in a "missing embedding" issue (as shown in Fig. 1). Thus, the limited amount of embeddings may impair the sample quality and the performance of DML. Based on the above analyses, we ask: "Can we overcome the inaccurate sampling issue brought by the absence of data points?"

Very recently, a few attempts [13,16,28,54,64] have been committed to answering this question by pseudo embedding generation. Hard example gen-

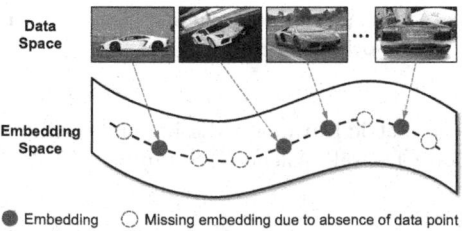

Fig. 1. Illustration of the "missing embedding" issue. The data points of similar semantics are mapped into the nearby embedding space that is often with barren area due to the absence of data points, resulting in the "missing embedding" issue

eration approaches [13,64] generate hard embeddings from easy embeddings with an additional generative adversarial network or auto-encoder. Embedding expansion [28] performs interpolation between embeddings to achieve augmentation in embedding space. Cross batch memory [54] maintains embeddings from previous iterations and considers them are still informative in the current batch in terms of sampling. However, these approaches either leverage additional sub-network [13,64], which introduce extra training cost, or need further modification to the sampling and loss computation process [28,54] in standard DML [18,20,42,45,53], which may limit their applicability to other tasks.

In this paper, we seek to densely produce embeddings without data points to alleviate the "missing embedding" issue. In this way, with the combination of embeddings with and without data points, we are able to provide more embeddings for sampling to improve the sample quality and achieve effective DML. Our motivation stems from a fundamental hypothesis of metric learning: *the embeddings that are close to each other in the embedding space have similar semantics.* Unfortunately, how to exploit the embedding space to produce effective embeddings without data points remains an unsolved problem. To this end, we propose a Densely-Anchored Sampling (DAS) scheme to consider the embedding with data point as "anchor" and densely exploit the anchor's nearby embedding space to produce embeddings that have no corresponding data points. The proposed DAS is consist of two modules, namely, Discriminative Feature Scaling (DFS) and Memorized Transformation Shifting (MTS), which exploit the embedding space around single and multiple embeddings respectively to produce effective embeddings with no corresponding data points. To be specific, based on observations that effective semantics for one embedding are highly activated features [2,3,14], DFS identifies these features and applies random scaling on them. In this sense, we are able to exploit the embedding space around a single embedding by enhancing or weakening its effective semantics to produce embeddings. Based on the fact that semantic differences (*i.e.,* transformations) of intra-class embeddings can be added to other embeddings to generate effective embeddings [31], we assume that they can be added in a way like word embeddings [34]: $Queen = Woman + (King - Man)$. Thus, our Memorized Transformation Shifting module exploits the embedding space among multiple embeddings by adding (*i.e.,* shift) intra-class embeddings' semantic differences to other embeddings of the same class to produce effective embeddings.

Our main contributions are summarized as follows. **First**, we propose a novel and plug-and-play Densely-Anchored Sampling (DAS) scheme that exploits embeddings' nearby embedding space and densely produces embeddings without data points to improve the sampling quality and performance of DML. **Second**, we propose two modules, namely Discriminative Feature Scaling (DFS) and Memorized Transformation Shifting (MTS) to exploit embedding space around a single and multiple embeddings to produce embeddings. **Last**, extensive experiments demonstrate the effectiveness of the proposed method.

2   Related Work

Sampling Methods in DML. Sampling informative and stable embeddings is vital to train the deep model in DML [41,42,56]. Thus, various sampling approaches [15,41,42,53,56] have been tailored to effectively sample the embeddings to train the deep model. To further improve sampling efficiency, some researchers propose to leverage a whole batch of embeddings [20,25,36,53,67]. Even though sophisticated sampling methods improve DML, due to the absence of data points, sampling embeddings that are often with "missing embedding" leads to inaccurate sampling, thereby degenerating the final performance. In this paper, we propose a DAS scheme to produce embeddings with no data points by exploiting embeddings' nearby embedding space to achieve effective DML.

Loss Functions for DML. Studies on DML losses can be grouped into two categories: pair-based and proxy-based. The pair-based losses [18,22,26,42,45,51–53,56,58] are constructed upon the pairwise distance between embeddings. Although pair-based approaches mine the rich information among vast embedding pairs, they typically encounter the sampling effective embedding pairs issues. Instead, proxy-based [1,10,25,33,36,40,60] losses introduce the concept of "proxy" as a class representation and avoid the sampling issue by optimizing the embedding close to its proxy. However, proxy-based methods are very difficult to train when the number of classes is extremely large [38], limiting their applicability to real-life scenarios. Thus, in this paper, we focus on developing an effective technique to alleviates the general data sampling issue for pair-based methods that have wider applicability and delivers boosted performance for them.

Pseudo Embedding Generation. Methods on synthesizing pseudo embedding have been recently shown as an important technique to improve DML [13, 28,31,54,62,64]. DAML [13] uses an additional generative adversarial network to generates only hard negatives to improve the model training. HDML [62] leverages the inter-class information for embedding generation on the sampled embeddings. DVML [31] apply extra generator and decoder to model the class centers that may have inaccurate distance estimation to the real embeddings and employs them to generate embeddings. Embedding expansion [28] linearly interpolates the embeddings to obtain more embeddings. Cross batch memory [54] stores embeddings from previous batches and considers them beneficial for the upcoming sampling process. However these approaches [28,54] suffer from the following limitations: **First**, the generated embeddings can only be considered as negative during sampling, which may limit the power of them. **Second**, the sampling or loss computation process need to be modified to dock with them, limiting their applicability. **Third**, an additional sub-network is introduced in order to generate embeddings, which brings heavy computation cost. **Last**, information source that may have inaccurate distance measurement to real embeddings such as class centers and inter-class differences are considered to produce embeddings. Different from them, DAS is a light-weight module, which produces embeddings by densely sampling around the "anchor" and serves as a plug-and-play component to facilitate the sampling process in standard DML.

Data Augmentation. Augmentation in data space such as image [44] has been widely studied and is considered an important technique to avoid overfitting. Recently, many efforts have been made to design effective augmentation methods [8,11,49,55,57] in feature space, aiming to provide more features for training when the source data (*e.g.,* images) is scarce. These methods often introduce complicated training processes [8,49]. Wang *et al.* [55] propose ISDA that estimates semantic differences with covariance matrices and develops an improved version of cross-entropy loss. The computation and memory consumption of covariance matrices are much heavier than DAS. Moreover, ISDA can not be trivially extended to pair-based DML loss. Yin *et al.* [57] introduce FTL that requires extra networks (*e.g.,* decoder and feature transfer module) and a carefully designed bi-stage training strategy to achieve feature translation, which is less efficient and general than DAS. Unlike these methods, we view the feature space augmentation as an approach to fill the "missing embedding" in the embedding space and propose a simpler solution under the context of DML.

3 Densely-Anchored Sampling

In this paper, we seek to improve DML by alleviating the "missing embedding" issue incurred in sampling. The overall process of DAS scheme is shown in Fig. 2.

Notation. Let $\mathbf{v} = f_\theta(\mathbf{I}) \in \mathbb{R}^d$ be an embedding with data point $\mathbf{I}$, where $f_\theta(\cdot)$ is a deep model (*e.g.,* CNNs) with learnable parameters θ. Let $y_\mathbf{v}$ be the label of the embedding $\mathbf{v}$. Let $\mathbf{v}'$ denote embedding without data point. Following previous methods [42], we normalize both $\mathbf{v}$ and $\mathbf{v}'$ to the d-dimensional hypersphere (*i.e.,* $\|\mathbf{v}\|_2, \|\mathbf{v}'\|_2 = 1$). We omit the normalization process for brevity. Let C denote the number of training classes.

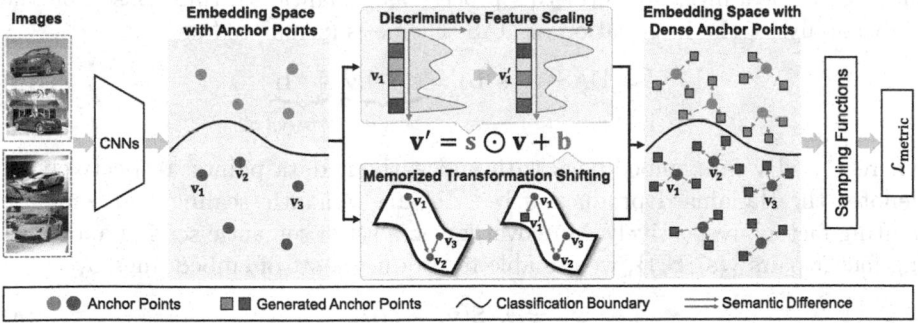

Fig. 2. Illustration of our Densely-Anchored Sampling (DAS) scheme, which leverages two modules to exploit anchors' (*i.e.,* embeddings with data points) nearby embedding space to densely produce embeddings without data points: DFS performs random scaling on the discriminative features to produce embeddings around a single embedding; MTS exploits the embedding space among multiple embeddings by adding the intraclass semantic differences to embeddings of the same class to produce embeddings. With DAS, we alleviate the "missing embedding" issue by providing more embeddings for sampling, thereby, achieving effective DML

3.1   Problem Definition and Motivation

DML seeks to learn a deep model that keeps similar data points close, and vice versa. Formally, we define the distance between two embeddings as follows [56]:

$$\mathbf{D}_{ij} = \|f_\theta(\mathbf{I}_i) - f_\theta(\mathbf{I}_j)\|, \tag{1}$$

where $\| \cdot \|$ denotes the ℓ_2 norm. For any positive pair of embeddings ($y_i = y_j$), the distance should be small; Whilst for negative pair ($y_i \neq y_j$), it should be large. In practice, limited by computing resources, it is infeasible to optimize every element in $\mathbf{D}_{ij}$. Therefore, it is necessary to sample effective embedding pair for the objective construction (take the contrastive loss as an example):

$$\mathcal{L} = \sum_{(i,j)\in\mathcal{Q}} \mathbb{I}\{y_i = y_j\} \, \mathbf{D}_{ij} + \mathbb{I}\{y_i \neq y_j\} \, [\alpha - \mathbf{D}_{ij}]_+, \tag{2}$$

where $\mathbb{I}\{\cdot\}$ is the indication function, α is a margin, $\mathcal{Q} = S(D)$ indicates indexes of the sampled embedding pairs and S denotes some sampling function.

Without causing ambiguity, we denote the points on the embedding space as "**anchor points**", based on which we will conduct sampling to train the deep model. Note that each data point shall have an anchor point on the embedding space. However, due to the absence of training data, the embedding space may have a lot of "barren area". Thus, it is very difficult to provide sufficient anchor points for sampling and learn a deep model with good performance. To this end, we propose to densely produce anchor points with no data points to facilitate the sampling, thereby improving the training in DML.

Specifically, we first propose to exploit the embedding space around a single embedding by enhancing or weakening its semantics. We term this process as semantic scaling. Second, we propose to add (*i.e.*, shift) intra-class differences (*i.e.*, transformations) to embeddings to exploit the embedding space among multiple embeddings. We term this process as semantic shifting. Based on the above analyses, the formulation of DAS scheme is formulated as

$$\mathbf{v}' = \mathrm{DAS}(\mathbf{v}; \, \mathbf{s}, \mathbf{b}) = \underbrace{\mathbf{s} \odot \mathbf{v}}_{scaling} + \underbrace{\mathbf{b}}_{shifting}, \tag{3}$$

where $\mathbf{v}$ and $\mathbf{v}'$ are embeddings with and without data points, respectively. $\odot$ denotes the Hadamard product. $\mathbf{s}, \mathbf{b} \in \mathbb{R}^d$ are semantic scaling and semantic shifting factors, respectively. Moreover, given a set of semantic scaling and shifting factor pairs $\{(\mathbf{s}_t, \mathbf{b}_t)\}$, we are able to produce a set of embeddings by

$$\mathbf{v}'_t = \mathrm{DAS}(\mathbf{v}; \, \mathbf{s}_t, \mathbf{b}_t). \tag{4}$$

Therefore, the semantic scaling and shifting factors is essential to the quality of the produced embeddings and we propose DFS and MTS to acquire them:

$$\mathbf{s} = \mathrm{DFS}(\{\mathbf{v} \mid y_\mathbf{v} = c\}), \tag{5}$$

$$\mathbf{b} = \mathrm{MTS}(\{\mathbf{v} \mid y_\mathbf{v} = c\}), \tag{6}$$

where DFS and MTS take embeddings from the same class as input and produce the semantic scaling and shifting factors, respectively.

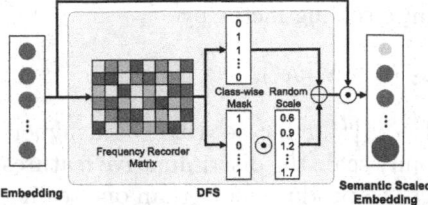

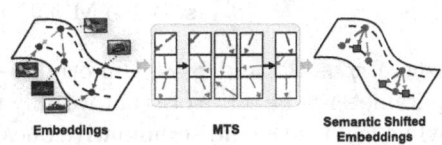

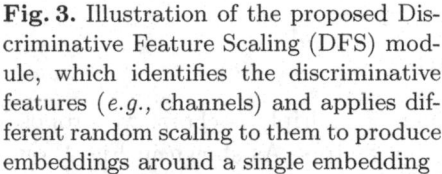

Embedding   **DFS**   **Semantic Scaled Embedding**

Embeddings   **MTS**   **Semantic Shifted Embeddings**

Fig. 3. Illustration of the proposed Discriminative Feature Scaling (DFS) module, which identifies the discriminative features (*e.g.*, channels) and applies different random scaling to them to produce embeddings around a single embedding

Fig. 4. Illustration of the proposed Memorized Transformation Shifting (MTS) module. MTS adds the intraclass transformations to embeddings of the same class to produce embeddings among multiple embeddings

3.2 Discriminative Feature Scaling

We seek to obtain effective semantic scaling factors to produce anchor points around a single anchor. Thus, as shown in Fig. 3, our Discriminative Feature Scaling (DFS) module carries out the semantic scaling mechanism by finding the discriminative features in an embedding and applying random scaling on them. The feasibility of DFS comes from two aspects. First, visual attributes can be predicted reliably using a sparse number of neurons from CNNs [14]. Second, in CNNs, neurons that match a diverse set of object concepts are highly activated [2,3]. In practice, the embedding typically occupies a high dimensional embedding space, which contains semantics for all training classes and semantics for each class are diverse. Thus, the semantics for one class are more likely to be noise for another. In this sense, it is very important to find out the effective *e.g.*, discriminative features for each class in order to perform semantic scaling. To this end, we propose to identify the effective semantics by counting the number of occurrences of the highly-activated neurons for each class.

To be specific, we first initialize a Frequency Recorder Matrix (FRM) $\mathbf{P} \in \mathbb{R}^{C \times d}$ as a zero matrix. Then, given a set of embeddings $\{\mathbf{v} \mid y_{\mathbf{v}} = c\}$ from class c, we update $\mathbf{P}$ as follows:

$$\mathbf{P}[c, k] = \begin{cases} \mathbf{P}[c, k] + 1, & \text{if } \mathbf{v}[k] \in \text{Top}(\mathbf{v}, K), \\ \mathbf{P}[c, k], & \text{otherwise}, \end{cases} \quad (7)$$

where $\text{Top}(\mathbf{v}, K)$ is an operator to select the top-K elements from the vector $\mathbf{v}$. During training, we constantly update the FRM by recording the position of highly-activated neurons from the embeddings of the same class. In this way, FRM[1] serves as a stable, accurate and effective semantics identifier for training classes. Given the FRM, we compute the class-wise binary channel mask $\mathbf{M} \in \mathbb{R}^{C \times d}$ by

$$\mathbf{M}[c, k] = \begin{cases} 1, & \text{if } \mathbf{P}[c, k] \in \text{Top}(\mathbf{P}[c], K), \\ 0, & \text{otherwise}. \end{cases} \quad (8)$$

---

[1] Visualization of the frequency recorder matrix is in the supplementary.

Given an embedding $\mathbf{v}$, we attain the semantic scaling factor by

$$\mathbf{s} = \boldsymbol{\gamma} \odot \mathbf{M}[y_{\mathbf{v}}] + \mathbf{1}^d \odot (1 - \mathbf{M}[y_{\mathbf{v}}]), \tag{9}$$

where $\boldsymbol{\gamma} \in \mathbb{R}^d$ and $\boldsymbol{\gamma} \sim \text{Uniform}[1 - r_s, 1 + r_s]^d$ and $r_s \in (0, 1)$ is a hyperparameter to be set. Note that we only randomly scale the discriminative features while leaving the indiscriminative ones intact. To produce more than one scaling factor, we repeatedly sample $\boldsymbol{\gamma}$ from the uniform distribution.

3.3   Memorized Transformation Shifting

To produce anchors without data points among multiple anchors, we propose a module to provide effective semantic shifting factors. As shown in Fig. 4, our Memorized Transformation Shifting (MTS) module exploit intra-class embeddings' nearby embedding space by leveraging the differences between embeddings and adding them to other embeddings of the same class. On the basis of that semantic differences of embeddings can be added to other embedding to generate effective embeddings [31], the motivation of our MTS comes from the semantic relations of word embedding [34]: $Woman + (King - Man) = Queen$, where a "woman" pluses "royal" semantics (*e.g.,* transformation) becomes a "Queen".

The transformations from both inter-class and intra-class embeddings are candidates for our design choices. However, the majority of the inter-class transformations typically are not transferable due to large inter-class differences. Thus, we only consider intra-class embeddings to attain the transformations. As suggested by the latest research [41], sampling only two images for each class in a batch consistently achieves good performance, which leads to very limited transformations we can obtain in one batch *i.e.,* two transformations. To address this issue, we construct a bank to memorize the transformations from previous iterations to ensure the diversity of the transformations. Specifically, we construct a transformation bank $\mathbf{B} \in \mathbb{R}^{C \times Z \times d}$, where Z is the bank capacity for each class. Then, during training, once we obtain a set of embeddings $\mathcal{V}_c = \{\mathbf{v} \mid y_{\mathbf{v}} = c\}$ from the class c, we calculate the transformations between them by

$$\mathbf{t}_z = \mathbf{v}_i - \mathbf{v}_j, \quad \mathbf{v}_i, \mathbf{v}_j \in \mathcal{V}_c, i \neq j. \tag{10}$$

Then, the transformations are en-queued into $\mathbf{B}$ according to the FIFO principle to ensure that the transformations in the bank are in a relatively fresh state:

$$\mathbf{B}[y_{\mathbf{v}}, z] = \mathbf{t}_z, \quad z \in \{1, 2, \dots, Z\}. \tag{11}$$

Note that z is reset to 1 when it reaches Z. Finally, with the assistance of the bank $\mathbf{B}$, given an embedding $\mathbf{v}$, we retrieve the semantic shifting factor as follow

$$\mathbf{b} = r_b \mathbf{t}, \quad \mathbf{t} \sim \{\mathbf{B}[y_{\mathbf{v}}, z] \mid z = 1, 2, \dots, Z\}. \tag{12}$$

r_b is a hyper-parameter. Multiple shifting factors are formed by repeat sampling.

Algorithm 1. Training method of DAS-based DML

Require: Training image-label pairs $\mathcal{S} = \{(\mathbf{I}_i, y_i)\}_{i=1}^N$; the embedding function f_θ; number of embeddings to produce T; number of training classes C; transformation bank capacity Z; learning rate α.
Ensure: Optimized embedding function f_θ^*.
1: Initialize θ from ImageNet pretrained model.
2: Initialize the frequency recorder matrix $\mathbf{P} \in \mathbb{R}^{C \times d} = \mathbf{0}$.
3: Initialize the transformation bank $\mathbf{B} \in \mathbb{R}^{C \times Z \times d} = \mathbf{0}$.
4: **while** not converge **do**
5:   Obtain a batch image-label pairs $\{(\mathbf{I}_i, y_i)\}_{i=1}^B$ from $\mathcal{S}$.
6:   Compute embeddings $\mathbf{v}_i \leftarrow f_\theta(\mathbf{I}_i), i = 1, 2, \cdots, B$.
7:   // *perform semantic scaling by Discriminative Feature Scaling*
8:   Update the frequency recorder matrix $\mathbf{P}$ by Eqn. (7).
9:   Acquire semantic scaling factors $\{\mathbf{s}_j\}_{j=1}^{B \times T}$ by Eqn. (9).
10:   // *perform semantic shifting by Memorized Transformation Shifting*
11:   Obtain intra-class transformations $\{\mathbf{t}\}$ by Eqn. (10).
12:   Update the transformation bank $\mathbf{B}$ by Eqn. (11).
13:   Attain semantic shifting factors $\{\mathbf{b}_j\}_{j=1}^{B \times T}$ by Eqn. (12).
14:   // *perform densely-anchored sampling*
15:   Produce embeddings $\{\mathbf{v}_j'\}_{j=1}^{B \times T}$ by Eqn. (4).
16:   Sample positive and negative embedding sets.
17:   Compute the training loss $\mathcal{L}_{\text{DAS-DML}}$ by Eqn. (13).
18:   Update the parameters θ by $\theta \leftarrow \theta - \alpha \nabla_\theta \mathcal{L}_{\text{DAS-DML}}$.
19: **end while**

3.4 DML with Densely-Anchored Sampling

The overall algorithm of integrating DAS into DML is detailed in Algorithm 1. Given anchor-label pairs $\{(\mathbf{v}, y_\mathbf{v})\}$, we produce embedding-label pairs $\{(\mathbf{v}', y_\mathbf{v}')\}$ with no data points by DAS scheme, where $y_\mathbf{v}' = y_\mathbf{v}$ since the class semantic is preserved. Then, embedding-label pairs with or without data points are fed into the sampling module to obtain the positive and negative embedding sets (*e.g.*, pairs, triplets, *etc.* specified by the sampling and loss functions): $\{(\mathcal{P}, \mathcal{N})\} = \text{Sample}(\{(\mathbf{v}, y_\mathbf{v})\} \cup \{(\mathbf{v}', y_\mathbf{v}')\})$. Last, given a DML loss function $\mathcal{L}_{\text{DML}}{}^2$, DAS-based DML objective function is formulated as:

$$\mathcal{L}_{\text{DAS-DML}} = \mathcal{L}_{\text{DML}}(\{(\mathcal{P}, \mathcal{N})\}). \tag{13}$$

4 Experiments

Datasets. We use three popular benchmarks: 1) CUB2011-200 (CUB) [50], a fine-grained bird dataset with the first 100 categories for training and another 100 categories for testing. 2) CARS196 (CARS) [29], a fine-grained vehicle dataset

---

^{2} See supplementary for detailed DML sampling methods and loss functions.

Table 1. Comparisons with SoTA methods on CUB, CARS and SOP. The best results are in **bold**. ∗ indicates the reimplementation by [4]. † denotes our reimplementation

Method	Backbone	CUB				CARS				SOP			
		R@1	R@2	R@4	R@8	R@1	R@2	R@4	R@8	R@1	R@10	R@100	R@1000
Margin [56]	R^{128}	63.60	74.40	83.10	90.00	79.60	86.50	91.90	95.10	72.70	86.20	93.80	98.00
HDC [59]	G^{384}	53.60	65.70	77.00	85.60	73.70	83.20	89.50	93.80	69.50	84.40	92.80	97.70
A-BIER [39]	G^{384}	57.50	68.70	78.30	86.20	82.00	89.00	93.20	96.10	74.20	86.90	94.00	97.80
ABE [27]	G^{512}	60.60	71.50	79.80	87.40	85.20	90.50	94.00	96.10	76.30	88.40	94.80	98.20
HTL [15]	IBN^{512}	57.10	68.80	78.70	86.50	81.40	88.00	92.70	95.70	74.80	88.30	94.80	98.40
RLL-H [52]	IBN^{512}	57.40	69.70	79.20	86.90	74.00	83.60	90.10	94.10	76.10	89.10	95.40	N/A
SoftTriple [40]	IBN^{512}	65.40	76.40	84.50	90.40	84.50	90.70	94.50	96.90	78.30	90.30	95.90	N/A
MS [53]	IBN^{512}	65.70	77.00	86.30	91.20	84.10	90.40	94.00	96.50	78.20	90.50	96.00	98.70
ProxyGML [67]	IBN^{512}	66.60	77.60	86.40	N/A	85.50	91.80	95.30	N/A	78.00	90.60	96.20	N/A
ProxyAnchor [25]	IBN^{512}	68.40	79.20	86.80	91.60	86.10	91.70	95.00	97.30	79.10	90.80	96.20	98.70
Contrastive + XBM [54]	IBN^{512}	65.80	75.90	84.00	89.90	82.00	88.70	93.10	96.10	79.50	90.80	96.10	98.70
MS∗ [53]	IBN^{512}	64.50	76.20	84.60	90.50	82.10	88.80	93.20	96.10	76.30	89.70	96.00	98.80
MS + EE∗ [28]	IBN^{512}	65.10	76.80	86.10	91.00	82.70	89.20	93.80	96.40	77.00	89.50	96.00	98.80
ProxyAnchor + MemVir [4]	IBN^{512}	69.00	79.20	86.80	91.60	86.70	92.00	95.20	97.40	79.70	91.00	96.30	98.60
MS† [53]	IBN^{512}	65.72	77.19	85.74	91.56	83.86	90.41	94.64	96.99	76.89	89.58	95.59	98.60
MS + DAS ($K = 8$) (ours)	IBN^{512}	67.07	78.11	86.43	91.88	85.66	91.60	95.27	97.37	78.16	90.26	95.99	98.76
MS† [53]	R^{512}	66.46	77.28	85.85	91.69	83.99	90.39	94.51	96.80	79.53	91.06	96.30	98.83
MS + DAS ($K = 8$) (ours)	R^{512}	**69.19**	**79.25**	**87.09**	**92.62**	**87.84**	**93.15**	**95.99**	**97.85**	**80.59**	**91.80**	**96.68**	**98.95**

with the first 98 classes for training and another 98 classes for testing. 3) Stanford Online Products (SOP) [38], a large-scale online products dataset with the train and test partitions as 11,318 classes and another 11,316 classes, respectively.

Implementation Details.[3] We leverage two popular backbones: ResNet50 [19] (R^d) and Inception BN [23] (IBN^d), where their parameters are initialized from ImageNet [9] pre-trained models and d denotes the embedding dimension. Note that some approaches also consider GoogleNet [46] (G^d) as the backbone. Here, we mainly consider the settings of $d = 128, 512$. R^{128} is used as the default backbone. The embedding layer is randomly initialized. Regarding evaluation metrics, Recall at k (R@k) [24], Normalized Mutual Information (NMI) [43] and F1 score (F1) [45] are used, where R@k measures the image retrieval performance while F1 and NMI measure the image clustering performance. For hyper-parameters in DAS, we set $(T, K, Z, r_s, r_b) = (3, 4, 10, 1e^{-2}, 1e^{-2})$ by default.[4] Our source code is publicly available at https://github.com/lizhaoliu-Lec/DAS.

4.1   Comparison with State-of-the-Arts

In this section, we compare our method with state-of-the-art competitors to investigate the effectiveness of DAS. The results are shown in Table 4. For fair comparisons, the results of the closely related baseline EE are from the reimplementation by [4] using the stronger IBN^{512} backbone (G^{512} in the original paper). Our approach is based on MS loss and achieves superior performance on all datasets and evaluation metrics. **First**, when combining the R^{512} backbone and DAS, we are able to boost the R@1 metrics by 3.49% on CUB and

---

[3] See supplementary for more details.

[4] Experiments on hyper-parameters T, r_s, r_b are in the supplementary.

Table 2. Comparisons with pair-based methods on CUB, CARS and SOP. [S] and [D] denote semi-hard and distance weighted sampling, respectively

Method	CUB			CARS			SOP		
	R@1	F1	NMI	R@1	F1	NMI	R@1	F1	NMI
Triplet [S] [42]	60.25	32.82	64.64	74.64	31.98	63.22	73.51	33.47	89.33
Triplet [S] + DAS	**60.82**	**33.86**	**65.67**	**77.21**	**33.88**	**64.84**	**73.99**	**33.91**	**89.42**
Triplet [D] [56]	62.68	36.39	67.03	78.86	35.80	65.85	77.54	37.10	90.05
Triplet [D] + DAS	**64.28**	**38.16**	**68.06**	**82.63**	**39.14**	**68.12**	**77.95**	**37.64**	**90.18**
Contrastive [D] [56]	61.65	35.23	66.58	76.03	32.77	64.09	73.13	35.60	89.78
Contrastive [D] + DAS	**63.67**	**36.25**	**67.15**	**80.74**	**36.07**	**65.93**	**74.80**	**36.21**	**89.89**
Margin [56]	62.61	37.33	67.58	80.10	37.85	67.15	78.69	39.20	90.50
Margin + DAS	**64.50**	**37.86**	**68.04**	**82.29**	**38.22**	**67.94**	**79.14**	**39.52**	**90.56**
GenLifted [20]	58.81	34.64	65.50	72.45	32.43	64.00	76.18	37.26	90.13
GenLifted + DAS	**59.94**	**35.09**	**66.07**	**73.55**	**32.85**	**64.11**	**76.92**	**37.64**	**90.21**
N-Pair [45]	60.55	36.94	67.19	77.35	36.26	66.74	77.71	37.13	90.15
N-Pair + DAS	**62.81**	**38.37**	**68.43**	**79.93**	**38.06**	**68.20**	**77.98**	**37.82**	**90.28**
MS [53]	62.63	38.88	68.19	82.04	40.85	69.45	78.89	37.53	90.12
MS + DAS	**64.13**	**39.18**	**69.08**	**83.31**	**42.78**	**70.77**	**79.44**	**38.77**	**90.40**

1.74% on CARS, which shows that DAS is able to deliver more accurate image retrieval results even with higher embedding dimension (*i.e.,* 512). **Second**, for our closely relative opponent, EE, its improvements on MS are marginal, showing that simply performing interpolation to generate embeddings is inferior to DAS. **Last**, even for a strong baseline, ProxyAnchor that leverages the advanced training techniques, and sophisticated loss, we still outperform it considerably.

4.2   Effectiveness of DAS on Pair-based Loss

Quantitative Results. To investigate the efficacy of DAS, we conduct experiments with R^{128} backbone on the widely used pair-based losses. We reimplement all baselines under the same settings for a fair comparison. The results are presented in Table 2. For considered pair-based losses, DAS is able to improve their performance on both image retrieval and clustering metrics. Notably, for approaches such as GenLifted and N-Pair that leverage the whole batch of embeddings for loss computation, DAS still improves their performance, showing its effectiveness. Last, even for a very strong baseline, MS, that considers different kinds of relationships among embedding pairs and designs sophisticated weighting mechanism, DAS is able to greatly improve it without bells and whistles.

Convergence Analyses. We provide the results of training loss and test set R@1 in Fig. 5 to analyze the training behaviors of DAS.[5] The loss curve with DAS

---

[5] Results on more pair-based losses are in the supplementary.

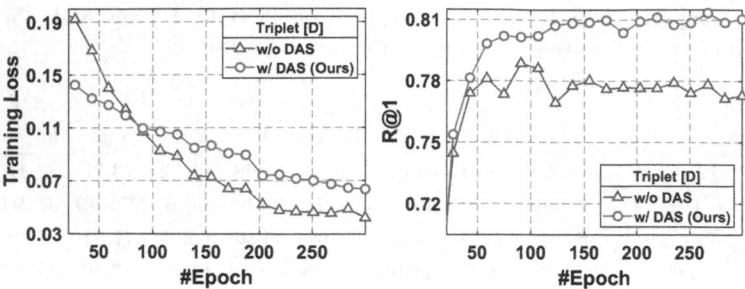

Fig. 5. The training loss and test set R@1 on CARS. The sampling method and loss function are triplet loss and distance weighted sampling, respectively

Table 3. Comparisons with various sampling methods on CARS

Method	Sampling	DAS	R@1	F1	NMI
Triplet	Random		74.21	33.41	64.28
		✓	**76.79**	**35.21**	**65.49**
	Semi-hard [42]		74.64	31.98	63.22
		✓	**77.10**	**33.82**	**65.03**
	Soft-hard [41]		79.20	35.55	66.08
		✓	**80.54**	**37.52**	**66.77**
	Distance [56]		78.86	35.80	65.85
		✓	**81.34**	**37.27**	**67.21**
Contrastive	Random		42.44	15.83	48.87
		✓	**50.79**	**19.40**	**52.71**
	Distance [56]		76.03	32.77	64.09
		✓	**80.70**	**35.47**	**66.01**

Table 4. Comparisons with more related works on CARS

Method	Backbone	R@1	R@2	R@4	R@8
N-Pair + HDML [63]	G^{512}	68.90	78.90	85.80	90.90
N-Pair + HDML-A [63]	G^{512}	81.10	88.80	93.70	96.70
N-Pair + DAS (ours)	G^{512}	**83.70**	**90.33**	**94.47**	**96.77**
MS + SEC [61]	IBN^{512}	85.73	91.96	95.51	97.54
MS + DAS (ours)	IBN^{512}	85.66	91.60	95.27	97.37
MS + SEC + DAS (ours)	IBN^{512}	**87.80**	**93.16**	**96.18**	**98.01**
Margin + DiVA [35]	IBN^{512}	83.10	90.00	N/A	N/A
Margin + DAS (ours)	IBN^{512}	**84.85**	**90.32**	93.99	96.40
ProxyNCA++ [47]	R^{512}	86.50	92.50	95.70	97.70
Margin + DiVA	R^{512}	82.20	89.00	N/A	N/A
Margin + DRML [66]	R^{512}	73.30	83.00	89.80	94.40
Margin + DCML [65]	R^{512}	85.20	91.80	**96.00**	**98.00**
Margin + DAS (ours)	R^{512}	**88.34**	**93.21**	95.92	97.59

decreases smoother than that without DAS, showing that DAS provides more embeddings to facilitate sampling, thereby, stabilizing the training. Moreover, with DAS, the training loss is higher than the baseline, one possible reason is that DAS is able to act as a regularizer to avoid overfitting, which is consistent with the result that DAS achieves a higher test set R@1. Similar phenomenon is also observed in other embeddings generation methods [28].

4.3 Effectiveness of DAS on Sampling Method

In this section, we investigate the effectiveness of DAS by evaluating it with different sampling approaches. We choose two popular loss functions: triplet and contrastive losses that are sensitive to the sampling methods. Therefore, various sampling approaches are tailored for them. The experiment results are presented in Table 3. For two loss functions, despite the choice of sampling approaches, DAS is able to improve them considerably on both image retrieval and clustering metrics. Notably, when applying DAS, triplet loss with random sampling outperform the one with the semi-hard sampling. This indicates that producing more embeddings for sampling is as important as the sampling approach.

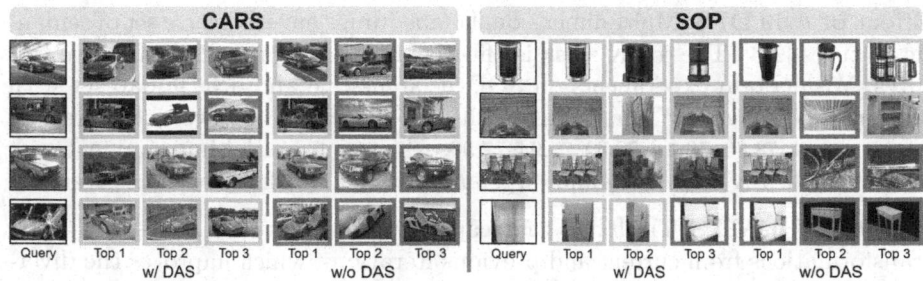

Fig. 6. Top 3 retrieved results from the R^{128} trained w/ or w/o DAS. green and red rectangles indicate desired and undesired results, respectively (Color figure online)

Table 5. Ablation studies on CARS

DFS	MTS	R@1	F1	NMI
		78.86	35.80	65.85
✓		81.28 (**+2.42**)	36.22 (**+0.42**)	66.84 (**+0.99**)
	✓	81.83 (**+2.97**)	38.26 (**+2.46**)	67.81 (**+1.96**)
✓	✓	82.63 (**+3.77**)	39.14 (**+3.34**)	68.12 (**+2.27**)

4.4 Qualitative Results

To better understand our method, we compare contrastive loss (with distance weighted sampling) w/ or w/o DAS and visualize image retrieval results on both CARS (Fig. 6) and SOP (Fig. 6) datasets.[6] On CARS, the model performs better with DAS despite the background noises or the interference from the car's color, demonstrating that DAS enforces the model to focus on real semantics. On SOP, the model with DAS is insensitive to drastic viewpoint changes. These results verify the generalization ability and robustness of DAS under various scenes.

4.5 Ablation Studies

Effect of DFS and MTS. In this section, we perform ablation studies to evaluate the performance gain by each module in DAS. The loss function and sampling method are triplet loss and distance weighted sampling, respectively. The results are in Table 5. First, DFS, alone, boosts R@1 by +2.42%, verifying that producing embeddings around a single embedding is able to force the model to focus on real semantics and achieve better image retrieval results. Second, with MTS only, the clustering metrics are greatly improved, indicating that producing embeddings among multiple embeddings are beneficial to the image clustering task. Last, with DFS and DAS, all metrics are further improved, suggesting that DFS and MTS reinforce and complement each other.

---

[6] More qualitative results are in the supplementary.

Effect of K in DFS. Multi-dimensional embeddings have a diverse set of semantic features [2,3]. The top-K mask is effective to discover the discriminative features. We perform experiments on SOP, a large-scale and diverse dataset with margin loss to support our claim. With $K = 1, 2, 4, 8, 16, 32$, we obtain results R@1 = 78.76, 78.86, **79.14**, 78.09, 77.94, 77.96, where substantial improvements are observed when $K = \{1, 2, 4\}$ and larger K (*i.e.*, $K > 4$) leads to worse results.

Effect of Z in MTS. The larger bank capacity (Z) allows us to access intra-class transformations from current and previous iterations, which improves the diversity of the produced embeddings. We conduct experiments on CARS with margin loss by setting $Z = 1, 2, 3, 4, 5$ and obtain R@1 = 82.35, 82.38, 82.42, **82.75**, 82.33, showing that history transformations ($Z > 2$) bring slight improvements.

4.6 Further Discussions

More Discussions on DFS. One may question whether the proposed DFS requires the linear assumption on high dimensional feature space. In fact, we do not make this assumption and our method is built on a very basic hypothesis of metric learning: the embeddings that are close to each other in the embedding space have similar semantics. More critically, DFS does not rely on the linearity assumption. Instead, DFS is based on the observations that effective semantics for one embedding are highly activated features [2,3].

More Discussions on MTS. Li *et al.* [30] also apply a memory module is leveraged to store abundant features and conduct neighborhood search upon them to enhance the discriminative power of a general CNN feature on the image search and few-shot learning tasks. Unlike them, DAS constructs a memory bank with the intra-class embedding transformations, which allows us to access intra-class transformations from current and previous iterations, and thus improves the diversity of produced embeddings for DML.

Comparisons with More Related Works. In Table 4, we compare DAS with HDML [63], SEC [61], DiVA [35], ProxyNCA++ [47], DRML [66], DCML [65] on CARS under the same settings. We can see that DAS outperforms HDML, DiVA, DRML and DCML, and achieves comparable performance to SEC. Note that DAS can be also incorporated into SEC. As a result, using MS loss, SEC + DAS outperforms SEC by 2.07% in R@1. These results further verify the applicability of DAS on some regularization techniques in DML.

5 Conclusion

In this paper, we propose a Densely-Anchored Sampling (DAS) scheme to alleviate the "missing embedding" issue incurred during DML sampling. To this end, we propose to produce embeddings with no data points by exploiting the embeddings' nearby embedding space. Specifically, we propose a DFS module that identifies an embedding's discriminative features and performs random scaling on them to exploit the embedding space around it. Moreover, we propose a MTS module to exploit embedding space among multiple embedding by adding the intra-class semantic differences to embeddings of the same class. By combining the embeddings with and without data points, DAS provides more embeddings for sampling to improve the sampling quality and achieve effective DML. Extensive experiments with various loss functions and sampling methods on three public available benchmarks show that DAS is effective. In the future, we plan to apply DAS to other areas such as self-supervised learning that require sampling.

Acknowledgements. This work was partially supported by Peng Cheng Laboratory Research Project No. PCL2021A07, National Natural Science Foundation of China (NSFC) 62072190, Program for Guangdong Introducing Innovative and Enterpreneurial Teams 2017ZT07X183.

References

1. Aziere, N., Todorovic, S.: Ensemble deep manifold similarity learning using hard proxies. In: Proceedings of the IEEE/CVF Conference on Computer Vision and Pattern Recognition, pp. 7299–7307 (2019)
2. Bau, D., Zhou, B., Khosla, A., Oliva, A., Torralba, A.: Network dissection: quantifying interpretability of deep visual representations. In: Proceedings of the IEEE Conference on Computer Vision and Pattern Recognition, pp. 6541–6549 (2017)
3. Bau, D., Zhu, J.Y., Strobelt, H., Lapedriza, A., Zhou, B., Torralba, A.: Understanding the role of individual units in a deep neural network. Proc. Natl. Acad. Sci. **117**(48), 30071–30078 (2020)
4. Ko, B., Gu, G., Kim, H.G.: Learning with memory-based virtual classes for deep metric learning. In: Proceedings of the IEEE/CVF International Conference on Computer Vision (2021)
5. Chen, P., et al.: RSPNet: relative speed perception for unsupervised video representation learning. In: AAAI Conference on Artificial Intelligence 2021 (2021)
6. Chen, P., Zhang, Y., Tan, M., Xiao, H., Huang, D., Gan, C.: Generating visually aligned sound from videos. IEEE Trans. Image Process. **29**, 8292–8302 (2020)
7. Chen, W., Chen, X., Zhang, J., Huang, K.: Beyond triplet loss: a deep quadruplet network for person re-identification. In: Proceedings of the IEEE Conference on Computer Vision and Pattern Recognition, pp. 403–412 (2017)
8. Chu, P., Bian, X., Liu, S., Ling, H.: Feature space augmentation for long-tailed data. In: Vedaldi, A., Bischof, H., Brox, T., Frahm, J.-M. (eds.) ECCV 2020. LNCS, vol. 12374, pp. 694–710. Springer, Cham (2020). https://doi.org/10.1007/978-3-030-58526-6_41
9. Deng, J., Dong, W., Socher, R., Li, L.J., Li, K., Fei-Fei, L.: ImageNet: a large-scale hierarchical image database. In: Proceedings of the IEEE Conference on Computer Vision and Pattern Recognition, pp. 248–255. IEEE (2009)
10. Deng, J., Guo, J., Xue, N., Zafeiriou, S.: ArcFace: additive angular margin loss for deep face recognition. In: Proceedings of the IEEE/CVF Conference on Computer Vision and Pattern Recognition, pp. 4690–4699 (2019)
11. DeVries, T., Taylor, G.W.: Dataset augmentation in feature space. arXiv preprint arXiv:1702.05538 (2017)

12. Ding, Z., Fu, Y.: Robust transfer metric learning for image classification. IEEE Trans. Image Process. **26**(2), 660–670 (2016)
13. Duan, Y., Zheng, W., Lin, X., Lu, J., Zhou, J.: Deep adversarial metric learning. In: Proceedings of the IEEE Conference on Computer Vision and Pattern Recognition, pp. 2780–2789 (2018)
14. Escorcia, V., Carlos Niebles, J., Ghanem, B.: On the relationship between visual attributes and convolutional networks. In: Proceedings of the IEEE Conference on Computer Vision and Pattern Recognition, pp. 1256–1264 (2015)
15. Ge, W., Huang, W., Dong, D., Scott, M.R.: Deep metric learning with hierarchical triplet loss. In: Ferrari, V., Hebert, M., Sminchisescu, C., Weiss, Y. (eds.) ECCV 2018. LNCS, vol. 11210, pp. 272–288. Springer, Cham (2018). https://doi.org/10.1007/978-3-030-01231-1_17
16. Gu, G., Ko, B., Kim, H.G.: Proxy synthesis: learning with synthetic classes for deep metric learning. In: Proceedings of the AAAI Conference on Artificial Intelligence, pp. 1460–1468 (2021)
17. Guo, X., Gao, L., Liu, X., Yin, J.: Improved deep embedded clustering with local structure preservation. In: International Joint Conference on Artificial Intelligence, pp. 1753–1759 (2017)
18. Hadsell, R., Chopra, S., LeCun, Y.: Dimensionality reduction by learning an invariant mapping. In: IEEE Computer Society Conference on Computer Vision and Pattern Recognition, vol. 2, pp. 1735–1742. IEEE (2006)
19. He, K., Zhang, X., Ren, S., Sun, J.: Deep residual learning for image recognition. In: Proceedings of the IEEE Conference on Computer Vision and Pattern Recognition, pp. 770–778 (2016)
20. Hermans, A., Beyer, L., Leibe, B.: In defense of the triplet loss for person re-identification. arXiv preprint arXiv:1703.07737 (2017)
21. Hoi, S.C., Liu, W., Chang, S.F.: Semi-supervised distance metric learning for collaborative image retrieval and clustering. ACM Trans. Multimed. Comput. Commun. Appl. **6**(3), 1–26 (2010)
22. Hu, J., Lu, J., Tan, Y.P.: Discriminative deep metric learning for face verification in the wild. In: Proceedings of the IEEE Conference on Computer Vision and Pattern Recognition, pp. 1875–1882 (2014)
23. Ioffe, S., Szegedy, C.: Batch normalization: accelerating deep network training by reducing internal covariate shift. In: International Conference on Machine Learning, pp. 448–456. PMLR (2015)
24. Jegou, H., Douze, M., Schmid, C.: Product quantization for nearest neighbor search. IEEE Trans. Pattern Anal. Mach. Intell. **33**(1), 117–128 (2010)
25. Kim, S., Kim, D., Cho, M., Kwak, S.: Proxy anchor loss for deep metric learning. In: Proceedings of the IEEE/CVF Conference on Computer Vision and Pattern Recognition, pp. 3238–3247 (2020)
26. Kim, S., Seo, M., Laptev, I., Cho, M., Kwak, S.: Deep metric learning beyond binary supervision. In: Proceedings of the IEEE/CVF Conference on Computer Vision and Pattern Recognition, pp. 2288–2297 (2019)
27. Kim, W., Goyal, B., Chawla, K., Lee, J., Kwon, K.: Attention-based ensemble for deep metric learning. In: Ferrari, V., Hebert, M., Sminchisescu, C., Weiss, Y. (eds.) ECCV 2018. LNCS, vol. 11205, pp. 760–777. Springer, Cham (2018). https://doi.org/10.1007/978-3-030-01246-5_45
28. Ko, B., Gu, G.: Embedding expansion: augmentation in embedding space for deep metric learning. In: Proceedings of the IEEE/CVF Conference on Computer Vision and Pattern Recognition, pp. 7255–7264 (2020)

29. Krause, J., Stark, M., Deng, J., Fei-Fei, L.: 3D object representations for fine-grained categorization. In: Proceedings of the IEEE International Conference on Computer Vision Workshops, pp. 554–561 (2013)

30. Li, S., Chen, D., Liu, B., Yu, N., Zhao, R.: Memory-based neighbourhood embedding for visual recognition. In: Proceedings of the IEEE/CVF International Conference on Computer Vision, pp. 6102–6111 (2019)

31. Lin, X., Duan, Y., Dong, Q., Lu, J., Zhou, J.: Deep variational metric learning. In: Ferrari, V., Hebert, M., Sminchisescu, C., Weiss, Y. (eds.) ECCV 2018. LNCS, vol. 11219, pp. 714–729. Springer, Cham (2018). https://doi.org/10.1007/978-3-030-01267-0_42

32. Liu, L., Cao, J., Liu, M., Guo, Y., Chen, Q., Tan, M.: Dynamic extension nets for few-shot semantic segmentation. In: Proceedings of the 28th ACM International Conference on Multimedia, pp. 1441–1449 (2020)

33. Liu, W., Wen, Y., Yu, Z., Li, M., Raj, B., Song, L.: SphereFace: deep hypersphere embedding for face recognition. In: Proceedings of the IEEE Conference on Computer Vision and Pattern Recognition, pp. 212–220 (2017)

34. Mikolov, T., Yih, W.T., Zweig, G.: Linguistic regularities in continuous space word representations. In: Proceedings of the 2013 Conference of the North American Chapter of the Association for Computational Linguistics: Human Language Technologies, pp. 746–751 (2013)

35. Milbich, T., et al.: DiVA: diverse visual feature aggregation for deep metric learning. In: Vedaldi, A., Bischof, H., Brox, T., Frahm, J.-M. (eds.) ECCV 2020. LNCS, vol. 12353, pp. 590–607. Springer, Cham (2020). https://doi.org/10.1007/978-3-030-58598-3_35

36. Movshovitz-Attias, Y., Toshev, A., Leung, T.K., Ioffe, S., Singh, S.: No fuss distance metric learning using proxies. In: Proceedings of the IEEE International Conference on Computer Vision, pp. 360–368 (2017)

37. Musgrave, K., Belongie, S., Lim, S.-N.: A metric learning reality check. In: Vedaldi, A., Bischof, H., Brox, T., Frahm, J.-M. (eds.) ECCV 2020. LNCS, vol. 12370, pp. 681–699. Springer, Cham (2020). https://doi.org/10.1007/978-3-030-58595-2_41

38. Oh Song, H., Xiang, Y., Jegelka, S., Savarese, S.: Deep metric learning via lifted structured feature embedding. In: Proceedings of the IEEE Conference on Computer Vision and Pattern Recognition, pp. 4004–4012 (2016)

39. Opitz, M., Waltner, G., Possegger, H., Bischof, H.: Deep metric learning with BIER: boosting independent embeddings robustly. IEEE Trans. Pattern Anal. Mach. Intell. **42**(2), 276–290 (2018)

40. Qian, Q., Shang, L., Sun, B., Hu, J., Li, H., Jin, R.: SoftTriple Loss: deep metric learning without triplet sampling. In: Proceedings of the IEEE/CVF International Conference on Computer Vision, pp. 6450–6458 (2019)

41. Roth, K., Milbich, T., Sinha, S., Gupta, P., Ommer, B., Cohen, J.P.: Revisiting training strategies and generalization performance in deep metric learning. In: International Conference on Machine Learning, pp. 8242–8252. PMLR (2020)

42. Schroff, F., Kalenichenko, D., Philbin, J.: FaceNet: a unified embedding for face recognition and clustering. In: Proceedings of the IEEE Conference on Computer Vision and Pattern Recognition, pp. 815–823 (2015)

43. Schütze, H., Manning, C.D., Raghavan, P.: Introduction to Information Retrieval, vol. 39. Cambridge University Press, Cambridge (2008)

44. Shorten, C., Khoshgoftaar, T.M.: A survey on image data augmentation for deep learning. J. Big Data **6**(1), 1–48 (2019)

45. Sohn, K.: Improved deep metric learning with multi-class n-pair loss objective. In: Proceedings of the 30th International Conference on Neural Information Processing Systems, pp. 1857–1865 (2016)
46. Szegedy, C., et al.: Going deeper with convolutions. In: Proceedings of the IEEE Conference on Computer Vision and Pattern Recognition, pp. 1–9 (2015)
47. Teh, E.W., DeVries, T., Taylor, G.W.: ProxyNCA++: revisiting and revitalizing proxy neighborhood component analysis. In: Vedaldi, A., Bischof, H., Brox, T., Frahm, J.-M. (eds.) ECCV 2020. LNCS, vol. 12369, pp. 448–464. Springer, Cham (2020). https://doi.org/10.1007/978-3-030-58586-0_27
48. Ustinova, E., Lempitsky, V.: Learning deep embeddings with histogram loss. In: Proceedings of the International Conference on Neural Information Processing Systems, pp. 4177–4185 (2016)
49. Volpi, R., Morerio, P., Savarese, S., Murino, V.: Adversarial feature augmentation for unsupervised domain adaptation. In: Proceedings of the IEEE Conference on Computer Vision and Pattern Recognition, pp. 5495–5504 (2018)
50. Wah, C., Branson, S., Welinder, P., Perona, P., Belongie, S.: The Caltech-UCSD Birds-200-2011 dataset (2011)
51. Wang, J., et al.: Learning fine-grained image similarity with deep ranking. In: Proceedings of the IEEE Conference on Computer Vision and Pattern Recognition, pp. 1386–1393 (2014)
52. Wang, X., Hua, Y., Kodirov, E., Hu, G., Garnier, R., Robertson, N.M.: Ranked list loss for deep metric learning. In: Proceedings of the IEEE/CVF Conference on Computer Vision and Pattern Recognition, pp. 5207–5216 (2019)
53. Wang, X., Han, X., Huang, W., Dong, D., Scott, M.R.: Multi-similarity loss with general pair weighting for deep metric learning. In: Proceedings of the IEEE/CVF Conference on Computer Vision and Pattern Recognition, pp. 5022–5030 (2019)
54. Wang, X., Zhang, H., Huang, W., Scott, M.R.: Cross-batch memory for embedding learning. In: Proceedings of the IEEE/CVF Conference on Computer Vision and Pattern Recognition, pp. 6388–6397 (2020)
55. Wang, Y., Pan, X., Song, S., Zhang, H., Huang, G., Wu, C.: Implicit semantic data augmentation for deep networks. In: Advances in Neural Information Processing Systems, vol. 32, pp. 12635–12644 (2019)
56. Wu, C.Y., Manmatha, R., Smola, A.J., Krahenbuhl, P.: Sampling matters in deep embedding learning. In: Proceedings of the IEEE International Conference on Computer Vision, pp. 2840–2848 (2017)
57. Yin, X., Yu, X., Sohn, K., Liu, X., Chandraker, M.: Feature transfer learning for face recognition with under-represented data. In: Proceedings of the IEEE/CVF Conference on Computer Vision and Pattern Recognition, pp. 5704–5713 (2019)
58. Yu, B., Tao, D.: Deep metric learning with tuplet margin loss. In: Proceedings of the IEEE/CVF International Conference on Computer Vision, pp. 6490–6499 (2019)
59. Yuan, Y., Yang, K., Zhang, C.: Hard-aware deeply cascaded embedding. In: Proceedings of the IEEE International Conference on Computer Vision, pp. 814–823 (2017)
60. Zhai, A., Wu, H.Y.: Classification is a strong baseline for deep metric learning (2019)
61. Zhang, D., Li, Y., Zhang, Z.: Deep metric learning with spherical embedding. In: Advances in Neural Information Processing Systems, vol. 33, pp. 18772–18783 (2020)

62. Zhao, Y., Jin, Z., Qi, G., Lu, H., Hua, X.: An adversarial approach to hard triplet generation. In: Ferrari, V., Hebert, M., Sminchisescu, C., Weiss, Y. (eds.) ECCV 2018. LNCS, vol. 11213, pp. 508–524. Springer, Cham (2018). https://doi.org/10.1007/978-3-030-01240-3_31
63. Zheng, W., Lu, J., Zhou, J.: Hardness-aware deep metric learning. IEEE Trans. Pattern Anal. Mach. Intell. **43**(9), 3214–3228 (2021)
64. Zheng, W., Chen, Z., Lu, J., Zhou, J.: Hardness-aware deep metric learning. In: Proceedings of the IEEE/CVF Conference on Computer Vision and Pattern Recognition, pp. 72–81 (2019)
65. Zheng, W., Wang, C., Lu, J., Zhou, J.: Deep compositional metric learning. In: Proceedings of the IEEE/CVF Conference on Computer Vision and Pattern Recognition, pp. 9320–9329 (2021)
66. Zheng, W., Zhang, B., Lu, J., Zhou, J.: Deep relational metric learning. In: Proceedings of the IEEE/CVF International Conference on Computer Vision, pp. 12065–12074 (2021)
67. Zhu, Y., Yang, M., Deng, C., Liu, W.: Fewer is more: a deep graph metric learning perspective using fewer proxies. In: Advances in Neural Information Processing Systems, vol. 33, pp. 17792–17803 (2020)

Learn from All: Erasing Attention Consistency for Noisy Label Facial Expression Recognition

Yuhang Zhang[ID], Chengrui Wang[ID], Xu Ling[ID], and Weihong Deng[(✉)][ID]

Beijing University of Posts and Telecommunications, Beijing, China
{zyhzyh,crwang,lingxu,whdeng}@bupt.edu.cn

Abstract. Noisy label Facial Expression Recognition (FER) is more challenging than traditional noisy label classification tasks due to the inter-class similarity and the annotation ambiguity. Recent works mainly tackle this problem by filtering out large-loss samples. In this paper, we explore dealing with noisy labels from a new feature-learning perspective. We find that FER models remember noisy samples by focusing on a part of the features that can be considered related to the noisy labels instead of learning from the whole features that lead to the latent truth. Inspired by that, we propose a novel Erasing Attention Consistency (EAC) method to suppress the noisy samples during the training process automatically. Specifically, we first utilize the flip semantic consistency of facial images to design an imbalanced framework. We then randomly erase input images and use flip attention consistency to prevent the model from focusing on a part of the features. EAC significantly outperforms state-of-the-art noisy label FER methods and generalizes well to other tasks with a large number of classes like CIFAR100 and Tiny-ImageNet. The code is available at https://github.com/zyh-uaiaaaa/Erasing-Attention-Consistency.

Keywords: Noisy label learning · Facial expression recognition · Erasing attention consistency

1 Introduction

Facial Expression Recognition (FER) has wide applications in the real world, such as driver fragile detection, service robots, and human-computer interaction [35]. The most common paradigm for FER is the end-to-end supervised manner, whose performance largely relies on the massive high-quality annotated data. However, collecting large-scale datasets with fully precise annotations is usually expensive and time-consuming, sometimes even impossible. Furthermore, facial expression images have inherent inter-class similarity (all classes are human

Supplementary Information The online version contains supplementary material available at https://doi.org/10.1007/978-3-031-19809-0_24.

faces) and annotation ambiguity (some expression images are quite confusing), making noisy label FER more challenging than traditional noisy label classification tasks. On the other hand, it is well-known that deep neural networks have enough capacity to memorize large-scale data with even completely random labels, leading to poor performance in generalization [2,19,48]. Therefore, robust FER with noisy labels has become an essential and challenging task in computer vision [4,7,9,18,35,38,47,49,50].

Mainstream noisy label FER methods can be mainly classified into two categories, sample selection and label ensembling. SCN [38] and RUL [50] can be viewed as sample selection methods, which learn more from clean samples and then relabel the noisy samples. SCN [38] uses a fully-connected layer to learn an importance weight for each sample and suppresses uncertain samples during the training phase. RUL [50] learns uncertainty weights through comparison between different samples. IPA2LT [35] and DMUE [35] are label ensembling methods, which provide several labels for a single sample to better mine the latent truth. IPA2LT [35] assigns each sample more than one labels with human annotations or model predictions while DMUE [35] uses a multi-branch model to better mine the latent distribution in the label space. All the aforementioned methods get good performances under noisy label FER while they still have defects. Specifically, sample selection methods are based on the small-loss assumption [2,48], which might confuse hard samples and noisy samples as both of them have large loss values during the training process. Sample selection methods also need the noise rate, which is non-trivial in large-scale real-world datasets. Label ensembling methods provide different views of the same sample using several networks, similar to crowdsourcing in real FER applications. However, the extra information gain they bring might be noisy. Label ensembling methods might bring great computation overhead, making them less preferable in real applications. Thus, the noisy label FER problem demands better methods that do not need to know the noise rate or train several models to perform well.

In this paper, instead of following the traditional path to detect noisy samples according to their loss values and then suppress them, we view noisy label learning from a new feature-learning perspective and propose a novel framework to deal with all the aforementioned defects. We find that the FER model remembers noisy samples by focusing on a part of the features that can be considered related to the noisy labels, shown in Fig. 1. The image in the first column is labeled as sad, while its latent truth is surprise. SCN [38] remembers this noisy sample by focusing on the frown feature which can be considered related to the noisy label of the sad expression. However, it neglects the open mouth feature, which is vital for the correct classification as an open mouth combined with a frown leads to the latent truth surprise instead of the noisy label sad. From the attention regions of the noisy samples, we conclude that the FER model only observes a part of the features that can be considered related to the noisy labels to remember noisy samples. It is intuitive as remembering noisy samples

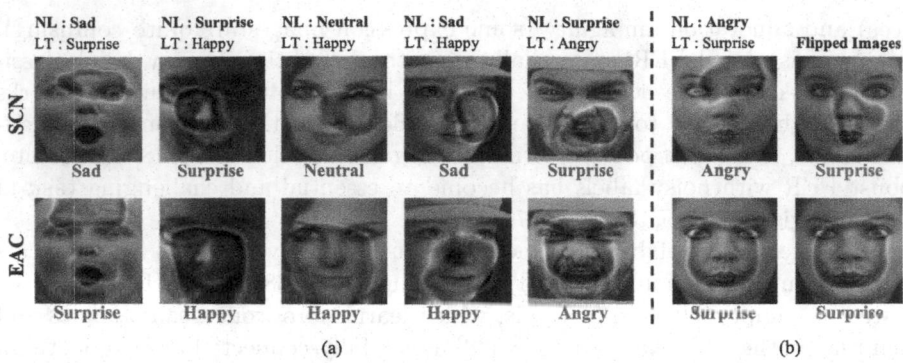

Fig. 1. (a) shows the attention regions of the noisy samples learned by SCN and EAC (ours). NL represents the noisy label, LT represents the latent truth. The prediction results are shown under the images. SCN only focuses on a part of the features that can be considered related to the noisy labels to remember the noisy samples. (b) shows SCN predicts differently on the flipped image. Our EAC forces the model to focus on similar parts before and after the flip to prevent the model from remembering noisy labels.

by focusing on a part of the features that can be considered related to the noisy labels does not contradict the other learned features from the clean samples. Inspired by this finding, we propose to deal with noisy label FER from a new feature-learning perspective. If the model can not focus on a part of the features and always learns from the whole features, then it cannot remember the noisy samples. Learning from the whole features from all training samples also means the model does not need to filter out large-loss samples like traditional methods which might confuse useful hard samples with noisy samples.

In this paper, we use Attention Consistency to implement the consistency regularization. Attention Consistency [11] assumes that the learned attention maps should follow the same transformation as the input images to achieve better multi-label classification performance. The attention maps denote the features that the model based on to make the predictions.

We find that the flip semantic consistency of facial expression images can help to detect noisy labels. Flip semantic consistency means the original image and its flipped counterpart should be classified into the same category. However, if we train a FER model with a noisy sample, the model might remember the noisy sample while it still predicts the latent truth on its flipped counterpart, shown as the images in the first row of Fig. 1. Inspired by that, we propose an imbalanced framework to prevent the model from remembering noisy samples. Specifically, we *only* compute classification loss on the original images and compute consistency loss between the attention maps extracted from the original images and their flipped counterparts. We utilize the consistency loss to prevent the model from remembering a part of the features of the original images. Such an imbalanced framework cannot help the model totally get rid of the noisy labels as the model can still gradually overfit the attention maps of the flipped images to keep the consistency loss small, which degrades the regularization effect. We further propose Erasing Attention Consistency (EAC) to increase the performance of the imbalanced framework. Before flipping, we first randomly erase the input images during the whole training phase. During the training phase, the dynamic changing of the erased area ensures that the model can not simply remember the attention maps before and after the flip to get small consistency loss values. When the model starts to overfit the noisy original samples by focusing on a part of the features related to the noisy labels, the attention maps of the original images will deviate largely from the attention maps of their flipped counterparts, which will lead to large consistency loss values. We set the weight of the consistency loss larger enough to ensure the model first optimizes the consistency loss. Thus, to get small consistency loss values, the model will automatically quit overfitting the noisy samples.

The main contributions of our work are as follows:

1. Instead of using traditional methods which deal with noisy labels from high-level small-loss selection, we cope with noisy labels from middle-level feature learning, which does not require the noise rate to perform well.
2. We propose a novel method named Erasing Attention Consistency (EAC) which automatically prevents the model from memorizing noisy samples.
3. We experimentally show that EAC significantly advances state-of-the-art results on multiple FER benchmarks with different levels of label noise. EAC also generalizes well to image classification tasks with a large number of classes.

2   Related Work

Noisy Label Learning. Learning with noisy labels has been well studied [1,13–15,17,19,20,24,25,29,31–33,37,41–43,45,46,51]. Current works can be mainly categorized into two groups: modifying the primary loss function or selecting clean samples for training.

The first type of method mainly focuses on estimating the noise transition matrix or proposing robust loss functions. Patrini et al. [32] estimate the transition matrix to model the relationship between noisy labels and the latent truth to prevent the model from overfitting noisy labels. Han et al. [13] propose a human-assisted approach that conveys human cognition of invalid class transitions to make estimating transition matrix easier. Both Thulasidasan et al. [37] and Zhang et al. [51] propose generalized cross-entropy loss functions to combat noisy labels. Xu et al. [43] design a new loss function based on mutual information which is information-monotone and robust to various kinds of label noise. Although these methods have theory guarantees, they are not suitable for challenging real-world settings or handling a large number of classes. Thus, recent works usually focus on the second type of method.

The second strand of approach is based on the memorization effect that DNNs fit the underlying clean distribution before overfitting the noisy labels [2]. They focus on reweighting or sample selection to suppress noisy samples. Jiang *et al.* [19] train a mentor net using clean samples to guide the student net by weighing the samples. Ren *et al.* [33] reweight samples according to their gradient directions. Arazo *et al.* [1] model per-sample loss by a mixture model to calculate a weight for each sample. Han *et al.* [14] train two models to select small loss samples for each other hoping to filter different types of error introduced by noisy labels. Malach *et al.* [29] improve co-teaching by updating only on instances with different predictions to keep the two models diverged. Wei *et al.* [41] train two models together and use their agreement degree to select small-loss samples. These methods select small-loss samples to eliminate the bad influence from the noisy samples. However, the useful hard samples are likely to have large loss values and might be filtered out as noisy samples. These methods also need to know the noise rate to get better performance. Different from them, our method automatically prevents the model from memorizing the noisy samples, which do not require the noise rate or selecting clean samples.

Facial Expression Recognition. Facial Expression Recognition (FER) aims at helping computers to understand human behavior or even interact with a human by recognizing human expression. In recent years, as the recognition accuracy is very high in the laboratory collected FER datasets, more attempts try to address the in-the-wild FER problem, which contains lots of label noise. Zeng *et al.* [47] first consider annotation inconsistency and assign each sample with more than one label to better mine the latent truth. Wang *et al.* [38] propose to learn an importance weight for each sample and suppress the uncertain images by relabeling. She *et al.* [35] train multi-branch models by leaving out one class for each branch in order to find the latent truth under label noise. Zhang *et al.* [50] propose to learn the uncertainty of different facial images by comparison and then suppress the uncertain images. They can be mainly categorized into two classes, sample selection [38,50] or label ensembling [35,47]. Sample selection methods select good samples and suppress noisy samples while label ensembling methods use crowdsourcing to improve performance. However, they either require the noise rate to better filter out noisy samples or bring extra computation overhead and cannot generalize well to classification tasks with a large number of classes. Our method automatically prevents the model from overfitting the noisy samples without the noise rate and generalizes well to classification tasks with a large number of classes.

3   Proposed Method

In this section, we illustrate the implementation details of our proposed Erasing Attention Consistency (EAC) method.

3.1   Preliminary

Class Activation Mapping. Class Activation Mapping (CAM) [53] is an attention method, which allows us to visualize the predicted class scores on the given images, highlighting the discriminative parts detected by the CNN.

In the CNN trained for classification, an attention map is the weighted sum of the feature maps from the last convolutional layer with the weights from a fully connected (FC) layer. By viewing the attention maps, we can know what the model is based on to make the predictions. We denote the feature map extracted from the last convolutional layer as $\mathbf{F} \in \mathbb{R}^{C \times H \times W}$, C, H, W respectively represent the number of channels, height, width of the feature map. We denote the weights of the FC layer as $\mathbf{W} \in \mathbb{R}^{L \times C}$, L represents the number of classes. The attention map computes as

$$\mathbf{M}_j(h, w) = \sum_{c=1}^{C} \mathbf{W}(j, c)\mathbf{F}_c(h, w), \tag{1}$$

$\mathbf{M}_j(h, w)$ is the attention value of location (h, w) for class index j, which is the weighted sum of feature maps over different channels. In our method, we use CAM to compute the attention maps from the input images to show the features that the model attends to.

Attention Consistency. Attention Consistency [11] is first proposed for achieving better visual perceptual plausibility and better multi-label image classification by considering visual attention consistency under spatial transforms. It assumes that the learned attention maps of the model should follow the same transformation as the input images.

3.2   Overview of Erasing Attention Consistency

In this paper, we design an imbalanced framework to help the model get rid of the negative effect of the noisy labels. We notice that the facial images before and after the flip have the same semantic meaning of the facial expression. We only compute classification loss with the original images and compute consistency loss between the attention maps of the original images and their flipped counterparts to prevent the model from remembering the original images with noisy labels. Simply using this imbalanced framework can not help the model totally get rid of the negative effect from noisy labels as the model can gradually remember the flipped images to always get small consistency loss, which degrades the regularization effect. We further propose Erasing Attention Consistency to enhance the performance of our proposed imbalanced framework. Before flipping the original images to generate their counterparts, we first randomly erase the images according to [52], which will generate different pairs of original images and their flipped counterparts during the training process. Thus, the model cannot remember the flipped images to get small consistency loss. If the model starts to remember the original images with noisy labels, the attention maps extracted

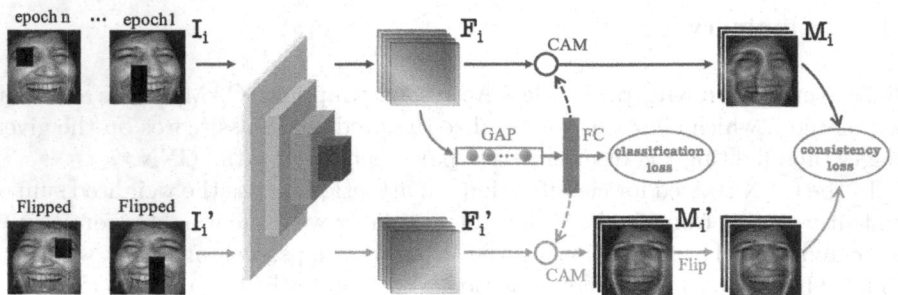

Fig. 2. The framework of the Erasing Attention Consistency (EAC). EAC randomly erases input images and then gets their flipped counterparts. EAC only computes the classification loss with the original images. The classification loss with the noisy labels might cause the model to overfit the noisy samples shown as M_i. EAC uses the consistency loss between the original images and their flipped counterparts to prevent the model from remembering noisy labels. The dotted lines mean no gradient propagation.

from them will focus on a part of the features, which deviate largely from the flipped attention maps extracted from their flipped counterparts leading to the increase of the consistency loss. Thus, the consistency loss can prevent the model from remembering noisy samples.

3.3 Framework of Erasing Attention Consistency

The overall framework of our proposed EAC is shown in Fig. 2. Given a batch of facial expression images, we first erase the input images according to [52] and get $\mathbf{I}$. We then flip these images to get their flipped counterparts $\mathbf{I}'$. $\mathbf{I}$ and $\mathbf{I}'$ are the input images. The feature maps are extracted from the last convolutional layer, denoted as $\mathbf{F} \in \mathbb{R}^{N \times C \times H \times W}$ and $\mathbf{F}' \in \mathbb{R}^{N \times C \times H \times W}$. N, C, H, W respectively represent the number of images, the number of channels, height, width of the feature maps. We *only* input $\mathbf{F}$ through the global average pooling (GAP) layer to get features $\mathbf{f} \in \mathbb{R}^{N \times C \times 1 \times 1}$. We resize features $\mathbf{f}$ to $N \times C$ and put them through fully connected (FC) layer to compute classification loss according to

$$l_{cls} = -\frac{1}{N} \sum_{i=1}^{N} (\log \frac{e^{\mathbf{W}_{\mathbf{y}_i} \mathbf{f}_i}}{\sum_{j}^{L} e^{\mathbf{W}_j \mathbf{f}_i}}), \tag{2}$$

$\mathbf{W}_{\mathbf{y}_i}$ is the $\mathbf{y}_i$-th weight from the FC layer with $\mathbf{y}_i$ as the given label of the i-th image. We compute attention maps $\mathbf{M}$ and $\mathbf{M}'$ for $\mathbf{I}$ and $\mathbf{I}'$ according to Eq. (1). Note that the weights used to compute attention maps come from the FC layer, while the FC layer only computes classification loss with the original feature maps $\mathbf{F}$. We use consistency loss to minimize the distance between the feature maps $\mathbf{M}$ and $Flip(\mathbf{M}')$ as

$$l_c = \frac{1}{NLHW} \sum_{i=1}^{N} \sum_{j=1}^{L} ||\mathbf{M}_{ij} - Flip(\mathbf{M}')_{ij}||_2. \tag{3}$$

The total loss is computed as follows,

$$l_{total} = l_{cls} + \lambda l_c. \tag{4}$$

λ is the weight of the erasing consistency loss. The ablation study of λ is in Sect. 4.8.

4   Experiments

In this section, we first describe 3 popular in-the-wild FER benchmarks and our implementation details. We then verify the proposed EAC on the FER datasets with different levels of label noise and study why EAC works. Visualization results of the learned features, attention maps and classification loss values are displayed to provide an intuitive understanding of EAC. We carry out an ablation study and also show the generalization ability of EAC by conducting experiments on CIFAR100 [22] and Tiny-ImageNet [34]. Finally, we compare EAC with other state-of-the-art FER methods.

4.1   Datasets

RAF-DB [26] is annotated with basic or compound expressions by 40 trained human coders. In our experiments, images with seven basic expressions (i.e. neutral, happy, surprise, sad, angry, disgust, fear) are used including 12,271 images for training and 3,068 images for testing.

FERPlus [3] is extended from FER2013 [10] with finer label annotations. It is collected by the Google search engine consisting of 28,709 training images and 3,589 test images. We use the most voting category as the annotation for a fair comparison [3,38,39].

AffectNet [30] is by far the largest FER dataset, which is collected from the Internet by querying expression-related keywords in three search engines containing more than one million images. There are 286,564 training images and 4,000 test images manually labeled to eight classes.

4.2   Implementation Details

By default, we use ResNet-18 [16] pre-trained on MS-Celeb-1M [12] as the backbone network with the same routine as [35,38,39,50] for fair comparisons. The facial images are aligned and cropped with three landmarks [40], resized to 224×224 pixels. We only use the horizontal flip and the random erasing without any other data augmentation tricks to evaluate the effectiveness of our proposed method. During training, the batch size is 256. The initial learning rate is 0.0002. We use Adam [21] optimizer with weight decay of 0.0001 and ExponentialLR [27] learning rate scheduler with the gamma of 0.9 to decrease the learning rate after each epoch. The training ends at epoch 60.

4.3 Evaluation of EAC on Noisy FER Datasets

We quantitatively evaluate the improvement of our proposed EAC against other state-of-the-art noisy label FER methods. We explore the robustness of EAC with three levels of label noise including the ratio of 10%, 20%, 30% on RAF-DB, FERPlus, and AffectNet datasets. We follow [35,38,50] to generate noisy labels. As the generation of label noise is random, we re-implement other state-of-the-art methods on our generated noisy datasets to make fair comparisons with them. We also consider the influence of the different backbones and backbones with or without pretraining.

Shown in Table 1, our method outperforms other state-of-the-art FER noisy label learning methods by a large margin. For example, EAC outperforms SCN under 30% label noise by 6.97%, 3.24%, 4.31% on RAF-DB, FERPlus, AffectNet respectively.

Table 1. Evaluation of EAC on noisy FER datasets. We re-implement other state-of-the-art methods and test all the methods with the same noisy datasets to make fair comparisons. Results are computed as the mean of the accuracy from the last 5 epochs

Method	Noise (%)	RAF-DB (%)	FERPlus (%)	AffectNet (%)
Baseline	10	81.01	83.29	57.24
SCN (CVPR20)	10	82.15	84.99	58.60
RUL (NeurIPS21)	10	86.17	86.93	60.54
EAC (ours)	10	88.02	87.03	61.11
Baseline	20	77.98	82.34	55.89
SCN (CVPR20)	20	79.79	83.35	57.51
RUL (NeurIPS21)	20	84.32	85.05	59.01
EAC (ours)	20	86.05	86.07	60.29
Baseline	30	75.50	79.77	52.16
SCN (CVPR20)	30	77.45	82.20	54.60
RUL (NeurIPS21)	30	82.06	83.90	56.93
EAC (ours)	30	84.42	85.44	58.91

Note that, unlike SCN [38] and RUL [50], EAC does not need to modify the labels of the training samples. Relabeling has the risk of changing right labels to wrong labels, which is less flexible than our method as EAC can automatically learn useful information from all training samples. EAC does not need to know the noise rate or tell apart hard samples and noisy samples, which fundamentally solves the defects of sample selection methods as sample selection methods require the noise rate to filter out large-loss samples, which might contain useful hard samples and useless noisy samples.

We also study EAC with different backbones. With different backbones, λ is set to 5 under 0 and 10% noise, 10 under 20% and 30% noise. As shown in Table 2, adding EAC to MobileNet or ResNet-50 can both improve their performance. Baselines are also trained with erase and flip for a fair comparison. EAC achieves better results in all settings using ResNet-50 as backbone compared with ResNet-18 in Table 1. The experiments of EAC using an unpretrained model as backbone are shown in the supplementary material.

4.4   Why EAC Works

We evaluate the three modules of the proposed EAC to find why EAC works well under label noise. The experiment results are shown in Table 3. Several observations are concluded as follows. Without the flip attention consistency module, the model can not use the same semantic meaning from the flipped counterparts to regularize the classification loss, which is shown in the second row. Without the erasing, the model will gradually remember the attention maps from the flipped images to get small consistency loss values, which degrades the regularization effect. Without the imbalanced framework, the noisy labels will affect the images before and after the flip together. The model can remember the noisy samples before and after the flip together, making the consistency loss useless. However, when we combine the three modules, the performance skyrockets.

Table 2. The influence of different backbones on EAC. We carry out experiments on RAF-DB. Results are computed as the mean of the accuracy from the last 5 epochs

Method	0 noise	10% noise	20% noise	30% noise
MobileNet	83.31%	77.80%	70.60%	62.48%
MobileNet + EAC	86.47%	82.63%	81.65%	79.82%
ResNet-50	88.75%	83.44%	79.11%	71.67%
ResNet-50 + EAC	90.35%	88.62%	87.35%	85.27%

We believe it is the dynamic erasing that prevents the model from remembering the attention maps. Thus, the model needs to learn flip consistent features to minimize the consistency loss. As we only compute the classification loss with the original images (the imbalanced framework), if the model tries to remember the noisy samples, the features learned from these samples will deviate largely from their flipped counterparts, making the consistency loss large. As we set the weight of the consistency loss large enough, the model will first minimize the consistency loss. Thus, it will quit remembering the noisy samples.

Table 3. Evaluation of the three modules of EAC on RAF-DB with 30% label noise

Flip attention consistency	Imbalanced framework	Erasing	RAF-DB
✗	✗	✗	75.50
✗	✓	✓	78.10
✓	✗	✓	78.29
✓	✓	✗	76.26
✓	✓	✓	84.42

4.5 Whether Flip and Erase Is Sufficiently Valid for EAC

We use flip because we need *spatial transforms* to enable attention consistency following [11]. Other spatial transforms like Rotate or Scale are not very effective for FER as FER test sets are mainly frontal faces with a similar scale. We utilize erasing as FER models fit noisy labels through remembering parts of the features. Erasing guides the model to focus on the whole feature as the remembered feature parts might be absent during the training. Other augments can not directly solve the part-view problem and are not very effective. We test them on noisy RAF-DB. Rotate and Scale is compared to Flip. Blur [36] and AutoAugment [5] (AutoAug.) is compared to Erasing. AutoAugment searches and combines many kinds of augments together while it is still inferior to erasing.

Table 4. Comparison with other augmentation methods. The experiments are carried out on noisy RAF-DB.

Noise	Rotate	Scale	Flip	Blur	AutoAug.	Erasing
10%	80.93%	85.98%	88.02%	86.80%	87.84%	88.02%
20%	79.63%	85.30%	86.05%	83.77%	85.82%	86.05%
30%	78.23%	82.01%	84.42%	76.92%	82.40%	84.42%

4.6 Feature Visualization

To understand EAC intuitively, we plot the learned features of EAC trained with 30% noisy labels on RAF-DB by t-SNE [28]. Figure 3(a) is the learned features displayed with the noisy training labels. It is shown that EAC does not remember noisy labels as features with different labels are clustered together. It is shown that the features with noisy labels are close to the classification boundary which means these samples are with large classification loss values. Thus, EAC separates clean and noisy samples effectively. We also plot the same learned features in Fig. 3(b), but displayed with the latent truth. Compared with Fig. 3(a), we can draw the conclusion that EAC can automatically prevent the

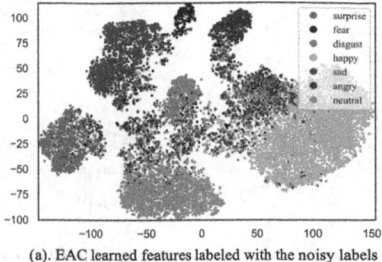 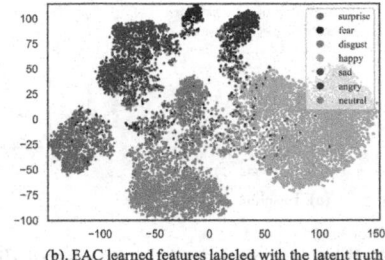

(a). EAC learned features labeled with the noisy labels   (b). EAC learned features labeled with the latent truth

Fig. 3. The learned features by EAC training with noisy labels. (a) is the learned features displayed with the noisy training labels, EAC does not overfit noisy labels as different classes mixed with each other. *Notice that noisy samples are pushed to the classification boundary by EAC.* (b) is the same learned features with (a), but displayed with the latent truth. Though we train EAC with noisy labels, it can still learn useful features related to the latent truth.

model from remembering noisy labels and learn useful features from both clean and noisy samples.

We plot the attention maps on images before and after the flip in Fig. 4 to show the effectiveness of EAC. We train SCN with the original images and test on their flipped counterparts. It is shown that SCN remembers the original images to the noisy labels, while it still gets correct predictions on their flipped counterparts after training. Inspired by that, EAC uses the attention maps of the flipped ones to regularize the classification loss and get correct prdictions on both the original images and their flipped counterparts. We display more results in the supplementary material.

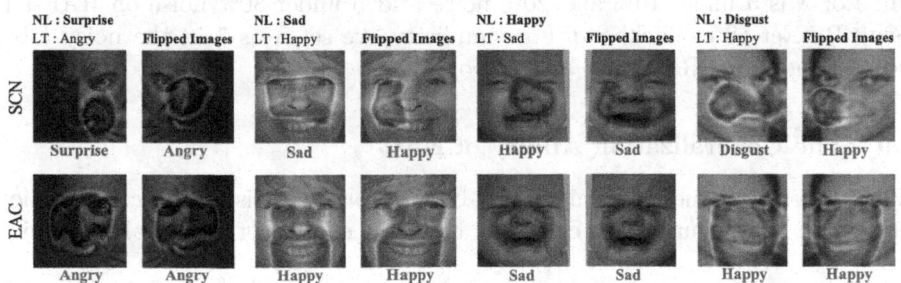

Fig. 4. The attention maps of SCN and EAC on the original images and their flipped counterparts.

4.7 Visualization of the Classification Loss Values

We plot the distribution of classification loss values after training for 60 epochs in Fig. 5 under the same setting as Sect. 4.6. We normalize the histogram of

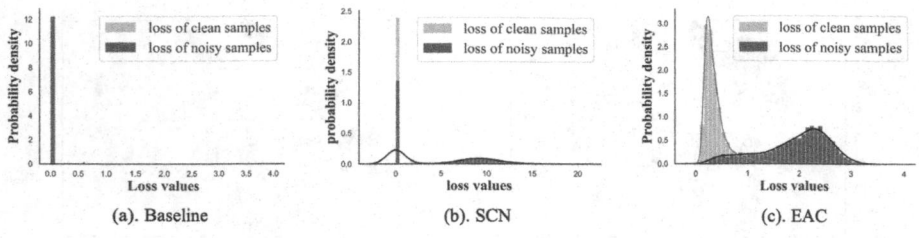

Fig. 5. The classification loss values of different methods after training for 60 epochs with noisy samples. The baseline remembers nearly all noisy samples. SCN avoids overfitting a part of the noisy samples, while EAC can still separate clean and noisy samples apart after training for 60 epochs.

loss values and plot it as the probability density. The baseline method overfits nearly all the noisy samples after training for 60 epochs as the loss values of all samples are around 0. SCN learns importance weights and uses relabeling to deal with noisy samples. However, lots of the noisy samples are not correctly relabeled during the training process as there are still lots of noisy samples with loss values close to 0. Our EAC prevents the model from remembering the noisy samples during the whole training process. After training for 60 epochs, the loss values of clean and noisy samples can still be separated clearly.

4.8 Ablation Study

We evaluate the consistency loss weight λ from 0.1 to 10.0 with different levels of label noise. The results are shown in the supplementary material. We can choose λ from a wide range to acquire state-of-the-art performance. The best value of λ is 3 under 10% and 20% noise and 5 under 30% noise on RAF-DB using ResNet-18 as backbone. For simplicity, we set λ as 5 in the noisy label experiments using ResNet-18 as backbone.

4.9 The Generalization Ability of EAC

Noisy label FER methods might not be suitable for noisy label classification tasks with a large number of classes as the class number of the facial expression

Table 5. CIFAR100 and Tiny-ImageNet label noise training

Methods	CIFAR100 noise rate			Tiny-ImageNet noise rate		
	Top-1/Top-5 (%)			Top-1/Top-5 (%)		
	10%	20%	30%	10%	20%	30%
Baseline	64.56/85.37	57.33/78.93	49.70/72.55	58.11/80.24	49.56/72.43	41.32/64.58
SCN [38]	65.18/86.60	60.38/82.11	56.19/78.30	62.22/85.89	55.23/80.21	47.39/72.56
EAC	70.93/90.15	66.73/87.01	60.59/82.84	70.22/90.23	67.23/89.01	63.51/87.18

Table 6. Comparison with other state-of-the-art results on different FER datasets. † denotes training with both AffectNet and RAF-DB datasets. ∗ denotes test with 7 classes on AffectNet.

RAF-DB		FERPlus		AffectNet	
Methods	Acc. (%)	Methods	Acc. (%)	Methods	Acc. (%)
IPA2LT† [47]	86.77	IPA2LT† [47]	–	IPA2LT† [47]	57.31
RAN [39]	86.90	RAN [39]	88.55	RAN [39]	59.50
SCN [38]	87.03	SCN [38]	88.01	SCN [38]	60.23
DACL [8]	87.78	DACL [8]	–	DACL∗ [8]	65.20
KTN [23]	88.07	KTN [23]	90.49	KTN∗ [23]	63.97
DMUE [35]	88.76	DMUE [35]	88.64	DMUE [35]	62.84
RUL [50]	88.98	RUL [50]	88.75	RUL [50]	61.43
EAC (ours)	89.99	EAC (ours)	89.64	EAC∗(ours)	65.32

is very small. For example, DMUE [35] needs to train a multi-branch model whose branch number equals the class number plus 1 to mine the latent truth, which is unaffordable when the class number is very large. However, EAC can generalize well to tasks with a large number of classes.

To show the generalization ability of EAC. We carry out experiments on CIFAR100 [22] and Tiny-ImageNet [34]. Due to the space limitation, the implementation details are illustrated in the supplementary material. As shown in Tabel 5, our EAC consistently improves the baseline by a large margin in both top-1 and top-5 accuracy. EAC outperforms the baseline by 6.37%, 9.40%, 10.89% on CIFAR100 and 12.11%, 17.67%, 22.19% on Tiny-ImageNet in top-1 accuracy with noise ratio 10%, 20%, 30%. Although SCN [38] also outperforms the baseline, it is clear that our EAC achieves much better results.

4.10   Comparison with Other State-of-the-Art FER Methods

EAC can also help the FER model achieve state-of-the-art performance on clean datasets as EAC encourages the model to learn flip consistent features from the input images which conforms to the human visual perceptual. The results are shown in Table 6. Besides the works mentioned in Sect. 2, RAN [39] utilizes attention weights to aggregate a varied number of face regions to recognize facial expression robustly. DACL [8] adaptively selects a subset of significant feature elements for enhanced discrimination. [23] utilizes a knowledgeable teacher network (KTN) and a self-taught student network (STSN) to transfer knowledge. Our EAC achieves the best performance than other state-of-the-art methods on RAF-DB and AffectNet (7 classes) while slightly lower than KTN [23] under FERPlus. We do not compare with [44] as it utilizes Vision Transformer [6] as backbone while we use ResNet-18 [16].

5   Conclusion

In this paper, we explore to deal with noisy label FER from a new feature-learning perspective and propose a novel and effective method named Erasing Attention Consistency (EAC). We design an imbalanced framework to utilize the erasing and flip consistency loss to prevent the model from remembering noisy labels. EAC does not require the noise rate or label ensembling. Extensive experiments verify that EAC outperforms other state-of-the-art noisy label FER methods on clean and noisy datasets. Furthermore, EAC generalizes well to noisy label classification tasks with a large number of classes.

Acknowledgments. This work was supported in part by the National Natural Science Foundation of China under Grant 62192784 and Grant 61871052.

References

1. Arazo, E., Ortego, D., Albert, P., O'Connor, N., McGuinness, K.: Unsupervised label noise modeling and loss correction. In: ICML (2019)
2. Arpit, D., et al.: A closer look at memorization in deep networks. In: ICML (2017)
3. Barsoum, E., Zhang, C., Ferrer, C.C., Zhang, Z.: Training deep networks for facial expression recognition with crowd-sourced label distribution. In: ICMI (2016)
4. Chen, S., Wang, J., Chen, Y., Shi, Z., Geng, X., Rui, Y.: Label distribution learning on auxiliary label space graphs for facial expression recognition. In: CVPR (2020)
5. Cubuk, E.D., Zoph, B., Mane, D., Vasudevan, V., Le, Q.V.: AutoAugment: learning augmentation policies from data. arXiv preprint arXiv:1805.09501 (2018)
6. Dosovitskiy, A., et al.: An image is worth 16 × 16 words: transformers for image recognition at scale. arXiv preprint arXiv:2010.11929 (2020)
7. Fan, X., Deng, Z., Wang, K., Peng, X., Qiao, Y.: Learning discriminative representation for facial expression recognition from uncertainties. In: ICIP (2020)
8. Farzaneh, A.H., Qi, X.: Facial expression recognition in the wild via deep attentive center loss. In: WACV (2021)
9. Gera, D., Balasubramanian, S.: Noisy annotations robust consensual collaborative affect expression recognition. In: ICCV (2021)
10. Goodfellow, I.J., et al.: Challenges in representation learning: a report on three machine learning contests. In: Lee, M., Hirose, A., Hou, Z.-G., Kil, R.M. (eds.) ICONIP 2013. LNCS, vol. 8228, pp. 117–124. Springer, Heidelberg (2013). https://doi.org/10.1007/978-3-642-42051-1_16
11. Guo, H., Zheng, K., Fan, X., Yu, H., Wang, S.: Visual attention consistency under image transforms for multi-label image classification. In: CVPR (2019)
12. Guo, Y., Zhang, L., Hu, Y., He, X., Gao, J.: MS-Celeb-1M: a dataset and benchmark for large-scale face recognition. In: Leibe, B., Matas, J., Sebe, N., Welling, M. (eds.) ECCV 2016. LNCS, vol. 9907, pp. 87–102. Springer, Cham (2016). https://doi.org/10.1007/978-3-319-46487-9_6
13. Han, B., et al.: Masking: a new perspective of noisy supervision. In: NIPS (2018)
14. Han, B., et al.: Co-teaching: robust training of deep neural networks with extremely noisy labels. In: NIPS (2018)
15. Han, J., Luo, P., Wang, X.: Deep self-learning from noisy labels. In: ICCV (2019)
16. He, K., Zhang, X., Ren, S., Sun, J.: Deep residual learning for image recognition. In: CVPR (2016)

17. Huang, J., Qu, L., Jia, R., Zhao, B.: O2U-Net: a simple noisy label detection approach for deep neural networks. In: ICCV (2019)
18. Jiang, J., Deng, W.: Boosting facial expression recognition by a semi-supervised progressive teacher. IEEE Trans. Affect. Comput. (2021)
19. Jiang, L., Zhou, Z., Leung, T., Li, L.J., Fei-Fei, L.: MentorNet: learning data-driven curriculum for very deep neural networks on corrupted labels. In: ICML (2018)
20. Kim, Y., Yim, J., Yun, J., Kim, J.: NLNL: negative learning for noisy labels. In: ICCV (2019)
21. Kingma, D.P., Ba, J.: Adam: a method for stochastic optimization. arXiv preprint arXiv:1412.6980 (2014)
22. Krizhevsky, A., et al.: Learning multiple layers of features from tiny images. Technical report (2009)
23. Li, H., Wang, N., Ding, X., Yang, X., Gao, X.: Adaptively learning facial expression representation via CF labels and distillation. TIP 30, 2016–2028 (2021)
24. Li, J., Socher, R., Hoi, S.C.: DIVIDEMIX: learning with noisy labels as semi-supervised learning. arXiv preprint arXiv:2002.07394 (2020)
25. Li, J., Xiong, C., Hoi, S.C.: Learning from noisy data with robust representation learning. In: ICCV (2021)
26. Li, S., Deng, W., Du, J.: Reliable crowdsourcing and deep locality-preserving learning for expression recognition in the wild. In: CVPR (2017)
27. Li, Z., Arora, S.: An exponential learning rate schedule for deep learning. arXiv preprint arXiv:1910.07454 (2019)
28. Van der Maaten, L., Hinton, G.: Visualizing data using t-SNE. J. Mach. Lear. Res. 9, 2579–2605 (2008)
29. Malach, E., Shalev-Shwartz, S.: Decoupling "when to update" from "how to update". In: NIPS (2017)
30. Mollahosseini, A., Hasani, B., Mahoor, M.H.: AffectNet: a database for facial expression, valence, and arousal computing in the wild. IEEE Trans. Affect. Comput. 10, 18–31 (2017)
31. Nguyen, D.T., Mummadi, C.K., Ngo, T.P.N., Nguyen, T.H.P., Beggel, L., Brox, T.: Self: learning to filter noisy labels with self-ensembling. arXiv preprint arXiv:1910.01842 (2019)
32. Patrini, G., Rozza, A., Krishna Menon, A., Nock, R., Qu, L.: Making deep neural networks robust to label noise: a loss correction approach. In: CVPR (2017)
33. Ren, M., Zeng, W., Yang, B., Urtasun, R.: Learning to reweight examples for robust deep learning. In: ICML (2018)
34. Russakovsky, O., et al.: ImageNet large scale visual recognition challenge. IJCV 115, 211–252 (2015). https://doi.org/10.1007/s11263-015-0816-y
35. She, J., Hu, Y., Shi, H., Wang, J., Shen, Q., Mei, T.: Dive into ambiguity: latent distribution mining and pairwise uncertainty estimation for facial expression recognition. In: CVPR (2021)
36. Shi, Y., Yu, X., Sohn, K., Chandraker, M., Jain, A.K.: Towards universal representation learning for deep face recognition. In: CVPR (2020)
37. Thulasidasan, S., Bhattacharya, T., Bilmes, J., Chennupati, G., Mohd-Yusof, J.: Combating label noise in deep learning using abstention. arXiv preprint arXiv:1905.10964 (2019)
38. Wang, K., Peng, X., Yang, J., Lu, S., Qiao, Y.: Suppressing uncertainties for large-scale facial expression recognition. In: CVPR (2020)
39. Wang, K., Peng, X., Yang, J., Meng, D., Qiao, Y.: Region attention networks for pose and occlusion robust facial expression recognition. IEEE Trans. Image Process. 29, 4057–4069 (2020)

40. Wang, X., Bo, L., Fuxin, L.: Adaptive wing loss for robust face alignment via heatmap regression. In: ICCV (2019)
41. Wei, H., Feng, L., Chen, X., An, B.: Combating noisy labels by agreement: a joint training method with co-regularization. In: CVPR (2020)
42. Xie, M.K., Huang, S.J.: Partial multi-label learning with noisy label identification. IEEE Trans. Pattern Anal. Mach. Intell. **44**(7), 3676–3687 (2022)
43. Xu, Y., Cao, P., Kong, Y., Wang, Y.: L_DMI: a novel information-theoretic loss function for training deep nets robust to label noise. In: NIPS (2019)
44. Xue, F., Wang, Q., Guo, G.: TransFER: learning relation-aware facial expression representations with transformers. In: ICCV (2021)
45. Ye, M., Yuen, P.C.: PurifyNet: a robust person re-identification model with noisy labels. TIFS **15**, 2655–2666 (2020)
46. Yi, K., Wu, J.: Probabilistic end-to-end noise correction for learning with noisy labels. In: CVPR (2019)
47. Zeng, J., Shan, S., Chen, X.: Facial expression recognition with inconsistently annotated datasets. In: Ferrari, V., Hebert, M., Sminchisescu, C., Weiss, Y. (eds.) ECCV 2018. LNCS, vol. 11217, pp. 227–243. Springer, Cham (2018). https://doi.org/10.1007/978-3-030-01261-8_14
48. Zhang, C., Bengio, S., Hardt, M., Recht, B., Vinyals, O.: Understanding deep learning (still) requires rethinking generalization. In: ICLR (2017)
49. Zhang, F., Xu, M., Xu, C.: Weakly-supervised facial expression recognition in the wild with noisy data. IEEE Trans. Multimed. **24**, 1800–1814 (2021)
50. Zhang, Y., Wang, C., Deng, W.: Relative uncertainty learning for facial expression recognition. In: NIPS (2021)
51. Zhang, Z., Sabuncu, M.: Generalized cross entropy loss for training deep neural networks with noisy labels. In: NIPS (2018)
52. Zhong, Z., Zheng, L., Kang, G., Li, S., Yang, Y.: Random erasing data augmentation. In: AAAI (2020)
53. Zhou, B., Khosla, A., Lapedriza, A., Oliva, A., Torralba, A.: Learning deep features for discriminative localization. In: CVPR (2016)

A Non-isotropic Probabilistic Take on Proxy-based Deep Metric Learning

Michael Kirchhof$^{(\boxtimes)}$ ⓘ, Karsten Roth ⓘ, Zeynep Akata ⓘ,
and Enkelejda Kasneci ⓘ

University of Tübingen, Tübingen, Germany
`michael.kirchhof@uni-tuebingen.de`

Abstract. Proxy-based Deep Metric Learning (DML) learns deep representations by embedding images close to their class representatives (*proxies*), commonly with respect to the angle between them. However, this disregards the embedding norm, which can carry additional beneficial context such as class- or image-intrinsic uncertainty. In addition, proxy-based DML struggles to learn class-internal structures. To address both issues at once, we introduce non-isotropic probabilistic proxy-based DML. We model images as directional von Mises-Fisher (vMF) distributions on the hypersphere that can reflect image-intrinsic uncertainties. Further, we derive non-isotropic von Mises-Fisher (nivMF) distributions for class proxies to better represent complex class-specific variances. To measure the proxy-to-image distance between these models, we develop and investigate multiple distribution-to-point and distribution-to-distribution metrics. Each framework choice is motivated by a set of ablational studies, which showcase beneficial properties of our probabilistic approach to proxy-based DML, such as uncertainty-awareness, better behaved gradients during training, and overall improved generalization performance. The latter is especially reflected in the competitive performance on the standard DML benchmarks, where our approach compares favourably, suggesting that existing proxy-based DML can significantly benefit from a more probabilistic treatment. Code is available at http://github.com/ExplainableML/Probabilistic_Deep_Metric_Learning.

Keywords: Deep metric learning · von Mises-Fisher · Non-isotropy · Probablistic embeddings · Uncertainty

1 Introduction

Understanding and encoding visual similarity is a key concept that drives applications ranging from image (video) retrieval [3, 27, 60, 65, 70] to clustering [1] and

M. kirchhof and K. Roth—Equal contribution.

Supplementary Information The online version contains supplementary material available at https://doi.org/10.1007/978-3-031-19809-0_25.

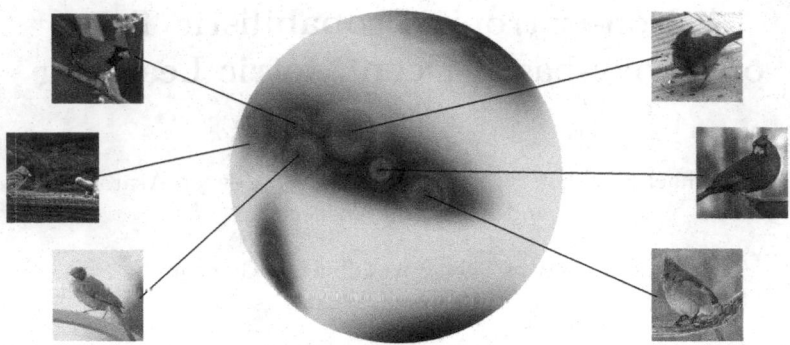

Fig. 1. Class proxy distributions (blue (Color figure online)) and image distributions (red) embedded on the 3D unit sphere. The central proxy has a non-isotropic variance, so it can represent the high variance in body color between male (left) and female (right) cardinals and the low variance in their beak shape (top to bottom). Ambiguous images (e.g. middle left) have higher variance than images that clearly show class-discriminating features (top left, middle right). Best viewed in color.

face re-identification [9,20,33,56]. Most commonly, approaches leverage Deep Metric Learning (DML) [40,52,56,60,70] to reformulate visual similarity learning into a surrogate, contrastive representation learning problem: Here, a deep network is tasked to embed images such that a simple predefined distance metric over pairs of embeddings represents their actual semantic relations. Similar contrastive learning is used for representation learning tasks s.a. supervised image classification [25] or self-supervised learning [5,18]. Common DML approaches are formulated as ranking tasks over data tuples (e.g. pairs [15], triplets [56] or quadruplets [6]) of similar and dissimilar samples. Unfortunately, the complexity of sampling such tuples grows exponentially with the tuples size [70]. This has motivated recent advances in DML to focus on *proxy-based* approaches, where the similar samples are summarized into learnable proxy representations [40,47] against which the sample embeddings are contrasted.

While this allows for fast convergence and reliable generalization, drawbacks may arise both in the treatment of proxies and samples: Firstly, the deterministic treatment of sample representations does not offer any degrees of freedom to address ambiguities and uncertainty (e.g., an image of a bird covered by branches). Secondly, isotropic distance scores between proxy-sample pairs (e.g., cosine similarity) provide only limited tools for the network to derive the similarity of samples within a class, as the distance to each proxy alone is insufficient to resolve relative sample placements around a proxy. This hinders class-specific variance and substructures to be successfully accounted for, which have been shown to notably benefit downstream generalization performance [37,52].

To address these issues, we propose a *probabilistic* interpretation of proxy-based DML. Driven by the fact that modern DML consistently operates on hyperspherical (i.e., normalized) representations [52,70], we derive hyperspherical von-Mises Fisher (vMF) distributions for each sample. A sample embedding's direction controls the placement on the hypersphere, and therefore its semantic content, and its norm parametrizes the certainty of the distribution. In conjunction, we also treat class proxies probabilistically, but through *non-isotropic* vMF distributions. This enforces the distributional prior over each class proxy to explicitly account for different, non-isotropic distributions, capturing more complex class-specific sample distributions (c.f. Figure 1). As this moves the DML training from point-based to distributional comparisons, we merge both components into a sound setup by motivating distribution-to-distribution matching metrics based on probabilistic product kernels. Our full framework is supported through an extensive set of derivations and experimental ablations that showcase and support how the extension to probabilistic proxy-based DML offers significant improvements, with competitive performance across the standard DML benchmarks – CUB200-2011 [64], CARS196 [30], and Stanford Online Products [42] – even when compared to much more complex training methods.

Overall, our contributions can be summarized as: (**1**) We propose and derive a novel probabilistic interpretation of proxy-based DML to account for sample and class ambiguities by reformulating the standard proxy-based metric learning approach to a distributional one on the hypersphere. (**2**) We extend the vMF model to a non-isotropical one for each class proxy to better incorporate and address intra-class substructures for better generalization. (**3**) We introduce various distribution-to-distribution metrics for DML and contrast them to traditional point-to-point metrics. (**4**) We support our proposed framework through various derivational and experimental ablations showcasing how a distributional treatment can positively impact the learned representation spaces. (**5**) Finally, we benchmark against standard DML approaches and provide further significant experimental support for our probabilistic approach to proxy-based DML.

2   Related Work

Deep Metric Learning comprises several conceptually different approaches. Firstly, one can define ranking tasks over data tuples such as pairs [15,70], triplets [56], quadruplets [6] or higher-order variants [42,60,67]. An underlying network then learns to solve each tuple presented by learning a representation space in which distances between embeddings correctly reflect their respective semantics/labelling. However, as the sizes of presented tuples increase, so does the tuple space each ranking task is sampled from, resulting in notable redundancy and impacted convergence behaviour [52,56,70]. As a result, a secondary branch evolved focusing on heuristics which target ranking tuples fulfilling a set of predefined [56,67,70,71] or learned [16,50] criteria. In a similar vein, DML research has also tried to address the sampling complexity issue through the replacement of tuple components with learned concept representations denoted as *proxies*, with some approaches leveraging proxies in a classification-style setting [9,73] or in a ranking fashion, where each sample is contrasted against a respective proxy [26,40,47,63]. Finally, benefits have also been found in orthogonal extensions and fundamental improvements to the general DML training pipeline, through various different approaches such as the usage of adversarial training [10], synthetic samples [32, 75], higher-order or curvilinear metric learning [4, 21], feature mining for ranking [37, 38, 49] or proxy-based [54] approaches, a breakdown of the overall metric space into subspaces [43, 44, 55], orthogonal modalities [53] or knowledge distillation [51]. Our proposed probabilistic proxy-based DML falls into this line of work, but is orthogonal to these other approaches, as these extensions can be applied in a method-agnostic fashion. In particular, we extend proxy-based DML by specifically accounting for sample and class ambiguity through a distributional treatment of samples and proxies, and by utilizing non-isotropic proxy distributions to encourage more complex intra-class distributions around each proxy, which has been shown to be beneficial for generalization [39, 52, 54].

Probabilistic Embeddings. Various approaches to DML can already be framed from a more probabilistic standpoint, where softmax-based approaches on the basis of cosine similarities [9, 63, 73] can be seen as analytical class posteriors if each class assumes a von Mises-Fisher (vMF) distribution [45, 74]. While these methods implicitly model classes as vMFs, probabilistic embedding approaches further model each sample as a distribution in the embedding space [31, 57, 58]. This allows the model to express uncertainty when images are ambiguous. Recent works argue that this ambiguity is captured in the image embedding's norm [31, 48, 57]: [57] argues that the embedding of an image that shows many class-discriminative features of one class consists of several vectors that all point in the same direction, resulting in a higher norm. On this basis, [31, 57] pioneered the use of embedding direction and norm to model each image as a vMF distribution, in particular for supervised classification. Utilizing vMF distributions, we are the first to introduce a full probabilistic proxy-based DML framework, yielding distribution-to-distribution metrics. Additionally, we propose a non-isotropic vMF for proxy distributions, which allows us to represent richer class structures in the embedding space beneficial to generalization [37, 52].

3   Non-isotropic Probabilistic Proxy-based DML

3.1   A Probabilistic Interpretation of Proxy-based DML

In this section, we extend the common DML framework to a probabilistic one. Fundamentally, DML aims to find embedding functions $e : \mathcal{X} \to \mathcal{E}$ from image $\mathcal{X} \subset \mathbb{R}^{H \times W \times 3}$ to M-dimensional metric embedding spaces $\mathcal{E} \subset \mathbb{R}^M$ such that a distance function $d : \mathcal{E} \times \mathcal{E} \to \mathbb{R}$ between embeddings $z_1 = e(x_1)$ and $z_2 = e(x_2)$ of images $x_1, x_2 \in \mathcal{X}$ reflects the semantic relation between them. The embedding space $\mathcal{E}$ is chosen to be the M-dimensional unit hypersphere $\mathcal{E} = \mathcal{S}^{M-1}$, i.e. $\|z\| = 1$. While an euclidean $\mathcal{E}$ might appear more natural, recent works in DML [26, 51, 52, 67, 70] and other contrastive learning domains like self-supervised learning [5, 8, 18, 66] have seen significant benefits in a directional treatment through normalization of embeddings to the unit hypersphere. This can in parts be attributed to better scaling with increased embedding dimensions [68] and semantic information being mostly directionally encoded [48]. To learn the respective embedding space $\mathcal{E}$, DML commonly employs ranking objectives over sample tuples. Based on the class assignments for each sample, an embedding network is tasked to minimize distances between same-class samples while maximizing them when classes differ. More recently, proxy-based approaches [26,40,47,63] directly model the class assignments by introducing class representatives during training – the proxies $p \in \mathcal{S}^{M-1}$. These are contrasted against the sample embeddings $e(x) = z$ using a NCA-like [14] formulation (ProxyNCA, [40]), which was slightly modified by [63] as a softmax-loss

$$\mathcal{L}_{\text{NCA++}} = \log \frac{\exp(-d(\text{p}^*, z)/t)}{\sum_{c=1}^{C} \exp(-d(\text{p}_c, z)/t)}. \tag{1}$$

Here, p^* denotes the ground-truth proxy associated with z, t a temperature, and d a distance metric, most commonly the negative cosine similarity $d = -s$ with $s(p_c, z) = (p_c z)/(\|p_c\|\|z\|)$. This implies a problematic assumption: Since only angles between samples and proxies are leveraged, class-specific distribution variances around each proxy cannot be accounted for. Second, the deterministic underlying network e induces a Dirac delta distribution over sample representations [59]. This treats all the input data the same regardless of the level of ambiguity, not accounting for sample-specific uncertainties.

Therefore, we suggest to represent samples and proxies as random variables Z and P with densities ζ and ρ on $\mathcal{S}^{M-1}$, which allows both samples and proxies to carry uncertainty context to address sample ambiguity while encouraging to account for more complex class distributions. This converts the above loss to

$$\mathcal{L} = \log \frac{\exp(-d(\rho^*, \zeta)/t)}{\sum_{c=1}^{C} \exp(-d(\rho_c, \zeta)/t)}. \tag{2}$$

Below in Sect. 3.2, we discuss how precisely ρ and ζ are parametrized, and in Sect. 3.3, we find a $d(\cdot, \cdot)$ suitable for distribution-to-distribution matching .

3.2   Probabilistic Sample and Proxy Representations

Sample Representations. A common distribution on $\mathcal{S}^{M-1}$ is the von Mises-Fisher (vMF) distribution [13,35,79]. It parametrizes the sample distribution ζ by a direction vector $\mu_z \in \mathcal{S}^{M-1}$ that points towards the mode of the distribution and a concentration parameter $\kappa_z \in \mathbb{R}_{\geq 0}$ that controls the spread around the mode, where a higher κ_z yields a sharper distribution. The density ζ of a vMF-distributed sample $Z \sim \text{vMF}(\mu_z, \kappa_z)$ at a point $\tilde{z} \in \mathcal{S}^{M-1}$ is

$$\zeta(\tilde{z}) = C_M(\kappa_z) \exp\left(\kappa_z \, s(\tilde{z}, \mu_z)\right). \tag{3}$$

C_M is the normalizing function which we approximate in high-dimensions (see Supp. ??). The advantage of the vMF is a duality to the un-normalized image embeddings $z = e(x) \in \mathbb{R}^M$: The natural parameter of the vMF is $\nu_z = \kappa_z \mu_z \in \mathbb{R}^M$, such that if we set $\mu_z = \frac{z}{\|z\|}$ and $\kappa_z = \|z\|$, the embedding norm gives the vMF concentration without needing to explicitly predict it (as necessary for normal distribution [7,58]). This is further motivated by recent findings indicating that CNNs encode the amount of visible class discriminative features in the norm of the embedding (e.g. [57]). We validate this assumption in Sect. 4.4.

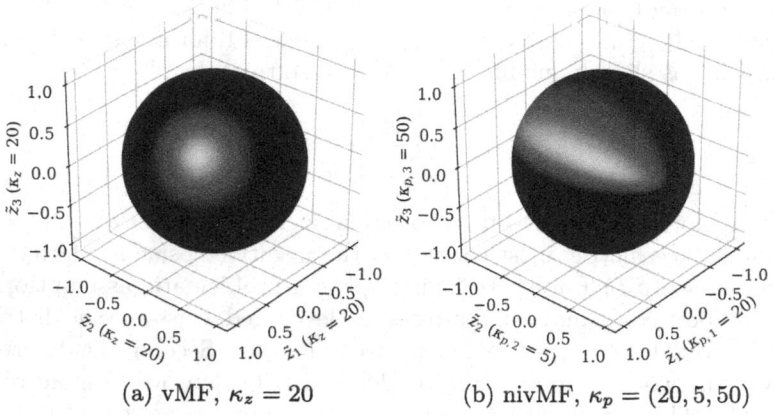

(a) vMF, $\kappa_z = 20$ (b) nivMF, $\kappa_p = (20, 5, 50)$

Fig. 2. Densities of (a) vMF and (b) non-isotropic vMF distributions on $\mathcal{S}^2$. The density is proportional to the color gradient from violet (zero) to yellow (high).

Proxy Representations. It is possible to analogously treat the proxy distributions ρ as vMF distributions with parameters $\nu_\rho = \kappa_\rho \mu_\rho$. However, a limiting factor owed to the simplicity of the vMF is its isotropy: The vMF is equivariant in all directions as shown in Fig. 2a. Proxies, however, need to account for more complex class distributions, i.e., non-isotropic ones (c.f. Figure 2b). Generalized families of vMF distributions, such as Fisher-Bingham or Kent distributions [24,35,36], are able to capture non-isotropy. However, they use covariance matrices with a quadratic number of parameters and constraints on their eigenvectors. This complicates their training via gradient descent, especially in high dimensions. Hence, we propose a low-parameter vMF extension called non-isotropic von Mises-Fisher distribution (nivMF). Just like the vMF, the M-dimensional nivMF of a proxy p is parametrized by a direction $\mu_p \in \mathcal{S}^{M-1}$, but its concentration is described by a concentration *matrix* $K_p \in \mathbb{R}^{(M \times M)}$. To reduce its parameters, we assume $K_p = \text{diag}(\kappa_p) = \text{diag}(\kappa_{p,1}, \dots, \kappa_{p,M})$ to be a diagonal matrix where $\kappa_{p,m} > 0, m = 1, \dots, M$, gives the concentration per dimension. They are treated as learnable parameters (see Supp.??). Then, we define the density ρ of a nivMF distributed proxy $P \sim \text{nivMF}(\mu_p, K_p)$ at a point $\tilde{z} \in \mathcal{S}^{M-1}$ as

$$\rho = f_P(\tilde{z}) := C_M(\|K_p\mu_p\|) \, D(K_p) \exp\left(\|K_p\mu_p\| \, s(K_p\tilde{z}, K_p\mu_p)\right). \tag{4}$$

with vMF normalizer C_M, and D approximating an additional normalizing constant (see Supp. ??). Intuitively, the nivMF is obtained from a vMF by a change-of-variable transformation: The unit sphere is stretched into an ellipsoid with axis lengths $\kappa_m, m = 1, \ldots, M$, before the angle to the mode μ_p is measured. Thus, distances of $\tilde{z}$ to μ_p along dimensions with high concentrations are emphasized and distances along dimensions with low concentrations are weighted less. In effect, the M-dim K_p is projected onto the $(M-1)$-dim tangential plane of μ_p and controls the density's spherical shape (see Fig. 2b). The remaining concentration projected on the μ_p-axis, i.e., $\|K_p\mu_p\|$, controls the density's peakedness, analogously to the κ parameter from a standard vMF. Thus, when $K_p = cI_M$ is the identity matrix scaled by some $c > 0$, the nivMF simplifies to a vMF (up to a constant due to an approximation, see Supp. ??).

3.3 Comparing Distributions Instead of Points

As proxies and images are no longer modeled as points but as distributions, we present several distribution-to-distribution metrics (in the sense of distance functions d in DML – formally, they are no metrics as they don't fulfill the triangle inequality) and contrast them to traditional distribution-to-point metrics.

Distribution-to-Distribution Metrics. Probability product kernels (PPK) [22] are a family of metrics to compare two distributions ρ and ζ by the product of their densities. One member of this family is the expected likelihood kernel (or mutual likelihood score [58]). Although there is no analytical solution for nivMFs, we can derive a Monte-Carlo approximation

$$d_{\text{EL-nivMF}}(\rho, \zeta) := -\log\left(\int_{\mathcal{E}} \rho(a)d\zeta(a)\right) \approx -\log\left(\frac{1}{N}\sum_{\substack{i=1,\ldots,N \\ z_i \sim \zeta}} \rho(z_i)\right), \quad (5)$$

where N is the number of samples. Similar to [57], we empirically found that a low number of samples ($N = 5$) is sufficient. We use [8] to sample from ζ.

The expected likelihood kernel is advantageous since it is easily Monte-Carlo approximated, but there are other distribution-to-distribution metrics we would like to survey. Hence, we derive them under a vMF assumption for ρ, where they have analytical solutions (see Supp. ??). Namely, these are an analogous expected likelihood kernel $d_{\text{EL-vMF}}$, a related PPK kernel $d_{\text{B-vMF}}$, and a Kullback-Leibler distance $d_{\text{KL-vMF}}$. All three implicitly use the norm of the image embeddings in their calculations to respect the ambiguity, but differ in performance (see Sect. 4.3).

Distribution-to-point Metrics. Classical metrics like the cosine distance of the loss in Eq. 1 implicitly assume a distribution for each proxy and evaluate its log-likelihood at each sample. Hence, we will refer to them as distribution-to-point metrics. E.g., the cosine metric used in Eq. 1 is equivalent to the log-likelihood of the normalized sample embedding under vMF-distributed proxies with equal concentration values [17], i.e., $d_{\text{Cos}}(\rho, \zeta) := -s(\mu_p, \mu_z) =$

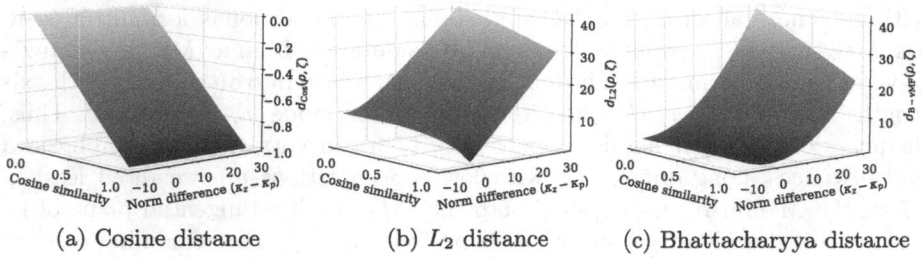

(a) Cosine distance   (b) L_2 distance   (c) Bhattacharyya distance

Fig. 3. Distances of a sample embedding to a vMF-distributed proxy with norm $\kappa_p = 10$. (a) and (b) treat the sample as a point and (c) as a vMF distribution.

$-\log(\rho(\mu_z))$. Another common example is the L2-distance $d_{\mathrm{L2}}(\rho, \zeta) := (\nu_p - \nu_z)^2 = -\log(\rho(\nu_z))$ which is obtained by an equivariance normal distribution assumption for ρ. We analogously define $d_{\mathrm{nivMF}}(\rho, \zeta) := -\log(\rho(\mu_z))$ under a nivMF assumption for ρ to benchmark it against the $d_{\mathrm{EL\text{-}nivMF}}$ distance.

3.4   Probabilistic Proxy-based Deep Metric Learning

Utilizing distributional proxies ρ, distributional sample presentations ζ and the Monte-Carlo approximated Expected Likelihood Kernel $d_{\mathrm{EL\text{-}nivMF}}(\rho, \zeta)$ we can fill in Eq. 2 and define the probabilistic extension to proxy-based DML, precisely of the basic ProxyNCA ([63]), as

$$\mathcal{L}_{\mathrm{NCA++}}^{\mathrm{EL\text{-}nivMF}} = \log \frac{\exp(-d_{\mathrm{EL\text{-}nivMF}}(\rho^*, \zeta)/t)}{\sum_{c=1}^{C} \exp(-d_{\mathrm{EL\text{-}nivMF}}(\rho_c, \zeta)/t)}. \tag{6}$$

While this can be used as standalone loss, it can also probabilistically enhance other proxy-based objectives $\mathcal{L}_{\mathrm{Proxy\text{-}DML}}$, such as ProxyAnchor [26]. For easy usage in practice, we thus also propose using it as a regularizer via

$$\mathcal{L}_{\mathrm{joint}}^{\mathrm{NCA++}} = \mathcal{L}_{\mathrm{NCA++}}^{\mathrm{EL\text{-}nivMF}}(\rho, \zeta) + \omega \cdot \mathcal{L}_{\mathrm{Proxy\text{-}DML}}(\mu_\rho, \mu_\zeta) \tag{7}$$

with regularization scale ω. Crucially, μ_ρ and μ_ζ of the proxy and sample distributions are shared parameters with the non-probabilistic objective's proxies. This ensures alignment between the two learned representations spaces. The scaling ω balances the orthogonal benefits of the two approaches: An increasing ω highlights the non-probabilistic objective that encourages a better global alignment of distribution modes, and a decreasing ω yields a continuously more distributional treatment. For the remainder of this work, we use **EL-nivMF** for the standalone probabilistic extension of ProxyNCA (Eq. 6), and $PANC+$**EL-nivMF** for the probabilistically regularized ProxyAnchor (Eq. 7).

3.5   How Uncertainty-awareness Impacts Training

Before the experimental evaluation, we provide an insight into *how* incorporating uncertainty into the training benefits it. For this, we take a closer look at the norms of sample embeddings that, by duality, yield the concentration κ_z of ζ.

Uncertainty as Sample-wise Temperature. Fig. 3 displays two distribution-to-point and one distribution-to-distribution metric with regard to the difference in norms and directions. We use the isotropic $d_{\text{B-vMF}}$ as a representative for distribution-to-distribution metrics since it has an analytical solution. While d_{Cos} ignores the difference in norms, d_{L2} and the similar, yet smoother, $d_{\text{B-vMF}}$ incorporate it as an sample-wise temperature: The larger the norm of the sample gets, the steeper the metrics rise with increasing cosine distance. Thus, when comparing a sample to several proxies of roughly the same norm, their distances to the sample will be more uniform when the sample embedding norm is low and become more contrasted when it is high. In other words, ambiguous images produce more similar logits across all proxies and thus flatter class posterior distributions whereas highly certain images produce sharp posteriors.

Uncertainty as Gradients Scale. κ_z has another influence on the training: Differentiating the losses $\mathcal{L}^{\text{Cos}}_{NCA++}$ and $\mathcal{L}^{\text{L2}}_{NCA++}$, obtained when using the norm-agnostic d_{Cos} or the norm-aware d_{L2} as distance functions in Eq. 1, w.r.t. the cosine similarity between μ_z and μ_p (as in [26]) reveals (see Supp. ??)

$$\frac{\delta \mathcal{L}^{\text{Cos}}_{NCA++}}{\delta \cos(\mu_p, \mu_z)} = \begin{cases} \frac{1}{t}\left(-1 + \frac{\exp(-d_{\text{Cos}}(\rho^*,\varsigma)/t)}{\sum_{c=1}^{C}\exp(-d_{\text{Cos}}(\rho_c,\varsigma)/t)}\right) & \text{if } p = p^* \\ \frac{1}{t}\frac{\exp(-d_{\text{Cos}}(\rho^*,\varsigma)/t)}{\sum_{c=1}^{C}\exp(-d_{\text{Cos}}(\rho_c,\varsigma)/t)} & \text{else} \end{cases} \tag{8}$$

$$\frac{\delta \mathcal{L}^{\text{L2}}_{NCA++}}{\delta \cos(\mu_p, \mu_z)} = \begin{cases} \frac{2\kappa_p\kappa_z}{t}\left(-1 + \frac{\exp(-d_{\text{L2}}(\rho^*,\varsigma)/t)}{\sum_{c=1}^{C}\exp(-d_{\text{L2}}(\rho_c,\varsigma)/t)}\right) & \text{if } p = p^* \\ \frac{2\kappa_p\kappa_z}{t}\frac{\exp(-d_{\text{L2}}(\rho^*,\varsigma)/t)}{\sum_{c=1}^{C}\exp(-d_{\text{L2}}(\rho_c,\varsigma)/t)} & \text{else} \end{cases}, \tag{9}$$

where p^* denotes the ground-truth class. Besides the sample-wise temperature in d_{L2}, the gradients differ in that the gradient of $\mathcal{L}^{\text{L2}}_{NCA++}$ scales proportionally to κ_z. This means that in batch-wise gradient descent, samples with a high embedding norm are pulled towards ground-truth proxies and pushed away from others stronger than samples with low norm. In other words, the impact of an image on the structuring process of the embedding space depends on its ambiguity. This holds similarly for the distribution-to-distribution metrics, but is harder to derive than for d_{L2}. This analysis unveils that using the Euclidean d_{L2} distance is adequate during training albeit switching to the hyperspherical d_{Cos} at retrieval-time, as it can be seen as a simple approximation to the uncertainty-aware training of hyperspherical distribution-to-distribution metrics.

4   Experiments

We now detail the experiments (Sect. 4.1) that benchmark our method (Sect. 4.2), before surveying different distr.-to-distr. metrics (Sect. 4.3) and the role of the norm (Sect. 4.4).

4.1   Experimental Details

Implementations. All experiments use PyTorch [46]. We follow standard DML protocols by leveraging ImageNet-pretrained ResNet50 [19] and Inception-V1 networks with Batch-Normalization [62] as encoders. Their weights are taken from torchvision [34] and timm [69]. To further ensure standardized training, we built upon the code and standardized DML protocols proposed in [52], using the Adam optimizer [28], a learning rate of 10^{-5} and weight decay of $4 \cdot 10^{-3}$. In the more open state-of-the-art comparison (Table 2), we additionally use step-wise learning rate scheduling. To ensure comparability and access to fast similarity search methods, all test-time retrieval uses cosine distances. To sample from vMF-distributions, we make use of [8] and respective implementations. Further details on our method and hyperparameters are provided in Supp. ??. All experiments were run on NVIDIA 2080Ti GPUs with 12GB VRAM.

Datasets. We benchmark on three standard datasets: CUB200-2011 [64] (has a 100/100 split of train and test bird classes with 11,788 images in total), CARS196 [30] (contains a 98/98 split of car classes and 16,185 images), and Stanford Online Products (SOP) [42] (covers 22,634 product categories and 120,053 images).

Table 1. We re-run various strong benchmarks in the *standardized comparison* setting of [52]. We find strong improvements both when enhancing simple ProxyNCA towards probabilistic DML (**EL-nivMF**) and when using our approach as a regularizer on top of more versatile approaches (*PANC* + **EL-nivMF**).

BENCHMARKS→	CUB200-2011		CARS196		SOP	
APPROACHES ↓	R@1	mAP@1000	R@1	mAP@1000	R@1	mAP@1000
Sample-based Baselines.						
Margin [70]	62.9 ± 0.4	32.7 ± 0.3	80.1 ± 0.2	32.7 ± 0.4	78.4 ± 0.1	46.8 ± 0.1
Multisimilarity [67]	62.8 ± 0.2	31.1 ± 0.3	81.6 ± 0.3	31.7 ± 0.1	76.0 ± 0.1	43.3 ± 0.1
Standard versus Probabilistic.						
ProxyNCA [40,63]	63.2 ± 0.2	33.4 ± 0.1	78.8 ± 0.2	31.9 ± 0.2	76.2 ± 0.1	43.0 ± 0.1
EL-nivMF	64.8 ± 0.4	34.3 ± 0.3	82.1 ± 0.3	33.4 ± 0.2	76.6 ± 0.2	43.3 ± 0.1
Probabilistic DML as Regularization.						
ProxyAnchor (*PANC*, [26])	64.4 ± 0.3	33.2 ± 0.3	82.4 ± 0.4	34.2 ± 0.3	78.0 ± 0.1	45.5 ± 0.1
PANC + **EL-nivMF**	66.5 ± 0.3	35.3 ± 0.1	83.6 ± 0.2	35.1 ± 0.1	78.2 ± 0.1	45.6 ± 0.1

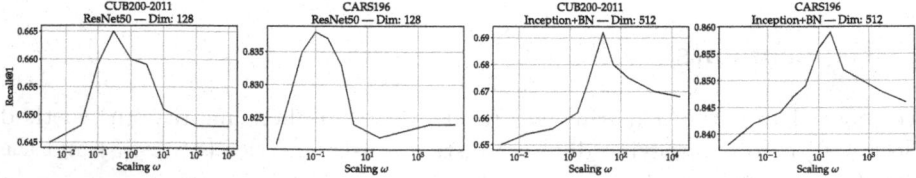

Fig. 4. *Probabilistic regularization as a function of the scaling factor* ω. We find a notable benefit when accounting for both orthogonal enhancements, i.e., the more probabilistic treatment (*decreasing* ω) and the better global alignment of the proxy distribution modes (*increasing* ω).

4.2 Quantitative Evaluation of Probabilistic Proxy-Based DML

Standardized Comparison. We first follow protocols proposed in [52], which suggest comparisons under equal pipeline and implementation settings (and no learning rate scheduling) to determine the true benefits of a proposed method, unbiased by external covariates. Particularily, we thus compare the standard ProxyNCA (see Eq. 1) against our proposed **EL-nivMF** extension of ProxyNCA that includes sample and proxy distributions with distribution-to-distribution metrics during training. We further apply **EL-nivMF** as a probabilistic regularizer on top of the strong, but hyperparameter-heavy ProxyAnchor objective. Here, we only optimize the scaling ω. Finally, we rerun the two strongest sample-based methods used in [52]. In all cases, Table 1 shows significant improvements in performance and outperforms the sample-based methods. First, converting from standard to probabilistic proxy-based DML (ProxyNCA $\rightarrow$ **EL-nivMF**) increases R@1 on CUB200-2011 by 1.6pp, 3.3pp on Cars196 and 0.4pp on SOP. This highlights the benefits of accounting for uncertainty and explicitly encouraging non-isotropic intra-class variance. However, due to the large number of proxies and low number of samples per class, on SOP benefits are limited when compared to datasets such as CUB200-2011 and CARS196, as the estimation of our proxy distributions becomes noticeably noisier. When using **EL-nivMF** as probabilistic regularization, we find boosts of over 2.1pp and 1.2pp on CUB200-2011 and CARS196, respectively, with expected smaller improvements of 0.2pp on SOP. Generally however, the consistent improvements, whether as a standalone objective or as a regularization method, highlight the versatility of a probabilistic take on DML, and offer a strong proof-of-concept for future DML research to built upon.

Impact of Different Scaling Factors. ω. Figure 4 showcases the generalization performance as a function of the scaling weight ω (see Eq. 7). Higher ω denotes a more non-probabilistic treatment to the point of ignoring the distributional aspects and returning to the auxiliary ProxyAnchor loss [26]. Lower ω indicates a higher emphasis on distributional treatment of proxies (and samples). Across benchmarks and backbones, the best performance is reached with an ω that is neither high nor 0. Thus, the results highlight that our probabilistic proxy-based DML helps the better global realignment of each proxy distribution mode via ProxyAnchor, and vice-versa. Overall, R@1 increases up to 4pp at the most suitable scaling choice. This optimum is reached robustly in a large area around the peak (note the logarithmic x-axes).

Comparison Against SOTA. After these strictly standardized comparisons, we now compare the combination of ProxyAnchor and **EL-nivMF**, which performed best in the previous study to the larger DML literature. The hyperparameters and pipeline components (e.g., learning rate, weight decay) differ between the approaches, and so the comparison should be taken with a grain of salt [41,52,57], but we still separate by the backbones and embedding dimensionalities, which are identified as the largest factors of variation [52]. Accounting

Table 2. *Comparison to Literature*, separated by backbones and embedding dimensions. **Bold** denotes best results for a respective Backbone/Dim. subset, **bold** the overall best. Results show that our probabilistically regularized ProxyAnchor method matches or beats previous, in parts notably more complex state-of-the-art methods.

BENCHMARKS →			CUB200 [64]			CARS196 [30]			SOP [42]		
METHODS ↓	Venue	Arch/Dim.	R@1	R@2	NMI	R@1	R@2	NMI	R@1	R@10	NMI
Margin [70]	ICCV '17	R50/128	63.6	74.4	69.0	79.6	86.5	69.1	72.7	86.2	**90.7**
Div&Conq [55]	CVPR '19	R50/128	65.9	76.6	69.6	**84.6**	**90.7**	**70.3**	75.9	88.4	90.2
MIC [49]	ICCV '19	R50/128	66.1	76.8	69.7	82.6	89.1	68.4	77.2	89.4	90.0
PADS [50]	CVPR '20	R50/128	**67.3**	**78.0**	69.9	83.5	89.7	68.8	76.5	89.0	89.9
RankMI [23]	CVPR '20	R50/128	66.7	77.2	**71.3**	83.3	89.8	69.4	74.3	87.9	90.5
PANC + EL-niVMF	-	R50/128	67.0	77.6	70.0	84.0	90.0	69.5	**78.6**	**90.5**	90.1
NormSoft [73]	BMVC '19	R50/512	61.3	73.9	–	84.2	90.4	–	78.2	90.6	–
EPSHN [72]	WACV '20	R50/512	64.9	75.3	–	82.7	89.3	–	78.3	90.7	–
Circle [61]	CVPR '20	R50/512	66.7	77.2	–	83.4	89.7	-	78.3	90.5	–
DiVA [37]	ECCV '20	R50/512	69.2	79.3	71.4	**87.6**	**92.9**	72.2	79.6	**91.2**	90.6
DCML-MDW [76]	CVPR '21	R50/512	68.4	77.9	71.8	85.2	91.8	**73.9**	**79.8**	90.8	**90.8**
PANC + EL-niVMF	–	R50/512	**69.3**	**79.3**	**72.1**	86.2	91.9	70.3	79.4	90.7	90.6
Group [12]	ECCV '20	IBN/512	65.5	77.0	69.0	85.6	91.2	**72.7**	75.1	87.5	**90.8**
DR-MS [11]	TAI '20	IBN/512	66.1	77.0	–	85.0	90.5	–	–	–	–
ProxyGML [78]	NeurIPS '20	IBN/512	66.6	77.6	69.8	85.5	91.8	72.4	78.0	90.6	90.2
DRML [77]	ICCV '21	IBN/512	68.7	78.6	69.3	**86.9**	**92.1**	72.1	71.5	85.2	88.1
PANC + MemVir [29]	ICCV '21	IBN/512	69.0	79.2	-	86.7	92.0	–	**79.7**	**91.0**	-
PANC + EL-niVMF	-	IBN/512	**69.5**	**80.0**	**71.0**	86.4	92.0	71.3	79.2	90.4	90.2

for that, we find competitive performance on all benchmarks (c.f. Table 2), even when compared against other, much more complex state-of-the-art methods relying on multitask learning (DiVA [37], MIC [49]) or reinforcement learning (PADS [50]). This makes our probabilistic take on proxy-based DML a generally attractive approach to DML, with further potential improvements down the line by implementing the probabilistic perspective into these orthogonal extensions.

Computational Overhead. We do note that training with **EL-nivMF** requires the differentiable drawing of samples from vMF-distributions (see Eq. 5 and [8]). This can increase the overall training time, but we found 2–5 samples to already be suitable, limiting the impact on overall walltime to $< 25\%$ against pure ProxyNCA. This is in line with other extensions of ProxyNCA (s.a. [21,37,49,50,55]). The retrieval walltime remains unaffected as cosine-similarity is deployed. As an alternative for rapid training, we provide further probabilistic distribution-to-distribution distances ($d_{\text{EL-vMF}}$, $d_{\text{B-vMF}}$, $d_{\text{KL-vMF}}$) along with analytical solutions (Supp. ??), so that no sampling is required and computational overhead is negligible. We study them in the next section.

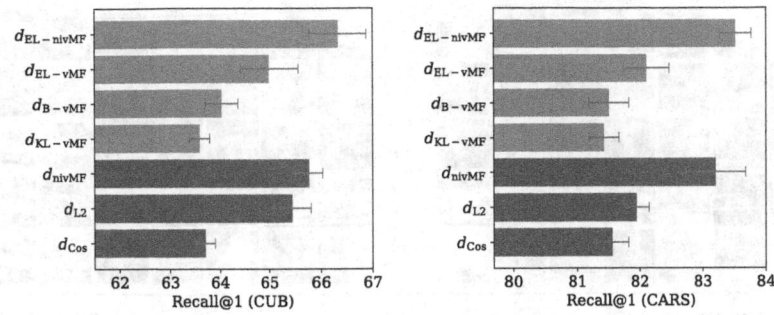

Fig. 5. Distance-to-point (blue) vs. distance-to-distance (green) metrics on CUB and CARS. Bars show average R@1 with standard deviation. (Color figure online)

4.3   Quantitative Comparison of Metrics

Sects. 3.3 and 3.2 provided numerous modeling choices for distributions and distance metrics that can be plugged into the probabilistic DML framework in Eq. 2. This section investigates these possibilities, ultimately motivating the particular choice of $d_{\text{EL-nivMF}}$, and also compares to more traditional distribution-to-point metrics. To ensure fair comparisons, we return to the standardized benchmark protocol of [52] using a 512-dimensional ResNet-50. All hyperparameters are fixed, except for the initial proxy norm and temperature, which are tuned via grid search on a validation set.

Figure 5 shows the R@1 of all three distribution-to-point and four distribution-to-distribution metrics on CUB and CARS. Comparing the distribution-to-point metrics, d_{L2} outperforms d_{Cos} on both datasets, but is dominated by d_{nivMF}. The non-isotropic approach also performs best within the distribution-to-distribution metrics. Within the three isotropic distribution-to-distribution metrics, $d_{\text{KL-vMF}}$ shows the worst performance, with a small gap to the Bhattacharyya and a larger gap to the expected likelihood PPKs. This stands in line with preliminary findings of [7]. The latter performs within one standard deviation of d_{L2}. Altogether, we find that adding non-isotropy to the standard d_{Cos} (i.e., using d_{nivMF}) increases the R@1 by $2.1pp$ on CUB and $1.7pp$ on CARS. Further considering the image norm (i.e., $d_{\text{EL-nivMF}}$) adds another $0.6pp$ on CUB and $0.3pp$ on CARS.

The enhancement by non-isotropic modeling can be seen as inductive bias towards better resolution of intra-class variances and substructures (see Supp. ??), which drives generalization performance [32,37,52,72,77]. The strong performance of d_{L2} is surprising as many current approaches use a d_{Cos}-based loss [9,26,63]. The crux is that d_{L2} in our setting still uses the cosine distance at retrieval-time, similar to, e.g., [2]. Using d_{L2} also as the retrieval metric would reduce the R@1 by up to $-5.34pp$ across all metrics and datasets, with the highest reduction appearing on the d_{L2}-trained model itself (see Supp. ??). This supports the usage of the norm only during training, discussed in Sect. 3.5, where d_{L2} shares the uncertainty-awareness of distribution-to-distribution metrics, explaining the small gap between d_{L2} and $d_{\text{EL-vMF}}$. Thus, ultimately, we conjecture

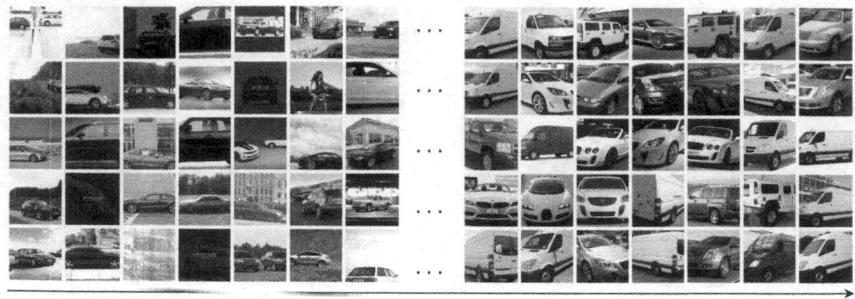

lowest norm   highest norm

Fig. 6. CARS train images with lowest (left) to highest (right) embedding norms.

that it doesn't matter whether an approach is motivated from a distribution-to-distribution or distribution-to-point perspective, as long as it considers the ambiguity of images (and proxies) during training.

4.4 Embedding Norms Encode Uncertainty

In the previous section, we found that considering the norms of embeddings during training leads to a higher performance. In this section, we qualitatively support that the learned norms actually correspond to a sample-wise ambiguity.

For this, we study the **EL-nivMF** model on CARS. Figure 6 shows the images with the lowest and highest embedding norm in the training set. In many samples with low norm, characteristic parts of the cars are cropped out by the data augmentation (this also happens in the test set, hindering perfect accuracy). Others are overlaid or portray multiple distracting objects. In high-norm images, illumination and camera angle facilitate the detection of class-discriminative features. A competing hypothesis could be that high-norm images comprise mostly car classes with more distinctive designs. However, the differences between low and high norm images also hold within classes, see Supp. ?? and ??. These findings are in line with [31,48,57] and support the hypothesis that the image norm indicates image certainties, motivated by being the sum of visible class-discriminative parts [57]. This justifies the $\kappa_z = \|z\|$ duality underlying the vMF assumption and is consistent with our analysis of uncertainty-aware training in Sect. 3.5.

5   Conclusion

This work proposes non-isotropic probabilistic proxy-based deep metric learning (DML) through uncertainty-aware training and non-isotropic proxy-distributions. Uncertainty-aware training is achieved by treating sample embeddings not as deterministic points but as directional distributions parametrized by embedding directions and, beyond popular DML approaches, norms. This allows semantic ambiguities to be decoupled from the directional semantic context, which mathematically manifests itself in sample-wise temperature scaling and certainty-weighed gradients. Additionally, our non-isotropic von Mises-Fisher distribution for proxies better models intra-class uncertainty, which introduces a low-parameter inductive prior for better generalizing embedding spaces. We support our approach through various ablation studies, which showcase that our proposed framework can operate both as a standalone objective and a probabilistic regularizer on top of existing proxy-based objectives. In both cases, we further found strong performances on the standard DML benchmarks, in parts matching or beating existing state-of-the-art methods. Our findings strongly indicate that a probabilistic treatment of proxy-based DML offers simple, orthogonal enhancements to existing DML methods and enables better generalization.

Limitations. We find that for applications with only few samples per class, the ability to estimate the non-isotropic proxy densities is limited (c.f. performance on SOP). For future work in such sparse settings, returning to the proposed isotropic distribution-to-distribution metrics or introducing across-class priors for the covariance matrices might serve as alternatives.

Acknowledgements. This work has been partially funded by the ERC (853489 - DEXIM) and DFG (2064/1 - Project number 390727645) under Germany's Excellence Strategy. Michael Kirchhof and Karsten Roth thank the International Max Planck Research School for Intelligent Systems (IMPRS-IS) for support. Karsten Roth further acknowledges his membership in the European Laboratory for Learning and Intelligent Systems (ELLIS) PhD program.

References

1. Bouchacourt, D., Tomioka, R., Nowozin, S.: Multi-level variational autoencoder: Learning disentangled representations from grouped observations. In: Thirty-Second AAAI Conference on Artificial Intelligence (AAAI) (2018)
2. Boudiaf, M., et al.: A unifying mutual information view of metric learning: cross-entropy vs. pairwise losses. In: Vedaldi, A., Bischof, H., Brox, T., Frahm, J.-M. (eds.) ECCV 2020. LNCS, vol. 12351, pp. 548–564. Springer, Cham (2020). https://doi.org/10.1007/978-3-030-58539-6_33
3. Brattoli, B., Tighe, J., Zhdanov, F., Perona, P., Chalupka, K.: Rethinking zero-shot video classification: End-to-end training for realistic applications. In: Proceedings of the IEEE/CVF Conference on Computer Vision and Pattern Recognition (CVPR) (2020)
4. Chen, S., Luo, L., Yang, J., Gong, C., Li, J., Huang, H.: Curvilinear distance metric learning. In: Advances in Neural Information Processing Systems 32, pp. 4223–4232. Curran Associates, Inc. (2019). https://papers.nips.cc/paper/8675-curvilinear-distance-metric-learning.pdf
5. Chen, T., Kornblith, S., Norouzi, M., Hinton, G.: A simple framework for contrastive learning of visual representations. In: Proceedings of the 37th International Conference on Machine Learning (ICML) (2020)

6. Chen, W., Chen, X., Zhang, J., Huang, K.: Beyond triplet loss: a deep quadruplet network for person re-identification. In: Proceedings of the IEEE Conference on Computer Vision and Pattern Recognition (CVPR) (2017)
7. Chun, S., Oh, S.J., De Rezende, R.S., Kalantidis, Y., Larlus, D.: Probabilistic embeddings for cross-modal retrieval. In: Proceedings of the IEEE/CVF Conference on Computer Vision and Pattern Recognition (CVPR) (2021)
8. Davidson, T.R., Falorsi, L., De Cao, N., Kipf, T., Tomczak, J.M.: Hyperspherical variational auto-encoders. In: 34th Conference on Uncertainty in Artificial Intelligence (UAI) (2018)
9. Deng, J., Guo, J., Xue, N., Zafeiriou, S.: ArcFace: Additive angular margin loss for deep face recognition. In: Proceedings of the IEEE/CVF Conference on Computer Vision and Pattern Recognition (CVPR) (2019)
10. Duan, Y., Zheng, W., Lin, X., Lu, J., Zhou, J.: Deep adversarial metric learning. In: Proceedings of the IEEE/CVF Conference on Computer Vision and Pattern Recognition (CVPR) (2018)
11. Dutta, U.K., Harandi, M., Sekhar, C.C.: Unsupervised deep metric learning via orthogonality based probabilistic loss. IEEE Trans.actions Artif. Intell. **1**(1), 74–84 (2020)
12. Elezi, I., Vascon, S., Torcinovich, A., Pelillo, M., Leal-Taixé, L.: The group loss for deep metric learning. In: Vedaldi, A., Bischof, H., Brox, T., Frahm, J.-M. (eds.) ECCV 2020. LNCS, vol. 12352, pp. 277–294. Springer, Cham (2020). https://doi.org/10.1007/978-3-030-58571-6_17
13. Fisher, R.A.: Dispersion on a sphere. Proc. Royal Society London. Series A. Math. Phys. Sci. **217** 295–305 (1953)
14. Goldberger, J., Hinton, G.E., Roweis, S., Salakhutdinov, R.R.: Neighbourhood components analysis. In: Advances in Neural Information Processing Systems (NeurIPS) (2004)
15. Hadsell, R., Chopra, S., LeCun, Y.: Dimensionality reduction by learning an invariant mapping. In: Proceedings of the IEEE Conference on Computer Vision and Pattern Recognition (2006)
16. Harwood, B., Kumar, B., Carneiro, G., Reid, I., Drummond, T., et al.: Smart mining for deep metric learning. In: Proceedings of the IEEE International Conference on Computer Vision (ICCV) (2017)
17. Hasnat, M.A., Bohné, J., Milgram, J., Gentric, S., Chen, L.: von Mises-Fisher mixture model-based deep learning: Application to face verification. arXiv preprint arXiv:1706.04264 (2017)
18. He, K., Fan, H., Wu, Y., Xie, S., Girshick, R.: Momentum contrast for unsupervised visual representation learning. In: Proceedings of the IEEE/CVF Conference on Computer Vision and Pattern Recognition (CVPR) (2020)
19. He, K., Zhang, X., Ren, S., Sun, J.: Deep residual learning for image recognition. In: Proceedings of the IEEE Conference on Computer Vision and Pattern Recognition (CVPR) (2016)
20. Hu, J., Lu, J., Tan, Y.: Discriminative deep metric learning for face verification in the wild. In: Proceedings of the IEEE Conference on Computer Vision and Pattern Recognition (CVPR) (2014)
21. Jacob, P., Picard, D., Histace, A., Klein, E.: Metric learning with horde: High-order regularizer for deep embeddings. In: The IEEE Conference on Computer Vision and Pattern Recognition (CVPR) (2019)
22. Jebara, T., Kondor, R.: Bhattacharyya and expected likelihood kernels. In: Learning Theory and Kernel Machines (2003)

23. Kemertas, M., Pishdad, L., Derpanis, K.G., Fazly, A.: RankMI: A mutual information maximizing ranking loss. In: Proceedings of the IEEE/CVF Conference on Computer Vision and Pattern Recognition (CVPR) (2020)
24. Kent, J.T.: The Fisher-Bingham distribution on the sphere. J. Royal Stat. Society: Series B (Methodological) **44**(1) 71–80 (1982)
25. Khosla, P., et al.: Supervised contrastive learning. Advances in Neural Information Processing Systems (NeurIPS) (2020)
26. Kim, S., Kim, D., Cho, M., Kwak, S.: Proxy anchor loss for deep metric learning. In: Proceedings of the IEEE/CVF Conference on Computer Vision and Pattern Recognition (CVPR) (2020)
27. Kim, S., Kim, D., Cho, M., Kwak, S.: Embedding transfer with label relaxation for improved metric learning. In: Proceedings of the IEEE/CVF Conference on Computer Vision and Pattern Recognition (CVPR) (2021)
28. Kingma, D.P., Ba, J.: Adam: A method for stochastic optimization. In: Bengio, Y., LeCun, Y. (eds.) 3rd International Conference on Learning Representations (ICLR) (2015)
29. Ko, B., Gu, G., Kim, H.G.: Learning with memory-based virtual classes for deep metric learning. In: Proceedings of the IEEE/CVF International Conference on Computer Vision (ICCV) (2021)
30. Krause, J., Stark, M., Deng, J., Fei-Fei, L.: 3d object representations for fine-grained categorization. In: Proceedings of the IEEE International Conference on Computer Vision Workshops (CVPR) (2013)
31. Li, S., Xu, J., Xu, X., Shen, P., Li, S., Hooi, B.: Spherical confidence learning for face recognition. In: Proceedings of the IEEE/CVF Conference on Computer Vision and Pattern Recognition (CVPR) (2021)
32. Lin, X., Duan, Y., Dong, Q., Lu, J., Zhou, J.: Deep variational metric learning. In: Proceedings of the European Conference on Computer Vision (ECCV) (2018)
33. Liu, W., Wen, Y., Yu, Z., Li, M., Raj, B., Song, L.: Sphereface: Deep hypersphere embedding for face recognition. Proceedings of the IEEE Conference on Computer Vision and Pattern Recognition (CVPR) (2017)
34. Marcel, S., Rodriguez, Y.: Torchvision the machine-vision package of torch. MM '10, Association for Computing Machinery (2010)
35. Mardia, K.V., Jupp, P.E.: Directional statistics (2009)
36. Mardia, K.V.: Statistics of directional data. J. Royal Stat. Society: Series B (Methodological) **37**(3), 349–393 (1975)
37. Milbich, T., et al.: DiVA: diverse visual feature aggregation for deep metric learning. In: Vedaldi, A., Bischof, H., Brox, T., Frahm, J.-M. (eds.) ECCV 2020. LNCS, vol. 12353, pp. 590–607. Springer, Cham (2020). https://doi.org/10.1007/978-3-030-58598-3_35
38. Milbich, T., Roth, K., Brattoli, B., Ommer, B.: Sharing matters for generalization in deep metric learning. IEEE Trans. Pattern Anal. Mach. Intell. **44**(1), 416–427 (2022). https://doi.org/10.1109/TPAMI.2020.3009620
39. Milbich, T., Roth, K., Sinha, S., Schmidt, L., Ghassemi, M., Ommer, B.: Characterizing generalization under out-of-distribution shifts in deep metric learning. In: Ranzato, M., Beygelzimer, A., Dauphin, Y., Liang, P., Vaughan, J.W. (eds.) Advances in Neural Information Processing Systems. vol. 34, pp. 25006–25018. Curran Associates, Inc. (2021), https://proceedings.neurips.cc/paper/2021/file/d1f255a373a3cef72e03aa9d980c7eca-Paper.pdf
40. Movshovitz-Attias, Y., Toshev, A., Leung, T.K., Ioffe, S., Singh, S.: No fuss distance metric learning using proxies. In: Proceedings of the IEEE International Conference on Computer Vision (ICCV) (2017)

41. Musgrave, K., Belongie, S., Lim, S.-N.: A metric learning reality check. In: Vedaldi, A., Bischof, H., Brox, T., Frahm, J.-M. (eds.) ECCV 2020. LNCS, vol. 12370, pp. 681–699. Springer, Cham (2020). https://doi.org/10.1007/978-3-030-58595-2_41

42. Oh Song, H., Xiang, Y., Jegelka, S., Savarese, S.: Deep metric learning via lifted structured feature embedding. In: Proceedings of the IEEE Conference on Computer Vision and Pattern Recognition (CVPR) (2016)

43. Opitz, M., Waltner, G., Possegger, H., Bischof, H.: Bier-boosting independent embeddings robustly. In: Proceedings of the IEEE International Conference on Computer Vision (ICCV) (2017)

44. Opitz, M., Waltner, G., Possegger, H., Bischof, H.: Deep metric learning with BIER: Boosting independent embeddings robustly. IEEE Trans. Pattern Analysis Mach. Intell. **42**(2), 276–290 (2018)

45. Park, J., Yi, S., Choi, Y., Cho, D.Y., Kim, J.: Discriminative few-shot learning based on directional statistics. arXiv preprint arXiv:1906.01819 (2019)

46. Paszke, A., et al.: Automatic differentiation in pytorch. In: NIPS Workshop on Automatic Differentiation (2017)

47. Qian, Q., Shang, L., Sun, B., Hu, J., Li, H., Jin, R.: Softtriple loss: Deep metric learning without triplet sampling. In: Proceedings of the IEEE/CVF International Conference on Computer Vision (ICCV) (2019)

48. Ranjan, R., Castillo, C.D., Chellappa, R.: L2-constrained softmax loss for discriminative face verification. arXiv preprint arXiv:1703.09507 (2017)

49. Roth, K., Brattoli, B., Ommer, B.: Mic: Mining interclass characteristics for improved metric learning. In: Proceedings of the IEEE International Conference on Computer Vision (ICCV) (2019)

50. Roth, K., Milbich, T., Ommer, B.: PADS: Policy-adapted sampling for visual similarity learning. In: Proceedings of the IEEE/CVF Conference on Computer Vision and Pattern Recognition (CVPR) (2020)

51. Roth, K., Milbich, T., Ommer, B., Cohen, J.P., Ghassemi, M.: Simultaneous similarity-based self-distillation for deep metric learning. In: Proceedings of the 38th International Conference on Machine Learning (ICML) (2021)

52. Roth, K., Milbich, T., Sinha, S., Gupta, P., Ommer, B., Cohen, J.P.: Revisiting training strategies and generalization performance in deep metric learning. In: Proceedings of the 37th International Conference on Machine Learning (ICML) (2020)

53. Roth, K., Vinyals, O., Akata, Z.: Integrating language guidance into vision-based deep metric learning. In: Proceedings of the IEEE/CVF Conference on Computer Vision and Pattern Recognition (CVPR), pp. 16177–16189 (June 2022)

54. Roth, K., Vinyals, O., Akata, Z.: Non-isotropy regularization for proxy-based deep metric learning. In: Proceedings of the IEEE/CVF Conference on Computer Vision and Pattern Recognition (CVPR), pp. 7420–7430 (2022)

55. Sanakoyeu, A., Tschernezki, V., Buchler, U., Ommer, B.: Divide and conquer the embedding space for metric learning. In: The IEEE Conference on Computer Vision and Pattern Recognition (CVPR) (2019)

56. Schroff, F., Kalenichenko, D., Philbin, J.: Facenet: A unified embedding for face recognition and clustering. In: Proceedings of the IEEE Conference on Computer Vision and Pattern Recognition (CVPR) (2015)

57. Scott, T.R., Gallagher, A.C., Mozer, M.C.: von Mises-Fisher loss: An exploration of embedding geometries for supervised learning. In: Proceedings of the IEEE/CVF International Conference on Computer Vision (ICCV) (2021)

58. Shi, Y., Jain, A.K.: Probabilistic face embeddings. In: Proceedings of the IEEE/CVF International Conference on Computer Vision (ICCV) (2019)

59. Sinha, S., et al.: Uniform priors for data-efficient learning. In: Proceedings of the IEEE/CVF Conference on Computer Vision and Pattern Recognition (CVPR) Workshops, pp. 4017–4028 (2022)
60. Sohn, K.: Improved deep metric learning with multi-class n-pair loss objective. In: Advances in Neural Information Processing Systems (NeurIPS) (2016)
61. l. Sun, Y., et al.: Circle loss: A unified perspective of pair similarity optimization. In: Proceedings of the IEEE/CVF Conference on Computer Vision and Pattern Recognition (CVPR) (2020)
62. Szegedy, C., et al.: Going deeper with convolutions. In: Computer Vision and Pattern Recognition (CVPR) (2015)
63. Teh, E.W., DeVries, T., Taylor, G.W.: ProxyNCA++: Revisiting and revitalizing proxy neighborhood component analysis. In: Proceedings of the European Conference on Computer Vision (ECCV) (2020)
64. Wah, C., Branson, S., Welinder, P., Perona, P., Belongie, S.: The Caltech-UCSD birds-200-2011 dataset. Tech. Rep. CNS-TR-2011-001, California Institute of Technology (2011)
65. Wang, J., Zhou, F., Wen, S., Liu, X., Lin, Y.: Deep metric learning with angular loss. In: Proceedings of the IEEE International Conference on Computer Vision (ICCV) (2017)
66. Wang, T., Isola, P.: Understanding contrastive representation learning through alignment and uniformity on the hypersphere. In: Proceedings of the 37th International Conference on Machine Learning (ICML) (2020)
67. Wang, X., Han, X., Huang, W., Dong, D., Scott, M.R.: Multi-similarity loss with general pair weighting for deep metric learning. In: Proceedings of the IEEE/CVF Conference on Computer Vision and Pattern Recognition (CVPR) (2019)
68. Weisstein, E.W.: Hypersphere (2002)
69. Wightman, R.: Pytorch image models. https://github.com/rwightman/pytorch-image-models (2019)
70. Wu, C.Y., Manmatha, R., Smola, A.J., Krahenbuhl, P.: Sampling matters in deep embedding learning. In: Proceedings of the IEEE International Conference on Computer Vision (ICCV) (2017)
71. Xuan, H., Stylianou, A., Pless, R.: Improved embeddings with easy positive triplet mining. In: Proceedings of the IEEE/CVF Winter Conference on Applications of Computer Vision (WACV) (March 2020)
72. Xuan, H., Stylianou, A., Pless, R.: Improved embeddings with easy positive triplet mining. In: Proceedings of the IEEE/CVF Winter Conference on Applications of Computer Vision (WACV) (March 2020)
73. Zhai, A., Wu, H.: Making classification competitive for deep metric learning. arXiv Preprint arXiv:1811.12649 (2018)
74. Zhe, X., Chen, S., Yan, H.: Directional statistics-based deep metric learning for image classification and retrieval. Pattern Recognition 93 (2018)
75. Zheng, W., Chen, Z., Lu, J., Zhou, J.: Hardness-aware deep metric learning. The IEEE Conference on Computer Vision and Pattern Recognition (CVPR) (2019)
76. Zheng, W., Wang, C., Lu, J., Zhou, J.: Deep compositional metric learning. In: Proceedings of the IEEE/CVF Conference on Computer Vision and Pattern Recognition (CVPR) (2021)
77. Zheng, W., Zhang, B., Lu, J., Zhou, J.: Deep relational metric learning. In: Proceedings of the IEEE/CVF International Conference on Computer Vision (ICCV) (2021)

78. Zhu, Y., Yang, M., Deng, C., Liu, W.: Fewer is more: A deep graph metric learning perspective using fewer proxies. In: Larochelle, H., Ranzato, M., Hadsell, R., Balcan, M.F., Lin, H. (eds.) Advances in Neural Information Processing Systems (NeurIPS) (2020)
79. Zimmermann, R.S., Sharma, Y., Schneider, S., Bethge, M., Brendel, W.: Contrastive learning inverts the data generating process. In: Proceedings of the 38th International Conference on Machine Learning (ICML) (2021)

TokenMix: Rethinking Image Mixing for Data Augmentation in Vision Transformers

Jihao Liu[1,2], Boxiao Liu[3], Hang Zhou[1], Hongsheng Li[1(✉)], and Yu Liu[2(✉)]

[1] CUHK, MMLab, Hong Kong, China
hsli@ee.cuhk.edu.hk
[2] SenseTime Research, Hong Kong, China
liuyuisanai@gmail.com
[3] SKLP, Institute of Computing Technology, CAS, Beijing, China

Abstract. CutMix is a popular augmentation technique commonly used for training modern convolutional and transformer vision networks. It was originally designed to encourage Convolution Neural Networks (CNNs) to focus more on an image's global context instead of local information, which greatly improves the performance of CNNs. However, we found it to have limited benefits for transformer-based architectures that naturally have a global receptive field. In this paper, we propose a novel data augmentation technique TokenMix to improve the performance of vision transformers. TokenMix mixes two images at token level via partitioning the mixing region into multiple separated parts. Besides, we show that the mixed learning target in CutMix, a linear combination of a pair of the ground truth labels, might be inaccurate and sometimes counter-intuitive. To obtain a more suitable target, we propose to assign the target score according to the content-based neural activation maps of the two images from a pre-trained teacher model, which does not need to have high performance. With plenty of experiments on various vision transformer architectures, we show that our proposed TokenMix helps vision transformers focus on the foreground area to infer the classes and enhances their robustness to occlusion, with consistent performance gains. Notably, we improve DeiT-T/S/B with +1% ImageNet top-1 accuracy. Besides, Token-Mix enjoys longer training, which achieves 81.2% top-1 accuracy on ImageNet with DeiT-S trained for 400 epochs.

Keywords: Data augmentation · Representation learning

1 Introduction

Deep neural networks dominate the learning of visual representations and show effectiveness on various downstream tasks, including image classification [9,11], object detection [18], semantic segmentation [37], etc. To further improve the performance, various data augmentation strategies were introduced, including

© The Author(s), under exclusive license to Springer Nature Switzerland AG 2022
S. Avidan et al. (Eds.): ECCV 2022, LNCS 13686, pp. 455–471, 2022.
https://doi.org/10.1007/978-3-031-19809-0_26

Dog 0.6 Cat 0.4   Dog 0.6 Cat 0.4
(a) CutMix

Input images   Dog 0.8 Cat 0.6   Dog 0.5 Cat 0.0
(b) TokenMix

Fig. 1. TokenMix and CutMix. TokenMix not only mixes images at token-level to encourage better learning of long-range dependency but also generates more reasonable target scores according to content-based neural activation maps from an (even imperfectly trained) teacher network.

hand-crafted [32,34] and automatically searched ones [7,8]. Recently, data augmentation based on mixing multiple images into single ones shows impressive performances on various vision tasks. The labels of such "mixed" images are created based on their original labels. Mixup [34] for the first time attempted to generate mixed training samples via linear combinations of pairs of samples. CutMix [32] proposed to mix pairs of samples on region level, which replaces a random local rectangular area in a source image with the contents of the corresponding area in a target image. In addition, a series of works attempted to improve CutMix with more complicated strategies on choosing rectangular sizes and locations to be used for mixing [15,16,29].

In general, CutMix and its variants use the region-level cut-and-paste mixing technique to enforce Convolution Neural Networks (CNNs) to pay more attention to the image's global context instead of just local information. While the CutMix augmentation can also be used for training vision transformers [11,25], the region-level mixing strategy becomes less effective.

We revisit the design of CutMix augmentation and argue that it is a suboptimal strategy for transformer-based architectures. On the one hand, the region-level mixing in CutMix cuts a rectangular area in a source image and mixes the contents into a target image. As CNNs are primarily designed to encode local image contents, the region-level mixing of CutMix can effectively prevent CNNs from over-focusing on local context. However, for transformer-based architectures that naturally have global receptive fields from the first layer, the region-level mixing is less beneficial. On the other hand, CutMix assigns a mixed label for the augmented image according to only the cropped area ratio between the source and target images, regardless of their cropped contents. However, the cut region and location of CutMix are randomly chosen, and the same label is assigned no matter whether the cut contents are foreground or background, which inevitably introduces label noise to the learning targets and causes unstable training (see Fig. 1(b)). There are recent works trying to mitigate this problem by attentively choosing the salient area for cutting [27,29] or using alternate optimization to determine the cutting region [15,16]. However, the label noise problem is still under-explored as the salient areas might not correctly correspond to the foreground regions.

In this paper, we propose TokenMix, a token-level augmentation technique that can be well applied to training various transformer-based architectures. In contrast to previous approaches, TokenMix directly mixes two images at the token level to promote the interactions of the input tokens and generates a more reasonable target with considering the images' semantic information. First, to train transformers for better encoding long-range dependency, we directly cut at token level and allow the cut region to be separated into multiple isolated parts. As a result, the cut area can be distributed all over the image, as shown in Fig. 1 (b). The token-level mixing encourages the transformer to better encode long-range dependency to correctly classify the mixed images with the augmented tokens inside. Instead of relying on alternate optimization or an extra network to determine which region to mix, all the mixing tokens in TokenMix are randomly determined as blocks, which is easier to implement with a small number of hyper-parameters.

Besides, previous methods usually assign a mixed target to the augmented image, which equals the linear combination of the ground truth labels of the source and target images. The linear combination ratio of the labels is determined as the area ratio between the cutting region of the source image and the total size of the target image. We found that such target scores can be highly inaccurate. As shown in Fig. 1 (a), the same target is assigned to both cases even the mixing area has significantly different semantic meanings.

Following the spirit of distillation, we propose to assign the target score to an augmented target image according to the content-based neural activation maps of the two mixing images. Specifically, we first obtain the neural activation maps of both the source and target images with a pre-trained neural network, which does not need to be perfectly trained. The scores of two mixing regions are calculated as the summation of the spatially normalized neural activation maps, which are combined as the final target. Our intuition is that the neural activation map of even a partially trained classification network can better localize some part of an object [4,36] than using naive score averaging. After spatial normalization of the neural activation map, the regions with rich semantic information would be assigned high scores and low scores would be assigned for other regions, leading to more robust targets. The neural activation maps are generated offline, so the extra training overhead introduced is negligible (+0.8%). In contrast, the distillation method used in DeiT [25] relies on the online inference of a teacher network to generate target scores from augmented images, which cannot generate target scores offline and therefore nearly doubles the training time. Although ReLabel [33] and TokenLabeling [14] also explored utilizing neural activation maps to generate training supervisions, their approaches use the patch-level activations as supervisions and is prone to suffer more from inaccurate activation maps of mix-based augmentations. In contrast, our proposed method sums up the activations from the cut regions as the image-level target scores and is less likely to be affected by individual tokens' incorrect activations. Experiments on combining our token cutting strategy and ReLabel or TokenLabeling validate our scoring strategy. We show that the resulted targets of our approach are more reasonable, which improve the performance and stabilize the training of not only our proposed TokenMix and also the original CutMix. Replacing the way to generate target scores in CutMix with our approach, we obtain a +0.7% top-1 accuracy gain on ImageNet with DeiT-S. In addition, as the generated target scores are more learning-friendly, we show that our approach enjoys longer training. Specifically, we achieve 81.2% top-1 accuracy on ImageNet with DeiT-S when training for 400 epochs.

In summary, our contributions are as follows:

- We propose TokenMix, a token-level augmentation technique that generalizes well across various transformer-based architectures.
- We propose to assign the target scores of the mixed images with content-based neural activation maps, which can benefit both TokenMix and CutMix augmentations.
- Experimental results show that TokenMix promotes transformer's capability on encoding image contents and robustness to the occlusions. We improve DeiT-S from 79.8% to 80.8% top-1 accuracy on ImageNet.

2 Related Works

Cutting-based Data Augmentation. The motivation behind cutting-based methods [6,10,23,35] is to make a network learn informative representations from the entire image. By masking some areas from the input image, it can alleviate the issue of overfitting and improve the occlusion robustness [10]. Cutout [10] is a pioneer of this idea, and proposes to randomly select a square patch of an image and set the inputs within as some consistent. The shape and size of the masked patch are manually designed. Random-erasing [35] works in a similar way with Cutout, but introduces more randomness into the augmentation. In every iteration, the erasing operation is performed under a probability, and the size and aspect ratio is randomly selected with predefined limits. Hide-and-seek [23] differs from the previous two methods in the number of masked patches. It divides an image into grids and masked each grid randomly and independently.

Mixing-based Data Augmentation. Mixing-based data augmentations [13,15,28,34] is another popular regularization method to help the optimization of deep neural networks. Mixup [34] proposes to mix the RGB values of two randomly selected images according to a mixing factor, which is drawn from a beta distribution. The target for the mixed image is also a linear combination of the targets of original images. Manifold Mixup [28] extends the mixed information from input images to intermediate feature maps of a network. Co-Mixup [15] and Puzzle Mix [16] consider the mixing process as an optimization problem, and propose to maximize the saliency in the mixed images. AugMix [13] generates mixed images from the original image and its transformed ones.

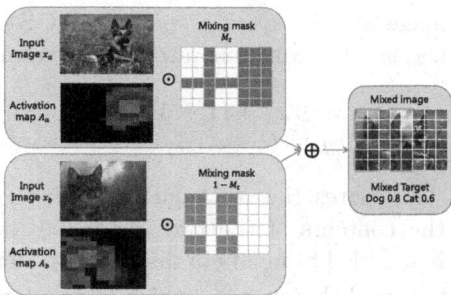

Fig. 2. The overall pipeline of TokenMix. TokenMix partitions the mask region into multiple separated parts. The target score of the mixed image is calculated according to the neural activation maps of the two input images.

Joint of Cutting and Mixing. One issue of cutting-based augmentation is the information in the cut area is lost, so recent researches [5,22,24,32] propose to combine cutting and mixing together to achieve better performance. As introduced in CutMix, a patch is replaced with that from another image instead of being deleted. Like Mixup, the target for the mixed image is computed as the proportion of the replaced area. Attentive CutMix [29] points out that the randomly selected patches may contain only background regions, and proposes to replace attentive regions identified by a pre-trained network. RICAP [24] introduces another way of stitching four rectangle patches from different images into one new image. The target of the new image is also determined according to the area of different patches. ResizeMix [22] argues the traditional cut-and-paste operation may lead to an unreasonable target when only the background part of one image is mixed. It solves this issue by using a resize-and-paste process. In this paper, we revisit the CutMix method for vision transformer and find that CutMix under-explores the ability of vision transformer to model long-range interaction and the assigned target is non-optimal. We further introduce our TokenMix augmentation with novel ways to select mixed parts and generate learning targets.

3 Method

In this section, we first revisit the general process of CutMix [32] and show the limitations of applying CutMix to transformers. We then present our proposed TokenMix, which conducts image augmentation via mixing images at token-level and assigns target scores with neural activation maps.

3.1 Revisiting CutMix Augmentation

To enhance the localization ability of CNNs, CutMix [32] proposed to mix pairs of samples with a random rectangular binary mask. Let $x \in \mathbb{R}^{H \times W \times C}$ and

y denote a training image and its label, respectively. Given a pair of training samples (x_a, y_a) and (x_b, y_b), CutMix generates a new training sample $(\tilde{x}, \tilde{y})$ as follows:

$$\tilde{x} = M \odot x_a + (1 - M) \odot x_b,$$
$$\tilde{y} = \lambda y_a + (1 - \lambda) y_b, \tag{1}$$

where $M \in \{0, 1\}^{H \times W}$ denotes the rectangular mask that decides where to drop out and fill in the contents of the two images, $\odot$ denotes element-wise multiplication, and λ is sampled from a beta distribution $\text{Beta}(\alpha, \alpha)$. The binary mask M is a randomly sampled rectangle, which guarantees $\frac{\sum M}{HW} = \lambda$. Similar to Mixup [34], CutMix assigns a mixed target for the generated image as a linear combination of y_a and y_b.

We argue that the region-level mixing in CutMix might not be suitable for transformer-based architectures. As CNNs are primarily designed to encode local image contents, training with CutMix effectively prevents CNNs from over-focusing on local context. However, transformer-based architectures might be less benefited from CutMix as all of its layers have global receptive fields. In addition, the label of the mixed image is a linear combination of y_a and y_b with mixing ratio λ being estimated only according to the size of the mask, which might be inappropriate in many cases as shown in Fig. 1 (b). Although there were recent methods on attempting to improve CutMix by choosing the salience regions to maximize the saliency in the mixed images [15,16,27,29], the salient areas might not correctly correspond to the target class [2], and the label noise problem is still serious.

3.2   TokenMix

In this paper, we propose TokenMix to mix a pair of images to generate a mixed image and learning target. We generate the mask M at token-level to encourage better learning of long-range dependency and assign the target score of the mixed image according to the content-based neural activation maps of the two mixing images, which follows the general spirit of distillation to create more robust targets.

Figure 2 shows an overview of our proposed TokenMix. We first partition the input image x into non-overlapping patches $x^p \in \mathbb{R}^{\frac{H}{P} \times \frac{W}{P} \times (P^2 \cdot C)}$, which are then linearly projected to visual tokens. We then generate a random mask $M_t \in \mathbb{R}^{\frac{H}{P} \times \frac{W}{P}}$ at token-level according to the mask-out ratio λ. The mixed new training sample $(\tilde{x}^p, \tilde{y})$ is created as follows:

$$\tilde{x}^p = M_t \odot x_a^p + (1 - M_t) \odot x_b^p,$$
$$\tilde{y} = \sum_{i \in \mathfrak{S}} M_{ti} \odot A_{ai} + \sum_{i \in \mathfrak{S}} (1 - M_{ti}) \odot A_{bi}, \tag{2}$$

where $\mathfrak{S}$ indicates the set of all tokens, $\odot$ denotes element-wise multiplication, M_{ti} denotes the i-th token of the mask M_t, A_{ai} and A_{bi} are the i-th token of the spatially normalized neural activation maps of x_a and x_b respectively. The neural activation maps are generated with pre-trained networks' last layer before the classification head [14,33].

Instead of masking a whole rectangular area, we partition the mask area into multiple separated parts. For each part, we randomly choose the number of masked tokens and the aspect ratio [1,32]. We set the minimum number of tokens to 14 and log-uniformly sample the aspect ratio in the range of $[0.3, \frac{1}{0.3}]$. We repeatedly mask a part of the image until the total number of masked tokens reaches the pre-defined ratio $\lambda \frac{HW}{P^2}$. Instead of sampling λ from a beta distribution, we set λ to 0.5 unless otherwise specified. Our intuition is that the distributed masking regions are easier to recognize compared with masking a whole rectangular area. For investigation, we also introduce a uniformly random version, where each masking part is only a single token. While totally random mixing is harmful to the performance of CNNs, we show that transformers are still benefited from the simplified version.

To solve the issue of inaccurate target scores generated by CutMix, we propose to set the target score with the content-based neural activation maps of the two mixing images, generated by a pre-trained teacher network. Our intuition is that not all regions correspond to the foreground object. Concretely, the regions with rich semantic information would have a bigger impact on the target score than other regions. Inspired by the distillation technique that sets the target score of an image by a teacher network, we extend the design to set the target score by combining a teacher network's neural activation maps of the two mixing images. As shown in Fig. 2, the target scores of two mixing regions are calculated as the summation of spatially normalized neural activation maps within the mask for x_a or outside the mask for x_b. We then combine the two target scores as the final target of the mixed image.

Compared to previous arts [15,16,29,32], our proposed TokenMix has two main advantages: 1) We explicitly encourage the transformer to better encode long-range dependency to correctly classify the image with the other image mixed inside. We show that our approach can lead to consistent accuracy gain when used in various vision transformers, and also enhances the occlusion robustness of the transformers. 2) The target label of the mixed image that is generated with content-based neural activation map is more robust than those of previous approaches, which takes advantage of the distillation technique. Besides, we show that our approach promotes transformers to better localize the discriminate regions, with attention weights.

4   Experiment

4.1   Datasets

We use ImageNet-1K [9] dataset to demonstrate the effectiveness of our method. The dataset contains 1.2 million images for training and 50K for validation. The top-1 accuracy is reported as the evaluation metric.

Table 1. ImageNet classification performances based on various transformer-based architectures. TokenMix consistently improves DeiT for ∼ 1% top-1 accuracy with nearly no extra training overhead.

Model	#FLOPs (G)	#Params (M)	CutMix	TokenMix
DeiT-T [25]	1.3	5.7	72.2	**73.2** (+1.0)
PVT-T [30]	1.9	13.2	75.1	**75.6** (+0.5)
CaiT-XXS-24 [26]	2.5	9.5	77.6	**78.0** (+0.4)
DeiT-S [25]	4.6	22.1	79.8	**80.8** (+1.0)
Swin T [19]	4.5	29	81.2	**81.6** (+0.4)
DeiT-B [25]	17.6	86.6	81.8	**82.9** (+1.1)

We also use ADE20K [37] to verify the transferability of our TokenMix pre-trained models. ADE20K is a widely-used semantic segmentation dataset, covering 150 semantic categories. The dataset has 25K images in total, with 20K for training, 2K for validation, and another 3K for testing.

4.2   Implementation Details

We evaluate our method on several recent vision transformer architectures, including DeiT [25], CaiT [26], PVT [30] and Swin Transformer [30]. We also test TokenMix on ResNet [12], which is representative of convolution models, as comparison. We follow the training recipe of DeiT [25]. The batch size is set to 1024. We use AdamW [17,20] as the optimizer and set the learning rate as 0.001 with 5 warm-up epochs. The learning rate is decayed following a cosine scheduler down to 10^{-6}. Without other specification, we train the models for 300 epochs. Rand Augment [8] and Mixup [34] are both used by default. Following [25], we switch TokenMix and Mixup with the probability of 0.5. For training architectures with smaller model sizes, e.g., DeiT-T [25], PVT-T [30], or CaiT-XXS [26], we sample the λ in Eq. 2 from a beta distribution Beta(1.0, 1.0). We use binary cross-entropy (BCE) loss instead of the typical cross-entropy (CE) loss by default following [2,31], as the mixed images are more likely to contain multiple labels. To generate the neural activation maps, we defaulty use NFNet-F6 [3] following [14].

For transferring to the ADE20K dataset, we follow the setting in BEiT [1], and fine-tune for 160K steps with Adam [17] optimizer. The detailed hyperparameters are described in supplementary materials.

5   Main Results

5.1   ImageNet Results

We report the results on ImageNet-1K dataset with our TokenMix. As shown in Table 1, TokenMix consistently improves CutMix on various transformer-based

Table 2. Comparisons with ReLabel and TokenLabeling with DeiT-T on ImageNet. GPU time refers to the increase of training time.

Augmentation	Supervision	Top-1 Acc.	GPU Time
CutMix	ImageNet	72.2	+0.0%
TokenMix	ImageNet	**72.7**	+0.0%
TokenMix	ReLabel	72.7	+0.8%
TokenMix	TokenLabeling	72.9	+0.8%
TokenMix	TokenMix	**73.2**	+0.8%

Table 3. Comparisons with previous mixing methods with DeiT-T on ImageNet.

Augmentation	Top-1 acc.
CutMix [32]	72.2
Co-Mix [15]	72.2
SaliencyMix [27]	71.8
Puzzle-Mix [16]	72.3
TokenMix	**72.7**

Table 4. Transferring the pre-trained models to downstream semantic segmentation task on ADE20K dataset. TL and RL denote TokenLabeling and ReLabel respectively. ✓+RL/TL represents row 3/4 in Table 2.

Model	TokenMix	mIoU (%)	mAcc (%)	+ms mIoU (%)	+ms mAcc(%)
DeiT-T	✗	36.4	46.7	37.5	47.1
	✓+RL	36.6	47.0	38.1	47.9
	✓+TL	36.9	47.1	38.3	48.1
	✓	**37.1**	**47.5**	**38.6**	**48.2**
DeiT-S	✗	42.3	52.8	43.7	53.8
	✓	**44.5**	**55.0**	**45.9**	**56.1**
DeiT-B	✗	46.3	56.5	47.7	57.6
	✓	**46.8**	**56.9**	**48.2**	**58.1**

architectures, i.e., DeiT [25], PVT [30], CaiT [26], and Swin Transformer [19]. Specifically, TokenMix outperforms CutMix [32] by +1% for DeiT, across DeiT-T to DeiT-B. We also improve popular hierarchical transformer architectures Swin-T and PVT-T for +0.4% and +0.5%, respectively. All the results demonstrate the effectiveness and generalization of the proposed TokenMix.

Our proposed TokenMix consists of two parts, i.e., token-level mixing and label refinement. We decouple the two parts and then compare them with the previous methods by fixing one part. In Table 2, we compare TokenMix to ReLabel [33] and TokenLabeling [14] with the same data augmentation method. The two methods utilize pixel-level supervision, but our TokenMix summarizes neural activations to create image-level target scores and is, therefore, more robust to individual pixel-level errors. Note that we use the same teacher network, i.e., NFNet-F6, to generate the offline targets. As shown in Table 2, TokenMix outperforms both ReLabel (+0.5%) and TokenLabeling (+0.3%) with the same training cost. We further compare TokenMix to previous mixing-based augmentation methods in Table 3. For a more fair comparison, we only use the labels from ImageNet. As shown in Table 3, TokenMix have performance advantages compared to other approaches. We see that the methods that introduce more foreground regions fail to improve CutMix on Vision Transformer. In contrast, our proposed TokenMix improves CutMix for +0.5% accuracy.

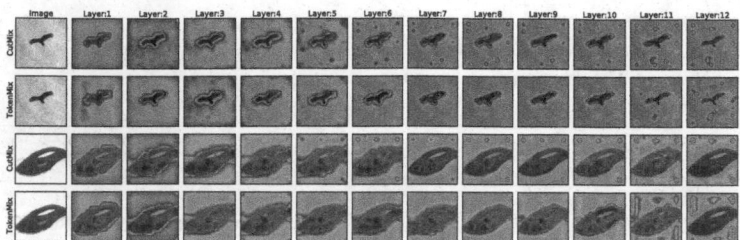

Fig. 3. Visualization of the attention maps of the class token in DeiT-S to attend to patch tokens at different layers. Using CutMix distracts the attention to background areas in the several middle layers. In contrast, the proposed TokenMix helps the class token focus more on foreground objects and leads to consistent performance gain.

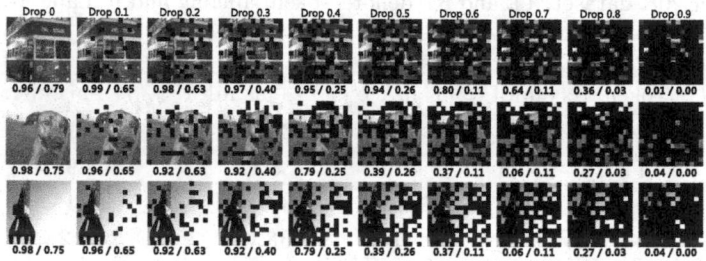

Fig. 4. Example images and the predicted confidences under different occlusion ratios. Red scores under the images are predicted by TokenMix (Color figure online), and green ones by CutMix. The model trained with TokenMix holds high confidence when a large number of patches are dropped, while the model trained with CutMix outputs low confidence.

5.2   Transfer to Downstream Task

Pre-training on ImageNet-1K then finetuning to the downstream tasks is a common practice for many visual recognition tasks. It is important to verify whether the better pre-train with TokenMix can boost the performance on the downstream task. To do so, we transfer our TokenMix pre-trained models to the semantic segmentation task and compare them with regular pre-train. Note that TokenMix does not introduce extra computation overhead in the transfer stage. As shown in Table 4, we find that better pre-train from TokenMix consistently improves the segmentation performance on the ADE20K dataset. Notably, we improve DeiT-T for +0.7% mIoU, DeiT-S for +2.2% mIoU, DeiT-B for +0.5% mIoU. We notice that the performance gap becomes even larger (e.g. +1.1% mIoU for DeiT-T) when using multi-scale testing. All the results demonstrate the transferability of our TokenMix pre-trained models.

5.3   Main Properties

Besides the performance gains, we find that our proposed TokenMix improves transformers to be robust to occlusion, and focus more on the foreground area. All the visualization and analysis are conducted on DeiT-S.

TokenMix Helps Transformers Focus on the Foreground Area. As discussed in Sect. 3, CutMix assigns targets of the mixed images based on linear combinations of labels of the pairs of mixing images, which might be inaccurate if the foreground region is cut. We find that the inaccurate labels make transformers pay incorrect attention to the input image. As shown in Fig. 3, using CutMix distracts the transformer's attention to background areas in several middle layers (layers 5–10). In comparison, TokenMix helps transformers learn to pay more attention to the foreground areas and leads to consistent performance gain.

TokenMix Enhances the Occlusion Robustness of Vision Transformers. After training converges, we construct a sequence of images with different occlusion ratios. Specifically, we gradually drop 10% more patches and set the pixels inside to zero, and use the images for testing. We report the top-1 accuracy on ImageNet under different drop ratios. As shown in Fig. 5, the model trained with TokenMix surpasses that with CutMix by increasingly larger margins as the drop ratio grows, demonstrating its better occlusion robustness.

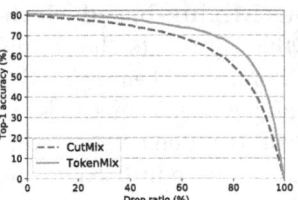

Fig. 5. ImageNet top-1 accuracy of DeiT-S under different drop ratios. The gap between the model trained with CutMix and that with TokenMix increases as the drop ratio grows.

Specifically, we notice a ~10% performance gap at the drop ratio of 80%. We further visualize some examples in Figure 4. It can be found that when about 40% tokens are dropped, the predicted ground-truth class confidences of the baseline model decrease to very low values (0.25 in the first row) while the model trained with our TokenMix holds higher confidences (0.95 in the first row).

6   Ablative Studies

In this section, we conduct various ablation studies to analyze our proposed TokenMix. We use DeiT-S as the backbone and train it on ImageNet for 300 epochs unless otherwise specified. All other training settings are the same as described in Sect. 4. We report the top-1 accuracy on ImageNet.

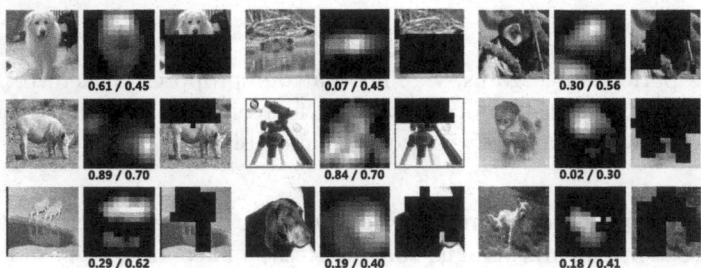

Fig. 6. The target scores generated by TokenMix (Color figure online) and CutMix. For each tripled sub-figure, the left is the input image, the middle is the neural activation map, and the right is the masked image. Our approach generates more reasonable target scores, especially when the foreground region is cropped.

Integrating TokenMix with Previous Mixing-based Methods. Table 5 presents the results of combining TokenMix with other mixing-based methods to train DeiT-B. When two mixing augmentations are utilized during training, one of them is randomly chosen to be used for data augmentation with a probability of 0.5 at each iteration. The baseline (row 1 in Table 5) does not use any mixing-based augmenta-

Table 5. Performances of using a single or randomly sampled one of the multiple mixing methods for training DeiT-B.

Mixup [34]	CutMix [32]	TokenMix	Top-1 Acc
✗	✗	✗	75.8
✗	✓	✗	78.7
✓	✗	✗	80.0
✗	✗	✓	**81.5**
✓	✓	✗	81.8
✗	✓	✓	82.0
✓	✗	✓	**82.9**

tions. Using only MixToken improves the baseline and CutMix by large margins. Specifically, TokenMix improves the baseline by +5.7% top-1 accuracy. Using both TokenMix and Mixup improves TokenMix-only by +1.4% top-1 accuracy. In contrast, using both CutMix and Mixup also improves top-1 accuracy to 81.8%, which, however, is still lower than TokenMix + Mixup.

Different Ways to Generate Neural Activation Maps. Table 6 presents the results of using different ways to generate neural activation maps. Besides our default choice of NFNet-F6, popular ResNet and hand-crafted saliency method are also compared. As shown in Table 6, TokenMix follows the general behavior of distillation techniques, i.e., if the performance of the teacher model is high, so is the student model. In addition, TokenMix is robust to different choices of teacher networks for generating target scores. Even when the performance of the teacher drops by 6.3%, only 0.3% performance drop is observed on DeiT trained with our proposed TokenMix. However, using neural networks to generate neural activation maps is consistently better than using scores from hand-crafted approaches [21] as the targets generated by a teacher model are generally better to learn than hand-crafted ones. We further visualized the target scores of the

Table 6. Comparison of different ways to generate neural activation maps. NFNet-F6 is used by default.

Teacher	Teacher top-1 acc.	Top-1 acc
NFNet-F6 [3]	86.1	80.8
ResNet101 [12]	82.3	80.7
ResNet26 [12]	79.8	80.5
Saliency [21]	N/A	80.1

Table 7. Ablation of the way to generate target scores. Our approach generates target scores with content-based neural activation maps (denoted as *refinement*).

Model	Refinement	Top-1 acc
DeiT-S [25]	✗	79.8
	✓	**80.5** (+0.7)
Swin-T [19]	✗	81.2
	✓	**81.5** (+0.3)
ResNet50 [12]	✗	79.3
	✓	**79.8** (+0.5)

Table 8. Ablation of mask sampling strategy. The *region-based* strategy works best on ResNet50, but degrades on DeiT-S.

Model	Region	Random	Block
DeiT-T [25]	72.2	**72.7**	**72.7**
DeiT-S [25]	79.8	**80.6**	**80.6**
ResNet50 [12]	79.3	78.3	**79.7**

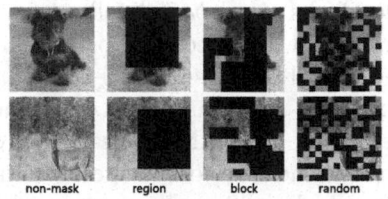

non-mask   region   block   random

Fig. 7. Illustration of different mask sampling strategies.

mixed images in Fig. 6. For each tripled sub-figure, the left is the input images, the middle is the neural activation maps, and the right is the masked images. The scores generated from CutMix are shown in green, while the red scores are generated by our approach. As shown in Fig. 6, the target scores generated by our approach are more reasonable, especially when the foreground is cut.

Our Neural-Activation Target Scores are Comptible with CutMix. To test whether our proposed target scores are compatible with CutMix, we conduct experiments of using CutMix to mix pairs of images but generating targets with our approach (denoted as *refinement* in Table 7), and train with various backbones, e.g., DeiT-S, Swin-T, and ResNet50. As shown in Table 7, we achieve consistent performance gains on those backbones. Specifically, we improve DeiT-S for +0.7%, Swin-T for +0.3%, and ResNet50 for +0.5% with nearly no extra computation cost during the training process. All the results verify the compatibility of our proposed target score assignment with CutMix.

Mask Sampling Strategy. Table 8 presents the impact of different sampling strategies on transformers and Convolution Neural Networks, as illustrated in Fig. 7. The *region-based* sampling, widely used in [21, 29,32], cuts a single large rectangular area from the mixing images. Our proposed TokenMix directly cuts at token-level. We compare two settings of our approach, masking multiple blocks (*block-based*) following our description in Sect. 3.2 or masking individual tokens separately (*random*). To better inspect the impact of sampling

Table 9. Ablation of mask sampling strategy. The *block-based* strategy obtains higher accuracy with label refinement.

Model	Mask	Refinement	Top-1 acc
DeiT-T	random	✗	72.7
		✓	**72.9** (+0.2)
	block	✗	72.7
		✓	**73.2** (+0.5)
DeiT-S	random	✗	80.6
		✓	80.6
	block	✗	80.6
		✓	**80.8** (+0.2)

strategies alone, in all the experiments in Table 8, we directly use target scores generated by CutMix, instead of ours. As shown in Table 8, the *region-based* strategy achieves decent performance on ResNet50, but degrades on transformers, which validates our argument on the sub-optimality of using region-based cut for training transformers. Compared to the *random* strategy, the *block-based* strategy achieves similar performances on transformers, but performs much better on ResNet50. When using our proposed target score assignment approach, we further compare the *random* and the *block-based* sampling strategies. As shown in Table 9, the *block-based* strategy used in our final solution consistently has higher accuracy. The results further verify the effectiveness of our proposed TokenMix.

Table 10. Ablation of training epochs. TokenMix enjoys longer training. The extra 100 epochs of training improve +0.4% accuracy.

Mixing Method	Epoch	Top-1 acc
CutMix [32]	300	79.8
	400	79.9 (+0.1)
TokenMix	300	80.8
	400	**81.2** (+0.4)

Table 11. Ablation of the loss function. Binary cross-entropy (BCE) improves TokenMix, compared with multi-class cross-entropy (CE).

Mixing Method	Loss Type	Top-1 acc
CutMix [32]	CE	79.8
	BCE	79.8
TokenMix	CE	80.3
	BCE	**80.8** (+0.5)

Training Epochs. Table 10 presents the results of longer training. As targets generated by a teacher network's neural activation maps can provide more appropriate scores and more challenging samples for training the transformers, which mitigates the risk of over-fitting scheme, our proposed TokenMix can enjoy longer training. As shown in Table 10, our TokenMix improves DeiT-S for +0.4% with additional 100 training epochs, while using CutMix for long training is less beneficial.

Loss Function. As the mixed images may contain multiple objects of different classes, we adopt the binary cross-entropy (BCE) loss instead of the typical cross-entropy (CE) loss [2,31]. Using BCE loss improves DeiT-S for +0.5% accuracy (Table 11) when training with our proposed TokenMix, as the cut-and-paste operation might generate a mixed image with multiple objects of different classes. It might be because the generated targets by CutMix are sub-optimal, we do not notice performance improvement of replacing CE with BCE when training DeiT-S with CutMix augmentation.

7   Conclusions

In this paper, we propose TokenMix, a token-level augmentation strategy that generalizes well across various transformer-based architectures. TokenMix is motivated by two key observations: 1) region-level mixing is less beneficial for transformer-based architectures, and 2) assigning target of mixed images with linear combination might be inaccurate and even counter-intuitive. Our proposed TokenMix directly cuts at token level and obtains the target of the mixed images with content-based neural activation maps. Empirical results show that Token-Mix has the properties of enhancing occlusion robustness and helping vision transformers focus on the foreground area of input images. Besides, TokenMix consistently improves various transformer-based architectures, including DeiT, PVT, and Swin Transformer.

Acknowledgment. Hongsheng Li is also a Principal Investigator of Centre for Perceptual and Interactive Intelligence Limited (CPII). This work is supported in part by CPII, in part by the General Research Fund through the Research Grants Council of Hong Kong under Grants (Nos. 14204021, 14207319), in part by CUHK Strategic Fund.

References

1. Bao, H., Dong, L., Wei, F.: Beit: Bert pre-training of image transformers. arXiv preprint arXiv:2106.08254 (2021)
2. Beyer, L., Hénaff, O.J., Kolesnikov, A., Zhai, X., Oord, A.v.d.: Are we done with imagenet? arXiv preprint arXiv:2006.07159 (2020)
3. Brock, A., De, S., Smith, S.L., Simonyan, K.: High-performance large-scale image recognition without normalization. arXiv preprint arXiv:2102.06171 (2021)
4. Chefer, H., Gur, S., Wolf, L.: Transformer interpretability beyond attention visualization. In: Proceedings of the IEEE/CVF Conference on Computer Vision and Pattern Recognition, pp. 782–791 (2021)
5. Chen, J., Sun, S., He, J., Torr, P.H.S., Yuille, A.L., Bai, S.: Transmix: Attend to mix for vision transformers. ArXiv abs/2111.09833 (2021)
6. Chen, P., Liu, S., Zhao, H., Jia, J.: Gridmask data augmentation. ArXiv abs/2001.04086 (2020)
7. Cubuk, E.D., Zoph, B., Mane, D., Vasudevan, V., Le, Q.V.: Autoaugment: Learning augmentation policies from data. arXiv preprint arXiv:1805.09501 (2018)

8. Cubuk, E.D., Zoph, B., Shlens, J., Le, Q.V.: Randaugment: Practical automated data augmentation with a reduced search space. In: Proceedings of the IEEE/CVF Conference on Computer Vision and Pattern Recognition Workshops, pp. 702–703 (2020)
9. Deng, J., Dong, W., Socher, R., Li, L.J., Li, K., Fei-Fei, L.: Imagenet: A large-scale hierarchical image database. In: 2009 IEEE conference on computer vision and pattern recognition, pp. 248–255. Ieee (2009)
10. Devries, T., Taylor, G.W.: Improved regularization of convolutional neural networks with cutout. ArXiv abs/1708.04552 (2017)
11. Dosovitskiy, A., et al.: An image is worth 16x16 words: Transformers for image recognition at scale. arXiv preprint arXiv:2010.11929 (2020)
12. He, K., Zhang, X., Ren, S., Sun, J.: Deep residual learning for image recognition. In: Proceedings of the IEEE conference on computer vision and pattern recognition, pp. 770–778 (2016)
13. Hendrycks, D., Mu, N., Cubuk, E.D., Zoph, B., Gilmer, J., Lakshminarayanan, B.: Augmix: A simple data processing method to improve robustness and uncertainty. ArXiv abs/1912.02781 (2020)
14. Jiang, Z., et al.: Token labeling: Training a 85.5% top-1 accuracy vision transformer with 56m parameters on imagenet. arXiv preprint arXiv:2104.10858 (2021)
15. Kim, J.H., Choo, W., Jeong, H., Song, H.O.: Co-mixup: Saliency guided joint mixup with supermodular diversity. arXiv preprint arXiv:2102.03065 (2021)
16. Kim, J.H., Choo, W., Song, H.O.: Puzzle mix: Exploiting saliency and local statistics for optimal mixup. In: International Conference on Machine Learning, pp. 5275–5285. PMLR (2020)
17. Kingma, D.P., Ba, J.: Adam: A method for stochastic optimization. arXiv preprint arXiv:1412.6980 (2014)
18. Lin, T.-Y., et al.: Microsoft COCO: common objects in context. In: Fleet, D., Pajdla, T., Schiele, B., Tuytelaars, T. (eds.) ECCV 2014. LNCS, vol. 8693, pp. 740–755. Springer, Cham (2014). https://doi.org/10.1007/978-3-319-10602-1_48
19. Liu, Z., et al.: Swin transformer: Hierarchical vision transformer using shifted windows. arXiv preprint arXiv:2103.14030 (2021)
20. Loshchilov, I., Hutter, F.: Decoupled weight decay regularization. arXiv preprint arXiv:1711.05101 (2017)
21. Montabone, S., Soto, A.: Human detection using a mobile platform and novel features derived from a visual saliency mechanism. Image and Vision Computing 28(3), 391–402 (2010)
22. Qin, J., Fang, J., Zhang, Q., Liu, W., gang Wang, X., Wang, X.: Resizemix: Mixing data with preserved object information and true labels. ArXiv abs/2012.11101 (2020)
23. Singh, K.K., Yu, H., Sarmasi, A., Pradeep, G., Lee, Y.J.: Hide-and-seek: A data augmentation technique for weakly-supervised localization and beyond. ArXiv abs/1811.02545 (2018)
24. Takahashi, R., Matsubara, T., Uehara, K.: Data augmentation using random image cropping and patching for deep cnns. IEEE Trans. Circ. Syst. Video Technol. 30, 2917–2931 (2020)
25. Touvron, H., Cord, M., Douze, M., Massa, F., Sablayrolles, A., Jégou, H.: Training data-efficient image transformers & distillation through attention. In: International Conference on Machine Learning, pp. 10347–10357. PMLR (2021)
26. Touvron, H., Cord, M., Sablayrolles, A., Synnaeve, G., Jégou, H.: Going deeper with image transformers. arXiv preprint arXiv:2103.17239 (2021)

27. Uddin, A., Monira, M., Shin, W., Chung, T., Bae, S.H., et al.: Saliencymix: A saliency guided data augmentation strategy for better regularization. arXiv preprint arXiv:2006.01791 (2020)
28. Verma, V., et al.: Manifold mixup: Better representations by interpolating hidden states. In: ICML (2019)
29. Walawalkar, D., Shen, Z., Liu, Z., Savvides, M.: Attentive cutmix: An enhanced data augmentation approach for deep learning based image classification. arXiv preprint arXiv:2003.13048 (2020)
30. Wang, W., et al.: Pyramid vision transformer: A versatile backbone for dense prediction without convolutions. arXiv preprint arXiv:2102.12122 (2021)
31. Wightman, R., Touvron, H., Jégou, H.: Resnet strikes back: An improved training procedure in timm. arXiv preprint arXiv:2110.00476 (2021)
32. Yun, S., Han, D., Oh, S.J., Chun, S., Choe, J., Yoo, Y.: Cutmix: Regularization strategy to train strong classifiers with localizable features. In: Proceedings of the IEEE/CVF International Conference on Computer Vision, pp. 6023–6032 (2019)
33. Yun, S., Oh, S.J., Heo, B., Han, D., Choe, J., Chun, S.: Re-labeling imagenet: from single to multi-labels, from global to localized labels. In: Proceedings of the IEEE/CVF Conference on Computer Vision and Pattern Recognition, pp. 2340–2350 (2021)
34. Zhang, H., Cisse, M., Dauphin, Y.N., Lopez-Paz, D.: mixup: Beyond empirical risk minimization. arXiv preprint arXiv:1710.09412 (2017)
35. Zhong, Z., Zheng, L., Kang, G., Li, S., Yang, Y.: Random erasing data augmentation. ArXiv abs/1708.04896 (2020)
36. Zhou, B., Khosla, A., Lapedriza, A., Oliva, A., Torralba, A.: Learning deep features for discriminative localization. In: Proceedings of the IEEE conference on computer vision and pattern recognition, pp. 2921–2929 (2016)
37. Zhou, B., Zhao, H., Puig, X., Fidler, S., Barriuso, A., Torralba, A.: Scene parsing through ade20k dataset. In: Proceedings of the IEEE conference on computer vision and pattern recognition, pp. 633–641 (2017)

UFO: Unified Feature Optimization

Teng Xi[✉], Yifan Sun, Deli Yu, Bi Li, Nan Peng, Gang Zhang[✉],
Xinyu Zhang, Zhigang Wang, Jinwen Chen, Jian Wang, Lufei Liu,
Haocheng Feng, Junyu Han, Jingtuo Liu, Errui Ding, and Jingdong Wang

Baidu Inc., Beijing, China
{xiteng01,zhanggang03}@baidu.com

Abstract. This paper proposes a novel Unified Feature Optimization
(UFO) paradigm for training and deploying deep models under real-world
and large-scale scenarios, which requires a collection of multiple AI functions. UFO aims to benefit each single task with a large-scale pretraining
on all tasks. Compared with existing foundation models, UFO has two
points of emphasis, *i.e.*, relatively smaller model size and NO adaptation
cost: 1) UFO squeezes a wide range of tasks into a moderate-sized unified
model in a multi-task learning manner and further trims the model size
when transferred to down-stream tasks. 2) UFO does not emphasize transfer to novel tasks. Instead, it aims to make the trimmed model dedicated
for one or more already-seen task. To this end, it directly selects partial
modules in the unified model, requiring completely NO adaptation cost.
With these two characteristics, UFO provides great convenience for flexible deployment, while maintaining the benefits of large-scale pretraining.
A key merit of UFO is that the trimming process not only reduces the
model size and inference consumption, but also even improves the accuracy on certain tasks. Specifically, UFO considers the multi-task training
and brings a two-fold impact on the unified model: some closely-related
tasks have mutual benefits, while some tasks have conflicts against each
other. UFO manages to reduce the conflicts and preserve the mutual benefits through a novel Network Architecture Search (NAS) method. Experiments on a wide range of deep representation learning tasks (*i.e.*, face
recognition, person re-identification, vehicle re-identification and product
retrieval) show that the model trimmed from UFO achieves higher accuracy than its single-task-trained counterpart and yet has smaller model
size, validating the concept of UFO. Besides, UFO also supported the
release of 17 billion parameters computer vision (CV) foundation model
which is the largest CV model in the industry. Code: https://github.com/
PaddlePaddle/VIMER/tree/main/UFO.

Keywords: Train and deploy · Foundation model · Multi-task
learning · Unified feature optimization

T. Xi, Y. Sun, D. Yu, B. Li and N. Peng—Equal contribution

Supplementary Information The online version contains supplementary material
available at https://doi.org/10.1007/978-3-031-19809-0_27.

1   Introduction

Training and deploying are two essential procedures for artificial intelligence (AI) applications based on deep learning. A realistic AI system usually consists of multiple tasks. The naive train-and-deploy strategy is to train a respective deep model on each single sub-task for individual deployment. Given that some sub-tasks are actually correlated, this naive strategy wastes their mutual benefits. A feasible approach to benefit individual tasks with the large-scale multi-task data is the foundation model. In this paper, we refer the foundation model as "a model that is trained on broad data at scale and can be adapted to a wide range of downstream tasks", according to [3]. However, foundation model has some burden for deployment, e.g., it maintains the huge foundation model size and requires additional adaptation costs when transferred to down-stream tasks.

This paper presents a novel train-and-deploy paradigm, named Unified Feature Optimization (UFO), to benefit down-stream tasks with large-scale multi-task pretraining. Compared to foundation model, UFO has two different points of emphasis, i.e., relatively smaller model size and NO adaptation cost. 1) *Small model size*. UFO does not use a tremendous network. Instead, it squeezes a wide range of tasks into a moderate-sized unified model, and further trims the model size for down-stream applications, so that the inference will be more efficient. 2) *No adaptation cost*. UFO does not emphasize transferring to novel tasks. Instead, it aims to make the trimmed model dedicated for already-seen sub-tasks. Without fine-tuning or prompt-based learning, UFO directly selects partial components from the already-learned unified model and thus requires completely no adaptation cost.

With the advantages of small model size and no adaptation cost, UFO provides great convenience for flexible deployment while maintaining the benefits of large-scale pretraining. Although the advantage of no adaptation cost is constrained to the already-seen sub-tasks, it does compromise great benefits for realistic AI development. For example, in the smart city prototype, like vision-based smart city, the system needs the collaboration of face, body and car to provide comprehensive understanding of the state of the city. Moreover, in spite that UFO lays no emphasis on the mode of transferring to novel down-stream tasks, it is compatible to this mode through existing foundation model techniques, which is not the major concern of this paper. Given their orthogonal advantages, we believe UFO and foundation model can well co-operate with each other to bring another wave of development.

As an early exploration, this paper presents the concept of UFO with focus on deep representation learning, as shown in Fig. 1. Deep representation learning is fundamental for a lot of AI applications, e.g., face recognition [2,7,24], person/vehicle re-identification [17–19,19,22] and fine-grained image retrieval [26]. We base our UFO on the vision transformer (ViT) [10] architecture. UFO first trains a unified model (i.e., the supernet) on a variety of deep representation tasks in a multi-task learning manner. Afterwards, UFO learns to trim the supernet to get a dedicated sub-net for partial sub-tasks. Given a ViT backbone, the trimming object can be sub-block of the transformer, attention heads

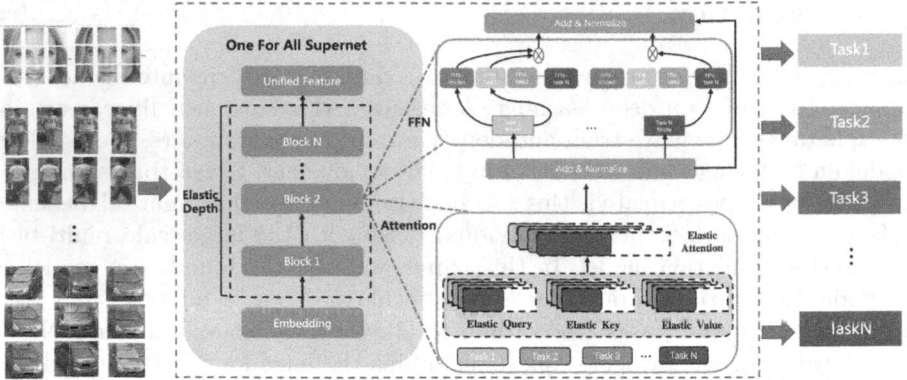

Fig. 1. Overview of the UFO paradigm.

and FFN channels from coarse granularity to fine granularity, as illustrated in Fig. 1. Moreover, UFO integrates another trimming strategy at the FFN path level. Following [12], UFO uses multiple FFN paths in parallel when training the supernet and allows trimming some FFN paths for down-stream tasks. Although these trimming strategies are popular, UFO is the first to integrate them and thus provides great trimming flexibility.

An important advantage of UFO is that the trimming process not only reduces the model size and inference consumption, but also improves the accuracy on its dedicated sub-tasks. It is non-trivial because trimming the model (without further fine-tuning) usually compromises the accuracy. To this end, UFO considers that the multi-task training brings two-fold impacts on the supernet. On the one hand, some tasks are closely related to each other and thus have mutual benefits. On the other hand, some tasks have significant divergence and thus have mutual conflicts. During the trimming, UFO manages to reduce the conflicts and to preserve the mutual benefits through a novel Network Architecture Search (NAS) method. Specifically, we design a search space for the UFO, which first introduces FFN paths together with the supernet. Accordingly, we propose an end-to-end training strategy for UFO, which is different from previous multi-stage approaches [4,20]. Meanwhile, we also propose a novel evaluation metric for UFO, which is flexible to any requirements of practical application.

Experiments on a wide range of deep representation learning tasks show that UFO achieves higher accuracy with the smaller trimmed model than the single-task-trained counterpart. It confirms that while UFO gains the additional advantage of flexible deployment, it maintains the benefits of large-scale pretraining.

The contributions of the paper are summarized as follows:

- We propose a novel train-and-deploy paradigm, named Unified Feature Optimization (UFO), to benefit down-stream tasks with large-scale pretraining. UFO emphasizes the advantage of small model size and no adaptation cost, which significantly promotes flexible deployment.

- We propose a novel trimming process in UFO, dedicated to preserve the mutual benefits and discard the mutual conflicts from the multi-task unified model by the proposed NAS method.
- We propose a novel evaluation metric to measure the correlations among tasks, which provides basic and effective analyses for the trimming process.
- We experiment on 10+ benchmarks from face, person, vehicle and product. Comprehensive analyses and extensive experiments clearly show the effectiveness of our UFO.

2   Related Work

The development of smart city has led to significant demand on the optimizations of multiple objectives to facility integrated solutions of diverse, real-world problems. With an overall increase in number of models and tasks, significant computing and inference cost are required for deploying specific models for specific tasks, especially deployed on embedded sensors or devices where computational and power resources may be limited. One way to solve this problem is the development of foundation models, which refer to models trained from broad data at scale that is capable of being adapted to a wide range of down-stream tasks. Existing works try to overcome these challenges from the following two aspects.

2.1   Training Strategy

Tuning weights of different task losses is an effective method. Kendall et al. [23] propose a principled approach to tune the weights of multiple loss functions by considering the homoscedastic uncertainty of each task. Dynamic Task Prioritization [14] automatically prioritizes more difficult tasks by adaptively adjusting the mixing weight of each task's loss objective. Other works adopt gradient-based methods to combat the challenge. GradNorm [6] automatically balances the training of different task losses in deep multi-task models by dynamically tuning their gradient magnitudes. Sener et al. [37] explicitly cast multi-task learning as gradient-based multi-objective optimization, with the overall objective of finding a Pareto optimal solution to minimizing all task losses. Based on the observation that models with lower variance in the angles between task gradients perform better, Suteu et al. [40] propose a novel gradient regularization of enforcing nearly orthogonal gradients. To avoid the interference of gradients from different losses, PCGrad [43] projects a task's gradient onto the normal plane of the gradient of other tasks that have a conflicting gradient.

In contrast to these methods, our method designs a novel model structure, which adaptively specifies correlations or conflicts among all tasks, and obtains competitive results even with ordinary training strategy.

2.2   Model Structure

Some works [11,13,29,34] adopts the manner of soft parameter sharing. They allow each task to have separate model and parameters, but enforce each model can access the information inside other models by regularizers [11,34] or NAS-searched structures [13].

Other works [30,31,33,39] use a shared part of backbone parameters with task-specific modules, which is called hard parameter sharing. The first five convolutional layers are shared and task-specific fully-connected layers are used for each task in the method of Deep Relationship Networks [31]. Lu et al. [33] starts with a thin network and dynamically grows it during the training phase by creating new branches for tasks. Besides the area of computer vision, [30,39] use shared encoders with task-specific layers across multiple NLP tasks.

Beyond the two kind of ways, Task-MOE [25] proposes an architecture which combines both the shared and task-specific modules for multi-task learning. Specifically, it shares the Self-Attention modules and selects task-specific FFN modules based on a task-level router.

All these works consider adding components by encouraging the information interaction between single tasks or introducing task-specific modules, but miss the idea of reducing modules. By contrast, we extract subnet by reducing incompatible weights and keeping complementary weights from a surpernet. Similar to Task-MOE, our method also adopts task-level routers to select specific FFNs. However, our method extracts the most suitable sub-weights of Self-Attention for each task, while Task-MOE share the complete one among all tasks.

3   Methodology

UFO consists of two steps, *i.e.*, training a multi-task supernet, and extracting a dedicated sub-network for down-stream task deployment. Under this novel training and deploying paradigm, UFO aims to preserve the mutual benefit of multi-task pretraining and remove the mutual conflict between different tasks. To this end, we employ a Neural Architecture Search (NAS) method to search for the sub-network from the supernet. Specifically, we introduce the architecture of UFO supernet as well as its search space in Sect. 3.1. We note that different from the search space for single task, the UFO search space is to accommodate multiple sub-networks for various downstream tasks. Given the architecture of UFO supernet, Sect. 3.2 explains how to train the supernet on all the tasks in a multi-task learning manner. Finally, Sect. 3.3 elaborates on learning the sub-network extraction based on NAS. It allows UFO to directly extract a corresponding sub-network through architecture prediction, given the desired down-stream tasks (as well as the model size and inference speed).

3.1   The Architecture and Search Space of UFO Supernet

As shown in Fig. 1, we base the UFO supernet on the vision transformer (ViT). Since the sub-network selects partial modules from the supernet and inherits the corresponding parameters during the deployment, it is important that the supernet provides a large space for searching and extracting the sub-networks.

Prior transformer-based NAS usually provides three searching directions, *i.e.*, elastic depths, elastic attention heads and elastic expansion ratios of the Feed Forward Networks (FFN) [25]. In addition to these commonly-used searching directions, we introduce a novel search direction, *i.e.*, flexible FFN paths. In other words, UFO combines three commonly-used search directions and a novel one, and thus provides a large searching space. Consequently, the sub networks can reduce FFN paths, FFN weights, attention weights or even the whole sub blocks of the vision transformer. We explain these searching directions in details as below.

The architecture space is consisted with a set of architectures, and is denoted as $\mathcal{A} = \{a_1, a_2, \cdots, a_{n_a}\}$, $n_a = |\mathcal{A}|$. Let $\mathcal{H}$ be set of head numbers and $\mathcal{M}$ be the set of mlp ratios in FFN, where $\mathcal{H} = \{h_1, h_2, \cdots, h_{n_h}\}$, $n_h = |\mathcal{H}|$ and $\mathcal{M} = \{m_1, m_2, \cdots, m_{n_m}\}$, $n_m = |\mathcal{M}|$. Let $\mathcal{T}$ be the set of target tasks, where $\mathcal{T} = \{t_1, t_2, \cdots, t_{n_t}\}$, $n_t = |\mathcal{T}|$. Let $\mathcal{G}$ be the set of gate choice of FFN paths, where $\mathcal{G} = \{g_0, g_1, \cdots, g_{n_g}\}$, $n_g = |\mathcal{G}|$. Finally, let $\mathcal{D} = \{0,1\}$ be the set of drop choice to denote whether the entire layer will be dropped. Then, the search space $\mathcal{A}$ can be denoted as follows: $\mathcal{A} = \{[[h_1, m_1, g_1, d_1], [h_2, m_2, g_2, d_2], \cdots, [h_l, m_l, g_l, d_l]], h_i \in \mathcal{H}, m_i \in \mathcal{M}, g_i \subseteq \mathcal{G}, d_i \in \mathcal{D}, \forall i \in \{1, 2, \cdots, l\}\}$, where l is the numbers of layers. In summary, $\mathcal{G}$ determines the FFN paths of different tasks of $\mathcal{T}$. Furthermore, $\mathcal{H}$ and $\mathcal{M}$ determine the model size of different sub networks. Besides, $\mathcal{D}$ controls the depth of sub networks to further reduce the model size.

Given the input $\mathbf{x}_i^t$ of task t, an arch a is sampled from $\mathcal{A}$, and then the consecutive blocks of the arch are computed as:

$$\hat{\mathbf{x}}_i^t = d_l * \text{MHSA}(\text{LN}(\mathbf{x}_i^t), h_l) + \mathbf{x}_i^t$$
$$\mathbf{x}_{i+1}^t = d_l * \text{FFNs}(\text{LN}(\hat{\mathbf{x}}_i^t), m_i, g_i^t) + \hat{\mathbf{x}}_i^t \tag{1}$$

3.2 Multi-task Training of the UFO Supernet

In this subsection, we will describe how to train multi-task supernet. As shown in Subsect. 3.1, the supernet in UFO is quite different from other single-task supernets. Accordingly, the training strategy of UFO is also different in two aspects of sub-network sampling and data sampling.

Sub-network Sampling. The sub-network sampling is involved with the sampling of (m_l, h_l, d_l, g_l). Similar to weight entanglement mechanism [5], the weights of the arch a are shared with the weight of supernet for their common parts with respect to the sampling of m_l and g_l. However, as the supernet do not have FFN-paths in the existing training strategies [5,20,41], there are serious competitions among shared attention weights. Thus, their supernet has to be trained in a step-by-step way. In the UFO, the FFN-paths relieve the competition of shared attention. Thus, the UFO can be trained in an end-to-end way.

However, the supernet is hard to converge if we directly sample sub-networks from $\mathcal{A}$ with respect to g_l, because the total number of FFN paths is $|\mathcal{T}| \times (2^{|\mathcal{G}|} -$

$1)^l$. Thus, we set constraint for the path gate of each task, where each task in $\mathcal{T}$ only has 3 choices for each layer, i.e. shared FFN only, task specific FFN only or both. To be specific, we use gumbel-softmax on learn-able gate weights to sample probability distribution for task t. Thus, the output of FFNs (we ignore layer/block idx i) can be defined as:

$$\text{FFNs}(\cdot) = p^t[0]\text{FFN}_{shared}(\cdot) + p^t[1]\text{FFN}^t_{task-specific}(\cdot) \tag{2}$$

After training, the learned gate weights determine the single choice of gates by argmax or choose both gates. In this way, the total number of FFN paths is reduced from $|\mathcal{T}| \times (2^{|\mathcal{G}|} - 1)^l$ to $|\mathcal{T}| \times |3|^l$.

Data Sampling. There are five existing data sampling strategies in [1]. The accumulating gradient strategy is the most promising among them. It accumulates gradients from all task data in one optimizer step, and can achieve better optimization trade-off between different tasks than other methods, e.g. task-by-task and alternating methods. Inspire by the thought, we propose a similar but different strategy of forming batch, and it is called heterogeneous batch type. To be specific, we sample some data from all tasks of $\mathcal{T}$ to form a mini batch with a weight roughly proportional to the size of the task datasets, respectively. Then, these mini batch is concatenated into a batch data, which is feed into the backbone. Next, the obtained features are separated and feed into $|\mathcal{T}|$ task-specific head networks, each of which is responsible for the output of a task. Finally, we calculate the loss of $|\mathcal{T}|$ tasks, sum it up for the shared transform backbone network, and finish a backward step to obtain gradients, which are used to update the shared parameters.

3.3   Extracting the Sub-network for Down-Stream Task Deploying

In this subsection, we will introduce how to select optimal dedicated models from supernet according to requirement of practical applications.

Our target is to find optimal architecture a of $\mathcal{A}$ under flops and parameter constraints and the average performance is maximized.

Let $f_t(a)$ be the performance of architecture a on task t, $\forall t \in \mathcal{T}$, $\forall a \in \mathcal{A}$. Then, let $f_{\mathbf{t}}(a)$ be the performance of architecture a on task set $\mathbf{t}$, $\forall \mathbf{t} \subset \mathcal{T}$, $\forall a \in \mathcal{A}$.

Except for the extreme performances for target tasks, we also care about the generalized performances on other tasks. Thus, let $avg\_f(\mathbf{t}, a)$ be the comprehensive performance of architecture on all tasks, where:

$$avg\_f(\mathbf{t}, a) = \lambda f_{\mathbf{t}}(a) + (1 - \lambda)f_{\mathcal{T}\backslash\mathbf{t}}(a) \tag{3}$$

$$= \lambda \sum_{t_1 \in \mathbf{t}} f_{t_1}(a) + (1 - \lambda) \sum_{t_2 \in \mathcal{T}\backslash\mathbf{t}} f_{t_2}(a) \tag{4}$$

$$, \forall \mathbf{t} \subset \mathcal{T}, \forall a \in \mathcal{A} \tag{5}$$

Algorithm 1: Multi-task Searching Algorithm (MSA)

Input: $\mathcal{T}$, $\mathcal{A}$, **t**;
Output: a_best;

1 Generate a sub set of architectures $\mathcal{S}$ from $\mathcal{A}$, $\mathcal{S} \subset \mathcal{A}$.
2 Initialize performance predictors $pre(a, t)$ for each task, $\forall t \in \mathcal{T}$, $\forall a \in \mathcal{A}$.
3 Initialize $ready\_flag\_t$ for each task, $\forall t \in \mathcal{T}$.
4 **for** $n = 1; n <= k; n + +$ **do**
5   Sample architectures from $\mathcal{S}$.
6   **for** $t \in \mathcal{T}$ **do**
7   Train predictor of task t.
8   Calculate predicted architectures ranks of task t.
9   Calculate Kendall tau between ground truth ranks and predicted ranks for task t, kd_t.
10   **if** $kd\_t >= thre\_t$ **then**
11 | $ready\_flag\_t = 1$;
12   **end**
13   **end**
14   **if** $ready\_flag\_t == 1, \forall t \in \mathcal{T}$ *or* $n == k$ **then**
15   Calculate objective function of ORP for all architectures in $\mathcal{S}$ according to Eq. 13.
16   Select best architecture a_best.
17   Return a_best.
18   **end**
19 **end**

λ is set to $1/|\mathcal{T}|$ by default, and can be flexibly adjusted according to different tasks.

Then, we can formulate as follows:

$$\max \lambda \sum_{t_1 \in \mathbf{t}} f_{t_1}(a) + (1 - \lambda) \sum_{t_2 \in \mathcal{T} \backslash \mathbf{t}} f_{t_2}(a) \tag{6}$$

$$\text{s.t.} a \in \mathcal{A}, \tag{7}$$

$$flops(a) <= constraint\_flops \tag{8}$$

$$parameters(a) <= constraint\_parameters \tag{9}$$

Nevertheless, as $avg\_f(\mathbf{t}, a)$ has different metrics for different tasks which can not be added directly, we use rank instead of performance.

Similarly, let $r_t(a)$ be the rank of performance of architecture a on task t, $\forall t \in \mathcal{T}$, $\forall a \in \mathcal{A}$. Then, let $r_\mathbf{t}(a)$ be the rank of performance of architecture a on task set $\mathbf{t}$, $\forall t \subset \mathcal{T}$, $\forall a \in \mathcal{A}$.

Similarly, we also care about the generalized rank on other tasks. Accordingly, let $avg\_r(\mathbf{t}, a)$ be the comprehensive rank of architecture on all tasks, where:

$$avg\_r(\mathbf{t}, a) = \lambda r_{\mathbf{t}}(a) + (1 - \lambda) r_{\mathcal{T} \backslash \mathbf{t}}(a) \tag{10}$$

$$= \lambda \sum_{t_1 \in \mathbf{t}} r_{t_1}(a) + (1 - \lambda) \sum_{t_2 \in \mathcal{T} \backslash \mathbf{t}} r_{t_2}(a) \tag{11}$$

$$, \forall \mathbf{t} \subset \mathcal{T}, \forall a \in \mathcal{A} \tag{12}$$

Finally, we formulate the optimal rank problem (ORP) as follows:

$$\min \ \lambda \sum_{t_1 \in \mathbf{t}} r_{t_1}(a) + (1 - \lambda) \sum_{t_2 \in \mathcal{T} \backslash \mathbf{t}} r_{l_2}(a) \tag{13}$$

$$\text{s.t. } a \in \mathcal{A}, \tag{14}$$

$$flops(a) <= constraint\_flops \tag{15}$$

$$parameters(a) <= constraint\_parameters \tag{16}$$

Then, a multi-task searching algorithm (MSA) is proposed to solve the ORP. Alogrithm 1 shows the pseudo code of MSA. As the search space is huge, we first generate a sub set of architectures $\mathcal{S}$ from $\mathcal{A}$, $\mathcal{S} \in \mathcal{A}$. Then, we sample architectures from $\mathcal{S}$ to train task specific performance predictors separately based on GP-NAS [27]. We utilize Kendall tau to measure the accuracy of the predictors. When the predictors are all well trained, we calculate the objective function of ORP for all architectures in $\mathcal{S}$ according to Eq. 13 and select best architecture a_best. In the experiment section, we will evaluate the performance of task specific predictors thoroughly.

4   Experiments

4.1   Settings

Training Dataset. MS1M-V3 (MS1M-RetinaFace) [8,9,15], Market1501-Train [44], MSMT17-Train [42], Veri-776-Train [28], VehicleID-Train [28], VeriWild-Train [32] and SOP-Train [36] are used as training dataset. The detailed information is shown in table 1.

Table 1. Trainning Dataset

Tasks	Datesets	Img number	ID number
Face	MS1M-V3	5,179,510	93,431
Person	Market1501-Train	12,936	751
Person	MSMT17-Train	30,248	1,041
Vehicle	Veri-776-Train	37,778	576
Vehicle	VehicleID-Train	113,346	13,164
Vehicle	VeriWild-Train	277,797	30,671
Products	SOP-Train	59,551	11,318

Table 2. Test Dataset

Tasks	Datesets	Img number	ID number
Face	LFW	12,000	–
Face	CPLFW	12,000	–
Face	CFP-FF	14,000	–
Face	CFP-FP	14,000	–
Face	CALFW	12,000	–
Face	AGEDB-30	12,000	–
Person	Market1501-Test	19,281	750
Person	MSMT17-Test	93,820	3,060
Vehicle	Veri-776-Test	13,257	200
Vehicle	VehicleID-Test	19,777	2,400
Vehicle	VeriWild-Test	138,517	10,000
Products	SOP-Test	60,502	11,316

Table 3. Training Configurations

	Face/Person/Vehicle/Products
Input Size	256×256
Batch Size	1024/512/512/512
Augmentation	Flipping + Random Erasing + AutoAug
Model	ViT-base
Feature Dim	768
Loss	CosFace Loss/(CosFace Loss + Triplet Loss)*3
Optimizer	SGD
Init LR	0.2
LR scheduler	Warmup + Cosine LR
Iterations	100,000

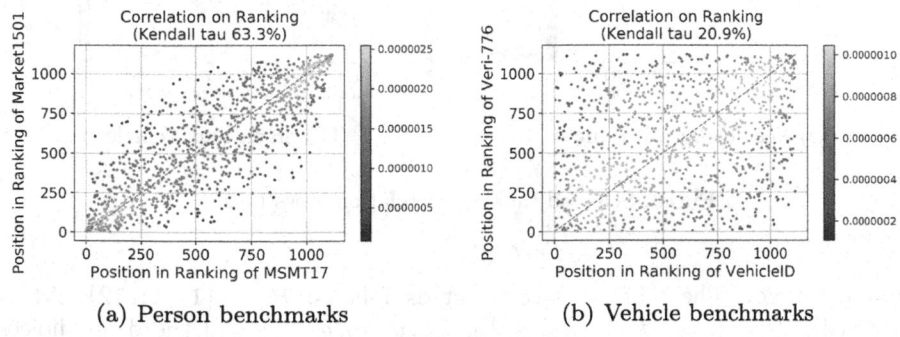

(a) Person benchmarks   (b) Vehicle benchmarks

Fig. 2. Ranking correlation within tasks.

Test Dataset. Accordingly, we use LFW [21], CPLFW [45], CFP [38], CALFW [46], AGEDB-30 [35], Market1501-Test [44], MSMT17-Test [42], Veri-776-Test [28], VehicleID-Test [28], VeriWild-Test [32] and SOP-Test [36] as test dataset. The detailed information is shown in table 2.

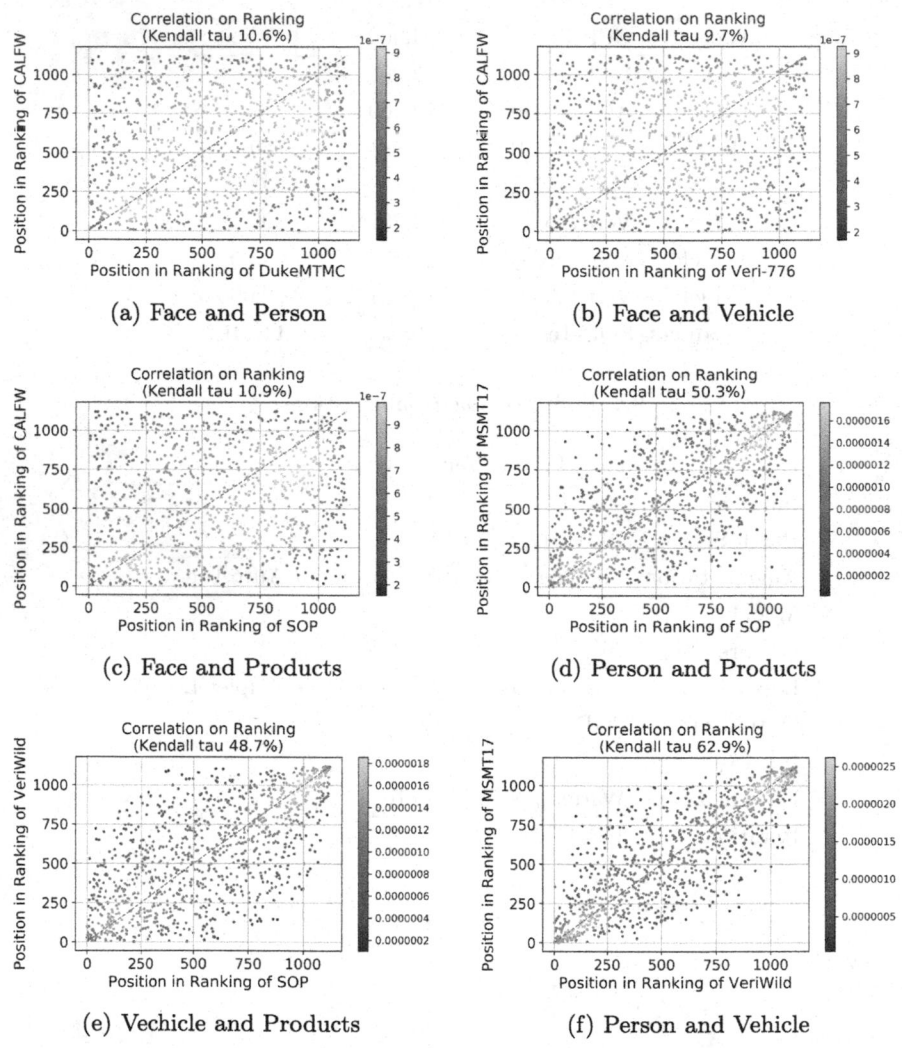

(a) Face and Person

(b) Face and Vehicle

(c) Face and Products

(d) Person and Products

(e) Vechicle and Products

(f) Person and Vehicle

Fig. 3. Selected ranking correlation cross tasks

Seach Space. The search space is set as follows: $\mathcal{H} = \{10, 11, 12\}$, $\mathcal{M} = \{3, 3.5, 4\}$, $\mathcal{T} = \{t_1, t_2, t_3, t_4\}$, $\mathcal{G} = \{g_{share}, g_1, g_2, g_3, g_4\}$ and the drop choices of the first 10 layers are all set to 1 and λ is set to 1/4. The subset size $|\mathcal{S}|$ is set to 10,0000 and we sample 500 sub networks from $\mathcal{S}$ for training where each sampled sub network is evaluated on all benchmarks. The sampled networks and $\mathcal{S}$ are released as one of the first multi-task NAS benchmark and has supported the performance prediction track of the second lightweight NAS challenge of CVPR 2022 (https://cvpr-nas.com/competition).

Sampling Strategy. We sample data from four tasks to form a batch, input the batch to the shared transformer backbone network, and finally separate four head networks, each of which is responsible for the output of a task. The four tasks separately calculate the loss and sum it up as the total loss.

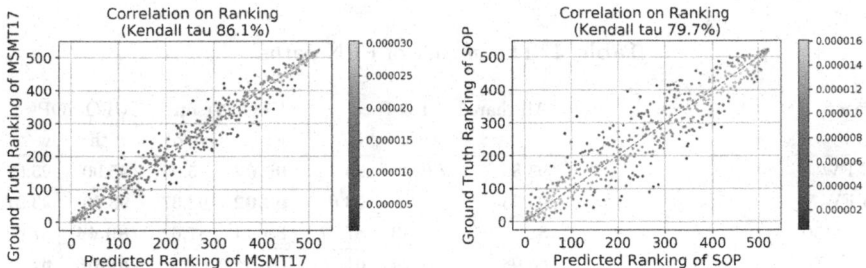

(a) Ranking correlation between ground truth and prediction on MSMT17.

(b) Ranking correlation between ground truth and prediction on SOP.

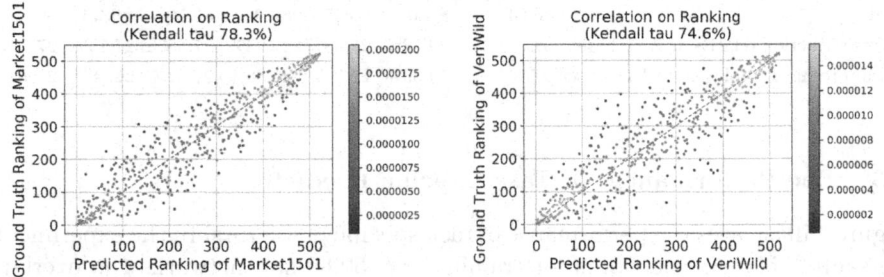

(c) Ranking correlation between ground truth and prediction on Market1501.

(d) Ranking correlation between ground truth and prediction on VeriWild.

Fig. 4. Performance of task specific predictors on selected benchmarks.

Training Configurations. Because the input size and model structure used by different tasks are quite different. From the model optimization level, the batch size, learning rate and even the optimizer are all different. In order to facilitate subsequent multi-task training, we first unify the model structure and optimization method of each task. In particular, we use transformer as the backbone network. The unified configurations are shown in table 3.

Experiments with bigger backbones and with more dataset can be found in https://github.com/PaddlePaddle/VIMER/tree/main/UFO.

4.2 Correlation Within and Cross Tasks

As different benchmark has different metric, we utilize Kendall tau to measure ranking correlation within and cross tasks. In this experiment, we have sampled 1000+ architectures from S with different reduced parameters and evaluated the performance of each architecture on all benchmarks.

We first conduct experiment on person benchmarks and vehicle benchmarks. As shown in Fig. 2, person benchmarks are highly correlated while, vehicle benchmark are sightly correlated.

Then, we conduct experiments on benchmarks between different tasks. As shown in Fig. 3, the benchmark of face is sightly correlated to all other tasks. While, certain benchmarks of person, vehicle and products are highly correlated.

Table 4. The impact of FFN paths.

Datasets	All shared	UFO-Face		UFO-Person		UFO-SOP	
		with	w/o	with	w/o	with	w/o
CALFW	95.86	**96.00**	95.95	**96.02**	95.92	95.90	95.92
CPLFW	93.53	93.62	93.65	**93.62**	93.37	93.30	93.37
Market1501	88.19	**89.33**	87.57	**89.44**	87.62	**89.44**	87.62
MSMT17	60.08	**64.24**	61.13	**64.84**	61.38	**64.66**	61.38
Veri-776	86.11	**87.90**	86.48	**88.03**	86.50	**87.95**	86.50
VehicleID	86.27	**85.43**	85.40	**87.00**	85.46	**86.41**	85.46
VeriWild	68.43	**69.60**	67.85	**69.72**	67.92	**69.69**	67.92
SOP	86.64	**86.09**	83.47	**86.19**	83.50	**86.24**	83.53
Flops reduction relative to ViT-base	0%	29.52%	27.38%	26.94%	27.38%	27.15%	27.38%
Param reduction relative to ViT-base	0%	29.39%	27.25%	26.88%	27.31%	26.88%	27.10%

4.3 The Performances of Task Specific Predictors

Figure 4 illustrates the performance of task specific predictors. In the experiment, we sample 500 sub networks for training and 500+ sub networks (no overlap) for testing where each sampled sub network is evaluated on all tasks. Then, we measure the correlation between the predicted rankings and ground truth rankings. As shown in the figure, the predictors are with very good accuracy.

4.4 The Impact of FFN Paths

As shown in table 4, FFN paths is of significant importance in multi-task learning, compared with all shared approach. The supernet with FFN paths can significantly improve the performances. One possible explanation is that, FFN paths relieve the competition of shared attention weights.

4.5 Compared with SOTA Results

In this subsection, we compare UFO with previous SOTA results[1] on 10 benchmarks, that are SOTA results on CALFW [2], CPLFW [24], CFP-FF [7], Market1501 [19], MSMT17 [18], Veri-776 [22], VehicleID [17], VeriWild [17] and SOP [26]. As shown in table 5, UFO reaches SOTA result on CFP-FF and creates 4 new SOTA results on CPLFW, Veri-776, VehicleID and SOP. We can averagely reduce 51.08% flops and 42.34% parameters (relative to supernet). Besides, we also compare UFO against two recent state-of-the-art multi-task methods, i.e., Switch Transformers [12] and DSelect-k [16] (based on their publicly available code). Our UFO surpasses Switch Transformers/DSelect-k by 1.28/1.05% (CALFW), 1.61/1.30% (CPLFW), 0.29/0.25% (CFP-FF), 1.43/0.98% (Market-1501), 1.79/2.18% (MSMT17), 5.39/6.27% (Veri-776), 6.28/6.47% (VehicleID), 12.32/12.57% (VeriWild), 0.03/0.62% (SOP), respectively.

Table 5. Compared with SOTA results

	SOTA	UFO for CPLFW	UFO for CFP-FF	UFO for Veri776	UFO for VehicleID	UFO for SOP
CALFW	96.20	95.78	95.98	95.95	95.83	95.95
CPLFW	93.37	93.65	93.40	93.60	93.47	93.63
CFP-FF	99.89	99.87	99.89	99.83	99.86	99.86
Market1501	91.50	89.45	89.52	89.46	89.51	89.50
MSMT17	69.40	64.84	64.86	64.87	65.03	65.06
Veri-776	87.10	88.03	88.01	88.18	88.09	88.06
VehicleID	80.50	85.26	86.32	86.18	87.04	86.44
VeriWild	77.30	69.74	69.71	69.73	69.82	69.74
SOP	85.90	86.19	86.22	86.21	86.25	86.39
Flops reduction relative to ViT-base	–	18.90%	25.00%	11.50%	20.00%	24.00%
Param reduction relative to ViT-base	–	17.60%	23.90%	10.30%	18.90%	22.80%
Flops reduction relative to supernet	–	50.84%	54.54%	46.36%	51.51%	53.93%
Param reduction relative to supernet	–	41.97%	46.40%	36.83%	42.88%	45.63%

5 Conclusions

This paper proposes a novel train-and-deploy paradigm named Unified Feature Optimization (UFO) to benefit down-stream tasks with large-scale pretraining. UFO maintains the benefit of large-scale pretraining and provides high convenience for flexible deployment: it transfers the multi-task trained supernet to a dedicated model for any already-seen sub-tasks without no adaptation cost and reduces the model size during adaptation. On deep representation learning tasks, we explore an early prototype of UFO based on Vision Transformer (ViT) and Neural Architecture Search (NAS) techniques. Specifically, UFO integrates multiple trimming strategies to enhance the trimming flexibility for ViT and employs a novel performance-ranking based method for NAS. Experimental results show that the sub-model trimmed from supernet surpasses its single-task-trained counterpart and has smaller model size. That being said, we also note that the accuracy improvement

---

[1] without rerank strategy and external data from https://paperswithcode.com/.

and the size reduction is still marginal and call for more efforts from the research community to explore UFO. Besides, UFO also supported the release of 17 billion parameters computer vision (CV) foundation model which is the largest CV model in the industry.

References

1. Abnar, S., Dehghani, M., Neyshabur, B., Sedghi, H.: Exploring the limits of large scale pre-training. arXiv preprint arXiv:2110.02095 (2021)
2. An, X., et al.: Partial fc: Training 10 million identities on a single machine. In: Proceedings of the IEEE/CVF International Conference on Computer Vision, pp. 1445–1449 (2021)
3. Bommasani, R., et al.: On the opportunities and risks of foundation models. arXiv preprint arXiv:2108.07258 (2021)
4. Cai, H., Gan, C., Wang, T., Zhang, Z., Han, S.: Once-for-all: Train one network and specialize it for efficient deployment. arXiv preprint arXiv:1908.09791 (2019)
5. Chen, M., Peng, H., Fu, J., Ling, H.: Autoformer: Searching transformers for visual recognition. In: Proceedings of the IEEE/CVF International Conference on Computer Vision, pp. 12270–12280 (2021)
6. Chen, Z., Badrinarayanan, V., Lee, C.Y., Rabinovich, A.: Gradnorm: Gradient normalization for adaptive loss balancing in deep multitask networks. In: International Conference on Machine Learning, pp. 794–803. PMLR (2018)
7. Chrysos, G.G., Moschoglou, S., Bouritsas, G., Deng, J., Panagakis, Y., Zafeiriou, S.P.: Deep polynomial neural networks. In: IEEE Transactions on Pattern Analysis and Machine Intelligence, pp. 7325–7335 (2021)
8. Deng, J., Guo, J., Ververas, E., Kotsia, I., Zafeiriou, S.: Retinaface: Single-shot multi-level face localisation in the wild. In: Proceedings of the IEEE/CVF Conference on Computer Vision and Pattern Recognition, pp. 5203–5212 (2020)
9. Deng, J., Guo, J., Zhang, D., Deng, Y., Lu, X., Shi, S.: Lightweight face recognition challenge. In: Proceedings of the IEEE/CVF International Conference on Computer Vision Workshops, pp. 0–0 (2019)
10. Dosovitskiy, A., et al.: An image is worth 16x16 words: Transformers for image recognition at scale. arXiv preprint arXiv:2010.11929 (2020)
11. Duong, L., Cohn, T., Bird, S., Cook, P.: Low resource dependency parsing: Cross-lingual parameter sharing in a neural network parser. In: Proceedings of the 53rd annual meeting of the Association for Computational Linguistics and the 7th international joint conference on natural language processing, vol. 2, pp. 845–850 (2015)
12. Fedus, W., Zoph, B., Shazeer, N.: Switch transformers: Scaling to trillion parameter models with simple and efficient sparsity. arXiv preprint arXiv:2101.03961 (2021)
13. Gao, Y., Bai, H., Jie, Z., Ma, J., Jia, K., Liu, W.: Mtl-nas: Task-agnostic neural architecture search towards general-purpose multi-task learning. In: Proceedings of the IEEE/CVF Conference on computer vision and pattern recognition, pp. 11543–11552 (2020)
14. Guo, M., Haque, A., Huang, D.A., Yeung, S., Fei-Fei, L.: Dynamic task prioritization for multitask learning. In: Proceedings of the European conference on computer vision (ECCV), pp. 270–287 (2018)
15. Guo, Y., Zhang, L., Hu, Y., He, X., Gao, J.: MS-Celeb-1M: a dataset and benchmark for large-scale face recognition. In: Leibe, B., Matas, J., Sebe, N., Welling, M. (eds.) ECCV 2016. LNCS, vol. 9907, pp. 87–102. Springer, Cham (2016). https://doi.org/10.1007/978-3-319-46487-9_6

16. Hazimeh, H., et al.: Dselect-k: differentiable selection in the mixture of experts with applications to multi-task learning. Adv. Neural. Inf. Process. Syst. **34**, 29335–29347 (2021)

17. He, L., Liao, X., Liu, W., Liu, X., Cheng, P., Mei, T.: Fastreid: A pytorch toolbox for general instance re-identification. arXiv preprint arXiv:2006.02631 (2020)

18. He, S., Luo, H., Wang, P., Wang, F., Li, H., Jiang, W.: Transreid: Transformer-based object re-identification. In: Proceedings of the IEEE/CVF International Conference on Computer Vision, pp. 15013–15022 (2021)

19. Herzog, F., Ji, X., Teepe, T., Hörmann, S., Gilg, J., Rigoll, G.: Lightweight multi-branch network for person re-identification. In: 2021 IEEE International Conference on Image Processing (ICIP), pp. 1129–1133. IEEE (2021)

20. Hou, L., Huang, Z., Shang, L., Jiang, X., Chen, X., Liu, Q.: Dynabert: dynamic bert with adaptive width and depth. Adv. Neural. Inf. Process. Syst. **33**, 9782–9793 (2020)

21. Huang, G.B., Mattar, M., Berg, T., Learned-Miller, E.: Labeled faces in the wild: A database forstudying face recognition in unconstrained environments. In: Workshop on faces in'Real-Life'Images: detection, alignment and recognition (2008)

22. Huynh, S.V.: A strong baseline for vehicle re-identification. In: Proceedings of the IEEE/CVF Conference on Computer Vision and Pattern Recognition, pp. 4147–4154 (2021)

23. Kendall, A., Gal, Y., Cipolla, R.: Multi-task learning using uncertainty to weigh losses for scene geometry and semantics. In: Proceedings of the IEEE conference on computer vision and pattern recognition, pp. 7482–7491 (2018)

24. Kim, Y., Park, W., Roh, M.C., Shin, J.: Groupface: Learning latent groups and constructing group-based representations for face recognition. In: Proceedings of the IEEE/CVF Conference on Computer Vision and Pattern Recognition, pp. 5621–5630 (2020)

25. Kudugunta, S., et al.: Beyond distillation: Task-level mixture-of-experts for efficient inference. arXiv preprint arXiv:2110.03742 (2021)

26. Lee, J., et al.: Compounding the performance improvements of assembled techniques in a convolutional neural network. arXiv preprint arXiv:2001.06268 (2020)

27. Li, Z., Xi, T., Deng, J., Zhang, G., Wen, S., He, R.: Gp-nas: Gaussian process based neural architecture search. In: Proceedings of the IEEE/CVF Conference on Computer Vision and Pattern Recognition, pp. 11933–11942 (2020)

28. Liu, H., Tian, Y., Yang, Y., Pang, L., Huang, T.: Deep relative distance learning: Tell the difference between similar vehicles. In: Proceedings of the IEEE conference on computer vision and pattern recognition, pp. 2167–2175 (2016)

29. Liu, P., Qiu, X., Huang, X.: Recurrent neural network for text classification with multi-task learning. arXiv preprint arXiv:1605.05101 (2016)

30. Liu, X., He, P., Chen, W., Gao, J.: Multi-task deep neural networks for natural language understanding. arXiv preprint arXiv:1901.11504 (2019)

31. Long, M., Wang, J.: Learning multiple tasks with deep relationship networks. arXiv preprint arXiv:1506.02117 2(1) (2015)

32. Lou, Y., Bai, Y., Liu, J., Wang, S., Duan, L.: Veri-wild: A large dataset and a new method for vehicle re-identification in the wild. In: Proceedings of the IEEE/CVF conference on computer vision and pattern recognition, pp. 3235–3243 (2019)

33. Lu, Y., Kumar, A., Zhai, S., Cheng, Y., Javidi, T., Feris, R.: Fully-adaptive feature sharing in multi-task networks with applications in person attribute classification. In: Proceedings of the IEEE conference on computer vision and pattern recognition, pp. 5334–5343 (2017)

34. Misra, I., Shrivastava, A., Gupta, A., Hebert, M.: Cross-stitch networks for multi-task learning. In: Proceedings of the IEEE conference on computer vision and pattern recognition, pp. 3994–4003 (2016)
35. Moschoglou, S., Papaioannou, A., Sagonas, C., Deng, J., Kotsia, I., Zafeiriou, S.: Agedb: the first manually collected, in-the-wild age database. In: proceedings of the IEEE conference on computer vision and pattern recognition workshops, pp. 51–59 (2017)
36. Oh Song, H., Xiang, Y., Jegelka, S., Savarese, S.: Deep metric learning via lifted structured feature embedding. In: Proceedings of the IEEE conference on computer vision and pattern recognition, pp. 4004–4012 (2016)
37. Sencr, O., Koltun, V · Multi-task learning as multi-objective optimization. In: Advances in Neural Information Processing Systems vol. 31 (2018)
38. Sengupta, S., Chen, J.C., Castillo, C., Patel, V.M., Chellappa, R., Jacobs, D.W.: Frontal to profile face verification in the wild. In: 2016 IEEE Winter Conference on Applications of Computer Vision (WACV), pp. 1–9. IEEE (2016)
39. Subramanian, S., Trischler, A., Bengio, Y., Pal, C.J.: Learning general purpose distributed sentence representations via large scale multi-task learning. arXiv preprint arXiv:1804.00079 (2018)
40. Suteu, M., Guo, Y.: Regularizing deep multi-task networks using orthogonal gradients. arXiv preprint arXiv:1912.06844 (2019)
41. Wang, H., et al.: Hat: Hardware-aware transformers for efficient natural language processing. arXiv preprint arXiv:2005.14187 (2020)
42. Wei, L., Zhang, S., Gao, W., Tian, Q.: Person transfer gan to bridge domain gap for person re-identification. In: Proceedings of the IEEE Conference on Computer Vision and Pattern Recognition, pp. 79–88 (2018)
43. Yu, T., Kumar, S., Gupta, A., Levine, S., Hausman, K., Finn, C.: Gradient surgery for multi-task learning. Adv. Neural. Inf. Process. Syst. 33, 5824–5836 (2020)
44. Zheng, L., Shen, L., Tian, L., Wang, S., Bu, J., Tian, Q.: Person re-identification meets image search. arXiv preprint arXiv:1502.02171 (2015)
45. Zheng, T., Deng, W.: Cross-pose lfw: A database for studying cross-pose face recognition in unconstrained environments. In: Beijing University of Posts and Telecommunications, Tech. Rep 5, 7 (2018)
46. Zheng, T., Deng, W., Hu, J.: Cross-age lfw: A database for studying cross-age face recognition in unconstrained environments. arXiv preprint arXiv:1708.08197 (2017)

Sound Localization by Self-supervised Time Delay Estimation

Ziyang Chen$^{(\boxtimes)}$, David F. Fouhey, and Andrew Owens

University of Michigan, Ann Arbor, USA
czyang@umich.edu

Abstract. Sounds reach one microphone in a stereo pair sooner than the other, resulting in an *interaural time delay* that conveys their directions. Estimating a sound's time delay requires finding correspondences between the signals recorded by each microphone. We propose to learn these correspondences through self-supervision, drawing on recent techniques from visual tracking. We adapt the contrastive random walk of Jabri et al. to learn a cycle-consistent representation from unlabeled stereo sounds, resulting in a model that performs on par with supervised methods on "in the wild" internet recordings. We also propose a multimodal contrastive learning model that solves a *visually-guided* localization task: estimating the time delay for a particular person in a multi-speaker mixture, given a visual representation of their face. Project site: https://ificl.github.io/stereocrw.

1 Introduction

Sounds in the world arrive at one of our two ears slightly sooner than the other. This *interaural time delay*, which generally lasts only a few hundred microseconds, indicates a sound's direction and thus provides an important cue for multimodal perception. In humans, for example, time delays convey the positions of objects that move out of sight, and are integrated with visual cues when localizing events [53]. Visual information can also guide the sound localization process, allowing us to find a particular event of interest through binaural cues, while ignoring the others.

While high-quality stereo sound recordings are now abundant, such as in the audio tracks of videos recorded by consumer phones, existing methods often struggle to localize sound sources within them, particularly when they contain correlated noise or multiple sound sources. The localization problem has typically been addressed by matching hand-crafted features [51,67] and, recently, by supervised learning [21,44,62]. However, the difficulty in acquiring natural labeled data has limited their effectiveness. Many approaches, consequently, resort to using simulated training data that may not be fully representative of the world.

We propose to address these problems by learning time delay estimation from real, unlabeled recordings. We take inspiration from work in self-supervised

Supplementary Information The online version contains supplementary material available at https://doi.org/10.1007/978-3-031-19809-0_28.

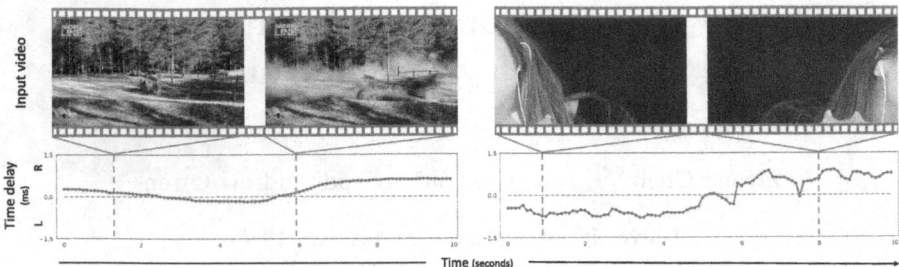

Fig. 1. Given a stereo audio recording, we estimate a sound's *interaural time delay*. Our model learns through self-supervision to find correspondences between the signals in each channel, from which the time delay can be estimated. We show time delay predictions for two scenes, along with their corresponding video frames (not used by the model). In both cases, the sound source changes its position in a scene, resulting in a corresponding change in time delay.

visual tracking that learns space-time correspondences from videos, such as through cycle consistency [5,46,78] and contrastive learning [79]. Analogously, our approach is based on learning audio embeddings that can be used to find *interaural correspondences*: pairs of sounds from different stereo channels that correspond to the same underlying events.

We introduce a model, inspired by the *contrastive random walk* of Jabri et al. [46], that learns cycle consistent features from unlabeled stereo sound. This model maximizes the return probability of a random walk on a graph whose nodes correspond to the audio samples in each channel. In this graph, edges connect samples between channels, and the walk's transition probabilities are defined by learned embeddings. We show examples of time delay estimates for two real-world videos in Fig. 1.

We also propose a model inspired by instance discrimination [12,23,40,81] that can perform a novel *visually-guided* time delay estimation task: localizing a speaker in a multi-speaker audio recording, given only their visual appearance. The resulting model is simple and can accurately localize speakers, without the need for explicitly separating sounds in the mixture. We also use this approach to train audio-based localization models solely from mono audio, which in some domains may be more readily available than stereo sound. This model uses data augmentation to incorporate knowledge about invariances to important sources of variation.

Through experiments on simulated environments with metrically accurate ground truth, and on internet videos with directional judgments annotated by human listeners, we show:

- Interaural time delays can be accurately estimated through self-supervised learning, using either unlabeled stereo and mono training data.
- Our models provide robustness to distracting sounds within a mixture, and perform well on real-world recordings, obtaining competitive performance with state-of-the-art supervised methods.
- Visual signals allow our models to localize specific speakers within mixtures.

2   Related Work

Human Binaural Localization. Humans use two main cues for estimating the azimuth of a sound: interaural time differences (ITD) and interaural intensity differences (IID), i.e., the difference in the loudness of the sounds entering both ears [64,75]. In practice, IID is primarily useful for high-frequency sounds that are close to the observer, while ITD is useful for low-frequency sounds and is relatively unaffected by distance [8]. Our work is thus complementary to methods that use IID cues. Humans can accurately estimate azimuth from multi-source mixtures [39,86], and integrate vision with binaural cues [53], motivating our work on multi-speaker time delay estimation.

Time Delay Estimation. Time delay estimation is a classic signal processing problem. In early work, Carter et al. [9] estimated time delays using generalized cross-correlation with phase transform (GCC-PHAT), which corresponds to a maximum likelihood estimate under low noise [7,51,87]. Other work uses beamforming [22] or subspace methods [67]. Comanducci et al. [18] trained a convolutional network (CNN) to denoise GCC-PHAT features. Other work trains a multi-layer perceptron to predict a time delay from a raw waveform [44], trains recurrent networks on hand-crafted features [1,62], and uses 3D CNNs [21]. Christensen et al. [14] used GCC-PHAT and echolocation to estimate depth maps from audio. In concurrent work, Chen et al. [13] localized multiple sounds by jointly solving source separation and time delay estimation problems. Time delay estimation also has a wide range of applications and modalities, such as oceanography [6], wireless networking [61,85], sonar [10], and possibly directional olfaction [63]. In contrast, we pose time delay estimation as a self-supervised learning problem, and we do not require hand-crafted features or labels.

Supervised Binaural Localization. Vecchiotti et al. [73] estimated sound direction directly from raw waveforms. Other work uses Short-time Fourier Transform [2,11,83] or beamforming features [65]. Due to the challenge in obtaining labeled data, these methods have largely been trained on synthetic or lab-collected data. In contrast to these approaches, we learn a specific (but widely useful) cue—the time delay—through self-supervision on natural data.

Audio-Visual Binaural Learning. Yang et al. [84] distinguished between audio-visual examples in which the stereo channels have (or have not been) swapped, resulting in a representation that can be finetuned to solve localization tasks. In contrast, our model can optionally be trained and deployed solely with audio, and produces an output—the time delay—that is directly correlated with sound direction, without the need for finetuning. Gan et al. [30] used a car detector to provide pseudo ground truth for a sound-based localization method. Since the training data comes from a supervised car detector, the model relies on labeled training data, whereas ours is self-supervised. Later work [19,72] extends this approach by distilling supervision from multiple visual classifiers and modalities. Other work generates stereo sound from mono audio using images [32, 34,82], largely by adjusting the relative volume of the channels to simulate IID cues.

Audio-Visual Sound Localization and Separation. A variety of methods have been proposed for using vision to localize and separate sounds. Classic work searches for cross-modal similarity in statistical models [28,42,49]. Later work uses contrastive learning to find image regions that are highly correlated with sound [4,58,59,70,88], and separates sounds from synthetic mixtures [3,26,29, 31,58]. Recent work has applied the contrastive random walk to localize multiple sounds within images [45]. This method learns correspondences between image patches and (mono) audio, whereas our model learns correspondences between the signals in each stereo channel.

Audio Self-supervision. A variety of methods have been proposed for learning audio representations through self-supervision, typically for semantic recognition tasks, such as music or speech understanding. These include contrastive learning [36,47,57,68,76,77], autoencoding [25], multi-task learning with pretext tasks [60], and generative autoregressive models [17]. In contrast, we learn a representation for learning interaural correspondence in binaural audio.

Learning Visual Correspondences. We take inspiration from methods that learn space-time correspondences from video. These include methods that colorize grayscale video [74], cycle-consistent feature representations [38,46,78] and slow features [37,80]. Other work [79] has shown that features learned through instance discrimination [12,24,40,81] are effective for tracking. However, these methods have not been applied to learning stereo audio correspondences. In our models, by contrast, vision is used to aid the audio matching process. We adapt several of these methods [5,12,37,46] to learn correspondences between temporal samples of audio for binaural matching.

3   Method

The goal of the time delay estimation problem is to determine how much sooner a sound reaches one microphone than another[1]. Given the two channels of a stereo recording, $\mathbf{x}_1, \mathbf{x}_2 \in \mathbb{R}^n$, represented as waveforms, and a function $h : \mathbb{R}^n \mapsto \mathbb{R}^{n \times d}$ that computes features for each temporal sample, a common solution is to choose a time delay τ that maximizes the generalized cross-correlation [51]:

$$R_{\mathbf{x}_1, \mathbf{x}_2}(\tau) = \mathbb{E}_t \left[\mathbf{h}_1(t) \cdot \mathbf{h}_2(t - \tau) \right], \tag{1}$$

where $\mathbf{h}_i = h(\mathbf{x}_i)$ are the features for $\mathbf{x}_i$, and $\mathbf{h}_i(t)$ is the d-dimensional feature embedding for time t.

Traditionally, the audio features, h, are defined using hand-crafted features. For example, the widely-used Generalized Cross Correlation with Phase Transform (GCC-PHAT) [51] whitens the audio by dividing by the magnitude of the cross-power spectral density. This approach provides the maximum likelihood solution under certain ideal, low-noise conditions [7,51,87].

---

[1] This quantity is also known as the *time difference of arrival* (TDOA) or alternatively as the *interaural time difference* or *delay* (ITD).

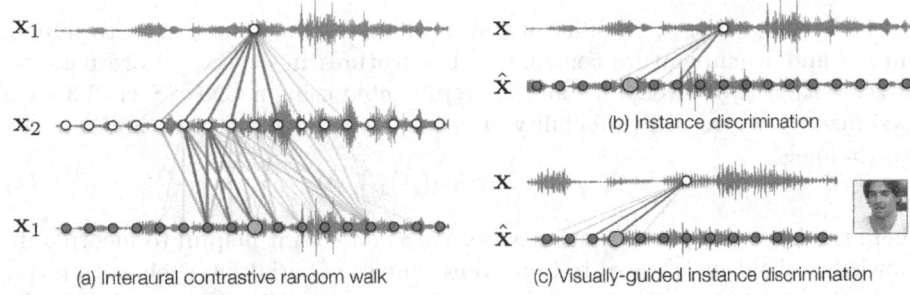

Fig. 2. Learning interaural correspondence. We consider several self-supervised models. (a) A random walk moves from one stereo channel to another, then back, with transition probabilities determined by our learned embeddings. We learn to maximize the probability that it returns to the node where it started (marked in green). (b) We apply data augmentation to mono audio, and learn embeddings that maximize the similarity of corresponding timesteps. (c) We learn to match audio for a single speaker from a multi-speaker mixture, given a visual input.

We propose, instead, to learn h through self-supervision from unlabeled data. These features ought to capture interaural correspondences: observations in both waveforms that were generated by the same underlying events should be close in embedding space. We consider models that can be trained solely from unlabeled stereo or mono sound (Sect. 3.1), or that learn to perform visually-guided estimation from audio-visual data (Sect. 3.2).

3.1   Learning Interaural Correspondence

We propose models that learn interaural correspondence from unlabeled data.

Contrastive Random Walks. Our embeddings should provide *cycle consistent* matches: the process of matching features from $\mathbf{x}_1$ to those in $\mathbf{x}_2$ should yield the same correspondences as matching in the opposite direction, from $\mathbf{x}_2$ to $\mathbf{x}_1$. We use this idea to learn a representation from unlabeled stereo sounds.

We adapt the contrastive random walk model of Jabri et al. [46] to binaural audio (Fig. 2a). We create a graph that contains nodes for each of the temporal sample $\mathbf{x}_i(t)$ from both channels, with edges connecting the nodes that come from different channels.[2] We then perform a random walk that transitions from nodes in $\mathbf{x}_1$ to those in $\mathbf{x}_2$, then back to $\mathbf{x}_1$, with transition probabilities that are defined by dot products between embedding vectors:

$$A_{ij}(s,t) = \frac{\exp(\mathbf{h}_i(s) \cdot \mathbf{h}_j(t)/c)}{\sum_{k=1}^{n} \exp(\mathbf{h}_i(s) \cdot \mathbf{h}_j(k)/c)}, \tag{2}$$

---

[2] Following visual tracking work [46], one could potentially extend this approach to microphone arrays with 3 or more channels by performing the walk over all channels.

where $A_{ij}(s,t)$ is the probability of transitioning from sample s in $\mathbf{x}_i$ to sample t in $\mathbf{x}_j$, and a temperature constant c. The features $\mathbf{h}_i = h(\mathbf{x}_i; \theta)$ are parameterized with network weights θ and are represented using a CNN (Sect. 3.3). We maximize the log return probability of a walk that moves between nodes in the two channels:

$$\mathcal{L}_{\mathtt{crw}} = -\frac{1}{n} \operatorname{tr}(\log(A_{12}A_{21})), \qquad (3)$$

where the log is computed element-wise. We also found it helpful to incorporate knowledge about invariances to important sources of variation, such as to noise. To do this, we also apply data augmentation to two audio channels during the walk similar to Hu et al. [45] (see supp. for details).

Slow Features. We also train a variation of the model that learns to associate embeddings that temporally co-occur, taking inspiration from methods that learn slow features in video [37,80] and audio-visual synchronization [16,52,58]. These pairs of embeddings are more likely (than misaligned timestamps) to correspond to the same events. We minimize:

$$\mathcal{L}_{\mathtt{zero}} = -\frac{1}{n} \operatorname{tr}(\log(A_{12})), \qquad (4)$$

where A_{12} is defined as in Eq. 2.

Instance Discrimination. We also consider models that can be trained solely with mono audio using *instance discrimination* [81]. In lieu of a second audio channel, we create synthetic views of mono audio, using data augmentation that encourages invariances that are likely to be useful for interaural matching. We minimize:

$$\mathcal{L}_{\mathtt{dis}} = -\log \frac{\exp(\mathbf{h}(t) \cdot \hat{\mathbf{h}}(t)/c)}{\sum_{k=1}^{n} \exp(\mathbf{h}(t) \cdot \hat{\mathbf{h}}(k)/c)}, \qquad (5)$$

over all timesteps t, where $\mathbf{h} = h(\mathbf{x})$ are the features for a mono audio $\mathbf{x}$, and $\hat{\mathbf{h}} = h(\hat{\mathbf{x}})$ are features computed from an augmented version of $\mathbf{x}$.

Unless otherwise specified, we perform two types of augmentation: time shifting and volume adjustment. To model the challenges in time delay estimation, we choose negative examples exclusively from $\mathbf{x}$, rather than other examples in the batch [16,52,58]. We ensure that augmented positive views are always taken from the corresponding timestep, i.e., we undo any time-shifting augmentation when indexing $\hat{\mathbf{h}}(t)$.

3.2   Visually-Guided Time Delay Estimation

We also apply our model to the novel problem of estimating the time delay for a single sound within a mixture using visual information. Given a sound mixture containing multiple simultaneous speakers, we estimate the time delay for one object, given a visual representation of its appearance (e.g., localizing a speaker using a visual representing their face). The visual input need not co-occur with the audio. For example, the object may be off-screen, or its visual features may have been extracted at an earlier time.

We adapt the instance discrimination variation of our model, with a training procedure that resembles the "mix-and-separate" [88] paradigm used in audio-visual source separation [3,26,29,31,58]. We create a mixture from two sounds, each with its own delay, and ask the model to estimate the delay from only the desired source. Given two audio tracks $\mathbf{u}$ and $\mathbf{v}$, we create a synthetic binaural sound mixture $\mathbf{x}_1 = \mathbf{u} + \mathbf{v}$ and $\mathbf{x}_2 = \text{shift}(\mathbf{u}, \tau_u) + \text{shift}(\mathbf{v}, \tau_v)$ for randomly sampled values τ_u and τ_v, where $\text{shift}(\mathbf{x}, \tau)$ shifts $\mathbf{x}$ by τ. The model is also provided with I_u, an image depicting $\mathbf{u}$. We learn audio-visual features by minimizing:

$$\mathcal{L}_{\text{av}} = -\log \frac{\exp(\mathbf{g}_1(t) \cdot \mathbf{g}_2(t - \tau_u)/c)}{\sum_{k=1}^{n} \exp(\mathbf{g}_1(t) \cdot \mathbf{g}_2(k)/c)}, \tag{6}$$

over all timesteps t, where $\mathbf{g}_i = g(\mathbf{x}_i, I_u)$ are the learned audio-visual features for channel $\mathbf{x}_i$. Here, g obtains its embedding by fusing audio from one channel with the input image. As in the instance discrimination model, we apply augmentation to $\mathbf{g}_2$. Note that this task cannot be solved without I_u: from audio alone, the model would be unable to determine whether the true delay is τ_u or τ_v.

3.3 Learning a Time Delay Estimation Model

We now describe how these self-supervised learning models can be trained, and how they can be used to estimate time delays.

Network Architectures. We implement the audio embedding h using a CNN that operates on spectrograms [43]. To compute the embedding for sample s, we extract a waveform of length T centered on s. We create a spectrogram representation of size $128 \times 128 \times 2$ using a Short-time Fourier transform (STFT). We keep both magnitude and phase and provide them as input to a ResNet [41], which extracts a $d = 128$ dimensional, ℓ_2-normalized embedding.

For our audio-visual model, we represent the visual information using (pre-trained) FaceNet [69]. This allows our model to estimate attributes of speakers from face crops, similar to the work in source separation that uses face embeddings [26]. We fuse the audio and visual features after the second convolution block of the audio subnetwork by concatenating the 128-dimensional visual features at each time-frequency position.

Datasets. We train our audio models on datasets of stereo sound: **FAIR-Play** [32], which has 1,871 videos (5.2 h) of lab-collected music performances from a small number of rooms and **Free-Music-Archive** (FMA) [20], a dataset of 101K (841 h) music recordings created by a large number of artists.

For the visually-guided model, we train our model on VoxCeleb2 [15] with 500 randomly selected identities. We randomly create training mixtures from mono sound, without the speaker identity labels and without using a simulator.

Training. We use the AdamW optimizer [50,55] with a learning rate $= 10^{-4}$, a cosine decay learning rate scheduler, a batch size of 48, a temperature $c = 0.05$ following [81], and early stopping. Please see supp. for more training details.

Self-supervised Learning Formulation. For all models, we extract our examples from a 1220-sample waveform, sampled at 16 Khz. We obtain our embeddings using a sliding window of size 0.064 s (1024 samples), with a step of 4 samples, yielding 49 audio clips. We apply random stereo channel swapping and channel-wise waveform rescaling for augmentation in all models. In some experiments, we also add random noise, add reverberation, and mix in other sounds as additional augmentation. At test time, we obtain a denser audio graph by using the step of 1 sample for the sliding window. Our model can use input sounds with a variety of durations without retraining, due to the fully-convolutional network architecture [54]. For the audio-visual task, we use a window length of 0.96 s or 2.55 s to obtain more temporal context, since this problem involves jointly solving a separation task.

Estimating Delays from Features. After learning our representation h, we can use it to estimate the time delay, such as by maximizing $R_{\mathbf{x}_1,\mathbf{x}_2}$ (Eq. 1). We have found that this procedure can affect the quality of the prediction for both learned and hand-crafted methods (e.g., due to outliers), so we evaluate a number of different variations in our experiments. In our approach, each embedding votes on a value for τ. We then choose a single time delay for the audio from these votes, either by taking the mean or by using a RANSAC-like [27] mode estimation method. In the latter, we first select the delay with the most votes, then average the inliers (those within a small threshold of the chosen value). This vote can be performed by the nearest neighbor search, or by treating the learned similarities as probabilities (Eq. 2) and taking the expectation, i.e., $\frac{1}{n}\sum_{s,\tau} \tau A_{12}(s,\tau)$ [5].

4   Experiments

We evaluate our methods using both simulated audio, where time delays can be measured exactly, and real-world binaural audio from unknown microphone geometry, where quantized sound direction categories are labeled by humans.

4.1   Evaluation with Simulated Sounds

Before considering real-world audio, we evaluate each model's performance on time delay estimation task using simulated environments, following [1]. While the resulting sounds are considerably simpler than real-world recordings, they allow us to obtain metrically accurate ground-truth time delays, and to systematically vary different experimental conditions, such as the amount of background noise.

Simulation. Following previous work [1], we simulate stereo sounds using Pyroomacoustics [66]. We create three simulated environments with rooms of different sizes and microphone positions. For our sound sources, we take speech sounds from TIMIT [35] (recorded in anechoic conditions) and place them at random angles sampled uniformly from $(-90°, 90°)$ and distances (0.5 m, 3.0 m) with respect to the microphone. We add independent Gaussian noise to create conditions with different signal-noise ratio (SNR) levels, and consider a variety of reverberation times (RT_{60}). The ground-truth time delay can straightforwardly be calculated from the sound source and the microphone pose. This simulated test set, which we call **TDE-Simulation**, contains approximately 6K audio samples total (please see the supplement for more details).

Models. We evaluated our audio-based learning methods: 1) **StereoCRW**, contrastive random walks trained on stereo sounds, 2) **ZeroNCE**, slow features trained on stereo sounds (named after VINCE [37]), and 3) **MonoCLR**, and instance discrimination trained on mono sounds (named after SimCLR [12]).

We compared our methods with the widely-used **GCC-PHAT** [51], a handcrafted audio feature. We also compared with the recent *supervised* method **Salvati et al.** [1], which trains a CNN on parameterized GCC-PHAT features to regress time delay. We trained this model on simulated stereo sounds, based on audio clips from VoxCeleb2 [15] to obtain human speech signals. To improve this baseline's performance, we make a modification: in addition to the noise and reverberation augmentations from [1], we train with synthetic sound mixtures, in which a background sound is added to the input waveform. We regard this supervised method as an approximate upper bound for the simulation-based experiments. We provide all methods with the same duration audio as input, and evaluate different post-processing methods.

Evaluation with Moderate Noise. We first evaluate our models on TDE-Simulation with SNR = 10 and RT_{60} = 0.5s, a condition with moderate amounts of noise and reverberation. This simulated setup is also well-suited for analyzing traditional techniques [51,87], which are designed to deal with unstructured, independent noise and reverberation. We evaluate three audio-based variations of our model, with and without augmentation, and on the different unlabeled training sets. For the instance discrimination model, we always include timeshifting, since the model cannot be trained without some form of augmentation.

To measure prediction accuracy, we use mean absolute error (MAE) and root mean

Table 1. Delay estimation on TDE-Simulation data. We use SNR = 10 and RT_{60} = 0.5 s. FAIR is FAIR-Play [32], FMA is FreeMusic-Archive [20]. *Vox-Sim* is the simulator [66]] with VoxCeleb2 [15] clips and *FMA-Sim* is the simulator with FreeMusic-Archive clips. Errors in ms. *Sup* refers to supervision, and *Aug* refers to augmentation.

Model	Variation	Data	Sup	Aug	MAE	RMSE
Salvati et al. [1]	Mean	Vox-Sim	✓		**0.126**	**0.254**
	Mean	Vox-Sim	✓	✓	0.169	0.294
	Mean	FMA-Sim	✓		0.135	0.256
	Mean	FMA-Sim	✓	✓	0.146	0.267
GCC-PHAT [51]	Mode	--			0.179	0.396
	Mean	--			**0.160**	**0.318**
Ours	Random	--			0.448	0.505
	MonoCLR	FAIR			0.395	0.566
	MonoCLR	FAIR		✓	0.202	0.340
	ZeroNCE	FAIR			0.241	0.362
	ZeroNCE	FAIR		✓	0.196	0.366
	StereoCRW	FAIR			0.241	0.364
	StereoCRW	FAIR		✓	0.174	0.322
	MonoCLR	FMA			0.430	0.648
	MonoCLR	FMA		✓	0.187	0.335
	ZeroNCE	FMA			0.227	0.347
	ZeroNCE	FMA		✓	0.174	0.319
	StereoCRW	FMA			0.434	0.654
	StereoCRW	FMA		✓	**0.133**	**0.259**

square error (RMSE) in milliseconds (ms). For all the methods, we provide 1024 (0.064 s) audio samples (at 16 Khz) as input and perform 128 time delay prediction votes (Sect. 3.3). For GCC-PHAT and Salvati et al., we combine the votes into a single prediction by computing the mode or mean. For our method, we use the mode. We provide an ablation study about post-process, input duration and data distribution gap in the supplement.

As shown in Table 1, the StereoCRW model substantially outperforms GCC-PHAT when it is trained on a large stereo dataset, FreeMusic-Archive, obtaining performance comparable with supervised models trained on synthetic data. While ZeroNCE is trained with real stereo sound, its loss implicitly assumes the true time delay is zero, which is violated in real scenes. The cycle consistency loss in StereoCRW does not make this assumption, allowing it to learn from more complex data and learn better representations. The ZeroNCE model outperforms MonoCLR, suggesting that stereo sounds are useful training signals. Augmentations are important for all the models. We also note that the data distribution between training and test cases is quite different (*i.e.*, training with music signals and testing on the human speech), suggesting that our approach is capable of generalization.

Robustness to Noise and Reverberation. Following [1], we evaluate our model's robustness to noise. We simulate sounds with the fixed reverberation time $RT_{60} = 0.1s$. We use the models trained on FreeMusic-Archive dataset and evaluate them with different SNR levels. In Fig. 3, we see that our methods trained with augmentation outperform GCC-PHAT, with a gap that widens as the amount of noise increases. This suggests that augmentation allows us to build in useful invariances that may not be captured by hand-crafted features.

We also evaluated robustness to reverberation. We fixed the SNR level to 30dB and used reverberation conditions RT_{60} in the range of $[0.1, 0.9]$ via the simulation. As shown in Fig. 4, our slow feature method outperforms the baseline under each reverberation condition while the other two approaches show similar overall performances as GCC-PHAT. The results suggest our approaches are robust to some amount of reverberation.

Robustness to Mixed-in Sounds. In the previous experiments, the noise in two channels is designed to be random and uncorrelated. However, in real-world audio, a major source of error comes from other sound sources (*e.g.*, background sounds). These sound sources are also present in the scene at some spatial position, thus generating a correlated error (and possibly time delay) in both channels.

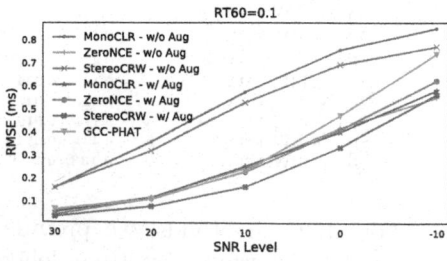

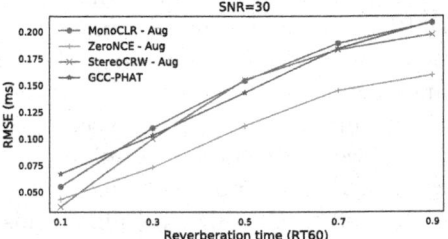

Fig. 3. Robustness to random noise.   **Fig. 4.** Robustness to reverberation.

Table 2. Sound mixtures on TDE-Simulation data. We evaluate time delay estimation with sound mixtures under simulator settings SNR = 30 and RT_{60} = 0.1 s. We report RMSE (ms).

Model	Variation	Aug	Dataset	Intensity level of distracting sound				
				0.1	0.3	0.5	0.7	0.9
Salvati et al. [1]	Mean		Vox-Sim	0.030	0.068	0.171	0.298	0.415
	Mean	✓	Vox-Sim	**0.027**	**0.055**	**0.092**	**0.200**	**0.370**
	Mean		FMA-Sim	0.047	0.091	0.196	0.326	0.423
	Mean	✓	FMA-Sim	0.051	0.073	0.102	0.217	**0.370**
GCC-PHAT [51]	Mean		–	**0.024**	0.177	0.304	0.395	0.459
Ours	MonoCLR		FMA	0.078	0.204	0.302	0.389	0.452
	MonoCLR	✓	FMA	0.055	0.103	0.185	0.306	0.427
	ZeroNCE		FMA	0.065	0.129	0.212	0.294	**0.369**
	ZeroNCE	✓	FMA	0.091	0.164	0.249	0.332	0.405
	StereoCRW		FMA	0.052	0.138	0.254	0.358	0.438
	StereoCRW	✓	FMA	0.041	**0.079**	**0.144**	**0.273**	0.417

We design experiments to investigate the model's ability to ignore distracting background sounds within a mixture. We create synthetic mixtures from TDE-Simulation by mixing two sounds with different angles and distances, using SNR = 30 and RT_{60} = 0.1 s. We set one sound source to be the "dominant" signal and rescale the distracting sound to be 10% – 90% loudness of the dominant source (such that the delay of the louder sound is considered to be the correct answer). We used the models from FMA and evaluate them with 0.5s audio to ensure that there is sufficient signal to identify the dominant sound.

In Table 2, we see that our proposed approaches significantly outperform GCC-PHAT when the distracting sounds became louder, suggesting that our model has obtained robustness to sound mixtures. For very quiet mixtures (10% the volume of the dominant source), GCC-PHAT outperforms our model, which is understandable, given that this domain resembles noise-free audio, which it is well-suited to [51]. The supervised model of Salvati et al. [1] performs worse than our method when distracting sounds have a high intensity level (above 50%) unless we explicitly add the same mixture augmentation used in our methods.

4.2   Evaluation with In-the-Wild Audio Recordings

Next, we ask how well our time delay estimation methods can localize sound directions in challenging real-world scenes, using audio collected from the internet.

Fig. 5. Qualitative results for in-the-wild audio. We provide an overview of our In-the-wild Binaural dataset along with predictions from our StereoCRW model. Green denotes the correct predictions and red means the wrong predictions. We show our failure cases in the last samples on each row. For clarity, we chose examples in which the sound source is evident from the video frame. Please see supp. for more videos. (Color figure online)

In-the-Wild Data. We collected 30 internet binaural videos, extracted 1K samples from them, and use human judgments to label sound directions. These videos contain a variety of sounds, including engine noise and human speech, which are often far from the viewer. Many also contain multiple sound sources and background noise. We provide examples of these videos in the supplement.

Since it is difficult for humans to describe sound directions in terms of time delay, we asked lis-

Table 3. In-the-wild evaluation. We evaluate our models' ability of localizing sounding objects on **in-the-wild** test cases.

Model	Variation	Aug	Dataset	Acc (%) ↑
Salvati et al. [1]	Mean		Vox-Sim	87.0
	Mean	✓	Vox-Sim	87.3
	Mean		FMA-Sim	87.9
	Mean	✓	FMA-Sim	**89.1**
Chance	–		–	50.0
IID	–		–	75.5
GCC-PHAT [51]	Mean		–	81.3
Ours	Random	–	–	72.5
	MonoCLR		FMA	84.2
	MonoCLR	✓	FMA	87.9
	ZeroNCE		FMA	86.0
	ZeroNCE	✓	FMA	86.0
	StereoCRW		FMA	82.5
	StereoCRW	✓	FMA	**88.7**

teners to annotate the direction of the loudest sound. The annotator (one of the authors) listened to the audio with headphones and labeled 5 directions: *left/right*, *center left/right*, and *center*. From these, we created binary *left/right* labels, which can be objectively evaluated by thresholding the delay: we discard the *center* label and merge the remaining directional labels (resulting in 885 examples). We measure the accuracy of the thresholded time delay using these labels. We balance the dataset by swapping stereo channels, such that chance is 50%. As in the mixture experiments, we provide models with 0.5s audio to ensure that they have sufficient context. We also compared with a method that uses interaural intensity difference (IID) cues, by comparing the root mean square (RMS) of each audio channel to determine which channel is louder to predict its left/right direction (equivalent to thresholding based on $\|\mathbf{x}\|$).

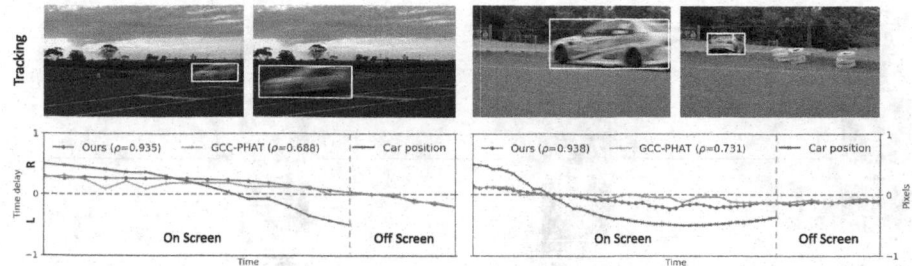

Fig. 6. Motion and time delays. We show the time delays for both our method and for GCC-PHAT, along with the x coordinate for a tracked vehicle. We also show their correlation. We continue showing the time delay when the car moves off-screen.

As shown in Table 3, our proposed approaches all substantially outperform GCC-PHAT. Interestingly, our top-performing model shows comparable results to a state-of-the-art *supervised* method, Salvati et al. We also found that augmentation generally improved results, perhaps due to the complexity of the scenes. The IID-based model performed poorly, which may be due to the fact that the sounds were often distant from the camera, and due to the presence of multiple sound sources. We show qualitative results in Fig. 5.

Correlation Between Visual Motion and Time Delay. To help understand how our predicted time delays vary with motion and change over time, we correlated the visual motions in our dataset with the predicted time delays. We tracked race cars in the subset of our in-the-wild dataset that contains them using CenterTrack [89], and manually removed erroneous tracks (obtaining 49 trajectories). We applied our StereoCRW model (with 1024 samples and 128 votes). In qualitative examples (Fig. 6), we see that the car's on-screen position is closely correlated with the time delay. Interestingly, our model continues to convey the car's position when it moves off-screen. We computed the Spearman rank correlation coefficient [71] between the x position of each track (using the center of the bounding box) and the time delay predictions (averaged over all video clips), yielding $\rho = 0.57$ for our model and $\rho = 0.48$ for GCC-PHAT. More video results are shown in the supplement.

Application to Phone Recordings. We also found that our model worked successfully on sounds from ordinary video recordings from recent iPhones. For qualitative results, please see the supplement.

4.3   Visually-Guided Time Delay Estimation

Instead of attending to a loud, dominant sound in a mixture (Sect. 4.1), we use vision to specify which, of several, sound sources to localize. The model solves this task by first learning to associate a voice with the given visual attribute of the speakers. Unlike audio spatialization and active speaker detection tasks, which provide temporal and spatial cues from the video, the audio-visual streams in our case are not necessarily temporally aligned (*e.g.*, modeling the challenges of tracking a speaker when they move out of sight).

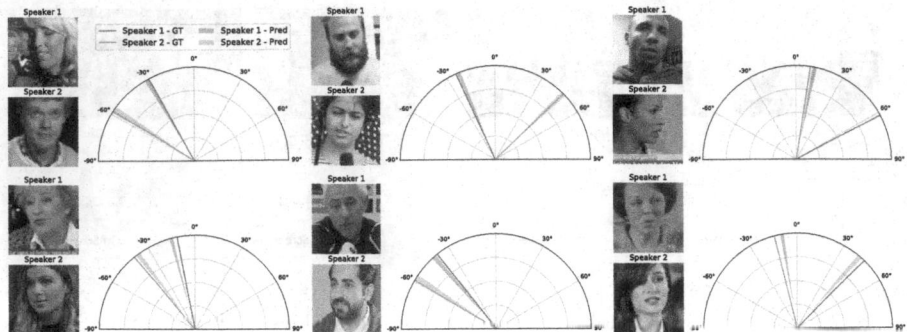

Fig. 7. Qualitative results for visually-guided localization. We estimate the azimuth of speakers by converting time delay predictions to angles. To convey uncertainty, we show the angular cone corresponding to ±0.25 samples of error. We show failure cases in the last example in each row. Please see supp. for more video results.

Evaluation Dataset. We evaluate the audio-visual model in a simulated environment. This allows us to control the positions of the speakers, and to remove other localization cues from the images and audio. We use audio clips from Vox-Celeb2 [15] with the simulation parameters from Sect. 4.1. We select 500 speakers from the database (same as training) and pair them with their corresponding face images. Following the work in source separation, we remove loudness cues by normalizing the volume of sound sources, and placing two speakers in the simulator at the same distance (but at different angles). Note that, since the position of the speakers is randomized, the visual signal does not provide localization cues (*e.g.*, via perspective). We also convert delay predictions to direction-of-arrival angles, using the known radius and microphone distance.

Comparisons. To provide points of comparison for this novel task, we compare our audio-visual approach with audio-only methods including GCC-PHAT. We also provide a (oracle) baseline which selects one of the two speakers' ground-truth time delay at random, thus simulating a method that perfectly solves the localization task but which is unable to match faces to voices. We also consider a two-stage method that first separates the speaker's voice for each channel using VisualVoice [33], a state-of-the-art audio-visual separation model, then applies audio-based time delay estimation methods to the separated

Table 4. Quantitative results of visual-guided time delay estimation on simulated data. We evaluate our models' ability of predicting ITD signals from mixtures with the aid of visual information.

Audio duration	0.96 s		2.55 s	
Model	RMSE	Err≤ 0.1 ↑	RMSE	Err≤ 0.1 ↑
GCC-PHAT [51]	0.503	56.6	0.504	56.9
Salvati et al. [1]	0.490	52.5	0.483	50.1
Random Oracle	0.502	56.9	0.502	56.9
Ours - Random	0.493	10.0	0.503	9.76
Ours - StereoCRW	0.493	56.8	0.488	55.7
Ours - AV	**0.304**	**72.5**	**0.295**	**76.1**
Sep [33] + GCC	0.361	77.6	0.323	82.2
Sep [33] + StereoCRW	**0.309**	**82.8**	**0.281**	**85.5**

sound. To ensure a fair comparison, we retrain the static-image based separation model [33] with input audio duration of 1.27 s and 2.55 s.

We evaluated the methods using two metrics: RMSE, and the percentage of predictions with less than 0.1 ms (1.6 samples) of error (Err≤ 0.1). We feed models 1.0 s or 2.55 s audio, resulting in 512 votes. We show results in Tab. 4. Our audio-visual model substantially outperforms the baselines. Interestingly, it outperforms the baseline that chooses one speaker's delay at random, an upper bound on audio-only performance. This suggests that our model successfully uses visual information. We found that the model that combines audio-visual separation with our learned audio representation performs best. Our audio-visual model (without separation) performs comparably to Sep+GCC-PHAT in regression metrics. We provide qualitative results (for the 0.96 s case) in Fig. 7.

Real-World Visually-Guided Localization. We perform visually-guided time delay estimation on a self-recorded video (Fig. 8). Two speakers talk concurrently while moving off-screen. Our model localizes each speaker in the mixture with a cropped image of their face. We show the mean and standard deviation of delay predictions in 2.0 s windows.

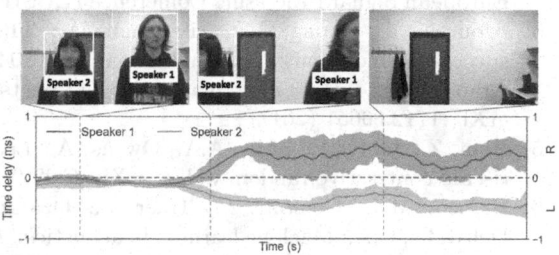

Fig. 8. Visually-guided localization for a real-world scene. Images are blurred to preserve privacy.

5 Discussion and Limitations

We have proposed to use *self-supervised time delay estimation* to localize sounds by learning interaural correspondence. We also introduced a novel visually-guided localization task. Our audio models obtain performance on par with supervised methods on real-world sound, while our audio-visual model successfully localizes speakers in mixtures. We see our work opening two directions: first, integrating more visual information for multisensory localization and, second, finding finer-grained delays using recent methods from optical flow [5, 48].

Limitations. Our audio-visual model associates the appearance of speakers with the sound of their voice. We tested on speakers that our model has been trained on, avoiding the need to generalize based solely on a person's appearance [56]. However, there is still a potential for the model to exhibit bias. Our sound-based models are trained on music, which may not be representative of all downstream tasks. We released code, data, and models on our project site.

Acknowledgments. We would like to thank Xixi Hu for her valuable suggestions about the augmentation idea on random walk graphs. We thank Justin Salamon for helpful discussions and Daniele Salvati for the help on the simulator setup. We thank

Zhaoying Pan and Matthew Sticha for the help recording real-world examples. We also thank Daniel Geng for his comments and feedback on the paper. This work was funded in part by DARPA Semafor and Cisco Systems. The views, opinions and/or findings expressed are those of the authors and should not be interpreted as representing the official views or policies of the Department of Defense or the U.S. Government.

References

1. Time delay estimation for speaker localization using cnn-based parametrized gcc-phat features
2. Adavanne, S., Politis, A., Virtanen, T.: Direction of arrival estimation for multiple sound sources using convolutional recurrent neural network. In: 2018 26th European Signal Processing Conference (EUSIPCO), pp. 1462–1466. IEEE (2018)
3. Afouras, T., Chung, J.S., Zisserman, A.: The conversation: deep audio-visual speech enhancement. arXiv preprint arXiv:1804.04121 (2018)
4. Arandjelović, R., Zisserman, A.: Objects that sound. arXiv preprint arXiv:1712.06651 (2017)
5. Bian, Z., Jabri, A., Efros, A.A., Owens, A.: Learning pixel trajectories with multiscale contrastive random walks. arXiv (2022)
6. Bianco, M.J., Gerstoft, P., Traer, J., Ozanich, E., Roch, M.A., Gannot, S., Deledalle, C.A.: Machine learning in acoustics: Theory and applications. The Journal of the Acoustical Society of America **146**(5), 3590–3628 (2019)
7. Brandstein, M.S., Silverman, H.F.: A practical methodology for speech source localization with microphone arrays. Comput. Speech Lang. **11**(2), 91–126 (1997)
8. Brungart, D.S.: Near-field auditory localization. Ph.D. thesis, Massachusetts Institute of Technology (1998)
9. Carter, G.C., Nuttall, A.H., Cable, P.G.: The smoothed coherence transform. Proc. IEEE **61**(10), 1497–1498 (1973)
10. Carter, G.: Time delay estimation for passive sonar signal processing. IEEE Trans. Acoust. Speech Signal Process. **29**(3), 463–470 (1981)
11. Chakrabarty, S., Habets, E.A.: Broadband doa estimation using convolutional neural networks trained with noise signals. In: 2017 IEEE Workshop on Applications of Signal Processing to Audio and Acoustics (WASPAA), pp. 136–140. IEEE (2017)
12. Chen, T., Kornblith, S., Norouzi, M., Hinton, G.: A simple framework for contrastive learning of visual representations. arXiv preprint arXiv:2002.05709 (2020)
13. Chen, Y., Liu, B., Zhang, Z., Kim, H.S.: An end-to-end deep learning framework for multiple audio source separation and localization. International Conference on Acoustics, Speech, and Signal Processing (ICASSP) (2022)
14. Christensen, J.H., Hornauer, S., Yu, S.: Batvision with gcc-phat features for better sound to vision predictions. arXiv preprint arXiv:2006.07995 (2020)
15. Chung, J.S., Nagrani, A., Zisserman, A.: Voxceleb2: Deep speaker recognition. arXiv preprint arXiv:1806.05622 (2018)
16. Chung, Joon Son, Zisserman, Andrew: Out of time: automated lip sync in the wild. In: Chen, Chu-Song., Lu, Jiwen, Ma, Kai-Kuang. (eds.) ACCV 2016. LNCS, vol. 10117, pp. 251–263. Springer, Cham (2017). https://doi.org/10.1007/978-3-319-54427-4_19
17. Chung, Y.A., Hsu, W.N., Tang, H., Glass, J.: An unsupervised autoregressive model for speech representation learning. arXiv preprint arXiv:1904.03240 (2019)

18. Comanducci, L., Cobos, M., Antonacci, F., Sarti, A.: Time difference of arrival estimation from frequency-sliding generalized cross-correlations using convolutional neural networks. In: ICASSP 2020–2020 IEEE International Conference on Acoustics, Speech and Signal Processing (ICASSP). pp. 4945–4949. IEEE (2020)
19. Dai, D., Vasudevan, A.B., Matas, J., Van Gool, L.: Binaural soundnet: predicting semantics, depth and motion with binaural sounds. arXiv preprint arXiv:2109.02763 (2021)
20. Defferrard, M., Benzi, K., Vandergheynst, P., Bresson, X.: Fma: a dataset for music analysis. arXiv preprint arXiv:1612.01840 (2016)
21. Diaz-Guerra, D., Miguel, A., Beltran, J.R.: Robust sound source tracking using srp-phat and 3d convolutional neural networks. IEEE/ACM Trans. Audio Speech Lang. Process. **29**, 300–311 (2020)
22. DiBiase, J.H.: A high-accuracy, low-latency technique for talker localization in reverberant environments using microphone arrays. Brown University (2000)
23. Dosovitskiy, A., Fischer, P., Springenberg, J.T., Riedmiller, M., Brox, T.: Discriminative unsupervised feature learning with exemplar convolutional neural networks. IEEE Trans. Pattern Anal. Mach. Intell. **38**(9), 1734–1747 (2015)
24. Dosovitskiy, A., Springenberg, J.T., Riedmiller, M., Brox, T.: Discriminative unsupervised feature learning with convolutional neural networks. In: Neural Information Processing Systems (NIPS) (2014)
25. Eloff, R., et al.: Unsupervised acoustic unit discovery for speech synthesis using discrete latent-variable neural networks. arXiv preprint arXiv:1904.07556 (2019)
26. Ephrat, A., et al.: Looking to listen at the cocktail party: a speaker-independent audio-visual model for speech separation. arXiv preprint arXiv:1804.03619 (2018)
27. Fischler, M.A., Bolles, R.C.: Random sample consensus: a paradigm for model fitting with applications to image analysis and automated cartography. Communications of the ACM (1981)
28. Fisher III, J.W., Darrell, T., Freeman, W.T., Viola, P.A.: Learning joint statistical models for audio-visual fusion and segregation. In: Neural Information Processing Systems (NIPS) (2000)
29. Gabbay, A., Ephrat, A., Halperin, T., Peleg, S.: Seeing through noise: visually driven speaker separation and enhancement. In: 2018 IEEE International Conference on Acoustics, Speech and Signal Processing (ICASSP), pp. 3051–3055. IEEE (2018)
30. Gan, C., Zhao, H., Chen, P., Cox, D., Torralba, A.: Self-supervised moving vehicle tracking with stereo sound. In: Proceedings of the IEEE International Conference on Computer Vision, pp. 7053–7062 (2019)
31. Gao, Ruohan, Feris, Rogerio, Grauman, Kristen: Learning to separate object sounds by watching unlabeled video. In: Ferrari, Vittorio, Hebert, Martial, Sminchisescu, Cristian, Weiss, Yair (eds.) ECCV 2018. LNCS, vol. 11207, pp. 36–54. Springer, Cham (2018). https://doi.org/10.1007/978-3-030-01219-9_3
32. Gao, R., Grauman, K.: 2.5 d visual sound. In: Proceedings of the IEEE/CVF Conference on Computer Vision and Pattern Recognition, pp. 324–333 (2019)
33. Gao, R., Grauman, K.: Visualvoice: audio-visual speech separation with cross-modal consistency. In: 2021 IEEE/CVF Conference on Computer Vision and Pattern Recognition (CVPR), pp. 15490–15500. IEEE (2021)
34. Garg, R., Gao, R., Grauman, K.: Geometry-aware multi-task learning for binaural audio generation from video. arXiv preprint arXiv:2111.10882 (2021)
35. Garofolo, J.S.: Timit acoustic phonetic continuous speech corpus. Linguistic Data Consortium, 1993 (1993)

36. Gong, Y., Lai, C.I.J., Chung, Y.A., Glass, J.: Ssast: Self-supervised audio spectrogram transformer. arXiv preprint arXiv:2110.09784 (2021)
37. Gordon, D., Ehsani, K., Fox, D., Farhadi, A.: Watching the world go by: Representation learning from unlabeled videos (2020)
38. Hadji, I., Derpanis, K.G., Jepson, A.D.: Representation learning via global temporal alignment and cycle-consistency. In: Proceedings of the IEEE/CVF Conference on Computer Vision and Pattern Recognition, pp. 11068–11077 (2021)
39. Hawley, M.L., Litovsky, R.Y., Colburn, H.S.: Speech intelligibility and localization in a multi-source environment. J. Acoustical Soc. Am. **105**(6), 3436–3448 (1999)
40. He, K., Fan, H., Wu, Y., Xie, S., Girshick, R.: Momentum contrast for unsupervised visual representation learning. arXiv preprint arXiv:1911.05722 (2019)
41. He, K., Zhang, X., Ren, S., Sun, J.: Deep residual learning for image recognition. In: Computer Vision and Pattern Recognition (CVPR) (2016)
42. Hershey, J.R., Movellan, J.R.: Audio vision: using audio-visual synchrony to locate sounds. In: Neural Information Processing Systems (NIPS) (1999)
43. Hershey, S., Chaudhuri, S., Ellis, D.P.W., Gemmeke, J.F., Jansen, A., Moore, C., Plakal, M., Platt, D., Saurous, R.A., Seybold, B., Slaney, M., Weiss, R., Wilson, K.: Cnn architectures for large-scale audio classification. In: International Conference on Acoustics, Speech and Signal Processing (ICASSP) (2017), https://arxiv.org/abs/1609.09430
44. Houegnigan, L., Safari, P., Nadeu, C., van der Schhaar, M., Solé, M., Andre, M.: Neural networks for high performance time delay estimation and acoustic source localization. In: Proceedings of the Second International Conference on Computer Science, Information Technology and Applications. pp. 137–146 (2017)
45. Hu, X., Chen, Z., Owens, A.: Mix and localize: Localizing sound sources in mixtures. Computer Vision and Pattern Recognition (CVPR) (2022)
46. Jabri, A., Owens, A., Efros, A.A.: Space-time correspondence as a contrastive random walk. arXiv (2020)
47. Jiang, D., Li, W., Cao, M., Zou, W., Li, X.: Speech simclr: Combining contrastive and reconstruction objective for self-supervised speech representation learning. arXiv preprint arXiv:2010.13991 (2020)
48. Jonschkowski, R., Stone, A., Barron, J.T., Gordon, A., Konolige, K., Angelova, A.: What matters in unsupervised optical flow. arXiv preprint arXiv:2006.04902 (2020)
49. Kidron, E., Schechner, Y.Y., Elad, M.: Pixels that sound. In: Computer Vision and Pattern Recognition (CVPR) (2005)
50. Kingma, D., Ba, J.: Adam: A method for stochastic optimization. International Conference on Learning Representation (2015)
51. Knapp, C., Carter, G.: The generalized correlation method for estimation of time delay. IEEE Trans. Acoust. Speech Signal Process. **24**(4), 320–327 (1976)
52. Korbar, B., Tran, D., Torresani, L.: Cooperative learning of audio and video models from self-supervised synchronization. In: Advances in Neural Information Processing Systems (2018)
53. Kumpik, D.P., Campbell, C., Schnupp, J.W., King, A.J.: Re-weighting of sound localization cues by audiovisual training. Front. Neurosci. **13**, 1164 (2019)
54. Long, J., Shelhamer, E., Darrell, T.: Fully convolutional networks for semantic segmentation. In: CVPR (2015)
55. Loshchilov, I., Hutter, F.: Decoupled weight decay regularization. arXiv preprint arXiv:1711.05101 (2017)

56. Nagrani, A., Albanie, S., Zisserman, A.: Seeing voices and hearing faces: cross-modal biometric matching. In: Proceedings of the IEEE Conference on Computer Vision and Pattern Recognition, pp. 8427–8436 (2018)

57. Van den Oord, A., Li, Y., Vinyals, O.: Representation learning with contrastive predictive coding. arXiv e-prints pp. arXiv-1807 (2018)

58. Owens, Andrew, Efros, Alexei A..: Audio-visual scene analysis with self-supervised multisensory features. In: Ferrari, Vittorio, Hebert, Martial, Sminchisescu, Cristian, Weiss, Yair (eds.) ECCV 2018. LNCS, vol. 11210, pp. 639–658. Springer, Cham (2018). https://doi.org/10.1007/978-3-030-01231-1_39

59. Owens, A., Wu, J., McDermott, J.H., Freeman, W.T., Torralba, A.: Learning sight from sound: Ambient sound provides supervision for visual learning. In: International Journal of Computer Vision (IJCV) (2018)

60. Pascual, S., Ravanelli, M., Serra, J., Bonafonte, A., Bengio, Y.: Learning problem-agnostic speech representations from multiple self-supervised tasks. arXiv preprint arXiv:1904.03416 (2019)

61. Patwari, N., Ash, J.N., Kyperountas, S., Hero, A.O., Moses, R.L., Correal, N.S.: Locating the nodes: cooperative localization in wireless sensor networks. IEEE Signal Process. Mag. 22(4), 54–69 (2005)

62. Pertilä, P., Parviainen, M.: Time difference of arrival estimation of speech signals using deep neural networks with integrated time-frequency masking. In: ICASSP 2019–2019 IEEE International Conference on Acoustics, Speech and Signal Processing (ICASSP). pp. 436–440. IEEE (2019)

63. Rajan, R., Clement, J.P., Bhalla, U.S.: Rats smell in stereo. Science 311(5761), 666–670 (2006)

64. Rayleigh, L.: Xii. on our perception of sound direction. The London, Edinburgh, and Dublin Philosophical Mag. J. Sci. 13(74), 214–232 (1907)

65. Salvati, D., Drioli, C., Foresti, G.L.: Exploiting cnns for improving acoustic source localization in noisy and reverberant conditions. IEEE Trans. Emerg. Top. Comput. Intell. 2(2), 103–116 (2018)

66. Scheibler, R., Bezzam, E., Dokmanić, I.: Pyroomacoustics: A python package for audio room simulation and array processing algorithms. In: 2018 IEEE International Conference on Acoustics, Speech and Signal Processing (ICASSP), pp. 351–355. IEEE (2018)

67. Schmidt, R.: Multiple emitter location and signal parameter estimation. IEEE Trans. Antennas Propag. 34(3), 276–280 (1986)

68. Schneider, S., Baevski, A., Collobert, R., Auli, M.: wav2vec: Unsupervised pre-training for speech recognition. arXiv preprint arXiv:1904.05862 (2019)

69. Schroff, F., Kalenichenko, D., Philbin, J.: Facenet: a unified embedding for face recognition and clustering. In: Proceedings of the IEEE Conference on Computer Vision and Pattern Recognition, pp. 815–823 (2015)

70. Senocak, A., Oh, T.H., Kim, J., Yang, M.H., Kweon, I.S.: Learning to localize sound source in visual scenes. In: Proceedings of the IEEE Conference on Computer Vision and Pattern Recognition, pp. 4358–4366 (2018)

71. Spearman, C.: The proof and measurement of association between two things. (1961)

72. Valverde, F.R., Hurtado, J.V., Valada, A.: There is more than meets the eye: Self-supervised multi-object detection and tracking with sound by distilling multimodal knowledge. In: Proceedings of the IEEE/CVF Conference on Computer Vision and Pattern Recognition, pp. 11612–11621 (2021)

73. Vecchiotti, P., Ma, N., Squartini, S., Brown, G.J.: End-to-end binaural sound local-isation from the raw waveform. In: ICASSP 2019–2019 IEEE International Conference on Acoustics, Speech and Signal Processing (ICASSP), pp. 451–455. IEEE (2019)
74. Vondrick, Carl, Shrivastava, Abhinav, Fathi, Alireza, Guadarrama, Sergio, Murphy, Kevin: Tracking emerges by colorizing videos. In: Ferrari, Vittorio, Hebert, Martial, Sminchisescu, Cristian, Weiss, Yair (eds.) ECCV 2018. LNCS, vol. 11217, pp. 402–419. Springer, Cham (2018). https://doi.org/10.1007/978-3-030-01261-8_24
75. Wang, D., Brown, G.J.: Computational auditory scene analysis: Principles, algorithms, and applications. Wiley-IEEE press (2006)
76. Wang, L., ct al.: Towards learning universal audio representations. arXiv preprint arXiv:2111.12124 (2021)
77. Wang, L., van den Oord, A.: Multi-format contrastive learning of audio representations. arXiv preprint arXiv:2103.06508 (2021)
78. Wang, X., Jabri, A., Efros, A.A.: Learning correspondence from the cycle-consistency of time. In: CVPR (2019)
79. Wang, Z., Zhao, H., Li, Y.L., Wang, S., Torr, P., Bertinetto, L.: Do different tracking tasks require different appearance models? NeruIPS (2021)
80. Wiskott, L., Sejnowski, T.J.: Slow feature analysis: unsupervised learning of invariances. Neural Comput. 14(4), 715–770 (2002)
81. Wu, Z., Xiong, Y., Yu, S.X., Lin, D.: Unsupervised feature learning via non-parametric instance discrimination. In: Proceedings of the IEEE Conference on Computer Vision and Pattern Recognition, pp. 3733–3742 (2018)
82. Xu, X., Zhou, H., Liu, Z., Dai, B., Wang, X., Lin, D.: Visually informed binaural audio generation without binaural audios. In: Proceedings of the IEEE/CVF Conference on Computer Vision and Pattern Recognition, pp. 15485–15494 (2021)
83. Yalta, N., Nakadai, K., Ogata, T.: Sound source localization using deep learning models. J. Robot. Mechatron. 29(1), 37–48 (2017)
84. Yang, K., Russell, B., Salamon, J.: Telling left from right: learning spatial correspondence of sight and sound. In: Proceedings of the IEEE/CVF Conference on Computer Vision and Pattern Recognition, pp. 9932–9941 (2020)
85. Yang, M., Chuo, L.X., Suri, K., Liu, L., Zheng, H., Kim, H.S.: ilps: local positioning system with simultaneous localization and wireless communication. In: IEEE INFOCOM 2019-IEEE Conference on Computer Communications, pp. 379–387. IEEE (2019)
86. Yost, W.A., Dye, R.H., Sheft, S.: A simulated "cocktail party" with up to three sound sources. Perception Psychophys. 58(7), 1026–1036 (1996)
87. Zhang, C., Florêncio, D., Zhang, Z.: Why does phat work well in lownoise, reverberative environments? In: 2008 IEEE International Conference on Acoustics, Speech and Signal Processing, pp. 2565–2568. IEEE (2008)
88. Zhao, Hang, Gan, Chuang, Rouditchenko, Andrew, Vondrick, Carl, McDermott, Josh, Torralba, Antonio: The sound of pixels. In: Ferrari, Vittorio, Hebert, Martial, Sminchisescu, Cristian, Weiss, Yair (eds.) ECCV 2018. LNCS, vol. 11205, pp. 587–604. Springer, Cham (2018). https://doi.org/10.1007/978-3-030-01246-5_35
89. Zhou, Xingyi, Koltun, Vladlen, Krähenbühl, Philipp: Tracking objects as points. In: Vedaldi, Andrea, Bischof, Horst, Brox, Thomas, Frahm, Jan-Michael. (eds.) ECCV 2020. LNCS, vol. 12349, pp. 474–490. Springer, Cham (2020). https://doi.org/10.1007/978-3-030-58548-8_28

X-Learner: Learning Cross Sources and Tasks for Universal Visual Representation

Yinan He[1], Gengshi Huang[2], Siyu Chen[3], Jianing Teng[4], Kun Wang[4], Zhenfei Yin[4], Lu Sheng[5], Ziwei Liu[6], Yu Qiao[1(✉)], and Jing Shao[4]

[1] Shanghai AI Laboratory, Shanghai, China
`{heyinan,qiaoyu}@pjlab.org.cn`
[2] Sun Yat-sen University, Guangzhou, China
`huanggsh3@mail2.sysu.edu.cn`
[3] Carnegie Mellon University, Pittsburgh, USA
`siyuche3@cs.cmu.edu`
[4] SenseTime Research, Sha Tin, Hong Kong
`{tengjianing,wangkun,yinzhenfei,shaojing}@senseauto.com`
[5] College of Software, Beihang University, Beijing, China
`lsheng@buaa.edu.cn`
[6] S-Lab, Nanyang Technological University, Singapore, Singapore
`ziwei.liu@ntu.edu.sg`

Abstract. In computer vision, pre-training models based on large-scale supervised learning have been proven effective over the past few years. However, existing works mostly focus on learning from individual task with single data source (*e.g.*, ImageNet for classification or COCO for detection). This restricted form limits their generalizability and usability due to the lack of vast semantic information from various tasks and data sources. Here, we demonstrate that jointly learning from heterogeneous tasks and multiple data sources contributes to universal visual representation, leading to better transferring results of various downstream tasks. Thus, learning how to bridge the gaps among different tasks and data sources is the key, but it still remains an open question. In this work, we propose a representation learning framework called **X-Learner**, which learns the universal feature of multiple vision tasks supervised by various sources, with expansion and squeeze stage: **1) Expansion Stage:** X-Learner learns the task-specific feature to alleviate task interference and enrich the representation by reconciliation layer. **2) Squeeze Stage:** X-Learner condenses the model to a reasonable size and learns the universal and generalizable representation for various tasks transferring. Extensive experiments demonstrate that X-Learner achieves strong performance on different tasks without extra annotations, modalities and computational

---

Y. He, G. Huang, S. Chen, J. Teng—Equal contribution.

Supplementary Information The online version contains supplementary material available at https://doi.org/10.1007/978-3-031-19809-0_29.

S. Avidan et al. (Eds.): ECCV 2022, LNCS 13686, pp. 509–528, 2022.
https://doi.org/10.1007/978-3-031-19809-0_29

costs compared to existing representation learning methods. Notably, a single X-Learner model shows remarkable gains of 3.0%, 3.3% and 1.8% over current pre-trained models on 12 downstream datasets for classification, object detection and semantic segmentation.

Keywords: Representation learning · Multi-source · Multi-task

1   Introduction

Substantial advances have been achieved in visual representation learning, such as those based on curated large-scale image datasets with supervised [30,59], weakly-supervised [29,41], semi-supervised [65,66], as well as self-supervised [7, 11,12,21,25] pre-training. These visual representations show promising abilities in improving the performance on downstream tasks.

Among these pre-training techniques, supervised pre-training is widely adopted for its clear objective and steady training process. Nevertheless, existing works in this direction only consider individual upstream task[1] (e.g., classification or detection) and most of them solely utilize one single data source (e.g., ImageNet [13] or COCO [39]). We argue this single-source single-task (SSST, Fig. 1 (a)) paradigm has several drawbacks: 1) The learned representation in SSST is specialized for one given task and is likely to have inferior performance on other tasks [19,26,44,55,56]. 2) It misses the potentials of a more robust representation by integrating characteristic semantic information from different tasks. Intuitively, we can opt to a simple hard-sharing method, i.e. single-source, multi-task (SSMT) paradigm, as described in Fig. 1 (b), by building many heads, each of which is specific for one task [24,55]. However, this over-simplified algorithm usually encounters task interference [43,73], especially for heterogeneous tasks, leading to a significant drop in performance. Besides, it requires the same image with a variety of labels [71,72], which is not scalable easily due to the high annotation cost. A recent self-training work [19] attempts to create a pseudo multi-task dataset to alleviate the data-scarcity issue of multi-task learning, which follows a similar spirit to other SSMT works.

In light of issues with previous settings, we focus on utilizing numerous data sources of multiple tasks to learn a universal visual representation which should transfer well to various downstream tasks like classification, object detection and semantic segmentation. To leverage cross-source, cross-task information and mitigate undesired task interference, we propose a new pre-training paradigm **X-Learner**, as shown in Fig. 1(c). The X-Learner contains two dedicated stages: **1) Expansion Stage:** It first trains a set of sub-backbones, each of which specifically exploits one task enriched with multiple sources. It then joins together

---

[1] To avoid ambiguity, we refer to a *task* as a general vision problem such as classification, detection or segmentation, and a *source* as a specific dataset or context within a certain *task*.

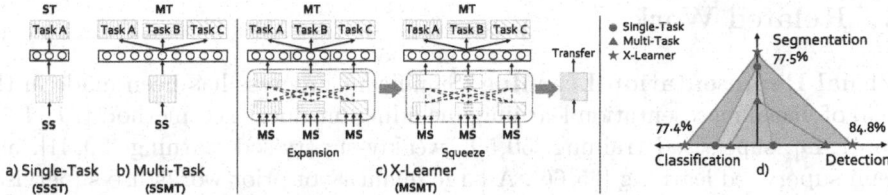

Fig. 1. a) Single-Source Single-Task; b) Single-Source Multi-Task; c) X-Learner: Multi-Source Multi-Task; d) Our proposed X-Learner achieves the best performances in Classification (average linear probe results across 10 classification datasets), Detection (Pascal VOC Detection [15]) and Segmentation (Pascal VOC Semantic Segmentation [15]).

these sub-backbones and combine their representational knowledge via our proposed *reconciliation layer*, forming an expanded backbone with enhanced modeling capacity. **2) Squeeze Stage**: Given the expanded backbone, this stage reduces the model complexity back to sub-backbone level and produces a unified and compact multi-task-aware representation. This new paradigm has two main advantages: **1)** It can effectively consolidate diverse knowledge from our new multi-source multi-task learning and avoid task conflicts. The resulting representation generalizes well to different types of tasks simultaneously. **2)** Compared to traditional multi-task methods, it is highly extensible with new tasks and sources, since we only require data sources annotated with single-task labels.

Our contributions are summarized as follows:

- We propose a new **multi-source multi-task learning** setting that only requires single-task label per datum, and is highly scalable with more tasks and sources without requiring any extra annotation effort.
- We present **X-Learner**, a general framework for learning a universal representation from supervised multi-source multi-task learning, with Expansion Stage and Squeeze Stage. Task interference can be well mitigated by Expansion Stage, while a compact and generalizable model is produced by Squeeze Stage. With X-Learner, heterogeneous tasks can be jointly learned, and the resulting single model renders a universal visual representation suitable for various tasks.
- We show the **strong transfer ability** of feature representations learned by our X-Learner. In terms of transfer learning performance, multi-source multi-task learning with our two-stage design outperforms traditional supervised single/multi-task training, self-supervised learning and self-training methods. As illustrated in Fig. 1(d), a model pre-trained with X-Learner exhibits significant gains (3.0%, 3.3% and 1.8%) over the ImageNet supervised counterpart on downstream image classification, object detection and semantic segmentation.
- We offer **several new insights** into representation learning and the framework design for multi-task and multi-source learning through extensive experiments.

2   Related Work

Visual Representation Learning. Significant progress has been made in the field of visual representation learning, including unsupervised method [10,11,14, 25,47,49], supervised training [30,59], weakly-supervised learning [29,41], and semi-supervised learning [65,66]. A large quantity of prior works use supervised datasets, including ImageNet1k [31], ImageNet-21K [52], IG-3.5B-17k [41] and JFT [30], for learning visual representations. In supervised pre-training, labeled training data provide significant improvement for transfer performance in the same task as the one for which the data are annotated. However, the ability of transferring across different tasks is not good enough [57]. In unsupervised learning, [49] focuses on multi-modal vision language pre-training to achieve strong performances in classification, but not do well in other visual tasks like detection [22]. In order to obtain uniformly high transfer performance on diverse task types, it is important to improve the task diversity of training data, justifying the necessity of multi-task pre-training.

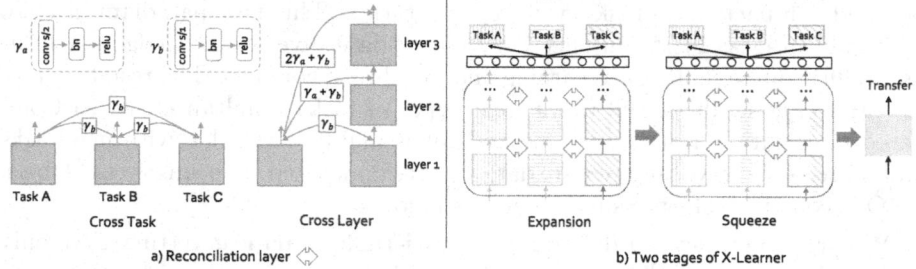

Fig. 2. Structure of X-Learner. a) illustrates how reconciliation layers make the features from different tasks interact with each other. We use γ to represent the reconciliation layer. We present two typical ways of connection by reconciliation layer: cross different tasks and cross multiple layers; b) Features for different tasks are learned in Expansion Stage and unified in Squeeze Stage. After the two stages, X-Learner obtains a general representation for transferring to downstream tasks.

Multi-task Learning. There has been substantial interest in multi-task learning [4,8,23,40,50,62,72,74,77] in the community. A common practice for multi-task learning is to share the hidden layers of a backbone model across different tasks, which is called "hard-sharing" in the literature. However, such sharing is not always beneficial, in many times hurting performance [23,63,69,70]. To alleviate this, there are several lines of works to solve the problem in different ways. One of them is the use of a split architecture with parallel backbones for different tasks [18,40,45]. [45] proposes a cross-stitch module, which intelligently combines task-specific networks, avoiding the need to brute-force search through numerous architectures. Another line of works is improving optimization during learning [35,63,69,70]. For example, [70] mitigates gradient interference by altering the gradients directly, i.e., performing "gradient surgery". [63] addresses interference by de-conflicting gradients via projection. [35,36] use distillation to avoid interference, but they are limited to a retrained setting, either single-task multi-source or single-source multi-task. Other works attempt to develop systematic techniques to determine which tasks should be trained together in a multi-task neural network to avoid harmful conflicts between non-affinitive tasks [1–3,17,34]. These methods perform multi-task learning to improve the performances of tasks involved, but they are not concerned with the transfer performance on downstream tasks. [37] applies vision transformer on multiple modalities and achieves impressive performance. For the image modality, it deals with the classification task only, and learns in a simple hard-sharing way. The problem of multi-task learning remains. A recent work [19] turns to semi-supervised learning and constructs cross-task pseudo labels with task-specific teachers, creating a complete multi-task dataset for pre-training. Yet it only considers the single-source setting, and its student training still follows a hard-sharing regime.

3   X-Learner

In this section, we introduce X-Learner, which leverages multiple vision tasks and various data sources to learn a unified representation that transfers well to a wide range of downstream tasks. It combines the superior modelling capacity of a split architecture design with the simplicity of hard parameter sharing. The whole two-stage framework is shown in Fig. 2. In Expansion Stage, we learn individual sub-backbones for different tasks with multi-source data in parallel. We further interconnect them to an expanded backbone that effectively alleviates interference among tasks. We then condense the expanded backbone to a normal-sized one in Squeeze Stage, producing the final general representation for downstream transfer.

3.1   Multi-Task and Multi-Source Learning

As illustrated in Fig. 1(a), the most common supervised learning setting involves only one task with a single source, i.e., a datum from the source has one label or annotation corresponding to the only task (SSST). There is no task interference during optimization, yet the generated representation is weak in terms of transferability to other tasks.

Traditional multi-task approaches in previous works concurrently learn multiple tasks within a single data source (SSMT), which is shown in Fig. 1(b). The single data source should have multiple sets of labels, each for one task. Such a data source is hardly scalable due to the high annotation cost.

To fix the drawbacks of previous setups, we propose our multi-source multi-task setting (MSMT), which is displayed in Fig. 1(c). More concretely, let T be the number of tasks, then for each task $t \in \{1, 2, ..., T\}$, there are N_t data sources $\mathcal{S}^t = \{(X_n^t, Y_n^t)\}_{n=1}^{N_t}$ with labels of the task. In this way, we only require $N = \sum_{t=1}^{T} N_t$ single-task data sources which are easily attainable, avoiding the

---

Algorithm 1. Expansion Stage

Input: Data sources of T tasks $\{\mathcal{S}^t\}_{t=1}^T$, where $\mathcal{S}^t = \{(X_n^t, Y_n^t)\}_{n=1}^{N_t}$; Sub-backbones
$\{\mathcal{E}^t\}_{t=1}^T$; Task losses $\{\ell_t\}_{t=1}^T$; Set of reconciliation layers γ; Total step number K;
Step threshold τ
Output: pre-trained expanded backbone $\mathcal{E}$
  Initialize $\{\mathcal{E}^t\}_{t=1}^T$ and γ
  for $k \leftarrow 1$ to K **do**
    for $t \leftarrow 1$ to T **do**
      Sample a batch $\mathcal{B}^t$ from $\mathcal{S}^t$ with N_t sources
      if $k \leq \tau$ **then**
        Forward with data $\mathcal{B}^t$ on sub-backbone $\mathcal{E}^t$, Compute task loss ℓ_t
        Update $\mathcal{E}^t$ separately with gradients from ℓ_t
      end if
    end for
    if $k > \tau$ **then**
      Forward with multi-task data $\{\mathcal{B}^t\}_{t=1}^T$ on expanded backbone $\{\mathcal{E}^t\}_{t=1}^T \cup \gamma$
      Compute averaged loss L with Eq. 1
      Jointly update $\{\mathcal{E}^t\}_{t=1}^T \cup \gamma$ with gradients from L
    end if
  end for
  return $\{\mathcal{E}^t\}_{t=1}^T \cup \gamma$

---

difficulty of multi-task annotation. Our setting is also highly extensible since adding new tasks or data sources becomes an effortless process. During training, the optimization objective of our multi-task and multi-source paradigm is to simply minimize the average loss over all the N data sources consisting of T different tasks:

$$\min_\theta L(\theta, \{\mathcal{S}^t\}_{t=1}^T) = \frac{1}{N} \sum_{t=1}^T \sum_{n=1}^{N_t} \ell_t(\theta, (X_n^t, Y_n^t)) \tag{1}$$

where θ denotes model parameters, and ℓ_t refers to the loss function for task t.

3.2 Expansion Stage

We aim to learn general representation from heterogeneous tasks while being least affected by the harmful interference among tasks. This motivates us to design this Expansion Stage to learn a split architecture combining multiple single-task networks. We first train T sub-backbones individually for the T tasks, leveraging their own data sources. We then join all T sub-backbones into one holistic architecture, integrating information learned from all tasks to form a general representation. Specifically, we introduce an expanded backbone composed of multiple sub-backbones corresponding to T tasks, along with several reconciliation layers for connecting them, which we describe in detail below. The expanded backbone learned in this pipeline largely 1) preserves the high precision of single-task training, and 2) combines advantages of all tasks to achieve better generalizability on downstream tasks. The full training process is summarized in Algorithm 1.

Reconciliation Layer. As shown in Fig. 2(a), each reconciliation layer is a link between two sub-backbones of two tasks. It obtains features from one task, transforms them with a few operations, and then fuses them into the features of another task at the same or a deeper layer.

Suppose each sub-backbone has D output layers, and we denote the original output of layer $i \in \{1, 2, ..., D\}$ from the sub-backbone for task $t \in \{1, 2, ..., T\}$ by $\mathcal{E}_i^t$. Let $\gamma_{j \to i}^{k \to t}$ ($j \leq i$, $k \neq t$) refer to the reconciliation layer taking $\mathcal{E}_j^k$ as input and providing its output to the ith layer of another task t. According to Fig. 2(a), $\gamma_{j \to i}^{k \to t}$ can be expressed as the composition of one γ_b and $i - j$ times of γ_a. Receiving all cross-task and cross-layer features, we take a summation to compute the final fused output F_i^t at layer i of the sub-backbone for task t:

$$F_i^t = \mathcal{E}_i^t + \sum_{\substack{k=1 \\ k \neq t}}^{T} \sum_{j=1}^{i} \gamma_{j \to i}^{k \to t} \left(\mathcal{E}_j^k \right). \tag{2}$$

Adding reconciliation layers directly facilitates interactions among information from different tasks. Thus it closely unifies all sub-backbones into one expanded backbone expressing an integrated and general representation. In practical implementation, to avoid task interference introduced by such cross-task communication, we detach inputs to all reconciliation layers from the computational graph to cut off further gradient propagation.

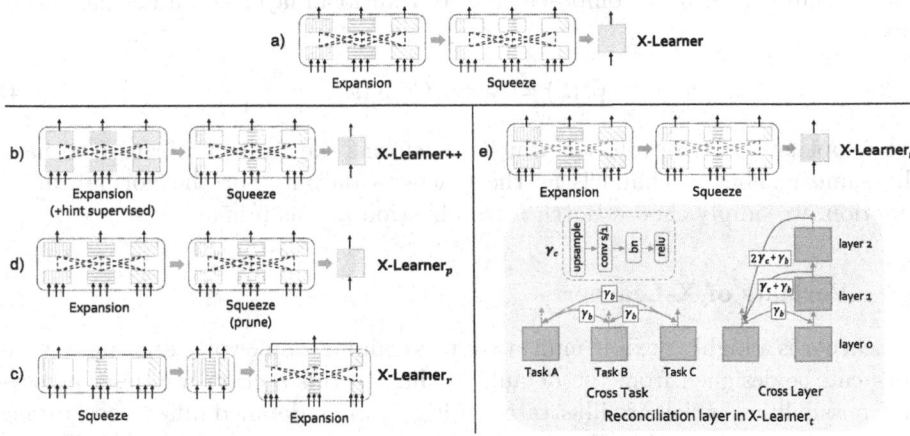

Fig. 3. Variants of X-Learner. (a) is the default form of **X-Learner**. (b) The expansion stage of **X-Learner++** is supervised by extra hints from single-task single-source pre-trained models. (c) X-Learner$_r$ is a Squeeze-Expansion version. (d) X-Learner$_p$ replace the distillation with pruning in the squeeze stage. (e) We switch to a new reconciliation layer in X-Learner$_t$. Differences between variants and the default X-Learner are highlighted in red.

3.3 Squeeze Stage

The previous Expansion Stage gives a concerted representation provided by the expanded backbone uniting all T sub-backbones of T tasks. However, it also introduces an undesirable T times increase in the number of model parameters and computational complexity. To maintain performance while reducing the expanded parameters, we present the Squeeze Stage. The final squeezed model remains highly generalizable for downstream transfer while sharing the same number of parameters with a single-task sub-backbone.

In Squeeze Stage, given an expanded backbone, we adopt distillation to consolidate the model. We employ the FitNets [53] approach, but with multiple targets (hints) from the expanded backbone as the student's supervision. Formally, given multiple outputs from the expanded teacher indexed by $t \in \{1, 2, ..., T\}$, we refer to F^t as the output feature of task t, and $\hat{F}$ as the feature of the student network. We perform distillation between the student model and the bunch of teacher outputs. Specifically, we project the single student feature $\hat{F}$ through a task-specific guidance layer $\mathcal{G}^t$, and expect the outcome to match the teacher's version F^t. Therefore, our distillation loss L_{squeeze} is simply the sum over squared L_2 losses of all teacher-student pairs:

$$L_{\text{squeeze}} = \sum_{t=1}^{T} ||F^t - \mathcal{G}^t(\hat{F})||_2^2. \tag{3}$$

The guidance layer $\mathcal{G}^t$ is composed of a convolutional layer and a normalization layer:

$$\mathcal{G}^t(x) = \text{Norm}(\text{Conv}(x)). \tag{4}$$

We adopt an 1×1 convolution which transforms the student's feature to have the same number of channels as the teacher's output. For the normalization function, we simply choose Batch Normalization [28] as in [53].

3.4 Variants of X-Learner

X-Learner is a highly flexible multi-task pre-training framework, and many variants can be designed from the default setting. In this section, we describe several possibilities, which are illustrated in Fig. 3. More detailed differences among those variants are listed in Fig. 4.

X-Learner$_r$. We notice that the number of parameters in each individual model is first rising and then declining in our default X-Learner. It is natural to also study the reversed order, i.e., Squeeze-Expansion. In the new squeeze stage, we use T task-specific teachers trained with multiple sources to distill T more lightweight sub-backbones. They are then combined into one network with normal computational complexity via reconciliation layers in the following expansion stage.

X-Learner$_t$. We make a modification on the reconciliation layers and let them take features from deeper layers of other sub-backbones as input and fuse to low-level features of a task. We also replace γ_a in cross-layer reconciliation layers with γ_c which is composed of an up-sampling layer and a convolutional layer.

X-Learner$_p$. We replace the distillation operation with unstructured pruning in Squeeze Stage. It is another way to reduce computation consumption while maintaining the performance of a network. We adopt a simple unstructured pruning method referencing [78].

X-Learner++. Inspired by [36], in the Expansion Stage, we add extra supervisions from single-task single-source pre-trained model in the form of hints besides the original supervision from labels of multiple data sources. This can be viewed as adding a pre-distillation process with multiple SSST teachers prior to training the expanded backbone.

Table 1. Datasets used for X-Learner pre-training. We grouped them into manually defined image domains according to [44].

Dataset	Task	Domain	Train size
ImageNet [54]	General CLS.	Websearch	1.3M
Places365 [75]	General CLS	Websearch	8.0M
iNat2021 [61]	Fine-Grained CLS	Consumer	2.7M
CompCars [67]	Fine-Grained CLS.	Close-ups	120k
Tsinghua Dogs [79]	Fine-Grained CLS.	Close-ups	65k
COCO [39]	General DET	Consumer	118k
Objects365 [56]	General DET	Consumer	609k
WIDER FACE [68]	Face DET	Websearch	13k
ADE20K [76]	Semantic SEG	Consumer	20k
COCO-Stuff [6]	Semantic SEG	Consumer	164k

4 Experiments

4.1 Pre-training Settings

Pre-Training Sources (Datasets). Table 1 summarizes the sources we use for experiments. Most of our experiments are conducted in a base setting, where we pre-train models with 2 tasks: classification and object detection. We use 3 sources for image classification: ImageNet [54], iNat2021 [61] and Places365 [75] (Challenge version), and 2 sources for object detection: COCO [39] and Objects365 [56]. We also consider two extended settings: 1) to investigate the effect of more sources on X-Learner, we add CompCars [67] as well as Tsinghua Dogs [79] as two extra classification sources, and select WIDER FACE [68] as a

Table 2. Comparison with supervised and self-supervised methods on classification, detection and segmentation. * represents the model is not pre-trained with semantic segmentation. We compare X-Learner to supervised pre-training, self-supervised learning, and a simple hard-sharing multi-task learning baseline. Relative gains are computed with respect to the ImageNet supervised baseline.

Method	AVG Cls	PASCAL det	PASCAL seg
ImageNet [54] Supervised	74.4	81.5	75.7*
SimCLR [10]	74.6	82.9	74.1*
Hard-sharing	73.2	83.7	70.5*
X-Learner	77.1 (+2.7)	84.4 (+2.9)	77.1* (+1.4)
X-Learner++	77.4 (+3.0)	**84.8** (+3.3)	**77.5*** (+1.8)
X-Learner w/ seg	**77.7** (+3.3)	84.3 (+2.8)	**77.6** (+1.9)

new object detection source; 2) we study the impact of adding a new task, which is semantic segmentation, with ADE20K [76] and COCO-Stuff [6] as its sources.

Implementation Details. We implement X-Learner and its variants described in Sect. 3.4 using ResNet-50 [27] as the basic backbone throughout our experiments unless otherwise specified. The weights of reconciliation layers are initialized with [20]. We use SGD optimizer with a momentum of 0.9 [60], 10^{-4} weight decay and a base learning rate of 0.2. We decay the learning rate three times by a multi-step schedule with factors 0.5, 0.2 and 0.1 at 50%, 70% and 90% of the total iterations respectively.

Experiment	Sub-Backbone	Expansion	Squeeze	Pre-Distillation	Parameters
Hard-sharing	ResNet-50	×	×	×	→
X-Learner	ResNet-50	✓	D	×	↗↘
X-Learner_r	HalfResNet-50	✓	D	×	↘↗
X-Learner_t	ResNet-50	✓	D	×	↗↘
X-Learner_p	ResNet-50	✓	P	×	↗↘
X-Learner++	ResNet-50	✓	D	✓	↗↘
X-Learner w/o Rec.	ResNet-50	×	D	×	↘

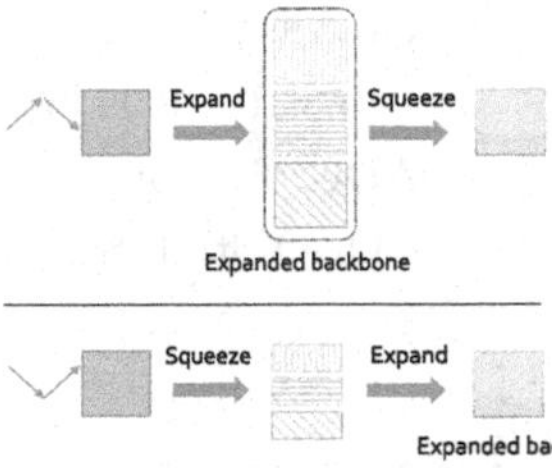

Fig. 4. Differences among X-learner variants. We conduct different ablation study of X-Learner. Pre-distillation refers to applying extra supervisions from single-task single-source pre-trained models as is introduced in X-Learner++. In the Squeeze column, we denote distillation by D and pruning by P if there is a squeeze stage present in the pipeline. The change of the parameter can refer to the figure on the right.

4.2 Downstream Task Settings

Classification. We select 10 datasets from the well-studied evaluation suite introduced by [31], including general object classification (CIFAR-10 [33], CIFAR-100 [33]); fine-grained object classification (Food-101 [5], Stanford Cars

[32], FGVC-Aircraft [42], Oxford-IIIT Pets [48], Oxford 102 Flower [46], Caltech-101 [16]), and scene classification (SUN397 [64]). We follow the linear probe evaluation setting used in [49]. We use the average accuracy of 10 classification datasets (AVG Cls) to represent the overall performance on the classification task. We train a logistic regression classifier using the L-BFGS optimizer, with a maximum of 1,000 iterations. We search the value for the L2 regularization strength λ over a set which distributes evenly over the range between 10^{-1} and 10^{-5}. We use images of resolution 224×224 for both training and evaluation.

Detection. We fine-tune our pre-trained model on PASCAL VOC07+12 (PASCAL Det) [15] for the detection task. We use Faster-RCNN [51] architecture in our experiments and run 24,000 iterations with a batch size of 16. We use SGD as the optimizer and search the best learning rate between 0.001 and 0.05. Weight decay is set to 10^{-4}, and momentum is set to 0.9. Evaluation is performed on the PASCAL VOC 2007 test set, with the shorter edges of images scaled to 800 pixels.

Semantic Segmentation. We evaluate models on PASCAL VOC 2012 (PASCAL Seg) [15]. We run 33,000 iterations with a batch size of 16. The architecture is based on Deeplab v3 [9]. We use SGD as the optimizer with a learning rate between 0.001 and 0.07. Weight decay is set to 10^{-4}, and momentum is set to 0.9. Images are scaled to 513×513.

4.3 Main Results

Pre-Training Paradigm Comparison. Table 2 compares our pre-training scheme X-Learner with supervised training and self-supervised learning (SimCLR [10]) on ImageNet [54], as well as a simple hard-parameter-sharing baseline (named as "Hard-sharing") on our multi-task and multi-source setting. We report performances on all three types of downstream tasks. Under the base setting, X-Learner uniformly outperforms all compared methods in terms of all evaluated metrics, especially AVG Cls. We also observe that the Hard-sharing model has better performance than the ImageNet-supervised model on PASCAL Det, but suffers a performance drop of 1.2% in AVG Cls. This suggests that the

Table 3. Comparison on extended settings with extra pre-training sources. By adding sources in different tasks (marked in bold italic), Hard-sharing suffers performance drops on both upstream and downstream tasks, while our X-Learner is stable across different settings, benefiting from the proposed *Expansion Stage*.

Experiments	Methods	Pre-train								Transfer	
		ImageNet	iNat2021	Places	*Cars*	*Dogs*	COCO	Objects365	*FACE*	AVG Cls	PASCAL Det
Base	Hard-sharing	75.0	75.3	53.0	–	–	35.5	17.4	–	73.2	83.7
	X-Learner	77.3	79.7	54.4	–	–	39.9	22.2	–	77.1	84.4
+ Cls Sources	Hard-sharing	73.7	73.6	52.3	98.5	85.3	35.4	17.6	–	77.5	83.1
	X-Learner	77.3	77.9	54.4	98.4	86.9	40.5	22.6	–	80.6	84.3
+ Cls & Det Sources	Hard-sharing	73.6	73.6	52.0	98.4	85.4	34.9	16.5	31.5	77.1	83.2
	X-Learner	76.9	78.6	54.6	98.6	85.9	40.1	22.1	33.6	80.5	84.3

Table 4. Comparison with self-training. PASCAL Seg is an unseen task for X-Learner++, which is marked with *. NYU-Depth V2 is an unseen task for X-Learner$_{R152}$, which is marked with *.

Method	Backbone	Pre-training settings	CIFAR-100 [33]	PASCAL Det [15]	PASCAL Seg [15]	NYU-Depth V2 [58]
MuST [19]	ResNet-152	ImageNet + DET. + SEG. + DEP	86.3	85.1	80.6	87.8
MuST [19]	ResNet-152	JFT300M + DET. + SEG. + DEP	88.3	87.9	**82.9**	89.5
X-Learner++	ResNet-50	ImageNet + DET	87.0 (+0.7)	87.3 (+2.2)	78.8* (-1.8)	89.0 (+1.2)
X-Learner$_{R152}$	ResNet-152	ImageNet + DET. + SEG	**89.7** (+3.4)	**88.6** (+3.5)	**82.6** (+2.0)	**91.3*** (+3.5)

Table 5. The effect of applying reconciliation layers in the Expand Stage. The reconciliation layer can significantly improve the performance in multi-task learning.

	AVG Cls	PASCAL Det
X-Learner w/o Rec	74.8	83.9
X-Learner	**77.1**	**84.4**

hard-sharing model benefits from multi-task pre-training with object detection sources included, but is harmed by task interference. In contrast, our X-Learner clearly overcomes the shortcoming and alleviates undesirable interference, leading to performance boosts on all considered tasks. Moreover, compared with training solely on ImageNet which is already specialized for classification, our approach still enjoys a 2.5% increase on AVG Cls. This result demonstrates that our setting of learning with multiple tasks simultaneously is beneficial for all involved pre-training tasks, such as classification here.

In addition, our X-Learner++ mentioned in Sect. 3.4 further enhances performance by means of its extra distillation process during sub-backbone training in the Expansion Stage, and achieves the best performance on all three downstream tasks.

We also compare our X-Learner++ with the multi-task self-training method MuST [19] in Table 4, For fair comparison, we fine-tune on the CIFAR-100 dataset instead of applying our default linear probe setting, evaluate PASCAL Det with pre-trained FPN [38], and set output stride to 8 in segmentation.

Our model surpasses MuST on classification and detection tasks despite using ResNet-50 instead of the more advanced ResNet-152 applied by MuST. To better show the effectiveness of our setting, we also conduct an experiment with the ResNet-152 backbone. Table 4 shows the performance of X-Learner$_{R152}$ as well as MuST on four different tasks. We observe that our framework outperforms the self-training method by significant margins on all evaluated downstream tasks. Moreover, it is worth mentioning that on NYU-Depth V2, our X-Learner, without any depth estimation pre-training, surpasses MuST which is learned with MiDaS, a mixture dataset with 10 depth-wise datasets. This zero-shot result further demonstrates the strong generalization capability of X-Learner.

We also compare our X-Learner$_{R152}$ with a stronger version of MuST model pre-trained with JFT-300M, which is much larger than our datasets. As our X-Learner achieves 89.7 and 88.6 in downstream classification and detection tasks. This comparison proves that the dataset size is not an important factor, and our design has its superiority.

Cross-task Generalization and Scalability. In Table 2, among methods that are not pre-trained on semantic segmentation, our X-Learner++ has the highest result on PASCAL Seg. This validates that our models produce more generalizable representations in terms of unseen tasks.

In addition to generalizability, our framework is also highly scalable and can incorporate extra tasks or sources effortlessly. As a demonstration, we add a semantic segmentation task according to the extended setting with ADE20K and COCO-Stuff. Results of "X-Learner w/seg" in Table 2 show improvement on PASCAL Seg by 0.5 mIoU compared to the basic X-Learner. Classification performance is also benefitted from the new task introduced, demonstrating the effectiveness of our multi-task learning approach.

Necessity of Reconciliation Layers. As shown in Table 5, we train an X-Learner without reconciliation layer to study the importance of the component. Compared to the default setting, removing reconciliation layers leads to significant performance drops at downstream transfer learning, especially on fine-grained datasets. We find that the feature from detection sub-backbone contains more detail, and it can be enhanced to a universal feature by the reconciliation layer. This phenomenon also verifies that reconciliation layers play a crucial role in coordinating multiple tasks towards the common goal of general representation learning.

4.4   In-Depth Studies

Multi-task and Multi-source Pre-training

Observation 1: Proper Multi-Task Learning Promotes Collaboration Instead of Bringing Interference. As is discussed in Sect. 4.3, X-Learner not only resolves the task interference issue encountered by the hard-sharing model, but also surpasses single-task pre-trained models such as the ImageNet baseline in terms of downstream results. This shows that with an appropriately designed learning scheme, multi-task training is able to collaboratively enhance performances on all pre-training tasks. This conclusion is again corroborated by the results of

Table 6. Comparison of various X-Learner variants. Pre-training tasks and downstream tasks are evaluated on X-Learner variants. Our framework always performs better than Hard-sharing.

Method	Pre-train					Transfer	
	ImageNet	iNat2021	Places	COCO	Objects365	AVG Cls	PASCAL det
Hard-sharing	75.0	75.3	53.0	35.5	17.4	73.2	83.7
X-Learner	77.3	79.7	54.4	39.9	22.2	77.1	84.4
X-Learner$_r$	73.9	76.6	52.5	41.1	21.7	73.9	84.1
X-Learner$_t$	76.3	79.9	53.3	42.5	22.0	74.5	83.5
X-Learner$_p$	76.1	78.6	53.5	42.4	23.4	77.2	83.1
X-Learner++	77.2	80.4	54.6	40.1	22.4	**77.4**	**84.8**

X-Learner++ in Table 2. With a more elaborated design, performances on all tasks are again consistently boosted.

Observation 2: Additional Sources Further Improve Multi-Task and Multi-Source Representation Learning If Task Conflicts are Well-Mitigated. We experiment on the extended setting with extra classification and detection sources. The added sources, such as CompCars [67] and WIDER FACE [68], have data in domains very different from existing sources. Ideally, including sources of complementary nature should help the overall multi-task and multi-source learning, since information available for pre-training is enriched and is more likely to cover downstream domains. However, this may also increase conflicts among tasks if not dealt with properly. In Table 3, we can see that the over-simplified hard-sharing baseline has considerably inferior results at both upstream and down-steam if more sources are added. In pre-training stage, there is slight decrease after adding classification sources. This is due to the increase in task conflict when introducing new data domains. Nonetheless, we can find that additional sources becomes beneficial to transfer learning tasks both in hard-sharing and X-Learner. Compared to hard-sharing, X-Learner has mitigated such detrimental conflict to a certain extent with the aid of our two-stage design. This suggests that when task interference is properly alleviated, new data sources can be fully utilized by the model to learn more diverse knowledge and enhance the final representation.

Design of X-Learner Framework

Observation 3: Expansion-Squeeze is better than Squeeze-Expansion. In Sect. 3.4, we have described the X-Learner$_r$ variant in which the order of the two stages within X-Learner is reversed. Performing squeezing first would result in smaller single-task sub-backbones with $1/T$ of the original size. Since $T = 2$ in our base setting, we should get two halved ResNet-50 models, corresponding to HalfResNet-50 in Fig. 4, which are to be joined in the further expansion process. HalfResNet-50 is a sub-backbone with only $1/\sqrt{2}$ of the original ResNet-50 channels. As shown in Table 6, X-Learner$_r$ has lower performance on most pre-training tasks and all downstream tasks than the default X-Learner. This finding is reasonable since by intuition, shrinking sub-backbones first is likely to cause unrecoverable information loss. It also validates our choice of Expansion-Squeeze for the default setup. Note that X-Learner$_r$ is still better than the hard-sharing model, which again highlights the importance of a two-stage paradigm to mitigate task interference.

Observation 4: Reconciliation Layers Should Receive Information from Lower Levels. We also evaluate the alternative design of X-Learner$_t$, where reconciliation layers take features from deeper layers instead of shallower ones. Experiments in Table 6 show that the modified and original setups are both competitive at upstream pre-training. However, X-Learner$_t$ is not as good as X-Learner in terms of downstream tasks. In conclusion, low-level features are more suitable to serve as complementary information among heterogeneous tasks.

Observation 5: Pruning May Replace Distillation in Squeeze Stage. In Table 6, X-Learner$_p$ achieves results similar to those of X-Learner. This shows that pruning is also a valid choice for squeezing the expanded backbone, and thus is able to substitute distillation in Squeeze Stage.

5 Discussion and Conclusion

In this paper, we propose a flexible multi-task and multi-source pre-training paradigm called X-Learner, the general framework for representation learning by supervised multi-task learning. Heterogeneous tasks and diverse sources can be jointly learned with the help of the Expansion Stage and Squeeze Stage. We validate that X-Learner mitigates the well-known task interference problem and learns unified general representation that generalizes well to multiple seen and unseen tasks. We also show that X-Learner is superior to traditional supervised and self-supervised learning methods, as well as self-training approaches. In addition, We also demonstrate that our framework is highly flexible and additional tasks or sources can be integrated in a "plug-and-play" manner. Moreover, we offer several insightful observations through our experiments. One possible limitation is that the representation capability of our current pre-training is confined by the scale of publicly available datasets. It is possible to study with larger sources and more tasks in our framework. We hope this work will encourage further researches towards creating general representations by performing multi-task and multi-source learning at scale.

Acknowledgements. This work is supported by NTU NAP, MOE AcRF Tier 2 (T2EP20221-0033), and under the RIE2020 Industry Alignment Fund - Industry Collaboration Projects (IAF-ICP) Funding Initiative, as well as cash and in-kind contribution from the industry partner(s) and the Shanghai Committee of Science and Technology (Grant No. 21DZ1100100).

References

1. Achille, A., Paolini, G., Mbeng, G., Soatto, S.: The information complexity of learning tasks, their structure and their distance. Inf. Inference J. IMA **10**(1), 51–72 (2021)
2. Baxter, J.: A model of inductive bias learning. J. Artif. Intell. Res. **12**, 149–198 (2000)
3. Ben-David, S., Schuller, R.: Exploiting task relatedness for multiple task learning. In: Schölkopf, B., Warmuth, M.K. (eds.) COLT-Kernel 2003. LNCS (LNAI), vol. 2777, pp. 567–580. Springer, Heidelberg (2003). https://doi.org/10.1007/978-3-540-45167-9_41
4. Bilen, H., Vedaldi, A.: Universal representations: the missing link between faces, text, planktons, and cat breeds. arXiv preprint arXiv:1701.07275 (2017)
5. Bossard, L., Guillaumin, M., Van Gool, L.: Food-101 – mining discriminative components with random forests. In: Fleet, D., Pajdla, T., Schiele, B., Tuytelaars, T. (eds.) ECCV 2014. LNCS, vol. 8694, pp. 446–461. Springer, Cham (2014). https://doi.org/10.1007/978-3-319-10599-4_29

6. Caesar, H., Uijlings, J., Ferrari, V.: Coco-stuff: thing and stuff classes in context. In: Proceedings of the IEEE Conference on Computer Vision and Pattern Recognition, pp. 1209–1218 (2018)

7. Caron, M., Misra, I., Mairal, J., Goyal, P., Bojanowski, P., Joulin, A.: Unsupervised learning of visual features by contrasting cluster assignments. arXiv preprint arXiv:2006.09882 (2020)

8. Caruana, R.: Multitask learning. Mach. Learn. **28**(1), 41–75 (1997)

9. Chen, L.C., Papandreou, G., Schroff, F., Adam, H.: Rethinking atrous convolution for semantic image segmentation. arXiv preprint arXiv:1706.05587 (2017)

10. Chen, T., Kornblith, S., Norouzi, M., Hinton, G.: A simple framework for contrastive learning of visual representations. In: International Conference on Machine Learning, pp. 1597–1607. PMLR (2020)

11. Chen, X., Fan, H., Girshick, R., He, K.: Improved baselines with momentum contrastive learning. arXiv preprint arXiv:2003.04297 (2020)

12. Chen, X., He, K.: Exploring simple siamese representation learning. In: Proceedings of the IEEE/CVF Conference on Computer Vision and Pattern Recognition, pp. 15750–15758 (2021)

13. Deng, J., Dong, W., Socher, R., Li, L.J., Li, K., Fei-Fei, L.: Imagenet: a large-scale hierarchical image database. In: 2009 IEEE Conference on Computer Vision and Pattern Recognition, pp. 248–255. IEEE (2009)

14. Dosovitskiy, A., Springenberg, J.T., Riedmiller, M., Brox, T.: Discriminative unsupervised feature learning with convolutional neural networks. Adv. Neural. Inf. Process. Syst. **27**, 766–774 (2014)

15. Everingham, M., Van Gool, L., Williams, C.K.I., Winn, J., Zisserman, A.: The pascal visual object classes (VOC) challenge. Int. J. Comput. Vision **88**(2), 303–338 (2010). Jun

16. Fei-Fei, L., Fergus, R., Perona, P.: Learning generative visual models from few training examples: an incremental bayesian approach tested on 101 object categories. In: CVPR workshop, pp. 178–178. IEEE (2004)

17. Fifty, C., Amid, E., Zhao, Z., Yu, T., Anil, R., Finn, C.: Efficiently identifying task groupings for multi-task learning. arXiv preprint arXiv:2109.04617 (2021)

18. Gao, Y., Ma, J., Zhao, M., Liu, W., Yuille, A.L.: Nddr-CNN: layerwise feature fusing in multi-task CNNs by neural discriminative dimensionality reduction. In: Proceedings of the IEEE/CVF Conference on Computer Vision and Pattern Recognition, pp. 3205–3214 (2019)

19. Ghiasi, G., Zoph, B., Cubuk, E.D., Le, Q.V., Lin, T.Y.: Multi-task self-training for learning general representations. In: Proceedings of the IEEE/CVF International Conference on Computer Vision, pp. 8856–8865 (2021)

20. Glorot, X., Bengio, Y.: Understanding the difficulty of training deep feedforward neural networks. In: Proceedings of the Thirteenth International Conference on Artificial Intelligence and Statistic, pp. 249–256. JMLR Workshop and Conference Proceedings (2010)

21. Grill, J.B., Strub, F., Altché, F., Tallec, C., Richemond, P.H., Buchatskaya, E., Doersch, C., Pires, B.A., Guo, Z.D., Azar, M.G., et al.: Bootstrap your own latent: A new approach to self-supervised learning. arXiv preprint arXiv:2006.07733 (2020)

22. Gu, X., Lin, T.Y., Kuo, W., Cui, Y.: Zero-shot detection via vision and language knowledge distillation. arXiv e-prints, pp. arXiv-2104 (2021)

23. Guo, Y., Li, Y., Wang, L., Rosing, T.: Depthwise convolution is all you need for learning multiple visual domains. In: Proceedings of the AAAI Conference on Artificial Intelligence, vol. 33, pp. 8368–8375 (2019)

24. Han, H., Jain, A.K., Wang, F., Shan, S., Chen, X.: Heterogeneous face attribute estimation: a deep multi-task learning approach. IEEE Trans. Pattern Anal. Mach. Intell. **40**(11), 2597–2609 (2017)
25. He, K., Fan, H., Wu, Y., Xie, S., Girshick, R.: Momentum contrast for unsupervised visual representation learning. In: Proceedings of the IEEE/CVF Conference on Computer Vision and Pattern Recognition, pp. 9729–9738 (2020)
26. He, K., Girshick, R., Dollár, P.: Rethinking imagenet pre-training. In: Proceedings of the IEEE/CVF International Conference on Computer Vision. pp. 4918–4927 (2019)
27. He, K., Zhang, X., Ren, S., Sun, J.: Deep residual learning for image recognition. In: Proceedings of the IEEE conference on computer vision and pattern recognition. pp. 770–778 (2016)
28. Ioffe, S., Szegedy, C.: Batch normalization: Accelerating deep network training by reducing internal covariate shift (2015)
29. Joulin, A., Van Der Maaten, L., Jabri, A., Vasilache, N.: Learning visual features from large weakly supervised data. In: European Conference on Computer Vision. pp. 67–84. Springer (2016)
30. Kolesnikov, A., et al.: Big transfer (BiT): general visual representation learning. In: Vedaldi, A., Bischof, H., Brox, T., Frahm, J.-M. (eds.) ECCV 2020. LNCS, vol. 12350, pp. 491–507. Springer, Cham (2020). https://doi.org/10.1007/978-3-030-58558-7_29
31. Kornblith, S., Shlens, J., Le, Q.V.: Do better imagenet models transfer better? In: Proceedings of the IEEE/CVF Conference on Computer Vision and Pattern Recognition, pp. 2661–2671 (2019)
32. Krause, J., Stark, M., Deng, J., Fei-Fei, L.: 3d object representations for fine-grained categorization. In: 4th International IEEE Workshop on 3D Representation and Recognition (3dRR-13), Sydney, Australia (2013)
33. Krizhevsky, A., Hinton, G., et al.: Learning multiple layers of features from tiny images (2009)
34. Kumar, A., Daume III, H.: Learning task grouping and overlap in multi-task learning. arXiv preprint arXiv:1206.6417 (2012)
35. Li, W.-H., Bilen, H.: Knowledge distillation for multi-task learning. In: Bartoli, A., Fusiello, A. (eds.) ECCV 2020. LNCS, vol. 12540, pp. 163–176. Springer, Cham (2020). https://doi.org/10.1007/978-3-030-65414-6_13
36. Li, Z., Ravichandran, A., Fowlkes, C., Polito, M., Bhotika, R., Soatto, S.: Representation consolidation for training expert students. arXiv preprint arXiv:2107.08039 (2021)
37. Likhosherstov, V., et al: Polyvit: co-training vision transformers on images, videos and audio. arXiv preprint arXiv:2111.12993 (2021)
38. Lin, T.Y., Dollár, P., Girshick, R., He, K., Hariharan, B., Belongie, S.: Feature pyramid networks for object detection. In: Proceedings of the IEEE Conference on Computer Vision and Pattern Recognition, pp. 2117–2125 (2017)
39. Lin, T.-Y., et al.: Microsoft COCO: common objects in context. In: Fleet, D., Pajdla, T., Schiele, B., Tuytelaars, T. (eds.) ECCV 2014. LNCS, vol. 8693, pp. 740–755. Springer, Cham (2014). https://doi.org/10.1007/978-3-319-10602-1_48
40. Liu, S., Johns, E., Davison, A.J.: End-to-end multi-task learning with attention. In: Proceedings of the IEEE/CVF Conference on Computer Vision and Pattern Recognition, pp. 1871–1880 (2019)

41. Mahajan, D., et al.: Exploring the limits of weakly supervised pretraining. In: Ferrari, V., Hebert, M., Sminchisescu, C., Weiss, Y. (eds.) ECCV 2018. LNCS, vol. 11206, pp. 185–201. Springer, Cham (2018). https://doi.org/10.1007/978-3-030-01216-8_12

42. Maji, S., Rahtu, E., Kannala, J., Blaschko, M., Vedaldi, A.: Fine-grained visual classification of aircraft. arXiv preprint arXiv:1306.5151 (2013)

43. Maninis, K.K., Radosavovic, I., Kokkinos, I.: Attentive single-tasking of multiple tasks. In: Proceedings of the IEEE/CVF Conference on Computer Vision and Pattern Recognition, pp. 1851–1860 (2019)

44. Mensink, T., Uijlings, J., Kuznetsova, A., Gygli, M., Ferrari, V.: Factors of influence for transfer learning across diverse appearance domains and task types. arXiv preprint arXiv:2103.13318 (2021)

45. Misra, I., Shrivastava, A., Gupta, A., Hebert, M.: Cross-stitch networks for multi-task learning. In: Proceedings of the IEEE Conference on Computer Vision and Pattern Recognition, pp. 3994–4003 (2016)

46. Nilsback, M.E., Zisserman, A.: A visual vocabulary for flower classification. In: CVPR, vol. 2, pp. 1447–1454. IEEE (2006)

47. van den Oord, A., Li, Y., Vinyals, O.: Representation learning with contrastive predictive coding. arXiv preprint arXiv:1807.03748 (2018)

48. Parkhi, O.M., Vedaldi, A., Zisserman, A., Jawahar, C.: Cats and dogs. In: CVPR, pp. 3498–3505. IEEE (2012)

49. Radford, A., et al.: Learning transferable visual models from natural language supervision. arXiv preprint arXiv:2103.00020 (2021)

50. Rebuffi, S.A., Bilen, H., Vedaldi, A.: Learning multiple visual domains with residual adapters. arXiv preprint arXiv:1705.08045 (2017)

51. Ren, S., He, K., Girshick, R., Sun, J.: Faster R-CNN: towards real-time object detection with region proposal networks. Adv. Neural. Inf. Process. Syst. **28**, 91–99 (2015)

52. Ridnik, T., Ben-Baruch, E., Noy, A., Zelnik-Manor, L.: Imagenet-21k pretraining for the masses. arXiv preprint arXiv:2104.10972 (2021)

53. Romero, A., Ballas, N., Kahou, S.E., Chassang, A., Gatta, C., Bengio, Y.: Fitnets: Hints for thin deep nets. arXiv preprint arXiv:1412.6550 (2014)

54. Russakovsky, O., et al.: Imagenet large scale visual recognition challenge. Int. J. Comput. Vision **115**(3), 211–252 (2015)

55. Sermanet, P., Eigen, D., Zhang, X., Mathieu, M., Fergus, R., LeCun, Y.: Overfeat: integrated recognition, localization and detection using convolutional networks. arXiv preprint arXiv:1312.6229 (2013)

56. Shao, S., et al.: Objects365: a large-scale, high-quality dataset for object detection. In: Proceedings of the IEEE/CVF International Conference on Computer Vision, pp. 8430–8439 (2019)

57. Shen, Z., Liu, Z., Li, J., Jiang, Y.G., Chen, Y., Xue, X.: Object detection from scratch with deep supervision. IEEE Trans. Pattern Anal. Mach. Intell. **42**(2), 398–412 (2019)

58. Silberman, N., Hoiem, D., Kohli, P., Fergus, R.: Indoor segmentation and support inference from RGBD images. In: Fitzgibbon, A., Lazebnik, S., Perona, P., Sato, Y., Schmid, C. (eds.) ECCV 2012. LNCS, vol. 7576, pp. 746–760. Springer, Heidelberg (2012). https://doi.org/10.1007/978-3-642-33715-4_54

59. Sun, C., Shrivastava, A., Singh, S., Gupta, A.: Revisiting unreasonable effectiveness of data in deep learning era. In: Proceedings of the IEEE International Conference on Computer Vision, pp. 843–852 (2017)

60. Sutskever, I., Martens, J., Dahl, G., Hinton, G.: On the importance of initialization and momentum in deep learning. In: International Conference on Machine Learning, pp. 1139–1147. PMLR (2013)
61. Van Horn, G., Cole, E., Beery, S., Wilber, K., Belongie, S., Mac Aodha, O.: Benchmarking representation learning for natural world image collections. In: CVPR, pp. 12884–12893 (2021)
62. Wang, X., Cai, Z., Gao, D., Vasconcelos, N.: Towards universal object detection by domain attention. In: Proceedings of the IEEE/CVF Conference on Computer Vision and Pattern Recognition, pp. 7289–7298 (2019)
63. Wang, Z., Tsvetkov, Y., Firat, O., Cao, Y.: Gradient vaccine: investigating and improving multi-task optimization in massively multilingual models. arXiv preprint arXiv:2010.05874 (2020)
64. Xiao, J., Ehinger, K.A., Hays, J., Torralba, A., Oliva, A.: Sun database: exploring a large collection of scene categories. IJCV **119**(1), 3–22 (2016)
65. Yalniz, I.Z., Jégou, H., Chen, K., Paluri, M., Mahajan, D.: Billion-scale semi-supervised learning for image classification. arXiv preprint arXiv:1905.00546 (2019)
66. Yan, X., Misra, I., Gupta, A., Ghadiyaram, D., Mahajan, D.: Clusterfit: improving generalization of visual representations. In: Proceedings of the IEEE/CVF Conference on Computer Vision and Pattern Recognition, pp. 6509–6518 (2020)
67. Yang, L., Luo, P., Change Loy, C., Tang, X.: A large-scale car dataset for fine-grained categorization and verification. In: Proceedings of the IEEE Conference on Computer Vision and Pattern Recognition, pp. 3973–3981 (2015)
68. Yang, S., Luo, P., Loy, C.C., Tang, X.: Wider face: a face detection benchmark. In: Proceedings of the IEEE Conference on Computer Vision and Pattern Recognition, pp. 5525–5533 (2016)
69. Yang, Y., Eriguchi, A., Muzio, A., Tadepalli, P., Lee, S., Hassan, H.: Improving multilingual translation by representation and gradient regularization. arXiv preprint arXiv:2109.04778 (2021)
70. Yu, T., Kumar, S., Gupta, A., Levine, S., Hausman, K., Finn, C.: Gradient surgery for multi-task learning. arXiv preprint arXiv:2001.06782 (2020)
71. Zamir, A.R., Sax, A., Cheerla, N., Suri, R., Cao, Z., Malik, J., Guibas, L.J.: Robust learning through cross-task consistency. In: Proceedings of the IEEE/CVF Conference on Computer Vision and Pattern Recognition, pp. 11197–11206 (2020)
72. Zamir, A.R., Sax, A., Shen, W., Guibas, L.J., Malik, J., Savarese, S.: Taskonomy: disentangling task transfer learning. In: Proceedings of the IEEE Conference on Computer Vision and Pattern Recognition, pp. 3712–3722 (2018)
73. Zhao, X., Li, H., Shen, X., Liang, X., Wu, Y.: A modulation module for multi-task learning with applications in image retrieval. In: Proceedings of the European Conference on Computer Vision, pp. 401–416 (2018)
74. Zhao, X., Schulter, S., Sharma, G., Tsai, Y.-H., Chandraker, M., Wu, Y.: Object detection with a unified label space from multiple datasets. In: Vedaldi, A., Bischof, H., Brox, T., Frahm, J.-M. (eds.) ECCV 2020. LNCS, vol. 12359, pp. 178–193. Springer, Cham (2020). https://doi.org/10.1007/978-3-030-58568-6_11
75. Zhou, B., Lapedriza, A., Khosla, A., Oliva, A., Torralba, A.: Places: a 10 million image database for scene recognition. IEEE Trans. Pattern Anal. Mach. Intell. **40**(6), 1452–1464 (2017)
76. Zhou, B., et al.: Semantic understanding of scenes through the ade20k dataset. Int. J. Comput. Vision **127**(3), 302–321 (2019)
77. Zhou, X., Koltun, V., Krähenbühl, P.: Simple multi-dataset detection. arXiv preprint arXiv:2102.13086 (2021)

78. Zhuang, L., Sun, M., Zhou, T., Gao, H., Darrell, T.: Rethinking the value of network pruning (2018)
79. Zou, D.-N., Zhang, S.-H., Mu, T.-J., Zhang, M.: A new dataset of dog breed images and a benchmark for finegrained classification. Comput. Visual Media **6**(4), 477–487 (2020). https://doi.org/10.1007/s41095-020-0184-6

SLIP: Self-supervision Meets Language-Image Pre-training

Norman Mu[1]([⊠]), Alexander Kirillov[2], David Wagner[1], and Saining Xie[2]

[1] UC Berkeley, Berkeley, USA
thenorm@berkeley.edu
[2] Meta AI, Menlo Park, USA

Abstract. Recent work has shown that self-supervised pre-training leads to improvements over supervised learning on challenging visual recognition tasks. CLIP, an exciting new approach to learning with language supervision, demonstrates promising performance on a wide variety of benchmarks. In this work, we explore whether self-supervised learning can aid in the use of language supervision for visual representation learning with Vision Transformers. We introduce SLIP, a multi-task learning framework for combining self-supervised learning and CLIP pre-training. After pre-training, we thoroughly evaluate representation quality and compare performance to both CLIP and self-supervised learning under three distinct settings: zero-shot transfer, linear classification, and end-to-end finetuning. Across ImageNet and a battery of additional datasets, we find that SLIP improves accuracy by a large margin. We validate our results further with experiments on different model sizes, training schedules, and pre-training datasets. Our findings show that SLIP enjoys the best of both worlds: better performance than self-supervision (+8.1% linear accuracy) and language supervision (+5.2% zero-shot accuracy). Our code is available at: github.com/facebookresearch/SLIP.

1 Introduction

Much of recent progress in deep learning has been driven by the paradigm of pre-training powerful, general-purpose representations that transfer well to a variety of specific applications. Within computer vision, supervised learning on image classification and self-supervised learning on unlabeled images comprise the two primary approaches to representation learning. After AlexNet [23], researchers soon realized that supervised pre-training yields a generic visual backbone which can be repurposed for many different tasks [13]. Today, most state-of-the-art results still depend on supervised pre-training, and scaling to massive amounts of data, such as Google's proprietary JFT dataset, remains one of the most reliable methods for improving downstream performance. Self-supervised learning, a form of unsupervised learning, found tremendous success first in the domain of

---

Supplementary Information The online version contains supplementary material available at https://doi.org/10.1007/978-3-031-19809-0_30.

language [9,29], but has also made significant recent progress in vision. A major motivation for studying self-supervised learning has been a desire to supersede supervised pre-training and its reliance on labor-intensive human annotation. Indeed, self-supervised pre-training has outperformed supervised learning for some time now on small datasets, but only recently with the development of contrastive methods [5,18] has it begun to improve performance on larger datasets such as ImageNet (Fig. 1).

Both supervised and self-supervised pre-training today rely heavily on ImageNet (i.e. ImageNet-1K) [30], a highly curated dataset with particular idiosyncrasies and biases [35]. The YFCC100M dataset [33] was released in 2015 and remains the largest publicly-accessible collection of images. To date, the field of representation learning has found much less use for this dataset. On the other hand, the full ImageNet dataset of 14M images (i.e. ImageNet-22K) has become very popular for its role in training Vision Transformer models which require a larger amount of data

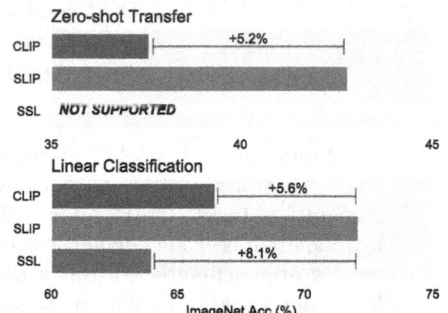

Fig. 1. SLIP pre-training on YFCC 15M. Combining image-only self-supervision and image-text supervision simultaneously improves zero-shot transfer and linear classification on ImageNet.

than ImageNet-1K [1,10]. Why are uncurated datasets not more common in the study of representation learning? There are a few possible reasons. Most immediately, uncurated datasets also lack labels and so long as supervised pre-training remains the simpler and more accessible option for most researchers, datasets like YFCC100M are a non-starter. As we confirm again in our work, the standard self-supervised evaluation task of ImageNet classification from frozen features heavily biases results against models not also pre-trained on ImageNet [2]. Finally, while progress on ImageNet has been encouraging, there has not been strong evidence that current self-supervised methods scale well to larger uncurated datasets [11,34].

Recently, CLIP [28] introduced an exciting new approach to representation learning. It re-examines language supervision for learning visual representations, and catapults it into contention with label supervision and self-supervision. CLIP requires only images and free-form text captions, thus revitalizing the use of YFCC100M in representation learning. In addition to no longer requiring label annotations, CLIP accuracy also scales well to large datasets and models. The best results for CLIP are achieved with big models on a curated dataset of 400M image-text pairs, though promising results are also shown on a subset of YFCC100M. CLIP also enables many exciting new applications with its flexible language-guided capabilities.

In this work, we explore whether the momentum of self-supervised learning on images carries into the setting of language supervision. In particular, we investigate whether language supervision in the form of CLIP also benefits from image self-supervision. We note that it is not immediately clear that jointly training on these two objectives should improve representation quality, since the objectives require the model to encode different and possibly conflicting information about the image.

In order to explore these questions, we introduce SLIP (**S**elf-supervision meets **L**anguage-**I**mage **P**re-training), a multi-task framework combining language supervision and self-supervision. We pre-train various SLIP models on a subset of YFCC100M, and thoroughly evaluate representation quality under three distinct settings: zero-shot transfer, linear classification, and end-to-end finetuning. We evaluate downstream performance on ImageNet, in addition to a battery of 25 other classification benchmarks. Additionally, we further validate our findings with experiments on different model sizes, training schedules, and pre-training datasets. Our findings conclusively show that SLIP improves performance across most evaluations by a significant margin, an encouraging signal for the general utility of self-supervision in the context of language supervision. Additionally, we analyze various components of our method in further detail such as the choices of pre-training dataset and data processing method. We conclude with a discussion of our evaluations.

2   Related Work

Language Supervision. Early work explored learning visual representations from image captions, even before the advent of deep learning [27]. DeViSE [12] jointly embeds images and textual class labels within a shared semantic space, allowing the model to recognize classes that were not explicitly trained for. Initial attempts at leveraging the YFCC100M dataset for representation learning included predicting the bag-of-words representation [22] or n-gram occurrence [24] from images. ICMLM [31] and VirTex [8] showed that language supervision on COCO Captions produced useful visual representations. Prior to CLIP, Multimodal Contrastive Training [38] adds contrastive image-image and language-image losses to VirTex which further improve performance. CLIP [28] quickly garnered significant attention for its simplicity, scale, and strong results. Developed concurrently, ALIGN [21], uses a larger but noisier uncurated dataset and shows similar results.

Self-supervised Learning. Earlier self-supervised learning methods have shown subpar scaling with dataset size [15]. Contrastive learning methods ushered in rapid progress [5,18,26,37] due to their simplicity and effectiveness. Recent methods for self-supervised learning also propose a variety of alternatives to the contrastive objective such as self-distillation [3,16], or input reconstruction [1,17].

Multi-modal Multi-task Learning. MURAL [20] extends ALIGN to the multi-lingual setting and introduces a cross-lingual objective to improve multilingual image and text retrieval. Concurrently to this work, DeCLIP [25] adds several additional training objectives and more data collected in-house to CLIP in order to improve data efficiency.

3   SLIP Framework

We introduce SLIP, a framework for combining language supervision and image self-supervision to learn visual representations without category labels. During pre-training, separate views of each input image are constructed for the language supervision and image self-supervision branches, then fed through a shared image encoder. Through the course of training, the image encoder learns to represent visual input in a semantically meaningful manner. We then measure the quality of these representations through performance on downstream tasks.

3.1   Contrastive Language-Image Pre-training

Radford et al. [28] demonstrated the ability of contrastive learning (CLIP) on corresponding images and captions to learn powerful representations. CLIP embeds images and text with separate modality-specific models. These vectors are then projected into a shared embedding space and normalized. The InfoNCE loss is computed using these embeddings, with corresponding images and captions as positive pairs and all non-matching images and captions as negative pairs.

Non-contrastive alternatives for language supervision include predicting a bag-of-words representation of the caption [22] or the original caption [8, 31] from the image. However, the authors of [29] find that these methods to be less effective than CLIP. The contrastive objective also enables image classification without re-training (zero-shot transfer).

3.2   Image Self-Supervision

View-based self-supervised learning, in which models are trained to represent different views or augmentations of the same image similarly, has yielded strong results across a variety of different formulations. In this work we primarily use an adaptation of SimCLR [5,6], a representative example of these methods, as the self-supervised objective in SLIP. However, other frameworks can be swapped in quite easily, and we explore this in Sect. 6. We focus on the Vision Transformer [10] architecture for its simplicity and good performance. We follow hyperparameter settings from MoCo v3 [7] for training self-supervised Vision Transformers, which will be described later in Sect. 4.1.

3.3   Our Method

We outline SLIP with SimCLR for self-supervision (i.e. SLIP-SimCLR). The pseudo-code for our algorithm can be found in the appendix. During each forward pass in SLIP, all images are fed through the image encoder. The CLIP and SSL objectives are computed on the relevant embeddings and then summed together into a single scalar loss. The two objectives can be balanced differently by rescaling the SSL objective. We find that a scale of 1.0 for the self-supervised objective, i.e. no re-scaling, works well for SimCLR. Unless otherwise noted, we refer to SLIP-SimCLR simply as SLIP.

SLIP increases the number of images processed which results in approximately 3× more activations. This expands the model's memory footprint and slows down the forward pass during training. See Sect. 7 for further discussion.

4   Improved Training Procedure

The authors of CLIP focus primarily on training with a large private dataset of 400M image-text pairs, where the large scale of data lessens the need for regularization and data augmentation. While re-implementing CLIP, we found some simple adjustments (mostly to data processing) which significantly improved model performance when pre-trained on YFCC15M. Our improved training procedure, detailed in the appendix, achieves 34.6% zero-shot transfer to ImageNet with a modified[1] ResNet-50, exceeding the original result of 31.3% [28]. Another re-implementation achieves 32.7% accuracy on ImageNet [19]. In our experiments we focus primarily on the Vision Transformer model family for their strong scaling behavior [10]. We train all Vision Transformer models with our improved procedure as well, in order to set strong baselines for comparing our methods.

4.1   Implementation Details

Datasets. We focus primarily on a 15M subset of YFCC100M [33] filtered by Radford et al. [28] consisting of English-only titles and descriptions, which we refer to as YFCC15M. We also evaluate on Conceptual Captions 3M (CC3M) [32] and Conceptual Captions 12M (CC12M) [4].

Data Augmentation. During training, we randomly sample a valid caption for each image (i.e. title or description for YFCC15M). Images for the CLIP branch are randomly resized and cropped to between 50% and 100% of the original image, which we refer to as global cropping. In the self-supervised branch we sample two views with the augmentation from MoCo v3 [5].

Architecture. We use the original ViT-B/16 and ViT-L/16 architectures from the ViT paper [10] for our image encoders, as well as a ViT-S/16 architecture [36] which is comparable to ResNet-50 in FLOPs and parameters. For our text encoders, we use the smallest text Transformer model from CLIP which contains 63M parameters and uses byte-pair encoding with a 49K token vocabulary, and maximum context length of 77.

For the CLIP objective, our model projects the image and caption embeddings into a 512-dim space with separate learned linear projections. In the self-supervised branch, we use the 3-layer MLP projection head with 4096-dim hidden layers to transform the image embeddings into a 256-dim output space.

Training. We train with a batch size of 4096 and the AdamW optimizer in all our experiments. Both the image and text encoders are randomly initialized.

---

[1] The initial 7×7 conv is replaced by three 3×3 convs; global average pooling is replaced by a self-attention pooling layer with 14M parameters.

Following CLIP, we set the $\beta_2 = 0.98$ to improve training stability, but we keep $\epsilon = 1e-8$. We use a weight decay of 0.5 for CLIP and 0.1 for SLIP. Instead of the custom mixed-precision recipe used in CLIP, we opt for the built-in automatic mixed precision library in PyTorch.

Zero-Shot Transfer Evaluation. We evaluate zero-shot transfer to various classification benchmarks including ImageNet. We perform prompt ensembling by averaging the caption embeddings for each class across the prompt templates. This average caption embedding is then used to compute cosine similarity with the image embeddings. CLIP provides prompt templates and class names for these benchmarks, which we use directly for ease of comparison.

Linear Classification Evaluation. We use the same setup as MoCo v3 to evaluate linear classification performance. We use SGD w/ momentum and no weight decay. On ImageNet, we use a learning rate of 0.01 and on the other downstream datasets we tune the learning rate and report the best result. We train for 100 epochs and perform standard cropping and flipping augmentations.

End-to-End Finetuning Evaluation. To finetune our models on ImageNet, we use the training procedure from BEiT [1]. This procedure employs strong regularization and data augmentation, as well as layerwise learning rate decay. We disable relative positional embedding, layer scaling, and average pooling across tokens. For ViT-B and ViT-S we train for 100 epochs, while on ViT-L we train for 50 epochs. For finetuning on smaller downstream datasets, we use the simpler DeiT training procedure [36].

5   Empirical Evaluations

5.1   ImageNet Classification

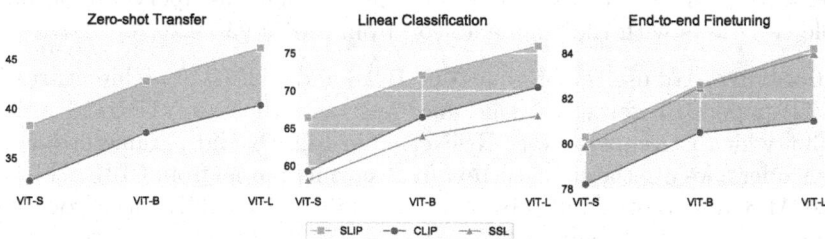

Fig. 2. ImageNet results. We evaluate the representation quality by testing the performance on ImageNet under different settings: zero-shot transfer using text prompts, linear classification, and end-to-end finetuning. SLIP improves upon the zero-shot transfer and linear classification performance of CLIP by significant margin across all vision Transformer model sizes.

We evaluate performance on ImageNet under three distinct settings: zero-shot transfer, linear classification, and end-to-end finetuning. The zero-shot transfer task evaluates model performance on classification benchmarks directly after pre-training without updating any of the model weights. A model trained with contrastive language supervision can be used as an image classifier by selecting the class whose caption embedding aligns most closely with the input image. Linear classification, also called linear probing, is a standard evaluation method used to evaluate unsupervised or self-supervised representations. A randomly initialized final classification layer is trained while all other model weights are frozen. Finally, another way of evaluating representation quality is whether a pre-trained model can improve upon the performance of supervised learning when finetuning the model end-to-end (Fig. 2).

Table 1. We train ViT-B/16 with two self-supervised frameworks. Both linear classification and end-to-end finetuning accuracy on ImageNet suffers when pre-training on YFCC15M instead of ImageNet. Accuracy drop show in (red).

Dataset	Method	Linear	Finetuning
ImageNet	SimCLR	74.5	82.8
	MoCo v3	76.6	83.1
YFCC15M	SimCLR	64.0 (-10.5)	82.5 (-0.3)
	MoCo v3	66.1 (-10.5)	82.8 (-0.3)

One common evaluation setup in the self-supervised learning literature is to train both the model and the linear classifier on ImageNet (i.e. ImageNet-1K), which even without labels is a highly curated and class-balanced dataset. In Table 1 we train ViT-B/16 with SimCLR and MoCo v3 on both YFCC15M and ImageNet. The resulting models are evaluated on ImageNet using linear classification and end-to-end finetuning. Both SimCLR and MoCo v3 experience a more than 10% drop in linear classification accuracy when pretrained on YFCC15M instead of ImageNet, a dramatic degradation in performance. For this reason, the baseline linear results in our experiments are lower than what is typically reported in the self-supervised literature. Similarly, we observe a less severe but consistent degradation for end-to-end finetuning results as well. We argue that training on uncurated data is a more realistic and informative setting, especially given the original motivations of learning vision from less supervision.

In Table 2, we provide evaluation results for CLIP, SimCLR, and SLIP across three sizes of Vision Transformer and on all three ImageNet settings. All models are trained for 25 epochs on YFCC15M. We find that language supervision and image self-supervision interact constructively in SLIP, improving upon the performance of both methods alone.

Zero-Shot Transfer. Self-supervised models do not support zero-shot transfer evaluation since there is no way to directly map the learned representations onto categorical labels. SLIP consistently outperforms CLIP by around +5% on zero-shot transfer across all three model sizes, a very large margin relative

Table 2. Full ImageNet results. SLIP significantly improves performance on ImageNet in the zero-shot transfer, linear classification, and end-to-end finetuning settings.Improvements over stronger baseline (underlined) shown in (green).

Model	Method	0-shot	Linear	Finetuned
ViT-S/16	CLIP	32.7	59.3	78.2
	SimCLR	–	58.1	79.9
	SLIP	**38.3** (+5.6)	**66.4** (+7.1)	**80.3** (+0.4)
ViT-B/16	CLIP	37.6	66.5	80.5
	SimCLR	–	64.0	82.5
	SLIP	**42.8** (+5.2)	**72.1** (+5.6)	**82.6** (+0.1)
ViT-L/16	CLIP	40.4	70.5	81.0
	SimCLR	–	66.7	84.0
	SLIP	**46.2** (+4.8)	**76.0** (+5.5)	**84.2** (+0.2)

to the original number. The gap between SLIP and CLIP does close slightly between ViT-Small (22M params) and ViT-Large (300M params) from +5.6% to +4.8%. This trend suggests that SLIP would continue to yield benefits over CLIP even for the largest Vision Transformer architectures currently in use. With ViT-Large SLIP achieves 46.2% top-1 accuracy, which is still significantly below the performance achieved with larger curated data [28]. In absolute terms however, this is a surprisingly strong result considering that YFCC15M contains very little data of the specific form seen during zero-shot transfer evaluation (i.e. object-centric, or iconic, images labeled with captions of the form "a photo of a class name.").

Linear Classification. In this setting we also observe the benefits of combining language supervision and image self-supervision. CLIP outperforms SimCLR, but by a much smaller margin than SLIP outperforms SimCLR. We see that SLIP significantly outperforms SimCLR in linear classification accuracy across all three model sizes. The gap between SLIP and SimCLR is largest with ViT-L at almost +10%, suggesting that SLIP continues to scale with larger models while SimCLR slightly saturates in performance.

End-to-End Finetuning. We see in Table 1 that finetuning performance is somewhat less affected by pre-training on YFCC15M than linear performance is affected, possibly because the model is allowed to adapt to the target distribution. Both SimCLR and MoCo v3 experience −0.3% drops in finetuning accuracy when pre-trained on YFCC15M instead of ImageNet, which is still quite significant for this setting. We re-iterate that the results in Table 2 are not directly comparable with methods which are pre-trained on ImageNet-1K.

When finetuning on ImageNet, CLIP is particularly weak: ViT-S and ViT-B performance is below even that of training from a random weight initialization [36]. The performance of CLIP does not scale well with model size either, as CLIP ViT-L performance is only +0.5% above CLIP ViT-B. On the other hand, self-supervised learning does quite well in this setting, especially with the larger models. SimCLR ViT-L enjoys a +3.0% gain in accuracy over CLIP ViT-L, and SLIP ViT-L does slightly better than SimCLR ViT-L, though by a very marginal amount. These results suggest that the low finetuning performance of CLIP is mostly solved with self-supervision.

5.2   Model and Compute Scaling

We also investigate the scaling behavior of SLIP with more compute (longer training) and larger vision models. We note that 100 epochs of training on YFCC15M corresponds to around 1200 epochs of training on ImageNet-1K. In Table 3 we experimented with holding model size fixed (ViT-B/16) and training for longer as well as training different model sizes for an extended training schedule (100 epochs). Our results indicate that SLIP scales well with both longer training and larger models. We show full results simultaneously varying model and compute scaling with SLIP in the appendix.

Table 3. SLIP pre-training performance (in terms of zero-shot transfer, linear classification, and end-to-end finetuning) can scale well with both model size and number of training epochs.

Model	#params.	0-shot	Linear	Finetuned
ViT-S	22M	39.5	68.3	80.7
ViT-B	86M	45.0	73.6	83.4
ViT-L	307M	47.9	75.1	84.8

(a) Comparing ViT model variants of different capacities (ViT-S/B/L). All models are pre-trained for 100 epochs.

Epochs	0-shot	Linear	Finetuned
25	42.8	72.1	82.6
50	44.1	73.0	82.9
100	45.0	73.6	83.4

(b) ViT-B with longer pre-training schedules (25/50/100 epochs).

5.3   Additional Benchmarks

Table 4. Zero-shot transfer evaluation with ViT S, B, and L on a variety of classification benchmarks. Best results in **bold**. SLIP outperforms CLIP on most of the tasks, frequently with a significant margin. With longer pre-training epochs, the performance can be further improved.

		Food-101	CIFAR-10	CIFAR-100	CUB	SUN397	Cars	Aircraft	DTD	Pets	Caltech-101	Flowers	MNIST	FER-2013	STL-10	EuroSAT	RESISC45	GTSRB	KITTI	Country211	PCAM	UCF101	Kinetics700	CLEVR	HatefulMemes	SST2	ImageNet	Average
ViT-S	CLIP	43.4	61.0	29.9	21.1	43.9	3.1	4.7	17.9	26.0	53.5	17.8	9.8	29.1	86.8	22.3	16.1	9.5	34.1	5.7	64.8	26.0	18.8	14.7	56.1	49.5	32.7	32.3
	SLIP (25 ep)	51.6	73.0	35.4	26.3	49.2	4.2	6.1	23.7	30.9	62.5	54.3	9.9	31.3	91.6	22.4	21.9	11.0	39.0	9.6	50.8	22.8	22.9	14.8	49.6	50.1	38.3	35.6
	SLIP (100 ep)	53.0	69.4	39.3	26.5	49.8	4.6	5.1	26.6	33.6	68.3	55.8	2.7	37.8	91.9	18.2	22.2	13.8	38.4	8.5	62.8	33.3	23.5	19.2	51.4	49.4	39.5	36.7
ViT-B	CLIP	50.6	66.0	34.5	28.5	51.1	4.0	5.4	21.2	28.5	60.9	53.3	8.4	17.3	90.5	30.2	21.5	6.1	35.1	10.5	55.5	28.5	22.1	10.8	52.4	50.7	37.6	34.2
	SLIP (25 ep)	59.5	78.6	45.2	38.7	53.4	5.4	5.7	26.1	31.1	71.0	56.6	9.8	19.6	94.4	20.3	28.9	14.5	34.0	11.6	55.4	37.7	26.9	17.5	52.6	51.1	42.8	38.0
	SLIP (100 ep)	63.9	79.2	50.4	44.7	52.0	8.1	8.4	26.2	34.7	74.0	61.5	17.1	40.8	95.4	20.9	27.8	11.7	35.2	11.5	52.1	37.1	28.8	13.0	55.1	43.9	45.0	40.0
ViT-L	CLIP	59.5	72.9	41.5	40.3	51.6	6.9	6.4	20.6	27.9	65.4	58.0	10.3	34.5	94.2	22.7	28.8	5.8	41.4	12.6	54.9	34.3	24.0	12.9	54.3	50.1	40.4	37.4
	SLIP (25 ep)	64.4	87.8	56.4	39.8	58.9	8.6	7.8	26.9	32.0	76.0	59.4	13.2	36.0	96.6	27.7	36.5	7.2	28.8	15.6	54.4	42.6	30.0	14.1	55.4	50.1	46.2	41.2
	SLIP (100 ep)	69.2	87.5	54.2	39.8	58.0	9.0	9.5	29.9	41.6	80.9	60.2	14.9	39.6	96.2	34.5	40.0	8.6	30.7	14.2	50.6	44.1	30.5	17.4	55.0	49.8	47.9	43.0

While evaluating classification performance on ImageNet gives a broad overview of representation quality, it is also informative to measure performance on a variety of narrowly targeted downstream datasets. In Table 4 we evaluate zero-shot transfer on a battery of downstream image classification tasks compiled by [28]. We also provide linear classification results on these benchmarks in the appendix. These datasets span many different domains including everyday scenes such as traffic signs, specialized domains such as medical and satellite imagery, video frames, rendered text with and without visual context, and more. We remove Pascal VOC and replace NABirds with CUB-200-2011. To preprocess the datasets into a unified pipeline we use the extra scripts included in VISSL [14]. We catalog chance performance along with short descriptions of the datasets in the appendix.

In the zero-shot setting, both CLIP and SLIP models perform well on datasets whose categories are well represented in YFCC15M, such as Food-101, Oxford Pets, Caltech-101, and STL-10. On these datasets we see that larger models and training for longer with SLIP more generally improve zero-shot transfer accuracy. Datasets with less overlap with the content in YFCC15M, such as Rendered SST2, KITTI depth, and PatchCamelyon (PCAM) is only around chance performance.

Zero-shot performance on the low-resolution datasets (MNIST, CIFAR-10, CIFAR-100) is also very poor. On many datasets performance is several times chance performance yet still much lower than what is achievable with a small supervised model. This suggests that language supervision alone is an inefficient way of training models for specific tasks of interest. Which method does best under the zero-shot setting is also somewhat inconsistent and variable across datasets, unlike the linear setting, and we note this as a caveat in evaluating representation quality with zero-shot evaluations.

5.4   Additional Pre-training Datasets

Table 5. ImageNet results with ViT-B/16 pre-trained on CC3M [32] and CC12M [4], two smaller datasets.

Dataset	Method	0-shot	Linear	Finetuned
CC3M	CLIP	17.1	53.3	79.5
	SimCLR	–	55.4	80.9
	SLIP	23.0	65.4	81.4
CC12M	CLIP	36.5	69.0	82.1
	SimCLR	–	62.2	82.6
	SLIP	40.7	73.7	83.1

In addition to YFCC15M, we experiment with two additional image-text datasets: CC3M and CC12M. In Table 5, we train ViT-B with CLIP, SimCLR, and SLIP. SLIP maintains its margin of improvement over CLIP and SimCLR in all ImageNet evaluation settings. Notably, pre-training SLIP on CC12M instead of YCC15M yields lower zero-shot accuracy but results in higher linear and finetuning performance. CLIP sees a boost to finetuning performance of +1.6%.

Our improved training recipe (see Sect. 4.1) alleviates overfitting by CLIP when trained on YFCC15M and CC12M, but on the smaller CC3M dataset CLIP overfits quite dramatically. This may also be due to the hypernymization and other aggressive text cleaning used in CC3M to make the captions more amenable to image captioning but reduces dataset difficulty. CLIP reaches its highest zero-shot ImageNet accuracy after just 15 out of 40 epochs of training on CC3M, after which we observe a steady decline in ImageNet zero-shot transfer accuracy. In contrast, on CC3M SLIP reaches its highest zero-shot ImageNet performance after 35 epochs.

5.5   Alternative Self-supervised Frameworks

Table 6. We evaluate ViT-B/16 with several SLIP variants using different self-supervised frameworks. SLIP works the best with SimCLR among several other self-supervised frameworks, but all variants outperform CLIP.

Method	0-shot	Linear	Finetuned
SLIP-SimCLR [5]	42.8	72.1	82.6
SLIP-MoCo v3 [7]	41.8	71.4	82.4
SLIP-BYOL [16]	41.3	71.1	82.2
SLIP-BEiT [1]	39.1	66.5	82.2
None (CLIP)	37.6	66.5	80.5

As noted in Sect. 3.2, SLIP enables the use of many different self-supervision methods. We ran several experiments on ViT-B/16 with different alternatives to SimCLR, in particular MoCo v3 [7], BYOL [16], and BEiT [1]. Similar to how we tuned the hyperparameters for SLIP-SimCLR, we largely keep the original self-supervised hyperparameters and add in the CLIP objective and text encoder. MoCo v3 and BEiT hyperparameters are already tuned for ViT, but with BYOL we tuned the learning rate and weight decay while copying the data augmentation and projector/predictor heads from MoCo v3. We also lightly tune different scaling parameters for the self-supervised loss. All models are trained for 25 epochs on YFCC15M.

Results in Table 6 show that all three alternatives underperform SLIP-SimCLR, despite being individually stronger self-supervised methods. Nonetheless, all SLIP variants still improve performance over CLIP.

6   Further Analysis

What Do Language Supervised Models Learn from YFCC15M? We probe the sources of the image classification abilities of CLIP and SLIP by visualizing nearest neighbor retrievals from the YFCC15M training data using each model's image encoder, shown in the appendix. Our visualizations reveal a surprising amount of specific and accurate category information in the captions (object names, plant and animal species, geographic location, etc.).

We also estimate an upper bound of zero-shot ImageNet classification performance using YFCC15M with a simple image retrieval baseline. With a strong ImageNet classifier (BEiT-Large @ 384px^2), we retrieve the 50 nearest neighbors of each validation image from the YFCC15M training images. We then map each caption of the retrieved images onto ImageNet classes by selecting the closest class text embedding as measured by the publicly released CLIP ViT-L/16 text encoder trained on 400M image-text pairs. We take the modal class as the classification prediction. Thus, each validation image can only be correctly classified if there exists similar training images in YFCC15M which are captioned in a way that describes the correct ImageNet category. This baseline achieves surprisingly high 74.4% top-1 accuracy, indicating a substantial amount of accurate, category-specific information in the captions.

What Does SLIP Gain from Self-supervision? We evaluate the image retrieval baseline from above using the image encoders from our SLIP and CLIP models, shown in Table 7. We also measure the average cosine similarity between ImageNet image embeddings (averaged across 50 validation images per class) and the corresponding class embedding (averaged across 7 prompts) for these two models, and find much higher similarity between image and text for SLIP than CLIP. We interpret these two results to support the conclusion that the self-supervision objective pushes SLIP to learn better visual features, which are then more easily indexed by the text encoder.

Table 7. Comparison of SLIP vs. CLIP feature quality with a image retrieval baseline and average cosine similarity between images and categories on ImageNet. Both methods use a ViT-B/16 model trained on YFCC15M.

Method	CLIP	SLIP
Image retrieval acc	26.3%	**29.1%**
Cosine similarity	0.343	**0.412**

Why Not Pre-train with SSL and Finetune with CLIP? An alternative to SLIP would be to simply initialize the image encoder of CLIP with SSL-trained weights. We try training CLIP ViT-B/16 under this setting but find worse performance than training jointly with CLIP and SSL. In Table 8, we see this approach underperforms SLIP in all three ImageNet evaluation settings.

---

[2] This model achieves 88.4% top-1 accuracy on ImageNet.

Table 8. Finetuning vs. multi-task training. One alternative to SLIP consists of initializing the image encoder of CLIP with weights trained through self-supervised learning. With ViT-B/16 trained for 25 epochs, finetuning with CLIP performs noticeably worse across all three ImageNet evaluating settings.

Method	0-shot	Linear	Finetuned
SimCLR → CLIP	41.1	68.2	82.3
SLIP-SimCLR	**42.8**	**72.1**	**82.6**

Is SLIP Just CLIP with Data Augmentation? We also examine the effects of adding further data augmentation to CLIP and whether this explains the performance improvements seen in SLIP. The SimCLR augmentation can be separated into two components: color (jitter or grayscale) + blur, and resize crop + flip. We train CLIP with these two components individually and also with the full SimCLR augmentation. When training with color + blur, we use the original CLIP cropping strategy from [28] in which we resize the shorter side to 224px then perform a random square crop. Our results are shown in Table 9. While augmentation and resize crop + flip hurt performance, color + blur do improve zero-shot transfer performance by +0.8% which is still far below the gain by SLIP.

Table 9. We train CLIP with different data augmentations and compare ImageNet performance to SLIP. Color + blur slightly improve performance over our improved training recipe using global image crops, but by a much smaller margin than SLIP does.

Augmentation	0-shot	Linear	Finetuned
Global crop (CLIP)	37.6	66.5	80.5
Color + blur	38.4	68.5	81.5
Resize crop + flip	36.0	66.1	80.5
Color + blur + resize crop + flip	36.3	65.2	80.6
SLIP	**42.8**	**72.1**	**82.6**

Can We Fully Decouple Self-supervision from Language Supervision? We experiment with a version of SLIP we call SLIP-decoupled in which the self-supervised objective is computed on a disjoint set of 15M images from the YFCC15M images used in the text supervision object. During training, the images are sampled independently from both sets, effectively decoupling the language-image supervision and self-supervision signals. In Table 10, we find that SLIP-decoupled does just as well as SLIP.

Table 10. Decoupling self-supervision and text-supervision has no effect on performance. We sampled an additional 15M images disjoint from the YFCC15M images to use only in the self-supervised objective and observe that this performs nearly identically.

Method	0-shot	Linear	Finetuned
SLIP	42.8	72.1	82.6
Decoupled SLIP	42.7	72.0	82.8

7   Discussion

Our results on ImageNet and other classification benchmarks show that language supervision and self-supervision are indeed highly synergistic. As shown in Table 2, SLIP improves zero-shot performance across model sizes by large margins of +4.8% to +5.6%. Similar gains can be seen in the linear classification setting, with consistent but marginal improvements in the end-to-end finetuning setting.

These trends remain consistent on longer training schedules with the exception of linear probe performance on SLIP ViT-L which actually decreases with more training. With SLIP ViT-L pre-trained on YFCC15M for 100 epochs, we achieve our strongest result of 47.9% zero-shot accuracy on ImageNet. SLIP also shows significant improvements on CC3M and CC12M. Finally, we also confirm our findings with zero-shot and linear evaluations on additional benchmarks.

Evaluating Representation Quality. Prior work on representation learning has argued against end-to-end finetuning for its sensitivity to optimization hyperparameters [15], and against linear classification for being too contrived [39]. We instead view zero-shot transfer, along with linear classification and end-to-end finetuning, as one cohesive paradigm for evaluating representation quality. Zero-shot transfer represents the strictest setting, where the exemplar vector for each class must be specified through natural language. Linear classification is a relaxation of zero-shot transfer, in which the class exemplars are optimized on training data. Finally, end-to-end finetuning represents a further relaxation where all model parameters are allowed to adapt to. Performance should be assessed across multiple settings, rather than a single setting.

Zero-Shot ImageNet Monitor. SLIP may also serve as a useful framework within which to evaluate new methods for self-supervised learning. Training loss on the pre-text task is a poor predictor of downstream performance, so a simple external metric like kNN accuracy is important for quickly estimating performance and diagnosing training issues such as overfitting or instability. However, kNN classification requires encoding and storing every single training image and naive inference requires very expensive matrix multiplications. The memory bank kNN monitor [7] alleviates this cost but is not feasible when pre-training on unlabeled datasets such as YFCC100M. Instead, zero-shot evaluations on ImageNet are virtually as fast as evaluating validation accuracy in the supervised setting.

Acknowledgements. This work was supported by BAIR, the Berkeley Deep Drive (BDD) project, and gifts from Meta and Open Philanthropy.

References

1. Bao, H., Dong, L., Wei, F.: Beit: bert pre-training of image transformers. ArXiv abs/2106.08254 (2021)
2. Caron, M., Bojanowski, P., Joulin, A., Douze, M.: Deep clustering for unsupervised learning of visual features. In: Ferrari, V., Hebert, M., Sminchisescu, C., Weiss, Y. (eds.) Computer Vision – ECCV 2018. LNCS, vol. 11218, pp. 139–156. Springer, Cham (2018). https://doi.org/10.1007/978-3-030-01264-9_9
3. Caron, M., et al.: Emerging properties in self-supervised vision transformers. ArXiv abs/2104.14294 (2021)
4. Changpinyo, S., Sharma, P.K., Ding, N., Soricut, R.: Conceptual 12m: Pushing web-scale image-text pre-training to recognize long-tail visual concepts. 2021 IEEE/CVF Conference on Computer Vision and Pattern Recognition (CVPR), pp. 3557–3567 (2021)
5. Chen, T., Kornblith, S., Norouzi, M., Hinton, G.E.: A simple framework for contrastive learning of visual representations. ArXiv abs/2002.05709 (2020)
6. Chen, T., Kornblith, S., Swersky, K., Norouzi, M., Hinton, G.E.: Big self-supervised models are strong semi-supervised learners. ArXiv abs/2006.10029 (2020)
7. Chen, X., Xie, S., He, K.: An empirical study of training self-supervised vision transformers. ArXiv abs/2104.02057 (2021)
8. Desai, K., Johnson, J.: Virtex: Learning visual representations from textual annotations. 2021 IEEE/CVF Conference on Computer Vision and Pattern Recognition (CVPR), pp. 11157–11168 (2021)
9. Devlin, J., Chang, M.W., Lee, K., Toutanova, K.: Bert: pre-training of deep bidirectional transformers for language understanding. In: NAACL (2019)
10. Dosovitskiy, A., et al.: An image is worth 16×16 words: transformers for image recognition at scale. ArXiv abs/2010.11929 (2021)
11. El-Nouby, A., Izacard, G., Touvron, H., Laptev, I., Jégou, H., Grave, E.: Are large-scale datasets necessary for self-supervised pre-training? ArXiv abs/2112.10740 (2021)
12. Frome, A., et al.: Devise: a deep visual-semantic embedding model. In: NIPS (2013)
13. Girshick, R.B., Donahue, J., Darrell, T., Malik, J.: Rich feature hierarchies for accurate object detection and semantic segmentation. In: 2014 IEEE Conference on Computer Vision and Pattern Recognition, pp. 580–587 (2014)
14. Goyal, P., et al.: Vissl (2021). https://github.com/facebookresearch/vissl
15. Goyal, P., Mahajan, D.K., Gupta, A., Misra, I.: Scaling and benchmarking self-supervised visual representation learning. In: 2019 IEEE/CVF International Conference on Computer Vision (ICCV), pp. 6390–6399 (2019)
16. Grill, J.B., et al.: Bootstrap your own latent: A new approach to self-supervised learning. ArXiv abs/2006.07733 (2020)
17. He, K., Chen, X., Xie, S., Li, Y., Doll'ar, P., Girshick, R.B.: Masked autoencoders are scalable vision learners (2021)
18. He, K., Fan, H., Wu, Y., Xie, S., Girshick, R.B.: Momentum contrast for unsupervised visual representation learning. 2020 IEEE/CVF Conference on Computer Vision and Pattern Recognition (CVPR), pp. 9726–9735 (2020)
19. Ilharco, G., et al.: Openclip (2021). https://doi.org/10.5281/zenodo.5143773

20. Jain, A., et al.: Mural: Multimodal, multitask retrieval across languages. ArXiv abs/2109.05125 (2021)
21. Jia, C., et al.: Scaling up visual and vision-language representation learning with noisy text supervision. In: ICML (2021)
22. Joulin, A., van der Maaten, L., Jabri, A., Vasilache, N.: Learning visual features from large weakly supervised data. In: Leibe, B., Matas, J., Sebe, N., Welling, M. (eds.) ECCV 2016. LNCS, vol. 9911, pp. 67–84. Springer, Cham (2016). https://doi.org/10.1007/978-3-319-46478-7_5
23. Krizhevsky, A., Sutskever, I., Hinton, G.E.: Imagenet classification with deep convolutional neural networks. Commun. ACM 60, 84–90 (2012)
24. Li, A., Jabri, A., Joulin, A., van der Maaten, L.: Learning visual n-grams from web data. In: 2017 IEEE International Conference on Computer Vision (ICCV), pp. 4193–4202 (2017)
25. Li, Y., et al.: Supervision exists everywhere: a data efficient contrastive language-image pre-training paradigm. ArXiv abs/2110.05208 (2021)
26. van den Oord, A., Li, Y., Vinyals, O.: Representation learning with contrastive predictive coding. ArXiv abs/1807.03748 (2018)
27. Quattoni, A., Collins, M., Darrell, T.: Learning visual representations using images with captions. In: 2007 IEEE Conference on Computer Vision and Pattern Recognition, pp. 1–8 (2007)
28. Radford, A., et al.: Learning transferable visual models from natural language supervision. In: ICML (2021)
29. Radford, A., Narasimhan, K.: Improving language understanding by generative pre-training (2018)
30. Russakovsky, O., Deng, J., Su, H., Krause, J., Satheesh, S., Ma, S., Huang, Z., Karpathy, A., Khosla, A., Bernstein, M.S., Berg, A.C., Fei-Fei, L.: Imagenet large scale visual recognition challenge. Int. J. Comput. Vis. 115, 211–252 (2015)
31. Sariyildiz, M.B., Perez, J., Larlus, D.: Learning visual representations with caption annotations. In: Vedaldi, A., Bischof, H., Brox, T., Frahm, J.-M. (eds.) ECCV 2020. LNCS, vol. 12353, pp. 153–170. Springer, Cham (2020). https://doi.org/10.1007/978-3-030-58598-3_10
32. Sharma, P., Ding, N., Goodman, S., Soricut, R.: Conceptual captions: a cleaned, hypernymed, image alt-text dataset for automatic image captioning. In: ACL (2018)
33. Thomee, B., Shamma, D.A., Friedland, G., Elizalde, B., Ni, K.S., Poland, D.N., Borth, D., Li, L.J.: Yfcc100m: the new data in multimedia research. Commun. ACM 59, 64–73 (2016)
34. Tian, Y., Henaff, O.J., Oord, A.v.d.: Divide and contrast: Self-supervised learning from uncurated data. arXiv preprint arXiv:2105.08054 (2021)
35. Torralba, A., Efros, A.A.: Unbiased look at dataset bias. In: CVPR 2011, pp. 1521–1528 (2011)
36. Touvron, H., Cord, M., Douze, M., Massa, F., Sablayrolles, A., J'egou, H.: Training data-efficient image transformers & distillation through attention. In: ICML (2021)
37. Wu, Z., Xiong, Y., Yu, S.X., Lin, D.: Unsupervised feature learning via non-parametric instance-level discrimination. ArXiv abs/1805.01978 (2018)
38. Yuan, X., et al.: Multimodal contrastive training for visual representation learning. In: 2021 IEEE/CVF Conference on Computer Vision and Pattern Recognition (CVPR), pp. 6991–7000 (2021)
39. Zhai, X., et al.: A large-scale study of representation learning with the visual task adaptation benchmark. arXiv: Computer Vision and Pattern Recognition (2019)

Discovering Deformable Keypoint Pyramids

Jianing Qian$^{(\boxtimes)}$, Anastasios Panagopoulos, and Dinesh Jayaraman

University of Pennsylvania, Philadelphia, USA
{jianingq,anpans,dineshj}@seas.upenn.edu

Abstract. The locations of objects and their associated landmark keypoints can serve as versatile and semantically meaningful image representations. In natural scenes, these keypoints are often hierarchically grouped into sets corresponding to coherently moving objects and their moveable and deformable parts. Motivated by this observation, we propose Keypoint Pyramids, an approach to exploit this property for discovering keypoints without explicit supervision. Keypoint Pyramids discovers multi-level keypoint hierarchies satisfying three desiderata: comprehensiveness of the overall keypoint representation, coarse-to-fine informativeness of individual hierarchy levels, and parent-child associations of keypoints across levels. On human pose and tabletop multi-object scenes, our experimental results show that Keypoint Pyramids jointly discovers object keypoints and their natural hierarchical groupings, with finer levels adding detail to coarser levels to more comprehensively represent the visual scene. Further, we show qualitatively and quantitatively that keypoints discovered by Keypoint Pyramids using its hierarchical prior bind more consistently, and are more predictive of manually annotated semantic keypoints, compared to prior flat keypoint discovery approaches. Code is at: https://github.com/jianingq/KeypointPyramids.

Keywords: Keypoint · Self-supervision · Hierarchical representations

1 Introduction

Object keypoint sets are particularly attractive in computer vision as compact and versatile representations of images. In common instantiations of this idea, each keypoint in an image is represented by pixel coordinates attached to a specific semantic object in the real scene, and usually to a specific landmark 3D position on its surface. When all such keypoints in a scene are combined, the resulting scene descriptor is succinct, easy to interpret semantically, and convenient for spatial reasoning and systematic generalization. These advantages have been explored by researchers over many years for a large number of applications spanning pose estimation for humans [3], animals [33], and objects [39], face recognition [34], tactile sensing [26], reinforcement learning in video games [24,35], and robotics [2,4,32,40] (Fig. 1).

Supplementary Information The online version contains supplementary material available at https://doi.org/10.1007/978-3-031-19809-0_31.

Fig. 1. Our method, Keypoint Pyramids, discovers multi-level keypoint hierarchies without explicit supervision, and represent information in a coarse-to-fine structure to represent the configurations of objects and their moving and deformable parts and subparts.

Early applications of keypoints [8,10,34] relied on pre-annotated fiducial keypoints for select object categories, such as the joints of a human skeleton. However, recent works [2,13,19,24,36,44,49] have targeted *discovering* object keypoint representations without such explicit supervision to extend the benefits of keypoint representations beyond only a few pre-annotated object categories. These approaches build off the recent successes of general unsupervised image representation learning that produce unstructured 2D feature maps or 1D vector representations of images. To inject keypoint structure into such representations, unsupervised keypoint discovery methods rely on two fundamental properties of object keypoints: sparsity and local associations with small neighborhoods in the image. This prior knowledge about keypoints is commonly represented through a representational bottleneck [5] that enforces sparse and local keypoints.

In this paper, we start by observing an additional, higher order property of keypoint sets: keypoints in natural scenes are often hierarchically grouped into nested subsets that are tied to coherently moving objects and their movable and deformable parts. In a multi-object scene, each object may coarsely be represented by a single keypoint to specify the location of that object as a whole. To capture more fine-grained detail such as its pose, each rigid object requires two additional keypoints (three in total) to specify its 6-degree-of-freedom pose. An articulated object containing multiple parts requires more keypoints for each part, and a continuously deformable object may be modeled as containing many local neighborhoods each containing many keypoints.

Motivated by this natural hierarchical organization, we argue for representing the configuration of objects in a scene in a hierarchical data structure containing nested groups of keypoints. We propose Keypoint Pyramids, an unsupervised approach that learns to represent images as coarse-to-fine keypoint hierarchies, improving upon current approaches that discover *flat* keypoint representations. Keypoints in the earlier coarser levels of this hierarchy capture only the gist of the scene. Later finer levels can then add new, more local keypoints to elaborate upon this and describe the scene more comprehensively. Each l-level keypoint in the pyramid is connected through spring connections to several children keypoints at its subsequent finer level $l + 1$. For example, a human may be represented at the coarsest level by a single keypoint to identify their location in a scene. In the next level, important joints determining overall body pose such as the shoulders, elbows, and knees may be represented. At subsequent levels, finer details such as the fingers on the hand, and facial keypoints determining facial expressions may be modeled.

Indeed, several prior works have established the utility of manually defined hierarchies over pre-annotated keypoints [11,17,22,37]. Our approach, Keypoint Pyramids, is the first to exploit this for *unsupervised* keypoint discovery, improving the quality of discovered keypoint representations, and providing a convenient coarse-to-fine representation for downstream use cases. Through quantitative and qualitative evaluations on several datasets of human and multi-object images, we establish that learned keypoint pyramids generate better descriptions of visual scenes, showing higher quality information retention and more consistent keypoint binding than prior approaches that all generate flat keypoint sets. Our results validate hierarchical organization as an important prior for keypoint discovery, and our Keypoint Pyramids approach as an effective technique to exploit this prior.

2   Related Work

Unsupervised Object-Centric Representations: Explicitly representing objects within the feature representation has many benefits, including improved ML generalization to novel compositions of similar objects [15,25]. To extend such benefits of object-centric representations and reasoning beyond just the tens of categories for which pre-annotated bounding boxes and segmentation masks exist, many recent works have aimed to discover self-supervised object-centric representations without any manual annotations. One class of such methods aims to partition the scene into object bounding boxes or segmentation masks [1,6,14,21,23,29,30,45,50]. To represent pose and other variations internal to the bounding boxes or contours of each discovered object, these methods rely on unstructured dense feature vectors. Instead, we aim to comprehensively represent the full object configuration of a multi-object visual scene through a versatile, sparse, and succinct collection of keypoints that can not only localize objects but also capture their pose, part articulations and deformations.

There is also work on object part discovery [38,42,43,47] by grouping local features into semantically consistent parts. For example, it is possible to exploit optical flow information for part discovery [47], or discover 3D shape primitives for a target mesh [38], or to spatially downsample object-based feature maps to represent hierarchies in simulated and simple scenes [43]. These methods all operate in simplified settings [38,43,47], rely on additional information for part discovery [42,47], and/or inherit dense feature vector-based representations of parts [42,43]. We avoid these pitfalls in our Keypoint Pyramids approach.

Unsupervised Keypoint Discovery: More relevant to us, unsupervised keypoint discovery methods represent an input image as a set of landmarks that describe the object configuration [2,13,19,24,36,44,49]. Zhang et al. [49] design an hourglass network that takes in a single image and outputs a set of landmarks that describe the object shapes. Lorenz et al. [31] designs part discovery network that aims to disentangled object shape and appearances. Thewlis et al. [44] constrain learned landmarks for an object category to be viewpoint-invariant. Jakab et al. [19] carefully design a network architecture that is now called KeyNet, which uses extracted keypoints as an information bottleneck [5] to reconstruct the input image. Since their work, many others have built on KeyNet, for example, using a spatial feature prediction error map as input to KeyNet [13], inputting additional pose prior images to KeyNet [20], or training the keypoint outputs to be predictive of future frames [35]. Kulkarni et al. [24] augment KeyNet with a feature map tied closely to keypoints by constructing a "transported feature map" bottleneck. We build upon these approaches, particularly the keypoint and transported feature map representations of [19] and [24], but unlike any prior approaches, we jointly discover not only a flat set of keypoints, but also their hierarchical organization, with different levels corresponding to objects and their articulated and deformable parts and subparts in a coarse-to-fine structure. As described in Sect. 1, prior approaches only exploit the sparsity and local association properties of individual keypoints, but we observe and exploit the joint hierarchical organization property of keypoint sets in an image. In our experiments, we compare against flat keypoint discovery methods and show superior results.

Supervised Hierarchies: Many previous works have shown benefits from modeling manually annotated hierarchies over keypoints or objects. The classic pictorial structures model [7,9,10] established the utility of predefined graphs over object parts for object recognition. For detecting supervised keypoints, [16] propose a coarse-to-fine training and detection process, yielding advantages across human and bird pose detection tasks. In this case, "coarse" detections are merely less accurate detections of *all* keypoints, to be refined afterwards. [41] use a predefined hierarchy of over 133 annotated human body keypoints to perform "hierarchical regression", proceeding in stages to regress finer keypoints such as facial features, conditioned on coarser keypoints that determine the body pose. [37] show how predefined dense particle-based models of rigid or deformable objects can be abstracted into clustered hierarchies to allow efficiently modeling complex physical dynamics such as non-rigid collisions from data. Broadly, these methods showcase the utility of keypoint hierarchies, but our method is different in that it operates without supervision for either the keypoints or their hierarchical relationships, and aims to discover both jointly from images alone.

3   Approach

Suppose we are given a dataset of unlabeled images from a domain, such as humans in varied poses, or rooms with various configurations of objects. With no prior annotations, can we automatically learn to succinctly represent new images from that domain in terms of their objects, object parts, and other useful landmarks?

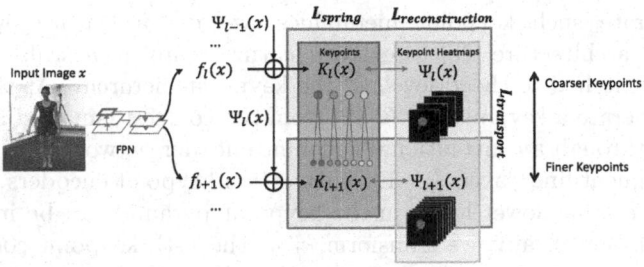

Fig. 2. The Keypoint Pyramids encoder generates a coarse to fine hierarchy of keypoints for an input image. This schematic illustrates two consecutive levels $K_l(x)$ and $K_{l+1}(x)$. Details in Sect. 3.1. The three training losses annotated on the right: "combined", "transport", and "spring" are described in detail in Sect. 3.2, 3.3, and 3.4.

Three Desiderata for Keypoint Hierarchies. To accomplish this, as motivated in Sect. 1, we would like to represent an image as a keypoint hierarchy that satisfies three desiderata:

1. It must permit comprehensively describing the configuration of the objects in the image i.e., their locations, poses, articulations, and deformations.
2. Individual levels in the hierarchy must proceed from coarse to fine, representing different trade-offs between compactness and informativeness.
3. Each keypoint at a coarse level must be tied to a set of "children" keypoints at the next finer level, which help provide more details about their parent keypoint.

We propose Keypoint Pyramids, an approach to learn representations that satisfy these desiderata from datasets of unlabeled images. Figure 2 illustrates the overall workflow of our method. In Sect. 3.1, we describe the Keypoint Pyramids neural architecture for encoding input images into keypoint hierarchies. Next, we describe how to train Keypoint Pyramids through a training objective that balances the three desiderata above, laid out in Sects. 3.2, 3.3, and 3.4. In addition to the input image and the encoding weights above, our training procedure for the encoder relies on auxiliary reference images for each training sample, and auxiliary network weights that aid in training. Finally, we summarize the overall objective and describe implementation and optimization details in Sect. 3.5.

3.1 Keypoint Pyramids Encoder Architecture

First, we define a neural network architecture for encoding images $x \in \mathbb{R}^{H \times W \times 3}$ to L-level keypoint hierarchies. Figure 2 shows a schematic. At each level $1 \leq l \leq L$, we wish to generate a new set of N_l keypoints $K_l(x) = [k_l^1(x), ..., k_l^{N_l}(x)]$. Each keypoint $k_l^n(x)$ is a 2-D vector representing pixel coordinates within the image.

To generate such keypoint hierarchies, we use a feature pyramid network (FPN) architecture [28] to extract feature maps at L scales, denoted as $\{f_l(x)\}_{l=1}^L$, matched to the L levels of the keypoint hierarchy. At the first level $l = 1$, we generate a keypoint set $K_1(x)$ from the coarsest, smallest scale feature maps $f_1(x)$ through a convolutional keypoint encoder network.

At subsequent finer layers $l > 1$, we condition keypoint encoders additionally on $K_{l-1}(x)$, so that lower levels in the keypoint pyramid can be influenced by higher levels. Specifically, we transform k_{l-1}^n, the n-th keypoint coordinates at level $l - 1$, to a heatmap representation $\Psi_{l-1}^n(x) \in \mathbb{R}^{H \times W}$ by applying a Gaussian function with a small fixed variance around the keypoint coordinates. Note that the heatmaps $\Psi_{l-1}^n(x)$ are lossless representations of the keypoint coordinates $k_{l-1}^n(x)$ and we will go back and forth between these two representations as convenient. The stack of all N_{l-1} heatmaps at level $l - 1$ is denoted Ψ_{l-1}. The inputs to the keypoint encoder for generating the l-th level $K_l(x)$ are then $[\Psi_{l-1}(x), f_l(x)]$. This architecture is shown in Fig. 2.

Keypoint encoders at each level l follow the popular KeyNet architecture [19]: a convolutional network takes $f_l(x)$ as input and generates N_l feature maps, to each of which a spatial softmax operation is applied followed by marginalization along the image dimensions to determine the keypoint coordinates $k_l^n(x)$.

3.2 Comprehensiveness of the Overall Keypoint Representation

Our first desideratum for the keypoint hierarchy is that it should permit a comprehensive description of the object configuration in the scene through keypoint coordinates alone. To achieve this, our objective includes a loss term that measures the pixelwise error for reconstructing the input image x from the combination of all levels of the keypoint hierarchy. The process of calculating this objective is shown in Fig. 3.

First, we convert all keypoints $k_l^n(x)$ across all levels to their corresponding heatmaps $\Psi_l^n(x)$ as described in Sect. 3.1. Stacking these heatmaps across all levels, we get $\Psi(x) \in \mathbb{R}^{H \times W \times \sum_l N_l}$. This keypoint heatmap stack $\Psi(x)$ is now fed into a decoder that is to be trained to reconstruct the input image x. However, keypoints only capture object configurations, and do not contain information about other aspects of the appearance of the scene such as the background, lighting, and colors. To provide this auxiliary information required for image reconstruction, following [19], we extract convolutional "appearance" features $\Phi(x_{\text{ref}}) \in \mathbb{R}^{H \times W \times C}$ from a reference image x_{ref} of the same scene as x, but with a different configuration of the objects. For example, x_{ref} could be a different video frame from the same static-camera video sequence as x.

Finally, we train a convolutional decoder network to map from the concatenation $[\Psi(x), \Phi(x_{\text{ref}})]$ to a reconstruction $\hat{x}$, minimizing the following combined reconstruction objective:

$$\mathcal{L}_{\text{reconstruction}}(\hat{x}, x) = ||\hat{x}([\Psi(x), \Phi(x_{\text{ref}})]) - x||_2^2. \tag{1}$$

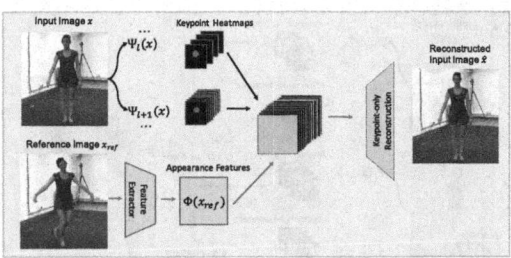

Fig. 3. To train a comprehensive keypoint representation, we reconstruct the input image from the combination of all levels of our hierarchy, generating a reconstruction loss. Details in Sect. 3.2. The gray areas in the figure show components that are required only to compute the training objectives; these are not used at test time.

3.3   Graded Informativeness of Keypoint Levels

To satisfy our second desideratum, individual levels in the keypoint hierarchy must each capture useful information, and finer levels must progressively capture more information. However, the combined reconstruction objective of Eq. 1 pools keypoints from all levels in the hierarchy and does not impose any requirements on individual levels. For example, it would suffice to minimize Eq. 1 if all of the information was represented in only one level, and all other levels captured no information at all.

Augmenting Keypoint Coordinates with Local Features. To incentivize meaningful coarse-to-fine keypoint hierarchies, we introduce level-wise objective terms requiring each level to be independently informative about the object configuration. However, note that merely the 2D pixel coordinates of keypoints at coarse levels cannot capture the fine-grained details of the object configuration. For example, just the coordinates of the centroid of a person cannot reasonably be sufficient to infer their full pose. To effectively capture the object configuration, keypoint coordinates at each level must therefore be augmented with some residual information from their local image neighborhoods, to substitute for missing finer-level keypoints.

For this purpose, we construct feature-augmented keypoints. Specifically, to represent missing fine-grained information from level l keypoints, we extract convolutional features from their neighborhoods. We compute feature maps $\Phi_l(x) \in \mathbb{R}^{H \times W \times C_l}$ from a new convolutional encoder operating on top of the FPN level l features $f_l(x)$. Then, local features around a keypoint $k_l^n(x)$ can be computed by masking these features through an elementwise product with the keypoint heatmap $\Psi_l^n(x)$. This produces the feature-augmented keypoints $[\Psi_l^n(x), \Phi_l(x)\Psi_l^n(x)]$.

Finally, to incentivize finer levels to capture more information within the keypoint coordinates, we augment the heatmaps for coarser levels with more information than for finer levels; accordingly, we set the number of channels C_l

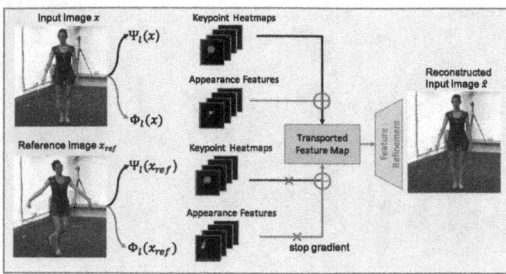

Fig. 4. While individual levels of the keypoint hierarchy need not be comprehensive, they should each capture useful information. We construct feature-augmented keypoints at each level, create "transported" feature maps and then use those to reconstruct the image, generating a transport loss. Details in Sect. 3.3.

in the feature maps $\Phi_l(x)$ to be higher for coarser levels, i.e., $C_{l_1} > C_{l_2}$ for $l_1 < l_2$.

Transport Loss. Recall that the combined reconstruction objective Eq. 1 aims to reconstruct the input image x using appearance features from a reference image x_{ref} and keypoints from the original input x. In similar spirit, we may now set up a level-wise image reconstruction objective using the feature-augmented keypoints above. In other words, we would like to compute appearance features $\Phi_l(x_{\text{ref}})$ from the reference image, inject augmented keypoint information from x, and train a decoder to produce a reconstruction $\hat{x}$. See Fig. 4.

We set up such layerwise reconstruction losses following the "keypoint transport" loss from [24]. At each level, we first compute a transported feature map:

$$\Phi_l'(x, x_{\text{ref}}) = \underbrace{\Phi_l(x_{\text{ref}})(1 - \Psi_l(x_{\text{ref}}))(1 - \Psi_l(x))}_{\text{Appearance features from reference image}}$$

$$+ \underbrace{\Phi_l(x)(1 - (1 - \Psi_l(x_{\text{ref}}))(1 - \Psi_l(x)))}_{\text{"Augmented" keypoints from input image}}. \tag{2}$$

This transport equation can be interpreted as follows. The first term effectively removes all keypoints from the reference image feature map to provide reference appearance information alone. The second term fills in those keypoint holes using augmented keypoints from the original image x. We can now reconstruct x from this transported feature at each level l, computing a transport objective:

$$\mathcal{L}_{\text{transport}} = \sum_{l=1}^{L} \lambda_l ||\hat{x}_l(\Phi_l'(x, x_{\text{ref}})) - x||_2^2. \tag{3}$$

3.4 Keypoint Associations Across Levels

Finally, how can we ensure a pyramidal association structure between higher and lower levels, as in our third desideratum? We pre-specify desired associations between keypoints across neighboring levels and use a spring loss to encourage children keypoints at finer levels to remain close to their parent.

For each "parent" keypoint $k_l^n \in K_l$ at level l, we specify a fixed disjoint subset $\delta_l^n \subset K_{l+1}$ of children keypoints at its finer level. In our experiments, we use $\delta_l^n = \{Ml + 1, Ml + 2, \ldots, M(l + 1) - 1\}$, where M specifies the number of children per parent keypoint. We would now like each parent keypoint k_l^n to serve as an anchor for its children. We therefore penalize the deviation between children keypoint coordinates and their parent. This is akin to minimizing the energy of a mechanical system of springs connecting each child to its parent. This produces the following spring loss:

$$\mathcal{L}_{\text{spring}} = \lambda_s \sum_{\text{levels } l<L} \sum_{\text{keypoints } n\leq N_l} \sum_{\text{children } m\in\delta_l^n} ||k_l^n - k_{l+1}^m||_2^2 \tag{4}$$

3.5 Implementation Details

The overall Keypoint Pyramids objective function is:

$$\mathcal{L}_{\text{total}} = \mathcal{L}_{\text{reconstruction}} + \mathcal{L}_{\text{transport}} + \mathcal{L}_{\text{spring}} \tag{5}$$

We minimize this objective end-to-end, jointly training the feature pyramid network, the keypoint encoders for all levels, as well as the auxiliary weights required during training, namely, the feature extractors and decoders. We use Adam optimizer with learning rate of 1e-4 for all experiments. During training, we randomly sampled a reference image x_{ref} from the same video sequence as the input image x, within 250 frames from it. In all of our experiments, we train Keypoint Pyramids with $L = 2$ levels, and with $N_1 = 10$ and $N_2 = 20$ keypoints on the first and second levels. Thus, our combined flattened representation has $\sum_l N_l = 30$ keypoints. We set $\lambda_s = 1$, $\lambda_1 = 0.1$ and $\lambda_2 = 1$ for all of our experiments. For the FPN network, we output feature maps at two levels and $l = 2$. At the coarsest level, the feature maps have size 16×16 and at the finest level the feature maps have size 32×32.

4   Experiments

Our experiments aim to answer the following questions: (1) Does Keypoint Pyramids discover semantically meaningful keypoint hierarchies? (2) Compared to prior flat keypoint discovery approaches, how well does a flattened Keypoint Pyramid recover the configurations of objects in the scene? (3) How important are the different components of our approach? (4) Is the Keypoint Pyramid representation suitable for downstream computer vision tasks? (Fig. 5).

4.1   Datasets

While many prior unsupervised keypoint and object discovery approaches have been evaluated in simulated settings, we focus on two real image datasets to evaluate Keypoint Pyramids on realistic scenes and objects.

Fig. 5. Sample images from the two datasets used in our experiments: **(left)** Human 3.6M (H3.6M) showing people enacting various actions, and **(right)** our new dataset Bot-and-Objects (B&O), containing a robot interacting with objects on a tabletop.

Human3.6M (H3.6M): Human3.6M [18] is a large-scale video dataset featuring 7 actors performing 16 categories of actions in an indoor environment. It contains 3.6M images. Following the conventions in [27], we use 5 human subjects (S1, S5, S6, S7, S8) for training and the remaining 2 human subjects (S9, S11) for testing. Image pairs (x, x_{ref}) are extracted from the same video sequence. We apply loose crops around the subject using ground-truth annotation following [19]. To focus on the full body pose, we omit 5 action categories (Sitting, Smoking, etc.) that involve largely seated poses, leaving 11 categories in our dataset. This dataset is challenging because it requires the network to learn to recognize common keypoints that generalize across actors with disparate appearances, clothing, and body shapes, set against different backgrounds[1] and non-ideal lighting conditions. Further, modeling the human body is challenging, because it is a complicated articulated and deformable object with many moving parts and other degrees of freedom. On the other hand, this dataset permits extensive quantitative evaluation: it contains exhaustive keypoint annotations for 17 human pose keypoints corresponding to the major joints for all images, and the action category labels also permit an action recognition task from discovered keypoint representations.

Bot-And-Objects (B&O): To evaluate Keypoint Pyramids on real-world multi-object scenes, we collect an object pushing dataset with an articulated 5-degree-of-freedom WidowX 200 robot arm and three plush toys. We collect a video dataset with 450 videos, each containing 30 frames (13500 images). Between any two frames, the robot arm performs random motions of its gripper up to 5 cm within its 50 by 50 cm workspace, frequently displacing or rotating objects, and thus generating diverse object configurations within our dataset. We train on 10800 images and test on the remaining 2700 images.

4.2   Baselines and Ablations

Recall that all prior keypoint discovery approaches produce flat keypoint sets. We pick two state-of-the-art approaches for comparison against Keypoint Pyramids:

- **KeyNet** [19]: This baseline uses a flat keypoint set output by an encoder as the bottleneck in a neural network autoencoder.

---

[1] different video sequences are shot against different backgrounds.

- **Transporter** [24]: This method trains convolutional feature maps alongside keypoints to permit reconstruction from a transported feature map.

These baselines are the most widely used object keypoint discovery method so far. [13,20,35] mentioned above all reuse the KeyNet encoder architecture, and many works reuse the Transporter loss [46,48]. A comparison with a more recent method [12] is in Sec A.3. For both baselines, we use the widely used KeyNet-based keypoint encoder network architecture (same as for our method), with inputs from the largest and final feature map from FPN, which has size 32×32. More architecture details are in Sec A.1. We train both baselines with varying numbers of keypoints for fair comparison against our Keypoint Pyramids approach. In addition to these baselines, we also evaluate several ablations of our approach to analyze the effects of its various components. First, we train without the combined reconstruction loss (**No-Reconstruction**), without the transport loss (**No-Transport**), and without the spring loss (**No-Spring**). Next, rather than use the keypoints-only reconstruction loss for the overall flattened representation (Eq. 1) and the augmented keypoints-based transport loss for the individual levels (Eq. 3), we try using the same type of loss for both, either keypoint-only reconstruction (**All-Reconstruction**) or transport loss (**All-Transport**). We also run an ablation without the architectural choice of conditioning the keypoint encoder at level l on the keypoints from the previous level $l - 1$ (**Unconditioned**). Note that Unconditioned still introduces dependencies between keypoint levels during training, through the reconstruction and spring losses. Finally, for our full method after training, we evaluate keypoints from its individual levels separately (**Level l=1 or 2**) to validate the coarse-to-fine representation.

4.3   Results

On H3.6M, which comes with exhaustive annotations for 17 major joints, we report the RMSE error for linear regression from discovered keypoints to annotated ground truth keypoint coordinates. This quantitatively evaluates keypoint representations for their ability to capture object configurations. We split the test data into two halves, fit the regression on one half and report errors on the other half. Table 1 shows the keypoint regression error for all methods for levels 1, 2, and for the combined flattened keypoint representation (level 1 + level 2). For comparison with flat approaches, we train them three times with 10, 20, and 30 keypoints. Flattened Keypoint Pyramids performs much better than intrinsically flat approaches, and shows a clear progression from level 1 to level 2 to the flattened representation. Our ablations further validate our algorithm design choices. All-Reconstruction which uses only keypoint information from source images works better than All-Transport which always augments keypoints with local feature information, but neither works as well as our choice to combine the overall reconstruction loss with the level-wise transport loss to allow graded information in the individual levels. Further, the No-X ablations show that all terms in the objective function are important to our performance: dropping any

Table 1. Keypoint regression error on H3.6M, compared to prior flat unsupervised keypoint discovery baselines and ablations. Lower is better.

	Methods ↓/Level (num. keypts.) →	level 1(10)	level 2(20)	flattened(30)
	Transporter	50.15	45.25	47.45
	KeyNet	56.51	53.28	46.71
	Keypoint Pyramids (Ours)	52.81	**43.97**	**43.30**
Ablations	(KP) No-Reconstruction	**49.09**	46.73	45.23
	(KP) No-Transport	50.52	46.29	45.85
	(KP) No-Spring	49.27	48.21	45.28
	(KP) All-Transport	54.72	50.07	49.53
	(KP) All-Reconstruction	50.83	48.15	46.93
	(KP) Unconditioned	49.37	44.73	**43.75**

Table 2. Action classification accuracy on H3.6M, compared to prior flat unsupervised keypoint discovery baselines. Higher is better.

Methods	Accuracy
Ground-truth Keypoints(17)	0.331
Keypoint Pyramids (Ours)(L1+L2)	**0.218**
Transporter(30)	0.177
KeyNet(30)	0.179
Keypoint Pyramids (Ours)(L2)	**0.193**
Transporter(20)	0.164
KeyNet(20)	0.168
Keypoint Pyramids (Ours)(L1)	**0.182**
Transporter(10)	0.152
KeyNet(10)	0.148

individual term deteriorates performance and all terms contribute nearly equally. Finally, removing forward connections from coarser to finer keypoints (Unconditioned) produces only a marginally worse flattened representation than our full approach, suggesting that the training objective already enforces the hierarchy even without this architectural bias. For reference, we train our keypoint encoder to minimize MSE loss with respect to ground-truth keypoints to show the upper-bound performance of our method. With the same number of keypoints (17) as ground-truth, this yields a RMSE error of 37.97.

On our new B&O dataset, which contains deformable objects, exhaustively annotating with all keypoints required to recover the full object configuration is intractable, since deformable objects have infinite degrees of freedom. We coarsely annotate a small test data subset and validate that Keypoint Pyramids performs better than baselines. We report these results in Sec A.2.

Utility for Downstream Tasks: H3.6M Action Category Recognition. Having established that Keypoint Pyramids discovers better keypoint representations than prior approaches, we now ask: how much do these representations contribute to downstream tasks? Towards evaluating this, we design an action classification task for recognizing activities from sequences of human poses. For H3.6M, where videos come with 11 action category labels, we evaluate discovered

Ours(l_1)   Ours(l_2)   Ours($l_{1+}l_2$)   T (10)   T (20)   T (30)   K (10)   K (20)   K (30)

Fig. 6. (Best seen in pdf) Visualizing discovered keypoints from our method and baselines Transporter [24] (T) and KeyNet [19] (K). Each row is a single image and each column is a method. For our method, parent and children keypoints are illustrated with the same color, and their connections are drawn in column 3. More results in appendices.

keypoint representations as inputs for training GRU-based recurrent networks for action classification. We describe the detail of these networks in Sect. A.5.

As shown in Table 2, Keypoint Pyramids performs substantially better than the two baselines for this task, either by using the full flattened keypoint representations(L1+L2) or by just using the individual levels of keypoints. The first row of Table 2 shows an upper bound for this task: the action classification accuracy when input features are the 17 ground-truth keypoints. These results show that the improved quality of our discovered keypoint representations confers benefits for downstream tasks that use those representations.

Keypoint Visualizations. Figure 6 visualizes discovered keypoints on both datasets for our method (levels 1, 2, and combined) and the baselines Transporter (T) and KeyNet (K) trained with varying keypoint counts. We observe that Keypoint Pyramids recovers meaningful keypoints and hierarchies. On H3.6M, it discovers one coarse keypoint on each knee (yellow, cyan), connected pyramidally to two fine keypoints above and below capturing the full leg pose, a similar elbow pyramid (green) to capture the configuration of an arm, and a pyramid centered at the hip (light blue) that captures the relative orientation of the torso to the lower body. Even when discovered keypoints do not map one-to-one to semantic keypoints, they are consistently located on the body, and bind to specific locations, for example, the green pyramid near the right shoulder, and the pink pyramid near the top of the head. On the other hand, the flat baselines bind less consistently: for example, Transporter scatters many keypoints around the body rather than on it (column 6), and KeyNet produces keypoints that switch positions between actors or poses. In addition to these visualizations, we also train separate decoders to map discovered keypoint coordinates to image reconstructions. On both datasets, we see a clear progression of image reconstruction quality from level 1 to 2 to combination. Details in Sec A.4.

5   Conclusions

We have presented Keypoint Pyramids, an approach to tackle the challenging task of discovering coarse-to-fine keypoint hierarchies from unlabeled images. Keypoint Pyramids is designed to meet three key desiderata of comprehensiveness, graded informativeness, and parent-child associations between levels. Our results show the first examples of successfully discovered keypoint hierarchies, and our flattened representations outperform prior state-of-the-art for keypoint discovery.

Acknowledgements. This work was partially supported by an Amazon Research Award to Dinesh Jayaraman.

References

1. Burgess, C.P., et al.: Monet: unsupervised scene decomposition and representation. ArXiv:abs/1901.11390 (2019)
2. Chen, B., Abbeel, P., Pathak, D.: Unsupervised learning of visual 3D keypoints for control, June 2021
3. Dang, Q., Yin, J., Wang, B., Zheng, W.: Deep learning based 2D human pose estimation: a survey. Tsinghua Sci. Technol. **24**(6), 663–676 (2019)
4. Das, N., Bechtle, S., Davchev, T., Jayaraman, D., Rai, A., Meier, F.: Model-based inverse reinforcement learning from visual demonstrations. CORL (2020)
5. Engelcke, M., Jones, O.P., Posner, I.: Reconstruction bottlenecks in Object-Centric generative models, July 2020
6. Engelcke, M., Kosiorek, A.R., Jones, O.P., Posner, I.: Genesis: generative scene inference and sampling with object-centric latent representations. ArXiv, abs/1907.13052 (2020)
7. Felzenszwalb, P., McAllester, D., Ramanan, D.: A discriminatively trained, multi-scale, deformable part model. In: 2008 IEEE Conference on Computer Vision and Pattern Recognition, pp. 1–8. IEEE (2008)
8. Felzenszwalb, P.F., Huttenlocher, D.P.: Pictorial structures for object recognition. Int. J. Comput. Vis. **61**(1), 55–79 (2005)
9. Felzenszwalb, P.F., Huttenlocher, D.P.: Pictorial structures for object recognition. Int. J. Comput. Vision **61**(1), 55–79 (2005)
10. Fischler, M.A., Elschlager, R.A.: The representation and matching of pictorial structures. IEEE Trans. Comput. **100**(1), 67–92 (1973)
11. Ghiasi, G., Fowlkes, C.C.: Occlusion coherence: localizing occluded faces with a hierarchical deformable part model. In: Proceedings of the IEEE Conference on Computer Vision and Pattern Recognition, pp. 2385–2392 (2014)
12. Gopalakrishnan, A., van Steenkiste, S., Schmidhuber, J.: Unsupervised object keypoint learning using local spatial predictability. arXiv:abs/2011.12930 (2021)
13. Gopalakrishnan, A., van Steenkiste, S., Schmidhuber, J.: Unsupervised object keypoint learning using local spatial predictability. In: International Conference on Learning Representations (2021). https://openreview.net/forum?id=GJwMHetHc73
14. Greff, K., et al.: Multi-object representation learning with iterative variational inference. arXiv:abs/1903.00450 (2019)
15. Greff, K., Van Steenkiste, S., Schmidhuber, J.: On the binding problem in artificial neural networks. arXiv preprint arXiv:2012.05208 (2020)
16. Huang, S., Gong, M., Tao, D.: A coarse-fine network for keypoint localization. In: 2017 IEEE International Conference on Computer Vision (ICCV), pages 3047–3056 (2017)
17. Huang, S., Gong, M., Tao, D.: A coarse-fine network for keypoint localization. In: Proceedings of the IEEE International Conference on Computer Vision, pp. 3028–3037 (2017)
18. Ionescu, C., Papava, D., Olaru, V., Sminchisescu, C.: Human3.6m: large scale datasets and predictive methods for 3D human sensing in natural environments. IEEE Trans. Pattern Anal. Mach. Intell. **36**(7), 1325–1339 (2014)
19. Jakab, T., Gupta, A., Bilen, H., Vedaldi, A.: Unsupervised learning of object landmarks through conditional image generation. In: NeurIPS (2018)
20. Jakab, T., Gupta, A., Bilen, H., Vedaldi, A.: Self-supervised learning of interpretable keypoints from unlabelled videos. In: 2020 IEEE/CVF Conference on Computer Vision and Pattern Recognition (CVPR), pp. 8784–8794 (2020)

21. Jiang, J., Janghorbani, S., de Melo, G., Ahn, S.: Scalable object-oriented sequential generative models. CoRR, abs/1910.02384 (2019). arxiv.org/abs/1910.02384
22. Jin, S., et al.: Differentiable hierarchical graph grouping for multi-person pose estimation. In: Vedaldi, A., Bischof, H., Brox, T., Frahm, J.-M. (eds.) ECCV 2020. LNCS, vol. 12352, pp. 718–734. Springer, Cham (2020). https://doi.org/10.1007/978-3-030-58571-6_42
23. Kipf, T., van der Pol, E., Welling, M.: Contrastive learning of structured world models. arXiv:abs/1911.12247 (2020)
24. Kulkarni, T.D., et al.: Unsupervised learning of object keypoints for perception and control. Advances in Neural Information Processing Systems, vol. 32 (2019)
25. Lake, B.M., Ullman, T.D., Tenenbaum, J.B., Gershman, S.J.: Building machines that learn and think like people. Behav. Brain Sci. **40**, e253 (2017)
26. Lambeta, M., et al.: Digit: a novel design for a low-cost compact high-resolution tactile sensor with application to in-hand manipulation. In: ICRA and IEEE RA-L (2020)
27. Li, S., Chan, A.B.: 3D human pose estimation from monocular images with deep convolutional neural network. In: ACCV (2014)
28. Lin, T.-Y., Dollár, P., Girshick, R., He, K., Hariharan, B., Belongie, S.: Feature pyramid networks for object detection. In: Proceedings of the IEEE Conference on Computer Vision and Pattern Recognition, pp. 2117–2125 (2017)
29. Lin, Z., et al.: SPACE: unsupervised object-oriented scene representation via spatial attention and decomposition. CoRR, abs/2001.02407 (2020). https://arxiv.org/abs/2001.02407
30. Locatello, F., et al.: Object-centric learning with slot attention. arXiv:abs/2006.15055 (2020)
31. Lorenz, D., Bereska, L., Milbich, T., Ommer, B.: Unsupervised part-based disentangling of object shape and appearance. In: 2019 IEEE/CVF Conference on Computer Vision and Pattern Recognition (CVPR), pp. 10947–10956 (2019)
32. Manuelli, L., Li, Y., Florence, P.R., Tedrake, R.: Keypoints into the future: Self-supervised correspondence in model-based reinforcement learning. In: CoRL (2020)
33. Mathis, A., et al.: Deeplabcut: markerless pose estimation of user-defined body parts with deep learning. Nat. Neurosci. **21**(9), 1281–1289 (2018)
34. Mian, A.S., Bennamoun, M., Owens, R.: Keypoint detection and local feature matching for textured 3D face recognition. Int. J. Comput. Vision **79**(1), 1–12 (2008)
35. Minderer, M., Sun, C., Villegas, R., Cole, F., Murphy, K., Lee, H.: Unsupervised learning of object structure and dynamics from videos, June 2019
36. Minderer, M., Sun, C., Villegas, R., Cole, F., Murphy, K.P., Lee, H.: Unsupervised learning of object structure and dynamics from videos. ArXiv:abs/1906.07889 (2019)
37. Mrowca, D., et al.: Flexible neural representation for physics prediction. In: Advances in Neural Information Processing Systems, vol. 31 (2018)
38. Paschalidou, D., Katharopoulos, A., Geiger, A., Fidler, S.: Neural parts: learning expressive 3D shape abstractions with invertible neural networks. In: 2021 IEEE/CVF Conference on Computer Vision and Pattern Recognition (CVPR), pp. 3203–3214 (2021)
39. Pavlakos, G., Zhou, X., Chan, A., Derpanis, K.G., Daniilidis, K.: 6-dof object pose from semantic keypoints. In: 2017 IEEE International Conference on Robotics and Automation (ICRA), pp. 2011–2018. IEEE (2017)
40. Qin, Z., Fang, K., Zhu, Y., Fei-Fei, L., Savarese, S.: Learning keypoint representations for tool manipulation, KETO, October 2019

41. Samet, N., Akbas, E.: Hprnet: hierarchical point regression for whole-body human pose estimation. arXiv:abs/2106.04269 (2021)
42. Siarohin, A., Roy, S., Lathuilière, S., Tulyakov, S., Ricci, E., Sebe, N.: Motion-supervised co-part segmentation. In: 2020 25th International Conference on Pattern Recognition (ICPR), pp. 9650–9657 (2021)
43. Stanić, A., van Steenkiste, S., Schmidhuber, J.: Hierarchical relational inference. arXiv preprint arXiv:2010.03635 (2020)
44. Thewlis, J., Bilen, H., Vedaldi, A.: Unsupervised learning of object landmarks by factorized spatial embeddings. In: 2017 IEEE International Conference on Computer Vision (ICCV), pp. 3229–3238 (2017)
45. Veerapaneni, R., et al.: Entity abstraction in visual model-based reinforcement learning. arXiv:abs/1910.12827 (2019)
46. Xiong, H., Li, Q., Chen, Y.-C., Bharadhwaj, H., Sinha, S., Garg, A.: Learning by watching: physical imitation of manipulation skills from human videos. In: 2021 IEEE/RSJ International Conference on Intelligent Robots and Systems (IROS), pp. 7827–7834 (2021)
47. Xu, Z., et al.: Unsupervised discovery of parts, structure, and dynamics. arXiv:abs/1903.05136 (2019)
48. Yang, J., Zhang, J., Settle, C., Rai, A., Antonova, R., Bohg, J.: Learning periodic tasks from human demonstrations. arXiv:abs/2109.14078 (2022)
49. Zhang, Y., Guo, Y., Jin, Y., Luo, Y., He, Z., Lee, H.: Unsupervised discovery of object landmarks as structural representations. In: 2018 IEEE/CVF Conference on Computer Vision and Pattern Recognition, pp. 2694–2703 (2018)
50. Zoran, D., Kabra, R., Lerchner, A., Rezende, D.J.: Parts: unsupervised segmentation with slots, attention and independence maximization. In: 2021 IEEE/CVF International Conference on Computer Vision (ICCV), pp. 10419–10427 (2021)

Neural Video Compression Using GANs for Detail Synthesis and Propagation

Fabian Mentzer[(✉)], Eirikur Agustsson, Johannes Ballé, David Minnen,
Nick Johnston, and George Toderici

Google Research,Zürich, Switzerland
mentzer@google.com

Abstract. We present the first neural video compression method based
on generative adversarial networks (GANs). Our approach significantly
outperforms previous neural and non-neural video compression methods in a user study, setting a new state-of-the-art in visual quality for
neural methods. We show that the GAN loss is crucial to obtain this
high visual quality. Two components make the GAN loss effective: we
i) synthesize detail by conditioning the generator on a latent extracted
from the warped previous reconstruction to then ii) propagate this detail
with high-quality flow. We find that user studies are required to compare
methods, i.e., none of our quantitative metrics were able to predict all
studies. We present the network design choices in detail, and ablate them
with user studies.

Keywords: Neural Video Compression · GANs

1 Introduction

Recently, there has been progress in neural video compression, leading to the
latest approaches being comparable to or even outperforming the non-learned
standard codec HEVC [17] in terms of PSNR [1,20,33,48] or outperforming it
in MS-SSIM [11,20,33]. However, as we navigate the rate-distortion trade-off
towards low bitrates, reconstructions become blurry (for neural approaches) or
blocky (for non-neural). This was also observed for images, where there has been
interest in instead optimizing the rate-distortion-realism trade-off [8,39,40,42].
In short, the goal is to add a realism constraint, forcing the decoder to make
sure that reconstructions are also looking "realistic" (in the sense that they are
indistinguishable from real images), while still staying close to the input. To
optimize this constraint, previous work [2,24,34,37] added a GAN [12] loss to
the rate distortion objective, thereby navigating the triple-tradeoff.

F. Mentzer and E. Agustsson—Equal contributions.

Supplementary Information The online version contains supplementary material
available at https://doi.org/10.1007/978-3-031-19809-0_32.

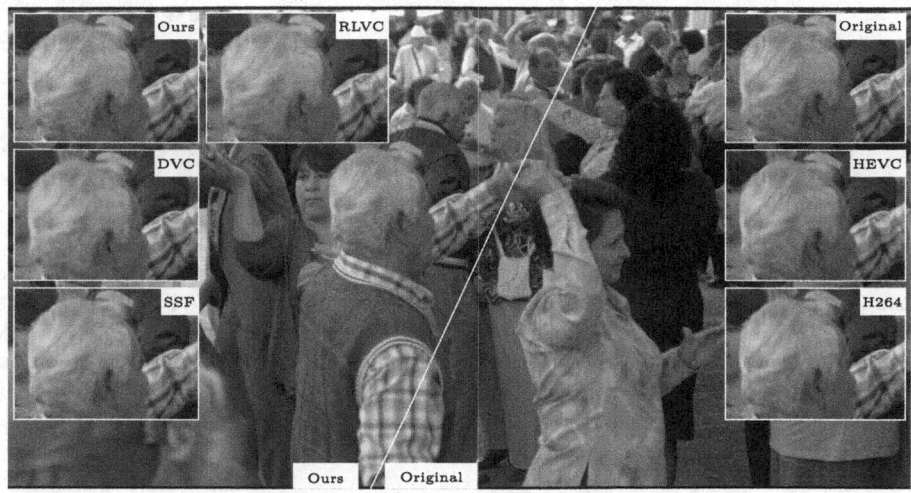

Fig. 1. Comparing our reconstruction to various baselines. On the left, we see crops from *neural* methods, where we compare to the published MSE-based methods RLVC [47], SSF [1], and DVC [23]. On the right we see the original and the non-neural methods, H.264 [4] and HEVC [17]. We see how high frequency texture is faithfully synthesized in our approach, while staying close to the input, where-as MSE-based methods suffer from blurryness. *Best viewed on screen.*

However, targeting realism remains largely unexplored for neural *video* compression. This is perhaps not surprising, as video compression brings various challenges [49], and GAN training is notoriously hard [12]. To apply rate-distortion-realism theory for video, we need to be able to synthesize detail whenever new content appears, and then we need to propagate this detail to future frames. With this in mind, we carefully design a *generative* neural video compression approach excelling at synthesizing and then preserving detail.

According to the theory [7,8], realism cannot be measured in terms of pair-wise distortions such as PSNR and MS-SSIM. In fact, theory predicts that these metrics must get worse as realism increases. Following previous work [2,24], we thus perform extensive user studies to evaluate our approach, where we ask raters to compare methods and chose which "is closest to the original" (see Sect. 4.2). We find that by trading-off just a little bit in PSNR ($\approx$0.6dB, see Sect. 5), we can significantly improve in realism, as measured by the study. This way, our approach manages to synthesize small scale detail while staying close to the original (see Fig. 1). Our main contributions are as follows:

1. We present the first GAN-based neural compression system and set a new state-of-the-art in subjective visual quality measured with user studies, where we significantly outperform previous neural compression systems ([1,23,47]), as well as the standard codecs H.264 [4] and HEVC [17]. We show that the GAN loss is crucial for this performance.
2. We show that two components are crucial to make the GAN loss effective: i) We condition the generator on a "free" (in terms of bits) latent obtained

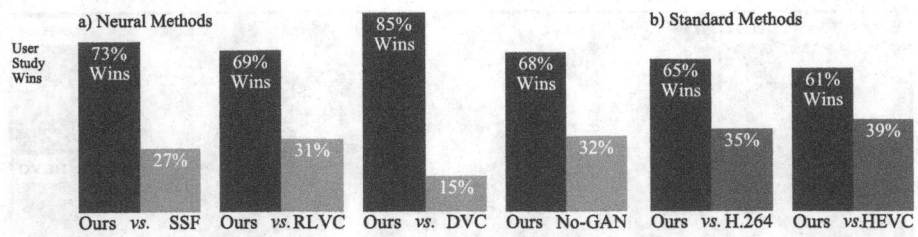

Fig. 2. Comparing 6 different pairs of methods in a *user study*, on MCL-JCV. We visualize how often each method is preferred in the user studies. We had 1639 ratings in total, with an average of 273 per method pair. *a)* Shows neural methods, SSF [1], RLVC [47], and DVC [23], seeing that our method significantly outperforms them in terms of visual quality. We compare *Ours* to our *no-GAN* baseline, where we see that a GAN clearly helps. *b)* We compare to the standard codecs H.264 [4] and HEVC [17], and see that our method is also preferred.

by feeding the warped previous reconstruction through the image encoder, and show that this is crucial to *synthesize* details. ii) To be able to *propagate* previously synthesized details, we rely on accurate optical flow provided by $Uflow$ [18], and warping with high-quality resampling kernels.

2   Related Work

Neural Video Compression. Wu *et al.* [46] use frame interpolation for video compression, compressing B-frames by interpolating between other frames. Djelouah *et al.* [10] also use interpolation, but additionally employ an optical flow predictor for warping frames. This approach of using future frames is commonly referred to as "B-frame coding" for "bidirectional prediction". Other neural video coding methods rely on only using predictive (P) frames, commonly referred to as the "low-delay" setting, since it is more suitable for streaming applications by not relying on future frames. Lu *et al.* [23] use previously decoded frames and a pretrained optical flow network. Habibian *et al.* [15] do not explicitly model motion, and instead rely on a 3D autoregressive entropy model to capture spatial and temporal correlations. Liu *et al.* [21] build temporal priors via LSTMs, while Liu *et al.* [22] condition entropy models on previous frames. Rippel *et al.* [35] support adapting the rate during encoding, and also do not explicitly model motion. Agustsson *et al.* [1] propose "scale-space flow" to avoid complex residuals by allowing the model to blur as needed via a pyramid of blurred versions of the image. Yang *et al.* [48] generalize various approaches by learning to adapt the residual scale, and conditioning residual entropy models on flow latents. Li *et al.* [20] use deep features as context for encoding, decoding and entropy coding. Golinsky *et al.* [11] recurrently connect decoders with subsequent unrolling steps, while Yang *et al.* [47] also add recurrent entropy models. Rippel and Anderson *et al.* [33] explore ways to make neural video compression more practical, with models that cover a range of bitrates and a focus on computational efficientcy, improving encode and decode time.

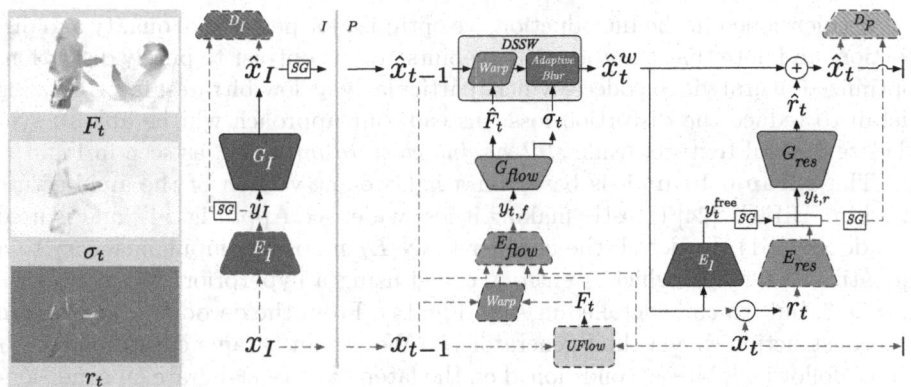

Fig. 3. Architecture overview, with some intermediate tensors visualized in the gray box. To the *left* of the gray line is the I-frame branch (learned CNNs in blue), to the *right* the P-frame branch (learned CNNs in green). Dashed lines are not active during decoding, and discriminators D_I, D_P are only active during training. The size of the CNN blocks roughly indicates their capacity. SG is a stop gradient operation. *DSSW* is our "decoupled scale-space warping" (Sect. 3.2), and *UFlow* is a frozen optical flow model from [18].

Non-Neural Video Compression. The combination of transform coding [14] using discrete cosine transforms [3] with spatial and/or temporal prediction, known as "Hybrid video coding", emerged in the 1980s s as the technology dominating video compression until the present day. Non-neural methods such as H.261 through H.265/HEVC [17], VP8 [6], VP9 [29] and AV1 [9] have all remained faithful to the hybrid coding principle, with extensive refinements, regarding more flexible pixel formats (*e.g.*, bit depth, chroma subsampling), more flexible temporal and spatial prediction (*e.g.*, I-, P-, B-frames, intra block copy), and many more. Thanks to the years of research that went into these codecs, they provide strong baselines for neural approaches.

3 Method

3.1 Overview

An overview of the architecture we use is given in Fig. 3, while a detailed view with all layers is provided in App. Fig. 14. Let $x = \{x_1, x_2, \dots\}$ be a sequence of frames, where x_1 is the initial (I) frame, denoted by x_I in the figure and below. Similar to previous work, we operate in the "low-delay" mode, and hence predict subsequent (P) frames from previous frames. Let $\hat{x} = \{\hat{x}_1, \hat{x}_2, \dots\}$ be the reconstructed video. We use the following strategy to obtain high-fidelity reconstructions:

(S1) Synthesize plausible details in the I-frame.
(S2) Propagate those details wherever possible and as sharp as possible.
(S3) For new content appearing in P-frames, we again want to synthesize plausible details.

As mentioned in the Introduction, we optimize for perceptual quality and distortion, and note that the above three points are in contrast to purely distortion-optimized neural video codecs, which, particularly at low bitrates, favor blurring detail to reduce the distortion loss. Instead, our approach will be able to synthesize faithful texture, while *still staying close to the input*, as seen in Fig. 1.

The **I-frame branch** is based on a lightweight version of the architecture used in "HiFiC" [24] (mostly making it less wide, see App. Fig. 14), and is used to address (S1). In detail, the encoder CNN E_I maps the input image x_I to a quantized latent y_I, which is entropy coded using a hyperprior [26] (not shown in Fig. 3, but which is detailed in App. Fig. 14). From the decoded y_I, we obtain a reconstruction $\hat{x}_I$ via the I-generator G_I. We use an I-frame discriminator D_I that—following [24]—is conditioned on the latent z_I (we elaborate on conditioning in Sect. 3.5).

The **P-frame branch** has two parts, an auto-encoder E_{flow}, G_{flow} for the flow, and an auto-encoder E_{res}, G_{res} for the residual, following previous video work (*e.g.* [1,23], *etc.*). To partially address (S2), similar to previous work, we employ a powerful optical flow predictor network on the encoder side, *Uflow* [18]. The resulting (backward) flow $F_t = UFlow(x_t, x_{t-1})$ is fed to the flow-encoder E_{flow}, which outputs the quantized and entropy-coded flow-latent $y_{t,f}$. From the flow-latent, the generator G_{flow} predicts both a reconstructed flow $\hat{F}_t$, as well as a mask σ_t. The mask σ_t has the same spatial dimensions as F_t, with each value in $[0, \sigma_{max}]$. Together, $(\hat{F}_t, \sigma_t)$ are used for our **decoupled scale-space warping**, a variant of *scale-space warping* [1], described in Sect. 3.2. Intuitively, for each pixel, the mask σ_t predicts how "correct" the flow at that pixel is (see the gray box in Fig. 3). We first warp the previous reconstruction $\hat{x}_{t-1}$ using $\hat{F}_t$, then we use σ_t to decide how much to blur each pixel. In practice, we observe σ_t predicts where new content that is not well captured by warping appears. Since the flow is in general relatively easy to compress, we employ shallow networks for E_{flow} and G_{flow} based on networks used in image compression [26]. We denote the resulting warped and potentially blurred previous reconstruction with $\hat{x}_t^w$.

Finally, we calculate the residual $r_t = x_t - \hat{x}_t^w$ and compress it with the **residual auto-encoder** E_{res}, G_{res}. To address the last point above, (S3), we again employ the light version of the HiFiC architecture for E_{res}, G_{res}. However, we introduce one important component. We observe that G_{res} is not able to synthesize high-frequency details from the sparse residual latent $E_{res}(r_t)$ alone. However, we found that additionally feeding a **"free"** latent extracted from the warped previous reconstruction $y_t^{free} = E_I(\hat{x}_t^w)$ significantly increased the amount of synthesized detail, possibly due to the additional information and context provided by $\hat{x}_t^w$. Note that this latent does not need to be encoded into the bitstream because the decoder already has $\hat{x}_t^w$ and can compute y_t^{free} directly (hence it is "free"), and thus also does not need to be quantized. Instead, we concatenate it to $E_{res}(r_t)$ as a source of information, forming $y_{t,r} = concat(y_t^{free}, E_{res}(r_t))$.

To train the P-frame branch, we employ a seperate P-frame discriminator D_P, with the same architecture as D_I, conditioned on the generator input $y_{t,r}$.

Bilinear Resampling Kernel   Bicubic Resampling Kernel

Fig. 4. To avoid blurry results when repeatedly warping, the quality of the resampling kernel is crucial. Here, we compare shifting an images 20 times with a fixed flow of 0.5px to the left for bilinear and bicubic.

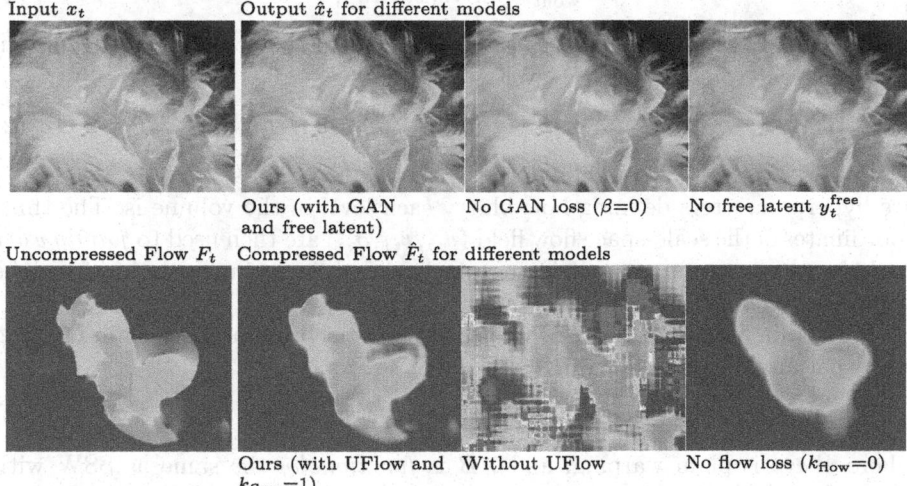

Fig. 5. Visual examples for our ablations, see Sect. 5.1 for details. *Top*: Our model faithfully reconstructs details of the input, whereas disabling the GAN loss or removing the free latent introduces blurryness like in MSE models. *Bottom*: Not using supervised optical flow (*UFlow*) gives poor quality flows. Not using the flow loss makes the flow slightly burrier.

3.2 Decoupled Scale-Space Warping

When warping previously reconstructed frames, we want to preserve detail as much as possible (whether real or synthesized, per (S2) above). Previous neural video compression approaches have commonly used bi-linear warping [10,23,35, 47], or tri-linear scale-space warping (SSW) [1,33,48]. However it is known from signal processing theory (see *e.g.* Nehab *et al.* [30][Fig. 10.6 on p. 64]) that for repeated applications of re-sampling, the quality of the interpolation kernel is crucial to avoid low-pass filtering the signal and blurring out details. We visualize this phenomenon in Fig. 4.

Motivated by these observations, we were interested in implementing the more powerful *bicubic* warping in SSW, but found that this makes the implementation significantly more complex when combined with the 3-D indexing of scale-space warping. Instead, to be able to efficiently use bicubic warping (and arbitrary other warping operations), we propose a variant of scale-space warping [1], where we *decouple* the operation into two steps: plain warping, followed by spatially adaptive blurring. We can then use off-the-shelf warping implementations for the first part.

Both variants, at their core, use the scale-space flow field $(\hat{F}, \sigma)$, which generalizes optical flow $\hat{F}$ by also specifying a "scale" σ, such that we get a triplet $(u_{ij}, v_{ij}, \sigma_{ij})$ for each target pixel (i, j), where u_{ij}, v_{ij} are the flow coordinates, and σ_{ij} is the blurring scale to use. We recall the method from [1]: To compute a *scale-space warped* result

$$x_{\text{out}} = \text{SSW}(x, \hat{F}, \sigma), \tag{1}$$

the source x is first repeatedly convolved with Gaussian blur kernels to obtain a "scale-space volume" with L levels,

$$V(x) = [x, x * G(s_1), \cdots, x * G(s_{L-1})], \tag{2}$$

where $G(s_i)$ is the Gaussian blur kernel with std. deviation s_i, and $\{s_1, \ldots, s_{L-1}\}$ are hyperparameters defining how blurry each level in the volume is. The three coordinates of the scale-space flow field $(u_{ij}, v_{ij}, \sigma_{ij})$ are then used to *jointly warp and blur* the source image, retrieving pixels via tri-linear interpolation from the scale-space volume.

We obtain a **Decoupled SSW (DSSW)** result by combining plain warping with spatially adaptive blurring (AB),

$$x'_{\text{out}} = \text{DSSW}(x, \hat{F}, \sigma) = \text{AB}(\text{Warp}(x, \hat{F}), \sigma), \tag{3}$$

where *Warp* is plain warping, and *AB* is *functionally* the same as SSW with a zero flow, *i.e.* $\text{AB}(y, \sigma) := \text{SSW}(y, 0, \sigma)$, but can be implemented with a few lines of code using simple multiplicative masks for each level in the scale-space volume to apply the 1-D linear interpolation for each pixel (code in App. A.3).

Together, bicubic warping and adaptive blurring help to propagate sharp detail when needed, while also facilitating smooth blurring when needed (*e.g.*, for focus changes in the video). See App. Fig. 12 for a visualization of how a given input and sigma field σ_t get blurred via scale-space blur.

We found that on a GPU, DSSW using an optimized warping implementation and our AB was 2−3× faster than a naive SSW implementation. In App. A.3, we validate our implementation by training models for MSE, and showing that DSSW with bilinear warping obtains similar PSNR as SSW, and DSSW with bicubic warping yields a better model.

3.3   Adaptive Proportional Rate Control

We train our system by optimizing the rate-distortion-perception trade-off [8,24], and we describe our formulation and loss in Sect. 3.5, but here we want to focus

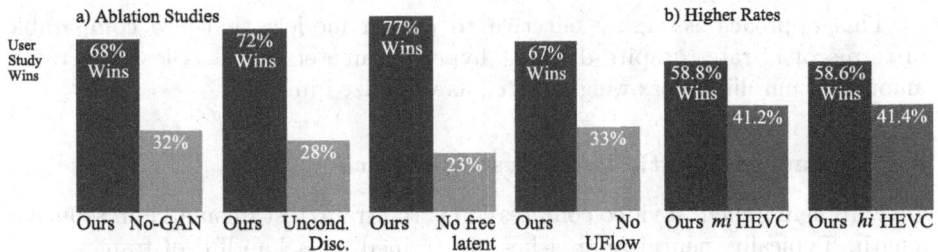

Fig. 6. *a)*User study for Ablations. We see that disabling the GAN loss (β=0), using an unconditional discriminator, or not using the free latent hurts performance. On the flow side, not using UFlow hurts. *b)* Comparing models at higher rates, targeting 0.14bpp (*mi*) and 0.22bpp (*hi*).

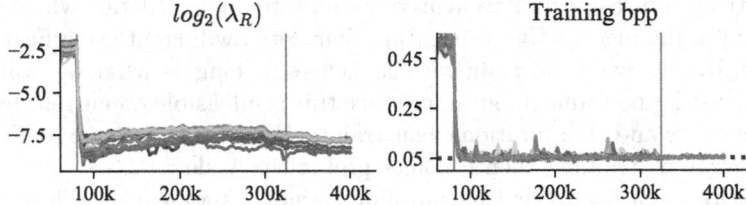

Fig. 7. Visualizing the effect of the rate controller for a broad family of models with different hyper parameters, trained for 400k steps. The rate parameter λ_R is automatically adapted during training (*left*) to match the target bpp of 0.05 for all models (*right*). At 80k steps we drop the target rate, at 325k steps we drop the learning rate.

on one hyper-parameter in this trade-off (that also typically appears in the rate-distortion trade-off optimized by previous work): the weight on the bitrate, λ_R. It controls the trade-off between bitrate and other loss terms (distortion, GAN loss, *etc.*). Unfortunately, since there is no direct relationship between λ_R and the bitrate of the model when we vary other hyper-parameters, comparison across models is practically impossible, since they end up at different rates if we vary other hyper parameters, in particular other loss weights.

Van Rozendaal *et al.* [36] also observe this and propose targeting a fixed distortion via constraint optimization. Another approach was used in [24], where λ_R was dynamically selected from a small λ_1 and a large λ_2, depending on whether the model bitrate was below or above a given target. This approach can be interpreted as an "on-off" controller, but still some requires tuning of λ_1, λ_2.

A natural generalization is to use a **proportional-controller**: We measure the error between the current mini-batch bitrate b to a target bitrate b_t (in log-space), and apply it with a proportional controller to update λ_R as follows:

$$\log_2(\lambda_R) \leftarrow \log_2(\lambda_R) + k_P(\log(b + \epsilon) - \log(b_t + \epsilon)), \qquad (4)$$

where $\epsilon = 1\mathrm{E}{-}9$ for stability and the "proportional gain" k_P is a hyperparameter. We note that if we ignore the log-reparameterization, this corresponds to the "Basic Differential Multiplier Method" [32].

This approach is highly effective to obtain models that are comparable in terms of bitrate, despite different hyper-parameters such as learning rates, amount of unrolling, loss weights, *etc.*, as visualized in Fig. 7.

3.4   Sequence Length Train/Test Mismatch

One problem in neural video compression is the train/test mismatch in sequence length: Typically, neural approaches are trained on a handful of frames (*e.g.*, three frames for [1] and five for [21]), and evaluated on hundreds of frames, which can lead to error patterns that emorge during evaluation. While the unrolling behavior is already a problem for MSE-optimized neural codecs (some previous works use small GOPs of 8–12 frames for evaluation to limit temporal error propagation), it requires even more care when detail is synthesized in a generative setting. Since we aim to synthesize high-frequency detail whenever new content appears, incorrectly propagating that detail will create significant visual artifacts. Ideally, we could train with sequences as long as what we evaluate on (*i.e.*, at least $T=60$ frames), but in practice this is infeasible on current hardware due to memory and computational constraints. While we can fit up to $T=12$ into our accelerators, training then becomes prohibitively slow.

To work towards preventing unrolling issues, as well as accelerating prototyping and training new models, we instead adopt the following scheme: 1) Train E_I, G_I, D_I only, on randomly selected frames, for 1 000 000 steps. 2) Freeze E_I, G_I, D_I and initialize the weights of E_{res}, G_{res} from E_I, G_I. Train E_{flow}, G_{flow}, E_{res}, G_{res}, D_P for 400 000 additional steps using **staged unrolling**, that is, use $T=2$ until 80k steps, $T=3$ until 300k, $T=4$ until 350k, and $T=6$ until 400k. This splitting into steps 1) and 2) means trained E_I, G_I can be re-used for many variants of the P-frame branch, and, as a bonus, sharing E_I, G_I across models makes them more comparable. For training times, see App. A.7.

Some error accumulation remains, which we address in two ways: We quantize the frame buffer at each step, *i.e.*, during inference, we always quantize $\hat{x}_t$, to be closer to the (8-bit quantized) input. Additionally, we randomly shift reconstructions in each step, to avoid overlapping larger-scale error patterns from accumulating. Together, these techniques help to get rid of most error patterns.

3.5   Formulation and Loss

We base our formulation on HiFiC [24] and optimize the rate-distortion-perception trade-off [8]. We use conditional GANs [12,28], where both the generator and the discriminator have access to additional labels. As a short recap, the general conditional GAN formulation assumes data points x and labels s following some joint distribution $p(x, s)$. The generator is supposed to map samples $s \sim p(s)$ to the distribution $p(x|s)$, and the discriminator is supposed to predict whether a given pair (x, s) is from the real distribution $p(x|s)$, or from the generator distribution $p(\hat{x}|s)$.

In contrast to HiFiC, we are working with *sequences* of frames and reconstructions, however, we aim for per-frame distribution matching, *i.e.*, for T-length video sequences, the goal is to obtain a model s.t.:

$$p(\hat{x}_t|y_t) = p(x_t|y_t) \quad \forall t \in \{1, \ldots, T\}, \tag{5}$$

where x_t are inputs, $\hat{x}_t$ reconstructions (as above), and we condition both the generators and the discriminators on latents y_t, using $y_1 = y_I$ for the I-frame, $y_t = y_{t,r}$ for P-frames ($t > 1$). To readers more familiar with conditional generative video synthesis (e.g., Wang et al. [44]), this simplification may seem suboptimal as it may lead to temporal consistency issues (i.e., you may imagine that reconstructions $\hat{x}_t, \hat{x}_{t+1}$ are inconsistent). We emphasize that since we are doing compression, we will also have a per-frame distortion loss (MSE), and we have information that we transmit to the decoder via a bitstream. So while the residual generator can in theory produce arbitrarily inconsistent reconstructions, in practice, these two points appear to be sufficient for preventing any temporal inconsistency issues in our models. We nevertheless explored variations where the discriminator is based on more frames, but this did not significantly alter reconstructions.

Continuing from Eq. 5, we define the overall loss for the I-frame branch and its discriminator D_I as follows. We use the "non-saturating" GAN loss [12]. To simplify notation, let $y_I = E_I(x_I), \hat{x}_I = G_I(y_I)$:

$$\mathcal{L}_{I\text{-}Frame} = \mathbb{E}_{x_I \sim p(x_I)} \left[\lambda_R^I r(y_I) + d(x_I, \hat{x}_I) - \beta \log(D_I(\hat{x}_I, y_I)) \right], \tag{6}$$

$$\mathcal{L}_{D_I} = \mathbb{E}_{x_I \sim p(x_I)} \left[-\log(1 - D_I(\hat{x}_I, y_I)) - \log(D_I(x_I, y_I)) \right], \tag{7}$$

where λ_R^I is the adaptive rate controller described in Sect. 3.3, β is the GAN loss weight, and d is a per-frame distortion. We use $d = $MSE, i.e., in contrast to HiFiC [24], we *do not use a perceptual distortion* such as LPIPS. We found no benefit in training with LPIPS, possibly due to a more balanced hyper-parameter selection, and removing it speeds up training by $\approx 35\%$.

For the P-frame branch, let $p(x_1^T)$ be the distribution of T-length clips, where we use x_1 as the I-frame, and let

$$\mathcal{L}_{P\text{-}Frame} = \mathbb{E}_{p(x_1^T)} \left[\sum_{t=2}^{T} \lambda_R^P r(y_{t,r}) + td(x_t, \hat{x}_t) - t\beta \log(D_P(\hat{x}_t, y_{t,r})) + \mathcal{L}_{reg} \right], \tag{8}$$

$$\mathcal{L}_{D_P} = \mathbb{E}_{p(x_1^T)} \left[\sum_{t=2}^{T} -t \log(1 - D_P(\hat{x}_t, y_{t,r})) - t \log(D_P(x_I, y_{t,r})) \right]. \tag{9}$$

Note that we scale the losses of the t-th frame with t. This is motivated by the observation that $\hat{x}_t$ influences all $T - t$ reconstructions following it, and hence earlier frames indirectly have more influence on the overall loss. Scaling with t ensures all frames have similar influence.

Additionally, we employ a simple regularizer for the P-frame branch:

$$\mathcal{L}_{reg} = k_{flow} \cdot \text{SG}(\sigma_t) \cdot L_2(F_t, \hat{F}_t) + k_{TV} TV(\sigma_t), \tag{10}$$

where the first part is an MSE on the flow, ensuring that E_{flow}, G_{flow} learn to reproduce the flow from *UFlow*. We mask it with the sigma field, since we only require consistent flow where the network actually uses the flow (but add a stop gradient, SG, to avoid minimizing the loss by just predicting $\sigma_t = 0$). *TV* is a total-variation loss [38] ensuring a smooth sigma field.

4   Experiments

4.1   Datasets

Our **training** data contains 992k spatio-temporal crops of dimension 256×256, each containing 12 frames, obtained from videos from YouTube. For training, we randomly choose a contiguous sub-sequence of length $T \in \{2, 3, 4, 5\}$, see Sect. 3.4. The videos are filtered to originally be at least 1080p in resolution, 16:9, 30fps. We omit content labeled as "video games" or "computer generated graphics", using YouTube's category system [50]. We **evaluate** our model on the 30 videos of MCL-JCV [43], which is available under a permissive license from USC, in contrast to, *e.g.*, the HEVC test sequences, which are not publicly available. MCL-JCV contains a broad variety of content types and difficulty, including a wide variety of motion from natural videos, computer animation and classical animation.

4.2   User Study

2AFC. We evaluate our method in a user study, where we ask human raters to rate pairs of methods, *i.e.*, our setup is "two alternatives, forced choice" (2AFC). We implement 2AFC by showing raters two videos *side-by-side*, where the right video is always the *original*. On the left, raters see either a video from method A or method B. They can toggle between A and B in-place. We always shuffle the methods, *i.e.*, *Ours* is not always method A. We use all 30 videos from MCL-JCV, and show the first 2 s (to avoid large file sizes, see below), playing in a loop, but raters are allowed to pause videos. Raters are asked to select the video "is closest to the original" (the GUI is shown in the inline figure, exact instructions in App. Fig. 8). This protocol is inspired by previous work in image compression [24,41], and ensures that differences between methods are easy to spot.

Several considerations went into these choices: For *generative* video compression, it is important to be able to compare to the original, as otherwise the method may, *e.g.*, completely change colors or content. However, we do not require pixel-perfect reconstructions, which is why we show the original on the right, and not in-place. Methods can be very similar, which is why we allow in-place switching *between methods* to be able to spot differences.

Rater Qualifications. Our raters are contracted through the "Google Cloud AI Labeling Service" [13]. For each pair of methods, raters are asked to rate all 30 videos of MCL-JCV. In order to make sure our ratings have a high quality, we intersperse **five golden questions** at random locations into each study, where we compare HEVC at quality factor $Q=27$ to $Q=35$ ($Q=27$ yields bitrates similar to what we study, and $Q=35$ is ≈0.023bpp and contains significant blurring artifacts). We filter out raters who do not correctly answer 4 out of 5 of these questions. Overall, this yields 8–14 raters per study. To ensure that our results are *repeatable*, we re-do the study after three days.

Shipping Videos to Raters. In order to play back the videos in a web browser we transcode all methods with VP9 [29], using a very high quality factor to avoid any new artifacts. To ensure consistency, and to be sure that the raters can fit the task in their web browser, we center-crop the videos to 1080 × 1080. This yields large file sizes, so to ensure smooth playback, we *focus on the first 2 s (60 frames) of each video.*

4.3 Metrics and Models

In order to assess how quantitative metrics predict the user study, we employ the well-known PSNR and MSSSIM [45]. We use LPIPS [51] (which measures a distance in AlexNet [19] features space) and PIM (an unsupervised quality metric), as well as FID [16]. Following HiFiC [24] we evaluate FID on non-overlapping 256×256 patches (see App. A.7 in [24]). Finally, we use VMAF [31], developed by Netflix to evaluate video codecs. We calculate these metrics on the exact sequences we ship to raters.

We refer to our model as **Ours**, and report all hyper-parameters in App. A.6. To assess the effect of the GAN loss, we train a **no-GAN** baseline, which uses exactly the same architecture and training schedule as *Ours*, but is trained without a GAN loss ($\beta=0$ in Eqs. (6), (8)). We compare to three neural codecs: **SSF**, by Agustsson *et al.* [1], CVPR'2020, **RLVC** by Yang *et al.* [47], J-STSP'2021, and **DVC** by Lu *et al.* [23], CVPR'2019. For SSF and RLVC, we obtained reconstructions from the authors, for DVC we ran the open-sourced code ourselves and verified that this does match their published numbers on the UVG dataset [25] (exact details in App. A.4). We ran user studies comparing all these models against our proposed GAN model. In contrast to most previous work, we do not constrain our model to use a small GoP size, and instead only use an I-frame for the first frame. For the neural models, we used the GoP from the respective papers (∞ for SSF, 10 for DVC, 12 for RLVC), and we do not constrain the GoP for H.264 and HEVC. The neural codecs we compare to do not densely cover the bitrate axis, so to ensure fair studies, we fix *Ours* to a model targeting $\approx$0.07bpp, and then select a different competing model for each video to match filesizes as closely as possible. The resulting average bpps are at most $\approx$3% smaller or at most $\approx$24% bigger than our method. We emphasize that we would have liked to compare to even more neural models, but found no additional code or reconstructions.

Furthermore, we compare against the non-neural standard codecs **H.264** and **HEVC**. We follow best practice and make sure to minimally constrain the codecs, thus using the default "medium" preset (note that some previous works used "fast" or even "veryfast"). Like our method, we run the codecs in the low-latency setting (disabling B-frames). The exact (short) ffmpeg commands are listed in App. A.1. We also run the codecs at $\approx$0.07bpp. To get an idea how models compare at higher rates, we fruther run *HEVC* at $\approx$0.14 and $\approx$0.22bpp.

On Padding and Bitrates. A problem faced by all CNN-based neural compression codecs is: what happens if the stride of the network does not divide the input resolution. For example, our encoder downscales 4 times, and thus needs the input resolution to divide 16. Like most previous work, we solve this by *padding* input frames (*e.g.*, 1080×1920 gets padded to 1088×1920), obtaining the bitstream of the padded image, obtaining the reconstruction, cropping the reconstruction back to the input resolution, and *calculating bpp w.r.t. the input resolution* (calculating it w.r.t. the padded resolution would amount to cheating). We note that the RLVC reconstructions were cropped to 1066 pixels, and we thus performed that user study in a cropped setting, and we had to add padding support to the DVC code, which may account for some differences in PSNR (DVC seems to have calculated on cropped images).

Table 1. We show metrics corresponding to the user studies, where the last row repeats the results from Fig. 2. We indicate whether each metric *predicts* the study, using *Yes* and *No*. If the values are within 1% of each other, the metric also *does not predict* the study, and we indicate this with $No_\approx$. ↑ indicates that higher is better for this row, ↓ the opposite. We can see that no metric predicts all user studies (since *Ours* is preferred in all studies).

	Ours	SSF Predicts?	RLVC Predicts?	DVC Predicts?	No-GAN Predicts?	H.264 Predicts?	HEVC Predicts?
PSNR↑	34.5	34.8 $No_\approx$	34.0 *Yes*	31.7 *Yes*	35.1 *No*	34.6 $No_\approx$	35.6 *No*
MS-SSIM↑	0.964	0.963 $No_\approx$	0.965 $No_\approx$	0.95 *Yes*	0.967 $No_\approx$	0.963 $No_\approx$	0.966 $No_\approx$
VMAF↑	87.3	84.8 *Yes*	83.1 *Yes*	81.9 *Yes*	86.9 $No_\approx$	87.7 $No_\approx$	91.1 *No*
PIM-1↓	3.34	4.69 *Yes*	4.93 *Yes*	6.91 *Yes*	4.17 *Yes*	3.17 *No*	2.62 *No*
LPIPS↓	0.168	0.224 *Yes*	0.224 *Yes*	0.26 *Yes*	0.194 *Yes*	0.169 $No_\approx$	0.147 *No*
FID/256↓	32.8	54.1 *Yes*	50.3 *Yes*	61.6 *Yes*	35.7 *Yes*	33.0 $No_\approx$	24.2 *No*
Preferred vs.	Ours↑	27%	31%	15%	32%	35%	39%

5 Results

We show visual results in Fig. 1. We can see how our approach faithfully synthesizes texture and looks very similar to the original, whereas MSE-based approaches suffer from blurryness. The quantitative results from our user study are shown in Fig. 2. At a high level, we see that *Ours* is preferred by the majority in all studies. Ours vs. no-GAN shows that the GAN loss significantly improves visual quality. The first three studies show that our method significantly outperforms all neural baselines. The standard codecs fare somewhat better, yet our method is clearly preferred overall. We show the comparison at higher rates in Fig. 6b, where the gap between methods gets smaller, but our method is still preferred.

In Table 1 we explore which metrics are able to predict the user study results from Fig. 2. We show values of all methods on all metrics, and indicate whether the metrics predicts the corresponding study. *E.g.*, we can see there that we are preferred over *no-GAN* in the user study, yet our method has 34.5 dB PSNR, while *no-GAN* has 35.1dB (better), thus PSNR does *not* predict this study correctly, and we write "No". Overall, none of the metrics are able to predict all studies. However, we find that the three "perceptual" metrics PIM, LPIPS, and FID/256 all predict the studies of the *neural codecs*. Unfortunately, none of them predicts the studies involving the standard codecs.

The table also shows how we trade-off distortion (PSNR) for improved realism/visual quality. In the comparison against *no-GAN*, we can see that 0.6dB in PSNR is traded for being preferred 68% of the time in the user study.

In App. A.2, we show that we were able to obtain the same overall results when running the studies with the same raters three days later, with an even wider gap, and more raters passing the golden study. We also present statistics: how long raters take to answer questions, how often they flip, and how often they pause. We split this data by experiment, by video, and by worker. Averaged over all studies, raters take 26.4s per comparison, flip 13.5 times, and pause 0.967 times. To facilitate further research, we provide links to **reconstructions and raw user study data** in App B.

5.1 Ablations

We ablate our main components, using a user study (shown in Fig. 6a) and visually (in Fig. 5). We do ablations by removing parts: In **No-GAN**, we disable the GAN loss ($\beta = 0$), for **No free latent** we train without the free latent y_t^{free}, and in **Uncond. Disc.**, we train with an unconditional discriminator (*i.e.*, D does not see any latents). We can see that all of these perform significantly worse in terms of visual quality (Fig. 6), and lead to blurry reconstruction (Fig. 5, uncond. disc. is not shown but looks similar to No-GAN). In **No UFlow**, we disable *UFlow*, *i.e.*, if we do not feed F_t to E_{flow}, and instead let E_{flow} learn flow unsupervised from frames, which performs significantly worse (Fig. 6).

6   Conclusion

We presented a GAN-based approach to neural video compression, that significantly outperforms previous neural and non-neural methods, as measured in a user study. With additional user studies, we showed that two components are crucial: i) conditioning the residual generator on a latent obtained from the warped previous reconstruction, and ii) leveraging accurate flow from an optical flow network. Furthermore, we showed how to decouple scale-space warping to be able to leverage high quality resampling kernels, and we used adaptive rate control to ensure consistent bitrates across a wide range of hyperparameters.

Limitations. As we saw, the quantitative metrics we currently have cannot be fully relied on, and hence we have to do user studies. However, this is expensive and not very scalable, and further research into perceptual metrics is needed. We hope that by releasing our reconstructions, we can encourage research in this direction.

References

1. Agustsson, E., Minnen, D., Johnston, N., Balle, J., Hwang, S.J., Toderici, G.: Scale-space flow for end-to-end optimized video compression. In: Proceedings of the IEEE/CVF Conference on Computer Vision and Pattern Recognition, pp. 8503–8512 (2020)
2. Agustsson, E., Tschannen, M., Mentzer, F., Timofte, R., Gool, L.V.: Generative adversarial networks for extreme learned image compression. In: The IEEE International Conference on Computer Vision (ICCV) (October 2019)
3. Ahmed, N., Natarajan, T., Rao, K.R.: Discrete cosine transform. IEEE Trans. Comput. **C-23**(1) (1974). https://doi.org/10.1109/T-C.1974.223784
4. ITU-T rec. H.264 & ISO/IEC 14496-10 AVC: Advanced video coding for generic audiovisual services (2003)
5. Ballé, J., Minnen, D., Singh, S., Hwang, S.J., Johnston, N.: Variational image compression with a scale hyperprior. In: International Conference on Learning Representations (ICLR) (2018)
6. Bankoski, J., Wilkins, P., Xu, Y.: Technical overview of vp8, an open source video codec for the web. In: 2011 IEEE International Conference on Multimedia and Expo, pp. 1–6. IEEE (2011)
7. Blau, Y., Michaeli, T.: The perception-distortion tradeoff. In: Proceedings of the IEEE Conference on Computer Vision and Pattern Recognition (CVPR), June 2018
8. Blau, Y., Michaeli, T.: Rethinking lossy compression: the rate-distortion-perception tradeoff. arXiv preprint arXiv:1901.07821 (2019)
9. Chen, Y., et al.: An overview of core coding tools in the av1 video codec. In: 2018 Picture Coding Symposium (PCS), pp. 41–45. IEEE (2018)
10. Djelouah, A., Campos, J., Schaub-Meyer, S., Schroers, C.: Neural inter-frame compression for video coding. In: Proceedings of the IEEE/CVF International Conference on Computer Vision, pp. 6421–6429 (2019)
11. Golinski, A., Pourreza, R., Yang, Y., Sautiere, G., Cohen, T.S.: Feedback recurrent autoencoder for video compression. In: Proceedings of the Asian Conference on Computer Vision (2020)
12. Goodfellow, I., et al.: Generative adversarial nets. In: Advances in Neural Information Processing Systems, pp. 2672–2680 (2014)
13. Google AI platform data labeling service. https://cloud.google.com/ai-platform/data-labeling/pricing. Accessed 01 May 2021
14. Goyal, V.K.: Theoretical foundations of transform coding. IEEE Signal Process. Mag. **18**(5) (2001). https://doi.org/10.1109/79.952802
15. Habibian, A., Rozendaal, T.v., Tomczak, J.M., Cohen, T.S.: Video compression with rate-distortion autoencoders. In: Proceedings of the IEEE/CVF International Conference on Computer Vision, pp. 7033–7042 (2019)
16. Heusel, M., Ramsauer, H., Unterthiner, T., Nessler, B., Hochreiter, S.: GANs trained by a two time-scale update rule converge to a local Nash equilibrium. In: Advances in Neural Information Processing Systems, pp. 6626–6637 (2017)
17. ITU-T rec. H.265 & ISO/IEC 23008-2: High efficiency video coding (2013)
18. Jonschkowski, R., Stone, A., Barron, J.T., Gordon, A., Konolige, K., Angelova, A.: What matters in unsupervised optical flow. 1(2), 3 arXiv preprint arXiv:2006.04902 (2020)
19. Krizhevsky, A., Sutskever, I., Hinton, G.E.: Imagenet classification with deep convolutional neural networks. In: Advances in Neural Information Processing Systems, pp. 1097–1105 (2012)

20. Li, J., Li, B., Lu, Y.: Deep contextual video compression. Adv. Neural. Inf. Process. Syst. **34**, 18114–18125 (2021)
21. Liu, H., Chen, T., Lu, M., Shen, Q., Ma, Z.: Neural video compression using spatio-temporal priors. arXiv preprint arXiv:1902.07383 (2019)
22. Liu, J., et al.: Conditional entropy coding for efficient video compression. arXiv preprint arXiv:2008.09180 (2020)
23. Lu, G., Ouyang, W., Xu, D., Zhang, X., Cai, C., Gao, Z.: DVC: an end-to-end deep video compression framework. In: Proceedings of the IEEE/CVF Conference on Computer Vision and Pattern Recognition, pp. 11006–11015 (2019)
24. Mentzer, F., Toderici, G.D., Tschannen, M., Agustsson, E.: High-fidelity generative image compression. In: Advances in Neural Information Processing Systems, vol. 33 (2020)
25. Mercat, A., Viitanen, M., Vanne, J.: UVG dataset: 50/120fps 4K sequences for video codec analysis and development. In: Proceedings of the 11th ACM Multimedia Systems Conference, pp. 297–302 (2020)
26. Minnen, D., Ballé, J., Toderici, G.D.: Joint autoregressive and hierarchical priors for learned image compression. In: Advances in Neural Information Processing Systems, pp. 10771–10780 (2018)
27. Minnen, D., Singh, S.: Channel-wise autoregressive entropy models for learned image compression. arXiv preprint arXiv:2007.08739 (2020)
28. Mirza, M., Osindero, S.: Conditional generative adversarial nets. arXiv preprint arXiv:1411.1784 (2014)
29. Mukherjee, D., et al.: The latest open-source video codec vp9-an overview and preliminary results. In: 2013 Picture Coding Symposium (PCS), pp. 390–393. IEEE (2013)
30. Nehab, D., Hoppe, H., et al.: A fresh look at generalized sampling. Citeseer (2014)
31. Netix: VMAF - Video Multi-Method Assessment Fusion. https://github.com/Netflix/vmaf/
32. Platt, J.C., Barr, A.H.: Constrained differential optimization for neural networks. Caltech (1988)
33. Rippel, O., Anderson, A.G., Tatwawadi, K., Nair, S., Lytle, C., Bourdev, L.: ELF-VC: efficient learned flexible-rate video Coding. arXiv preprint arXiv:2104.14335 (2021)
34. Rippel, O., Bourdev, L.: Real-time adaptive image compression. In: Proceedings of the 34th International Conference on Machine Learning. Proceedings of Machine Learning Research, vol. 70, pp. 2922–2930. PMLR, International Convention Centre, Sydney, Australia, 06–11 August 2017
35. Rippel, O., Nair, S., Lew, C., Branson, S., Anderson, A.G., Bourdev, L.: Learned video compression. In: Proceedings of the IEEE/CVF International Conference on Computer Vision, pp. 3454–3463 (2019)
36. van Rozendaal, T., Sautiere, G., Cohen, T.S.: Lossy compression with distortion constrained optimization. In: Proceedings of the IEEE/CVF Conference on Computer Vision and Pattern Recognition Workshops, pp. 166–167 (2020)
37. Santurkar, S., Budden, D., Shavit, N.: Generative compression. arXiv preprint arXiv:1703.01467 (2017)
38. Shulman, D., Herve, J.Y.: Regularization of discontinuous flow fields. In: Proceedings of the Workshop on Visual Motion, pp. 81–86. IEEE Computer Society Press (1989)
39. Theis, L., Agustsson, E.: On the advantages of stochastic encoders. arXiv preprint arXiv:2102.09270 (2021)

40. Theis, L., Wagner, A.B.: A coding theorem for the rate-distortion-perception function. arXiv preprint arXiv:2104.13662 (2021)
41. Toderici, G., et al.: CLIC 2020: Challenge on Learned Image Compression (2020). http://compression.cc
42. Tschannen, M., Agustsson, E., Lucic, M.: Deep generative models for distribution-preserving lossy compression. In: Advances in Neural Information Processing Systems, pp. 5929–5940 (2018)
43. Wang, H., et al.: MCL-JCV: a JND-based H.264/AVC video quality assessment dataset. In: 2016 IEEE International Conference on Image Processing (ICIP), pp. 1509–1513. IEEE (2016)
44. Wang, T.C., et al.: Video-to-video synthesis. In: Advances in Neural Information Processing Systems (NeurIPS) (2018)
45. Wang, Z., Simoncelli, E.P., Bovik, A.C.: Multiscale structural similarity for image quality assessment. In: The Thrity-Seventh Asilomar Conference on Signals, Systems & Computers, vol. 2, pp. 1398–1402. IEEE (2003)
46. Wu, C.-Y., Singhal, N., Krähenbühl, P.: Video compression through image interpolation. In: Ferrari, V., Hebert, M., Sminchisescu, C., Weiss, Y. (eds.) Video compression through image interpolation. LNCS, vol. 11212, pp. 425–440. Springer, Cham (2018). https://doi.org/10.1007/978-3-030-01237-3_26
47. Yang, R., Mentzer, F., Van Gool, L., Timofte, R.: Learning for video compression with recurrent auto-encoder and recurrent probability model. IEEE J. Sel. Topics Signal Process. 15, 388–401 (2020)
48. Yang, R., Yang, Y., Marino, J., Mandt, S.: Hierarchical autoregressive modeling for neural video compression. arXiv preprint arXiv:2010.10258 (2020)
49. Yang, Y., Mandt, S., Theis, L.: An introduction to neural data compression. arXiv preprint arXiv:2202.06533 (2022)
50. YouTube Data API (2021). https://www.googleapis.com/youtube/v3/videoCategories
51. Zhang, R., Isola, P., Efros, A.A., Shechtman, E., Wang, O.: The unreasonable effectiveness of deep features as a perceptual metric. In: Proceedings of the IEEE Conference on Computer Vision and Pattern Recognition, pp. 586–595 (2018)

A Contrastive Objective for Learning Disentangled Representations

Jonathan Kahana[✉] and Yedid Hoshen

Hebrew University of Jerusalem, Jerusalem, Israel
`jonathan.kahana@mail.huji.ac.il`

Abstract. Learning representations of images that are invariant to sensitive or unwanted attributes is important for many tasks including bias removal and cross domain retrieval. Here, our objective is to learn representations that are invariant to the domain (sensitive attribute) for which labels are provided, while being informative over all other image attributes, which are unlabeled. We present a new approach, proposing a new domain-wise contrastive objective for ensuring invariant representations. This objective crucially restricts negative image pairs to be drawn from the same domain, which enforces domain invariance whereas the standard contrastive objective does not. This domain-wise objective is insufficient on its own as it suffers from shortcut solutions resulting in feature suppression. We overcome this issue by a combination of a reconstruction constraint, image augmentations and initialization with pre-trained weights. Our analysis shows that the choice of augmentations is important, and that a misguided choice of augmentations can harm the invariance and informativeness objectives. In an extensive evaluation, our method convincingly outperforms the state-of-the-art in terms of representation invariance, representation informativeness, and training speed. Furthermore, we find that in some cases our method can achieve excellent results even without the reconstruction constraint, leading to a much faster and resource efficient training (Our Code is available at https://github.com/jonkahana/DCoDR).

1 Introduction

Representing the attributes of an image that are independent of its domain (e.g. imaging modality, geographic location, sensitive attribute or object identity) is key for many computer vision tasks. For instance, consider the following toy example: assume that we observe images of faces, each image is specified by the identity and pose but only labels of the identity are provided. The goal is to learn a representation that captures the unlabeled pose attribute, and carry no information about the identity attribute. This task has many other applications, including: learning to make fair decisions, cross domain matching, model anonymization, image translation etc. It is a part of the fundamental machine learning problem of representation disentanglement. We note that

---

Supplementary Information The online version contains supplementary material available at https://doi.org/10.1007/978-3-031-19809-0_33.

S. Avidan et al. (Eds.): ECCV 2022, LNCS 13686, pp. 579–595, 2022.
https://doi.org/10.1007/978-3-031-19809-0_33

the most ambitious disentanglement setting, i.e. unsupervised disentanglement where no labels are provided, was proven by Locatello et al. [25] to be impossible without inductive biases. Luckily, our setting is easier than unsupervised disentanglement as the domain label is provided for all training images. This setting has attracted much research e.g. DRNET [10], ML-VAE [1] and LORD [13].

We begin by defining the desired properties for domain disentanglement. This task has two objectives: i) *Invariance*: the learned representation should be invariant to the domain ii) *Informativeness*: the learnt representation should include the information about all of the attributes which are independent of the domain. The invariance requirement is challenging, but it can *in-principle* be directly optimized as the domain label is provided, e.g. using an adversarial discriminator. The informativeness requirement, however, is not generally possible to directly optimize without additional inductive biases as the attributes are unlabeled. This was theoretically demonstrated by [20,40]. Nonetheless, recent methods have been able to achieve meaningful representations in many cases, by enforcing a reconstruction term, which optimizes a related objective.

We present a new method, **DCoDR: D**omain-wise **C**ontrastive **D**isentangled **R**epresentations, that significantly improves both representation domain invariance and informativeness. To enforce the domain invariance, we propose a per-domain contrastive loss, that requires the representations of each domain to be uniformly distributed across the unit sphere. Differently from standard contrastive losses [4], our objective only considers negative examples from the *same* domain. As shown in Sect. 5.2, this seemingly simple change is crucial for learning domain invariant representations. Unfortunately, we find that encoders which satisfy this invariance constraint alone, are often uninformative over the desired attributes. This is a case of the documented phenomenon of *feature suppression* [6,24,32]. In line with previous methods [1,10,13], we optimize the informative-

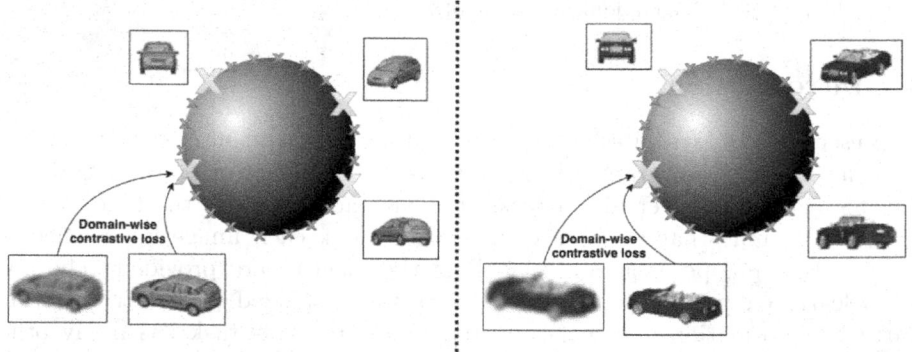

Fig. 1. An illustration of our method. The representations are domain invariant as the representations of each domain follow a spherically uniform distribution (encouraged by our domain-wise contrastive objective). Image augmentations (here Gaussian blurring) are used to assign similar images to nearby representations which indirectly improves informativeness. The reconstruction objective and encoder pre-trained weights initialization are not shown in this diagram.

ness of the representations indirectly by a reconstruction constraint. As we find this may be insufficient for learning informative representations in some cases, we propose two other techniques: i) Similarly to several self-supervised objectives (e.g. the one in SimCLR [4]), we enforce representations of images to be similar to those of their augmentations. Despite being common among self-supervised methods, we show that standard choices of augmentations (specifically, those used by SimSiam [8]) can harm the domain invariance of the representation. We analyse the effectiveness of different augmentations for domain invariant representation learning. ii) Initializing the image encoder using weights pre-trained with self-supervision on an external dataset, which we empirically find to learn both more informative and invariant representations.

We evaluate our method on five popular benchmarks. Our method significantly exceeds the state-of-the-art in terms of invariance and informativeness. We investigate a fully discriminative version and find that in many cases it is competitive with the previous state-of-the-art while being much faster.
A summary of our contributions:

1. A non-adversarial and non-generative, domain invariance objective.
2. Analysing the benefits and pitfalls of image augmentations for informativeness and domain invariance of the learned representations.
3. A new approach, DCoDR, which significantly outperforms the state-of-the-art in domain invariant representation learning.
4. A discriminative only variant, which is 5X faster than existing approaches.
5. An extensive evaluation on five datasets.

2 Related Work

Learning Domain Disentangled Representations. Much research was done on separating between labeled and unlabelled attributes. Several methods use adversarial training [11,26,34]. Other methods use non-adversarial approaches, e.g. cycle consistency [16], group accumulation [1] or latent optimization [13,14]. Our method improves upon this body of work.

Contrastive Representation Learning. Significant progress in self-supervised representation learning was achieved by methods relying on pairs of augmented samples. Most recent methods use the constraint that the neural representations of different augmentations of the same image should be equal. Non-contrastive methods [8,15,31] use the above constraint with various other tricks for learning representations. As the above formulation is prone to collapse, contrastive methods [4,5,7,17,18,18,27,29,36,38] add an additional uniformity constraint that prohibits collapse of the representation to a single point. We propose a per-domain contrastive objective, tailored for domain disentanglement.

Contrastive Approaches for Disentanglement. Recently, Zimmerman et al. [42] proposed a seminal approach for contrastive learning of disentangled representations. They tackle the ambitious setting of unsupervised disentanglement, and therefore make strong assumptions on the distribution of the true factors of variation as well as requiring temporal sequences of images at training time. Our method applies to the different (and less ambitious) setting of domain disentanglement - assuming domain labels for training data, but not having image sequences or strong assumptions on the evolution of unlabeled true factors. Our technical approaches are consequently very different.

Applications of Disentangled Representations. Learning disentangled representations has many applications including: controllable image generation [41], image manipulation [13,14,37] and domain adaptation [30]. Furthermore, it is believed that better disentangled representations will have future impact on model interpretability [19], abstract reasoning [33] and fairness [9].

3   Domain Invariant Representation Learning

3.1   Preliminaries

We receive as input a set of training samples $\mathcal{X}_t = \{x_1, x_2, .., x_N\}$. Each training sample $x \in \mathcal{X}_t$ has a labeled domain d and unlabelled attributes y which are uncorrelated to d. We assume that the labeled domain d is a single categorical variable. The objective is to learn an encoder E, which encodes each image x as code $z = E(x)$ satisfying the criteria in Sect. 3.2.

3.2   Criteria

The domain disentanglement task requires satisfying the following two criteria:

Invariance: We require that the representation z should not be predictive of the domain d. This can be written as:

$$P(d|z) = P(d) \tag{1}$$

Informativeness: We require that the representation z should encapsulate as much information on attributes y as possible. Note that z cannot hold more information about y than the original image x, as there exists a deterministic encoder E which maps x to z. It therefore follows by the data processing inequality, that the maximally informative representation z should be as informative as the original image about the attributes y:

$$I(y, z) = I(y, x) \tag{2}$$

In our setting, only the domain labels d are provided but not the attribute labels of y. The objective in Eq. 2 cannot therefore be optimized directly. Saying that, in line with previous methods, we optimize informativeness by training a conditional generator through a reconstruction objective. Unlike previous methods, we use additional techniques which increase informativeness significantly. Our proposed approach will be detailed in Sect. 4.3.

3.3   Existing Approaches for Invariance Optimization

Current methods optimize the invariance criterion using two main approaches:

Adversarial Methods [10]. Many disentanglement methods rely on adversarial domain confusion constraints to ensure representation invariance. They are often written in the following form:

$$L_{adv} = \max_{D} \ell_{CE}(D(E(x)), d) \tag{3}$$

where ℓ_{CE} is the cross-entropy loss. The discriminator D measures how informative the representation $z = E(x)$ is over the original domain d. An encoder that satisfies this constraint will indeed be domain invariant $P(d|z) = P(d)$. Unfortunately, adversarial training is challenging and the optimization often fails to minimize this loss perfectly.

Variational-Autoencoders (VAE) [1,13]. Given the weaknesses of adversarial methods, variational methods were proposed that ensure the representations are normally distributed $P(z|d) = N(0; I)$. The encoder in this case outputs the parameters of a Gaussian distribution of the posterior $p(z|x)$. Using the ELBO criterion, the objective becomes:

$$L_{vae} = \ell_{KL}(E(x), N(0, I)) \tag{4}$$

However, LORD [13] found that simply optimizing this criterion does not converge to disentangled representations. Furthermore, they showed that randomly initialized encoders are highly entangled and variational losses were insufficient for removing this entanglement. Instead, they suggested using latent optimization rather than deep encoders at first, for directly learning the representation z of each training image x. This indeed improves the domain invariance of the representations, but is more sensitive to hyper-parameter choices. It also requires an inconvenient second stage for learning an image to representation encoder.

4   DCoDR: Learning Domain-wise Contrastive Disentangled Representation

4.1   Overview

We introduce a new approach, DCoDR, for learning informative, domain invariant representations. In Sect. 4.2, a new per-domain contrastive loss is proposed to enforce invariance directly. It does not, by itself, require the representation to be maximally informative. To overcome this issue, we optimize informativeness indirectly by *reconstruction* and *image augmentation* objectives as well as *encoder pre-trained weights initialization*. We investigate an additional, fully discriminative variant of our method, which is much faster than existing methods at the price of lower informativeness.

4.2   Representation Invariance with Domain-wise Contrastive Losses

Learning an invariant representation requires the domain d to be unpredictable from the learned representation z. We present a non-adversarial method for encouraging domain invariance. Our approach enforces the probability distribution of representations z to follow a uniform spherical distribution (denoted U_S) regardless of the domain d: $P(z|d) = U_S$. It follows from Bayes' law that the representation z does not provide any information about the domain, $\forall z : P(d|z) = P(d)$. This also yields that mutual information between the domain and representation is zero $I(d, z) = 0$.

The above analysis requires that $P(z|d) = U_S$ for every domain d. We do so by training a separate contrastive loss for every domain d. It was highlighted by Wang and Isola [35] that the denominator of the contrastive objective encourages the representations follow a uniform spherical distribution. Learning a contrastive loss *separately* over image representations from different domains, ensures that the representations z are distributed as U_S regardless of the domain d. For an image x from domain d, this can be written as follows:

$$\mathcal{L}_{inv}(x, d) = \log \sum_{(x', d') \in \mathbb{X}} \mathbf{1}_{d'=d} e^{sim(E(x'), E(x))} \tag{5}$$

sim is a similarity function, cosine similarity in our case. The objective only considers image pairs drawn from the *same* domain. Unlike previous methods in Sect. 3.3 (e.g. [10,13,28]), it does not rely on adversarial or variational approximations.

4.3   Improving Representation Informativeness

Beyond invariance, the representations z should encapsulate the information about all of the image attributes y except the domain label d. In Eq. 2 this was shown to imply $I(y, x) = I(y, z)$. We cannot directly optimize this constraint, as the attributes y for image x are not provided in our setting. In line with previous methods presented in Sect. 3.3, we optimize the informativeness indirectly by a reconstruction constraint. Furthermore, we present two algorithmic choices that empirically further increase informativeness significantly.

Reconstruction: Reconstruction constraints are an established way to improve the informativeness of the representation d. They have been used in many previous methods [1,10,13]. In line with previous methods, we include a reconstruction constraint in our method. Specifically, we learn a conditional generator G that takes as input the domain d and representation z and outputs an image $G_d(z)$. The reconstruction objective requires that the output image is as close as possible to the input image x. The difference between the reconstruction and original images is measured using the function ℓ. In practice, we use the same perceptual loss as in LORD [13] in Eq. 6

$$L_{rec} = \sum_{d \in \mathcal{D}} \sum_{x \in \mathcal{X}_d} \ell_{perc}(G_d(E(x)), x) \tag{6}$$

Augmentations: Contrastive objectives are susceptible to shortcut solutions that lower informativeness, also known as *feature suppression* [32]. This occurs by (inadvertently) learning an encoder that maps nuisance image attributes (or noise) to the spherical uniform distribution. This representation ignores the other image attributes, therefore being insufficiently informative. Ensuring that image augmentations have similar representations to the original image can help reduce this collapse, for suitably well selected augmentations:

$$\mathcal{L}_{aug} = \sum_{x \in \mathcal{X}_t} -sim(E(A_1(x)), E(A_2(x))) \tag{7}$$

Where $A_1(x)$ and $A_2(x)$ are two random augmentations of image x. Unfortunately, poorly selected augmentations can make the representation z invariant to the desired attributes y, which is harmful. E.g. when y is pose, and the augmentation is horizontal flip, the representation z

Table 1. Evaluation of our method's discriminative variant, DCoDR-norec, with 2 different augmentations on Cars3D.

	Inv.	Inform.
Blur	0.002	0.960
H. Flip	0.003	0.725

will be invariant to flip direction, therefore less informative over the pose. To test this hypothesis, we trained our method's discriminative variant, DCoDR-norec, using blur or flip augmentations on Cars3D. We measure each metric as explained in Sect. 5.2. Table 1 shows flipping significantly reduced the informativeness.

It is clear from the discussion above that augmentations can be highly desirable for improving informativeness, while their choice is important. We discovered that the standard augmentations used by state-of-the-art contrastive methods e.g. [4,8,15] are not optimal for our task. The reason is that they are designed to keep information only about the object's 'class' while being invariant to all other attributes. This may, in some cases, also require invariance on the attributes of interest y. Instead, we selected a much smaller set of augmentations which we empirically show to be effective on a set of datasets that we considered. There selected augmentations are: i) Cropping, ii) Gaussian Blurring, iii) Increase of contrast iv) Increase in saturation. For Edges2Shoes [39] dataset, we find it more effective to include gaussian blurring alone. In Sect. 5.2 we show the selected augmentations significantly outperform the standard set of SimSiam [8].

Encoder Initialization with Unsupervised Pre-Trained Weights: Although the constraints proposed in this section are effective for learning domain disentangled representations, we empirically find they are not always sufficient. In order to improve generalization [12], we propose to initialize the encoder with the weights of a network pre-trained in an **unsupervised** manner (MoCo-V2 [7]) on the ImageNet dataset. Using the inductive bias from pre-trained weights in this setting is common, e.g. LORD [13] uses an ImageNet pre-trained perceptual loss. Note, this initialization is not beneficial for LORD as it does not use an encoder in the first stage.

4.4 Our Complete Method: DCoDR

DCoDR optimizes the combination of the 3 objectives presented in this section:

$$\min_{E,G} L_{DCoDR} = L_{inv} + L_{aug} + L_{rec} \tag{8}$$

We use the augmentations from Sect. 4.3. We initialize the encoder E with the weights of an MoCo-V2 encoder pre-trained on ImageNet (without labels).

Discriminative DCoDR (DCoDR-norec). We present a discriminative variant of our method, by simply dropping the reconstruction constraint:

$$\min_{E} L_{DCoDR-norec} = L_{inv} + L_{aug} \tag{9}$$

The lack of a reconstruction constraint, makes this variant typically learn less informative representations than DCoDR. However, as this variant does not train a generator, it is several times faster than DCoDR which by itself is considerably faster than previous state-of-the-art LORD.

4.5 Differences from SimCLR

Although a part of our method is motivated by the SimCLR [4] objective, it is significantly different and attempts to obtain satisfy different criteria compared to SimCLR (the first 3 apply for DCoDR-norec as well):

- **Domain-wise Loss.** DCoDR learns a contrastive loss over each domain separately whereas SimCLR learns a single loss over all the data.
- **Choice of Augmentations.** DCoDR learns a reduced set of augmentations rather than the standard set used in SimCLR.
- **Pre-Training.** DCoDR initializes the encoders weights by *unsupervised* pre-training on ImageNet using of MoCo-V2 [7], which does *not* use any labels.
- **Reconstruction** DCoDR uses a reconstruction term for increasing the informativeness of its representations, which does not exist in SimCLR.

Tables 2 and 3 show that although the differences from SimCLR might look superficially simple, each of them is essential for the success of our method, on the described domain disentanglement setup.

5 Experiments

In this section, we evaluate our method against (variational and adversarial) state-of-the-art domain disentanglement approaches. We evaluate the invariance and informativeness of the learned representations. We then demonstrate cross domain retrieval of our method compared to the other baselines in Sect. 5.3.

Benchmark Datasets. We report results on Cars3D [21], SmallNorb [22], Shapes3D [3], CelebA [23] and Edges2Shoes [39]. All datasets are used in 64×64 resolution. Due to the large number of samples in the full Shapes3D and the limited variation between them, we randomly sample $50,000$ images for training, while keeping the test set size at 10% of the original size.

5.1   Implementation Details

Architecture and Optimization. We used a ResNet50 encoder, trained for 200 epochs using a batch size of 128. Each batch was composed from 32 images drawn from 4 different classes. In line with other methods e.g. LORD, the reconstruction loss is computed using a VGG based perceptual loss pre-trained on ImageNet.

Baselines. We use the default parameters of ML-VAE [1] and DRNET [10]. We tried to replace their encoders by larger ResNet architectures but it resulted in degraded performance. We therefore kept the original architectures and hyperparameters for all runs. We use a ResNet50 architecture for LORD's second stage and SimCLR's encoders, training each for 200 epochs. We do not compare to OverLORD [14] as in our evaluated datasets it is exactly the same as LORD.

Augmentations. As mentioned in Sect. 4.3, we used cropping, Gaussian blurring, high contrast and high saturation transformations as our positive augmentations, except for Edges2Shoes where we use only Gaussian blurring.

5.2   Representation Evaluation

Experimental Setup. For each dataset, we evaluate both *Invariance* and *Informativeness* of the representations. To do so, we train a deep classifier to predict all image attributes from the learned representations, including the domain d and the other factors y. For the synthetic datasets, we compute each of the two objectives over each factor separately. Since some of the datasets have multiple factors, we present the average of the informativeness over all factors, while the full results are presented in the SM. For CelebA we use the location of the 68 landmarks [2] as the uncorrelated attribute. As the landmarks are numeric rather than categorical, we train an MLP regression model to predict the landmark locations. We measure the L_1 error of the MLP regressor where lower errors are better. To understand how far the results are from the theoretical limit, we present the frequency of the most common domain value as a lower bound on the invariance. Note that since we use a probabilistic estimator to evaluate our metrics, in some cases (especially when performance is close to optimal limit) the invariance may be slightly lower than the theoretical limit. This can happen when the classifier slightly overfits its training data, hence the small gap. To ensure a fair comparison is made, we train each classifier with several regularization strengths and present the one that is able to generalize best.

Results. The results on all datasets are presented in Table 2. We observe that on Cars3D, even though LORD is a strong baseline, both discriminative and complete variants of DCoDR are able to surpass it, and achieve nearly perfect results. ML-VAE, DRNET and SimCLR do not perform as well on this dataset, inline with the observations in [13]. On SmallNorb, it is clear that LORD fails to disentangle the domain. Both our methods outperforms it on both metrics, achieving much more disentangled representations than any other method. As

Table 2. Content Invariance (↓) (Content to Domain) and Representation Quality (↑) (Average Prediction Accuracy). For CelebA we use extracted landmarks as attributes, and compute the regression L1 (↓) error.

	Cars3D		SmallNorb		Shapes3D		CelebA	
	Inv. ↓	Inf. ↑	Inv. ↓	Inf. ↑	Inv. ↓	Inf. ↑	Inv. ↓	L1 ↓
SimCLR	0.885	0.443	0.956	0.758	1	0.99	0.116	1.286
LORD	0.009	0.940	0.393	0.670	0.703	0.995	0.019	0.862
DRNET	0.504	0.909	0.953	0.899	0.892	1	0.084	0.795
ML-VAE	0.697	0.930	0.968	0.944	0.999	1	0.136	0.723
DCoDR-norec	0.005	0.970	0.071	0.730	0.246	0.997	0.015	1.127
DCoDR	0.005	0.980	0.143	0.785	0.245	0.999	0.017	0.858
Optimal	0.005	1	0.021	1	0.251	1	0.002	0

the representations learned by ML-VAE and DRNET are not domain invariant, they have higher informativeness but do not satisfy the main requirement of disentanglement. Note that we used the original version of the SmallNorb benchmark rather than the simplified version presented in the LORD paper. In this setting, the domain is defined as the object category alone whereas *both* pose and lighting are unknown. On Shapes3D, again both variants of DCoDR achieve almost perfect results while all other methods suffer from lack of domain invariance. LORD achieves very limited invariance while ML-VAE, DRNET and SimCLR learn representations that are not invariant at all. CelebA is challenging for our per-domain contrastive loss, as it contains very few images per each domain, meaning the estimation of a uniform distribution for each domain is limited. That being said, we observe DCoDR performs better than LORD. It has an additional advantage over LORD of not requiring 2-stage optimization. CelebA is a failure case for our discriminative variant. Although presenting stronger invariance than the other methods, it is not sufficiently informative.

Generally, DCoDR demonstrated state-of-the-art results in invariance and informativeness. In some cases (e.g. CelebA), DCoDR-norec fails to learn sufficiently informative representations, while being more invariant than previous methods as well as DCoDR itself. We emphasize that a key advantage of DCoDR-norec is its training time, as shown in Sect. 5.4.

Ablation Study. We ablate our method on the SmallNorb dataset (Table 3). First, we observe that removal of the unsupervised MoCo-V2 pre-trained weight initialization significantly hurts all metrics. Removal of per-domain negative pairs i.e. using a single contrastive loss for all domains (the loss used in SimCLR), makes the representations entangled. We also tested removing the positive augmentations, using the objective in Eq. 5. Removing the positive augmentations has different effects in to DCoDR and DCoDR-norec. DCoDR's informativeness was reduced while invariance improved. DCoDR-norec fails without the positive augmentations as they are its only objective that enforces informativeness. Lastly, we consider the standard set of augmentations used in SimSiam [8]. This choice significantly harms both invariance and informativeness in both variants.

Table 3. Ablation analysis on SmallNorb.

	DCoDR		DCoDR-norec	
	Inv. ($\downarrow$)	Inform. ($\uparrow$)	Inv. ($\downarrow$)	Inform. ($\uparrow$)
No Domain Negatives	0.863	0.829	0.879	0.754
No Positive Augmentations	0.057	0.555	0.021	0.166
No Pre-Training	0.253	0.701	0.298	0.716
SimSiam [8] Augmentations	0.244	0.643	0.246	0.658
Complete Method	0.143	0.785	0.071	0.730
Optimal	0.020	1	0.020	1

5.3 Cross Domain Retrieval Evaluation

Experimental Setup. To evaluate cross-domain retrieval, we first extract representation $z = E(x)$ for each image x from domain d in the test set. Than, we retrieve its nearest neighbors (using L_2 distance) from each domain d' so that $d' \neq d$ and average the results over all domains. Finally, results are averaged over all test images. We present both quantitative and qualitative analyses. For our quantitative analysis, we use the labels of the attributes y for deciding weather a match was found or not. Since many attributes are naturally ordered we would like to consider more than just perfect matches in all attributes. To do so, we allow a match for small changes in some numeric attributes, as detailed in the SM. Here we present the accuracy of matching over all attributes. The accuracy of matching individual attributes is presented in the SM. We also visually present the 5 nearest-neighbor images for several test set images - using the representations learned by our and baseline methods. Here, we search for neighbors *in all domains at once*, contrary to the previous quantitative retrieval evaluation, which was performed for each domain separately, then averaged. The analysis highlights leakage of domain information in the representations.

Quantitative Analysis. Our numerical retrieval results are presented in Fig. 4. Similarly to the earlier probing experiments on Cars3D, LORD achieves the highest retrieval scores among all the baseline methods on this dataset. Our method, convincingly outperforms it, both with and without reconstruction.

Table 4. Retrieval Accuracies Comparison.

	Cars3D	SmallNorb	Shapes3D	Edges2Shoes
SimCLR	0.07	0.02	< 0.01	0.40
LORD	0.88	0.06	0.76	0.66
DRNET	0.64	0.09	0.86	0.66
ML-VAE	0.50	0.06	0.63	0.65
DCoDR-norec	0.96	0.22	0.99	0.41
DCODR	**0.97**	**0.26**	1	**0.90**

DRNET and ML-VAE achieve acceptable results, but underperform DCoDR and LORD due to their lack of invariance. SimCLR fails to retrieve accurately since, as Table 2 suggests, it prefers representing the domain over the pose. SmallNORB is a much harder task, all baseline methods struggle on this dataset achieving poor retrieval accuracy. We showed in Table 2 that these methods have high informativeness and poor invariance on this dataset. This shows that invariance is important for succeeding in cross domain retrieval. DCoDR (with and without reconstruction) is able to retrieve much better matches as it is considerably less biased by the domain. This is backed up by the qualitative analysis of SmallNorb in Fig. 2. Results on Shapes3D describe a similar case. Although all methods achieve strong informativeness, DCoDR and DCoDR-norec only are able to retrieve nearly perfect matches due to domain invariance. Surprisingly, on this dataset DRNET was able to retrieve strong matches from different domains, despite not being domain invariant at all. Finally, Edges2Shoes showcases a failure of DCoDR-norec, as the augmentations do not provide a strong enough inductive bias for learning informative representations. Saying that, when given the inductive bias of a generator, DCoDR exceeds previous methods significantly.

Qualitative Analysis. We present retrieval results on SmallNorb [22] and Edges2Shoes [39] datasets in Figs. 2 and 3 respectively. We present DCoDR-norec on SmallNorb, and DCoDR on Edges2Shoes (as the reconstruction loss is needed there). On SmallNorb, DRNET and ML-VAE retrieve images from the same domain at the expense of changing the pose, achieving poor retrieval results. While LORD does select images from other domains, the domains are typically similar to the source. DCoDR-norec retrieves images from a variety of domains while preserving the pose. Both LORD and DCoDR-norec struggle with

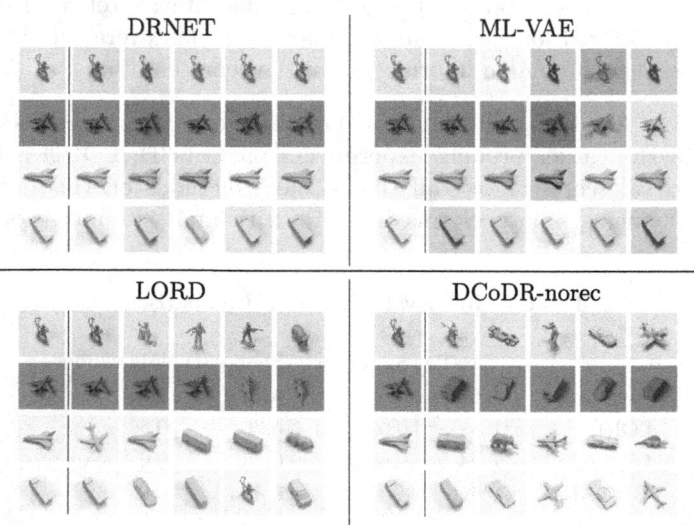

Fig. 2. Retrieval examples from SmallNorb.

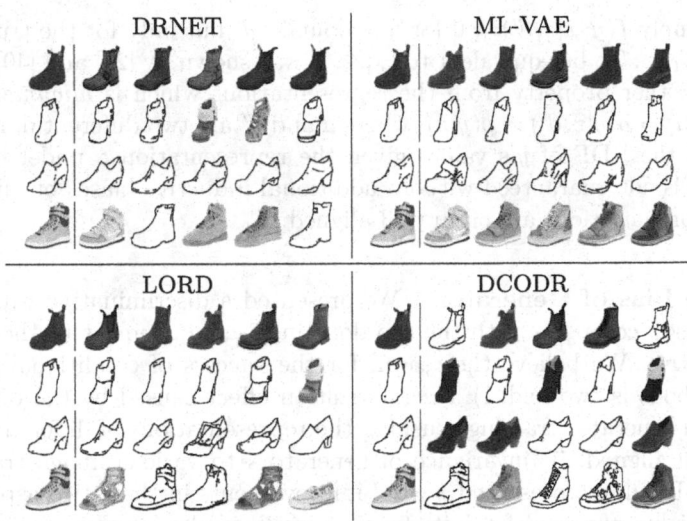

Fig. 3. Retrieval examples from Edges2Shoes.

Table 5. Training Times (↓) In Hours.

	Cars3D	SmallNorb	Shapes3D (50K)	CelebA
LORD	7.5	15.5	18	160
DCODR	5.5	9.5	11.5	30
DCoDR-norec	**1.5**	**3.5**	**3.5**	**9**

180° flips. For Edges2Shoes, ML-VAE clearly shows lack of domain invariance. DCoDR retrieves more accurate images than DRNET and LORD.

5.4   Runtime Comparison

We compared our method's runtime with LORD [13], the top baseline. All methods were run on a single NVIDIA-RTX6000 for 200 epochs for all datasets (note that LORD has two stages). Results are presented in Table 5. Both DCoDR and DCoDR-norec are faster than LORD. DCoDR-norec is **5–10 times faster** than LORD as it does not train a generator nor require perceptual loss computation.

6   Discussion

The Mismatch Between Conditional Reconstruction Constraints and Informativeness. By the data processing inequality, the existence of a deterministic mappings $x = G_{d_{true}}(z)$ (and accordingly $x = E(z)$) implies that $I(y; x | z, d_{true}) = 0$. In other words, all the information about y which exists in x, exists in the combination of z and the domain label d_{true} as well. Note this does not imply $I(y; x|z, d') = 0$ for any domain d' but only for the true domain of x, $d' = d_{true}$. To be equivalent to Eq. 2, it was shown by [20] and [40] that this requires another property from the representations which is *alignment*. Meaning, $p(y|z, d) = p(y|z, d') = p(y|z)$, where d and d' are two different domains and $p(y|z, d)$ is the PDF of y's values given the representation z under domain d. Alignment is not guaranteed without additional inductive biases but in practice learned representations are often well aligned.

Inductive Bias of Generators. We presented a discriminative variant that, in some cases, competes with the top domain disentanglement methods, which are generative. We believe the reason for the success of conditional generator based methods is two-fold: i) a regularization effect caused by the difficulty of conditional generator training, pushing the representations of different domains to be more aligned. ii) invariance of generators to various image transformations. DCoDR-norec presented *partial* improvements in these two aspects. Pre-trained weights are used for initialization, we hypothesize this acts as a regularizer although not as strong as a conditional generator. Image augmentations are used, *most of which* are encapsulated in the invariance of generators. To test the invariance of generators to different augmentations, we performed an experiment where we trained autoencoders on several datasets and compared their reconstruction for images with and without augmentations. This motivated our choice of augmentations. For more details, see the SM. Despite DCoDR-norec showing promising results of in some cases, we find that all components of our method are needed for sufficient informativeness. We expect that future research will find other augmentations which will result in further improvements.

Limitations. Our method has a few limitations which we leave for future work:
(i) *Discrete Domains.* As required by our per-domain invariance objective.
(ii) *Pre-Training.* We showed in Sect. 5.2 that using unsupervised pre-training (MoCo-V2 trained on ImageNet) significantly improves both invariance and informativeness. Although requiring an external dataset is a limitation, we do not believe it is a very serious one for two reasons. Firstly, previous methods, e.g. LORD, often use supervised pre-trained features in their perceptual loss as well. Secondly, these weights are available to all and identical for all new datasets.
(iii) *Image-Specific Augmentations.* Our method rely on image augmentations, which are not always transferable to other modalities e.g. audio or text. Nevertheless, we believe other helpful augmentations can be found in each modality.

7 Conclusion

We presented a new approach for learning domain disentangled representations from images. It uses a per-domain contrastive loss, a reconstruction objective, image augmentations and self-supervised pre-trained encoder initialization. Our method demonstrated results that are better in both invariance and informativeness metrics over the state-of-the-art.

Acknowledgement. Jonathan Kahana was partially supported by grants from the Israeli Prime Minister Office and the Council for Higher Learning.

References

1. Bouchacourt, D., Tomioka, R., Nowozin, S.: Multi-level variational autoencoder: learning disentangled representations from grouped observations. In: AAAI (2018)
2. Bulat, A., Tzimiropoulos, G.: How far are we from solving the 2D & 3D face alignment problem? (and a dataset of 230,000 3D facial landmarks). In: International Conference on Computer Vision (2017)
3. Burgess, C., Kim, H.: 3D shapes dataset. https://github.com/deepmind/3dshapesdataset/ (2018)
4. Chen, T., Kornblith, S., Norouzi, M., Hinton, G.E.: A simple framework for contrastive learning of visual representations. In: ICML (2020)
5. Chen, T., Kornblith, S., Swersky, K., Norouzi, M., Hinton, G.: Big self-supervised models are strong semi-supervised learners. In: NeurIPS (2020)
6. Chen, T., Luo, C., Li, L.: Intriguing properties of contrastive losses. In: Advances in Neural Information Processing Systems 34 (2021)
7. Chen, X., Fan, H., Girshick, R., He, K.: Improved baselines with momentum contrastive learning. arXiv preprint arXiv:2003.04297 (2020)
8. Chen, X., He, K.: Exploring simple Siamese representation learning. In: CVPR (2020)
9. Creager, E., et al.: Flexibly fair representation learning by disentanglement. In: International Conference on Machine Learning (2019)
10. Denton, E., Birodkar, V.: Unsupervised learning of disentangled representations from video. In: Proceedings of the 31st International Conference on Neural Information Processing Systems, pp. 4417–4426 (2017)
11. Denton, E.L., et al.: Unsupervised learning of disentangled representations from video. In: Advances in neural information processing systems, pp. 4414–4423 (2017)
12. Erhan, D., Bengio, Y., Courville, A., Manzagol, P.A., Vincent, P., Bengio, S.: Why does unsupervised pre-training help deep learning? J. Mach. Learn. Res. **11**(19), 625–660 (2010). http://jmlr.org/papers/v11/erhan10a.html
13. Gabbay, A., Hoshen, Y.: Demystifying inter-class disentanglement. In: International Conference on Learning Representations (ICLR) (2020)
14. Gabbay, A., Hoshen, Y.: Scaling-up disentanglement for image translation. In: ICCV (2021)
15. Grill, J.B., et al.: Bootstrap your own latent: a new approach to self-supervised learning. In: NeurIPS (2020)
16. Jha, A.H., Anand, S., Singh, M., Veeravasarapu, V.S.R.: Disentangling factors of variation with cycle-consistent variational auto-encoders. In: Ferrari, V., Hebert, M., Sminchisescu, C., Weiss, Y. (eds.) ECCV 2018. LNCS, vol. 11207, pp. 829–845. Springer, Cham (2018). https://doi.org/10.1007/978-3-030-01219-9_49

17. He, K., Fan, H., Wu, Y., Xie, S., Girshick, R.: Momentum contrast for unsupervised visual representation learning. In: CVPR (2020)
18. Hjelm, R.D., Fedorov, A., Lavoie-Marchildon, S., Grewal, K., Trischler, A., Bengio, Y.: Learning deep representations by mutual information estimation and maximization. In: ICLR (2019)
19. Hsu, W.N., Zhang, Y., Glass, J.: Unsupervised learning of disentangled and interpretable representations from sequential data. In: Advances in neural information processing systems, pp. 1878–1889 (2017)
20. Johansson, F.D., Sontag, D., Ranganath, R.: Support and invertibility in domain-invariant representations. In: The 22nd International Conference on Artificial Intelligence and Statistics, pp. 527–536. PMLR (2019)
21. Krause, J., Stark, M., Deng, J., Fei-Fei, L.: 3d object representations for fine-grained categorization. In: 4th International IEEE Workshop on 3D Representation and Recognition (3dRR-13). Sydney, Australia (2013)
22. LeCun, Y., Huang, F.J., Bottou, L.: Learning methods for generic object recognition with invariance to pose and lighting. In: Proceedings of the 2004 IEEE Computer Society Conference on Computer Vision and Pattern Recognition 2, II-104, vol. 2 (2004)
23. Lee, C.H., Liu, Z., Wu, L., Luo, P.: MaskGAN: towards diverse and interactive facial image manipulation. In: IEEE Conference on Computer Vision and Pattern Recognition (CVPR) (2020)
24. Li, T., Fan, L., Yuan, Y., He, H., Tian, Y., Katabi, D.: Information-preserving contrastive learning for self-supervised representations. CoRR abs/2012.09962 (2020). https://arxiv.org/abs/2012.09962
25. Locatello, F., et al.: Challenging common assumptions in the unsupervised learning of disentangled representations. In: International Conference on Machine Learning, pp. 4114–4124. PMLR (2019)
26. Mathieu, M.F., Zhao, J.J., Zhao, J., Ramesh, A., Sprechmann, P., LeCun, Y.: Disentangling factors of variation in deep representation using adversarial training. In: NIPS (2016)
27. Misra, I., van der Maaten, L.: Self-supervised learning of pretext-invariant representations. In: CVPR (2020)
28. Moyer, D., Gao, S., Brekelmans, R., Steeg, G.V., Galstyan, A.: Invariant representations without adversarial training. In: Proceedings of the 32nd International Conference on Neural Information Processing Systems, pp. 9102–9111 (2018)
29. van den Oord, A., Li, Y., Vinyals, O.: Representation learning with contrastive predictive coding. arXiv preprint arXiv:1807.03748 (2018)
30. Peng, X., Huang, Z., Sun, X., Saenko, K.: Domain agnostic learning with disentangled representations. In: International Conference on Machine Learning, pp. 5102–5112. PMLR (2019)
31. Richemond, P.H., et al.: Byol works even without batch statistics. arXiv preprint arXiv:2010.10241 (2020)
32. Robinson, J., Sun, L., Yu, K., Batmanghelich, K., Jegelka, S., Sra, S.: Can contrastive learning avoid shortcut solutions? In: Advances in Neural Information Processing Systems 34 (2021)
33. van Steenkiste, S., Locatello, F., Schmidhuber, J., Bachem, O.: Are disentangled representations helpful for abstract visual reasoning? In: Advances in Neural Information Processing Systems. pp. 14245–14258 (2019)
34. Szabó, A., Hu, Q., Portenier, T., Zwicker, M., Favaro, P.: Challenges in disentangling independent factors of variation. In: ICLRW (2018)

35. Wang, T., Isola, P.: Understanding contrastive representation learning through alignment and uniformity on the hypersphere. In: International Conference on Machine Learning, pp. 9929–9939. PMLR (2020)
36. Wu, Z., Xiong, Y., Yu, S., Lin, D.: Unsupervised feature learning via nonparametric instance discrimination. In: CVPR (2018)
37. Wu, Z., Lischinski, D., Shechtman, E.: Stylespace analysis: disentangled controls for stylegan image generation. In: IEEE Conference on Computer Vision and Pattern Recognition (CVPR) (2021)
38. Ye, M., Zhang, X., Yuen, P.C., Chang, S.F.: Unsupervised embedding learning via invariant and spreading instance feature. In: CVPR (2019)
39. Yu, A., Grauman, K.: Fine-grained visual comparisons with local learning. In: Proceedings of the IEEE Conference on Computer Vision and Pattern Recognition, pp. 192–199 (2014)
40. Zhao, H., Des Combes, R.T., Zhang, K., Gordon, G.: On learning invariant representations for domain adaptation. In: International Conference on Machine Learning, pp. 7523–7532. PMLR (2019)
41. Zhu, J.Y., et al.: Visual object networks: image generation with disentangled 3D representations. In: Advances in Neural Information Processing Systems, pp. 118–129 (2018)
42. Zimmermann, R.S., Sharma, Y., Schneider, S., Bethge, M., Brendel, W.: Contrastive learning inverts the data generating process. In: ICML (2021)

PT4AL: Using Self-supervised Pretext Tasks for Active Learning

John Seon Keun Yi[1], Minseok Seo[2,4], Jongchan Park[3],
and Dong-Geol Choi[4(✉)]

[1] Georgia Institute of Technology, Atlanta, USA
[2] SI Analytics, Mainz, Germany
[3] Lunit Inc, Seoul, South Korea
[4] Hanbat National University, Daejeon, South Korea
dgchoi@hanbat.ac.kr

Abstract. Labeling a large set of data is expensive. Active learning aims to tackle this problem by asking to annotate only the most informative data from the unlabeled set. We propose a novel active learning approach that utilizes self-supervised pretext tasks and a unique data sampler to select data that are both difficult and representative. We discover that the loss of a simple self-supervised pretext task, such as rotation prediction, is closely correlated to the downstream task loss. Before the active learning iterations, the pretext task learner is trained on the unlabeled set, and the unlabeled data are sorted and split into batches by their pretext task losses. In each active learning iteration, the main task model is used to sample the most uncertain data in a batch to be annotated. We evaluate our method on various image classification and segmentation benchmarks and achieve compelling performances on CIFAR10, Caltech-101, ImageNet, and Cityscapes. We further show that our method performs well on imbalanced datasets, and can be an effective solution to the cold-start problem where active learning performance is affected by the randomly sampled initial labeled set. Code is available at https://github.com/johnsk95/PT4AL

Keywords: Active learning · Self-supervised learning · Pretext task

1 Introduction

The recent success in deep learning has shown remarkable advancements in computer vision tasks such as classification [12,19] and semantic segmentation [7,30]. This has been possible due to the advent of deep convolutional neural networks (CNNs) and large annotated datasets such as ImageNet [12] and COCO [27].

J. S. K. Yi and M. Seo—Equal contribution.

Supplementary Information The online version contains supplementary material available at https://doi.org/10.1007/978-3-031-19809-0_34.

As deep learning models are trained in a data-driven manner, having a large enough training set is crucial to achieve high performance. However, building a large labeled dataset is prohibitively time-consuming and expensive. Labeling costs increase with the size of data and complexity of the tasks. Instead of labeling the entire data, active learning (AL) [39] aims to select informative subsets to label that achieve the highest performance within a fixed labeling budget.

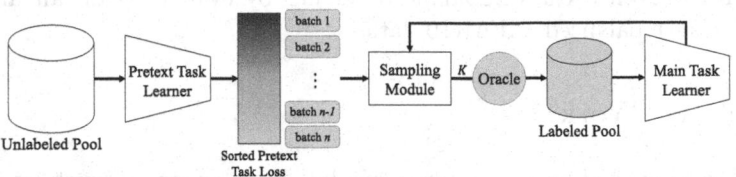

Fig. 1. The overall framework of the proposed method. Unlabeled data are sorted by pretext task losses, split into batches, and sampled for training

Existing AL approaches can be divided into two main groups: distribution-based and uncertainty-based methods. Distribution-based methods [5,38] aim to sample data that well covers the distribution of the feature space. The advantage of such methods is that they can sample *representative* points: data points from high density regions that well represent the overall feature distribution. However, distribution-based sampling fails to select data that are placed near the decision boundary (i.e. high uncertainty data points). Uncertainty-based approaches [26] resolve this problem by sampling the most uncertain points. Simple approaches that utilize class posterior probabilities [25,26], entropy [21,40], and loss prediction [23,46] were revealed to perform well on various settings. While these approaches effectively sample *uncertain* or *difficult* data near decision boundaries in the feature space, they do not capture the overall distribution of the data, according to our qualitative analysis in Fig. 4. Our method aims to capture the best of both worlds by sampling both representative and difficult data.

This paper proposes Pretext Tasks for Active Learning (PT4AL), a novel active learning framework that utilizes self-supervised pretext tasks combined with an uncertainty-based sampler. We train a pretext task model [16,48] with unlabeled data, and the pretext task loss is highly correlated to the main task loss. In order to sample diversely from both representative and difficult data, the unlabeled data are sorted in descending order by their pretext task loss, and split into batches to be used for each AL iteration. Starting from the batch containing data with the highest losses, the most uncertain K data points are sampled from each batch, based on the posterior class probability of the previous main task learner. The uncertainty-based sampler enables PT4AL to sample difficult data, while the batch split allows balanced sampling across the entire data distribution.

PT4AL also resolves the innate problem in active learning: the cold start problem. Existing approaches start from a randomly sampled set of labeled data, rendering the overall performance highly dependent on the distribution of the initial set. Since our method learns the representation of the unlabeled set in advance, we can sample informative data from the first iteration. This approach avoids the issue of high variance and decrease in performance that can stem from randomly sampling the initial labeled set.

We validate our proposed method on various image classification and semantic segmentation datasets and achieve state-of-the-art or compelling results across different datasets and tasks. Additionally, we demonstrate the robustness of PT4AL on a class imbalanced setting by evaluating on an artificially created class-imbalanced CIFAR10 dataset.

2   Related Work

Active Learning. Various AL approaches has been proposed, such as information theoretical approaches [32], ensemble approaches [15,33], uncertainty based methods [21,43] and Bayesian AL methods [22]. However, these traditional methods have not been verified in large-scale datasets for large-scale models, such as in the field of CNN-based deep learning, which has achieved state-of-the-art in various computer vision tasks.

Recent AL methods have been centered on large-scale settings for CNN-based deep learning models. Sener & Savarese [38] proposed a core-set selection method, which chooses data points that cover all data with high diversity based on the feature distribution. This method targets two problems of the previous uncertainty-based methods. First, uncertainty-based methods select only hard samples, resulting in redundant, overlapping data points. Second, the existing methods are not suitable for batch processing on CNNs. The core-set algorithm aims to sample diverse data points in a batch manner. Yoo & Kweon [46] proposed a sub-task module to predict the main task loss of unlabeled data, and sample the high-loss samples from the unlabeled pool. This method samples from a subset of the unlabeled pool to avoid selecting redundant data points when sampling consecutively from the most uncertain data [4]. However, in our qualitative analysis in Fig. 4, uncertainty-based methods like Yoo & Kweon sample data points from decision boundaries with less diversity in distribution. Recently, using a variational autoencoder architecture [41], the discriminator adversarially trains the input data to be unlabeled or labeled. In the data sampling phase, a method that first labels the sample predicted as unlabeled with the lowest confidence was proposed.

Our active learning method uses a self-supervised pretext task to supplement the flaws of the data distribution-based method and the uncertainty-based method. As described above, AL is largely divided into data distribution-based methods [5,29,38] and uncertainty-based methods [10,23,41,46]. The data distribution-based method has the disadvantage that it cannot extract hard samples, and the uncertainty-based method has the possibility to sample overlapping data points and it is difficult to extract the representation of the entire data distribution. Other works [1,20,45] sample from both representative and difficult data by utilizing variance maximization between labeled and unlabeled data or using separate sampling criteria for data in each category. Our method uses pretext task-based batch split which allows us to select representative samples across the semantic distribution, and an uncertainty-based in-batch sampler which allows us to select difficult samples.

Representation Learning with Pretext Tasks. Representation learning aims to learn good pre-trained weights by learning self-supervised pretext tasks with unlabeled data. The pre-trained weights are fine-tuned with a small amount of labeled data to achieve high performance on downstream tasks. The key assumption and the findings in representation learning is that pretext tasks provide enough learning signals without any labels (i.e. direct supervision) provided. Using these assumptions, Liu *et al.* [28] proposed unsupervised neural architecture search (NAS) using self-supervised pretext tasks [16,34,48] and achieved similar performance to supervised NAS baselines. Zhang *et al.* [48] proposed a pretext task to restore the color of the original image through a network after transforming the input image to gray scale. Noroozi and Favaro [34] improved the performance of representation learning in image classification through the task of dividing input images into grids, mixing them with each other, and inputting each grid into the network. Gidaris *et al.* [16] proposed a pretext task that rotates the input image by 0°, 90°, 180°, and 270° and training the network to match the rotated angle of the transformed input image. This method achieved the highest performance among representation learning methods utilizing data structures. Recently proposed representation learning methods use contrastive learning [6,8,9,18,35] to minimize the distance between different pairwise augmentations of the same image, and repel from augmentations of different images. Contrastive learning is proved to be robust on different downstream tasks and provide state-of-the-art results by far.

There have been several efforts to use self-supervised pretext tasks in active learning. Zhu *et al.* [49] uses graph contrastive learning [47] for active learning on graph neural networks. [2,17,37] utilizes self-supervised learning to pretrain the main task model, which is then fine-tuned on labeled data. Bhatnagar *et al.* [3] presents a multi-task active learner trained for both pretext task and main task, while being robust to mislabeled samples. Although these methods help justify the use of pretext tasks in active learning, they are limited to specific domains [17,37,49], fail to sample both difficult and representative data [2], and does not solve the cold start problem [2,3,49].

As pretext tasks provide good initializations for downstream tasks, we assume that the information learned through these tasks is highly correlated to the semantic data distribution. We analyze and identify the correlation between the pretext task loss and the supervised loss in downstream tasks in Sect. 3. Finally, we propose an active learning method using pretext tasks in Sect. 4.

3   Using Pretext Tasks for Active Learning

The success of representation learning with self-supervised pretext tasks [8,9,18, 28], leads us to believe that there is a high correlation between self-supervised pretext tasks and downstream tasks, and thus pretext tasks can be utilized for active learning. Rather than utilizing the feature distribution after the pretext task training, we resort to a simpler metric for active learning - *the pretext task loss*. In this section, we propose and validate a hypothesis, and use these evidences to formulate our AL algorithm. Our hypothesis is that:

H1: *Pretext task loss is correlated with the main task loss.*

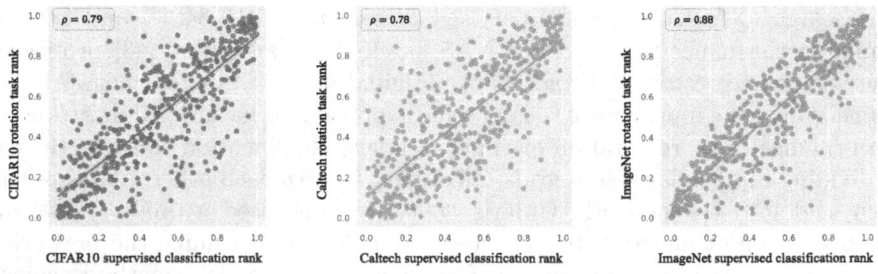

Fig. 2. (From left to right) The loss rank correlation plots for the main task loss and the pretext task loss in CIFAR10, Caltech-101 and ImageNet. The x and y axes represent the normalized rank of the two losses, respectively

We think that if a pretext task is correlated or representative of the main task, images that are *hard* (i.e. having high loss values) for the pretext task will also be *hard* for the main task.

Figure 2 presents scatter plots of the pretext task loss and the main task loss in three benchmark datasets. The x-axis is the normalized rank of the main task loss, and the y-axis is the normalized rank of the pretext task loss. The pretext task and the main task are independently trained with the training set, and the losses are computed in the test set. For ease of interpretation, we visualized 1,000 random samples on the plots. Spearman's rank correlation [42] denoted as ρ is calculated on the full test set.

As illustrated in Fig. 2, the pretext and main task losses have a strong positive correlation. That is, if a data sample has high loss for a pretext task, it is likely for it to have high loss for the main task, and vice versa. We observe high ρ values for all three datasets: CIFAR10 ($\rho = 0.79$), Caltech-101 ($\rho = 0.78$), and ImageNet ($\rho = 0.88$). Note that these datasets vary in image size, number of classes, and class balance. The strong correlation between the pretext task loss and the main task loss across diverse datasets validates our hypothesis, and thus is a strong evidence for using pretext task losses for active learning. However, there is one caveat to the hypotheses: methods that use contrastive loss as the pretext task [8,9,18] do not have a strong loss correlation. ($\rho = -0.001$ for SimSiam) We contribute this result to two main reasons: class bias of the contrastive loss and strong reliance to augmentations. Details are explained in the supplementary material. Even if we could find a way to achieve close correspondence with the main loss, we decide not to use contrastive methods since the large batch size and long training time generally required for these methods beat our purpose of a simple and quick AL model. Details are explained in the supplementary material.

Throughout this work, we validate the efficacy of PT4AL with 4 different pretext tasks: Rotation prediction [16], colorization [48], solving jigsaw puzzles [34], and SimSiam [9]. We compare and analyze the efficacy of different pretext tasks on classification and semantic segmentation in Sect. 6.2. Since rotation prediction [16] performs best in CIFAR10 and colorization [48] performs the best in Cityscapes, we use rotation prediction for image classification main tasks, and colorization for semantic segmentation.

4 Method

In this section, we introduce the specifics of PT4AL. First, we provide a brief overview of our active learning algorithm. Then we provide details of the pretext task learning for batch split and in-batch sampling in the following sections.

4.1 Overview

In a typical active learning scenario, we are initially provided with a pool of unlabeled data $x_U \in X_U$. The objective of AL is to achieve the best performance in the main task model $F_m(\cdot)$ with a limited amount of labeled data. In specific, we follow the *batch mode* active learning scheme: in the i-th AL iteration, we select K samples from X_U^i, add them into labeled pool (X_L^i, Y_L^i) with oracle, train and evaluate $F_m^i(\cdot)$ with (X_L^i, Y_L^i). The iterations are repeated until the specified labeling budget is reached.

The overall framework of PT4AL is illustrated in Fig. 1. PT4AL is split into two parts: pretext task learning for batch split and in-batch sampling. Pretext task learning is done prior to the AL iterations. We train a pretext task learner with X_U. The unlabeled samples are sorted in descending order of their pretext task losses, and split into batches. The in-batch sampling is done at each AL iteration. At the i-th iteration, the sampling module selects K samples from the i-th batch, according to the uncertainty of the main task learner in these samples. The main task learner $F_m^i(\cdot)$ is trained with (X_L^i, Y_L^i) and evaluated on the test set.

4.2 Pretext Task Learning for Batch Split

In this section, we explain how a pretext task is used for active learning batch split. The term *batch* refers to a pool of unlabeled data to be sampled in an AL iteration. While any pretext task can be used in our method, we use the widely used rotation prediction task [16] for the explanation. For the rotation prediction task, the backbone neural network [19] is trained on all four orientations (0°, 90°, 180°, 270° degrees) of the input image. The loss function is defined as the average of the losses for each orientation:

$$loss(x_i, \theta_p) = \frac{1}{k} \sum_{y=1}^{k} \mathcal{L}_{CE}(F_p(g(x_i \mid y) \mid \theta_p), y) \tag{1}$$

where $\mathcal{L}_{CE}$ is the cross-entropy loss. The rotation operator $g(\cdot \mid y)$ yields the rotated input image according to the orientation label y. We define $k = 4$ since we predict four different rotations. F_p represents the probability distribution of the input image rotated by label y. Note that the rotation label y is unknown to F_p. In inference, four orientations of each image is fed into the trained network F_p and the extracted loss is the same averaged loss $loss(x_i, \theta_p)$ used in training. F_p is trained and tested on the same unlabeled set X_U. The model weights θ_p with the best test accuracy is used for loss extraction.

After training the pretext task learner, we extract pretext task loss values from X_U and split them into batches. Given the pretext task loss values of the unlabeled data $loss_{X_U}$ in the pretext task learning phase, we first sort the losses in descending order. The sorted data $\mathcal{X}_U$ is then divided into I batches of equal size. The number of I is equal to the number of AL iterations: if there are ten iterations($I = 10$), there will be ten batches $\mathcal{B} = \{b_i\}_{i=1}^{I=10}$.

4.3 In-batch Sampling

The in-batch sampler selects K samples at each AL iteration. At the i-th iteration, the in-batch sampler $\phi(\cdot)$ selects K samples from the i-th batch to be annotated by the oracle. The sampler computes the top-1 posterior probability in the given batch using the previous main task learner F_m^{i-1}, and K data points with the lowest confidence scores are selected. In the first iteration, K points are sampled from the first batch b_0 at even intervals. Equation 2 summarizes the sampler $\phi(\cdot)$. The sampling makes use of the main task model from the previous iteration, F_m^{i-1}.

$$\phi(b_i, F_m^{i-1}) = min_K\{max(F_m^{i-1}(b_i \mid \theta_m))\} \tag{2}$$

Algorithm 1 illustrates our overall sampling algorithm including batch splitting and in-batch sampling. In the first iteration when we do not have F_m^0, we uniformly select samples in the first batch, based on our empirical observation that visually similar samples have similar pretext task loss values. Sampled data have two main traits: difficult and representative. Difficult or uncertain data refers to data that the main task model cannot easily distinguish because it is near a decision boundary. Conversely, representative data well defines the distribution in the feature space. Our intuition is that if we can sample data from both categories, we can form a labeled pool with the most informative data. This is

---

Algorithm 1. Sampling Strategy

Input: Unlabeled X_U, labeled X_L, pretext task losses $loss_{X_U}$, main task model F_m

$\mathcal{X}_U = sort(loss_{X_U})$ ▷ Sort losses in descending order

Split $\mathcal{X}_U$ into batches $\mathcal{B}$

for b_i in $\mathcal{B}$ **do**

     if i == 1, $X_K = uniform(b_i, loss^i_{X_U})$ ▷ For the first batch, uniformly sample

     else, $X_K = \phi(b_i, F^{i-1}_m)$ ▷ For other batches, sample top-K uncertain data

     $X_U \leftarrow X_U - X_k$ ▷ Remove from unlabeled pool

     $X_L \leftarrow X_L \cup X_k$ ▷ Add to labeled pool

     train F^i_m with X_L

end for

---

empirically verified through query analysis in Sect. 5. Our batch split method combined with the sampler samples both representative and difficult data. Our method is much simpler and well performing compared to previous works that sample data from both traits [1, 20, 45].

5 Experiments

We evaluate the efficacy of our method on two commonly used visual recognition tasks: image classification and semantic segmentation. We choose CIFAR10 [24], Caltech-101 [14], ImageNet [12] benchmarks for image classification, and Cityscapes [11] for semantic segmentation. To further demonstrate our method's efficacy in a more challenging class-imbalanced setting, we additionally use a class-imbalanced version of CIFAR10. Finally, we show the use of PT4AL as an effective solution to the cold start problem. Unless otherwise specified, all the experiment results are reproduced by ourselves, averaged over multiple runs with different random seeds.

5.1 Image Classification

Dataset. We perform experiments on three image classification datasets with varying size and number of classes. CIFAR10 contains 50,000 training and 10,000 testing images of size 32×32 with 10 object categories. We start with 1,000 labeled images, and 1,000 images are added for each iteration. Caltech-101 has 9,144 images of size around 300×200 distributed around 101 classes. We divide the data into 8,046 for training and 1,098 for testing. Similar to CIFAR10 we also start with 1,000 labeled images with increments of 1,000 per iteration. ImageNet consists of over 1.3M images of 1,000 classes. 1,279,867 and 49,950 images are used for the training and testing set. For ease of experimentation and to avoid noise from similar class labels, ImageNet classes are reduced to 67 based on the WordNet [36] superclasses. ImageNet starts with $K \approx 128,000$ labeled samples, and the same K samples are selected for each iteration. Due to heavy computation, each ImageNet performance is the average of 3 runs.

Baselines and Implementation Details. We compare PT4AL with random sampling, Core-Set [38], Variational Adversarial Active Learning (VAAL) [41], Learning Loss [46], CoreGCN [5], and PAL [3]. For CIFAR10 we add "Learning loss(detached)", where the loss prediction task is detached during supervised learning to avoid influences from multi-task learning. ResNet-18 [19] is used as the backbone network for the pretext task and the main task learner. The final linear layer of the pretext task learner is converted to (512,4) to account for the four orientations of the rotation task. For Caltech-101 and ImageNet, input images are resized into 224 × 224. No data augmentation is applied in the pretext task learning phase. Random resized crop and horizontal flip is applied in the main task phase. The main task is trained for 200 epochs in CIFAR10 and Caltech-101, and 100 epochs in ImageNet. SGD with a multi-stage learning rate is applied. Detailed hyper-parameters are described in the supplement material.

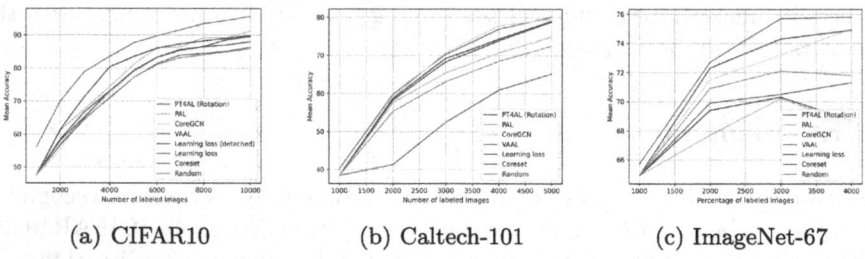

(a) CIFAR10   (b) Caltech-101   (c) ImageNet-67

Fig. 3. Comparison of image classification performance on CIFAR10, Caltech-101, ImageNet-67. Best viewed in color (Color figure online)

Results. Figure 3a demonstrates the results for CIFAR10. PT4AL clearly outperforms other methods across all AL iterations by a noticeable margin. The accuracy of PT4AL in the final iteration of 10,000 labeled points is 95.13% (↑ 8.91%), while the second-best performing learning loss scores 89.93% (↑ 3.71%). Note that detached learning loss [46] performs significantly worse than the original multi-task learning approach, where the main task model is simultaneously trained with auxiliary tasks. The significant drop in performance due to the detachment indicates that the multi-task approaches [5,41,46] may benefit from multi-task learning. To strictly measure the benefit of AL to select informative samples, we need to compare the detached setting across all methods. Our method also has a significant advantage from the first iteration, achieving an accuracy of 55.83% (↑ 9.81%) compared to the other methods' 46.02%. This emphasizes the advantage of PT4AL sampling informative points in the first iteration, instead of random sampling in other AL frameworks. Further details of PT4AL solving the cold-start problem is described in Sect. 5.4.

Similar results can also be observed in Caltech-101 and ImageNet, in Figs. 3b and c. Our method outperforms other methods across most of the iterations with a considerable advantage from the start.

Query Analysis. Figure 4 illustrates t-SNE [31] embeddings of the CIFAR10 data points sampled by random, learning loss [46] and ours. For a fair comparison, we use embeddings extracted from a ResNet-18 model trained with fully labeled CIFAR10. To visualize the sampled data in different methods across the AL iterations, each of the 1,000 samples from the first iteration are marked in circle, fifth iteration in triangle, and tenth (last) iteration as square. Figure 4a shows that random sampling queries evenly from the embedding space, but fails to sample difficult data points along the decision boundaries. As shown in Fig. 4b, learning loss [46] has most of its queries concentrated on the border regions. While this may be effective for the labeled classifier to learn difficult points, it does not query points that represent the classes well. Figure 4c shows that PT4AL queries from both difficult and representative regions. The sampled points are either concentrated on the class boundaries or evenly located in the class distributions. Since PT4AL initially samples from batches with higher pretext loss values, selected points from the first iteration are concentrated on the decision boundaries of the embedding space. As the sampler progresses to batches with lower loss values, we can see that the sampled points propagate to the remaining regions of the class clusters. Such sampling behavior is a mix of both distribu-

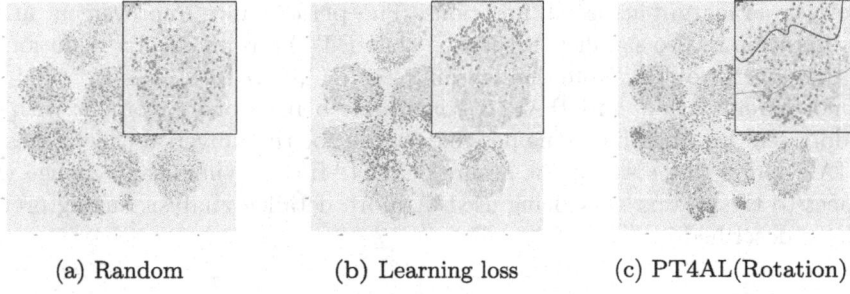

(a) Random   (b) Learning loss   (c) PT4AL(Rotation)

Fig. 4. t-SNE visualization of the CIFAR10 dataset for random, learning loss [46] and PT4AL. Vivid points are sampled for labeling. Best viewed in color (Color figure online)

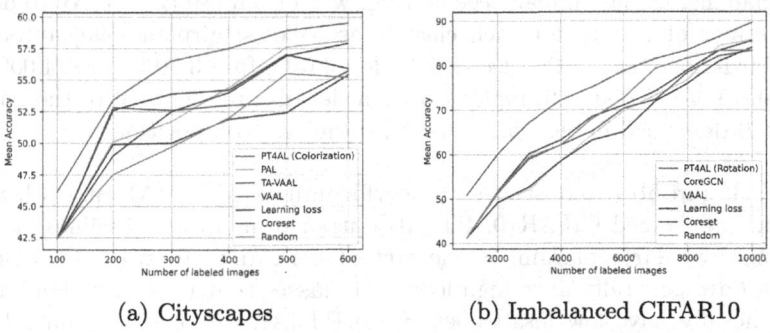

(a) Cityscapes   (b) Imbalanced CIFAR10

Fig. 5. Comparison of cityscapes semantic segmentation and imbalanced cifar10 classification. Best viewed in color (Color figure online)

tion and uncertainty-based methods, mitigating their flaws while sampling both difficult and representative data points.

5.2 Semantic Segmentation

Dataset. We choose Cityscapes [11], a public benchmark dataset widely used in semantic segmentation. The dataset consists of 2,975 training and 500 validation images. At each AL iteration, 100 images are sampled for the labeled training set. The original training set is set as the unlabeled set.

Baselines and Implementation Details. We choose the state-of-the-art active learning methods for this experiment: Core-Set [38], Learning loss [46], VAAL [41], TA-VAAL [23], and PAL [3]. We choose a widely-used semantic segmentation architecture, DeepLab [7] with a ResNet-101 [19] backbone. The model is initialized with ImageNet [13] pre-trained weights. The input images are resized to (1024,512) and no data augmentation is applied. The training batch size is 1, and all hyper-parameters follow the original paper [7], unless otherwise specified.

Results. Figure 5a demonstrates that PT4AL outperforms all other methods by a noticeable margin across all iterations. The performance improvement at the first iteration is also significant, showing that PT4AL is an effective solution for the cold start problem. Note that learning loss [46], VAAL [41] and Core-Set [38] are not as effective as in CIFAR10, sometimes being worse or on-par with the random selection baseline. One possible reason for the universal effectiveness of PT4AL across tasks is that the nature of PT4AL can dynamically change with respect to the pretext task being used. A more detailed analysis among pretext tasks is described in Sect. 6.2.

5.3 Image Classification on an Imbalanced Dataset

Dataset and Experiment Details. To evaluate the efficacy of PT4AL on a more challenging class-imbalanced setting, we recompose the CIFAR10 dataset. The number of images for each class is as follows: airplane-500, automobile-1,000, bird-1,500, cat-2,000, deer-2,500, dog-3,000, frog-3,500, horse-4,000, ship-4,500 and truck-5,000. All implementation details are identical to the balanced CIFAR10 described in Sect. 5.1, except for dataset composition.

Results. Figure 5b demonstrates the performances of PT4AL and other baselines on imbalanced CIFAR10. PT4AL outperforms other baselines across all iterations by a large margin. In the pretext task, data from classes with little training data generally have high loss, and classes that have abundant training data generally have low loss values. Since PT4AL samples from data batches with high to low loss, it can sample in a class-balanced way even in imbalanced settings. Also, unlike other methods using only the main task model related metrics, PT4AL utilizes the pretext task loss which is completely independent from the main task model. Interestingly, unlike the experiment results in balanced CIFAR10, data distribution-based AL methods (Core-Set, CoreGCN) obtains higher performance than the uncertainty-based methods (VAAL, learning loss). These results empirically show that uncertainty-based methods are more negatively affected by the class-imbalanced setting than the distribution-based methods. PT4AL outperforms other methods by a margin, showing robustness on a more challenging class-imbalanced setting. Furthermore, we observe that PT4AL samples data in a more class-balanced way. Details on the class distribution of the sampled data are in the supplementary material.

5.4 Cold Start Problem in Active Learning

Since most AL approaches require a trained main task model, the first AL iteration starts with randomly selected labeled data. This is what we call *the cold start problem in active learning*. To thoroughly validate the efficacy of our method as a solution to the cold start problem, we take a closer look into the first AL iteration in the CIFAR10 benchmark. Note that all other methods use random selection for the first iteration. For PT4AL, after training the pretext task learner, the unlabeled data are sorted by pretext task loss in a descending order, split into 10 batches, and 1,000 data points are uniformly selected from the first batch. The experiment is repeated 20 times with different random seeds. All implementation details are identical to Sect. 5.1.

Table 1 summarizes the experiment results. PT4AL displays more stable performance compared with random sampling in the first iteration, as the standard deviation is smaller, and the gap between the max/min accuracy is smaller than that of the random baseline. PT4AL significantly outperforms random in the average accuracy, indicating that more informative data points are sampled for the main task model. These results indicate that PT4AL is a good solution to the cold start problem, and can be used as a good starting point for existing AL methods [5,23,29,41,46]. More details are in the supplement material.

Table 1. Results of the first active learning iteration in CIFAR10

Method	Mean accuracy	Min/Max
Random	$47.49 \pm 3.15\%$	43.06/53.74 %
PT4AL(Rotation)	55.20 ± 1.95 %	52.00/57.71 %

5.5 Computational Overheads

As described in Sect. 4, the extra computation for PT4AL, apart from the main task model training, is the pretext task learning for batch split, and the unlabeled data inference for uncertainty measurement in in-batch sampling. To fairly compare the computational overheads of different approaches, we measure the wall-clock time of the methods compared in CIFAR10 experiment under the same environment. In Fig. 3a and Table 2, we can observe that PT4AL achieves the best performance while having on-par computational overheads with others. Core-Set [38] has similar computations as the random selection baseline.

Table 2. The wall-clock time of each algorithm in the CIFAR10 experiment

Method	Random Selection	PT4AL	Learning Loss [46]	VAAL [41]	CoreGCN [5]
Time	2 hr 16 min	3 hr 30 min	2 hr 37 min	14 hr 9 min	3 hr 48 min

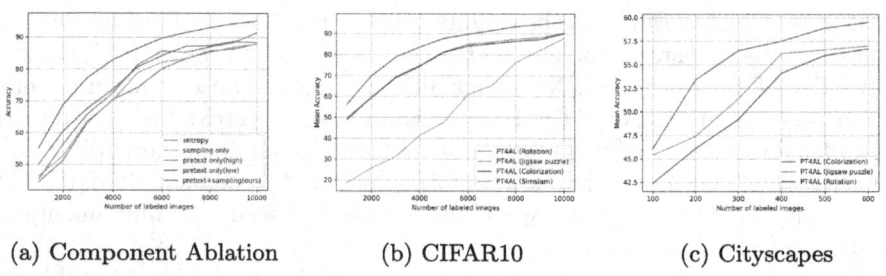

(a) Component Ablation   (b) CIFAR10   (c) Cityscapes

Fig. 6. (a) Ablation on two components of PT4AL. (b),(c) PT4AL with different pretext tasks on CIFAR10 and Cityscapes

6 Ablation Study

6.1 Ablation on Sampling Strategy and Pretext Task Loss

Figure 6a shows the ablations results of the two core components of PT4AL. Instead of the pretext task loss, "Sampling only" uses the main task model's entropy. Batches are made by randomly segmenting the unlabeled data. Data in the first iteration are randomly sampled as there is no main task model to begin with. "Pretext only" replaces our proposed sampling method with a naive sampling of high-loss samples or low-loss samples. Compared with PT4AL which uses both heuristics, the two variations display inferior performance. Using both components is imperative to a well-performing model.

6.2 Pretext Tasks

Figures 6b and c presents active learning performance of PT4AL using different pretext tasks. Rotation prediction [16], colorization [48], solving jigsaw puzzles [34], and SimSiam [9] are compared in CIFAR10 and Cityscapes benchmarks.

The experiment settings are identical to Sects. 5.1 and 5.2. The inferior performance of SimSiam is analyzed in detail in the supplement material. The rotation prediction task shows the best performance in CIFAR10, and the colorization task performs best in Cityscapes. The best performing pretext task differs by the main task. Since rotation prediction is an image-level task and colorization is a pixel-level task, it is intuitive to match rotation prediction with image classification and colorization with segmentation.

6.3   Sampling Strategy

Sampling in the First Iteration. In the first iteration, we do not have access to the main task model for uncertainty measurement. Thus, sampling within the first batch resorts to sampling with the pretext task losses. We compare three simple sampling methods in CIFAR10: top-K, random, and uniform. The performances for top-K loss, random, and uniform sampling are 44.65%, 51.88%, and 55.20%, respectively. As the uniform sampling outperforms the other two sampling methods, we choose it as our in-batch sampling method for the first iteration. We observe that the samples with similar loss values are visually similar, indicating overlapping semantic information in the top-K sampling. This observation is also coherent with the best performance of uniform sampling, as it avoids selecting data points with visually too similar data points. More details are in the supplementary material.

High Loss First vs Low Loss First Batch Split. We examine two different strategies for batch split: high loss batch first or low loss batch first. *High loss batch first* method starts the first iteration with the batch containing the highest pretext task losses, then moves to batches with lower losses for consecutive iterations. *Low loss batch first* is in reverse. On the CIFAR10 experiment, the high loss first strategy displays slightly better results with 55.20% accuracy in the first iteration and 95.13% from the last iteration. Low loss first strategy scores 53.47% and 94.59% in the first and last iterations. We attribute the small performance difference between the two batch split methods to a finding in curriculum learning [44]. Low loss batch first and high loss batch first are analogous to curriculum learning and anti-curriculum learning, respectively. Wu *et al.* [44] concludes that curriculum or anti-curriculum is not effective in standard settings, which explains the small performance gap. As the high loss first method performs better across all iterations, we choose it as our batch split method.

7   Conclusion

In this paper we introduce PT4AL, a novel active learning method based on pretext tasks. We demonstrate the correlation between pretext tasks and semantic recognition tasks, and utilize the pretext task losses to split unlabeled samples into batches. In the query analysis in Sect. 5, we show that the batches are scattered across the whole semantic distribution. Combined with the uncertainty-based in-batch sampler, PT4AL samples both difficult and representative data from the unlabeled pool. We thoroughly examine our method on two widely used vision tasks across various datasets. Our method demonstrates compelling results on datasets with varying resolution, scale and class distribution. We also show that PT4AL is an effective solution for the cold start problem. Although our proposed method performs well on different tasks and datasets, performance varies by the pretext task being used and some tasks such as SimSiam [9] perform poorly. Future research directions may include designing a pretext task that is universal across various recognition tasks.

Acknowledgments. This research was supported by the National Research Foundation of Korea(NRF) grant funded by the Korea government(MSIT) (No. 2022R1F1A1075019, No. 2021M3E8A2100446) and partially supported by the IITP grant funded by the MSIT (No. 2014–3–00123).

References

1. Behpour, S., Liu, A., Ziebart, B.: Active learning for probabilistic structured prediction of cuts and matchings. In: International Conference on Machine Learning, pp. 563–572. PMLR (2019)
2. Bengar, J.Z., van de Weijer, J., Twardowski, B., Raducanu, B.: Reducing label effort: self-supervised meets active learning. In: Proceedings of the IEEE/CVF International Conference on Computer Vision, pp. 1631–1639 (2021)
3. Bhatnagar, S., Goyal, S., Tank, D., Sethi, A.: Pal: pretext-based active learning. arXiv preprint arXiv:2010.15947 (2020)
4. Birodkar, V., Mobahi, H., Bengio, S.: Semantic redundancies in image-classification datasets: the 10% you don't need. arXiv preprint arXiv:1901.11409 (2019)
5. Caramalau, R., Bhattarai, B., Kim, T.K.: Sequential graph convolutional network for active learning. In: Proceedings of the IEEE/CVF Conference on Computer Vision and Pattern Recognition, pp. 9583–9592 (2021)
6. Caron, M., Misra, I., Mairal, J., Goyal, P., Bojanowski, P., Joulin, A.: Unsupervised learning of visual features by contrasting cluster assignments. arXiv preprint arXiv:2006.09882 (2020)
7. Chen, L.C., Papandreou, G., Kokkinos, I., Murphy, K., Yuille, A.L.: DeepLab: semantic image segmentation with deep convolutional nets, atrous convolution, and fully connected CRFs. IEEE Trans. Pattern Anal. Mach. Intell. **40**(4), 834–848 (2017)
8. Chen, T., Kornblith, S., Norouzi, M., Hinton, G.: A simple framework for contrastive learning of visual representations. In: International Conference on Machine Learning, pp. 1597–1607. PMLR (2020)
9. Chen, X., He, K.: Exploring simple Siamese representation learning. In: Proceedings of the IEEE/CVF Conference on Computer Vision and Pattern Recognition, pp. 15750–15758 (2021)
10. Cho, J.W., Kim, D.J., Jung, Y., Kweon, I.S.: MCDAL: maximum classifier discrepancy for active learning. In: IEEE Transactions on Neural Networks and Learning Systems (2022)
11. Cordts, M., et al.: The cityscapes dataset for semantic urban scene understanding. In: Proceedings of the IEEE Conference on Computer Vision and Pattern Recognition, pp. 3213–3223 (2016)

12. Deng, J., Dong, W., Socher, R., Li, L.J., Li, K., Fei-Fei, L.: ImageNet: a large-scale hierarchical image database. In: 2009 IEEE Conference on Computer Vision and Pattern Recognition, pp. 248–255. IEEE (2009)

13. Deng, J., Dong, W., Socher, R., Li, L.J., Li, K., Fei-Fei, L.: ImageNet: a large-scale hierarchical image database. In: 2009 IEEE Conference on Computer Vision and Pattern Recognition, pp. 248–255 (2009). https://doi.org/10.1109/CVPR.2009.5206848

14. Fei-Fei, L., Fergus, R., Perona, P.: Learning generative visual models from few training examples: an incremental Bayesian approach tested on 101 object categories. In: 2004 Conference on Computer Vision and Pattern Recognition Workshop, pp. 178–178. IEEE (2004)

15. Freund, Y., Seung, H.S., Shamir, E., Tishby, N.: Selective sampling using the query by committee algorithm. Mach. Learn. **28**(2), 133–168 (1997)

16. Gidaris, S., Singh, P., Komodakis, N.: Unsupervised representation learning by predicting image rotations. arXiv preprint arXiv:1803.07728 (2018)

17. Hacohen, G., Dekel, A., Weinshall, D.: Active learning on a budget: opposite strategies suit high and low budgets. arXiv preprint arXiv:2202.02794 (2022)

18. He, K., Fan, H., Wu, Y., Xie, S., Girshick, R.: Momentum contrast for unsupervised visual representation learning. In: Proceedings of the IEEE/CVF Conference on Computer Vision and Pattern Recognition, pp. 9729–9738 (2020)

19. He, K., Zhang, X., Ren, S., Sun, J.: Deep residual learning for image recognition. In: Proceedings of the IEEE conference on computer vision and pattern recognition, pp. 770–778 (2016)

20. Huang, S.J., Jin, R., Zhou, Z.H.: Active learning by querying informative and representative examples. In: Advances in Neural Information Processing Systems 23 (2010)

21. Joshi, A.J., Porikli, F., Papanikolopoulos, N.: Multi-class active learning for image classification. In: 2009 IEEE Conference on Computer Vision and Pattern Recognition, pp. 2372–2379. IEEE (2009)

22. Kapoor, A., Grauman, K., Urtasun, R., Darrell, T.: Active learning with Gaussian processes for object categorization. In: 2007 IEEE 11th International Conference on Computer Vision, pp. 1–8. IEEE (2007)

23. Kim, K., Park, D., Kim, K.I., Chun, S.Y.: Task-aware variational adversarial active learning. In: Proceedings of the IEEE/CVF Conference on Computer Vision and Pattern Recognition, pp. 8166–8175 (2021)

24. Krizhevsky, A., et al.: Learning multiple layers of features from tiny images (2009)

25. Lewis, D.D., Catlett, J.: Heterogeneous uncertainty sampling for supervised learning. In: Machine Learning Proceedings 1994, pp. 148–156. Elsevier (1994)

26. Lewis, D.D., Gale, W.A.: A sequential algorithm for training text classifiers. In: Croft, B.W., van Rijsbergen, C.J. (eds.) SIGIR 1994, pp. 3–12. Springer (1994). https://doi.org/10.1007/978-1-4471-2099-5_1

27. Lin, T.-Y., et al.: Microsoft COCO: common objects in context. In: Fleet, D., Pajdla, T., Schiele, B., Tuytelaars, T. (eds.) ECCV 2014. LNCS, vol. 8693, pp. 740–755. Springer, Cham (2014). https://doi.org/10.1007/978-3-319-10602-1_48

28. Liu, C., Dollár, P., He, K., Girshick, R., Yuille, A., Xie, S.: Are labels necessary for neural architecture search? In: Vedaldi, A., Bischof, H., Brox, T., Frahm, J.-M. (eds.) ECCV 2020. LNCS, vol. 12349, pp. 798–813. Springer, Cham (2020). https://doi.org/10.1007/978-3-030-58548-8_46

29. Liu, Z., Ding, H., Zhong, H., Li, W., Dai, J., He, C.: Influence selection for active learning. In: Proceedings of the IEEE/CVF International Conference on Computer Vision, pp. 9274–9283 (2021)

30. Long, J., Shelhamer, E., Darrell, T.: Fully convolutional networks for semantic segmentation. In: Proceedings of the IEEE Conference on Computer Vision and Pattern Recognition, pp. 3431–3440 (2015)
31. Van der Maaten, L., Hinton, G.: Visualizing data using t-SNE. J. Mach. Learn. Res. **9**(11), 2579–2605 (2008)
32. MacKay, D.J.: Information-based objective functions for active data selection. Neural Comput. **4**(4), 590–604 (1992)
33. McCallumzy, A.K., Nigamy, K.: Employing EM and pool-based active learning for text classification. In: Proceedings of the International Conference on Machine Learning (ICML), pp. 359–367. CiteSeer (1998)
34. Noroozi, M., Favaro, P.: Unsupervised learning of visual representations by solving jigsaw puzzles. In: Leibe, B., Matas, J., Sebe, N., Welling, M. (eds.) ECCV 2016. LNCS, vol. 9910, pp. 69–84. Springer, Cham (2016). https://doi.org/10.1007/978-3-319-46466-4_5
35. van den Oord, A., Li, Y., Vinyals, O.: Representation learning with contrastive predictive coding. arXiv preprint arXiv:1807.03748 (2018)
36. Pedersen, T., et al.: Wordnet: similarity-measuring the relatedness of concepts. In: AAAI, vol. 4, pp. 25–29 (2004)
37. Pourahmadi, K., Nooralinejad, P., Pirsiavash, H.: A simple baseline for low-budget active learning. arXiv preprint arXiv:2110.12033 (2021)
38. Sener, O., Savarese, S.: Active learning for convolutional neural networks: a core-set approach. arXiv preprint arXiv:1708.00489 (2017)
39. Settles, B.: Active learning literature survey (2009)
40. Shannon, C.E.: A mathematical theory of communication. Bell Syst. Tech. J. **27**(3), 379–423 (1948)
41. Sinha, S., Ebrahimi, S., Darrell, T.: Variational adversarial active learning. In: Proceedings of the IEEE/CVF International Conference on Computer Vision, pp. 5972–5981 (2019)
42. Spearman, C.: The proof and measurement of association between two things. (1961)
43. Tong, S., Koller, D.: Support vector machine active learning with applications to text classification. J. Mach. Learn. Res. **2**(1), 45–66 (2001)
44. Wu, X., Dyer, E., Neyshabur, B.: When do curricula work? arXiv preprint arXiv:2012.03107 (2020)
45. Yang, Y., Loog, M.: A variance maximization criterion for active learning. Pattern Recogn. **78**, 358–370 (2018)
46. Yoo, D., Kweon, I.S.: Learning loss for active learning. In: Proceedings of the IEEE/CVF Conference on Computer Vision and Pattern Recognition, pp. 93–102 (2019)
47. You, Y., Chen, T., Sui, Y., Chen, T., Wang, Z., Shen, Y.: Graph contrastive learning with augmentations. Adv. Neural. Inf. Process. Syst. **33**, 5812–5823 (2020)
48. Zhang, R., Isola, P., Efros, A.A.: Colorful image colorization. In: Leibe, B., Matas, J., Sebe, N., Welling, M. (eds.) ECCV 2016. LNCS, vol. 9907, pp. 649–666. Springer, Cham (2016). https://doi.org/10.1007/978-3-319-46487-9_40
49. Zhu, Y., Xu, W., Liu, Q., Wu, S.: When contrastive learning meets active learning: a novel graph active learning paradigm with self-supervision. arXiv preprint arXiv:2010.16091 (2020)

ParC-Net: Position Aware Circular Convolution with Merits from ConvNets and Transformer

Haokui Zhang[✉], Wenze Hu, and Xiaoyu Wang

Intellifusion, Shenzhen, China
hkzhang1991@mail.nwpu.edu.cn

Abstract. Recently, vision transformers started to show impressive results which outperform large convolution based models significantly. However, in the area of small models for mobile or resource constrained devices, ConvNet still has its own advantages in both performance and model complexity. We propose ParC-Net, a pure ConvNet based backbone model that further strengthens these advantages by fusing the merits of vision transformers into ConvNets. Specifically, we propose position aware circular convolution (ParC), a light-weight convolution op which boasts a global receptive field while producing location sensitive features as in local convolutions. We combine the ParCs and squeeze-excitation ops to form a meta-former like model block, which further has the attention mechanism like transformers. The aforementioned block can be used in plug-and-play manner to replace relevant blocks in ConvNets or transformers. Experiment results show that the proposed ParC-Net achieves better performance than popular light-weight ConvNets and vision transformer based models in common vision tasks and datasets, while having fewer parameters and faster inference speed. For classification on ImageNet-1k, ParC-Net achieves 78.6% top-1 accuracy with about 5.0 million parameters, saving 11% parameters and 13% computational cost but gaining 0.2% higher accuracy and 23% faster inference speed (on ARM based Rockchip RK3288) compared with MobileViT, and uses only 0.5× parameters but gaining 2.7% accuracy compared with DeIT. On MS-COCO object detection and PASCAL VOC segmentation tasks, ParC-Net also shows better performance. Source code is available at https://github.com/hkzhang91/ParC-Net.

Keywords: Light-weight · Edge devices · Pure ConvNet · Vision transformer

Supplementary Information The online version contains supplementary material available at https://doi.org/10.1007/978-3-031-19809-0_35.

S. Avidan et al. (Eds.): ECCV 2022, LNCS 13686, pp. 613–630, 2022.
https://doi.org/10.1007/978-3-031-19809-0_35

1   Introduction

Recently, various vision transformers (ViTs) models have achieved remarkable results in many vision tasks, forming strong alternatives to convolutional neural networks (ConvNets) [5,21,33].

However, we believe both ViTs and ConvNets are indispensable for the following reasons: 1) From application perspective, both ViTs and ConvNets have their advantages and disadvantages. ViT models generally have better performance but usually suffer from high computational cost and are difficult to train [33]. Compared with ViTs, ConvNets may show inferior performance, but they still have some unique advantages. For instance, ConvNets have better hardware support and are easy to train. In addition, as is summarized in [9] and our experiments, ConvNets still dominate in the area of small models for mobile or edge devices. 2) From the information processing perspective, both ViTs and ConvNets have unique features. ViTs are good at extracting global information and use attention mechanism to extract information from different locations driven by input data [3,25]. ConvNets focus on modeling local relationships and have strong prior by inductive bias [4]. The above analysis naturally raise a question: *can we learn from ViTs to improve ConvNets for mobile or edge computing applications?*.

In this paper, we aim to design new light-weight pure ConvNets that further enhance its strength in the area of mobile and edge computing friendly models.

Pure convolution is more mobile friendly because convolutions are highly optimized by existing tool chains that are widely used to deploy model into these resource constrained devices. Even more, because of the huge popularity of ConvNets in the past few years, some existing neural network accelerators are designed mainly around convolution style operations, and the complex non-linear operations such as softmax and data bus bandwidth demanding large matrix multiplications are not efficiently supported. These hardware and software constraints make a pure convolutional light-weight model more preferable even if a ViT based model is equally competitive in other aspects.

To design such a ConvNet, we compare ConvNets with ViTs and summarize three main differences between them: 1) ViTs are good at extracting global features [3,4,25]; 2) ViTs adopt Meta-former block [40]; 3) Information aggregations in ViTs are data driven (data dependent dynamic computation). Corresponding to these three points, we design our ParC block. 1) We propose the position aware circular convolution (ParC) to extract global features; 2) Based on the proposed ParC, we build a pure ConvNet Meta-former block as the basic outer structure; 3) We add channel wise attention module to the feature forward network (FFN) part of meta-former, which makes our proposed ParC block adapt kernel weights according inputs. Finally, inspired by CoatNet [4] and Mobile-ViT [25], we use a bifurcate structure (Sect. 3.2) as the outer frame to build a complete network ParC-Net.

Experiment results show that the proposed ParC-Net achieves solid performance on three popular vision tasks, including image classification, object detection and semantic segmentation. Taking experiment results of image classification as an example, ParC-Net achieves 78.6% top-1 accuracy with about 5.0 million parameters, saving 11% parameters and 13% computational cost but gaining 0.2% higher accuracy and 23% faster inference speed (on Rockchip RK3288) compared with MobileViT [25]. For experiments of object detection and semantic segmentation, compared with other light-weight models, the proposed ParC-Net achieves higher mAP and mIOU, while having fewer parameters.

Our main contributions are summarized as follows:

- To overcome the restriction that traditional convolutions have limited perception fields, we propose position aware circular convolution (ParC), where base-instance kernel and position embedding strategies are used to handle input size variations and inject location information to output feature maps respectively. We jointly use the proposed ParC and conventional convolution operations to extract local-global features, which brings higher accuracy.
- We propose ParC-Net, a pure ConvNet for mobile and edge computing applications. The proposed ParC-Net inherits advantages of ConvNets and ViTs. To our knowledge, this is the first attempt that combines strengths of ConvNets and ViTs to design a light-weight ConvNet.
- We apply the proposed ParC-Net on three vision tasks. Compared with the baseline model, the proposed ParC-Net achieves better performance on all three tasks, while having fewer parameters, lower computational cost and higher inference speed.

2   Related Work

2.1   Vision Transformers

Vaswani et al. firstly proposed transformer [34] for natural language processing (NLP) tasks. Compared with recurrent neural network (RNN) models, transformer has much higher computational efficiency and it is good at capturing relationship from any pair of elements in the input sequence. As a result, transformers replaced RNNs and dominate the NLP field.

In 2020, Dosovitskiy et al. introduced transformer into vision tasks and proposed vision transformer (ViT) [5], where each image is cropped into a sequence of patches to meet the input requirement of transformer and PE is adopted to ensure the model is sensitive to position information of the input patches. With pre-training on huge datasets such as JFT-300M [29], ViT achieves impressive performance on various vision tasks. However, the original ViT model has some restrictions, for instance, it is heavy-weight, having low computational efficiency and hard to train. Subsequent variants of ViTs are proposed to overcome these problems. From the point of improving training strategy, Touvron et al. [33] proposed to use knowledge distillation to train ViT models, and achieved competitive accuracy with less pre-training data. To further improve the model architecture, some researchers attempted to optimize ViTs by learning from ConvNets. Among them, PVT [35] and CVT [37] insert convolutional operations into each stage of ViT model to reduce the number of tokens, and build hierarchical multi-stage structures. Swin transformer [21] computes self attention within shifted local windows. PiT [11] jointly use pooling layer and depth wise convolution layer to achieve channel multiplication and spatial reduction. CCNet [15] propose a simplified version of self attention mechanism criss-cross attention and inserted it into ConvNet to build ConvNet which has global receptive field. These papers clearly show that some techniques of ConvNets can be applied on vision transformers to design better vision transformer models.

2.2 Hybrid Structures Combining ConvNet and Vision Transformers

Another popular line of research is combining elements of ViTs and ConvNets to design new backbones. Graham et al. mixed ConvNet and transformer in their LeVit model, which significantly outperforms previous ConvNet and ViT models with respect to the speed/accuracy tradeoff [8]. BoTNet [28] replaces the standard convolution with multi-head attention in the last several blocks of ResNet. ViT-C [38] adds early convolutional stem to vanilla ViT. ConViT [6] incorporates soft convolutional inductive biases via a gated positional self-attention. The CMT [9] block consists of depth wise convolution based local perception unit and a light-weight transformer module. CoatNet [4] merges convolution and self-attention to design a new transformer module, which focuses on both local and global information. After comprehensive comparison, we find that these hybrid models simultaneously employed similar structure, that is using convolutional stem to extract local features in the beginning stages and transformer style models later to extract global or local-global features. We choose a similar structure when designing our pure convolutional model.

2.3 Light-Weight ConvNets and ViTs

Since 2017, light-weight ConvNets attract much attentions as more and more applications needs to run ConvNet models on mobile devices. Now, there are a lot of light-weight ConvNets, such as ShuffleNets [24,24], MobileNets [12,13,27], MicroNet [18], GhostNet [10], EfficientNet [32], TinyNet [2] and MnasNet [31]. Compared with standard ConvNets, light-weight ConvNets have fewer parameters, lower computational cost and faster inference speed. In addition, light-weight ConvNets can be applied on a wide range of devices. Despite these benefits, these light-weight models have inferior performance compared with heavy-weight models. Very recently, following the research line of combining strengths of ConvNet and ViT, some researcher attempted to build light-weight hybrid models for mobile vision tasks. Mobile-Former presents a parallel design of MobileNet and transformer, which leverages the advantages of MobileNet at extracting local features and transformer at capturing global information [3]. Mehta and Rastegari proposed MobileViT, where the upper stages of MobileNetv2 [27] are replaced with MobileViT block [25]. In MobileViT block, local representations extracted by convolution and global representations are concatenated to generate local-global representations.

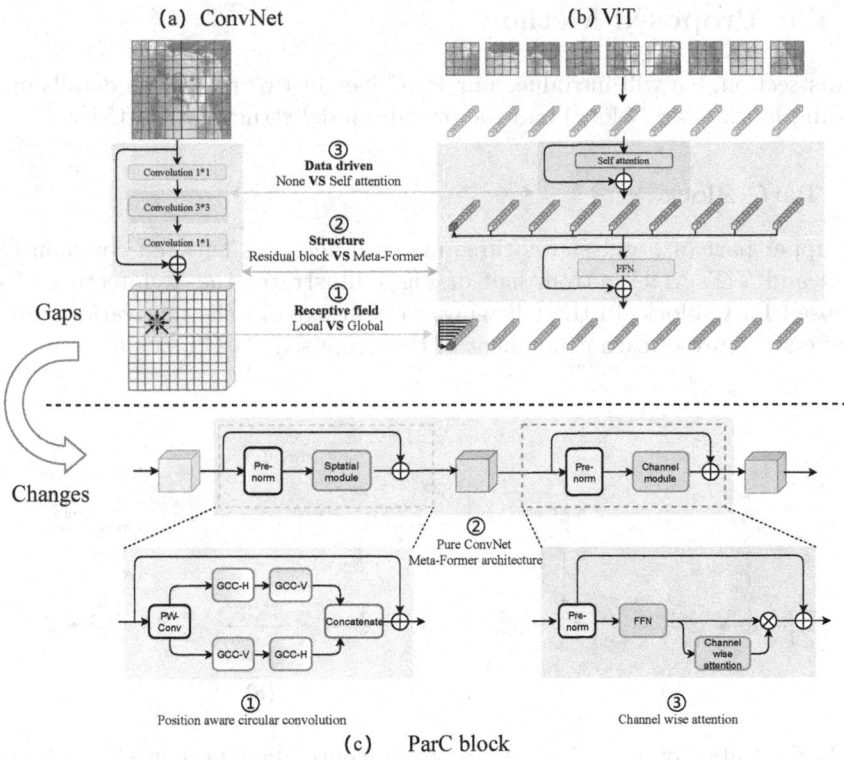

Fig. 1. ParC block. (a) A residual block that is widely used in ConvNets; (b) A ViT block; (c) An ParC block

In terms of purpose, our proposed ParC-Net is related to Mobile-Former and MobileViT. Different from these two models which still keep transformer blocks, our proposed ParC-Net is pure ConvNet, which makes our proposed ParC-Net more mobile friendly. Our experiments of deploying models on low power platform confirm this point. In terms of designing a pure ConvNet via learning from ViTs, our work is most closely related to a parallel work ConvNext [22]. The two major differences are: 1) Ideas and architectures are different. The ConvNext modernizes a standard ResNet toward the design of a vision transformer by introducing a series (more than ten) of incremented but effective designs. Our proposed ParC-Net starts from three main differences between ConvNets and ViTs and fills the gaps from macro level. As the ideas are different, the corresponding structures are also different; 2) They are proposed for different purposes. Our ParC-Net is proposed for mobile devices. Compared with ConvNext, the proposed ParC-Net shows advantages when constraining models as light-weight models.

3   The Proposed Method

In this section, we will introduce our ParC-Net in two parts, the details of the building block (ParC block) and the overall model structure (ParC-Net).

3.1   ParC Block

The upper part of Fig. 1 shows three major differences between common ConvNets and ViTs. The bottom half of Fig. 1 illustrates the architecture of our proposed ParC block. In the following, we will explain the motivation and the specific structure of each component of the proposed ParC block.

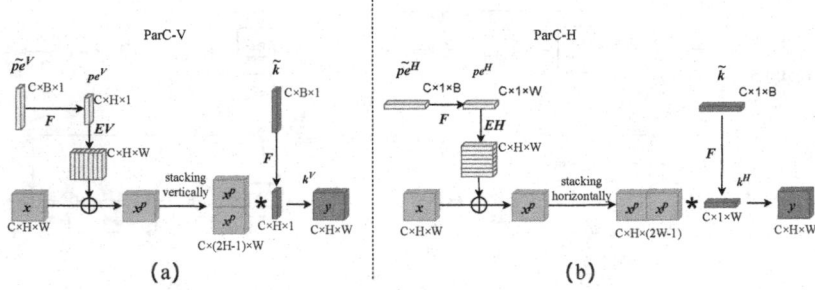

Fig. 2. Illustration of the position aware circular convolution. (a) ParC-V; (b) ParC-H. F, EV and EH are explained in Eqs. 1 and 2

Extracting Global Features with ParC. In ConvNets, feature is calculated as $y_i = \sum_{j \in \mathcal{L}(i)} w_{i-j} x_j$, where x_i, y_i are the input and output at position i respectively, and $\mathcal{L}(i)$ denotes a local neighborhood of i. In ViTs, self-attention modules extracts features based on formula $y_i = \sum_{j \in \mathcal{G}} \frac{e^{(x_i^T x_j)}}{\sum_{k \in \mathcal{G}} e^{(x_i^T x_k)}} x_j$, where $\mathcal{G}$ means the global spatial space. Comparing these two formulas, we can see that self attention learns global features from the entire spatial locations but convolution gathers information from a local receptive field.

To overcome this issue, we propose the position aware circular convolution (ParC). As shown in Fig. 2, our proposed ParC has two types, one is ParC of vertical direction (ParC-V) and the other one is ParC of horizontal direction (ParC-H). The receptive field of the ParC-V and ParC-H covers all pixel in the same column and the same row, respectively. Jointly using ParC-V and ParC-H can extract global features from all input pixels. For notational simplicity, we assume the input x has only one channel and the corresponding shape is $1 \times h \times w$.

The output of ParC-V at location (i, j) is computed with:

$$
\begin{aligned}
pe^V &= F(\widetilde{pe}^V) = [pe_0^V, pe_1^V, \cdots, pe_{h-1}^V]^T \\
pe_e^V &= EV(pe^V, w) \\
k^V &= F(\widetilde{k}) = [k_0^V, k_1^V, \cdots, k_{h-1}^V] \\
x^p &= x + pe_e^V \\
y_{i,j} &= \sum_{t \in (0, h-1)} k_t^V x_{((i+t)\bmod h, j)}^p
\end{aligned}
\tag{1}
$$

where, pe^V is instance position embedding (PE) and it is generated from a base embedding $\widetilde{pe}^V$ via bilinear interpolation function $F()$. Here $F()$ is used to adapt the size of position embedding to the size of input features. pe_e^V is expanded PE. k^V is instance kernel. $EV()$ is an expand function of vertical direction. After copying the input vector w times, $EV()$ concatenates these copied vectors along horizontal direction to generate a $h \times w$-sized PE matrix. Similarly, the output of ParC-H at location (i, j) can be expressed as:

$$
\begin{aligned}
x^p &= x + pe_e^H \\
y_{i,j} &= \sum_{t \in (0, w-1)} k_t^H x_{(i, (j+t)\bmod w)}^p
\end{aligned}
\tag{2}
$$

where $pe_e^H = EH(pe^H, h)$ and $EH()$ is an expand function. $EH()$ expands input vector along the vertical direction. Implementing the ParC in modern deep learning libraries is straightforward. Taking the most complicated part $y_{i,j} = \sum_{t \in (0, w-1)} k_t^H x_{(i, (j+t)\bmod w)}^p$ as an example, it can be implemented with one line of code: $y = F.conv2D(torch.cat(x^p, x^p, dim = 3), k^H)$. Figure 3 illustrates the computational process in the case that the input is an one dimensional vector. From Fig. 3, we can see that ParC-H perform convolutions along a circle generated by connecting the start and the end of the input. So, we name the proposed convolution as the circular convolution. The proposed ParC introduces three modifications:

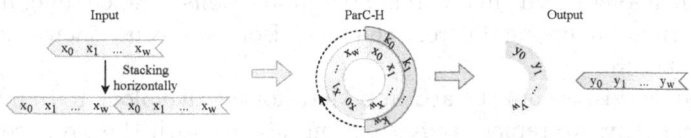

Fig. 3. Illustration of global circular convolution on horizontal direction.

– The receptive field is increased to global spatial space. Note that, increasing
  the kernel size of tradition local convolution to full input size does not extract
  global features. In local convolution, zero padding is usually used to keep the
  size of convolutional feature the same with that of the input. Even if we
  increase the kernel size to global size, the global kernel only covers part pixels
  coming from input. Especially for extracting feature in edge portion, only
  about half of pixels that covered by global kernel are from input actual input,
  while others are simply zeros.
– The PE is used to keep the output feature sensitive to spatial location. Circular convolution can extract global features, but it disturbed the spatial
  structure of the original input. For classification, keeping spatial structure
  may not be a big issue. But, as is shown in ablation study, for location sensitive tasks such as segmentation and detection, keeping spatial structure does
  matter. Here, following the design in ViTs, we introduce PE to keep spatial
  structure. Experiment results in ablation study show that PE is useful in
  segmentation and detection tasks
– The kernel and PE are dynamically generated according to the input size.
  In ParC, the sizes of kernels and PE codes must be consistent with that of
  instance inputs. To handle the case that inputs have different spatial resolution, we generate instance kernels and PE codes via interpolation functions.

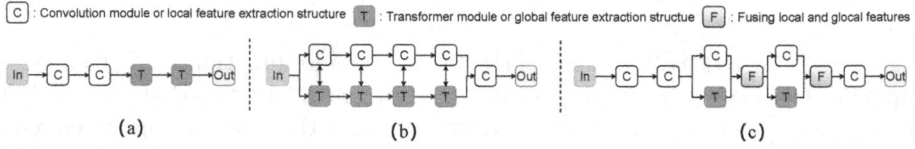

(a)   (b)   (c)

Fig. 4. Three main hybrid structures. (a) serial structure; (b) parallel structure; (c)
bifurcate structure

Designing ParC block with ParC. From ConvNets to ViTs, a considerable
modification is meta-former block replaced residual block (the blue two-way
arrow). A Meta-former block generally consists of a sequence of two components: a token mixer and a channel mixer. The token mixer is for exchanging
information among tokens in different spatial locations. The channel mixer is for
mixing information among different channels. Both two components use residual
learning structure.

Inspired by this, we insert ParC into Meta-former like block to build our ParC
block. Specifically, we replace self-attention module with the proposed ParC to
build an new spatial module to replace token mixer part. Here, we do this for
two main reasons: 1) ParC can extract global features and interacts information
among pixels from global space, which meets the requirement of token mixer
module; 2) the computation complexity of self attention module is quadratic.
Replacing this part with ParC can reduce computational cost significantly, which
is helps achieving our goal of designing a light-weight ConvNet. Based on the
proposed ParC, we build a pure ConvNet meta-former like block.

Adding Channel Wise Attention in Channel Mixer Part.
In ViTs, self attention module can adapt weights according input, which makes ViTs data driven models. By adopting attention mechanism, data driven models can focus on important features and suppress unnecessary ones, which brings better performance. Previous literature [14,16,36] already explained the importance of keep model data driven.

By replacing the self-attention with the proposed global circular convolution, we get a pure ConvNet which can extract global features. But the replaced model is no longer a data driven model. To compensate, we insert channel wise attention module into channel mixer part, as shown in Fig. 1(c). Following SENet [14], we first aggregate spatial information of input features $x \in \mathbb{R}^{c \times h \times w}$ via global average pooling and get aggregated feature $x_a \in \mathbb{R}^{c \times 1 \times 1}$; Then we feed x_a into a multi-layer perceptron to generate channel wise weight $a \in \mathbb{R}^{c \times 1 \times 1}$. The a is multiplied with x channel wise to generate the final output.

3.2 ParC-Net

In Sect. 3.1, we have presented the ParC block, which is a basic block and can be inserted into most of the current existing models. In this section, we select an outer frame for it and build the complete network ParC-Net.

Currently, as shown in Fig. 4, existing hybrid structures can be basically divided into three main structures, including serial structure (Fig. 4(a)) [8,38], parallel structure (Fig. 4(b)) [3] and bifurcate structure (Fig. 4(c)) [4,25]. Among all three structures, the third one achieves best performance for now. At present, bifurcate model CoatNet [4] achieves the highest classification accuracy on Imagenet-1k. Mobile device aimed model MobileViT [25] also adopts the third structure.

Inspired by this, we adopt bifurcate structure as our outer frame and build our final outer frame based on MobileViT. Specifically, taking the outer frame adopted in MobileViT as baseline, we further make some improvements:

- MobileViT consists of two major types of modules. Shallow stages consist of MobileNetV2 blocks, which have local receptive field. Deep stages are made up of ViT blocks, which enjoy global receptive field. We keep all MobileNetV2 blocks and replacing ViT blocks with corresponding ParC blocks. This replacement converts the model from hybrid structure to pure ConvNet.
- We appropriately increase the widths of ParC blocks. Even so, the replaced model still has fewer parameters and less computational cost.
- As show in Fig. 4(c), the bifurcate structure contains some interaction modules, which are in charge of interacting information between local and global feature modules. In the original MobileViT, ViT blocks are the most heavy modules. After replacing ViT blocks with ParC blocks, the cost of these interaction modules becomes prominent. So, we introduce group convolution and point wise convolution into these modules, which decreases number of parameters without hurting performance.

4   Experiment Results

In experiments, we show the overall advantages of the proposed ParC-Net on three typical vision tasks, and then conduct detailed study to show the value of our design choices, the model scaling characteristics, and its speed advantage on low power devices.

4.1   Image Classification

We conduct image classification experiments on ImageNet-1k, the most widely used benchmark dataset for this task. We train the proposed ParC-Net models on the training set of ImageNet-1K, and report top-1 accuracy on the validation set.

Training Setting. As we adopt MobileViT like structure as our outer framework, we train our model using a very similar training strategy as well. To be specific, we train each model for 300 epochs on 8 V100 or A100 GPUs with AdamW optimizer [23], where the maximum learning rate, minimum learning rate, weight decay and batchsize are set to 0.004, 0.0004, 0.025 and 1024 respectively. Optimizer momentum β_1 and β_2 of the AdamW optimizer are set to 0.9 and 0.999 respectively. We use the first 3000 iterations as warm up stage. We adjust learning rate following the cosine schedule. For data augmentation, we use random cropping, horizontal flipping and multi-scale sampler. We use label smoothing [30] to regularize the networks and set smoothing factor to 0.1. We use Exponential Moving Average (EMA) [26]. More details of the training settings and *link to source code will be provided in supplementary materials.*

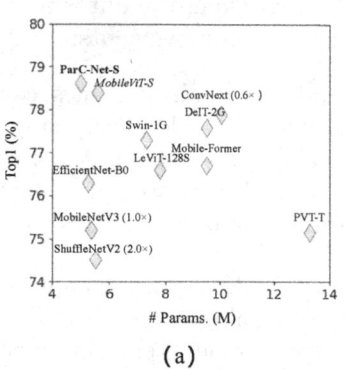

(a)

Frameworks	Models	Date	# params (M)	Top1(%)
Pre-ConvNets	ShuffleNetV2 (2.0×)	ECCV 2018	5.5	74.5
	MobileNetV3 (1.0×)	ICCV 2019	5.4	75.2
	EfficientNet-B0	ICML 2019	5.3	76.3
	DenseNet-169	CVPR 2017	14.0	76.2
	ResNet-101-SE	CVPR 2018	49.3	77.6
ViTs	PVT-T	ICCV 2021	13.2	75.1
	T2T-ViT-12	ICCV 2021	6.9	76.5
	T2T-T	ICCV 2021	6.9	76.5
	Swin-1G	ICCV 2021	7.3	77.3
	DeIT-2G	ICML 2021	9.5	77.6
Hybrid structures (ConvNet+ViT)	ConViT-T	ICML 2021	6.0	73.1
	ViTC	NeurIPS 2021	4.6	75.3
	CoaT-Lite-T	ICCV 2021	5.7	76.6
	LeViT-128S	ICCV 2021	7.8	76.6
	Mobile-Former	CVPR 2022	9.4	76.7
Post-ConvNets	MobileViT-S (baseline)	ICLR 2022	5.6	78.4
	ConvNext-T (0.5 ×)*	CVPR 2022	7.4	77.5
	ParC-Net-S (Ours)	-	5.0	**78.6**

(b)

Fig. 5. Classification experiment results on ImageNet-1K. (a) Accuracy vs model size. Here we only keep part of comparison models for clarity. (b) Comparison of results on image classification. * indicates our implementation. Pre-ConvNets indicate classical ConvNets appeared before ViTs. Post-ConvNets denote ConvNets which integrate merits of ViTs but still keep pure ConvNet structures.

Comparison Results. The experiment results of image classification are listed in Fig. 5. Figure 5 (a) shows that ParC-Net-S and MobileViT-S beat other model by a clear margin. Figure 5 (b) shows comparison with more models. The proposed ParC-Net-S achieves highest classification accuracy, and have fewer parameters than most models. Compared with the second best model MobileViT-S, our ParC-Net-S decreases the number of parameters by 11% and increases the top 1 accuracy by 0.2% points.

Light-Weight Models. Table 1 shows comparison results among light-weight models, which confirms our ideas and answers the question proposed in introduction.

Firstly, comparing results of light-weight ConvNets with that of ViTs, light-weight ConvNets show much better performance.

Secondly, comparing the popular ConvNets before ViT appears (pre-ConvNets), ViTs and hybrid structures, hybrid structures achieve the best performance. Therefore improving ConvNets by learning from the merits of ViT is feasible.

Finally, the proposed ParC-Net achieves the best performance among all comparison models. So indeed by learning from ViT design, performance of pure light-weight ConvNets can be improved significantly.

Table 1. Comparisons of light-weight models on ImageNet-1K classification

Frameworks	Models	Date	# params (M)	Top1(%)
Pre-CNNs	ShuffleNetV2(2.0×)	ECCV 2018	5.5	74.5
	MobileNetV3(1.0×)	ICCV 2019	5.4	75.2
	EfficientNet-B0	ICML 2019	5.3	76.3
ViTs	T2T-ViT-7	ICCV 2021	4.3	71.7
	DeiT-T	ICML 2021	5.7	72.2
Hybrid structures	ViT-C	NeurIPS 2021	4.6	75.3
	CoaT-Lite-T	ICCV 2021	5.7	76.6
	MobileViT-S	ICLR 2022	5.6	78.4
Post-CNN	ParC-Net-S	–	5.0	78.6

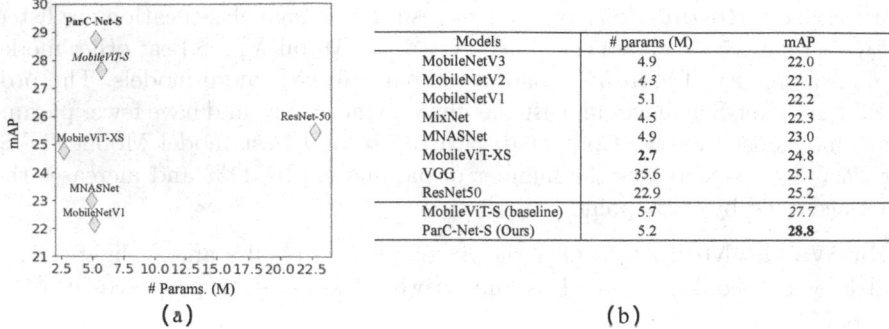

(a)

Models	# params (M)	mAP
MobileNetV3	4.9	22.0
MobileNetV2	4.3	22.1
MobileNetV1	5.1	22.2
MixNet	4.5	22.3
MNASNet	4.9	23.0
MobileViT-XS	2.7	24.8
VGG	35.6	25.1
ResNet50	22.9	25.2
MobileViT-S (baseline)	5.7	27.7
ParC-Net-S (Ours)	5.2	28.8

(b)

Fig. 6. Object detection results on MS-COCO. (a) mAP vs model size. (b) Comparison results

4.2   Object Detection

We use MS-COCO [19] datasets and its evaluation protocol for object detection experiments. Following [25, 27], we take single shot object detection (SSD) [20] as the detection framework and use separable convolution to replace the standard convolutions in the detection head.

Experiment Setting. Taking models pretrained on ImageNet-1K as backbone, we finetune detection models on training set of MS-COCO with AdamW optimizer for 200 epochs. Batchsize and weight decay are set to 128 and 0.01. We use the first 500 iterations as warm up stage, where the learning rate is increased from 0.000001 to 0.0009. Both label smoothing and EMA are used during training.

Comparison Results. Figure 6 lists the corresponding results. Similar to results in image classification, MobileViT-S and ParC-Net-S achieve the second best and the best in terms of mAP. Compared with the second best model, ParC-Net-S shows advantages in both model size and detection accuracy (Table 2).

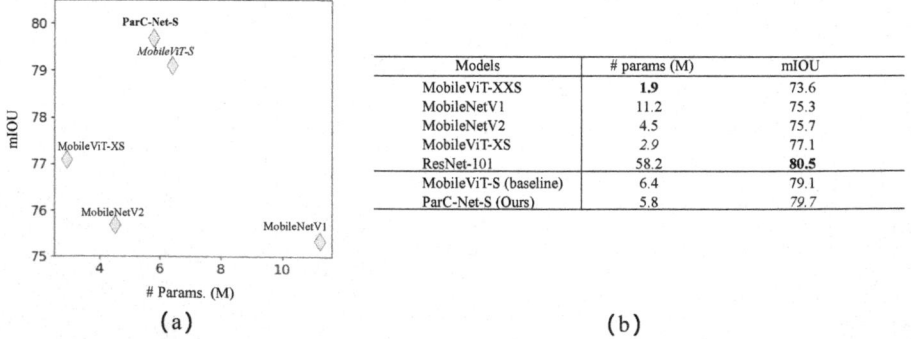

(a)

Models	# params (M)	mIOU
MobileViT-XXS	1.9	73.6
MobileNetV1	11.2	75.3
MobileNetV2	4.5	75.7
MobileViT-XS	2.9	77.1
ResNet-101	58.2	80.5
MobileViT-S (baseline)	6.4	79.1
ParC-Net-S (Ours)	5.8	79.7

(b)

Fig. 7. Semantic segmentation experiments on PASCAL VOC. (a) mIOU vs model size.(b) Comparison results with more models.

Table 2. Ablation study. BK, MF, CA and PE denote big kernel, meta-former architecture, channel wise attention and position embedding. BK 1/4 and BK 1/2 means the kernel size is set to 1/4 and 1/2 of the input features, respectively.

Row	Task	Kernel	MF	CA	PE	# params (M)	Top1/mAP/mIOU
1	Classification	Baseline	–	–	–	5.6	78.35
2	Classification	BK 1/4	Y	Y	N	5.0	78.46
3	Classification	BK 1/2	Y	Y	N	5.0	78.45
4	Classification	ParC	N	Y	Y	5.3	76.00
5	Classification	ParC	Y	N	Y	5.0	78.50
6	Classification	ParC	Y	Y	N	5.0	78.63
7	Classification	ParC	Y	Y	Y	5.0	78.63
8	Detection	Baseline	–	–	–	5.7	27.7
9	Detection	ParC	Y	Y	N	5.2	27.5
10	Detection	ParC	Y	Y	Y	5.2	28.5
11	Segmentation	Baseline	–	–	–	6.4	79.1
12	Segmentation	ParC	Y	Y	N	5.8	79.2
13	Segmentation	ParC	Y	Y	Y	5.8	79.7

4.3 Semantic Segmentation

Experiment Settings. DeepLabV3 is adopted as the semantic segmentation framework. We fine tune segmentation models on training set of PASCAL VOC [7] and COCO dataset, then evaluate trained models on validation set of PASCAL VOC using mean intersection over union (mIOU) and report the final results for comparison. We fine tune each model for 50 epochs with AdamW. Readers may refer to more details about training settings in supplementary materials.

Comparison Results. Results are summarized in Fig. 7. We can see that MobileViT-S and ParC-Net-S have the best trade-off between model scale and mIOU. Compared with ResNet-101, MobileViT-S and ParC-Net-S achieve competitive mIOU, while having much fewer parameters.

4.4 Ablation Study

Using the MobileViT as a baseline model, we further conduct ablation analysis on three components proposed in our ParC-Net.

- **Position aware circular convolution.** The proposed ParC has two major characteristics: 1) Circular convolution brings global receptive field; 2) PE keeps spatial structure information. Experiment results confirm that both characteristics are important. 1) Results in rows 1–3 show that, using big kernel can also improve accuracy, but the benefit of it reaches a saturation point when kernel size reaches a certain level. This results are consistent with the statement claimed in [22]. Using ParC can further improve accuracy, as shown in rows 2–3 and 6–7. 2) Introducing PE to ParC is necessary. As we explained in Sect. 3.1, using circular convolution alone can indeed capture global features but it disturbs the original spatial structures. For classification task, PE has no impact (rows 6 and 7). However, for detection and segmentation tasks which are sensitive to spatial location, abandoning PE hurts performances (rows 9–10 and 12–13).

- **Meta-former architecture.** In experiments of abandoning Meta-former architecture, we integrate ParC with the ResNeXt block [39] to replace Meta-former architecture. By comparing row 4 and 7, we can see that using the proposed pure ConvNet meta-former architecture is useful.
- **Channel wise attention.** Results in rows 5 and 7 show that using channel wise attention can improves performance. Compared with ParC, channel wise attention brings less benefit.

In summary, all three components are useful. Connecting them as a whole achieves the best performance.

4.5 Inference Speed on Low Power Devices

In this section, we conduct experiments to verify two points: 1) as we mentioned in introduction, the ParC-Net is proposed for edge computing devices. To verify whether the proposed ParC-Net meets our requirements, we deploy the proposed ParC-Net on a widely used low power chip Rockchip RK3288 and an in house low power neural network processor DP2000, compare it with baseline. We use

Table 3. Applying ParC-Net designs on different backbones. CPU used here is Xeon E5-2680 v4. DP2000 is the code name of a in house unpublished low power neural network processor that highly optimizes the convolutions. *denotes the models are trained under convnext hyperparameters settings, which may not be the optimal. W means network width. Latency is measured with batch size 1.

Row	Models	# param	FLOPs	Devices	Speed (ms)	Top1 (%)
1	MobileViT-S	5.6M	4.0G	RK3288	457	78.4
2	ParC-Net-S	5.0M	3.5G	RK3288	353	78.6
3	MobileViT-S	5.6M	4.0G	DP2000	368	78.4
4	ParC-Net-S	5.0M	3.5G	DP2000	98	78.6
5	ResNet50*	26 M	4.1G	CPU	98	78.8
6	ParC-ResNet50*	24 M	4.0G	CPU	98	79.6
7	MobileNetV2*	3.5M	0.6G	CPU	24	70.2
8	ParC-MobileNetV2*	3.5M	0.6G	CPU	27	71.1
9	ConvNext-T$(0.5 \times W)$*	7.4M	1.1G	CPU	47	77.5
10	ParC-ConvNext-T$(0.5 \times W)$*	7.4M	1.1G	CPU	48	78.3

ONNX [1] and MNN [17] to port these models to chips and time each model for 100 iterations to measure the average inference speed; 2) The proposed ParC block is an plug-and-play block, it can be inserted into other models. We replaced convolutions in the last few blocks of typical CNNs with our proposed ParC (with PE and kernel generation etc.) Comparison results are listed in Table 3.

As shown in rows 1–4 of Table 3, compared with baseline, ParC-Net is 23% faster on Rockchip RK3288 and 3.77× faster On DP2000. Besides less FLOPs operations, we believe this speed improvement is also brought by two factors: 1) Convolutions are highly optimized by existing tool chains that are widely used to deploy models into these resource constrained devices; 2) Compared with convolutions, transformers are more data bandwidth demanding as computing the attention map involves two large matrices K and Q, whereas in convolutions the kernel is a rather small matrix compared with the input feature map. In case the bandwith requirement exceeds that of the chip design, the CPU will be left idle waiting for data, resulting in lower CPU utilization and overall slower inference speed;

Results in rows 3–10 show that our ParC-Net universally improves performances of typical light weight models. MobileViT-S has much higher FLOPs but achieves good trade-off between model size and accuracy, which excels in its own application purpose. By applying our ParC-Net designs on MobileViT-S, ParC-Net-S achieves better balance between model size, FLOPs and accuracy. Results on ResNet50, MobileNetV2 and ConvNext-T shows that models which focus on optimizing FLOPs-accuracy trade-offs can also benefit from ParC-Net designs.

5 Conclusion

In this paper, for edge computing devices, we present ParC-Net, a pure ConvNet, which inherits advantages of ConvNet and integrated structure characteristics of ViT. To evaluate the performances, we apply the proposed model on three popular vision tasks, image classification, object detection and semantic segmentation. The proposed model achieves better performance on all three tasks, while having fewer parameters compared with other ConvNet, ViT and hybrid models. Experimental results on low power devices Rockchip RK3288 and our in house processor DP2000 show that the proposed ParC-Net does inherit ConvNets and it is well supported by edge computing devices.

References

1. Bai, J., Lu, F., Zhang, K., et al.: ONNX: open neural network exchange (2019). https://github.com/onnx/onnx
2. Chen, G., Wang, Y., Li, H., Dong, W.: TinyNet: a lightweight, modular, and unified network architecture for the Internet of Things. In: Proceedings of the ACM SIGCOMM 2019 Conference Posters and Demos, pp. 9–11 (2019)

3. Chen, Y., et al.: Mobile-former: bridging MobileNet and transformer. In: Proceedings of the IEEE/CVF Conference on Computer Vision and Pattern Recognition, pp. 5270–5279 (2022)
4. Dai, Z., Liu, H., Le, Q., Tan, M.: CoAtNet: marrying convolution and attention for all data sizes. In: Advances in Neural Information Processing Systems 34 (2021)
5. Dosovitskiy, A., et al.: An image is worth 16×16 words: transformers for image recognition at scale. arXiv preprint arXiv:2010.11929 (2020)
6. d'Ascoli, S., Touvron, H., Leavitt, M.L., Morcos, A.S., Biroli, G., Sagun, L.: ConViT: improving vision transformers with soft convolutional inductive biases. In: International Conference on Machine Learning, pp. 2286–2296. PMLR (2021)
7. Everingham, M., Eslami, S., Gool, L.V., Williams, C., Winn, J., Zisserman, A.: The pascal visual object classes challenge: a retrospective. Int. J. Comput. Vis. 111(1), 98–136 (2015)
8. Graham, B., et al.: LeViT: a vision transformer in ConvNet's clothing for faster inference. In: Proceedings of the IEEE/CVF International Conference on Computer Vision, pp. 12259–12269 (2021)
9. Guo, J., et al.: CMT: convolutional neural networks meet vision transformers. arXiv preprint arXiv:2107.06263 (2021)
10. Han, K., Wang, Y., Tian, Q., Guo, J., Xu, C., Xu, C.: GhostNet: more features from cheap operations. In: Proceedings of the IEEE/CVF Conference on Computer Vision and Pattern Recognition, pp. 1580–1589 (2020)
11. Heo, B., Yun, S., Han, D., Chun, S., Choe, J., Oh, S.J.: Rethinking spatial dimensions of vision transformers. In: Proceedings of the IEEE/CVF International Conference on Computer Vision, pp. 11936–11945 (2021)
12. Howard, A., et al.: Searching for MobileNetV3. In: Proceedings of the IEEE/CVF International Conference on Computer Vision, pp. 1314–1324 (2019)
13. Howard, A.G., et al.: MobileNets: efficient convolutional neural networks for mobile vision applications. arXiv preprint arXiv:1704.04861 (2017)
14. Hu, J., Shen, L., Sun, G.: Squeeze-and-excitation networks. In: Proceedings of the IEEE Conference on Computer Vision and Pattern Recognition, pp. 7132–7141 (2018)
15. Huang, Z., Wang, X., Huang, L., Huang, C., Wei, Y., Liu, W.: CCNet: criss-cross attention for semantic segmentation. In: Proceedings of the IEEE/CVF International Conference on Computer Vision, pp. 603–612 (2019)
16. Jaderberg, M., Simonyan, K., Zisserman, A., et al.: Spatial transformer networks. In: Advances in Neural Information Processing Systems 28 (2015)
17. Jiang, X., et al.: MNN: a universal and efficient inference engine. In: Proceedings of Machine Learning and Systems, vol. 2, pp. 1–13 (2020)
18. Li, Y., et al.: MicroNet: improving image recognition with extremely low flops. In: Proceedings of the IEEE/CVF International Conference on Computer Vision, pp. 468–477 (2021)
19. Lin, T.-Y., et al.: Microsoft COCO: common objects in context. In: Fleet, D., Pajdla, T., Schiele, B., Tuytelaars, T. (eds.) ECCV 2014. LNCS, vol. 8693, pp. 740–755. Springer, Cham (2014). https://doi.org/10.1007/978-3-319-10602-1_48
20. Liu, W., et al.: SSD: single shot MultiBox detector. In: Leibe, B., Matas, J., Sebe, N., Welling, M. (eds.) ECCV 2016. LNCS, vol. 9905, pp. 21–37. Springer, Cham (2016). https://doi.org/10.1007/978-3-319-46448-0_2
21. Liu, Z., et al.: Swin transformer: hierarchical vision transformer using shifted windows. In: Proceedings of the IEEE/CVF International Conference on Computer Vision, pp. 10012–10022 (2021)

22. Liu, Z., Mao, H., Wu, C.Y., Feichtenhofer, C., Darrell, T., Xie, S.: A ConvNet for the 2020s. In: Proceedings of the IEEE/CVF Conference on Computer Vision and Pattern Recognition, pp. 11976–11986 (2022)
23. Loshchilov, I., Hutter, F.: Decoupled weight decay regularization. ICLR (2019)
24. Ma, N., Zhang, X., Zheng, H.-T., Sun, J.: ShuffleNet V2: practical guidelines for efficient CNN architecture design. In: Ferrari, V., Hebert, M., Sminchisescu, C., Weiss, Y. (eds.) Computer Vision – ECCV 2018. LNCS, vol. 11218, pp. 122–138. Springer, Cham (2018). https://doi.org/10.1007/978-3-030-01264-9_8
25. Mehta, S., Rastegari, M.: MobileViT: light-weight, general-purpose, and mobile-friendly vision transformer. ICLR (2022)
26. Polyak, B.T., Juditsky, A.B.: Acceleration of stochastic approximation by averaging. SIAM J. Control Optim. **30**(4), 838–855 (1992)
27. Sandler, M., Howard, A., Zhu, M., Zhmoginov, A., Chen, L.C.: MobileNetV2: inverted residuals and linear bottlenecks. In: Proceedings of the IEEE Conference on Computer Vision and Pattern Recognition, pp. 4510–4520 (2018)
28. Srinivas, A., Lin, T.Y., Parmar, N., Shlens, J., Abbeel, P., Vaswani, A.: Bottleneck transformers for visual recognition. In: Proceedings of the IEEE/CVF Conference on Computer Vision and Pattern Recognition, pp. 16519–16529 (2021)
29. Sun, C., Shrivastava, A., Singh, S., Gupta, A.: Revisiting unreasonable effectiveness of data in deep learning era. In: Proceedings of the IEEE International Conference on Computer Vision, pp. 843–852 (2017)
30. Szegedy, C., Vanhoucke, V., Ioffe, S., Shlens, J., Wojna, Z.: Rethinking the inception architecture for computer vision. In: Proceedings of the IEEE Conference on Computer Vision and Pattern Recognition, pp. 2818–2826 (2016)
31. Tan, M., et al.: MnasNet: platform-aware neural architecture search for mobile. In: Proceedings of the IEEE/CVF Conference on Computer Vision and Pattern Recognition, pp. 2820–2828 (2019)
32. Tan, M., Le, Q.: EfficientNet: rethinking model scaling for convolutional neural networks. In: International Conference on Machine Learning, pp. 6105–6114. PMLR (2019)
33. Touvron, H., Cord, M., Douze, M., Massa, F., Sablayrolles, A., Jégou, H.: Training data-efficient image transformers & distillation through attention. In: International Conference on Machine Learning, pp. 10347–10357. PMLR (2021)
34. Vaswani, A., et al.: Attention is all you need. In: Advances in Neural Information Processing Systems, pp. 5998–6008 (2017)
35. Wang, W., et al.: Pyramid vision transformer: a versatile backbone for dense prediction without convolutions. In: Proceedings of the IEEE/CVF International Conference on Computer Vision, pp. 568–578 (2021)
36. Woo, S., Park, J., Lee, J.-Y., Kweon, I.S.: CBAM: convolutional block attention module. In: Ferrari, V., Hebert, M., Sminchisescu, C., Weiss, Y. (eds.) ECCV 2018. LNCS, vol. 11211, pp. 3–19. Springer, Cham (2018). https://doi.org/10.1007/978-3-030-01234-2_1
37. Wu, H., et al.: CVT: introducing convolutions to vision transformers. In: Proceedings of the IEEE/CVF International Conference on Computer Vision, pp. 22–31 (2021)
38. Xiao, T., Dollar, P., Singh, M., Mintun, E., Darrell, T., Girshick, R.: Early convolutions help transformers see better. In: Advances in Neural Information Processing Systems 34 (2021)

39. Xie, S., Girshick, R., Dollár, P., Tu, Z., He, K.: Aggregated residual transformations for deep neural networks. In: Proceedings of the IEEE Conference on Computer Vision and Pattern Recognition, pp. 1492–1500 (2017)
40. Yu, W., et al.: Metaformer is actually what you need for vision. arXiv preprint arXiv:2111.11418 (2021)

DualPrompt: Complementary Prompting for Rehearsal-Free Continual Learning

Zifeng Wang[1]([✉]), Zizhao Zhang[2], Sayna Ebrahimi[2], Ruoxi Sun[2], Han Zhang[3],
Chen-Yu Lee[2], Xiaoqi Ren[2], Guolong Su[3], Vincent Perot[3], Jennifer Dy[1],
and Tomas Pfister[2]

[1] Northeastern University, Boston, USA
zifengwang@ece.neu.edu
[2] Google Cloud AI, Sunnyvale, USA
[3] Google Research, Mountain View, USA

Abstract. Continual learning aims to enable a single model to learn a
sequence of tasks without catastrophic forgetting. Top-performing methods
usually require a rehearsal buffer to store past pristine examples for experience replay, which, however, limits their practical value due to privacy and
memory constraints. In this work, we present a simple yet effective framework, DualPrompt, which learns a tiny set of parameters, called *prompts*,
to properly instruct a pre-trained model to learn tasks arriving sequentially
without buffering past examples. DualPrompt presents a novel approach to
attach complementary prompts to the pre-trained backbone, and then formulates the objective as learning task-invariant and task-specific "instructions". With extensive experimental validation, DualPrompt consistently
sets state-of-the-art performance under the challenging class-incremental
setting. In particular, DualPrompt outperforms recent advanced continual
learning methods with relatively large buffer sizes. We also introduce a more
challenging benchmark, Split ImageNet-R, to help generalize *rehearsal-free*
continual learning research. Source code is available at https://github.com/
google-research/l2p.

Keywords: Continual learning · Rehearsal-free · Prompt-based
learning

1 Introduction

The central goal of continual learning (CL) is to learn a sequence of tasks with
a single model without suffering from *catastrophic forgetting* [38] – a significant
deterioration in performance on previously seen data. Many existing methods

---

Z. Wang—Work done while the author was an intern at Google Cloud AI Research.

Supplementary Information The online version contains supplementary material
available at https://doi.org/10.1007/978-3-031-19809-0_36.

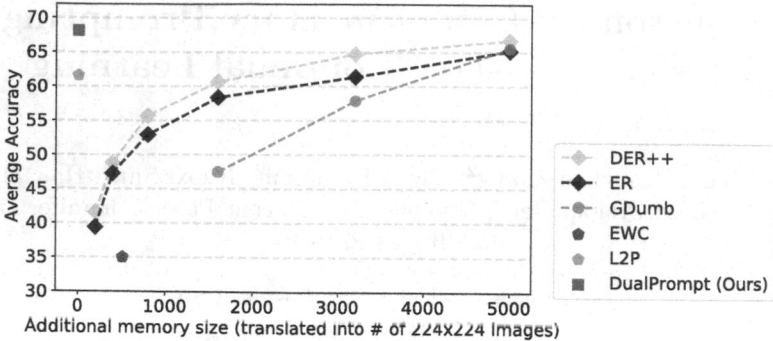

Fig. 1. The average accuracy comparison on Split ImageNet-R, suggesting that the accuracy degradation is significant for representative rehearsal-based methods like DER++ [3] and ER [7] when buffer size shrinks. Notably, they require a large rehearsal buffer (5000 images ≈ 20% of the whole training set) to close the gap to our method. In contrast, GDumb [45] matches their result by training only on the i.i.d sampled buffer, without continual learning. The additional parameters size required by Dual-Prompt is only about the bytes of one 224×224 RGB image. See Experiments section for discussion on compared methods.

aim at preserving and extending the acquired knowledge during the continual learning process [11,33]. Architecture-based methods assign isolated parameters to encode learned knowledge from different tasks [25,30,35,52,57]. However, they often introduce a substantial number of additional parameters and sometimes involve simplified assumption like known test time task identity [10,34,35], which falls into the setting of task-incremental learning. However, the task-incremental setting is usually considered over-simplified [3,33,36], since task identity is not known at test time in the real world. Our work focuses on more difficult class-incremental setting with unknown test-time task identity. Another line of work, rehearsal-based CL methods, preserve past knowledge directly by keeping data from prior tasks in a rehearsal buffer [3,4,43]. Due to their conceptual simplicity, generalizability to various settings, and superior ability to mitigate catastrophic forgetting, rehearsal-based methods have been widely recognized as the reigning state-of-the-art [3,5] in the challenging class-incremental setting. Nevertheless, the dependence on rehearsal buffer has been criticised in the community [11, 29,45,52]. While the performance of these methods is sensitive to the size of the buffer, GDumb [45] argues that performing supervised training directly on a relatively large buffer already surpasses most recent CL methods. Critically, these methods cannot be used in applications with privacy concerns [53] or when memory budget is highly constrained [54]. Thus, it is desirable to develop a parsimonious, rehearsal-free continual learning method that can achieve similar or higher level of performance.

A recent method, Learning to Prompt (L2P) [58] approaches this problem from a brand-new perspective – it proposes to leverage learnable *prompt* parameters to encode knowledge in a much more succinct way (i.e. prompt pool) than buffer, thus a rehearsal buffer is no longer necessary. Prompt techniques are originally introduced in natural language processing (NLP) for task adaptation [27] of large-scale pre-trained models by attaching fixed or learnable "instructions", since prompts are designed to instruct the model to properly reuse learned representations, instead of learning new representations from scratch. L2P successfully formulates the problem of learning new tasks as training small prompt parameters attached to a pre-trained frozen model. L2P takes an exciting step towards rehearsal-free continual learning, although the performance is still lower than rehearsal-based methods.

In L2P, one single prompt pool is designed to transfer knowledge from one task to another without distinguishing between the common features among all tasks versus the features that are unique to each task. We argue such a design could be sub-optimal from the perspective of theory of Complementary Learning Systems (CLS) [21,37], an intuition that many recent advanced CL methods are based on [3,7,43]. CLS suggests that humans learn continually via the synergy between two learning systems: the hippocampus focuses on learning pattern-separated representation on specific experiences, and the neocortex focuses on learning more general and transferable representation from past experience sequences. Thus, they are able to learn task-specific knowledge separately without interference while leveraging task-invariant knowledge to have greater learning capacity to learn future tasks better. However, previous CLS-driven methods still decouple or expand the backbone parameters learn the two kinds of knowledge [10,43,44]. Thus, they still rely on constructing a rehearsal buffer repeatedly to consolidate decoupled knowledge to prevent catastrophic forgetting.

In this paper, we present DualPrompt, a rehearsal-free continual learning approach to explicitly learn two sets of disjoint prompt spaces, *G(eneral)-Prompt* and *E(xpert)-Prompt*, that encode task-invariant and task-specific instructions, respectively. DualPrompt directly decouples the higher-level prompt space, which turns out to be more effective and memory efficient that conventional methods which focus on the lower-level latent representation space. We further explore where and how to attach both types of prompts is crucial to steer the backbone model to learn with less forgetting and to achieve effective knowledge sharing, thus significantly enhancing the effectiveness of continual learning.

Moreover, we introduce Split ImageNet-R, a new CL benchmark based on ImageNet-R [14] to the community. The intra-class diversity for each task in Split ImageNet-R is large (see Appendix E for representative examples), thus a small buffer is not sufficient to represent past experiences. Figure 1 showcases that the size of rehearsal buffer needed is non-trivial for even advanced methods to perform well. While rehearsal-based methods require a large buffer (up to 20% of total training data) to achieve a competitive average accuracy, our method DualPrompt shows superior performance despite not using any rehearsal buffer.

In summary, our work makes the following contributions:

- We propose DualPrompt, a simple and effective rehearsal-free CL method, comprised of G-Prompt and E-Prompt for learning task-invariant and task-specific knowledge, respectively. The method is fairly simple to apply without data or memory access concerns which is favorable for real-world CL scenarios.

- DualPrompt explores various design choices to incorporate these two types of prompts into the pre-trained models. For the first time, we empirically discover that properly attaching prompts to the backbone model is crucial to the effectiveness of continual learning.
- We introduce a new CL benchmark, Split ImageNet-R to help validate the method. DualPrompt sets new state-of-the-art performance on multiple benchmarks under the challenging class-incremental setting, and beats rehearsal-based methods with relatively large buffer size.

2   Related Work

Continual Learning. We discuss three related categories of continual learning methods: regularization-based, rehearsal-based and architecture-based methods.

Regularization-based methods [1,18,26,65] address catastrophic forgetting by regularizing important parameters for learned tasks. Although these methods mitigate forgetting under simpler task-incremental setting, their performance under more challenging class-incremental setting [33], or more challenging datasets [60] is not satisfactory.

Architecture-based methods assign isolated parameters for each task. These methods can be further categorized as expanding the model [25,30,51,63,67], or dividing the model [10,16,35,52,57]. However, a major part of the work is limited to the task-incremental setting [16,34,35,52], while other work only considers specific convolutional-based architectures [10,44,59]. However, Dual-Prompt aims at more challenging class-incremental setting, and focus on pre-trained transformer-based models. Moreover, architecture-based method generally require substantially large amount of additional parameters to assist model separation [16,57,62]. On the contrary, DualPrompt is much lightweight and only require negligible amount of parameters (0.2%–0.6% of full model size).

Rehearsal-based methods save data from learned tasks in a rehearsal buffer to train with the current task. Although these methods share this quite simple idea, they are very effective even in the class-incremental setting. Several advanced rehearsal-base methods achieve state-of-the-art performance [3,4]. However, rehearsal-based methods deteriorates when buffer size [4] decreases, and are eventually not applicable to data privacy sensitive scenarios [53]. Some recent methods are inspired from the Complementary Learning Systems (CLS). However, ACL [10] is limited to the task-incremental setting, DualNet [43] requires specific architecture design, and both methods still rely on a rehearsal buffer to work well. Our DualPrompt tackles continual learning from a rehearsal-free perspective, standing upon a wise utilization of pre-trained models, thus getting rid of the shortcomings of rehearsal-based methods.

Prompt-Based Learning. As an emerging transfer learning technique in natural language processing (NLP), prompt-based learning (or prompting), applies a fixed function to condition the model, so that the language model gets additional instructions to perform the downstream task. However, the design of a prompting function is challenging and requires heuristics. To this end, recent work propose to apply prompts as learnable parameters, achieving outstanding performance on transfer learning [23,24]. Prompts capture task-specific knowledge with much smaller additional parameters, than its competitors, such as Adapter [42,56] and LoRA [15]. As discussed above, L2P [58] is the only work that connects prompting and continual learning. Differently, DualPrompt takes inspiration from CLS and presents a different approach to attach complementary prompts to the pre-trained backbone to learn task-invariant and task-specific instructions. We show DualPrompt outperforms L2P consistently.

3   Prerequisites

3.1   Continual Learning Problem Setting

Continual learning is defined as training machine learning models on a continuum of data from a sequence of tasks. We denote the sequence of tasks as $\mathcal{D} = \{\mathcal{D}_1, \cdots, \mathcal{D}_T\}$, where the t-th task $\mathcal{D}_t = \{(\boldsymbol{x}_{i,t}, y_{i,t})\}_{i=1}^{n_t}$ contains tuples of the input sample $\boldsymbol{x}_{i,t} \in \mathcal{X}$ and its corresponding label $y_{i,t} \in \mathcal{Y}$. The model $f_\theta : \mathcal{X} \rightarrow \mathcal{Y}$ is parameterized by θ, such that it predicts the label $y = f_\theta(\boldsymbol{x}) \in \mathcal{Y}$ given an unseen test sample $\boldsymbol{x}$ from arbitrary tasks. Data from the previous tasks is not available when training future tasks.

We use the widely-adopted assumption that the task boundaries are clear and the task switch is sudden at training time [6,43]. Moreover, we consider the more challenging class-incremental learning [6] setting, i.e., task identity is unknown for each example at test time. Also, following the settings in prior work [58], we assume a pre-trained sequence model, e.g., a vision transformer (ViT) [9] on ImageNet, is available, a wide-used assumption in recent literature of the computer vision community. Unlike many rehearsal-based methods [3,7], we do not assume any form of rehearsal buffer as a prerequisite.

3.2   Prompt-Based Learning

Prompt-based learning (or prompting) was first proposed in NLP for transfer learning. The main idea of prompting is to add extra instruction for pre-trained models to perform downstream tasks conditionally [27]. Prompt Tuning [23], one of the recent emerging techniques, proposes to attach a set of prompt parameters to frozen transformer-based language models [46] to perform downstream NLP tasks. The prompts are usually prepended to the input sequence to instruct the model prediction. We briefly illustrate the idea of Prompt Tuning below.

As we mainly focus on vision-related continual learning setting, here we introduce the definition of Prompt Tuning using the vision transformer (ViT) based sequence models [9,55]. In ViT, the input embedding layer transforms the input image into a sequence-like output feature $\boldsymbol{h} \in \mathbb{R}^{L \times D}$, where L is the sequence length and D is the embedding dimension. When solving downstream tasks, the pre-trained backbone is kept frozen as a general feature extractor, and the prompt parameters $\boldsymbol{p} \in \mathbb{R}^{L_p \times D}$ with sequence length L_p and embedding dimension D are prepended to the embedding feature along the sequence length dimension to form the extended embedding feature. Finally, the extended feature is sent to the rest of the model for performing classification tasks. Prompt serves as a lightweight module to encode high-level instruction to instruct the backbone to leverage pre-trained representations for downstream tasks.

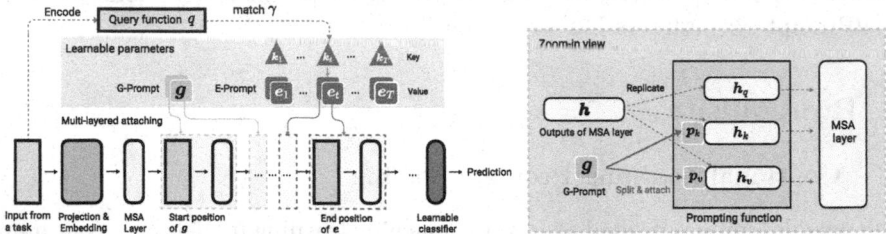

Fig. 2. Overview of DualPrompt. **Left:** At test time, an input is transformed by a query function to match the closest task key $\boldsymbol{k}_t$ and the corresponding E-Prompt $\boldsymbol{e}_t$. Then the shared G(eneral)-Prompt $\boldsymbol{g}$ and the matched E(xpert)-Prompt $\boldsymbol{e}_t$ are attached to multiple MSA layers of a pre-trained transformer. At training time, the E-Prompt is selected by task identity and the selected E-Prompt and G-Prompt are trained together with the classifier. **Right:** A prompting function is illustrated where the G-prompt is split equally and attached to the key and value replicas of the hidden feature (see Sect. 4.2) before passing them to the preceding MSA layer.

4 DualPrompt

Our proposed method, DualPrompt is illustrated in Fig. 2. We first introduce the complementary learning components, G- and E-prompts, in Sect. 4.1 by showcasing how they work with a single multi-head self-attention (MSA) layer. We then explore design choices of attaching prompts to the backbone Sect. 4.2. We finally present the overall objective for DualPrompt in Sect. 4.3.

4.1 Complementary G-Prompt and E-Prompt

Given a pre-trained ViT f with N consecutive MSA layers, we further extend the notations introduced in Sect. 3.2 by denoting the input embedding feature of the i-th MSA layer as $\boldsymbol{h}^{(i)}, i = 1, 2, \cdots, N$.

G-Prompt: $\boldsymbol{g} \in \mathbb{R}^{L_g \times D}$ with sequence length L_g and embedding dimension D, is a shared parameter for all tasks. Suppose we would like to attach G-Prompt to the i-th MSA layer, G-Prompt transforms $\boldsymbol{h}^{(i)}$ via a *prompting function*:

$$\boldsymbol{h}_g^{(i)} = f_{\text{prompt}}\left(\boldsymbol{g}, \boldsymbol{h}^{(i)}\right), \tag{1}$$

where f_{prompt} defines the approach how to attach the prompts to the hidden embeddings. Section 4.2 discusses the details.

E-Prompt: $\mathbf{E} = \{e_t\}_{t=1}^{T}$ is a set of task-dependent parameters, where $e_t \in \mathbb{R}^{L_e \times D}$ has a sequence length of L_e and the same embedding dimension D as the G-Prompt, and T is the total number of tasks. Different from the shared G-Prompt, each e_t is associated with a task-specific key $k_t \in \mathbb{R}^D$, which is also a learnable parameter that aims to capture representative features of a task. For an input example from the t-th task, to attach E-Prompt to the j-th MSA layer, we apply the prompting function in a similar way:

$$h_e^{(j)} = f_{\text{prompt}}\left(e_t, h^{(j)}\right). \tag{2}$$

Moreover, we update the corresponding k_t to match the feature of the input instance via a matching loss $\mathcal{L}_{\text{match}}$, such that k_t becomes "closer" to examples from the t-th task than other keys. At test time, inspired by the strategy proposed in [58], we propose to adopt a query function q on the test sample to search for the best match from the task keys, and select the corresponding E-Prompt to use. Although it is interesting to design various matching and query strategies by introducing additional components, it actually violates the principle of parsimony in continual learning [11,57]. Fortunately, as suggested in [58], we can directly use the whole pre-trained model as the query function: $q(\boldsymbol{x}) = f(\boldsymbol{x})[0]$ (the feature vector corresponding to [class] token [9]), and cosine similarity as γ. Thus, the matching loss takes the following form:

$$\mathcal{L}_{\text{match}}(\boldsymbol{x}, k_t) = \gamma(q(\boldsymbol{x}), k_t), \quad \boldsymbol{x} \in \mathcal{D}_t. \tag{3}$$

For a test example $\boldsymbol{x}$, we simply choose the best matched task key index via $\text{argmin}_t \, \gamma(q(\boldsymbol{x}), k_t)$. We show the relationship between query accuracy and final performance in Appendix I. We empirically discover this matching loss and the corresponding query mechanism works fairly well for all benchmarks.

4.2 Prompt Attaching: Where and How?

G- and E-prompts encode respective type of instructions during training with the backbone and cooperatively instruct the model to make predictions at inference. We have showcased how to attach them to a single MSA layer in Sect. 4.1. Most existing prompt-related work simply place prompts only at the first MSA [23,58], or at every MSA layer [24,28]. However, we argue that it is crucial to explore *where* and *how* to attach both types of prompts.

Where: Decoupled Prompt Positions. Intuitively, different layers of the backbone have different levels of feature abstraction [47]. Therefore, when learning tasks sequentially, some layers of representations can have higher responses to task-specific knowledge than others, vise versa for task-invariant knowledge. This motivates us to give the two types of prompts more flexibility to attach to the most proper positions in a decoupled way, thus different instructions can interact with the corresponding representations more effectively.

With a slight abuse of notation, we introduce the multi-layered extension of both types of prompts: $g = \{g^{(l)}\}_{l=\text{start}_g}^{\text{end}_g}$, where $g^{(l)} \in \mathbb{R}^{L_g \times D}$ is the G-Prompt to be attached to the l-th MSA layer. We also define $e_t = \{e_t^{(l)}\}_{l=\text{start}_e}^{\text{end}_e}$ similarly. In this way, we are able to attach the G-Prompt $g^{(l)}$ from the start_g-th to the end_g-th MSA layers, and attach the E-Prompt $e_t^{(l)}$ from the start_e-th to the end_e-th MSA layers. And most importantly, $(\text{start}_g, \text{end}_g)$ and $(\text{start}_e, \text{end}_e)$ could be totally different or non-overlapping. In our experiments, we empirically search for a certain set of $\text{start}_g, \text{end}_g, \text{start}_e, \text{end}_e$ on a validation set and discover that it performs consistently well across different benchmarks. Note that we make a simplified assumption that the chosen indices of MSA layers to attach prompts are contiguous, which already achieves state-of-the-art performance in our empirical evaluation. However, there could be more advanced ways to auto-search the configuration, which we treat as valuable future work.

How: Configurable Prompting Function. The prompting function f_{prompt} controls the way we combine prompts with the embedding features. From another perspective, f_{prompt} directly affects how the high-level instructions in prompts interact with low-level representations. Thus, we believe a well-designed prompting function is also vital for the overall continual learning performance. Although DualPrompt is compatible with various prompting functions, here we exemplify and study two mainstream realizations in the NLP community - Prompt Tuning (Pro-T) [23] and Prefix Tuning (Pre-T) [24].

Specifically, applying a prompting function can be viewed as modifying the inputs of the MSA layers [55]. Let the input to the MSA layer be $h \in \mathbb{R}^{L \times D}$, and we further denote the input query, key, and values for the MSA layer to be h_Q, h_K, h_V, respectively. Recall that the MSA layer is proposed by [55]:

$$\text{MSA}(h_Q, h_K, h_V) = \text{Concat}(h_1, \dots, h_m) W^O$$

$$\text{where } h_i = \text{Attention}\left(h_Q W_i^Q, h_K W_i^K, h_V W_i^V\right),$$

where W^O, W_i^Q, W_i^K, and W_i^V are projection matrices. m is the number of heads. In ViT, $h_Q = h_K = h_V$. For simplicity, we define a unified prompt parameter $p \in \mathbb{R}^{L_p \times D}$ (p could be either single-layered G or E-Prompt).

Prompt Tuning (Pro-T) prepends prompts to the input tokens, which is equivalent to concatenate the same prompt parameter p to h_Q, h_K, and h_V,

$$f_{\text{prompt}}^{\text{Pro-T}}(p, h) = \text{MSA}([p; h_Q], [p; h_K], [p; h_V]), \tag{4}$$

where $[\cdot; \cdot]$ defines the concatenation operation along the sequence length dimension. The output length increases, resulting the output dimension as $\mathbb{R}^{(L+L_p) \times D}$. The operation is equivalent to how [class] is added [9] at the first MSA layer.

Prefix Tuning (Pre-T) splits p into $p_K, p_V \in \mathbb{R}^{L_p/2 \times D}$, and prepends them to to h_K and h_V respectively, while keep h_Q as-is:

$$f_{\text{prompt}}^{\text{Pre-T}}(p, h) = \text{MSA}(h_Q, [p_k; h_K], [p_v; h_V]). \tag{5}$$

Compared with Pro-T, the output sequence length remains the same as input $h \in \mathbb{R}^{L \times D}$. Section 5.4 studies both versions empirically and discusses the intuition behind their difference in performance from a continual learning perspective.

4.3 Overall Objective for DualPrompt

The full picture of DualPrompt at training and test time is described in Algorithm 1 and 2, respectively, in Appendix A. Following the design patterns discussed in Sect. 4.2, we denote the architecture with prompts attached by f_{g,e_t}. Then we transform our input x from the t-th task via f_{g,e_t} and send it to the classification head f_ϕ parametrized by ϕ for prediction. Finally, we train both types of prompts, the task keys, as well as the newly-initialized classification head in an end-to-end fashion:

$$\min_{g,e_t,k_t,\phi} \mathcal{L}(f_\phi(f_{g,e_t}(x)), y) + \lambda \mathcal{L}_{\text{match}}(x, k_t), \quad x \in \mathcal{D}_t, \tag{6}$$

where $\mathcal{L}$ is the cross-entropy loss, $\mathcal{L}_{\text{match}}$ is the matching loss defined in (3), and λ is a scalar balancing factor.

5 Experiments

5.1 Evaluation Benchmarks

Split ImageNet-R. The Split ImageNet-R benchmark is build upon ImageNet-R [14] by dividing the 200 classes randomly into 10 tasks with 20 classes per task. We split the dataset into training and test set with 24,000 and 6,000 images respectively. We further sample 20% from the training set as validation data for prompt attaching design search. The original ImageNet-R includes newly collected data of different styles, such as cartoon, graffiti and origami, as well as hard examples from ImageNet [8] that standard models, *e.g.*, ResNet [13], fail to classify. We believe the Split ImageNet-R is of great importance to the continual learning community, for the following reasons: 1) Split ImageNet-R contains classes with different styles, which is closer to the complicated real-world problems. 2) The significant intra-class diversity (see Appendix E) poses a great challenge for rehearsal-based methods to work effectively with a small buffer size (see Fig. 1), thus encouraging the development of more practical, rehearsal-free methods. 3) Pre-trained vision models are useful in practice for many fields [19,50], including continual learning. However, their training set usually includes ImageNet. Thus, Split ImageNet-R serves as a relative fair and challenging benchmark, and an alternative to ImageNet-based benchmarks [49, 60] for continual learning that uses pre-trained models.

Split CIFAR-100. Split CIFAR-100 is a widely-used benchmark in continual learning literature. It splits the original CIFAR-100 [20] into 10 disjoint tasks, with 10 classes per task. Although it is a relatively simple task for image classification under the i.i.d. setting, it sufficiently makes advanced CL methods expose large forgetting rate in class-incremental learning.

We use Split ImageNet-R and Split CIFAR-100 to demonstrate our main results in Sect. 5.2, and additionally conduct experiments on 5-datasets for completeness in the Appendix H.

5.2 Comparison with State-of-the-Arts

We compare DualPrompt against representative baselines and state-of-the-art methods. Please refer to Appendix B for experimental details. We use the widely-used *Average accuracy* (higher is better) and *Forgetting* (lower is better) [6,31, 33] as our evaluation metrics. The definitions of both metrics are in Appendix C.

Table 1. Results on class-incremental learning (i.e., task identity is unknown at test time). We compare and group methods by buffer sizes. 0 means no rehearsal is used, when most SOTA methods are not applicable anymore. Note that the chosen buffer sizes here are considered sufficiently large sizes that are used in prior works for Split CIFAR-100 [3,6]. They are large enough even for training a supervised counterpart – e.g. GDumb [45] trains on the i.i.d sampled buffer with this size and demonstrated competitive results, making continual training unnecessary.

Method	Buffer size	Split CIFAR-100		Buffer size	Split ImageNet-R	
		Avg. Acc (↑)	Forgetting (↓)		Avg. Acc (↑)	Forgetting (↓)
ER [7]	1000	67.87 ± 0.57	33.33 ± 1.28	1000	55.13 ± 1.29	35.38 ± 0.52
BiC [60]		66.11 ± 1.76	35.24 ± 1.64		52.14 ± 1.08	36.70 ± 1.05
GDumb [45]		67.14 ± 0.37	–		38.32 ± 0.55	–
DER++ [3]		61.06 ± 0.87	39.87 ± 0.99		55.47 ± 1.31	34.64 ± 1.50
Co^{2}L [4]		72.15 ± 1.32	28.55 ± 1.56		53.45 ± 1.55	37.30 ± 1.81
ER [7]	5000	82.53 ± 0.17	16.46 ± 0.25	5000	65.18 ± 0.40	23.31 ± 0.89
BiC [60]		81.42 ± 0.85	17.31 ± 1.02		64.63 ± 1.27	22.25 ± 1.73
GDumb [45]		81.67 ± 0.02	–		65.90 ± 0.28	–
DER++ [3]		83.94 ± 0.34	14.55 ± 0.73		66.73 ± 0.87	20.67 ± 1.24
Co^{2}L [4]		82.49 ± 0.89	17.48 ± 1.80		65.90 ± 0.14	23.36 ± 0.71
FT-seq	0	33.61 ± 0.85	86.87 ± 0.20	0	28.87 ± 1.36	63.80 ± 1.50
EWC [18]		47.01 ± 0.29	33.27 ± 1.17		35.00 ± 0.43	56.16 ± 0.88
LwF [26]		60.69 ± 0.63	27.77 ± 2.17		38.54 ± 1.23	52.37 ± 0.64
L2P [58]		83.86 ± 0.28	7.35 ± 0.38		61.57 ± 0.66	9.73 ± 0.47
DualPrompt		$\mathbf{86.51 \pm 0.33}$	$\mathbf{5.16 \pm 0.09}$		$\mathbf{68.13 \pm 0.49}$	$\mathbf{4.68 \pm 0.20}$
Upper-bound	–	90.85 ± 0.12	–	–	79.13 ± 0.18	–

To make the comparison fair and precise, we first compare DualPrompt with regularization-, rehearsal- and prompt-based methods, which are compatible with transformer-based models, in Table 1. We then compare DualPrompt with architecture-based methods, which are mostly compatible with ConvNets, using a different protocol in Table 2.

– **Comparing methods.** We select representative methods including EWC [18], LwF [26], ER [7,12], GDumb [45], BiC [60], DER++ [3], Co^{2}L [4] and L2P [58], from all categories. Please see Appendix D for details.

- **Naive baselines.** For better demonstration of the relative effectiveness of all methods, we also include: FT-seq, the naive sequential training, and Upper-bound, the usual supervised finetuning on the i.i.d. data of all tasks.

Table 1 reports the performance of all comparing methods on Split CIFAR-100 and Split ImageNet-R. Our proposed method, DualPrompt, outperforms all methods consistently, including non-rehearsal based methods and rehearsal-based methods with a large buffer size. When the buffer size is 5000 (10% of the CIFAR-100 training set and >20% of the ImageNet-R training set), all rehearsal-based methods are fairly close to GDumb, indicating that performing rehearsal-based continual learning likely provide no performance gain than supervised training on the buffered data as GDumb does. *DualPrompt achieves better performance without any buffered data.* Moreover, from Table 1, as well as Fig. 1, we can observe the performance of rehearsal-based methods drops sharply when the buffer size shrinks. This again suggests the clear advantage of DualPrompt as a rehearsal-free method. For the non-rehearsal based methods, only L2P performs close to our methods. Nevertheless, DualPrompt still beats L2P significantly by a 3%-7% margin on Average accuracy, thanks to our novel design of the two complementary prompts, which successfully reduces catastrophic forgetting.

Table 2. Comparison with architecture-based methods on Split CIFAR-100. We use Diff = Upper-Bound Acc - Method Acc (lower is better), to measure how close the performance to the upper-bound of the used backbone.

Method	Backbone	Avg. Acc ($\uparrow$)	Diff ($\downarrow$)	Buffer size	Additional Parameters	
					MB	%
Upper-bound	ResNet18	$80.41^{\dagger}$	–	–	–	–
SupSup [59]		$28.34 \pm 2.45^{\ddagger}$	52.07	0	3.0	6.5%
DualNet [43]		$40.14 \pm 1.64^{\ddagger}$	40.27	1000	5.04	10.9%
RPSNet [48]		$68.60^{\dagger}$	11.81	2000	181	404%
DynaER [62]		$74.64^{\dagger}$	5.77	2000	19.8	43.8%
Upper-bound	ResNet152	$88.54^{\dagger}$	–	–	–	–
DynaER [62]		$71.01 \pm 0.58^{\ddagger}$	17.53	2000	159	68.5%
Upper-bound	ViT-B/16	$90.85 \pm 0.12^{\ddagger}$	–	–	–	–
L2P [58]		$83.86 \pm 0.28^{\ddagger}$	6.99	0	1.94	0.56%
DualPrompt		$\mathbf{86.51 \pm 0.33}$	**4.34**	0	**1.90**	**0.55%**

†Reported by the original papers. ‡ Reproduced using their original codebases

Architecture-Based Methods. We compare against representative class-incremental learning methods, including DualNet [43], SupSup [59], DynaER [62] and RPSNet [48]. Please see Appendix D for details.

Prior architecture-based methods, which are based on ConvNet, are not trivial to migrate to transformer-based models. Moreover, different architecture-based methods usually add different amount of additional parameters. To enable a relative fair comparison between these methods, we introduce a metric to measure how close the performance of a certain method is to the upper-bound performance, *i.e.* trained under the i.i.d. setting, of a given architecture. Table 2 shows the results on Split-CIFAR100. DualPrompt achieves the best accuracy and its difference to upper-bound is only 4.34%, with minimal additional parameters and no buffer. The strongest competitor on ResNet, DynaER, on the contrary, requires a buffer of 2,000 images and include 43.8% additional parameters.

5.3   Does Stronger Backbones Naively Improve CL?

Our method builds upon more advanced yet bigger backbones than many previous methods. We think understand this question is very important for fair comparison and future research. Although pre-trained ViT is a stronger backbone than common ConvNets, it is not necessarily translate to continual learning performance. The observations we shown here are similar to what reported in a very recent study about how large architecture help continual learning [40]. First, this fact can be seen from Table 1, where well-known general methods still suffer large forgetting rate given this backbone. We have tried to use ImageNet pre-trained ResNet for competing methods in Table 2, which leads to no improvement upon the reported numbers in Table 2. This further indicates that a pre-trained model is not a "panacea" for continual learning without being leveraged properly. We also equip best-performing DynaER [62] with ImageNet pre-trained ResNet152 (60M parameters), which has close upper-bound performance to ViT-B/16 (86M). DynaER learns weight masks, a popular strategy for architecture-based methods [59], to dynamically expand architectures. However, results in Table 2 show worse performance (we sweep their suggested hyperparameters to report the best performance), a similar observation is shown in their original paper when scaling DynaER to ResNet32. That being said, how to effectively utilize large models under traditional architecture-based methods remains an open question. DualPrompt is novel at wisely leveraging the state-of-the-art vision backbones to solve challenges in continual learning.

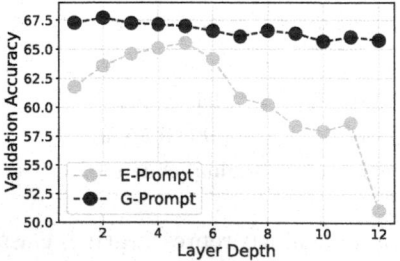

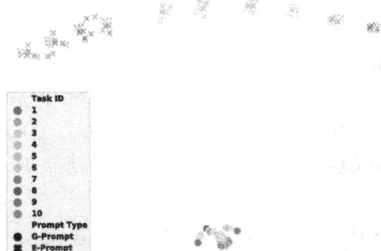

Fig. 3. Effects of position to attach prompts on Split ImageNet-R validation set. We empirically observe that attaching G- and E-Prompts to the 2nd and 5th MSA layer results in the best performance.

Fig. 4. t-SNE visualization of G- and E-prompts. Each point represents a prompt vector of dimension 768. E-Prompts are taken from the final model, while G-Prompts are taken from model snapshots after trained on each task.

5.4 Exploration of Where and How to Attach Prompts

We have shown the best performing model of DualPrompt in Sect. 5.2. In this section, we explore *where and how* to attach prompts and enhance their influences to the overall performance. We also present critical empirical observations that lead to interesting future research.

Position of Prompts. To explore the most proper position to insert the G-Prompt and E-Prompt, we use a heuristic search strategy on the validation set of Split ImageNet-R. We first set $start_e = end_e$, *i.e.*, only insert E-Prompt at a single MSA layer. The lower line of Fig. 3 shows that placing E-Prompt at the 5th MSA layer leads to the best performance. We then search extend E-Prompt to multi-layer and found that $start_e = 3, end_e = 5$ performs the best (see Appendix F). We then study the case of $start_g = end_g$ based on the optimal setting of E-Prompt. Interestingly, the upper line of Fig. 3 shows that placing G-Prompt at the 2nd MSA layer leads to the best performance. We also extend G-Prompt into its multi-layered counterparts and conduct searching experiments and find the best choice to be $start_g = 1, end_g = 2$ (see Appendix F).

Table 3. Comparison of different prompting functions: Prompt Tuning (Pro-T) v.s. Prefix Tuning (Pre-T).

Prompting function		Pro-T	Pre-T
Split	Avg. Acc (↑)	83.81	**86.51**
CIFAR-100	Forgetting (↓)	5.94	**5.16**
Split	Avg. Acc (↑)	64.99	**68.13**
ImageNet-R	Forgetting (↓)	6.81	**4.68**

Table 4. Ablation study on Split ImageNet-R. ML means multi-layered.

G-P	E-P	ML	Split ImageNet-R	
			Avg. Acc (↑)	Forgetting (↓)
			27.01	7.57
✓			63.41	6.52
	✓		65.10	5.52
✓	✓		66.77	5.74
✓		✓	63.85	7.50
	✓	✓	66.91	4.77
✓	✓	✓	**68.13**	**4.68**

Interestingly, we observe that the best depth are different, and the final layers to attach G- and E-Prompts are non-overlapping. In particular, $start_g > start_e$, which suggests that G-Prompt captures task-invariant knowledge better at shallower layer, while E-Prompt captures task-specific knowledge better at deeper layer. This observation also fits the intuition that different layers in deep learning models capture different types of knowledge [47,64], and thus naturally fit different prompts. This also justifies decoupling positions of G- and E-Prompts as a reasonable option. Moreover, when attaching them to top layers, both E-Prompt and G-Prompt exhibit the worst performance. We speculate prompts need to be attached to shallower layers in order to condition more layers of the pre-trained model and thereby offer effective instructions.

Prompting Function: Prompt v.s. Prefix. We further study the role of prompting function on Split CIFAR-100 and Split ImageNet-R. In prior prompt-based CL work, L2P, only Pro-T is applied without further investigation. In Table 3, we observe that Pre-T version leads to a better performance on both datasets. Besides its empirically better performance, Pre-T is actually more scalable and efficient when attached to multiple layers, since it results in unchanged sequence length. Nevertheless, prompting function is a flexible component of our method, and designing better prompting function is also an open research question, so we can easily plug-in any newly proposed prompting function to DualPrompt and evaluate its effectiveness on given continual learning tasks.

5.5   Ablation Study

Based on the optimal parameters searched in the previous section, we present the ablation study results in Table 4 to show the importance of each component of DualPrompt on Split ImageNet-R. Note that G-P (G-Prompt) and E-P (E-Prompt) alone represent the optimal single-layered version for each type of prompts ($\text{start}_g = \text{end}_g = 2, \text{start}_e = \text{end}_e = 5$), while ML represents the optimal multi-layered version ($\text{start}_g = 1, \text{end}_g = 2, \text{start}_e = 3, \text{end}_e = 5$). When all components are absent, we simply have a naive baseline with a frozen pre-trained backbone and trainable classification head.

In general, all components contribute to the final performance. Interestingly, adding a single-layered G-Prompt alone brings substantial improvement upon the baseline, indicating that the task-invariant knowledge obtained by G-Prompt generalizes pretty well across tasks. However, simply sharing knowledge between tasks introduces inevitable forgetting, due to the fact that task-specific knowledge is not properly decoupled. Thus, E-Prompt alone consistently outperforms G-Prompt alone, since E-Prompt mitigates forgetting by separating knowledge learned from different tasks. However, only applying E-Prompt ignores the task-invariant knowledge, which helps to learn future tasks. Thus, when adding G-Prompt and E-Prompt together to the backbone, it further enhances the overall performance by selectively decoupling the task-invariant knowledge into G-Prompt and task-specific knowledge into E-Prompt. We also observe that extending both prompts to its multi-layered counterparts helps consistently in all cases, due to the fact that properly adding more prompt parameters through different layers offers more representation power.

Visualization of G- and E-Prompts. To further understand different types of instructions learned within G- and E-prompts, we visualize these two types of prompts using t-SNE [32] in Fig. 4. For a prompt with shape $L \times D$, we treat it as L prompts with dimension D. E-Prompts are taken from the final model after trained on the sequence of all tasks, while the G-Prompts are taken from different model snapshots after training on each task. We can observe that E-Prompts are well-separated, indicating they are learning task-specific knowledge. Meanwhile, the G-Prompts are quite centered and only differ slightly between tasks, which suggests they are learning task-invariant knowledge.

6   Conclusion

In this paper, we present a novel method, DualPrompt, that achieves rehearsal-free continual learning under the challenging class-incremental setting. Dual-Prompt presents a novel way to attach complementary prompts to a pre-trained model to learn decoupled knowledge. To comprehensively validate the proposed method, we propose a new continual learning benchmark, Split ImageNet-R, besides study on the widely-used benchmarks. DualPrompt sets state-of-the-art performance in all metrics, surprisingly needs much lower additional memory compared with previous architecture-based and rehearsal-based methods. Empirical investigations are conducted to understand the inner-workings. Since large-scale pre-trained models are widely used in practice for their great representation power, we believe DualPrompt serves as a starting point for real-world rehearsal-free continual learning systems. Moreover, we recommend DualPrompt as a unified framework for future prompt-based continual learning research, for its simplicity, flexibility, and strong performance.

References

1. Aljundi, R., Babiloni, F., Elhoseiny, M., Rohrbach, M., Tuytelaars, T.: Memory aware synapses: learning what (not) to forget. In: Ferrari, V., Hebert, M., Sminchisescu, C., Weiss, Y. (eds.) ECCV 2018. LNCS, vol. 11207, pp. 144–161. Springer, Cham (2018). https://doi.org/10.1007/978-3-030-01219-9_9
2. Bulatov, Y.: notMNIST dataset (2011). http://yaroslavvb.blogspot.com/2011/09/notmnist-dataset.html
3. Buzzega, P., Boschini, M., Porrello, A., Abati, D., Calderara, S.: Dark experience for general continual learning: a strong, simple baseline. In: NeurIPS (2020)
4. Cha, H., Lee, J., Shin, J.: Co^{2}L: contrastive continual learning. In: ICCV (2021)
5. Chaudhry, A., Gordo, A., Dokania, P.K., Torr, P., Lopez-Paz, D.: Using hindsight to anchor past knowledge in continual learning. arXiv preprint arXiv:2002.08165 2(7) (2020)
6. Chaudhry, A., Ranzato, M., Rohrbach, M., Elhoseiny, M.: Efficient lifelong learning with A-GEM. arXiv preprint arXiv:1812.00420 (2018)
7. Chaudhry, A., et al.: On tiny episodic memories in continual learning. arXiv preprint arXiv:1902.10486 (2019)
8. Deng, J., Dong, W., Socher, R., Li, L.J., Li, K., Fei-Fei, L.: ImageNet: a large-scale hierarchical image database. In: CVPR, pp. 248–255. IEEE (2009)
9. Dosovitskiy, A., et al.: An image is worth 16 × 16 words: transformers for image recognition at scale. In: ICLR. OpenReview.net (2021). https://openreview.net/forum?id=YicbFdNTTy
10. Ebrahimi, S., Meier, F., Calandra, R., Darrell, T., Rohrbach, M.: Adversarial continual learning. In: Vedaldi, A., Bischof, H., Brox, T., Frahm, J.-M. (eds.) ECCV 2020. LNCS, vol. 12356, pp. 386–402. Springer, Cham (2020). https://doi.org/10.1007/978-3-030-58621-8_23
11. Hadsell, R., Rao, D., Rusu, A.A., Pascanu, R.: Embracing change: continual learning in deep neural networks. Trends Cogni. Sci. **24**, 1028–1040 (2020)
12. Hayes, T.L., Cahill, N.D., Kanan, C.: Memory efficient experience replay for streaming learning. In: ICRA (2019)

13. He, K., Zhang, X., Ren, S., Sun, J.: Deep residual learning for image recognition. In: CVPR, pp. 770–778 (2016)
14. Hendrycks, D., et al.: The many faces of robustness: a critical analysis of out-of-distribution generalization. arXiv preprint arXiv:2006.16241 (2020)
15. Hu, E.J., et al.: LoRa: low-rank adaptation of large language models. arXiv preprint arXiv:2106.09685 (2021)
16. Ke, Z., Liu, B., Huang, X.: Continual learning of a mixed sequence of similar and dissimilar tasks. In: NeurIPS 33 (2020)
17. Kingma, D.P., Ba, J.: Adam: a method for stochastic optimization. arXiv preprint arXiv:1412.6980 (2014)
18. Kirkpatrick, J., et al.: Overcoming catastrophic forgetting in neural networks. PNAS **114**(13), 3521–3526 (2017)
19. Kolesnikov, A., Beyer, L., Zhai, X., Puigcerver, J., Yung, J., Gelly, S., Houlsby, N.: Big Transfer (BiT): general visual representation learning. In: Vedaldi, A., Bischof, H., Brox, T., Frahm, J.-M. (eds.) ECCV 2020. LNCS, vol. 12350, pp. 491–507. Springer, Cham (2020). https://doi.org/10.1007/978-3-030-58558-7_29
20. Krizhevsky, A., Hinton, G., et al.: Learning multiple layers of features from tiny images (2009)
21. Kumaran, D., Hassabis, D., McClelland, J.L.: What learning systems do intelligent agents need? Complementary learning systems theory updated. Trends Cogn. Sci. **20**(7), 512–534 (2016)
22. LeCun, Y.: The MNIST database of handwritten digits (1998). http://yann.lecun.com/exdb/mnist/
23. Lester, B., Al-Rfou, R., Constant, N.: The power of scale for parameter-efficient prompt tuning. arXiv preprint arXiv:2104.08691 (2021)
24. Li, X.L., Liang, P.: Prefix-tuning: optimizing continuous prompts for generation. arXiv preprint arXiv:2101.00190 (2021)
25. Li, X., Zhou, Y., Wu, T., Socher, R., Xiong, C.: Learn to grow: a continual structure learning framework for overcoming catastrophic forgetting. In: ICML, pp. 3925–3934. PMLR (2019)
26. Li, Z., Hoiem, D.: Learning without forgetting. TPAMI **40**(12), 2935–2947 (2017)
27. Liu, P., Yuan, W., Fu, J., Jiang, Z., Hayashi, H., Neubig, G.: Pre-train, prompt, and predict: A systematic survey of prompting methods in natural language processing. arXiv preprint arXiv:2107.13586 (2021)
28. Liu, X., Ji, K., Fu, Y., Du, Z., Yang, Z., Tang, J.: P-tuning v2: prompt tuning can be comparable to fine-tuning universally across scales and tasks. arXiv preprint arXiv:2110.07602 (2021)
29. Lomonaco, V., Maltoni, D., Pellegrini, L.: Rehearsal-free continual learning over small non-IID batches. In: CVPR Workshops, pp. 989–998 (2020)
30. Loo, N., Swaroop, S., Turner, R.E.: Generalized variational continual learning. arXiv preprint arXiv:2011.12328 (2020)
31. Lopez-Paz, D., Ranzato, M.: Gradient episodic memory for continual learning. NeurIPS (2017)
32. Van der Maaten, L., Hinton, G.: Visualizing data using t-SNE. JMLR **9**(11), 2579–2605 (2008)
33. Mai, Z., Li, R., Jeong, J., Quispe, D., Kim, H., Sanner, S.: Online continual learning in image classification: an empirical survey. arXiv preprint arXiv:2101.10423 (2021)
34. Mallya, A., Davis, D., Lazebnik, S.: Piggyback: adapting a single network to multiple tasks by learning to mask weights. In: Ferrari, V., Hebert, M., Sminchisescu, C., Weiss, Y. (eds.) ECCV 2018. LNCS, vol. 11208, pp. 72–88. Springer, Cham (2018). https://doi.org/10.1007/978-3-030-01225-0_5

35. Mallya, A., Lazebnik, S.: PackNet: adding multiple tasks to a single network by iterative pruning. In: CVPR (2018)
36. Masana, M., Liu, X., Twardowski, B., Menta, M., Bagdanov, A.D., van de Weijer, J.: Class-incremental learning: survey and performance evaluation on image classification. arXiv preprint arXiv:2010.15277 (2020)
37. McClelland, J.L., McNaughton, B.L., O'Reilly, R.C.: Why there are complementary learning systems in the hippocampus and neocortex: insights from the successes and failures of connectionist models of learning and memory. Psychol. Rev. **102**(3), 419 (1995)
38. McCloskey, M., Cohen, N.J.: Catastrophic interference in connectionist networks: The sequential learning problem. Psychol. Learn. Motiv. **24**, 109–165 (1989)
39. Mehta, S.V., Patil, D., Chandar, S., Strubell, E.: An empirical investigation of the role of pre-training in lifelong learning. In: ICML Workshop (2021)
40. Mirzadeh, S.I., et al.: Architecture matters in continual learning. arXiv preprint arXiv:2202.00275 (2022)
41. Netzer, Y., Wang, T., Coates, A., Bissacco, A., Wu, B., Ng, A.Y.: Reading digits in natural images with unsupervised feature learning. In: NIPS (2011)
42. Pfeiffer, J., Kamath, A., Rücklé, A., Cho, K., Gurevych, I.: AdapterFusion: non-destructive task composition for transfer learning. arXiv preprint arXiv:2005.00247 (2020)
43. Pham, Q., Liu, C., Hoi, S.: DualNet: continual learning, fast and slow. In: NeurIPS 34 (2021)
44. Pham, Q., Liu, C., Sahoo, D., et al.: Contextual transformation networks for online continual learning. In: ICLR (2020)
45. Prabhu, A., Torr, P.H.S., Dokania, P.K.: GDumb: a simple approach that questions our progress in continual learning. In: Vedaldi, A., Bischof, H., Brox, T., Frahm, J.-M. (eds.) ECCV 2020. LNCS, vol. 12347, pp. 524–540. Springer, Cham (2020). https://doi.org/10.1007/978-3-030-58536-5_31
46. Raffel, C., et al.: Exploring the limits of transfer learning with a unified text-to-text transformer. JMLR **21**, 1–67 (2020)
47. Raghu, M., Unterthiner, T., Kornblith, S., Zhang, C., Dosovitskiy, A.: Do vision transformers see like convolutional neural networks? In: NeurIPS 34 (2021)
48. Rajasegaran, J., Hayat, M., Khan, S.H., Khan, F.S., Shao, L.: Random path selection for continual learning. In: NeurIPS 32 (2019)
49. Rebuffi, S.A., Kolesnikov, A., Sperl, G., Lampert, C.H.: iCaRL: incremental classifier and representation learning. In: CVPR, pp. 2001–2010 (2017)
50. Ridnik, T., Ben-Baruch, E., Noy, A., Zelnik-Manor, L.: ImageNet-21k pretraining for the masses. arXiv preprint arXiv:2104.10972 (2021)
51. Rusu, A.A., et al.: Progressive neural networks. arXiv preprint arXiv:1606.04671 (2016)
52. Serra, J., Suris, D., Miron, M., Karatzoglou, A.: Overcoming catastrophic forgetting with hard attention to the task. In: ICML, pp. 4548–4557 (2018)
53. Shokri, R., Shmatikov, V.: Privacy-preserving deep learning. In: Proceedings of SIGSAC Conference on Computer and Communications Security (2015)
54. Smith, J., Balloch, J., Hsu, Y.C., Kira, Z.: Memory-efficient semi-supervised continual learning: the world is its own replay buffer. arXiv preprint arXiv:2101.09536 (2021)
55. Vaswani, A., et al.: Attention is all you need. In: NeurIPS (2017)
56. Wang, R., et al.: K-adapter: Infusing knowledge into pre-trained models with adapters. arXiv preprint arXiv:2002.01808 (2020)

57. Wang, Z., Jian, T., Chowdhury, K., Wang, Y., Dy, J., Ioannidis, S.: Learn-prune-share for lifelong learning. In: ICDM (2020)
58. Wang, Z., et al.: Learning to prompt for continual learning. In: CVPR (2022)
59. Wortsman, M., et al.: Supermasks in superposition. arXiv preprint arXiv:2006.14769 (2020)
60. Wu, Y., et al.: Large scale incremental learning. In: CVPR, pp. 374–382 (2019)
61. Xiao, H., Rasul, K., Vollgraf, R.: Fashion-MNIST: a novel image dataset for benchmarking machine learning algorithms. arXiv preprint arXiv:1708.07747 (2017)
62. Yan, S., Xie, J., He, X.: DER: dynamically expandable representation for class incremental learning. In: CVPR, pp. 3014–3023 (2021)
63. Yoon, J., Yang, E., Lee, J., Hwang, S.J.: Lifelong learning with dynamically expandable networks. arXiv preprint arXiv:1708.01547 (2017)
64. Zeiler, M.D., Fergus, R.: Visualizing and understanding convolutional networks. In: Fleet, D., Pajdla, T., Schiele, B., Tuytelaars, T. (eds.) ECCV 2014. LNCS, vol. 8689, pp. 818–833. Springer, Cham (2014). https://doi.org/10.1007/978-3-319-10590-1_53
65. Zenke, F., Poole, B., Ganguli, S.: Continual learning through synaptic intelligence. In: ICML (2017)
66. Zeno, C., Golan, I., Hoffer, E., Soudry, D.: Task agnostic continual learning using online variational bayes. arXiv preprint arXiv:1803.10123 (2018)
67. Zhao, T., Wang, Z., Masoomi, A., Dy, J.: Deep Bayesian unsupervised lifelong learning. Neural Netw. **149**, 95–106 (2022)

Unifying Visual Contrastive Learning for Object Recognition from a Graph Perspective

Shixiang Tang[1,3], Feng Zhu[3], Lei Bai[1,2(✉)], Rui Zhao[3,4], Chenyu Wang[1], and Wanli Ouyang[1,2]

[1] University of Sydney, Camperdown, Australia
stan3906@uni.sydney.edu.au , baisanshi@gmail.com
[2] Shanghai AI Laboratory, Shanghai, China
[3] Sensetime Research, Hong Kong, China
[4] Qing Yuan Research Institute, Shanghai Jiao Tong University, Shanghai, China

Abstract. Recent contrastive based unsupervised object recognition methods leverage a Siamese architecture, which has two branches composed of a backbone, a projector layer, and an optional predictor layer in each branch. To learn the parameters of the backbone, existing methods have a similar projector layer design, while the major difference among them lies in the predictor layer. In this paper, we propose to Unify existing unsupervised Visual Contrastive Learning methods by using a GCN layer as the predictor layer (UniVCL), which deserves two merits to unsupervised learning in object recognition. First, by treating different designs of predictors in the existing methods as its special cases, our fair and comprehensive experiments reveal the critical importance of neighborhood aggregation in the GCN predictor. Second, by viewing the predictor from the graph perspective, we can bridge the vision self-supervised learning with the graph representation learning area, which facilitates us to introduce the augmentations from the graph representation learning to unsupervised object recognition and further improves the unsupervised object recognition accuracy. Extensive experiments on linear evaluation and the semi-supervised learning tasks demonstrate the effectiveness of UniVCL and the introduced graph augmentations.

1 Introduction

Self-supervised learning (SSL) [1,11,23,28,36,50,54,62] has recently attracted much research interest in the computer vision community. Contrastive learning [5,7–9,16,18,20,51,59,65], which is an important framework of recent unsupervised learning methods, aims to reduce the distance between augmented views from the same image (positive samples) and push apart views from different

Supplementary Information The online version contains supplementary material available at https://doi.org/10.1007/978-3-031-19809-0_37.

images (negative samples). It has shown the potential to extract powerful visual representations that are competitive with supervised learning and delivered superior performance on multiple visual tasks when models are pre-trained without labels.

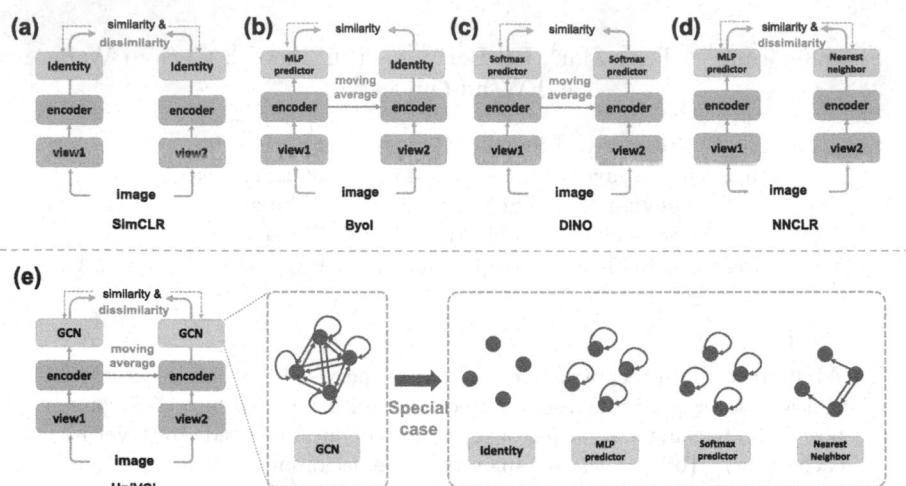

Fig. 1. (a-d): Existing self-supervised learning methods share the similar encoder designs, but have highly different designs in their predictors. The encoder in the picture includes a backbone and a projector. (e): Our UniVCL unifies different designs by a GCN layer, which has a neighborhood aggregation term and a self-loop term. The arrow denotes the aggregation operation. Specifically, the MLP predictor and Softmax predictor are the self-loop terms with different activation functions. The nearest neighbor retrieval can be viewed the neighborhood aggregation term in GCN layer.

Recent contrastive-based SSL methods leverage a Siamese architecture, which has two branches, i.e., an online branch and a target branch. Each branch is composed of a backbone, a projector layer, and an optional predictor layer. While the processes in the backbone and projector layer are similar for these works, there are major difference in their predictor layer designs as shown in Fig. 1(a-d). Specifically, there are four types of predictor layers. 1) SimCLR [5], MOCOv1 [18], MOCOv2 [7] do not have any operation after the projector layer, which is mathematically equivalent to using an identity layer as the predictor. 2) BYOL [16], SimSiam [8], and MOCOv3 [9] use a MLP predictor on the online branch; 3) DINO [4], SEED [14], and TWIST [49] leverage a softmax layer on both online branch and target branch; 4) recent states-of-the-art methods, *e.g.,* NNCLR [13] and MSF [27], retrieve the K nearest neighboring samples (K-nearest neighbor layer) in the feature space on the target branch for contrastive learning. While these designs seem to be highly different in how to learn representations, we advocate that they can be viewed as a unified framework by simply modifying the predictor design from the perspective of graph neural network.

In this work, we propose a Unified Vison Contrastive Learning (UniVCL) framework that is a unified representation of the aforementioned four typical types of contrastive-based SSL methods from a graph perspective. By modeling the projection feature and its K nearest neighbors in the feature space as the graph nodes, Graph Convolution Network (GCN) layer [24, 46, 55], which consists of a self-loop term and a neighborhood aggregation term, can formulate different predictor designs as its special variant (see the second row of Fig. 1). Specifically, the identity mapping, the MLP layer, and the softmax layer can be viewed as the self-loop term only with different activation functions, and the K-nearest neighbor retrieval can be viewed as the neighborhood aggregation term in the GCN layer. From this perspective, we benchmark different predictor designs in existing methods under the same learning schedules, data augmentations, and objective functions. Our detailed and fair experiments lead to three interesting observations. Firstly, the neighborhood aggregation term in the GCN layer can significantly improves the linear evaluation performances by $+2.1\%$. Secondly, the activation function can fairly influence the linear evaluation performance. The non-linear activation function can boost about $+0.4\%$ performance gain than identity activation function. Thirdly, the performance difference between different non-linear activation functions are quite small if other GCN layer components are well-designed, indicating the non-linear activation function selection to be a less important factor.

With this unified framework from the graph perspective, we can further link vision SSL with graph SSL, another active SSL research topic, and explore the effectiveness of different pretext tasks in graph SSL for vision SSL. Specifically, the new data augmentation, i.e. graph augmentation, found to be effective in graph SSL can be leveraged for vision SSL. Graph augmentation adds variations to features according to the graph structure to regularize the network optimization. Our studies on ImageNet-1K uncover that the graph augmentation that uses message passing throughout the network can improve the self-supervised learning methods in image classification by $+1.0\%$. Our in-depth analysis by the purity metric [27] verifies that these augmentations can add the edge noise in the GCN predictor, and regularize the encoder to learn more robustness image features.

To conclude, our contributions are three-folds: **(1)** We propose a general framework (UniVCL) to unify recent states-of-the-art contrastive learning methods in the vision SSL domain. **(2)** We illustrate the importance of neighborhood aggregation term and the non-linear activation function of GCN layer in UniVCL by conducting fair and detailed experimental comparisons. **(3)** Owing to graph design of UniVCL, we bridge vision SSL and graph SSL, and introduce typical graph augmentations into self-supervised image classification, which is empirically verified to be beneficial to linear evaluation and semi-supervised learning performances.

2   Related Work

2.1   Self-supervised Learning on Vision

A typical unsupervised learning framework for contrastive learning consists of a Siamese network. The two branches of the Siamese network are named as the online branch and the target branch [5,16] (also named as the query branch and the key branch in some literature [7,13,18]), respectively, where each includes a backbone, a projector layer and an optional predictor layer. Recent states-of-the-art vision SSL methods share similar designs of backbone network and projector layer, but they differs in the predictor designs. Typical predictor designs can be divided into four categories. The first type of the predictor layer is the identity mapping, which is adopted in SimCLR [5], MOCOv2 [7], and the target branch of MOCOv3 [9], BYOL [16], and other self-supervised contrastive learning methods [59]. The second type is the MLP predictor. The MLP predictor is initially proposed to avoid network collapse by BYOL. Some following contrastive learning based papers, *e.g.,* MOCOv3, also append the predictor layer after the projector layer to improve the self-supervised learning performance instead of avoid network collapse. The third type of the predictor is the softmax layer, which is a softmax activation function applied in methods equipped with KL-divergence loss. The representative methods include DINO [4], SEED [14], and TWIST [49]. The recent states-of-the-art methods retrieve the k-nearest sample in the feature space. Experimental results illustrate the contrastive learning by using nearest samples as the positive sample can improve the linear evaluation compared with using the different augmented view of the same sample as its positive samples. Although these methods have highly different designs for predictors, our method unifies them with a Graph Convolution Layer, which can 1) represent lots of existing works and 2) include graph self-supervised learning designs (unification of self-loop and neighborhood aggregation and graph augmentation) that are not covered in these works.

2.2   Self-supervised Learning on Graph

Recent years witness the development of deep learning on graphs [21,25,33,48, 58], since the graph-structured is ubiquitous in numerous domains, including e-commence [31], traffic [52], and knowledge base [32]. The biggest challenge of self-supervised learning on graphs lies in learning the topology information in the existing network. Contrastive learning methods are also cornerstones for self-supervised learning on graphs [2,37,40,41,47]. In particular, the contrastive loss uses two different augmented views of the same graph as the positive samples to maximize their mutual information. Typical augmentation methods include Node Feature Masking [21,64], Edge Modification [22,57], and Graph Diffusion [17,26]. However, self-supervised Learning on graph has not been investigated for unsupervised object recognition. In this paper, by incorporating GCN layers as the predictor in the deep models for object recognition, we can introduce and verify the effectiveness of graph augmentations that are widely adopted in the graph self-supervised learning on the unsupervised object recognition.

3 UniVCL

We are interested in using the Graph Convolution Network (GCN) to unify different predictor designs in different methods. Specifically, we maintain a support queue $\mathcal{S} = \{\mathbf{s}_i | i \in [1, \cdots, m]\} \in \mathbb{R}^{m \times d}$ in the same way as [13], where m is the size of the support queue, and d is the feature dimension. We only use embeddings from the target view to update the support set. As shown in Fig. 2, our proposed UniVCL has the following steps.

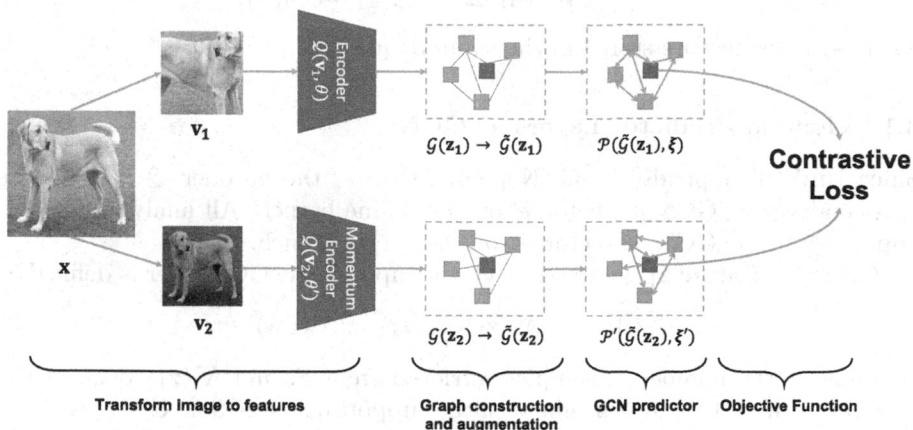

Fig. 2. The framework of UniVCL. It includes four steps. First, Given an image $\mathbf{x}$, two augmented views $\mathbf{v}_1$ and $\mathbf{v}$ are generated. Then the features $\mathbf{z}_1$ and $\mathbf{z}_2$ are extracted by encoder $\mathcal{Q}(*, \theta)$ and $\mathcal{Q}(*, \theta')$, respectively. Second, we retrieve the K nearest neighborhood samples of $\mathbf{z}_1$ and $\mathbf{z}_2$ from the support queue $\mathcal{S}$, forming graph $\mathcal{G}(\mathbf{z}_1)$ and $\mathcal{G}(\mathbf{z}_2)$ respectively. Then, we implement the graph augmentation on $\mathcal{G}(\mathbf{z}_1)$ and $\mathcal{G}(\mathbf{z}_2)$, generating augmented graphs $\widetilde{\mathcal{G}}(\mathbf{z}_1)$ and $\widetilde{\mathcal{G}}(\mathbf{z}_2)$. Third, we input the augmented graph into the GCN predictor layer, generating the predicted features $\mathbf{q}_1$ and $\mathbf{q}_2$. Last, we compute the alignment loss based on $\mathbf{q}_1$ and $\mathbf{q}_2$. The encoder denotes both the backbone network and the projector layer.

Step1: Transform Image to Features. Specifically, given two different augmented views $(\mathbf{v}_1, \mathbf{v}_2)$ of an image $\mathbf{x}$, the features of two views can be computed by $\mathbf{z}_1 = \mathcal{Q}(\mathbf{v}_1, \theta)$ and $\mathbf{z}_2 = \mathcal{Q}(\mathbf{v}_2, \theta')$, respectively. Following [7,9,16,18], the online branch $\mathcal{Q}(*, \theta)$ is a neural network updated by backward propagation, while the target branch $\mathcal{Q}(*, \theta')$ is a network with the same architecture as the online branch but with parameters obtained from the moving average of $\mathcal{Q}(*, \theta)$.

Step2: Graph Construction and Augmentation (Sect. 3.3). Give $\mathbf{z}_1$ and $\mathbf{z}_2$ from Step 1, we respectively construct the fully connected graph $\mathcal{G}(\mathbf{z}_1)$ and $\mathcal{G}(\mathbf{z}_2)$, where nodes in $\mathcal{G}(\mathbf{z}_1)$ and $\mathcal{G}(\mathbf{z}_2)$ are K nearest neighbors of $\mathbf{z}_1$ and $\mathbf{z}_2$ in support queue $\mathcal{S}$, respectively. Then we implement typical graph augmentations (Sect. 3.3) to generate the augmented graphs $\widetilde{\mathcal{G}}(\mathbf{z}_1)$ and $\widetilde{\mathcal{G}}(\mathbf{z}_2)$.

Step 3: GCN Predictor (Sect. 3.1). The augmented graphs $\widetilde{\mathcal{G}}(\mathbf{z}_1)$ and $\widetilde{\mathcal{G}}(\mathbf{z}_2)$ are respectively transformed to prediction features $\mathbf{q}_1$ and $\mathbf{q}_2$ through GCN predictors $\mathcal{P}(*, \xi)$ and $\mathcal{P}'(*, \xi')$.

Step 4: Backward propagation using the alignment loss. Given the prediction features $\mathbf{q}_1$ and $\mathbf{q}_2$, the parameters θ in $\mathcal{Q}(*, \theta)$ and the parameters ξ, ξ' in $\mathcal{P}(*, \xi)$, $\mathcal{P}'(*, \xi')$ are learned by using alignment loss. In our design, the alignment loss is implemented as the contrastive, *i.e.*,

$$\mathcal{L} = -\log \frac{\exp(\mathbf{q}_1^\top \mathbf{q}_2)}{\exp(\mathbf{q}_1^\top \mathbf{q}_2) + \sum_{i=1}^{m} \exp(\mathbf{q}_1^\top \mathbf{s}_i)}, \tag{1}$$

where $\mathbf{s}_i$ is the feature stored in the support queue $\mathcal{S}$.

3.1   General Predictor Layers as GCNs

Since UniVCL appends the GCN predictor after the encoder $\mathcal{Q}$ and $\mathcal{Q}'$, we only analyze the GCN predictor $\mathcal{P}$ on the online branch. All analysis below is applicable to the GCN predictor $\mathcal{P}'$ on the target branch.

Given the feature $\mathbf{z}_1$ obtained by $\mathcal{Q}$, the input of the GCN layer is defined as

$$\mathcal{G}(\mathbf{z}_1) = (\mathbf{z}_1, \mathcal{N}_1(\mathbf{z}_1), \mathcal{N}_2(\mathbf{z}_1), ..., \mathcal{N}_K(\mathbf{z}_1)) \tag{2}$$

where K is the number of samples retrieved from $\mathcal{S}$, and $\mathcal{N}_i(\mathbf{z}_1)$ denotes the features of the i-th nearest neighbor in the support queue $\mathcal{S}$. The GCN predictor $\mathbf{q}_1 = \mathcal{P}(\mathcal{G}(\mathbf{z}_1))$ can be represented as a stack of graph convolution layers $\mathcal{F}_l$, where l is the layer index, *i.e.*, $\mathcal{P}(\mathcal{G}(\mathbf{z}_1), \theta) = \mathcal{F}_L(\mathcal{F}_{L-1} \cdots (\mathcal{F}_2(\mathcal{F}_1(\mathcal{G}(\mathbf{z}_1))))),$ where L is the number of stacked GCN layers. Here, $\mathcal{F}_l$ is presented as

$$\mathbf{F}_{l+1} = \mathcal{F}_l(\mathbf{F}_l) = \sigma_l(\underbrace{\mathbf{W}_l \mathbf{A} \mathbf{F}_l}_{\text{neighborhood aggregation}} + \underbrace{\mathbf{W}_l' \mathbf{F}_l}_{\text{self-loop}}), \tag{3}$$

where the affinities $\mathbf{A} = \{a_{i,j}\} \in \mathbb{R}^{(K+1)\times(K+1)}, 0 \le i, j \le K$ are defined as

$$a_{i,j} = \begin{cases} \mathcal{N}_i(\mathbf{z}_1)^\top \mathcal{N}_j(\mathbf{z}_1), & i \ne j, \\ 0, & i = j, \end{cases} \tag{4}$$

where $e_{i,j}$ is the affinity between $\mathcal{N}_i(\mathbf{z}_1)$ and $\mathcal{N}_j(\mathbf{z}_1)$, and we denote $\mathcal{N}_0(\mathbf{z}_1) = \mathbf{z}_1$.

3.2   Unifying Unsupervised Contrastive Learning Methods in UniVCL

As UniGrad [42] has explored the equivalence of different objective functions in the existing methods both theoretically and experimentally, we focus on the predictor designs among these different self-supervised learning methods.

As shown in Table 1 and Fig. 1(a-d), the predictor designs of different self-supervised learning methods can be categorized into four types: the identity predictor, the MLP predictor, the Softmax predictor, and the nearest neighbor

Table 1. The implementation of predictor layer the existing self-supervised learning methods. We omit the comparison of objective functions in different methods because they are not the focus of our paper. The type number here denotes one of the four types described in Sect. 1 and Fig. 1(a-d).

Method	Venue	Type	Online branch	Target branch
MOCOv2	Arxiv'21	a	Identity	Identity
SimCLR	ICML'20	a	Identity	Identity
Barlow Twins	ICML'21	a	Identity	Identity
MOCOv3	ICCV'21	b	MLP	Identity
BYOL	NeurIPS'20	b	MLP	Identity
SimSiam	CVPR'21	b	MLP	Identity
DINO	ICCV'21	c	Softmax	Softmax
SEED	ICLR'21	c	Softmax	Softmax
TWIST	Arxiv'21	c	Softmax	Softmax
NNCLR	ICCV'21	d	MLP	K nearest
MSF	ICCV'21	d	MLP	K nearest

Table 2. Illustrate the simplification to different predictor layers based the formal formulation of Graph Convolution predictor in Eq. 3.

Method	Activation	Neighborhood aggregation		Self-loop	
	σ	Existence	$\mathbf{A}$ $\mathbf{W}$	Existence	$\mathbf{W}'$
Identity	$\mathbf{I}$	x	$-$ $\mathbf{0}$	✓	$\mathbf{I}$
Percepton	ReLU(BN)	x	$-$ $\mathbf{0}$	✓	Train
fc	$\mathbf{I}$	x	$-$ $\mathbf{0}$	✓	Train
Softmax	Softmax	x	$-$ $\mathbf{0}$	✓	$\mathbf{I}$
Nearest neighbors	$\mathbf{I}$	✓	$\mathbf{1}$ $\mathbf{I}$	x	$\mathbf{0}$

predictor. Based on the the formal formulation of a graph convolution layer in Eq. 3, Table 2 shows that these different designs are special cases of Eq. 3. The detailed derivation for Table 2 is presented below.

The Identity Predictor (Fig. 1(a)). SimCLR [5] and MOCOv2 [7] do not append an explicit predictor after the projector, which is mathematically equivalent to appending an identity predictor. In this case, the predictor can be formulated as

$$\mathbf{F}_{l+1} = \mathbf{F}_l. \tag{5}$$

The formulation above can be obtained by setting $\sigma_l = \mathbf{I}$, $\mathbf{W}_l = \mathbf{0}$, $\mathbf{W}'_l = \mathbf{I}$ in Eq. 3 for our unified graph convolution predictor. In this case, the neighborhood aggregation term is ignored, and the self-loop term is exactly the identity mapping.

The MLP Predictors (Fig. 1(b)). Popular unsupervised learning methods such as MOCOv3 [9], BYOL [16] and Simsiam [5] use MLP layers as predictors. The typical MLP is a stack of *fc-bn-relu* layers (perception layer), where *fc-bn-relu* layer can be formulated as

$$F_{l+1} = \text{ReLU}(\text{BN}(W'_l F_l)). \tag{6}$$

The *fc-relu-bn* above can be obtained by setting $\sigma_l = \text{ReLU}(\text{BN})$ in Eq. 3. In this case, the neighborhood aggregation term is also ignored and only the self-loop term is presented. Some unsupervised learning methods such as MOCOv3, BYOL and Simsiam uses the fully-connected layer as the last layer in the constructed MLP predictor, which can be obtained by setting the activation function as the identity matrix, *i.e.*, $\sigma_l = I$.

The Softmax Predictors (Fig. 1(c)). DINO presents a softmax predictor to obtain the logits for the following KL-divergence loss. The softmax operation can be presented as

$$F_{l+1} = \text{Softmax}(W'_l F_l). \tag{7}$$

The softmax predictor above can be achieved by setting $\sigma_l = \text{Softmax}$ for the graph convolution predictor (Eq. 3). In this case, the neighborhood aggregation term is ignored and only the self-loop term is presented.

The K Nearest Neighbors Predictors (Fig. 1(d)). Recent states-of-the-art methods treats the sample and its K nearest neighbors in the feature space as the positive samples. Given $F_l = (f_l^0, f_l^1, ..., f_l^K)$. The K nearest neighbor predictor can be presented as

$$\begin{aligned}
f_{l+1}^i &= \frac{1}{K}(\mathcal{N}_1(f_l^i) + \mathcal{N}_2(f_l^i) + ... + \mathcal{N}_K(f_l^i)) \\
&= \frac{1}{K}(0, 1, 1, ..., 1)^\top (f_l^i, \mathcal{N}_1(f_l^i), \mathcal{N}_2(f_l^i), ..., \mathcal{N}_K(f_l^i)) \\
&= \frac{1}{K}(0, 1, 1, ..., 1)^\top (f_l^0, f_l^1, ..., f_l^K) \\
&= \frac{1}{K}(0, 1, 1, ..., 1)^\top F_l.
\end{aligned} \tag{8}$$

Therefore, the output of the l-th GCN predictor can be formulated as

$$F_{l+1} = \frac{1}{K}(0, 1, 1, ..., 1)^\top (f_{l+1}^1, f_{l+1}^2, ..., f_{l+1}^K) = \frac{1}{K}(0, 1, 1, ..., 1)^\top F_{l+1}. \tag{9}$$

Compared with typical graph convolution layer (Eq. 3), the K-nearest-neighbor layer can be obtained by setting $\sigma_l = I$ and the affinity matrix $A = \frac{1}{K}(0, 1, 1, ..., 1)^\top \in \mathbb{R}^{(K+1)\times(K+1)}$. In this case, only neighborhood aggregation term is considered and the self-loop term is ignored.

3.3   Graph Augmentations for Unsupervised Visual Learning

To better take advantage of pretext tasks in graph contrastive learning, the proposed GCN predictor layer leverages an augmented graph $\widetilde{\mathcal{G}}(z_1)$ as the input [2,37,47,63]. Given an input graph $\mathcal{G}(\mathbf{z})$ defined by Eq. 2, we implement the typical graph augmentations in self-supervised graph contrastive learning on $\mathcal{G}(\mathbf{z}_1)$, achieving $\widetilde{\mathcal{G}}(\mathbf{z}_1) = (\widetilde{\mathcal{V}}, \widetilde{\mathbf{A}}) = (t(\mathcal{V}), s(\mathbf{A}))$, where t and s are augmentations on the node features $\mathcal{V}$ and affinities $\mathbf{A}$, respectively. After graph augmentation, we will change the input node features and affinity as $\widetilde{\mathcal{V}}$ and $\widetilde{\mathbf{A}}$ in Eq. 3 as the input of the GCN predictor.

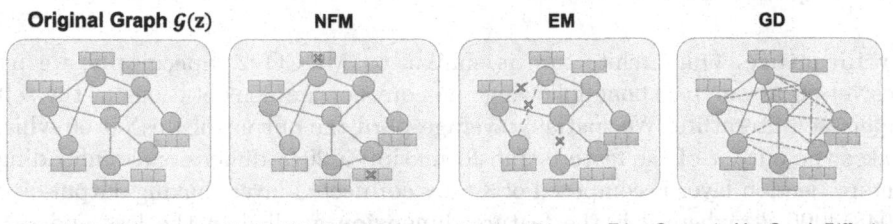

Fig. 3. Graph augmentations. There are three typical graph augmentations, *i.e.,* node feature masking (NFM), edge modification (EM), and graph diffusion (GD).

Node Feature Masking (NFM). As shown in Fig. 3, Node Feature Masking (NFM) randomly masks the features of a portion of nodes within $\mathcal{G}(\mathbf{z})$. In particular, we can completely mask seleceted feature vectors with zeros, or partially mask a number of selected feature channels with zeros. This operation can be formulated as

$$\widetilde{\mathcal{V}} = t(\mathcal{V}) = \mathbf{M}_f \circ \mathcal{V}, \quad \widetilde{\mathbf{A}} = s(\mathbf{A}) = \mathbf{A}, \tag{10}$$

where $\mathbf{M}_f$ is the feature masking matrix with the same shape of $\mathcal{V}$, and $\circ$ denotes the Hadamard (element-wise) product. The elements in $\mathbf{M}_f$ are initialized to one and masking entries are 30% randomly assigned to zero.

Edge Modification (EM). Edge modification (EM) randomly drops the affinities, which means setting the affinities to zeros. This process is formulated as

$$\widetilde{\mathcal{V}} = t(\mathcal{V}) = \mathcal{V}, \quad \widetilde{\mathbf{A}} = s(\mathbf{A}) = \mathbf{M}_e \circ \mathbf{A}, \tag{11}$$

where $\mathbf{M}_e$ is the edge dropping matrix, and $\circ$ denotes the Hadamard product.

Graph Diffusion (GD). Graph diffusion is also a type of affinity augmentations, which injects the global affinity information to the given affinity by recomputing the affinity with diffusion operations. The overall diffusion operation can be formulated as

$$\widetilde{\mathcal{V}} = t(\mathcal{V}) = \mathcal{V}, \quad \widetilde{\mathbf{A}} = s(\mathbf{A}) = \sum_{n=0}^{\infty} \Theta_n \mathbf{T}^n, \tag{12}$$

where Θ_n and $\mathbf{T}$ are weighing coefficient and transition matrix, respectively. The diffusion above have two common instantiations: heat diffusion [26,43] and PPR diffusion [12,15]. The heat diffusion formulates $\Theta_n = \frac{\exp(-\eta)t^n}{n!}$, and $\mathbf{T} = \mathbf{A}\mathbf{D}^{-1}$, achieving $\widetilde{\mathbf{A}} = \exp(\eta \mathbf{A}\mathbf{D}^{-1} - \eta)\mathbf{A}$, where $\mathbf{A}$ is the affinity matrix, $\mathbf{D}$ is the diagonal degree matrix, $\eta \in (0,1)$ is the diffusion time. The PPR diffusion formulates $\Theta_n = \gamma(1-\gamma)^n$, and $\mathbf{T} = \mathbf{D}^{-1/2}\mathbf{A}\mathbf{D}^{-1/2}$, achieving $\widetilde{\mathbf{A}} = \gamma(\mathbf{I} - (1-\gamma)\mathbf{D}^{-1/2}\mathbf{A}\mathbf{D}^{-1/2})\mathbf{A}$, where $\gamma \in (0,1)$ is the teleport probability in random walk.

4 Experiment

4.1 Implementation Details

Architecture. Our architecture is similar to MOCOv2. Specifically, we use ResNet-50 as our backbone following the common implementations in the self-supervised literature. We spatially average pool the output of ResNet-50 which makes the output of the feature transformation a 2048-dimensional embedding. The projection layer is composed of 3 fully connected layers having output sizes $[2048, 4096, d]$, where d is the feature dimension applied in the loss and $d = 2048$ if not specified. Besides, batch normalization and ReLU activation function is employed in the projection layer following other SSL works [8,9,16]. The architecture of the predictor is the GCN layers, which is formulated in Eq. 3.

Training. For a fair comparison, we train our method on the ImageNet2012 dataset, which contains 1,281,167 images without using any annotation or class labels. In the training stage, we train for 200 and 800 epochs with a warm-up of 10 epochs and cosine annealing schedule using the LARS optimizer. The

Table 3. Ablation of the importance of parameters in the GCN predictor. $\mathbf{I}^*$ denotes the centering operation proposed in DINO which is used to avoid network collapse. "train" denotes the trainable parameters. "ema" denotes exponential moving average of the parameters in the online branch.

Method	Online branch				Target branch				Linear
	Act.	Neigh. Agg.		Self-loop	Act.	Neigh. Agg.		Self-loop	
	σ	$\mathbf{A}$	$\mathbf{W}$	$\mathbf{W}'$	σ	$\mathbf{A}$	$\mathbf{W}$	$\mathbf{W}'$	
Baseline									
MOCOv2	I	–	0	I	I	–	0	I	68.6
Effectiveness of activation function									
Exp.(a)	I	–	0	Train	I	–	0	I	68.5
Exp.(b)	Re(BN)	–	0	Train	I	–	0	I	69.3
Exp.(c)	Re(BN)	–	–	I	I	–	–	I	67.5
Exp.(d)	Softmax	–	0	I	Softmax	–	0	I	69.3
Exp.(e)	Softmax	–	0	Train	Softmax	–	0	I*	69.4
Effectiveness of neighborhood aggregation									
Exp.(f)	Re(BN)	–	0	Train	I	1	I	0	71.4
Exp.(g)	Re(BN)	–	0	Train	I	1	I	I	71.8
Exp.(h)	Re(BN)	1	Train	Train	I	1	I	Ema	71.9

base learning rate is set to 0.3. Weight decay of 10^{-6} is applied during training. As is common practice, we do not use weight decay on the bias. The training details above are the same as MOCOv2. We also use the basic data augmentation scheme (i.e., random crop, color jittering) as MOCOv2 and do not include the multi-crop strategy [3] for a fair comparison with the most majority of works.

4.2   Ablation Study

Exploring the Critical Factors in GCN Predictor. Previous self-supervised learning methods have different predictor designs in activation functions, and the using of neighborhood aggregation. For example, MOCOv2 [7] and SimCLR [5,6] uses the linear activation, MOCOv3 [9] and BYOL [16] use the ReLU(BN) as the activation function in the online branch, DINO [4] uses Softmax layer as the activation function. Furthermore, the recent state-of-the-art methods, *i.e.*, MSF and NNCLR, retrieve the nearest neighbors in the feature space in the target branch, which can be mathematically viewed as the neighborhood aggregation as analyzed in Table 1. To strictly ablate the importance of different components in the GCN predictor layer, we keep the batch size, objective function, learning rate schedule, optimizer exactly the same, and then train the ImageNet-1K for 200 epochs. For the MLP predictor, we stack three GCN layers as the common practice with ReLU(BN) being its activation function except the last GCN layer.

Effectiveness of Activation Function σ. We have three findings from Table 3. First, comparing Exp. (a) and Exp. (b,e), we can see that with a learnable transformation matrix $\mathbf{W}'$, the non-linear activation is better than the identity activation by about +0.9%, which is consistent with the finding in MOCOv3 [9]. Second, the trainable transformation $\mathbf{W}'$ plays an important role when the activation function is ReLU(BN), but plays an unimportant role when the activation function is Softmax and Identity mapping. We consider the difference may result from the information loss of ReLU. Third, comparing Exp. (b) and Exp. (e), we find the performance between the GCN layer with different activation functions are quite small if other components are well-designed, which indicates the activation function is a less important factor.

Effectiveness of Neighborhood Aggregation. Different from self-supervised learning methods that do not use supervision from other samples, neighborhood based methods uses K nearest neighbors as their positive samples. This can be achieved by using the neighborhood aggregation term in Eq. 3 in GCN predictor. As shown in Table 3, we have three findings. First, the linear evaluation performances of using neighboring information on the target branch are significantly higher than those self-supervised learning methods by a considerable 2.1% gain by comparing Exp.(b) and Exp. (f). Second, comparing Exp.(f) and Exp.(g), we can see adding the self-loop term in the target branch can only boost the performance by 0.4%. Third, when adding the neighborhood aggregation and self-loop term in both online branch and the target branch, the performance can be further improved by 0.1%, which is not significant by comparing Exp.(g) and Exp.(h).

Evaluating Graph Augmentation in Unsupervised Image Classification. Owing to the GCN predictor, we can naturally bridge the vision SSL with graph SSL, which benefit us to introduce the graph augmentations on the constructed graph $\mathcal{G}(\mathbf{z})$ before the GCN predictor. Refer to Table 3, we use the Exp (h) as the baseline (using a GCN predictor in both online branch and target branch) in this part and extend it with diverse graph augmentations. Specifically, we explore the effectiveness of three common graph augmentations in the following.

Node Feature Masking (NFM) and Edge Masking (EM).   According   to the mechanism of NFM and EM described in [33], we randomly remove the node features or edges in both $\mathcal{G}(\mathbf{z})$ and $\mathcal{G}(\mathbf{z}')$ with different drop probabilities. As shown in Table 4, the performance first increases from 71.9 to 72.1 with NFM and 72.2 with EM, respectively, when we increase the dropping probability from 0 to 0.3. Further increasing the drop probability (e.g., to 0.7) will harm the performance. The results demonstrate that both node and edge masking graph augmentations are beneficial for vision SSL with a proper drop probability.

Table 4. Ablation study of node feature masking and edge modification with different drop probabilities.

Drop probability	NFM	EM
0	71.9	71.9
0.1	72.1	72.0
0.3	72.1	**72.2**
0.5	71.3	71.7
0.7	70.1	70.5

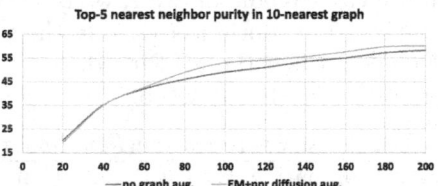

Fig. 4. Top-5 neighbor purity evolution by graph augmentations.

Graph Diffusion (GD). The graph diffusion propagates the global information in the graph to affinities by diffusion. Based on the results about masking-based augmentations, we further integrate the diffusion-based augmentations with EM (drop probability is 0.3) and explore the influence of heat diffusion and PPR diffusion on both online and target branches. The experimental results are presented in Table 5. We can observe that using graph diffusion to incorporate the graph information can significantly improve the the performance baseline by 0.9%. In detail, both heat diffusion and PPR diffusion can benefit vision SSL above the EM augmentation. Besides, using graph diffusion in both branches is more powerful than only using the diffusion in the target branch.

Analysis. In this section, we explain why the graph diffusion operation can improve the unsupervised learning performance empirically. We find the graph diffusion operation can correct the affinity of some visually different but semantically same samples in $\mathcal{G}(\mathbf{z})$. To better illustrate this, we utilize the setting

Table 5. Ablation study of different graph diffusion methods on the online branch and the target branch.

Method	Online branch	Target branch	Linear eval
Exp. (i)	No	No	72.2
Exp. (j)	No	Heat diffusion	72.6
Exp. (k)	No	PPR diffusion	72.8
Exp. (l)	Heat diffusion	Heat diffusion	72.4
Exp. (m)	PPR diffusion	PPR diffusion	72.5
Exp. (n)	Heat diffusion	PPR diffusion	**72.9**
Exp. (o)	PPR diffusion	Heat diffusion	72.8

Table 6. Comparison with other self-supervised learning methods under the linear evaluation protocol [18] on ImageNet. We omit the result for SwAV with multi-crop for fair comparion with other methods.

Method	Architecture	Epochs	Top1	Top5
ODC [61]	ResNet-50	100	57.6	–
InstDisc [51]	ResNet-50	200	58.5	–
LocalAgg [65]	ResNet-50	200	58.8	–
MOCOv2 [7]	ResNet-50	200	68.6	–
MSF [39]	ResNet-50	200	71.4	–
MSF w/s [39]	ResNet-50	200	72.4	–
CPC v2 [19]	ResNet-50	200	63.8	85.3
DINO [19]	VIT-S/16	300	72.5	–
CMC [44]	ResNet-50	240	66.2	87.0
Adco [36]	ResNet-50	200	68.6	–
NNCLR [13]	ResNet-50	200	70.7	–
UniVCL	ResNet-50	200	72.9	–
PIRL [34]	ResNet-50	800	63.6	–
MOCOv2 [7]	ResNet-50	800	71.1	–
SimSiam [8]	ResNet-50	800	71.3	90.7
SimCLR [5]	ResNet-50	800	69.3	89.0
SwAV [3]	ResNet-50	800	71.8	–
InfoMin Aug. [45]	ResNet-50	800	73.0	91.1
BYOL [16]	ResNet-50	1000	74.3	91.6
Adco [36]	ResNet-50	800	72.8	–
Barlow Twins [59]	ResNet-50	1000	73.2	91.0
MoCov3 [9]	ResNet-50	800	73.8	–
NNCLR [13]	ResNet-50	800	75.4	92.4
UniVCL	ResNet-50	800	75.7	93.1

in Exp.(e). Inspired by [39], we compare the **top-5** purity in different epochs between the original 10-nearest graph $\mathcal{G}(\mathbf{z}_2)$ and the 10-nearest augmented graph $\widetilde{\mathcal{G}}(\mathbf{z}_2)$. The purity for a single feature $\mathbf{z}$ is the percentage of $\mathcal{N}_1$ to $\mathcal{N}_K$ in the top-K nearest neighbors which have the same class as $\mathbf{z}$. Final purity is calculated by averaging the purities of all samples. The results are presented in Fig. 4. We find the purity of top-5 nearest neighbor in the augmented graph is higher than that in the original graph. By using affinity as the aggregation weight in GCN layer, we can conclude that the features can be aggregated with more accurate neighbors by using graph augmentations and therefore provided better target predictions for the online branch to learn.

4.3   Comparison with State-of-the-Art Methods

In this section, we utilize the optimal hyperparameters explored in the previous sections. Specifically, we apply the edge masking, followed by heat diffusion on the online brach and PPR diffusion on the target branch. For GCN predictor, we apply the setting in Exp. (h), where we add a GCN predictor in both online branch and target branch, and the parameters of GCN layers in the target branch are updated from the online branch in a momentum update manner. The results of transfer experiments are presented in supplementary materials.

Linear Evaluations. Following the standard linear evaluation protocol [7,18, 51,65], we train a linear classifier for 90 epochs on the frozen 2048-dimensional embeddings from the ResNet-50 encoder using LARS [56] with cosine annealed learning rate of 1 with Nesterov momentum of 0.9 and batch size of 4096. Comparison with state-of-the-art methods is presented in Table 6. Firstly, UniVCL achieves better performance compared to the state-of-the-art methods, using a ResNet-50 backbone without multi-crops augmentations. In 200 epochs training setting, UniVCL improves MOCOv2 by 4.3%, which uses the identity layer in both online branch and target branch. UniVCL still improves the DINO by 0.4% although standard DINO [4] leverages more powerful backbone (VIT-S/16) and more training epochs (300 epochs). The significant improvements by Uni-VCL verifies the significance of our GCN predictor in the unsupervised vision contrastive learning. Secondly, MSF and NNCLR also leverage the neighboring information, but not in a GCN way. The results of our UniVCL is also higher than MSF and NNCLR [13] by 0.5% and 2.2%, respectively, because of grpah formulation and the introducing of graph augmentations from the graph SSL domain with negligible additional computational cost (less than 2%).

Semi-Supervised Learning Evaluations. We conduct experiments in a semi-supervised setting on ImageNet following the standard evaluation protocol [5,6], which fine-tunes the whole base network on 1% or 10% labeled ImageNet data without regularization after unsupervised pre-training. The experimental results are presented in Table 7.

Table 7. Comparison with the state-of-the-art methods for semi-supervised learning. Pseudo Label, UDA, FixMatch and MPL are semi-supervised learning methods. † denotes using random augment [10]. We follow the exact data split in SwAV [3].

Method	ImageNet 1%		ImageNet 10%	
	Top1	Top5	Top1	Top5
Supervised baseline [60]	25.4	48.4	56.4	80.4
Pseudo label [29]	–	–	51.6	82.4
UDA [53]	–	–	68.8†	88.5†
FixMatch [38]	–	–	71.5†	89.1†
MPL [35]	–	73.5†	–	–
InstDisc [51]	–	39.2	–	77.4
PIRL [34]	–	57.2	–	83.8
PCL [30]	–	75.6	–	86.2
SimCLR [5]	48.3	75.5	65.6	87.8
BYOL [16]	53.2	78.4	68.8	89.0
SwAV (multicrop) [3]	53.9	78.5	70.2	89.9
Barlow Twins [59]	55.0	79.2	69.7	89.3
NNCLR	56.4	80.7	69.8	89.3
UniVCL	58.6	81.8	71.8	91.4

5 Conclusions and Discussions

In this paper, we unify the recent state-of-the-art methods in our proposed Uni-VCL. Specifically, we propose the GCN predictor to unify the diverse structural designs of predictor layers in various self-supervised learning methods. Then, fairly and comprehensively experiments are conducted to explore the critical factors in the GCN predictor, revealing the key point of a good predictor is to aggregate neighboring information in the feature space. Owing to the graph perspective, we further verify the effectiveness of graph augmentations in the vision contrastive learning. In the future, we will extend UniVCL from two perspectives, 1) further link the graph self-supervised learning and vision self-supervised learning by exploring other non-contrastive frameworks with graph self-supervised learning, such as reconstruction, attribute prediction, and 2) validating the effectiveness on other vision tasks, *e.g.*, detection, segmentation.

Acknowledgement. This work was supported by the Australian Research Council Grant DP200103223, Australian Medical Research Future Fund MRFAI000085, CRC-P Smart Material Recovery Facility (SMRF) - Curby Soft Plastics, and CRC-P ARIA - Bionic Visual-Spatial Prosthesis for the Blind.

References

1. Agrawal, P., Carreira, J., Malik, J.: Learning to see by moving. In: Proceedings of the IEEE International Conference on Computer Vision, pp. 37–45 (2015)
2. Cao, J., Lin, X., Guo, S., Liu, L., Liu, T., Wang, B.: Bipartite graph embedding via mutual information maximization. In: Proceedings of the 14th ACM International Conference on Web Search and Data Mining, pp. 635–643 (2021)
3. Caron, M., Misra, I., Mairal, J., Goyal, P., Bojanowski, P., Joulin, A.: Unsupervised learning of visual features by contrasting cluster assignments. arXiv preprint arXiv:2006.09882 (2020)
4. Caron, M., et al · Emerging properties in self-supervised vision transformers. In: Proceedings of the IEEE/CVF International Conference on Computer Vision, pp. 9650–9660 (2021)
5. Chen, T., Kornblith, S., Norouzi, M., Hinton, G.: A simple framework for contrastive learning of visual representations. In: International Conference on Machine Learning, pp. 1597–1607. PMLR (2020)
6. Chen, T., Kornblith, S., Swersky, K., Norouzi, M., Hinton, G.: Big self-supervised models are strong semi-supervised learners. arXiv preprint arXiv:2006.10029 (2020)
7. Chen, X., Fan, H., Girshick, R., He, K.: Improved baselines with momentum contrastive learning. arXiv preprint arXiv:2003.04297 (2020)
8. Chen, X., He, K.: Exploring simple Siamese representation learning. In: Proceedings of the IEEE/CVF Conference on Computer Vision and Pattern Recognition, pp. 15750–15758 (2021)
9. Chen, X., Xie, S., He, K.: An empirical study of training self-supervised vision transformers. In: Proceedings of the IEEE/CVF International Conference on Computer Vision, pp. 9640–9649 (2021)
10. Cubuk, E.D., Zoph, B., Shlens, J., Le, Q.V.: Randaugment: practical automated data augmentation with a reduced search space. In: Proceedings of the IEEE/CVF Conference on Computer Vision and Pattern Recognition Workshops, pp. 702–703 (2020)
11. Doersch, C., Gupta, A., Efros, A.A.: Unsupervised visual representation learning by context prediction. In: Proceedings of the IEEE International Conference on Computer Vision, pp. 1422–1430 (2015)
12. Donoser, M., Bischof, H.: Diffusion processes for retrieval revisited. In: Proceedings of the IEEE Conference on Computer Vision and Pattern Recognition, pp. 1320–1327 (2013)
13. Dwibedi, D., Aytar, Y., Tompson, J., Sermanet, P., Zisserman, A.: With a little help from my friends: nearest-neighbor contrastive learning of visual representations. In: Proceedings of the IEEE/CVF International Conference on Computer Vision, pp. 9588–9597 (2021)
14. Fang, Z., Wang, J., Wang, L., Zhang, L., Yang, Y., Liu, Z.: Seed: self-supervised distillation for visual representation. arXiv preprint arXiv:2101.04731 (2021)
15. Gao, Y., Yu, X., Zhang, H.: Graph clustering using triangle-aware measures in large networks. Inf. Sci. **584**, 618–632 (2022)
16. Grill, J.B., et al.: Bootstrap your own latent-a new approach to self-supervised learning. Adv. Neural Inf. Process. Syst. **33**, 21271–21284 (2020)
17. Hassani, K., Khasahmadi, A.H.: Contrastive multi-view representation learning on graphs. In: International Conference on Machine Learning, pp. 4116–4126. PMLR (2020)

18. He, K., Fan, H., Wu, Y., Xie, S., Girshick, R.: Momentum contrast for unsupervised visual representation learning. In: Proceedings of the IEEE/CVF Conference on Computer Vision and Pattern Recognition, pp. 9729–9738 (2020)
19. Henaff, O.: Data-efficient image recognition with contrastive predictive coding. In: International Conference on Machine Learning, pp. 4182–4192. PMLR (2020)
20. Hu, Q., Wang, X., Hu, W., Qi, G.J.: AdCo: adversarial contrast for efficient learning of unsupervised representations from self-trained negative adversaries. In: Proceedings of the IEEE/CVF Conference on Computer Vision and Pattern Recognition, pp. 1074–1083 (2021)
21. Hu, W., et al.: Strategies for pre-training graph neural networks. arXiv preprint arXiv:1905.12265 (2019)
22. Hu, Z., Dong, Y., Wang, K., Chang, K.W., Sun, Y.: GPT-GNN: generative pre-training of graph neural networks. In: Proceedings of the 26th ACM SIGKDD International Conference on Knowledge Discovery & Data Mining, pp. 1857–1867 (2020)
23. Kim, D., Cho, D., Yoo, D., Kweon, I.S.: Learning image representations by completing damaged jigsaw puzzles. In: 2018 IEEE Winter Conference on Applications of Computer Vision (WACV), pp. 793–802. IEEE (2018)
24. Kipf, T.N., Welling, M.: Semi-supervised classification with graph convolutional networks. arXiv preprint arXiv:1609.02907 (2016)
25. Kipf, T.N., Welling, M.: Variational graph auto-encoders. arXiv preprint arXiv:1611.07308 (2016)
26. Klicpera, J., Weißenberger, S., Günnemann, S.: Diffusion improves graph learning. In: Advances in Neural Information Processing Systems, vol. 32 (2019)
27. Koohpayegani, S.A., Tejankar, A., Pirsiavash, H.: Mean shift for self-supervised learning. In: Proceedings of the IEEE/CVF International Conference on Computer Vision, pp. 10326–10335 (2021)
28. Larsson, G., Maire, M., Shakhnarovich, G.: Learning representations for automatic colorization. In: Leibe, B., Matas, J., Sebe, N., Welling, M. (eds.) ECCV 2016. LNCS, vol. 9908, pp. 577–593. Springer, Cham (2016). https://doi.org/10.1007/978-3-319-46493-0_35
29. Lee, D.H., et al.: Pseudo-label: the simple and efficient semi-supervised learning method for deep neural networks. In: Workshop on Challenges in Representation Learning, ICML, vol. 3, p. 896 (2013)
30. Li, J., Zhou, P., Xiong, C., Socher, R., Hoi, S.C.: Prototypical contrastive learning of unsupervised representations. arXiv preprint arXiv:2005.04966 (2020)
31. Li, Z., et al.: Hierarchical bipartite graph neural networks: towards large-scale e-commerce applications. In: 2020 IEEE 36th International Conference on Data Engineering (ICDE), pp. 1677–1688. IEEE (2020)
32. Liu, Q., Allamanis, M., Brockschmidt, M., Gaunt, A.: Constrained graph variational autoencoders for molecule design. In: Advances in Neural Information Processing Systems, vol. 31 (2018)
33. Liu, X., et al.: Self-supervised learning: generative or contrastive. IEEE Tran. Knowl. Data Eng. (2021)
34. Misra, I., Maaten, L.V.D.: Self-supervised learning of pretext-invariant representations. In: Proceedings of the IEEE/CVF Conference on Computer Vision and Pattern Recognition, pp. 6707–6717 (2020)
35. Pham, H., Dai, Z., Xie, Q., Le, Q.V.: Meta pseudo labels. In: Proceedings of the IEEE/CVF Conference on Computer Vision and Pattern Recognition, pp. 11557–11568 (2021)

36. Qi, G.J., Zhang, L., Lin, F., Wang, X.: Learning generalized transformation equivariant representations via autoencoding transformations. IEEE Trans. Pattern Anal. Mach. Intell. **44**(4), 2045–2057 (2020)
37. Robinson, J., Chuang, C.Y., Sra, S., Jegelka, S.: Contrastive learning with hard negative samples. arXiv preprint arXiv:2010.04592 (2020)
38. Sohn, K., et al.: FixMatch: simplifying semi-supervised learning with consistency and confidence. arXiv preprint arXiv:2001.07685 (2020)
39. Soroush Abbasi, K., Tejankar, A., Pirsiavash, H.: Mean shift for self-supervised learning. In: International Conference on Computer Vision (ICCV) (2021)
40. Subramonian, A.: Motif-driven contrastive learning of graph representations. In: Proceedings of the AAAI Conference on Artificial Intelligence, vol. 35, pp. 15980–15981 (2021)
41. Sun, Q., et al.: Sugar: subgraph neural network with reinforcement pooling and self-supervised mutual information mechanism. In: Proceedings of the Web Conference 2021, pp. 2081–2091 (2021)
42. Tao, C., et al.: Exploring the equivalence of Siamese self-supervised learning via a unified gradient framework. arXiv preprint arXiv:2112.05141 (2021)
43. Thanou, D., Dong, X., Kressner, D., Frossard, P.: Learning heat diffusion graphs. IEEE Trans. Sig. Inf. Process. Netw. **3**(3), 484–499 (2017)
44. Tian, Yonglong, Krishnan, Dilip, Isola, Phillip: Contrastive multiview coding. In: Vedaldi, Andrea, Bischof, Horst, Brox, Thomas, Frahm, Jan-Michael. (eds.) ECCV 2020. LNCS, vol. 12356, pp. 776–794. Springer, Cham (2020). https://doi.org/10.1007/978-3-030-58621-8_45
45. Tian, Y., Sun, C., Poole, B., Krishnan, D., Schmid, C., Isola, P.: What makes for good views for contrastive learning. arXiv preprint arXiv:2005.10243 (2020)
46. Veličković, P., Cucurull, G., Casanova, A., Romero, A., Lio, P., Bengio, Y.: Graph attention networks. arXiv preprint arXiv:1710.10903 (2017)
47. Wang, C., Liu, Z.: Learning graph representation by aggregating subgraphs via mutual information maximization. arXiv preprint arXiv:2103.13125 (2021)
48. Wang, C., Pan, S., Long, G., Zhu, X., Jiang, J.: MGAE: marginalized graph autoencoder for graph clustering. In: Proceedings of the 2017 ACM on Conference on Information and Knowledge Management, pp. 889–898 (2017)
49. Wang, F., Kong, T., Zhang, R., Liu, H., Li, H.: Self-supervised learning by estimating twin class distributions. arXiv preprint arXiv:2110.07402 (2021)
50. Wei, C., Wang, H., Shen, W., Yuille, A.: Co2: consistent contrast for unsupervised visual representation learning. arXiv preprint arXiv:2010.02217 (2020)
51. Wu, Z., Xiong, Y., Yu, S.X., Lin, D.: Unsupervised feature learning via non-parametric instance discrimination. In: Proceedings of the IEEE Conference on Computer Vision and Pattern Recognition, pp. 3733–3742 (2018)
52. Wu, Z., Pan, S., Long, G., Jiang, J., Zhang, C.: Graph wavenet for deep spatial-temporal graph modeling. arXiv preprint arXiv:1906.00121 (2019)
53. Xie, Q., Dai, Z., Hovy, E., Luong, M.T., Le, Q.V.: Unsupervised data augmentation for consistency training. arXiv preprint arXiv:1904.12848 (2019)
54. Xie, Z., Lin, Y., Zhang, Z., Cao, Y., Lin, S., Hu, H.: Propagate yourself: exploring pixel-level consistency for unsupervised visual representation learning. In: Proceedings of the IEEE/CVF Conference on Computer Vision and Pattern Recognition, pp. 16684–16693 (2021)
55. Xu, K., Hu, W., Leskovec, J., Jegelka, S.: How powerful are graph neural networks? arXiv preprint arXiv:1810.00826 (2018)
56. You, Y., Gitman, I., Ginsburg, B.: Large batch training of convolutional networks. arXiv preprint arXiv:1708.03888 (2017)

57. You, Y., Chen, T., Sui, Y., Chen, T., Wang, Z., Shen, Y.: Graph contrastive learning with augmentations. Adv. Neural Inf. Process. Syst. **33**, 5812–5823 (2020)
58. You, Y., Chen, T., Wang, Z., Shen, Y.: When does self-supervision help graph convolutional networks? In: International Conference on Machine Learning, pp. 10871–10880. PMLR (2020)
59. Zbontar, J., Jing, L., Misra, I., LeCun, Y., Deny, S.: Barlow twins: self-supervised learning via redundancy reduction. In: International Conference on Machine Learning, pp. 12310–12320. PMLR (2021)
60. Zhai, X., Oliver, A., Kolesnikov, A., Beyer, L.: S4l: self-supervised semi-supervised learning. In: Proceedings of the IEEE/CVF International Conference on Computer Vision, pp. 1476–1485 (2019)
61. Zhan, X., Xie, J., Liu, Z., Ong, Y.S., Loy, C.C.: Online deep clustering for unsupervised representation learning. In: Proceedings of the IEEE/CVF Conference on Computer Vision and Pattern Recognition, pp. 6688–6697 (2020)
62. Zhang, L., Qi, G.J., Wang, L., Luo, J.: AAET vs. AED: unsupervised representation learning by auto-encoding transformations rather than data. In: Proceedings of the IEEE/CVF Conference on Computer Vision and Pattern Recognition, pp. 2547–2555 (2019)
63. Zhu, Q., Yang, C., Xu, Y., Wang, H., Zhang, C., Han, J.: Transfer learning of graph neural networks with ego-graph information maximization. Adv. Neural Inf. Process. Syst. **34**, 1766–1779 (2021)
64. Zhu, Y., Xu, Y., Yu, F., Liu, Q., Wu, S., Wang, L.: Deep graph contrastive representation learning. arXiv preprint arXiv:2006.04131 (2020)
65. Zhuang, C., Zhai, A.L., Yamins, D.: Local aggregation for unsupervised learning of visual embeddings. In: Proceedings of the IEEE/CVF International Conference on Computer Vision, pp. 6002–6012 (2019)

Decoupled Contrastive Learning

Chun-Hsiao Yeh[1,2], Cheng-Yao Hong[1], Yen-Chi Hsu[1,3], Tyng-Luh Liu[1(✉)],
Yubei Chen[4], and Yann LeCun[4,5]

[1] IIS, Academia Sinica, Taipei City, Taiwan
{sensible,yenchi,liutyng}@iis.sinica.edu.tw
[2] UC Berkeley, Berkeley, USA
daniel_yeh@berkeley.edu
[3] National Taiwan University, New Taipei, Taiwan
[4] Meta AI Research, New York, USA
{yubeic,yann}@fb.com
[5] New York University, New York, USA

Abstract. Contrastive learning (CL) is one of the most successful paradigms for self-supervised learning (SSL). In a principled way, it considers two augmented "views" of the same image as *positive* to be pulled closer, and all other images as *negative* to be pushed further apart. However, behind the impressive success of CL-based techniques, their formulation often relies on heavy-computation settings, including large sample batches, extensive training epochs, etc. We are thus motivated to tackle these issues and establish a simple, efficient, yet competitive baseline of contrastive learning. Specifically, we identify, from theoretical and empirical studies, a noticeable *negative-positive-coupling* (NPC) effect in the widely used InfoNCE loss, leading to unsuitable learning efficiency concerning the batch size. By removing the NPC effect, we propose decoupled contrastive learning (DCL) loss, which removes the positive term from the denominator and significantly improves the learning efficiency. DCL achieves competitive performance with less sensitivity to sub-optimal hyperparameters, requiring neither large batches in SimCLR, momentum encoding in MoCo, or large epochs. We demonstrate with various benchmarks while manifesting robustness as much less sensitive to suboptimal hyperparameters. Notably, SimCLR with DCL achieves 68.2% ImageNet-1K top-1 accuracy using batch size 256 within 200 epochs pre-training, outperforming its SimCLR baseline by 6.4%. Further, DCL can be combined with the SOTA contrastive learning method, NNCLR, to achieve 72.3% ImageNet-1K top-1 accuracy with 512 batch size in 400 epochs, which represents a new SOTA in contrastive learning. We believe DCL provides a valuable baseline for future contrastive SSL studies.

Keywords: Contrastive learning · Self-supervised learning

Supplementary Information The online version contains supplementary material available at https://doi.org/10.1007/978-3-031-19809-0_38.

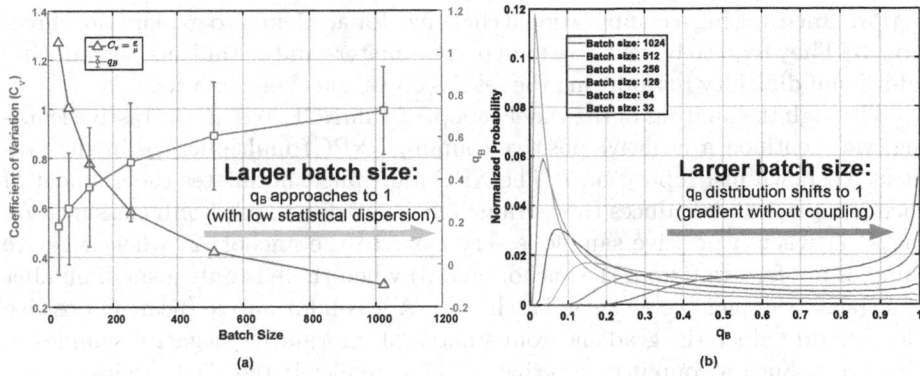

Fig. 1. An overview of the batch size issue is that general contrastive approaches need large batch sizes to perform better: (a) shows the NPC multiplier q_B in different batch sizes. As the batch size gradually increases, the q_B will approach to 1 with a small coefficient of variation ($C_v = \sigma/\mu$); and (b) illustrates the distribution of q_B with various batch sizes and indicates that the mode value of q_B will shift towards 1 when the batch size increases. Note that the σ and μ are the standard deviation and mean of q_B, respectively. The coefficient of variation, C_v, measures the dispersion of a frequency distribution.

1 Introduction

As a fundamental task in machine learning, representation learning aims to extract useful information from the raw data for the downstream tasks. It has been regarded as a long-acting goal over the past decades. Recent progress on representation learning has achieved a significant milestone over self-supervised learning (SSL), facilitating feature learning with its competence in exploiting massive raw data without any annotated supervision. In the early stage of SSL, representation learning has focused on exploiting pretext tasks, which are addressed by generating pseudo-labels to the unlabeled data through different transformations, such as solving jigsaw puzzles [20], colorization [36] and rotation prediction [12]. Though these approaches succeed in computer vision, there is a large gap between these methods and supervised learning. Recently, there has been a significant advancement in using contrastive learning [7,15,21,26,31] for self-supervised pre-training, which significantly closes the gap between the SSL method and supervised learning. Contrastive SSL methods, e.g., SimCLR [7], in general, try to pull different views of the same instance close and push different instances far apart in the representation space.

Despite the evident progress of the state-of-the-art contrastive SSL methods, there have been facing several challenges into future development in this direction, including 1) The SOTA models, *e.g.*, [15] may require specific structures such as the momentum encoder and large memory queues, which may complicate the underlying representation learning. 2) The contrastive SSL models, *e.g.*, [7] often depend on large batch size and huge epoch numbers to achieve competitive performance, posing a computational challenge for academia to explore this direction. 3) They tend to be sensitive to hyperparameters and optimizers, introducing additional difficulty reproducing the results on various benchmarks.

Through the analysis of the widely adopted InfoNCE loss in contrastive learning, we identified a negative-positive-coupling (NPC) multiplier q_B in the gradient as shown in Proposition 1. The NPC multiplier modulates the gradient of each sample, and it reduces the learning efficiency due to easy SSL classification tasks: 1) when a positive sample is very close to the anchor; 2) when negative samples are far away from the anchor; and 3) when there is only a small number of negative samples (i.e., a small batch size). A less-informative (nearby) positive view would reduce the gradient from a batch of informative negative samples or vice versa. Such a coupling exacerbates when smaller batch sizes are used.

Meanwhile, we also investigate the relationship between q_B and batch size through the baseline, SimCLR. As can be seen in Fig. 1, the distribution of q_B has a strong positive correlation with the batch size. Figure 1(a) shows that when batch size gradually increases, q_B not only approaches 1 but also reduces the coefficient of variation C_v. The distribution with larger C_v has low statistical dispersion and vice versa. Figure 1(b) indicates that the mode value of q_B will also shift from 0 to 1 when the batch size becomes larger. Hence, it is reasonable to fix the value of q_B, alleviating the influence of batch size.

By removing the coupling term from the Info-NCE loss, we reach a new formulation, the *decoupled contrastive learning* (DCL). The new objective function significantly improves the training efficiency with less sensitivity to sub-optimal hyper-parameters requires neither large batches, momentum encoding, or large epochs to achieve competitive performance on various benchmarks. The main contributions of the proposed DCL can be characterized as follows:

1) We provide both theoretical analysis and empirical evidence to show the NPC effect in the InfoNCE-based contrastive learning;
2) We introduce DCL objective, which casts off the NPC coupling phenomenon, significantly improves the training efficiency, and it is less sensitive to sub-optimal hyper-parameters;
3) Extensive experiments are provided to show the effectiveness of the proposed method that DCL achieves competitive performance **without** large batch sizes, large training epochs, momentum encoding, or additional tricks such as stop-gradient and multi-cropping, etc. This leads to a plug-and-play improvement to the widely adopted InfoNCE-based contrastive learning;
4) We show that DCL can be easily combined with the SOTA contrastive methods, e.g. NNCLR [10], to achieve further improvements.

2   Related Work

Contrastive Learning. Contrastive learning (CL) constructs positive and negative sample pairs to extract information from the data itself. In CL, each anchor image in a batch has only one positive sample to construct a positive sample pair [7,14,15]. CPC [21] predicts the future output of sequential data by

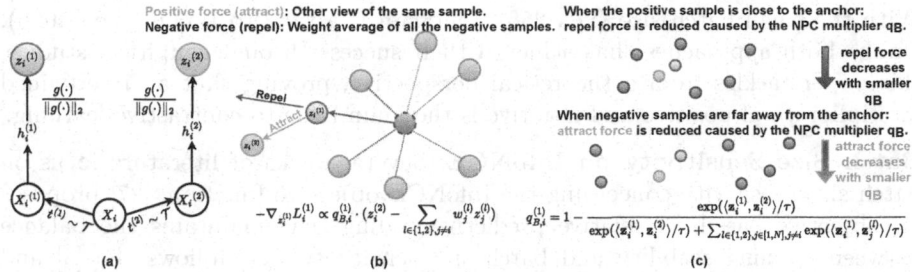

Fig. 2. Contrastive learning and negative-positive coupling (NPC). (a) In SimCLR, each sample $\mathbf{x}_i$ has two augmented views $\{\mathbf{x}_i^{(1)}, \mathbf{x}_i^{(2)}\}$. They are encoded by the same encoder f and further projected to $\{\mathbf{z}_i^{(1)}, \mathbf{z}_i^{(2)}\}$ by a normalized MLP. (b) According to Eq. 4. For the view $\mathbf{x}_i^{(1)}$, the cross-entropy loss $L_i^{(1)}$ leads to a positive force $\mathbf{z}_i^{(2)}$, which comes from the other view $\mathbf{x}_i^{(2)}$ of $\mathbf{x}$ and a negative force, which is a weighted average of all the negative samples, i.e. $\{\mathbf{z}_j^{(l)} | l \in \{1,2\}, j \neq i\}$. However, the gradient $-\nabla_{\mathbf{z}_i^{(2)}} L_i^{(1)}$ is proportional to the NPC multiplier. (c) We show two cases when the NPC term affects learning efficiency. The positive sample is close to the anchor and less informative on the top. However, the gradient from the negative samples is also reduced. On the bottom, when the negative samples are far away and less informative, the learning rate from the positive sample is mistakenly reduced. In general, the NPC multiplier from the InfoNCE loss makes the SSL task simpler to solve, leading to reduced learning efficiency.

using current output as prior knowledge, which can improve the feature representing the ability of the model. Instance discrimination [31] proposes a non-parametric cross-entropy loss to optimize the model at the instance level. Inv. spread [32] makes use of data augmentation invariant and the spread-out property of instance to learn features. MoCo [15] proposes a dictionary to maintain a negative sample set, thus increasing the number of negative sample pairs. Different from the aforementioned self-supervised CL approaches, [19] proposes a supervised CL that considers all the same categories as positive pairs to increase the utility of images.

Collapsing Issue on the Number of Negatives. In CL, the objective is to maximize the mutual information between the positive pairs. However, to avoid the *"collapsing output"*, vast quantities of negative samples are needed so that the learning objectives obtain the maximum similarity and have the minimum similarity with negative samples. For instance, in SimCLR [7], training requires many negative samples, leading to a large batch size (i.e., 4096). Furthermore, to optimize such a huge batch, a specially designed optimizer LARS [33] is used. Similarly, MoCo [15] needs a vast queue (i.e., 65536) to achieve competitive performance. BYOL [13] does not collapse output without using any negative samples by considering all the images are positive and to maximize the similarity of "projection" and "prediction" features. On the other hand, SimSiam [9] leverages the Siamese network to introduce inductive biases for modeling invariance.

With the small batch size (i.e., 256), SimSiam is a rival to BYOL (i.e., 4096). Unlike both approaches that achieved their success through empirical studies, this paper tackles from a theoretical perspective, proving that an intertwined multiplier q_B of positive and negative is the main issue to contrastive learning.

Batch Size Sensitivity on InfoNCE. Several works of literature focus on batch size sensitivity concerning the InfoNCE objective function. [27] proposes an objective based on relative predictive coding that maintains the balance between training stability and batch size sensitivity. [17] follows the [3] and extends the idea between the local and global features. [22] proposes a Wasserstein distance to prevent the encoder from learning any other differences between unpaired samples. [18] and [25] learn better representation by sampling hard negatives, particularly for small batches. Other recent works [11,37] aim to mitigate the issue of small batch size in InfoNCE loss. Although the basic principle of recent works and DCL is derived from InfoNCE objective function, we provide a novel perspective to support the decoupling between positive and negative terms in InfoNCE loss is essential. Simply removing the term from the denominator pre-training to positive pairs can drastically improve the performance and keep the objective function invariant to batch size sensitivity.

3   Decouple Negative and Positive Samples in Contrastive Learning

We choose to start from SimCLR because of its conceptual simplicity. Given a batch of N samples (e.g. images), $\{\mathbf{x}_1, \ldots, \mathbf{x}_N\}$, let $\mathbf{x}_i^{(1)}, \mathbf{x}_i^{(2)}$ be two augmented views of the sample x_i and B be the set of all of the augmented views in the batch, i.e. $B = \{\mathbf{x}_i^{(k)} | k \in \{1, 2\}, i \in [\![1, N]\!]\}$. As shown by Fig. 2(a), each of the views $\mathbf{x}_i^{(k)}$ is sent into the same encoder network f and the output $\mathbf{h}_i^{(k)} = f(\mathbf{x}_i^{(k)})$ is then projected by a normalized MLP projector that $\mathbf{z}_i^{(k)} = g(\mathbf{h}_i^{(k)})/\|g(\mathbf{h}_i^{(k)})\|$. For each augmented view $\mathbf{x}_i^{(k)}$, SimCLR solves a classification problem by using the rest of the views in B as targets, and assigns the only positive label to $\mathbf{x}_i^{(u)}$, where $u \neq k$. So SimCLR creates a cross-entropy loss function $L_i^{(k)}$ for each view $\mathbf{x}_i^{(k)}$, and the overall loss function is $L = \sum_{k \in \{1,2\}, i \in [\![1,N]\!]} L_i^{(k)}$.

$$L_i^{(k)} = -\log \frac{\exp(\langle \mathbf{z}_i^{(1)}, \mathbf{z}_i^{(2)} \rangle / \tau)}{\exp(\langle \mathbf{z}_i^{(1)}, \mathbf{z}_i^{(2)} \rangle / \tau) + U_{i,k}}, \tag{1}$$

where

$$U_{i,k} = \sum_{l \in \{1,2\}, j \in [\![1,N]\!], j \neq i} \exp(\langle \mathbf{z}_i^{(k)}, \mathbf{z}_j^{(l)} \rangle / \tau) \tag{2}$$

means the summation of negative terms for the view k of the sample i.

Proposition 1 : *There exists a negative-positive coupling (NPC) multiplier $q_{B,i}^{(1)}$ in the gradient of $L_i^{(1)}$:*

$$
\begin{cases}
-\nabla_{\mathbf{z}_i^{(1)}} L_i^{(1)} = \\
\quad \frac{q_{B,i}^{(1)}}{\tau}\left(\mathbf{z}_i^{(2)} - \sum_{l\in\{1,2\},j\in[1,N],j\neq i} \frac{\exp\langle\mathbf{z}_i^{(1)},\mathbf{z}_j^{(l)}\rangle/\tau}{U_{i,1}} \cdot \mathbf{z}_j^{(l)}\right) \\
-\nabla_{\mathbf{z}_i^{(2)}} L_i^{(1)} = \frac{q_{B,i}^{(1)}}{\tau}\cdot\mathbf{z}_i^{(1)} \\
-\nabla_{\mathbf{z}_j^{(l)}} L_i^{(1)} = -\frac{q_{B,i}^{(1)}}{\tau}\frac{\exp\langle\mathbf{z}_i^{(1)},\mathbf{z}_j^{(l)}\rangle/\tau}{U_{i,1}}\cdot\mathbf{z}_i^{(1)}
\end{cases}
\tag{3}
$$

where the NPC multiplier $q_{B,i}^{(1)}$ is:

$$
q_{B,i}^{(1)} = 1 - \frac{\exp(\langle\mathbf{z}_i^{(1)},\mathbf{z}_i^{(2)}\rangle/\tau)}{\exp(\langle\mathbf{z}_i^{(1)},\mathbf{z}_i^{(2)}\rangle/\tau) + U_{i,1}}
\tag{4}
$$

and $U_{i,1} = \sum_{l\in\{1,2\},j\in[1,N],j\neq i}\exp(\langle\mathbf{z}_i^{(1)},\mathbf{z}_j^{(l)}\rangle/\tau)$. Due to the symmetry, a similar NPC multiplier $q_{B,i}^{(k)}$ exists in the gradient of $L_i^{(k)}$, $k\in\{1,2\}, i\in[1,N]$.

As we can see, all of the partial gradients in Eq. 3 are modified by the common NPC multiplier $q_{B,i}^{(k)}$ in Eq. 4. Equation 4 makes intuitive sense: when the SSL classification task is easy, the gradient would be reduced by the NPC term. However, the positive samples and negative samples are strongly coupled. When the negative samples are far away and less informative (easy negatives), the gradient from an informative, positive sample would be reduced by the NPC multiplier $q_{B,i}^{(1)}$. On the other hand, when the positive sample is close (easy positive) and less informative, the gradient from a batch of informative negative samples would also be reduced by the NPC multiplier. When the batch size is smaller, the SSL classification problem can be significantly simpler to solve. As a result, the learning efficiency can be significantly reduced with a small batch size setting.

Figure 1(b) shows the NPC multiplier q_B distribution shift w.r.t. different batch sizes for a pre-trained SimCLR baseline model. While all of the shown distributions have prominent fluctuation, the smaller batch size makes q_B cluster towards 0, while the larger batch size pushes the distribution towards $\delta(1)$. Figure 1(a) shows the averaged NPC multiplier $\langle q_B\rangle$ changes w.r.t. the batch size and the relative fluctuation. The small batch sizes introduce significant NPC fluctuation. Based on this observation, we propose to remove the NPC multipliers from the gradients, which corresponds to the case $q_{B,N\to\infty}$. This leads to the decoupled contrastive learning formulation. [29] also proposes an alignment & uniformity loss which does not have the NPC. However, a similar analysis introduces negative-negative coupling from different positive samples. In other words, [29] considers all the negative samples in the batch together, which may cause the gradient to be dominated by a specific negative pair. In Appendix 5, we provide a thorough discussion and demonstrate the advantage of DCL loss against [29].

Proposition 2 the DCL Loss: *Removing the positive pair from the denominator of Eq. 1 leads to a decoupled contrastive learning loss. If we remove the NPC multiplier $q_{B,i}^{(k)}$ from Eq. 3, we reach a decoupled contrastive learning loss* $L_{DC} = \sum_{k \in \{1,2\}, i \in [\![1,N]\!]} L_{DC,i}^{(k)}$, *where $L_{DC,i}^{(k)}$ is:*

$$L_{DC,i}^{(k)} = -\log \frac{\exp(\langle \mathbf{z}_i^{(1)}, \mathbf{z}_i^{(2)} \rangle / \tau)}{\exp(\langle \mathbf{z}_i^{(1)}, \mathbf{z}_i^{(2)} \rangle / \tau) + U_{i,k}} \tag{5}$$

$$= -\langle \mathbf{z}_i^{(1)}, \mathbf{z}_i^{(2)} \rangle / \tau + \log U_{i,k} \tag{6}$$

The proofs of Proposition 1 and 2 are given in Appendix. Further, we can generalize the loss function L_{DC} to L_{DCW} by introducing a weighting function for the positive pairs i.e. $L_{DCW} = \sum_{k \in \{1,2\}, i \in [\![1,N]\!]} L_{DCW,i}^{(i,k)}$.

$$L_{DCW,i}^{(k)} = -w(\mathbf{z}_i^{(1)}, \mathbf{z}_i^{(2)})(\langle \mathbf{z}_i^{(1)}, \mathbf{z}_i^{(2)} \rangle / \tau) + \log U_{i,k} \tag{7}$$

where we can intuitively choose w to be a negative von Mises-Fisher weighting function that $w(\mathbf{z}_i^{(1)}, \mathbf{z}_i^{(2)}) = 2 - \frac{\exp(\langle \mathbf{z}_i^{(1)}, \mathbf{z}_i^{(2)} \rangle / \sigma)}{E_i [\exp(\langle \mathbf{z}_i^{(1)}, \mathbf{z}_i^{(2)} \rangle / \sigma)]}$ and $E[w] = 1$. L_{DC} is a special case of L_{DCW} and we can see that $\lim_{\sigma \to \infty} L_{DCW} = L_{DC}$. The intuition behind $w(\mathbf{z}_i^{(1)}, \mathbf{z}_i^{(2)})$ is that there is more learning signal when a positive pair of samples are far from each other, and $E\left[w(\mathbf{z}_i^{(1)}, \mathbf{z}_i^{(2)}) \langle \mathbf{z}_i^{(1)}, \mathbf{z}_i^{(2)} \rangle \right] \approx E\left[\langle \mathbf{z}_i^{(1)}, \mathbf{z}_i^{(2)} \rangle \right]$. Other similar weight functions also provide similar results. In general, we find such a weighting function, which gives a larger weight to the hard positives tend to increase the representation quality.

4   Experiments

This section empirically evaluates the proposed decoupled contrastive learning (DCL) and compares it to general contrastive learning methods. We summarize the experiments and analysis as the following: (1) the proposed work significantly outperforms the general InfoNCE-based contrastive learning on both large-scale and small-scale vision benchmarks; (2) we show that the enhanced version of DCL, DCLW, could further improve the representation quality; and (3) we further analyze DCL with ablation studies on ImageNet-1K, hyperparameters, and few learning epochs, which shows fast convergence of the proposed DCL. Note that all the experiments are conducted with 8 Nvidia V100 GPUs on a single machine.

4.1   Implementation Details

ImageNet. For a fair comparison on ImageNet data, we implement the proposed decoupled structure, DCL, by following SimCLR [7] with ResNet-50 [16] as the encoder backbone and use cosine annealing schedule with SGD optimizer. We

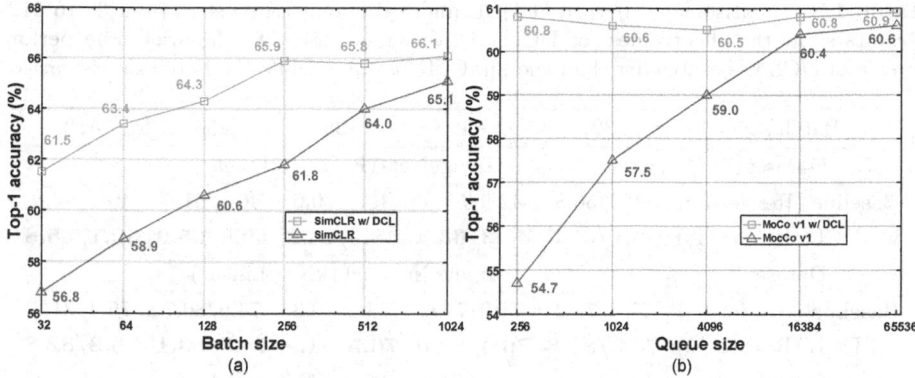

Fig. 3. Comparisons on ImageNet-1K with/without DCL under different numbers of (a): batch sizes for SimCLR and (b): queues for MoCo. Without DCL, the top-1 accuracy significantly drops when batch size (SimCLR) or queues (MoCo) becomes very small. Note that the temperature τ is 0.1 for SimCLR and 0.07 for MoCo in the comparison.

set the temperature τ to 0.1 and the latent vector dimension to 128. Following the OpenSelfSup benchmark [35], we evaluate the pre-trained models by training a linear classifier with frozen learned embedding on ImageNet data. We further consider evaluating DCL on ImageNet-100, a selected subset of 100 classes of ImageNet-1K. Note that all models on ImageNet are trained for 200 epochs.

CIFAR and STL10. For CIFAR10, CIFAR100, and STL10, ResNet-18 [16] is used as the encoder architecture. Following the small-scale benchmark [30], we set the temperature τ to 0.07. All models are trained for 200 epochs with SGD optimizer, a base $lr = 0.03 * batchsize/256$, and evaluated by k nearest neighbor (kNN) classifier. Note that on STL10, we include both the *train* and *unlabeled* set for model pre-training. We further use ResNet-50 as a stronger backbone by following the implementation [24], using the same backbone and hyperparameters.

4.2 Experiments and Analysis

DCL on ImageNet. This section illustrates the effect of DCL against InfoNCE-based approaches under different batch sizes and queues. The initial setup is to have 1024 batch size (SimCLR) and 65536 queues (MoCo [15]) and gradually reduce the batch size (SimCLR) and queue (MoCo) to show the corresponding top-1 accuracy by linear evaluation. Figure 3 indicates that without DCL, the top-1 accuracy drastically drops when batch size (SimCLR) or queue (MoCo) becomes very small. While with DCL, the performance keeps steadier than baselines (SimCLR: -4.1% vs. -8.3%, MoCo: -0.4% vs. -5.9%).

Specifically, Fig. 3 further shows that in SimCLR, the performance with DCL improves from 61.8% to 65.9% under 256 batch size; MoCo with DCL improves

Table 1. Comparisons with/without DCL under different batch sizes from 32 to 512. Results show the effectiveness of DCL on five widely used benchmarks. The performance of DCL keeps steadier than the SimCLR baseline while the batch size is varied.

Batch size	32	64	128	256	512
Dataset	ImageNet-1K (kNN/Linear)				
Baseline (ResNet-50)	40.2/56.8	42.9/58.9	45.1/60.6	46.3/61.8	49.4/64.0
w/ DCL (ResNet-50)	**43.7/61.5**	**46.3/63.4**	**48.5/64.3**	**49.8/65.9**	**50.1/65.8**
Dataset	ImageNet-100 (kNN/Linear)				
Baseline (ResNet-50)	67.8/74.2	71.9/77.6	73.2/79.3	74.6/80.7	75.4/81.3
w/ DCL (ResNet-50)	**74.9/80.8**	**76.3/82.0**	**76.5/81.9**	**76.9/83.1**	**76.8/82.8**
Dataset	CIFAR-10 (kNN/Linear)				
Baseline (ResNet-18)	78.9/79.8	80.4/81.3	81.1/82.8	81.4/83.0	81.3/83.3
w/ DCL (ResNet-18)	**83.7/85.1**	**84.4/85.9**	**84.4/85.7**	**84.2/85.3**	**83.5/84.7**
Dataset	CIFAR-100 (kNN/Linear)				
Baseline (ResNet-18)	49.4/51.3	50.3/53.8	51.8/55.3	52.0/56.3	52.4/56.8
w/ DCL (ResNet-18)	**51.1/55.4**	**54.3/58.3**	**54.6/58.9**	**54.9/58.5**	**55.0/58.4**
Dataset	STL-10 (kNN/Linear)				
Baseline (ResNet-18)	74.1/76.2	77.6/77.8	79.3/80.0	80.7/81.3	81.3/81.5
w/ DCL (ResNet-18)	**82.0/85.2**	**82.8/86.3**	**81.8/86.1**	**81.2/85.7**	**81.0/85.6**

from 54.7% to 60.8% under 256 queues. The comparison fully demonstrates the necessity of DCL, especially when the number of negatives is small. Although batch size increases to 1024, DCL (66.1%) still improves over the SimCLR baseline (65.1%).

We further observe the same phenomenon on ImageNet-100 data. Table 1 shows that, with DCL, the top-1 linear performance only drops 2.3% compared to the InfoNCE baseline (SimCLR) of 7.1% when the batch size is varied.

In summary, it is worth noting that, while the batch size is small, the strength of $q_{B,i}$, which is used to push the negative samples away from the positive sample, is also relatively weak. This phenomenon tends to reduce the efficiency of learning representation. While taking advantage of DCL alleviates the performance gap between small and large batch sizes. Hence, through the analysis, we find out DCL can simply tackle the batch size issue in contrastive learning. With this considerable advantage given by DCL, general SSL approaches can be implemented with fewer computational resources or lower standard platforms. Compared to InfoNCE, DCL is more applicable across all large-scale SSL applications.

DCL on CIFAR and STL10. For STL10, CIFAR10, and CIFAR100, we implement DCL with ResNet-18 as encoder backbone. In Table 1, it is observed that DCL also demonstrates its strong effectiveness on small-scale benchmarks. In the evaluation (kNN/Linear) summary, DCL outperforms its baseline by 4.8%/5.3%

Table 2. Comparisons between SimCLR baseline, DCL, and DCLW. The linear and kNN top-1 (%) results indicate that DCL improves baseline performance, and DCLW further provides an extra boost. Note that results are under batch size 256 and epoch 200. All models are both trained and evaluated with the same experimental settings. The backbones are ResNet-18 and ResNet-50 for CIFAR and ImageNet, respectively.

Dataset	CIFAR10 (kNN)	CIFAR100 (kNN)	ImageNet-100 (linear)	ImageNet-1K (linear)
SimCLR	81.4	52.0	80.7	61.8
DCL	84.2 (+2.8)	54.9 (+2.9)	83.1 (+2.4)	65.9 (+4.1)
DCLW	**84.8** (+3.4)	**55.2** (+3.2)	**84.2** (+3.5)	**66.9** (+5.1)

Table 3. Improve the DCL model performance on ImageNet-1K with tuned hyperparameters: temperature and learning rate, and stronger image augmentation. Note that models are trained with 256 batch size and 200 epochs.

ImageNet-1K (256 Batch size; 200 epoch)	Linear Top-1 Accuracy (%)
DCL	65.9
+ optimal $(\tau, l_r) = (0.2, 0.07)$	67.8 (+1.9)
+ asymmetric augmentation [13]	68.2 (+0.4)

(CIFAR10) and 1.7%/4.4% (CIFAR100) under a small batch size 32. The accuracy (kNN/Linear) of the SimCLR baseline on STL10 is also improved significantly by 7.9%/9.0%.

Decoupled Objective with Re-weighting DCLW. We only replace L_{DC} with L_{DCW} with no possible advantage from additional tricks. Both DCL and the baselines apply the same training instruction of the OpenSelfSup benchmark for fairness. Note that we empirically choose $\sigma = 0.5$ in the experiments. Results in Table 2 indicates that, DCLW achieves extra 5.1% (ImageNet-1K), 3.5% (ImageNet-100) gains compared to the baseline. For CIFAR data, an extra 3.4% (CIFAR10) 3.2% is gained from the addition of DCLW. It is worth noting that, trained with 200 epochs, DCLW reaches 66.9% with batch size 256, surpassing the SimCLR baseline: 66.2% with batch size 8192.

4.3 Ablations

We perform extensive ablations on the hyperparameters of DCL on both ImageNet data and other small-scale data, i.e., CIFAR and STL10. By seeking better configurations empirically, we see that DCL gives consistent gains over the standard InfoNCE baselines (SimCLR and MoCo-v2). In other ablations, we see that DCL achieves more gains over both SimCLR and MoCo-v2, i.e., InfoNCE-based baselines, also when training for 100 epochs only.

DCL Ablations on ImageNet. In Table 3, we have slightly improved the DCL model performance on ImageNet-1K: 1) tuned hyperparameters, temperature τ and learning rate ; 2) asymmetric image augmentation (e.g., BYOL). To obtain

Table 4. The comparisons with/without DCL under various batch sizes from 32 to 512 on ResNet-50.

Architecture@epoch	ResNet-50@500 epoch									
Dataset	CIFAR10 (kNN)					CIFAR100 (kNN)				
Batch size	32	64	128	256	512	32	64	128	256	512
SimCLR	82.2	85.9	88.5	88.9	89.1	49.8	55.3	59.9	60.6	61.1
SimCLR w/DCL	**86.1**	**88.3**	**89.9**	**90.1**	**90.3**	**54.3**	**58.4**	**61.6**	**62.0**	**62.2**

Table 5. Linear top-1 accuracy (%) comparison with MoCo-V2 on ImageNet-1K and ImageNet-100.

Queue size	32	64	128	256	8192	64	256	65536
Dataset	ImageNet-100 (Linear)					ImageNet-1K (Linear)		
MoCo-v2 Baseline (ResNet-50)	73.7	76.4	78.7	78.7	79.8	63.9	67.1	67.5
MoCo-v2 w/DCL (ResNet-50)	**76.2**	**78.3**	**79.6**	**79.6**	**80.5**	**65.8**	**67.6**	**67.7**

a stronger baseline, we conduct an empirical hyperparameter search with batch size 256 and 200 epochs. This improves DCL from 65.9% to 67.8% top-1 accuracy on ImageNet-1K. We further adopt the asymmetric augmentation policy from BYOL and improve DCL from 67.8% to 68.2% top-1 accuracy on ImageNet-1K.

DCL Ablations on CIFAR. Further experiments are conducted based on the ResNet-50 backbone and large learning epochs (i.e., 500 epochs). The DCL model with kNN eval, batch size 32, and 500 epochs of training could reach 86.1% compared to 82.2%. For the following experiments in Table 4, we show DCL ResNet-50 performance on CIFAR10 and CIFAR100. In these comparisons, we vary the batch size to show the effectiveness of DCL.

MoCo-v2 with DCL. We are aware that it is more convincing to compare the proposed DCL against a more compelling version, MoCo-v2. Comparisons on both ImageNet-1K and ImageNet-100 in Table 5 indicate that DCL becomes significantly more effective than MoCo-v2 when the queue size gets smaller.

Few Learning Epochs. DCL can alleviate the shortcoming of the traditional contrastive learning framework, which needs a large batch size long learning epochs to achieve higher performance. The previous state-of-the-art, SimCLR, heavily relies on large quantities of learning epochs to obtain high top-1 accuracy. (e.g., 69.3% with up to 1000 epochs). DCL aims to achieve higher learning efficiency with few learning epochs. We demonstrate the effectiveness of DCL in InfoNCE-based frameworks SimCLR and MoCo-v2 [8]. We choose the batch size of 256 (queue of 65536) as the baseline and train the model with only 100 epochs. We make sure other parameter settings are the same for a fair comparison. Table 6 shows the result on ImageNet-1K using linear evaluation. With DCL, SimCLR can achieve 64.6% top-1 accuracy with only 100 epochs compared to SimCLR baseline: 57.5%; MoCo-v2 with DCL reaches 64.4% compared to MoCo-v2 baseline: 63.6% with 100 epochs pre-training.

Table 6. ImageNet-1K top-1 accuracy (%) on SimCLR and MoCo-v2 with/without DCL under few training epochs. We further list results under 200 epochs for clear comparison. With DCL, the performance of SimCLR trained under 100 epochs nearly reaches its performance under 200 epochs. The MoCo-v2 with DCL also reaches higher accuracy than the baseline under 100 epochs.

	SimCLR	SimCLR w/ DCL	MoCo-v2	MoCo-v2 w/ DCL
100 epoch	57.5	64.6	63.6	64.4
200 epoch	61.8	65.9	67.5	67.7

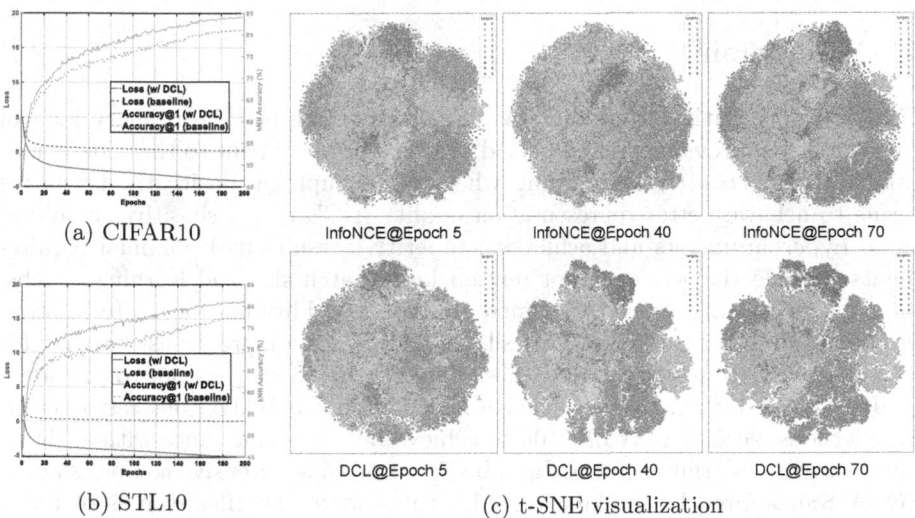

(a) CIFAR10   InfoNCE@Epoch 5   InfoNCE@Epoch 40   InfoNCE@Epoch 70

(b) STL10   DCL@Epoch 5   DCL@Epoch 40   DCL@Epoch 70   (c) t-SNE visualization

Fig. 4. Comparisons between DCL and InfoNCE-based baseline (SimCLR) on (a) CIFAR10 and (b) STL10 data. DCL speeds up the model convergence during the SSL pre-training and provides better performance than the baseline on CIFAR and STL10 data. (c) t-SNE visualization of CIFAR-10 with 32 batch size. DCL shows a stronger separation force between the features than SimCLR.

We further demonstrate that, with DCL, learning representation becomes faster during the early stage of training compared to the InfoNCE-based learning scheme. The reason is that DCL successfully solves the decoupled issue between positive and negative pairs. Figure 4 on (a) CIFAR10 and (b) STL10 shows that DCL improves the speed of convergence and reaches higher performance than the baseline on CIFAR and STL10 data. The t-SNE visualization in Fig. 4 (c) also supports the proposed theoretical derivation that removing the batch-size dependent impact (i.e., NPC multiplier) should improve representation learning abilities over the InfoNCE-based learning scheme.

Table 7. Linear top-1 accuracy (%) comparison of SSL approaches on ImageNet-1K. Given lower computational budget, DCL model are better than recent SOTA approaches. Its effectiveness **does not rely on** large batch size and epochs (Sim-CLR [7], NNCLR [10]), momentum encoding (BYOL [13], MoCo-v2 [8]), or other tricks such as stop-gradient (SimSiam [9]) and multi-cropping (SwAV [5]).

ResNet-50 w/	SimCLR	BYOL	SwAV	MoCo-v2	SimSiam	Barlow twins	NNCLR	NNCLR +DCL
Epoch		400		400	300	1000	400	
Batch size		4096		256	256	256/512	256/512	
ImageNet-1K (Linear)	69.8	73.2	70.7	71.0	70.8	70.7	68.7/71.7	**71.1/72.3**

5 Discussion

Comparison with Other SOTA SSL Approaches. The primary goal of this work is to provide an efficient and effective improvement to the widely used InfoNCE-based contrastive learning, where we decouple the positive and negative terms to achieve better representation quality. DCL is less sensitive to suboptimal hyperparameters and achieves competitive results with minimal requirements. Its effectiveness does not rely on large batch size and learning epochs, momentum encoding, negative sample queues, or additional tactics (e.g., stop-gradient and multi-cropping). Overall, DCL provides a more robust baseline for the contrastive-based SSL approaches. Though this work aims not to provide a SOTA SSL approach, DCL can be combined with the SOTA contrastive learning methods, such as NNCLR [10], to achieve better performance without large batch size and learning epochs. In Table 7, we provide extensive comparisons to SOTA SSL approaches on ImageNet-1K to validate the effectiveness of DCL. In Table 8, we further show that DCL achieves competitive results compared to VICReg [2], Barlow Twins [34], SimSiam [9], SwAV [4], and DINO [6] on ImageNet-100 and CIFAR-10.

Generalization of DCL to Different Domains. DCL can be easily adapted to different domains (e.g., speech and language models) to achieve competitive performance. We demonstrate that DCL can be combined with SOTA SSL speech models, e.g., wav2vec 2.0 [1] which uses transformer backbone and requires enormous computation resources. We evaluate wav2vec 2.0 on its downstream tasks and perform better by applying the DCL method. Detailed results and discussion can be found in Appendix. To the best of our knowledge, DCL can be potentially combined with a transformer-based language model, CLIP [23], which uses a very large batch size of 32768. With DCL, CLIP shall maintain its complexity and achieve huge learning efficiency when the batch size becomes smaller. Note that it has been implemented by [28].

DCL Convergence for Large Batch Sizes. The performance of DCL appears to have less gain compared to InfoNCE-based baseline when the batch size is large. According to Fig. 1 and the theoretical analysis, the reason is that the NPC multiplier $q_B \to 0$ when the batch size is large (e.g., 1024). As shown in the analysis, InfoNCE loss converges to the DCL loss as the batch size approaches infin-

Table 8. kNN & linear top-1 accuracy (%) comparison of SSL approaches on CIFAR10 and ImageNet-100.

ResNet-18 @ 256 batch size	DINO	SwAV	SimSiam	VICReg	Barlow twins	NNCLR	NNCLR+DCL
CIFAR-10, 1000 Epoch (kNN)	89.5	89.2	90.5	92.1	92.1	91.8	**92.3**
ImageNet-100, 400 Epoch (Linear)	74.9	74.0	74.5	79.2	80.2	79.8	**80.6**

Table 9. Results of DCL and SimCLR with large batch size and learning epochs.

ImageNet-1K (ResNet-50)	Batch size	Epoch	Top-1 accuracy (%)
SimCLR	256	200	61.8
SimCLR	256	400	64.8
SimCLR	1024	400	67.3
SimCLR w/ DCL	256	200	67.8 (+6.0)
SimCLR w/ DCL	256	400	69.5 (+4.7)
SimCLR w/ DCL	1024	400	69.9 (+2.6)

ity. With 400 training epochs, the ImageNet-1K top-1 accuracy slightly increases from 69.5% to 69.9% when the batch size increases from 256 to 1024. Please refer to Table 9.

6 Conclusion

This paper identifies the negative-positive-coupling (NPC) effect in the widely used InfoNCE loss, making the SSL task significantly easier to solve with smaller batch size. By removing the NPC effect, we reach a new objective function, *decoupled contrastive learning* (DCL). The proposed DCL loss function requires minimal modification to the SimCLR baseline and provides efficient, reliable, and nontrivial performance improvement on various benchmarks. Given the conceptual simplicity of DCL and that it requires neither momentum encoding, large batch size, or long epochs to reach competitive performance. Notably, DCL can be combined with the SOTA contrastive learning method, NNCLR, to achieve 72.3% ImageNet-1K top-1 accuracy with 512 batch size in 400 epochs. We wish that DCL can serve as a strong baseline for the contrastive-based SSL methods. Further, an important lesson from the DCL loss is that a more efficient SSL task shall maintain its complexity when the batch size becomes smaller.

Acknowledgements. This work was supported in part by the MOST grants 110-2634-F-007-027, 110-2221-E-001-017 and 111-2221-E-001-015 of Taiwan. We are grateful to National Center for High-performance Computing and Meta AI Research for providing computational resources and facilities.

References

1. Baevski, A., Zhou, Y., Mohamed, A., Auli, M.: wav2vec 2.0: a framework for self-supervised learning of speech representations. In: Advances in Neural Information Processing Systems (NeurIPS) (2020)
2. Bardes, A., Ponce, J., LeCun, Y.: VICReg: variance-invariance-covariance regularization for self-supervised learning. CoRR abs/2105.04906 (2021)
3. Belghazi, M.I., et al.: Mutual information neural estimation. In: Proceedings of the International Conference on Machine Learning (ICML) (2018)
4. Caron, M., Bojanowski, P., Joulin, A., Douze, M.: Deep clustering for unsupervised learning of visual features. In: Ferrari, V., Hebert, M., Sminchisescu, C., Weiss, Y. (eds.) Computer Vision – ECCV 2018. LNCS, vol. 11218, pp. 139–156. Springer, Cham (2018). https://doi.org/10.1007/978-3-030-01264-9_9
5. Caron, M., Misra, I., Mairal, J., Goyal, P., Bojanowski, P., Joulin, A.: Unsupervised learning of visual features by contrasting cluster assignments. In: Advances in Neural Information Processing Systems (NeurIPS) (2020)
6. Caron, M., et al.: Emerging properties in self-supervised vision transformers. CoRR abs/2104.14294 (2021)
7. Chen, T., Kornblith, S., Norouzi, M., Hinton, G.E.: A simple framework for contrastive learning of visual representations. In: Proceedings of the International Conference on Machine Learning (ICML) (2020)
8. Chen, X., Fan, H., Girshick, R.B., He, K.: Improved baselines with momentum contrastive learning. CoRR abs/2003.04297 (2020)
9. Chen, X., He, K.: Exploring simple Siamese representation learning. In: IEEE Conference on Computer Vision and Pattern Recognition (CVPR) (2021)
10. Dwibedi, D., Aytar, Y., Tompson, J., Sermanet, P., Zisserman, A.: With a little help from my friends: Nearest-neighbor contrastive learning of visual representations. In: Proceedings of the IEEE/CVF International Conference on Computer Vision, pp. 9588–9597 (2021)
11. Ermolov, A., Siarohin, A., Sangineto, E., Sebe, N.: Whitening for self-supervised representation learning. In: International Conference on Machine Learning (ICML) (2021)
12. Gidaris, S., Singh, P., Komodakis, N.: Unsupervised representation learning by predicting image rotations. In: International Conference on Learning Representations (ICLR) (2018)
13. Grill, J., et al.: Bootstrap your own latent - a new approach to self-supervised learning. In: Advances in Neural Information Processing Systems (NeurIPS) (2020)
14. Hadsell, R., Chopra, S., LeCun, Y.: Dimensionality reduction by learning an invariant mapping. In: IEEE Computer Society Conference on Computer Vision and Pattern Recognition (CVPR) (2006)
15. He, K., Fan, H., Wu, Y., Xie, S., Girshick, R.: Momentum contrast for unsupervised visual representation learning. In: Proceedings of the IEEE/CVF Conference on Computer Vision and Pattern Recognition (CVPR) (2020)
16. He, K., Zhang, X., Ren, S., Sun, J.: Deep residual learning for image recognition. In: IEEE Conference on Computer Vision and Pattern Recognition (CVPR) (2016)
17. Hjelm, R.D., et al.: Learning deep representations by mutual information estimation and maximization. In: International Conference on Learning Representations (ICLR) (2019)
18. Kalantidis, Y., Sariyildiz, M.B., Pion, N., Weinzaepfel, P., Larlus, D.: Hard negative mixing for contrastive learning. In: Advances in Neural Information Processing Systems (NeurIPS) (2020)

19. Khosla, P., et al.: Supervised contrastive learning. In: Advances in Neural Information Processing Systems (NeurIPS) (2020)
20. Noroozi, M., Favaro, P.: Unsupervised learning of visual representations by solving Jigsaw puzzles. In: Leibe, B., Matas, J., Sebe, N., Welling, M. (eds.) ECCV 2016. LNCS, vol. 9910, pp. 69–84. Springer, Cham (2016). https://doi.org/10.1007/978-3-319-46466-4_5
21. van den Oord, A., Li, Y., Vinyals, O.: Representation learning with contrastive predictive coding. CoRR abs/1807.03748 (2018)
22. Ozair, S., Lynch, C., Bengio, Y., van den Oord, A., Levine, S., Sermanet, P.: Wasserstein dependency measure for representation learning. In: Advances in Neural Information Processing Systems (NeurIPS) (2019)
23. Radford, A., et al.: Learning transferable visual models from natural language supervision. In: Meila, M., Zhang, T. (eds.) Proceedings of the 38th International Conference on Machine Learning, ICML 2021, 18–24 July 2021, Virtual Event. Proceedings of Machine Learning Research, vol. 139, pp. 8748–8763. PMLR (2021)
24. Ren, H.: A PyTorch implementation of SimCLR (2020). https://github.com/leftthomas/SimCLR
25. Robinson, J.D., Chuang, C., Sra, S., Jegelka, S.: Contrastive learning with hard negative samples. In: International Conference on Learning Representations (ICLR) (2021)
26. Tian, Y., Krishnan, D., Isola, P.: Contrastive multiview coding. In: Vedaldi, A., Bischof, H., Brox, T., Frahm, J.-M. (eds.) ECCV 2020. LNCS, vol. 12356, pp. 776–794. Springer, Cham (2020). https://doi.org/10.1007/978-3-030-58621-8_45
27. Tsai, Y.H., Ma, M.Q., Yang, M., Zhao, H., Morency, L., Salakhutdinov, R.: Self-supervised representation learning with relative predictive coding. In: International Conference on Learning Representations (ICLR) (2021)
28. Wang, P.: x-clip (2021). https://github.com/lucidrains/x-clip
29. Wang, T., Isola, P.: Understanding contrastive representation learning through alignment and uniformity on the hypersphere. In: International Conference on Machine Learning (ICML) (2020)
30. Wang, X., Liu, Z., Yu, S.X.: Unsupervised feature learning by cross-level instance-group discrimination. In: IEEE Conference on Computer Vision and Pattern Recognition (CVPR) (2021)
31. Wu, Z., Xiong, Y., Yu, S.X., Lin, D.: Unsupervised feature learning via non-parametric instance discrimination. In: Proceedings of the IEEE Conference on Computer Vision and Pattern Recognition (CVPR) (2018)
32. Ye, M., Zhang, X., Yuen, P.C., Chang, S.F.: Unsupervised embedding learning via invariant and spreading instance feature. In: Proceedings of the IEEE Conference on Computer Vision and Pattern Recognition (CVPR) (2019)
33. You, Y., Gitman, I., Ginsburg, B.: Large batch training of convolutional networks. arXiv preprint arXiv:1708.03888 (2017)
34. Zbontar, J., Jing, L., Misra, I., LeCun, Y., Deny, S.: Barlow twins: self-supervised learning via redundancy reduction. In: International Conference on Machine Learning, pp. 12310–12320. PMLR (2021)
35. Zhan, X., Xie, J., Liu, Z., Lin, D., Change Loy, C.: OpenSelfSup: open MMLab self-supervised learning toolbox and benchmark (2020). https://github.com/open-mmlab/openselfsup

36. Zhang, R., Isola, P., Efros, A.A.: Colorful image colorization. In: Leibe, B., Matas, J., Sebe, N., Welling, M. (eds.) ECCV 2016. LNCS, vol. 9907, pp. 649–666. Springer, Cham (2016). https://doi.org/10.1007/978-3-319-46487-9_40
37. Zhu, B., Huang, J., Li, Z., Zhang, X., Sun, J.: EqCo: equivalent rules for self-supervised contrastive learning. arXiv preprint arXiv:2010.01929 (2020)

Joint Learning of Localized Representations from Medical Images and Reports

Philip Müller[1]([✉])[iD], Georgios Kaissis[1,2,3][iD], Congyu Zou[4],
and Daniel Rueckert[1,3][iD]

[1] Institute of Artificial Intelligence in Medicine, Technical University of Munich,
81675 Munich, Germany
philip.j.mueller@tum.de
[2] Institute of Radiology, Technical University of Munich, 81675 Munich, Germany
[3] Department of Computing, Imperial College London, London SW7 2BX, UK
[4] Department for Internal Medicine I, Klinikum Rechts der Isar, Technical University
of Munich, 81675 Munich, Germany

Abstract. Contrastive learning has proven effective for pre-training
image models on unlabeled data with promising results for tasks such as
medical image classification. Using paired text (like radiological reports)
during pre-training improves the results even further. Still, most existing methods target image classification downstream tasks and may not
be optimal for localized tasks like semantic segmentation or object
detection. We therefore propose *Lo*calized *representation learning from
*V*ision and *T*ext (LoVT), a text-supervised pre-training method that
explicitly targets localized medical imaging tasks. Our method combines
instance-level image-report contrastive learning with local contrastive
learning on image region and report sentence representations. We evaluate LoVT and commonly used pre-training methods on an evaluation
framework of 18 localized tasks on chest X-rays from five public datasets.
LoVT performs best on 10 of the 18 studied tasks making it the preferred
method of choice for localized tasks.

Keywords: Representation learning · Contrastive learning · Text
supervision

1 Introduction and Motivation

In medical applications of computer vision, high-quality annotated data is scarce
and expensive to acquire, as it typically requires trained physicians to manually label samples [37]. Therefore, the requirement for large labeled datasets can
become quite problematic and may limit the applications of deep learning in this

---

Supplementary Information The online version contains supplementary material
available at https://doi.org/10.1007/978-3-031-19809-0_39.

field. One approach to overcome this problem is to utilize radiological reports that are paired with medical images. Such reports are produced routinely in clinical practice and are typically written by medical experts (e.g. radiologists). They thus provide a valuable source of semantic information that is available with little additional cost. Rule-based Natural Language Processing (NLP) models like CheXpert [19] extract labels from these reports allowing the automatic creation of large datasets but they also have some significant limitations. Most importantly, such approaches are typically limited to classification tasks. They generate overall labels for reports (and therefore the paired images) but relating these labels to specific image regions is nontrivial so they cannot be used for localized tasks like semantic segmentation or object detection. Also, rule-based NLP models have to be manually created and cannot generalize to different classification tasks or even different report writing styles [19]. Instead of using these reports to generate classification labels, the reports can be utilized directly in the pre-training method, as was first proposed in the ConVIRT method [51]. Here, the semantic information contained in the reports is used as weak supervision to pre-train image models that are then fine-tuned on labeled downstream tasks, where results can be improved or the number of labeled samples can be reduced. We argue that while this approach is quite promising it is not designed for localized downstream tasks. For example, ConVIRT [51] only works on per-sample image representations and does not explicitly provide more localized representations that might be beneficial for localized tasks like semantic segmentation and object detection. In this work, we therefore propose *Localized representation learning from Vision and Text (LoVT)*, a pre-training method that utilizes the structure of radiological reports (where each sentence typically describes a single property of the image) to pre-train image models for localized tasks. It extends ConVIRT [51] and outperforms it on most localized downstream tasks.

Our contributions are as follows:

- We split each report into sentences and each image into regions (i.e. patches), jointly encode all sentences of the report to get representations per sentence and jointly encode all patches to get region representations.
- We align sentence and region representations using an attention mechanism and local contrastive learning.
- We show that this can be effectively achieved using our novel local contrastive loss that encourages spatial smoothness and sensitivity.
- We evaluate our method trained using MIMIC-CXR [13,22–24] on a downstream evaluation framework [30] with 18 localized tasks on chest X-rays, including object detection and semantic segmentation on five public datasets. We compare it with several self- and text-supervised methods and with transfer from classification in more than 1400 evaluation runs. Our method LoVT proves as the most successful method outperforming all other methods on 10 out of 18 tasks.

2   Related Work

In recent years, contrastive learning [2–4, 6, 7, 11, 14, 15, 17, 18, 25, 29, 31, 47, 50], has become the state-of-the-art approach for self-supervised representation learning on images. It has been successfully applied as pre-training method in medical imaging including downstream tasks such as image classification on chest X-rays [12, 41, 42].

Most contrastive learning approaches use, unlike our method, only instance-level contrast, i.e. represent each view of the image by a single vector. While the resulting representations are well-suited for global downstream tasks, they are not designed for localized downstream tasks. Therefore, there is a number of recent approaches that use region-level contrast [5, 28, 32, 46, 48, 49], i.e. they act on representations of image regions. Unlike our method, these methods do not utilize paired text.

Recently however, there is much focus on self-supervised representation learning methods that pre-train image models for downstream tasks by taking advantage of the companion text [8, 21, 27, 33, 38, 51]. VirTex [8] and ICMLM [38] use image captioning tasks (generative tasks). ConVIRT [51], CLIP [33] and ALIGN [21] on the other hand use multiview contrastive learning [1]. These approaches have been found to be more effective for discriminative downstream tasks [33]. ConVIRT, CLIP, and ALIGN all follow the same general framework where an image and a text encoder are trained jointly using the NT-Xent loss (which is also used in SimCLR) on image and text views. The text views are based on single sentences from companion text, in the case of ConVIRT it is a sentence sampled from the radiology report. The main difference between these methods is the datasets they are studied on, ConVIRT is trained on chest X-rays while the other methods use natural images. Additionally, CLIP uses attention pooling to compute image representations from feature maps while the other methods use the default pooling method from the image encoder (average pooling in the case of ResNet50 [16]). Our method follows a similar framework but adds local contrastive losses for better performance on localized tasks. Also, it encodes the whole report instead of sampling a single sentence and uses attention pooling in the image and text encoders. LocTex [27] does localized pre-training on natural images with companion text and predicts alignment of text and image regions. Unlike our method, it uses supervision generated by mouse gazes instead of learning the alignment implicitly using a local contrastive loss. Most related to our work is the recently published local Mutual Information approach [26] that performs contrastive learning on report sentences and image regions but targets classification instead of localized tasks and does therefore neither encourage contrast between regions nor spatial smoothness.

3   Method

3.1   Assumptions and Intuition

As shown in Fig. 1, a radiology report is typically split into several sections, including a *Findings* section, describing related radiological images, and an *Assessment* section, interpreting the findings. As these sections describe medical aspects observed (*Findings*) in one or more related images and conclusions (*Assessment*) drawn from it, they provide supervision for identifying relevant patterns in the images and interpretations of these patterns. Both sections can be split into sentences and each of these sentences typically describes one or a few aspects of which we assume that most are related to one or a few very localized regions in a paired image. We randomly sample one of the images related to a given report and split it into 7×7 equally-sized regions. More precisely, we augment and resize the image to a size of 224×224, feed it into a convolutional neural network, and use the output feature map of size 7×7 as region representations. A language model encodes the tokens of the report as contextualized (i.e. considering their meaning in the whole report) vector representations from which we compute sentence representations. A many-to-many alignment model is then used to compute *cross-modal representations* from *uni-modal representations*, i.e. image region representations from sentence representations and vice-versa. We argue that by aligning cross-modal and uni-modal representations, the image region representations are encouraged to contain the high-level semantics present in the report.

EXAMINATION: CHEST (PA and LAT)
INDICATION: ___ year old woman with ?pleural effusion
FINDINGS: Cardiac size cannot be evaluated. Large left pleural effusion is new. Small right effusion is new. The upper lungs are clear. Right lower lobe opacities are better seen in prior CT. There is no pneumothorax. There are mild degenerative changes in the thoracic spine.
IMPRESSION: Large left pleural effusion.

Fig. 1. Example radiology report describing chest X-Rays. Taken from the MIMIC-CXR [13, 23, 24] dataset.

3.2   Model Overview

Figure 2 shows the general architecture of our proposed LoVT model. Each training sample x_i is a pair of an image $x_i^{\mathcal{I}} \in \mathbb{R}^{224 \times 224}$ and the related report $x_i^{\mathcal{R}}$

consisting of M_i sentences. Both, $x_i^{\mathcal{I}}$ and $x_i^{\mathcal{R}}$, are encoded independently into two global representations, for image and report respectively, and multiple local representations per sample, corresponding to image regions and report sentences, respectively. An attention-based alignment model then computes cross-modal representations (i.e. sentence representations from image regions and vice-versa) which are aligned with the local uni-modal representations using local contrastive losses. Additionally, the global representations are aligned using a global contrastive loss. The encoders and the alignment model are trained jointly on batches of image-report pairs x_i. The details of the model and the loss function will be described in the following sections.

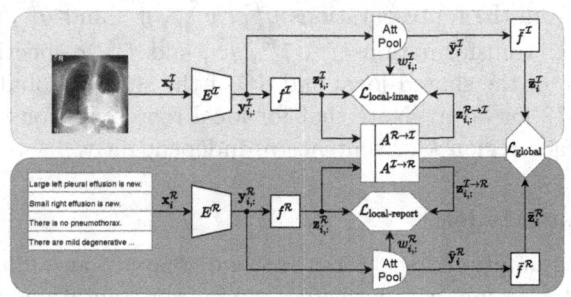

Fig. 2. Architecture of LoVT. Given an image $x_i^{\mathcal{I}}$ and the related report $x_i^{\mathcal{R}}$, the encoders $E^{\mathcal{I}}$ and $E^{\mathcal{R}}$ compute image region and report sentence representations, respectively, which are projected using $f^{\mathcal{I}}$ and $f^{\mathcal{R}}$. The alignment models $A^{\mathcal{R}\to\mathcal{I}}$ and $A^{\mathcal{I}\to\mathcal{R}}$ compute cross-modal report-to-image ($z_{i,k}^{\mathcal{R}\to\mathcal{I}}$) and image-to-report ($z_{i,m}^{\mathcal{I}\to\mathcal{R}}$) representations which are aligned with the uni-modal representations ($z_{i,k}^{\mathcal{I}}$ and $z_{i,m}^{\mathcal{R}}$) using the local losses $\mathcal{L}_{\text{local-image}}$ and $\mathcal{L}_{\text{local-report}}$, respectively. Global image ($\bar{y}_i^{\mathcal{I}}$) and report ($\bar{y}_i^{\mathcal{R}}$) representations are computed using attention pooling on the local representations, are then projected using $\bar{f}^{\mathcal{I}}$ and $\bar{f}^{\mathcal{R}}$ and aligned using the global loss $\mathcal{L}_{\text{global}}$.

3.3 Encoding

Each image $x_i^{\mathcal{I}}$ is encoded into $K = H \times W$ (we use $K = 7 \times 7$) region representations $y_{i,k}^{\mathcal{I}} \in \mathbb{R}^{d^{\mathcal{I}}}$ using the image encoder $E^{\mathcal{I}}$, where k is the index of the image region, and $d^{\mathcal{I}}$ is the dimension of the image region representation space. Our approach is encoder agnostic, i.e. any model encoding image regions into vector representations can be used for $E^{\mathcal{I}}$. We use a ResNet50 [16] and take the feature map before global average pooling as region representations. Similarly, each report $x_i^{\mathcal{R}}$ is encoded into M_i sentence representations $y_{i,m}^{\mathcal{R}} \in \mathbb{R}^{d^{\mathcal{R}}}$ using the report encoder $E^{\mathcal{R}}$. Here M_i is the number of sentences of report sample i, m is the index of the sentence, and $d^{\mathcal{R}}$ is the dimension of the report sentence representation space. Note that while K is constant, M_i may be different for each sample. Any model encoding sentences into vector representations can be used for $E^\mathcal{R}$. We use BERT_base [10] to jointly encode the tokens of the concatenated sentences of each report and then perform max pooling over the token representations of each sentence to get sentence representations.

The global (i.e. per-sample) representations $\bar{\boldsymbol{y}}_i^\mathcal{I}$ and $\bar{\boldsymbol{y}}_i^\mathcal{R}$ are each computed by an attention pooling layer (not shared between modalities) on the region and sentence representations, respectively. It is implemented using multi-head query-key-value attention [44] where the query is computed from the globally averaged region or sentence representations. This pooling approach was first proposed for the image encoder of CLIP [33].

Following previous works [6,14,51], we compute projected local representations $\boldsymbol{z}_{i,k}^\mathcal{I} \in \mathbb{R}^{d^\mathcal{Z}}$ and $\boldsymbol{z}_{i,m}^\mathcal{K} \in \mathbb{R}^{d^\mathcal{Z}}$, and projected global representations $\bar{\boldsymbol{z}}_i^\mathcal{I} \in \mathbb{R}^{\bar{d}^\mathcal{Z}}$ and $\bar{\boldsymbol{z}}_i^\mathcal{R} \in \mathbb{R}^{\bar{d}^\mathcal{Z}}$ from the representations $\boldsymbol{y}_{i,k}^\mathcal{I}$, $\boldsymbol{y}_{i,m}^\mathcal{R}$, $\bar{\boldsymbol{y}}_i^\mathcal{I}$, and $\bar{\boldsymbol{y}}_i^\mathcal{R}$, using the (non-shared) nonlinear transformations $f^\mathcal{I}$, $f^\mathcal{R}$, $\bar{f}^\mathcal{I}$, and $\bar{f}^\mathcal{R}$, respectively, where $d^\mathcal{Z}$ is the dimension of the shared local and $\bar{d}^\mathcal{Z}$ of the shared global representation space (we use 512 for both). Note that for local representations the projections are applied to each region k or sentence m independently.

3.4 Alignment Model

Following our assumptions (see Sect. 3.1), we compute an alignment of image regions and sentences and compute cross-modal representations using the alignment models $A^{\mathcal{I} \to \mathcal{R}}$ and $A^{\mathcal{R} \to \mathcal{I}}$, which are based on single-head query-key-value attention [44].

For each sentence m the cross-modal representation $\boldsymbol{z}_{i,m}^{\mathcal{I} \to \mathcal{R}}$ is computed by letting $\boldsymbol{z}_{i,m}^\mathcal{R}$ attend to all image region representations $\boldsymbol{z}_{i,k}^\mathcal{I}$ (of the related image). We therefore compute the probability $\alpha_{i,m,k}^{\mathcal{I} \to \mathcal{R}}$ that sentence m is aligned with region k based on the scaled dot product scores of their projected representations, i.e. $\alpha_{i,m,k}^{\mathcal{I} \to \mathcal{R}} = \text{softmax}_k \left(\frac{(\boldsymbol{Q} \boldsymbol{z}_{i,m}^\mathcal{R})^T (\boldsymbol{Q} \boldsymbol{z}_{i,k}^\mathcal{I})}{\sqrt{d^\mathcal{Z}}} \right)$, where the linear query-key projection $\boldsymbol{Q}$ is a learned matrix. Then the alignment model $A^{\mathcal{I} \to \mathcal{R}}$ uses $\alpha_{i,m,k}^{\mathcal{I} \to \mathcal{R}}$ to compute $\boldsymbol{z}_{i,m}^{\mathcal{I} \to \mathcal{R}}$ as projected weighted sum of the image region representations $\boldsymbol{z}_{i,k}^\mathcal{I}$:

$$\boldsymbol{z}_{i,m}^{\mathcal{I} \to \mathcal{R}} = \boldsymbol{O} \left(\sum_{k=1}^{K} \alpha_{i,m,k}^{\mathcal{I} \to \mathcal{R}} \left(\boldsymbol{V} \boldsymbol{z}_{i,k}^\mathcal{I} \right) \right), \tag{1}$$

where the value projection $\boldsymbol{V}$, and the output projection $\boldsymbol{O}$ are learned matrices.

In a similar fashion the cross-modal representations $\boldsymbol{z}_{i,k}^{\mathcal{R} \to \mathcal{I}}$ are computed by $A^{\mathcal{R} \to \mathcal{I}}$:

$$\boldsymbol{z}_{i,k}^{\mathcal{R} \to \mathcal{I}} = \boldsymbol{O} \left(\sum_{m=1}^{M_i} \alpha_{i,k,m}^{\mathcal{R} \to \mathcal{I}} \left(\boldsymbol{V} \boldsymbol{z}_{i,m}^\mathcal{R} \right) \right), \tag{2}$$

with $\alpha_{i,k,m}^{\mathcal{R} \to \mathcal{I}} = \text{softmax}_m \left(\frac{(\boldsymbol{Q} \boldsymbol{z}_{i,k}^\mathcal{I})^T (\boldsymbol{Q} \boldsymbol{z}_{i,m}^\mathcal{R})}{\sqrt{d^\mathcal{Z}}} \right)$. Note that as $A^{\mathcal{R} \to \mathcal{I}}$ and $A^{\mathcal{I} \to \mathcal{R}}$ share the same matrices $\boldsymbol{Q}$, $\boldsymbol{V}$, and $\boldsymbol{O}$, the only difference between $\alpha_{i,k,m}^{\mathcal{R} \to \mathcal{I}}$ and $\alpha_{i,m,k}^{\mathcal{I} \to \mathcal{R}}$ is transposition and the index over which softmax is applied.

3.5 Loss Function

Global Alignment. For global alignment we follow ConVIRT [51] and maximize the cosine similarity between paired image and report representations while minimizing the similarity between non-paired (i.e. from different samples) representations. The loss consists of a image-report part, where all non-paired report representations from the batch are used as negatives:

$$\ell_{\text{global}}^{\mathcal{I}\|\mathcal{R}} = -\log \frac{e^{\cos(\bar{z}_i^{\mathcal{I}}, \bar{z}_i^{\mathcal{R}})/\tau}}{\sum_j e^{\cos(\bar{z}_i^{\mathcal{I}}, \bar{z}_j^{\mathcal{R}})/\tau}}, \tag{3}$$

and a report-image part, defined analogously:

$$\ell_{\text{global}}^{\mathcal{R}\|\mathcal{I}} = -\log \frac{e^{\cos(\bar{z}_i^{\mathcal{R}}, \bar{z}_i^{\mathcal{I}})/\tau}}{\sum_j e^{\cos(\bar{z}_i^{\mathcal{R}}, \bar{z}_j^{\mathcal{I}})/\tau}}, \tag{4}$$

where τ is the similarity temperature (we use 0.1) and all logarithms are natural. Both parts are combined using the hyperparameter $\lambda \in [0,1]$ (we use 0.75):

$$\mathcal{L}_{\text{global}} = \frac{1}{N} \sum_{i=1}^{N} \left[\lambda \cdot \ell_{\text{global}}^{\mathcal{I}\|\mathcal{R}} + (1-\lambda) \cdot \ell_{\text{global}}^{\mathcal{R}\|\mathcal{I}} \right]. \tag{5}$$

Local Alignment. The global alignment loss does not only align the global representations but it also prevents the global representations from collapsing to a constant vector using negative samples to contrast the positive pairs. Similarly, we propose local alignment losses encouraging spatial (sentence) sensitivity through negatives from the same sample, i.e. preventing the local representations to be similar for all regions (sentences) of an image (report). We use two NT-Xent-based [6] local losses: $\mathcal{L}_{\text{local-image}}$, aligning region representations $z_{i,k}^{\mathcal{I}}$ with $z_{i,k}^{\mathcal{R}\to\mathcal{I}}$, and $\mathcal{L}_{\text{local-report}}$, aligning sentence representations $z_{i,m}^{\mathcal{R}}$ with $z_{i,m}^{\mathcal{I}\to\mathcal{R}}$.

Some regions or sentences may not be relevant for aligning a sample (e.g. background regions or sentences not related to the image). Therefore, we introduce region weights $w_{i,k}^{\mathcal{I}}$ and sentence weights $w_{i,m}^{\mathcal{R}}$, which are computed as the attention probabilities from the respective attention pooling layer (which was used to compute global representations), averaged over all attention heads. These weights are used in the local loss functions such that irrelevant representations do not have to be aligned. Note that we do not backpropagate through the region or sentence weights.

The loss $\mathcal{L}_{\text{local-image}}$ allows for having multiple positive pairs within each sample by giving each pair of regions (k, l) a positiveness probability $p_{k,l}^{\mathcal{I}} \in [0,1]$. We then treat each positive pair as its own (weighted) example and contrast it with all other pairs (again all logarithms are natural):

$$\ell_{\text{local-image}}^{\mathcal{I}\|\mathcal{R}\to\mathcal{I}} = -\sum_{l=1}^{K} p_{k,l}^{\mathcal{I}} \log \frac{e^{\cos(z_{i,k}^{\mathcal{I}}, z_{i,l}^{\mathcal{R}\to\mathcal{I}})/\tau'}}{\sum_{k'} e^{\cos(z_{i,k}^{\mathcal{I}}, z_{i,k'}^{\mathcal{R}\to\mathcal{I}})/\tau'}} \tag{6}$$

$$\ell_{\text{local-image}}^{\mathcal{R}\to\mathcal{I}\|\mathcal{I}} = -\sum_{l=1}^{K} p_{k,l}^{\mathcal{I}} \log \frac{e^{\cos\left(z_{i,k}^{\mathcal{R}\to\mathcal{I}}, z_{i,l}^{\mathcal{I}}\right)/\tau'}}{\sum_{k'} e^{\cos\left(z_{i,k}^{\mathcal{R}\to\mathcal{I}}, z_{i,k'}^{\mathcal{I}}\right)/\tau'}} \tag{7}$$

$$\mathcal{L}_{\text{local-image}} = \frac{1}{2N} \sum_{i=1}^{N} \sum_{k=1}^{K} w_{i,k}^{\mathcal{I}} \cdot \left[\ell_{\text{local-image}}^{\mathcal{I}\|\mathcal{R}\to\mathcal{I}} + \ell_{\text{local-image}}^{\mathcal{R}\to\mathcal{I}\|\mathcal{I}} \right]. \tag{8}$$

Here τ' is the similarity temperature and is set to 0.3. We assume that nearby image regions are often similar and that therefore nearby regions are more likely to be positives while distant regions are more likely to be negatives. Thus, we define the positiveness probability $p_{k,l}^{\mathcal{I}}$ of two image regions as the complementary cumulative exponential distribution of d_x (their spatial ℓ_2-distance in 2D space normalized by the length of the diagonal $\sqrt{H^2 + W^2}$) and set $p_{k,l}^{\mathcal{I}}$ to zero above cutoff threshold $T \in [0, \infty)$:

$$p_{k,l}^{\mathcal{I}} = \frac{\mathbb{1}_{[d_x(k,l)\le T]} \cdot e^{-d_x(k,l)/\beta}}{\sum_{k'} \mathbb{1}_{[d_x(k,k')\le T]} \cdot e^{-d_x(k,k')/\beta}}. \tag{9}$$

Here $\beta \in (0, \infty)$ is a sharpness hyperparameter. We set $\beta = 1$ and $T = 0.5$. Note that the normalization of d_x is equal to rescaling T and β, i.e. it allows us to define both hyperparameters independently of the image size.

The definition of $p_{k,l}^{\mathcal{I}}$ is derived by modeling the occurrence of related features at specific distances in the image as a Poisson point process, such that the ℓ_2-distance of related features follows the exponential distribution. We assume a Poisson process due to its property of being memoryless, i.e. knowing that a feature is already related to another feature at some distance does not change how distant additional related features can be found. Also, the probability density function of the exponential distribution is decreasing (with support on the interval $[0, \infty)$), which seems reasonable as it is typically more likely that related features are near than far. Its cumulative distribution function then describes the probability that two related features are within a given radius and its complementary function that of being outside a given radius. The threshold T assures that very distant pairs do not count as positives. The loss $\mathcal{L}_{\text{local-image}}$ thus encourages spatial smoothness of image regions while maintaining spatial sensitivity through negative samples. Note that it is related to the pixel-contrast loss proposed in [49], where the main novelty of our work is the partly smooth definition of $p_{k,l}^{\mathcal{I}}$ based on the exponential distribution.

The local report loss $\mathcal{L}_{\text{local-report}}$ is defined similarly but we do not assume prior knowledge about the similarity of sentences and therefore only have a single positive pair per sentence (again all logarithms are natural):

$$\ell_{\text{local-report}}^{\mathcal{R}\|\mathcal{I}\to\mathcal{R}} = -\log \frac{e^{\cos\left(z_{i,m}^{\mathcal{R}}, z_{i,m}^{\mathcal{I}\to\mathcal{R}}\right)/\tau'}}{\sum_{m'} e^{\cos\left(z_{i,m}^{\mathcal{R}}, z_{i,m'}^{\mathcal{I}\to\mathcal{R}}\right)/\tau'}} \tag{10}$$

$$\ell_{\text{local-report}}^{\mathcal{I}\to\mathcal{R}\|\mathcal{R}} = -\log \frac{e^{\cos\left(z_{i,m}^{\mathcal{I}\to\mathcal{R}}, z_{i,m}^{\mathcal{R}}\right)/\tau'}}{\sum_{m'} e^{\cos\left(z_{i,m}^{\mathcal{I}\to\mathcal{R}}, z_{i,m'}^{\mathcal{R}}\right)/\tau'}} \tag{11}$$

$$\mathcal{L}_{\text{local-report}} = \frac{1}{2N} \sum_{i=1}^{N} \sum_{m=1}^{M_i} w_{i,m}^{\mathcal{R}} \cdot \left[\ell_{\text{local-report}}^{\mathcal{R}\|\mathcal{I}\rightarrow\mathcal{R}} + \ell_{\text{local-report}}^{\mathcal{T}\rightarrow\mathcal{R}\|\mathcal{R}} \right] \quad (12)$$

Total Loss. The total loss $\mathcal{L}$ is computed as the weighted sum of global and local losses:

$$\mathcal{L} = \gamma \cdot \mathcal{L}_{\text{global}} + \mu \cdot \mathcal{L}_{\text{local-image}} + \nu \cdot \mathcal{L}_{\text{local-report}}, \quad (13)$$

where γ, μ, and ν are loss weights to balance the individual losses and are set to 1.0, 0.75, and 0.75, respectively. We determined these loss weights by running small grid searches (see supplementary material for details).

4   Evaluation

4.1   Downstream Tasks and Experimental Setup

We evaluate our method on a downstream evaluation framework [30] with 18 localized tasks on chest X-rays, which we will shortly describe here. For more details, we refer to the supplementary material.

Evaluation Protocols. We only evaluate the pre-trained ResNet50 (from the image encoder). For semantic segmentation tasks we use the following evaluation protocols: (i) **U-Net Finetune**, where the ResNet50 is used as the backbone of a U-Net [35] and is finetuned jointly with all other layers, (ii) **U-Net Frozen**, where the ResNet50 is used as the frozen backbone of a U-Net [35] and only the non-backbone layers are trained, and (iii) **Linear**, where an element-wise linear layer is trained that is applied to the feature map of the frozen ResNet50, and then results are upsampled to the segmentation resolution.

For object detection tasks we use the following protocols: (i) **YOLOv3 Finetune**, where the ResNet50 is used as the backbone of a YOLOv3 [34] model and is finetuned jointly with all other layers, (ii) **YOLOv3 Frozen**, where the ResNet50 is used as the frozen backbone of a YOLOv3 [34] model and only the non-backbone layers are trained, and (iii) **Linear**, where the object detection ground truth is converted to segmentation masks and the *Linear* evaluation protocol is applied.

Downstream Datasets. We evaluate the pre-trained ResNet50 on several medical datasets, namely (i) **RSNA Pneumonia Detection** [39,45], with more than 260000 frontal-view chest X-rays with detection targets for pneumonia opacities. We use the *YOLOv3 Finetune, YOLOv3 Frozen,* and *Linear* protocols, each with 1%, 10%, and 100% of the training samples; (ii) **COVID Rural** [9,43], with more than 200 frontal-view chest X-rays with segmentation masks for COVID-19 lung opacity regions. We use the *UNet Finetune, UNet Frozen,* and *Linear* protocols; (iii) **SIIM-ACR Pneumothorax Segmentation** [40], with more than 12000 frontal-view chest X-rays with segmentation masks for pneumothorax. We use the *UNet Finetune, UNet Frozen* protocols, but due not use *Linear* due to the fine-grained nature of the segmentation masks; (iv) **Object CXR** [20] with

9000 frontal-view chest X-rays with detection targets for foreign objects. We use the *YOLOv3 Finetune, YOLOv3 Frozen,* and *Linear* protocols; (v) **NIH CXR** [45], with almost 1000 frontal-view chest X-rays with detection targets for eight pathologies (Atelectasis, Cardiomegaly, Effusion, Infiltrate, Mass, Nodule, Pneumonia, and Pneumothorax). Due to the limited data per class, we only use the *Linear* protocol. The different evaluation protocols are complementary to each other, where the *U-Net Finetune* and *YOLOv3 Finetune* protocols evaluate how well suited the pre-trained image models are for fine-tuning as used in practical applications and the *Linear* protocols evaluate the quality of learned local representations (i.e. feature maps) while adding only a few parameters and therefore mostly omitting the variance introduced by random initialization during downstream evaluation. The *U-Net Frozen* and *YOLOv3 Frozen* protocols are a trade-off, where representations are frozen but evaluated in a more practical setting (with several randomly initialized layers).

Tuning and Evaluation Procedure. All baselines and our models have been tuned only on a single downstream task, *RSNA YOLOv3 Frozen 10%*, where a single fixed downstream learning rate was used (determined in preliminary experiments) and the results of five runs have been averaged. Other downstream tasks have not been evaluated during tuning to make sure that models are not biased towards the downstream tasks. After tuning, we evaluated each model on all downstream tasks: The learning rates were tuned individually per model and task (using single evaluation runs) before running five evaluations per task (all using the tuned learning rate). We report the average results of these five runs and their 95%-confidence interval (where each evaluation run is considered a sample).

Pre-Training Dataset. We train our method on MIMIC-CXR [13, 22–24] (version 2) as, to our best knowledge, it is the largest and most commonly used dataset of this kind. Since all downstream tasks contain only frontal views, we remove all lateral views, such that roughly 21000 training samples remain, each with a report and one or more frontal images.

Baselines. We compare our method against several baseline methods:

- **Random Init.**: The ResNet50 is initialized using its default random initialization
- **ImageNet** [36] **Init.**: The ResNet50 is initialized with weights pre-trained on the ImageNet ILSVRC-2012 task [36];
- **CheXpert** [19]: The ResNet50 is pre-trained using supervised multi-label binary classification with CheXpert [19] labels on frontal chest X-rays of MIMIC-CXR
- **Global image pre-training methods**: The ResNet50 is pre-trained using the self-supervised pre-training methods SimCLR [6] or BYOL [14] on frontal chest X-rays of MIMIC-CXR. We decided to include SimCLR as is uses a similar loss function as LoVT and we include BYOL because of its widespread use.
- **Local image pre-training methods**: The ResNet50 is pre-trained using the self-supervised pre-training method PixelPro [49] on frontal chest X-rays

Table 1. Results on the RSNA pneumonia detection tasks with different training set sizes. All results are averaged over five evaluation runs and the 95%-confidence interval is shown. The best results per task are underlined, the second-best results are dash-underlined and the best results per pre-training category (general initialization, pre-training on 30% and 100%) are highlighted in bold. Note that the *YOLOv3 Frozen 10%* task (task 5) was used for tuning of all methods and may therefore not be representative as methods may overfit on this task.

	RSNA YOLOv3 Finetune mAP (%)			RSNA YOLOv3 Frozen mAP (%)			RSNA Lin. Seg. Dice (%)		
	1%	10%	100%	1%	10%	100%	1%	10%	100%
General initialization methods									
Random	2.4±0.5	5.1±1.2	14.9±1.7	1.0±0.2	4.0±0.3	8.9±0.9	21.9±1.2	5.3±0.0	5.3±0.0
ImageNet [36]	**5.0±0.7**	**12.4±0.8**	**19.0±0.2**	**3.6±1.4**	**8.0±0.1**	**15.7±0.3**	**27.5±0.6**	**38.3±0.0**	**43.3±0.0**
Pre-Training on 30 % of frontal MIMIC-CXR									
CheXpert [19]	**8.3±0.8**	12.4±1.6	**21.3±0.3**	7.0±1.0	14.8±0.8	18.8±0.4	38.9±0.2	45.5±0.2	48.1±0.0
BYOL [14]	7.0±1.0	11.9±1.1	18.8±0.2	9.6±0.2	14.0±1.2	**21.0±0.2**	42.9±0.1	47.8±0.2	50.0±0.0
SimCLR [6]	6.7±0.5	**12.9±0.5**	20.4±1.8	7.9±1.0	11.9±0.1	19.9±0.2	43.1±0.0	46.0±0.0	48.2±0.0
PixelPro [49]	4.8±0.6	12.6±1.2	19.8±0.4	3.1±0.2	6.4±0.5	13.4±0.3	25.9±0.2	34.6±0.0	39.8±0.1
ConVIRT [51]	7.4±1.3	12.7±1.5	18.3±0.4	**9.8±0.3**	14.8±1.1	18.4±1.1	42.1±0.1	47.1±0.2	50.2±0.0
CLIP [33]*	7.2±0.8	12.8±1.2	19.7±0.5	9.3±0.4	16.1±1.1	19.6±1.4	44.3±0.1	48.8±0.1	50.7±0.0
LoVT (Ours)	7.7±1.0	11.7±0.5	17.2±1.3	8.6±1.5	**17.9±0.4**	18.0±0.1	**46.0±0.0**	**49.4±0.0**	**51.5±0.0**
Pre-Training on 100 % of frontal MIMIC-CXR									
CheXpert [19]	**10.0±1.9**	12.4±0.9	**22.2±0.4**	5.8±0.4	11.9±0.7	20.0±0.2	40.0±0.1	44.3±0.0	46.9±0.0
BYOL [14]	5.6±0.8	11.0±0.2	17.3±1.1	6.8±1.6	12.1±1.1	15.9±0.6	41.9±0.0	45.1±0.0	46.8±0.0
SimCLR [6]	7.1±0.7	12.2±0.8	18.8±1.0	5.4±0.2	13.1±0.2	17.3±1.6	43.0±0.0	45.1±0.0	47.0±0.0
PixelPro [49]	4.8±0.3	11.0±1.5	17.4±1.7	4.6±1.6	5.4±1.1	12.6±1.3	23.9±0.4	34.8±0.2	40.2±0.1
ConVIRT [51]	**10.7±1.1**	**13.3±0.8**	18.5±0.4	8.2±0.9	15.6±1.2	17.9±0.3	44.6±0.1	48.5±0.0	50.4±0.3
CLIP [33]*	7.0±1.5	10.7±1.1	19.9±0.8	**11.9±0.7**	15.0±1.1	18.7±0.0	45.2±0.0	49.3±0.1	51.1±0.0
LoVT (Ours)	8.5±0.8	13.2±0.6	18.1±3.2	9.6±1.2	**16.4±1.3**	**20.5±1.0**	**46.3±0.0**	**50.1±0.0**	**51.8±0.0**
Task Nr.	1	2	3	4	5	6	7	8	9

* Modified to use the same image and text encoders as ConVIRT and LoVT.

of MIMIC-CXR. We include PixelPro to study the effect of local contrastive losses when using only images.

- **Global image-text pre-training methods**: The ResNet50 is pre-trained using the image-text methods ConVIRT [51] or CLIP [33] on frontal MIMIC-CXR. Note that for comparability we adapted CLIP to use the same image and text encoders as ConVIRT such that the main difference between CLIP and ConVIRT is that CLIP uses attention pooling to compute the scan representation while ConVIRT uses average pooling. We include both methods as LoVT builds upon a similar general framework, where we include ConVIRT because it targets chest X-rays (like LoVT) and include CLIP because of its widespread use and as it uses (like LoVT) attention pooling in the image encoder. We decided not to include VirTex [8] and ICMLM [38] as they use generative tasks, which have been found to be less effective for discriminative downstream tasks [33].

4.2 Downstream Results

We present the downstream results of our model LoVT and the baselines, with pre-training on 100% and 30% of MIMIC-CXR. Table 1 shows the results on

Table 2. Results on downstream tasks on the COVID Rural, SIIM Pneumothorax, Object CXR, and NIH CXR datasets. All results are averaged over five evaluation runs and the 95%-confidence interval is shown. The best results per task are underlined, the second-best results are dash-underlined and the best results per pre-training category (general initialization, pre-training on 30% and 100%) are highlighted in bold.

| | COVID Rural | | | SIIM-ACR Pneumoth. | | | | Object CXR | | NIH CXR |
| | UNet Finetune | UNet Frozen | Linear | UNet Finetune | UNet Frozen | YOLOv3 Finetune | YOLOv3 Frozen | Linear | | Linear |
	Dice (%)	Dice (%)	Dice (%)	Dice (%)	Dice (%)	fROC (%)	fROC (%)	Dice (%)		Avg Dice (%)
General initialization methods										
Random	34.0±1.1	32.2±1.8	6.0±0.0	23.2±1.0	23.9±1.6	49.5±1.2	28.4±1.4	6.9±0.0		0.5±0.4
ImageNet [36]	**43.9±2.0**	**41.9±1.7**	**32.6±0.7**	**38.5±0.9**	**36.9±0.7**	**62.5±0.4**	**52.7±1.3**	**37.8±0.0**		**2.6±1.6**
Pre-Training on 30 % of frontal MIMIC-CXR										
CheXpert [19]	43.5±4.9	44.1±3.2	32.1±2.0	38.9±0.9	40.7±0.7	62.2±0.6	46.3±1.9	16.5±7.7		8.7±0.6
BYOL [14]	46.2±1.6	47.5±1.6	36.9±1.7	43.1±0.6	42.9±0.3	59.6±1.0	55.7±1.0	32.3±0.1		6.0±0.1
SimCLR [6]	44.9±2.9	41.4±3.7	33.0±0.0	42.6±0.4	39.2±0.7	61.9±0.8	54.3±1.0	33.2±0.1		13.3±0.5
PixelPro [49]	47.0±3.4	38.5±3.9	26.6±0.4	39.3±0.8	39.1±0.3	**63.1±0.7**	46.3±0.2	29.9±0.2		1.8±0.0
ConVIRT [51]	48.8±2.2	44.2±3.1	45.0±3.0	42.5±1.0	42.5±0.2	62.5±0.1	54.0±0.7	37.7±0.1		11.4±0.8
CLIP [33]*	49.3±2.0	46.5±2.3	46.2±0.3	42.8±1.5	42.5±0.6	62.9±0.8	55.5±2.1	**39.0±0.0**		12.5±1.0
LoVT (Ours)	**49.5±1.3**	**49.2±4.6**	**49.2±0.2**	43.4±0.7	43.1±0.6	61.0±1.3	55.8±1.1	37.6±0.2		13.4±0.8
Pre-Training on 100 % of frontal MIMIC-CXR										
CheXpert [19]	46.2±1.7	45.9±3.9	37.7±0.4	34.2±0.8	37.7±0.3	57.5±1.1	39.8±2.4	19.4±0.1		15.2±0.0
BYOL [14]	50.7±2.7	42.0±3.0	32.9±0.0	42.6±0.7	40.7±0.7	60.6±1.1	53.1±0.8	21.8±0.1		5.7±0.0
SimCLR [6]	48.1±2.5	44.1±2.1	35.3±0.0	41.2±0.8	38.7±0.5	61.1±0.7	48.7±0.5	30.0±0.0		11.8±0.0
PixelPro [49]	42.4±4.4	37.7±1.0	18.9±6.4	39.4±1.2	38.7±0.6	**65.0±0.5**	46.2±1.2	29.7±0.1		1.8±0.0
ConVIRT [51]	47.9±0.7	46.0±1.1	42.7±2.0	39.3±0.3	43.1±0.3	60.6±1.2	52.5±1.0	36.0±0.0		**18.6±0.1**
CLIP [33]*	48.6±2.4	45.8±4.1	41.7±0.1	44.0±0.7	**45.0±0.5**	62.8±0.5	56.9±1.4	39.4±0.0		11.4±0.8
LoVT (Ours)	**51.2±2.5**	46.2±2.4	44.0±0.8	**44.1±0.3**	43.9±0.7	62.1±0.5	**57.4±0.5**	**39.9±0.0**		9.4±0.5
Task Nr.	10	11	12	13	14	15	16	17		18

* Modified to use the same image and text encoders as ConVIRT and LoVT.

different subsets of the RSNA dataset and Table 2 shows the results on the remaining downstream datasets, i.e. on COVID Rural, SIM-ACR Pneumothorax, Object CXR, and NIH CXR.

Comparison of Methods. We found that there is no single pre-training method performing best on all evaluated downstream tasks. On most tasks (15 out of 18) image-text self-supervised methods (i.e. LoVT, CLIP, or ConVIRT) outperform the other methods, such that they should be preferred if paired text is available.

Our model LoVT is the best method (over all pre-training settings) on 10 of 18 tasks, and significantly outperforms all other methods in 6 of these tasks, while the second-best method CLIP significantly outperforms all other methods only on 2 tasks. LoVT outperforms image-only methods (i.e. BYOL, SimCLR, and PixelPro) on 14 tasks, where the localized image-only method PixelPro outperforms LoVT only on one task (task 15). On 11 tasks LoVT outperforms other text-supervised methods (i.e. ConVIRT and CLIP), on 14 tasks it outperforms CheXpert classification and on all but two tasks it outperforms ImageNet initialization. When using 100% of the pre-training data LoVT is the best pre-training method on 11 tasks (better by at least the confidence interval on 5 tasks) and when using 30% on 11 tasks (significantly the best on 4 tasks). LoVT performs

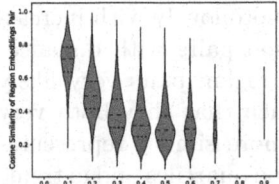 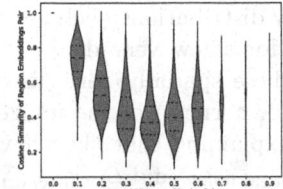 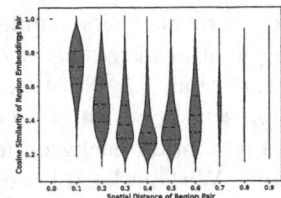

Fig. 3. Spatial smoothness and sensitivity of image region representations. **Left:** LoVT (Ours). **Middle:** No local losses. **Right:** No local losses and no attention pooling. Cosine similarities of image region pairs $y_{i,k}^{\mathcal{I}}, y_{i,k'}^{\mathcal{I}}$ (each from the same sample) plotted as violin plots (with their width representing the number of pairs and quartiles shown as dashed lines) over their spatial distance in the 7×7 image space (normalized and rounded to one decimal digit). We trained all models on 30% of the data and computed the representations on the test set.

best on all COVID Rural tasks, best on most *Linear* tasks, and quite well on the *Frozen* protocol, but does not perform well on the NIH CXR dataset and when finetuned on the RSNA dataset. As there is no single method performing best on all tasks and LoVT performs best in the majority of tasks, this makes LoVT the default method of choice for localized downstream tasks.

Relevance of Pre-Training Dataset Size. We do not observe a consistent benefit of using roughly 210000 pre-training samples (i.e. 100% of the data) over using roughly 63000 samples (i.e. 30%). While on some datasets like RSNA and Object CXR many methods often perform better when pre-trained on 210000 samples (100%), on other datasets like COVID Rural, methods often perform better when pre-trained on 63000 samples (30%). When comparing LoVT pre-trained on 30% of the data with other methods pre-trained in both settings (i.e. 30% and 100%), we observe that LoVT outperforms image-only methods (i.e. BYOL, SimCLR, and PixelPro) on 12 tasks, other text-supervised methods (i.e. ConVIRT and CLIP) on 7 tasks and CheXpert classification on 12 tasks, showing that LoVT effectively reduces the number of required pre-training samples.

Relevance of Downstream Dataset Size. The results shown in Table 1 suggest that, as expected, larger downstream training sets lead to better results. However, we observe that for text-supervised methods (i.e. LoVT, CLIP, and ConVIRT), the downstream training set size is often less relevant compared to other methods. On the *RSAN YOLOv3 Frozen* tasks, LoVT (100%) outperforms ImageNet initialization by 31% when using 100% of the downstream samples, while it outperforms ImageNet initialization by even 167% when only using 1% of the samples.

Spatial Smoothness and Sensitivity. We analyze the influence of the local losses and attention pooling on the spatial smoothness and sensitivity of image region representations and therefore plot in Fig. 3 the distributions of the cosine similarity of image region pairs over their spatial distances. For our LoVT model spatial smoothness and sensitivity can be observed as the quartiles and extreme points of the cosine similarity distributions decrease monotonously with increasing spatial distance, except for a few very distant region pairs with distances larger than 0.6. Note that these spatially very distant region pairs very likely represent opposite borders (or corners) of the image such that they both very likely contain background, explaining that they have more similar representations. Without local losses $\mathcal{L}_{\text{local-image}}$ and $\mathcal{L}_{\text{local-report}}$, the quartiles and extreme points decrease only for small spatial distances while increasing again for points further away, showing that spatial smoothness is only present for nearby regions and spatial sensitivity of more distant region is not optimal. When additionally replacing attention pooling with average (for image regions) and max (for sentences) pooling, similar results can be observed except that the quartiles are decreasing faster and the maximum points do not decrease for nearby regions. We can therefore deduce that the local losses effectively encourage spatial smoothness and sensitivity while attention pooling alone has only little effect.

Analysis of LoVT and Ablation Study. We refer to the supplementary material for a detailed analysis of our method LoVT, including an ablation study (focusing on local weighting, global and local losses, and attention pooling), an analysis of the distribution and alignment of learned representations, and an analysis of the region weights $w_{i,k}^{\mathcal{I}}$.

5   Discussion

Limitations of Our Evaluation Procedure. In the evaluation procedure, we did not apply extensive hyperparameter tuning, resized all inputs to a resolution of only 224×224, and applied no data augmentation. The presented downstream results are therefore below results typically reported on these datasets. We followed [30] and kept the evaluation procedure simple to limit computational resources and avoid bias induced by tuning to allow for a fair comparison of our method with the baselines.

Limitations of LoVT. LoVT learns its alignment model implicitly based only on latent representations and instance-level pairing information. This makes the model sensitive to hyperparameters and hard to train. Also, it only uses local negatives from the same sample which restricts the number of negatives and may therefore limit its performance. Additionally, the alignment model is restricted to a simple attention mechanism and the regions are based on fixed patches that are not adaptive to the contents of the image. This may restrict the capabilities of the model and therefore of the pre-training method. For a detailed discussion of these limitations as well as of the potential negative societal impact we refer to the supplementary material.

Conclusion. We study pre-training for localized medical imaging on chest X-rays and propose a novel text-supervised method called LoVT, that combines instance-level contrastive learning with local contrastive learning. We evaluate our method on 18 localized tasks on chest X-rays and compare it with typically used pre-training and initialization methods. While there is no single best method for all tasks, our method LoVT is the best method on 10 out of 18 studied tasks making it the method of choice for localized tasks.

We hope that our work provides valuable insights that encourage using pre-training for localized medical imaging and that our method inspires future work on localized text-supervised pre-training.

References

1. Bachman, P., Hjelm, R., Buchwalter, W.: Learning representations by maximizing mutual information across views. In: NeurIPS (2019)
2. Bardes, A., Ponce, J., LeCun, Y.: VICReg: variance-invariance-covariance regularization for self-supervised learning. In: ICLR (2022)
3. Caron, M., Misra, I., Mairal, J., Goyal, P., Bojanowski, P., Joulin, A.: Unsupervised learning of visual features by contrasting cluster assignments. In: NeurIPS (2020)
4. Caron, M., et al.: Emerging properties in self-supervised vision transformers. In: ICCV, pp. 9630–9640 (2021). https://doi.org/10.1109/ICCV48922.2021.00951
5. Chaitanya, K., Erdil, E., Karani, N., Konukoglu, E.: Contrastive learning of global and local features for medical image segmentation with limited annotations. In: NeurIPS (2020)
6. Chen, T., Kornblith, S., Norouzi, M., Hinton, G.: A simple framework for contrastive learning of visual representations. In: ICML (2020)
7. Chen, X., He, K.: Exploring simple Siamese representation learning. In: CVPR, pp. 15745–15753 (2021). https://doi.org/10.1109/CVPR46437.2021.01549
8. Desai, K., Johnson, J.: VirTex: learning visual representations from textual annotations. In: CVPR, pp. 11157–11168 (2021). https://doi.org/10.1109/CVPR46437.2021.01101
9. Desai, S., et al.: Data from chest imaging with clinical and genomic correlates representing a rural COVID-19 positive population [data set]. The Cancer Imaging Archive (2020). https://doi.org/10.7937/tcia.2020.py71-5978
10. Devlin, J., Chang, M.W., Lee, K., Toutanova, K.: BERT: pre-training of deep bidirectional transformers for language understanding. In: NAACL, pp. 4171–4186 (2019). https://doi.org/10.18653/v1/N19-1423
11. Ermolov, A., Siarohin, A., Sangineto, E., Sebe, N.: Whitening for self-supervised representation learning. In: ICML, pp. 3015–3024 (2021)
12. Gazda, M., Plavka, J., Gazda, J., Drotár, P.: Self-supervised deep convolutional neural network for chest x-ray classification. IEEE Access, 151972–151982 (2021). https://doi.org/10.1109/ACCESS.2021.3125324
13. Goldberger, A., Amaral, L., Glass, L., Hausdorff, J., et al.: PhysioBank, PhysioToolkit, and PhysioNet: components of a new research resource for complex physiologic signals. Circulation [Online] 101(23), 215–220 (2000)
14. Grill, J.B., et al.: Bootstrap your own latent - a new approach to self-supervised learning. In: NeurIPS (2020)
15. He, K., Fan, H., Wu, Y., et al.: Momentum contrast for unsupervised visual representation learning. In: CVPR, pp. 9726–9735 (2020). https://doi.org/10.1109/CVPR42600.2020.00975
16. He, K., Zhang, X., Ren, S., Sun, J.: Deep residual learning for image recognition. In: CVPR, pp. 770–778 (2016). https://doi.org/10.1109/CVPR.2016.90
17. Hjelm, R.D., et al.: Learning deep representations by mutual information estimation and maximization. In: ICLR (2019)

18. Hénaff, O.J., Srinivas, A., et al.: Data-efficient image recognition with contrastive predictive coding. In: ICML, pp. 4182–4192 (2019)
19. Irvin, J., et al.: CheXpert: a large chest radiograph dataset with uncertainty labels and expert comparison. In: AAAI, pp. 590–597 (2019)
20. JF-Healthcare: object-CXR - automatic detection of foreign objects on chest x-rays. MIDL (2020). https://jfhealthcare.github.io/object-CXR/
21. Jia, C., et al.: Scaling up visual and vision-language representation learning with noisy text supervision. In: ICML (2021)
22. Johnson, A., Lungren, M., Peng, Y., et al.: MIMIC-CXR-JPG - chest radiographs with structured labels (version 2.0.0). PhysioNet (2019). https://doi.org/10.13026/8360-t248
23. Johnson, A., Pollard, T., Berkowitz, S., et al.: MIMIC-CXR, a de-identified publicly available database of chest radiographs with free-text reports. Sci. Data 6(317) (2019). https://doi.org/10.1038/s41597-019-0322-0
24. Johnson, A., Pollard, T., Mark, R., Berkowitz, S., Horng, S.: MIMIC-CXR database (version 2.0.0). PhysioNet (2019). https://doi.org/10.13026/C2JT1Q
25. Li, J., Zhou, P., Xiong, C., Hoi, S.C.H.: Prototypical contrastive learning of unsupervised representations. In: ICLR (2021)
26. Liao, R., et al.: Multimodal representation learning via maximization of local mutual information. In: de Bruijne, M., et al. (eds.) MICCAI 2021. LNCS, vol. 12902, pp. 273–283. Springer, Cham (2021). https://doi.org/10.1007/978-3-030-87196-3_26
27. Liu, Z., Stent, S., Li, J., Gideon, J., Han, S.: LocTex: learning data-efficient visual representations from localized textual supervision. In: ICCV, pp. 2147–2156 (2021). https://doi.org/10.1109/ICCV48922.2021.00217
28. Mahendran, A., Thewlis, J., Vedaldi, A.: Cross pixel optical-flow similarity for self-supervised learning. In: Jawahar, C.V., Li, H., Mori, G., Schindler, K. (eds.) ACCV 2018. LNCS, vol. 11365, pp. 99–116. Springer, Cham (2019). https://doi.org/10.1007/978-3-030-20873-8_7
29. Misra, I., van der Maaten, L.: Self-supervised learning of pretext-invariant representations. In: CVPR, pp. 6706–6716 (2020). https://doi.org/10.1109/CVPR42600.2020.00674
30. Müller, P., Kaissis, G., Zou, C., Rueckert, D.: Radiological reports improve pre-training for localized imaging tasks on chest x-rays. In: Wang, L., Dou, Q., Fletcher, P.T., Speidel, S., Li, S. (eds.) MICCAI 2022. LNCS, vol. 13435, pp. 647–657. Springer, Cham (2022). https://doi.org/10.1007/978-3-031-16443-9_62
31. van den Oord, A., Li, Y., Vinyals, O.: Representation learning with contrastive predictive coding. arXiv preprint arXiv: 1807.03748 (2019)
32. Pinheiro, P.O., Almahairi, A., Benmalek, R.Y., Golemo, F., Courville, A.: Unsupervised learning of dense visual representations. In: NeurIPS (2020)
33. Radford, A., et al.: Learning transferable visual models from natural language supervision. In: ICML, pp. 8748–8763 (2021)
34. Redmon, J., Farhadi, A.: YOLOv3: an incremental improvement. arXiv preprint arXiv: 1804.02767 (2018)
35. Ronneberger, O., Fischer, P., Brox, T.: U-Net: convolutional networks for biomedical image segmentation. In: Navab, N., Hornegger, J., Wells, W.M., Frangi, A.F. (eds.) MICCAI 2015. LNCS, vol. 9351, pp. 234–241. Springer, Cham (2015). https://doi.org/10.1007/978-3-319-24574-4_28
36. Russakovsky, O., et al.: ImageNet large scale visual recognition challenge. Int. J. Comput. Vision 115(3), 211–252 (2015). https://doi.org/10.1007/s11263-015-0816-y

37. Saraf, V., Chavan, P., Jadhav, A.: Deep learning challenges in medical imaging. In: Vasudevan, H., Michalas, A., Shekokar, N., Narvekar, M. (eds.) Advanced Computing Technologies and Applications. AIS, pp. 293–301. Springer, Singapore (2020). https://doi.org/10.1007/978-981-15-3242-9_28

38. Sariyildiz, M.B., Perez, J., Larlus, D.: Learning visual representations with caption annotations. In: Vedaldi, A., Bischof, H., Brox, T., Frahm, J.-M. (eds.) ECCV 2020. LNCS, vol. 12353, pp. 153–170. Springer, Cham (2020). https://doi.org/10.1007/978-3-030-58598-3_10

39. Shih, G., et al.: Augmenting the national institutes of health chest radiograph dataset with expert annotations of possible pneumonia. Radiol. Artif. Intell. 1 (2019). https://doi.org/10.1148/ryai.2019180041

40. Society for Imaging Informatics in Medicine: SIIM-ACR pneumothorax segmentation (2019). https://www.kaggle.com/c/siim-acr-pneumothorax-segmentation

41. Sowrirajan, H., Yang, J., Ng, A.Y., Rajpurkar, P.: MoCo pretraining improves representation and transferability of chest x-ray models. In: MIDL (2021)

42. Sriram, A., et al.: COVID-19 prognosis via self-supervised representation learning and multi-image prediction. arXiv preprint arXiv: 2101.04909 (2021)

43. Tang, H., Sun, N., Li, Y.: Segmentation model of the opacity regions in the chest X-rays of the COVID-19 patients in the us rural areas and the application to the disease severity. medRxiv (2020). https://doi.org/10.1101/2020.10.19.20215483

44. Vaswani, A., et al.: Attention is all you need. In: NIPS (2017)

45. Wang, X., Peng, Y., Lu, L., et al.: ChestX-ray8: hospital-scale chest x-ray database and benchmarks on weakly-supervised classification and localization of common thorax diseases. In: CVPR, pp. 3462–3471 (2017). https://doi.org/10.1109/CVPR.2017.369

46. Wang, X., Zhang, R., Shen, C., Kong, T., Li, L.: Dense contrastive learning for self-supervised visual pre-training. In: CVPR, pp. 3023–3032 (2021). https://doi.org/10.1109/CVPR46437.2021.00304

47. Wu, Z., Xiong, Y., Yu, S., Lin, D.: Unsupervised feature learning via non-parametric instance discrimination. In: CVPR, pp. 3733–3742 (2018). https://doi.org/10.1109/CVPR.2018.00393

48. Xie, E., et al.: DetCo: unsupervised contrastive learning for object detection. In: ICCV, pp. 8372–8381 (2021). https://doi.org/10.1109/ICCV48922.2021.00828

49. Xie, Z., Lin, Y., Zhang, Z., Cao, Y., Lin, S., Hu, H.: Propagate yourself: exploring pixel-level consistency for unsupervised visual representation learning. In: CVPR, pp. 16679–16688 (2021). https://doi.org/10.1109/CVPR46437.2021.01641

50. Zbontar, J., Jing, L., Misra, I., LeCun, Y., Deny, S.: Barlow twins: self-supervised learning via redundancy reduction. In: ICML (2021)

51. Zhang, Y., Jiang, H., Miura, Y., Manning, C.D., Langlotz, C.P.: Contrastive learning of medical visual representations from paired images and text. arXiv preprint arXiv: 2010.00747 (2020)

The Challenges of Continuous Self-Supervised Learning

Senthil Purushwalkam[1]([⊠]), Pedro Morgado[1,2], and Abhinav Gupta[1]

[1] Carnegie Mellon University, Pittsburgh, USA
spurushw@andrew.cmu.edu
[2] University of Wisconsin-Madison, Madison, USA
https://www.senthilpurushwalkam.com/publication/continuoussl/

Abstract. Self-supervised learning (SSL) aims to eliminate one of the major bottlenecks in representation learning - the need for human annotations. As a result, SSL holds the promise to learn representations from data in-the-wild, i.e., without the need for finite and static datasets. Instead, SSL should exploit the continuous stream of data being generated on the internet or by agents exploring their environments. In this work, we investigate whether traditional self-supervised learning approaches would be effective deployed in-the-wild by conducting experiments on the *continuous self-supervised learning problem*. In this setup, models should learn from a continuous (infinite) non-IID data stream that follows a non-stationary distribution of visual concepts. The goal is to learn representations that are robust, adaptive yet not forgetful of concepts seen in the past. We show that a direct application of current methods to continuous SSL is 1) inefficient both computationally and in the amount of data required, 2) leads to inferior representations due to temporal correlations (non-IID data) in the streaming sources and 3) exhibits signs of catastrophic forgetting when trained on sources with non-stationary data distributions. We study the use of replay buffers to alleviate the issues of inefficiency and temporal correlations, and enhance them by actively maintaining the least redundant samples in the buffer. We show that minimum redundancy (MinRed) buffers allow us to learn effective representations even in the most challenging streaming scenarios (*e.g.*, sequential frames obtained from a single embodied agent), and alleviates the problem of catastrophic forgetting.

1 Introduction

We are witnessing yet another paradigm shift in the field of computer vision: from supervised to self-supervised learning (SSL). This shift promises to unleash the true potential of data, as we are no longer bound by the cost of manual labeling.

S. Purushwalkam and P. Morgado—Equal contribution.

Supplementary Information The online version contains supplementary material available at https://doi.org/10.1007/978-3-031-19809-0_40.

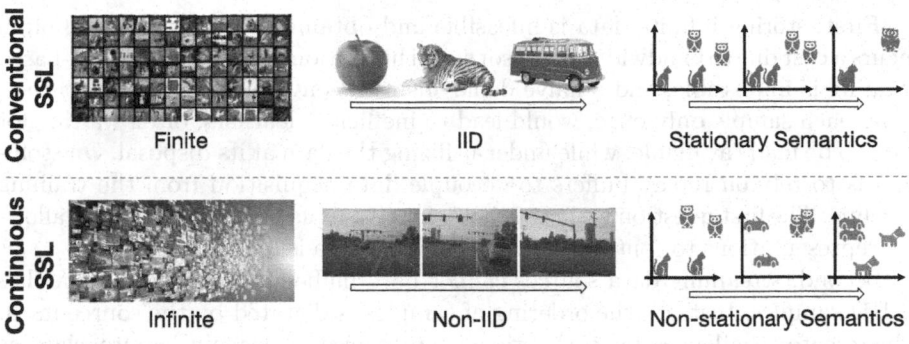

Fig. 1. Conventional vs. Continuous Self-Supervised Learning. The conventional setup of fixed datasets for SSL violates key properties exhibited by data continuously gathered in-the-wild: infinite, non-IID and non-stationary semantics. Hence, the conventional setup serves as a poor benchmark for SSL methods that aim to be deployed in-the-wild. In this work, we introduce the problem of continuous self-supervised learning to facilitate the evaluation of such methods and expose novel challenges.

Unsurprisingly, recent work has begun to scale current methods to extremely large datasets of up to 1 billion images [8,9,24–26] with the hope of learning better representations. In this paper, we pose the question: *Are we ready to deploy SSL in-the-wild to harness the full potential of unlimited data?*

While SSL promises to exploit the infinite stream of data generated on the internet or by a robotic agent, current practices in SSL still rely on the traditional dataset setup. Images and videos are accumulated to create a training corpus, followed by optimization on hundreds of shuffled passes through the data. The primary reason for working with datasets is the need for reproducible benchmarks, but one question remains: is this traditional static learning setup right for benchmarking self-supervised learning? Does this setup accurately reflect the challenges of a self-supervised system deployed in the wild? We believe the answer is NO. For example, consider a self-supervised system attempting to learn representations of cars over the years from the web. Current setups only evaluate static learning and do not evaluate the ability to adapt representations to new car models (and not forget old ones). Another example is to consider a deployed robotic self-supervised learning agent that actively collects frames from its video feed. This data is heavily structured and correlated due to temporal coherence. However, existing SSL benchmarks do not reflect this challenge since they rely on datasets that can be randomly sampled to produce *IID* samples.

In this paper, we move past dataset-driven SSL and investigate the efficacy of existing methods on the **Continuous Self-Supervised Learning** problem. We explore the challenges faced in two possible deployment scenarios: (a) an internet-based SSL model which relies on continuously acquired images/videos; (b) an agent-based SSL system that learns directly from an agent's sensors. As summarized in Fig. 1, both settings rely on a streaming data source that continuously generates new data, presenting three unique challenges that should be reflected when benchmarking SSL approaches.

First, storing infinite data is infeasible and obtaining data in the wild often incurs a cost due to bandwidth or sensor speed limitations. As a result, epoch-based training is impossible, and a naive deployment of conventional SSL approaches, using each sample only once, would lead to inefficient learners, often waiting for data to be made available, while under-utilizing the data at its disposal. One solution is to rely on replay buffers to decouple data acquisition from the training pipeline. The first question we pose is how effective replay mechanism are at allowing representations to continue to improve while data is being collected?

Second, streaming data sources cannot be "shuffled" to create mini-batches of IID samples. Instead, the ordering of samples is dictated by the source itself. This creates challenges for conventional representation learning approaches, as training data is not necessarily IID. Hence, we pose the question of how to adapt existing SSL methods to learn under non-IID conditions?

Third, real-world data is non-stationary. For example, a higher number of football-related images are seen during the world cup. Also, robots exploring indoor environments observe temporally clustered semantic distributions - a sequence of bedroom objects, followed by kitchen objects, and so on. An intelligent lifelong learning system should be able to continuously learn new concepts without forgetting old ones from non-stationary data distributions. However, we show empirically that conventional contrastive learning approaches can overfit to the current distribution, displaying signs of forgetting. We thus pose the question of how to design SSL methods that learn under non-stationary conditions?

Overall, the main contributions of this work are the following. We identify three critical challenges that arise in the continuous self-supervised learning setup, namely, training efficiency, robustness to non-IID data streams and learning under non-stationary semantic distributions. For each challenge, we construct a curated data stream that simulates this challenge and quantitatively demonstrates the shortcomings of existing SSL methods. We also propose initial solutions to these problems (Fig. 2), with the goal of encouraging further research along these directions. We explore the idea of Buffered SSL, which involves augmenting existing approaches with a *replay buffer* to improve training efficiency. Second, we propose a novel method to handle non-IID data streams by minimizing redundancy among stored samples. Finally, we show that *minimum redundancy buffers* prevent forgetting and improve continual learning under non-stationary data distributions.

2   Related Work

Self-supervised visual representation learning is a mature research area, capable of producing models that outperform fully supervised methods when transferred to a variety of downstream tasks [9,13,27,29]. Despite not relying on labeled data, these methods are still trained on fixed-size curated datasets originally developed for the supervised setting. This paper explores the various challenges of deploying self-supervised learning systems truly in-the-wild.

Self-supervised Learning has a long history in computer vision [7,35,42, 50,70,71] aiming to learn representations of visual data by solving tasks that can be defined without human annotations. A breadth of methodologies has

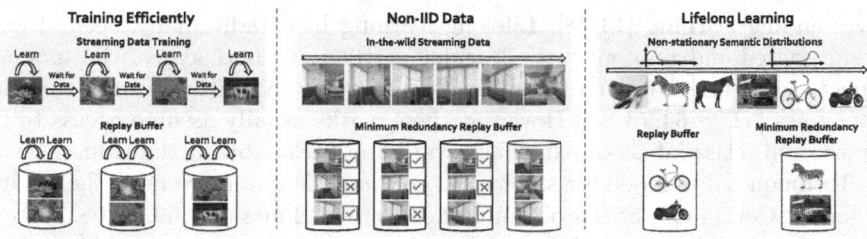

Fig. 2. Overview: We investigate continuous self-supervised learning, exposing three challenges faced by SSL methods deployed in-the-wild. First, representations should be learned in a single pass, as streaming sources do not repeat data samples. We show that augmenting an existing SSL method [13] with replay buffers can significantly alleviate data and computational inefficiencies of training in a single pass. Second, data gathered continuously in-the-wild is often temporally correlated and non IID. We show that actively maintaining minimally redundant samples in the replay buffers yields less correlated training data. Finally, semantic distributions of data gathered in-the-wild are non-stationary. This can cause models to "forget" concepts seen in past distributions. We show that minimizing redundancy also mitigates "forgetting" by focusing on unique samples from various semantic groups.

been proposed from generative models such as denoising auto-encoders [78], sparse coding [36,54,55], inpainting [59] and colorization [18,34,86], to methods that learn representations predictive of spatial context [19,22,53], temporal context [21,47,58,61,79,80], or concurrent modalities like audio [4,52,57,70], text [17,23,62] or speech [43,44]. One successful approach is to learn transformation invariant representations [12,20,28,29,46,56,65,81]. After relentless improvements in image augmentations [12,46], backbone models [10,24], stable (slow-moving) learning targets [9,15,29], and transformation invariant loss functions [10,13,27,56,84], augmentation invariance has produced impressive models that improve state-of-the-art on a diverse set of downstream tasks like recognition [9,10], detection [29] and video object segmentation [10].

Given its success, a few attempts have been made to scale SSL to large uncurated datasets, such as YFCC-100M [8,26] and Instagram-1B [9,24]. Goyal et al. [26] showed that tasks such as colorization [86], context prediction [53] and rotation [22] have diminishing returns on large datasets, due to the low complexity of the task, and argued for the development of more complex tasks. Transformation invariance objectives, coupled with heavy data augmentations, have increased the task's complexity substantially. As a result, recent attempts of scaling up augmentation invariance [9,24,25] have seen some performance gains. However, we argue that these methods are still not ready to be deployed truly in-the-wild. Beyond the difficulties of training on uncurated data, already studied in prior work [9,24], training on fixed datasets ignores important challenges of streaming data, such as the non-iid nature of streaming sources, data acquisition costs, and model saturation due to its fixed capacity.

Continual and Lifelong Learning: The ability to continuously learn new concepts or tasks over time is often referred to as lifelong learning [75] or never-ending learning [14,48]. Lifelong learning has traditionally been studied in supervised and reinforcement learning settings. In both cases, the model is expected to learn distinct tasks presented sequentially, without forgetting previous ones [32,38,64,76,85]. However, these works usually assume access to full supervision (class labels or external rewards) not available in the wild.

Techniques developed for supervised continual learning are nevertheless useful for the Continuous SSL problem. Rehearsal techniques [2,6,60,67,68,73] store and replay a small set of training samples from previous tasks to avoid forgetting previously learned skills or concepts. While there is no notion of well-defined tasks in Continuous SSL, we show that replay buffers help improve training efficiency. We also propose replay buffers that minimize the redundancy of stored memories to decorrelate highly correlated streaming sources. Beyond rehearsal techniques, expandable models [69,83] have also been used to reduce catastrophic forgetting. This is often accomplished either by progressively growing the model each time a new task is added [37,69,83], or adapting a common backbone model to each task separately using small task-specific adaptation blocks [41,51,67]. The lack of well-defined tasks in streaming SSL makes lifelong learning more challenging, as it needs to learn from data distributions that may shift over time.

Lifelong Generative Models: Discriminative self-supervised representation learning has never been investigated in the continuous learning setup (streaming, non-IID and non-stationary data). However, recent works [1,63,66,82] have attempted to address a sub-problem of ours, *i.e.*, learning self-supervised representations using generative models in a continual learning setting where the domain of data exhibits significant shifts during training. These works present approaches to locate domain shifts in order to avoid the problem of catastrophic forgetting. These techniques are made possible by the fact that training data is constructed by collecting samples from images in significantly different datasets - for example, [82] uses Celeb-A [40] faces followed by 3D-Chair [5] images). In contrast, we consider a more realistic setting of ImageNet images with a smoothly changing distribution of classes. Furthermore, as highlighted above, these works do not address other critical challenges of deploying SSL in-the-wild, as they are limited to epoch-based optimization, do not consider non-curated and/or high correlated streaming sources, data efficiency, or the issue of early convergence.

3   Problem Setup and Challenges

Our goal is to investigate the efficacy of self-supervised representation learning on a naturally occurring source of streaming data, which we refer to as the *continuous self-supervised learning problem*. First, we describe the distinction between conventional training and the continuous self-supervised learning setup. We then discuss the various unique challenges that appear in the continuous case.

3.1   Streaming vs Conventional Self-Supervised Learning

Existing self-supervised learning methods rely on fixed-size datasets. These datasets $\mathcal{D} = \{\mathbf{x}_1, \ldots, \mathbf{x}_N\}$ are finite (*i.e.*, $N << \infty$), immutable (*i.e.*, $\mathcal{D}$ does

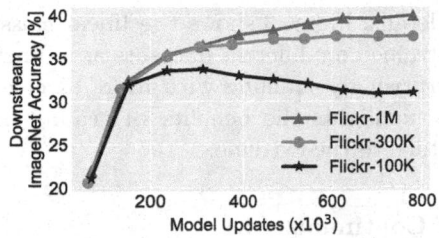

Fig. 3. ImageNet downstream accuracy of a SimSiam model trained on datasets of different sizes with a ResNet-18 backbone.

not change) and readily available (*i.e.*, all its samples $\mathbf{x}_i$ can be easily accessed at all times). Due to these properties, samples can be indexed, shuffled, and accessed at any point in training. Conventional SSL takes advantage of these possibilities by iterating over the datasets multiple times (epochs).

In contrast, Continuous SSL relies on a *streaming source* $\mathcal{S}$, defined as a time-series of unlabeled sensory data $\mathcal{S} = (\mathbf{x}_1, \mathbf{x}_2, \ldots, \mathbf{x}_T)$, potentially of infinite length $T \to \infty$. At any given moment in time t, fetching data from a streaming source $\mathcal{S}$ yields the current sample $\mathbf{x}_t$. Future samples $\{\mathbf{x}_\tau \forall \tau > t\}$ are not accessible at time t, and past samples $\{\mathbf{x}_\tau \forall \tau < t\}$ are only accessible if stored when fetched.

In the Continuous SSL setup, one important parameter is the ratio between the data loading time t_{data} and the time taken to perform one optimization step t_{opt}. In most deployment setups $t_{\mathrm{data}} > t_{\mathrm{opt}}$, due to slower data transfer speed or low sensor frame rates. Therefore, even with parallelization, optimization algorithms can wait idle for $t_{\mathrm{idle}} = t_{\mathrm{data}} - t_{\mathrm{opt}}$. Therefore, SSL methods developed for the continuous setup should be able to efficiently and continually build better representations, while training on samples obtained from a streaming source.

3.2 Why Continuous SSL? Does Scaling the Number of Unique Images Help Representation Learning?

To understand the effect of increasing the scale of training data (potentially to infinite), we indexed all Creative Commons images uploaded to the photo-sharing website Flickr.com between 2008 and 2021. We then used this index to create datasets of varying sizes, and train visual representations through self-supervision over multiple epochs in the Conventional SSL setup.

We adopt SimSiam [13] as a prototypical example of contrastive learning methods, which have been shown to be effective for Conventional SSL. SimSiam learns representations by optimizing the augmentation invariance loss

$$\mathcal{L}(x_1, x_2) = -\mathbf{sg}(\mathbf{z}_1)^T g(\mathbf{z}_2) - \mathbf{sg}(\mathbf{z}_2)^T g(\mathbf{z}_1) \tag{1}$$

where x_1 and x_2 are two random transformations of an image x, $\mathbf{z}_i = f(x_i)$ is the model output representations, $\mathbf{sg}(\cdot)$ the stop gradient and $g(\cdot)$ a prediction head.

Refer to [13] for full details. Figure 3 shows the linear classification accuracy on ImageNet for models trained on different datasets as a function of the number of model updates. Unsurprisingly, training with more diverse data leads to better representations. This highlights the benefits of scaling *unique* images, which Continuous SSL will take to the extreme.

3.3 Challenges of Continuous SSL

Streaming sources available in the wild do not allow revisiting past samples. Since storing the full data stream is infeasible due to the potentially infinite length, Continuous SSL methods should learn representations in a single pass over the data (instead of learning over multiple epochs). This setup poses novel challenges that Conventional SSL methods do not face.

Computational and Data Efficiency: Sampling data from streaming sources in the real world can be significantly slower (when compared to sampling from static datasets) due to sensor frame rates or bandwidth limitations. Thus, current SSL approaches could become inefficient learners, as optimization algorithms may have to wait idly while waiting for new data to be made available, while under-utilizing the data at their disposal.

Correlated Samples: Many streaming sources in the wild exhibit temporal coherence. For example, consecutive frames from online videos or from a robot exploring its environment display minimal changes. Such correlations break the *IID* assumption on which conventional optimization algorithms rely.

Lifelong Learning: Access to infinite streams of data provides us the opportunity to continuously improve visual representations. However, the non-stationary nature of data streams in the wild cause conventional SSL methods to quickly forget features that are no longer relevant for the current distribution. Continuous SSL methods should therefore be able to integrate new concepts in their representations without forgetting previously learned ones.

While all these challenges co-exist in the wild, our goal is to analyze each one comprehensively and in isolation. Therefore, we disentangled each challenge by designing a set of data streams that highlight each problem separately, and assess its effect on existing SSL methods. This helps us building a thorough characterization of each challenge and inform us on how to tackle them. We believe a disentangled analysis will help the community build intuitions about the impact of each challenge on continuous SSL as a whole. Section 4 introduces the challenge of one pass training and computational efficiency. Section 5 introduces the non-iid data setup, and Sect. 6 analyses the lifelong learning setting.

4 Efficient Training

Computational and data efficiency are two challenges that currently prevent SSL from being deployed on continuous data streams in-the-wild. For most practical applications, $t_{data} : t_{optim}$ might be high, so SSL methods should use idle time to improve the models. Second, fetching new samples can still be costly.

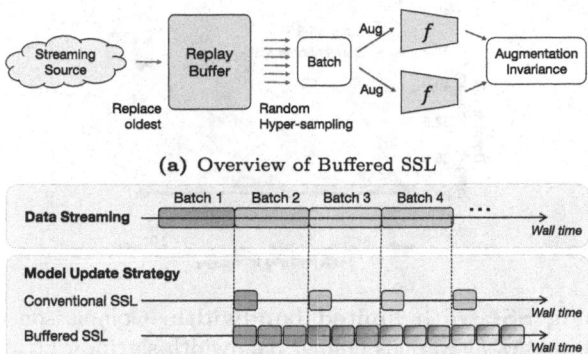

(a) Overview of Buffered SSL

(b) Optimization under limited streaming bandwidth.

Fig. 4. Buffered Self-Supervised Learning. Buffered SSL introduces a replay buffer, which allows the model to continuously train even under limited bandwidth settings.

For example, exploration robots often run on batteries, and web crawlers are limited by network bandwidths. Trivially deploying current SSL methods to the streaming setup would discard each batch of data after being used once. However, current deep learning optimization practices show that iterating over the same samples over multiple epochs helps learn better representations. For example, supervised learning on ImageNet [30,33] iterates over the dataset 100 times, and SSL approaches [12] have been shown to keep improving even after seeing each sample 800 times. Therefore, we would like to answer the question of how to improve data efficiency while still following the streaming setting.

4.1 Buffered Self-Supervised Learning

We present a simple solution to the challenges above. The key idea is to maintain a fixed-size *replay buffer* that stores a small number of recent samples. This idea is inspired by experience replay [39] commonly used in reinforcement learning [3, 49,72] and supervised continual learning [31,68]. As shown in Fig. 4a, the replay buffer decouples the streaming source from the training pipeline. The streaming data can be added to the replay buffer when available, replacing the oldest samples (*i.e.* first-in-first-out (FIFO) update rule). Simultaneously, mini-batches of training data can be generated at any time by randomly sampling from the buffer. As shown in Fig. 4b, replay buffers allow us to continue training during the otherwise idle wait time t_{idle}. Replay buffers also allow us to reuse samples by sampling them multiple times, hence reducing the total data cost. We refer to this approach as *Buffered Self-Supervised Learning*.

4.2 Single-pass Training Experiments

We study the effectiveness of replay buffers when training with a single pass of the data. We trained ResNet-18 SimSiam models with and without replay

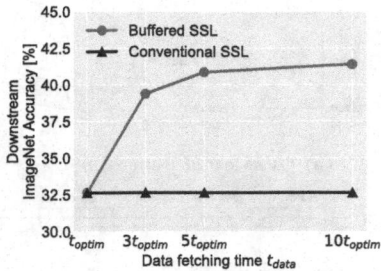

Fig. 5. Streaming SSL with limited bandwidth. Comparison of buffered and non-buffered approaches for various limited bandwidth settings. $t_{data} : t_{optim}$ denotes the ratio of data acquisition time to the optimization time. Buffered SSL can take advantage of the idle time to effectively improve the learned representations instead of waiting idly for new data.

Table 1. Data Efficiency: Augmenting SSL methods with replay buffers can improve efficiency allowing us to train on data streams with one pass. We show that Buffered SSL methods outperform the Conventional SSL methods and achieve performances close to training for multiple epochs.

	Epochs	Hyper sampling	Memory size	ImageNet Top1 Acc	iNaturalist Top1 Acc
Training DB: Flickr 20M					
Conventional SSL	1	–	–	32.2	12.2
Buffered SSL	1	10	16K	41.4	16.7
Buffered SSL	1	10	64K	41.8	17.4
Buffered SSL	1	10	256K	41.5	17.5
Epoch-based SSL*	10	–	–	41.7	17.3
Training DB: Flickr 5M					
Conventional SSL	1	–	–	14.5	2.8
Buffered SSL	1	40	16K	39.9	16.1
Buffered SSL	1	40	64K	41.0	17.1
Buffered SSL	1	40	256K	41.5	17.3
Epoch-based SSL*	40	–	–	41.8	17.0
Training DB: Flickr 1M					
Conventional SSL	1	–	–	8.0	1.5
Buffered SSL	1	200	16K	30.5	9.5
Buffered SSL	1	200	64K	36.4	14.3
Buffered SSL	1	200	256K	38.8	15.5
Epoch-based SSL*	200	–	–	41.7	17.3

Epoch-based SSL violates the streaming setting (reference only).

buffers, with various amounts of idle time $t_{idle} = t_{data} - t_{optim}$. All models were trained using the first 20 million images in our Flickr index as the streaming source.

Figure 5 shows the ImageNet linear classification performance for increasing t_{data}. By maintaining a small replay buffer (containing only the most recent 64k images), Buffered SSL was able to make good use of the idle time and improve representations significantly (41.4% accuracy on ImageNet) over the bottlenecked Conventional SSL approach (32.5% ImageNet accuracy). Replay buffers also improve data efficiency in the Continuous SSL setup, as each sample can be reused multiple times. Data usage is proportional to the hyper-sampling rate K, defined as the ratio between the number of mini-batches generated for training and acquired from the streaming source.

To understand the limits of hyper-sampling, we trained a ResNet-18 SimSiam model with a replay buffer for a fixed amount of updates (780 000 iterations). Table 1 shows a comparison of Buffered SSL at varying hyper-sampling rates K, to Conventional SSL trained on the same amount of data, and Epoch-based SSL methods trained for K epochs. Epoch-based SSL and Buffered SSL are optimized with the same number of updates, but the former violates the streaming setup. Despite being required to train on a single pass of the data, Buffered SSL with a hyper-sampling rate of $K = 10$ achieved similar performance to epoch-based training, even for buffers as small as 64K images (0.3% of the 20M unique images seen). Table 1 also shows that, as hyper-sampling rates increase, the size of the replay buffer becomes critical. For example, for $K = 200$, Buffered SSL still improves significantly over Conventional SSL on the same amount of data, regardless of buffer size. However, better representations are learned as the buffer size increases. Since, in high hyper-sampling regimes, the buffer is updated slowly with new images from the streaming source, increasing the buffer size prevents the model from quickly overfitting to the samples in the buffer.

5 Correlated Data Sources

Visual data obtained in-the-wild is often correlated and non-*IID*. For example, video feed from a self-driving car collects very similar consecutive frames. This is in stark contrast to the data used in Conventional SSL methods. For example, the ImageNet dataset allows sampling images from a collection of 1000 uniformly distributed object classes. Even methods trained on larger datasets like Instagram-1B [24,26] are less likely to encounter heavily correlated samples in the mini-batches. However, the constant flow of data in the Continuous SSL setup generally violates these assumptions even in the static image setup (images uploaded near events are likely to be highly correlated).

Let $(x_i : i \in \mathcal{D})$ be a sequence of samples. When x_i is generated by randomly sampling from a large dataset, samples are close to IID. Hence, the probability p_c that two samples x_i and x_j are highly correlated is low, $p_c \approx 0$. Correlated samples may indicate images that are visually very similar or visually dissimilar but depict similar semantic content. However, in the Continuous SSL setup, the IID assumption is generally violated, leading to $p_c \gg 0$. Under the assumption that consecutive samples in a continuous stream of data have the same correlation probability p_c, the likelihood of a random pair in a batch $(x_i, \ldots, x_{i+b})$ of size b being correlated (*correlation likelihood*) is large, and given by

$$\mathcal{L}_{\text{Seq}} = P_c(b, p_c) = \frac{2}{b(b-1)} \sum_{i=1}^{b-1} \sum_{j=i+1}^{b} p_c^{j-1} = \frac{2p_c}{b(b-1)} \left(\frac{p_c^b - 1}{(1-p_c)^2} + b\frac{p_c}{1-p_c} \right). \quad (2)$$

Introducing a replay buffer of size $B >> b$, as proposed in Sect. 4.1, lowers the correlation likelihood to $\mathcal{L}_{\text{FIFO}} = P_c(B, p_c) \approx \frac{b}{B}\mathcal{L}_{\text{Seq}} < P_c(b, p_c)^1$, and enables more effective representation learning.

5.1   Minimum Redundancy Replay Buffer

While replay buffers are able to reduce the correlation likelihood, prohibitively large replay buffers $(B >> b)$ are required to significantly lower $\mathcal{L}_{\text{FIFO}}$ in heavily correlated setups $(p_c \approx 1)$. In order to overcome this, we propose a modified replay buffer to only retain de-correlated samples, thereby actively reducing p_c. We call this the Minimum Redundancy Replay Buffer (MinRed).

To accomplish this, we rely on the learned embedding space to identify redundant samples. Consider a replay buffer $\mathcal{B}$ with a maximum capacity of B, already containing B samples with representation $\bar{z}_i$. To add a new sample x to $\mathcal{B}$, we rely on the cosine distance between all pairs of samples to discard the most redundant:

$$\mathcal{B} \leftarrow \mathcal{B} \backslash i^* \cup \{x\}   \text{where}   i^* = \arg\min_{i \in \mathcal{B}} \min_{j \in \mathcal{B}} d_{\cos}(\bar{z}_i, \bar{z}_j). \tag{3}$$

In other words, we discard the sample with minimum distance to its nearest neighbor. To represent instances, we track the features $\bar{z}_i$ of all samples in the buffer using a moving average $\bar{z}_i = \alpha\bar{z}_i + (1 - \alpha)z_i$, where $z_i = f(x_i)$ is the current feature of the ith sample, and α the moving average coefficient. Since redundant samples are dropped from the buffer, the probability p_c of two consecutive samples in the buffer being correlated decreases. If this probability decreases from p_c to ηp_c where $\eta << 1$, the correlation likelihood is lowered to $\mathcal{L}_{\text{MinRed}} = P_c(B, \eta p_c) < P_c(B, p_c)$, which facilitates representation learning.

5.2   Experiments with Non-IID Data Streams

We assess the performance of SSL methods on two data streams with heavy temporal coherence. The first is created by concatenating video frames from the Kinetics dataset [11]. From each video, we sample N_{seq} frames at random and add them sequentially to the data stream. The second data stream is composed by consecutive frames from the KrishnaCAM dataset[2] [74] which records egocentric videos spanning nine months in the life of a computer vision graduate student. On each stream, we train the baseline SimSiam (Conventional SSL), SimSiam augmented with replay buffers (Buffered SSL) and SimSiam augmented with MinRed buffers (Buffered SSL (MinRed)). We evaluate these representations by training a linear classifier on ImageNet [16] and iNaturalist [77]. Results are shown in Table 2. We observe that the correlated nature of the data heavily disrupts training of conventional models. While regular replay buffers alleviate the issue to some extent, the learned representations still suffer when trained

---

[1] Approximation holds for large values of B and b, and $p_c \neq 1$.
[2] Concatenated videos are looped over 10 times to create a larger stream.

on heavy correlated data streams (as in Kinetics $N_{seq} = 64$ and KrishaCAM). Finally, MinRed buffers are very effective in these setups, learning representations that perform similarly to the "oracle" IID setting (*i.e.*, by randomly sampling from the collection of all frames from all videos, violating the streaming assumption).

Correlation of Training Samples: One of the benefits of Buffered SSL is the ability to generate training samples with low correlation likelihood and thus closer to *IID*. We analyzed the contents of the replay buffer during training to track the correlation likelihood (see Fig. 6). We confirmed that the contents of MinRed replay buffers are significantly less correlated than FIFO buffers. In KrishnaCAM, MinRed buffers tend to maintain memories of past unique frames for longer periods of time. In Kinetics, MinRed buffers also yield mini-batches with frames from a larger number of unique videos.

Table 2. Visually Correlated SSL: Linear classification performance of buffered and unbuffered SimSiam representations trained on data sources with high temporal coherence. MinRed buffers learns better representations by decorrelating the data.

	Epochs	Hyper sampling	Memory size	ImageNet Top1 Acc	iNaturalist Top1 Acc
Streaming source: Kinetics ($N_{seq}=16$)					
Conventional SSL	5	–	–	17.7	3.0
Buffered SSL	1	5	64K	25.9	8.4
Buffered SSL (MinRed)	1	5	64K	26.2	7.9
Decorrelated source*	5	–	–	25.9	7.9
Streaming source: Kinetics ($N_{seq}=64$)					
Conventional SSL	5	–	–	8.0	0.8
Buffered SSL	1	5	64K	9.8	0.8
Buffered SSL (MinRed)	1	5	64K	30.6	9.6
Decorrelated source*	5	–	–	31.4	10.6
Streaming source: Krishna CAM					
Conventional SSL	5	–	–	0.4	0.03
Buffered SSL	1	5	16K	0.5	0.05
Buffered SSL (MinRed)	1	5	16K	15.2	3.43
Buffered SSL	1	5	64K	1.7	0.07
Buffered SSL (MinRed)	1	5	64K	17.9	5.91
Decorrelated source*	5	–	–	19.2	6.94

Decorrelated sources violate the streaming setting (reference only).

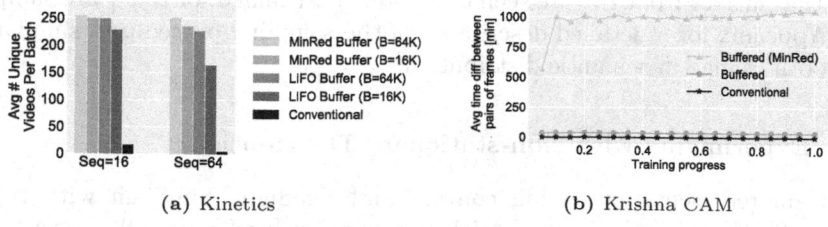

(a) Kinetics   (b) Krishna CAM

Fig. 6. Estimate of within batch correlation while training w/ and w/o replay buffers.

6   Lifelong Self-Supervised Learning

As we explore the world, we encounter different distributions of object classes, some previously seen and some unseen. For example, we see furniture and appliances every day. But we also encounter novel concepts like zebras when we visit a zoo. This suggests that the distribution of semantic classes is often correlated in time with occasional changes in distribution. However, Conventional SSL methods learn from a limited vocabulary of concepts that is repeatedly seen thousands of times (often uniformly). This provides a simplification of the learning setup that does not reflect the non-stationary nature of concepts in-the-wild.

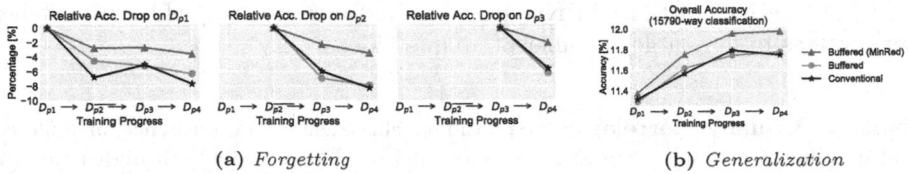

(a) *Forgetting*   (b) *Generalization*

Fig. 7. Continual unsupervised representation learning on full ImageNet (14M images). The dataset is partitioned in 4 separate tasks which are seen in sequence $D_{p1} \rightarrow D_{p2} \rightarrow D_{p3} \rightarrow D_{p4}$. Forgetting (a) is measured by computing the relative accuracy drop on each task after training on data of the task itself. Generalization (b) is measured as the overall accuracy across all 15790 full ImageNet classes. All results are averaged over 3 different sequences p_i.

6.1   A Non-stationary Data Stream to Benchmark SSL

To evaluate deployable SSL, we must use benchmarks that simulate the non-stationary semantic distributions encountered in-the-wild. Inspired by supervised continual learning [32,38], we created a stream with smooth shifting semantics.

First, we create four datasets $\mathcal{D}_1, \mathcal{D}_2, \mathcal{D}_3, \mathcal{D}_4$ by splitting the classes of the ImageNet-21K dataset [16]. We create the splits based on the Wordnet [45] hierarchy such that each $\mathcal{D}_i$ contains images from semantically similar classes. For each class, we hold out 25 images per class for evaluation. The training stream is created by sampling images from the four splits $\{\mathcal{D}_{p_1}, \mathcal{D}_{p_2}, \mathcal{D}_{p_3}, \mathcal{D}_{p_4}\}^3$ such that images from $\mathcal{D}_{p_i}$ are seen only after most images of $\mathcal{D}_{p_{i-1}}$ are sampled (see Appendix for a detailed description of the sampling procedure), simulating a smooth change in semantic distribution.

6.2   Experiments with Non-stationary Distributions

We train representations using conventional SimSiam, SimSiam with replay buffers (Sect. 4.1) and SimSiam with minimum redundancy buffers (Sect. 5.1)

---

[3] $[p_1, p_2, p_3, p_4]$ denotes a permutation of the sequence $[1, 2, 3, 4]$.

on a single pass of this stream of data. These models are initialized from Sim-Siam trained on Flickr200M. During evaluation, we train a linear classifier on the learned representations to recognize all classes in the ImageNet-21k dataset, and measure the accuracy on the held-out set of each $\mathcal{D}_{p_i}$ separately. All results are averaged over 3 permutations of $p_1, \ldots, p_4$.

Figure 7a shows the drop in classification accuracy on each dataset D_{p_i} after the representation is trained on new data $D_{p_{i+1}}, D_{p_{i+2}}$, etc., relative to the initial accuracy at the end of D_{p_i}. This serves as a measure of forgetting - a larger drop indicates that the representation lost its ability to discriminate older classes. As can be seen, all methods suffer from forgetting. However, SimSiam with MinRed buffers displays less forgetting compared to conventional and buffered SimSiam. Intuitively, this can be attributed to the MinRed criteria which naturally retains instances from previous semantic distributions. Figure 7b also depicts the accuracy on all classes as training progresses, showing that SimSiam with MinRed buffers also yields slightly better overall generalization, consistently throughout training. In supplementary material, we also evaluated the learned representations on unseen classes, by testing only on future data streams $D_{p_{i+t}}$. Since MinRed buffers maintain training buffers with wider coverage of semantics, the learned representations were also shown to generalize better to unseen concepts.

7   Discussion and Future Work

In this work, we exposed three challenges that require investigation to build robust deployable self-supervised learners. We improve the efficiency of Continuous SSL by leveraging replay buffers to revisit old samples. In future work, developing approaches for quickly rejecting samples by preemptively evaluating their value might yield improved data efficiency. We also propose a novel minimum redundancy buffer to discard correlated samples allowing us to mimic the generation of IID training data, even in highly correlated settings. An alternative future direction could focus on learning representations that take advantage of the correlated nature of the data stream to learn from fine-grained discrepancies.

In data streams with non-stationary semantic distributions, we show that MinRed buffers alleviate the issue of catastrophic forgetting, as they are capable of maintaining unique samples from past distributions. However, we observed signs of saturating generalization as new concepts are introduced. Some possible reasons could be: 1) the cosine decay learning rate schedule and 2) the fixed capacity of our models that prohibits learning a large sequence of novel concepts. In preliminary experiments (see supplementary material), we saw that training with a constant learning rate (on 100M images from Flickr) does not lead to significant improvements in performance. We also observed that trivially expanding the architecture at regular intervals does not lead to noticeable improvements. However, we believe that further exploration in this direction is required to continually learning novel concepts in a self-supervised manner.

8   Conclusion

One of the grand goals of self-supervised learning is to build systems capable of continually learning from unlimited sources of unlabelled data. However, due to the need for benchmarking, existing SSL methods have primarily focused on curated datasets of limited size. Unfortunately, while the existing approaches work well in the dataset setup, we are still not close to deployable continual self-supervised methods. In this work, we advocate for a more realistic SSL setup that will facilitate deployment, while retaining the benefits of benchmarking. To this end, we identified three broad challenges of deployable SSL - training efficiency, correlated data, and lifelong learning, - and proposed potential solutions to address them. We believe however that further research is needed to develop deployable systems that deliver on the promise of self-supervised learning, and hope future efforts in SSL research focus on these challenges.

References

1. Achille, A., et al.: Life-long disentangled representation learning with cross-domain latent homologies. In: Advances in Neural Information Processing Systems 31 (2018)
2. Aljundi, R., Lin, M., Goujaud, B., Bengio, Y.: Gradient based sample selection for online continual learning. Adv. Neural. Inf. Process. Syst. **32**, 11816–11825 (2019)
3. Andrychowicz, M., et al.: Hindsight experience replay. arXiv preprint arXiv:1707.01495 (2017)
4. Arandjelovic, R., Zisserman, A.: Look, listen and learn. In: Proceedings of the IEEE/CVF International Conference on Computer Vision, pp. 609–617 (2017)
5. Aubry, M., Maturana, D., Efros, A.A., Russell, B.C., Sivic, J.: Seeing 3D chairs: exemplar part-based 2D–3D alignment using a large dataset of CAD models. In: Proceedings of the IEEE/CVF Conference on Computer Vision and Pattern Recognition, pp. 3762–3769 (2014)
6. Buzzega, P., Boschini, M., Porrello, A., Abati, D., Calderara, S.: Dark experience for general continual learning: a strong, simple baseline. In: Advances in Neural Information Processing Systems (2020)
7. Caron, M., Bojanowski, P., Joulin, A., Douze, M.: Deep clustering for unsupervised learning of visual features. In: Ferrari, V., Hebert, M., Sminchisescu, C., Weiss, Y. (eds.) Computer Vision – ECCV 2018. LNCS, vol. 11218, pp. 139–156. Springer, Cham (2018). https://doi.org/10.1007/978-3-030-01264-9_9
8. Caron, M., Bojanowski, P., Mairal, J., Joulin, A.: Unsupervised pre-training of image features on non-curated data. In: Proceedings of the IEEE/CVF International Conference on Computer Vision, pp. 2959–2968 (2019)
9. Caron, M., Misra, I., Mairal, J., Goyal, P., Bojanowski, P., Joulin, A.: Unsupervised learning of visual features by contrasting cluster assignments. In: Thirty-fourth Conference on Neural Information Processing Systems (NeurIPS) (2020)
10. Caron, M., et al.: Emerging properties in self-supervised vision transformers. In: Proceedings of the IEEE/CVF International Conference on Computer Vision (2021)
11. Carreira, J., Zisserman, A.: Quo Vadis, action recognition? A new model and the kinetics dataset. In: Proceedings of the IEEE/CVF Conference on Computer Vision and Pattern Recognition, pp. 6299–6308 (2017)

12. Chen, T., Kornblith, S., Norouzi, M., Hinton, G.: A simple framework for contrastive learning of visual representations. In: Proceedings of the International Conference on Machine Learning, pp. 1597–1607. PMLR (2020)
13. Chen, X., He, K.: Exploring simple Siamese representation learning. In: Proceedings of the IEEE/CVF Conference on Computer Vision and Pattern Recognition, pp. 15750–15758 (2021)
14. Chen, X., Shrivastava, A., Gupta, A.: NEIL: extracting visual knowledge from web data. In: Proceedings of the IEEE/CVF International Conference on Computer Vision, pp. 1409–1416 (2013)
15. Chen*, X., Xie*, S., He, K.: An empirical study of training self-supervised vision transformers. In: Proceedings of the IEEE/CVF International Conference on Computer Vision (2021)
16. Deng, J., Dong, W., Socher, R., Li, L.J., Li, K., Fei-Fei, L.: ImageNet: a large-scale hierarchical image database. In: Proceedings of the IEEE/CVF Conference on Computer Vision and Pattern Recognition, pp. 248–255. IEEE (2009)
17. Desai, K., Johnson, J.: VirTex: learning visual representations from textual annotations. In: Proceedings of the IEEE/CVF Conference on Computer Vision and Pattern Recognition, pp. 11162–11173 (2021)
18. Deshpande, A., Rock, J., Forsyth, D.: Learning large-scale automatic image colorization. In: Proceedings of the IEEE/CVF International Conference on Computer Vision, pp. 567–575 (2015)
19. Doersch, C., Gupta, A., Efros, A.A.: Unsupervised visual representation learning by context prediction. In: Proceedings of the IEEE/CVF International Conference on Computer Vision, pp. 1422–1430 (2015)
20. Dosovitskiy, A., Fischer, P., Springenberg, J.T., Riedmiller, M., Brox, T.: Discriminative unsupervised feature learning with exemplar convolutional neural networks. IEEE Trans. Pattern Anal. Mach. Intell. 38(9), 1734–1747 (2015)
21. Fernando, B., Bilen, H., Gavves, E., Gould, S.: Self-supervised video representation learning with odd-one-out networks. In: Proceedings of the IEEE/CVF Conference on Computer Vision and Pattern Recognition, pp. 3636–3645 (2017)
22. Gidaris, S., Singh, P., Komodakis, N.: Unsupervised representation learning by predicting image rotations. In: International Conference on Learning Representations (2018)
23. Gomez, L., Patel, Y., Rusiñol, M., Karatzas, D., Jawahar, C.: Self-supervised learning of visual features through embedding images into text topic spaces. In: Proceedings of the IEEE/CVF Conference on Computer Vision and Pattern Recognition, pp. 4230–4239 (2017)
24. Goyal, P., et al.: Self-supervised pretraining of visual features in the wild. arXiv preprint arXiv:2103.01988 (2021)
25. Goyal, P., et al.: Vision models are more robust and fair when pretrained on uncurated images without supervision. arXiv preprint arXiv:2202.08360 (2022)
26. Goyal, P., Mahajan, D., Gupta, A., Misra, I.: Scaling and benchmarking self-supervised visual representation learning. In: Proceedings of the IEEE/CVF International Conference on Computer Vision, pp. 6391–6400 (2019)
27. Grill, J.B., et al.: Bootstrap your own latent: a new approach to self-supervised learning. In: Advances in Neural Information Processing Systems (2020)
28. Hadsell, R., Chopra, S., LeCun, Y.: Dimensionality reduction by learning an invariant mapping. In: Proceedings of the IEEE/CVF Conference on Computer Vision and Pattern Recognition, vol. 2, pp. 1735–1742. IEEE (2006)

29. He, K., Fan, H., Wu, Y., Xie, S., Girshick, R.: Momentum contrast for unsupervised visual representation learning. In: Proceedings of the IEEE/CVF Conference on Computer Vision and Pattern Recognition, pp. 9729–9738 (2020)
30. He, K., Zhang, X., Ren, S., Sun, J.: Deep residual learning for image recognition. In: Proceedings of the IEEE/CVF Conference on Computer Vision and Pattern Recognition, pp. 770–778 (2016)
31. Hsu, Y.C., Liu, Y.C., Ramasamy, A., Kira, Z.: Re-evaluating continual learning scenarios: a categorization and case for strong baselines. arXiv preprint arXiv:1810.12488 (2018)
32. Kirkpatrick, J., et al.: Overcoming catastrophic forgetting in neural networks. Proc. Natl. Acad. Sci. 114(13), 3521–3526 (2017)
33. Krizhevsky, A., Sutskever, I., Hinton, G.E.: Imagenet classification with deep convolutional neural networks. Adv. Neural. Inf. Process. Syst. 25, 1097–1105 (2012)
34. Larsson, G., Maire, M., Shakhnarovich, G.: Learning representations for automatic colorization. In: Leibe, B., Matas, J., Sebe, N., Welling, M. (eds.) ECCV 2016. LNCS, vol. 9908, pp. 577–593. Springer, Cham (2016). https://doi.org/10.1007/978-3-319-46493-0_35
35. Le, Q.V.: Building high-level features using large scale unsupervised learning. In: Proceeding of the IEEE International Conference on Acoustics, Speech and Signal Processing, pp. 8595–8598. IEEE (2013)
36. Lee, H., Battle, A., Raina, R., Ng, A.Y.: Efficient sparse coding algorithms. In: Advances in Neural Information Processing Systems, pp. 801–808 (2007)
37. Li, X., Zhou, Y., Wu, T., Socher, R., Xiong, C.: Learn to grow: a continual structure learning framework for overcoming catastrophic forgetting. In: Proceedings of the International Conference on Machine Learning, pp. 3925–3934. PMLR (2019)
38. Li, Z., Hoiem, D.: Learning without forgetting. IEEE Trans. Pattern Anal. Mach. Intell. 40(12), 2935–2947 (2017)
39. Lin, L.J.: Reinforcement Learning for Robots Using Neural Networks. Carnegie Mellon University, Pittsburgh (1992)
40. Liu, Z., Luo, P., Wang, X., Tang, X.: Deep learning face attributes in the wild. In: Proceedings of the IEEE/CVF International Conference on Computer Vision, pp. 3730–3738 (2015)
41. Mallya, A., Davis, D., Lazebnik, S.: Piggyback: adapting a single network to multiple tasks by learning to mask weights. In: Ferrari, V., Hebert, M., Sminchisescu, C., Weiss, Y. (eds.) ECCV 2018. LNCS, vol. 11208, pp. 72–88. Springer, Cham (2018). https://doi.org/10.1007/978-3-030-01225-0_5
42. Masci, J., Meier, U., Cireşan, D., Schmidhuber, J.: Stacked convolutional auto-encoders for hierarchical feature extraction. In: Honkela, T., Duch, W., Girolami, M., Kaski, S. (eds.) ICANN 2011. LNCS, vol. 6791, pp. 52–59. Springer, Heidelberg (2011). https://doi.org/10.1007/978-3-642-21735-7_7
43. Miech, A., Alayrac, J.B., Smaira, L., Laptev, I., Sivic, J., Zisserman, A.: End-to-end learning of visual representations from uncurated instructional videos. In: Proceedings of the IEEE/CVF Conference on Computer Vision and Pattern Recognition, pp. 9879–9889 (2020)
44. Miech, A., Zhukov, D., Alayrac, J.B., Tapaswi, M., Laptev, I., Sivic, J.: HowTo100M: learning a text-video embedding by watching hundred million narrated video clips. In: Proceedings of the IEEE/CVF International Conference on Computer Vision, pp. 2630–2640 (2019)
45. Miller, G.A.: WordNet: An Electronic Lexical Database. MIT Press, Cambridge (1998)

46. Misra, I., Maaten, L.v.d.: Self-supervised learning of pretext-invariant representations. In: Proceedings of the IEEE/CVF Conference on Computer Vision and Pattern Recognition, pp. 6707–6717 (2020)
47. Misra, I., Zitnick, C.L., Hebert, M.: Shuffle and learn: unsupervised learning using temporal order verification. In: Leibe, B., Matas, J., Sebe, N., Welling, M. (eds.) ECCV 2016. LNCS, vol. 9905, pp. 527–544. Springer, Cham (2016). https://doi. org/10.1007/978-3-319-46448-0_32
48. Mitchell, T., et al.: Never-ending learning. Commun. ACM **61**(5), 103–115 (2018)
49. Mnih, V., et al.: Human-level control through deep reinforcement learning. Nature **518**(7540), 529–533 (2015)
50. Mobahi, H., Collobert, R., Weston, J.: Deep learning from temporal coherence in video. In: Proceedings of the International Conference on Machine Learning, pp. 737–744 (2009)
51. Morgado, P., Vasconcelos, N.: NetTailor: tuning the architecture, not just the weights. In: Proceedings of the IEEE/CVF Conference on Computer Vision and Pattern Recognition, pp. 3044–3054 (2019)
52. Morgado, P., Vasconcelos, N., Misra, I.: Audio-visual instance discrimination with cross-modal agreement. In: Proceedings of the IEEE/CVF Conference on Computer Vision and Pattern Recognition, pp. 12475–12486 (2021)
53. Noroozi, M., Favaro, P.: Unsupervised learning of visual representations by solving Jigsaw puzzles. In: Leibe, B., Matas, J., Sebe, N., Welling, M. (eds.) ECCV 2016. LNCS, vol. 9910, pp. 69–84. Springer, Cham (2016). https://doi.org/10.1007/978-3-319-46466-4_5
54. Olshausen, B.A.: Sparse coding of time-varying natural images. In: Proceedings of the International Conference on Independent Component Analysis and Blind Source Separation, vol. 2. Citeseer (2000)
55. Olshausen, B.A., Field, D.J.: Emergence of simple-cell receptive field properties by learning a sparse code for natural images. Nature **381**(6583), 607–609 (1996)
56. Oord, A.v.d., Li, Y., Vinyals, O.: Representation learning with contrastive predictive coding. arXiv preprint arXiv:1807.03748 (2018)
57. Owens, A., Efros, A.A.: Audio-visual scene analysis with self-supervised multisensory features. In: Ferrari, V., Hebert, M., Sminchisescu, C., Weiss, Y. (eds.) ECCV 2018. LNCS, vol. 11210, pp. 639–658. Springer, Cham (2018). https://doi.org/10. 1007/978-3-030-01231-1_39
58. Pathak, D., Girshick, R., Dollár, P., Darrell, T., Hariharan, B.: Learning features by watching objects move. In: Proceedings of the IEEE/CVF Conference on Computer Vision and Pattern Recognition, pp. 2701–2710 (2017)
59. Pathak, D., Krahenbuhl, P., Donahue, J., Darrell, T., Efros, A.A.: Context encoders: feature learning by inpainting. In: Proceedings of the IEEE/CVF Conference on Computer Vision and Pattern Recognition, pp. 2536–2544 (2016)
60. Prabhu, A., Torr, P.H.S., Dokania, P.K.: GDumb: a simple approach that questions our progress in continual learning. In: Vedaldi, A., Bischof, H., Brox, T., Frahm, J.-M. (eds.) ECCV 2020. LNCS, vol. 12347, pp. 524–540. Springer, Cham (2020). https://doi.org/10.1007/978-3-030-58536-5_31
61. Qian, R., et al.: Spatiotemporal contrastive video representation learning. In: Proceedings of the IEEE/CVF Conference on Computer Vision and Pattern Recognition, pp. 6964–6974 (2021)
62. Radford, A., et al.: Learning transferable visual models from natural language supervision. arXiv preprint arXiv:2103.00020 (2021)
63. Ramapuram, J., Gregorova, M., Kalousis, A.: Lifelong generative modeling. Neurocomputing **404**, 381–400 (2020)

64. Rannen, A., Aljundi, R., Blaschko, M.B., Tuytelaars, T.: Encoder based lifelong learning. In: Proceedings of the IEEE/CVF International Conference on Computer Vision, pp. 1320–1328 (2017)
65. Ranzato, M., Huang, F.J., Boureau, Y.L., LeCun, Y.: Unsupervised learning of invariant feature hierarchies with applications to object recognition. In: Proceedings of the IEEE/CVF Conference on Computer Vision and Pattern Recognition, pp. 1–8. IEEE (2007)
66. Rao, D., Visin, F., Rusu, A., Pascanu, R., Teh, Y.W., Hadsell, R.: Continual unsupervised representation learning. Adv. Neural. Inf. Process. Syst. **32**, 7647–7657 (2019)
67. Rebuffi, S.A., Kolesnikov, A., Sperl, G., Lampert, C.H.: iCaRL: incremental classifier and representation learning. In: Proceedings of the IEEE/CVF Conference on Computer Vision and Pattern Recognition, pp. 2001–2010 (2017)
68. Rolnick, D., Ahuja, A., Schwarz, J., Lillicrap, T.P., Wayne, G.: Experience replay for continual learning. In: Advances in Neural Information Processing Systems, pp. 350–360 (2019)
69. Rusu, A.A., et al.: Progressive neural networks. arXiv preprint arXiv:1606.04671 (2016)
70. de Sa, V.R.: Learning classification with unlabeled data. In: Advances in Neural Information Processing Systems, pp. 112–119. Citeseer (1994)
71. Salakhutdinov, R., Hinton, G.: Deep Boltzmann machines. In: Artificial Intelligence and Statistics, pp. 448–455. PMLR (2009)
72. Schaul, T., Quan, J., Antonoglou, I., Silver, D.: Prioritized experience replay. In: Proceedings of the International Conference on Learning Representations (2016)
73. Shin, H., Lee, J.K., Kim, J., Kim, J.: Continual learning with deep generative replay. In: Advances in Neural Information Processing Systems, pp. 2994–3003 (2017)
74. Singh, K.K., Fatahalian, K., Efros, A.A.: KrishnaCam: using a longitudinal, single-person, egocentric dataset for scene understanding tasks. In: 2016 IEEE Winter Conference on Applications of Computer Vision (WACV), pp. 1–9. IEEE (2016)
75. Thrun, S.: A lifelong learning perspective for mobile robot control. In: Intelligent Robots and Systems, pp. 201–214. Elsevier (1995)
76. Titsias, M.K., Schwarz, J., Matthews, A.G.d.G., Pascanu, R., Teh, Y.W.: Functional regularisation for continual learning with gaussian processes. arXiv preprint arXiv:1901.11356 (2019)
77. Van Horn, G., et al.: The iNaturalist species classification and detection dataset. In: Proceedings of the IEEE/CVF Conference on Computer Vision and Pattern Recognition, pp. 8769–8778 (2018)
78. Vincent, P., Larochelle, H., Bengio, Y., Manzagol, P.A.: Extracting and composing robust features with denoising autoencoders. In: Proceedings of the International Conference on Machine Learning, pp. 1096–1103 (2008)
79. Wang, J., Jiao, J., Liu, Y.-H.: Self-supervised video representation learning by pace prediction. In: Vedaldi, A., Bischof, H., Brox, T., Frahm, J.-M. (eds.) ECCV 2020. LNCS, vol. 12362, pp. 504–521. Springer, Cham (2020). https://doi.org/10.1007/978-3-030-58520-4_30
80. Wang, X., Gupta, A.: Unsupervised learning of visual representations using videos. In: Proceedings of the IEEE/CVF International Conference on Computer Vision, pp. 2794–2802 (2015)
81. Wu, Z., Xiong, Y., Yu, S.X., Lin, D.: Unsupervised feature learning via non-parametric instance discrimination. In: Proceedings of the IEEE/CVF Conference on Computer Vision and Pattern Recognition, pp. 3733–3742 (2018)

82. Ye, F., Bors, A.G.: Learning latent representations across multiple data domains using lifelong VAEGAN. In: Vedaldi, A., Bischof, H., Brox, T., Frahm, J.-M. (eds.) ECCV 2020. LNCS, vol. 12365, pp. 777–795. Springer, Cham (2020). https://doi.org/10.1007/978-3-030-58565-5_46

83. Yoon, J., Yang, E., Lee, J., Hwang, S.J.: Lifelong learning with dynamically expandable networks. arXiv preprint arXiv:1708.01547 (2017)

84. Zbontar, J., Jing, L., Misra, I., LeCun, Y., Deny, S.: Barlow twins: self-supervised learning via redundancy reduction. In: Proceedings of the International Conference on Machine Learning (2021)

85. Zenke, F., Poole, B., Ganguli, S.: Continual learning through synaptic intelligence. In: Proceedings of the International Conference on Machine Learning, pp. 3987–3995. PMLR (2017)

86. Zhang, R., Isola, P., Efros, A.A.: Colorful image colorization. In: Leibe, B., Matas, J., Sebe, N., Welling, M. (eds.) ECCV 2016. LNCS, vol. 9907, pp. 649–666. Springer, Cham (2016). https://doi.org/10.1007/978-3-319-46487-9_40

Conditional Stroke Recovery for Fine-Grained Sketch-Based Image Retrieval

Zhixin Ling⬤, Zhen Xing⬤, Jian Zhou⬤, and Xiangdong Zhou$^{(\boxtimes)}$⬤

Fudan University, Shanghai, China
{20212010005,zxing20,19212010009,xdzhou}@fudan.edu.cn

Abstract. The key to Fine-Grained Sketch Based Image Retrieval (FG-SBIR) is to establish fine-grained correspondence between sketches and images. Since sketches only consist of abstract strokes, stroke recognition ability plays an important role in FG-SBIR. However, existing works usually ignore the unique feature of sketches and treat images and sketches equally. Targeting at this problem, we propose Conditional Stroke Recovery (CSR) to enhance stroke recognition ability for FG-SBIR, in which we introduce an auxiliary task that requires the network recover the strokes using the paired image as condition. In this way, the network learns better to match the strokes with corresponding image elements. To complete the auxiliary task, we propose an unsupervised stroke disorder algorithm, which does well in stroke extraction and sketch augmentation. In addition, we figure out two weaknesses of the common triplet loss and propose double-anchor InfoNCE loss to reduce cosine distances between sketch-image pairs. Comprehensive experiments using various backbones are conducted on four datasets (*i.e.*, QMUL-Shoe, QMUL-Chair, QMUL-ShoeV2, and Sketchy). In terms of acc@1, our method outperforms previous works by a great margin.

Keywords: Fine-Grained · SBIR · FG-SBIR · Double-anchor InfoNCE

1 Introduction

Compared with text description, sketches interpret the information need of users more accurately in some real applications like product retrieval. As a result, the research of Sketch-Based Image Retrieval (SBIR) has received increasing attention recently. According to the retrieval granularity, SBIR can be categorized into Coarse-Grained category-level SBIR (CG-SBIR) [1,4,18] and Fine-Grained instance-level SBIR (FG-SBIR) [3,17,22,38,44]. CG-SBIR retrieves an image in the gallery based on the category of query sketch while FG-SBIR retrieves

Supplementary Information The online version contains supplementary material available at https://doi.org/10.1007/978-3-031-19809-0_41.

a specific image that shares the same pose and outline. FG-SBIR has a wide range of applications in many fields such as searching online images or products. The key to FG-SBIR is to establish fine-grained correspondence between sketches and images. Considering that sketches only consists of strokes, to establish the fine-grained correspondence is mainly to match each sketch stroke with the corresponding image element (*e.g.*, a minute hand of a clock matched with an arrowed line in an sketch). We refer to the ability to recognize the arrowed line as stroke recognition. However, the unique stroke characteristic is not well stressed in previous works [16,29,31].

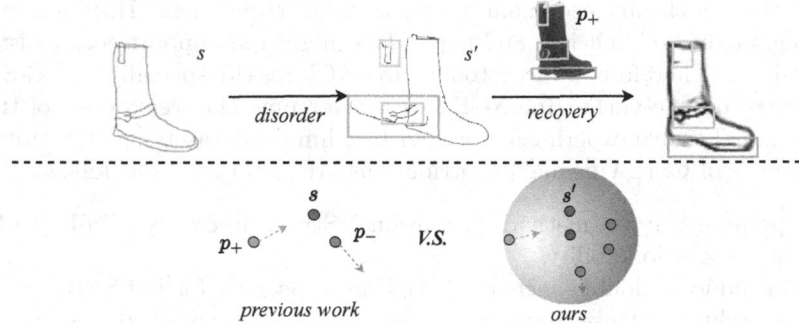

Fig. 1. 1) The top part shows an auxiliary recovery task conditioned by the paired image p_+. The task recovers a sketch s from a disordered one s'. The recovery process learns to match each stroke with its corresponding image element and place the stroke back to the right position. **2)** The bottom part compares triplet loss with our double-anchor InfoNCE loss. The former usually optimizes the L2 distance and samples negative images p_- inefficiently. The latter optimizes cosine similarity and take s' as an augmented auxiliary anchor, therefore enhancing robustness of our model.

Several previous works notice the problem. SaN [41,42] feeds strokes of different drawing stages into the network to enhance stroke recognition ability. Whereas, stroke annotations could be unavailable in real-world applications, limiting application scenarios of SaN. A jigsaw pretraining strategy [23] was proposed to boost the ability of the network to capture fine-grained correspondence. However, the jigsaw game requires that the backgrounds of input images should be clean. A generative model [39] reconstruct sketch feature based on the paired image feature. In this way, the network interprets different image elements into sketch stroke precisely. However, uncertainties in manually created sketch make the method only available for coarse-grained SBIR.

To eliminate the uncertainties, we propose Conditional Stroke Recovery (CSR). We introduce an auxiliary task that recovers sketches. At first, we randomly move the strokes elsewhere within the sketch to obtain a corresponding disordered sketch. After that, conditioned on the image feature, we recover the original sketch from the feature of the disordered sketch. Intuitively, based on observation on the image, the network learns to decide which strokes are misplaced in the disordered sketch and place the misplaced strokes back. To decide the misplaced strokes is necessary for *stroke recovery*, so we take this intermediate recovery step as *misplaced stroke distinguishing* (MSD) for simplicity. In this way, the network learns to decide the right image element and match it with the corresponding sketch stroke, therefore enhancing stroke recognition ability. Besides, the disordering process is completed by our proposed unsupervised stroke disorder algorithm. Compared with previous works, CSR locates stroke recognition ability of the network to establish fine-grained correspondence between paired images and sketches. CSR does not require side information (*e.g.*, other pretraining datasets, stroke annotations and text descriptions), making it available in all kinds of scenarios. In addition, the existing works on FG-SBIR [16,29,31,33] reduce the sketch-image domain gap mainly by triplet loss. However, triplet sampling might be inefficient and triplet loss might not support cosine distance retrieval well. Therefore, by accustoming InfoNCE loss [5] specially for FG-SBIR, we propose double-anchor InfoNCE loss to overcome the weaknesses of triplet loss. Comprehensive experiments on four benchmark datasets [29,41] verify the effectiveness of CSR. Our main contributions are summarized as follows,

- We propose a novel method, Conditional Stroke Recovery (CSR), to learn stroke recognition ability.
- We introduce a double-anchor InfoNCE loss specially for FG-SBIR.
- We introduce a stroke disorder algorithm that can be applied to sketch augmentation without sequential information of pixels.
- Comprehensive results on four popular benchmark datasets demonstrate the advantage of our proposed CSR method over state-of-the-art methods.

2   Related Works

Coarse-grained SBIR. Coarse-grained SBIR (CG-SBIR) is firstly proposed by [14]. CG-SBIR aims to learn a feature space that reduces the gap between sketch domain and image domain. Early CG-SBIR works usually extract edges maps from images and then design hand-crafted features to match the query sketches with images [8,11,12,28]. In recent years, deep-learning based methods using variants of siamese losses [33] and ranking losses [43] are proposed for the CG-SBIR. Bui *et. al.* [4] applies a siamese loss and a triplet loss in different training stages to learn detailed features. A graph-based searching method [1] is proposed to re-rank the retrieved images.

Fine-grained SBIR. Fine-grained SBIR (FG-SBIR) is firstly defined as retrieving the images with the same attributes (*e.g.*, viewpoint and body configuration) as the query sketch [15]. Qian *et. al.* [41] further extend the definition, requiring the retrieved image instance to be right corresponding to the query sketch. Since attribute annotations are usually unavailable in real-world applications, we follow the latter definition [41] like most of existing FG-SBIR works [3,16,22,26,37]. Apart from the huge domain gap in CG-SBIR, FG-SBIR also needs to capture fine-grained correspondence between images and sketches, making the task much more challenging. Li *et. al.* [15] adopt DPM [9] to learn different parts of objects and perform graph matching between sketches and images. Other existing FG-SBIR works [16,29,31,33] are mostly based on a contrastive loss that captures fine-grained correspondence. Among these works, DSSA [33] proposes an attention mechanism to locate the most discrminative regions. GN Triplet [29] applies a classification loss to distinguish objects from different categories. Quadruplet [31] extends triplet loss to quadruplet loss. Radenovi et. al. [26] converts images to edge maps for shape matching. A reinforcement learning method [3] is proposed to support on-the-fly retrieval. TC-Net [16] further introduces various classification losses. Although SaN Triplet [41,42] improve stroke recognition ability by incorporating strokes of different drawing phases into different input channels, but it requires expensive stroke annotations. Besides, converting images to edge maps [23,41,42] for pre-training helps little for FG-SBIR [16] since edge maps can remove helpful information (e.g., color and texture).

Sketch Reconstruction from Images. Bhunia et. al. [2] propose an image-to-sketch translation method. But it requires coordinate sequences and is only used for generation of more training sketch-image pairs. Pang et. al. [23] design a jigsaw game where edge maps are divided into grids and mixed into real image to form jigsaw tiles. However, simply dividing edge maps into grids might do great harm to semantic completeness of strokes. Yelamarthi et. al. [39] employ CVAE and CAAE to reconstruct sketch features from features of paired images. Since one image can correspond to more than one sketches, the generation process is not unique for the same image and therefore these generative frameworks do not work in FG-SBIR.

InfoNCE Loss. Information Noise Contrastive Estimation loss (InfoNCE loss) is first proposed for Contrastive Predictive Coding [21], which learns robust representations by predicting the future in latent space. In SimCLR [5] and SimCLRv2 [6], InfoNCE loss aimes to minimize the distance between paired augmented images. Chen et. al. [5] verify the advantage of InfoNCE loss over triplet loss on self-supervised image classification tasks. In this paper, based on InfoNCE loss, we introduce a double-anchor InfoNCE loss and prove its effectiveness on FG-SBIR as well.

3   Our Method

3.1   Overview

A fine-grained sketch-image dataset basically consists of paired sketch-image pairs. We denote a sketch by s and an image by p. For a given s, we represent the paired image by p_+, an unpaired one by p_-, and a disordered sketch by s'. Our proposed CSR mainly consists of two networks: a feature extraction network E^f and a stroke recovery network E^r, as illustrated in Fig. 2. E^f fuses multi-level features for retrieval. We give up the common triplet loss and propose double-anchor InfoNCE loss which supports cosine distance retrieval and samples negative images more efficiently. To learn stroke recognition ability, we design a recovery task by E^r. Given retrieval features of a disordered sketch and its paired image, E^r recovers the original sketch using a recovery loss.

3.2 Stroke Disorder Algorithm

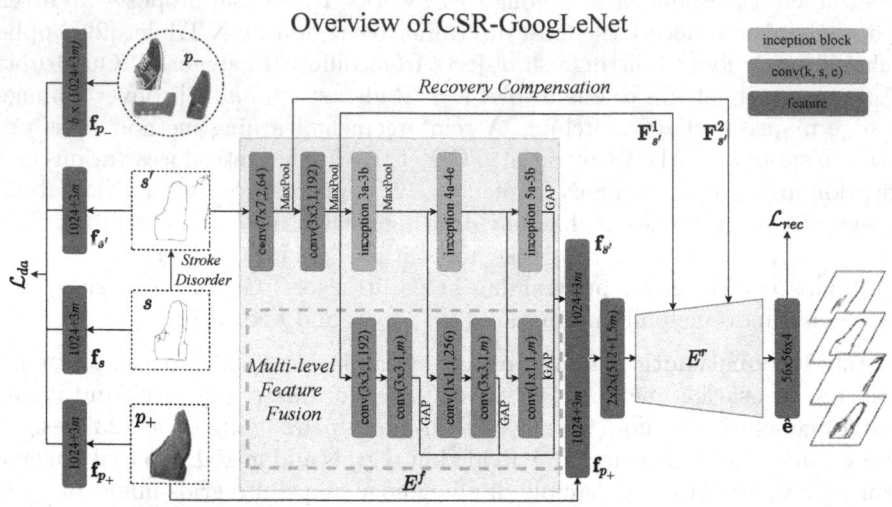

Fig. 2. Overview of CSR-GoogLeNet (refer to Supplementary [3]. for details). CSR consists of E^f and E^R. All of images, sketches and disordered sketches share the same E^f. In E^r, intermmediate feature maps are converted to m-dimensional feature vectors and then concatenated to the final 1024-dim output vector as a retrieval feature. An double-anchor InfoNCE loss $\mathcal{L}_{da}$ is applied on the retrieval feature. The retrieval features of a sketch s and its paired image p_+ are concatenated and sent into E^R. A recovery loss $\mathcal{L}_{rec}$ is applied on a 4-channel recovered extended map **e**.

A disordered sketch s' is created by stroke disorder Algorithm 1 in an unsupervised way. Algorithm 1 consists of two parts: *stroke extraction* (SE, Ln1-8) and *stroke disorder* (SD, Ln9-15). The whole algorithm runs as the following steps: **1)** Ln1 initializes the strokes as unconnected pixels; **2)** Ln3 obtains the longest stroke; **3)** Ln4 find a chokepoint where several strokes might join; **4)** Ln5-8 cut the stroke into n_m parts with a direct line. We want the line to be perpendicular to the variance of neighborhood pixels to avoid the line coinciding with the stroke. **5)** Ln9-15 disorders the selected strokes. The pixels removed in Ln6 into any stroke are stroke end points. We do not reassign them to any other strokes to prevent the network from taking a shortcut for stroke recovery [20]. The algorithm results are visualized in Fig. 3. p_d is a hyper-parameter and a larger p_d makes s' messier. Instead of simply dividing strokes into grids [23], the algorithm tries to preserve stroke completeness and independence. The SD process can be used as a sketch augmentation technique. The obtained sketch strokes can also be used for other augmentation approaches, (*e.g.*, stroke removal and stroke deformation in SaN [30,41]). Supplementary also presents more details.

Algorithm 1: Stroke disorder algorithm.

Input: A $w \times h$ binary matrix s, where 0/1 is stroke/background color; A disorder probability p_d. The target strokes n_s, an integer.

Output: Strokes of the disordered sketch.

1 Group 0-valued pixels in s into n sets, say $\mathcal{P}_1, \mathcal{P}_2, \cdots, \mathcal{P}_n$, where only pixels in the same set are connected, $\mathcal{S} \leftarrow \{\mathcal{P}_1, \mathcal{P}_2, \cdots, \mathcal{P}_n\}$; // $\mathcal{P}_i$ forms a stroke

2 **while** $n < n_s$ **do** // Stroke extraction

3 | $\mathcal{P}_m \leftarrow argmax_{\mathcal{P}_i \in \mathcal{S}} |\mathcal{P}_i|$;

4 | $c_m \leftarrow argmax_{c_i \in \mathcal{P}_m} |Adj(c_i) \cap \mathcal{P}_m|$; // Adj yields neighborhood pixels.

5 | $\mathbf{v} \leftarrow var(Adj(c_m)), \mathcal{P}_l \leftarrow Ln(c_m, \frac{\mathbf{v}}{|\mathbf{v}|})$; // var is the direction that maximizes neighbor variance. $Ln(point, normal)$ is a parameterized line

6 | $\mathcal{P}_m \leftarrow \mathcal{P}_m - \mathcal{P}_l$; // Remove intersection pixels

7 | Group pixels in $\mathcal{P}_m$ as Line-1 and obtain n_m sets, say $\mathcal{P}_1, \mathcal{P}_2, \cdots, \mathcal{P}_{n_m}$;

8 | $\mathcal{S} \leftarrow \mathcal{S} \cup \{\mathcal{P}_1, \mathcal{P}_2, \cdots, \mathcal{P}_{n_m}\} - \{\mathcal{P}_m\}, n \leftarrow n - 1 + n_m$;

9 **end**

10 Randomly select a subset $\mathcal{S}' \subset \mathcal{S}$, where $|\mathcal{S}'| = \lceil n \times p_d \rceil$;

11 **for** $\mathcal{P} \in \mathcal{S}'$ **do** // Stroke Disorder

12 | $x_t \sim N(0, (w \times p_d)^2), y_t \sim N(0, (h \times p_d)^2), r \sim N(0, \pi^2 \times p_d^4)$;

13 | Clip x_t, y_t, r to constrain processed pixel coordinates in a valid value scope;

14 | Rotate $\mathcal{P}$ by r and translate $\mathcal{P}$ by (x_t, y_t);

15 **end**

16 **return** $\mathcal{S}$

3.3 Feature Extraction

All of s, p_+, p_- and s' shares the same feature extraction procedure. We take s for example. Original output of E^f is a 1024-dimensional vector, mainly containing high-level information (*e.g.*, semantic information). We fuse multi-level features to enrich the output with low-level information (*e.g.*, contours, texture and color). We refer to this step as *Multi-level Feature Fusion*. Specifically, CNNs are utilized to encode intermmediate feature maps into m-dimensional vectors. They are fused to be a vector of $1024 + 3m$ dimensions, $\mathbf{f}_s$, which is taken as the final output of E^f. The procedure is formulated as $\mathbf{f}_s = E^f(\mathbf{x}_s)$. $\mathbf{f}_s$ is used for retrieval, so the distances between $\mathbf{f}_s$ and $\mathbf{f}_{p_+}$ should be reduced.

A Common Approach: Triplet Loss. A common approach is to employ a triplet loss $\mathcal{L}_{trp}$ on the retrieval feature:

$$\mathcal{L}_{trp} = max(d(\mathbf{f}_s, \mathbf{f}_{p_-}) - d(\mathbf{f}_s, \mathbf{f}_{p_+}) + r, 0), \tag{1}$$

where d is a distance metric and r is triplet margin. Empirically, $\mathcal{L}_{trp}$ should satisfy two rules: **1)** the triplet anchor should be a sketch for sketch is the query. **2)** negative samples of $\mathcal{L}_{trp}$ should all be images. These two rules are adopted by most previous works [16,23,29,31,41]. Despite broad application of $\mathcal{L}_{trp}$, there exists two problems: **1)** Naive triplet sampling is inefficient: a batch of $b \times 3$ samples contains only b triplets. **2)** $\mathcal{L}_{trp}$ usually targets at L2 distance [16,23,31,33] while cosine distance might produce better retrieval performance.

Most of existing works [16, 23, 26, 29, 31, 41] adopt L2 distance as d for $\mathcal{L}_{trp}$. Cosine distance disagrees with d because **(1)** cosine distance in $\mathcal{L}_{trp}$ leads to insignificant gradients; **(2)** cosine distance has a certain value scope and thus makes $\mathcal{L}_{trp}$ very sensitive to r. However, cosine distance performs better in retrieval since it avoids variations introduced by the vector norm [19]. Consequently, the inconsistency between training distance and retrieval distance might cause a performance bottleneck.

Our Solution: Double-anchor InfoNCE. Inspired by InfoNCE loss [5], we propose a loss that overcomes weaknesses of $\mathcal{L}_{trp}$ while following the above rules:

$$\mathcal{L}_{sa} = -\log \frac{e^{sim(\mathbf{f}_s, \mathbf{f}_{p_+})}}{e^{sim(\mathbf{f}_s, \mathbf{f}_{p_+})} + \sum_{p_-} e^{sim(\mathbf{f}_s, \mathbf{f}_{p_-})}}, \tag{2}$$

where sim yields amplified cosine similarity: $sim(x, y) = \frac{cos(x,y)}{\tau}$. τ controls temperature. Different from the original InfoNCE loss that targets at similarity of single-domain features, $\mathcal{L}_{sa}$ refers to the success of triplet loss and is designed to optimize cross-modality distances.

To further improve robustness of our model, the distance between s' and p_+ should be taken into consideration. Although s' is not strictly aligned with p_+, s' is more similar to p_+ than to p_-. At the same time, s should always be the closest to p_+. We therefore propose a double-anchor InfoNCE loss:

$$\mathcal{L}_{da} = -\log \frac{e^{sim(\mathbf{f}_s, \mathbf{f}_{p_+})} + \alpha e^{sim(\mathbf{f}_{s'}, \mathbf{f}_{p_+})}}{e^{sim(\mathbf{f}_s, \mathbf{f}_{p_+})} + \alpha e^{sim(\mathbf{f}_{s'}, \mathbf{f}_{p_+})} + \sum_{p_-} (e^{sim(\mathbf{f}_s, \mathbf{f}_{p_-})} + \alpha e^{sim(\mathbf{f}_{s'}, \mathbf{f}_{p_-})})}, \tag{3}$$

where $0 \le \alpha < 1$. In $\mathcal{L}_{da}$, s' is an auxiliary anchor and regarded as an augmented sketch from s. A larger α encourages $\mathbf{f}_{p_+}$ to move towards $\mathbf{f}_{s'}$. To collect a b-sized training batch, we fill it with b triplets of (s, s', p_+). For a specific s or s', other $b-1$ images in the same batch are regarded as as p_-. Although $\mathcal{L}_{trp}$ can also

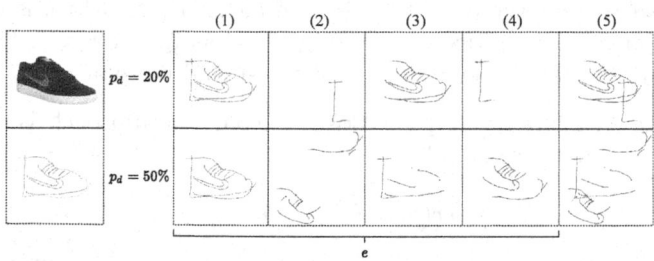

Fig. 3. Visualization of the stroke disorder Algorithm 1. The leftmost two subfigures are an image and visualization of different groups of its paired sketch. The 5 columns on the right are: (1) the original sketch s; (2) disorder strokes, i.e., $\mathcal{P} \in \mathcal{S}'$ after rotation and translation; (3) fixed strokes, i.e., the unselected strokes $\mathcal{P} \in \mathcal{S} - \mathcal{S}'$; (4) selected strokes, i.e., $\mathcal{P} \in \mathcal{S}'$ before rotation and translation; (5) the disorder sketch s'. We use column (1)-(4) to compose a 4-channel extended recovery map $\mathbf{e}$.

adopt a similar *efficient triplet collection* (ETC) approach, where $b \times (b-1)$ triplets can be collected in a batch, $\mathcal{L}_{da}$ is still superior to $\mathcal{L}_{trp}$ since it directly optimizes cosine distances. Supplementary also analyzes an alternative of $\mathcal{L}_{da}$.

3.4 Stroke Recovery

The stroke recovery network E^r takes the input of $\mathbf{f}_{s'}$ and $\mathbf{f}_{p_+}$. The aim of E^r is to recover the paired sketch from its disordered style. To stabilize the training of E^r, we add another three maps to compose a 4-channel extended recovery map $\mathbf{e}$ as the recovery target, as illustrated in Fig. 3. Intuitively, the network first learns to distinguish misplaced and well-placed strokes (channel 2 and channel 3). After that, misplaced strokes are moved to their right places (channel 4) and then the sketch is recovered (channel 1).

CSR does not intend to recover high-resolution sketch, so we downsample $\mathbf{e}$ to 56×56. It simplifies E^r and prevent the risk that $\mathbf{f}_{s'}$ contains over-detailed pixel-level information. We compensate $\mathbf{f}_{s'}$ and $\mathbf{f}_{p_+}$ by two low-level feature maps of s from E^f [27], denoted by $\mathbf{F}_{s'}^1$ and $\mathbf{F}_{s'}^2$. We refer to the trick as *recovery compensation*. The whole recovery process is formulated as: $\hat{\mathbf{e}} = E^r(\mathbf{f}_{s'}, \mathbf{f}_{p_+}, \mathbf{F}_{s'}^1, \mathbf{F}_{s'}^2)$. Then we derive a recovery loss on the output $\hat{\mathbf{e}}$: $\mathcal{L}_{rec} = CE(\hat{\mathbf{e}}, \mathbf{e})$, where CE is the cross entropy loss. Although additional losses (*e.g.*, adversarial losses) might improve the quality of the recovered sketch, these losses turn out to be helpless for FG-SBIR when complicating our proposed framework.

3.5 Optimization

After obtaining $\mathcal{L}_{da}$ and $\mathcal{L}_{rec}$, we derive the total loss:

$$\mathcal{L}_{total} = w \times \mathcal{L}_{da} + \mathcal{L}_{rec}, \tag{4}$$

where w is the weight to balance $\mathcal{L}_{da}$ and $\mathcal{L}_{rec}$. All of s, p_+, p_- and s' share the same E^f. The parameters of both of E^f and E^r are optimized simultaneously.

4   Experiments

4.1 Experimental Setup

We briefly introduce the experimental setup in this section. Details can be seen in Supplementary. We report main results on GoogLeNet [34], InceptionV3 [35], DenseNet169 [13] and ResNet18 [10], which are adopted by the FG-SBIR works in the last three years [2,3,7,16,23,38]. We conduct all other experiments based on GoogLeNet. Empirically, we set $m = 64, b = 96, w = 10.0, \tau = 0.005, n_s = 10$. p_d starts at 0.1 and linearly grows to 0.3. We dynamically set $\alpha = 1 - \alpha_p p_d, \alpha_p = 2$. We evaluate CSR on four fine-grained sketch-image datasets: Sketchy [29], QMUL-Shoe [41], QMUL-Chair [41], and QMUL-ShoeV2 [41]. Following Qian *et. al.* [41], we report top-1 accuracy (acc@1) and top-10 accuracy (acc@10).

4.2 Comparison with Existing Works

We compare CSR with 12 baseline methods and report results in Table 1.

Table 1. Comparison of CSR and baselines on Sketchy, QMUL-Chair, QMUL-Shoe and QMUL-ShoeV2. Column "Side" shows side information used by existing works. "E" and "D" are short for extra annotations (*e.g.*, text descriptions and attributes) and other datasets [23–25,36,40]. Results are grouped by backbone. The best within each group are denoted in **boldface** and the best across different groups are <u>underlined</u>.

Method	Backbone	Side	Sketchy(%) acc@1	acc@10	QMUL-Chair(%) acc@1	acc@10	QMUL-Shoe(%) acc@1	acc@10	QMUL-ShoeV2(%) acc@1	acc@10
Song *et. al.* [32](BMVC'16)	SaN	E	-	-	78.4	99.0	50.4	91.3	-	-
SaN Triplet [41](CVPR'16)	SaN	DE	25.9	-	69.1	**97.9**	39.1	87.8	30.9	-
DSSA [33](ICCV'17)	SaN	E	-	-	81.4	95.9	**61.7**	**94.8**	**33.7**	-
Radenovi *et. al.* [26](ECCV'18)	VGG16	D	-	-	**85.6**	**97.9**	54.8	92.2	-	-
GN Triplet [29](TOG'16)	GoogLeNet	-	37.1	-	-	-	-	-	-	-
DCCRM [38](PR'19)	GoogLeNet	DE	46.2	**96.5**	-	-	-	-	-	-
Pang *et. al.* [23](CVPR'20)	GoogLeNet	D	-	-	86.0	-	56.5	-	36.5	-
CSR (ours)	GoogLeNet	-	**50.8**	85.4	**93.8**	**99.0**	**58.3**	**90.5**	**48.7**	**84.8**
Ayan *et. al.* [3] (CVPR'20)	InceptionV3	E	-	-	-	-	-	-	-	79.6
Bhunia *et. al.* [2] (CVPR'21)	InceptionV3	D	-	-	-	-	-	-	39.1	87.5
CSR (ours)	InceptionV3	-	<u>**58.9**</u>	**89.7**	**94.8**	<u>**100.0**</u>	**64.4**	**91.3**	<u>**52.1**</u>	**87.9**
Quadruplet [31] (ACMMM'17)	ResNet18	-	42.2	-	-	-	-	-	-	-
AE-Net [7](PR'22)	ResNet18	-	46.0	-	-	-	-	-	-	-
CSR (ours)	ResNet18	-	**47.6**	**82.9**	**93.8**	**97.9**	**55.5**	**89.1**	**45.1**	**85.5**
TC-Net [16](ACMMM'19)	Densnet169	E	40.8	-	95.9	**100.0**	63.5	94.8	40.2	-
CSR (ours)	Densenet169	-	**56.2**	**88.6**	<u>**97.9**</u>	**100.0**	<u>**67.8**</u>	<u>**97.4**</u>	47.6	**85.0**

acc@1 Comparison: CSR outperforms previous works within each backbone group respectively. Compared with TC-Net [16], CSR yields better performance gain on large datasets, (*i.e.*, Sketchy and QMUL-ShoeV2). For small datasets (*i.e.*, QMUL-Chair and QMUL-Shoe), it is not important to collect more negative samples, so advantage of $\mathcal{L}_{da}$ is not obvious and the performance gain is smaller. Compared with previous works, CSR-Densenet169 achieves the best acc@1 on all four datasets, outperforming previous works by 10.0% on Sketchy, 2.0% on QMUL-Chair, 4.3% on QMUL-Shoe and 7.4% on QMUL-ShoeV2.

acc@10 Comparison: CSR achieves the best performance except on Sketchy, where DCCRM [38] reports 96.5%. We suspect that side information (*e.g.*, text descriptions in DCCRM [38]) provides rich references for matching similar images. However, the side information can be ambiguous and help little to target at the exact image paired with the query. Therefore, acc@1 of DCCRM [38] is lower than CSR. Beside Sketchy, CSR achieves 100% on QMUL-Shoe Chair. CSR outperforms TC-Net [16] by 2.6% on QMUL-Shoe and Bhunia *et. al.* by 0.4% on QMUL-ShoeV2.

Side Information Comparison: As shown in column "Side", several works [2,3,23,38] rely on side information. These methods dug into side information in one or two specific fine-grained sketch-image datasets. However, in some other scenarios where such information is unavailable, these methods might suffer from performance drop. On the contrary, since CSR relaxes the requirement for side information, it certainly paves the way for further applications.

To observe how side information can work on CSR, we conducted an extra experiment: we pretrain CSR-GoogLeNet with $\mathcal{L}_{da}$ on the pretraining dataset used by Pang et. al. [23]. acc@1 on QMUL-Shoe improves from 64.4% to 68.7% and acc@1 on QMUL-ShoeV2 improves from 48.7% to 51.0%. The result shows the performance gain from side information.

Table 2. acc@1/acc@10 results on QMUL-ShoeV2 and Sketchy. MF stands for multi-level feature fusion. RC stands for recovery compensation. S0 reports results obtained from a pretrained backbone. "SE+SD": we adopt the stroke disorder approach as a sketch augmentation technique by setting $p_d = 0.05$. "GridD": we divide the sketch into grids and then rotate and translate the grids to obtain a disordered sketch.

Setting	MF	RC	Total loss	Sketchy(%)		QMUL-ShoeV2(%)	
				acc@1	acc@10	acc@1	acc@10
S0	×	-	×	0.7	3.6	0.6	9.6
S1	×	-	$\mathcal{L}_{sa}$	42.6	80.2	42.2	82.9
S2	×	-	$\mathcal{L}_{sa}$ w/ SE+SD	43.4	81.4	44.2	83.2
S3	×	-	$\mathcal{L}_{da}$	44.9	81.6	43.7	83.0
S4	√	-	$\mathcal{L}_{da}$	48.2	82.4	45.9	84.3
S5	×	×	$\mathcal{L}_{rec} + \mathcal{L}_{da}$	45.2	82.5	44.0	83.7
S6	×	√	$\mathcal{L}_{rec} + \mathcal{L}_{da}$	47.7	84.8	46.6	**85.3**
S7	√	×	$\mathcal{L}_{rec} + \mathcal{L}_{da}$	48.9	84.4	46.7	83.5
S8	√	√	$\mathcal{L}_{rec} + \mathcal{L}_{da}$ w/ GridD	41.9	80.8	43.5	81.7
S9	√	√	$\mathcal{L}_{rec} + \mathcal{L}_{da}$	**50.8**	**85.4**	**48.7**	84.8

4.3 Ablation Study

We conduct ablation experiments on both QMUL-ShoeV2 and Sketchy bacause 1) QMUL-ShoeV2 is the largest clean dataset; 2) Sketchy is the largest and most diversified among the introduced four FG-SBIR datasets. Experiments on these two datasets can be representative.

Module Ablation. We report ablation study results in Table 2. S2 outperforms S1 by 0.4/2.2 acc@1 performance gain on Sketchy/QMUL-ShoeV2, implying that our disorder algorithm work well for sketch augmentation. Also, S1 is inferior to S3, which proves that $\mathcal{L}_{da}$ can effectively make the advantage of s' to enhance robustness of our model. Comparison between S4 and S3 shows importance of MF in FG-SBIR. Moreover, MF contributes a greater performance gain when $\mathcal{L}_{rec}$ is introduced (S5 v.s. S7). It is also observed that $\mathcal{L}_{rec}$ does not work when ablating MF and RC, which produce important low-level information to support the recovery process (S5 v.s. S3). S8 shows that simply dividing the sketch into grids is not viable because it destroys semantic completeness of sketch strokes. S9 is the best setting, demonstrating the effectiveness of our method.

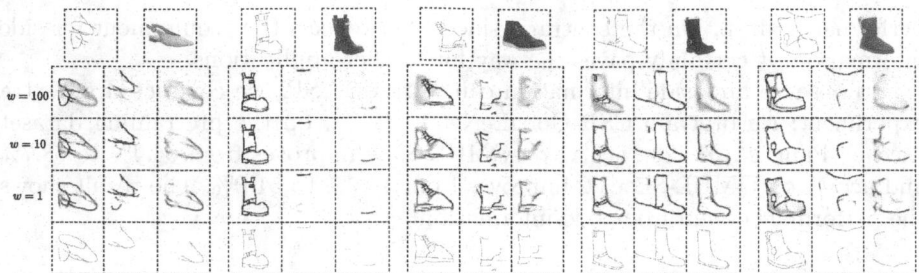

Fig. 4. Visualization of recovered sketches and retrieval features towards different w on QMUL-ShoeV2 test set. Within each group of figures bordered by dotted lines, the top two are the disordered sketch and the paired image. The rest three columns illustrate the original sketch, disordered strokes and selected strokes (refer to Fig. 3).

Effect of w. We study effect of w in Fig. 4. The recovered sketches in QMUL-ShoeV2 using different w are visualized in Fig. 6. The results reveal that a smaller w yields clearer recovered sketches. An over small w will overemphasize $\mathcal{L}_{rec}$ so that retrieval feature contains too much pixel-level information. These information is unnecessary for retrieval. On the other hand, overvaluing w leads to performance drop. Based on the low quality of the recovered sketches with a large w, we suspect that $\mathcal{L}_{rec}$ is ignored during training so the model fails to learn stroke recognition ability.

Table 3. acc@1 results by ablating each channel of **e** . "ablated" stands for the disenabled channel.

ablated	-	1	2	3	4
QMUL-ShoeV2	**48.7**	44.7	45.5	46.3	43.9
Sketchy	50.8	**51.0**	49.6	49.4	50.8

Table 4. acc@1 results by setting different α_p. Note that $\alpha = 1 - \alpha_p p_d$ and p_d linearly grows to 0.3.

α_p	0	1	2	3
QMUL-ShoeV2	38.8	48.3	**48.7**	47.3
Sketchy	36.7	50.3	**50.8**	49.6

Misplaced Stroke Distinguishing. The visualization in Fig. 4 shows that recovery of disordered strokes (column 2) is better than that of selected strokes(column 3). Largely due to the complete pixel-level information, misplaced stroke distinguishing(MSD) is easier than stroke recovery. To further investigate the role MSD plays in stroke recovery in Table 3, we ablate each channel of **e**. That is, we remove the channel from **e** and study the retrieval performance. We report results in Table 3. On QMUL-ShoeV2, each channel shows its necessity since sketch-image pairs are well aligned and recovery is well performed. Whereas, in Sketchy, the image object can be occluded and the paired sketch can be misaligned. Then stroke recovery cannot complete but MSD is still achievable. Therefore, channel 2 abd channel 3 are more important than channel 1 and channel 4 on Sketchy and ablating channel 1 and channel 4 does not make much difference. In conclusion, when stroke recovery is unable to complete, we can resort to MSD to enhance stroke recognition ability.

$\mathcal{L}_{trp}$ **v.s.** $\mathcal{L}_{sa}$ **v.s.** $\mathcal{L}_{da}$ We compare variants of $\mathcal{L}_{trp}$, $\mathcal{L}_{da}$ and $\mathcal{L}_{da}$. Results are reported in Table. 5. Differences among some typical settings are visualized in Fig. 5. In this paper, we define as $\lambda(1 - cos(\cdot, \cdot))$, where λ is a scale hyperparameter. Besides results in the Table. 5, we also conduct experiments of $\mathcal{L}_{trp} + dot$ and $\mathcal{L}_{da} + L2$ but their results are not comparable.

Table 5. acc@1 results with variants of $\mathcal{L}_{trp}$ and $\mathcal{L}_{da}$. Column "loss" omits $\mathcal{L}_{rec}$. CSR adopts **A5** while A4 is the original InfoNCE loss [5]. "ETC" stands for efficient triplet collection (refer to Sect. 3.3). n_t is the number of triplets in a batch. "anchor" stands for the anchor modality.

Setting	Loss	Anchor	ETC	n_t	$Metric$	$b = 16$		$b = 96$	
						Sketchy	QMUL-ShoeV2	Sketchy	QMUL-ShoeV2
T1	$\mathcal{L}_{trp}$	s	×	b	L2	38.9	26.6	39.2	27.0
T2	$\mathcal{L}_{trp}$	p	×	b	L2	28.8	14.2	30.1	14.3
T3	$\mathcal{L}_{trp}$	$p\&s$	×	$2b$	L2	35.0	37.3	35.2	38.2
T4	$\mathcal{L}_{trp}$	s	√	$b(b-1)$	L2	45.8	43.0	46.5	45.2
T5	$\mathcal{L}_{trp}$	p	√	$b(b-1)$	L2	37.8	37.1	38.9	39.6
T6	$\mathcal{L}_{trp}$	$p\&s$	√	$4b(b-1)$	L2	45.2	42.0	46.2	44.5
T7	$\mathcal{L}_{trp}$	s	√	$b(b-1)$	cos	29.5	40.1	30.5	42.9
A1	$\mathcal{L}_{sa}$	s	-	-	cos	46.9	44.0	48.6	47.1
A2	$\mathcal{L}_{sa}$	s	-	-	dot	30.4	29.5	31.8	32.8
A3	$\mathcal{L}_{sa}$	p	-	-	cos	42.0	35.6	44.0	37.4
A4	$\mathcal{L}_{sa}$	$p\&s$	-	-	cos	46.8	37.5	48.7	39.0
A5	$\mathcal{L}_{da}$	$s\&s'$	-	-	cos	**48.3**	**44.7**	**50.8**	**48.7**
A6	$\mathcal{L}_{da}$	$s\&s'$	-	-	dot	30.0	30.1	32.7	32.8

Results show that **1)** sketches serve as anchors better than images (T1 *v.s.* T2, T4 *v.s.* T5, A1 *v.s.* A3); **2)** negative samples should be all images and a sketch-image mixture does not help model performance (T4 *v.s.* T6, A1 *v.s.* A3) **3)** ETC is consistently superior to the naive triplet collection approach(T1-T3 *v.s.* T4-T6); **4)** $\mathcal{L}_{trp}$ is inconsistent with with cosine distance (T4 *v.s.* T7) ; **5)** $\mathcal{L}_{sa}/\mathcal{L}_{da}$ are inconsistent with dot similarity (A1 *v.s.* A3,A5 *v.s.* A6).

These results are reported according to retrieval with cosine distance. To ensure that the comparison is fair for $\mathcal{L}_{trp}$, we perform retrieval using L2 distance. In setting T4($b = 96$), the resultant acc@1 is 46.3/45.2 on Sketchy/QMUL-ShoeV2, which almost remains the same. We also compare $\mathcal{L}_{trp}$ acc@1-r curves using cosine and L2 distance in Fig. 8. The curves show that $\mathcal{L}_{trp} + cos$ is sensitive to margin r and is not a feasible combination. These results verify that our $\mathcal{L}_{sa}$ and $\mathcal{L}_{da}$ are superior to $\mathcal{L}_{trp}$. Besides, enlarging the batch size leads to greater performance gain in T4-T6, A1 and A2-A4. This is because these settings can collect more negative samples.

Augmentation via Stroke Disorder. To further investigate how our proposed stroke disorder algorithm works for sketch augmentation, we reproduce

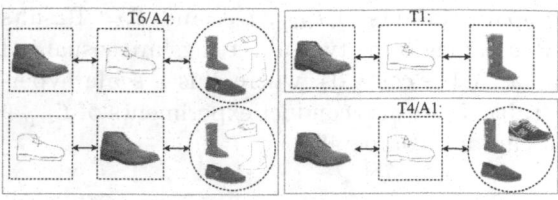

Fig. 5. Illustration of some settings in Table 5.

Table 6. Acc@1 using different augmentation methods on Sketchy.

Augmentation	[29]	[31]	[16]	$\mathcal{L}_{sa}$
baselines	37.1	42.2	40.8	42.6
SE+SD	37.6	44.1	41.4	43.4
SE+SaN	39.0	43.9	41.7	43.6
SE+SD+SaN	39.3	44.4	42.2	44.0

several existing worksGN Triplet [29] and Quadruplet [31] and TC-Net [16] and employ different sketch augmentation methods in the training stage. The results are reported in Table. 6. In this section, SaN stands for the augmentation methods applied in SaN [41], including stroke removal and stroke deformation. p_d is set to 0.05. Column "$\mathcal{L}_{sa}$" reports results of setting S2 in Tab. 2. Results show that **1)** SE+SD outperforms baselines, verifying that SD can improve diversity of training samples and prevent the risk of overfitting; **2)** both of SE+SaN and SE+SD+SaN outperform baselines, implying that extracted strokes are effective; **3)** SaN works as an augmentation method better than SD. Compared with rotation and translation of SD, removal and deformation can provide more natural augmented sketches. But we do not disorder a sketch via removal and deformation since sketches augmented in this way are found difficult for recovery.

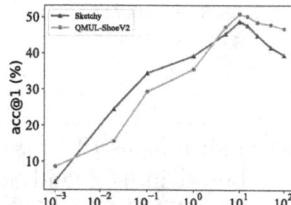

Fig. 6. acc@1-w curves of CSR.

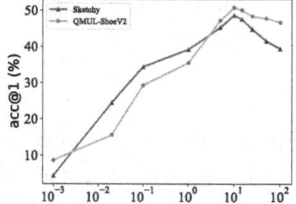

Fig. 7. acc@1-τ curves of CSR with different sim.

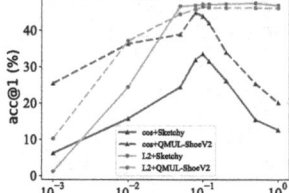

Fig. 8. acc@1-r curves using $\mathcal{L}_{trp}$ with different d.

Effect of τ. We plot acc@1-τ curves in Fig. 7. The results show that cosine similarity works better than dot product. An extremely small τ can lead good model performance, which is subtly different from observation in SimCLR [5]. SimCLR [5] aims at self-supervised learning task, where a pair of positive samples are augmented from the same image and their cosine similarity is very high, approximating one. In FG-SBIR, a sketch-image pair belongs to two different domains and their features are likely to be mutually orthogonal. Therefore, a small τ is required to amplify the similarity between a sketch-image pair.

5 Case Study

Retrieval results are visualized in Fig. 9. In most cases, the first retrieved image is correctly hit. The failure case of row (4) results from misalignment between the sketch and target images. The failure case of row (7) is due to the noises from image background. Recovered sketches are presented in Fig. 10. Recovery results are generally satisfactory and most of poor-quality recovery results come from Sketchy. For example, the duck in row (2) is not well recovered for **1)** the feather in the sketch is abstract and does not match any image element; **2)** bottom of the duck is obstructed by water, making stroke recovery unfeasible. These two problems are common in Sketchy. Sketchy therefore benefits less from $\mathcal{L}_{rec}$ than QMUL-ShoeV2. Moreover, compared with row(10), we mannually erase the knot of the image in row (8) and the knot of the disordered sketch in row (9). In both circumstances of row (8) and row (9), the knot cannot be recovered. These three cases imply that the recovery process does not rely on memorizing category characteristics. Instead, the recovery needs to match each sketch stroke with the corresponding image element.

 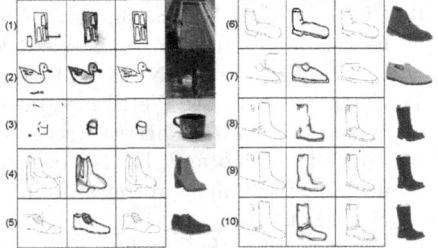

Fig. 9. Top-10 retrievals on QMUL-ShoeV2 (row (1)-(4)) and Sketchy (row (5)-(7)). Green/red borders indicate the correct/incorrect retrieved images. (Color figure online)

Fig. 10. Recovery visualization on Sketchy (row (1)-(3)) and QMUL-ShoeV2 (row (4)-(6)). The four columns are the disordered sketch, the recovered sketch, the original sketch and the paired image.

6 Conclusion

In this paper, we investigate the task of fine-grained sketch-based image retrieval (FG-SBIR) from a new perspective. We highlight stroke recognition ability of the network and propose Conditional Stroke Recovery(CSR). CSR introduce an auxiliary task that recovers a sketch from its disordered style with its paired image as condition. Moreover, targeting at the weaknesses of triplet loss, we propose double-anchor InfoNCE loss specially for FG-SBIR. A unsupervised stroke disorder algorithm is also proposed along with CSR. The algorithm can work as a new sketch augmentation approach. In terms of acc@1, CSR outperforms previous works by a great margin on four datasets.

Acknowledgment. This work was supported by the National Key Research and Development Program of China, No.2018YFB1402600.

References

1. Bhattacharjee, S.D., Yuan, J., Hong, W., Ruan, X.: Query adaptive instance search using object sketches. In: ACM International Conference on Multimedia (ACM MM), pp. 1306–1315 (2016)
2. Bhunia, A.K., Chowdhury, P.N., Sain, A., Yang, Y., Xiang, T., Song, Y.: More photos are all you need: semi-supervised learning for fine-grained sketch based image retrieval. In: Computer Vision and Pattern Recognition (CVPR) (2021)
3. Bhunia, A.K., Yang, Y., Hospedales, T.M., Xiang, T., Song, Y.Z.: Sketch less for more: on-the-fly fine-grained sketch-based image retrieval. In: Computer Vision and Pattern Recognition (CVPR) (2020)
4. Bui, T., Ribeiro, L.S.F., Ponti, M., Collomosse, J.P.: Sketching out the details: sketch-based image retrieval using convolutional neural networks with multi-stage regression. Comput. Graph. (CAG) **71**, 77–87 (2018)
5. Chen, T., Kornblith, S., Norouzi, M., Hinton, G.E.: A simple framework for contrastive learning of visual representations. In: International Conference on Machine Learning, (ICML) (2020)
6. Chen, T., Kornblith, S., Swersky, K., Norouzi, M., Hinton, G.E.: Big self-supervised models are strong semi-supervised learners. In: Advances in Neural Information Processing Systems (NIPS) (2020)
7. Chen, Y., et al.: AE-Net: Fine-grained sketch-based image retrieval via attention-enhanced network. Pattern Recognition(PR) (2022)
8. Eitz, M., Hildebrand, K., Boubekeur, T., Alexa, M.: An evaluation of descriptors for large-scale image retrieval from sketched feature lines. Comput. Graph. **34**(5), 482–498 (2010)
9. Felzenszwalb, P.F., Girshick, R.B., McAllester, D., Ramanan, D.: Object detection with discriminatively trained part-based models. IEEE Trans. Pattern Anal. Mach. Intell. (TPAMI) **32**(9), 1627–1645 (2010)
10. He, K., Zhang, X., Ren, S., Sun, J.: Deep residual learning for image recognition. In: Computer Vision and Pattern Recognition (CVPR) (2016)
11. Hu, R., Collomosse, J.: A performance evaluation of gradient field hog descriptor for sketch based image retrieval. Computer Vision and Image Understanding (CVIU) (2013)
12. Hu, R., Wang, T., Collomosse, J.: A bag-of-regions approach to sketch-based image retrieval. In: IEEE International Conference on Image Processing (ICIP) (2011)
13. Huang, G., Liu, Z., van der Maaten, L., Weinberger, K.Q.: Densely connected convolutional networks. In: Computer Vision and Pattern Recognition (CVPR), pp. 2261–2269 (2017)
14. Kato, T., Kurita, T., Otsu, N., Hirata, K.: A sketch retrieval method for full color image database-query by visual example. In: IAPR International Conference on Pattern Recognition (ICPR), pp. 530–533 (1992)
15. Li, Y., Hospedales, T.M., Song, Y.Z., Gong, S.: Intra-category sketch-based image retrieval by matching deformable part models. In: British Machine Vision Conference (BMVC), pp. 115.1-115.12 (2014)
16. Lin, H., Fu, Y., Lu, P., Gong, S., Xue, X., Jiang, Y.G.: TC-Net for iSBIR: triplet classification network for instance-level sketch based image retrieval. In: ACM International Conference on Multimedia (ACM MM) (2019)

17. Ling, Z., Xing, Z., Li, J., Niu, L.: Multi-level region matching for fine-grained sketch-based image retrieval. In: ACM International Conference on Multimedia (ACM MM) (2022)
18. Liu, L., Shen, F., Shen, Y., Liu, X., Shao, L.: Deep sketch hashing: fast free-hand sketch-based image retrieval. In: Computer Vision and Pattern Recognition (CVPR), pp. 2862–2871 (2017)
19. Liu, Q., Xie, L., Wang, H., Yuille, A.: Semantic-aware knowledge preservation for zero-shot sketch-based image retrieval. In: ICCV (2019)
20. Noroozi, M., Favaro, P.: Unsupervised learning of visual representations by solving jigsaw puzzles. In: European Conference on Computer Vision (ECCV) (2016)
21. van den Oord, A., Li, Y., Vinyals, O.: Representation learning with contrastive predictive coding. CoRR abs/1807.03748 (2018)
22. Pang, K., et al.: Generalising fine-grained sketch-based image retrieval. In: Computer Vision and Pattern Recognition (CVPR), pp. 677–686 (2019)
23. Pang, K., Yang, Y., Hospedales, T.M., Xiang, T., Song, Y.: Solving mixed-modal jigsaw puzzle for fine-grained sketch-based image retrieval. In: Computer Vision and Pattern Recognition (CVPR) (2020)
24. Peng, C., Gao, X., Wang, N., Li, J.: Face recognition from multiple stylistic sketches: scenarios, datasets, and evaluation. Pattern Recognit. **84**, 262–272 (2018)
25. Radenovic, F., Tolias, G., Chum, O.: CNN image retrieval learns from bow: unsupervised fine-tuning with hard examples. In: Proceedings of the European Conference on Computer Vision (ECCV), pp. 3–20 (2016)
26. Radenovic, F., Tolias, G., Chum, O.: Deep shape matching. In: European Conference on Computer Vision (ECCV), pp. 751–767 (2018)
27. Ronneberger, O., Fischer, P., Brox, T.: U-Net: convolutional networks for biomedical image segmentation. In: Navab, N., Hornegger, J., III, W.M.W., Frangi, A.F. (eds.) Medical Image Computing and Computer-Assisted Intervention MICCAI, vol. 9351, pp. 234–241 (2015)
28. Saavedra, J.M., Barrios, J.M., Orand, S.: Sketch based image retrieval using learned keyshapes (LKS). In: British Machine Vision Conference (BMVC), pp. 164.1-164.11 (2015)
29. Sangkloy, P., Burnell, N., Ham, C., Hays, J.: The sketchy database: learning to retrieve badly drawn bunnies. ACM Transactions on Graphics (TOG) (2016)
30. Schaefer, S., McPhail, T., Warren, J.D.: Image deformation using moving least squares. ACM Trans. Graph. **25**, 533–540 (2006)
31. Seddati, O., Dupont, S., Saïd, M.: Quadruplet networks for sketch-based image retrieval. In: ACM International Conference on Multimedia (ACM MM) (2017)
32. Song, J., Song, Y.Z., Xiang, T., Hospedales, T., Xiang, R.: Deep multi-task attribute-driven ranking for fine-grained sketch-based image retrieval. In: British Machine Vision Conference (BMVC), vol. 1, p. 3 (2016)
33. Song, J., Yu, Q., Song, Y.Z., Xiang, T., Hospedales, T.M.: Deep spatial-semantic attention for fine-grained sketch-based image retrieval. In: International Conference on Computer Vision (ICCV), pp. 5551–5560 (2017)
34. Szegedy, C., et al.: Going deeper with convolutions. In: Computer Vision and Pattern Recognition (CVPR), pp. 1–9 (2015)
35. Szegedy, C., Vanhoucke, V., Ioffe, S., Shlens, J., Wojna, Z.: Rethinking the inception architecture for computer vision. In: Computer Vision and Pattern Recognition (CVPR), pp. 2818–2826 (2016)
36. Xu, P., et al.: SketchMate: deep hashing for million-scale human sketch retrieval. In: Computer Vision and Pattern Recognition (CVPR), pp. 8090–8098 (2018)

37. Xu, P., et al.: Instance-level coupled subspace learning for fine-grained sketch-based image retrieval. In: Proceedings of the European Conference on Computer Vision (ECCV), pp. 19–34 (2016)
38. Yanfei, W., Fei, H., Yuejie, Z., Rui, F., Tao, Z., Weiguo, F.: Deep cascaded cross-modal correlation learning for fine-grained sketch-based image retrieval. Pattern Recognition(PR) (2019)
39. Yelamarthi, S.K., Reddy, S.K., Mishra, A., Mittal, A.: A zero-shot framework for sketch based image retrieval. In: ECCV (2018)
40. Yu, A., Grauman, K.: Fine-grained visual comparisons with local learning. In: Computer Vision and Pattern Recognition (CVPR), pp. 192–199 (2014)
41. Yu, Q., Liu, F., Song, Y.Z., Xiang, T., Hospedales, T.M., Loy, C.C.: Sketch me that shoe. In: Computer Vision and Pattern Recognition (CVPR) (2016)
42. Yu, Q., Yang, Y., Liu, F., Song, Y.Z., Xiang, T., Hospedales, T.M.: Sketch-a-Net: a deep neural network that beats humans. Int. J. Comput. Vis. (IJCV) **122**(3), 411–425 (2017)
43. Zhu, H., Long, M., Wang, J., Cao, Y.: Deep hashing network for efficient similarity retrieval. In: Proceedings of the AAAI Conference on Artificial Intelligence (AAAI), pp. 2415–2421 (2016)
44. Zhu, M., Chen, C., Wang, N., Tang, J., Bao, W.: Gradually focused fine-grained sketch-based image retrieval. PLoS ONE **14**(5), e0217168 (2019)

Identifying Hard Noise in Long-Tailed Sample Distribution

Xuanyu Yi[1]([⊠]), Kaihua Tang[1], Xian-Sheng Hua[2], Joo-Hwee Lim[3],
and Hanwang Zhang[1]

[1] Nanyang Technological University, Singapore, Singapore
xuanyu001@e.ntu.edu.sg, kaihua.tang@ntu.edu.sg, hanwangzhang@ntu.edu.sg
[2] Damo Academy, Alibaba Group, Hangzhou, China
[3] Institute for Infocomm Research, Singapore, Singapore
joohwee@i2r.a-star.edu.sg

Abstract. Conventional de-noising methods rely on the assumption that all samples are independent and identically distributed, so the resultant classifier, though disturbed by noise, can still easily identify the noises as the outliers of training distribution. However, the assumption is unrealistic in large-scale data that is inevitably long-tailed. Such imbalanced training data makes a classifier less discriminative for the tail classes, whose previously "easy" noises are now turned into "hard" ones—they are almost as outliers as the clean tail samples. We introduce this new challenge as Noisy Long-Tailed Classification (NLT). Not surprisingly, we find that most de-noising methods fail to identify the hard noises, resulting in significant performance drop on the three proposed NLT benchmarks: ImageNet-NLT, Animal10-NLT, and Food101-NLT. To this end, we design an iterative noisy learning framework called Hard-to-Easy (H2E). Our bootstrapping philosophy is to first learn a classifier as noise identifier *invariant* to the class and context distributional changes, reducing "hard" noises to "easy" ones, whose removal further improves the invariance. Experimental results show that our H2E outperforms state-of-the-art de-noising methods and their ablations on long-tailed settings while maintaining a stable performance on the conventional balanced settings. Datasets and codes are available at https://github.com/yxymessi/H2E-Framework.

Keywords: Denoising · Long-tailed classification · Debiasing

1 Introduction

Any visual model should learn to co-exist with noise because any real-world dataset is imperfect [33]. During data collection, noise such as sensory failure (*e.g.*, low-quality or corrupted images) and human error (*e.g.*, mislabeling or

Supplementary Information The online version contains supplementary material available at https://doi.org/10.1007/978-3-031-19809-0_42.

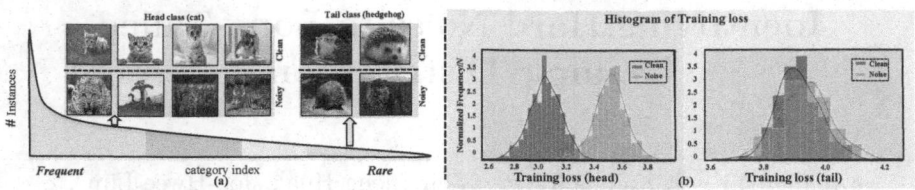

Fig. 1. (a) Large-scale datasets are both long-tailed and noisy. For instance, a head category "cat" may contain noisy samples such as "leopard" and "cartoon tiger" while noise like "porcupine" and "spiny horse" in tail category "hedgehog" (b) The identification of noise based on classifier confidence (or training loss) is no longer applicable in tail classes for most de-noise algorithms

ambiguous annotation) may hurt model training. In general, noise can be understood as a small population of training samples whose image contents differ from the ground-truth classes [13]. Therefore, if the data is independent and identically distributed (IID) regardless of class [12,36,38], noise samples can be identified as the outliers of the classifier confidence [8,9,15]. Specifically, we first learn the classifier on noisy data, then identify the noises as outliers, and finally remove them for a cleaner data that improves the classifier—a virtuous cycle [25,52]. In particular, we term the noise that can be identified as outliers as "easy" noise.

On a dataset with the balanced number of diverse training samples per class—the conventional settings as in most de-noise literature [10,25,32]—the IID assumption is easy to be satisfied. The key reason is that such dataset can guarantee a robust classifier that only focuses on the context-invariant class feature (or causal feature) [3,34,37,45]. Therefore, after learning to exclude all the varying contexts (non-causal features), the class features of clean and noisy samples are indeed different. For example, even if the noise is as tricky as a "leopard" sample mislabeled as "cat" that is visually similar to "leopard", after removing the context, "cat" feature is still different from "leopard" feature, who is an "easy" outlier of "cat". So, the premise of the IID assumption is the disentanglement of the class and context features.

However, should a dataset be at scale, long-tailed distribution will be inevitable [23,55], and thus disentangling class and context becomes challenging. The reasons are due to the following two folds that make the classifier dependent on **class prior** and **context distribution**. *First*, as head has more samples than tail, the classifier will be biased to head [44]. *Second*, head samples have more diverse contexts than tail, *i.e.*, contexts are not shared by all the classes and some contexts are unique to certain tail classes due to sample scarcity. So, the resultant classifier fails to learn context-invariant class features, but entangling context with class [46]. As shown in Fig. 1(a), the "spine" context is highly correlated to "hedgehog" and thus "spine" is a confusing context to mis-recognize the noise "porcupine" and "spiny horse" as "hedgehog". Thus the long-tailed distribution will turn "easy" noise into "hard", especially for the tail classes. Figure 1(b) illustrate such an example: the noises in tail class are almost as outliers as the tail samples. We leave a more detailed analysis in Sect. 3.

In this paper, we present a new challenge for noisy learning at scale, called Noisy Long-Tailed classification (NLT), which unifies the long-tailed distribution with realistic noisy data, completing the pioneering work with only synthetic noise on imbalanced data [6,21,50]. For rigorous and reproducible evaluations in the community, we introduce three benchmarks: ImageNet-NLT, Animal10-NLT, and Food101-NLT, with various noise and imbalance ratio for comprehensive diagnosis (Sect. 5). Not surprisingly, most of the existing de-noise methods degrade significantly on the benchmarks, especially for those who heavily rely on outlier detection [19,25,51,52].

One may wonder if we could first learn a balanced classifier on the noisy data by using long-tailed classification methods [20,44,56], and then apply the conventional outlier detection for noise identification. The answer is "No" because those methods can only mitigate the class bias but not the context bias in long-tailed data. Figure 2 demonstrates that with the increase of noise ratio, the performance of a SOTA long-tailed method [31] decreases significantly.

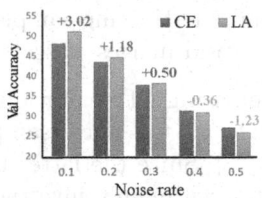

Fig. 2. The comparison of CE (cross-entropy) [39] and Logit-Adjustment [31] in CIFAR-100 with different noise ratios.

To this end, we propose an iterative Hard-to-Easy (H2E) framework for NLT. It has two stages: 1) A noise identifier that is invariant to the class and context distributional change caused by long-tailed distribution (Sect. 4.1). Such invariance can reduce "hard" noises to "easy" ones. Specifically, we sample three data distribution: long-tailed, balanced, and reversed long-tailed, as three context environments, and then apply Invariant Risk Minimization (IRM) [3] to learn a long-tailed classifier as the noise identifier invariant to these environments. Note that this stage is iterative as "clearner" data improves training better backbones. 2) Thanks to the noise identifier, we can eventually learn a robust classifier.

Our contributions are summarized as follows:

- We present the task: Noisy Long-Tailed classification (NLT) with non-synthetic real-world noises. NLT is challenging because it turns "easy" noises into "hard" ones that cannot be identified by prior work.
- We propose a strong NLT baseline: Hard-to-Easy (H2E) noisy learning framework. The success of H2E is based on learning a noise identifier invariant to the class and context changes introduced by long-tailed data.
- We introduce three NLT benchmarks: ImageNet-NLT, Animal10-NLT, and Food101-NLT. Extensive experimental results on them show the limitations of existing de-noise method and the potential of learning invariance for noisy learning.

2   Related Work

Long-Tailed Classification. Most existing long-tailed methods can be categorized into three types: 1) class-wise re-balancing using re-sampling strategies [20,56], re-weighted losses [17,35,40], and post-hoc adjustments [31,44], 2) data augmentation [11,27], and 3) model ensembling [47,54]. Since the latter two aim to boost the overall performance by directly increasing the model capability, which is generally suitable for all classification tasks, rather than focusing on tackling the imbalance between head and tail, we mainly focus on the class-wise re-balancing methods in this paper. Besides, the performance of conventional long-tailed algorithms may significantly degrade in the noisy environment, as they assume the training samples to be annotated correctly, which is impractical in real-world images at scale.

Noisy Learning. The previous learning with noise algorithms can be summarized into 1) the noisy sample selection [15,19,25] and 2) the regularization [1,22,28]. Since the latter methods are generally applicable for all classification tasks, we mainly investigate the former in this paper, as they are more related to the proposed H2E framework. Most of the noisy sample selection methods filter out noisy samples by adopting the *small-loss trick*, which treats samples with small training losses as correct-annotated. In particular, Co-teaching [15] trains two networks simultaneously where each network selects small-loss samples in a mini-batch to train the other. Beta Mixture Model (BMM) [2] separates the clean and noise samples during training based on the loss value of each sample. Similarly, Divide-Mix [25] fits a Gaussian mixture model on per-sample loss distribution to divide the training samples into clean set and noisy set. However, in the existence of the class imbalance, most of these methods may not work well since the training loss converges easier in major classes than minor classes, resulting in the risk of discarding most samples in the minor classes.

3   Noisy Long-Tailed Classification

The classification of an image x as class c can be defined as predicting $p(y = c|x)$ based on a dataset of image and ground-truth label pairs $\{(x, y)\}$ [14], where the noise is caused by the wrong label assignment $\widetilde{y} \to x$ ($\widetilde{y} \neq y$). By Bayes theorem [4], we can decompose the predictive model as $p(y = c|x) = \frac{p(x|y=c) \cdot p(y=c)}{p(x)}$, where $p(y = c)$ is the class distribution, $p(x)$ is the marginal distribution of images. In the independent and identical distribution (IID) assumption of uniform $p(x)$ and $p(y = c)$, it is relatively easy to obtain an *ideal* noise identifier: the classifier $p(y = c|x)$ *per se*, which will be explained later.

Unfortunately, the IID assumption is not practical in general as large-scale dataset is usually imbalanced in not only class distribution, but also context distribution. We assume that any image x is generated by a set of hidden semantics $z = \{z_1, z_2, z_3, ...\}$, which includes two disjoint subsets: class-specific attributes

z_c (*e.g.*, the cat-like shape in the "cat" category) and context-specific environmental attributes z_e (*e.g.*, the fur color). So, we can further decompose the predictive model $p(y = c|x = (z_c, z_e))$ as follows:

$$p(y = c|z_c, z_e) = \frac{p(z_c|y = c)}{p(z_c, z_e)} \cdot \overbrace{p(z_e|y = c, z_c)}^{context\ bias} \cdot \overbrace{p(y = c)}^{class\ bias}. \tag{1}$$

From Eq. (1), the noise identifier $p(y = c|z_c, z_e)$ is affected by the variations of 1) class bias $p(y = c)$: the distribution shift caused by class imbalance, and 2) context bias $p(z_e|y = c, z_c)$: spurious correlation[1] between context attributes and class. Such negative effect motivates us to introduce the concept of "hard" and "easy" noise, which has not been addressed in the de-noise literature yet. **Noise** is defined as training samples with a mismatch between the ground-truth label y and class-specific (causal) features z_c.

"Easy" Noise could be easily detected by the ideal identifier $p(y = c|z_c, z_e)$, regardless of the influence by $p(z_e|y = c, z_c) \cdot p(y = c)$. That is to say z_e is independent of y, *i.e.*, $p(z_e|y = c, z_c)$ approaching $p(z_e|z_c)$ and z_e can be eliminated by $p(z_e|z_c)/p(z_e, z_c) = 1/p(z_c)$. Meanwhile, $p(y = c)$ is uniformly distributed under IID assumption in the conventional de-noise setting [15,19,25]. Since the above $1/p(z_c)$ and $p(y = c)$ could be both considered as constant, noise can be easily identified because $p(y = c|z_c, z_e)$ is directly calculated through the observation of $p(z_c|y = c)$.

"Hard" Noise is elusive as $p(y = c|z_c, z_e)$ is affected by the negative impact of $p(z_e|y = c, z_c) \cdot p(y = c)$, leading to erroneous abnormal identification.

The proposed Noisy Long-Tailed classification aims to learn from the training data that possesses two joint phenomena: 1) the class distribution $p(y = c)$ is long-tailed; 2) part of the training samples (noise) are wrongly annotated. Some previous "easy" noises are thus turned into "hard" ones, resulting in that most of the conventional noise removal algorithms [2,9,33] are no longer reliable in NLT since the outlier samples can be either caused by the noisy labels with lower $p(z_c|y = c)$ or rare contexts and classes with lower $p(z_e|y = c, z_c) \cdot p(y = c)$. Therefore, we propose the following Hard-to-Easy framework, aiming to learn a fair noise identifier invariant to the change of $p(z_e|y = c, z_c) \cdot p(y = c)$, so the "hard" noises can thus be converted into "easy" ones.

4 Hard-to-Easy (H2E) Framework

As shown in Algorithm 1, our H2E framework is composed of two stages with an initial warm-up stage, where **Stage 1** (Sect. 4.1) obtains a fairer identifier

---

[1] For a thought example based on Eq. (1), if a class-specific attribute "body" and a context-specific attribute "spine" have strong co-occurrence under the "hedgehog" class, the wrong annotation "hedgehog" of a "porcupine" image with "spine" could be imperceptible for the identifier due to the high spurious correspondence $p(z_e = $ "*spine*"$|y = $ "*hedgehog*", $z_c = $ "*body*").

Algorithm 1. H2E Framework

Input: NLT-Dataset $\{(x, y)\}$, # Iteration T, Confidence Threshold τ.
1: **Stage0** (Input: $\{\{(x, y)\}, \tau\}$) → Output: $\{\Phi_0(\cdot), f_0(\cdot)\}$
        Initialize backbone $\Phi_0(\cdot)$, linear classifier $f_0(\cdot)$ by Part A in Appendix.

2: **for** $t = 1, 2, \ldots T$ **do**
3:       **Stage1** (Input: $\{\{(x, y)\}, \Phi_{t-1}(\cdot), f_{t-1}(\cdot), g_{t-1}(\cdot)\}$) → Output: $\{\Phi_t(\cdot), f_t(\cdot), g_t(\cdot)\}$
          // Learn Noise Identifier.
          $\{e_1, e_2, \cdots\}$ generated multiple environments with Sec. 4.1.
          $g_t(\cdot) \leftarrow g_{t-1}(\cdot)$ by learning parameters w through IRM with Eq.(2).
          // Easy Noise Removal.
          $\{(\tilde{x}, \tilde{y})\} \leftarrow \{(x, y)\}$ by commensurate Mixup with Eq.(3).
          $\Phi_t(\cdot) \leftarrow \Phi_{t-1}(\cdot)$, $f_t(\cdot) \leftarrow f_{t-1}(\cdot)$ by fine-tuning on $\{(\tilde{x}, \tilde{y})\}$.
4: **end for**

5: **Stage2** (Input: $\{\{(x, y)\}, \Phi_T(\cdot), f_T(\cdot), g_T(\cdot)\}$) → Output: updated $f_T(\cdot)$
       // Robust classifier tackling class imbalance.
       Update $f_T(\cdot)$ by reweighted Balance-softmax from Eq.(4).
Output: The final robust model $f_T(\Phi_T(\cdot))$.

---

by turning "hard" noise into "easy" through invariant muti-environment learning, thus obtaining a "cleaner" representation by removing the identified "easy" noise. An iterative virtuous circle is conducted to progressively identify "harder" noises and learn better representations. Eventually, in **Stage 2** (Sect. 4.2), a long-tailed loss, *e.g.*, a balanced loss [35], is attached to the clean backbone from Stage 1 to learn a robust classifier.

4.1 Stage 1: Hard-to-Easy Noise Converter

Input: An initialized model containing backbone $\Phi(\cdot)$ and projection layer $f(\cdot)$, the training dataset $\{(x, y)\}$.

Output: A fair noise identifier $g(\cdot)$ invariant to environments, a fine-tuned cleaner backbone $\Phi(\cdot)$ and projection layer $f(\cdot)$.

As we discussed in Sect. 3, the imbalanced $p(z_e | y = c, z_c) \cdot p(y = c)$ turns "easy" noise into "hard", since the noise identifier $p(z_c | y = c)$ cannot be disentangled from the context and class bias. To better adapt to the long-tailed classification, the proposed noise identifier combines the previous LWS [20] and Logit Adjustment [31] classifiers as $g(\cdot) = f(\Phi(\cdot)) - w \cdot \log \pi$, where $\Phi(\cdot)$ is the frozen backbone extracting the image feature; $f(\cdot)$ projects feature vectors to the logit space; w is learnable parameters; π is the class distribution $p(y)$. However, the above $g(\cdot)$ can only remove the class bias $p(y = c)$ but not the context bias $p(z_e | y = c, z_c)$.

Intuitively, the crux for mitgating context bias $p(z_e | y = c, z_c)$ is to directly eliminate the impact of certain context z_e distribution, making $g(\cdot)$ an invariant identifier by capturing the class-specific attributes z_c. Inspired by Invariant Risk Minimization (IRM) [3], we construct a set of environments $\mathcal{E} = \{e_1, e_2, \ldots\}$, ensuring the diverse $p(z_e | y = c, z_c)$ in different environments. Then, IRM essentially regularizes $g(\cdot)$ to be equally optimal across environments with different context-distribution, thus removing the influence of context bias. The objective function of the proposed noise identifier invariant across $\mathcal{E}$ is thus defined as follows:

$$\min_g \sum_{e \in \mathcal{E}} R^e(x, y; f(\Phi(\cdot)), g) \tag{2}$$
$$\text{subject to } g \in \arg\min_g R^e(x, y; f(\Phi(\cdot)), g) \text{ for all } e \in \mathcal{E},$$

where $R^e(x, y; f(\Phi(\cdot)), g)$ is the risk under environment e; $g \in \arg\min_g R^e(x, y; M, g)$ for all $e \in \mathcal{E}$ means that the invariant identifier g should minimize the risk under all environments simultaneously. The implementation of IRM loss is in Appendix. Detailed process of Hard-to-Easy transformation is as below:

Environment Construction. A set of diverse environments $\{e_1, e_2, ...\}$ are constructed which ensure the variance of $p(z_e|y = c, z_c)$. The criterion of ideal environment construction is the orthogonality of context distribution; however, considering the computation consumption, we only construct three learning environments with classical sampling strategies and provide further ablations of the settings of environment construction in Sect. 5.4. As illustrated in Fig. 3, each learning envi-

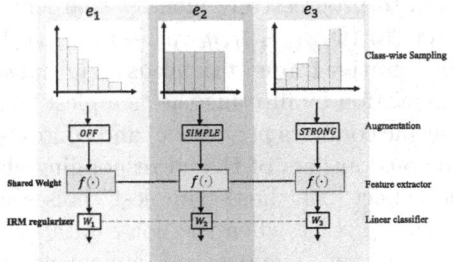

Fig. 3. Multi-environment with diverse class and context distributions are built, then an IRM optimization [3] is applied to obtain an invariant identifier across environments

ronments adopts a different class-wise sampling strategy: 1) the instance-balanced sampler maintains the raw distribution of dataset, 2) the class-balanced sampler ensures the equal probability of being selected for each class, and 3) the class-reversed sampler aims to over-correct the imbalanced $p(y)$ by deliberately picking samples of class $y = c$ with the probability negatively correlated with class size. Then, in order to generate diverse distributions of $p(z_e|y = c, z_c)$ to avoid the over-sampling that generates a lot of duplicate samples (especially in tail categories), we adopt different data augmentation methods for each environment: e_3 with class-reversed sampler is equipped with the **"Strong"** augmentation [11] as it has the most number of duplicate samples, e_2 with class-balanced sampler uses **"Simple"** Random Flip and Resized Crop, as it has less duplicates, and e_1 is without augmentation (**"OFF"**) as it has no duplicate samples.

Easy Noise Removal. After obtaining the robust noise identifier $g(\cdot)$, in order to learn a better backbone with less contamination from the noise and prevent those clean images from being mistakenly penalized, we adopt a soft noisy removal strategy that uses Mixup [53] to dynamically augment samples according to the confidence generated by the noise identifier $g(\cdot)$. Specifically, we fine-tune $\Phi(\cdot)$ and $f(\cdot)$ with the generation of training pair $(\tilde{x}_{ij}, \tilde{y}_{ij})$ through conducting linear mixture of each two images as follows:

$$\tilde{x}_{ij} = \delta_{ij}x_i + (1 - \delta_{ij})x_j,$$
$$\tilde{y}_{ij} = \delta_{ij}y_i + (1 - \delta_{ij})y_j,$$
(3)

where x_i and x_j are two images with labels y_i and y_j, respectively; δ_{ij} is the denoise weight in proportion to the confidences $g(x_i)/g(x_j)$. Intuitively, the sample with a higher probability of being noise will have smaller weight in the mixed image $\tilde{x}_{ij}$. Such commensurate Mixup strategy alleviates the noise memorization effect [26] and prevent the overfitting of the already-detected easy noises. Moreover, the long-tailed effect can also be better eliminated by the Mixup, compared with other noise identification methods [15,19,25].

Iterative Refinement. As both the noise identifier and the easy noise removal can benefit from the improvement of each other, we introduce an iterative framework to progressively identify "harder" noises and learn better representations, refers to $(\Phi_{t-1}, f_{t-1}, g_{t-1}) \rightarrow (\Phi_t, f_t, g_t)$ in Algorithm 1. It's worth noting that the iterative framework needs an initial step to learn a relatively pure feature representation by filtering the "simplest" noises, i.e., those samples that both class-specific contents $p(z_c|y = c)$ and context-specific environments $p(z_e|y = c, z_c)$ are obvious outliers of the corresponding class $y = c$. Due to the model memorization effect [26], those "simplest" noises can be identified by a commonly adopted warm-up stage when the noisy data haven't affected the learning of generalized patterns yet. The detailed implementation of this step is in Appendix.

4.2   Stage 2: Robust Classifier

Input : The last-iteration model $f(\Phi(\cdot))$ in Stage 1, noise identifier $g(\cdot)$, and training dataset $\{(x, y)\}$.
Output : The final robust model $f(\Phi(\cdot))$.

For the sake of simplicity of symbol, we omit all the subscript in this section. After obtaining purified representation from the iterative H2E, we assume the network has already modeled the underline $p(x|y = c)$. Therefore, we only need to tackle the class bias $p(y = c)$ in the cleaner data by any existing long-tailed classification algorithms. Without loss of generality, we resort to the balanced softmax loss [35], which can be defined as: $\mathcal{L}(x, y) = -y \log CE\left(f(\Phi(x)) + \log \pi\right)$, where CE denotes the cross-entropy loss; π is the distribution of $p(y)$ in the training data; $f(\cdot)$ is the learnable linear classifier initialized from the last-iteration in Stage 1. Noted that the noise identifier $g(\cdot)$ is not directly selected as the initialized classifier since there is a trade-off between the robustness of noise identification and performance of classification.

Besides, to eliminate all the noises detected by $g(\cdot)$, the final robust classifier is thus optimized by re-weighting all samples from the training data according to $\theta(x, y)$ as follows:

$$\mathcal{L}_{overall} = \frac{1}{N} \sum_{(x,y)} \theta(x, y) \cdot \mathcal{L}(x, y),$$
(4)

where N refers to the batch size, $\theta(x, y)$ is the weight parameter generated by $g_I(\cdot)$; $\theta(x, y) = p(y|x)$ when $p(y|x)$ is larger than any other $p(y'|x)$ and $\theta(x, y) = \eta$, a hyper-parameter threshold otherwise in order to make noisy samples contribute less to the loss.

5   Experiments

5.1   Benchmarks

We constructed three benchmarks for Noisy Long-Tailed (NLT) classification using both synthetic and realistic noise with class imbalance to imitate the real-world dataset at scale. As conventions [18], we call them **blue** (synthetic) and **red** (realistic), respectively. Our benchmarks: ImageNet-NLT, Animal10-NLT and Food101-NLT are built on top of three standard image classification dataset : Red Mini-ImageNet [18], Animal-10N [41] and Food-101N [24].

Dataset Construction. During the dataset construction, we adopted the standard rule of first building a balanced but noisy dataset and then transforming them into the long-tailed distribution to simulate the real distribution of noisy labels. To be specific, as for ImageNet-NLT, we augmented the vanilla Mini-ImageNet by adding correct-annotated samples from ImageNet with the same taxonomy. Then we followed the construction of Red Mini-ImageNet to replace ρ proportion of the original training images with noisy images from the web where ρ denotes the noise rate that is uniform across classes. Blue noises in ImageNet-NLT were generated by randomly sampling ρ training images from each class and substituting their labels uniformly drawn from other classes. The above process is not necessary for the construction of Animal10-NLT and Food101-NLT since their original datasets have already contained various real-world noises. After obtaining the balanced but noisy datasets, we simulated the long-tailed distribution in the real-world following the same setting as LDAM [7] to clip the size of each class: the long-tailed imbalance follows an exponential decay in the number of training samples across different classes. The imbalance ratio η denotes the ratio between the size of the maximum and minimum class.

Before sampling the long-tailed subsets of the original datasets, the balanced Red Mini-ImageNet contains 60,000 images from the original Mini-ImageNet [42] and 54,400 images with incorrect labels collected from the web. Animal-10N is a real-world noisy dataset of human-annotated online images of ten bewildering animals, with 50,000 training and 5,000 testing images in an estimated 8 % noise rate. Food-101N is a webly noisy food dataset containing 310,000 images from Google, Yelp, Bing and other search engines using the Food-101 [5] taxonomy. Table 1 summarizes our benchmarks and further description are in Appendix.

Table 1. Overview of three NLT benchmarks with controlled noise level and imbalance ratio

Dataset	#Class	Train size	Val size	Noise levels(%)	Imbalance ratio
Red ImageNet-NLT	100	31,817	5,000	10,20,30	0,20
Blue ImageNet-NLT	100	31,817	5,000	10,20,30	0,20
Food101-NLT	101	63,460	25,000	≃8.0	20,50,100,200
Animal10-NLT	10	17,023	5,000	≃18.4	20,50,100,200

5.2 Implementation Details

We compared the proposed H2E with previous state-of-the-art methods in both fields of learning with noise and long-tailed classification. Moreover, since noisy long-tailed classification is rarely explored and the number of algorithms designed to fit our setting is small, we further proposed several joint algorithms that combine both long-tailed algorithms and de-noise methods for ablation.

LT Baselines: 1) LWS [20] decouples the learning procedure into representation learning and classifier fine-tuning, that re-scales the magnitude of classifier after obtaining the model capable of recognizing all classes; 2) The post-hoc logit adjustment (LA) [31] is another widely-used algorithm to compensate the long-tailed distribution by adding a class-dependent offset to each logit; 3) BBN [56] uses a framework of Bilateral-Branch network with a cumulative learning strategy; 5) LDAM [7] is a label-distribution-aware margin loss designed to re-balance the distribution.

De-noise Baselines: 1) Co-teaching+ [52] trains two networks then predict first, and selects small-loss data to teach its peer by keeping the data with prediction disagreement only; 2) Nested Co-teaching (N-Coteaching) [10] conducts adaptive data compression to train two separate networks and is further fine-tuned with Co-teaching (iii). 3) Co-Learning [43] further predigests these co-training methods through a shared feature encoder; 4) MentorMix [18] minimizes the empirical risk using curriculum learning to overcome both synthetic and realistic web noises; 5) Normalized Loss (NL) [30] combines passive and active loss to prevent over-fitting to noise labels. 6) Confident Learning (CL) [33] is a muti-round learning method which refines the selected set of clean samples by repeating the training round. (7) Two well-known SOTA denoise algorithms JoCoR [48] and DivideMix [25] are also included.

Joint Baselines: 1) HAR [6] is the first algorithm to tackle the long-tailed distribution with label noises (synthetic ones), that applies a Lipschitz regularizer with varying regularization to deal with noisy and rare examples in a unified way; 2) Co-teaching-WBL (Co-WBL) conducts a temperature weight to offset the tail classes in the procedure of Co-teaching [15] and fine-tunes with the balanced softmax loss [35]; 3) We also intuitively add Re-sampling strategy into the MentorMix [18], denoted as MentorMix-RS, to re-balance before curricu-

Fig. 4. The example of iterative hard-to-easy transformation on Red ImageNet-NLT, presenting H2E gradually detects harder noises and improve overall robustness

lum learning; 4) A distribution-robust loss function [7] and a noise-robust loss function [30] is also combined, denoted as LDAM+NL.

Experimental Details. ResNet-18 [16] backbone was adopted for all methods in ImageNet-NLT and Animal10-NLT, and ResNet-50 [16] for Food101-NLT. They were all trained *from scratch* by SGD with weight decay of 1×10^{-4} and momentum of 0.9. All models were implemented in PyTorch and on NVIDIA Tesla A100 GPUs for 200 epochs with batch size of 512, except for Co-teaching+ [52] and Co-teaching-WBL with the batch size of 256. The initial learning rate was set to 0.2 and the default learning rate decay strategy is Cosine Annealing scheduler except for [7,18,56], which we followed the original setting to apply the multi-step scheduler, and we also maintained the warm-up stage and their backbone variations based on the corresponding papers. It's worth noting that we reported the version of single iteration H2E as well for fair comparison, which is conducted straightforwardly with 200 epochs. Further experiment on the ablation of iteration is included in Appendix.

5.3 Main Results

Evaluation on ImageNet-NLT. We conducted extensive experiments on ImageNet-NLT with three different noise ratios including both synthetic noises and realistic web noises, denoted as blue noises and red noises, respectively, following the setting of Jiang *et al* [18]. Figure 4 presents that the iterative noise detection can better transfer hard noises into easy ones thus improving the model robustness step by step. We compared our method with several popular LT, de-noise baselines and a few joint baselines were also proposed in our experiments to intuitively combine LT algorithms with de-noise methods. As presented in Table 1, the proposed H2E consistently outperforms the baseline methods across different noise rates and noise types (red and blue). In particular, compared with MentorMix [18], which achieves the best performance among selected de-noise methods, H2E improves the test accuracy by 6.1% on average.

Table 2. The evaluation (Top-1 Accuracy%) on ImageNet-NLT: we reported both blue (synthetic) and red (realistic) noises with three different noise rates: 10%, 20%, and 30%. Experiments demonstrate the effectiveness of the proposed H2E on all settings. The reported H2E-iter has the same number of total epochs with others

Category	Methods	10% ρ		20% ρ		30% ρ	
		Red	Blue	Red	Blue	Red	Blue
Baseline	CE	54.36	45.80	50.20	40.66	46.90	34.80
Denoise	Co-teaching+ [52]	45.58	53.16	44.14	49.43	43.16	37.47
	CL [33]	52.44	48.26	51.42	44.23	48.62	38.21
	MentorMix [18]	59.26	54.60	55.18	50.20	54.68	45.84
	NL [30]	56.36	52.48	53.84	44.80	51.28	39.14
	Co-learning [43]	50.19	49.72	48.77	42.65	44.37	37.20
LT	LWS [20]	57.05	52.36	53.62	44.78	49.15	36.54
	LA [31]	58.92	51.34	54.50	45.24	51.94	37.86
	BBN [56]	57.83	52.24	54.88	45.76	51.58	41.35
	LDAM [7]	59.24	53.02	55.98	46.60	54.38	42.76
Joint	HAR [6]	57.14	53.24	54.04	47.14	52.13	43.92
	NL+LA	59.80	51.88	57.21	46.52	53.56	37.40
	Co-WBL	61.44	54.98	57.62	52.40	54.08	45.81
	LDAM+NL	60.06	52.90	56.24	48.14	54.03	43.62
	MentorMix-RS	62.20	55.44	56.14	52.85	55.91	48.27
Ours	H2E	64.86	58.12	60.92	55.84	58.38	51.52
	H2E-iter	**65.29**	**59.42**	**62.12**	**56.31**	**60.66**	**52.57**

Besides, we can see from Table 2 that vanilla long-tailed methods outperform de-noise baselines in most lower noisy situations, while their performance gap is narrowed in a higher noise level. Intriguingly, some de-noise methods such as CL [33] and Co-teaching+ [52] are built upon the strong assumption of class balance and highly rely on the *small-loss trick*, so their performance degrades dreadfully in NLT, even worse than Cross-Entropy in many cases. As for the combined methods, we intuitively followed the essence of de-noise and long-tailed algorithms, and proposed MentorMix-RS and Co-teaching-WBL that outperform their counterparts and each individual component in most cases. However, for other strategies such as NL+LA, the improvement is limited and unstable with the contradiction of their re-balance strategies.

Not surprisingly, when we compared results between the red and blue noise settings under the same ratios, all the methods perform much better in red than blue noise except for Co-teaching+ [52], which applies strong intervention on blue noises. This finding is consistent with Jiang *et al* [18] 's conclusion and extends it into a more realistic situation. We believe the underlying reason behind is that blue noises corrupted by label flipping hurts the representation of

Table 3. Evaluations (Top-1 Accuracy%) on Food101-NLT and Animal10-NLT

Dataset	Food101-NLT			Animal10-NLT		
Methods/ η	20	50	100	20	50	100
CE	57.21	49.94	44.71	66.10	59.94	53.02
NL [30]	60.13	53.42	46.29	48.20	33.46	22.08
N-Coteaching [10]	52.44	40.21	29.78	57.54	41.40	39.04
DivideMix [25]	69.46	57.15	42.80	72.43	65.77	47.60
Co-learning [43]	53.76	45.92	35.10	61.70	52.76	43.23
JoCoR [48]	49.07	32.98	33.49	51.29	44.02	37.19
LDAM [7]	61.35	59.29	48.61	75.40	72.82	**68.21**
LA [31]	62.81	55.42	52.30	69.08	67.78	61.89
BBN [56]	63.44	57.89	53.16	72.14	70.26	60.08
LWS [20]	61.29	54.42	51.10	71.16	69.35	62.40
CL +LA	50.16	42.18	39.13	54.14	46.23	41.92
HAR [6]	59.95	52.45	46.12	71.92	68.43	62.19
Co-teaching-WBL	58.04	52.12	53.97	72.43	71.06	66.60
H2E	**70.35**	**63.69**	**58.66**	**77.04**	**74.94**	66.58

the DNN more seriously than those open-set [49] and label-dependent red noises, which share more context-specific and class-related attributes. Further analysis of the combination of realistic noise and synthetic noise is given in Appendix.

Evaluation on Animal10-NLT and Food101-NLT. We further investigated the performance of H2E and other methods in Animal10-NLT and Food101-NLT with various imbalance ratios $\eta \in \{10, 20, 50\}$. As shown in Table 3, our method retains the most robust performance and outperforms other approaches in most cases as the imbalance ratio increase while most de-noise methods [10, 30] suffer from class imbalance and even perform worse than the Cross-Entropy. Long-tailed methods [7, 56] perform much better than de-noise methods in Animal10-NLT, attributes to the relatively low noise rate (estimated as 8%) and their specific design on network structures, e.g. cosine classifier in LDAM [7] and extra blocks in BBN [56]. Note that H2E is still comparable with state-of-art de-noise algorithms in a strictly balance training set, with 85.1% test accuracy in Animal-10N [41] and 73.4% test accuracy in Food-101N [24] from scratch.

5.4 Ablation Studies and Further Analysis

Q1: *Why H2E outperforms other methods in NLT?* To better diagnose the improvement of H2E, we followed [29] and further recorded test accuracy and the precision of noise identification on three splits of classes: Many-shot(the top 25%), Medium-shot(the middle 50%) and Few-shot(the last 25%).

A1: Specifically in Fig. 5(b), the proposed H2E surpasses MentorMix [18] and LDAM [7] in few-shot by 20 % and 8% on average, which concretely demonstrates the robustness of H2E under imbalance distribution. It is clear from Fig. 5(a) that considering the precision of noise detection, H2E outperforms all of the selected methods in tail classes, which highlights its power to identify hard noises. From these two aspects, we could give a conclusion: the higher performance of H2E indeed attributes to its comparatively better hard noise identification capability and less hurt on correct-annotated but rare samples, especially on tail classes.

Table 4. Ablation studies of **env**

Settings/ ρ		10%		20%		30%	
#env	Aug	Red	Blue	Red	Blue	Red	Blue
2		61.40	54.68	57.78	55.18	55.78	48.22
2	✓	62.15	55.70	59.66	55.38	56.02	49.10
3		62.79	57.40	60.64	55.06	57.14	49.38
3	✓	64.86	58.12	60.92	55.84	58.38	51.52
4		62.49	55.78	60.18	55.40	56.22	49.30
4	✓	65.38	56.52	60.42	55.96	57.56	49.78

Table 5. Effectiveness for each component

Component/ ρ		10%		20%		30%	
Stage1	Stage2	Red	Blue	Red	Blue	Red	Blue
CF	CE+RW	56.54	48.40	51.29	43.60	48.09	38.77
CF	H2E	63.90	56.10	60.08	54.76	57.80	49.30
LDAM	H2E	61.94	56.42	57.10	55.69	54.31	48.46
H2E	ERM+RW	60.20	57.02	58.54	50.94	56.27	46.24

Q2: *What impact performance of H2E considering environment construction?* We conducted two ablation experiments on ImageNet-NLT: one is to analyze the number of environments and the other is to unify the augmentation strategies in each environment to so-called "OFF" augmentation.

A2: From Table 4, we found out that the overall improvement is converged to the number of environments when $e > 2$; Moreover, H2E will averagely degrade by *1.14*% without handling the duplication in tail classes , *i.e.*, not augmentations, but it still largely outperforms other baselines in most settings comparing with the result in Table 2, which shows the power of the proposed H2E.

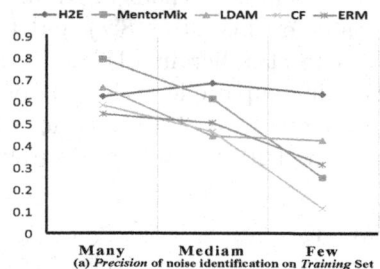
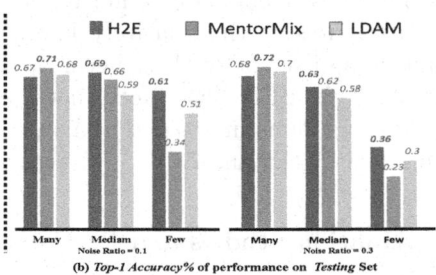

Fig. 5. (a) Evaluation(Precision) of noise identification capability on Blue ImageNet-NLT. The proposed H2E indeed significantly improves the Few-shot(tail) categories by better identifying hard noises. (b)Evaluations (Top-1 Accuracy%) on Red ImageNet-NLT. We compare test accuracy in Many, Medium and Few shots among different methods

Q3: *How effective is each individual component in H2E?* In Table 4, we replaced and modified each individual stage in H2E with other feasible methods to examine the effectiveness of the each stage.

A3: Considering a muti-stage framework, substituting any part of H2E caused the performance dropping to some extent. In detail, if we replace one component with other baselines, the Top-1 Accuracy will averagely degrade by *2.81%*.

Q4: *What's the justification of augmentation strategies in environment construction?*

A4: (1) All methods in Sect. 5 contains the so-called strong augmentation in the stage of data prepossessing for fair comparison, **so we don't take any unfair advantage**. (2) Different augmentations are introduced only to construct environments with context-wise distribution shift. It's directly derived from our formulation, so IRM can focus on class-specific attributes, making it easier to converge and avoid both class and context bias.

6 Conclusion

We presented a novel noisy learning algorithm, Hard-to-Easy (H2E) for Noisy Long-Tailed Classification (NLT). We motivated from the observation that the tail class confidence boundary between clean and noisy samples are not clear, rendering conventional noise identification methods ineffective. Our analysis shows that it is because the class and context imbalance in long-tailed data that turn the "easy" noises into "hard" ones. The highlight of H2E is that it learns a robust noise identifier invariant to the class and context environmental changes. On three newly proposed NLT benchmarks: ImageNet-NLT, Animal10-NLT, and Food101-NLT, we demonstrated that H2E significantly outperforms existing denoise methods, which do not take the imbalance into account. In future, we will conduct further analysis on NLT settings and more effective environment-invariant learning algorithms.

Acknowledgment. This project is partially supported by Alibaba-NTU Singapore Joint Research Institute (JRI), AI Singapore (AISG) Research Programme and the Agency for Science, Technology AND Research (A*STAR).

References

1. Amid, E., Warmuth, M.K., Anil, R., Koren, T.: Robust Bi-Tempered logistic loss based on Bregman divergences. arXiv preprint arXiv:1906.03361 (2019)
2. Arazo, E., Ortego, D., Albert, P., O'Connor, N., McGuinness, K.: Unsupervised label noise modeling and loss correction. In: International Conference on Machine Learning, pp. 312–321. PMLR (2019)
3. Arjovsky, M., Bottou, L., Gulrajani, I., Lopez-Paz, D.: Invariant risk minimization. arXiv preprint arXiv:1907.02893 (2019)
4. Bernardo, J.M., Smith, A.F.: Bayesian Theory, vol. 405. Wiley, Chichester (2009)

5. Bossard, L., Guillaumin, M., Van Gool, L.: Food-101 – mining discriminative components with random forests. In: Fleet, D., Pajdla, T., Schiele, B., Tuytelaars, T. (eds.) ECCV 2014. LNCS, vol. 8694, pp. 446–461. Springer, Cham (2014). https://doi.org/10.1007/978-3-319-10599-4_29

6. Cao, K., Chen, Y., Lu, J., Arechiga, N., Gaidon, A., Ma, T.: Heteroskedastic and imbalanced deep learning with adaptive regularization. arXiv preprint arXiv:2006.15766 (2020)

7. Cao, K., Wei, C., Gaidon, A., Arechiga, N., Ma, T.: Learning imbalanced datasets with label-distribution-aware margin loss. NeurIPS (2019)

8. Chen, P., Liao, B.B., Chen, G., Zhang, S.: Understanding and utilizing deep neural networks trained with noisy labels. In: International Conference on Machine Learning, pp. 1062–1070. PMLR (2019)

9. Chen, X., Gupta, A.: Webly supervised learning of convolutional networks. In: Proceedings of the IEEE International Conference on Computer Vision, pp. 1431–1439 (2015)

10. Chen, Y., Shen, X., Hu, S.X., Suykens, J.A.: Boosting co-teaching with compression regularization for label noise. In: Proceedings of the IEEE/CVF Conference on Computer Vision and Pattern Recognition, pp. 2688–2692 (2021)

11. Cubuk, E.D., Zoph, B., Shlens, J., Le, Q.V.: RandAugment: practical automated data augmentation with a reduced search space. In: Proceedings of the IEEE/CVF Conference on Computer Vision and Pattern Recognition Workshops, pp. 702–703 (2020)

12. Fawzi, A., Moosavi-Dezfooli, S.M., Frossard, P.: Robustness of classifiers: from adversarial to random noise. arXiv preprint arXiv:1608.08967 (2016)

13. Frénay, B., Verleysen, M.: Classification in the presence of label noise: a survey. IEEE Trans. Neural Netw. Learn. Syst. **25**(5), 845–869 (2013)

14. Goodfellow, I., et al.: Generative adversarial nets. NeurIPS (2014)

15. Han, B., et al.: Co-teaching: robust training of deep neural networks with extremely noisy labels. arXiv preprint arXiv:1804.06872 (2018)

16. He, K., Zhang, X., Ren, S., Sun, J.: Deep residual learning for image recognition. In: Proceedings of the IEEE Conference on Computer Vision and Pattern Recognition, pp. 770–778 (2016)

17. Jamal, M.A., Brown, M., Yang, M.H., Wang, L., Gong, B.: Rethinking class-balanced methods for long-tailed visual recognition from a domain adaptation perspective. In: Proceedings of the IEEE/CVF Conference on Computer Vision and Pattern Recognition, pp. 7610–7619 (2020)

18. Jiang, L., Huang, D., Liu, M., Yang, W.: Beyond synthetic noise: deep learning on controlled noisy labels. In: International Conference on Machine Learning, pp. 4804–4815. PMLR (2020)

19. Jiang, L., Zhou, Z., Leung, T., Li, L.J., Fei-Fei, L.: MentorNet: learning data-driven curriculum for very deep neural networks on corrupted labels. In: International Conference on Machine Learning, pp. 2304–2313. PMLR (2018)

20. Kang, B., et al.: Decoupling representation and classifier for long-tailed recognition. arXiv preprint arXiv:1910.09217 (2019)

21. Karthik, S., Revaud, J., Chidlovskii, B.: Learning from long-tailed data with noisy labels. arXiv preprint arXiv:2108.11096 (2021)

22. Kumar, H., Manwani, N., Sastry, P.: Robust learning of multi-label classifiers under label noise. In: Proceedings of the 7th ACM IKDD CoDS and 25th COMAD, pp. 90–97 (2020)

23. Lee, J., Kim, E., Lee, J., Lee, J., Choo, J.: Learning debiased representation via disentangled feature augmentation. arXiv preprint arXiv:2107.01372 (2021)

24. Lee, K.H., He, X., Zhang, L., Yang, L.: CleanNet: transfer learning for scalable image classifier training with label noise. In: Proceedings of the IEEE Conference on Computer Vision and Pattern Recognition, pp. 5447–5456 (2018)
25. Li, J., Socher, R., Hoi, S.C.: DivideMix: learning with noisy labels as semi-supervised learning. arXiv preprint arXiv:2002.07394 (2020)
26. Li, M., Soltanolkotabi, M., Oymak, S.: Gradient descent with early stopping is provably robust to label noise for overparameterized neural networks. In: International Conference on Artificial Intelligence and Statistics, pp. 4313–4324. PMLR (2020)
27. Liu, J., Sun, Y., Han, C., Dou, Z., Li, W.: Deep representation learning on long-tailed data: a learnable embedding augmentation perspective. In: CVPR (2020)
28. Liu, Y., Guo, H.: Peer loss functions: learning from noisy labels without knowing noise rates. In: International Conference on Machine Learning, pp. 6226–6236. PMLR (2020)
29. Liu, Z., Miao, Z., Zhan, X., Wang, J., Gong, B., Yu, S.X.: Large-scale long-tailed recognition in an open world. In: Proceedings of the IEEE/CVF Conference on Computer Vision and Pattern Recognition, pp. 2537–2546 (2019)
30. Ma, X., Huang, H., Wang, Y., Romano, S., Erfani, S., Bailey, J.: Normalized loss functions for deep learning with noisy labels. In: International Conference on Machine Learning, pp. 6543–6553. PMLR (2020)
31. Menon, A.K., Jayasumana, S., Rawat, A.S., Jain, H., Veit, A., Kumar, S.: Long-tail learning via logit adjustment. arXiv preprint arXiv:2007.07314 (2020)
32. Mirzasoleiman, B., Cao, K., Leskovec, J.: Coresets for robust training of neural networks against noisy labels. arXiv preprint arXiv:2011.07451 (2020)
33. Northcutt, C., Jiang, L., Chuang, I.: Confident learning: estimating uncertainty in dataset labels. J. Artif. Intell. Res. **70**, 1373–1411 (2021)
34. Qi, J., Tang, K., Sun, Q., Hua, X.S., Zhang, H.: Class is invariant to context and vice versa: on learning invariance for out-of-distribution generalization. In: ECCV (2022)
35. Ren, J., et al.: Balanced meta-softmax for long-tailed visual recognition. arXiv preprint arXiv:2007.10740 (2020)
36. Rolnick, D., Veit, A., Belongie, S., Shavit, N.: Deep learning is robust to massive label noise. arXiv preprint arXiv:1705.10694 (2017)
37. Rosenfeld, E., Ravikumar, P., Risteski, A.: The risks of invariant risk minimization. arXiv preprint arXiv:2010.05761 (2020)
38. Sastry, P., Manwani, N.: Robust learning of classifiers in the presence of label noise. In: Pattern Recognition and Big Data, pp. 167–197. World Scientific (2017)
39. Shore, J., Johnson, R.: Properties of cross-entropy minimization. IEEE Trans. Inf. Theor. **27**(4), 472–482 (1981)
40. Shu, J., et al.: Meta-Weight-Net: learning an explicit mapping for sample weighting. arXiv preprint arXiv:1902.07379 (2019)
41. Song, H., Kim, M., Lee, J.G.: SELFIE: refurbishing unclean samples for robust deep learning. In: ICML (2019)
42. Sun, Q., Liu, Y., Chua, T.S., Schiele, B.: Meta-transfer learning for few-shot learning. In: Proceedings of the IEEE/CVF Conference on Computer Vision and Pattern Recognition, pp. 403–412 (2019)
43. Tan, C., Xia, J., Wu, L., Li, S.Z.: Co-learning: learning from noisy labels with self-supervision. In: Proceedings of the 29th ACM International Conference on Multimedia, pp. 1405–1413 (2021)
44. Tang, K., Huang, J., Zhang, H.: Long-tailed classification by keeping the good and removing the bad momentum causal effect. arXiv preprint arXiv:2009.12991 (2020)

45. Wang, T., Sun, Q., Pranata, S., Jayashree, K., Zhang, H.: Equivariance and invariance inductive bias for learning from insufficient data. In: European Conference on Computer Vision (ECCV) (2022)

46. Wang, T., Yue, Z., Huang, J., Sun, Q., Zhang, H.: Self-supervised learning disentangled group representation as feature. arXiv preprint arXiv:2110.15255 (2021)

47. Wang, X., Lian, L., Miao, Z., Liu, Z., Yu, S.X.: Long-tailed recognition by routing diverse distribution-aware experts. ICLR (2020)

48. Wei, H., Feng, L., Chen, X., An, B.: Combating noisy labels by agreement: a joint training method with co-regularization. In: Proceedings of the IEEE/CVF Conference on Computer Vision and Pattern Recognition, pp. 13726–13735 (2020)

49. Wei, H., Tao, L., Xie, R., An, B.: Open-set label noise can improve robustness against inherent label noise. arXiv preprint arXiv:2106.10891 (2021)

50. Wei, T., Shi, J.X., Tu, W.W., Li, Y.F.: Robust long-tailed learning under label noise. arXiv preprint arXiv:2108.11569 (2021)

51. Wu, P., Zheng, S., Goswami, M., Metaxas, D., Chen, C.: A topological filter for learning with label noise. arXiv preprint arXiv:2012.04835 (2020)

52. Yu, X., Han, B., Yao, J., Niu, G., Tsang, I., Sugiyama, M.: How does disagreement help generalization against label corruption? In: International Conference on Machine Learning, pp. 7164–7173. PMLR (2019)

53. Zhang, H., Cisse, M., Dauphin, Y.N., Lopez-Paz, D.: mixup: Beyond empirical risk minimization. arXiv preprint arXiv:1710.09412 (2017)

54. Zhang, Y., Hooi, B., Hong, L., Feng, J.: Test-agnostic long-tailed recognition by test-time aggregating diverse experts with self-supervision. arXiv preprint arXiv:2107.09249 (2021)

55. Zhang, Y., Kang, B., Hooi, B., Yan, S., Feng, J.: Deep long-tailed learning: a survey. arXiv preprint arXiv:2110.04596 (2021)

56. Zhou, B., Cui, Q., Wei, X.S., Chen, Z.M.: BBN: bilateral-branch network with cumulative learning for long-tailed visual recognition. In: Proceedings of the IEEE/CVF Conference on Computer Vision and Pattern Recognition, pp. 9719–9728 (2020)

Author Index

Printed in the United States
by Baker & Taylor Publisher Services